TO
BELANNA, ARIEL AND ANNIKA
JACQUELINE AND REBECCA
CATHERINE, NICHOLAS AND PETER

micro

PRINCIPLES OF
ECONOMICS

Joshua GANS
Stephen KING
Robin STONECASH
N. Gregory MANKIW

5e

Principles of Economics
5th Edition
Joshua Gans
Stephen King
Robin Stonecash
N. Gregory Mankiw

Publishing manager: Dorothy Chiu
Senior publishing editor: Michelle Aarons
Developmental editor: Kylie McInnes
Senior project editor: Ronald Chung
Permissions research manager: Corrina Tauschke
Cover designer: Leigh Ashforth
Text designer: Olga Lavecchia
Editor: Greg Alford
Proofreader: Craig MacKenzie
Indexer: Russell Brooks
Cover: Getty Images
Typeset by S4 Carlisle Publishing Services

Any URLs contained in this publication were checked for
currency during the production process. Note, however,
that the publisher cannot vouch for the ongoing currency
of URLs.

First Australian edition published in 1999 by Harcourt
Australia Pty Limited
Second edition published in 2002 by Cengage Learning
Australia
Third edition published in 2005
Fourth edition published in 2009
Fifth edition published in 2012

© 2012 Cengage Learning Australia Pty Limited

For product information and technology assistance,
in Australia call **1300 790 853**;
in New Zealand call **0800 449 725**

For permission to use material from this text or product, please email
aust.permissions@cengage.com

National Library of Australia Cataloguing-in-Publication Data
Title: Principles of economics / Joshua Gans ... [et al.]
Edition: 5th ed.
ISBN: 9780170191722 (pbk.)
Notes: Includes index.
Previous ed: 2009.
Subjects:
        Economics.
        Economics--Textbooks.
Other Authors/Contributors:
        Gans, Joshua
Dewey Number: 330

Cengage Learning Australia
Level 7, 80 Dorcas Street
South Melbourne, Victoria Australia 3205

Cengage Learning New Zealand
Unit 4B Rosedale Office Park
331 Rosedale Road, Albany, North Shore 0632, NZ

For learning solutions, visit **cengage.com.au**

Printed in China by China Translation & Printing Services.
1 2 3 4 5 6 7 15 14 13 12 11

Brief Contents

Contents

Preface to this edition

Studying economics should invigorate and enthral. It should challenge students' preconceptions and provide them with a powerful, coherent framework for analysing the world they live in. Yet, all too often, economics textbooks are dry and confusing. Rather than highlighting the important foundations of economic analysis, these books focus on the 'ifs' and 'buts'. The motto underlying this book is that it is 'the rule, not the exception' that is important. Our aim is to show the power of economic tools and the importance of economic ideas.

This book has been designed particularly for students in Australia and New Zealand. However, we are keenly aware of the diverse mix of students studying in these countries. When choosing examples and applications, we have kept an international focus. Whether the issue is sauce tariffs in the EU, rent control in Mumbai, DVD prices in the USA or the gas industry in Australia, examples have been chosen for their relevance and to highlight that the same economic questions are being asked in many countries. The specific context in which economics is applied may vary, but the lessons and insights offered by the economic way of thinking are universal.

To boil economics down to its essentials, we had to consider what is truly important for students to learn in their first course in economics. As a result, this book differs from others not only in its length but also in its orientation.

It is tempting for professional economists writing a textbook to take the economist's point of view and to emphasise those topics that fascinate them and other economists. We have done our best to avoid that temptation. We have tried to put ourselves in the position of students seeing economics for the first time. Our goal is to emphasise the material that students should and do find interesting about the study of the economy.

One result is that more of this book is devoted to applications and policy, and less is devoted to formal economic theory, than is the case with many other books written for the principles course. For example, after students learn about the market forces of supply and demand in chapters 4 to 6, they immediately apply these tools in chapters 7 to 9 to consider three important questions facing our society: Why is the free market a good way to organise economic activity? How does taxation interfere with the market mechanism? Who are the winners and losers from international trade? These kinds of questions resonate with the concerns and interests that students hear about in the news and bring from their own lives.

In another example, after students learn about the demand for and supply of loanable funds in chapter 27, they immediately apply these tools to answer important macroeconomic questions facing the Australian economy, such as: How do changes in government tax policy affect the nation's ability to invest in new capital equipment? These principles are extended to the open economy in chapter 32, where students learn about the demand for and supply of foreign exchange and immediately apply the new tools to explain capital flight from Indonesia during the Asian economic crisis.

Throughout this book we have tried to return to applications and policy questions as often as possible. Most chapters include case studies illustrating how the principles of economics are applied. In addition, 'In the news' boxes offer excerpts from newspaper and magazine articles showing how economic ideas shed light on the current issues facing society. It is our hope that after students finish their first course in economics, they will think about news stories from a new perspective and with greater insight.

To write a brief and student-friendly book, we had to consider new ways to organise the material. This book includes all the topics that are central to a first course in economics, but the topics are not always arranged in the traditional order. What follows is a whirlwind tour of this text. This tour will, we hope, give instructors some sense of how the pieces fit together.

Chapter 1, 'Ten lessons from economics', introduces students to the economist's view of the world. It previews some of the big ideas that recur throughout economics, such as opportunity cost, marginal decision making, the role of incentives, the gains from trade and the efficiency of market allocations. Throughout the book, we refer regularly to the Ten Lessons from Economics in chapter 1 to remind students that these lessons are the foundation for most economic analysis. A key icon in the margin calls attention to these references.

Chapter 2, 'Thinking like an economist', examines how economists approach their field of study. It discusses the role of assumptions in developing a theory and introduces the concept of an economic model. It also discusses the role of economists in making policy. The appendix to this chapter offers a brief refresher course on how graphs are used and how they can be abused.

Chapter 3, 'Interdependence and the gains from trade', presents the theory of comparative advantage. This theory explains why individuals trade with their neighbours, and why nations trade with other nations. Much of economics is about the coordination of economic activity through market forces. As a starting point for this analysis, students see in this chapter why economic interdependence can benefit everyone. This is done using a familiar example of trade in household chores among flatmates.

The next three chapters introduce the basic tools of supply and demand. Chapter 4, 'The market forces of supply and demand', develops the supply curve, the demand curve and the notion of market equilibrium. Chapter 5, 'Elasticity and its application', introduces the concept of elasticity and uses it in three applications to quite different markets. Chapter 6, 'Supply, demand and government policies', uses these tools to examine price controls, such as rent control and the award wage system, and tax incidence.

Attention then turns to welfare analysis using the tools of supply and demand. Chapter 7, 'Consumers, producers and the efficiency of markets', extends the analysis of supply and demand using the concepts of consumer surplus and producer surplus. It begins by developing the link between consumers' willingness to pay and the demand curve and the link between producers' costs of production and the supply curve. It then shows that the market equilibrium maximises the sum of the producer and consumer surplus. In this book, students learn about the efficiency of market allocations early in their studies.

The next two chapters apply the concepts of producer and consumer surplus to questions of policy. Chapter 8, 'Application: The costs of taxation', examines the deadweight loss of taxation. Chapter 9, 'Application: International trade', examines the winners and losers from international trade and the debate about protectionist trade policies.

Having examined why market allocations are often desirable, the book then considers how the government can sometimes improve on market allocations. Chapter 10, 'Externalities', examines why external effects such as pollution can render market outcomes inefficient. It also examines the possible public and private solutions to those inefficiencies. This has become highly relevant as policymakers attempt to deal with mitigating the causes of climate change. Chapter 11, 'Public goods and common resources', considers the inefficiencies that arise for goods that have no market price, such as national defence. Chapter 12, 'The design of the tax system', examines how the government raises the revenue necessary to pay for public goods. It presents some institutional background about the tax system and then discusses how the goals of efficiency and equity come into play in the design of a tax system.

The next five chapters examine firm behaviour and industrial organisation. Chapter 13, 'The costs of production', discusses what to include in a firm's costs and introduces cost curves. Chapter 14, 'Firms in competitive markets', analyses the behaviour of price-taking firms and derives the market supply curve. Chapter 15, 'Monopoly', discusses the behaviour of a firm that is the sole seller in its market. It discusses the inefficiency of monopoly pricing and the value of price discrimination. Chapter 16, 'Business strategy', examines markets when there are only a few sellers and so strategic interactions are important. It uses the prisoners' dilemma as the model for examining strategic interaction. Chapter 17, 'Competition policy' describes the policy instruments used by governments to control monopoly power and preserve competition in markets. Chapter 18, 'Monopolistic competition', examines behaviour in a market in which many sellers offer similar but differentiated products. It also discusses the debate about the effects of advertising.

Microeconomic reform is discussed throughout the chapters on firm behaviour and industrial organisation rather than as a separate topic. For instance, the role of privatisation is included in chapter 15, and competition and trade practices issues are discussed in chapter 17. Also, note that chapter 16 includes an appendix that can be used to teach students about the differences between price and quantity competition in oligopoly. This appendix makes the latest game-theoretic thinking on these issues accessible to introductory economics students.

The next three chapters examine issues related to labour markets. Chapter 19, 'The markets for the factors of production', emphasises the link between factor prices and marginal productivity. It includes an appendix on the firm demand for labour under imperfect competition and monopoly. Chapter 20, 'Earnings, unions and discrimination', discusses the determinants of equilibrium wages, including compensating differentials, human capital, unions, efficiency wages and discrimination. The union discussion goes beyond simplistic analyses of unions and monopolists, introducing union behaviour as part of a bargaining equilibrium in bilateral monopoly. The discussion of human capital and efficiency wages proves a convenient point to introduce students to the concepts of signalling and asymmetric information. Chapter 21, 'Income inequity and poverty,' examines the degree of inequality in Australian society, the alternative views about the government's role in changing the distribution of income, and the various policies aimed at helping society's poorest members.

Chapter 22, 'The theory of consumer choice', analyses individual decision making using budget constraints and indifference curves. Finally, Chapter 23 goes beyond standard microeconomics to examine cutting-edge issues such as the role of information, political economy and behavioural economics; all of which help explain more of what happens in the real world. These last two chapters cover material that is somewhat more advanced than the rest of the book. Some instructors may want to skip this chapter, depending on the emphases of their courses and the interests of their students.

Instructors who do cover this material may want to move it earlier, and we have written this chapter so that it can be covered any time after the basics of supply and demand have been introduced.

Beginning in chapter 24, the book turns to the topics of macroeconomics. The coverage starts with the issues of measurement. Chapter 24, 'Measuring a nation's income', discusses the meaning of gross domestic product and related statistics from the national income accounts. Chapter 25, 'Measuring the cost of living', discusses the measurement and use of the consumer price index.

The next three chapters describe the behaviour of the real economy in the long run over which wages and prices are flexible. Chapter 26, 'Production and growth', examines the determinants of the large variation in living standards over time and across countries. Chapter 27, 'Saving, investment and the financial system', discusses the types of financial institutions in our economy and examines the role of these institutions in allocating resources. Chapter 28, 'The natural rate of unemployment', considers the long-run determinants of the unemployment rate, including minimum-wage laws, the market power of unions, the role of efficiency wages and the efficacy of job search.

Having described the long-run behaviour of the real economy, the book then turns to the long-run behaviour of money and prices. Chapter 29, 'The monetary system', introduces the economist's concept of money and the role of the central bank in influencing the amount of money in the economy. Chapter 30, 'Inflation: Its causes and costs', develops the link between money growth and inflation and discusses the social costs of inflation.

The next two chapters present the macroeconomics of open economies. Chapter 31, 'Open-economy macroeconomics: Basic concepts', explains the relationship among saving, investment and the trade balance, the distinction between the nominal and real exchange rate, and the theory of purchasing-power parity. Chapter 32, 'A macroeconomic theory of the open economy', presents a classical model of the international flow of goods and capital. The model sheds light on various issues, including the link between budget deficits and trade deficits and the macroeconomic effects of trade policies. Because instructors differ in how much they emphasise this material, these chapters were written so they could be used in different ways. Some instructors may choose to cover chapter 31 but not chapter 32; others may skip both chapters; and others may choose to defer the analysis of open-economy macroeconomics until the end of their courses.

After fully developing the long-run theory of the economy in chapters 26 to 32, the book turns its attention to explaining short-run fluctuations around the long-run trend. This organisation simplifies the teaching of the theory of short-run fluctuations because, at this point in the course, students have a good grounding in many basic macroeconomic concepts. Chapter 33, 'Aggregate demand and aggregate supply', begins with some facts about the business cycle and then introduces the model of aggregate demand and aggregate supply. Chapter 34, 'The influence of monetary and fiscal policy on aggregate demand', explains how policymakers can use the tools at their disposal to shift the aggregate-demand curve. Chapter 35, 'The short-run trade-off between inflation and unemployment', explains why policymakers who control aggregate demand face a trade-off between inflation and unemployment. It examines why this trade-off exists in the short run, why it shifts over time, and why it does not exist in the long run.

The book concludes with chapter 36, 'Five debates over macroeconomic policy'. This capstone chapter considers five controversial issues facing policymakers: the proper degree of policy activism in response to the business cycle, the choice between rules and discretion in the conduct of monetary policy, the desirability of reaching zero inflation, the importance of balancing the government's budget, and the need for tax reform to encourage saving. For each issue, the chapter presents both sides of the debate and encourages students to make their own judgements.

Joshua S. Gans
Stephen P. King
Robin E. Stonecash

Preface to the original edition

During my twenty-year career as a student, the course that excited me most was the two-semester sequence on the principles of economics I took during my freshman year in college. It is no exaggeration to say that it changed my life.

I had grown up in a family that often discussed politics over the dinner table. The pros and cons of various solutions to society's problems generated fervent debate. But, in school, I had been drawn to the sciences. Whereas politics seemed vague, rambling and subjective, science was analytic, systematic and objective. While political debate continued without end, science made progress.

My freshman course on the principles of economics opened my eyes to a new way of thinking. Economics combines the virtues of politics and science. It is, truly, a social science. Its subject matter is society – how people choose to lead their lives and how they interact with one another. But it approaches its subject with the dispassion of a science. By bringing the methods of science to the questions of politics, economics tries to make progress on the fundamental challenges that all societies face.

I was drawn to write this book in the hope that I could convey some of the excitement about economics that I felt as a student in my first economics course. Economics is a subject in which a little knowledge goes a long way. (The same cannot be said, for instance, of the study of physics or the Japanese language.) Economists have a unique way of viewing the world, much of which can be taught in one or two semesters. My goal in this book is to transmit this way of thinking to the widest possible audience and to convince readers that it illuminates much about the world around them.

I am a firm believer that everyone should study the fundamental ideas that economics has to offer. One of the purposes of general education is to make people more informed about the world in order to make them better citizens. The study of economics, as much as any discipline, serves this goal. Writing an economics textbook is, therefore, a great honor and a great responsibility. It is one way that economists can help promote better government and a more prosperous future. As the great economist Paul Samuelson put it, 'I don't care who writes a nation's laws, or crafts its advanced treaties, if I can write its economics textbooks.'

N. Gregory Mankiw
July 2000

To the students

'Economics is a study of mankind in the ordinary business of life.' So wrote Alfred Marshall, the great nineteenth-century economist, in his textbook, *Principles of Economics*. Although we have learned much about the economy since Marshall's time, this definition of economics is as true today as it was in 1890, when the first edition of his text was published.

Why should you, as a student entering the twenty-first century, embark on the study of economics? There are three reasons.

The first reason to study economics is that it will help you understand the world in which you live. There are many questions about the economy that might spark your curiosity. Why are houses more expensive in Sydney than in Perth? Why do airlines charge less for a return ticket if the traveller stays over a Saturday night? Why are some people paid so much to play tennis? Why are living standards so meagre in many African countries? Why do some countries have high rates of inflation while others have stable prices? Why are jobs easy to find in some years and hard to find in others? These are just a few of the questions that a course in economics will help you answer.

The second reason to study economics is that it will make you a more astute participant in the economy. As you go about your life, you make many economic decisions. While you are a student, you decide how many years you will continue with your studies. Once you take a job, you decide how much of your income to spend, how much to save and how to invest your savings. Someday you may find yourself running a small business or a large corporation, and you will decide what prices to charge for your products. The insights developed in the coming chapters will give you a new perspective on how best to make these decisions. Studying economics will not by itself make you rich, but it will give you some tools that may help in that endeavour.

The third reason to study economics is that it will give you a better understanding of the potential and limits of economic policy. As a voter, you help choose the policies that guide the allocation of society's resources. When deciding which policies to support, you may find yourself asking various questions about economics. What are the burdens associated with alternative forms of taxation? What are the effects of free trade with other countries? What is the best way to protect the environment? How does a government budget deficit affect the economy? These and similar questions are always on the minds of policymakers whether they work for a local council or the prime minister's office.

Thus, the principles of economics can be applied in many of life's situations. Whether the future finds you reading the newspaper, running a business or running a country, you will be glad that you studied economics.

Robin E. Stonecash
Joshua S. Gans
Stephen P. King
N. Gregory Mankiw
June 2011

About the authors

Joshua Gans holds the Skoll Chair in Innovation and Entrepreneurship at the Rotman School of Management, University of Toronto. He studied economics at the University of Queensland and Stanford University. He currently teaches network and digital market strategy. Professor Gans's research ranges over many fields of economics including economic growth, game theory, regulation and the economics of technological change and innovation. His work has been published in academic journals including the *American Economic Review, Journal of Economic Perspectives, Journal of Political Economy* and the *Rand Journal of Economics*. Joshua also has written the popular book, Parentonomics (published by MIT Press) and founded the Core Economics blog (economics.com.au). Currently, he is an associate editor at *Management Science* and the *Journal of Industrial Economics*. He has also undertaken consulting activities (through his consulting firm, CoRE Research), advising governments and private firms on the impact of microeconomic reform and competition policy in Australia. In 2007, he was awarded the Economic Society of Australia's Young Economist Award for the Australian economist under 40 who has made the most significant contribution to economic knowledge. In 2008, he was elected as a Fellow of the Academy of Social Sciences Australia.

Professor Gans lives in Toronto with his spouse and three children.

Stephen King is Professor of Economics at Monash University and a Member of the Economic Regulation Authority of Western Australia. Prior to joining Monash, Stephen was a Commissioner at the Australian Competition and Consumer Commission. After starting (and stopping) studying Forestry and Botany, Stephen completed an economics degree at the Australian National University. He completed his PhD at Harvard University in 1991. Stephen has taught a variety of courses, including introductory courses at Harvard University and the University of Melbourne.

Professor King specialises in industrial economics, although his research has covered a wide range of areas, including game theory, corporate finance, privatisation and tax policy. His work has been published in academic journals such as the *Journal of Industrial Economics, European Economic Review and Journal of Political Economy*. Stephen regularly provides advice to both government and private firms on a range of issues relating to regulation and competition policy. He is a Lay Member of the High Court of New Zealand and a Fellow of the Academy of Social Sciences in Australia.

Professor King lives in Melbourne with his wife. Their two children have run away from home to study at university.

Robin Stonecash is Director of Executive Education at the Business School at the University of Technology Sydney and Director of Stonecash Associates, a boutique consulting firm. She studied economics at Swarthmore College, the University of Wisconsin, and the University of New South Wales. She has taught a variety of courses in microeconomics, macroeconomics and international trade to undergraduates and graduates. She currently consults on strategy and negotiation as well as teaching economics, strategy and negotiation to MBA and executive students.

Dr Stonecash's research interests cover a wide range of topics, including competition policy, privatisation, and international trade and development. Her work has been published in several journals, including the *Economic Record*, *Prometheus* and *Public Performance and Management Review*. Dr Stonecash has also done several studies on the efficiency gains from outsourcing. She has consulted widely for private companies and government organisations such as AusAID and the Departments of Ageing and Disability and Community Services.

Dr Stonecash lives in Sydney with her husband, Mark.

N. Gregory Mankiw is Professor of Economics at Harvard University. As a student, he studied economics at Princeton University and MIT. As a teacher, he has taught macroeconomics, microeconomics, statistics and principles of economics. He even spent one summer long ago as a sailing instructor on Long Beach Island.

Professor Mankiw is a prolific writer and a regular participant in academic and policy debates. His work has been published in scholarly journals, such as the *American Economic Review*, *Journal of Political Economy* and *Quarterly Journal of Economics*, and in more popular forums, such as the *New York Times*, *Boston Globe* and the *Wall Street Journal*. He is also the author of the best-selling intermediate-level textbook *Macroeconomics* (Worth Publishers). In addition to his teaching, research and writing, Professor Mankiw is a research associate of the National Bureau of Economic Research, an adviser to the Federal Reserve Bank of Boston and the Congressional Budget Office, and a member of the ETS test development committee for the advanced placement exam in economics.

Professor Mankiw lives in Wellesley, Massachusetts, with his wife and three children.

Acknowledgements

In adapting this book, we have benefited from the input of a wide range of talented people. We would like to thank all those people who helped us with this task. We would like to thank Professor Lance Fisher of the Macquarie University, Ian Macfarlane and Glenn Stevens, former and current Governors of the Reserve Bank of Australia, Trevor Stegman of the University of New South Wales and Ian Harper of the University of Melbourne for useful discussions. We would also like to thank those economists who read and commented on portions of this manuscript, including:

Don Adams, Macquarie University

Jayanath Ananda, La Trobe University

Steven Barrett, University of Adelaide

Jeff Borland, University of Melbourne

Vivek Chaudhri, University of Melbourne

George S. Chen, University of New England

Mark Crosby, University of Melbourne

Peter Dawkins, University of Melbourne

Laurel Dawson, Deakin University

Sarath Delpachitra, University of Southern Queensland

Robert Dixon, University of Melbourne

James Farrell, University of Western Sydney

Lance Fisher, Macquarie University

Paul Flatau, Murdoch University

Cathy Fletcher, Monash University

John Forster, Griffith University

Michael Francis, University of Canberra

John Freebairn, University of Melbourne

Chris Geller, Deakin University

Mary Graham, Deakin University

Bob Gregory, Australian National University

Ian Harper, Melbourne Business School and Deloitte Access Economics

Ian Harriss, Charles Sturt University

John Hicks, Charles Sturt University

Sarah Jennings, University of Tasmania

Paul Jensen, Melbourne Institute of Applied Economics and Social Research

Chris Jones, Australian National University

Steven Kemp, Curtin University

Geoff Kelly, University of Western Australia

Monica Keneley, Deakin University

Micheal Kowalik, Australian Defence Force Academy

Radhika Lahiri, Queensland University of Technology

Boon Lee, Queensland Institute of Technology

Andrew Leigh, Australian National University

Bruce Littleboy, University of Queensland

Bernd Luedecke, Macquarie University

Rod Maddock, La Trobe University

Jakob Madsen, Monash University

Gary Magee, Latrobe University

Ian McDonald, University of Melbourne

Margaret McKenzie, Deakin University

Alan Morris, Victoria University of Technology

Mark Morrison, Charles Sturt University

Owen Nguyen, Australian Maritime College

Nilss Olekalns, University of Melbourne

Glen Otto, University of New South Wales

David Owens, Swinburne University of Technology

Greg Parry, Edith Cowan University

John Perkins, University of New South Wales

Clive Reynoldson, Edith Cowan University

John Rodgers, University of Western Australia

Sue Richardson, University of Adelaide

Amal Sanyal, Lincoln University

John Searle, University of Southern Queensland

Martin Shanahan, University of South Australia

Sharshi Sharma, Victoria University of Technology

Leanne Smith, Massey University

Lindsay Smyrk, Victoria University of Technology

Rod St Hill, University of Southern Queensland

Max Tani Bertuol, Macquarie University

Judy Taylor, Monash University

Judy Tennant, Monash University

Di Thomson, Deakin University

John Tressler, University of Waikato

Thea Vinnicombe, Bond University

Neil Warren, University of New South Wales

Philip Williams, University of Melbourne

Ed Wilson, University of Wollongong

John Wood, Edith Cowan University

Steffen Ziss, Sydney University

Finally, we give special acknowledgement to our team of research assistants – Teresa Fels, Richard Hayes, Richard Scheelings, Anna Kim and Kimberly Jin – who worked on this project. Special acknowledgement also to Sue Hornby, formerly of the Australian Graduate School of Management Frank Lowy Library, now head librarian for the Reserve Bank of Australia. She provided excellent research assistance. Thanks also to Pat Matthews.

Resources guide

FOR THE STUDENT

As you read this text you will find a wealth of features in every chapter to enhance your study of economics and help you understand how it is applied in the real world.

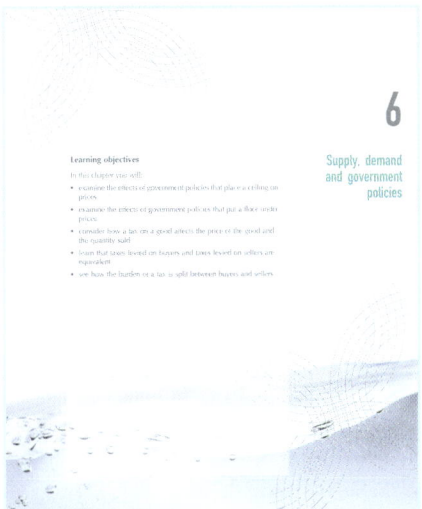

Learning objectives are listed at the start of each chapter giving you a clear sense of what the chapter will cover.

The *Introduction* is a short story, focused on the chapter topic, about how economics affects you on a daily basis without you even noticing.

Where you see this symbol, you should refer to the *Ten lessons from economics* found in chapter 1 of this text.

When *key terms* are used in the text for the first time, they are bolded, coloured and defined in the margins. This will help you identify key concepts throughout the text.

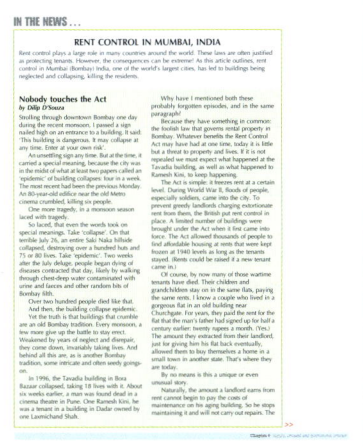

Current economic news and events are presented as *In the news*. This selection of media and journal clippings will explore how economic ideas shed light on current affairs.

IN THE NEWS . . .

Throughout the chapter there are quick quizzes to assess your knowledge and comprehension of key topics.

Useful economic facts can be found in the *FYI* boxes. They will provide you with additional information and material to support key concepts within each chapter.

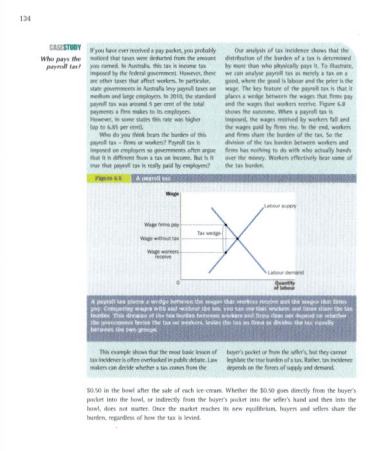

Case studies throughout the book will help you conceptualise key issues in the text, demonstrating how your knowledge can be applied to real-world situations.

CASESTUDY

At the end of each chapter there are several learning tools that will help you review the chapter and key concepts.

The *Conclusion* puts the content into perspective.

The end of chapter *Summary* provides you with key bullet points from the chapter.

All *Key concepts* referred to in the chapter are listed and page-referenced to guide your revision.

Questions for review ensure you have a complete understanding of the chapter's key concepts.

Problems and applications enable you to apply the theory you have learned and encourage group discussion.

Online resources

Visit **http://login.cengagebrain.com** and login using the code card at the front of this book for access to the **Principles of Economics Coursemate website**. You will find an ebook, quizzing, flashcards, crosswords, graphing workshops, videos and more tools to help you excel in your studies.

From **http://login.cengagebrain.com** you can also access *Search me! economics*. Fast and convenient, this resource is updated daily and provides you with 24-hour access to full-text articles from hundreds of scholarly and popular journals, ebooks and newspapers, including *The Australian* and *The New York Times*.

Use the *Search me! economics* keywords provided in the margins of each chapter to explore topics further and find current references. These terms will get you started, then try your own search terms to expand your knowledge.

For the instructor

Cengage Learning is pleased to provide you with a selection of resources that have been developed to supplement the fifth edition of **Principles of Economics**. These resources are available on the instructor's companion website accessible via **http://login.cengage.com**.

Instructor's manual

The **Instructor's manual** provides you with a wealth of content to help set up and administer an introductory Economics course. It includes learning objectives, chapter outlines, key points, figures from the text, adjunct teaching and warm-up activities as well as solutions to problems in the text.

PowerPoint presentations

Chapter-by-chapter **PowerPoint presentations** cover the main concepts addressed within the text and can be edited to suit your own requirements. Use these slides to enhance your lecture presentations and to reinforce the key principles of your subject, or for student handouts.

ExamView test bank

ExamView helps you to create, customise and deliver tests in minutes for both print and online applications. The Quick Test Wizard and Online Test Wizard guide you step by step through the test-creation process. With ExamView's complete word-processing abilities, you can add an unlimited number of new questions to the bank, edit existing questions and build tests of up to 250 questions using up to 12 question types. You can also export the files into Blackboard or WebCT.

Artwork

These digital files of graphs, tables and exhibits from the book can be used in a variety of media. Add them into your course management system, use them within student handouts or copy them into lecture presentations.

PART ONE
Introduction

1

Ten lessons from economics

Learning objectives

In this chapter you will:

- learn that economics is about the allocation of scarce resources
- examine some of the trade-offs that people face
- learn the meaning of opportunity cost
- see how to use marginal reasoning when making decisions
- discuss how incentives affect people's behaviour
- consider why trade among people or nations can be good for everyone
- discuss why markets are a good, but not perfect, way to allocate resources
- learn what determines some trends in the overall economy.

The word *economy* comes from the Greek word for 'one who manages a household'. At first, this origin might seem peculiar. But, in fact, households and economies have much in common.

A household faces many decisions. It must decide which members of the household do which tasks and what each member gets in return. Who cooks dinner? Who does the laundry? Who gets the extra dessert at dinner? Who chooses what TV show to watch? In short, the household must allocate its scarce resources among its various members, taking into account each member's abilities, efforts and desires.

Like a household, a society faces many decisions. A society must decide what jobs will be done and who will do them. It needs some people to grow food, other people to make clothing, and still others to design computer software. Once society has allocated people (as well as land, buildings and machines) to various jobs, it must also allocate the output of the goods and services that they produce. It must decide who will eat caviar and who will eat potatoes. It must decide who will drive a Porsche and who will take the bus.

The management of society's resources is important because resources are scarce. **Scarcity** means that society has limited resources and therefore cannot produce all the goods and services people wish to have. Just as each member of a household cannot get everything he or she wants, each individual in society cannot attain the highest standard of living to which he or she might aspire.

scarcity
the limited nature of society's resources

Economics is the study of how society manages its scarce resources. In most societies, resources are allocated not by an all-powerful dictator but through the combined actions of millions of households and firms. Economists, therefore, study how people make decisions – how much they work, what they buy, how much they save and how they invest their savings. Economists also study how people interact with one another. For instance, they examine how the buyers and sellers of a good interact to determine the price at which the good is sold and the quantity that is sold. Finally, economists analyse forces and trends that affect the economy as a whole, including the growth in average income, the fraction of the population that cannot find work and the rate at which prices are rising.

economics
the study of how society manages its scarce resources

The study of economics has many facets, but it is unified by several central ideas. In the rest of this chapter, we look at *Ten Lessons from Economics*. Don't worry if you don't understand them all at first or if you are not completely convinced. We will explore these ideas more fully in later chapters. The 10 lessons are introduced here to give you an overview of what economics is all about.

How people make decisions

There is no mystery about what an 'economy' is. Whether we are talking about the economy of Sydney, of Australia or of the whole world, an economy is just a group of people interacting with one another as they go about their lives. Because the behaviour of an economy reflects the behaviour of the individuals who make up the economy, we begin our study of economics with four lessons on individual decision making.

Lesson 1: People face trade-offs

You may have heard the saying: 'There is no such thing as a free lunch'. To get one thing that we like, we usually have to give up another thing that we like. Making decisions requires trading off one goal against another.

Consider a student who must decide how to allocate her most valuable resource – her time. She can spend all her time studying economics; she can spend all her time studying psychology; or she can divide her time between the two fields. For every hour she studies one subject, she gives up an hour she could have used studying the other. And for every hour she spends studying, she gives up an hour that she could have spent sleeping, bike riding, watching TV or working at her part-time job for some extra spending money.

Or consider parents deciding how to spend their family income. They can buy food or clothing, or have a holiday. Or they can save some of the family income for retirement or the children's education. When they choose to spend an extra dollar on one of these goods, they have one less dollar to spend on some other good.

When people are grouped into societies, they face different kinds of trade-offs. The classic trade-off is between 'guns and butter'. The more we spend on defence to protect our shores from foreign aggressors (guns), the less we can spend on personal goods to raise our standard of living at home (butter). Also important in modern society is the trade-off between a clean environment and a high level of income. Laws that require firms to reduce pollution usually raise the cost of producing goods and services. Because of the higher costs, these firms end up earning smaller profits, paying lower wages, charging higher prices or some combination of these three. Thus, while pollution regulations give us the benefit of a cleaner environment and the improved health that comes with it, they have the cost of reducing the incomes of the regulated firms' owners, workers and customers.

Another trade-off society faces is between efficiency and equity. **Efficiency** means that society is getting the most it can from its scarce resources. **Equity** means that the benefits of those resources are distributed fairly among society's members. In other words, efficiency refers to the size of the economic pie, and equity refers to how the pie is divided. Often, when government policies are being designed, these two goals conflict.

Consider, for instance, policies aimed at achieving a more equitable distribution of economic wellbeing. Some of these policies, such as the age pension or unemployment benefits, try to help those members of society who are most in need. Others, such as the individual income tax, ask the financially successful to contribute more than others to support the government. Although these policies have the benefit of achieving greater equity, they have a cost in terms of reduced efficiency. When the government redistributes income from the rich to the poor, it can reduce the reward for working hard; as a result, people may work less and produce fewer goods and services. In other words, as the government tries to cut the economic pie into more equitable slices, the pie may get smaller.

Recognising that people face trade-offs does not by itself tell us what decisions they will or should make. A student should not abandon the study of psychology just because doing so would increase the time available for the study of economics. Society should not stop protecting the environment just because environmental regulations reduce our material standard of living. The poor should not be ignored just because helping them distorts work incentives. Nonetheless, acknowledging life's trade-offs is important because people are likely to make good decisions only if they understand the options that they have available. Our study of economics starts by acknowledging life's trade-offs.

Lesson 2: The cost of something is what you give up to get it

Because people face trade-offs, making decisions requires comparing the costs and benefits of alternative courses of action. In many cases, however, the cost of some action is not as obvious as it might first appear.

efficiency
the property of society getting the most it can from its scarce resources

equity
the property of distributing economic prosperity fairly among the members of society

Consider, for example, the decision whether to go to university. The benefits include intellectual enrichment and a lifetime of better job opportunities. But what is the cost? To answer this question, you might be tempted to add up the money you or your parents spend on fees, books, rent and food. Yet this total does not truly represent what you give up to spend a year at university.

There are two problems with this calculation. First, it includes some things that are not really costs of university education. Even if you quit university, you would need a place to sleep and food to eat. Rent and food are costs of going to university only to the extent that they are more expensive because you are going to university. For instance, you might have to move cities to attend university and live away from home. Indeed, the cost of your room and food at your residential college or home might be less than the rent and food expenses that you would pay living on your own. In this case, the savings on the room and food are a benefit of going to university.

Second, this calculation ignores the largest cost of going to university – your time. When you spend a year listening to lectures, reading textbooks and writing assignments, you cannot spend that time working at a job. For most students, the wages given up to attend university are the largest single cost of their education.

The **opportunity cost** of an item is what you give up to get that item. When making any decision, such as whether to attend university, decision makers should be aware of the opportunity costs that accompany each possible action. In fact, they usually are. For example, some young athletes can earn millions if they forgo university and play professional sports. Their opportunity cost of university is very high. It is not surprising that they often decide that the benefit of a university education is not worth the opportunity cost.

opportunity cost
whatever must be given up to obtain some item

Lesson 3: Rational people think at the margin

Economists normally assume that people are rational. Rational people systematically and purposefully do the best they can do to achieve their objectives, given the opportunities they have. As you study economics, you will encounter firms that decide how many workers to hire and how much of their product to manufacture and sell to maximise profits. You will encounter individuals who decide how much time to spend working, and what goods and services to buy with the resulting income to achieve the highest possible level of satisfaction.

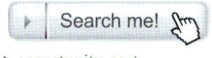
▸ opportunity cost

Rational people know that decisions in life are rarely black and white but usually involve shades of grey. At dinnertime, the decision you face is not between fasting or eating like a pig but whether to take that extra spoonful of mashed potatoes. When exams roll around, your decision is not between blowing them off or studying 24 hours a day but whether to spend an extra hour reviewing your notes instead of watching TV. Economists use the term **marginal change** to describe a small incremental adjustment to an existing plan of action. Keep in mind that *margin* means 'edge', so marginal changes are adjustments around the edges of what you are doing. Rational people often make decisions by comparing *marginal benefits* and *marginal cost*.

marginal change
a small incremental adjustment to a plan of action

For example, consider an airline deciding how much to charge passengers who fly standby. Suppose that flying a 200-seat plane from Brisbane to Perth costs the airline $100 000. In this case, the average cost of each seat is $100 000/200, which is $500. One might be tempted to conclude that the airline should never sell a ticket for less than $500. Actually, the airline can often raise its profits by thinking at the margin. Imagine that a plane is about to take off with 10 empty seats and a standby passenger waiting at the gate will pay $300 for a seat. Should the airline sell the ticket? Of course it should. If the plane has empty seats, the cost of adding one more passenger is tiny. Although the *average* cost of flying a passenger is $500, the *marginal* cost is merely the cost of the sandwich and coffee that the extra passenger will consume. As long as the standby passenger pays more than the marginal cost, selling the ticket is profitable.

Marginal decision making can help explain some otherwise puzzling economic phenomena. Here is a classic question: Why is water so cheap, while diamonds are so expensive? Humans need water to survive, while diamonds are unnecessary; but for some reason, people are willing to pay much more for a diamond than for a cup of water. The reason is that a person's willingness to pay for a good is based on the marginal benefit that an extra unit of the good would yield. The marginal benefit, in turn, depends on how many units a person already has. Although water is essential, the marginal benefit of an extra cup is small because water is plentiful. By contrast, no one needs diamonds to survive, but because diamonds are so rare, people consider the marginal benefit of an extra diamond to be large.

A rational decision maker takes an action if and only if the marginal benefit of the action exceeds the marginal cost. This principle can explain why airlines are willing to sell a ticket below the average cost and why people are willing to pay more for diamonds than for water. It can take some time to get used to the logic of marginal thinking, but the study of economics will give you ample opportunity to practice.

Lesson 4: People respond to incentives

An incentive is something that induces a person to act., such as the prospect of a punishment or a reward. Because rational people make decisions by comparing costs and benefits, they respond to incentives. You will see that incentives play a central role in the study of economics. One economist went so far as to suggest that the entire field could be summarised simply: 'People respond to incentives. The rest is commentary'.

Incentives are crucial to analysing how markets work. For example, when the price of an apple rises, for instance, people decide to eat fewer apples. At the same time, apple orchards decide to hire more workers and harvest more apples. In other words, a higher price in a market provides an incentive for buyers to consume less and an incentive for sellers to produce more. As we will see, the influence of prices on the behaviour of consumers and producers is crucial for understanding how the economy allocates scarce resources.

Public policymakers should never forget about incentives. Many policies change the costs or benefits that people face and, therefore, alter their behaviour. A tax on petrol, for instance, encourages people to drive smaller, more fuel-efficient cars. That is one reason people drive smaller cars in Europe and Australia, where petrol taxes are higher, than in the United States, where petrol taxes are low. A petrol tax also encourages people to take public transportation rather than drive, and to live closer to where they work. If the tax were larger, more people would be driving hybrid cars, and if it were large enough, they would switch to electric cars.

When policymakers fail to consider how behaviour might change as a result, their policies can have effects that they did not intend. For example, consider public policy toward seat belts and car safety. In the 1950s, few cars had seat belts. Today all cars do, and in Australia it is compulsory to wear seat belts. The reason for the change is public policy. In the late 1960s, the rising death toll from motor vehicle accidents in Australia generated much public concern over car safety. State governments responded and in December 1970 the Victorian State Government passed legislation requiring car drivers and passengers to wear seat belts. Other states followed and by 1973 it was compulsory throughout Australia to wear seat belts.

How does a seat belt law affect car safety? The direct effect is obvious. When wearing seat belts is compulsory, more people wear seat belts, and the probability of surviving a major car accident rises. In this sense, seat belts save lives. This direct impact of seat belts on safety is what motivated Australian governments to change the law.

But that is not the end of the story because the law also affects behaviour by changing incentives. In this case, the relevant behaviour is the speed and care with which drivers operate their cars. Driving slowly and carefully is costly because it uses the driver's time and energy. When deciding how safely to drive, rational people compare the marginal benefit from safer driving with the marginal cost. They drive more slowly and carefully when the benefit of increased safety is high. This explains why people drive more slowly and carefully when roads are wet and slippery than when roads are clear.

Now consider how a seat belt law alters a driver's cost–benefit calculation. Seat belts make accidents less costly because they reduce the probability of injury or death. In other words, wearing a seat belt reduces the benefits of slow and careful driving. People respond to wearing seat belts as they would to an improvement in road conditions – by driving faster and less carefully. The result of a seat belt law, therefore, is a larger number of accidents. The decline in safe driving has a clear, adverse impact on pedestrians who are more likely to find themselves in an accident but, unlike the drivers, are not protected by a seat belt. Thus, a seat belt law tends to increase the number of pedestrian deaths.

At first, this discussion of incentives and seat belts might seem like idle speculation. Yet in a classic 1975 study, economist Sam Peltzman argued that car safety laws in the United States have, in fact, had many of these effects. According to Peltzman's evidence, US laws produced both fewer deaths per accident and more accidents. He concluded that the net result was little change in the number of driver deaths and an increase in the number of pedestrian deaths.

Peltzman's analysis of car safety is an offbeat and controversial example of the general principle that people respond to incentives. It implies that more recent changes to car safety laws, such as requiring air bags and advanced braking systems in new cars, may mean more deaths for pedestrians and cyclists. When analysing any policy, we must consider not only the direct effects but also the less obvious, indirect effects that work through incentives. If the policy changes incentives, it will cause people to alter their behaviour.

List and briefly explain the four lessons of individual decision making.
Describe an important trade-off you recently faced.
Describe an incentive your parents offered you in an effort to influence your behaviour.

CASESTUDY

Choosing when the stork comes

The Australian government now pays $5000 for every baby born. It is an open issue whether this encourages more babies but the story of the 'baby bonus', as it is called, has lessons for how people might respond to incentives and why governments (and others) need to anticipate those responses.

In May 2004, the then Treasurer, Peter Costello, announced a $3000 payment (rising to $5000 in 2008) for every child born after 1 July 2004. This meant that the parents of someone whose birthday was 30 June 2004 or earlier would receive nothing. But hold off a day or so, and they would get $3000. This created an incentive for parents to delay births if they could. And by agreeing with their doctors to schedule planned caesareans and inducements a little later, births could be moved.

>>

The following graph shows what happened.

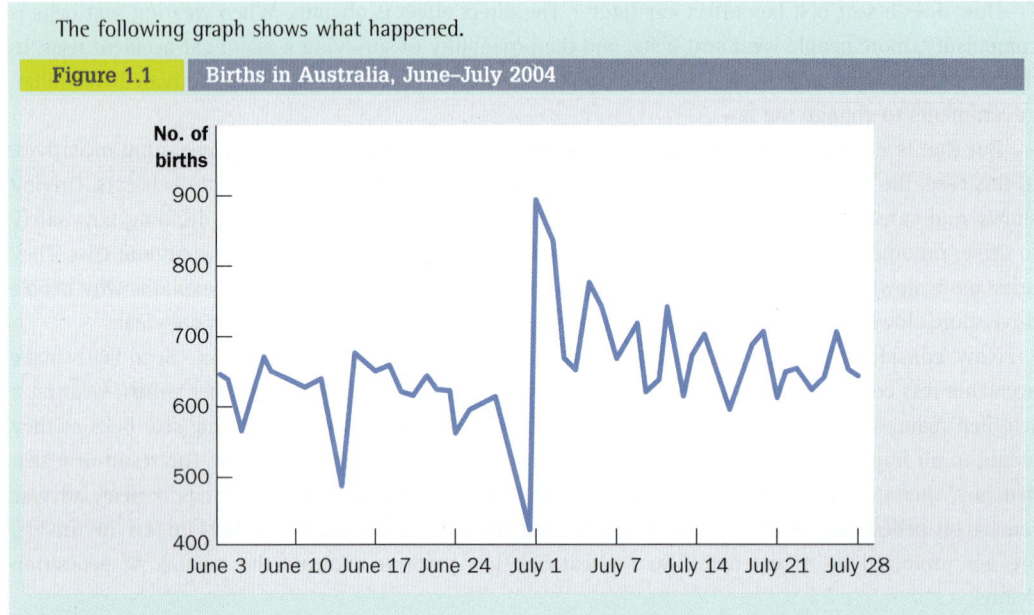

Figure 1.1   **Births in Australia, June–July 2004**

Notice that there was a dip in births in the last week of June followed by a sharp rise on 1 July 2004. Indeed, that day had the most number of recorded births on a single day in Australian history. And if you think this might just be 'fiddling the books', 2 July had the seventh-highest number of births.

In their paper, 'Born on the First of July', Joshua Gans and Andrew Leigh estimated that 1167 births were shifted from June to July that year, all as a result of the baby bonus. Medical organisations raised concerns about the health consequences of maternity hospital congestion caused by this, while economists argued that the policy should have been 'phased-in' so there were no big jumps in payments on any given day.

Nonetheless, the Howard government did not heed those warnings and raised the baby bonus by $834 on 1 July 2006. Gans and Leigh discovered that shifts in birth timing occurred again then but of a lower magnitude (around 700 births).

Joshua Gans and Andrew Leigh, 'Born on the First of July', *Journal of Public Economics*, Vol. 93, Nos 1–2, February 2009, pp. 246–63.

How people interact

The first four lessons discussed how individuals make decisions. As we go about our lives, many of our decisions affect not only ourselves but other people as well. The next three lessons present some key ideas about how people interact with one another.

Lesson 5: Trade can make everyone better off

You may have heard on the news how Australian workers compete with overseas workers for jobs and Australian businesses compete with overseas firms for sales. In some ways, this competition is real because Australian workers and firms produce many of the same goods that are produced overseas. Holden and Mazda compete for the same customers in the market for cars. Clothing firms in Victoria compete with those in Taiwan to sell shirts.

Yet it is easy to be misled when thinking about competition among countries. Trade between Australia and another country is not like a sports contest, where one side wins and the other side loses. In fact, the opposite is true – trade between two countries can make each country better off and, hence, workers (on average) better off.

To see why, consider how trade affects your family. When a member of your family looks for a job, he or she competes against members of other families who are looking for jobs. Families also compete against one another when they go shopping, because each family wants to buy the best goods at the lowest prices. So, in a sense, each family in the economy is competing with all other families.

Despite this competition, your family would not be better off isolating itself from all other families. If it did, your family would need to grow its own food, make its own clothes and build its own home. Clearly, your family gains much from its ability to trade with others. Trade allows each person to specialise in the activities he or she does best, whether it is farming, sewing or home building. By trading with others, people can buy a greater variety of goods and services at lower cost.

Countries as well as families benefit from the ability to trade with one another. Trade allows countries to specialise in what they do best and to enjoy a greater variety of goods and services. The Japanese, the French, the Saudi Arabians and the Vietnamese are as much our partners in the world economy as they are our competitors.

Lesson 6: Markets are usually a good way to organise economic activity

The collapse of communism in the Soviet Union and Eastern Europe in the 1980s may be the most important change in the world during the past 50 years. Communist countries worked on the premise that government workers were in the best position to guide economic activity. These workers, called central planners, decided what goods and services were produced, how much was produced and who produced and consumed these goods and services. The theory behind central planning was that only the government could organise economic activity in a way that promoted economic wellbeing for the country as a whole.

Most countries that once had centrally planned economies have abandoned this system and are instead developing market economies. In a **market economy**, the decisions of a central planner are replaced by the decisions of millions of firms and households. Firms decide whom to hire and what to make. Households decide which firms to work for and what to buy with their incomes. These firms and households interact in the marketplace, where prices and self-interest guide their decisions.

market economy
an economy that allocates resources through the decentralised decisions of many firms and households as they interact in markets for goods and services

At first glance, the success of market economies is puzzling. In a market economy, no one is looking out for the economic wellbeing of society as a whole. Decisions are made by millions of self-interested households and firms. It might sound like chaos. Yet this is not the case. Market economies have proven remarkably successful in organising economic activity to promote overall economic wellbeing.

In his 1776 book *An Inquiry into the Nature and Causes of the Wealth of Nations*, economist Adam Smith explained the success of market economies. He noted that households and firms interacting in markets act as if they are guided by an 'invisible hand' that leads them to desirable market outcomes. One of our goals in this book is to understand how this **invisible hand** works its magic.

invisible hand
The idea that buyers and sellers freely interacting in a market economy will create an outcome that allocates goods and services to those people who value them most highly and makes the best use of our scarce resources

As you study economics, you will learn that prices are the instrument with which the invisible hand directs economic activity. In any market, buyers look at the price when determining how much to demand, and sellers look at the price when deciding how much to supply. As a result of the decisions that buyers and sellers make, prices reflect both the value of a good to society and the cost to society of making the good. Smith's great insight was that prices adjust to guide these individual buyers and sellers to reach outcomes that, in many cases, maximise the wellbeing of society as a whole.

Smith's insight has an important corollary: When the government prevents prices from adjusting naturally to supply and demand, it impedes the invisible hand's ability to coordinate the millions of households and firms that make up the economy. This corollary explains why taxes adversely affect the allocation of resources. Taxes distort prices and thus the decisions of households and firms. It also explains the great harm caused by policies that directly control prices, such as rent control. And it explains the failure of communism. In communist countries, prices were not determined in the marketplace but were dictated by government central planners. These planners lacked the necessary information about consumers' tastes and producers' costs, which in a market economy is reflected in prices. Central planners failed because they tried to run the economy with one hand tied behind their backs – the invisible hand of the marketplace.

---

fyi

Adam Smith and the role of markets

Adam Smith

Adam Smith is often seen as the founder of modern economics. When his great book *An Inquiry into the Nature and Causes of the Wealth of Nations* was published in 1776, England and Europe were going through a period of major social, political and economic upheaval. The industrial revolution was changing the economic landscape just as the American and the French revolutions were to change the political and social landscape. Smith's book reflects a point of view that was gaining importance at the time – that individuals are usually best left to their own devices, without the heavy hand of government guiding their actions. This political philosophy provides the intellectual basis for the market economy, and for free society more generally.

To Smith, individuals interacting through the marketplace, guided only by their self-interest, promote general economic wellbeing. This view was based on three principles that contradicted the conventional wisdom of Smith's day. First, it involves a view that the individual is best able to determine the value of a product. This theory of value opposed the mercantilist view of the time that certain goods, such as gold, were intrinsically valuable and that successful commercial policy for a nation involved the hoarding of these intrinsically valuable goods. Second, Smith argued that individual specialisation is a key way to create value. This idea led to the theory of comparative advantage that we will discuss in chapter 3. Third, Smith argued that market-based interaction can not only replace centrally coordinated commercial interaction but is likely to be superior to centrally planned systems. While a monarch or a parliament could organise trade and commerce through laws that set prices and restricted certain types of market interactions, this is likely to result in less value creation and national wealth than the relatively unfettered interaction of individuals in the marketplace. We discuss the interaction between government policies and economic welfare throughout this book.

Considerable advances in economics have been made since 1776. But many of Smith's insights remain at the centre of modern economics. Our analysis in the coming chapters will allow us to express Smith's ideas and conclusions more precisely and to analyse fully the strengths and weaknesses of a market-based economy.

Lesson 7: Governments can sometimes improve market outcomes

If the invisible hand of the market is so great, why do we need government? One purpose of studying economics is to refine your view about the proper role and scope of government policy.

One reason we need government is that the invisible hand can work its magic only if government enforces the rules and maintains the institutions that are key to a market economy. Most important, markets work only if property rights are enforced so individuals can own and control scarce resources. A farmer won't grow food if he expects his crop to be stolen; a restaurant won't serve meals unless it is assured that customers will pay before they leave; and an entertainment company won't produce DVDs if too many potential customers avoid paying by making illegal copies. We all rely on government-provided police and courts to enforce our rights over the things we produce.

Yet there is another reason we need government. While markets are usually a good way to organise economic activity, this rule has some important exceptions. There are two broad reasons for a government to intervene in the economy and change the allocation of resources that people would choose on their own: to promote efficiency and to promote equity. That is, most policies aim either to enlarge the economic pie or to change how the pie is divided.

Consider first the goal of efficiency. Although the invisible hand usually leads markets to allocate resources to maximise the size of the economic pie, this is not always the case. Economists use the term **market failure** to refer to a situation in which the market on its own fails to allocate resources efficiently.

One possible cause of market failure is an externality. An **externality** is the impact of one person's actions on the wellbeing of a bystander. Pollution is a classic example. If a chemical factory does not bear the entire cost of the smoke it emits, it is likely to emit too much. In this case, the government can raise economic wellbeing through environmental regulation.

Another possible cause of market failure is **market power**, which refers to the ability of a single person (or small group of people) to unduly influence market prices. For example, suppose that everyone in town needs water but there is only one well. The owner of the well has market power over the sale of water. He is not subject to the rigorous competition with which the invisible hand normally keeps self-interest in check. In this case, regulating the price that the monopolist charges may improve economic efficiency.

Now consider the goal of equity. Even when the invisible hand is yielding efficient outcomes, it can nonetheless leave big differences in economic wellbeing. A market economy rewards people according to their ability to produce things that other people are willing to pay for. The world's best soccer player earns more than the world's best chess player simply because people are willing to pay more to see soccer than chess. The invisible hand does not ensure that everyone has sufficient food, decent clothing and adequate health care. Many public policies, such as the tax and social welfare systems, aim to achieve a more equitable distribution of economic wellbeing.

To say that the government can improve on market outcomes at times does not mean that it always *will*. Public policy is made by politicians operating in a political process that is far from perfect. Sometimes policies are designed simply to reward the politically powerful. Sometimes they are made by well-intentioned leaders who are not fully informed. As you study economics, you will become a better judge of when a government policy is justifiable because it promotes efficiency or equity and when it is not.

market failure
a situation in which a market left on its own fails to allocate resources efficiently

externality
the uncompensated impact of one person's actions on the wellbeing of a bystander. A positive externality makes the bystander better off. A negative externality makes the bystander worse off.

market power
the ability of a single economic actor (or small group of actors) to have a substantial influence on market prices

Lesson 7: Governments can sometimes
improve market outcomes

Q List and briefly explain the three lessons concerning economic interactions.

Why is a country better off not isolating itself from all other countries?

Why do we have markets and, according to economists, what roles should governments play in them?

fyi

Why markets make us better off

Australia's Productivity Commission is a government agency that investigates ways to improve Australia's economic prosperity. As this excerpt from a speech by Gary Banks, the head of the Productivity Commission, shows, the answer is simple: markets!

It's easy to lose sight of the simple function of markets. They are a means of connecting willing buyers and sellers to their mutual benefit. That's all they do. Of course, if they do it well, they achieve a lot. But, like the old saying about oils, 'markets ain't markets': some operate a lot better than others. History tells us that those societies with better functioning markets have been the most successful economically, and often the most successful socially as well.

Indeed, the economic progress of mankind is broadly coextensive with the evolution of markets: from localised barter, to monetised transactions encompassing large numbers of people over large distances. How rapidly and effectively markets have developed has depended in turn on the development of institutions and rules to facilitate them and to reduce the costs of transactions in particular. The key ones are how well property rights are defined; how effectively suppliers compete; how well informed are buyers; and the nature and reach of mechanisms for legal redress when things go wrong.

Through the medium of prices, competitive markets ensure that a country's resources get put to use where they can do the most good – taking account of what value people place on different goods and services, and how much those goods and services cost to produce. Competitive markets also ensure that the 'better mousetrap' gets appropriately rewarded, in turn providing incentives for innovation and lower cost production which underpin the growth process.

The logic of markets is that all this happens in a decentralised way, with the actions of many unrelated individuals coordinated spontaneously through the prices they face – Adam Smith's 'invisible hand'. Importantly, emerging shortages and surpluses, which are inherent to any economic system, can be signalled automatically in a competitive market through price movements, precipitating spontaneous actions by both buyers and sellers that eventually serve to eliminate them. If a queue persists, whether it be for taxis or hospital beds, you can be sure that a well-functioning market does not.

As noted, not all societies have been persuaded by the logic of markets. However, experiments around the world with alternative systems have only served to demonstrate their value. And indeed we've seen a progressive shift towards, or back to, markets across the globe in recent decades; a move which has generally paid off for the countries concerned. Since 1980, world GDP has risen by two and a half times, or an unprecedented 40 per cent per capita, with millions of people rising out of extreme poverty.

For example, China's performance since the end of the Cultural Revolution, when it tentatively began to open the door to markets, speaks for itself. Since the beginning of the reforms in China in 1978, we've seen real GDP in that country grow by more than 10 per cent a year. That in turn has seen dramatic reductions in poverty, rises in life expectancy and gains in other indicators of wellbeing and capability, like literacy and health. The OECD has described China's advance to a market economy as among the greatest economic success stories of modern times.

The power of markets to produce prosperity has also been reaffirmed within market economies themselves, wherever impediments to the functioning of particular markets have been reduced, or markets have been introduced to industries or activities where none had previously existed.

Australia itself illustrates how important it is to a country's economic performance to make use of markets in a way that achieves the right balance between freedom and intervention. For much of the previous century, that balance shifted decidedly in favour of intervention. Successive governments imposed policies that impeded competition, distorted prices, constrained business and raised its costs.

For many years, the costs of the inefficiencies that multiplied under that regime were masked by the performance of our broadacre agriculture and mining sectors. But by 1983, when the Hawke government came to power, Australia was falling off the sheep's back. Productivity and income growth were low, deficits had become relatively high, and our per capita GDP had slipped from fifth to fifteenth in the OECD. The 'banana republic' loomed, in Treasurer Keating's evocative phrase.

The fact that we were able to reverse our economic decline, unlike those Latin American countries that shared top billing with us on the global GDP ladder at the beginning of last century, was largely due to the structural reforms set in train by the Hawke/Keating government. Key strands of those reforms were directed at freeing up markets, exposing industry to international competition and allowing prices to perform

their proper allocative role, while undertaking reforms to make government infrastructure services more efficient and labour markets more flexible.

The consequent transformation of Australia's economy, from one that was inward looking, high cost and inflexible, to an innovative, adaptable and competitive one, brought a resurgence in productivity and income growth. Australia climbed back to eighth in the OECD's per capita GDP rankings by the end of the century.

Source: *Markets: How free?*, A presentation to the Whitlam Institute by Gary Banks, Chairman, Productivity Commission, 30/11/2009. Copyright Commonwealth of Australia, Productivity Commission. Reproduced by permission.

How the economy as a whole works

We started by discussing how individuals make decisions and then looked at how people interact with one another. All these decisions and interactions together make up 'the economy'. The last three lessons concern the workings of the economy as a whole.

Lesson 8: A country's standard of living depends on its ability to produce goods and services

The differences in living standards around the world are staggering. In 2009, the average Australian had an income (in US dollars) of about $39 000. In the same year, the average South Korean earned $28 000, the average New Zealander earned $27 000 and the average Indian earned $3000. Not surprisingly, this large variation in average income is reflected in various measures of the quality of life. Citizens of high-income countries have more TV sets, more cars, better nutrition, better health care and longer life expectancy than citizens of low-income countries.

Changes in living standards over time are also large. In Australia, incomes have historically grown about 2 per cent per year (after adjusting for changes in the cost of living). At this rate, average real income doubles every 35 years. In some countries, economic growth has been even more rapid. In South Korea, for instance, average income has doubled in the past 15 years. In China, average income has been growing at around 8 per cent per year since 2000, a rate of growth that will see it double in just under 10 years.

What explains these large differences in living standards among countries and over time? The answer is surprisingly simple. Almost all variation in living standards is attributable to differences in countries' **productivity** – that is, the amount of goods and services produced from each hour of a worker's time. In nations where workers can produce a large quantity of goods and services per unit of time, most people enjoy a high standard of living; in nations where workers are less productive, most people must endure a more meagre existence. Similarly, the growth rate of a nation's productivity determines the growth rate of its average income.

productivity
the quantity of goods and services produced from each hour of a worker's time

The fundamental relationship between productivity and living standards is simple, but its implications are far-reaching. If productivity is the primary determinant of living standards, other explanations must be of secondary importance. For example, it might be tempting to credit labour unions or award wage laws for the rise in living standards of Australian workers over the past century. Yet the real hero of Australian workers is their rising productivity.

The relationship between productivity and living standards also has profound implications for public policy. When thinking about how any policy will affect living standards, the key question is how it will affect our ability to produce goods and services. To boost living standards, policymakers need to raise productivity by ensuring that workers are well educated, have the tools needed to produce goods and services and have access to the best available technology.

Over the past decade, for example, much debate in Australia has centred on the government's budget deficit – the excess of government spending over government revenue. The major parties in the 2010 federal election campaign both stated that they would reduce the government budget deficit. As we will see, concern over the budget deficit is based largely on its adverse impact on productivity. When the government needs to finance a budget deficit, it does so by borrowing in financial markets, much as a student might borrow to pay for postgraduate education or a firm might borrow to finance a new factory. As the government borrows to finance its deficit, it reduces the quantity of funds available for other borrowers. The budget deficit thereby reduces investment both in human capital (the student's education) and physical capital (the firm's factory). Because lower investment today means lower productivity in the future, budget deficits are generally thought to depress growth in living standards.

Lesson 9: Prices rise when the government prints too much money

In January 1921, a daily newspaper in Germany cost 0.30 of a mark. Less than two years later, in November 1922, the same newspaper cost 70 000 000 marks. All other prices in the economy rose by similar amounts. This episode is one of history's most spectacular examples of **inflation**, an increase in the overall level of prices in the economy.

inflation
an increase in the overall level of prices in the economy

Although Australia and New Zealand have never experienced inflation even close to that in Germany in the 1920s, inflation has at times been an economic problem. During the 1970s, for instance, the overall level of prices more than doubled, and political leaders lived under the catchcry 'Fight Inflation First!' In contrast, in the first decade of the 21st century, inflation has run at about 2.5 per cent per year; at this rate it would take almost 30 years for prices to double. Because high inflation imposes various costs on society, keeping inflation at a low level is a goal of economic policymakers around the world.

What causes inflation? While there is some disagreement among economists about inflation in the short term, the answer in the long term is clear. In most cases of large or persistent inflation, the culprit turns out to be the same – growth in the quantity of money. When a government creates large quantities of the nation's money, the value of the money falls. In Germany in the early 1920s, when prices were, on average, tripling every month, the quantity of money was also tripling every month. Although less dramatic, the economic history of Australia, New Zealand and the United States points to a similar conclusion – the high inflation of the 1970s was associated with rapid growth in the quantity of money, and the low inflation of the 1990s and 2000s has been associated with slow growth in the quantity of money.

Lesson 10: Society faces a short-term trade-off between inflation and unemployment

If long-term inflation is so easy to explain, why do policymakers sometimes have trouble ridding the economy of it? One reason is that reducing inflation is often thought to cause a temporary rise in unemployment. This trade-off between inflation and unemployment is called the **Phillips curve**, after the economist who first examined this relationship.

Phillips curve
the short-term trade-off between inflation and unemployment

The Phillips curve remains a controversial topic among economists, but most economists today accept the idea that there is a short-term trade-off between inflation and unemployment. According to a common explanation, this trade-off arises because some prices are slow to adjust. Suppose, for example, that the government reduces the quantity of money in the economy. In the long term, the only result of this policy change will be a fall in the overall level of prices. Yet not all prices will adjust immediately. It may take several years before all firms issue new catalogues, all unions make wage concessions, and all restaurants print new menus. That is, prices are said to be *sticky* in the short term.

"WELL IT MAY HAVE BEEN 68 CENTS WHEN YOU GOT IN LINE, BUT IT'S 74 CENTS NOW!"

Source: © Tribune Media Services, Inc. All Rights Reserved. Reprinted with permission.

Because prices are sticky, various types of government policy have short-term effects that differ from their long-term effects. When the government reduces the quantity of money, for instance, it reduces the amount that people spend. Lower spending, together with prices that are stuck too high, reduces the quantity of goods and services that firms sell. Lower sales, in turn, cause firms to lay off workers. Thus, the reduction in the quantity of money raises unemployment temporarily until prices have fully adjusted to the change.

The trade-off between inflation and unemployment is only temporary, but it can last for several years. The Phillips curve is, therefore, crucial for understanding many developments in the economy.

In particular, policymakers can exploit this trade-off using various policy instruments. By changing the amount that the government spends, the amount it taxes and the amount of money it prints, policymakers can, in the short term, influence the combination of inflation and unemployment that the economy experiences. Because these instruments of monetary and fiscal policy are potentially so powerful, how policymakers should use these instruments to control the economy, if at all, is a subject of continuing debate.

List and briefly explain the three lessons that describe how the economy as a whole works.

Conclusion

You now have a taste of what economics is all about. In the coming chapters we will develop many specific insights about people, markets and economies. Mastering these insights will take some effort, but it is not an overwhelming task. The field of economics is based on a few basic ideas that can be applied in many different situations.

Throughout this book we will refer to the *Ten Lessons from Economics* highlighted in this chapter and summarised in Table 1.1. Whenever we do so, a 'key' icon will show up in the margin, as it does now. But even when that icon is absent, you should keep these keys in mind. Often, even the most sophisticated economic analysis is built using the 10 key ideas introduced here.

Table 1.1 Ten lessons from economics	
How people make decisions	1: People face trade-offs
	2: The cost of something is what you give up to get it
	3: Rational people think at the margin
	4: People respond to incentives
How people interact	5: Trade can make everyone better off
	6: Markets are usually a good way to organise economic activity
	7: Governments can sometimes improve market outcomes
How the economy as a whole works	8: A country's standard of living depends on its ability to produce goods and services
	9: Prices rise when the government prints too much money
	10: Society faces a short-term trade-off between inflation and unemployment

Summary

- The fundamental lessons about individual decision making are that people face trade-offs among alternative goals, that the cost of any action is measured in terms of forgone opportunities, that rational people make decisions by comparing marginal costs and marginal benefits, and that people change their behaviour in response to the incentives they face.
- The fundamental lessons about interactions among people are that trade can be mutually beneficial, that markets are usually a good way of coordinating trade among people, and that the government can potentially improve market outcomes if there is some market failure or if the market outcome is inequitable.
- The fundamental lessons about the economy as a whole are that productivity is the ultimate source of living standards, that money growth is the ultimate source of inflation, and that society faces a short-term trade-off between inflation and unemployment.

Key concepts

economics	invisible hand	opportunity cost
efficiency	marginal change	Phillips curve
equity	market economy	productivity
externality	market failure	scarcity
inflation	market power	

Questions for review

1 Give three examples of important trade-offs that you face in your life.
2 What is the opportunity cost of seeing a movie?
3 Water is necessary for life. Is the marginal benefit of a glass of water large or small?
4 Why should policymakers think about incentives?
5 Why isn't trade among countries like a game with some winners and some losers?
6 What does the 'invisible hand' of the marketplace do?
7 What are 'efficiency' and 'equity', and what do they have to do with government policy?
8 Why is productivity important?
9 What is inflation, and what causes it?
10 How are inflation and unemployment related in the short term?

Problems and applications

1 Describe some of the trade-offs faced by each of the following:
   a a family deciding whether to buy a new car
   b a politician deciding whether to increase spending on national parks
   c a company director deciding whether to open a new factory
   d a professor deciding whether to prepare for a lecture.
2 You are trying to decide whether to take a holiday. Most of the costs of the holiday (airfare, hotel, forgone wages) are measured in dollars, but the benefits of the holiday are psychological. How can you compare the benefits with the costs?

3 You were planning to spend Saturday working at your part-time job, but a friend asks you to go swimming. What is the true cost of going swimming? Now suppose that you had been planning to spend the day studying at the library. What is the cost of going swimming in this case? Explain.

4 You win $100 in a lottery. You have a choice between spending the money now or putting it away for a year in a bank account that pays 5 per cent interest. What is the opportunity cost of spending the $100 now?

5 The company that you manage has invested $5 million in developing a new product, but the development is not quite finished. At a recent meeting, your salespeople report that the introduction of competing products has reduced the expected sales of your new product to $3 million. If it would cost $1 million to finish development, should you go ahead and do so? What is the most that you should pay to complete development?

6 The pension system provides income for people when they retire. Recipients with more income from other sources receive smaller pension benefits (after taxes) than recipients with less income from other sources.
    a   How does the provision of pensions affect people's incentive to save while working?
    b   How does the reduction in after-tax pension benefits associated with higher income affect people's incentive to work past retirement age?

7 There has been some discussion about changes to unemployment benefits that will result in payments being withdrawn after two years for those able to work.
    a   How do these changes in the laws affect the incentives for working?
    b   How might these changes represent a trade-off between equity and efficiency?

8 Your flatmate is a better cook than you are, but you can clean more quickly than your flatmate can. If your flatmate did all of the cooking and you did all of the cleaning, would your chores take you more or less time than if you divided each task evenly? Give a similar example of how specialisation and trade can make two countries both better off.

9 Suppose Australia adopted central planning for its economy and you became the chief planner. Among the millions of decisions that you need to make for next year are how many DVDs to produce, what videos to record and who should receive the discs.
    a   To make these decisions intelligently, what information would you need about the DVD industry? What information would you need about each person in Australia?
    b   How would your decisions about DVDs affect some of your other decisions, such as how many DVD players to make or television sets to produce? How might some of your other decisions about the economy change your views about DVDs?

10 Explain whether each of the following government activities is motivated by a concern about equity or a concern about efficiency. In the case of efficiency, discuss the type of market failure involved.
    a   Regulating local telephone prices
    b   Providing some poor people with vouchers that can be used to buy food
    c   Prohibiting smoking in public places
    d   Breaking up the electricity industry into smaller generating companies
    e   Imposing higher personal income tax rates on people with higher incomes
    f   Instituting laws against driving while intoxicated.

11 'Everyone in society should be guaranteed the best health care possible.' Discuss this point of view from the standpoints of equity and efficiency.

12 In what ways is your standard of living different from that of your parents or grandparents when they were your age? Why have these changes occurred?

13 Suppose Australians decided to save more of their incomes. If banks lend this money to businesses, which use the money to build new factories, how might higher saving lead to faster productivity growth? Who do you suppose benefits from higher productivity? Is society getting a free lunch?

14 Suppose that when people wake up tomorrow, they discover that the government has given them an additional amount of money equal to the amount they already had. Explain what effect this doubling of the money supply is likely to have on:

   a the total amount spent on goods and services

   b the quantity of goods and services purchased if prices are sticky

   c the prices of goods and services if prices can adjust.

15 Imagine that you are a policymaker trying to decide whether to reduce the rate of inflation. To make an intelligent decision, what would you need to know about inflation, unemployment and the trade-off between them?

16 On 1 July 1979, Australia eliminated inheritance taxes. These taxes were a portion of the estate of the wealthiest deceased. What do you think this did to the pattern of deaths around June and July 1979?

Search me!

When accessing information about economics use the following keywords in any combinations you require:

- opportunity cost

CourseMate

For more multimedia resources and activities on economics, visit the Economics CourseMate website.

2

Thinking like an economist

Learning objectives

In this chapter you will:

- see how economists apply the methods of science

- consider how assumptions and models can shed light on the world

- learn two simple models – the circular-flow diagram and the production possibilities frontier

- distinguish between microeconomics and macroeconomics

- learn the difference between positive and normative statements

- examine the role of economists in making policy

- consider why economists sometimes disagree with one another.

Every field of study has its own language and its own way of thinking. Mathematicians talk about axioms, integrals and vector spaces. Psychologists talk about ego, id and cognitive dissonance. Lawyers talk about premeditation, torts and promissory estoppel.

Economics is no different. Supply, demand, elasticity, comparative advantage, consumer surplus, deadweight loss – these terms are part of the economist's language. In the coming chapters, you will encounter many new terms and some familiar words that economists use in specialised ways. At first, this new language may seem needlessly obscure. But, as you will see, its value lies in its ability to provide you with a new and useful way of thinking about the world in which you live.

The purpose of this book is to help you learn the economist's way of thinking. Just as you cannot become a mathematician, psychologist or lawyer overnight, learning to think like an economist will take some time. Yet with a combination of theory, case studies and examples of economics in the news, this book will give you ample opportunity to develop and practise this skill.

Before delving into the substance and details of economics, it is helpful to have an overview of how economists approach the world. This chapter, therefore, discusses the field's methodology. What is distinctive about how economists confront a question? What does it mean to think like an economist?

The economist as scientist

Economists try to tackle their subject with a scientist's objectivity. They approach the study of the economy in much the same way as a physicist approaches the study of matter and a biologist approaches the study of life – they devise theories, collect data and then analyse these data in an attempt to verify or refute their theories.

To beginners, it can seem odd to claim that economics is a science. After all, economists do not work with test tubes or telescopes. The essence of science, however, is the *scientific method* – the dispassionate development and testing of theories about how the world works. This method of inquiry is as applicable to studying a nation's economy as it is to studying the earth's gravity or a species' evolution. As Albert Einstein once put it: 'The whole of science is nothing more than the refinement of everyday thinking'.

Although Einstein's comment is as true for social sciences such as economics as it is for natural sciences such as physics, most people are not accustomed to looking at society through the eyes of a scientist. So let's discuss some of the ways in which economists apply the logic of science to examine how an economy works.

The scientific method: Observation, theory and more observation

Isaac Newton, the famous seventeenth-century scientist and mathematician, allegedly became intrigued one day when he saw an apple fall from an apple tree. This observation motivated Newton to develop a theory of gravity that applies not only to an apple falling to the earth but also to any two objects in the universe. Subsequent testing of Newton's theory has shown that it works well in many (but not all) circumstances. Because Newton's theory has been so successful at explaining observation, the theory is still taught today in undergraduate physics courses around the world.

22

Peanuts

"THOUSANDS OF PEOPLE PARADED HAPPILY THROUGH THE STREETS, BUT ECONOMISTS PREDICT THE CLEANUP WILL BE COSTLY"

"SKIES WERE SUNNY TODAY, BUT ECONOMISTS WARN THAT THIS COULD CAUSE AN INCREASE IN THE PRICE OF SUNGLASSES..."

"ALTHOUGH AUDIENCES ACROSS THE COUNTRY LOVE THE FILM, ECONOMISTS ARE SAYING IT WILL PROBABLY LOSE MONEY"

This interplay between theory and observation also occurs in the field of economics. An economist might live in a country experiencing rapid increases in prices and be moved by this observation to develop a theory of inflation. The theory might assert that high inflation arises when the government prints too much money. (As you may recall, this was one of the *Ten Lessons from Economics* in chapter 1.) To test this theory, the economist could collect and analyse data on prices and money from many different countries. If growth in the quantity of money were not at all related to the rate at which prices are rising, the economist would start to doubt the validity of his theory of inflation. If money growth and inflation were strongly correlated in international data, as in fact they are, the economist would gain confidence in his theory.

Although economists use theory and observation like other scientists, they do face an obstacle that makes their task especially challenging – experiments are often difficult in economics. Physicists studying gravity can drop many objects in their laboratories to generate data to test their theories. By contrast, economists studying inflation are not allowed to control a nation's monetary policy simply to generate useful data. Economists, like astronomers and evolutionary biologists, usually have to make do with whatever data the world happens to give them.

To find a substitute for laboratory experiments, economists pay close attention to the natural experiments offered by history. When a war in the Middle East interrupts the flow of crude oil, for instance, oil prices around the world skyrocket. For consumers of oil and oil products, such an event depresses living standards. For economic policymakers, it poses a difficult choice about how best to respond. But for economic scientists, the event provides an opportunity to study the effects of a key natural resource on the world's economies and this opportunity persists long after the wartime increase in oil prices is over. Throughout this book, therefore, we consider many historical episodes. These episodes are valuable to study because they give us insight into the economy of the past and, more importantly, because they allow us to illustrate and evaluate economic theories of the present.

The role of assumptions

If you ask a physicist how long it would take for a marble to fall from the top of a 10-storey building, she will answer the question by assuming that the marble falls in a vacuum. Of course, this assumption is false. In fact, the building is surrounded by air, which exerts friction on the falling marble and slows it down. Yet the physicist will correctly point out that friction on the marble is so small that its effect is negligible. Assuming the marble falls in a vacuum greatly simplifies the problem without substantially affecting the answer.

Economists make assumptions for the same reason – assumptions can make the world easier to understand. To study the effects of international trade, for example, we may assume that the world consists of only two countries and that each country produces only two goods. Of course, the real world consists of dozens of countries, each of which produces thousands of different types of goods. But by assuming two countries and two goods, we can focus our thinking. Once we understand international trade in an imaginary world with two countries and two goods, we are in a better position to understand international trade in the more complex world in which we live.

The art in scientific thinking – whether in physics, biology or economics – is deciding which assumptions to make. Suppose, for instance, that we were dropping a beach ball rather than a marble from the top of the building. Our physicist would realise that the assumption of no friction is far less accurate in this case: Friction exerts a greater force on a beach ball than on a marble. The assumption that gravity works in a vacuum is reasonable for studying a falling marble but not for studying a falling beach ball.

Similarly, economists use different assumptions to answer different questions. Suppose that we want to study what happens to the economy when the government changes the number of dollars in circulation. An important piece of this analysis, it turns out, is how prices respond. Many prices in the economy change infrequently; the newsagency prices of magazines, for instance, change only every few years. Knowing this fact may lead us to make different assumptions when studying the effects of the policy change over different time horizons. For studying the short-term effects of the policy, we may assume that prices do not change much. We may even make the extreme and artificial assumption that all prices are completely fixed. For studying the long-term effects of the policy, however, we may assume that all prices are completely flexible. Just as a physicist uses different assumptions when studying falling marbles and falling beach balls, economists use different assumptions when studying the short-term and long-term effects of a change in the quantity of money.

Economic models

Secondary school biology teachers teach basic anatomy with plastic replicas of the human body. These models have all the major organs – the heart, the liver, the kidneys and so on. The models allow teachers to show their students in a simple way how the important parts of the body fit together. Of course, these plastic models are not actual human bodies, and no one would mistake the model for a real person. These models are stylised and they omit many details. Yet despite this lack of realism – indeed, because of this lack of realism – studying these models is useful for learning how the human body works.

Economists also use models to learn about the world, but instead of being made of plastic, they are most often composed of diagrams and equations. Like a biology teacher's plastic model, economic models omit many details to allow us to see what is truly important. Just as the biology teacher's model does not include all of the body's muscles and capillaries, an economist's model does not include every feature of the economy.

As we use models to examine various economic issues throughout this book, you will see that all the models are built on assumptions. Just as a physicist begins the analysis of a falling marble by assuming away the existence of friction, economists assume away many of the details of the economy that are irrelevant for studying the question at hand. All models – in physics, biology or economics – simplify reality in order to improve our understanding of it.

Our first model: The circular-flow diagram

The economy consists of millions of people engaged in many activities – buying, selling, working, hiring, manufacturing and so on. To understand how the economy works, we must find some way to simplify our thinking about all these activities. In other words, we need a model that explains, in general terms, how the economy is organised and how participants in the economy interact with one another.

circular-flow diagram
a visual model of the economy that shows how dollars flow through markets among households and firms

Figure 2.1 presents a visual model of the economy, called a **circular-flow diagram**. In this model, the economy has two types of decision makers – households and firms. Firms produce goods and services using various inputs, such as labour, land and capital (buildings and machines). These inputs are called the *factors of production*. Households own the factors of production and consume all the goods and services that the firms produce.

Figure 2.1	The circular flow

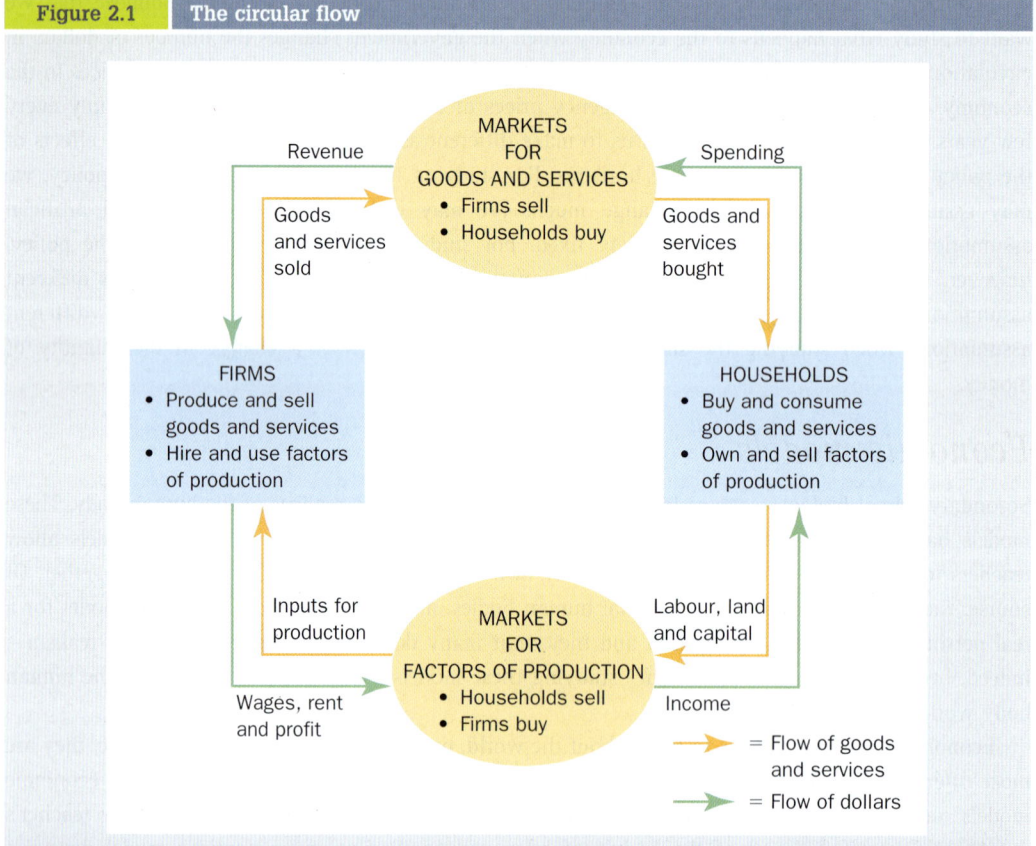

This diagram is a schematic representation of the organisation of the economy. Decisions are made by households and firms. Households and firms interact in the markets for goods and services (where households are buyers and firms are sellers) and in the markets for the factors of production (where firms are buyers and households are sellers). The outer set of arrows shows the flow of dollars and the inner set of arrows shows the corresponding flow of goods and services.

Households and firms interact in two types of markets. In the *markets for goods and services*, households are buyers and firms are sellers. In particular, households buy the output of goods and services that firms produce. In the *markets for the factors of production*, households are sellers and firms are buyers. In these markets, households provide firms with the inputs that the firms use to produce goods and services. The circular-flow diagram offers a simple way of organising all the economic transactions that occur between households and firms in the economy.

The two loops in the circular-flow diagram are distinct but related. The inner loop of the circular-flow diagram represents the flows of goods and services between households and firms. The households sell the use of their labour, land and capital to the firms in the markets for the factors of production. The firms then use these factors to produce goods and services, which in turn are sold to households in the markets for goods and services. Hence, the factors of production flow from households to firms, and goods and services flow from firms to households.

The outer loop of the circular-flow diagram represents the corresponding flow of dollars. The households spend money to buy goods and services from the firms. The firms use some of the revenue from these sales to pay for the factors of production, such as the wages of their workers. What is left is the profit of the firm owners, who themselves are members of households. Hence, spending on goods and services flows from households to firms, and income in the form of wages, rent and profit flows from firms to households.

Let's take a tour of the circular flow by following a dollar coin as it makes its way from person to person through the economy. Imagine that the dollar begins at a household, sitting in, say, your pocket. If you want to buy a cup of coffee, you take the dollar to one of the economy's markets for goods and services, such as your local café. There you spend it on your favourite drink. When the dollar moves into the café's cash register, it becomes revenue for the firm. The dollar doesn't stay at the café for long, however, because that firm uses it to buy inputs in the markets for factors of production. For instance, the café might use the dollar to pay rent to its landlord for the space it occupies or to pay the wages of its workers. In either case, the dollar enters the income of some household and, once again, is back in someone's pocket. At that point, the story of the economy's circular flow starts again.

The circular-flow diagram is a very simple model of the economy. It dispenses with various details that, for some purposes, are significant. A more complex and realistic circular-flow model would include, for instance, the roles of government and international trade. Yet these details are not crucial for a basic understanding of how the economy is organised. Because of its simplicity, this circular-flow diagram is useful to keep in mind when thinking about how the pieces of the economy fit together.

Our second model: The production possibilities frontier

Most economic models, unlike the circular-flow diagram, are built using the tools of mathematics. Here we consider one of the simplest models, called the production possibilities frontier, and see how this model illustrates some basic economic ideas.

Although real economies produce thousands of goods and services, let's imagine an economy that produces only two goods – cars and computers. Together the car industry and the computer industry use all of the economy's factors of production. The **production possibilities frontier** is a graph that shows the various combinations of output – in this case, cars and computers – that the economy can

production possibilities frontier
a graph that shows the various combinations of output that the economy can possibly produce given the available factors of production and the available production technology

Figure 2.2 | **The production possibilities frontier**

The production possibilities frontier shows the combinations of output – in this case, cars and computers – that the economy can possibly produce. The economy can produce any combination on or inside the frontier. Points outside the frontier are not feasible given the economy's resources.

possibly produce given the available factors of production and the available production technology that firms can use to turn these factors into output.

Figure 2.2 is an example of a production possibilities frontier. In this economy, if all resources were used in the car industry, the economy would produce 1000 cars and no computers. If all resources were used in the computer industry, the economy would produce 3000 computers and no cars. The two end points of the production possibilities frontier represent these extreme possibilities.

More likely, the economy divides its resources between the two industries, producing some cars and some computers. For example, it could produce 700 cars and 2000 computers, shown in the figure by point A. Or, by moving some of the factors of production to the computer industry from the car industry, the economy can produce 600 cars and 2200 computers, represented by point C.

Because resources are scarce, not every conceivable outcome is feasible. For example, no matter how resources are allocated between the two industries, the economy cannot produce the amount of cars and computers represented by point D. Given the technology available for manufacturing cars and computers, the economy does not have the factors of production to support that level of output. With the resources it has, the economy can produce at any point on or inside the production possibilities frontier, but it cannot produce at points outside the frontier.

An outcome is said to be *efficient* if the economy is getting all it can from the scarce resources it has available. Points on (rather than inside) the production possibilities frontier

▸ production possibilities frontier

represent efficient levels of production. When the economy is producing at such a point, say point A, there is no way of producing more of one good without producing less of the other. The same holds for point C. But, point B represents an *inefficient* outcome. For some reason, perhaps widespread unemployment, the economy is producing less than it could from the resources it has available – it is producing only 300 cars and 1000 computers. If the source of the inefficiency was eliminated, the economy could move from point B to either point A or point C, increasing production of both cars and computers.

One of the *Ten Lessons from Economics* discussed in chapter 1 is that people face trade-offs. The production possibilities frontier shows one trade-off that society faces. Once we have reached the efficient points on the frontier, the only way of producing more of one good is to produce less of the other. When the economy moves from point A to point C, for instance, society produces more computers but at the expense of producing fewer cars.

This trade-off helps us to understand another of the *Ten Lessons from Economics*: The cost of something is what you give up to get it. This is called the *opportunity cost.* The production possibilities frontier shows the opportunity cost of one good as measured in terms of the other good. When society reallocates some of the factors of production from the computer industry to the car industry, moving the economy from point C to point A, it gives up 200 computers to get 100 additional cars. In other words, when the economy is at point C, the opportunity cost of 100 cars is 200 computers.

Notice that the production possibilities frontier in Figure 2.2 is bowed outwards. This means that the opportunity cost of cars in terms of computers depends on how much of each good the economy is producing. When the economy is using most of its resources to make computers, the production possibilities frontier is relatively flat. Workers and machines best suited to making cars, like skilled autoworkers, are being used to make computers. If some of these skilled autoworkers are moved from computer production to the car industry, the economy will not have to lose much computer production to increase car production. Each computer the economy gives up yields a substantial increase in the number of cars. The opportunity cost of a car, in terms of computers forgone, is small. In contrast, when the economy is using most of its resources to make cars, the production possibilities frontier is quite steep. In this case, the resources best suited to making cars are already in the car industry. Producing an additional car means moving some of the best computer technicians out of the computer industry and making them autoworkers. As a result, producing an additional car will mean a substantial loss of computer output. The opportunity cost of a car is high, and the production possibilities frontier is steep.

The production possibilities frontier shows the trade-off between the production of different goods at a given time, but the trade-off can change over time. For example, suppose a technological advance in the computer industry raises the number of computers that a worker can produce each week. This advance expands society's set of opportunities. For any given number of cars, the economy can make more computers. If the economy does not make any computers, it can still only produce 1000 cars, so one endpoint of the frontier stays the same. But the rest of the production possibilities frontier shifts outwards, as in Figure 2.3.

This figure illustrates economic growth. Society can move production from a point on the old frontier to a point on the new frontier. Which point it chooses depends on its preferences for the two goods. In this example, society moves from point A to point E, enjoying more computers (2100 instead of 2000) and more cars (750 instead of 700).

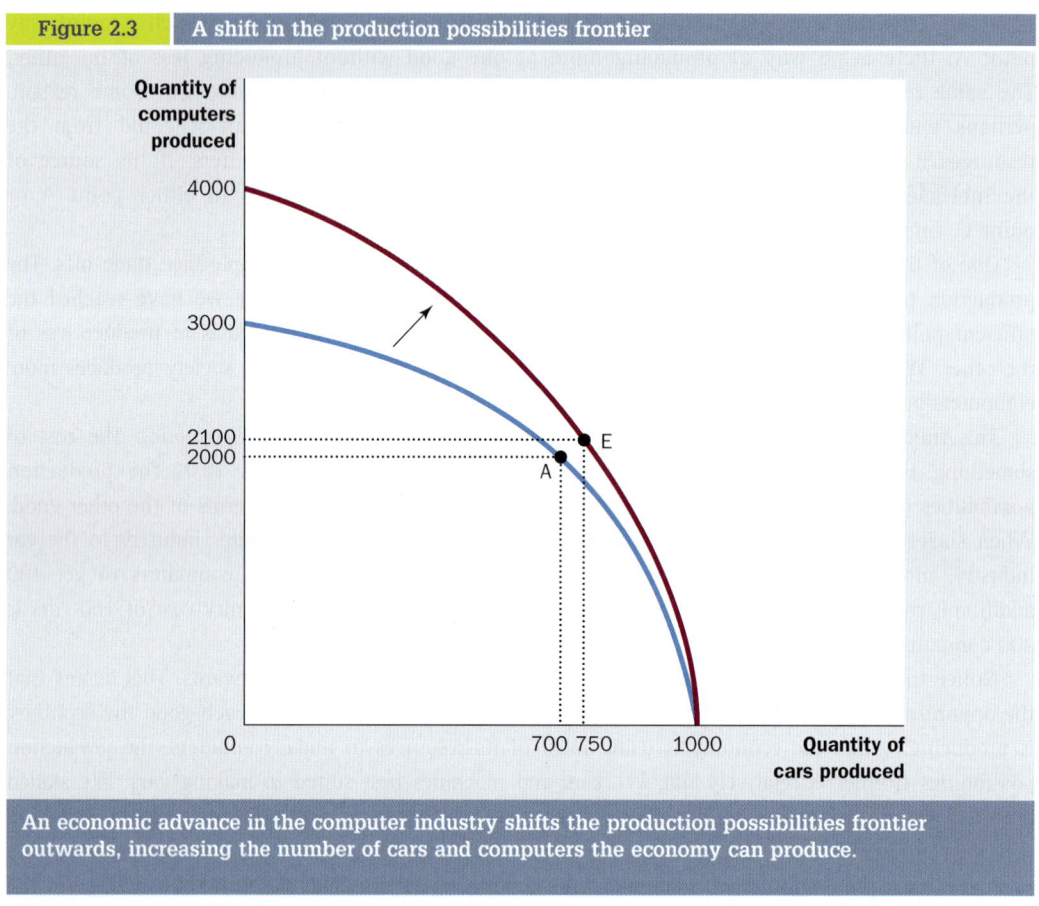

Figure 2.3 | **A shift in the production possibilities frontier**

An economic advance in the computer industry shifts the production possibilities frontier outwards, increasing the number of cars and computers the economy can produce.

The production possibilities frontier simplifies a complex economy to highlight some basic but powerful ideas: scarcity, efficiency, trade-offs, opportunity cost and economic growth. As you study economics, these ideas will recur in various forms. The production possibilities frontier offers one simple way of thinking about them.

Microeconomics and macroeconomics

Many subjects are studied on various levels. Consider biology, for example. Molecular biologists study the chemical compounds that make up living things. Cellular biologists study cells, which are made up of many chemical compounds and, at the same time, are themselves the building blocks of living organisms. Evolutionary biologists study the many varieties of animals and plants and how species change gradually over the centuries.

Economics is also studied on various levels. We can study the decisions of individual households and firms. We can study the interaction of households and firms in markets for specific goods and services. Or we can study the operation of the economy as a whole, which is just the sum of the activities of all these decision makers in all these markets.

The field of economics is traditionally divided into two broad subfields. **Microeconomics** is the study of how households and firms make decisions and how they interact in specific markets.

microeconomics
the study of how households and firms make decisions and how they interact in markets

Macroeconomics is the study of economy-wide phenomena. A microeconomist might study the effects of the discovery of a new gas reserve in Queensland on energy production, the impact of foreign competition on the domestic car industry or the effects of compulsory school attendance on workers' earnings. A macroeconomist might study the effects of borrowing by the federal government, the changes over time in the economy's rate of unemployment or alternative policies to raise growth in national living standards.

Microeconomics and macroeconomics are closely intertwined. Because changes in the overall economy arise from the decisions of millions of individuals, it is impossible to understand macroeconomic developments without considering the associated microeconomic decisions. For example, a macroeconomist might study the effect of a cut in income tax on the overall production of goods and services. To analyse this issue, the macroeconomist must consider how the tax cut affects the decisions of households about how much to spend on goods and services.

Despite the inherent link between microeconomics and macroeconomics, the two fields are distinct. Because microeconomics and macroeconomics tackle different questions, each field has its own set of models, which are often taught in separate courses.

> In what sense is economics like a science? Define *microeconomics* and *macroeconomics*.

The economist as policy adviser

Often, economists are asked to explain the causes of economic events. Why, for example, is unemployment higher for teenagers than for older workers? Sometimes economists are asked to recommend policies to improve economic outcomes. What, for instance, should the government do to improve the economic wellbeing of teenagers? When economists are trying to explain the world, they are scientists. When they are trying to improve it, they are policy advisers.

Positive versus normative analysis

To help clarify the two roles that economists play, let's examine the use of language. Because scientists and policymakers have different goals, they use language in different ways.

For example, suppose that two people are discussing minimum-wage laws. Here are two statements you might hear:

Polly: Minimum-wage laws cause unemployment.

Norma: The government should raise the minimum wage.

Ignoring for now whether you agree with these statements, notice that Polly and Norma differ in what they are trying to do. Polly is speaking like a scientist – she is making a claim about how the world works. Norma is speaking like a policymaker – she is making a claim about how she would like to change the world.

In general, statements about the world are of two types. One type, such as Polly's, is positive. **Positive statements** are descriptive. They make a claim about how the world *is*. A second type of statement, such as Norma's, is normative. **Normative statements** are prescriptive. They make a claim about how the world *ought to be*.

macroeconomics
the study of economy-wide phenomena, including inflation, unemployment and economic growth

positive statements
claims that attempt to describe the world as it is

normative statements
claims that attempt to prescribe how the world should be

Who studies economics?

As a university student, you might be asking yourself: How many economics classes should I take? How useful will this stuff be to me later in life? Economics can seem abstract at first, but the field is fundamentally very practical, and the study of economics is useful in many different career paths. Here is a small sampling of some well-known people who majored in economics when they were at university.

Donald Trump	Business and TV mogul
Meg Witman	Former Chief Executive Officer, eBay
Budiono	Vice President of Indonesia
Cate Blanchett	Actor
Arnold Schwarzenegger	Former actor and politician
Kofi Annan	Former Secretary General, United Nations
Gary Banks	Head of Australian Productivity Commission
Danny Glover	Actor
Warren Buffett	Financier
Manmohan Singh	Prime Minister of India
Lionel Richie	Singer
Sam Walton	Founder of WalMart
Mari Pangestu	Indonesian Minister of Trade
Tiger Woods	Golfer
Steve Ballmer	Chief Executive Officer, Microsoft
Lara Dutta	Miss Universe 2000 and actor
Duck-Woo Nam	Former Prime Minister of South Korea
Scott Adams	Cartoonist (creator of Dilbert)
Mick Jagger	Singer for the Rolling Stones

Having studied at the London School of Economics may not help Mick Jagger hit the high notes, but it has probably given him some insight about how to invest the substantial sums he has earned during his rock-'n'-roll career.

When asked in 2005 why the Rolling Stones were going on tour again, former economics major Mick Jagger replied, 'Supply and demand'. Keith Richards added, 'If the demand's there, we'll supply'.

Source: photos.com/Getty Images.

Source: AAP Image/AP Photo/Risto Bozovic.

A key difference between positive and normative statements is how we judge their validity. We can, in principle, confirm or refute positive statements by examining evidence. An economist might evaluate Polly's statement by analysing data on changes in minimum wages and changes in unemployment over time. In contrast, evaluating normative statements involves values as well as facts. Norma's statement cannot be judged using data alone. Deciding what is good or bad policy is not merely a matter of science. It also involves our views on ethics, religion and political philosophy.

Of course, positive and normative statements may be related. Our positive views about how the world works affect our normative views about what policies are desirable. Polly's claim that the minimum wage causes unemployment, if true, might lead us to reject Norma's conclusion that the government should raise the minimum wage. Yet our normative conclusions cannot come from positive analysis alone. Instead, they require both positive analysis and value judgements.

As you study economics, keep in mind the distinction between positive and normative statements. Much of economics just tries to explain how the economy works. Yet often the goal of economics is to improve how the economy works. When you hear economists making normative statements, you know they have crossed the line from scientist to policy adviser.

Economists in government

Former US President Harry Truman once said that he wanted to find a one-armed economist. When he asked his economists for advice, they always answered, 'On the one hand, ... On the other hand, ...'

Truman was right in realising that economists' advice is not always straightforward. This tendency is rooted in one of the *Ten Lessons from Economics* in chapter 1 – people face trade-offs. Economists are aware that trade-offs are involved in most policy decisions. A policy might increase efficiency at the cost of equity. It might help future generations but hurt current generations. An economist who says that all policy decisions are easy is an economist not to be trusted.

Nonetheless, economists play an important role in many areas of governmental decision making. In Australia, economists work in the Treasury and the Department of Finance to provide advice on taxation and fiscal policy. They give the government advice on microeconomic reform through research conducted at the Productivity Commission. Economists help construct statistical information at the Australian Bureau of Statistics (ABS) and assess competition policy issues at the Australian Competition and Consumer Commission (ACCC). Economists skilled in macroeconomic, monetary and financial issues are employed at all levels of the Reserve Bank. Table 2.1 lists the websites of some of these agencies.

Similar roles are undertaken by economists in many countries. The president of the United States appoints a Council of Economic Advisers, which has three members and a staff of several dozen economists. The council has no duty other than to advise the president and to write the annual *Economic Report of the President*. Perhaps the most influential economist in the world is the person who chairs the Federal Reserve – the central bank of the United States. Financial markets around the world hang on any word, or indeed thought, of the current chairperson who has direct control over monetary policy in the United States.

Table 2.1 Websites	
Commonwealth Treasury	www.treasury.gov.au
Reserve Bank of Australia	www.rba.gov.au
Australian Competition and Consumer Commission	www.accc.gov.au
Australian Bureau of Statistics	www.abs.gov.au
Productivity Commission	www.pc.gov.au
Here are the websites for a few of the government agencies that are responsible for collecting economic data and making economic policy.	

The influence of economists on policy goes beyond their role as advisers and policymakers; their research and writings often affect policy indirectly. Economist John Maynard Keynes offered this observation:

> The ideas of economists and political philosophers, both when they are right and when they are wrong, are more powerful than is commonly understood. Indeed, the world is ruled by little else. Practical men, who believe themselves to be quite exempt from intellectual influences, are usually the slaves of some defunct economist. Madmen in authority, who hear voices in the air, are distilling their frenzy from some academic scribbler of a few years back.

Although these words were written in 1935, they remain true today. Indeed, the 'academic scribbler' now influencing public policy is often Keynes himself.

Q Give an example of a positive statement and an example of a normative statement. Name three parts of government that regularly rely on advice from economists.

Why economists disagree

'If all economists were laid end to end, they would not reach a conclusion.' This quip from George Bernard Shaw is revealing. Economists as a group are often criticised for giving conflicting advice to policymakers. Former US President Ronald Reagan once joked that if the game Trivial Pursuit were designed for economists, it would have 100 questions and 3000 answers.

Why do economists so often appear to give conflicting advice to policymakers? There are two basic reasons:

- Economists may disagree about the validity of alternative positive theories about how the world works.
- Economists may have different values and, therefore, different normative views about what policies should try to accomplish.

Let's discuss each of these reasons.

Differences in scientific judgements

Several centuries ago, astronomers debated whether the earth or the sun was at the centre of the heavens. More recently, meteorologists have debated whether the earth is experiencing 'global warming'. Science is a search for understanding about the world around us. It is not surprising that, as the search continues, scientists can disagree about the direction in which truth lies.

Economists often disagree for the same reason. Economics is a young science and there is still much to be learned. Economists sometimes disagree because they have different hunches about the validity of alternative theories or about the size of important parameters.

For example, economists disagree about whether the government should levy taxes based on a household's income or its consumption (spending). In Australia, advocates of a switch from the old income tax system to the goods and services tax (GST) introduced in 2000 believed that the change would encourage households to save more, because income that is saved would not be taxed. Higher saving, in turn, would lead to more rapid growth in productivity and living standards. Those against the GST believed that household saving would not respond much to a change in the tax laws. These two groups of economists held (and continue to hold) different views about the tax system because they have different positive views about the responsiveness of saving to tax incentives.

Differences in values

Suppose that Peter and Paula both take the same amount of water from the town well. To pay for maintaining the well, the town taxes its residents. Peter has income of $50 000 and is taxed $5000, or 10 per cent of his income. Paula has income of $10 000 and is taxed $2000, or 20 per cent of her income.

Is this policy fair? If not, who pays too much and who pays too little? Does it matter whether Paula's low income is due to a medical disability or to her decision to pursue a career in acting? Does it matter whether Peter's high income is due to a large inheritance or to his willingness to work long hours at a dreary job?

These are difficult questions on which people are likely to disagree. If the town hired two experts to study how the town should tax its residents to pay for the well, we would not be surprised if they offered conflicting advice.

This simple example shows why economists sometimes disagree about public policy. As we learned earlier in our discussion of normative and positive analysis, policies cannot be judged on scientific grounds alone. Economists give conflicting advice sometimes because they have different values. Perfecting the science of economics will not tell us whether Peter or Paula pays too much.

Perception versus reality

Because of differences in scientific judgements and differences in values, some disagreement among economists is inevitable. Yet one should not overstate the amount of disagreement. Economists agree with one another far more than is sometimes understood.

Table 2.2 contains 10 propositions about economic policy. In a survey of economics professors in Australia, these propositions were endorsed by an overwhelming majority of respondents. The views of these economists reflect those generated by similar surveys around the world. However, by contrast, most of these propositions would fail to command a similar consensus among the general public.

The first proposition in the table is about rent control, a policy that sets a legal maximum on the amount landlords can charge for their properties. For reasons we will discuss in chapter 6, almost all economists believe that rent control adversely affects the availability and quality of housing and is a very costly way of helping the most needy members of society. Nonetheless, governments in many countries choose to ignore the advice of economists and place ceilings on the rents that landlords may charge their tenants.

The second proposition in the table concerns tariffs and import quotas, two policies that restrict trade among nations. For reasons we will discuss in chapter 3 and more fully in chapter 9, almost all economists oppose such barriers to free trade. Nonetheless, over the years, governments in Australia and elsewhere have chosen to restrict the import of certain goods. Attempts to secure trade agreements, such as the North American Free Trade Agreement (between the United States, Canada and Mexico), the European Union, and APEC (Asia Pacific Economic Cooperation), faced considerable

Table 2.2 Ten propositions with which most economists agree

	Proposition	Percentage of economists who agree
1	A ceiling on rents reduces the quantity and quality of housing available.	96%
2	Tariffs and import quotas usually reduce general economic welfare.	92%
3	Flexible and floating exchange rates offer an effective international monetary arrangement.	77%
4	Fiscal policy (e.g., tax cut and/or government expenditure increase) has a significant stimulative impact on a less than fully employed economy.	81%
5	In the short term, unemployment can be reduced by increasing the rate of inflation.	60%
6	Cash payments increase the welfare of recipients to a greater degree than do transfers-in-kind of equal cash value.	75%
7	Trade practices laws should be used vigorously to reduce monopoly power in Australia.	81%
8	A minimum wage increases unemployment among young and unskilled workers.	85%
9	The government should restructure the social security system along the lines of a 'negative income tax'.	77%
10	Effluent taxes and marketable pollution permits represent a better approach to pollution control than imposition of pollution ceilings.	87%

Source: Adapted from Malcolm Anderson and Richard Blandy, 'What Australian economics professors think', *Australian Economic Review*, no. 100, 1992, pp. 17–40.

domestic opposition in the respective countries, despite overwhelming support from economists. In these cases, economists did offer united advice, but many politicians chose to ignore it.

Why do policies such as rent control and import quotas persist if the experts are united in their opposition? The reason may be that economists have not yet convinced the general public that these policies are undesirable. One of the purposes of this book is to help you understand the economist's view of these and other subjects and, perhaps, to persuade you that it is the right one.

Give two reasons why two economic advisers to the federal government might disagree about a question of policy.

Let's get going

The first two chapters of this book have introduced you to the ideas and methods of economics. We are now ready to get to work. In the next chapter we start learning in more detail about the principles of economic behaviour and economic policy.

As you proceed through this book, you will be asked to draw on many of your intellectual skills. It may be helpful to keep in mind some advice from the great economist John Maynard Keynes:

> The study of economics does not seem to require any specialised gifts of an unusually high order. Is it not ... a very easy subject compared with the higher branches of philosophy or pure science? An easy subject, at which very few excel! The paradox finds its explanation, perhaps, in that the master-economist must possess a rare *combination* of gifts. He must be mathematician, historian, statesman, philosopher – in some degree. He must understand symbols and speak in words. He must contemplate the particular in terms of the general, and touch abstract and concrete in the same flight of thought. He must study the present in the light of the past for the purposes of the future. No part of man's nature or his institutions must lie entirely outside his regard. He must be purposeful and disinterested in a simultaneous mood; as aloof and incorruptible as an artist, yet sometimes as near the earth as a politician.

It is a tall order. But with practice, you will become more and more accustomed to thinking like an economist.

Summary

- Economists try to approach their subject with a scientist's objectivity. Like all scientists, they make appropriate assumptions and build simplified models in order to understand the world around them.
- The field of economics is divided into two subfields – microeconomics and macroeconomics. Microeconomists study decision making by households and firms and the interaction among households and firms in the marketplace. Macroeconomists study the forces and trends that affect the economy as a whole.
- A positive statement is an assertion about how the world *is*. A normative statement is an assertion about how the world *ought to be*. When economists make normative statements, they are acting more as policymakers than scientists.
- Economists who advise policymakers offer conflicting advice either because of differences in scientific judgements or because of differences in values. At other times, economists are united in the advice they offer, but policymakers may choose to ignore it.

Key concepts

circular-flow diagram
macroeconomics
microeconomics

normative statements
positive statements

production possibilities
frontier

Questions for review

1. How is economics like a science?
2. Why do economists make assumptions?
3. Should an economic model describe reality exactly?
4. Draw and explain a production possibilities frontier for an economy that produces milk and biscuits. What happens to this frontier if a disease kills half of the economy's cow population?
5. What are the two subfields into which economics is divided? Explain what each subfield studies.
6. What is the difference between a positive and a normative statement? Give an example of each.
7. Why do economists sometimes offer conflicting advice to policymakers?

Problems and applications

1. Describe some unusual language used in one of the other fields that you are studying. Why are these special terms useful?
2. One common assumption in economics is that the products of different firms in the same industry are indistinguishable. For each of the following industries, discuss whether this is a reasonable assumption:
   a steel
   b novels
   c wheat
   d fast food.
3. Draw a circular-flow diagram. Identify the parts of the model that correspond to the flow of goods and services and the flow of dollars for each of the following activities:

    a   Sam pays a shopkeeper $1 for a litre of milk.

    b   Terry earns $4.50 per hour working at a fast-food restaurant.

    c   Uma spends $7 to see a film.

    d   Violet earns $10 000 from her 10 per cent ownership of Acme Industrial.

4   Imagine a society that produces military goods and consumer goods, which we'll call 'guns' and 'butter'.

    a   Draw a production possibilities frontier for guns and butter. Explain why it most likely has a bowed-out shape.

    b   Show a point that is impossible for the economy to achieve. Show a point that is feasible but inefficient.

    c   Imagine that the society has two political parties, call them the Hawks (who want a strong military) and the Doves (who want a smaller military). Show a point on your production possibilities frontier that the Hawks might choose and a point the Doves might choose.

    d   Imagine that an aggressive neighbouring country reduces the size of its military. As a result, both the Hawks and the Doves reduce their desired production of guns by the same amount. Which party would get the bigger 'peace dividend', measured by the increase in butter production? Explain.

5   The first lesson from economics discussed in chapter 1 is that people face trade-offs. Use a production possibilities frontier to illustrate society's trade-off between a clean environment and high incomes. What do you suppose determines the shape and position of the frontier? Show what happens to the frontier if engineers develop a car engine with almost no emissions.

6   An economy consists of three workers: Larry, Moe and Curly. Each works 10 hours a day and can produce two services: mowing lawns and washing cars. In an hour, Larry can either mow one lawn or wash one car; Moe can either mow one lawn or wash two cars; and Curly can either mow two lawns or wash one car.

    a   Calculate how much of each service is produced under the following circumstances, which we label A, B, C, and D:

        i   All three spend all their time mowing lawns. (A)

        ii   All three spend all their time washing cars. (B)

        iii   All three spend half their time on each activity. (C)

        iv   Larry spends half his time on each activity, while Moe only washes cars and Curly only mows lawns. (D)

    Graph the production possibilities frontier for this economy. Using your answers to part (a), identify points A, B, C and D on your graph.

    b   Explain why the production possibilities frontier has the shape it does.

    c   Are any of the allocations calculated in part (a) inefficient? Explain.

7   Classify the following topics as relating to microeconomics or macroeconomics:

    a   a family's decision about how much income to save

    b   the effect of government regulations on car emissions

    c   the impact of higher saving on economic growth

    d   a firm's decision about how many workers to hire

    e   the relationship between the inflation rate and changes in the quantity of money.

8   Classify each of the following statements as positive or normative. Explain.

    a   Society faces a short-term trade-off between inflation and unemployment.

    b   A reduction in the rate of growth of money will reduce the rate of inflation.

    c   The Reserve Bank should reduce the rate of growth of money.

    d   Society ought to require people on social security benefits to look for jobs.

    e   Lower tax rates encourage more work and more saving.

9 If you were prime minister, would you be more interested in your economic advisers' positive views or their normative views? Why?

10 Would you expect economists to disagree less about public policy as time goes on? Why or why not? Can their differences be completely eliminated? Why or why not?

Search me!

When accessing information about economics use the following keywords in any combinations you require:

- production possibilities
  frontier

CourseMate

For more multimedia resources and activities on economics, visit the Economics CourseMate website.

APPENDIX

Graphing – a brief review

Many of the concepts that economists study can be expressed with numbers – the price of bananas, the quantity of bananas sold, the cost of growing bananas and so on. Often these economic variables are related to one another. When the price of bananas rises, people buy fewer bananas. One way of expressing the relationships among variables is with graphs.

Graphs serve two purposes. First, when economists develop economic theories, graphs offer a way to express visually ideas that might be less clear if described with equations or words. Second, when economists analyse economic data, graphs provide a way of finding how variables are, in fact, related in the world. Whether we are working with theory or with data, graphs provide a lens through which a recognisable forest emerges from a multitude of trees.

Numerical information can be expressed graphically in many ways, just as a thought can be expressed in words in many ways. A good writer chooses words that will make an argument clear, a description pleasing or a scene dramatic. An effective economist chooses the type of graph that best suits the purpose at hand.

In this appendix we discuss how economists use graphs to study the mathematical relationships among variables. We also discuss some of the pitfalls that can arise in the use of graphical methods.

Graphs of a single variable

Three common graphs are shown in Figure 2A.1. The *pie chart* in panel (a) shows the sources of tax revenue for the federal government. A slice of the pie represents each source's share of the total. The *bar graph* in panel (b) compares how much various large corporations are worth. The height of each bar represents the dollar value of each firm. The *time-series graph* in panel (c) traces the Australian–US dollar exchange rate over time. The height of the line shows the number of US dollars that can be bought by one Australian dollar in each year. You have probably seen similar graphs presented in newspapers and magazines.

Graphs of two variables: The coordinate system

The three graphs in Figure 2A.1 are useful in showing how a variable changes over time or across individuals, but they are limited in how much they can tell us. These graphs display information only on a single variable. Economists are often concerned with the relationships between variables. Thus, they need to be able to display two variables on a single graph. The *coordinate system* makes this possible.

Figure 2A.1   Types of graphs

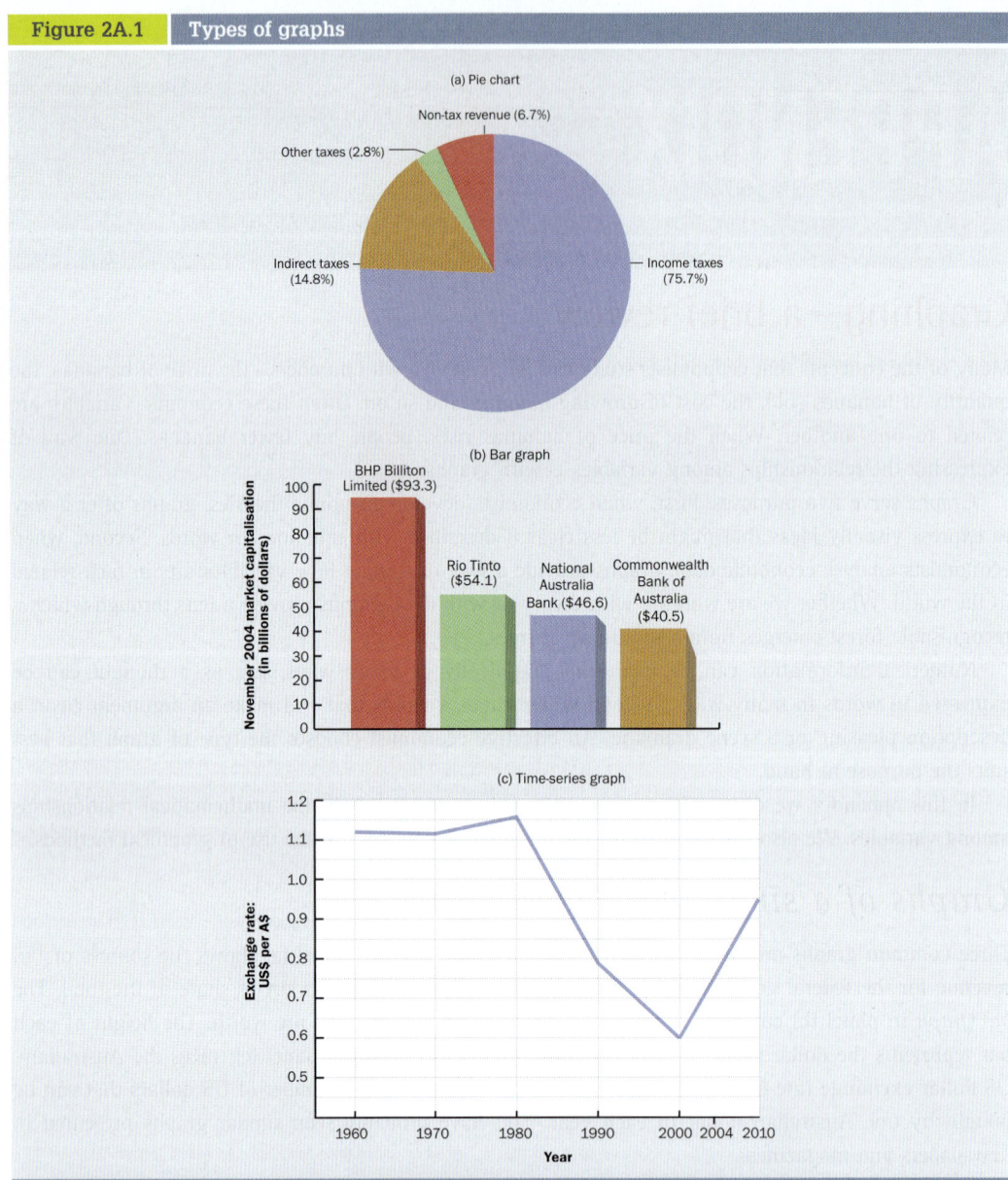

The pie chart in panel (a) shows the sources of revenue for the federal government. The bar graph in panel (b) compares how much various large corporations are worth. The time-series graph in panel (c) traces the Australian–US dollar exchange rate over time.

Source: (a) Department of the Treasury: www.budget.gov.au/2003–04/fbo/html/fbo-02.htm, 2003–04 Final Budget Outcome plus Appendix; (b) *Personal Investor*, January 2005, vol. 23, no. 1; (c) Reserve Bank of Australia Bulletin, June figures.

Suppose you want to examine the relationship between study time and average mark. For each student in your class, you could record a pair of numbers – hours per week spent studying and average mark. These numbers could then be placed in parentheses as an *ordered pair* and appear as a single point on the graph. Albert, for instance, is represented by the ordered pair (25 hours per week, 75 per cent average), and his 'what-me-worry?' classmate Alfred is represented by the ordered pair (five hours per week, 40 per cent average).

We can graph these ordered pairs on a two-dimensional grid. The first number in each ordered pair, called the *x-coordinate*, tells us the horizontal location of the point. The second number, called the *y-coordinate*, tells us the vertical location of the point. The point with both an *x*-coordinate and a *y*-coordinate of zero is known as the *origin*. The two coordinates in the ordered pair tell us where the point is located in relation to the origin – *x* units to the right of the origin and *y* units above it.

Figure 2A.2 graphs average marks against study time for Albert, Alfred and their classmates. This type of graph is called a *scatterplot* because it plots scattered points. Looking at this graph, we immediately notice that points further to the right also tend to be higher. Because higher study time

Figure 2A.2 | Using the coordinate system

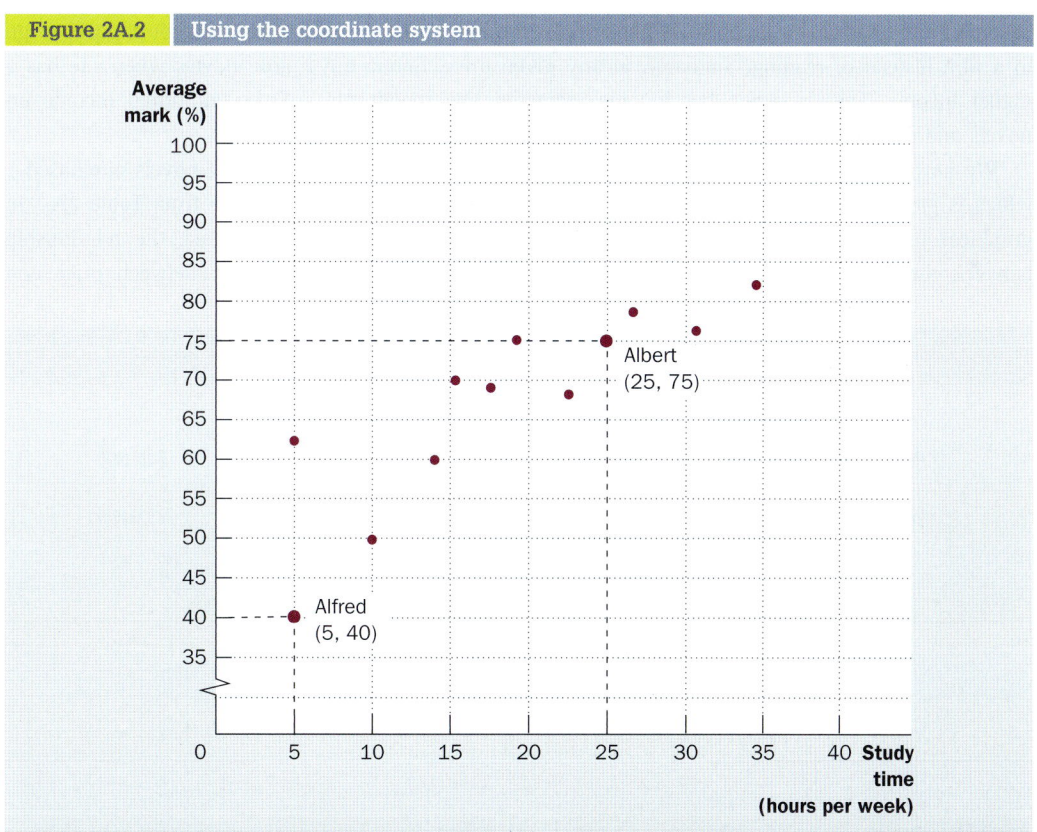

Average mark is measured on the vertical axis and study time on the horizontal axis. Albert, Alfred and their classmates are represented by various points. We can see from the graph that students who study more tend to get higher marks.

is associated with higher marks, we say that these two variables have a *positive correlation*. In contrast, if we were to graph party time and marks, it is likely that we would find that higher party time is associated with lower marks, and we would call this a *negative correlation*. In either case, the coordinate system makes the correlation between the two variables easy to see.

Curves in the coordinate system

Students who study more do tend to get higher marks, but other factors also influence a student's mark. Previous preparation is an important factor, for instance, as are talent, attention from teachers, even eating a good breakfast. A scatterplot like Figure 2A.2 does not attempt to isolate the effect that study has on marks from the effects of other variables. Often, however, economists prefer looking at how one variable affects another, holding everything else constant.

To see how this is done, let's consider one of the most important graphs in economics – the *demand curve*. The demand curve traces the effect of a good's price on the quantity of the good consumers want to buy. Table 2A.1 shows how the number of novels that Emma buys depends on her income and on the price of novels. When novels are cheap, Emma buys them in large quantities. As they become more expensive, she borrows books from the library instead of buying them or chooses to go to a film instead of reading. Similarly, at any given price, Emma buys more novels when she has a higher income. That is, when her income increases, she spends part of the additional income on novels and part on other goods.

We now have three variables – the price of novels, income and the number of novels purchased – which is more than we can represent in two dimensions. To put the information from Table 2A.1 in graphical form, we need to hold one of the three variables constant and trace the relationship between the other two. Because the demand curve represents the relationship between price and

Table 2A.1 Novels purchased by Emma			
	Income		
Price	$20 000	$30 000	$40 000
$10	2 novels	5 novels	8 novels
9	6	9	12
8	10	13	16
7	14	17	20
6	18	21	24
5	22	25	28
	Demand curve, D_3	Demand curve, D_1	Demand curve, D_2

This table shows the number of novels Emma buys at various incomes and prices. For any given level of income, the data on price and quantity demanded can be graphed to produce Emma's demand curve for novels.

quantity demanded, we hold Emma's income constant and show how the number of novels she buys varies with the price of novels.

Suppose that Emma's income is $30 000 per year. If we place the number of novels Emma purchases on the *x*-axis and the price of novels on the *y*-axis, we can graphically represent the third column of Table 2A.1. When the points that represent these entries from the table – (five novels, $10), (nine novels, $9) and so on – are connected, they form a line. This line, shown in Figure 2A.3, is known as Emma's demand curve for novels; it tells us how many novels Emma purchases at any given price. The demand curve is downward-sloping, indicating that the quantity of novels demanded is negatively related to the price.

Now suppose that Emma's income rises to $40 000 per year. At any given price, Emma will purchase more novels than she did at her previous level of income. Just as earlier we drew Emma's demand curve for novels using the entries from the third column of Table 2A.1, we now draw a new demand curve using the entries from the fourth column of the table. This new demand curve (curve D_2) is shown alongside the old one (curve D_1) in Figure 2A.4; the new curve is a similar line drawn further to the right. We therefore say that Emma's demand curve for novels *shifts* to the right when her income increases. Likewise, if Emma's income were to fall to $20 000 per year, she would buy fewer novels at any given price and her demand curve would shift to the left (to curve D_3).

Figure 2A.3	Demand curve

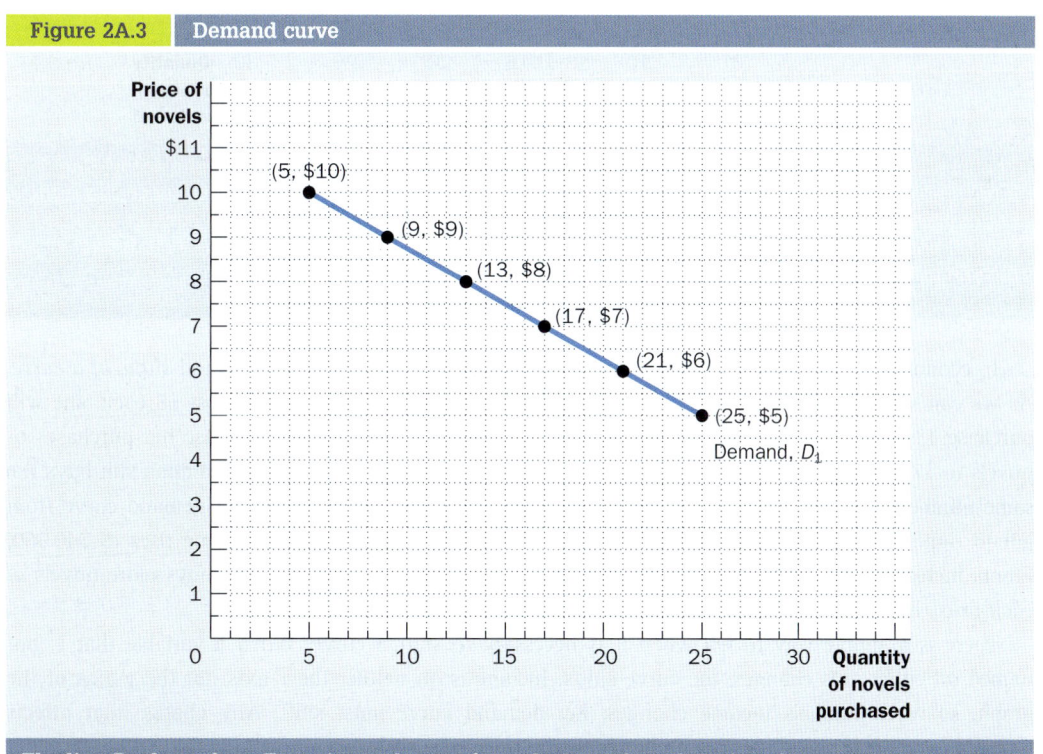

The line D_1 shows how Emma's purchases of novels depend on the price of novels when her income is held constant. Because the price and the quantity demanded are negatively related, the demand curve slopes downwards.

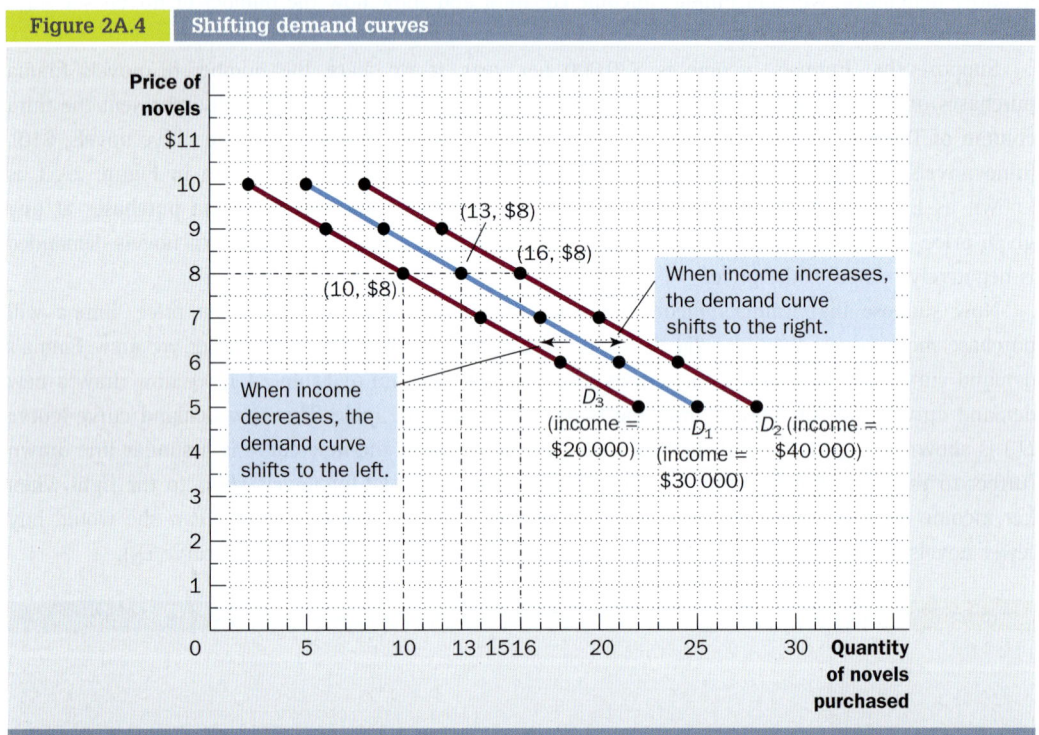

Figure 2A.4 | Shifting demand curves

The location of Emma's demand curve for novels depends on how much income she earns. The more she earns, the more novels she will purchase at any given price, and the further to the right her demand curve will lie. Curve D_1 represents Emma's original demand curve when her income is $30 000 per year. If her income rises to $40 000 per year, her demand curve shifts to D_2. If her income falls to $20 000 per year, her demand curve shifts to D_3.

In economics, it is important to distinguish between *movements along a curve* and *shifts of a curve*. As we can see from Figure 2A.3, if Emma earns $30 000 per year and novels cost $8 each, she will purchase 13 novels per year. If the price of novels falls to $7, Emma will increase her purchases of novels to 17 per year. The demand curve, however, stays fixed in the same place. Emma still buys the same number of novels *at each price*, but as the price falls she moves along her demand curve from left to right. In contrast, if the price of novels remains fixed at $8 but her income rises to $40 000, Emma increases her purchases of novels from 13 to 16 per year. Because Emma buys more novels *at each price*, her demand curve shifts out, as shown in Figure 2A.4.

There is a simple way to tell when it is necessary to shift a curve. When a variable that is not named on either axis changes, the curve shifts. Income is on neither the *x*-axis nor the *y*-axis of the graph, so when Emma's income changes, her demand curve must shift. Any change that affects Emma's purchasing habits besides a change in the price of novels will result in a shift in her demand curve. If, for instance, the public library closes and Emma must buy all the books she wants to read, she will demand more novels at each price and her demand curve will shift to the right. Or if the price of films falls and Emma spends more time at the pictures and less time reading, she will demand fewer novels at each price, and her demand curve will shift to the left. In contrast, when a variable on an axis of the graph changes, the curve does not shift. We read the change as a movement along the curve.

Slope and elasticity

One question we might want to ask about Emma is how much her purchasing habits respond to price. Look at the demand curve shown in Figure 2A.5. If this curve is very steep, Emma purchases nearly the same number of novels regardless of whether they are cheap or expensive. If this curve is much flatter, the number of novels Emma purchases is more sensitive to changes in the price. To answer questions about how much one variable responds to changes in another variable, we can use the concept of *slope*.

The slope of a line is the ratio of the vertical distance covered to the horizontal distance covered as we move along the line. This definition is usually written out in mathematical symbols as follows:

$$\text{Slope} = \frac{\Delta y}{\Delta x}$$

Figure 2A.5	Calculating the slope of a line

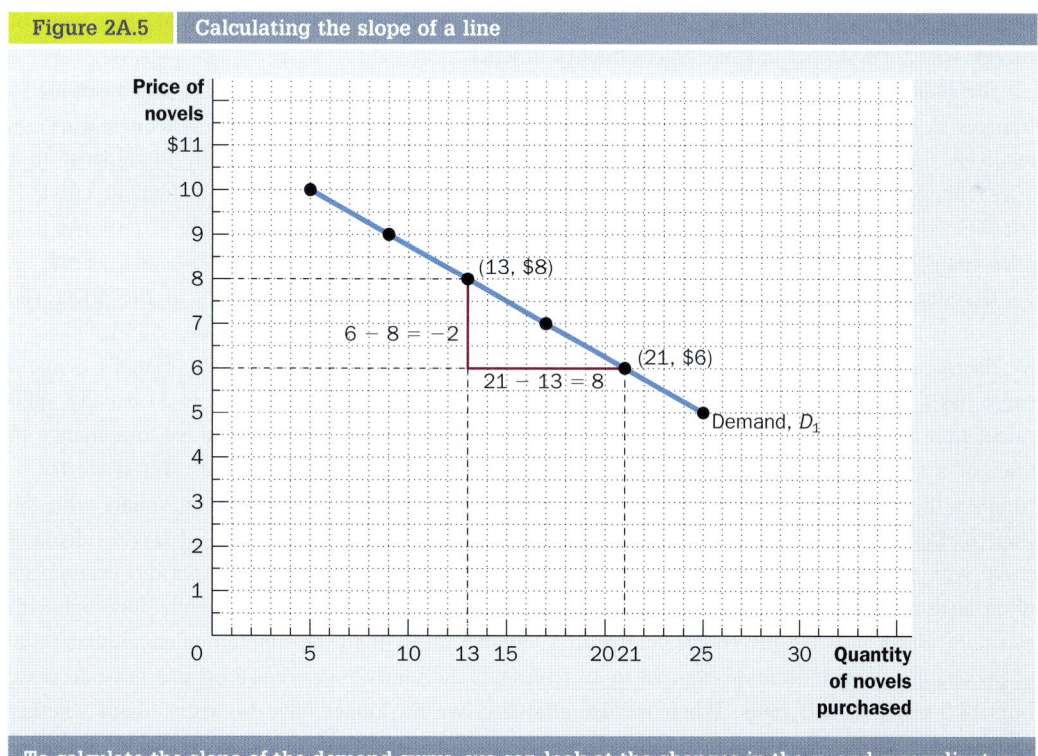

To calculate the slope of the demand curve, we can look at the changes in the x- and y-coordinates as we move from the point (21 novels, $6) to the point (13 novels, $8). The slope of the line is the ratio of the change in the y-coordinate (–2) to the change in the x-coordinate (+8), which equals –¼.

45

where the Greek letter Δ (delta) stands for the change in a variable. In other words, the slope of a line is equal to the 'rise' (change in y) divided by the 'run' (change in x). The slope will be a small positive number for a fairly flat upward-sloping line, a large positive number for a steep upward-sloping line, and a negative number for a downward-sloping line. A horizontal line has a slope of zero because in this case the y-variable never changes; a vertical line is defined to have an infinite slope because the y-variable can take any value without the x-variable changing at all.

What is the slope of Emma's demand curve for novels? First of all, because the curve slopes down, we know the slope will be negative. To calculate a numerical value for the slope, we must choose two points on the line. With Emma's income at \$30 000, she will purchase 21 novels at a price of \$6 or 13 novels at a price of \$8. When we apply the slope formula, we are concerned with the change between these two points; in other words, we are concerned with the difference between them, which lets us know that we will have to subtract one set of values from the other, as follows:

$$\text{Slope} = \frac{\text{first y-coordinate} - \text{second y-coordinate}}{\text{first x-coordinate} - \text{second x-coordinate}} = \frac{6-8}{21-13} = \frac{-2}{8} = \frac{-1}{4}$$

Figure 2A.5 shows graphically how this calculation works. Try calculating the slope of Emma's demand curve using two different points. You should get exactly the same result, $-\frac{1}{4}$. One of the properties of a straight line is that it has the same slope everywhere. This is not true of other types of curves, which are steeper in some places than in others.

The slope of Emma's demand curve tells us something about how responsive her purchases are to changes in the price. A small slope (a number close to zero) means that Emma's demand curve is relatively flat; in this case, she adjusts the number of novels she buys substantially in response to a price change. A larger slope (a number further from zero) means that Emma's demand curve is relatively steep; in this case, she adjusts the number of novels she buys only slightly in response to a price change.

The slope, however, is not a perfect measure of how much Emma responds to the price. The problem is that the slope depends on the units used to measure the variables on the x and y axes. If we measured the price of novels in cents instead of dollars, we would find that Emma's demand curve has a slope of $-100/4$ or -25, rather than $-\frac{1}{4}$ as we found originally. This is an equally valid calculation and tells us a useful fact – that Emma's demand for novels is less sensitive to a change in price of a certain number of cents than a change of the same number of dollars. Yet if we try to compare the slope of Emma's demand curve for novels with the price measured in dollars with the slope of Don's demand curve with the price measured in pesos or with the slope of David's demand curve with the price measured in pounds, great confusion will ensue. For this reason, economists often measure the sensitivity of one variable to changes in another variable not with slope but with *elasticity*, which uses the *percentage* change in a variable rather than the simple numerical magnitude of the change. A price decrease from \$8 to \$6 represents the same 25 per cent drop as a price decrease from 800 cents to 600 cents. When we use elasticity, we no longer have to worry about whether variables are always expressed in the same units because percentage changes are the same no matter what units are used. We examine elasticities in more detail in chapter 5.

Cause and effect

Economists often use graphs to advance an argument about how the economy works. In other words, they use graphs to argue about how one set of events causes another set of events. With a graph like the demand curve, there is no doubt about cause and effect. Because we are varying price and holding all other variables constant, we know that changes in the price of novels cause changes in the quantity Emma demands. Remember, however, that our demand curve came from a hypothetical example. When graphing data from the real world, it is often more difficult to establish how one variable affects another.

The first problem is that it is difficult to hold everything else constant when measuring how one variable affects another. If we are not able to hold variables constant, we might decide that one variable on our graph is causing changes in the other variable when actually those changes are caused by a third *omitted variable* not pictured on the graph. Even if we have identified the correct two variables to look at, we might run into a second problem – *reverse causality*. In other words, we might decide that A causes B when in fact B causes A. The omitted-variable and reverse-causality traps require us to proceed with caution when using graphs to draw conclusions about causes and effects.

Omitted variables

To see how omitting a variable can lead to a deceptive graph, let's consider an example. Imagine that the government, spurred by public concern about the large number of deaths from cancer, commissions an exhaustive study from Big Brother Statistical Services. Big Brother examines many of the items found in people's homes to see which of them are associated with the risk of cancer. Big Brother reports a strong relationship between two variables – the number of cigarette lighters that a household owns and the probability that someone in the household will develop cancer. Figure 2A.6 shows this relationship.

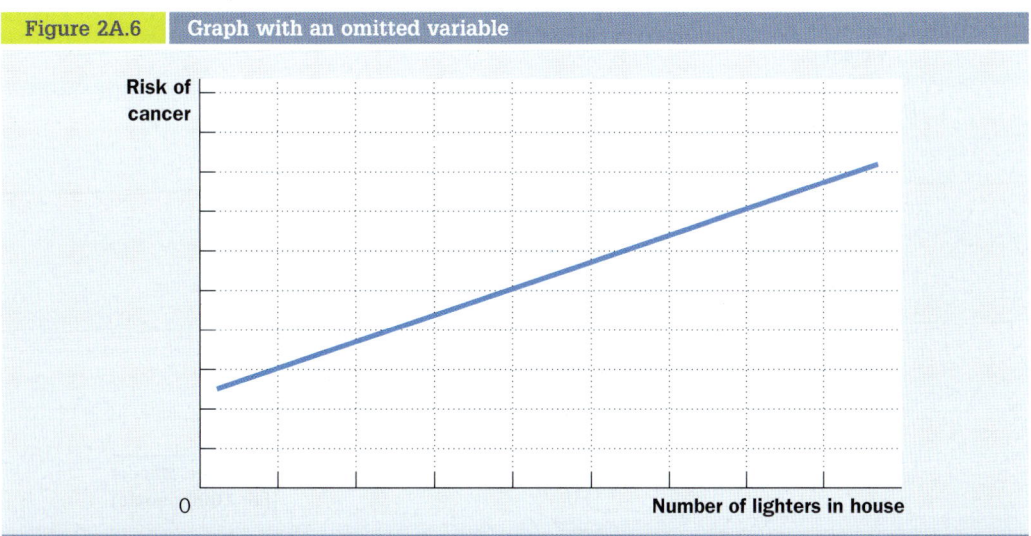

| Figure 2A.6 | Graph with an omitted variable |

The upward-sloping curve shows that households with more cigarette lighters are more likely to develop cancer. Yet we should not conclude that ownership of lighters causes cancer because the graph does not take into account the number of cigarettes smoked.

What should we make of this result? Big Brother advises a quick policy response. It recommends that the government discourage the ownership of cigarette lighters by taxing their sale. It also recommends that the government require warning labels: 'Big Brother has determined that this lighter is dangerous to your health'.

In judging the validity of Big Brother's analysis, one question is paramount. Has Big Brother held constant every relevant variable except the one under consideration? If the answer is no, the results are suspect. An easy explanation for Figure 2A.6 is that people who own more cigarette lighters are more likely to smoke cigarettes and that cigarettes, not lighters, cause cancer. If Figure 2A.6 does not hold constant the amount of smoking, it does not tell us the true effect of owning a cigarette lighter.

This story illustrates an important principle – when you see a graph being used to support an argument about cause and effect, it is important to ask whether the movements of an omitted variable could explain the results you see.

Reverse causality

Economists can also make mistakes about causality by misreading its direction. To see how this is possible, suppose the Association of Australian Anarchists commissions a study of crime in Australia and arrives at Figure 2A.7, which plots the number of violent crimes per thousand people in major cities against the number of police officers per thousand people. The anarchists note the curve's upward slope and argue that since police increase rather than decrease the amount of urban violence, law enforcement should be abolished.

If we could run a controlled experiment, we would avoid the danger of reverse causality. To run an experiment, we would set the number of police officers in different cities randomly and then examine

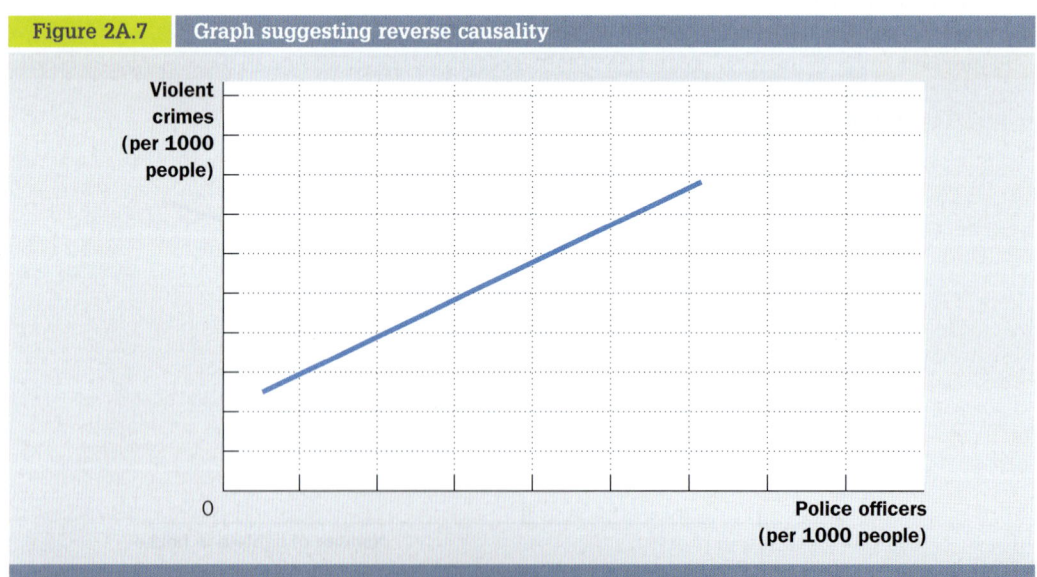

| Figure 2A.7 | Graph suggesting reverse causality |

The upward-sloping curve shows that cities with a higher concentration of police are more dangerous. Yet the graph does not tell us whether police cause crime or crime-plagued cities hire more police.

the correlation between police and crime. Figure 2A.7, however, is not based on such an experiment. We simply observe that more dangerous cities have more police officers. The explanation for this may be that more dangerous cities hire more police. In other words, rather than police causing crime, crime may cause police. Nothing in the graph itself allows us to establish the direction of causality.

It might seem that an easy way to determine the direction of causality is to examine which variable moves first. If we see crime increase and then the police force expand, we reach one conclusion. If we see the police force expand and then crime increase, we reach the other. Yet there is also a flaw with this approach – often people change their behaviour not in response to a change in their present conditions but in response to a change in their *expectations* of future conditions. A city that expects a major crime wave in the future, for instance, might well hire more police now. This problem is even easier to see in the case of babies and station wagons. Couples often buy a station wagon in anticipation of the birth of a child. The station wagon comes before the baby, but we would not want to conclude that the sale of station wagons causes the population to grow!

There is no exhaustive set of rules that specifies when it is appropriate to draw causal conclusions from graphs. Yet just keeping in mind that cigarette lighters don't cause cancer (omitted variable) and station wagons don't cause babies (reverse causality) will keep you from falling for many faulty economic arguments.

3

Interdependence and the gains from trade

Learning objectives

In this chapter you will:

- consider how everyone can benefit when people trade with one another
- learn the meaning of absolute advantage and comparative advantage
- see how comparative advantage explains the gains from trade
- apply the theory of comparative advantage to everyday life and national policy.

Consider your typical day. You wake up in the morning and you pour yourself juice from oranges grown in the Riverina District of New South Wales and coffee from beans grown in Indonesia. Over breakfast, you watch a news program broadcast from Sydney on your television made in China. You get dressed in clothes made from cotton grown in the United States and sewn in factories in Thailand. You drive to university in a car made of parts manufactured in more than a dozen countries around the world. Then you open up your economics textbook written by one author living in Massachusetts and two others in Melbourne, published by a company located in Melbourne, and printed on paper made from trees grown in Tasmania.

Every day you rely on many people from around the world, most of whom you have never met, to provide you with the goods and services that you enjoy. Such interdependence is possible because people trade with one another. Those people who provide you with goods and services are not acting out of generosity. Nor is some government agency directing them to satisfy your desires. Instead, people provide you and other consumers with the goods and services they produce because they get something in return.

In subsequent chapters we will examine how our economy coordinates the activities of millions of people with varying tastes and abilities. As a starting point for this analysis, here we consider the reasons for economic interdependence. One of the *Ten Lessons from Economics* highlighted in chapter 1 is that trade can make everyone better off. This lesson explains why people trade with their neighbours and why nations trade with other nations. In this chapter we examine this idea more closely. What exactly do people gain when they trade with one another? Why do people choose to become interdependent?

A parable for the modern economy

To understand why people choose to depend on others for goods and services and how this choice improves their lives, let's look at a simple economy – the economy inside a household. Imagine that there are two tasks that need to be completed in the household – cooking and laundry. And there are two people living in the house – Mitchell and Cameron – each of whom like to eat and to wear clean and neatly ironed clothes.

The gains from trade are most obvious if Mitchell can only cook and Cameron can only do the laundry. In one scenario, Mitchell and Cameron could choose to have nothing to do with each other. Mitchell would cook for himself and Cameron would wash and iron his own clothes. Mitchell's clothes would never be cleaned. But after several months of eating cold meat and biscuits, Cameron might decide that self-sufficiency is not all it's cracked up to be. Mitchell, whose clothing could not have a worse odour, would be likely to agree. It is easy to see that trade would allow them to enjoy greater variety – each could eat well and wear clean clothes.

Although this scene illustrates very simply how everyone can benefit from trade, the gains would be similar if Mitchell and Cameron were each capable of doing the other task, but only at great cost. Suppose, for example, that Mitchell is able to wash and iron clothes, but that he is not very good at it. Similarly, suppose that Cameron is able to cook but has not had the experience and so can prepare only a few basic dishes. In this case, it is easy to see that Mitchell and Cameron can each benefit by specialising in what he does best and then trading with the other.

The gains from trade are less obvious, however, when one person is better at producing *every* good. For example, suppose that Mitchell is better at cooking *and* better at washing and ironing than Cameron. In this case, should Mitchell choose to remain self-sufficient? Or is there still reason for him to trade with Cameron? To answer this question, we need to look more closely at the factors that affect such a decision.

Production possibilities

Suppose that Mitchell and Cameron each have 12 spare hours a week to work on household tasks and can devote this time to cooking, laundry or a combination of the two. Table 3.1 shows the amount of time each person requires to produce one unit of each good – a decent meal and a basket of clean clothes. Cameron can wash and iron a basket of clothes in four hours and cook a meal in two hours. Mitchell, who is more productive in both activities, needs only half an hour to cook a meal and can wash and iron a basket of clothes in three hours.

Panel (a) of Figure 3.1 illustrates the amounts of laundry and cooking that Cameron can produce. If Cameron devotes all 12 hours of his time to laundry, he cleans three baskets of clothes but does not cook. If he devotes all his time to cooking, he produces six meals and washes no clothes. If Cameron spends four hours doing laundry and eight hours cooking, he cooks four meals and washes and irons one basket of clothes. The figure shows these three possible outcomes and all others in between.

Table 3.1 The production opportunities of Cameron and Mitchell

	Hours needed to make:		Maximum amount produced in 12 hours:	
	1 meal	1 basket	Meals	Baskets
Cameron	2	4	6	3
Mitchell	½	3	24	4

Figure 3.1   The production possibilities frontier

Panel (a) shows the combinations of meals and laundry that Cameron can produce. Panel (b) shows the combinations of meals and laundry that Mitchell can produce. Both production possibilities frontiers are derived from table 3.1 and the assumption that Cameron and Mitchell each work 12 hours per week on domestic chores.

The graph (a) is Cameron's production possibilities frontier. As we discussed in chapter 2, a production possibilities frontier shows the various mixes of output that an economy can produce. It illustrates one of the *Ten Lessons from Economics* in chapter 1 – people face trade-offs. Here Cameron faces a trade-off between time spent cooking and doing laundry. You may recall that the production possibilities frontier in chapter 2 was drawn bowed out; in this case, the trade-off between the two goods depends on the amounts being produced. Here, however, Cameron's 'technology' (as summarised in Table 3.1) allows him to switch between one task and the other at a constant rate. In this case, the production possibilities frontier is a straight line.

Panel (b) of Figure 3.1 shows the production possibilities frontier for Mitchell. If Mitchell devotes all 12 hours of his time to cooking, he produces 24 meals but does no laundry. If he devotes all his time to laundry, he washes four baskets but cooks no meals. If Mitchell divides his time equally, spending six hours on each activity, he cooks 12 meals and washes two baskets of clothes per week. Once again, the production possibilities frontier shows all the possible outcomes.

If Mitchell and Cameron choose to go it alone, rather than trade with each other, then each consumes exactly what he produces. In this case, the production possibilities frontier is also the consumption possibilities frontier. That is, without trade, Figure 3.1 shows the possible combinations of cooking and laundry that Mitchell and Cameron can each produce and then consume.

Although these production possibilities frontiers are useful in showing the trade-offs that Mitchell and Cameron face, they do not tell us what they will actually choose to do. To determine their choices, we need to know the tastes of Mitchell and Cameron. Let's suppose they choose the combinations identified by points A and B in Figure 3.1 – Cameron produces and consumes four meals and washes one basket while Mitchell produces and consumes 12 meals and washes two baskets of clothing.

Specialisation and trade

After several months of combination B, Mitchell gets an idea and talks to Cameron:

Mitchell: Cameron, have I got a deal for you! I know how to improve life for both of us. I think you should stop cooking altogether and devote all your time to laundry. According to my calculations, if you work 12 hours a week washing and ironing, you'll get three baskets done every week. If you do one basket of laundry for me each week and an extra one every second week, then I'll cook you five meals a week. In the end, you'll be able to eat cooked meals more often and you will get your clothes cleaner as well. Indeed, another half basket. If you go along with my plan, you'll eat well and look better! *[To illustrate his point, Mitchell shows Cameron panel (a) of* Figure 3.2.]

Cameron: *(sounding sceptical)* That seems like a good deal for me. But I don't understand why you are offering it. If the deal is so good for me, it can't be good for you too.

Mitchell: Oh, but it is! If I spend nine hours a week cooking and three hours doing laundry, I'll make 18 meals and also have time spare to wash another basket. After I give you five meals in exchange for the extra basket-and-a-half you wash and iron, I'll be able to eat 13 meals at home but I'll have more clean shirts, trousers and, most importantly, socks and underwear. In the end, I will be much happier than I am now. *[He points out panel (b) of* Figure 3.2.]

Cameron: I don't know ... This sounds too good to be true. I don't want you coming back to me next week and complaining about having to do all the cooking.

Mitchell: It's really not as complicated as it seems at first. Here – I've summarised my proposal for you in a simple table. *[Mitchell hands Cameron a copy of Table 3.2.]*

Cameron: (*after pausing to study the table*) These calculations seem correct, but I'm puzzled. How can this deal make us both better off?

Mitchell: We can both benefit because trade allows each of us to specialise in doing what we do best. You will spend more time doing laundry and less time cooking. I will spend more time cooking and less time washing and ironing. I like to iron my clothes but I am, you must admit, a much better cook. As a result of specialisation and trade, each of us can consume more of the great meals that I cook and wear cleaner clothes without taking more time out of our other activities. What could be better?

Figure 3.2   **How trade expands the set of consumption opportunities**

The proposed trade between Cameron and Mitchell offers each a combination of meals and baskets of clean clothes that would be impossible in the absence of trade. In panel (a), Cameron gets to consume at point A* rather than point A. In panel (b), Mitchell gets to consume at point B* rather than point B. Trade allows each to consume more meals and have more clean clothes.

Table 3.2   **The gains from trade: A summary**

	Without trade:			With trade:	
	Production and consumption	Production	Trade	Consumption	Gains from trade
Cameron	4 meals	0 meals	Gets 5 meals	5 meals	1 meal
	1 basket	3 baskets	for 1½ baskets	1½ baskets	½ basket
Mitchell	12 meals	18 meals	Gives 5 meals	13 meals	1 meal
	2 baskets	1 basket	for 1½ baskets	2½ baskets	½ basket

Draw an example of a production possibilities frontier for Robinson Crusoe, a shipwrecked sailor who spends his time gathering coconuts and catching fish. Does this frontier limit Crusoe's consumption of coconuts and fish if he lives by himself? Does he face the same limits if he can trade with native residents on the island?

The principle of comparative advantage

Mitchell's explanation of the gains from trade, though correct, poses a puzzle – if Mitchell is better at both cooking and laundry, how can Cameron ever specialise in doing what he does best? Cameron doesn't seem to do anything best. To solve this puzzle, we need to look at the principle of *comparative advantage.*

As a first step in developing this principle, consider the following question. In our example, who does the laundry at lower cost – Cameron or Mitchell? There are two possible answers and in these two answers lie both the solution to our puzzle and the key to understanding the gains from trade.

Absolute advantage

One way to answer the question about the cost of doing the laundry is to compare the inputs required by the two housemates. Economists use the term **absolute advantage** when comparing the productivity of one person, firm or nation with that of another. The producer that requires a smaller quantity of inputs to produce a good is said to have an absolute advantage in producing that good.

In our example, time is the only input, so we can determine absolute advantage by looking at how much time each type of production takes. Mitchell has an absolute advantage both in laundry and cooking, because he requires less time than Cameron to produce a unit of either good. Mitchell needs only three hours to do a basket of laundry, whereas Cameron needs four hours. Similarly, Mitchell needs only half an hour to cook a meal whereas Cameron needs two hours. Based on this information, we can conclude that Mitchell has the lower cost of laundry and a lower cost of cooking, if we measure cost by the quantity of inputs.

absolute advantage
the comparison among producers of a good according to their productivity

▸ absolute advantage

Opportunity cost and comparative advantage

There is another way to look at the cost of laundry. Rather than comparing inputs required, we can compare the opportunity costs. Recall from chapter 1 that the opportunity cost of some item is what we give up to get that item. In our example, we assumed that Cameron and Mitchell each spend 12 hours a week on household tasks. Time spent doing laundry, therefore, takes away from time available for cooking. When reallocating time between the two goods, Mitchell and Cameron give up units of one good to produce units of the other good, moving along their production possibility frontiers. The opportunity cost measures the trade-off between the two goods that each faces.

Let's first consider Mitchell's opportunity cost. According to Table 3.1, doing a basket of clothes takes Mitchell three hours of work. When Mitchell spends that three hours doing laundry, he spends three hours less cooking. Because Mitchell needs only half an hour to produce one meal, three hours of work would yield six meals. Hence, Mitchell's opportunity cost of one basket is six meals.

Table 3.3 The opportunity cost of meals and baskets of clean clothes		
	Opportunity cost of one:	
	Meal (in terms of baskets given up)	**Basket (in terms of meals given up)**
Cameron	½	2
Mitchell	⅙	6

Mitchell's production possibilities frontier reflects this opportunity cost – the downward-sloping line in panel (b) of Figure 3.1 has a slope ('rise over run') equal to –6.

Now consider Cameron's opportunity cost. Washing and ironing one basket takes him four hours. Because he needs two hours to cook a meal, four hours would yield two meals. Hence, Cameron's opportunity cost of doing one basket of laundry is two meals. Cameron's production possibilities frontier in panel (a) of Figure 3.1 reflects this opportunity cost by having a slope of –2.

Table 3.3 shows the opportunity cost of cooking and laundry for Cameron and Mitchell. Notice that the opportunity cost of cooking is the inverse of the opportunity cost of laundry. Because one clean basket of laundry costs Mitchell six meals, one meal costs Mitchell one-sixth of a basket of laundry. Similarly, because doing one basket of laundry costs Cameron two meals, one meal costs Cameron half a basket of laundry.

Economists use the term **comparative advantage** when describing the opportunity cost of two producers. The producer who has the smaller opportunity cost of producing a good is said to have a comparative advantage in producing that good. In our example, Cameron has a lower opportunity cost of laundry than Mitchell (two versus six meals). Mitchell has a lower opportunity cost of cooking than Cameron (1/6 rather than ½ of a basket). Thus, Cameron has a comparative advantage in laundry, and Mitchell has a comparative advantage in cooking.

Although it is possible for one person to have an absolute advantage in both goods (as Mitchell does in our example), it is impossible for the same person to have a comparative advantage in both goods. Because the opportunity cost of one good is the inverse of the opportunity cost of the other, if a person's opportunity cost of one good is relatively high, his opportunity cost of the other good must be relatively low. Comparative advantage reflects the relative opportunity cost. Unless two people have exactly the same opportunity cost, one person will have a comparative advantage in one good and the other person will have a comparative advantage in the other good.

Comparative advantage and trade

Differences in opportunity cost and comparative advantage create the gains from trade. When each person specialises in producing the good for which he or she has a comparative advantage, total production in the economy rises. This increase in the size of the economic pie can be used to make everyone better off.

In our example, Cameron spends more time doing laundry and Mitchell spends more time cooking meals. As a result the total production of laundry rises from 3 to 4 baskets and the total production of cooked meals rises from 16 to 18. Mitchell and Cameron can share the benefits of this increased production.

comparative advantage
the comparison among producers of a good according to their opportunity cost

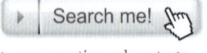

▸ comparative advantage

We can also look at the gains from trade in terms of the price that each person pays the other. Because Mitchell and Cameron have different opportunity costs, they can both get a 'bargain'. That is, each benefits from trade by obtaining a good at a price that is lower than his opportunity cost of that good.

Consider the proposed deal from Cameron's viewpoint. Cameron gets five meals in exchange for cleaning an extra one-and-a-half baskets of laundry. In other words, Cameron buys each meal for a price of 3/10 of a basket of laundry. This price of a meal is lower than his opportunity cost of cooking, which is 1/2 a basket. Thus, Cameron benefits from the deal because he gets to buy meals at a good price.

Now consider the deal from Mitchell's viewpoint. Mitchell buys a basket of laundry for a price of just over three meals. This price of laundry is lower than his opportunity cost of laundry, which is six meals. Thus, Mitchell benefits because he gets to buy a laundry service at a good price.

These benefits arise because each person concentrates on the activity for which he has the lower opportunity cost – Cameron spends more time doing laundry and Mitchell spends more time cooking. As a result, the total production of clean clothing and the total production of meals both rise, and Cameron and Mitchell share the benefits of this increased production.

The moral of the story of Mitchell and Cameron should now be clear – *trade can benefit everyone in society because it allows people to specialise in activities in which they have a comparative advantage.*

Robinson Crusoe can gather 10 coconuts or catch one fish per hour. His friend Friday can gather 30 coconuts or catch two fish per hour. What is Crusoe's opportunity cost of catching one fish? What is Friday's? Who has an absolute advantage in catching fish? Who has a comparative advantage in catching fish?

Applications of comparative advantage

The principle of comparative advantage explains interdependence and the gains from trade. Because interdependence is so prevalent in the modern world, the principle of comparative advantage has many applications. Here are two examples, one fanciful and one of great practical importance.

Should Roger Federer mow his own lawn?

Roger Federer is a great athlete. He is one of the best tennis players in the world and has 16 grand slam titles – more than any other male tennis player. Very likely, he is better at other activities, too. For example, Roger can probably mow his lawn faster than anyone else. But just because he can mow his lawn fast, does this mean he *should*?

To answer this question, we can use the concepts of opportunity cost and comparative advantage. Let's say that Roger can mow his lawn in two hours. In that same two hours, he could film a television commercial for sports shoes and earn $1 000 000. In contrast, Becky, the girl next door, can mow Roger's lawn in four hours. In that same four hours, she could work at Coles supermarket and earn $40.

In this example, Roger's opportunity cost of mowing the lawn is $1 000 000, and Becky's opportunity cost is $40. Roger has an absolute advantage in mowing lawns because he can do the work in less time. Yet Becky has a comparative advantage in mowing lawns because she has the lower opportunity cost.

The gains from trade in this example are tremendous. Rather than mowing his own lawn, Roger should make the commercial and hire Becky to mow the lawn. As long as he pays her more than $40 and less than $1 000 000, both of them are better off.

Should a country trade with other countries?

imports
goods produced abroad and sold domestically

exports
goods produced domestically and sold abroad

Just as individuals can benefit from specialisation and trade with one another, as Mitchell and Cameron did, so can populations of people in different countries. Many of the goods that Australians enjoy are produced abroad and many of the goods produced in Australia are sold abroad. Goods produced abroad and sold domestically are called **imports**. Goods produced domestically and sold abroad are called **exports**.

To see how countries can benefit from trade, suppose there are two countries, Australia and Japan, and two goods, food and cars. Imagine that the two countries produce cars equally well – an Australian worker and a Japanese worker can each produce one car per month. In contrast, because Australia has more and better land, it is better at producing food – an Australian worker can produce two tonnes of food per month, whereas a Japanese worker can produce only one tonne of food per month.

The principle of comparative advantage states that each good should be produced by the country that has the smaller opportunity cost of producing that good. Because the opportunity cost of a car is two tonnes of food in Australia but only one tonne of food in Japan, Japan has a comparative advantage in producing cars. Japan should produce more cars than it wants for its own use and export some of them to Australia. Similarly, because the opportunity cost of a tonne of food is one car in Japan but only half a car in Australia, Australia has a comparative advantage in producing food. Australia should produce more food than it wants to consume and export some of it to Japan. Through specialisation and trade, both countries can have more food and more cars.

In reality, of course, the issues involved in trade among nations are more complex than this example suggests, as we will see in chapter 9. Most important among these issues is that each country has many citizens with different interests. International trade can make some individuals worse off, even as it makes the country as a whole better off. When Australia exports food and imports cars, the impact on an Australian farmer is not the same as the impact on an Australian car worker. Yet contrary to the opinions sometimes voiced by politicians and political commentators, international trade is not like war, in which some countries win and others lose. Trade allows all countries to achieve greater prosperity.

IN THE NEWS . . .

WHO HAS A COMPARATIVE ADVANTAGE IN SLAYING OGRES?

A decade ago, no one would have asked which nation has a comparative advantage in slaying ogres. But technology is changing the goods and services that are traded between countries.

Ogre to slay? Outsource it to Chinese
by David Barboza

Fuzhou, China – One of China's newest factories operates here in the basement of an old warehouse. Posters of World of Warcraft and Magic Land hang above a corps of young people glued to their computer screens, pounding away at their keyboards in the latest hustle for money.

The people working at this clandestine locale are 'gold farmers'. Every day, in 12-hour shifts, they 'play' computer games by killing onscreen monsters and winning battles, harvesting artificial gold coins and other virtual goods as rewards that, as it turns out, can be transformed into real cash.

That is because, from Seoul to San Francisco, affluent online gamers who lack the time and patience to work their way up to the higher levels of gamedom are willing to pay the young Chinese here to play the early rounds for them.

'For 12 hours a day, 7 days a week, my colleagues and I are killing monsters', said a 23-year-old gamer who works here in this makeshift factory and goes by the online code name Wandering. 'I make about $250 a month, which is pretty good compared with the other jobs I've had. And I can play games all day.'

He and his comrades have created yet another new business out of cheap Chinese labor. They are tapping into the fast-growing world of 'massively multiplayer online games', which involve role playing and often revolve around fantasy or warfare in medieval kingdoms or distant galaxies …

For the Chinese in game-playing factories like these, though, it is not all fun and games. These workers have strict quotas and are supervised by bosses who equip them with computers, software and Internet connections to thrash online trolls, gnomes and ogres.

As they grind through the games, they accumulate virtual currency that is valuable to game players around the world. The games allow players to trade currency to other players, who can then use it to buy better armor, amulets, magic spells and other accoutrements to climb to higher levels or create more powerful characters.

The Internet is now filled with classified advertisements from small companies – many of them here in China – auctioning for real money their powerful figures, called avatars …

'It's unimaginable how big this is', says Chen Yu, 27, who employs 20 full-time gamers here in Fuzhou. 'They say that in some of these popular games, 40 or 50 percent of the players are actually Chinese farmers.'

fyi

The legacy of Adam Smith and David Ricardo

Economists have long understood the principle of comparative advantage. Here is how the great economist Adam Smith put the argument:

> It is a maxim of every prudent master of a family, never to attempt to make at home what it will cost him more to make than to buy. The tailor does not attempt to make his own shoes, but buys them off the shoemaker. The shoemaker does not attempt to make his own clothes but employs a tailor. The farmer attempts to make neither the one nor the other, but employs those different artificers. All of them find it for their interest to employ their whole industry in a way in which they have some advantage over their neighbours, and to purchase with a part of its produce, or what is the same thing, with the price of part of it, whatever else they have occasion for.

This quotation is from Smith's 1776 book *An Inquiry into the Nature and Causes of the Wealth of Nations.* This book was a landmark in the analysis of trade and economic interdependence. Many economists consider Smith to be the founder of modern economics.

Smith's book inspired David Ricardo, a millionaire stockbroker, to become an economist. In his 1817 book *Principles of Political Economy and Taxation*, Ricardo developed the principle of comparative advantage as we know it today. His defence of free trade was not a mere academic exercise. Ricardo put his economic beliefs to work as a member of the British Parliament, where he opposed the Corn Laws, which restricted the import of grain.

David Ricardo

The conclusions of Adam Smith and David Ricardo on the gains from trade have held up well

>>

over time. Although economists often disagree on questions of policy, they are united in their support of free trade. Moreover, the central argument for free trade has not changed much in the past two centuries. Even though the field of economics has broadened its scope and refined its theories since the time of Smith and Ricardo, economists' opposition to trade restrictions is still based largely on the principle of comparative advantage.

Q Suppose that the world's fastest typist happens to be trained in brain surgery. Should that person type for herself or hire a secretary? Explain.

Conclusion

You should now understand more fully the benefits of living in an interdependent economy. When Chinese companies buy Australian iron ore, when residents of Tasmania buy a mango grown in the Northern Territory, and when you spend Friday night babysitting for neighbours rather than going out, the same economic forces are at work. The principle of comparative advantage shows that trade can make everyone better off.

Having seen why interdependence is desirable, you might naturally ask how it is possible. How do free societies coordinate the diverse activities of all the people involved in their economies? What ensures that goods and services will go from those who should be producing them to those who should be consuming them?

In a world with only two people, such as Mitchell and Cameron, the answer is simple – these two people can directly bargain and allocate resources between themselves. In the real world with millions of people, the answer is less obvious. We take up this issue in the next chapter, where we see that free societies allocate resources through the market forces of supply and demand.

Summary

- Each person consumes goods and services produced by many other people both in our country and around the world. Interdependence and trade are desirable because they allow everyone to enjoy a greater quantity and variety of goods and services.
- There are two ways to compare the ability of two people in producing a good. The person who can produce the good with the smaller quantity of inputs is said to have an *absolute advantage* in producing the good. The person who has the smaller opportunity cost of producing the good is said to have a *comparative advantage*. The gains from trade are based on comparative advantage, not absolute advantage.
- Trade makes everyone better off because it allows people to specialise in those activities in which they have a comparative advantage.
- The principle of comparative advantage applies to countries as well as to people. Economists use the principle of comparative advantage to advocate free trade among countries.

Key concepts

absolute advantage   exports
comparative advantage   imports

Questions for review

1   Explain how absolute advantage and comparative advantage differ.
2   Give an example in which one person has an absolute advantage in doing something but another person has a comparative advantage.
3   Is absolute advantage or comparative advantage more important for trade? Explain your answer using the example in your answer to question 2.
4   Will a nation tend to export or import goods for which it has a comparative advantage? Explain.
5   Why do economists oppose policies that restrict trade among nations?

Problems and applications

1   Consider Cameron and Mitchell from our example in this chapter. Explain why Cameron's opportunity cost of producing one basket of clean clothing is two meals. Explain why Mitchell's opportunity cost of producing one meal is 1/6 of a washed and ironed basket of clothing.
2   Maria can read 20 pages of economics in an hour. She can also read 50 pages of sociology in an hour. She spends five hours per day studying.
    a   Draw Maria's production possibilities frontier for reading economics and sociology.
    b   What is Maria's opportunity cost of reading 100 pages of sociology?
3   Australian and Japanese workers can each produce four cars a year. An Australian worker can produce 10 tonnes of grain a year, whereas a Japanese worker can produce five tonnes of grain a year. To keep things simple, assume that each country has 100 million workers.
    a   For this situation, construct a table similar to Table 3.1.
    b   Graph the production possibilities frontier of the Australian and Japanese economies.

  c   For Australia, what is the opportunity cost of a car? Of grain? For Japan, what is the opportunity cost of a car? Of grain? Put this information in a table similar to Table 3.3.

  d   Which country has an absolute advantage in producing cars? In producing grain?

  e   Which country has a comparative advantage in producing cars? In producing grain?

  f   Without trade, half of each country's workers produce cars and half produce grain. What quantities of cars and grain does each country produce?

  g   Starting from a position without trade, give an example in which trade makes each country better off.

4   Monica and Rachel are flatmates. They spend most of their time working, but they leave some time for their favourite activities – making pizza and fine coffee. Monica takes five minutes to make a pot of coffee and half an hour to make a pizza. Rachel takes 15 minutes to make a pot of coffee and one hour to make a pizza.

  a   What is each flatmate's opportunity cost of making a pizza? Who has the absolute advantage in making pizza? Who has the comparative advantage in making pizza?

  b   If Rachel and Monica trade foods with each other, who will trade away pizza in exchange for coffee?

  c   The price of pizza can be expressed in terms of pots of coffee. What is the highest price at which pizza can be traded that would make both flatmates better off? What is the lowest price? Explain.

5   Suppose that there are 10 million workers in South Korea and that each of these workers can produce either two cars or 30 bags of wheat in a year.

  a   What is the opportunity cost of producing a car in South Korea? What is the opportunity cost of producing a bag of wheat in South Korea? Explain the relationship between the opportunity costs of the two goods.

  b   Draw South Korea's production possibilities frontier. If South Korea chooses to consume 10 million cars, how much wheat can it consume without trade? Label this point on the production possibilities frontier.

  c   Now suppose that Thailand offers to buy 10 million cars from South Korea in exchange for 20 bags of wheat per car. If South Korea continues to consume 10 million cars, how much wheat does this deal allow South Korea to consume? Label this point on your diagram. Should South Korea accept the deal?

6   Consider a professor who is writing a book. The professor can both write the chapters and gather the needed data faster than anyone else at her university. Still, she pays a student to collect data at the library. Is this sensible? Explain.

7   England and Scotland both produce scones and jumpers. Suppose that an English worker can produce 50 scones per hour or one jumper per hour. Suppose that a Scottish worker can produce 40 scones per hour or two jumpers per hour.

  a   Which country has the absolute advantage in the production of each good? Which country has the comparative advantage?

  b   If England and Scotland decide to trade, which commodity will Scotland trade to England? Explain.

  c   If a Scottish worker could produce only one jumper per hour, would Scotland still gain from trade? Would England still gain from trade? Explain.

8 The following table describes the production possibilities of two cities in the country of Footballia:

	Maroon shirts per worker per hour	Blue shirts per worker per hour
Brisbane	3	3
Sydney	2	1

    a Without trade, what is the price of blue shirts (in terms of maroon shirts) in Brisbane? What is the price in Sydney?

    b Which city has an absolute advantage in the production of each colour shirt? Which city has a comparative advantage in the production of each colour shirt?

    c If the cities trade with each other, which colour shirt will each export?

    d What is the range of prices at which trade can occur?

9 Suppose that all goods can be produced with fewer worker hours in Germany than in France.

    a In what sense is the cost of all goods lower in Germany than in France?

    b In what sense is the cost of some goods lower in France?

    c If Germany and France traded with each other, would both countries be better off as a result? Explain in the context of your answers to parts (a) and (b).

10 Are the following statements true or false? Explain in each case.

    a 'Two countries can achieve gains from trade even if one of the countries has an absolute advantage in the production of all goods.'

    b 'Certain very talented people have a comparative advantage in everything they do.'

    c 'If a certain trade is good for one person, it can't be good for the other one.'

Search me!

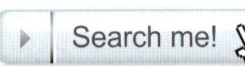

When accessing information about economics use the following keywords in any combinations you require:

- absolute advantage
- comparative advantage

CourseMate

For more multimedia resources and activities on economics, visit the Economics CourseMate website.

PART TWO
Supply and demand I: How markets work

4

The market forces of supply and demand

Learning objectives

In this chapter you will:

- learn what a competitive market is
- examine what determines the demand for a good in a competitive market
- examine what determines the supply of a good in a competitive market
- see how supply and demand together set the price of a good and the quantity sold
- consider the key role of prices in allocating scarce resources in market economies.

When a cyclone hits Queensland, the price of bananas rises in supermarkets throughout the country. On Tuesdays, movie theatres discount tickets. When a war breaks out in the Middle East, the price of petrol in Australia and elsewhere rises, and the price of a used Ford Falcon falls. What do these events have in common? They all show the workings of supply and demand.

Supply and *demand* are the two words that economists use most often – and for good reason. Supply and demand are the forces that make market economies work. They determine the quantity of each good produced and the price at which it is sold. If you want to know how any event or policy will affect the economy, you must think first about how it will affect supply and demand.

This chapter introduces the theory of supply and demand. It considers how buyers and sellers behave and how they interact with one another. It shows how supply and demand determine prices in a market economy and how prices, in turn, allocate the economy's scarce resources.

Markets and competition

The terms *supply* and *demand* refer to the behaviour of people as they interact with one another in competitive markets. Before discussing how buyers and sellers behave, let's first consider more fully what we mean by the terms *market* and *competition*.

What is a market?

A **market** is a group of buyers and sellers of a particular good or service. The buyers as a group determine the demand for the product and the sellers as a group determine the supply of the product. Before discussing how buyers and sellers behave, let's first consider more fully what we mean by the terms *market* and *competition*.

market
a group of buyers and sellers of a particular good or service

Markets take many forms. Sometimes markets are highly organised, such as the sharemarket or the market for some agricultural commodities, like the Sydney fish market. In these markets, buyers and sellers meet at a specific time and place, where an auctioneer helps set prices and arrange sales.

More often, markets are less organised. For example, consider the market for ice-cream in a particular town. Buyers of ice-cream do not meet together at any one time. The sellers of ice-cream are in different locations and offer somewhat different products. There is no auctioneer calling out the price of ice-cream. Each seller posts a price for an ice-cream and each buyer decides how much ice-cream to buy at each store. Nonetheless, these consumers and producers of ice-cream are closely connected. The ice-cream buyers are choosing from the various ice-cream sellers to satisfy their cravings and the ice-cream sellers are all trying to appeal to the same ice-cream buyers to make their businesses successful. Even though it is not as organised, the group of ice-cream buyers and ice-cream sellers forms a market.

What is competition?

The market for ice-cream, like most markets in the economy, is highly competitive. Each buyer knows that there are several sellers from which to choose. Each seller is aware that their product is similar to that offered by other sellers. As a result, the price of ice cream and the quantity of ice cream sold are not determined by any single buyer or seller. Rather, price and quantity are determined by all buyers and sellers as they interact in the marketplace.

Economists use the term **competitive market** to describe a market in which there are so many buyers and so many sellers that each has a negligible impact on the market price. Each seller has limited control over the price because other sellers are offering similar products. A seller has little

competitive market
a market in which there are many buyers and many sellers so that each has a negligible impact on the market price

reason to charge less than the going price and if more is charged then buyers will make their purchases elsewhere. Similarly, no single buyer of ice-cream can influence the price of ice-cream because each buyer purchases only a small amount.

In this chapter, we assume that markets are *perfectly competitive*. To reach this highest form of competition, a market must have two characteristics:

1 The goods offered for sale are all exactly the same.
2 The buyers and sellers are so numerous that no single buyer or seller has any influence over the market price.

Because buyers and sellers in a perfectly competitive market must accept the price the market determines, they are said to be *price takers*. At the market price, buyers can buy all they want and sellers can sell all they want.

There are some markets in which the assumption of perfect competition applies perfectly. In the international wheat market, for example, there are thousands of farmers who sell wheat and millions of consumers who use wheat and wheat products. Because no single buyer or seller can influence the price of wheat, each takes the price as given.

Not all goods and services, however, are sold in perfectly competitive markets. Some markets have only one seller and this seller sets the price. Such a seller is called a *monopoly*. Your local water company, for instance, may be a monopoly. Residents of your town probably have only one company from which to buy tap water. Still other markets fall between the extremes of perfect competition and monopoly.

Despite the diversity of market types we find in the world, assuming perfect competition is a useful simplification and, therefore, a natural place to start. Perfectly competitive markets are easier to analyse because everyone participating in the market takes the price as given by market conditions. Moreover, because some degree of competition is present in most markets, many of the lessons that we learn by studying supply and demand under perfect competition apply in more complicated markets as well.

> **Q** What is a market? What are the characteristics of a perfectly competitive market?

Demand

We begin our study of markets by examining the behaviour of buyers. To focus our thinking, let's keep in mind a particular good – ice-cream.

The demand curve: The relationship between price and quantity demanded

quantity demanded
the amount of a good that buyers are willing and able to purchase

The **quantity demanded** of any good is the amount of the good that buyers are willing and able to purchase. As we will see, many things determine the quantity demanded of any good, but in our analysis of how markets work, one determinant plays a central role – the price of the good. If the price of ice-cream rose to $20 per scoop, you would buy less ice-cream. You might buy frozen yoghurt instead. If the price of ice-cream fell to $0.20 per scoop, you would buy more. Because the quantity demanded falls as the price rises and rises as the price falls, we say that the quantity demanded is *negatively related* to the price. This relationship between price and quantity demanded is true for most goods in the economy and, in fact, is so pervasive that economists call it the **law of demand**. Other things being equal, when the price of a good rises, the quantity demanded of the good falls and when the price falls, the quantity demanded rises.

Table 4.1 shows how many ice-creams Catherine buys each month at different prices of ice-cream. If ice-creams are free, Catherine eats 12 ice-creams per month. At $0.50 each, Catherine buys

law of demand
the claim that, other things being equal, the quantity demanded of a good falls when the price of the good rises

Table 4.1 Catherine's demand schedule

Price of an ice-cream	Quantity of ice-creams demanded
$0.00	12
0.50	10
1.00	8
1.50	6
2.00	4
2.50	2
3.00	0

Figure 4.1 Catherine's demand curve

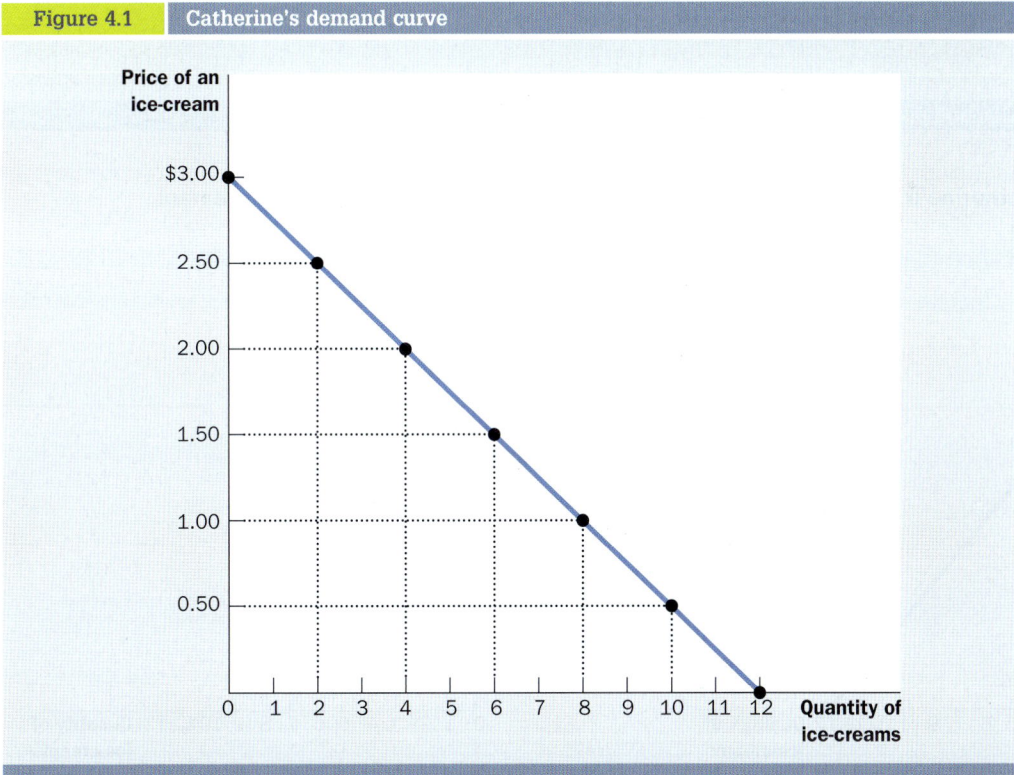

This demand curve, which graphs the demand schedule in Table 4.1, shows how the quantity demanded of the good changes as its price varies. Because a lower price increases the quantity demanded, the demand curve slopes downwards.

demand schedule
a table that shows the
relationship between the price
of a good and the quantity
demanded

10 ice-creams per month. As the price rises further, she buys fewer and fewer ice-creams. When the price reaches $3.00, Catherine doesn't buy any ice-cream at all. Table 4.1 is a **demand schedule**, a table that shows the relationship between the price of a good and the quantity demanded, holding constant everything else that influences how much of the good consumers want to buy.

The graph in Figure 4.1 uses the numbers from the table to illustrate the law of demand. By convention, the price of ice-cream is on the vertical axis and the quantity of ice-cream demanded is on the horizontal axis. The downward-sloping line relating price and quantity demanded is called the **demand curve**.

demand curve
a graph of the relationship
between the price of a good
and the quantity demanded

Table 4.2 Individual and market demand schedules

Price of an ice-cream	Catherine		Nicholas		Market
$0.00	12	+	7	=	19
0.50	10		6		16
1.00	8		5		13
1.50	6		4		10
2.00	4		3		7
2.50	2		2		4
3.00	0		1		1

Figure 4.2   Market demand as the sum of individual demands

The market demand curve is found by adding horizontally the individual demand curves. At a price of $2, Catherine demands four ice-creams, and Nicholas demands three ice-creams. The quantity demanded in the market at this price is seven ice-creams.

Market demand versus individual demand

The demand curve in Figure 4.1 shows an individual's demand for a product. To analyse how markets work, we need to determine the *market demand*, which is the sum of all the individual demands for a particular good or service.

The table in Figure 4.2 shows the demand schedules for ice-cream of two people – Catherine and Nicholas. At any price, Catherine's demand schedule tells us how much ice-cream she buys, and Nicholas's demand schedule tells us how much ice-cream he buys. The market demand is the sum of the two individual demands.

The graph in Figure 4.2 shows the demand curves that correspond to these demand schedules. Notice that we add the individual demand curves *horizontally* to obtain the market demand curve. That is, to find the total quantity demanded at any price, we add the individual quantities found on the horizontal axis of the individual demand curves. Because we are interested in analysing how markets work, we will work most often with the market demand curve. The market demand curve shows how the total quantity demanded of a good varies as the price of the good varies, while all other factors that affect how much consumers want to buy are held constant.

Shifts in the demand curve

Because the market demand curve holds other things constant, it need not be stable over time. If something happens to alter the quantity demanded at any given price, the demand curve shifts. For example, suppose that medical researchers suddenly announce a new discovery – people who regularly

Figure 4.3 | **Shifts in the demand curve**

Any change that raises the quantity that buyers wish to purchase at a given price shifts the demand curve to the right. Any change that lowers the quantity that buyers wish to purchase at a given price shifts the demand curve to the left.

eat ice-cream live longer, healthier lives. The discovery would raise the demand for ice-cream. At any given price, buyers would now want to purchase a larger quantity of ice-cream and the demand curve for ice-cream would shift.

Figure 4.3 illustrates shifts in demand. Any change that increases the quantity demanded at any given price, such as our imaginary discovery by medical researchers, shifts the demand curve to the right and is called *an increase in demand*. Any change that reduces the quantity demanded at every price shifts the demand curve to the left and is called *a decrease in demand*.

There are many variables that can shift the demand curve. Here are the most important:

Income

What would happen to your demand for ice-cream if you lost your job one summer? Most likely, it would fall. A lower income means that you have less to spend in total, so you would have to spend less on some – and probably most – goods. If the demand for a good falls when income falls, the good is called a **normal good**.

Not all goods are normal goods. If the demand for a good rises when income falls, the good is called an **inferior good**. An example of an inferior good might be bus rides. As your income falls, you are less likely to buy a car or take a taxi and more likely to take the bus.

Prices of related goods

Suppose that the price of frozen yoghurt falls. The law of demand says that you will buy more frozen yoghurt. At the same time, you will probably buy less ice-cream. Because ice-cream and frozen yoghurt are both cold, sweet, creamy desserts, they satisfy similar desires. When a fall in the price of one good reduces the demand for another good, the two goods are called **substitutes**. Substitutes are often pairs of goods that are used in place of each other, like hot dogs and hamburgers, butter and margarine, and movie tickets and DVD rentals.

normal good
a good for which, other things being equal, an increase in income leads to an increase in quantity demanded

inferior good
a good for which, other things being equal, an increase in income leads to a decrease in quantity demanded

substitutes
two goods for which a decrease in the price of one good leads to a decrease in the demand for the other good

Now suppose that the price of chocolate topping falls. According to the law of demand, you will buy more chocolate topping. Yet, in this case, you will buy more ice-cream as well, since ice-cream and topping are often used together. When a fall in the price of one good raises the demand for another good, the two goods are called **complements**. Complements are often pairs of goods that are used together, such as petrol and cars, computers and software, and skis and ski-lift tickets.

complements
two goods for which a decrease in the price of one good leads to an increase in the demand for the other good

Tastes

The most obvious determinant of your demand is your tastes. If you like ice-cream, you buy more of it. Economists normally do not try to explain people's tastes because tastes are based on historical and psychological forces that are beyond the realm of economics. Economists do, however, examine what happens when tastes change.

Expectations

Your expectations about the future may affect your demand for a good or service today. If you expect to earn a higher income next month, you may choose to save less now and spend more of your current income buying ice-cream. If you expect the price of ice-cream to fall tomorrow, you may be less willing to buy an ice-cream at today's price.

Number of buyers

In addition to the preceding factors, which influence the behaviour of individual buyers, market demand depends on the number of these buyers. If Peter, another consumer of ice-cream, were to join Catherine and Nicholas, the quantity demanded in the market would be higher at every price and the demand curve would shift to the right.

Summary

The demand curve shows what happens to the quantity demanded of a good when its price varies, holding constant all the other variables that influence buyers. When one of these other variables changes, the demand curve shifts. Table 4.3 lists all the variables that influence how much consumers choose to buy of a good.

Table 4.3 Variables that influence buyers	
Variables that affect quantity demanded	**A change in this variable …**
Price	Represents a movement along the demand curve
Income	Shifts the demand curve
Prices of related goods	Shifts the demand curve
Tastes	Shifts the demand curve
Expectations	Shifts the demand curve
Number of buyers	Shifts the demand curve

fyi

Ceteris paribus

ceteris paribus
a Latin phrase, translated as 'other things being equal', used as a reminder that all variables other than the ones being studied are assumed to be constant

Whenever you see a demand curve, remember that it is drawn holding many things fixed. Catherine's demand curve in Figure 4.1 shows what happens to the quantity of ice-cream Catherine wants to buy when only the price of ice-cream varies. The curve is drawn assuming that Catherine's income, tastes, expectations and the prices of related products are not changing.

Economists use the term *ceteris paribus* to signify that all the relevant variables, except those being studied at that moment, are held constant.

This Latin phrase means 'other things being equal'. The demand curve slopes downwards because, *ceteris paribus*, lower prices mean a greater quantity demanded.

Although the term *ceteris paribus* refers to a hypothetical situation in which some variables are assumed to be constant, in the real world many things change at the same time. For this reason, when we use the tools of supply and demand to analyse events or policies, it is important to keep in mind what is being held fixed and what is not.

CASESTUDY

Two ways to reduce the quantity of smoking demanded

Public policymakers often want to reduce the amount that people smoke because of smoking's adverse health effects. There are two ways that policy can attempt to achieve this goal.

One way to reduce smoking is to shift the demand curve for cigarettes and other tobacco products. Public service announcements, mandatory health warnings on cigarette packets and the prohibition of cigarette advertising on television are all policies aimed at reducing the quantity of cigarettes demanded at any given price. If successful, these policies shift the demand curve for cigarettes to the left, as in panel (a) of figure 4.4.

Alternatively, policymakers can try to raise the price of cigarettes. If the government taxes the manufacture of cigarettes, for example, cigarette companies pass much of this tax on to consumers in the form of higher prices. A higher price encourages smokers to reduce the amount of cigarettes they smoke. In this case, the reduced amount of smoking does not represent a shift in the demand curve. Instead, it represents a movement along the same demand curve to a point with a higher price and lower quantity, as in panel (b) of figure 4.4.

How much does the amount of smoking respond to changes in the price of cigarettes? Economists have attempted to answer this question by studying what happens when the tax on cigarettes changes. They have found that a

10 per cent increase in the price causes a 4 per cent reduction in the quantity demanded. Teenagers are found to be especially sensitive to the price of cigarettes – a 10 per cent increase in the price causes a 12 per cent drop in teenage smoking.

A related question is how the price of cigarettes affects the demand for illicit drugs, such as marijuana. Opponents of cigarette taxes often argue that tobacco and marijuana are substitutes, so that high cigarette prices encourage marijuana use. By contrast, many experts on substance abuse view tobacco as a 'gateway drug' leading the young to experiment with other harmful substances. Most studies of the data are consistent with this view – they find that higher cigarette prices are associated with reduced use of marijuana. In other words, tobacco and marijuana appear to be complements rather than substitutes.

What is the best way to stop this?

Source: photos.com/Getty Images.

Figure 4.4 — Shifts in the demand curve versus movements along the demand curve

(a) A shift in the demand curve

(b) A movement along the demand curve

If warnings on cigarette packets convince smokers to smoke less, the demand curve for cigarettes shifts to the left. In panel (a), the demand curve shifts from D_1 to D_2. At a price of $4 per packet, the quantity demanded falls from 20 to 10 cigarettes per day, as reflected by the shift from point A to point B. In contrast, if a tax raises the price of cigarettes, the demand curve does not shift. Instead, we observe a movement to a different point on the demand curve. In panel (b), when the price rises from $4 to $8, the quantity demanded falls from 20 to 12 cigarettes per day, as reflected by the movement from point A to point C.

List the determinants of the demand for pizza. Give an example of a demand schedule for pizza, and graph the implied demand curve. Give an example of something that would shift this demand curve. Would a change in the price of pizza shift this demand curve?

Notice the special role that the price of the good plays: A change in the good's price represents a movement along the demand curve, whereas a change in one of the other variables shifts the demand curve.

If you have trouble remembering whether you need to shift or move along the demand curve, it helps to recall a lesson from the appendix to chapter 2. A curve shifts when there is a change in a relevant variable that is not measured on either axis. Because the price is on the vertical axis, a change in price represents a movement along the demand curve. By contrast, income, the prices of related goods, tastes, expectations and the number of buyers are not measured on either axis, so a change in one of these variables shifts the demand curve.

Supply

We now turn to the other side of the market and examine the behaviour of sellers. Once again, to focus our thinking, let's consider the market for ice-cream.

The supply curve: The relationship between price and quantity supplied

quantity supplied
the amount of a good that sellers are willing and able to sell

law of supply
the claim that, other things being equal, the quantity supplied of a good rises when the price of the good rises

supply schedule
a table that shows the relationship between the price of a good and the quantity supplied

supply curve
a graph of the relationship between the price of a good and the quantity supplied

The **quantity supplied** of any good or service is the amount that sellers are willing and able to sell. There are many determinants of quantity supplied, but once again price plays a special role in our analysis. When the price of ice-cream is high, selling ice-cream is profitable and so the quantity supplied is large. The sellers of ice-cream work long hours, buy many ice-cream machines and hire many workers. In contrast, when the price of ice-cream is low, selling ice-cream is less profitable, so sellers produce less ice-cream. At a low price, some sellers may even choose to shut down and their quantity supplied falls to zero. This relationship between price and quantity supplied is called the **law of supply** – other things being equal, when the price of a good rises, the quantity supplied of the good also rises, and when the price falls, the quantity supplied falls as well.

Table 4.4 shows the quantity supplied by Tony, an ice-cream seller, at various prices of ice-cream. At a price below $1.00, Tony does not supply any ice-cream at all. As the price rises, he supplies a greater and greater quantity. This is the **supply schedule**, a table that shows the relationship between the price of a good and the quantity supplied, holding constant everything else that influences how much producers of the good want to sell.

The graph in Figure 4.5 uses the numbers from the table to illustrate the law of supply. The curve relating price and quantity supplied is called the **supply curve**. The supply curve slopes upwards because, other things being equal, a higher price means a greater quantity supplied.

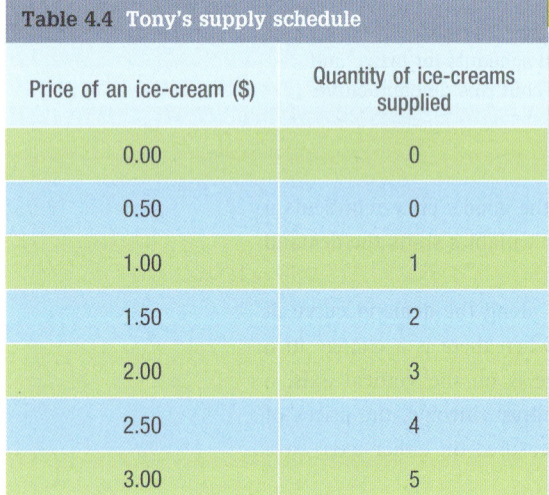

Table 4.4 Tony's supply schedule

Price of an ice-cream ($)	Quantity of ice-creams supplied
0.00	0
0.50	0
1.00	1
1.50	2
2.00	3
2.50	4
3.00	5

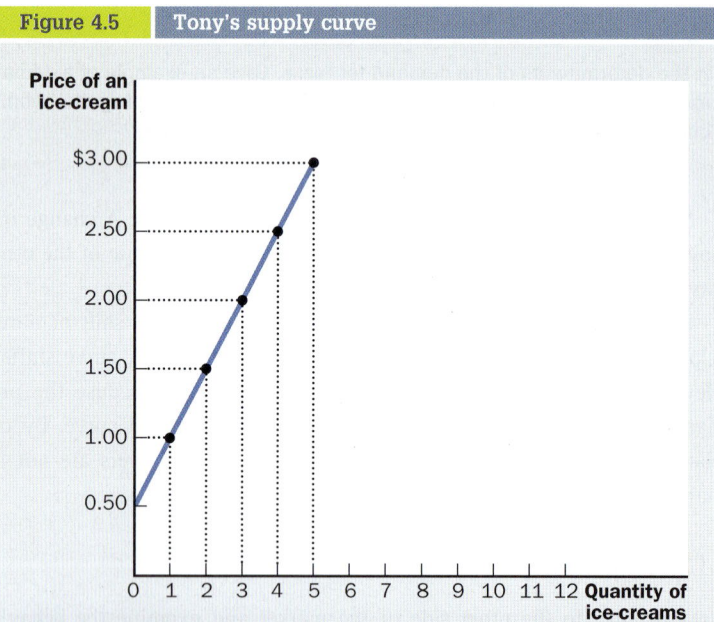

Figure 4.5 Tony's supply curve

This supply curve, which graphs the supply schedule in Table 4.4, shows how the quantity supplied of the good changes as its price varies. Because a higher price increases the quantity supplied, the supply curve slopes upwards.

Market supply versus individual supply

Just as market demand is the sum of the demands of all buyers, market supply is the sum of the supplies of all sellers. Table 4.5 shows the supply schedules for two ice-cream producers – Tony and Sonia. At any price, Tony's supply schedule tells us how much ice-cream Tony supplies, and Sonia's supply schedule tells us how much ice-cream Sonia supplies. The market supply is the sum of the two individual supplies.

The graph in Figure 4.6 shows the supply curves that correspond to the supply schedules. As with demand curves, we add the individual supply curves *horizontally* to obtain the market supply curve. That is, to find the total quantity supplied at any price, we add the individual quantities found on the horizontal axis of the individual supply curves. The market supply curve shows how the total quantity supplied varies as the price of the good varies, holding constant all the other factors beyond price that influence producers' decisions about how much to sell.

Shifts in the supply curve

Because the market supply curve holds other things constant, the curve shifts when one of these other factors changes. For example, suppose that the price of sugar falls. Because sugar is an input into producing ice-cream, the fall in the price of sugar makes selling ice-cream more profitable. This raises the supply of ice-cream; at any given price sellers are now willing to produce a larger quantity. Thus, the supply curve for ice-cream shifts to the right.

Figure 4.7 illustrates shifts in supply. Any change that raises quantity supplied at every price, such as a fall in the price of sugar, shifts the supply curve to the right and is called *an increase in supply*. Similarly, any change that reduces the quantity supplied at every price shifts the supply curve to the left and is called *a decrease in supply*.

There are many variables that can shift the supply curve. Here are some of the most important:

Input prices

To produce their output of ice-cream, sellers use various inputs – cream, sugar, flavouring, ice-cream machines, the buildings in which the ice-cream is made, and the labour of workers to mix the ingredients and operate the machines. When the price of one or more of these inputs rises, producing ice-cream is less profitable and sellers supply less ice-cream. If input prices rise substantially, some sellers might shut down and supply no ice-cream at all. Thus, the quantity supplied of a good is negatively related to the price of the inputs used to make the good.

Technology

The technology for turning the inputs into ice-cream is yet another determinant of the quantity supplied. The invention of the mechanised ice-cream machine, for example, reduced the amount of labour necessary to make ice-cream. By reducing sellers' costs, the advance in technology raised the quantity of ice-cream supplied.

Expectations

The quantity of ice-cream a seller supplies today may depend on its expectations about the future. For example, if a seller expects the price of ice-cream to rise in the future, it may put some of its current production into storage and supply less to the market today.

Number of sellers

In addition to the preceding factors, which influence the behaviour of individual sellers, market supply depends on the number of sellers. If Tony or Sonia were to retire from the ice-cream business, the supply in the market would fall.

Table 4.5 Individual and market supply schedule

Price of an ice-cream	Tony		Sonia		Market
$0.00	0	+	0	=	0
0.50	0		0		0
1.00	1		0		1
1.50	2		2		4
2.00	3		4		7
2.50	4		6		10
3.00	5		8		13

Figure 4.6 Market supply as the sum of individual supplies

The market supply curve is found by adding horizontally the individual supply curves. At a price of $2, Tony supplies three ice-creams and Sonia supplies four ice-creams. The quantity supplied in the market at this price is seven ice-creams.

Summary

The supply curve shows what happens to the quantity supplied of a good when its price varies, holding constant all the other variables that influence sellers. When one of these other variables changes, the supply curve shifts.

Table 4.6 lists the variables that affect how much producers choose to sell of any good. Again, notice the special role that the price of the good plays – a change in the good's price represents a movement along the supply curve, whereas a change in one of the other variables shifts the supply curve.

List the determinants of the supply of pizza. Give an example of a supply schedule for pizza, and graph the implied supply curve. Give an example of something that would shift this supply curve. Would a change in the price of pizza shift this supply curve?

Supply and demand together

Having analysed supply and demand separately, we now combine them to see how they determine the quantity of a good sold in a market and its price.

Figure 4.7   Shifts in the supply curve

Any change that raises the quantity that sellers wish to produce at a given price shifts the supply curve to the right. Any change that lowers the quantity that sellers wish to produce at a given price shifts the supply curve to the left.

Table 4.6 Variables that influence sellers

Variables that affect quantity supplied	A change in this variable …
Price	Represents a movement along the supply curve
Input prices	Shifts the supply curve
Technology	Shifts the supply curve
Expectations	Shifts the supply curve
Number of sellers	Shifts the supply curve

Equilibrium

Figure 4.8 shows the market supply curve and market demand curve together. Notice that there is one point at which the supply and demand curves intersect. This point is called the market's **equilibrium**. The price at this intersection is called the **equilibrium price** and the quantity is called the **equilibrium quantity**. Here the equilibrium price is $2.00 per ice-cream, and the equilibrium quantity is seven ice-creams.

Equilibrium is defined by the dictionary as a situation in which various forces are in balance – and this also describes a market's equilibrium. *At the equilibrium price, the quantity of the good that buyers are willing and able to buy exactly balances the quantity that sellers are willing and able to sell.* The equilibrium price is sometimes called the market-clearing price because, at this price, everyone in the market has been satisfied – buyers have bought all they want to buy, and sellers have sold all they want to sell.

equilibrium
a situation in which supply and demand have been brought into balance

equilibrium price
the price that balances supply and demand

equilibrium quantity
the quantity supplied and the quantity demanded when the price has adjusted to balance supply and demand

Figure 4.8	The equilibrium of supply and demand

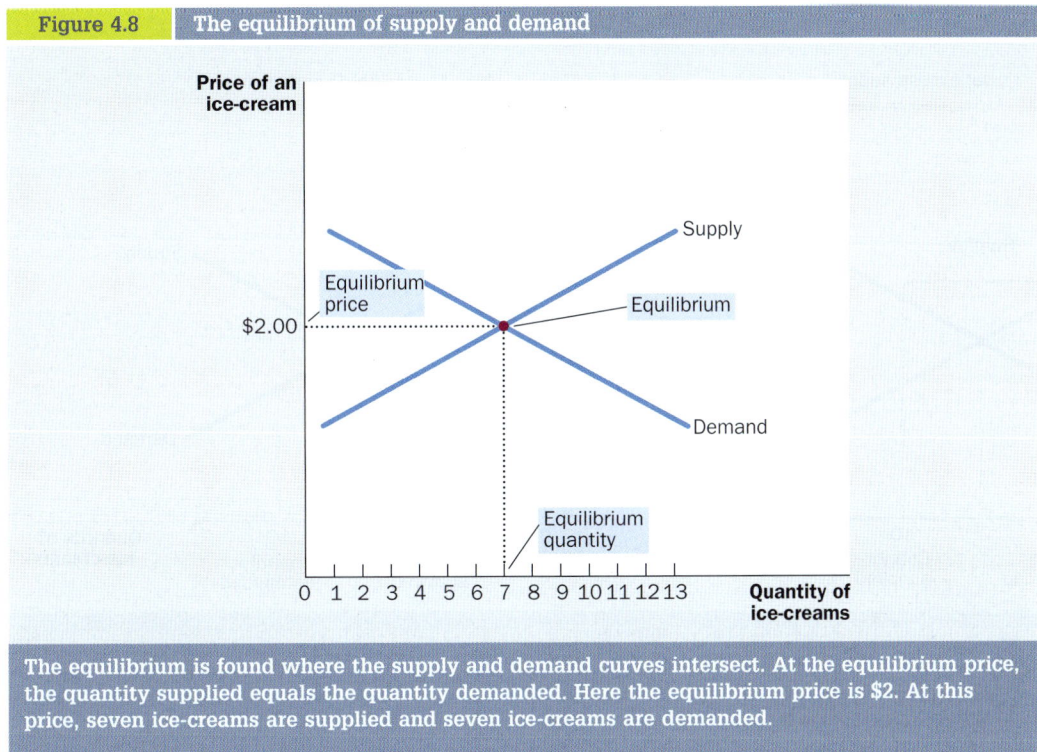

The equilibrium is found where the supply and demand curves intersect. At the equilibrium price, the quantity supplied equals the quantity demanded. Here the equilibrium price is $2. At this price, seven ice-creams are supplied and seven ice-creams are demanded.

The actions of buyers and sellers naturally move markets towards the equilibrium of supply and demand. To see why, consider what happens when the market price is not equal to the equilibrium price.

Suppose first that the market price is above the equilibrium price, as in panel (a) of Figure 4.9. At a price of $2.50 per ice-cream, the quantity of the good supplied (10 ice-creams) exceeds the quantity demanded (four ice-creams). There is a **surplus** of the good – suppliers are unable to sell all they want at the going price. A surplus is sometimes called a situation of *excess supply*. When there is a surplus in the ice-cream market, for instance, sellers of ice-cream find their freezers increasingly full of ice-cream they would like to sell but cannot. They respond to the excess supply by cutting their prices. Falling prices, in turn, increase the quantity demanded and decrease the quantity supplied. These changes represent movements *along* the supply and demand curves (not shifts in the curves). Prices continue to fall until the market reaches the equilibrium.

Suppose now that the market price is below the equilibrium price, as in panel (b) of Figure 4.9. In this case, the price is $1.50 per ice-cream and the quantity of the good demanded exceeds the quantity supplied. There is a **shortage** of the good – demanders are unable to buy all they want at the going price. A shortage is sometimes called a situation of *excess demand*. When a shortage occurs in the ice-cream market, buyers have to wait in long lines for a chance to buy the few ice-creams that are available. With too many buyers chasing too few goods, sellers can respond to excess demand by raising their prices without losing sales. These price increases cause the quantity demanded to fall and the quantity supplied to rise. Once again, these changes represent movements *along* the supply and demand curves and they move the market towards the equilibrium.

surplus
a situation in which quantity supplied is greater than quantity demanded

▶ equilibrium price

shortage
a situation in which quantity demanded is greater than quantity supplied

Figure 4.9 Markets not in equilibrium

(a) Excess supply

(b) Excess demand

In panel (a), there is excess supply. Because the market price of $2.50 is above the equilibrium price, the quantity supplied (10 ice-creams) exceeds the quantity demanded (four ice-creams). Suppliers try to increase sales by cutting the price of an ice-cream and this moves the price towards its equilibrium level. In panel (b), there is excess demand. Because the market price of $1.50 is below the equilibrium price, the quantity demanded (10 ice-creams) exceeds the quantity supplied (four ice-creams). Because too many buyers are chasing too few goods, suppliers can take advantage of the shortage by raising the price. Hence, in both cases, the price adjustment moves the market towards the equilibrium of supply and demand.

Thus, regardless of whether the price starts off too high or too low, the activities of the many buyers and sellers automatically push the market price towards the equilibrium price. Once the market reaches its equilibrium, all buyers and sellers are satisfied and there is no upward or downward pressure on the price. How quickly equilibrium is reached varies from market to market, depending on how quickly prices adjust. In most free markets, however, surpluses and shortages are only temporary because prices eventually move towards their equilibrium levels. Indeed, this phenomenon is so pervasive that it is sometimes called the **law of supply and demand** – the price of any good adjusts to bring the supply and demand for that good into balance.

law of supply and demand
the claim that the price of any good adjusts to bring the supply and demand for that good into balance

Three steps for analysing changes in equilibrium

So far we have seen how supply and demand together determine a market's equilibrium, which in turn determines the price of the good and the amount of the good that buyers purchase and sellers produce. The equilibrium price and quantity depend on the position of the supply and demand curves. When some event shifts one of these curves, the equilibrium in the market changes, resulting in a new price and a new quantity exchanged between buyers and sellers. The analysis of such a change is called *comparative statics* because it involves comparing an old equilibrium and a new equilibrium.

When analysing how some event affects a market, we proceed in three steps. First, we decide whether the event shifts the supply curve, the demand curve or, in some cases, both curves. Second, we decide whether the curve shifts to the right or to the left. Third, we use the supply-and-demand

▸ Search me!

▸ law of supply and demand

Table 4.7 A three-step program for doing comparative statics
1 Decide whether the event shifts the supply or demand curve (or perhaps both).
2 Decide in which direction the curve shifts.
3 Use the supply-and-demand diagram to see how the shift changes the equilibrium.

diagram to compare the initial and the new equilibrium, which shows how the shift affects the equilibrium price and quantity. Table 4.7 summarises these three steps. To see how this recipe is used, let's consider various events that might affect the market for ice-cream.

Example: A change in market equilibrium due to a shift in demand

Suppose that one summer the weather is very hot. How does this event affect the market for ice-cream? To answer this question, let's follow our three steps.

1   The hot weather affects the demand curve by changing people's taste for ice-cream. That is, the weather changes the amount of ice-cream that people want to buy at any given price. The supply curve is unchanged because the weather does not directly affect the firms that sell ice-cream.
2   Because hot weather makes people want to eat more ice-cream, the demand curve shifts to the right. Figure 4.10 shows this increase in demand as the shift in the demand curve from D_1 to D_2. This shift indicates that the quantity of ice-cream demanded is higher at every price.
3   At the old price of $2, there is now an excess demand for ice-cream and this shortage induces sellers to raise the price. As Figure 4.10 shows, the increase in demand raises the equilibrium price from $2.00 to $2.50 and the equilibrium quantity from seven to 10 ice-creams. In other words, the hot weather increases the price of ice-cream and the quantity of ice-cream sold.

Shifts in curves versus movements along curves

Notice that when hot weather drives up the price of ice-cream, the amount of ice-cream that firms supply rises, even though the supply curve remains the same. In this case, economists say there has been an increase in 'quantity supplied' but no change in 'supply'.

'Supply' refers to the position of the supply curve, whereas the 'quantity supplied' refers to the amount suppliers wish to sell. In this example, supply does not change because the weather does not alter firms' desire to sell at any given price. Instead, the hot weather alters consumers' desire to buy at any given price and thereby shifts the demand curve. The increase in demand causes the equilibrium price to rise. When the price rises, the quantity supplied rises. This increase in quantity supplied is represented by the movement along the supply curve.

To summarise, a shift *in* the supply curve is called a 'change in supply' and a shift *in* the demand curve is called a 'change in demand'. A movement *along* a fixed supply curve is called a 'change in the quantity supplied', and a movement *along* a fixed demand curve is called a 'change in the quantity demanded'.

Example: A change in supply

Suppose that, during another summer, a bushfire destroys several ice-cream factories. How does this event affect the market for ice-cream? Once again, to answer this question, we follow our three steps.

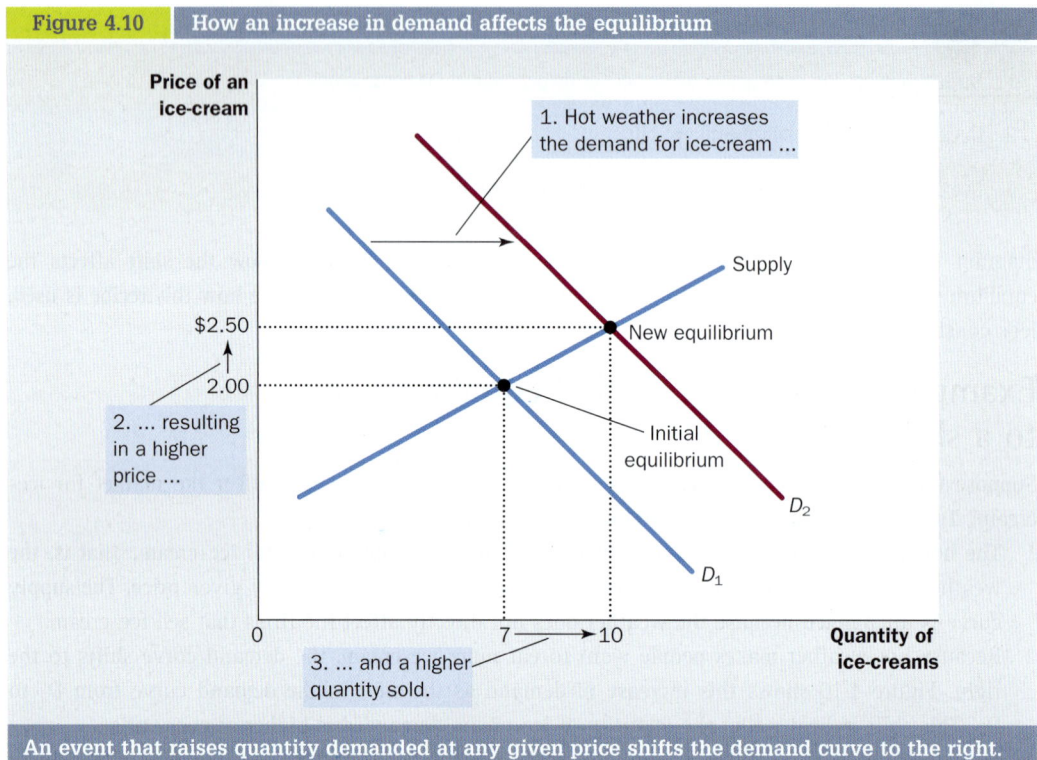

Figure 4.10 | **How an increase in demand affects the equilibrium**

Price of an ice-cream

1. Hot weather increases the demand for ice-cream ...

Supply

$2.50 ..... New equilibrium

2. ... resulting in a higher price ...

2.00

Initial equilibrium

D_2

D_1

0

7 → 10

3. ... and a higher quantity sold.

Quantity of ice-creams

An event that raises quantity demanded at any given price shifts the demand curve to the right. The equilibrium price and the equilibrium quantity both rise. Here, an abnormally hot summer causes buyers to demand more ice-cream. The demand curve shifts from D_1 to D_2, which causes the equilibrium price to rise from $2.00 to $2.50 and the equilibrium quantity to rise from seven to 10 ice-creams.

1   The fire affects the supply curve. By reducing the number of sellers, the fire changes the amount of ice-cream that firms produce and sell at any given price. The demand curve is unchanged because the fire does not directly change the amount of ice-cream households wish to buy.

2   The supply curve shifts to the left because, at every price, the total amount that firms are willing and able to sell is reduced. Figure 4.11 illustrates this decrease in supply as a shift in the supply curve from S_1 to S_2.

3   At the old price of $2.00 there is now an excess demand for ice-cream. This shortage causes ice-cream sellers to raise the price. As Figure 4.11 shows, the shift in the supply curve raises the equilibrium price from $2.00 to $2.50 and lowers the equilibrium quantity from seven to four ice-creams. As a result of the fire, the price of ice-cream rises and the quantity of ice-cream sold falls.

Example: A change in both supply and demand

Now suppose that the hot weather and the fire occur at the same time. To analyse this combination of events, we again follow our three steps.

1   We determine that both curves must shift. The hot weather affects the demand curve because it alters the amount of ice-cream that households want to buy at any given price. At the same time, the fire alters the supply curve because it changes the amount of ice-cream that firms want to sell at any given price.

Figure 4.11 How a decrease in supply affects the equilibrium

An event that reduces quantity supplied at a given price shifts the supply curve to the left. The equilibrium price rises, and the equilibrium quantity falls. Here, a bushfire causes sellers to supply less ice-cream. The supply curve shifts from S_1 to S_2, which causes the equilibrium price to rise from $2.00 to $2.50 and the equilibrium quantity to fall from seven to four ice-creams.

2   The curves shift in the same directions as they did in our previous analysis – the demand curve shifts to the right and the supply curve shifts to the left. Figure 4.12 illustrates these shifts.

3   As Figure 4.12 shows, there are two possible outcomes that might result, depending on the relative size of the demand and supply shifts. In both cases, the equilibrium price rises. In panel (a), where demand increases substantially and supply falls just a little, the equilibrium quantity also rises. In contrast, in panel (b), where supply falls substantially and demand rises just a little, the equilibrium quantity falls. Thus, these events certainly raise the price of ice-cream, but their impact on the amount of ice-cream sold is ambiguous.

Analyse what happens to the market for pizza if the price of tomatoes rises. Analyse what happens to the market for pizza if the price of hamburgers falls.

Conclusion: How prices allocate resources

This chapter has analysed supply and demand in a single market. Although our discussion has centred around the market for ice-cream, the lessons learned here apply in most other markets as well. Whenever you go to a shop to buy something, you are contributing to the demand for that item.

Figure 4.12 — A shift in both supply and demand

Here we observe a simultaneous increase in demand and decrease in supply. Two outcomes are possible. In panel (a), the equilibrium price rises from P_1 to P_2, and the equilibrium quantity rises from Q_1 to Q_2. In panel (b), the equilibrium price again rises from P_1 to P_2, but the equilibrium quantity falls from Q_1 to Q_2.

Whenever you look for a job, you are contributing to the supply of labour services. Because supply and demand are such pervasive economic phenomena, the model of supply and demand is a powerful tool for analysis. We will be using this model repeatedly in the following chapters.

One of the *Ten Lessons from Economics* discussed in chapter 1 is that markets are usually a good way to organise economic activity. Although it is still too early to judge whether market outcomes are good or bad, in this chapter we have begun to see how markets work. In any economic system, scarce resources have to be allocated among competing uses. Market economies harness the forces of supply and demand to serve that end. Supply and demand together determine the prices of the economy's many different goods and services; prices in turn are the signals that guide the allocation of resources.

'Two dollars.'   '– and seventy-five cents.'

Source: Day, J. Robert © Robert J. Day/The New Yorker Collection/www.cartoonbank.com.

For example, consider the allocation of beachfront land. Because the amount of this land is limited, not everyone can enjoy the luxury of living by the beach. Who gets this resource? The answer is: Whoever is willing to pay the price. The price of beachfront land adjusts until the quantity of land demanded exactly balances the quantity supplied. Thus, in market economies, prices are the mechanism for rationing scarce resources.

Similarly, prices determine who produces each good and how much is produced. For instance, consider farming. Because we need food to survive, it is crucial that some people work on farms. What determines who is a farmer and who is not? In a free society, there is no government planning agency making this decision and ensuring an adequate supply of food. Instead, the allocation of workers to farms is based on the job decisions of millions of workers. This decentralised system works well because these decisions depend on prices. The prices of food and the wages of farm workers (the price of their labour) adjust to ensure that enough people choose to be farmers.

If a person had never seen a market economy in action, the whole idea might seem preposterous. Economies are large groups of people engaged in many interdependent activities. What prevents decentralised decision making from degenerating into chaos? What coordinates the actions of the millions of people with their varying abilities and desires? What ensures that what needs to get done does, in fact, get done? The answer, in a word, is *prices*. If market economies are guided by an invisible hand, as Adam Smith famously suggested, then the price system is the baton that the invisible hand uses to conduct the economic orchestra.

IN THE NEWS ...

MOTHER NATURE SHIFTS THE SUPPLY CURVE

In this chapter we have seen three examples of how to use supply and demand curves to analyse a change in equilibrium. Whenever an event shifts the supply curve, the demand curve, or perhaps both curves, you can use these tools to predict how the event will alter the price and quantity sold in equilibrium. This article provides another example of how a natural disaster that reduces supply reduces the quantity sold and raises the price.

Bananas to recover quickly
by Tony Koch

Banana prices, which have risen because of crop devastation caused by Cyclone Yasi, will not stay high for long because of lessons learned by progressive farmers when Cyclone Larry caused similar havoc in 2006.

The advance notice of Yasi to growers in the Tully and Innisfail areas allowed a frenzied few days of picking mature fruit and storing it in packing sheds, ensuring at least two weeks' supply.

As well, farmers deleafed young trees, leaving just the stems standing, and these were not knocked over by the cyclonic winds as were the mature trees.

Australian banana production is 286 000 tonnes a year, or about 25 million cartons, each with 13 kg of fruit.

Gross value of the produce is $500 million based on an average wholesale price of $20 a carton.

The industry is estimated to be worth more than $870m to the broader economy through the employment it provides and ancillary services. North Queensland has 12 000ha of plantations, producing about 85 per cent of Australia's crop.

More than 3000 people are employed directly in the banana industry in the cyclone-affected areas.

>>

The Australian Banana Growers Council reported last week that 95 per cent of the crop in Tully and Innisfail was lost, or about 10 200ha, as well as 10 per cent on the Atherton Tableland (1350ha) and 100 per cent at Cardwell (630ha). Council chief executive Jonathan Eccles said about 5 per cent of crops in the Innisfail-Tully area had been deleafed, which will mean those crops can be harvested four months or so earlier than crops that must be planted now.

'Banana supply from Innisfail and Tully will not be back to normal for at least six months, with full supply not expected before December 2011,' he said.

'As well as the deleafing helping some get back into production quicker, Cyclone Yasi affected crops differently from the way Larry did.

'This time the stems were broken off higher up, about a metre and a half, and that stem is being left to provide nourishment for the adjoining sucker.

'The third thing working for farmers is that Yasi has come at the end of January and Larry hit towards the end of March, so there is a difference of six or seven weeks of summer growing season available.

'If we get another warm winter like last year, the plants will also grow faster, so there are some positives to come from all this.'

Mr Eccles said there was a lot less damage to farm infrastructure this time.

The big winners in the supply and demand for bananas are the few growers with 308ha under production at Lakeland on the Atherton Tableland. They suffered no loss from Yasi.

Source: Tony Koch/*The Australian*, 21 Feb 2011.

Summary

- Economists use the model of supply and demand to analyse competitive markets. In a competitive market, there are many buyers and sellers, each of whom has little or no influence on the market price.
- The demand curve shows how the quantity of a good demanded depends on the price. According to the law of demand, as the price of a good falls, the quantity demanded rises. Therefore, the demand curve slopes downwards.
- In addition to price, other determinants of the quantity demanded include income, tastes, expectations, and the prices of substitutes and complements. If one of these other determinants changes, the demand curve shifts.
- The supply curve shows how the quantity of a good supplied depends on the price. According to the law of supply, as the price of a good rises, the quantity supplied rises. Therefore, the supply curve slopes upwards.
- In addition to price, other determinants of the quantity supplied include input prices, technology and expectations. If one of these other determinants changes, the supply curve shifts.
- The intersection of the supply and demand curves determines the market equilibrium. At the equilibrium price, the quantity demanded equals the quantity supplied.
- The behaviour of buyers and sellers naturally drives markets towards their equilibrium. When the market price is above the equilibrium price, there is excess supply, which causes the market price to fall. When the market price is below the equilibrium price, there is excess demand, which causes the market price to rise.
- To analyse how any event influences a market, we use the supply-and-demand diagram to examine how the event affects the equilibrium price and quantity. To do this we follow three steps. First, we decide whether the event shifts the supply curve or the demand curve. Second, we decide in which direction the curve shifts. Third, we compare the new equilibrium with the old equilibrium.
- In market economies, prices are the signals that guide economic decisions and thereby allocate scarce resources. For every good in the economy, the price ensures that supply and demand are in balance. The equilibrium price then determines how much of the good buyers choose to purchase and how much sellers choose to produce.

Key concepts

ceteris paribus	inferior good	quantity supplied
competitive market	law of demand	shortage
complements	law of supply and	substitutes
demand curve	demand	supply curve
demand schedule	law of supply	supply schedule
equilibrium price	market	surplus
equilibrium quantity	normal good	
equilibrium	quantity demanded	

Questions for review

1 What is a competitive market?
2 What determines the quantity of a good that buyers demand?
3 What are the demand schedule and the demand curve, and how are they related?
4 Why does the demand curve slope downwards?
5 Does a change in consumers' tastes lead to a movement along the demand curve or a shift in the demand curve? Does a change in price lead to a movement along the demand curve or a shift in the demand curve?
6 What determines the quantity of a good that sellers supply?
7 What are the supply schedule and the supply curve, and how are they related?
8 Why does the supply curve slope upwards?
9 Does a change in producers' technology lead to a movement along the supply curve or a shift in the supply curve? Does a change in price lead to a movement along the supply curve or a shift in the supply curve?
10 Define the equilibrium of a market. Describe the forces that move a market towards its equilibrium.
11 Beer and pies are complements because they are often enjoyed together. When the price of beer rises, what happens to the supply, demand, quantity supplied, quantity demanded and the price in the market for pies?
12 Describe the role of prices in market economies.

Problems and applications

1 Explain each of the following statements using supply-and-demand diagrams.
   a When a cyclone hits Queensland, the price of bananas rises in supermarkets throughout the country.
   b On Tuesdays, picture theatres discount tickets.
   c When a war breaks out in the Middle East, the price of petrol rises and the price of a used Ford Falcon falls.
2 'An increase in the demand for notebooks raises the quantity of notebooks demanded, but not the quantity supplied.' Is this statement true or false? Explain.
3 Consider the market for station wagons. For each of the events listed here, identify which of the determinants of demand or supply are affected. Also indicate whether demand or supply is increased or decreased.
   a People decide to have more children.
   b A strike by steelworkers raises steel prices.
   c Engineers develop new automated machinery for the production of station wagons.
   d The price of mini-vans rises.
   e A stock market crash lowers people's wealth.
4 During the 1990s, technological advance reduced the cost of computer chips. How do you think this affected the market for computers? For computer software? For typewriters?
5 Using supply-and-demand diagrams, show the effect of the following events on the market for woollen jumpers:
   a an outbreak of 'foot-and-mouth' disease hits sheep farms in New Zealand
   b the price of leather jackets falls

c Lily Allen appears in a woollen jumper in her latest video

d new knitting machines are invented.

6 Suppose that in the year 2005 the number of births is temporarily high. How does this baby boom affect the price of baby-sitting services in 2010 and 2020? (*Hint:* five-year-olds need baby-sitters, whereas 15-year-olds can be baby-sitters.)

7 Tomato sauce is a complement (as well as a condiment) for hot dogs. If the price of hot dogs rises, what happens to the market for tomato sauce? For tomatoes? For tomato juice? For orange juice?

8 The case study presented in the chapter discussed cigarette taxes as a way to reduce smoking. Now think about the markets for other tobacco products such as cigars and pipe tobacco.

a Are these goods substitutes or complements for cigarettes?

b Using a supply-and-demand diagram, show what happens in the markets for cigars and pipe tobacco if the tax on cigarettes is increased.

c If policymakers wanted to reduce total tobacco consumption, what policies could they combine with the cigarette tax?

9 The market for pizza has the following demand and supply schedules:

Price ($)	Quantity demanded	Quantity supplied
4	135	26
5	104	53
6	81	81
7	68	98
8	53	110
9	39	121

Graph the demand and supply curves. What is the equilibrium price and quantity in this market? If the actual price in this market were above the equilibrium price, what would drive the market towards the equilibrium? If the actual price in this market were below the equilibrium price, what would drive the market towards the equilibrium?

10 In July 2010, vandals in North Queensland poisoned four million tomato seedlings by putting herbicide into the irrigation water. The seedlings were killed. These seedlings would have produced many of the tomatoes that were planned to be sold in Australia in October 2010.

a Using the tools of supply and demand, consider the effect of the poisoning of the tomato seedlings on the market for tomatoes in Australia in October 2010.

b Tomatoes are a major ingredient in salads. News reports suggested that the poisoning would lead to a 'salad surcharge' with restaurants raising the price of salads. Do you agree with this prediction? Why or why not?

c Lettuce is also an ingredient in salads. How will the poisoning of the tomato seedlings affect the price of lettuce and the quantity of lettuce sold? Does your answer depend on whether or not chefs can change the mix of lettuce and tomatoes in a salad?

d News reports suggested that the price of tomatoes would only rise in October. There would not be an effect in August. Do you think this is correct? Does your answer depend on whether or not tomatoes can be stored?

11 Suppose that the price of tickets at your local picture theatre is determined by market forces. Currently, the demand and supply schedules are as follows:

Price ($)	Quantity demanded	Quantity supplied
4	1000	800
8	800	800
12	600	800
16	400	800
20	200	800

  a Draw the demand and supply curves. What is unusual about this supply curve? Why might this be true?
  b What are the equilibrium price and quantity of tickets?
  c Demographers tell you that next year there will be more film goers in the area. The additional people will have the following demand schedule:

Price ($)	Quantity demanded
4	400
8	300
12	200
16	100

   Now add the old demand schedule and the demand schedule for the new people to calculate the new demand schedule for the entire area. What will be the new equilibrium price and quantity?

12 An article in *The New York Times* (18 October 1990) described a successful marketing campaign by the French champagne industry. The article also noted: 'Many executives felt giddy about the stratospheric champagne prices. But they also feared that such sharp price increases would cause demand to decline, which would then cause prices to plunge.' What mistake are the executives making in their analysis of the situation? Illustrate your answer with a graph.

13 (This question requires the use of secondary school algebra.) Market research has revealed the following information about the market for bars of chocolate – the demand schedule can be represented by the equation $Q_D = 1600 - 300P$, where Q_D is the quantity demanded and P is the price. The supply schedule can be represented by the equation $Q_S = 1400 + 700P$, where Q_S is the quantity supplied. Calculate the equilibrium price and quantity in the market for bars of chocolate.

Search me!

  Search me!

When accessing information about economics use the following keywords in any combinations you require:

- equilibrium price
- law of supply and demand

CourseMate

 CourseMate

For more multimedia resources and activities on economics, visit the Economics CourseMate website.

5

Elasticity and its application

Learning objectives

In this chapter you will:

- learn the meaning of the elasticity of demand
- examine what determines the elasticity of demand
- learn the meaning of the elasticity of supply
- examine what determines the elasticity of supply
- apply the concept of elasticity in three very different markets.

Imagine that some event drives up the price of petrol in Australia. It could be a war in the Middle East that disrupts the world supply of oil, a booming Chinese economy that boosts the world demand for oil, or a new tax on petrol passed by parliament. How would Australian consumers respond to the higher price?

It is easy to answer this question in broad fashion: Consumers would buy less. That is simply the law of demand we learned in the previous chapter But you might want a precise answer. By how much would consumption of petrol fall? This question can be answered using a concept called *elasticity*, which we develop in this chapter.

Elasticity is a measure of how much buyers and sellers respond to changes in market conditions. When studying how some event or policy affects a market, we can discuss not only the direction of the effects but their magnitude as well. Elasticity is useful in many applications, as we see later in this chapter.

Before proceeding, however, you might be curious about the answer to the petrol question. Many studies have examined consumers' response to petrol prices in developed countries like Australia. They typically find that the quantity demanded responds more in the long run than it does in the short run. A 10 per cent increase in petrol prices reduces petrol consumption by about 2.5 per cent after a year and about 6 per cent after five years. About half of the long-run reduction in quantity demanded arises because people drive less and half arises because they switch to more fuel-efficient cars. Both responses are reflected in the demand curve for petrol and its elasticity.

The elasticity of demand

When we introduced demand in chapter 4, we noted that buyers usually demand more of a good when its price is lower, when their incomes are higher, when the prices of substitutes for the good are higher or when the prices of complements of the good are lower. Our discussion of demand was qualitative, not quantitative. That is, we discussed the direction in which quantity demanded moves, but not the size of the change. To measure how much demand responds to changes in its determinants, economists use the concept of **elasticity**.

elasticity
a measure of the responsiveness of quantity demanded or quantity supplied to one of its determinants

The price elasticity of demand and its determinants

The law of demand states that a fall in the price of a good raises the quantity demanded. The **price elasticity of demand** measures how much the quantity demanded responds to a change in price. Demand for a good is said to be elastic if the quantity demanded responds substantially to changes in the price. Demand is said to be inelastic if the quantity demanded responds only slightly to changes in the price.

The price elasticity of demand for any good measures how willing consumers are to buy less of the good as its price rises. Because the demand curve reflects the many economic, social and psychological forces that shape consumers' preferences, there is no simple, universal rule for what determines the demand curve's elasticity. Based on experience, however, we can state some general rules about what influences the price elasticity of demand.

price elasticity of demand
a measure of how much the quantity demanded of a good responds to a change in the price of that good, calculated as the percentage change in quantity demanded divided by the percentage change in price

Availability of close substitutes

Goods with close substitutes tend to have more elastic demand because it is easier for consumers to switch from that good to others. For example, butter and margarine are easily substitutable. A small increase in the price of butter, assuming the price of margarine is held fixed, causes the quantity of butter sold to fall by a large amount. In contrast, because eggs are a food without a close substitute, the demand for eggs is probably less elastic than the demand for butter.

▸ price elasticity of demand

Necessities versus luxuries

Necessities tend to have inelastic demands, whereas goods that are luxuries have elastic demands. When the price of a visit to the doctor rises, people will not dramatically alter the number of times they go to the doctor, although they might go a little less often. In contrast, when the price of yachts rises, the quantity demanded falls substantially. The reason is that most people view visits to the doctor as a necessity and yachts as a luxury. Whether a good is a necessity or a luxury depends not on the intrinsic properties of the good but on the preferences of the buyer. For an avid sailor with few health concerns, a yacht might be a necessity with inelastic demand and visits to the doctor a luxury with elastic demand.

Definition of the market

The elasticity of demand in any market depends on how we draw the boundaries of the market. Narrowly defined markets tend to have more elastic demand than broadly defined markets, since it is easier to find close substitutes for narrowly defined goods. For example, food, a broad category, has a fairly inelastic demand because there are no good substitutes for food. Ice-cream, a more narrow category, has a more elastic demand because it is easy to substitute other desserts for ice-cream. Vanilla ice-cream, a very narrow category, has a very elastic demand because other flavours of ice-cream are almost perfect substitutes for vanilla.

Time horizon

Goods tend to have more elastic demand over longer time horizons. When the price of petrol rises, the quantity of petrol demanded falls only slightly in the first few months. Over time, however, people buy more fuel-efficient cars, switch to public transport or move closer to where they work. Within several years, the quantity of petrol demanded falls more substantially.

Computing the price elasticity of demand

Now that we have discussed the price elasticity of demand in general terms, let's be more precise about how it is measured. Economists calculate the price elasticity of demand as the percentage change in the quantity demanded divided by the percentage change in the price. That is:

$$\text{Price elasticity of supply} = \frac{\text{Percentage change in quantity demanded}}{\text{Percentage change in price}}$$

For example, suppose that a 10 per cent increase in the price of an ice-cream causes the amount of ice-cream you buy to fall by 20 per cent. We calculate your elasticity of demand as:

$$\text{Price elasticity of demand} = \frac{20\%}{10\%} = 2$$

In this example, the elasticity is 2, reflecting that the change in the quantity demanded is proportionately twice as large as the change in the price.

Because the quantity demanded of a good is negatively related to its price, the percentage change in quantity will always have the opposite sign to the percentage change in price. In this example, the percentage change in price is a *positive* 10 per cent (reflecting an increase), and the percentage change in quantity demanded is a *negative* 20 per cent (reflecting a decrease). For this reason, price elasticities of demand are sometimes reported as negative numbers. In this book we follow the common practice of dropping the minus sign and reporting all price elasticities as positive numbers. (Mathematicians call this the *absolute value*.) With this convention, a larger price elasticity implies a greater responsiveness of quantity demanded to a change in price.

The variety of demand curves

Economists classify demand curves according to their elasticity. Demand is *elastic* when the elasticity is greater than 1, so that quantity moves proportionately more than the price. Demand is *inelastic* when the elasticity is less than 1, so that quantity moves proportionately less than the price. If the elasticity is exactly 1, so that quantity moves the same amount proportionately as price, demand is said to have *unit elasticity*.

Because the price elasticity of demand measures how much quantity demanded responds to the price, it is closely related to the slope of the demand curve. (For a discussion of slope and elasticity, see the appendix to chapter 2.) The following rule of thumb is a useful guide: The flatter the demand curve that passes through a given point, the greater the price elasticity of demand; the steeper the demand curve that passes through a given point, the smaller the price elasticity of demand.

Figure 5.1 shows five cases. In the extreme case of a zero elasticity, demand is *perfectly inelastic*, and the demand curve is vertical. In this case, regardless of the price, the quantity demanded stays

---

fyi

The midpoint method: A better way to calculate percentage changes and elasticities

If you try calculating the price elasticity of demand between two points on a demand curve, you will quickly notice an annoying problem: The elasticity from point A to point B seems different from the elasticity from point B to point A. For example, consider these numbers:

Point A: Price = $4   Quantity = 120
Point B: Price = $6   Quantity = 80

Going from point A to point B, the price rises by 50 per cent, and the quantity falls by 33 per cent, indicating that the price elasticity of demand is 33/50, or 0.66. By contrast, going from point B to point A, the price falls by 33 per cent, and the quantity rises by 50 per cent, indicating that the price elasticity of demand is 50/30, or 1.5.

One way to avoid this problem is to use the *midpoint method* for calculating elasticities. Rather than computing a percentage change using the standard way (by dividing the change by the initial level), the midpoint method computes a percentage by dividing the change by the midpoint of the initial and final levels. For instance, $5 is the midpoint of $4 and $6. Therefore, according to the midpoint method, a change from $4 to $6 is considered a 40 per cent rise, because (6 − 4)/5 × 100 = 40. Similarly, a change from $6 to $4 is considered a 40 per cent fall.

Because the midpoint method gives the same answer regardless of the direction of change, it is often used when calculating the price elasticity of demand between two points. In our example, the midpoint between point A and point B is:

Midpoint: Price = $5   Quantity = 100

According to the midpoint method, when going from point A to point B, the price rises by 40 per cent and the quantity falls by 40 per cent. Similarly, when going from point B to point A, the price falls by 40 per cent and the quantity rises by 40 per cent. In both directions, the price elasticity of demand equals 1.

We can express the midpoint method with the following formula for the price elasticity of demand between two points, denoted (Q_1, P_1) and (Q_2, P_2):

$$\text{Price elasticity of demand} = \frac{[Q_2 - Q_1]/[[Q_2 + Q_1]/2]}{[P_2 - P_1]/[[P_2 + P_1]/2]}$$

The numerator is the percentage change in quantity computed using the midpoint method, and the denominator is the percentage change in price computed using the midpoint method. If you ever need to calculate elasticities, you should use this formula.

Throughout this book, however, we only rarely need to perform such calculations. For our purposes, what elasticity represents – the responsiveness of quantity demanded to price – is more important than how it is calculated.

Figure 5.1   The price elasticity of demand

The price elasticity of demand determines whether the demand curve is steep or flat. Note that all percentage changes are calculated using the midpoint method.

the same. As the elasticity rises, the demand curve gets flatter and flatter. At the opposite extreme, demand is *perfectly elastic.* This occurs as the price elasticity of demand approaches infinity and the demand curve becomes horizontal, reflecting the fact that very small changes in the price lead to huge changes in the quantity demanded.

Finally, if you have trouble keeping straight the terms *elastic* and *inelastic,* here's a memory trick for you: *I*nelastic curves, such as in panel (a) of Figure 5.1, look like the letter I. *E*lastic curves, as in panel (e), look like the letter E. This may not be a deep insight, but it might help on your next exam.

Total revenue and the price elasticity of demand

When studying changes in supply or demand in a market, one variable we often want to study is **total revenue (in a market)**, the amount paid by buyers and received by sellers of the good. In any market, total revenue is $P \times Q$, the price of the good times the quantity of the good sold. We can show total revenue graphically, as in Figure 5.2. The height of the box under the demand curve is P, and the width is Q. The area of this box, $P \times Q$, equals the total revenue in this market. In Figure 5.2, where $P = \$4$ and $Q = 100$, total revenue is $\$4 \times 100$, or $\$400$.

How does total revenue change as one moves along the demand curve? The answer depends on the price elasticity of demand. If demand is inelastic, as in Figure 5.3, then an increase in the price causes an increase in total revenue. Here an increase in price from $1 to $3 causes the quantity demanded to fall only from 100 to 80, and so total revenue rises from $100 to $240. An increase in price raises $P \times Q$ because the fall in Q is proportionately smaller than the rise in P.

We obtain the opposite result if demand is elastic – an increase in the price causes a decrease in total revenue. In Figure 5.4, for instance, when the price rises from $4 to $5, the quantity demanded falls from

total revenue (in a market)
the amount paid by buyers and received by sellers of a good, calculated as the price of the good times the quantity sold

Figure 5.2	Total revenue

The total amount paid by buyers, and received as revenue by sellers, equals the area of the box under the demand curve, $P \times Q$. Here, at a price of $4, the quantity demanded is 100, and total revenue is $400.

Figure 5.3 How total revenue changes when price changes: inelastic demand

With an inelastic demand curve, an increase in the price leads to a decrease in quantity demanded that is proportionately smaller. Therefore, total revenue (the product of price and quantity) increases. Here, an increase in the price from $1 to $3 causes the quantity demanded to fall from 100 to 80, and total revenue rises from $100 to $240.

Figure 5.4 How total revenue changes when price changes: elastic demand

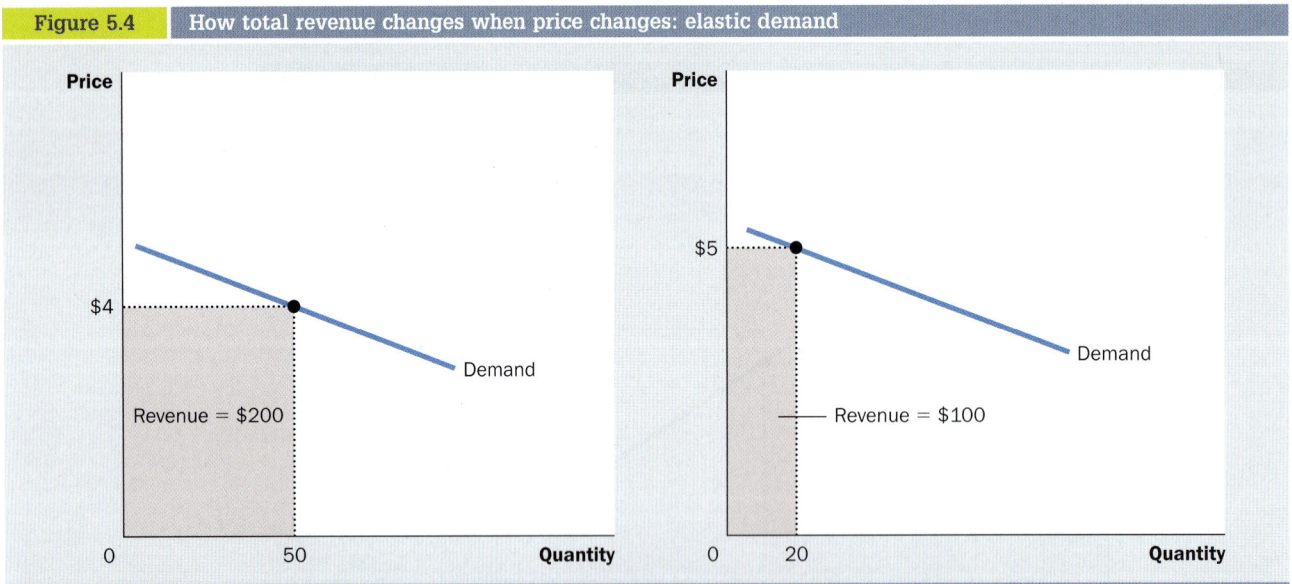

With an elastic demand curve, an increase in the price leads to a decrease in quantity demanded that is proportionately larger. Therefore, total revenue (the product of price and quantity) decreases. Here, an increase in the price from $4 to $5 causes the quantity demanded to fall from 50 to 20, so total revenue falls from $200 to $100.

50 to 20, and so total revenue falls from $200 to $100. Because demand is elastic, the reduction in the quantity demanded is so great that it more than offsets the increase in the price. That is, an increase in price reduces $P \times Q$ because the fall in Q is proportionately greater than the rise in P.

Although the examples in these two figures are extreme, they illustrate some general rules:

- When a demand curve is inelastic (a price elasticity less than 1), a price increase raises total revenue and a price decrease reduces total revenue.
- When a demand curve is elastic (a price elasticity greater than 1), a price increase reduces total revenue and a price decrease raises total revenue.
- In the special case of unit elastic demand (a price elasticity exactly equal to 1), a change in the price does not affect total revenue.

CASESTUDY

Pricing admission to an art gallery

You are curator of a major art gallery. Your financial controller tells you that the gallery is running short of funds and suggests that you consider altering the price of admission to increase total revenue. What do you do? Do you raise the price of admission, or do you lower it?

The answer depends on the elasticity of demand. If the demand for visits to the gallery is inelastic, then an increase in the price of admission would increase total revenue. But if the demand is elastic, then an increase in price would cause the number of visitors to fall by so much that total revenue would decrease. In this case, you should cut the price. The number of visitors would rise by so much that total revenue would increase.

To estimate the price elasticity of demand, you would need to turn to your statisticians. They might use historical data to study how gallery attendance varied from year to year as the admission price changed. Or they might use data on attendance at various galleries around the country to see how the admission price affects attendance. In studying either of these sets of data, the statisticians would need to take account of other factors that affect

If the price of admission were higher, how much smaller would this crowd be?

Source: iStockphoto.

attendance – weather, population, size of collection and so on – in order to isolate the effect of price. In the end, such data analysis would provide an estimate of the price elasticity of demand, which you could use in deciding how to respond to your financial problem.

Other demand elasticities

In addition to the price elasticity of demand, economists also use other elasticities to describe the behaviour of buyers in a market.

The income elasticity of demand

Economists use the **income elasticity of demand** to measure how the quantity demanded changes as consumer income changes. The income elasticity is the percentage change in quantity demanded divided by the percentage change in income. That is:

$$\text{Income elasticity of demand} = \frac{\text{Percentage change in quantity demanded}}{\text{Percentage change in income}}$$

income elasticity of demand
a measure of how much the quantity demanded of a good responds to a change in consumers' income, calculated as the percentage change in quantity demanded divided by the percentage change in income

▸ income elasticity of demand

As we discussed in chapter 4, most goods are normal goods – higher income raises quantity demanded. Because quantity demanded and income move in the same direction, normal goods have positive income elasticities. A few goods, such as second-hand clothes, are inferior goods – higher income lowers the quantity demanded. Because quantity demanded and income move in opposite directions, inferior goods have negative income elasticities.

Even among normal goods, income elasticities vary substantially in size. Necessities, such as food and clothing, tend to have small income elasticities because consumers, regardless of how low their incomes, choose to buy some of these goods. Luxuries, such as caviar and furs, tend to have large income elasticities because consumers feel that they can do without these goods altogether if their income is too low.

The cross-price elasticity of demand

cross-price elasticity of demand
a measure of how much the quantity demanded of one good responds to a change in the price of another good, computed as the percentage change in quantity demanded of the first good divided by the percentage change in the price of the second good.

Economists use the **cross-price elasticity of demand** to measure how the quantity demanded of one good changes as the price of another good changes. It is calculated as the percentage change in quantity demanded of good 1 divided by the percentage change in the price of good 2. That is:

$$\text{Cross–price elasticity of demand} = \frac{\text{Percentage change in quantity of good 1}}{\text{Percentage change in price of good 2}}$$

fyi

Elasticity and total revenue along a linear demand curve

Although some demand curves have an elasticity that is the same along the entire curve, that is not always the case. An example of a demand curve along which elasticity changes is a straight line, as shown in Figure 5.5. A linear demand curve has a constant slope. Recall that slope is defined as 'rise over run', which here is the ratio of the change in price ('rise') to the change in quantity ('run'). In this case, the demand curve's slope is constant because each $1 increase in price causes the same 2-unit decrease in the quantity demanded.

Even though the slope of a linear demand curve is constant, the elasticity is not. The reason is that the slope is the ratio of *changes* in the two variables, whereas the elasticity is the ratio of *percentage changes* in the two variables. You can see this most easily by looking at Table 5.1. This table shows the demand schedule for the linear demand curve in Figure 5.5 and calculates the price elasticity of demand using the midpoint method discussed earlier. At points with low price and high quantity, the demand curve is inelastic. At points with a high price and low quantity, the demand curve is elastic.

Table 5.1 also presents total revenue at each point on the demand curve. These numbers illustrate the relationship between total revenue and elasticity. When the price is $1, for instance, demand is inelastic and a price increase to $2 raises total revenue. When the price is $5, demand is elastic and a price increase to $6 reduces total revenue. Between $3 and $4, demand is exactly unit elastic and total revenue is the same at these two prices.

Figure 5.5 A linear demand curve

Elasticity is larger than 1.

Elasticity is smaller than 1.

The slope of a linear demand curve is constant, but its elasticity is not.

Price($)	Quantity	Total revenue (price × quantity)	% change in price	% change in quantity	Elasticity	Description
0	14	$0				
1	12	12	200	15	0.1	Inelastic
2	10	20	67	18	0.3	Inelastic
3	8	24	40	22	0.6	Inelastic
4	6	24	29	29	1.0	Unit elastic
5	4	20	22	40	1.8	Elastic
6	2	12	18	67	3.7	Elastic
7	0	0	15	200	13.0	Elastic

Table 5.1 Calculating the elasticity of a linear demand curve

Whether the cross-price elasticity is a positive or negative number depends on whether the two goods are substitutes or complements. As we discussed in chapter 4, substitutes are goods that are typically used in place of one another, such as hamburgers and hot dogs. Because the price of hot dogs and the quantity of hamburgers demanded move in the same direction, the cross-price elasticity is positive. Conversely, complements are goods that are typically used together, such as computers and software. In this case, the cross-price elasticity is negative, indicating that an increase in the price of computers reduces the quantity of software demanded.

IN THE NEWS . . .

ON THE ROAD WITH ELASTICITY

How should a firm that operates a private toll road set a price for its service? This article considers the problem of pricing for the City Link toll road in Melbourne. Answering the question of pricing requires an understanding of the demand curve and its elasticity.

City Link to lift tolls 11%
by Sushi Das

City Link tolls will jump a staggering 11 per cent after July 1 – a move the road's owner conceded yesterday was likely to lead to motorists avoiding the tollway and putting further pressure on local roads.

The increase takes into account the Federal Government's GST and a regular quarterly toll increase of more than 1 per cent.

Transurban managing director Kim Edwards said motorists were likely to divert off the link in the short-term to avoid the GST, but would return once they factored in income tax cuts.

'I suspect that like all businesses there will be some impact for a short term but I don't think it will be sustained,' Mr Edwards said.

The Victorian Government and the RACV believe tolls are too high and cheaper packages are needed to attract more motorists.

>>

Under Transurban's contract with the state, it may increase tolls every three months to a maximum of 4.5 per cent annually or the CPI rate – whichever is higher.

Transport Minister Peter Batchelor said the GST would mean that some people would find it hard to pay for City Link tolls, and might turn to residential streets.

'It (the GST) is going to make the tolls more expensive, it's going to make it more difficult for people to use the tollway. It stands to reason,' Mr Batchelor said.

RACV spokesman David Cumming said he was concerned motorists had been slugged with such a large increase in tolls so early in City Link's operation.

'It's bad news because next time Transurban has the right to take in whatever inflation is … we all know that on projections

the GST will lead to about an 8 per cent increase in CPI,' he said. 'There is no doubt that Transurban intends to take the maximum allowed increase every time it occurs. They are doing that to keep faith with their shareholders.'

While Transurban is pleased with strong growth in the use of the southern link, the numbers of vehicles using the western link are below expectations.

VicRoads figures show there has been a significant traffic increase on roads in Melbourne's north west, especially on Mount Alexander and Pascoe Vale roads.

Mr Cumming said motorists would decide if their tax cuts were enough to pay for additional costs in petrol and tolls.

Source: Sushi Das/*The Age*, 17 June 2000.

Define *price elasticity of demand*. Explain the relationship between total revenue and the price elasticity of demand.

IN THE NEWS ...

CAN YOU MEASURE PRICE ELASTICITY WITHOUT UPSETTING YOUR CUSTOMERS?

In order to determine your customer's price elasticity, you need to see what they will choose to buy at different prices. As this story shows, trying that experiment can have unintended consequences.

On the web, price tags blur; what you pay could depend on who you are
by David Streitfeld

Few things stir up a consumer revolt quicker than the notion that someone else is getting a better deal. That's a lesson Amazon.com has just learned.

Amazon, the largest and most potent force in e-commerce, was recently revealed to be selling the same DVD movies for different prices to different customers. It was the first

major Web test of a strategy called 'dynamic pricing', which gauges a shopper's desire, measures his means and then charges accordingly.

The Internet was supposed to empower consumers, letting them compare deals with the click of a mouse. But it is also supplying retailers with information about their customers that they never had before, along with the technology to use all this accumulated data. While prices have always varied by geography, local competition and whim, retailers were never able to effectively target individuals until the Web.

'Dynamic pricing is the new reality, and it's going to be used by more and more retailers,' said Vernon Keenan, a San Francisco Internet consultant. 'In the future, what you pay will be determined by where you live and who you are. It's unfair, but that doesn't mean it's not going to happen.'

With its detailed records on the buying habits of 23 million consumers, Amazon is perfectly situated to employ dynamic pricing on a massive scale. But its trial ran into a snag early this month when the regulars discussing DVDs at the Web site DVDTalk.com noticed something odd.

One man recounted how he ordered the DVD of Julie Taymor's 'Titus', paying $24.49. The next week he went back to Amazon and saw that the price had jumped to $26.24. As an experiment, he stripped his computer of the electronic tags that identified him to Amazon as a regular customer. Then the price fell to $22.74.

'Amazon was trying to figure out how much their loyal customers would pay', said Barrett Ladd, a retail analyst with Gomez Advisors. 'And the customers found out.'

A number of DVDTalk.com visitors were particularly distressed to find that prices seemed to be higher for regular customers. 'They must figure that with repeat Amazon customers they have "won" them over and they can charge them slightly higher prices since they are loyal and "don't mind and/or don't notice" that they are being charged three to five per cent more for some items,' wrote a user whose online handle is Deep Sleep.

Amazon says the pricing variations, which it stopped as soon as the complaints began coming in from DVDTalk members, were completely random.

'It was done to determine consumer responses to different discount levels,' said spokesman Bill Curry. 'This was a pure and simple price test. This was not dynamic pricing. We don't do that and have no plans ever to do that.'

But an Amazon customer service representative called it exactly that in an e-mail to a DVDTalk member.

'I would first like to send along my most sincere apology for any confusion or frustration caused by our dynamic price test,' wrote the company's Galen Sather. 'Dynamic testing of a customer base is a common practice among both brick & mortar and internet companies.'

Indeed, physical stores have always had varied pricing. Prices might be higher in an affluent neighborhood or lower, depending on the goods being sold. A stereo system or camera purchased in certain neighborhoods of Manhattan would almost always be cheaper than in a small town with only one electronics store. Industries as basic as airlines and automobiles routinely adjust their prices because of the consumer's negotiating skills and general savvy.

Still, these traditional methods used to calculate prices are sledgehammers compared with the Internet's scalpel. For one thing, the Web provides a continuous feedback loop: The more the consumer buys from a Web site, the more the site knows about him and the weaker his bargaining position is. It's as if the corner drugstore could see you coming down the sidewalk, clutching your fevered brow, and then double the price of aspirin.

'Any retailer would love to do dynamic pricing if they could,' said analyst Ladd. 'If you could make the optimum amount of money from a consumer who's willing to pay more, that's a beautiful thing.'…

Amazon swears it won't happen there again. 'Dynamic pricing is stupid, because people will find out,' said spokesman Curry. 'Fortunately, it only took us two instances to see this.'

The retailer has worked very hard, and largely successfully, to build an image of itself as the most consumer-centric business ever. Technology writers have penned love songs to the site, while analysts routinely commend it for excellent customer relations.

No wonder Amazon hasn't exactly been issuing news releases about its tests of dynamic pricing.

'It's not the kind of communication you can offer to your customers and expect them to accept,' said Jupiter analyst May. 'This is an initiative that can only be undertaken in a clandestine manner. No customer, no matter what their net worth, is going to be willing to pay more than anyone else.'

>>

The elasticity of supply

When we introduced supply in chapter 4, we noted that sellers of a good increase the quantity supplied when the price of the good rises, when their input prices fall or when their technology improves. To turn from qualitative to quantitative statements about supply, we once again use the concept of elasticity.

The price elasticity of supply and its determinants

price elasticity of supply
a measure of how much the quantity supplied of a good responds to a change in the price of that good, calculated as the percentage change in quantity supplied divided by the percentage change in price

The law of supply states that higher prices raise the quantity supplied. The **price elasticity of supply** measures how much the quantity supplied responds to changes in the price. Supply of a good is said to be *elastic* if the quantity supplied responds substantially to changes in the price. Supply is said to be *inelastic* if the quantity supplied responds only slightly to changes in the price.

The price elasticity of supply depends on the flexibility of sellers to change the amount of the good they produce. For example, beachfront land has an inelastic supply because it is almost impossible to produce more of it. In contrast, manufactured goods, such as books, cars and televisions, have elastic supplies because the firms that produce them can run their factories longer in response to a higher price.

In most markets, a key determinant of the price elasticity of supply is the time period being considered. Supply is usually more elastic in the long run than in the short run. Over short periods of time, firms cannot easily change the size of their factories to make more or less of a good. Thus, in the short run, the quantity supplied is not very responsive to the price. In contrast, over longer periods, firms can build new factories or close old ones. In addition, new firms can enter a market and old firms can shut down. Thus, in the long run, the quantity supplied can respond substantially to the price.

Computing the price elasticity of supply

Now that we have some idea about what the price elasticity of supply is, let's be more precise. Economists calculate the price elasticity of supply as the percentage change in the quantity supplied divided by the percentage change in the price. That is:

$$\text{Price elasticity of supply} = \frac{\text{Percentage change in quantity supplied}}{\text{Percentage change in price}}$$

For example, suppose that an increase in the price of milk from $1.00 to $1.10 a litre raises the amount that dairy farmers produce from 10 000 to 11 500 litres per month. We calculate the percentage change in price as:

$$\text{Percentage change in price} = (1.10 - 1.00)/1.00 \times 100 = 10\%$$

Similarly, we calculate the percentage change in quantity supplied as:

Percentage change in quantity supplied = (11 500 − 10 000)/10 000 × 100 = 15%

In this case, the price elasticity of supply is:

$$\text{Price elasticity of supply} = \frac{15\%}{10\%} = 1.5$$

In this example, the elasticity of 1.5 is greater than 1, which reflects the fact that the quantity supplied moves proportionately more than the price.

The variety of supply curves

Because the price elasticity of supply measures the responsiveness of quantity supplied to the price, it is reflected in the appearance of the supply curve. Figure 5.6 shows five cases. In the extreme case of a zero elasticity, supply is *perfectly inelastic*, and the supply curve is vertical. In this case, the quantity supplied is the same regardless of the price. As the elasticity rises, the supply curve gets flatter, which shows that the quantity supplied responds more to changes in the price. At the opposite extreme, supply is *perfectly elastic*. This occurs as the price elasticity of supply approaches infinity and the supply curve is horizontal, meaning that very small changes in the price lead to very large changes in the quantity supplied.

In some markets, the elasticity of supply is not constant but varies over the supply curve. Figure 5.7 shows a typical case for an industry in which firms have factories with a limited capacity for production. For low levels of quantity supplied, the elasticity of supply is high, indicating that firms respond substantially to changes in the price. In this region, firms have capacity for production that is not being used, such as plant and equipment sitting idle for all or part of the day. Small increases in price make it profitable for firms to begin using this idle capacity. As the quantity supplied rises, firms begin to reach capacity. Once capacity is fully used, increasing production further requires the construction of new factories. To induce firms to incur this extra expense, the price must rise substantially, so supply becomes less elastic.

Figure 5.7 presents a numerical example of this phenomenon. When the price rises from $3 to $4 (a 29 per cent increase according to the midpoint method), the quantity supplied rises from 100 to 200 (a 67 per cent increase). Because quantity supplied moves proportionately more than the price, the supply curve has elasticity greater than 1. In contrast, when the price rises from $12 to $15 (a 22 per cent increase), the quantity supplied rises from 500 to 525 (a 5 per cent increase). In this case, quantity supplied moves proportionately less than the price, so the elasticity is less than 1.

Define *price elasticity of supply*. Explain why the price elasticity of supply might be different in the long run than in the short run.

Three applications of supply, demand and elasticity

Can good news for farming be bad news for farmers? Why would the Organization of Petroleum Exporting Countries (OPEC) fail to keep the price of oil high? Does greater enforcement of drug laws

Figure 5.6 The price elasticity of supply

(a) Perfectly inelastic supply: elasticity equals 0

Price

Supply

$5
4

1. An increase in price …

0   100   **Quantity**

2. … leaves the quantity supplied unchanged.

(b) Inelastic supply: elasticity is less than 1

Price

Supply

$5
4

1. A 22% increase in price …

0   100 → 110   **Quantity**

2. … leads to a 10% increase in quantity supplied.

(c) Unit elastic supply: elasticity equals 1

Price

Supply

$5
4

1. A 22% increase in price …

0   100 → 125   **Quantity**

2. … leads to a 22% increase in quantity supplied.

(d) Elastic supply: elasticity is greater than 1

Price

Supply

$5
4

1. A 22% increase in price …

0   100 → 200   **Quantity**

2. … leads to a 67% increase in quantity supplied.

(e) Perfectly elastic supply: elasticity equals infinity

Price

1. At any price above $4, quantity supplied is infinite.

$4   Supply

2. At exactly $4, producers will supply any quantity.

0   **Quantity**

3. At a price below $4, quantity supplied is zero.

The price elasticity of supply determines whether the supply curve is steep or flat. Note that all percentage changes are calculated using the midpoint method.

| Figure 5.7 | How the price elasticity of supply can vary |

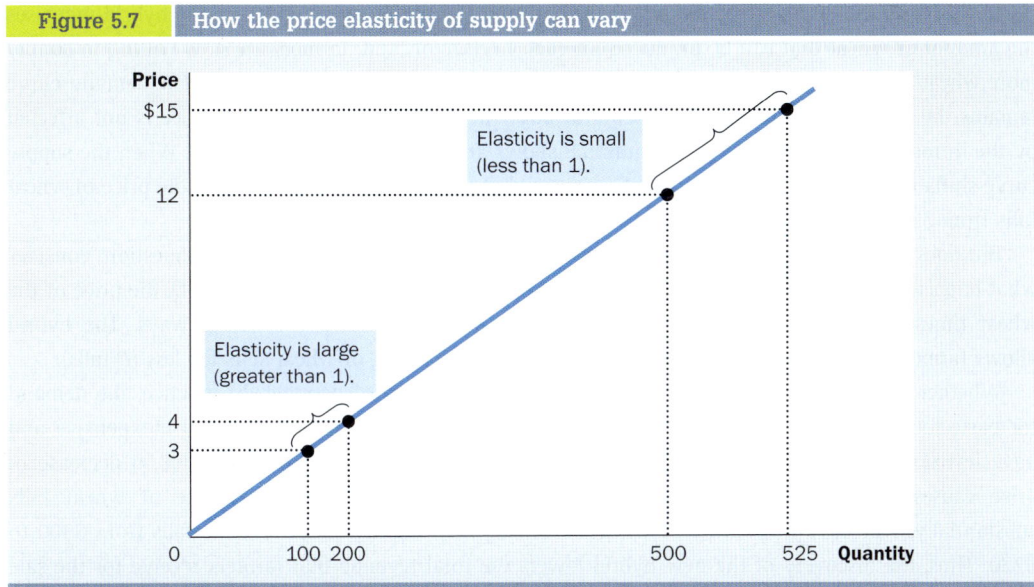

Because firms often have a maximum capacity for production, the elasticity of supply may be very high at low levels of quantity supplied and very low at high levels of quantity supplied. Here, an increase in price from $3 to $4 increases the quantity supplied from 100 to 200. Because the increase in quantity supplied of 100 per cent is larger than the increase in price of 33 per cent, the supply curve is elastic in this range. In contrast, when the price rises from $12 to $15, the quantity supplied rises from 500 to only 525. Because the increase in quantity supplied of 5 per cent is smaller than the increase in price of 25 per cent, the supply curve is inelastic in this range.

increase or decrease drug-related crime? At first, these questions might seem to have little in common. Yet all three questions are about markets and all markets are subject to the forces of supply and demand. Here we apply the versatile tools of supply, demand and elasticity to answer these seemingly complex questions.

Can good news for farming be bad news for farmers?

Imagine yourself as a West Australian wheat farmer. Because you earn all your income from selling wheat, you devote much effort to making your land as productive as possible. You monitor weather and soil conditions, check your fields for pests and disease and study the latest advances in farm technology. You know that the more wheat you grow, the more you will have to sell after the harvest and the higher will be your income and your standard of living.

One day, the University of Western Australia announces a major discovery. Researchers in its agronomy department have devised a new hybrid of wheat that raises the amount farmers can produce from each acre of land by 20 per cent. How should you react to this news? Does this discovery make you better off or worse off than you were before?

Recall from chapter 4 that we answer such questions in three steps. First, we examine whether the supply or demand curve shifts. Second, we consider in which direction the curve shifts. Third, we use the supply-and-demand diagram to see how the market equilibrium changes.

110

In this case, the discovery of the new hybrid affects the supply curve. Because the hybrid increases the amount of wheat that can be produced on each hectare of land, farmers are now willing to supply more wheat at any given price. In other words, the supply curve shifts to the right. The demand curve remains the same because consumers' desire to buy wheat products at any given price is not affected by the introduction of a new hybrid. Figure 5.8 shows an example of such a change. When the supply curve shifts from S_1 to S_2, the quantity of wheat sold increases from 100 to 110 and the price of wheat falls from $3 to $2.

But does this discovery make farmers better off? As a first cut to answering this question, consider what happens to the total revenue received by farmers. Farmers' total revenue is $P \times Q$, the price of the wheat times the quantity sold. The discovery affects farmers in two conflicting ways. The hybrid allows farmers to produce more wheat (Q rises), but now each bag of wheat sells for less (P falls).

Whether total revenue rises or falls depends on the elasticity of demand. In practice, the demand for basic foodstuffs such as wheat is usually inelastic, for these items are relatively inexpensive and have few good substitutes. When the demand curve is inelastic, as it is in Figure 5.8, a decrease in price causes total revenue to fall. You can see this in the figure – the price of wheat falls substantially, whereas the quantity of wheat sold rises only slightly. Total revenue falls from $300 to $220. Thus, the discovery of the new hybrid lowers the total revenue that farmers receive for the sale of their crops.

If farmers are made worse off by the discovery of this new hybrid, why do they adopt it? The answer to this question goes to the heart of how competitive markets work. Because each farmer is a

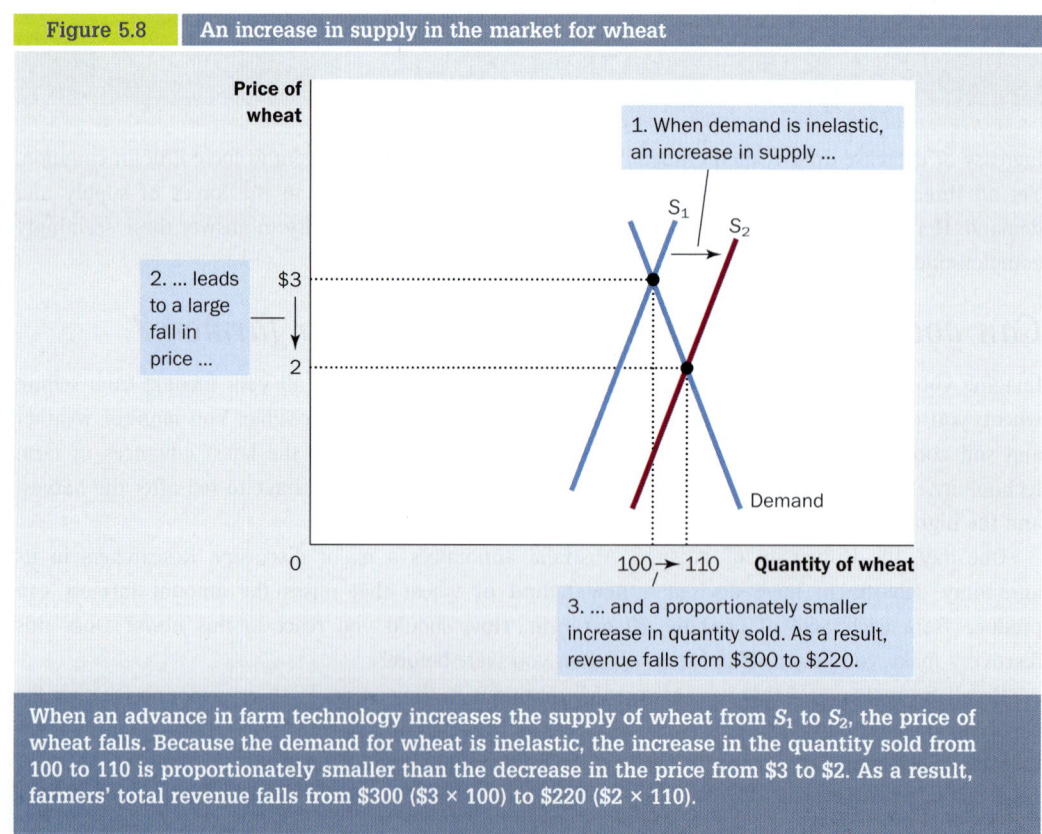

Figure 5.8   An increase in supply in the market for wheat

1. When demand is inelastic, an increase in supply ...

S_1

S_2

2. ... leads to a large fall in price ...

$3

2

Demand

0

100 → 110   **Quantity of wheat**

3. ... and a proportionately smaller increase in quantity sold. As a result, revenue falls from $300 to $220.

When an advance in farm technology increases the supply of wheat from S_1 to S_2, the price of wheat falls. Because the demand for wheat is inelastic, the increase in the quantity sold from 100 to 110 is proportionately smaller than the decrease in the price from $3 to $2. As a result, farmers' total revenue falls from $300 ($3 × 100) to $220 ($2 × 110).

small part of the market for wheat, he or she takes the price of wheat as given. For any given price of wheat, it is better to use the new hybrid in order to produce and sell more wheat. Yet when all farmers do this, the supply of wheat rises, the price falls and farmers are worse off.

This analysis of the market for farm products also helps to explain a seeming paradox of public policy – certain farm policies try to help farmers by getting farmers to destroy some of their crops. For example, in the 1980s the Australian government paid winemakers to pull up their grape vines. The purpose of these programs is to reduce the supply of farm products and thereby raise prices. Because demand is inelastic, farmers as a group receive greater total revenue if they supply a smaller crop to the market. No single farmer would choose to destroy crops alone, since each takes the market price as given. But if all farmers do so together, each can be better off.

When analysing the effects of farm technology or farm policy, it is important to keep in mind that what is good for farmers is not necessarily good for society as a whole. Improvement in farm technology can be bad for farmers who become increasingly unnecessary, but it is surely good for consumers who pay less for food. Similarly, a policy aimed at reducing the supply of farm products may raise the incomes of farmers, but it does so at the expense of consumers.

Why did OPEC fail to keep the price of oil high?

Many of the most disruptive events for the world's economies over the past several decades have originated in the world market for oil. In the 1970s, members of OPEC decided to raise the world price of oil in order to increase their incomes. These countries accomplished this goal by jointly reducing the amount of oil they supplied. From 1973 to 1974, the price of oil (adjusted for overall inflation) rose more than 50 per cent. Then, a few years later, OPEC did the same thing again. The price of oil rose 14 per cent in 1979, followed by 34 per cent in 1980 and 34 per cent in 1981.

Yet OPEC found it difficult to maintain a high price. From 1982 to 1985, the price of oil steadily declined by about 10 per cent per year. Dissatisfaction and disarray soon prevailed among the OPEC countries. In 1986, cooperation among OPEC members completely broke down and the price of oil plunged 45 per cent. In 1990, the price of oil (adjusted for overall inflation) was back to where it was in 1970, and stayed at that low level throughout most of the 1990s. (In the first decade of the 21st century, the price of oil fluctuated substantially once again, but the main driving force was changes in world demand rather than OPEC supply restrictions. Early in the decade, oil demand and prices spiked up, in part because of a large and rapidly growing Chinese economy. They plunged in 2008–09 as the world economy fell into a deep recession and then started rising once again as the world economy started to recover.)

The OPEC episodes of the 1970s and 1980s show how supply and demand can behave differently in the short run and in the long run. In the short run, both the supply and demand for oil are relatively inelastic. Supply is inelastic because the quantity of known oil reserves and the capacity for oil extraction cannot be changed quickly. Demand is inelastic because buying habits do not respond immediately to changes in price. Many drivers with old cars that 'guzzle' petrol and oil, for instance, will just pay the higher price. Thus, as panel (a) of Figure 5.9 shows, the short-run supply and demand curves are steep. When the supply of oil shifts from S_1 to S_2, the price increase from P_1 to P_2 is large.

The situation is very different in the long run. Over long periods of time, producers of oil outside of OPEC respond to high prices by increasing oil exploration and by erecting new drilling rigs. Consumers respond with greater conservation, for instance by replacing old inefficient cars with newer efficient

112

Figure 5.9 | A reduction in supply in the world market for oil

(a) The oil market in the short run

Price of oil

1. In the short run, when supply and demand are inelastic, a shift in supply …

2. … leads to a large increase in price.

S_2 S_1 P_2 P_1

Demand

Quantity of oil

(b) The oil market in the long run

Price of oil

1. In the long run, when supply and demand are elastic, a shift in supply …

2. … leads to a small increase in price.

S_2 S_1 P_2 P_1

Demand

Quantity of oil

When the supply of oil falls, the response depends on the time horizon. In the short run, supply and demand are relatively inelastic, as in panel (a). Thus, when the supply curve shifts from S_1 to S_2, the price rises substantially. In contrast, in the long run, supply and demand are relatively elastic, as in panel (b). In this case, the same size shift in the supply curve (S_1 to S_2) causes a smaller increase in the price.

ones. Thus, as panel (b) of Figure 5.9 shows, the long-run supply and demand curves are more elastic. In the long run, the shift in the supply curve from S_1 to S_2 causes a much smaller increase in the price.

This analysis shows why OPEC succeeded in maintaining a high price of oil only in the short run. When OPEC countries agreed to reduce their production of oil, they shifted the supply curve to the left. Even though each OPEC member sold less oil, the price rose by so much in the short run that OPEC's incomes rose. In contrast, in the long run when supply and demand are more elastic, the same reduction in supply, measured by the horizontal shift in the supply curve, caused a smaller increase in the price. Thus, OPEC's coordinated reduction in supply proved less profitable in the long run.

OPEC still exists today and it has from time to time succeeded at reducing supply and raising prices. The cartel now seems to understand that raising prices is easier in the short run than in the long run.

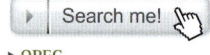

Search me!

▸ OPEC

Do drug bans increase or decrease drug-related crime?

A persistent problem facing our society is the use of illegal drugs, such as heroin, cocaine and crack. Drug use has several adverse effects. One is that drug dependency can ruin the lives of drug users and their families. Another is that drug addicts often turn to robbery and other violent crimes to obtain the money needed to support their habit. To discourage the use of illegal drugs, many governments devote billions of dollars each year to reduce the flow of drugs into their countries. Let's use the tools of supply and demand to examine this policy of drug prohibition.

Suppose the Australian government increases the number of customs inspectors and police officers devoted to preventing imports of drugs. What happens in the market for illegal drugs? As is usual, we answer this question in three steps. First, we consider whether the supply or demand curve shifts. Second, we consider the direction of the shift. Third, we see how the shift affects the equilibrium price and quantity.

Although the purpose of drug prohibition is to reduce drug use, its direct impact is on the sellers of drugs rather than the buyers. When the government stops some drugs from entering the country and arrests more smugglers, it raises the cost of selling drugs and, therefore, reduces the quantity of drugs supplied at any given price. The demand for drugs – the amount buyers want at any given price – is not changed. As panel (a) of Figure 5.10 shows, prohibition shifts the supply curve to the left from S_1 to S_2 and leaves the demand curve the same. The equilibrium price of drugs rises from P_1 to P_2, and the equilibrium quantity falls from Q_1 to Q_2. The fall in the equilibrium quantity shows that drug prohibition does reduce drug use.

But what about the amount of drug-related crime? To answer this question, consider the total amount that drug users pay for the drugs they buy. Because few drug addicts are likely to break their destructive habits in response to a higher price, it is likely that the demand for drugs is inelastic, as it is drawn in the figure. If demand is inelastic, then an increase in price raises total revenue in the drug market. That is, because drug prohibition raises the price of drugs proportionately more than it reduces drug use, it raises the total amount of money that drug users pay for drugs. Addicts who already had

Figure 5.10   **Policies to reduce the use of illegal drugs**

(a) Drug prohibition

(b) Drug education

Drug prohibition reduces the supply of drugs from S_1 to S_2, as in panel (a). If the demand for drugs is inelastic, then the total amount paid by drug users rises, even as the amount of drug use falls. In contrast, drug education reduces the demand for drugs from D_1 to D_2, as in panel (b). Because both price and quantity fall, the amount paid by drug users falls.

114

to steal to support their habits would have an even greater need for quick cash. Thus, drug bans could increase drug-related crime.

Because of this adverse effect of drug prohibition, some analysts argue for alternative approaches to the drug problem. Rather than trying to reduce the supply of drugs, policymakers might try to reduce the demand by pursuing a policy of drug education. Successful drug education has the effects shown in panel (b) of Figure 5.10. The demand curve shifts to the left from D_1 to D_2. As a result, the equilibrium quantity falls from Q_1 to Q_2, and the equilibrium price falls from P_1 to P_2. Total revenue, which is price times quantity, also falls. Thus, in contrast to drug prohibition, drug education can reduce both drug use and drug-related crime.

Advocates of drug prohibition might argue that the effects of this policy are different in the long run than in the short run, because the elasticity of demand may depend on the time horizon. The demand for drugs is probably inelastic over short periods of time because higher prices do not substantially affect drug use by established addicts. But demand may be more elastic over longer periods of time because higher prices would discourage experimentation with drugs among the young and, over time, lead to fewer drug addicts. In this case, drug prohibition would increase drug-related crime in the short run but decrease it in the long run.

 How might a drought that destroys half of all farm crops be good for farmers? If such a drought is good for farmers, why don't farmers destroy their own crops in the absence of a drought?

Conclusion

According to an old quip, even a parrot can become an economist simply by learning to say 'supply and demand'. The last two chapters should have convinced you that there is much truth in this statement. The tools of supply and demand allow you to analyse many of the most important events and policies that shape the economy. You are now well on your way to becoming an economist (or, at least, a well-educated parrot).

Summary

- The price elasticity of demand measures how much the quantity demanded responds to changes in the price. Demand tends to be more elastic if the good is a luxury rather than a necessity, if close substitutes are available, if the market is narrowly defined, or if buyers have substantial time to react to a price change.
- The price elasticity of demand is calculated as the percentage change in quantity demanded divided by the percentage change in price. If the elasticity is less than 1, so that quantity demanded moves proportionately less than the price, demand is said to be inelastic. If the elasticity is greater than 1, so that quantity demanded moves proportionately more than the price, demand is said to be elastic.
- Total revenue, the total amount paid for a good, equals the price of the good times the quantity sold. For inelastic demand curves, total revenue rises as price rises. For elastic demand curves, total revenue falls as price rises.
- The income elasticity of demand measures how much the quantity demanded responds to changes in consumers' income. The cross-price elasticity of demand measure how much the quantity demanded of one good responds to the price of another good.
- The price elasticity of supply measures how much the quantity supplied responds to changes in the price. This elasticity often depends on the time horizon under consideration. In most markets, supply is more elastic in the long run than in the short run.
- The price elasticity of supply is calculated as the percentage change in quantity supplied divided by the percentage change in price. If the elasticity is less than 1, so that quantity supplied moves proportionately less than the price, supply is said to be inelastic. If the elasticity is greater than 1, so that quantity supplied moves proportionately more than the price, supply is said to be elastic.
- The tools of supply and demand can be applied in many different kinds of markets. This chapter uses them to analyse the market for wheat, the market for oil and the market for illegal drugs.

Key concepts

cross-price elasticity
of demand
elasticity

income elasticity of
demand
price elasticity of
demand

price elasticity of supply
total revenue

Questions for review

1 Define the price elasticity of demand and the income elasticity of demand.
2 List and explain some of the determinants of the price elasticity of demand.
3 If the elasticity is greater than 1, is demand elastic or inelastic? If the elasticity equals 0, is demand perfectly elastic or perfectly inelastic?
4 On a supply-and-demand diagram, show total spending by consumers. How does this compare with total revenue received by producers?
5 If demand is elastic, how will an increase in price change total revenue? Explain.
6 What do we call a good whose income elasticity is less than 0?
7 What is the formula for the price elasticity of supply? Explain what this measures.
8 What is the price elasticity of supply of Picasso paintings?

9 Is the price elasticity of supply usually larger in the short run or in the long run? Why?
10 In the 1970s, OPEC caused a dramatic increase in the price of oil. What prevented the organisation from maintaining this high price through the 1980s?

Problems and applications

1 For each of the following pairs of goods, which good would you expect to have more elastic demand and why?
   a required textbooks or mystery novels
   b beethoven recordings or classical music recordings in general
   c bus trips during the next six months or bus trips during the next five years
   d lemonade or water.
2 Suppose that business travellers and holiday-makers have the following demand for airline tickets from Sydney to Melbourne:

Price ($)	Quantity demanded (business travellers)	Quantity demanded (holiday-makers)
150	2100	1000
200	2000	800
250	1900	600
300	1800	400

   a As the price of tickets rises from $200 to $250, what is the price elasticity of demand for (i) business travellers and (ii) holiday-makers?
   b Why might holiday-makers have a different elasticity than business travellers?
3 Suppose that your demand schedule for compact discs is as follows:

Price ($)	Quantity demanded (income = $10 000)	Quantity demanded (income = $12 000)
8	40	50
10	32	45
12	24	30
14	16	20

   a Calculate your price elasticity of demand as the price of compact discs increases from $8 to $10 if (i) your income is $10 000, and (ii) your income is $12 000.
   b Calculate your income elasticity of demand as your income increases from $10 000 to $12 000 if (i) the price is $12, and (ii) the price is $16.

4 Emily has decided always to spend one-third of her income on clothing.
   a What is her income elasticity of clothing demand?
   b What is her price elasticity of clothing demand?
   c If Emily's tastes change and she decides to spend only a quarter of her income on clothing, how does her demand curve change? What is her income elasticity and price elasticity now?

5 *The New York Times* (17 February 1996) reported that subway use declined after a fare increase: 'There were nearly four million fewer riders in December 1995, the first full month after the price of a token increased 25 cents to $1.50, than in the previous December, a 4.3 per cent decline.'
   a Use these data to estimate the price elasticity of demand for subway rides.
   b According to your estimate, what happens to the revenue when the fare rises?
   c Why might your estimate of the elasticity be unreliable?

6 Two drivers – Tom and Jerry – each drive up to a petrol station. Before looking at the price and starting to pump petrol, Tom says: 'I will buy 10 litres of petrol'. Jerry says: 'I will buy $10 of petrol'. What is each driver's price elasticity of demand?

7 Economists have observed that spending on restaurant meals declines more during economic downturns than does spending on food to be eaten at home. How might the concept of elasticity help to explain this phenomenon?

8 Consider public policy aimed at smoking.
   a Studies indicate that the price elasticity of demand for cigarettes is about 0.4. If a packet of cigarettes currently costs $8 and the government wants to reduce smoking by 20 per cent, by how much should it increase the price?
   b If the government permanently increases the price of cigarettes, will the policy have a larger effect on smoking one year from now or five years from now?
   c Studies also find that teenagers have a higher price elasticity than do adults. Why might this be true?

9 Would you expect the price elasticity of *demand* to be larger in the market for all ice-cream or the market for vanilla ice-cream? Would you expect the price elasticity of *supply* to be larger in the market for all ice-cream or the market for vanilla ice-cream? Be sure to explain your answers.

10 Pharmaceutical drugs have an inelastic demand, and computers have an elastic demand. Suppose that technological advance doubles the supply of both products (that is, the quantity supplied at each price is twice what it was).
   a What happens to the equilibrium price and quantity in each market?
   b Which product experiences a larger change in price?
   c Which product experiences a larger change in quantity?
   d What happens to total consumer spending on each product?

11 Beachfront resorts have an inelastic supply and cars have an elastic supply. Suppose that a rise in population doubles the demand for both products (that is, the quantity demanded at each price is twice what it was).
   a What happens to the equilibrium price and quantity in each market?
   b Which product experiences a larger change in price?
   c Which product experiences a larger change in quantity?
   d What happens to total consumer spending on each product?

12 Flooding in the Queensland Granite Belt destroyed thousands of hectares of grapevines.
   a Vineyard owners whose vines were destroyed by the floods were much worse off, but those whose vines were not destroyed benefited from the floods. Why?
   b What information would you need about the market for wine in order to assess whether vineyard owners as a group were hurt or helped by the floods?

13 Explain why the following might be true. A drought around the world raises the total revenue that farmers receive from the sale of grain, but a drought only in Queensland reduces the total revenue that Queensland farmers receive.

14 Because better weather makes farmland more productive, farmland in regions with good weather conditions is more expensive than farmland in regions with bad weather conditions. Over time, however, as advances in technology have made all farmland more productive, the price of farmland (adjusted for overall inflation) has fallen. Use the concept of elasticity to explain why productivity and farmland prices are positively related across space but negatively related over time.

15 In the 1980s, the government imposed a sales tax on the purchase of luxury cars. The revenue collected from the tax equals the tax rate multiplied by total spending on such cars. There have been suggestions that the government could earn more tax revenue by increasing the tax rate on luxury cars. Would such an increase necessarily raise tax revenue? Explain.

Search me!

When accessing information about economics use the following keywords in any combinations you require:

- price elasticity of demand
- income elasticity of demand
- OPEC

CourseMate

For more multimedia resources and activities on economics, visit the Economics CourseMate website.

6

Supply, demand and government policies

Learning objectives

In this chapter you will:

- examine the effects of government policies that place a ceiling on prices

- examine the effects of government policies that put a floor under prices

- consider how a tax on a good affects the price of the good and the quantity sold

- learn that taxes levied on buyers and taxes levied on sellers are equivalent

- see how the burden of a tax is split between buyers and sellers.

Economists have two roles. As scientists, they develop and test theories to explain the world around them. As policy advisors, they use their theories to try to change the world for the better. The focus of the past two chapters has been scientific. We have seen how supply and demand determine the price of a good and the quantity of the good sold. We have also seen how various events shift supply and demand and thereby change the equilibrium price and quantity.

This chapter offers our first look at policy. Here we analyse various types of government policies using only the tools of supply and demand. As you will see, the analysis yields some surprising results. Policies often have effects that their architects did not intend or anticipate.

We begin by considering policies that directly control prices. For example, rent-control laws dictate a maximum rent that landlords may charge tenants. Minimum-wage laws dictate the lowest wage that firms may pay workers. Price controls are usually imposed when policymakers believe that the market price of a good or service is unfair to buyers or sellers. Yet, as we will see, these policies can generate inequities of their own.

After our discussion of price controls, we next consider the impact of taxes. Policymakers use taxes both to influence market outcomes and to raise revenue for public purposes. Although the prevalence of taxes in our economy is obvious, their effects are not. For example, when the government levies a tax on the amount that firms pay their workers, do the firms or the workers bear the burden of the tax? The answer is not at all clear – until we apply the powerful tools of supply and demand.

Controls on prices

To see how price controls affect market outcomes, let's look once again at the market for ice-cream. As we saw in chapter 4, if ice-cream is sold in a competitive market free of government regulation, the price of ice-cream adjusts to balance supply and demand – at the equilibrium price, the quantity of ice-cream that buyers want to buy exactly equals the quantity that sellers want to sell. To be concrete, suppose the equilibrium price is $3 per ice-cream.

Not everyone may be happy with the outcome of this free-market process. Let's say the Australian Association of Ice-cream Eaters complains that the $3 price is too high for everyone to enjoy an ice-cream a day (their recommended daily allowance). Meanwhile, the National Organisation of Ice-cream Makers complains that the $3 price – the result of 'cutthroat competition' – is depressing the incomes of its members. Each of these groups lobbies the government to pass laws that alter the market outcome by directly controlling prices.

Because buyers of any good always want a lower price and sellers want a higher price, the interests of the two groups conflict. If the Ice-cream Eaters are successful in their lobbying, the government imposes a legal maximum on the price at which ice-cream can be sold, called a **price ceiling**. If the Ice-cream Makers are successful, the government imposes a legal minimum on the price, called a **price floor**. Let us consider the effects of these policies in turn.

How price ceilings affect market outcomes

When the government, moved by the complaints of the Ice-cream Eaters, imposes a price ceiling on the market for ice-cream, two outcomes are possible. In panel (a) of Figure 6.1, the

price ceiling
a legal maximum on the price
at which a good can be sold

price floor
a legal minimum on the price
at which a good can be sold

▸ price ceiling
▸ price floor

Figure 6.1 — A market with a price ceiling

(a) A price ceiling that is not binding

(b) A price ceiling that is binding

In panel (a), the government imposes a price ceiling of $4. Because the price ceiling is above the equilibrium price of $3, the price ceiling has no effect and the market can reach the equilibrium of supply and demand. In this equilibrium, quantity supplied and quantity demanded both equal 100 ice-creams. In panel (b), the government imposes a price ceiling of $2. Because the price ceiling is below the equilibrium price of $3, the market price equals $2. At this price, 125 ice-creams are demanded and only 75 are supplied, so there is a shortage of 50 ice-creams.

government imposes a price ceiling of $4 per ice-cream. In this case, because the price that balances supply and demand ($3) is below the ceiling, the price ceiling is *not binding*. Market forces naturally move the economy to the equilibrium and the price ceiling has no effect on the price or the quantity sold.

Panel (b) of figure 6.1 shows the other, more interesting, possibility. In this case, the government imposes a price ceiling of $2 per ice-cream. Because the equilibrium price of $3 is above the price ceiling, the ceiling is a *binding constraint* on the market. The forces of supply and demand tend to move the price towards the equilibrium price, but when the market price hits the ceiling, it can, by law, rise no further. Thus, the market price equals the price ceiling. At this price, the quantity of ice-cream demanded (125 ice-creams in the figure) exceeds the quantity supplied (75 ice-creams). There is a shortage of ice-cream, so some people who want to buy ice-cream at the going price are unable to do so.

When a shortage of ice-cream develops because of this price ceiling, some mechanism for rationing ice-cream will naturally develop. The mechanism could be long lines – buyers who are willing to arrive early and wait in line get an ice-cream, whereas those unwilling to wait do not. Alternatively, sellers could ration ice-cream according to their own personal biases, selling it only to friends, relatives or members of their own racial or ethnic group. Notice that even though the price ceiling was motivated by a desire to help buyers of ice-cream, not all buyers benefit from the policy. Some buyers do get to pay a lower price, although they may have to wait in line to do so, but other buyers cannot get any ice-cream at all.

This example in the market for ice-cream shows a general result – *when the government imposes a binding price ceiling on a competitive market, a shortage of the good arises and sellers must ration the scarce goods among the large number of potential buyers.* The rationing mechanisms that develop under price ceilings are rarely desirable. Long lines are inefficient, because they waste buyers' time. Discrimination according to seller bias is both inefficient (because the good does not go to the buyer who values it most highly) and potentially unfair. In contrast, the rationing mechanism in a free, competitive market is both efficient and impersonal. When the market for ice-cream reaches its equilibrium, anyone who wants to pay the market price can get an ice-cream. Free markets ration goods with prices.

CASESTUDY

Lines at the petrol station

Most major Australian cities receive their petrol from a single refinery. When the refinery reduces output, owing to a labour dispute, for example, then the supply of petrol to the city is cut. Long lines at petrol stations become commonplace, and motorists often have to wait for hours to buy only a few litres of petrol. A similar phenomenon occurred in the United States in 1973. Then, as we discussed in the last chapter, the Organization of Petroleum Exporting Countries (OPEC) raised the price of crude oil in world oil markets. Because crude oil is the major component used in making petrol, the higher oil prices reduced the supply of petrol. This also led to long lines for petrol in the United States.

Who is responsible for such long lines at petrol stations? If the supply of petrol has been cut because of a strike, most people blame either the oil companies or the unions. But the industrial dispute explains the cut in the supply of petrol, not the long lines. Similarly, the OPEC action also explains the reduction in the supply of petrol, but not the queues. These, most economists would argue, are due to government regulations that prevent petrol stations from raising the price they can charge for petrol.

Figure 6.2 shows what happens. As panel (a) shows, before the labour dispute, the supply of petrol is given by S_1 and the equilibrium price is P_1. But panel (b) shows that the dispute at the refinery cuts the supply of petrol back to S_2. If the petrol market were unregulated, the price of petrol

would rise to P_2 and there would be no shortage. Instead, state governments prevent petrol stations from significantly raising the price of petrol. It is claimed that any significant price rises would be unfair to customers. The petrol stations are forced to charge below P_2. At this price, the petrol stations are willing to sell Q_S and consumers are willing to buy Q_D. Thus, the shift in the supply curve causes a severe shortage.

The ban on price rises not only creates long lines at petrol stations, it also reduces the incentive for producers to ship petrol in from other states. If the price of petrol increased to P_2, it would pay enterprising petrol station owners to buy petrol in an area unaffected by the dispute and have it delivered to their stations. By not allowing the price to rise, the government eliminates this incentive to bring in petrol supplies.

When the government prevents the price of petrol from rising during an industrial dispute, it says that it is protecting customers from 'price gouging' (increases in prices after strikes or disasters). Governments also prevent price gouging after natural disasters, when the supply of food and water is cut and the equilibrium price of these goods rises sharply. While governments prevent prices from rising for equity reasons – so that poorer people trapped by the disaster are not forced to pay higher prices – the laws against price gouging create shortages and reduce the incentives to ship more food and water into the affected regions.

Figure 6.2 **The market for petrol with a price ceiling**

(a) The pre-dispute equilibrium in the petrol market

(b) The petrol market during a labour dispute with a price ceiling

1. When supply falls …

2. … the government prevents prices from rising significantly …

3. … resulting in a shortage.

Panel (a) shows the petrol market when there is no price ceiling. The equilibrium price is P_1 and petrol sales are Q_1. Panel (b) shows the petrol market during an industrial dispute. The supply curve shifts to the left from S_1 to S_2. In the absence of government intervention, the price would have risen from P_1 to P_2. If the government imposes a price ceiling, this cannot happen. At the binding price ceiling, consumers are willing to buy Q_D, but producers of petrol are willing to sell only Q_S. The difference between quantity demanded and quantity supplied, $Q_D - Q_S$, measures the petrol shortage.

One common example of a price ceiling is rent control. In many cities around the world, local governments place a ceiling on rents that landlords may charge their tenants. The goal of this policy is to help the poor by making housing more affordable. Economists often criticise rent control, arguing that it is a highly inefficient way to help the poor raise their standard of living. One economist called rent control 'the best way to destroy a city, other than bombing'.

The adverse effects of rent control are less apparent to the general population because these effects occur over many years. In the short run, landlords have a fixed number of flats to rent and they cannot adjust this number quickly as market conditions change. Moreover, the number of people searching for housing in a city may not be highly responsive to rents in the short run because people take time to adjust their housing arrangements. Therefore, the short run supply of and demand for housing are relatively inelastic.

Panel (a) of Figure 6.3 shows the effects in the short run of rent control on the housing market. As with any price ceiling, rent control causes a shortage. Yet because supply and demand are inelastic in the short run, the initial shortage caused by rent control is small. The main effect in the short run is to reduce rents.

In the long run, the story is very different because the buyers and sellers of rental housing respond more to market conditions as time passes. On the supply side, landlords respond to low rents by not building new flats and by failing to maintain existing ones. On the demand side, low rents encourage people to find their own

CASESTUDY

Rent control in the short run and long run

accommodation (rather than living with their parents or sharing flats with friends) and induce more people to move into a city. Therefore, both supply and demand are more elastic in the long run.

Panel (b) of Figure 6.3 illustrates the housing market in the long run. When rent control depresses rents below the equilibrium level, the quantity of flats supplied falls substantially and the quantity of flats demanded rises substantially. The result is a large shortage of housing.

In cities with rent control, landlords use various mechanisms to ration housing. Some landlords keep long waiting lists. Others give a preference to tenants without children. Still others discriminate on the basis of race. Sometimes, flats are allocated to those willing to offer under-the-table payments to real estate agents. In essence, these bribes bring the total price of a flat (including the bribe) closer to the equilibrium price.

To understand fully the effects of rent control, we have to remember one of the *Ten Lessons from Economics* from chapter 1 –people respond to incentives. In free markets, landlords try to keep their buildings clean and safe because desirable flats or home units command higher prices. In contrast, when rent control creates shortages and waiting lists, landlords lose their incentive to be responsive to tenants' concerns. Why should a landlord spend money to maintain and improve the property when people are waiting to get in as it is? In the end, tenants get lower rents, but they also get lower quality housing.

Policymakers often react to the effects of rent control by imposing additional regulations. For example, there are laws that make racial discrimination in housing illegal and require landlords to provide minimally adequate living conditions. These laws, however, are difficult and costly to enforce. In contrast, when rent control is eliminated and the market for housing is regulated by the forces of competition, such laws are less necessary. In a free market, the price of housing adjusts to eliminate the shortages that give rise to undesirable landlord behaviour.

Figure 6.3   Rent control in the short run and in the long run

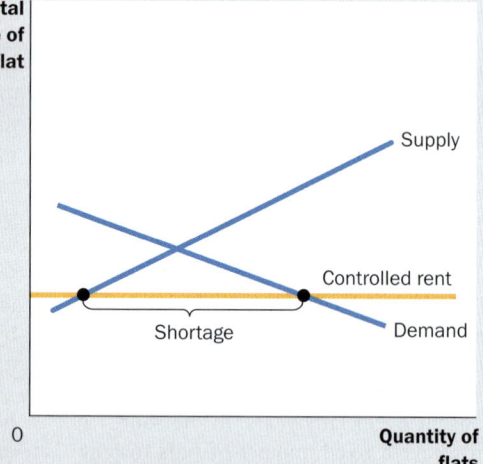

Panel (a) shows the effects in the short run of rent control – because the supply of and demand for flats are relatively inelastic, the price ceiling imposed by a rent-control law causes only a small shortage of housing. Panel (b) shows the effects in the long run of rent control – because the supply of and demand for flats are more elastic, rent control causes a large shortage.

IN THE NEWS . . .

RENT CONTROL IN MUMBAI, INDIA

Rent control plays a large role in many countries around the world. These laws are often justified as protecting tenants. However, the consequences can be extreme! As this article outlines, rent control in Mumbai (Bombay) India, one of the world's largest cities, has led to buildings being neglected and collapsing, killing the residents.

Nobody touches the Act
by Dilip D'Souza

Strolling through downtown Bombay one day during the recent monsoon, I passed a sign nailed high on an entrance to a building. It said: 'This building is dangerous. It may collapse at any time. Enter at your own risk'.

An unsettling sign any time. But at the time, it carried a special meaning, because the city was in the midst of what at least two papers called an 'epidemic' of building collapses: four in a week. The most recent had been the previous Monday. An 80-year-old edifice near the old Metro cinema crumbled, killing six people.

One more tragedy, in a monsoon season laced with tragedy.

So laced, that even the words took on special meanings. Take 'collapse'. On that terrible July 26, an entire Saki Naka hillside collapsed, destroying over a hundred huts and 75 or 80 lives. Take 'epidemic'. Two weeks after the July deluge, people began dying of diseases contracted that day, likely by walking through chest-deep water contaminated with urine and faeces and other random bits of Bombay filth.

Over two hundred people died like that.

And then, the building collapse epidemic.

Yet the truth is that buildings that crumble are an old Bombay tradition. Every monsoon, a few more give up the battle to stay erect. Weakened by years of neglect and disrepair, they come down, invariably taking lives. And behind all this are, as is another Bombay tradition, some intricate and often seedy goings-on.

In 1996, the Tavadia building in Bora Bazaar collapsed, taking 18 lives with it. About six weeks earlier, a man was found dead in a cinema theatre in Pune. One Ramesh Kini, he was a tenant in a building in Dadar owned by one Laxmichand Shah.

Why have I mentioned both these probably forgotten episodes, and in the same paragraph?

Because they have something in common: the foolish law that governs rental property in Bombay. Whatever benefits the Rent Control Act may have had at one time, today it is little but a threat to property and lives. If it is not repealed we must expect what happened at the Tavadia building, as well as what happened to Ramesh Kini, to keep happening.

The Act is simple: it freezes rent at a certain level. During World War II, floods of people, especially soldiers, came into the city. To prevent greedy landlords charging extortionate rent from them, the British put rent control in place. A limited number of buildings were brought under the Act when it first came into force. The Act allowed thousands of people to find affordable housing at rents that were kept frozen at 1940 levels as long as the tenants stayed. (Rents could be raised if a new tenant came in.)

Of course, by now many of those wartime tenants have died. Their children and grandchildren stay on in the same flats, paying the same rents. I know a couple who lived in a gorgeous flat in an old building near Churchgate. For years, they paid the rent for the flat that the man's father had signed up for half a century earlier: twenty rupees a month. (Yes.) The amount they extracted from their landlord, just for giving him his flat back eventually, allowed them to buy themselves a home in a small town in another state. That's where they are today.

By no means is this a unique or even unusual story.

Naturally, the amount a landlord earns from rent cannot begin to pay the costs of maintenance on his aging building. So he stops maintaining it and will not carry out repairs. The

>>

building becomes steadily weaker. In the end, it falls down, killing several of its tenants.

By no means is that a unique or unusual story either.

The strange thing about this state of affairs is not just that tenants pay absurdly low rents. They also want their landlords to carry out repairs and keep their buildings in shape. They also are unwilling to pay for the repairs themselves.

For example, one of the tenants of the Tavadia building told the press that she was paying a rent of Rs 100. But, as the *Times of India* reported, 'she felt that the tragedy could have been averted had the landlord … not ignored their repeated pleas to repair the building'. It was in such bad shape, she went on, that 'anyone walking with heavy steps would set off a tremor'.

The lady lost her father in the collapse. I wish she and her fellow tenants had offered to pay to maintain the building. Her father might still be alive. I hope she understands that now.

But there is a more sinister side to the Act too. Real estate prices are so inflated in this city that many tenants can never hope to move from their rent-controlled flats. (Unless they move, like my Churchgate friends did, to a small town). So they have no option but to stay. Landlords, meanwhile, know how lucrative it would be to sell their property, particularly to a builder. But what's to be done with tenants who won't leave?

Landlords try persuasion. They try pleading. They try the courts, but that takes years.

Eventually, some landlords turn to threats and force. That's what Ramesh Kini had to face. Eventually, he may have killed himself. Or he may have been done in by thugs. His death really remains a mystery, but in a profound way, Rent Control had a lot to do with it.

Everyone knows the damage the Rent Control Act does. But why isn't something done about it?

The simple answer: numbers. Tenants outnumber landlords. The low rent the Act has them paying outweighs all other considerations – they want to keep paying it. Politicians know all about numbers. They are aware that the first of their breed who makes a move on the Rent Control Act will promptly lose the votes of millions of tenants. He will probably gain the votes of landlords, but that's poor compensation.

Which means: nobody touches the Act.

But there's a more complex answer as well. The Act can't be seen in isolation. The high price of real estate; the well known corrupt, violent but mutually beneficial connection between politicians and builders; the steps we have deliberately ignored that would have served to keep land prices down – all of these have played roles in the persistence of this pernicious law. All have also flourished because of the Act. All will have to be taken into account in any review of the Act.

Which also means: nobody touches the Act.

Source: Dilip d'Souza/*India Together* Magazine, 24 November 2005.

How price floors affect market outcomes

To examine the effects of another kind of government price control, let's return to the market for ice-cream. Imagine now that the government is persuaded by the pleas of the National Organisation of Ice-cream Makers whose members feel that the $3 equilibrium price is too low. In this case, the government might institute a price floor. Price floors, like price ceilings, are an attempt by the government to maintain prices at other than equilibrium levels. Whereas a price ceiling places a legal maximum on prices, a price floor places a legal minimum.

When the government imposes a price floor on the ice-cream market, two outcomes are possible. If the government imposes a price floor of $2 per ice-cream when the equilibrium price is $3, we obtain the outcome in panel (a) of Figure 6.4. In this case, because the equilibrium price is above the floor, the price floor is not binding. Market forces naturally move the economy to the equilibrium and the price floor has no effect.

Figure 6.4 A market with a price floor

(a) A price floor that is not binding

(b) A price floor that is binding

In panel (a), the government imposes a price floor of $2. Because this is below the equilibrium price of $3, the price floor has no effect. The market price adjusts to balance supply and demand. At the equilibrium, quantity supplied and quantity demanded both equal 100 ice-creams. In panel (b), the government imposes a price floor of $4, which is above the equilibrium price of $3. Therefore, the market price equals $4. Because 120 ice-creams are supplied at this price and only 80 are demanded, there is a surplus of 40 ice-creams.

Panel (b) of Figure 6.4 shows what happens when the government imposes a price floor of $4 per ice-cream. In this case, because the equilibrium price of $3 is below the floor, the price floor is a binding constraint on the market. The forces of supply and demand tend to move the price towards the equilibrium price, but when the market price hits the floor, it can fall no further. The market price equals the price floor. At this floor, the quantity of ice-cream supplied (120 ice-creams) exceeds the quantity demanded (80). Some people who want to sell ice-cream at the going price are unable to. Thus, *a binding price floor causes a surplus*.

Just as the shortages resulting from price ceilings can lead to undesirable rationing mechanisms, so can the surpluses resulting from price floors. In the case of a price floor, some sellers are unable to sell all they want at the market price. The sellers who appeal to the personal biases of the buyers, perhaps because of racial or familial ties, are better able to sell their goods than those who do not. In contrast, in a free market, the price serves as the rationing mechanism and sellers can sell all they want at the equilibrium price.

CASE STUDY

Minimum wage rates

An important example of a price floor is a minimum wage. Minimum-wage laws dictate the lowest price for labour that any employer may pay. In Australia, a federal government body, Fair Work Australia, sets **awards** which include the minimum wage rates that can be paid to particular workers in particular industries. (Until 2009, this role was fulfilled by the Fair Pay Commission.) Unlike other countries, such as the United States, Australia does not have a single minimum wage but a system of awards.

To examine the effects of a minimum wage or award rate, we must consider the market for labour in a particular industry. Panel (a) of Figure 6.5 shows the labour market which, like all markets, is

awards
the minimum wage rates that can be paid to particular workers in particular industries

>>

subject to the forces of supply and demand. Workers determine the supply of labour, and firms determine the demand. In the absence of government intervention, the wage adjusts to balance labour supply and labour demand.

Panel (b) of Figure 6.5 shows the labour market with a minimum or award wage. If the minimum wage is above the equilibrium level, as it is here, the quantity of labour supplied exceeds the quantity demanded. The result is unemployment. Thus, the minimum wage raises the incomes of those workers who have jobs, but it lowers the incomes of those workers who cannot find jobs.

To fully understand the minimum or award wage, it is important to keep in mind that the economy contains not a single labour market, but many labour markets for different types of workers. The impact of the minimum wage depends on the skill and experience of the worker. Workers with high skills and much experience are not affected, because their equilibrium wages are well above the minimum. For these workers, award wage rates are not binding.

Minimum wages have their greatest impact on the market for teenage labour. The equilibrium wages of teenagers tend to be low because teenagers are among the least skilled and least experienced members of the labour force. In addition, teenagers are often willing to accept a lower wage in exchange for on-the-job training. This effect is recognised in Australia where there is a separate minimum wage for teenagers – the 'junior' award. Even so, teenagers are more likely to be paid at this minimum rate, whereas other members of the labour force may be paid above-award wages.

Many economists have examined how minimum-wage laws affect the teenage labour market. These researchers compare the changes in the minimum wage over time with the changes in teenage employment. Although there is some debate about how much the minimum wage affects employment, the typical study finds that a 10 per cent increase in the minimum wage depresses teenage employment between 1 per cent and 3 per cent. In interpreting this estimate, note that a 10 per cent increase in the minimum wage does not raise the average wage of teenagers by 10 per cent. A change in the law does not directly affect those teenagers who are already paid well above the minimum. Moreover, enforcement of minimum-wage laws is not perfect. Thus, the estimated drop in employment of 1 per cent to 3 per cent is substantial.

In addition to altering the quantity of labour demanded, the minimum wage also alters the quantity supplied. Because the minimum wage raises the wage that teenagers can earn, it increases the number of teenagers who choose to look for jobs. Studies have found that a higher minimum wage influences which teenagers are employed. When the minimum wage rises, some teenagers who are still attending school choose to drop out and take jobs. These new drop-outs displace other teenagers who had already dropped out of school and who now become unemployed.

The minimum wage is a frequent topic of political debate. Advocates of the minimum wage view the policy as one way to raise the income of the working poor. They correctly point out that workers who earn the minimum wage can afford only a meagre standard of living. In 2010, for instance, the Australian Council of Trade Unions – representing employees – argued to Fair Work Australia that the minimum wage applying to all workers should be increased by $27 per week. Their argument was based on the idea that there should be community standards for minimum wages and that low wage workers need sufficient income to meet their needs. Many advocates of the minimum wage admit that it potentially has some adverse effects, including unemployment, but they believe that these effects are small and that, all things considered, a higher minimum wage makes the poor better off.

Opponents of the minimum wage contend that it is not the best way to combat poverty. They note that high minimum wages and junior wages cause unemployment, encourage teenagers to drop out of school and prevent some unskilled workers from getting the on-the-job training they need. Moreover, opponents of the minimum wage point out that the minimum wage is a poorly targeted policy. Not all award-wage workers are heads of households trying to help their families escape poverty. Many award-wage earners are teenagers from middle-class homes working at part-time jobs for extra spending money.

In June 2010, Fair Work Australia concluded its first annual wage review. It accepted the argument that minimum wages provide a fair safety net for workers and raised the award minimum wages by $26 per week, resulting in a national minimum wage of $15 per hour.

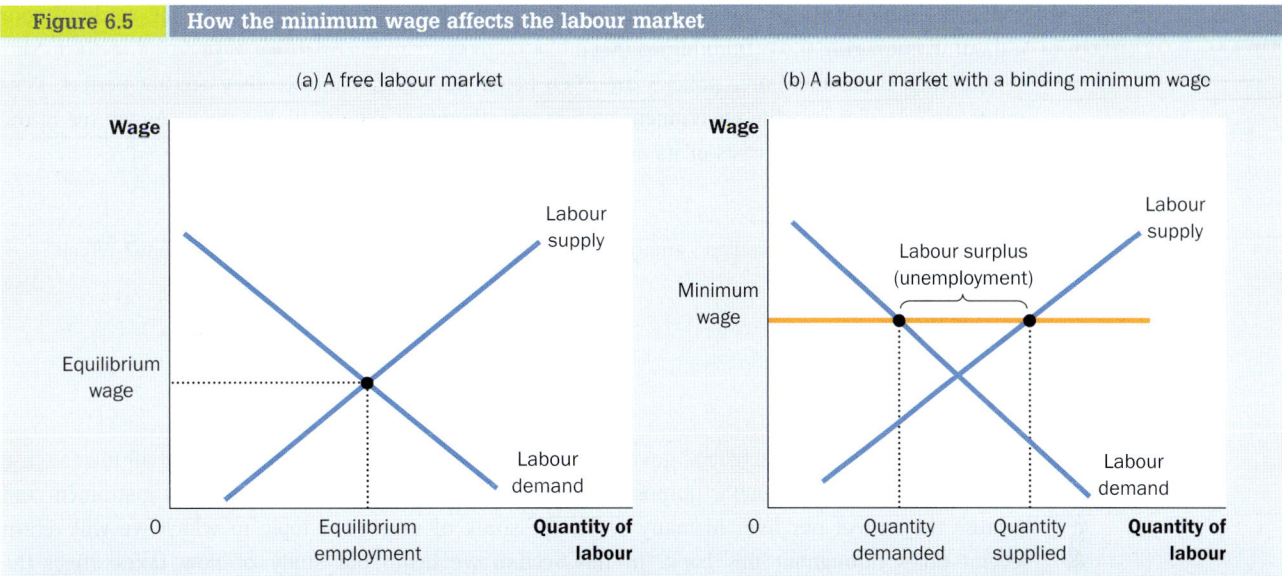

Figure 6.5 How the minimum wage affects the labour market

Panel (a) shows a labour market in which the wage adjusts to balance labour supply and labour demand. Panel (b) shows the impact of a binding minimum or award wage. Because the minimum wage is a price floor, it causes a surplus – the quantity of labour supplied exceeds the quantity demanded. The result is unemployment.

Evaluating price controls

One of the *Ten Lessons from Economics* discussed in chapter 1 is that markets are usually a good way to organise economic activity. That lesson explains why economists almost always oppose price ceilings and price floors. To economists, prices are not the outcome of some haphazard process. Prices, they contend, are the result of the millions of business and consumer decisions that lie behind the supply and demand curves. Prices have the crucial job of balancing supply and demand and, thereby, coordinating economic activity. When policymakers set prices by legal decree, they obscure the signals that normally guide the allocation of society's resources.

Another one of the *Ten Lessons from Economics* is that governments can sometimes improve market outcomes. Indeed, policymakers are led to control prices because they view the market's outcome as unfair. Price controls are often aimed at helping the poor. For instance, rent-control laws try to make housing affordable for everyone and minimum-wage laws try to help people escape poverty.

Yet price controls often hurt those they are trying to help. Rent control may keep rents low, but it also discourages landlords from maintaining their buildings and makes housing hard to find. Minimum-wage laws may raise the incomes of some workers, but they also cause other workers to be unemployed.

Helping those in need can be accomplished in ways other than controlling prices. For instance, the government can make housing more affordable by paying a fraction of the rent for poor families. In Australia, low-income families are eligible for rent assistance of up to around $75 per week. Unlike rent control, such rent subsidies do not reduce the quantity of housing supplied and, therefore, do not lead to housing shortages. Similarly, wage subsidies raise the living standards of the working poor without discouraging firms from hiring them.

Although these alternative policies are often better than price controls, they are not perfect. Rent and wage subsidies cost the government money and, therefore, require higher taxes. As we see in the next section, taxation has costs of its own.

Define price ceiling and price floor, and give an example of each. Which leads to a shortage? Which leads to a surplus? Why?

Taxes

All governments – from the federal government in Canberra to local governments in small towns – use taxes to raise revenue for public purposes. Because taxes are such an important policy instrument and because they affect our lives in many ways, the study of taxes is a topic to which we will return several times throughout this book. In this section we begin our study of how taxes affect the economy.

To set the stage for our analysis, imagine that a local government decides to hold an annual ice-cream celebration – with a parade, fireworks and speeches by town officials. To raise revenue to pay for the event, it decides to place a $0.50 tax on the sale of ice-creams. When the plan is announced, our two lobbying groups swing into action. The National Organisation of Ice-cream Makers claims that its members are struggling to survive in a competitive market and it argues that *buyers* of ice-cream should have to pay the tax. The Australian Association of Ice-cream Eaters claims that consumers of ice-cream are having trouble making ends meet and it argues that *sellers* of ice-cream should pay the tax. The mayor, hoping to reach a compromise, suggests that half the tax be paid by the buyers and half be paid by the sellers.

To analyse these proposals, we need to consider a simple but subtle question. When the government levies a tax on a good, who bears the burden of the tax – the people buying the good or the people selling the good? Or, if buyers and sellers share the tax burden, what determines how the burden is divided? Can the government simply legislate the division of the burden, as the mayor is suggesting, or is the division determined by more fundamental forces in the economy? Economists use the term **tax incidence** to refer to these questions about the distribution of a tax burden. As we will see, we can learn some surprising lessons about tax incidence just by applying the tools of supply and demand.

tax incidence
the study of who bears the burden of taxation

▸ tax incidence

How taxes on buyers affect market outcomes

We begin by considering a tax levied on buyers of a good. Suppose, for instance, that our local government passes a law requiring buyers of ice-creams to send $0.50 to the government for each ice-cream they buy. How does this law affect the buyers and sellers of ice-cream? To answer this question, we can follow the three steps in chapter 4 for analysing supply and demand:

1 we decide whether the law affects the supply or demand curve
2 we decide which way the curve shifts
3 we examine how the shift affects the equilibrium.

Step one

The initial impact of the tax is on the demand for ice-cream. The supply curve is not affected because, for any given price of ice-cream, sellers have the same incentive to provide ice-cream to the market. In contrast, buyers now have to pay a tax to the government (as well as the price to the sellers) whenever they buy ice-cream. Thus, the tax shifts the demand curve for ice-cream.

Step two

We next determine the direction of the shift. Because the tax on buyers makes buying ice-cream less attractive, buyers demand a smaller quantity of ice-cream at every price. As a result, the demand curve shifts to the left (or, equivalently, downwards), as shown in Figure 6.6.

In addition to determining the direction in which the demand curve shifts, we can also be precise about the size of the shift. Because of the $0.50 tax levied on buyers, the effective price to buyers is now $0.50 higher than the market price (whatever the market price happens to be). For example, if the market price of an ice-cream happened to be $2.00, the effective price to buyers would be $2.50. Because buyers look at their total cost including the tax, they demand a quantity of ice-cream as if the market price were $0.50 higher than it actually is. In other words, to induce buyers to demand any given quantity, the market price must now be $0.50 lower to make up for the effect of the tax. Thus, the tax shifts the demand curve *downward* from D_1 to D_2 by exactly the size of the tax ($0.50).

Figure 6.6	A tax on buyers

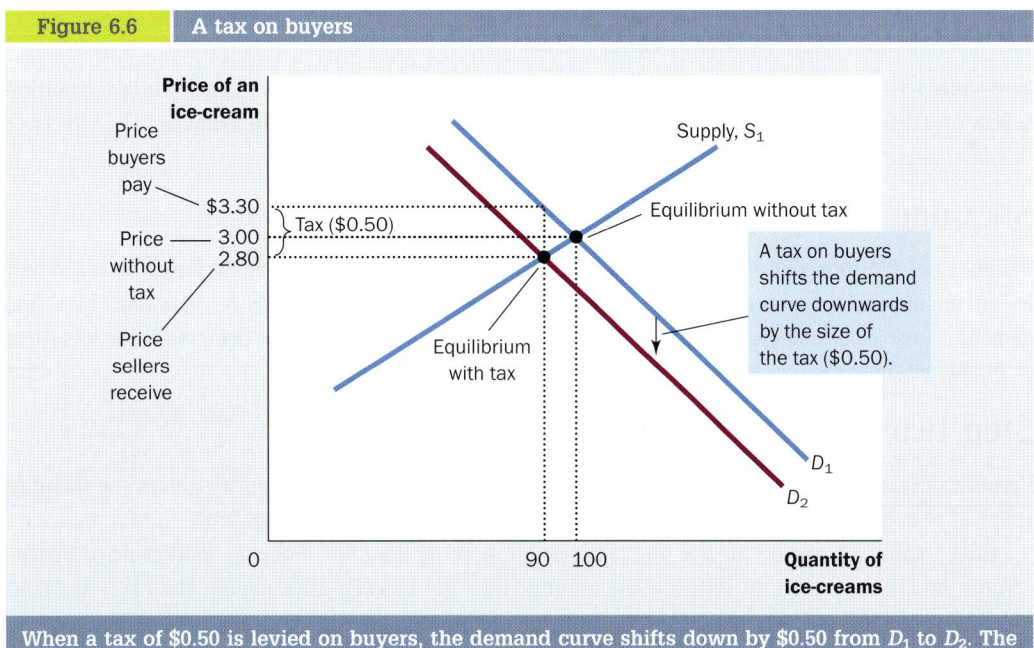

When a tax of $0.50 is levied on buyers, the demand curve shifts down by $0.50 from D_1 to D_2. The equilibrium quantity falls from 100 to 90 ice-creams. The price that sellers receive falls from $3.00 to $2.80. The price that buyers pay (including the tax) rises from $3.00 to $3.30. Even though the tax is levied on buyers, buyers and sellers share the burden of the tax.

Step three

Having determined how the demand curve shifts, we can now see the effect of the tax by comparing the initial equilibrium and the new equilibrium. You can see in the figure that the equilibrium price of ice-cream falls from $3.00 to $2.80 and the equilibrium quantity falls from 100 to 90 ice-creams. Because sellers sell less and buyers buy less in the new equilibrium, the tax on ice-cream reduces the size of the ice-cream market.

Implications

We can now turn to the question of tax incidence: Who pays the tax? Although buyers send the entire tax to the government, buyers and sellers share the burden. Because the market price falls from $3.00 to $2.80 when the tax is introduced, sellers receive $0.20 less for each ice-cream than they did without the tax. Thus, the tax makes sellers worse off. Buyers pay sellers a lower price ($2.80), but the effective price including the tax rises from $3.00 before the tax to $3.30 with the tax ($2.80 + $0.50 = $3.30). Thus, the tax also makes buyers worse off.

To sum up, this analysis yields two lessons:

- Taxes discourage market activity. When a good is taxed, the quantity of the good sold is smaller in the new equilibrium.
- Buyers and sellers share the burden of taxes. In the new equilibrium, buyers pay more for the good and sellers receive less.

How taxes on sellers affect market outcomes

Now consider a tax levied on sellers of a good. Suppose the local government passes a law requiring sellers of ice-creams to send $0.50 to the government for each one they sell. What are the effects of this law? Again, we apply our three steps.

Step one

In this case, the immediate impact of the tax is on the sellers of ice-cream. Because the tax is not levied on buyers, the quantity of ice-cream demanded at any given price is the same; thus, the demand curve does not change. By contrast, the tax on sellers makes the ice-cream business less profitable at any given price, so it shifts the supply curve.

Step two

Because the tax on sellers raises the cost of producing and selling ice-cream, it reduces the quantity supplied at every price. The supply curve shifts to the left (or equivalently, upward).

Once again, we can be precise about the magnitude of the shift. For any market price of ice-cream, the effective price to sellers – the amount they get to keep after paying the tax – is $0.50 lower. For example, if the market price of an ice-cream happened to be $2.00, the effective price received by sellers would be $1.50. Whatever the market price, sellers will supply a quantity of ice-cream as if the price were $0.50 lower than it is. Put differently, to induce sellers to supply any given quantity, the market price must now be $0.50 higher to compensate for the effect of the tax. Thus, as shown in Figure 6.7, the supply curve shifts *upward* from S_1 to S_2 by exactly the size of the tax ($0.50).

Figure 6.7 | A tax on sellers

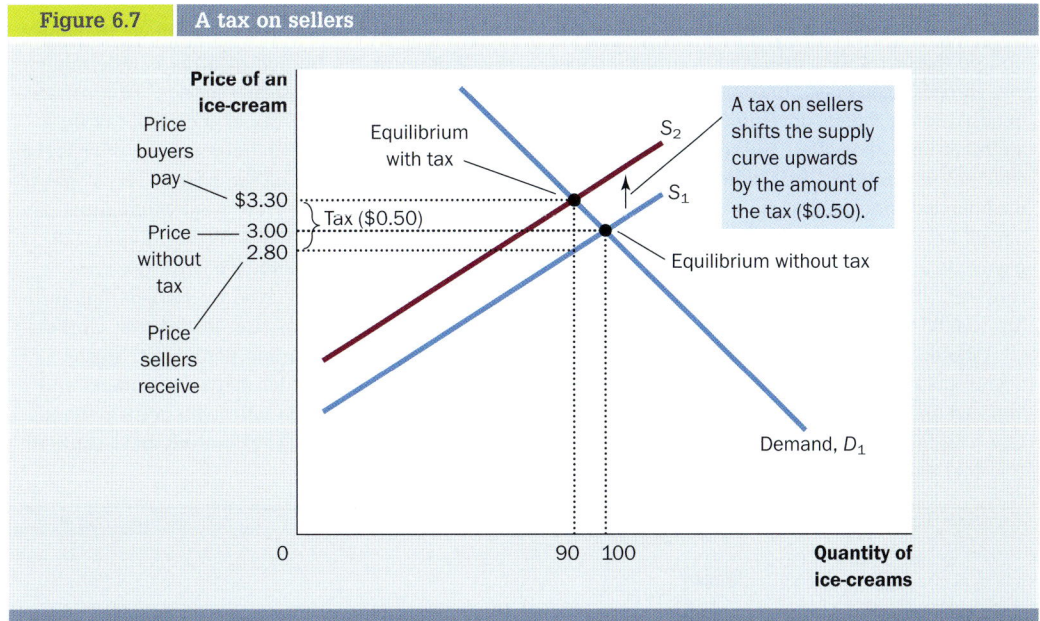

When a tax of $0.50 is levied on sellers, the supply curve shifts up by $0.50 from S_1 to S_2. The equilibrium quantity falls from 100 to 90 ice-creams. The price that buyers pay rises from $3.00 to $3.30. The price that sellers receive (after paying the tax) falls from $3.00 to $2.80. Even though the tax is levied on sellers, buyers and sellers share the burden of the tax.

Step three

Having determined how the supply curve shifts, we can now compare the initial and the new equilibrium. The figure shows that the equilibrium price of ice-cream rises from $3.00 to $3.30, and the equilibrium quantity falls from 100 to 90 ice-creams. Once again, the tax reduces the size of the ice-cream market. And once again, buyers and sellers share the burden of the tax. Because the market price rises, buyers pay $0.30 more for each ice-cream than they did before the tax was enacted. Sellers receive a higher price than they did without the tax, but the effective price (after paying the tax) falls from $3.00 to $2.80.

Implications

If you compare Figures 6.6 and 6.7, you will notice a surprising conclusion – *taxes on buyers and taxes on sellers are equivalent*. In both cases, the tax places a wedge between the price that buyers pay and the price that sellers receive. The wedge between the buyers' price and the sellers' price is the same, regardless of whether the tax is levied on buyers or sellers. In either case, the wedge shifts the relative position of the supply and demand curves. In the new equilibrium, buyers and sellers share the burden of the tax. The only difference between taxes on buyers and taxes on sellers is who sends the money to the government.

The equivalence of these two taxes is perhaps easier to understand if we imagine that the government collects the $0.50 ice-cream tax in a bowl on the counter of each ice-cream shop. When the government levies the tax on buyers, the buyer is required to place $0.50 in the bowl every time an ice-cream is bought. When the government levies the tax on sellers, the seller is required to place

CASE STUDY

Who pays the payroll tax?

If you have ever received a pay packet, you probably noticed that taxes were deducted from the amount you earned. In Australia, this tax is income tax imposed by the federal government. However, there are other taxes that affect workers. In particular, state governments in Australia levy payroll taxes on medium and large employers. In 2010, the standard payroll tax was around 5 per cent of the total payments a firm makes to its employees. However, in some states this rate was higher (up to 6.85 per cent).

Who do you think bears the burden of this payroll tax – firms or workers? Payroll tax is imposed on employers so governments often argue that it is different from a tax on income. But is it true that payroll tax is really paid by employers?

Our analysis of tax incidence shows that the distribution of the burden of a tax is determined by more than who physically pays it. To illustrate, we can analyse payroll tax as merely a tax on a good, where the good is labour and the price is the wage. The key feature of the payroll tax is that it places a wedge between the wages that firms pay and the wages that workers receive. Figure 6.8 shows the outcome. When a payroll tax is imposed, the wages received by workers fall and the wages paid by firms rise. In the end, workers and firms share the burden of the tax. So the division of the tax burden between workers and firms has nothing to do with who actually hands over the money. Workers effectively bear some of the tax burden.

| Figure 6.8 | A payroll tax |

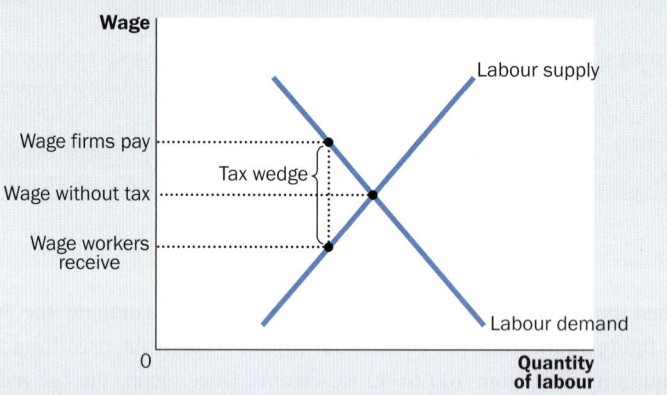

A payroll tax places a wedge between the wages that workers receive and the wages that firms pay. Comparing wages with and without the tax, you can see that workers and firms share the tax burden. This division of the tax burden between workers and firms does not depend on whether the government levies the tax on workers, levies the tax on firms or divides the tax equally between the two groups.

This example shows that the most basic lesson of tax incidence is often overlooked in public debate. Law makers can decide whether a tax comes from the buyer's pocket or from the seller's, but they cannot legislate the true burden of a tax. Rather, tax incidence depends on the forces of supply and demand.

$0.50 in the bowl after the sale of each ice-cream. Whether the $0.50 goes directly from the buyer's pocket into the bowl, or indirectly from the buyer's pocket into the seller's hand and then into the bowl, does not matter. Once the market reaches its new equilibrium, buyers and sellers share the burden, regardless of how the tax is levied.

Elasticity and tax incidence

When a good is taxed, buyers and sellers of the good share the burden of the tax. But how exactly is the tax burden divided? Only rarely will it be shared equally. To see how the burden is divided, consider the impact of taxation in the two markets in Figure 6.9. In both cases, the figure shows the initial demand curve, the initial supply curve and a tax that drives a wedge between the amount paid by buyers and the amount received by sellers. (Not drawn in either panel of the figure is the new supply or demand curve. Which curve shifts depends on whether the tax is levied on buyers or sellers. As we have seen, this is irrelevant for the incidence of the tax.) The difference in the two panels is the relative elasticity of supply and demand.

Panel (a) of Figure 6.9 shows a tax in a market with very elastic supply and relatively inelastic demand – that is, sellers are very responsive to the price of the good, whereas buyers are not very responsive. When a tax is imposed on a market with these elasticities, the price received by sellers does not fall much, so sellers bear only a small burden. In contrast, the price paid by buyers rises substantially, indicating that buyers bear most of the burden of the tax.

Panel (b) of Figure 6.9 shows a tax in a market with relatively inelastic supply and very elastic demand. In this case, sellers are not very responsive to the price, whereas buyers are very responsive. The figure shows that when a tax is imposed, the price paid by buyers does not rise much and the price received by sellers falls substantially. Thus, sellers bear most of the burden of the tax.

The two panels of Figure 6.9 show a general lesson about how the burden of a tax is divided – *a tax burden falls more heavily on the side of the market that is less elastic*. Why is this true? In essence, the elasticity measures the willingness of buyers or sellers to leave the market when conditions become unfavourable. A small elasticity of demand means that buyers do not have good alternatives to consuming this particular good. A small elasticity of supply means that sellers do not have good alternatives to producing this particular good. When the good is taxed, the side of the market with

Figure 6.9	How the burden of a tax is divided

In panel (a), the supply curve is elastic and the demand curve is inelastic. In this case, the price received by sellers falls only slightly and the price paid by buyers rises substantially. Thus, buyers bear most of the burden of the tax. In panel (b), the supply curve is inelastic and the demand curve is elastic. In this case, the price received by sellers falls substantially and the price paid by buyers rises only slightly. Thus, sellers bear most of the burden of the tax.

fewer good alternatives cannot easily leave the market and must, therefore, bear more of the burden of the tax.

We can apply this logic to the payroll tax, which was discussed in the previous case study: Most labour economists believe that the supply of labour is much less elastic than the demand. This means that workers, rather than firms, bear most of the burden of the payroll tax. In other words, the distribution of the tax burden is far from falling wholly on employers as the lawmakers may have intended.

In a supply-and-demand diagram, show how a tax on car buyers of $1000 per car affects the quantity of cars sold and the price of cars. In another diagram, show how a tax on car sellers of $1000 per car affects the quantity of cars sold and the price of cars. In both diagrams, show the change in the price paid by car buyers and the change in the price received by car sellers.

Conclusion

The economy is governed by two kinds of laws – the laws of supply and demand and the laws enacted by governments. In this chapter we have begun to see how these laws interact. Price controls and taxes are common in various markets in the economy and their effects are frequently debated in the press and among policymakers. Even a little bit of economic knowledge can go a long way towards understanding and evaluating these policies.

In subsequent chapters we will analyse many government policies in greater detail. We examine the effects of taxation more fully and consider a broader range of policies than we considered here. Yet the basic lessons of this chapter will not change – when analysing government policies, supply and demand are the first and most useful tools of analysis.

Summary

- A price ceiling is a legal maximum on the price of a good or service. An example is rent control. If the price ceiling is below the equilibrium price, so the price ceiling is binding, the quantity demanded exceeds the quantity supplied. Because of the resulting shortage, sellers must in some way ration the good or service among buyers.
- A price floor is a legal minimum on the price of a good or service. An example is a minimum or award wage. If the price floor is above the equilibrium price, so the price floor is binding, the quantity supplied exceeds the quantity demanded. Because of the resulting surplus, buyers' demands for the good or service must in some way be rationed among sellers.
- When the government levies a tax on a good, the equilibrium quantity of the good falls. That is, a tax on a market shrinks the size of the market.
- A tax on a good places a wedge between the price paid by buyers and the price received by sellers. When the market moves to the new equilibrium, buyers pay more for the good and sellers receive less for it. In this sense, buyers and sellers share the tax burden. The incidence of a tax (that is, the division of the tax burden) does not depend on whether the tax is levied on buyers or sellers.
- The incidence of a tax depends on the price elasticities of supply and demand. The burden tends to fall on the side of the market that is less elastic because that side of the market can respond less easily to the tax by changing the quantity bought or sold.

Key concepts

awards
price ceiling

price floor
tax incidence

Questions for review

1 Give an example of a price ceiling and of a price floor.
2 Which causes a shortage of a good – a price ceiling or a price floor? Which causes a surplus?
3 What mechanisms allocate resources when the price of a good is not allowed to bring supply and demand into equilibrium?
4 Explain why economists usually oppose controls on prices.
5 What is the difference between a tax paid by buyers and a tax paid by sellers?
6 How does a tax on a good affect the price paid by buyers, the price received by sellers and the quantity sold?
7 What determines how the burden of a tax is divided between buyers and sellers? Why?

Problems and applications

1 Lovers of classical music persuade the government to impose a price ceiling of $50 per concert ticket. As a result of this policy, do more or fewer people attend classical music concerts?
2 The government has decided that the free-market price of cheese is too low.
  a Suppose the government imposes a binding price floor in the cheese market. Use a supply-and-demand diagram to show the effect of this policy on the price of cheese and the quantity of cheese sold. Is there a shortage or surplus of cheese?
  b Farmers complain that the price floor has reduced their total revenue. Is this possible? Explain.

c   In response to farmers' complaints, the government agrees to purchase all of the surplus cheese at the price floor. Compared with the basic price floor, who benefits from this new policy? Who loses?

3   A recent study found that the demand and supply schedules for frisbees are as follows:

Price per frisbee	Quantity demanded	Quantity supplied
$11	1 million	15 million
10	2	12
9	4	9
8	6	6
7	8	3
6	10	1

a   What are the equilibrium price and quantity of frisbees?

b   Frisbee manufacturers persuade the government that frisbee production improves scientists' understanding of aerodynamics and thus is important for national security. A concerned government votes to impose a price floor $2 above the equilibrium price. What is the new market price? How many frisbees are sold?

c   Irate university students march on Canberra and demand a reduction in the price of frisbees. An even more concerned parliament votes to repeal the price floor and impose a price ceiling $1 below the former price floor. What is the new market price? How many frisbees are sold?

4   Suppose the federal government requires beer drinkers to pay a $2 tax on each carton of beer purchased. (In fact, both the federal and state governments impose beer taxes of some sort.)

a   Draw a supply-and-demand diagram of the market for beer without the tax. Show the price paid by consumers, the price received by producers and the quantity of beer sold. What is the difference between the price paid by consumers and the price received by producers?

b   Now draw a supply-and-demand diagram for the beer market with the tax. Show the price paid by consumers, the price received by producers and the quantity of beer sold. What is the difference between the price paid by consumers and the price received by producers? Has the quantity of beer sold increased or decreased?

5   If the government places a $500 tax on luxury cars, will the price paid by consumers rise by more than $500, less than $500 or exactly $500? Explain.

6   The federal government decides that Australia should reduce air pollution by reducing its use of petrol. The government imposes a $0.50 tax for each litre of petrol sold.

a   Should this tax be imposed on producers or consumers? Explain carefully using a supply-and-demand diagram.

b   If the demand for petrol were more elastic, would this tax be more effective or less effective in reducing the quantity of petrol consumed? Explain using both words and a diagram.

c   Are consumers of petrol helped or hurt by this tax? Why?

d   Are workers in the oil industry helped or hurt by this tax? Why?

7   A case study in this chapter discusses minimum or award wages.
    a   Suppose the award wage in a particular industry is above the equilibrium wage in the market
        for unskilled labour. Using a supply-and-demand diagram of the market for unskilled labour,
        show the market wage, the number of workers who are employed and the number of workers
        who are unemployed. Also show the total wage payments to unskilled workers.
    b   Now suppose that Fair Work Australia proposes an increase in the award wage. What effect
        would this increase have on employment? Does the change in employment depend on the
        elasticity of demand, the elasticity of supply, both elasticities or neither?
    c   What effect would this increase in the award wage have on unemployment? Does the change
        in unemployment depend on the elasticity of demand, the elasticity of supply, both elasticities
        or neither?
    d   If the demand for unskilled labour were inelastic, would the proposed increase in the award
        wage raise or lower total wage payments to unskilled workers? Would your answer change if
        the demand for unskilled labour were elastic?
8   An alcopop is a sweet pre-mixed alcoholic drink. Consider the following policies, each of which is
    aimed at reducing the amount of alcopops consumed by people in Australia. Illustrate each of
    these proposed policies in a supply-and-demand diagram of the alcopop market.
    a   a tax on alcopop buyers
    b   a tax on alcopop sellers
    c   a price floor on alcopops.
9   The Australian government administers two programs that affect the market for cigarettes. Media
    campaigns and labelling requirements are aimed at making the public aware of the dangers of
    cigarette smoking. At the same time, there is a tax on cigarettes.
    a   How do these two programs affect cigarette consumption? Use a graph of the cigarette market
        in your answer.
    b   What is the combined effect of these two programs on the price of cigarettes?
10 In 2001, the Australian government, in response to political pressure, cut the excise (or wholesale)
    tax on petrol by 1.5 cents per litre.
    a   In the absence of other policies (for example, price controls), do you think that the price of
        petrol that consumers pay (that is, the price at the pump) will fall by 1.5 cents?
    b   Who, apart from consumers, is likely to benefit from this tax cut?
    c   To ensure that the price consumers paid for petrol fell by the full 1.5 cents, the government
        attempted to enforce this through its competition regulator, the ACCC. Will producer profits
        rise, fall or stay the same if this price control is effective?
11 (This question requires the use of secondary school algebra.) Suppose the demand curve for pizza can be
    represented by the equation $Q^D = 20 - 2P$, where Q^D is the quantity demanded and P is the price. The
    supply curve for pizza can be represented by the equation $Q^S = P - 1$, where Q^S is the quantity supplied.
    Suppose the government imposes a $3 tax per pizza. How much more will consumers now pay for a pizza?
    (*Hint:* The prices in the demand and supply equations are no longer equal. The price that determines
    quantity demanded now equals the price that determines quantity supplied plus $3.)
12 A subsidy is the opposite of a tax. With a $0.50 tax on the buyers of ice-creams, the government
    collects $0.50 for each ice-cream purchased; with a $0.50 subsidy for the buyers of ice-creams,
    the government pays buyers $0.50 for each ice-cream purchased.
    a   Show the effect of a $0.50 subsidy per ice-cream on the demand curve for ice-creams, the
        effective price paid by consumers, the effective price received by sellers and the quantity of
        ice-creams sold.
    b   Do consumers gain or lose from this policy? Do producers gain or lose? Does the government
        gain or lose?

Search me!

 Search me!

When accessing information about economics use the following keywords in any combinations you require:

- price ceiling
- price floor
- tax incidence

CourseMate

 CourseMate

For more multimedia resources and activities on economics, visit the Economics CourseMate website.

PART THREE
Supply and demand II: Markets and welfare

7

Consumers, producers and the efficiency of markets

Learning objectives

In this chapter you will:

- examine the link between buyers' willingness to pay for a good and the demand curve

- learn how to define and measure consumer surplus

- examine the link between sellers' costs of producing a good and the supply curve

- learn how to define and measure producer surplus

- see that the equilibrium of supply and demand maximises total surplus in a market.

When consumers go to florists to buy roses and other types of flowers for Valentine's Day or Mother's Day, they may be disappointed that the price of a bunch is as high as it is. At the same time, when flower growers bring to market the flowers they have grown, they wish that the price of flowers were even higher. These views are not surprising; buyers always want to pay less and sellers always want to get paid more. But is there a 'right price' for flowers from the standpoint of society as a whole?

In previous chapters we saw how, in market economies, the forces of supply and demand determine the prices of goods and services and the quantities sold. So far, however, we have described the way markets allocate scarce resources without directly considering the question of whether these market allocations are desirable. In other words, our analysis has been positive (what is) rather than normative (what should be). We know that the price of a bunch of roses adjusts to ensure that the quantity of roses supplied equals the quantity of roses demanded. But, at this equilibrium, is the quantity of roses produced and consumed too small, too large or just right?

In this chapter we take up the topic of **welfare economics**, the study of how the allocation of resources affects economic wellbeing. We begin by examining the benefits that buyers and sellers receive from taking part in a market. We then examine how society can make these benefits as large as possible. This analysis leads to a profound conclusion – the equilibrium of supply and demand in a market maximises the total benefits received by buyers and sellers.

> **welfare economics**
> the study of how the allocation of resources affects economic wellbeing

As you may recall from chapter 1, one of the *Ten Lessons from Economics* discussed how markets are usually a good way to organise economic activity. The study of welfare economics explains this idea more fully. It also answers our question about the right price of flowers; the price that balances the supply and demand for flowers is, in a particular sense, the best one because it maximises the total welfare of flower consumers and flower producers. No consumer or producer of flowers aims to achieve this goal, but their joint actions, directed by market prices, moves them towards a welfare-maximising outcome – as if led by an invisible hand.

Consumer surplus

We begin our study of welfare economics by looking at the benefits buyers receive from participating in a market.

Willingness to pay

Imagine that you own a mint-condition recording of Michael Jackson's first solo album. Because you are not a Michael Jackson fan, you decide to sell it. One way to do so is to hold an auction.

Four Jackson fans show up for your auction: John, Paul, George and Ringo. Each of them would like to own the album, but there is a limit to the amount that each is willing to pay for it. Table 7.1

Table 7.1 Four possible buyers' willingness to pay	
Buyer	Willingness to pay
John	$100
Paul	80
George	70
Ringo	50

144

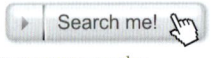
shows the maximum price that each of the four possible buyers would pay. Each buyer's maximum is called his **willingness to pay** and it measures how much that buyer values the good. Each buyer would be eager to buy the album at a price less than his willingness to pay, would refuse to buy the album at a price more than his willingness to pay and would be indifferent about buying the album at a price exactly equal to his willingness to pay.

To sell your album, you begin the bidding at a low price, say $10. Because all four buyers are willing to pay much more, the price rises quickly. The bidding stops when John bids $80 (or slightly more). At this point, Paul, George and Ringo have dropped out of the bidding, because they are unwilling to bid any more than $80. John pays you $80 and gets the album. Note that the album has gone to the buyer who values the album most highly.

What benefit does John receive from buying the Michael Jackson album? In a sense, John has found a real bargain – he is willing to pay $100 for the album but pays only $80 for it. We say that John receives consumer surplus of $20. **Consumer surplus** is the amount a buyer is willing to pay for a good minus the amount the buyer actually pays for it.

Consumer surplus measures the benefit to buyers of participating in a market. In this example, John receives a $20 benefit from participating in the auction because he pays only $80 for a good he values at $100. Paul, George and Ringo get no consumer surplus from participating in the auction, because they left without the album and without paying anything.

Now consider a somewhat different example. Suppose that you had two identical Michael Jackson albums to sell. Again, you auction them off to the four possible buyers. To keep things simple, we assume that both albums are to be sold for the same price and that no buyer is interested in buying more than one album. Therefore, the price rises until two buyers are left.

In this case, the bidding stops when John and Paul bid $70 (or slightly higher). At this price, John and Paul are each happy to buy an album, and George and Ringo are not willing to bid any higher. John and Paul each receive consumer surplus equal to his willingness to pay minus the price. John's consumer surplus is $30 and Paul's is $10. John's consumer surplus is higher now than it was previously, because he gets the same album but pays less for it. The total consumer surplus in the market is $40.

Using the demand curve to measure consumer surplus

Consumer surplus is closely related to the demand curve for a product. To see how they are related, let's continue our example and consider the demand curve for this rare Michael Jackson album.

We begin by using the willingness to pay of the four possible buyers to find the demand schedule for the album. Table 7.2 shows the demand schedule that corresponds to Table 7.1. If the price is above

Table 7.2 The demand schedule for the buyers in Table 7.1		
Price	Buyers	Quantity demanded
More than $100	None	0
$80 to $100	John	1
$70 to $80	John, Paul	2
$50 to $70	John, Paul, George	3
$50 or less	John, Paul, George, Ringo	4

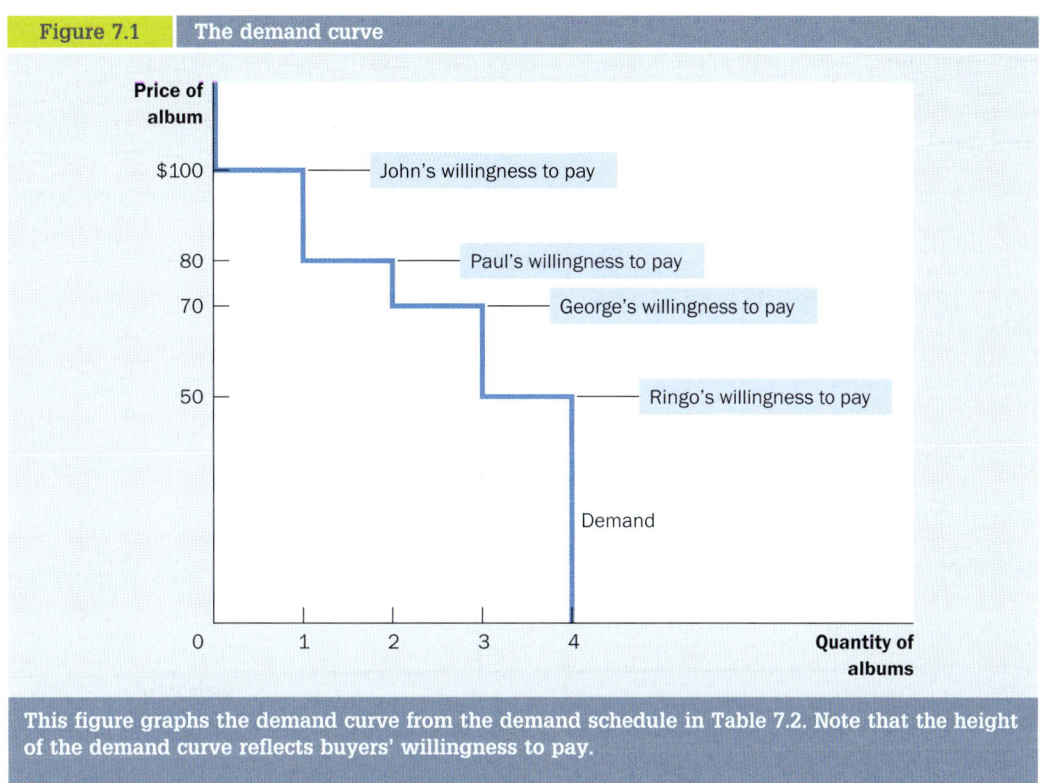

Figure 7.1 | **The demand curve**

This figure graphs the demand curve from the demand schedule in Table 7.2. Note that the height of the demand curve reflects buyers' willingness to pay.

$100, the quantity demanded in the market is 0, because no buyer is willing to pay that much. If the price is between $80 and $100, the quantity demanded is one, because only John is willing to pay such a high price. If the price is between $70 and $80, the quantity demanded is two, because both John and Paul are willing to pay the price. We can continue this analysis for other prices as well. In this way, the demand schedule is derived from the willingness to pay of the four possible buyers.

Figure 7.1 graphs the demand curve that corresponds to this demand schedule. Note the relationship between the height of the demand curve and the buyers' willingness to pay. At any quantity, the price given by the demand curve shows the willingness to pay of the marginal buyer, the buyer who would leave the market first if the price were any higher. At a quantity of four albums, for instance, the demand curve has a height of $50, the price that Ringo (the marginal buyer) is willing to pay for an album. At a quantity of three albums, the demand curve has a height of $70, the price that George (who is now the marginal buyer) is willing to pay.

Because the demand curve reflects buyers' willingness to pay, we can also use it to measure consumer surplus. Figure 7.2 uses the demand curve to calculate consumer surplus in our example. In panel (a), the price is $80 (or slightly above), and the quantity demanded is one. Note that the area above the price and below the demand curve equals $20. This amount is exactly the consumer surplus we calculated earlier when only one album is sold.

Panel (b) of Figure 7.2 shows consumer surplus when the price is $70 (or slightly above). In this case, the area above the price and below the demand curve equals the total area of the two rectangles; John's consumer surplus at this price is $30 and Paul's is $10. This area equals a total of $40. Once again, this amount is the consumer surplus we calculated earlier.

Figure 7.2 Measuring consumer surplus with the demand curve

(a) Price = $80

Price of album

$100 — John's consumer surplus ($20)

80

70

50

Demand

0   1   2   3   4   Quantity of albums

(b) Price = $70

Price of album

$100 — John's consumer surplus ($30)

80 — Paul's consumer surplus ($10)

70

Total consumer surplus ($40)

50

Demand

0   1   2   3   4   Quantity of albums

In panel (a), the price of the good is $80 and the consumer surplus is $20. In panel (b), the price of the good is $70 and the consumer surplus is $40.

The lesson from this example holds for all demand curves – the area below the demand curve and above the price measures the consumer surplus in a market. The reason is that the height of the demand curve measures the value buyers place on the good, as measured by their willingness to pay for it. The difference between this willingness to pay and the market price is each buyer's consumer surplus. Thus, the total area below the demand curve and above the price is the sum of the consumer surplus of all buyers in the market for a good or service.

How a lower price raises consumer surplus

Because buyers always want to pay less for the goods they buy, a lower price makes buyers of a good better off. But how much does buyers' wellbeing rise in response to a lower price? We can use the concept of consumer surplus to answer this question precisely.

Figure 7.3 shows a typical downward-sloping demand curve. Although this demand curve appears somewhat different in shape from the steplike demand curves in our previous two figures, the ideas we have just developed apply nonetheless – consumer surplus is the area above the price and below the demand curve. In panel (a), consumer surplus at a price of P_1 is the area of triangle ABC.

Now suppose that the price falls from P_1 to P_2, as shown in panel (b). The consumer surplus now equals area ADF. The increase in consumer surplus attributable to the lower price is the area BCFD.

This increase in consumer surplus is composed of two parts. First, those buyers who were already buying Q_1 of the good at the higher price P_1 are better off because they now pay less. The increase in consumer surplus of existing buyers is the reduction in the amount they pay; it equals the area of the rectangle BCED. Second, some new buyers enter the market because they are now willing to buy the good at the lower price and some existing buyers may decide to buy more of the good at the lower price. As a result, the quantity demanded in the market increases from Q_1 to Q_2. The consumer surplus from these new sales of the good is the area of the triangle CEF.

What does consumer surplus measure?

Our goal in developing the concept of consumer surplus is to make normative judgements about the desirability of market outcomes. Now that you have seen what consumer surplus is, let's consider whether it is a good measure of economic wellbeing.

Imagine that you are a policymaker trying to design a good economic system. Would you care about the amount of consumer surplus? Consumer surplus, the amount that buyers are willing to pay for a good minus the amount they actually pay for it, measures the benefit that buyers receive from a good *as the buyers themselves perceive it*. Thus, consumer surplus is a good measure of economic wellbeing if policymakers want to respect the preferences of buyers.

In some circumstances, policymakers might choose not to care about consumer surplus because they do not respect the preferences that drive buyer behaviour. For example, drug addicts are willing to pay a high price for heroin. Yet we would not say that addicts get a large benefit from being able to buy heroin at a low price (even though addicts might say they do). From the standpoint of society, willingness to pay in this instance is not a good measure of the buyers' benefit, and consumer surplus is not a good measure of economic wellbeing, because addicts are not looking after their own best interests.

In most markets, however, consumer surplus does reflect economic wellbeing. Economists normally presume that buyers are rational when they make decisions and that their preferences should be

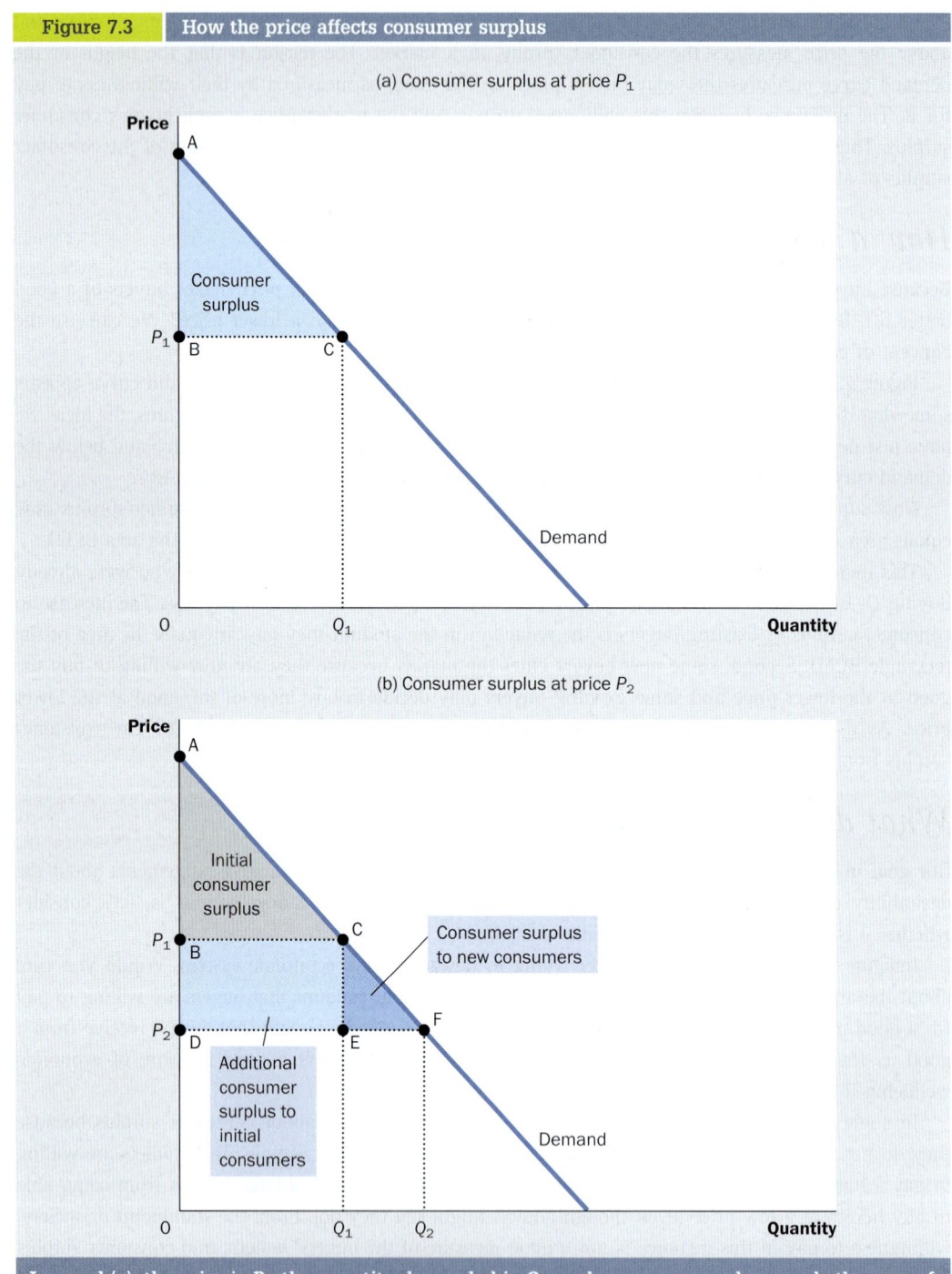

Figure 7.3 How the price affects consumer surplus

(a) Consumer surplus at price P_1

Price

A

Consumer
surplus

P_1 B   C

Demand

0   Q_1 Quantity

(b) Consumer surplus at price P_2

Price

A

Initial
consumer
surplus

P_1 B   C

Consumer surplus
to new consumers

P_2 D   E   F

Additional
consumer
surplus to
initial
consumers

Demand

0   Q_1 Q_2 Quantity

In panel (a), the price is P_1, the quantity demanded is Q_1, and consumer surplus equals the area of
the triangle ABC. When the price falls from P_1 to P_2, as in panel (b), the quantity demanded rises
from Q_1 to Q_2, and the consumer surplus rises to the area of the triangle ADF. The increase in
consumer surplus (area BCFD) occurs in part because existing consumers now pay less (area
BCED) and in part because new consumers enter the market at the lower price (area CEF).

respected. In this case, consumers are the best judges of how much benefit they receive from the goods they buy.

Draw a demand curve for a bunch of roses. In your diagram, show a price for a bunch and the consumer surplus that results from this price. Explain in words what this consumer surplus measures.

Producer surplus

We now turn to the other side of the market and consider the benefits sellers receive from participating in a market. As you will see, our analysis of sellers' welfare is similar to our analysis of buyers' welfare.

Cost and the willingness to sell

Imagine now that you are a homeowner and you need to get your house painted. You turn to four sellers of painting services: Alice, Emmett, Rosalie and Jasper. Each painter is willing to do the work for you if the price is right. You decide to take bids from the four painters and auction off the job to the painter who will do the work for the lowest price.

Each painter is willing to take the job if the price they receive exceeds their cost of doing the work. Here the term **cost** should be interpreted as the painters' opportunity cost; it includes both the painters' out-of-pocket expenses (for paint, brushes and so on) and the value that the painters place on their own time. Table 7.3 shows each painter's cost. Because a painter's cost is the lowest price they would accept for their work, cost is a measure of their willingness to sell their services. Each painter would be eager to sell their services at a price greater than their cost and each would refuse to sell their services at a price that is less than their cost. At a price exactly equal to their cost, each painter would be indifferent about selling their services: each would be equally happy getting the job or using their time and energy for another purpose.

When you take bids from the painters, the price might start off high, but it quickly falls as the painters compete for the job. Once Jasper has bid $600 (or slightly less), he is the sole remaining bidder. Jasper is happy to do the job for this price, because his cost is only $500. Alice, Emmett and Rosalie are unwilling to do the job for less than $600. Note that the job goes to the painter who can do the work at the lowest cost.

cost
the value of everything a seller must give up to produce a good

Table 7.3 The costs of four possible sellers	
Seller	Cost ($)
Alice	900
Emmett	800
Rosalie	600
Jasper	500

150

producer surplus
the amount a seller is paid for
a good minus the seller's cost

► producer surplus

What benefit does Jasper receive from getting the job? Because he is willing to do the work for $500 but gets $600 for doing it, we say that he receives producer surplus of $100. **Producer surplus** is the amount a seller is paid minus the cost of production. Producer surplus measures the benefit to sellers of participating in a market.

Now consider a somewhat different example. Suppose that you have two houses that need painting. Again, you auction off the jobs to the four painters. Let's assume that no painter is able to paint both houses and that you will pay the same amount to paint each house. Therefore, the price falls until two painters are left.

In this case, the bidding stops when Rosalie and Jasper each offer to do the job for a price of $800 (or slightly less). At this price, Rosalie and Jasper are willing to do the work and Alice and Emmett are not willing to bid a lower price. At a price of $800, Jasper receives producer surplus of $300 and Rosalie receives producer surplus of $200. The total producer surplus in the market is $500.

Using the supply curve to measure producer surplus

Just as consumer surplus is closely related to the demand curve, producer surplus is closely related to the supply curve. To see how, let's continue our example.

We begin by using the costs of the four painters to find the supply schedule for painting services. Table 7.4 shows the supply schedule that corresponds to the costs in Table 7.3. If the price is below $500, none of the four painters is willing to do the job, so the quantity supplied is 0. If the price is between $500 and $600, only Jasper is willing to do the job, so the quantity supplied is one. If the price is between $600 and $800, Rosalie and Jasper are willing to do the job, so the quantity supplied is two, and so on. Thus, the supply schedule is derived from the costs of the four painters.

Figure 7.4 graphs the supply curve that corresponds to this supply schedule. Note that the height of the supply curve is related to the sellers' costs. At any quantity, the price given by the supply curve shows the cost of the marginal seller, the seller who would leave the market first if the price were any lower. At a quantity of four houses, for instance, the supply curve has a height of $900, the cost that Alice (the marginal seller) incurs to provide her painting services. At a quantity of three houses, the supply curve has a height of $800, the cost that Emmett (who is now the marginal seller) incurs.

Because the supply curve reflects sellers' costs, we can use it to measure producer surplus. Figure 7.5 uses the supply curve to calculate producer surplus in our example. In panel (a), we assume that the price is $600. In this case, the quantity supplied is one. Note that the area below the price and above the supply curve equals $100. This amount is exactly the producer surplus we calculated earlier for Jasper.

Table 7.4 The supply schedule for the sellers in Table 7.3		
Price	Sellers	Quantity supplied
$900 or more	Alice, Emmett, Rosalie, Jasper	4
$800 to $900	Emmett, Rosalie, Jasper	3
$600 to $800	Rosalie, Jasper	2
$500 to $600	Jasper	1
Less than $500	None	0

Figure 7.4 | The supply curve

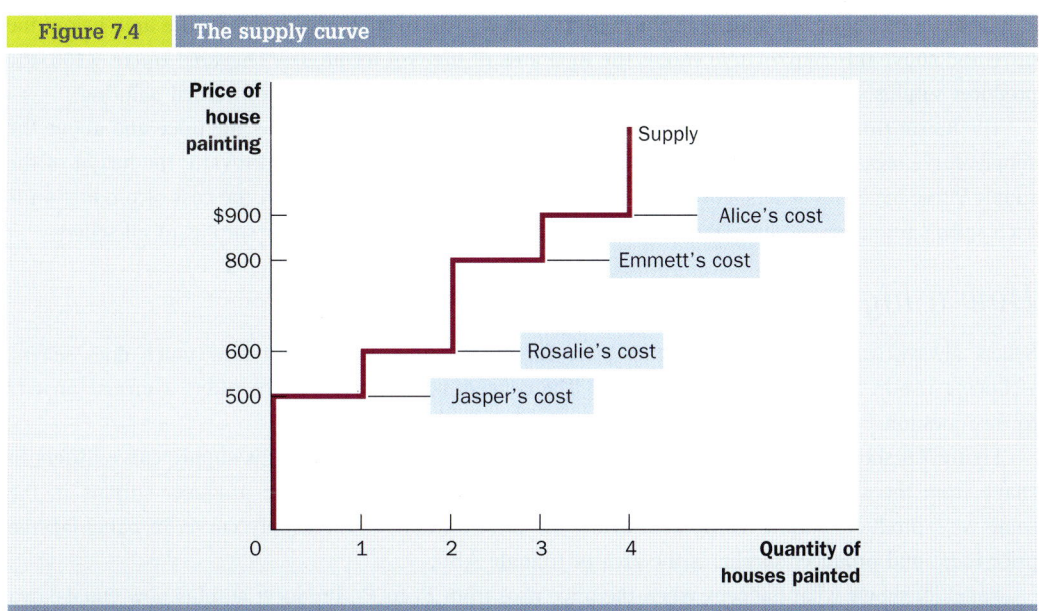

This figure graphs the supply curve from the supply schedule in Table 7.4. Note that the height of the supply curve reflects sellers' costs.

Figure 7.5 | Measuring producer surplus with the supply curve

In panel (a), the price of the good is $600 and the producer surplus is $100. In panel (b), the price of the good is $800 and the producer surplus is $500.

Panel (b) of Figure 7.5 shows producer surplus at a price of $800. In this case, the area below the price and above the supply curve equals the total area of the two rectangles. This area equals $500, the producer surplus we calculated earlier for Rosalie and Jasper when two houses needed painting.

The lesson from this example applies to all supply curves – the area below the price and above the supply curve measures the producer surplus in a market. The logic is straightforward; the height of the supply curve measures sellers' costs, and the difference between the price and the cost of production is each seller's producer surplus. Thus, the total area is the sum of the producer surplus of all sellers.

How a higher price raises producer surplus

Sellers always want to receive a higher price for the goods they sell. But how much does sellers' wellbeing rise in response to a higher price? The concept of producer surplus offers a precise answer to this question.

Figure 7.6 shows a typical upward-sloping supply curve. Even though this supply curve differs in shape from the steplike supply curves in the previous figure, we measure producer surplus in the same way; producer surplus is the area below the price and above the supply curve. In panel (a), the price is P_1, and producer surplus is the area of triangle ABC.

Panel (b) shows what happens when the price rises from P_1 to P_2. Producer surplus now equals area ADF. This increase in producer surplus has two parts. First, those sellers who were already selling Q_1 of the good at the lower price P_1 are better off because they now get more for what they sell. The increase in producer surplus for existing sellers equals the area of the rectangle BCED. Second, some existing

Figure 7.6	How the price affects producer surplus

In panel (a), the price is P_1, the quantity demanded is Q_1, and producer surplus equals the area of the triangle ABC. When the price rises from P_1 to P_2, as in panel (b), the quantity supplied rises from Q_1 to Q_2, and the producer surplus rises to the area of the triangle ADF. The increase in producer surplus (area BCFD) occurs in part because existing producers now receive more (area BCED) and in part because new producers enter the market at the higher price (area CEF).

sellers choose to sell more and some new sellers enter the market because they are now willing to produce the good at the higher price, resulting in an increase in the quantity supplied from Q_1 to Q_2. The producer surplus from this increase in production and sales is the area of the triangle CEF.

As this analysis shows, we use producer surplus to measure the wellbeing of sellers in much the same way as we use consumer surplus to measure the wellbeing of buyers. Because these two measures of economic welfare are so similar, it is natural to use them together. And, indeed, that is exactly what we do in the next section.

Draw a supply curve for a bunch of roses. In your diagram, show a price for a bunch of roses and the producer surplus that results from this price. Explain in words what this producer surplus measures.

Market efficiency

Consumer surplus and producer surplus are the basic tools that economists use to study the welfare of buyers and sellers in a market. These tools can help us consider a fundamental economic question: Is the allocation of resources determined by free markets in any way desirable?

The benevolent social planner

To evaluate market outcomes, we introduce into our analysis a new, hypothetical character, called the benevolent social planner. The benevolent social planner is an all-knowing, all-powerful, well-intentioned dictator. The planner wants to maximise the economic wellbeing of everyone in society. What do you suppose this planner should do? Should he just leave buyers and sellers at the equilibrium that they reach naturally on their own? Or can he increase economic wellbeing by altering the market outcome in some way?

To answer this question, the planner must first decide how to measure the economic wellbeing of a society. One possible measure is the sum of consumer and producer surplus, which we call *total surplus*. Consumer surplus is the benefit that buyers receive from participating in a market and producer surplus is the benefit that sellers receive. It is therefore natural to use total surplus as a measure of society's economic wellbeing.

To better understand this measure of economic wellbeing, recall how we measure consumer and producer surplus. We define consumer surplus as:

$$\text{consumer surplus} = \text{Value to buyers} - \text{Amount paid by buyers}$$

Similarly, we define producer surplus as:

$$\text{Producer surplus} = \text{Amount received by sellers} - \text{Costs of sellers}$$

When we add consumer and producer surplus together, we obtain:

$$\text{Total surplus} = \text{Value to buyers} - \text{Amount paid by buyers} + \text{Amount received by sellers} - \text{Costs of sellers}$$

The amount paid by buyers equals the amount received by sellers, so the middle two terms in this expression cancel each other. As a result, we can write total surplus as:

$$\text{Total surplus} = \text{Value to buyers} - \text{Costs of sellers}$$

Total surplus in a market is the total value to buyers of the goods, as measured by their willingness to pay, minus the costs to sellers of providing those goods.

If an allocation of resources maximises total surplus, we say that the allocation exhibits *efficiency*. If an allocation is not efficient, then some of the gains from trade among buyers and sellers are not being realised. For example, an allocation is inefficient if a good is not being produced by the sellers with lowest cost. In this case, moving production from a high-cost producer to a low-cost producer will lower the total costs of sellers and raise total surplus. Similarly, an allocation is inefficient if a good is not being consumed by the buyers who value it most highly. In this case, moving consumption of the good from a buyer with a low valuation to a buyer with a high valuation will raise total surplus.

In addition to efficiency, the social planner might also care about *equity* – the fairness of the distribution of wellbeing among the various buyers and sellers. In essence, the gains from trade in a market are like a pie to be distributed among the market participants. The question of efficiency is whether the pie is as big as possible. The question of equity is whether the pie is divided fairly. Evaluating the equity of a market outcome is more difficult than evaluating the efficiency. Whereas efficiency is an objective goal that can be judged on strictly positive grounds, equity involves normative judgements that go beyond economics and enter into the realm of political philosophy.

In this chapter we concentrate on efficiency as the social planner's goal. Keep in mind, however, that real policymakers often care about equity as well. That is, they care about both the size of the economic pie and how the pie gets sliced and distributed among members of society.

fyi

The invisible hand of the marketplace

The efficiency of free markets is, at first, a surprising idea. After all, no one is looking out for the general economic welfare. Free markets contain many buyers and sellers, and all of them are interested primarily in their own wellbeing. Yet despite decentralised decision making and self-interested decision makers, the result is not chaos but efficiency.

The virtue of free markets was well understood by the great economist Adam Smith. Here is what he wrote in his 1776 classic, *An Inquiry into the Nature and Causes of the Wealth of Nations*:

Man has almost constant occasion for the help of his brethren, and it is vain for him to expect it from their benevolence only. He will be more likely to prevail if he can interest their self-love in his favour, and show them that it is for their own advantage to do for him what he requires of them … It is not from the benevolence of the butcher, the brewer, or the baker that we expect our dinner, but from their regard to their own interest …

Every individual … neither intends to promote the public interest, nor knows how much he is promoting it … He intends only his own gain, and he is in this, as in many other cases, led by an invisible hand to promote an end which was no part of his intention. Nor is it always the worse for the society that it was no part of it. By pursuing his own interest he frequently promotes that of the society more effectually than when he really intends to promote it.

Smith is saying that participants in the economy are motivated by self-interest and that the 'invisible hand' of the marketplace guides this self-interest into promoting general economic wellbeing.

Smith's insights remain true today. Indeed, our analysis in this chapter allows us to express Smith's view more precisely by showing that the equilibrium of supply and demand maximises the sum of consumer and producer surplus.

Evaluating the market equilibrium

Figure 7.7 shows consumer and producer surplus when a market reaches the equilibrium of supply and demand. Recall that consumer surplus equals the area above the price and under the demand curve

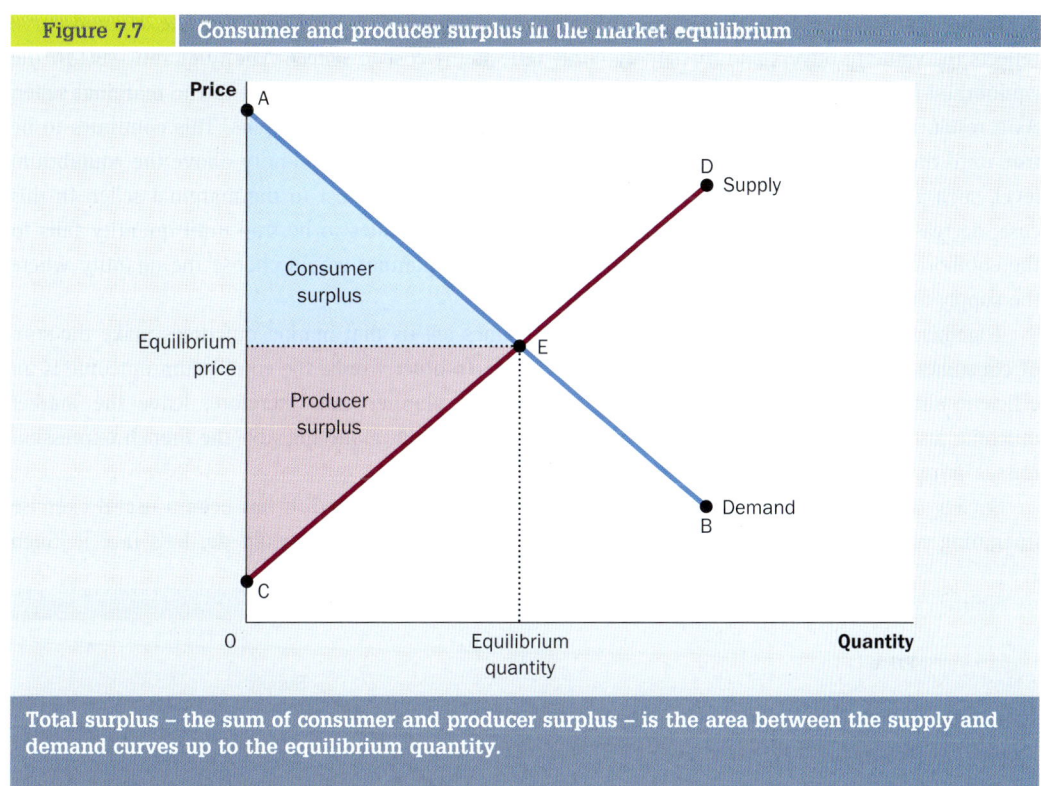

Figure 7.7   Consumer and producer surplus in the market equilibrium

Total surplus – the sum of consumer and producer surplus – is the area between the supply and demand curves up to the equilibrium quantity.

and producer surplus equals the area below the price and above the supply curve. Thus, the total area between the supply and demand curves up to the point of equilibrium represents the total surplus from this market.

Is this equilibrium allocation of resources efficient? Does it maximise total surplus? To answer these questions, keep in mind that when a market is in equilibrium the price determines which buyers and sellers participate in the market. Those buyers who value the good more than the price (represented by the segment AE on the demand curve) choose to buy the good; those buyers who value it less than the price (represented by the segment EB) do not. Similarly, those sellers whose costs are less than the price (represented by the segment CE on the supply curve) choose to produce and sell the good; those sellers whose costs are greater than the price (represented by the segment ED) do not.

These observations lead to two insights about market outcomes:

1   Free markets allocate the supply of goods to the buyers who value them most highly, as measured by their willingness to pay.
2   Free markets allocate the demand for goods to the sellers who can produce them at lowest cost.

Thus, given the quantity produced and sold in a market equilibrium, the social planner cannot increase economic wellbeing by changing the allocation of consumption among buyers or the allocation of production among sellers.

But can the social planner raise total economic wellbeing by increasing or decreasing the quantity of the good? The answer is no, as stated in this third insight about market outcomes:

3   Free markets produce the quantity of goods that maximises the sum of consumer and producer surplus.

Figure 7.8 illustrates why this is true. To interpret this figure, keep in mind that the demand curve reflects the value to buyers and the supply curve reflects the cost to sellers. At any quantity below the equilibrium level, such as Q_1, the value to the marginal buyer exceeds the cost to the marginal seller. As a result, increasing the quantity produced and consumed raises total surplus. This continues to be true until the quantity reaches the equilibrium level. Similarly, at any quantity above the equilibrium level, such as Q_2, the value to the marginal buyer is less than the cost to the marginal seller. In this case, decreasing the quantity raises total surplus and this continues to be true until quantity falls to the equilibrium level. To maximise total surplus, the social planner would choose the quantity where the supply and demand curves intersect.

Together, these three insights about market outcomes tell us that market outcomes make the sum of consumer and producer surplus as large as it can be. In other words, the equilibrium outcome is an efficient allocation of resources. The benevolent social planner can, therefore, leave the market outcome just as one finds it. This policy of leaving well enough alone goes by the French expression *laissez-faire*, which literally translated means 'allow them to do'.

Society is lucky that the planner doesn't need to intervene. Although it has been a useful exercise imagining what an all-knowing, all-powerful, well-intentioned dictator would do, let's face it: Such

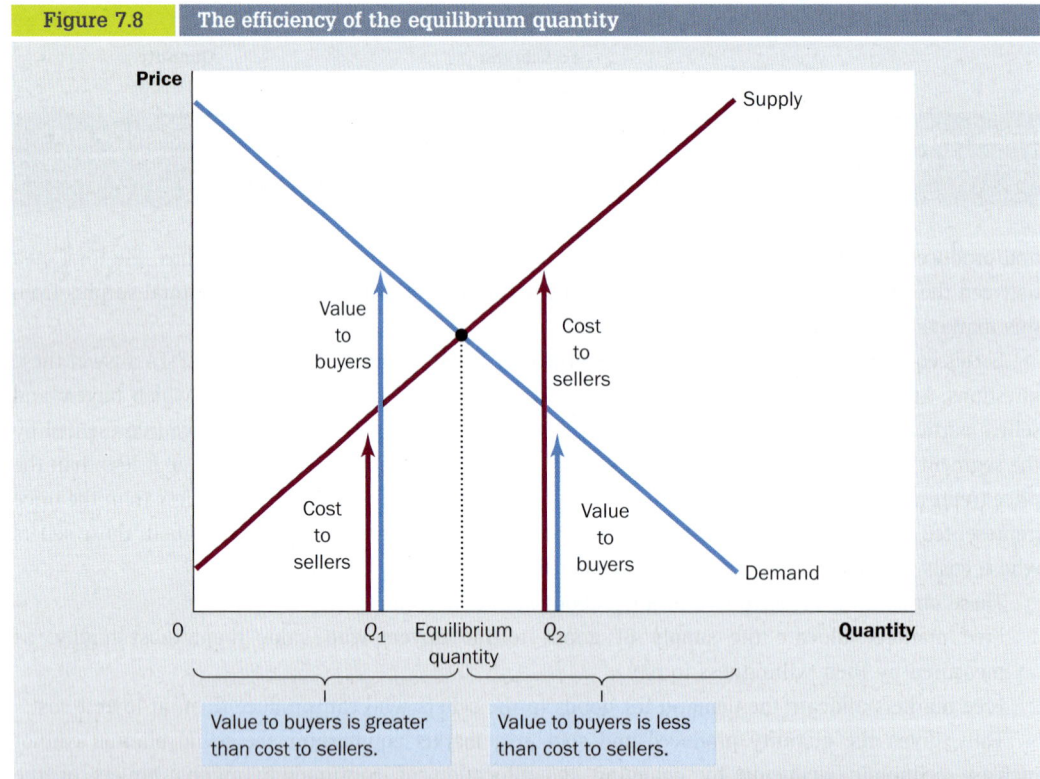

Figure 7.8   **The efficiency of the equilibrium quantity**

At quantities less than the equilibrium quantity, such as Q_1, the value to buyers exceeds the cost to sellers. At quantities greater than the equilibrium quantity, such as Q_2, the cost to sellers exceeds the value to buyers. Therefore, the market equilibrium maximises the sum of producer and consumer surplus.

characters are hard to come by. Dictators are rarely benevolent and even if we found someone so virtuous he would lack crucial information.

Suppose our social planner tried to choose an efficient allocation of resources on his own, instead of relying on market forces. To do so, he would need to know the value of a particular good to every potential consumer in the market and the cost of every potential producer. And he would need this information not only for this market but for every one of the many thousands of markets in the economy. The task is practically impossible, which explains why centrally planned economies never work very well.

The planner's job becomes easy, however, once he takes on a partner: Adam Smith's invisible hand of the marketplace. The invisible hand takes all the information about buyers and sellers into account and guides everyone in the market to the best outcome as judged by the standard of economic efficiency. It is, truly, a remarkable feat. That is why economists so often advocate free markets as the best way to organise economic activity.

Some years ago, a Boston newspaper reported the story of Susan Stephens, a woman whose son needed a kidney transplant. When the doctor learned that the mother's kidney was not compatible, he proposed a novel solution: If Stephens donated one of her kidneys to a stranger, her son would move to the top of the kidney waiting list. The mother accepted the deal and soon two patients had the transplant they were waiting for.

The ingenuity of the doctor's proposal and the nobility of the mother's act cannot be doubted. But the story raises many intriguing questions. If the mother could trade a kidney for a kidney, would the hospital allow her to trade a kidney for an expensive, experimental cancer treatment that she could not afford otherwise? Should she be allowed to exchange her kidney for free tuition for her son at the hospital's medical school? Should she be able to sell her kidney so she can use the cash to trade in her old Toyota for a new Lexus?

In many countries, including Australia, it is illegal for a person to sell their organs. In essence, in the market for organs, the government has imposed a price ceiling of zero. The result, as with any binding price ceiling, is a shortage of the good. The deal in the Stephens case did not fall under this prohibition because no cash exchanged hands.

Some countries, however, have illicit markets in organs. The World Health Organization estimates that 10 per cent of all organ transplants, including around 15 000 kidneys each year, involve a patient from a rich country buying an illegal organ from a citizen of a poorer nation. The temptation to the world's poorest people to sell their 'spare' organs is high. A kidney can sell for around $1500 or more in the illegal trade. This may not sound like much to you or me. But it can be many years income to a person living in dire poverty.

Some economists believe that there would be large benefits to allowing a free market in organs. People are born with two kidneys, but they usually need only one. Meanwhile, a few people suffer from illnesses that leave them without any working kidneys. Despite the obvious gains from trade, the current situation is dire. In Australia, the average wait for a kidney transplant is 3.8 years and there are up to 50 deaths a year from people on the waiting list because a kidney cannot be found. In Europe, on average 12 people die each day waiting for an organ transplant. If those needing a kidney were allowed to buy one from those who have two, the price would rise to balance supply and demand. Sellers would be better off with the extra cash in their pockets. Buyers would be better off with the organ they need to save their lives. The shortage of kidneys would disappear.

Such a market would lead to an efficient allocation of resources, but critics of this plan worry about fairness. A market for organs, they argue, would benefit the rich at the expense of the poor, because organs would then be allocated to those most willing and able to pay. But you can also question the fairness of the current system. Now, most of us walk around with an extra organ that we don't really need, while some of our fellow citizens are dying to get one. Is that fair?

Draw the supply and demand for roses. In the equilibrium, show producer and consumer surplus. Explain why producing more roses would lower total surplus.

Conclusion: Market efficiency and market failure

This chapter introduced the basic tools of welfare economics – consumer and producer surplus – and used them to evaluate the efficiency of free markets. We showed that the forces of supply and demand allocate resources efficiently. That is, even though buyers and sellers in a market are concerned only about their own welfare, they are together led by an invisible hand to an equilibrium that maximises the total benefits to buyers and sellers.

A word of warning is in order. To conclude that markets are efficient, we made several assumptions about how markets work. When these assumptions do not hold, our conclusion that the market equilibrium is efficient may no longer be true. As we close this chapter, let's consider briefly two of the most important of these assumptions.

First, our analysis assumed that markets are perfectly competitive. In the world, however, competition is sometimes far from perfect. In some markets, a single buyer or seller (or a small group of them) may be able to control market prices. This ability to influence prices is called *market power*. Market power can cause markets to be inefficient because it keeps the price and quantity away from the equilibrium of supply and demand.

Second, our analysis assumed that the outcome in a market matters only to the buyers and sellers in that market. Yet, in the real world, the decisions of buyers and sellers sometimes affect people who are not participants in the market at all. Pollution is the classic example of a market outcome that affects people not in the market. Such side effects, called *externalities*, cause welfare in a market to depend on more than just the value to the buyers and the costs of the sellers. Because buyers and sellers do not take these side effects into account when deciding how much to consume and produce, the equilibrium in a market can be inefficient from the standpoint of society as a whole.

Market power and externalities are examples of a general phenomenon called *market failure* – the inability of some unregulated markets to allocate resources efficiently. When markets fail, public policy can potentially remedy the problem and increase economic efficiency. Microeconomists devote much effort to studying when market failure is likely and what sorts of policies are best at correcting market failures. As you continue your study of economics, you will see that the tools of welfare economics developed here are readily adapted to that endeavour.

Despite the possibility of market failure, the invisible hand of the marketplace is extraordinarily important. In many markets, the assumptions we made in this chapter work well and the conclusion of market efficiency applies directly. Moreover, our analysis of welfare economics and market efficiency can be used to shed light on the effects of various government policies. In the next two chapters we apply the tools we have just developed to study two important policy issues – the welfare effects of taxation and of international trade.

IN THE NEWS . . .

TICKET SCALPING

If an economy is to allocate its scarce resources efficiently, goods must get to those consumers who value them most highly. Ticket scalping is one example of how markets reach efficient outcomes. Scalpers buy tickets to plays, concerts and sports events and then sell the tickets at a price above their original cost. By charging the highest price the market will bear, scalpers help ensure that consumers with the greatest willingness to pay for the tickets actually do get them. But scalping is usually illegal in Australia, unlike the United States. This article looks at the incentives behind this ban on scalping and how it hurts Australian sports fans.

▸ ticket scalping

The ticket-scalping myth
by Gareth Parker

Tonight I'm going to a baseball game at Citi Field – the home of my beloved New York Mets – a brand new ballpark that opened this year in the car park of adjacent old Shea Stadium.

We've got great seats behind home plate, and we paid less than half of the face value on the ticket to obtain them. How? Ticket scalpers.

In Australia, scalping is a dirty word that inspires revulsion in 'real fans' and is outlawed by State Governments. In the United States, the practice is, with a few minor exceptions, completely legal and, thanks to the internet, a quick, safe and convenient way to obtain tickets to any sporting, concert or theatre event you could wish to see.

Online ticket brokers, like StubHub.com, have created an efficient and transparent market for tickets of every stripe. Sellers are usually individual ticket holders (but also professional speculators) and prices are driven by supply and demand.

For a game like tonight's, between the Mets and the Atlanta Braves, prices are cheap because it's late in the season and both teams are out of playoff contention. Good news for buyers like us, because we can get great seats at a discount. Some seats for tonight's game, in the Upper Deck of the stadium, are literally being offered for sale for a dollar, substantially below their face value of $15.

A series this coming weekend however, between fierce rivals the New York Yankees and Boston Red Sox, is a different story. The teams, whose fans despise each other, are locked in a deathly serious fight for the American League East title and the three game series to be played on Friday, Saturday and Sunday will be crucial in deciding the race.

As such, tickets on StubHub.com are being offered for substantially higher than face value, in most cases, because the demand from fans supports the premium.

Either way, it's fans – both buyers and sellers – who decide how much each seat is worth through an efficient mechanism made possible by a willingness on the part of American lawmakers to let markets do what they do.

StubHub.com and the other ticket brokers make their money by charging a service fee on each transaction, a practice that would be familiar to anyone who has bought or sold shares on the Australian Stock Exchange.

Which brings us to the AFL grand final, and the annual outrageous fraud that is perpetuated on the average football fan.

The face value price for tickets to Saturday's clash between Geelong and St Kilda ranges from $142.50 to $245. But only a fraction of the 100 000 people who pack the MCG will have been fortunate enough to obtain a ticket at those prices.

As was reported on thewest.com.au this week, just one quarter of the tickets available were allocated for sale to the members of the competing clubs.

Twenty-one thousand tickets will go to AFL Members, 23 000 to members of the MCC, 7500 to AFL sponsors, invitees and corporates, 5000 to members of Etihad Stadium's pricey Medallion Club and 1000 each to the 14 non-competing AFL clubs.

The allocations to MCC and AFL members are eminently defensible given the game and

>>

160

where it is played, but it's what happens to all those other tickets controlled by the AFL and the non-competing clubs where things get outrageous.

Thanks to a handy bit of law passed by the Victorian Labor Government a few years ago (when former Carlton ruckman Justin Madden was Sports Minister) the grand final is a so-called 'declared event' under Victoria's anti-scalping legislation.

This means that no-one may re-sell grand final tickets at a premium without written approval from the league. And conveniently, the league only gives that approval to itself, its clubs and a select band of corporate resellers, who package up the $142.50 – $250 tickets with a lunch and/or accommodation and sell them for up to $2000 a pop.

In effect, Victoria's anti-scalping law, which in theory is meant to protect fans from being ripped off, in fact enables and authorises the AFL and its clubs to perpetrate the annual bald-faced fleecing of football fans desperate to see the biggest game of the year.

Yet somehow, every year, we read stories like this one in the Melbourne *Herald Sun* under the headline:

SCALP AT YOUR PERIL

Grand Final ticket scalpers outside the MCG will find themselves up against a crack team on Saturday.

Police, Melbourne City Council bylaws officers and State Government officials will all be looking to apprehend unscrupulous sellers.

How good of the State to protect the real scalpers from competition. The inspectors should start right at AFL House in the Docklands.

Enjoy the weekend's game. In the local parlance, I'll be rooting for the Saints!

Source: Gareth Parker/*The West Australian*, 23 September 2009. © The West Australian.

Summary

- Consumer surplus equals buyers' willingness to pay for a good minus the amount they actually pay for it and it measures the benefit buyers get from participating in a market. Consumer surplus can be calculated by finding the area below the demand curve and above the price.
- Producer surplus equals the amount sellers receive for their goods minus their costs of production and it measures the benefit sellers get from participating in a market. Producer surplus can be calculated by finding the area below the price and above the supply curve.
- An allocation of resources that maximises the sum of consumer and producer surplus is said to be efficient. Policymakers are often concerned with the efficiency, as well as the equity, of economic outcomes.
- The equilibrium of supply and demand maximises the sum of consumer and producer surplus. That is, the invisible hand of the marketplace leads buyers and sellers to allocate resources efficiently.
- Markets do not allocate resources efficiently in the presence of market failures such as market power or externalities.

Key concepts

consumer surplus
cost

producer surplus
welfare economics

willingness to pay

Questions for review

1. Explain how buyers' willingness to pay, consumer surplus and the demand curve are related.
2. Explain how sellers' costs, producer surplus and the supply curve are related.
3. In a supply-and-demand diagram, show producer and consumer surplus in the market equilibrium.
4. What is efficiency? Is it the only goal of economic policymakers?
5. What does the invisible hand do?
6. Name two types of market failure. Explain why each may cause market outcomes to be inefficient.

Problems and applications

1. Lanlan buys an iPod for $120 and gets consumer surplus of $80.
   a. What is her willingness to pay?
   b. If she had bought the iPod on sale for $90, what would her consumer surplus have been?
   c. If the price of an iPod were $250, what would her consumer surplus have been?
2. A plant disease in South Australia damages the grape crop. What happens to consumer surplus in the market for grapes? What happens to consumer surplus in the market for wine? Illustrate your answers with diagrams.
3. Suppose the demand for French bread rises. What happens to producer surplus in the market for French bread? What happens to producer surplus in the market for flour? Illustrate your answer with diagrams.

4   It is a hot day, and Bert is very thirsty. Here is the value he places on a bottle of water:

Value of first bottle	$7
Value of second bottle	5
Value of third bottle	3
Value of fourth bottle	1

   a   From this information, derive Bert's demand schedule. Graph his demand curve for bottled water.
   b   If the price of a bottle of water is $4, how many bottles does Bert buy? How much consumer surplus does Bert get from his purchases? Show Bert's consumer surplus in your graph.
   c   If the price falls to $2, how does quantity demanded change? How does Bert's consumer surplus change? Show these changes in your graph.

5   Ernie owns a water pump. Because pumping large amounts of water is harder than pumping small amounts, the cost of producing a bottle of water rises as he pumps more. Here is the cost he incurs to produce each bottle of water:

Cost of first bottle	$1
Cost of second bottle	3
Cost of third bottle	5
Cost of fourth bottle	7

   a   From this information, derive Ernie's supply schedule. Graph his supply curve for bottled water.
   b   If the price of a bottle of water is $4, how many bottles does Ernie produce and sell? How much producer surplus does Ernie get from these sales? Show Ernie's producer surplus in your graph.
   c   If the price rises to $6, how does quantity supplied change? How does Ernie's producer surplus change? Show these changes in your graph.

6   Consider a market in which Bert from problem 4 is the buyer and Ernie from problem 5 is the seller.
   a   Use Ernie's supply schedule and Bert's demand schedule to find the quantity supplied and quantity demanded at prices of $2, $4 and $6. Which of these prices brings supply and demand into equilibrium?
   b   What are consumer surplus, producer surplus and total surplus in this equilibrium?
   c   If Ernie produced and Bert consumed one less bottle of water, what would happen to total surplus?
   d   If Ernie produced and Bert consumed one additional bottle of water, what would happen to total surplus?

7   The cost of producing flat screen TVs has fallen substantially over the past decade. Let's consider some implications of this fact.
   a   Use a supply-and-demand diagram to show the effect of falling production costs on the price and quantity of flat screen TVs sold.
   b   In your diagram, show what happens to consumer surplus and producer surplus.

   c Suppose the supply of flat screen TVs is very elastic. Who benefits most from falling production costs – consumers or producers of these TVs?

8 There are four consumers willing to pay the following amounts for haircuts:

Dave: $14; Charlie: $4; Alice: $16; Kitty: $10

There are four hairdressing salons with the following costs:

Firm A: $6; Firm B: $12; Firm C: $8; Firm D: $4

   Each firm has the capacity to produce only one haircut. For efficiency, how many haircuts should be given? Which businesses should cut hair and which consumers should have their hair cut? How large is the maximum possible total surplus?

9 A friend of yours is considering two providers of mobile phone services. Provider A charges $120 per month for the service regardless of the number of phone calls made. Provider B does not have a fixed service fee but instead charges $1 per minute for calls. Your friend's monthly demand for minutes of calling is given by the equation $Q^D = 150 - 50P$, where P is the price of a minute.

   a With each provider, what is the cost to your friend of an extra minute on the phone?

   b In light of your answer to (a), how many minutes would your friend spend on the phone with each provider?

   c How much would he end up paying each provider every month?

   d How much consumer surplus would he obtain with each provider? (*Hint*: Graph the demand curve and recall the formula for the area of a triangle.)

   e Which provider would you recommend that your friend choose? Why?

10 Consider how private health insurance affects the quantity of health care services performed. Suppose that the typical medical procedure has a cost of $100, yet a person with private health insurance pays only $20 out-of-pocket when she chooses to have an additional procedure performed. Her health fund pays the remaining $80. (The health fund will recoup the $80 through higher premiums for everybody, but the share paid by this individual is small.)

   a Draw the demand curve in the market for private medical care. (In your diagram, the horizontal axis should represent the number of medical procedures.) Show the quantity of procedures demanded if each procedure has a price of $100.

   b On your diagram, show the quantity of procedures demanded if consumers pay only $20 per procedure. If the cost of each procedure to society is truly $100, and if individuals have private health insurance as just described, will the number of procedures performed maximise total surplus? Explain.

   c Economists often blame the health insurance system for excessive use of medical care. Given your analysis, why might the use of care be viewed as 'excessive'?

   d What sort of policies might prevent this excessive use?

11 Many parts of eastern Australia experienced a severe drought in recent years.

   a Use a diagram of the water market to show the effects of the drought on the equilibrium price and quantity of water.

   b Many communities did not allow the price of water to change, however. What is the effect of this policy on the water market? Show on your diagram any surplus or shortage that arises.

   c Suppose, instead, that the price of water was allowed to increase until the quantity demanded equalled the quantity supplied. Would the resulting allocation of water be more efficient? In your view, would it be more or less fair than the proportionate reductions in water use? What could be done to make the market solution more fair?

Search me!

  Search me!

When accessing information about economics use the following keywords in any combinations you require:

- consumer surplus
- producer surplus
- ticket scalping
- willingness to pay

CourseMate

For more multimedia resources and activities on economics, visit the Economics CourseMate website.

8

Application: The costs of taxation

Learning objectives

In this chapter you will:

- examine how taxes reduce consumer and producer surplus

- learn the meaning and causes of the deadweight loss of a tax

- consider why some taxes have larger deadweight losses than others

- examine how tax revenue and deadweight loss vary with the size of a tax.

Taxes are often a source of heated political debate. In 1808, William Bligh, Governor of colonial Australia, was thrown out of office over taxation concerns in the infamous Rum Rebellion. Two hundred years later, in 2010, Kevin Rudd, Prime Minister of Australia, was thrown out of office, in large part due to his handling of a government proposal for a super-profit tax on the mining industry. Yet few people would deny that some level of taxation is necessary to help fund government expenditure.

Because taxation has such a major impact on the modern economy, we return to the topic several times throughout this book as we expand the set of tools we have at your disposal. We began our study of taxes in chapter 6. There we saw how a tax on a good affects its price and the quantity sold and how the forces of supply and demand divide the burden of a tax between buyers and sellers. In this chapter we extend this analysis and look at how taxes affect welfare, the economic wellbeing of participants in a market.

The effects of taxes on welfare might at first seem obvious. The government imposes taxes to raise revenue and that revenue must come out of someone's pocket. As we saw in chapter 6, both buyers and sellers are worse off when a good is taxed; a tax raises the price buyers pay and lowers the price sellers receive. Yet to understand fully how taxes affect economic wellbeing, we must compare the reduced welfare of buyers and sellers with the amount of revenue the government raises. The tools of consumer and producer surplus allow us to make this comparison. The analysis will show that the costs of taxes to buyers and sellers exceed the revenue raised by the government.

The deadweight loss of taxation

We begin by recalling one of the surprising lessons from chapter 6 – it does not matter whether a tax on a good is levied on buyers or on sellers of the good. When a tax is levied on buyers, the demand curve shifts downwards by the size of the tax; when it is levied on sellers, the supply curve shifts upwards by that amount. In either case, when the tax is imposed, the price paid by buyers rises and the price received by sellers falls. In the end, the elasticities of supply and demand determine how the tax burden is distributed between producers and consumers. This distribution is the same, regardless of how the tax is levied.

Figure 8.1 shows these effects. To simplify our discussion, this figure does not show a shift in either the supply or demand curve, although one curve must shift. Which curve shifts depends on whether the tax is levied on sellers (the supply curve shifts) or buyers (the demand curve shifts). In this chapter, we can keep the analysis general and simplify the graphs by not bothering to show the shift. The key result is that the tax places a wedge between the price buyers pay and the price sellers receive. Because of this tax wedge, the quantity sold falls below the level that would be sold without a tax. In other words, a tax on a good causes the size of the market for the good to shrink. These results should be familiar from chapter 6.

How a tax affects market participants

Let's use the tools of welfare economics to measure the gains and losses from a tax on a good. To do this, we must take into account how the tax affects buyers, sellers and the government. The benefit received by buyers in a market is measured by consumer surplus – the amount buyers are willing to pay for the good minus the amount they actually pay for it. The benefit received by sellers in a market is measured by producer surplus – the amount sellers receive for the good minus their costs. These are precisely the measures of economic welfare we used in chapter 7.

Figure 8.1   **The effects of a tax**

A tax on a good places a wedge between the price that buyers pay and the price that sellers receive. The quantity of the good sold falls.

What about the third interested party, the government? If T is the size of the tax and Q is the quantity of the good sold, then the government gets total tax revenue of $T \times Q$. It can use this tax revenue to provide services, such as roads, police and education, or to help the needy. Therefore, to analyse how taxes affect economic wellbeing, we use tax revenue to measure the government's benefit from the tax. Keep in mind, however, that this benefit actually accrues not to the government but to those on whom the revenue is spent.

Figure 8.2 shows that the government's tax revenue is represented by the rectangle between the supply and demand curves. The height of this rectangle is the size of the tax, T, and the width of the rectangle is the quantity of the good sold, Q. Because a rectangle's area is its height times its width, this rectangle's area is $T \times Q$, which equals the tax revenue.

Welfare without a tax

To see how a tax affects welfare, we begin by considering welfare before the government has imposed a tax. Figure 8.3 shows the supply-and-demand diagram and marks the key areas with the letters A to F.

Without a tax, the price and quantity are found at the intersection of the supply and demand curves. The price is P_1, and the quantity sold is Q_1. Because the demand curve reflects buyers' willingness to pay, consumer surplus is the area between the demand curve and the price, A + B + C. Similarly, because the supply curve reflects sellers' costs, producer surplus is the area between the supply curve and the price, D + E + F. In this case, because there is no tax, tax revenue equals zero.

Total surplus, the sum of consumer and producer surplus, equals the area A + B + C + D + E + F. In other words, as we saw in chapter 7, total surplus is the area between the supply and demand curves up to the equilibrium quantity. The 'Without tax' column of Table 8.1 summarises these conclusions.

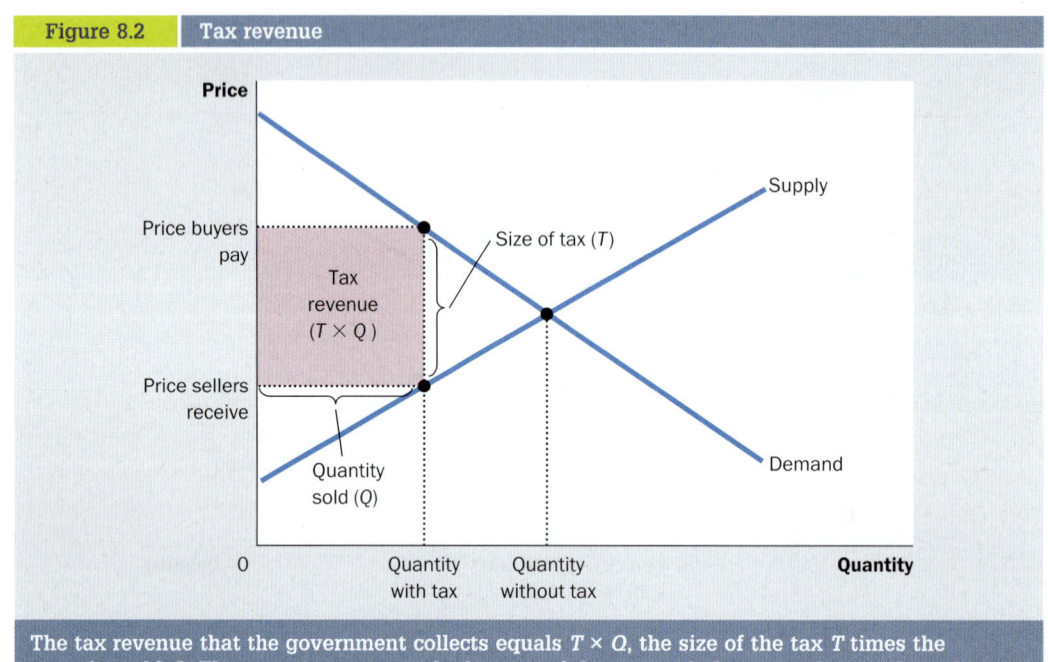

Figure 8.2 Tax revenue

The tax revenue that the government collects equals $T \times Q$, the size of the tax T times the quantity sold Q. Thus, tax revenue equals the area of the rectangle between the supply and demand curves.

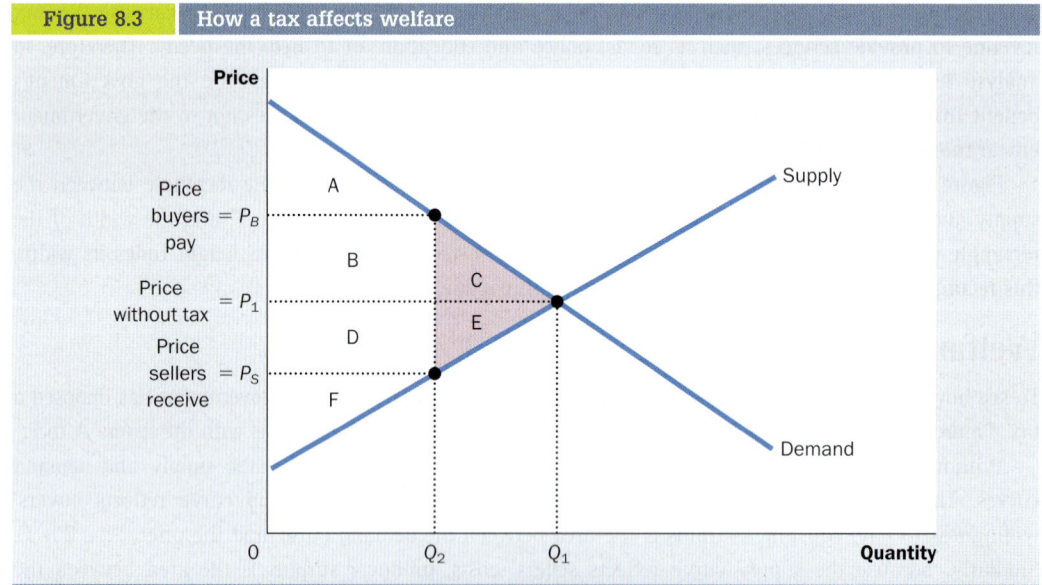

Figure 8.3 How a tax affects welfare

A tax on a good reduces consumer surplus (by the area B + C) and producer surplus (by the area D + E). Because the fall in producer and consumer surplus exceeds tax revenue (area B + D), the tax is said to impose a deadweight loss (area C + E).

Table 8.1 Changes in welfare from a tax			
	Without tax	With tax	Change
Consumer surplus	A+B+C	A	−(B+C)
Producer surplus	D+E+F	F	−(D+E)
Tax revenue	None	B+D	+(B+D)
Total surplus	A+B+C+D+E+F	A+B+D+F	−(C+E)

This table refers to the areas marked in Figure 8.3 to show how a tax affects the welfare of buyers and sellers in a market.

Welfare with a tax

Now consider welfare after the tax is imposed. The price paid by buyers rises from P_1 to P_B, so consumer surplus now equals only area A (the area below the demand curve and above the buyers' price). The price received by sellers falls from P_1 to P_S, so producer surplus now equals only area F (the area above the supply curve and below the sellers' price). The quantity sold falls from Q_1 to Q_2, and the government collects tax revenue equal to the area B + D.

To calculate total surplus with the tax, we add consumer surplus, producer surplus and tax revenue. Thus, we find that total surplus is area A + B + D + F. The 'With tax' column of Table 8.1 provides a summary.

Changes in welfare

We can now see the effects of the tax by comparing welfare before and after the tax is imposed. The last column in Table 8.1 shows the changes. The tax causes consumer surplus to fall by the area B + C and producer surplus to fall by the area D + E. Tax revenue rises by the area B + D. Not surprisingly, the tax makes buyers and sellers worse off and the government better off.

The change in total welfare includes the change in consumer surplus (which is negative), the change in producer surplus (which is also negative) and the change in tax revenue (which is positive). When we add these three pieces together, we find that total surplus in the market falls by the area C + E. *Thus, the losses to buyers and sellers from a tax exceed the revenue raised by the government.* The reduction in total surplus that results when a tax (or some other policy) distorts a market is called the **deadweight loss**. The area C + E measures the size of the deadweight loss.

To understand why taxes impose deadweight losses, recall one of the *Ten Lessons from Economics* in chapter 1 – people respond to incentives. In chapter 7 we saw that markets normally allocate scarce resources efficiently. That is, the equilibrium of supply and demand maximises the total surplus of buyers and sellers in a market. When a tax raises the price to buyers and lowers the price to sellers, however, it gives buyers an incentive to consume less and sellers an incentive to produce less than they would in the absence of the tax. As buyers and sellers respond to these incentives, the size of the market shrinks below its optimum (as shown in Figure 8.3 by the movement from Q_1 to Q_2). Thus, because taxes distort incentives, they cause markets to allocate resources inefficiently.

deadweight loss
the reduction in total surplus that results from a market distortion such as a tax or a monopoly price

▸ deadweight loss

Deadweight losses and the gains from trade

To gain some insight into why taxes result in deadweight losses, consider an example. Imagine that Joe cleans Jane's house each week for $100. The opportunity cost of Joe's time is $80 and the value of a clean house to Jane is $120. Thus, Joe and Jane each receive a $20 benefit from their deal. The total surplus of $40 measures the gains from trade in this particular transaction.

Now suppose that the government levies a $50 tax on the providers of cleaning services. There is now no price that Jane can pay Joe that will leave both of them better off after paying the tax. The most Jane would be willing to pay is $120, but then Joe would be left with only $70 after paying the tax, which is less than his $80 cost. Conversely, for Joe to receive his opportunity cost of $80, Jane would need to pay $130, which is above the $120 value she places on a clean house. As a result, Jane and Joe cancel their arrangement. Joe goes without the income and Jane lives in a dirtier house.

The tax has made Joe and Jane worse off by a total of $40, because they have each lost $20 of surplus. At the same time, the government collects no revenue from Joe and Jane because they decide to cancel their arrangement. The $40 is pure deadweight loss; it is a loss to buyers and sellers in a market not offset by an increase in government revenue. From this example, we can see the ultimate source of deadweight losses – *taxes cause deadweight losses because they prevent buyers and sellers from realising some of the gains from trade.*

The area of the triangle between the supply and demand curves (area C + E in Figure 8.3) measures these losses. This loss can be seen more easily in Figure 8.4 by recalling that the demand curve reflects the value of the good to consumers and that the supply curve reflects the costs of producers. When the

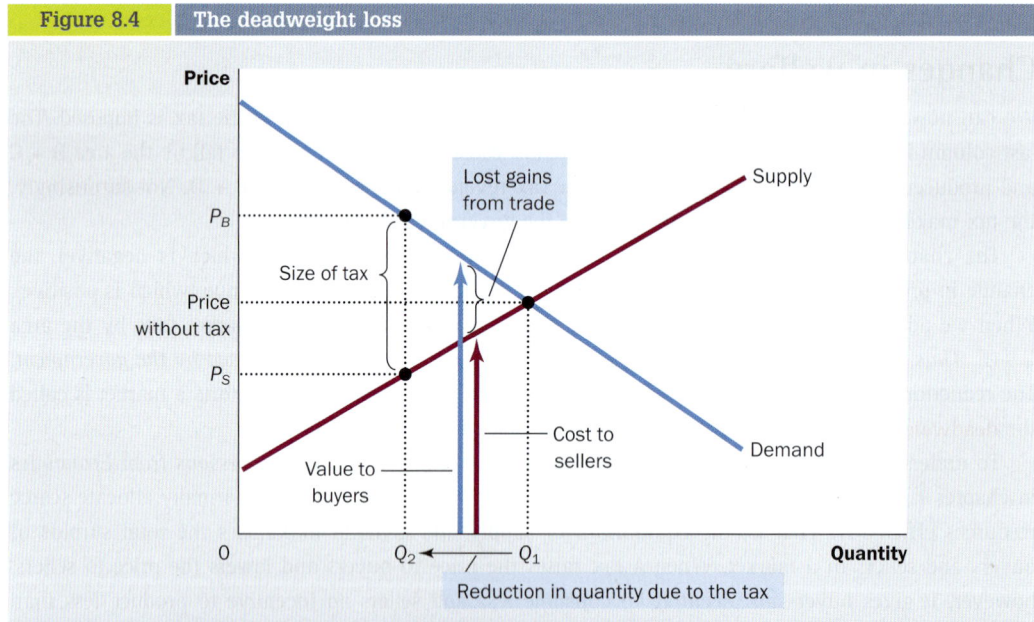

Figure 8.4 **The deadweight loss**

When the government imposes a tax on a good, the quantity sold falls from Q_1 to Q_2. As a result, some of the potential gains from trade among buyers and sellers do not get realised. These lost gains from trade create the deadweight loss.

tax raises the price to buyers to P_B and lowers the price to sellers to P_S, the marginal buyers and sellers leave the market, so the quantity sold falls from Q_1 to Q_2. Yet, as the figure shows, the value of the good to these buyers still exceeds the cost to these sellers. At every quantity between Q_1 to Q_2 the situation is the same as in our example with Joe and Jane. The gains from trade – the difference between buyers' value and sellers' cost – are less than the tax. As a result, these trades do not get made once the tax is imposed. The deadweight loss is the surplus lost because the tax discourages these mutually advantageous trades.

Draw the supply and demand curve for ice-cream. If the government imposes a tax on ice-cream, show what happens to the quantity sold, the price paid by buyers and the price paid by sellers. In your diagram, show the deadweight loss from the tax. Explain the meaning of the deadweight loss.

The determinants of the deadweight loss

What determines whether the deadweight loss from a tax is large or small? The answer is the price elasticities of supply and demand, which measure how much the quantity supplied and quantity demanded respond to changes in the price.

Let's consider first how the elasticity of supply affects the size of the deadweight loss. In the top two panels of Figure 8.5, the demand curve and the size of the tax are the same. The only difference in these figures is the elasticity of the supply curve. In panel (a), the supply curve is relatively inelastic – quantity supplied responds only slightly to changes in the price. In panel (b), the supply curve is relatively elastic – quantity supplied responds substantially to changes in the price. Notice that the deadweight loss, the area of the triangle between the supply and demand curves, is larger when the supply curve is more elastic.

Similarly, the bottom two panels of Figure 8.5 show how the elasticity of demand affects the size of the deadweight loss. Here the supply curve and the size of the tax are held constant. In panel (c), the demand curve is relatively inelastic and the deadweight loss is small. In panel (d), the demand curve is more elastic and the deadweight loss from the tax is larger.

The lesson from this figure is easy to explain. A tax has a deadweight loss because it induces buyers and sellers to change their behaviour. The tax raises the price paid by buyers, so they consume less. At the same time, the tax lowers the price received by sellers, so they produce less. Because of these changes in behaviour, the size of the market shrinks below the optimum. The elasticities of supply and demand measure how much sellers and buyers respond to the changes in the price and, therefore, determine how much the tax distorts the market outcome. *Hence, the greater the elasticities of supply and demand, the greater the deadweight loss of a tax.*

Figure 8.5 Tax distortions and elasticities

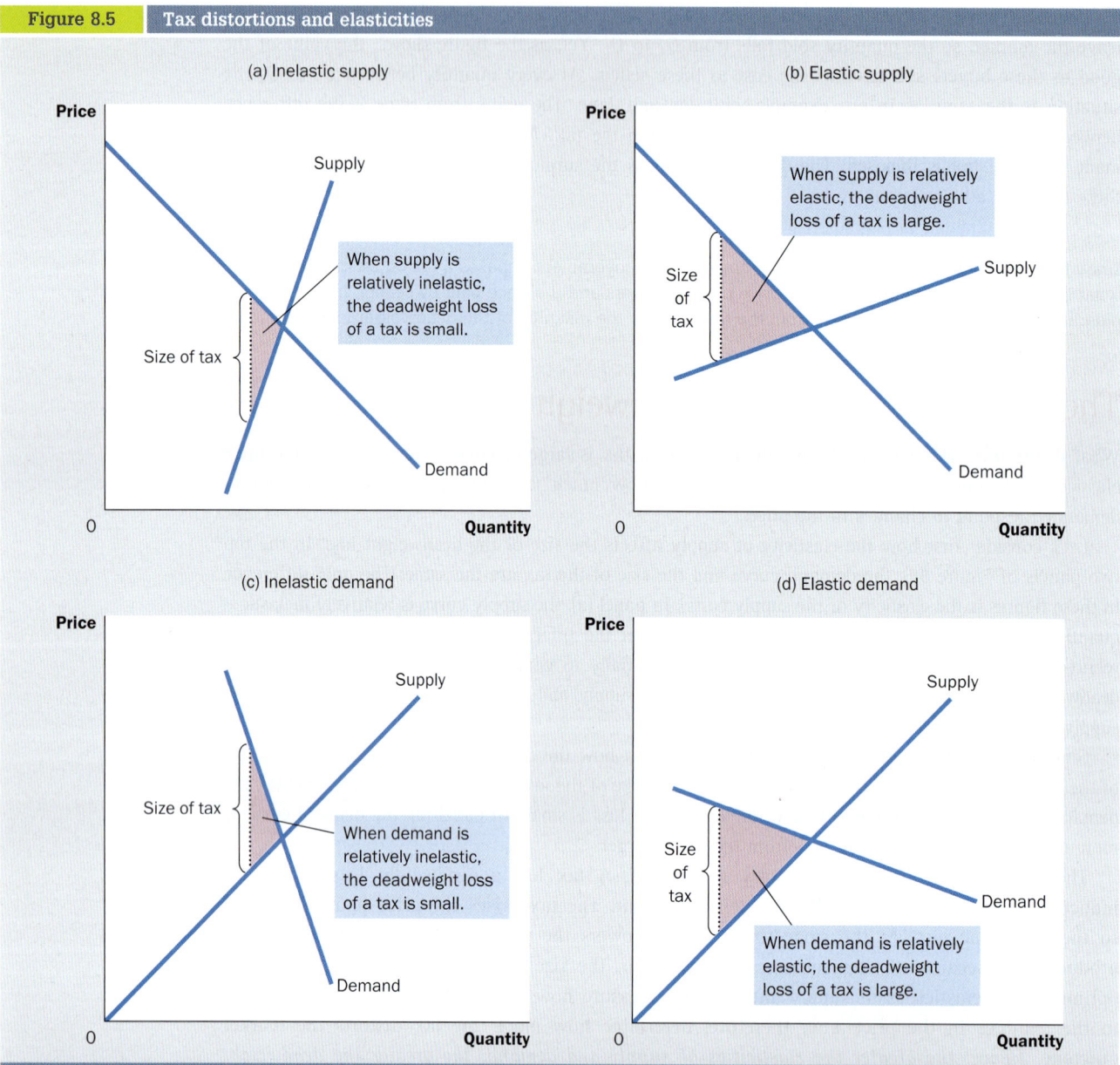

(a) Inelastic supply

Price

Supply

When supply is relatively inelastic, the deadweight loss of a tax is small.

Size of tax

Demand

0   Quantity

(b) Elastic supply

Price

When supply is relatively elastic, the deadweight loss of a tax is large.

Size of tax

Supply

Demand

0   Quantity

(c) Inelastic demand

Price

Supply

Size of tax

When demand is relatively inelastic, the deadweight loss of a tax is small.

Demand

0   Quantity

(d) Elastic demand

Price

Supply

Size of tax

Demand

When demand is relatively elastic, the deadweight loss of a tax is large.

0   Quantity

In panels (a) and (b), the demand curve and the size of the tax are the same, but the price elasticity of supply is different. Notice that the more elastic the supply curve, the larger the deadweight loss of the tax. In panels (c) and (d), the supply curve and the size of the tax are the same, but the price elasticity of demand is different. Notice that the more elastic the demand curve, the larger the deadweight loss of the tax.

Supply, demand, elasticity, deadweight loss – all this economic theory is enough to make your head spin. But believe it or not, these ideas go to the heart of a profound political question: How big should the government be? The reason the debate hinges on these concepts is that the larger the deadweight loss of taxation, the larger the cost of any government program. If taxation entails very large deadweight losses, then these losses are a strong argument for a leaner government that does less and taxes less. By contrast, if taxes impose only small deadweight losses, then government programs are less costly than they otherwise might be.

So how big are the deadweight losses of taxation? This is a question about which economists disagree. To see the nature of this disagreement, consider the most important tax in the Australian economy – the tax on labour. The most important example of this is income taxes. Many state governments also tax the payrolls of firms. Even a goods and services tax (nominally a tax on consumption) taxes labour because so much income is consumed. A labour tax places a wedge between the wages that firms pay and the wages that workers receive. If we add all forms of labour taxes together, the *marginal tax rate* on labour income – the tax on the last dollar of earnings – is almost 50 per cent for many workers.

Although the size of the labour tax is easy to determine, the deadweight loss of this tax is less straightforward. Economists disagree on whether labour taxes have a large or small deadweight loss. The disagreement arises from different views about the elasticity of labour supply.

Economists who argue that labour taxes are not very distorting believe that labour supply is fairly inelastic. Most people, they claim, would work full time regardless of the wage. If so, the labour supply curve is almost vertical and a tax on labour has a small deadweight loss.

Economists who argue that labour taxes are highly distorting believe that labour supply is more elastic. They admit that some groups of workers may supply their labour inelastically but claim that many other groups respond more to incentives. Here are some examples:

- Many workers can adjust the number of hours they work – for instance, by working overtime. The higher the wage, the more hours they choose to work.
- Some families have second wage earners – often married women with children – with some discretion over whether to do unpaid work at home or paid work in the marketplace. When deciding whether to take a job, these second wage earners compare the benefits of being at home (including savings on the cost of child care) with the wages they could earn.
- Many of the elderly can choose when to retire, and their decisions are partly based on the wage. Once they are retired, the wage determines their incentive to work part time.

In each of these cases, the quantity of labour supplied responds to the wage (the price of labour). Thus, the decisions of these workers are distorted when their labour earnings are taxed. Labour taxes encourage workers to work fewer hours, second wage earners to stay at home and the elderly to retire early.

These two views on labour taxation persist to this day. Indeed, whenever you see two political candidates debating whether the government should provide more services or reduce the tax burden, keep in mind that part of the disagreement may rest on different views about the elasticity of labour supply and the deadweight loss of taxation.

The demand for beer is more elastic than the demand for milk. Would a tax on beer or a tax on milk have a larger deadweight loss? Why?

Deadweight loss and tax revenue as taxes vary

Taxes rarely stay the same for long periods of time. Policymakers in local, state and federal governments are always considering raising one tax or lowering another. Here we consider what happens to the deadweight loss and tax revenue when the size of a tax changes.

Figure 8.6 shows the effects of a small, medium and large tax, holding constant the market's supply and demand curves. The deadweight loss – the reduction in total surplus that results when the tax reduces the size of a market below the optimum – equals the area of the triangle between the supply and demand curves. For the small tax in panel (a), the area of the deadweight loss triangle is quite small. But as the size of a tax rises in panels (b) and (c), the deadweight loss grows larger and larger.

Figure 8.6	Deadweight loss and tax revenue from three taxes of different size

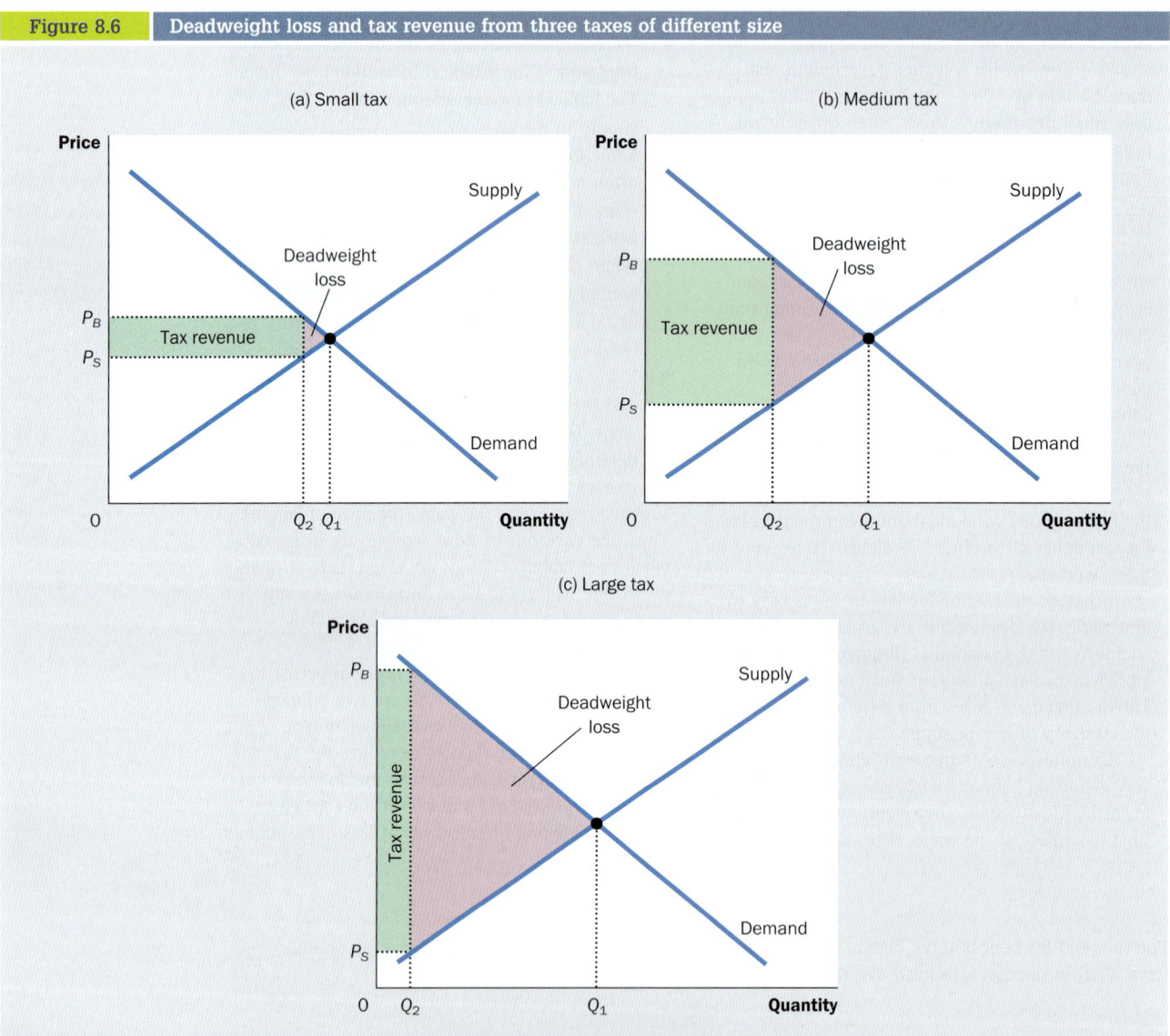

The deadweight loss is the reduction in total surplus due to the tax. Tax revenue is the amount of the tax times the amount of the good sold. In panel (a), a small tax has a small deadweight loss and raises a small amount of revenue. In panel (b), a somewhat larger tax has a larger deadweight loss and raises a larger amount of revenue. In panel (c), a very large tax has a very large deadweight loss, but because it has reduced the size of the market so much, the tax raises only a small amount of revenue.

Indeed, the deadweight loss of a tax rises even more rapidly than the size of the tax. The reason is that the deadweight loss is an area of a triangle, and an area of a triangle depends on the *square of* the size of the tax. If we double the size of a tax, for instance, the base and height of the triangle double, so the deadweight loss rises by a factor of 4. If we triple the size of a tax, the base and height triple, so the deadweight loss rises by a factor of 9.

The government's tax revenue is the size of the tax times the amount of the good sold. As Figure 8.6 shows, tax revenue equals the area of the rectangle between the supply and demand curves. For the small tax in panel (a), tax revenue is small. As the size of a tax rises from panel (a) to panel (b), tax revenue grows. But as the size of the tax rises further from panel (b) to panel (c), tax revenue falls because the higher tax drastically reduces the size of the market. For a very large tax, no revenue would be raised, because people would stop buying and selling the good altogether.

Figure 8.7 summarises these results. In panel (a) we see that, as the size of a tax increases, its deadweight loss quickly gets larger. In contrast, panel (b) shows that tax revenue first rises with the size of the tax; but then, as the tax gets larger, the market shrinks so much that tax revenue starts to fall.

| Figure 8.7 | How deadweight loss and tax revenue vary with the size of a tax |

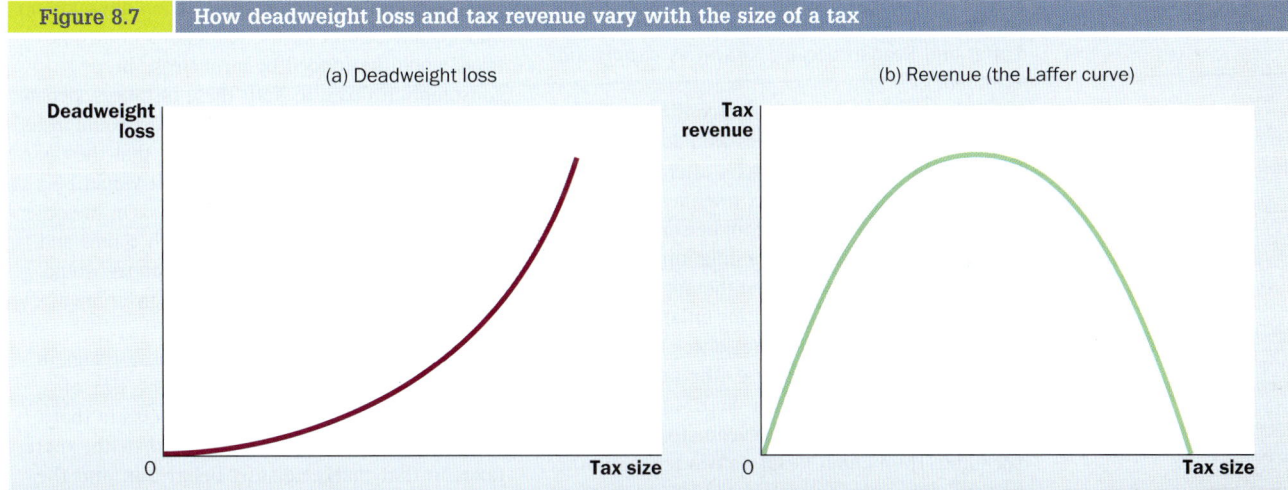

(a) Deadweight loss (b) Revenue (the Laffer curve)

Panel (a) shows that as the size of a tax grows larger, the deadweight loss grows larger. Panel (b) shows that tax revenue first rises, then falls. This relationship is sometimes called the Laffer curve.

CASE**STUDY**

The Laffer curve and supply-side economics

One day in 1974, economist Arthur Laffer sat in a Washington restaurant with some prominent journalists and politicians. He took out a serviette and drew a figure on it to show how tax rates affect tax revenue. It looked much like panel (b) of our Figure 8.7. Laffer then suggested that the United States was on the downward-sloping side of this curve. Tax rates were so high, he argued, that reducing them would actually raise tax revenue.

Few economists took Laffer's suggestion seriously. The idea that a cut in tax rates could raise tax revenue was correct as a matter of economic theory, but there was more doubt about whether it would do so in practice. There was no evidence for Laffer's view that US tax rates had in fact reached such extreme levels.

Nonetheless, the *Laffer curve* (as it became known) captured the imagination of Ronald

>>

Reagan, who became US President in the 1980s. David Stockman, budget director in the first Reagan administration, offers the following story:

> [Reagan] had once been on the Laffer curve himself. 'I came into the Big Money making pictures during World War II,' he would always say. At that time the wartime income surtax hit 90 per cent. 'You could only make four pictures and then you were in the top bracket,' he would continue. 'So we all quit working after four pictures and went off to the country.' High tax rates caused less work. Low tax rates caused more. His experience proved it.

When Reagan ran for president in 1980, he made cutting taxes part of his platform. Reagan argued that taxes were so high that they were discouraging hard work. He argued that lower taxes would give people the proper incentive to work, which would raise economic wellbeing and perhaps even tax revenue. Because the cut in tax rates was intended to encourage people to increase the quantity of labour they supplied, the views of Laffer and Reagan became known as *supply-side economics*.

Subsequent history failed to confirm Laffer's conjecture that lower tax rates would raise tax revenue. When Reagan cut taxes after he was elected, the result was less tax revenue, not more. In the United States, revenue from personal income taxes (per person, adjusted for inflation) fell by 9 per cent from 1980 to 1984, even though average income (per person, adjusted for inflation) grew by 4 per cent over this period. Yet once the policy was in place, it was hard to reverse. The tax cut helped begin a long period in which the US government failed to collect enough tax revenue to pay for all its spending. Throughout Reagan's two terms in office, and for many years thereafter, the US government ran large budget deficits.

Yet Laffer's argument is not completely without merit. Although an overall cut in tax rates does reduce revenue, there is evidence that some taxpayers may be on the wrong side of the Laffer curve. In the 1980s, tax revenue collected from the richest Americans, who face the highest tax rates, did rise when their taxes were cut. The idea that cutting taxes can raise revenue may be correct if applied to those taxpayers facing the highest tax rates. In addition, Laffer's argument may be more plausible when applied to other countries, where tax rates are much higher than in the United States. In Sweden in the early 1980s, for instance, the typical worker faced a marginal tax rate of about 80 per cent. Such a high tax rate provides a substantial disincentive to work. Studies have suggested that Sweden would indeed have raised more tax revenue if it had lowered its tax rates.

These ideas have also played a role in political debate in Australia. In 1990, the Liberal Party, under Andrew Peacock, had as a key part of its platform a simplification and reduction of marginal tax rates. Similarly, such reductions and simplifications were part of the Liberal Party's 'Fightback' policy in the 1993 election although, in that instance, some of the reductions in income taxes would be funded by an increase in consumption taxes. In both these instances, debate raged as to what change in tax revenue would result from the policy. The Liberals argued that the tax revenue change would be minor as it would be offset by Laffer-style incentive effects. On the other hand, Labor was sceptical about such claims and argued, successfully, that the tax changes would have to be accompanied by cuts to government spending.

Policymakers disagree about these issues in part because they disagree about the size of the relevant elasticities. The more elastic that supply and demand are in any market, the more taxes in that market distort behaviour, and the more likely it is that a tax cut will raise tax revenue. There is no debate, however, about the general lesson – how much revenue the government gains or loses from a tax change cannot be calculated just by looking at tax rates; it also depends on how the tax change affects people's behaviour.

IN THE NEWS . . .

TAX REFORM AND THE HENRY REPORT

On 2 May 2010, the federal government released the final report of an inquiry called *Australia's Future Tax System* – the so-called 'Henry report'. This report led to significant debate about tax reform in the lead up to the 2010 federal election. Despite the wide-ranging reforms proposed in the report, debate focused on one particular aspect, a recommended super-profit tax on the mining industry. This tax was controversial and was one of the reasons why, on 24 June 2010, Prime Minister Kevin Rudd resigned and was replaced by Australia's first female Prime Minister, Julia Gillard.

The really hard work on tax reform starts now

In September last year, Kevin Rudd publicly put himself in the shoes of the reformist Labor prime ministers Bob Hawke and Paul Keating. At the Canberra launch of Paul Kelly's book *The March of Patriots*, the Prime Minister declared Labor the true party of reform. Now, with the release of the Henry tax report, Mr Rudd has the opportunity to get with the program and make good his claim of being a reforming leader. Of course, Labor faces challenges in an election year, but it must not drop the ball on tax. There is room for real vision in responding to the Henry review. Just imagine, for example, what Mr Hawke would have done, given access to the $9 billion in annual revenue that will flow from the super-profits tax on miners? Mr Rudd is applying the revenue to useful projects such as superannuation but he has missed the opportunity to use it to manage the boom-and-bust cycle in resources by pouring it into a sovereign fund.

The Henry report is rich in ideas on how to deliver a fairer, simpler approach to tax that would also drive economic activity. The report sets out a 'tax and transfer system that would position Australia to deal with the demographic, economic and environmental challenges of the 21st century and would enhance community wellbeing'. Led by Treasury Secretary Ken Henry, the review group has taken a long-term perspective, up to 2050, recommending an overhaul of the architecture to create a system that 'would be robust, capable of supporting large structural change, dealing with unforeseeable external shocks and encouraging patterns of economic activity that prove fiscally and environmentally sustainable'. That represents a big national project and, as George Megalogenis writes today, implementing Henry lock, stock and barrel would leave us with a very different nation.

There are two areas in particular, personal tax rates and state taxes, that should continue to be debated. The recommendation for a flatter personal tax system is radical but would deliver a more transparent and efficient system. All income under $25 000 would be tax-free; all other income up to $180 000 would attract tax of 35 per cent (in effect, a flat tax for the great bulk of taxpayers); income beyond $180 000 would be taxed at 45 per cent. Pensions, allowances and other transfer payments would be tax free, thus removing the inefficient transfers that create wasteful tax-welfare churn. The report argues that while personal income is the most important means of raising revenue in developed countries, contributing 37 per cent of Australian tax revenue, it discourages workforce participation and savings. The flatter system would go some way to address this problem. A $25 000 threshold would help remove disincentives to move from welfare to work by ensuring that recipients are not punitively taxed as benefits are withdrawn.

Streamlining the messy and inefficient patchwork of state taxes ought to be a prominent goal of tax reform. Under the Henry vision, stamp duty on property could be replaced with consumption taxes or a land tax on the family home (the latter ruled out by Wayne Swan); and other inefficient taxes such as payroll tax would give way to a low-rate destination cash flow tax, in effect a state consumption tax (still on the table but not picked up by the Treasurer). While the politics of one-off stamp duty paid by the purchaser versus an annual land tax paid by the

>>

owner might appear to make this reform difficult to sell, the aim of property taxes should be to avoid distorting price signals, while favouring home ownership. Affordable housing and worker mobility are important economic goals, yet there is evidence that stamp duty can act as a deterrent to house purchase. The idea of a cash flow tax to replace payroll tax is evidence of the Dr Henry's shrewdness. The government ruled out any changes to the rate or the base of GST but the cash flow tax has slipped under the radar, giving the states the opportunity to impose a consumption tax of their own and create a more flexible revenue stream for themselves.

For the moment, the resource super-profits tax on mining dominates debate. This newspaper is broadly supportive of the tax, believing minerals belong to the nation, not the companies that extract them. The estimated $9 billion will cut company tax, give superannuation assistance to low-income earners and fund infrastructure. There are good arguments for these, but the government has missed the chance to pay down debt or create some form of sovereign fund for smoothing the economy in a resources downturn. It justified its tax on miners by arguing Australia has a two-speed economy: mining and the rest. It opted to address that imbalance by immediate spending. It should take a leaf out of the Henry report and recognise real tax reform sometimes requires a much longer time perspective.

Source: Opinion, *The Australian*, 4 May 2010.

If the government doubles the tax on petrol, can you be sure that revenue from the petrol tax will rise? Can you be sure that the deadweight loss from the petrol tax will rise? Explain.

Conclusion

It has been said that taxes are the price we pay for a civilised society. Indeed, our society cannot exist without some form of taxes. We all expect the government to provide us with certain services, such as roads, parks, police and defence. These public services require tax revenue.

This chapter has shed some light on how high the price of civilised society can be. One of the *Ten Lessons from Economics* discussed in chapter 1 is that markets are usually a good way to organise economic activity. Here we have seen that when the government imposes taxes on buyers or sellers of a good, however, society loses some of the benefits of market efficiency. Taxes are costly to market participants not only because taxes transfer resources from those participants to the government, but also because they alter incentives and distort market outcomes.

The analysis presented here and in chapter 6 should give you a good basis for understanding the economic impact of taxes, but this is not the end of the story. Microeconomists study how best to design a tax system, including how to strike the right balance between equity and efficiency. Macroeconomists study how taxes influence the overall economy and how policymakers can use the tax system to stablise economic activity and to achieve more rapid economic growth. So don't be surprised that, as you continue your study of economics, the subject of taxation comes up yet again.

Summary

- A tax on a good reduces the welfare of buyers and sellers of the good, and the reduction in consumer and producer surplus usually exceeds the revenue raised by the government. The fall in total surplus – the sum of consumer surplus, producer surplus and tax revenue – is called the deadweight loss of the tax.
- Taxes have deadweight losses because they cause buyers to consume less and sellers to produce less, and this change in behaviour shrinks the size of the market below the level that maximises total surplus. Because the elasticities of supply and demand measure how much market participants respond to market conditions, larger elasticities imply larger deadweight losses.
- As a tax grows larger it distorts incentives more and its deadweight loss grows larger. Because a tax reduces the size of the market, however, tax revenue does not continually increase. It first rises with the size of a tax, but if a tax gets large enough, tax revenue starts to fall.

Key concept

deadweight loss

Questions for review

1   What happens to consumer and producer surplus when the sale of a good is taxed? How does the change in consumer and producer surplus compare with the tax revenue? Explain.
2   Draw a supply-and-demand diagram with a tax on the sale of the good. Show the deadweight loss. Show the tax revenue.
3   How do the elasticities of supply and demand affect the deadweight loss of a tax? Why do they have this effect?
4   Why do experts disagree about whether labour taxes have small or large deadweight losses?
5   What happens to the deadweight loss and tax revenue when a tax is increased?

Problems and applications

1   The market for meat pies is characterised by a downward-sloping demand curve and an upward-sloping supply curve.
    a   Draw the competitive market equilibrium. Label the price, quantity, consumer surplus and producer surplus. Is there any deadweight loss? Explain.
    b   Suppose that the government forces each pie shop to pay a $1 tax on each pie sold. Illustrate the effect of this tax on the pie market, being sure to label the consumer surplus, producer surplus, government revenue and deadweight loss. How does each area compare with the pre-tax case?
    c   If the tax were removed, pie-eaters and sellers would be better off, but the government would lose tax revenue. Suppose that consumers and producers voluntarily transferred some of their gains to the government. Could all parties (including the government) be better off than they were with a tax? Explain using the labelled areas in your graph.
2   Evaluate the following two statements. Do you agree? Why or why not?
    a   'A tax that has no deadweight loss cannot raise any revenue for the government.'
    b   'A tax that raises no revenue for the government cannot have any deadweight loss.'

3 Consider the market for rubber bands.
  a If this market has very elastic supply and very inelastic demand, how would the burden of a tax on rubber bands be shared between consumers and producers? Use the tools of consumer surplus and producer surplus in your answer.
  b If this market has very inelastic supply and very elastic demand, how would the burden of a tax on rubber bands be shared between consumers and producers? Contrast your answer with your answer to part (a).

4 Suppose that the government imposes a tax on natural gas.
  a Is the deadweight loss from this tax likely to be greater in the first year after it is imposed or in the fifth year? Explain.
  b Is the revenue collected from this tax likely to be greater in the first year after it is imposed or in the fifth year? Explain.

5 After an economics lecture one day, your friend suggests that taxing food would be a good way to raise revenue because the demand for food is quite inelastic. In what sense is taxing food a 'good' way to raise revenue? In what sense is it not a 'good' way to raise revenue?

6 The government places a tax on the purchase of socks.
  a Illustrate the effect of this tax on equilibrium price and quantity in the sock market. Identify the following areas both before and after the imposition of the tax: total spending by consumers, total revenue for producers and government tax revenue.
  b Does the price received by producers rise or fall? Can you tell whether total receipts for producers rise or fall? Explain.
  c Does the price paid by consumers rise or fall? Can you tell whether total spending by consumers rises or falls? Explain carefully. (*Hint:* Think about elasticity.) If total consumer spending falls, does consumer surplus rise? Explain.

7 Suppose the government currently raises $100 million through a $0.01 tax on widgets and another $100 million through a $0.10 tax on gadgets. If the tax rate on widgets was doubled and the tax on gadgets was eliminated, would the government raise more money than today, less money or the same amount of money? Explain.

8 Most states tax the purchase of new cars. Suppose that Victoria currently requires car dealers to pay the state $100 for each car sold and plans to increase the tax to $150 per car next year.
  a Illustrate the effect of this tax increase on the quantity of cars sold in Victoria, the price paid by consumers and the price received by producers.
  b Create a table that shows the levels of consumer surplus, producer surplus, government revenue and total surplus both before and after the tax increase.
  c What is the change in government revenue? Is it positive or negative?
  d What is the change in deadweight loss? Is it positive or negative?
  e Give one reason that the demand for cars in Victoria might be fairly elastic. Does this make the additional tax more or less likely to increase government revenue? How might states try to reduce the elasticity of demand?

9 About 30 years ago the British government imposed a 'poll tax' that required each person to pay a flat amount to the government independent of his or her income or wealth. What is the effect of such a tax on economic efficiency? What is the effect on economic equity? Do you think this was a popular tax?

10 This chapter analysed the welfare effects of a tax on a good. Consider now the opposite policy. Suppose that the government subsidises a good – for each unit of the good sold, the government pays $2 to the buyer. How does the subsidy affect consumer surplus, producer surplus, tax revenue and total surplus? Does a subsidy lead to a deadweight loss? Explain.

11 Suppose that a market is described by the following supply and demand equations:

$$Q^S = 2P$$

$$Q^D = 300 - P$$

    a Solve for the equilibrium price and the equilibrium quantity.

    b Suppose that a tax of T is placed on buyers, so the new demand equation is:

$$Q^D = 300 - (P + T)$$

       Solve for the new equilibrium. What happens to the price received by sellers, the price paid by buyers and the quantity sold?

    c Tax revenue is $T \times Q$. Use your answer to part (b) to solve for tax revenue as a function of T. Graph this relationship for T between 0 and 300.

    d The deadweight loss of a tax is the area of the triangle between the supply and demand curves. Recalling that the area of a triangle is ½ × base × height, solve for deadweight loss as a function of T.

       Graph this relationship for T between 0 and 300. (*Hint:* Looking sideways, the base of the deadweight loss triangle is T, and the height is the difference between the quantity sold with the tax and the quantity sold without the tax.)

    e The government now levies a tax on this good of $200 per unit. Is this a good policy? Why or why not? Can you propose a better policy?

Search me!

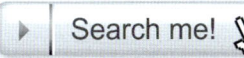

When accessing information about economics use the following keywords in any combinations you require:

- deadweight loss

CourseMate

For more multimedia resources and activities on economics, visit the Economics CourseMate website.

9

Application: International trade

Learning objectives

In this chapter you will:

- consider what determines whether a country imports or exports a good

- examine who wins and who loses from international trade

- learn that the gains to winners from international trade exceed the losses to losers

- analyse the welfare effects of tariffs and import quotas

- examine the arguments people use to advocate trade restrictions.

If you check the labels on the clothes you are now wearing, you will probably find that some of your clothes were made in another country. A century ago, textiles and clothing in Australia were mostly produced locally, but that is no longer the case. Faced with foreign competitors that could produce quality goods at low cost, many Australian firms found it increasingly difficult to produce and sell textiles and clothing at a profit. As a result, they laid off their workers and shut down their factories. Today, much of the textiles and clothing that Australians consume are imported from abroad.

The story of the textiles industry raises important questions for economic policy. How does international trade affect economic wellbeing? Who gains and who loses from free trade among countries, and how do the gains compare with the losses?

Chapter 3 introduced the study of international trade by applying the principle of comparative advantage. According to this principle, all countries can benefit from trading with one another because trade allows each country to specialise in doing what it does relatively best. But the analysis in chapter 3 was incomplete. It did not explain how the international marketplace achieves these gains from trade or how the gains are distributed among various economic participants.

We now return to the study of international trade and take up these questions. Over the past several chapters, we have developed many tools for analysing how markets work – supply, demand, equilibrium, consumer surplus, producer surplus and so on. With these tools we can learn more about the effects of international trade on economic wellbeing.

The determinants of trade

Consider the market for steel. The steel market is well suited to examining the gains and losses from international trade – steel is made in many countries around the world and there is much world trade in steel. Moreover, the steel market is one in which policymakers often consider (and sometimes implement) trade restrictions in order to protect domestic steel producers from foreign competitors. We examine here the steel market in the imaginary country of Isoland.

The equilibrium without trade

As our story begins, the Isolandian steel market is isolated from the rest of the world. By government decree, no one in Isoland is allowed to import or export steel and the penalty for violating the decree is so large that no one dares try.

Because there is no international trade, the market for steel in Isoland consists of Isolandian buyers and sellers. As Figure 9.1 shows, the domestic price adjusts to balance the quantity supplied by domestic sellers and the quantity demanded by domestic buyers. The figure shows the consumer and producer surplus in the equilibrium without trade. The sum of consumer and producer surplus measures the total benefits that buyers and sellers receive from the steel market.

Now suppose that, in an election upset, Isoland elects a new prime minister. The prime minister campaigned on a platform of 'change' and promised the voters bold new ideas. Her first act is to assemble a team of economists to evaluate Isolandian trade policy. She asks them to report back on three questions:

- If the government allowed Isolandians to import and export steel, what would happen to the price of steel and the quantity of steel sold in the domestic steel market?

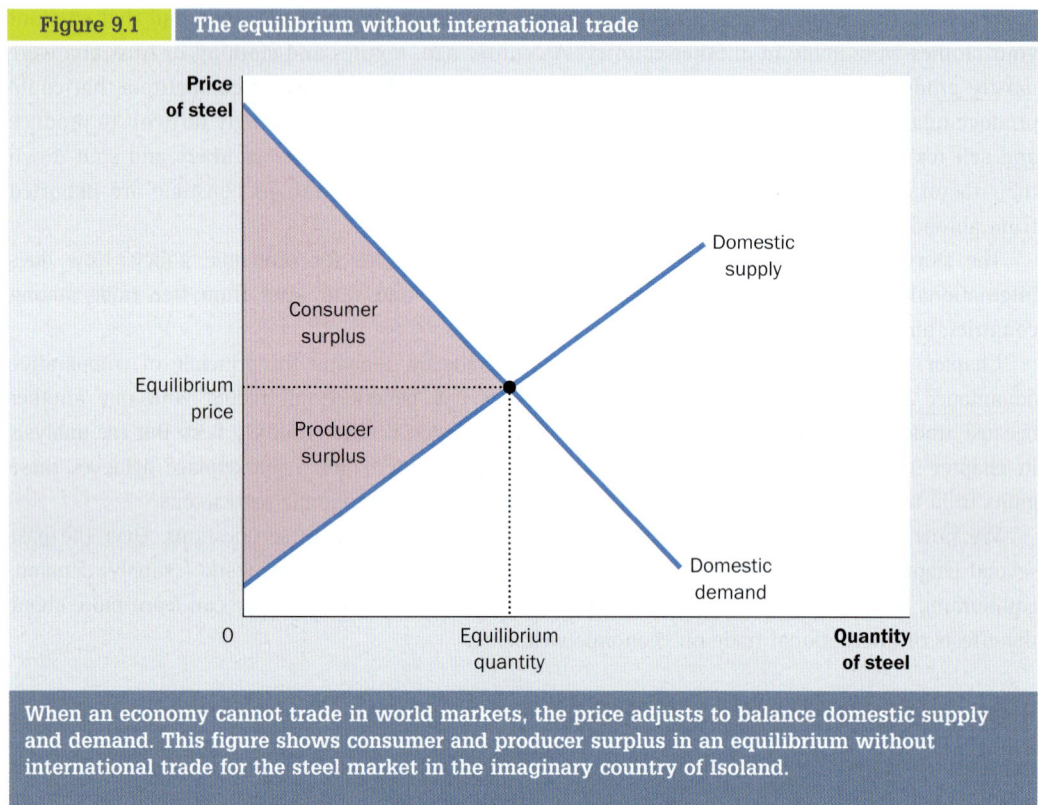

Figure 9.1 | **The equilibrium without international trade**

When an economy cannot trade in world markets, the price adjusts to balance domestic supply and demand. This figure shows consumer and producer surplus in an equilibrium without international trade for the steel market in the imaginary country of Isoland.

- Who would gain from free trade in steel and who would lose, and would the gains exceed the losses?
- Should a tariff (a tax on steel imports) or an import quota (a limit on steel imports) be part of the new trade policy?

After reviewing supply and demand in their favourite textbook (this one, of course), the Isolandian economics team begins its analysis.

The world price and comparative advantage

The first issue our economists take up is whether Isoland is likely to become a steel importer or a steel exporter. In other words, if free trade were allowed, would Isolandians end up buying or selling steel in world markets?

To answer this question, the economists compare the current Isolandian price of steel with the price of steel in other countries. We call the price prevailing in world markets the **world price**. If the world price of steel is higher than the domestic price, then Isoland would become an exporter of steel once trade is permitted. Isolandian steel producers would be eager to receive the higher prices available abroad and would start selling their steel to buyers in other countries. Conversely, if the world price of steel is lower than the domestic price, then Isoland would become an importer of steel. Because foreign sellers offer a better price, Isolandian steel consumers would quickly start buying steel from other countries.

world price
the price of a good that prevails in the world market for that good

In essence, comparing the world price and the domestic price before trade indicates whether Isoland has a comparative advantage in producing steel. The domestic price reflects the opportunity cost of steel – it tells us how much an Isolandian must give up to get one unit of steel. If the domestic price is low, the cost of producing steel in Isoland is low, suggesting that Isoland has a comparative advantage in producing steel relative to the rest of the world. If the domestic price is high, then the cost of producing steel in Isoland is high, suggesting that foreign countries have a comparative advantage in producing steel.

As we saw in chapter 3, trade among nations is ultimately based on comparative advantage. That is, trade is beneficial because it allows each nation to specialise in doing what it does relatively best. By comparing the world price and the domestic price before trade, we can determine whether Isoland is better or worse at producing steel than the rest of the world.

The country of Autarka does not allow international trade. In Autarka, you can buy a pure wool suit for 3 ounces of gold. Meanwhile, in neighbouring countries, you can buy the same suit for 2 ounces of gold. If Autarka were to allow free trade, would it import or export wool suits? Why?

The winners and losers from trade

To analyse the welfare effects of free trade, the Isolandian economists begin with the assumption that Isoland is a small economy compared with the rest of the world, so its actions have a negligible effect on world markets. The small-economy assumption has a specific implication for analysing the steel market – if Isoland is a small economy, then the change in Isoland's trade policy will not affect the world price of steel. The Isolandians are said to be *price takers* in the world economy. That is, they take the world price of steel as given. They can sell steel at this price and be exporters or buy steel at this price and be importers.

The small-economy assumption is not necessary to analyse the gains and losses from international trade. But the Isolandian economists know from experience that this assumption greatly simplifies the analysis. They also know that the basic lessons do not change in the more complicated case of a large economy.

fyi
Comparing prices and comparative advantages

When comparing prices of goods in different countries, it is important to pay attention to the units in which prices are quoted. One country may quote prices in dollars, whereas another quotes them in pesos. To compare prices, we need to measure them in terms of some item valued in both countries – ounces of gold, barrels of crude oil or bags of wheat. The price of a good measured in terms of another good is called a *relative price*. Because relative prices measure opportunity costs, they determine comparative advantage and patterns of trade.

Here is an example. In Isoland, the price of steel is $1000 a tonne and the price of wheat is $200 a bag. In Neighbourland, the price of steel is 10 000 pesos a tonne and the price of wheat is 1000 pesos a bag. Now consider these questions: Which country has cheaper steel? Which country has cheaper wheat?

To answer these questions, we can express the price of steel in terms of wheat. This relative price gives us the amount of wheat that a person must give up to obtain 1 tonne of steel. In Isoland, the price of a tonne of steel is five bags of wheat. In Neighbourland, the price of a tonne of steel is 10 bags of wheat. Thus, the price of steel (measured in bags of wheat) is lower in Isoland than in Neighbourland, indicating that Isoland has a comparative advantage in producing steel.

We can similarly compare the price of wheat in the two countries. In Isoland, the price of a bag of wheat is 1/5 tonne of steel. In Neighbourland, the

>>

price of a bag of wheat is 1/10 tonne of steel. The price of wheat (measured in tonnes of steel) is lower in Neighbourland, indicating that Neighbourland has a comparative advantage in producing wheat.

Notice that the price of wheat in terms of steel is the inverse of the price of steel in terms of wheat. If the price of steel (in terms of wheat) is lower in one country, the price of wheat (in terms of steel) must be lower in the other. Thus, unless the prices are exactly the same, one country must have a comparative advantage in one good and the other country must have a comparative advantage in the other good.

The gains and losses of an exporting country

Figure 9.2 shows the Isolandian steel market when the domestic equilibrium price before trade is below the world price. Once free trade is allowed, the domestic price rises to equal the world price. No seller of steel would accept less than the world price and no buyer would pay more than the world price.

With the domestic price now equal to the world price, the domestic quantity supplied differs from the domestic quantity demanded. The supply curve shows the quantity of steel supplied by Isolandian sellers. The demand curve shows the quantity of steel demanded by Isolandian buyers. Because the domestic quantity supplied is greater than the domestic quantity demanded, Isoland sells steel to other countries. Thus, Isoland becomes a steel exporter.

Although domestic quantity supplied and domestic quantity demanded differ, the steel market is still in equilibrium because there is now another participant in the market – the rest of the world. One

Figure 9.2   **International trade in an exporting country**

Once trade is allowed, the domestic price rises to equal the world price. The supply curve shows the quantity of steel produced domestically and the demand curve shows the quantity consumed domestically. Exports from Isoland equal the difference between the domestic quantity supplied and the domestic quantity demanded at the world price.

can view the horizontal line at the world price as representing the demand for steel from the rest of the world. This demand curve is perfectly elastic because Isoland, as a small economy, can sell as much steel as it wants at the world price.

Now consider the gains and losses from opening up trade. Clearly, not everyone benefits. Trade forces the domestic price to rise to the world price. Domestic producers of steel are better off because they can now sell steel at a higher price, but domestic consumers of steel are worse off because they have to buy steel at a higher price.

To measure these gains and losses, we look at the changes in consumer and producer surplus, which are shown in Figure 9.3 and summarised in Table 9.1. Before trade is allowed, the price of steel

---

Figure 9.3 | **How free trade affects welfare in an exporting country**

When the domestic price rises to equal the world price, sellers are better off (producer surplus rises from C to B + C + D), and buyers are worse off (consumer surplus falls from A + B to A). Total surplus rises by an amount equal to area D, indicating that trade raises the economic wellbeing of the country as a whole.

Table 9.1 Changes in welfare from free trade: The case of an exporting country

	Before trade	After trade	Change
Consumer surplus	A + B	A	− B
Producer surplus	C	B + C + D	+ (B + D)
Total surplus	A + B + C	A + B + C + D	+ D

The area D shows the increase in total surplus and represents the gains from trade.

This table examines changes in economic welfare resulting from opening up a market to international trade. Letters refer to the regions marked in figure 9.3.

adjusts to balance domestic supply and domestic demand. Consumer surplus, the area between the demand curve and the before-trade price, is area A + B. Producer surplus, the area between the supply curve and the before-trade price, is area C. Total surplus before trade, the sum of consumer and producer surplus, is area A + B + C.

After trade is allowed, the domestic price rises to the world price. Consumer surplus is area A (the area between the demand curve and the world price). Producer surplus is area B + C + D (the area between the supply curve and the world price). Thus, total surplus with trade is area A + B + C + D.

These welfare calculations show who wins and who loses from trade in an exporting country. Sellers benefit, since producer surplus increases by the area B + D. Buyers are worse off, since consumer surplus decreases by the area B. Because the gains of sellers exceed the losses of buyers by the area D, total surplus in Isoland increases.

This analysis of an exporting country yields two conclusions:

- When a country allows trade and becomes an exporter of a good, domestic producers of the good are better off and domestic consumers of the good are worse off.
- Trade raises the economic wellbeing of a nation, for the gains of the winners exceed the losses of the losers.

The gains and losses of an importing country

Now suppose that the domestic price before trade is above the world price. Once again, after free trade is allowed, the domestic price must equal the world price. As Figure 9.4 shows, the domestic quantity supplied is less than the domestic quantity demanded. The difference between the domestic quantity

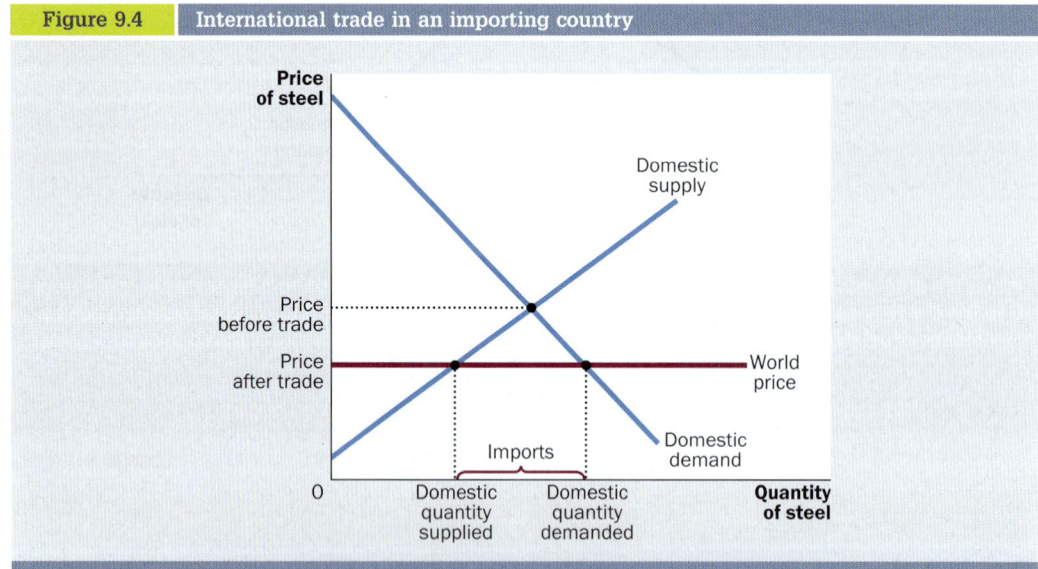

Figure 9.4   International trade in an importing country

Once trade is allowed, the domestic price falls to equal the world price. The supply curve shows the amount produced domestically and the demand curve shows the amount consumed domestically. Imports equal the difference between the domestic quantity demanded and the domestic quantity supplied at the world price.

demanded and the domestic quantity supplied is bought from other countries, and Isoland becomes a steel importer.

In this case, the horizontal line at the world price represents the supply of the rest of the world. This supply curve is perfectly elastic because Isoland is a small economy and, therefore, can buy as much steel as it wants at the world price.

Now consider the gains and losses from trade. Once again, not everyone benefits. When trade forces the domestic price to fall, domestic consumers are better off (they can now buy steel at a lower price), and domestic producers are worse off (they now have to sell steel at a lower price). Changes in consumer and producer surplus measure the size of the gains and losses, as shown in Table 9.2 and Figure 9.5. Before trade, consumer surplus is area A, producer surplus is area B + C, and total surplus is area A + B + C. After trade is allowed, consumer surplus is area A + B + D, producer surplus is area C, and total surplus is area A + B + C + D.

Figure 9.5	How free trade affects welfare in an importing country

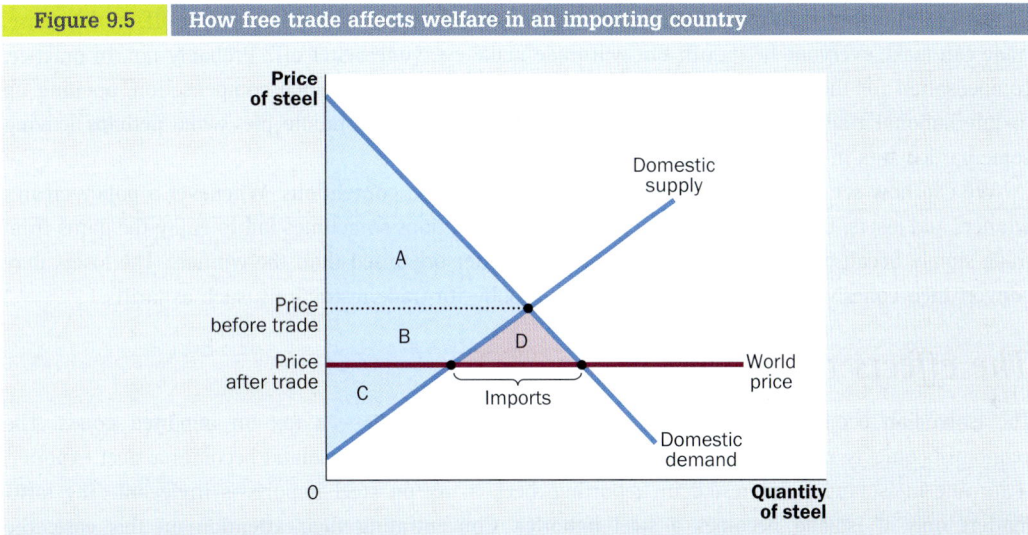

When the domestic price falls to equal the world price, buyers are better off (consumer surplus rises from A to A + B + D), and sellers are worse off (producer surplus falls from B + C to C). Total surplus rises by an amount equal to area D, indicating that trade raises the economic wellbeing of the country as a whole.

Table 9.2 Changes in welfare from free trade: The case of an importing country

	Before trade	After trade	Change
Consumer surplus	A	A + B + D	+ (B + D)
Producer surplus	B + C	C	− B
Total surplus	A + B + C	A + B + C + D	+ D

The area D shows the increase in total surplus and represents the gains from trade.

The table examines changes in economic welfare resulting from opening up a market to international trade. Letters refer to the regions marked in figure 9.5.

These welfare calculations show who wins and who loses from trade in an importing country. Buyers benefit because consumer surplus increases by the area B + D. Sellers are worse off because producer surplus falls by the area B. The gains of buyers exceed the losses of sellers and total surplus increases by the area D.

This analysis of an importing country yields two conclusions parallel to those for an exporting country:

- When a country allows trade and becomes an importer of a good, domestic consumers of the good are better off and domestic producers of the good are worse off.
- Trade raises the economic wellbeing of a nation, for the gains of the winners exceed the losses of the losers.

Now that we have completed our analysis of trade, we can better understand one of the *Ten Lessons from Economics* in chapter 1 – trade can make everyone better off. If Isoland opens up its steel market to international trade, that change will create winners and losers, regardless of whether Isoland ends up exporting or importing steel. In either case, however, the gains of the winners exceed the losses of the losers, so the winners could compensate the losers and still be better off. In this sense, trade can make everyone better off. But will trade make everyone better off? Probably not. In practice, compensation for the losers from international trade is rare. Without such compensation, opening up to international trade is a policy that expands the size of the economic pie, while perhaps leaving some participants in the economy with a smaller slice.

We can now see why the debate over trade policy is often contentious. Whenever a policy creates winners and losers, the stage is set for a political battle. Nations sometimes fail to enjoy the gains from trade simply because the losers from free trade are better organised than the winners. The losers may convert their cohesiveness into political clout and lobby for trade restrictions, such as tariffs.

The effects of a tariff

tariff
a tax on goods produced abroad and sold domestically

▸ tariff

The Isolandian economists next consider the effects of a **tariff** – a tax on imported goods. The economists quickly realise that a tariff on steel will have no effect if Isoland becomes a steel exporter. If no one in Isoland is interested in importing steel, a tax on steel imports is irrelevant. The tariff matters only if Isoland becomes a steel importer. Concentrating their attention on this case, the economists compare welfare with and without the tariff.

The graph in Figure 9.6 shows the Isolandian market for steel. Under free trade, the domestic price equals the world price. A tariff raises the price of imported steel above the world price by the amount of the tariff. Domestic suppliers of steel, who compete with suppliers of imported steel, can now sell their steel for the world price plus the amount of the tariff. Thus, the price of steel – both imported and domestic – rises by the amount of the tariff and is, therefore, closer to the price that would prevail without trade.

The change in price affects the behaviour of domestic buyers and sellers. Because the tariff raises the price of steel, it reduces the domestic quantity demanded from Q_1^D to Q_2^D and raises the domestic quantity supplied from Q_1^S to Q_2^S *Thus, the tariff reduces the quantity of imports and moves the domestic market closer to its equilibrium without trade.*

Now consider the gains and losses from the tariff. Because the tariff raises the domestic price, domestic sellers are better off and domestic buyers are worse off. In addition, the government raises revenue. To measure these gains and losses, we look at the changes in consumer surplus, producer surplus and government revenue. These changes are summarised in Table 9.3.

Before the tariff, the domestic price equals the world price. Consumer surplus, the area between the demand curve and the world price, is area A + B + C + D + E + F. Producer surplus, the area between the supply curve and the world price, is area G. Government revenue equals zero. Total surplus, the sum of consumer surplus, producer surplus and government revenue, is area A + B + C + D + E + F + G.

Once the government imposes a tariff, the domestic price exceeds the world price by the amount of the tariff. Consumer surplus is now area A + B. Producer surplus is area C + G. Government revenue,

Figure 9.6 **The effects of a tariff**

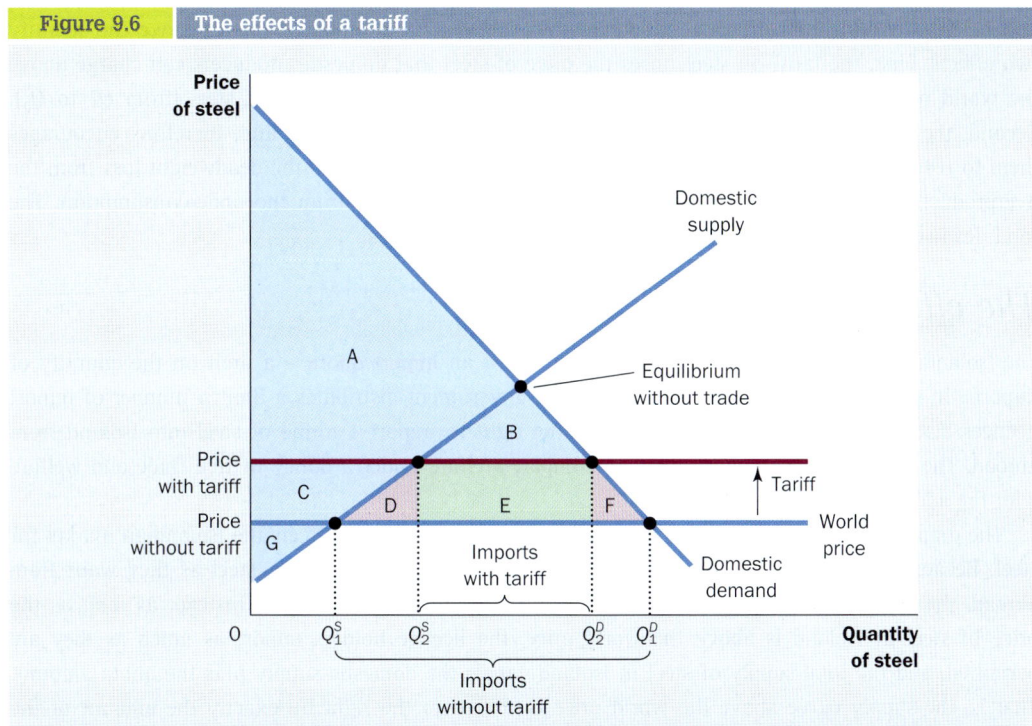

A tariff reduces the quantity of imports and moves a market closer to the equilibrium that would exist without trade. Total surplus falls by an amount equal to area D + F. These two triangles represent the deadweight loss from the tariff.

Table 9.3 Changes in welfare from a tariff

	Before tariff	After tariff	Change
Consumer surplus	A + B + C + D + E + F	A + B	− (C + D + E + F)
Producer surplus	G	C + G	+ C
Government revenue	None	E	+ E
Total surplus	A + B + C + D + E + F + G	A + B + C + E + G	− (D + F)

The area D + F shows the fall in total surplus and represents the deadweight loss of the tariff.

This table compares economic welfare when trade is unrestricted and when trade is restricted with a tariff. Letters refer to the regions marked in figure 9.6.

which is the quantity of after-tariff imports times the size of the tariff, is area E. Thus, total surplus with the tariff is area A + B +C + E + G.

To determine the total welfare effects of the tariff, we add the change in consumer surplus (which is negative), the change in producer surplus (positive) and the change in government revenue (positive). We find that total surplus in the market decreases by the area D + F. This fall in total surplus is called the *deadweight loss* of the tariff.

A tariff causes a deadweight loss because it is a type of tax. Like most taxes, it distorts incentives and pushes the allocation of scarce resources away from the optimum. In this case, we can identify two effects. First, the tariff on steel raises the price of steel that domestic producers can charge above the world price and, as a result, encourages them to increase production of steel (from Q_1^S to Q_2^S). Second, the tariff raises the price that domestic steel buyers have to pay and, therefore, encourages them to reduce consumption of steel (from Q_1^D to Q_2^D). Area D represents the deadweight loss from the overproduction of steel, and area F represents the deadweight loss from the underconsumption. The total deadweight loss of the tariff is the sum of these two triangles.

The effects of an import quota

import quota
a limit on the quantity of a good produced abroad that can be sold domestically

The Isolandian economists next consider the effects of an **import quota** – a limit on the quantity of imports. In particular, imagine that the Isolandian government distributes a limited number of import licences. Each licence gives the licence holder the right to import 1 tonne of steel into Isoland from abroad. The Isolandian economists want to compare welfare under a policy of free trade and welfare with the addition of this import quota.

The graph in Figure 9.7 and Table 9.4 show how an import quota affects the Isolandian market for steel. Because the import quota prevents Isolandians from buying as much steel as they want from abroad, the supply of steel is no longer perfectly elastic at the world price. Instead, as long as the price of steel in Isoland is above the world price, the licence holders import as much as they are permitted, and the total supply of steel in Isoland equals the domestic supply plus the quota amount. That is, the supply curve above the world price is shifted to the right by exactly the amount of the quota. (The supply curve below the world price does not shift because, in this case, importing is not profitable for the licence holders.)

The price of steel in Isoland adjusts to balance supply (domestic plus imported) and demand. As the figure shows, the quota causes the price of steel to rise above the world price. The domestic quantity demanded falls from Q_1^D to Q_2^D, and the domestic quantity supplied rises from Q_1^S to Q_2^S. Not surprisingly, the import quota reduces steel imports.

Now consider the gains and losses from the quota. Because the quota raises the domestic price above the world price, domestic sellers are better off and domestic buyers are worse off. In addition, the licence holders are better off because they make a profit from buying at the world price and selling at the higher domestic price. To measure these gains and losses, we look at the changes in consumer surplus, producer surplus and licence-holder surplus.

Before the government imposes the quota, the domestic price equals the world price. Consumer surplus, the area between the demand curve and the world price, is area A + B + C + D + E' + E" + F. Producer surplus, the area between the supply curve and the world price, is area G. The surplus of licence holders equals zero because there are no licences. Total surplus, the sum of consumer, producer and licence-holder surplus, is area A + B + C + D + E' + E" + F + G.

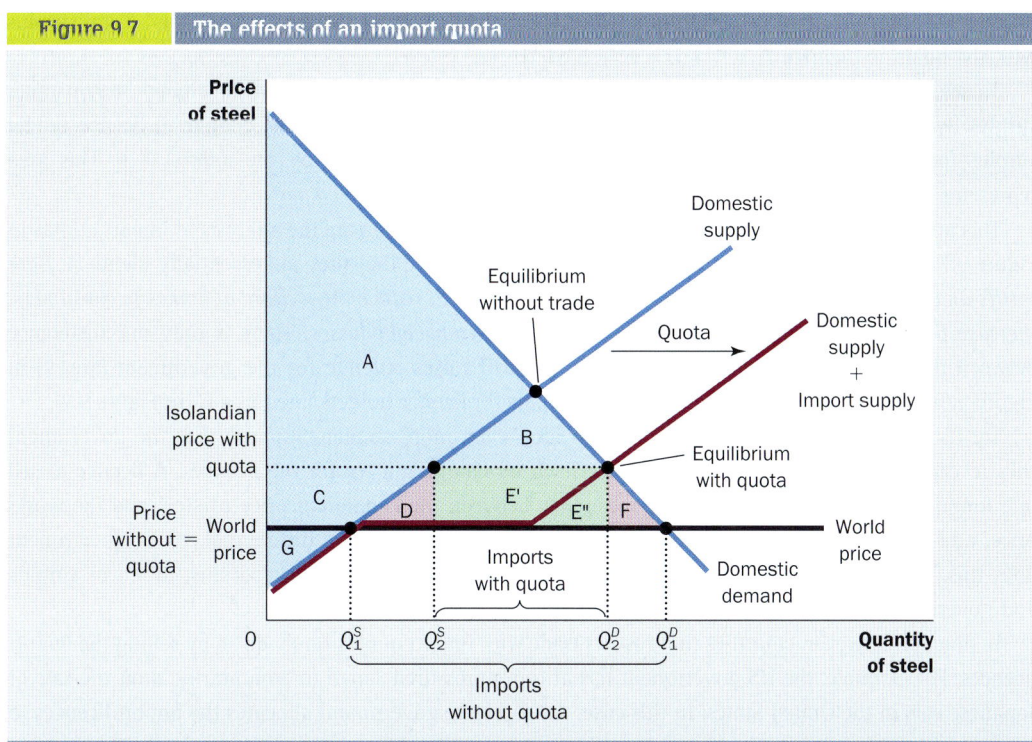

Figure 9.7   **The effects of an import quota**

An import quota, like a tariff, reduces the quantity of imports and moves a market closer to the equilibrium that would exist without trade. Total surplus falls by an amount equal to area D + F. These two triangles represent the deadweight loss from the quota. In addition, the import quota transfers E' + E" to whoever holds the import licences.

Table 9.4   Changes in welfare from an import quota

	Before quota	After quota	Change
Consumer surplus	A + B + C + D + E'+ E"+ F	A + B	– (C + D + E'+ E"+ F)
Producer surplus	G	C + G	+ C
Licence-holder surplus	None	E' + E"	+ (E' + E")
Total surplus	A + B + C + D + E' + E" F + G	A + B + C + E' + E" + G	– (D + F)

The area D + F shows the fall in total surplus and represents the deadweight loss of the quota.

The table compares economic welfare when trade is unrestricted and when trade is restricted with an import quota. Letters refer to the regions marked in figure 9.7.

After the government imposes the import quota and issues the licences, the domestic price exceeds the world price. Domestic consumers get surplus equal to area A + B and domestic producers get surplus equal to area C + G. The licence holders make a profit on each unit imported equal to the difference between the Isolandian price of steel and the world price. Their surplus equals this price differential times the quantity of imports. Thus, it equals the area of the rectangle E' + E". Total surplus with the quota is the area A + B + C + E' + E" + G.

To see how total welfare changes with the imposition of the quota, we add the change in consumer surplus (which is negative), the change in producer surplus (positive) and the change in licence-holder surplus (positive). We find that total surplus in the market decreases by the area D + F. This area represents the deadweight loss of the import quota.

This analysis should seem somewhat familiar. Indeed, if you compare the analysis of import quotas in Figure 9.7 with the analysis of tariffs in Figure 9.6, you will see that they are essentially identical. *Both tariffs and import quotas raise the domestic price of the good, reduce the welfare of domestic consumers, increase the welfare of domestic producers and cause deadweight losses.* There is only one difference between these two types of trade restrictions – a tariff raises revenue for the government (area E in Figure 9.6), whereas an import quota creates a surplus for licence holders (area E' + E" in Figure 9.7).

Tariffs and import quotas can be made to look even more similar. Suppose that the government tries to capture the licence-holder surplus for itself by charging a fee for the licences. A licence to sell one tonne of steel is worth exactly the difference between the Isolandian price of steel and the world price, and the government can set the licence fee as high as this price differential. If the government does this, the licence fee for imports works exactly like a tariff; consumer surplus, producer surplus and government revenue are exactly the same under the two policies.

In practice, however, countries that restrict trade with import quotas rarely do so by selling the import licences. For example, the US government has at times pressured Japan to 'voluntarily' limit the sale of Japanese cars in the United States. In this case, the Japanese government allocates the import licences to Japanese firms and the surplus from these licences (area E' + E") accrues to those firms. This kind of import quota is, from the standpoint of US welfare, strictly worse than a US tariff on imported cars. Both a tariff and an import quota raise prices, restrict trade and cause deadweight losses, but at least the tariff produces revenue for the US government rather than for Japanese car companies.

Although in our analysis so far import quotas and tariffs appear to cause similar deadweight losses, a quota can potentially cause an even larger deadweight loss, depending on the mechanism used to allocate the import licences. Suppose that when Isoland imposes a quota, everyone understands that the licences will go to those who spend the most resources lobbying the Isolandian government. In this case, there is an implicit licence fee – the cost of lobbying. The revenues from this fee, however, rather than being collected by the government, are spent on lobbying expenses. The deadweight losses from this type of quota include not only the losses from overproduction (area D) and underconsumption (area F) but also whatever part of the licence-holder surplus (area E' + E") is wasted on the cost of lobbying.

The lessons for trade policy

The team of Isolandian economists can now write to the new prime minister:

> Dear Prime Minister,
>
> You asked us three questions about opening up trade. After much hard work, we have the answers.
>
> *Question:* If the government allowed Isolandians to import and export steel, what would happen to the price of steel and the quantity of steel sold in the domestic steel market?
>
> *Answer:* Once trade is allowed, the Isolandian price of steel would be driven to equal the price prevailing around the world.
>
> If the world price is now higher than the Isolandian price, our price would rise. The higher price would reduce the amount of steel Isolandians

consume and raise the amount of steel that Isolandians produce. Isoland would, therefore, become a steel exporter. This occurs because, in this case, Isoland would have a comparative advantage in producing steel.

Conversely, if the world price is now lower than the Isolandian price, our price would fall. The lower price would raise the amount of steel that Isolandians consume and lower the amount of steel that Isolandians produce. Isoland would, therefore, become a steel importer. This occurs because, in this case, other countries would have a comparative advantage in producing steel.

Question: Who would gain from free trade in steel and who would lose, and would the gains exceed the losses?

Answer: The answer depends on whether the price rises or falls when trade is allowed. If the price rises, producers of steel gain and consumers of steel lose.

If the price falls, consumers gain, and producers lose. In both cases, the gains are larger than the losses. Thus, free trade raises the total welfare of Isolandians.

Question: Should a tariff or an import quota be part of the new trade policy?

Answer: A tariff, like most taxes, has deadweight losses – the revenue raised would be smaller than the losses to the buyers and sellers. In this case, the deadweight losses occur because the tariff would move the economy closer to our current no-trade equilibrium. An import quota works much like a tariff and would cause similar deadweight losses. The best policy, from the standpoint of economic efficiency, would be to allow trade without a tariff or an import quota.

We hope you find these answers helpful as you decide on your new policy.

Your faithful servants,

Isolandian economics team

fyi

Other benefits of international trade

Our conclusions so far have been based on the standard analysis of international trade. As we have seen, there are winners and losers when a nation opens itself up to trade, but the gains to the winners exceed the losses to the losers. Yet the case for free trade can be made even stronger. There are several other economic benefits of trade beyond those emphasised in the standard analysis.

Here, in a nutshell, are some of these other benefits:

- *Increased variety of goods:* Goods produced in different countries are not exactly the same. German beer, for instance, is not the same as Australian beer. Free trade gives consumers in all countries greater variety from which to choose.
- *Lower costs through economies of scale:* Some goods can be produced at low cost only if they are produced in large quantities – a phenomenon called *economies of scale.* A firm in a small country cannot take full advantage of economies of scale if it can sell only in the domestic market. Free trade gives firms access to larger world markets and allows them to realise economies of scale more fully.

- *Increased competition:* A company shielded from foreign competitors is more likely to have market power, which in turn gives it the ability to raise prices above competitive levels. This is a type of market failure. Opening up trade fosters competition and gives the invisible hand a better chance to work its magic.
- *Enhanced flow of ideas:* The transfer of technological advances around the world is often thought to be linked to international trade in the goods that embody those advances. The best way for a poor, agricultural nation to learn about the computer revolution, for instance, is to buy some computers from abroad, rather than trying to make them domestically.

Thus, free international trade increases variety for consumers, allows firms to take advantage of economies of scale, makes markets more competitive and facilitates the spread of technology. If the Isolandian economists thought these effects were important, their advice to their prime minister would be even more forceful.

Draw the supply and demand curve for pure wool suits in the country of Autarka. When trade is allowed, the price of a suit falls from 3 to 2 ounces of gold. In your diagram, what is the change in consumer surplus, the change in producer surplus and the change in total surplus? How would a tariff on suit imports alter these effects?

The arguments for restricting trade

The letter from the economics team persuades the new prime minister of Isoland to consider opening up trade in steel. She notes that the domestic price is now high compared with the world price. Free trade would, therefore, cause the price of steel to fall and hurt domestic steel producers. Before implementing the new policy, she asks Isolandian steel companies to comment on the economists' advice.

Not surprisingly, the steel companies are opposed to free trade in steel. They believe that the government should protect the domestic steel industry from foreign competition. Let's consider some of the arguments they might give to support their position and how the economics team would respond.

The jobs argument

Opponents of free trade often argue that trade with other countries destroys domestic jobs. In our example, free trade in steel would cause the price of steel to fall, reducing the quantity of steel produced in Isoland and thus reducing employment in the Isolandian steel industry. Some Isolandian steel workers would lose their jobs.

Yet free trade creates jobs at the same time that it destroys them. When Isolandians buy steel from other countries, other countries obtain the resources to buy other goods from Isoland. Isolandian workers would move from the steel industry to those industries in which Isoland has a comparative advantage. Although the transition may impose hardship on some workers initially, it allows Isolandians as a whole to enjoy a higher standard of living.

Opponents of trade are often sceptical that trade creates jobs. They might respond that *everything* can be produced more cheaply abroad. Under free trade, they might argue, Isolandians could not be profitably employed in any industry. As chapter 3 explains, however, the gains from trade are based on comparative advantage, not absolute advantage. Even if one country is better than another country at producing everything, each country can still gain from trading with the other. Workers in each country will eventually find jobs in the industry in which that country has a comparative advantage.

The national security argument

When an industry is threatened with competition from other countries, opponents of free trade often argue that the industry is vital for national security. In our example, Isolandian steel companies might point out that steel is used to make guns and tanks. With free trade, Isoland could become dependent on foreign countries to supply steel. If a war later broke out, Isoland might be unable to produce enough steel and weapons to defend itself.

Economists acknowledge that protecting key industries may be appropriate when there are legitimate concerns over national security. Yet they fear that this argument may be used too quickly by producers eager to gain at consumers' expense. The US watchmaking industry, for instance, long argued that it was vital for national security, claiming that its skilled workers would be necessary in wartime. Certainly, it is tempting for those in an industry to exaggerate their role in national defence in order to obtain protection from foreign competition.

IN THE NEWS ...

SHOULD THE WINNERS FROM FREE TRADE COMPENSATE THE LOSERS?

Politicians and pundits often say that the government should help workers made worse off by international trade by, for example, paying for their retraining. In this opinion piece, an economist makes the opposite case.

What to expect when you're free trading

by Steven E. Landsburg

All economists know that when American jobs are outsourced, Americans as a group are net winners. What we lose through lower wages is more than offset by what we gain through lower prices. In other words, the winners can more than afford to compensate the losers. Does that mean they ought to? Does it create a moral mandate for taxpayer-subsidized retraining programs? …

Um, no. Even if you've just lost your job, there's something fundamentally churlish about blaming the very phenomenon that's elevated you above the subsistence level since the day you were born. If the world owes you compensation for enduring the downside of trade, what do you owe the world for enjoying the upside?

I doubt there's a human being on earth who hasn't benefited from the opportunity to trade freely with his neighbors. Imagine what your life would be like if you had to grow your own food, make your own clothes and rely on your grandmother's home remedies for health care. Access to a trained physician might reduce the demand for grandma's home remedies, but – especially at her age – she's still got plenty of reason to be thankful for having a doctor.

Some people suggest, however, that it makes sense to isolate the moral effects of a single new trading opportunity or free trade agreement. Surely we have fellow citizens who are hurt by those agreements, at least in the limited sense that they'd be better off in a world where trade flourishes, except in this one instance. What do we owe those fellow citizens?

One way to think about that is to ask what your moral instincts tell you in analogous situations. Suppose, after years of buying shampoo at your local pharmacy, you discover you can order the same shampoo for less money on the Web. Do you have an obligation to compensate your pharmacist? If you move to a cheaper apartment, should you compensate your landlord? When you eat at McDonald's, should you compensate the owners of the diner next door? Public policy should not be designed to advance moral instincts that we all reject every day of our lives.

In what morally relevant way, then, might displaced workers differ from displaced pharmacists or displaced landlords? You might argue that pharmacists and landlords have always faced cutthroat competition and therefore knew what they were getting into, while decades of tariffs and quotas have led manufacturing workers to expect a modicum of protection. That expectation led them to develop certain skills, and now it's unfair to pull the rug out from under them.

Once again, that argument does not mesh with our everyday instincts. For many decades, schoolyard bullying has been a profitable occupation. All across America, bullies have built up skills so they can take advantage of that opportunity. If we toughen the rules to make bullying unprofitable, must we compensate the bullies?

Bullying and protectionism have a lot in common. They both use force (either directly or through the power of the law) to enrich someone else at your involuntary expense. If you're forced to pay $20 an hour to an American for goods you could have bought from a Mexican for $5 an hour, you're being extorted. When a free trade agreement allows you to buy from the Mexican after all, rejoice in your liberation.

National security concerns in Australia led to the introduction of tariffs to protect manufacturing industries after the Second World War. This policy was tied to immigration – it was argued that protecting manufacturing industries would create jobs for immigrant workers. Raising Australia's population through immigration would help protect the country from future invasion. As a result, between the 1950s and 1970s, Australia had some of the highest manufacturing tariffs among industrial countries.

The infant industry argument

New industries sometimes argue for temporary trade restrictions in order to help them get started. After a period of protection, the argument goes, these industries will mature and be able to compete with foreign competitors.

Similarly, older industries sometimes argue that they need temporary protection in order to help them adjust to new conditions. For example, Australia introduced quotas on imported motor vehicles, clothing, footwear and textiles in 1975 to give the local industries time to 'adjust' to increasing foreign competition. These restrictions lasted until the late 1980s and early 1990s.

Economists are often sceptical about such claims. The main reason is that the infant industry argument is difficult to implement in practice. To apply protection successfully, the government would need to decide which industries will eventually be profitable and decide whether the benefits of establishing these industries exceed the costs to consumers of protection. Yet 'picking winners' is extraordinarily difficult. It is made even more difficult by the political process, which often awards protection to those industries that are politically powerful. And once a powerful industry is protected from foreign competition, the 'temporary' policy is hard to remove.

In addition, many economists are sceptical about the infant industry argument even in principle. Suppose, for instance, that the Isolandian steel industry is young and unable to compete profitably against foreign rivals. Yet there is reason to believe that the industry can be profitable in the long run. In this case, the owners of the firms should be willing to incur temporary losses in order to obtain the eventual profits. Protection is not necessary for an industry to grow. Firms in various industries – such as many biotechnology firms today – incur temporary losses in the hope of growing and becoming profitable in the future. And many of them succeed, even without protection from foreign competition.

The unfair competition argument

A common argument is that free trade is desirable only if all countries play by the same rules. If firms in different countries are subject to different laws and regulations, then it is unfair (the argument goes) to expect the firms to compete in the international marketplace. For instance, in 2010, independent senator Bob Katter was reported by the *Cairns Post* as supporting protection for Australian farmers due to 'unfair' foreign competition:

> The government is closing down agriculture in this country. Four years ago Australia became the net importer of fruit and vegetables. This nation will be a net importer of food ... we will be the begging bowl of Australia, not the fruit bowl of Asia. If you are a poor damn Australian farmer you have no subsidy at all. We can't compete giving our competitor a 30m start over a 100m race.

Source: Kylie Regenzani, 'Katter opens up on agriculture',
Cairns Post, 15 October 2010.

Suppose that the government of Neighbourland subsidises wheat production by giving wheat farmers large tax breaks. Isolandian wheat farmers might argue that they should be protected from this foreign competition because Neighbourland is not competing fairly.

Would it, in fact, hurt Isoland to buy wheat from another country at a subsidised price? Certainly, Isolandian wheat producers would suffer, but Isolandian wheat consumers would benefit from the low price. Moreover, the case for free trade is no different; the gains of the consumers from buying at the low price would exceed the losses of the producers. Neighbourland's subsidy to its wheat farmers may be a bad policy, but it is the taxpayers of Neighbourland who bear the burden. Isoland can benefit from the opportunity to buy wheat at a subsidised price.

The protection-as-a-bargaining-chip argument

Another argument for trade restrictions concerns the strategy of bargaining. Many policymakers claim to support free trade but, at the same time, argue that trade restrictions can be useful when we bargain with our trading partners. They claim that the threat of a trade restriction can help remove a trade restriction already imposed by a foreign government. For example, Isoland might threaten to impose a tariff on steel unless Neighbourland removes its tariff on wheat. If Neighbourland responds to this threat by removing its tariff, the result can be freer trade.

The problem with this bargaining strategy is that the threat may not work. If it doesn't work, the country has a difficult choice. It can carry out its threat and implement the trade restriction, which would reduce its own economic welfare. Or it can back down from its threat, which would cause it to lose prestige in international affairs. Faced with this choice, the country would probably wish that it had never made the threat in the first place.

▸ free trade agreement

CASE**STUDY**

Trade agreements and the World Trade Organization

A country can take one of two approaches to achieving free trade. It can take a unilateral approach and remove its trade restrictions on its own. This is the approach that Great Britain took in the nineteenth century and that Chile and South Korea have taken in recent years. Alternatively, a country can take a *multilateral* approach and reduce its trade restrictions while other countries do the same. In other words, it can bargain with its trading partners in an attempt to reduce trade restrictions around the world. In recent times, the Australian government has favoured this approach.

One important example of a multilateral approach is the free trade agreement negotiated between Australia and the US. That agreement removed 97 per cent of US tariffs on non-agricultural goods (excluding textiles and clothing, which will be duty free from 2015). The agreement will result in consumer benefits in cars, metals, paper and chemicals. Two-thirds of agricultural tariffs will be removed, including those on lamb but not the important crop of sugar. It would also harmonise intellectual property laws, something that caused political tension, especially with regard to pharmaceuticals and copyright.

Another example of a multilateral deal is the General Agreement on Tariffs and Trade (GATT), which is a continuing series of negotiations among many of the world's countries with the goal of promoting free trade. GATT was founded after the Second World War as a response to the high tariffs imposed during the Great Depression of the 1930s. Many economists believe these tariffs contributed to the economic hardship during that period. GATT has successfully reduced the average tariff among member countries from about 40 per cent after the Second World War to about 5 per cent today.

The rules established under GATT are now enforced by an international institution called the World Trade Organization (WTO). The WTO was established in 1995 and has its headquarters in Geneva, Switzerland. As of January 2009, 153 countries have joined the organisation, accounting for more than 97 per cent of world trade. The functions of the WTO are to administer trade agreements, provide a forum for negotiations and handle disputes that arise among member countries.

>>

What are the pros and cons of the multilateral approach to free trade? One advantage is that the multilateral approach has the potential to result in freer trade than a unilateral approach because it can reduce trade restrictions abroad as well as at home. At the same time, however, if international negotiations fail, the result could be more restricted trade than under a unilateral approach.

In addition, the multilateral approach may have a political advantage. In most markets, producers are fewer and better organised than consumers – and thus wield greater political influence. Reducing the Islandian tariff on steel, for example, may be politically difficult if considered by itself. The steel companies would oppose free trade and the users of steel who would benefit are so numerous that organising their support would be difficult. Yet suppose that Neighbourland promises to reduce its tariff on wheat at the same time that Isoland reduces its tariff on steel. In this case, the Islandian wheat farmers, who are also politically powerful, would back the agreement. Thus, the multilateral approach to free trade can sometimes win political support when a unilateral reduction cannot.

Q The textile industry of Autarka advocates a ban on the import of pure wool suits. Give five arguments its lobbyists might make. Respond to each of these arguments.

Conclusion

Economists and the general public often disagree about free trade. In 1997, the Industry Commission released a report recommending the reduction and removal of Australian tariffs on textiles and clothing. The federal government decided not to implement the recommendations. Opponents viewed the freer trade as a threat to job security and the living standards of Australians currently employed in the textile industry. In contrast, economists overwhelmingly supported the report's recommendations. They viewed the tariff reductions as a way of reducing the relative prices paid for clothing and, hence, improving the consumption possibilities of Australians. Recently, similar debates have raged over cars, CDs and books, with varying outcomes. However, in each debate there was widespread agreement among economists that such tariff reductions were desirable.

IN THE NEWS . . .

EU SAUCE POLICY

Enforcing tariff protection can be a difficult task. The following article documents how vegetable producers became concerned that vegies were slipping under trade barriers by dosing themselves in sauce.

One lump or two? A saucy tale from Europe

Brussels: How many lumps are allowed in a sauce before it can be considered a vegetable? This question – to be considered by a European Union committee on January 10th – may sound absurd. But trade worth hundreds of millions of euros rests on the answer.

The reason: whereas the EU tariff on imported sauce is only 20%, the tariff on an imported vegetable is 288%. Protectionists in the EU – mainly vegetable producers from the south – fear that vegetables may sneak into Europe disguised as tinned sauces. They have argued that, if a sauce is more than 20% made up of lumps of fruit or vegetable, it should be considered a vegetable. That hits such culinary delights as Unilever's

Chicken Tonight, Heinz's Teletubbies pasta in sauce and Dolmio's Pasta Gusto.

Of course any multinational food producer worth its sauce has already shifted production to within the EU so as to get round the tariffs. The €200m of sauce that EU countries still import is thus mainly lump-free. But other sauce markets now apply the lump test too, and their tariffs hit about half of the EU's annual sauce exports of around €244m.

Big food producers such as Mars, Unilever and Nestlé were so irritated by these rules that they took a case against the EU to the World Customs Organisation. But, although the ruling went against the EU, there is no provision for sanctions. The EU has, however, graciously agreed to reconsider its rules. The European Commission is proposing raising the lump threshold to 30%. Still too low, scream the food companies, arguing – reasonably enough – that consumer perception should be the test; and that most people can tell the difference between a turnip and a tin of Teletubbies pasta in sauce. But the EU seems unlikely to change its mind. So the food companies may just have to lump it.

Source: *The Economist*, 3 January 2002. © The Economist Newspaper Limited, London 2002.

In many ways, Australia itself is an ongoing experiment that confirms the virtues of free trade. At the turn of the century, Australia made an important commitment to unrestricted trade among the states, and the country as a whole has benefited from the specialisation that trade allows. Bananas are grown in Queensland, oil is pumped from Bass Strait, wine is made in the Hunter and Barossa valleys, and so on. Australians would not enjoy the high standard of living they do today if people could consume only those goods and services produced in their own states. The world could similarly benefit from free trade among countries.

IN THE NEWS . . .

AUSTRALIA AND FREE TRADE

Over the past 40 years, Australia has significantly reduced its self-imposed impediments to international trade. Tariffs on imports have been reduced and quotas have been removed in a variety of areas. This article reviews some of these reforms and considers the pressure on the government to restrict imports.

Free trade push should boost economic activity

It is reassuring then that the new Trade minister, Craig Emerson, is confidently putting free trade at the top of the agenda, even though it is unlikely to yield many photo opportunities in the current political climate. Sandwiched between the regulatory policies of the Greens and independents like Bob Katter, who wants to block foreign bananas and manipulate exchange rates, it is an encouraging sign that the Gillard government might not throw up the white flag and surrender to the pre-modern tendencies of those who hold the balance of power. It is no coincidence that Dr Emerson's political career began as a senior adviser to the Hawke administration. Alongside Resources Minister Martin Ferguson and Regional Australia Minister Simon Crean, Dr Emerson's elevation to Cabinet has strengthened the government's ability to foster investment and jobs by making Australia more competitive.

The free trade challenge should not be underestimated. The international trade liberalisation process that began in Doha, Qatar, in 2001 ground to a halt in mid-2008 as the global financial crisis unfolded. But after a tentative recovery in Europe and the US, the time is right for nations to re-engage with this vexed yet vital reform. Major opportunities to

>>

kick-start the process will arise at the G20 summit in Seoul and at APEC in November.

It augurs well that faced with high unemployment and unpopularity, the Obama administration has recognised that the US will rebuild prosperity faster by boosting economic activity through trade than by raising the protectionist shutters. In particular, the US needs to rebalance its one-sided trading relationship with China, in which the US is incurring monthly deficits of $US25 billion, driven by the low value of the Chinese currency.

Australia also has a great deal to gain from the process. Re-building tariff walls would be a bad mistake. The experience of the past 20 years shows Australians benefit from reduced protection even when other countries maintain their own barriers, as imported equipment becomes cheaper. Since the Doha collapse, our trade officials have concentrated on pursuing bilateral agreements with China, Japan, Korea and Malaysia. But such initiatives do not preclude Australia from being proactive in wider trade liberalisation. This nation has vast opportunities to increase the export of services, which account for three-quarters of GDP but little more than 20 per cent of exports.

Dr Emerson is following a well-trodden path for Labor, the party responsible for much of the reform that opened up the Australian economy to the world, beginning with Gough Whitlam's tariff cuts in 1973. The process picked up pace in the Hawke/Keating years with more cuts in 1988 and 1991 and Australia leading the way in forming the Cairns group of 19 free trading agricultural export nations in response to spiralling EU agricultural trade barriers. We would urge Dr Emerson to stand firm against any push from the EU and the US to include more environmental and labour standards in bilateral or multilateral trade deals which amount to back-door protection.

As Australia's average industry assistance fell from more than 30 per cent in 1970 to less than five per cent, *The Australian* supported the transformation consistently for the prosperity it brought. For at least two centuries, economic theory has recognised the power of 'comparative advantage', or the dividend that flows from each country focusing on what it produces best and trading for the rest. In practice, real-world experience has confirmed the truth of the theory repeatedly.

Source: *The Australian*, 24 September 2010.

To better understand economists' view of trade, let's continue our parable. Suppose that the country of Isoland ignores the advice of its economics team and decides not to allow free trade in steel. The country remains in the equilibrium without international trade.

Then, one day, some Isolandian inventor discovers a new way to make steel at very low cost. The process is quite mysterious, however, and the inventor insists on keeping it a secret. What is odd is that the inventor doesn't need any workers or iron ore to make steel. The only input required by this process is wheat.

The inventor is hailed as a genius. Because steel is used in so many products, the invention lowers the cost of many goods and allows all Isolandians to enjoy a higher standard of living. Workers who had previously produced steel do suffer when their factories close, but eventually they find work in other industries. Some become farmers and grow the wheat that the inventor turns into steel. Others enter new industries that emerge as a result of higher Isolandian living standards. Everyone understands that the displacement of these workers is an inevitable part of progress.

After several years, a newspaper reporter decides to investigate this mysterious new steel process. She sneaks into the inventor's factory and learns that the inventor is a fraud. The inventor has not been making steel at all. Instead, he has been illegally shipping wheat abroad and importing steel from other countries. The only thing that the inventor had discovered was the gains from international trade.

When the truth is finally revealed, the government shuts down the inventor's operation. The price of steel rises and workers return to jobs in steel factories. Living standards in Isoland fall back to their former levels. The inventor is jailed and held up to public ridicule. After all, he was no inventor. He was just an economist.

Summary

- The effects of free trade can be determined by comparing the domestic price without trade with the world price. A low domestic price indicates that the country has a comparative advantage in producing the good and that the country will become an exporter. A high domestic price indicates that the rest of the world has a comparative advantage in producing the good and that the country will become an importer.
- When a country allows trade and becomes an exporter of a good, producers of the good are better off and consumers of the good are worse off. When a country allows trade and becomes an importer of a good, consumers are better off and producers are worse off. In both cases, the gains from trade exceed the losses.
- A tariff – a tax on imports – moves a market closer to the equilibrium that would exist without trade and, therefore, reduces the gains from trade. Although domestic producers are better off and the government raises revenue, the losses to consumers exceed these gains.
- An import quota has effects that are similar to those of a tariff. Under a quota, however, the holders of the import licences receive the revenue that the government would collect with a tariff.
- There are various arguments for restricting trade – protecting jobs, defending national security, helping infant industries, preventing unfair competition and responding to foreign trade restrictions. Although some of these arguments have some merit in some cases, economists believe that free trade is usually the better policy.

Key concepts

import quota   tariff   world price

Questions for review

1   What does the domestic price that prevails without international trade tell us about a nation's comparative advantage?
2   When does a country become an exporter of a good? An importer?
3   Draw the supply-and-demand diagram for an importing country. What is consumer surplus and producer surplus before trade is allowed? What is consumer surplus and producer surplus with free trade? What is the change in total surplus?
4   Describe what a tariff is, and describe its economic effects.
5   What is an import quota? Compare its economic effects with those of a tariff.
6   List five arguments often given to support trade restrictions. How do economists respond to these arguments?
7   What is the difference between the unilateral and multilateral approaches to achieving free trade? Give an example of each.

Problems and applications

1   Australia represents a small part of the world banana market.
    a   Draw a diagram depicting the equilibrium in the Australian banana market without international trade. Identify the equilibrium price, equilibrium quantity, consumer surplus and producer surplus.

    b Suppose that the world banana price is below the Australian price before trade and that the Australian banana market is now opened to trade. Identify the new equilibrium price, quantity consumed, quantity produced domestically and quantity imported. Also show the change in the surplus of domestic consumers and producers. Has domestic total surplus increased or decreased?

    c In 2011, Cyclone Yasi devastated the banana crop in Queensland. Prices rose but the government resisted pressure to allow banana imports from the Philippines. What impact did that have on consumers in Australia?

2 The world price of wine is below the price that would prevail in India in the absence of trade.

    a Assuming that Indian imports of wine are a small part of total world wine production, draw a graph for the Indian market for wine under free trade. Identify consumer surplus, producer surplus and total surplus in an appropriate table.

    b Australia is a major wine exporter. Suppose that a virulent disease destroys much of the grape harvest in Australia. What effect does this shock have on the world price of wine? Using your graph and table from part (a), show the effect on consumer surplus, producer surplus and total surplus in India. Who are the winners and losers? Is India as a whole better or worse off?

3 The world price of cotton is below the no-trade price in Country A and above the no-trade price in Country B. Using supply-and-demand diagrams and welfare tables such as those in the chapter, show the gains from trade in each country. Compare your results for the two countries.

4 If the world price of a good is above the no-trade price in a country, what is the effect of a tariff on that good? If the world price is below the no-trade price, what is the effect of a tariff that exceeds the difference between those prices?

5 Suppose that the federal government imposes a tariff on imported cars to protect the Australian car industry from foreign competition. Assuming that Australia is a price taker in the world car market, show on a diagram the change in the quantity of imports, the loss to Australian consumers, the gain to Australian manufacturers, government revenue and the deadweight loss associated with the tariff. The loss to consumers can be separated into three parts: a transfer to domestic producers, a transfer to the government and a deadweight loss. Use your diagram to identify these three parts.

6 The following table presents the demand and supply schedules for watches in Australia and Switzerland (which we assume are the only two countries in the world).

Price per watch	Q^D in Australia (thousands)	Q^S in Australia (thousands)	Q^D in Switzerland (thousands)	Q^S in Switzerland (thousands)
$10	110	0	80	30
20	90	20	50	50
30	70	40	35	65
40	60	60	20	80
50	50	80	5	95
60	40	95	0	105
70	30	105	0	110
80	20	110	0	115

    a   With no international trade, what are the equilibrium price and quantity in the Australian watch market and in the Swiss watch market?

    b   Now suppose that trade is opened between Australia and Switzerland only. What is the new equilibrium price in the world market for watches? How does it compare with the no-trade prices of watches in the two countries?

    c   What is the total quantity of watch production at the new equilibrium in the two countries? Which country exports watches? How many?

    d   When trade opens, what happens to the quantity of watches produced, and thus employment, in the Australian watch industry? In the Swiss watch industry? Who benefits and who loses from the opening of trade?

7 Imagine that winemakers in New South Wales petitioned the state government to tax wines imported from South Australia. They argue that this tax would raise both tax revenue for the state government and employment in the New South Wales wine industry. Do you agree with these claims? Is it a good policy?

8 Many developing countries have less restrictive labour laws than Australia. For example, child labour is common in parts of Asia. Some commentators argue that trade with these countries is undesirable. It encourages exploitation of workers and provides unfair competition to Australian producers. Other commentators argue that this trade helps the poor. Without trade, the poor in developing countries would not even have their current jobs and would be worse off.

  List three arguments for and against Australia trading with developing countries that have weak labour laws. Which arguments do you think are stronger? Why?

9 When the government of Tradeland decides to impose an import quota on foreign cars, three proposals are suggested: (1) sell the import licences in an auction; (2) distribute the licences randomly in a lottery; (3) let people wait in line and distribute the licences on a first-come, first-served basis. Compare the effects of these policies. Which policy do you think has the largest deadweight losses? Which policy has the smallest deadweight losses? Why? (*Hint:* The government's other ways of raising tax revenue all cause deadweight losses themselves.)

10 In a press release on 17 April 1997, the Australian Democrats announced their support for a tariff on sugar imports into Australia. The tariff on sugar at the time was $55 per tonne.

    a   Illustrate the effect of this tariff on the Australian sugar market. Label the relevant prices and quantities under free trade and under the tariff.

    b   Analyse the effects of the sugar tariff using the tools of welfare analysis.

    c   The Cairns Council claimed that the removal of the sugar tariff would lead to a loss of $2 million in revenue to five local sugar mills and the loss of many jobs. Do you think that these claims justify maintaining the tariff?

    d   Many overseas countries also protect their local sugar industries. The *Wall Street Journal* (26 June 1990) stated that the protection of the US sugar industry 'has helped make possible the spectacular rise of the high-fructose corn syrup industry'. Why would protecting the sugar industry have this effect? (*Hint:* Do you think sugar and corn syrup are substitutes or complements?)

11 (This question is challenging.) Consider a small country that exports steel. Suppose that a 'pro-trade' government decides to subsidise the export of steel by paying a certain amount for each tonne sold abroad. How does this export subsidy affect the domestic price of steel, the quantity of steel produced, the quantity of steel consumed and the quantity of steel exported? How does it affect consumer surplus, producer surplus, government revenue and total surplus? (*Hint:* The analysis of an export subsidy is similar to the analysis of a tariff.)

Search me!

 When accessing information about economics use the following keywords in any combinations you require:

- free trade agreement
- tariff

CourseMate

CourseMate

For more multimedia resources and activities on economics, visit the Economics CourseMate website.

PART FOUR
The economics of the public sector

10

Externalities

Learning objectives

In this chapter you will:

- learn what an externality is
- see why externalities can make market outcomes inefficient
- examine how people can sometimes solve the problem of externalities on their own
- consider why private solutions to externalities sometimes do not work
- examine the various government policies aimed at solving the problem of externalities.

Firms that make and sell paper also create, as a by-product of the manufacturing process, a chemical called dioxin. Scientists believe that once dioxin enters the environment, it raises the population's risk of cancer, birth defects and other health problems.

Is the production and release of dioxin a problem for society? In chapters 4 to 9 we examined how markets allocate scarce resources with the forces of supply and demand, and we saw that the equilibrium of supply and demand is typically an efficient allocation of resources. To use Adam Smith's famous metaphor, the 'invisible hand' of the marketplace leads self-interested buyers and sellers in a market to maximise the total benefit that society derives from that market. This insight is the basis for one of the *Ten Lessons from Economics* in chapter 1 – markets are usually a good way to organise economic activity. Should we conclude, therefore, that the invisible hand prevents firms in the paper market from emitting too much dioxin?

Markets do many things well, but they do not do everything well. In this chapter we begin our study of another one of the *Ten Lessons from Economics* – governments can sometimes improve market outcomes. We examine why markets sometimes fail to allocate resources efficiently, how government policies can potentially improve the market's allocation and what kinds of policies are likely to work best.

The market failures examined in this chapter fall under a general category called *externalities*. An **externality** arises when a person engages in an activity that influences the wellbeing of a bystander but the person neither pays nor receives any compensation for that effect. If the effect on the bystander is adverse, it is called a *negative externality*; if it is beneficial, it is called a *positive externality*. In the presence of externalities, society's interest in a market outcome extends beyond the wellbeing of buyers and sellers in the market; it also includes the wellbeing of bystanders who are affected. Because buyers and sellers neglect the external effects of their actions when deciding how much to demand or supply, the market equilibrium is not efficient in the presence of externalities. That is, the equilibrium fails to maximise the total benefit to society as a whole. The release of dioxin into the environment, for instance, is a negative externality. Self-interested paper firms will not consider the full cost of the pollution they create and, therefore, will emit too much unless the government prevents or discourages them from doing so.

externality
the uncompensated impact of one person's actions on the wellbeing of a bystander

Externalities come in many varieties, as do the policy responses that try to deal with the market failure. Here are some examples:

- The exhaust from cars is a negative externality because it creates smog that other people have to breathe. As a result of this externality, drivers tend to pollute too much. Governments attempt to solve this problem by setting emission standards for cars. They also tax petrol in order to reduce the amount that people drive.

- Restored historic buildings convey a positive externality because people who walk or drive by them enjoy their beauty and the sense of history that these buildings provide. Building owners do not get the full benefit of restoration and, therefore, tend to discard older buildings too quickly. In Australia, state governments can declare designated buildings as historic buildings. Private owners of these buildings generally cannot demolish them and must maintain them, at least to a minimum standard.

- Lawn-mowers create a negative externality when neighbours are disturbed by the noise. The person using the lawn-mower does not bear the full cost of the noise and, therefore, does not fully consider the noise created when choosing a time to mow the lawn. Local governments overcome this problem by limiting the times people can use lawn-mowers and other noisy equipment.

- Research into new technologies provides a positive externality because it creates knowledge that other people can use. Because inventors cannot capture the full benefits of their inventions, they tend to devote too few resources to research. The federal government tackles this problem partially through the patent system, which gives inventors an exclusive use of their inventions for a period of time, and also by providing tax breaks for research.

In each case, decision makers are failing to take account of the external effects of their behaviour. The government responds by trying to influence this behaviour to protect the interests of bystanders.

Externalities and market inefficiency

In this section we use the tools from chapter 7 to examine how externalities affect economic wellbeing. The analysis shows precisely why externalities cause markets to allocate resources inefficiently. Later in the chapter we examine various ways in which private actors and public policymakers may remedy this type of market failure.

Welfare economics: A recap

We begin by recalling the key lessons of welfare economics from chapter 7. To make our analysis concrete, we will consider a specific market – the market for aluminium. Figure 10.1 shows the supply and demand curves in the market for aluminium.

As you should recall from chapter 7, the supply and demand curves contain important information about costs and benefits. The demand curve for aluminium reflects the value of aluminium to consumers, as measured by the prices they are willing to pay. At any given quantity, the height of the demand curve shows the willingness to pay of the marginal buyer. In other words, it shows the value of the last unit of aluminium bought. Similarly, the supply curve reflects the costs of

| Figure 10.1 | The market for aluminium |

The demand curve reflects the value to buyers and the supply curve reflects the costs of sellers. The equilibrium quantity, Q_{MARKET}, maximises the total value to buyers minus the total costs of sellers. In the absence of externalities, therefore, the market equilibrium is efficient.

aluminium producers. At any given quantity, the height of the supply curve shows the cost to the marginal seller. In other words, it shows the cost of the last unit of aluminium sold.

In the absence of government intervention, the price adjusts to balance the supply and demand for aluminium. The quantity produced and consumed in the market equilibrium, shown as Q_{MARKET} in Figure 10.1, is efficient in the sense that it maximises the sum of producer and consumer surplus. That is, the market allocates resources in a way that maximises the total value to the consumers who buy and use aluminium minus the total costs to the producers who make and sell aluminium.

Negative externalities in production

Now let's suppose that aluminium factories emit pollution. For each unit of aluminium produced, a certain amount of smoke enters the atmosphere. Because this smoke creates a health risk for those who breathe the air, it is a negative externality. How does this externality affect the efficiency of the market outcome?

Because of the externality, the cost to society of producing aluminium is larger than the cost to the aluminium producers. For each unit of aluminium produced, the social cost includes the private costs of the aluminium producers plus the costs to those bystanders adversely affected by the pollution. Figure 10.2 shows the social cost of producing aluminium. The social-cost curve is above the supply curve because it takes into account the external costs imposed on society by aluminium production. At any given quantity, the height of the social-cost curve shows the private cost of the marginal seller and the extra social cost of the pollution created when the marginal unit of aluminium is produced. The difference between these two curves reflects the cost of the pollution emitted.

Figure 10.2	Pollution and the social optimum

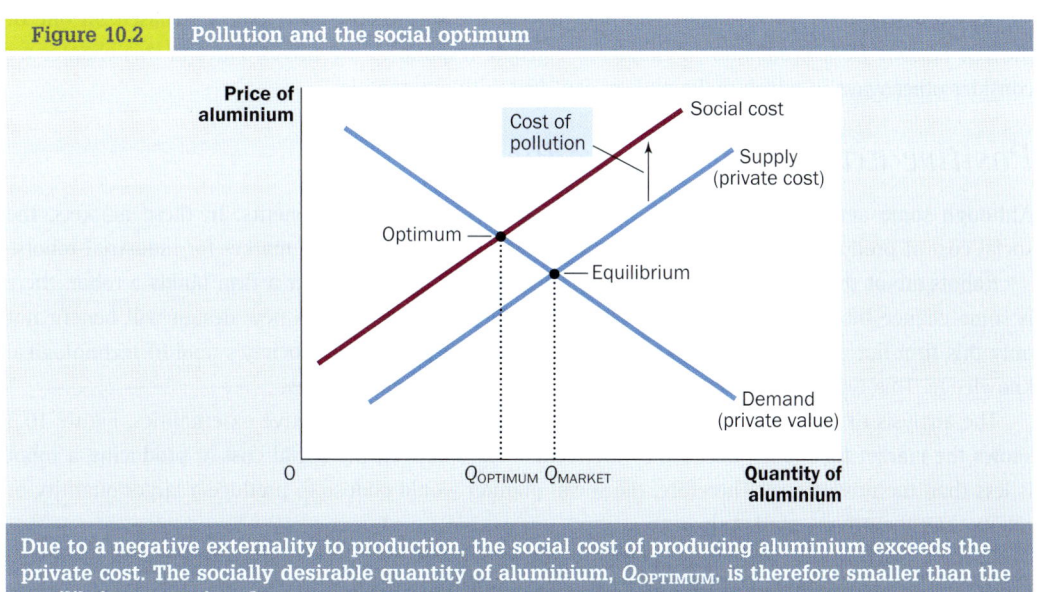

Due to a negative externality to production, the social cost of producing aluminium exceeds the private cost. The socially desirable quantity of aluminium, $Q_{OPTIMUM}$, is therefore smaller than the equilibrium quantity, Q_{MARKET}.

What quantity of aluminium should be produced? To answer this question, we once again consider what a benevolent social planner would do. The planner wants to maximise the total surplus derived from the market – the value to consumers of aluminium minus the cost of producing aluminium. The planner understands, however, that the cost of producing aluminium includes the external costs of the pollution.

The planner would choose the level of aluminium production at which the demand curve crosses the social-cost curve. This intersection determines the optimal amount of aluminium from the standpoint of society as a whole. Below this level of production, the value of the aluminium to consumers (as measured by the height of the demand curve) exceeds the social cost of producing it (as measured by the height of the social-cost curve). The planner does not produce more than this level because the social cost of producing additional aluminium exceeds the value to consumers.

Note that the equilibrium quantity of aluminium, Q_{MARKET}, is larger than the socially desirable quantity, $Q_{OPTIMUM}$. The reason for this inefficiency is that the market equilibrium reflects only the private costs of production. In the market equilibrium, the marginal consumer values aluminium at less than the social cost of producing it. That is, at Q_{MARKET} the demand curve lies below the social-cost curve. Thus, reducing aluminium production and consumption below the equilibrium level raises total economic wellbeing.

How can the social planner achieve the optimal outcome? One way would be to tax aluminium producers for each tonne of aluminium sold. The tax would shift the supply curve for aluminium upwards by the size of the tax. If the tax accurately reflected the social cost of pollutants released into the atmosphere, the new supply curve would coincide with the social-cost curve. In the new market equilibrium, aluminium producers would produce the socially desirable quantity of aluminium.

internalising an externality
altering incentives so that people take into account the external effects of their actions

The use of such a tax is said to be **internalising an externality** because it gives buyers and sellers in the market an incentive to take into account the external effects of their actions. Aluminium producers would, in essence, take the costs of pollution into account when deciding how much aluminium to supply because the tax now makes them pay for these external costs. The policy is based on one of the *Ten Lessons from Economics in* chapter 1 – people respond to incentives. Later in this chapter we consider other ways in which policymakers can deal with externalities.

Positive externalities in production

Although some activities impose costs on third parties, others yield benefits. In these markets, the social cost of production is less than the private cost. One example is the market for industrial robots.

Robots are at the frontier of a rapidly changing technology. Whenever a firm builds a robot, there is some chance that the firm will discover a new and better design. This new design will benefit not only this firm but also society as a whole because the design will enter society's pool of technological knowledge. This type of positive externality is called a *technology spillover*.

The analysis of positive externalities is similar to the analysis of negative externalities. Figure 10.3 shows the market for robots. Because of the technology spillover, the social cost of producing a robot is less than the private cost. Therefore, the social planner would choose to produce a larger quantity of robots than the private market does.

In this case, the government can internalise the externality by subsidising the production of robots. If the government paid firms for each robot produced, the supply curve would shift down by the amount of the subsidy and this shift would increase the equilibrium quantity of robots. To ensure that the market equilibrium equals the social optimum, the subsidy should equal the value of the technology spillover.

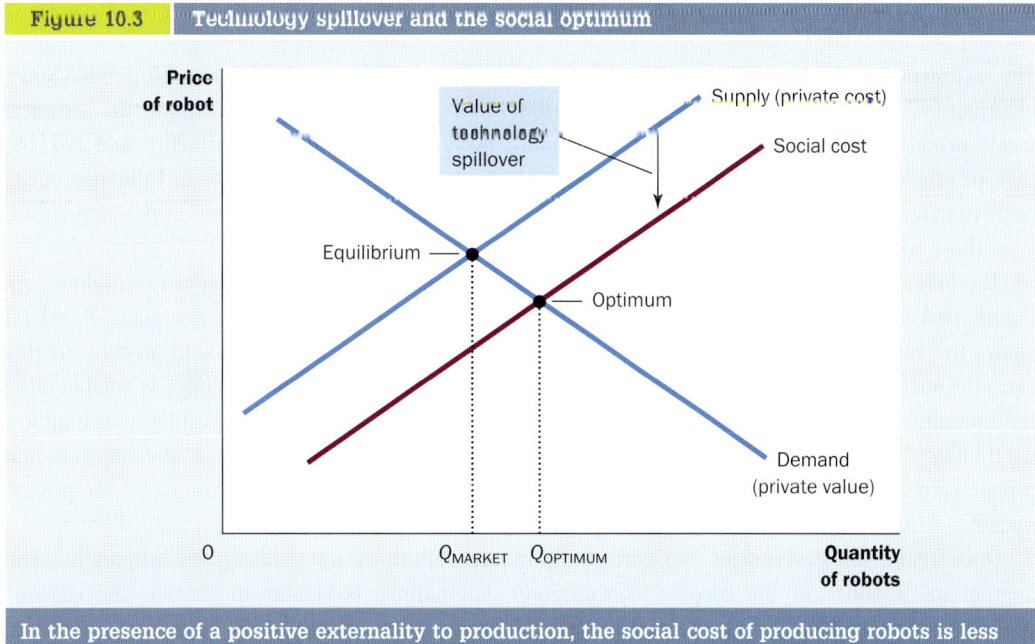

Figure 10.3 Technology spillover and the social optimum

In the presence of a positive externality to production, the social cost of producing robots is less than the private cost. The socially desirable quantity of robots, $Q_{OPTIMUM}$, is therefore larger than the equilibrium quantity, Q_{MARKET}.

CASESTUDY

The debate about technology policy

On 31 October 2010, ASIMO, a humanoid robot created in Japan by Honda, celebrated its 10th anniversary. While ASIMO probably is the best-known humanoid robot – its birthday was even celebrated with a new smartphone app – other companies have developed similar robots. For example, GM has developed Robonaut 2, a humanoid robot that could be used on the International Space Station.

How large are technology spillovers from inventions like ASIMO and what do they imply for public policy? This is an important question because technological progress is the key to why living standards rise from generation to generation. Yet it is also a difficult question on which economists often disagree.

Some economists believe that technology spillovers are pervasive and that the government should encourage those industries that yield the largest spillovers. For instance, these economists argue that if making computer chips yields greater spillovers than making potato chips, then the government should use the tax laws to encourage the production of computer chips relative to the production of potato chips. Government intervention in the economy that aims to promote technology-enhancing industries is called *technology policy*.

Other economists are sceptical about technology policy. Even if technology spillovers are common, the success of a technology policy requires that the government be able to measure the size of the spillovers from different markets. This measurement problem is difficult at best. Moreover, without precise measurements, the political system may end up subsidising those industries with the most political clout, rather than those that yield the largest positive externalities.

Another way to deal with technology spillovers is patent protection. The patent laws protect the rights of inventors by giving them exclusive use of their inventions for a period of time. When a firm makes a technological breakthrough, it can patent the idea and capture much of the economic benefit for itself. The patent is said to internalise the externality by giving the firm a property right over its invention. If other firms want to use the new technology, they have to obtain permission from the inventing firm and pay it a royalty. Thus, the patent system gives firms a greater incentive to engage in research and other activities that advance technology.

Externalities in consumption

The externalities we have discussed so far are associated with the production of goods. Some externalities, however, are associated with consumption. The consumption of alcohol, for instance, yields negative externalities if consumers are more likely to drive under its influence and risk the lives of others. Similarly, vaccination against a contagious disease such as measles or influenza yields positive externalities because it lowers the risk of catching the disease for everyone in the population, even those who are not vaccinated.

The analysis of consumption externalities is similar to the analysis of production externalities. As Figure 10.4 shows, the demand curve no longer reflects the social value from the good. Panel (a) shows the case of a negative consumption externality, such as that associated with alcohol. In this case, the social value is less than the private value, and the socially optimal quantity is smaller than the quantity determined by the private market. Panel (b) shows the case of a positive consumption externality, like that associated with a vaccine. In this case, the social value is greater than the private value, and the socially optimal quantity is greater than the quantity determined by the private market.

Once again, the government can correct the market failure by internalising the externality. The appropriate response in the case of consumption externalities is similar to that in the case of production externalities. To move the market equilibrium closer to the social optimum, a negative externality requires a tax and a positive externality requires a subsidy. In fact, that is exactly the policy the government follows; alcoholic beverages are among the most highly taxed goods in our economy and vaccination is heavily subsidised through preschool programs and the medical system.

As you may have noticed by now, these examples of externalities lead to some general lessons: *Negative externalities in production or consumption lead markets to produce a larger quantity than is*

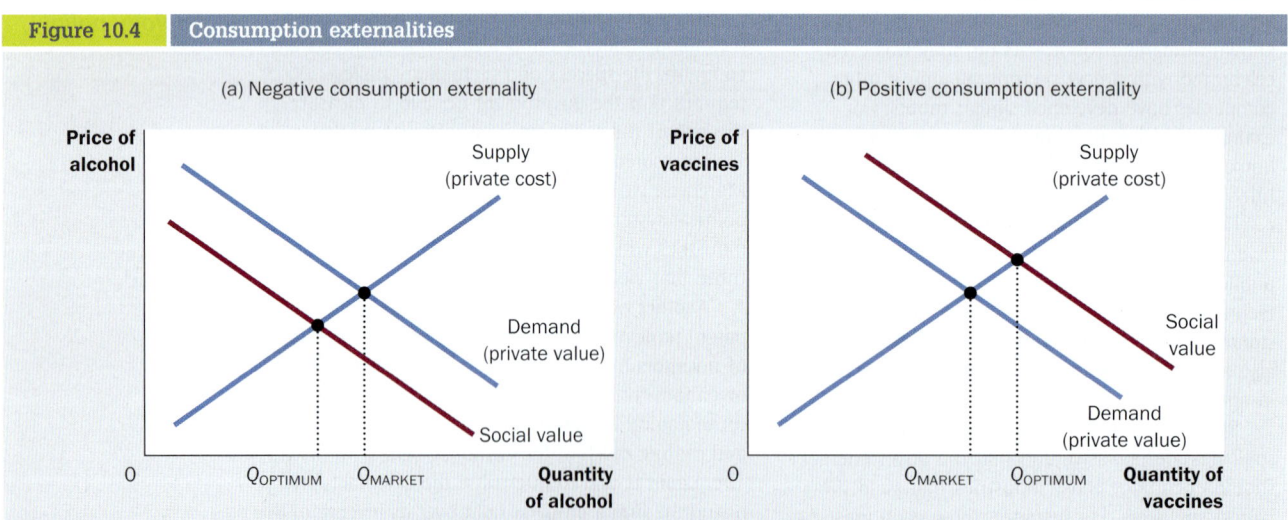

Figure 10.4 **Consumption externalities**

Panel (a) shows a market with a negative consumption externality, such as the market for alcoholic beverages. The curve representing social value is lower than the demand curve, and the socially desirable quantity, $Q_{OPTIMUM}$, is less than the equilibrium quantity, Q_{MARKET}. Panel (b) shows a market with a positive consumption externality, such as the market for vaccines. The curve representing social value is above the demand curve, and the socially desirable quantity, $Q_{OPTIMUM}$, is greater than the equilibrium quantity, Q_{MARKET}.

socially desirable. Positive externalities in production or consumption lead markets to produce a smaller quantity than is socially desirable. To remedy the problem, the government can internalise the externality by taxing goods that have negative externalities and subsidising goods that have positive externalities.

Give an example of a negative externality and a positive externality. Explain why market outcomes are inefficient in the presence of externalities.

CASESTUDY

Externalities and global warming

In 1936, a Swedish chemist suggested that carbon dioxide released from burning coal could create a 'greenhouse effect' in the atmosphere, leading to global warming. In October 2006, a report for the British government on global warming (the Stern report) concluded that there is now overwhelming scientific evidence that climate change is a serious global threat. The report urged immediate action to reduce emissions of greenhouse gases such as carbon dioxide.

The Stern report was authored, not by a climate scientist, but by an economist, Nicholas Stern. While science can tell us the source and extent of the problem, greenhouse gas pollution is a classic case of a negative externality in production. Greenhouse gases are produced whenever fossil fuels are burnt to provide energy, whether it is to light our houses, make paper to write on or take us to the shopping mall. As the Stern report noted, the producers of greenhouse gases face little or no economic incentive to reduce emissions and do not have to compensate those who lose out because of climate change. Because producers do not face the external cost of burning fossil fuels, too much of this fuel is burnt from society's perspective.

To solve the problems of climate change, we need to understand the best ways to deal with negative externalities. We discuss these solutions in the remainder of this chapter.

Private solutions to externalities

We have discussed why externalities lead markets to allocate resources inefficiently, but have mentioned only briefly how this inefficiency can be remedied. In practice, both private individuals and public policymakers respond to externalities in various ways. All of the remedies share the goal of moving the allocation of resources closer to the social optimum. In this section we examine private solutions.

The types of private solutions

Although externalities tend to cause markets to be inefficient, government action is not always needed to solve the problem. In some circumstances, people can develop private solutions.

Sometimes, the problem of externalities is solved by moral codes and social sanctions. Consider, for instance, why most people do not litter. Although there are laws against littering, these laws are not vigorously enforced. Most people do not litter simply because it is the wrong thing to do. The Golden Rule taught to most children says: 'Do unto others as you would have them do unto you'. This moral injunction tells us to take account of how our actions affect other people. In economic terms, it tells us to internalise externalities.

Another private solution to externalities is charities, many of which are established to deal with externalities. For example, Greenpeace, whose goal is to protect the environment, is a non-profit organisation funded by private donations. As another example, private individuals and corporations sometimes sponsor scholarships and prizes for university students, in part because education has positive externalities for society.

The private market can often solve the problem of externalities by relying on the self-interest of the relevant parties. Sometimes the solution takes the form of integrating different types of business. For example, consider an apple grower and a beekeeper located next to each other. Each business confers a positive externality on the other – by pollinating the flowers on the trees, the bees help the orchard produce apples. At the same time, the bees use the nectar they get from the apple trees to produce honey. Nonetheless, when the apple grower is deciding how many trees to plant and the beekeeper is deciding how many bees to keep, they neglect the positive externality. As a result, the apple grower plants too few trees and the beekeeper keeps too few bees. These externalities could be internalised if the beekeeper bought the apple orchard or if the apple grower bought the beehive; both activities would then take place within the same firm and this single firm could choose the right number of trees and bees. Internalising externalities is one reason that some firms are involved in different types of business.

Another way for the private market to deal with external effects is for the interested parties to enter into a contract. In the example above, a contract between the apple grower and the beekeeper can solve the problem of too few trees and too few bees. The contract can specify the number of trees, the number of bees and perhaps a payment from one party to the other. By setting the right number of trees and bees, the contract can solve the inefficiency that normally arises from these externalities and make both parties better off.

The Coase theorem

Coase theorem
the proposition that if private parties can bargain without cost over the allocation of resources, they can solve the problem of externalities on their own

How effective is the private market in dealing with externalities? A famous result, called the **Coase theorem** after economist Ronald Coase, suggests that it can be very effective in some circumstances. According to the Coase theorem, if private parties can bargain without cost over the allocation of resources, then the private market will always solve the problem of externalities and allocate resources efficiently.

To see how the Coase theorem works, consider an example. Suppose that Fred owns a dog that barks and disturbs Barney, Fred's neighbour. Fred gets a benefit from owning the dog, but his dog confers a negative externality on Barney. Should Fred be forced to send his dog to the pound, or should Barney have to suffer sleepless nights because of the dog's barking?

Consider first what outcome is socially efficient. A social planner, considering the two alternatives, would compare the benefit that Fred gets from the dog with the cost that Barney bears from the barking. If the benefit exceeds the cost, it is efficient for Fred to keep the dog and for Barney to live with the barking. Yet if the cost exceeds the benefit, then Fred should get rid of the dog.

According to the Coase theorem, the private market will reach the efficient outcome on its own. How? Barney can simply offer to pay Fred to get rid of the dog. Fred will accept the deal if the amount of money Barney offers is greater than the benefit of keeping the dog.

By bargaining over the price, Fred and Barney can always reach the efficient outcome. For instance, suppose that Fred gets a $500 benefit from the dog and Barney bears an $800 cost from the barking. In this case, Barney can offer Fred $600 to get rid of the dog and Fred will gladly accept. Both parties are better off than they were before and the efficient outcome is reached.

▸ Coase theorem

It is possible, of course, that Barney would not be willing to offer any price that Fred would accept. For instance, suppose that Fred gets a $1000 benefit from the dog and Barney bears an $800 cost from the barking. In this case, Fred would turn down any offer below $1000 and Barney would not offer any amount above $800. Therefore, Fred ends up keeping the dog. Given these costs and benefits, however, this outcome is efficient.

So far, we have assumed that Fred has the legal right to keep a barking dog. In other words, we have assumed that Fred can keep his dog unless Barney pays him enough to induce him to give up the dog voluntarily. How different would the outcome be, on the other hand, if Barney had the legal right to peace and quiet?

According to the Coase theorem, the initial distribution of rights does not matter for the market's ability to reach the efficient outcome. For instance, suppose that Barney can legally compel Fred to get rid of the dog. Although having this right works to Barney's advantage, it probably will not change the outcome. In this case, Fred can offer to pay Barney to allow him to keep the dog. If the benefit of the dog to Fred exceeds the cost of the barking to Barney, then Fred and Barney will strike a bargain in which Fred keeps the dog.

Although Fred and Barney can reach the efficient outcome regardless of how rights are initially distributed, the distribution of rights is not irrelevant; it determines the distribution of economic wellbeing. Whether Fred has the right to a barking dog or Barney has the right to peace and quiet determines who pays whom in the final bargain. But, in either case, the two parties can bargain with each other and solve the externality problem. Fred will end up keeping the dog only if the benefit exceeds the cost.

To sum up: *The Coase theorem says that private economic actors can potentially solve the problem of externalities among themselves. Whatever the initial distribution of rights, the interested parties can reach a bargain in which everyone is better off and the outcome is efficient.*

Why private solutions do not always work

Despite the appealing logic of the Coase theorem, private individuals on their own often fail to resolve the problems caused by externalities. The Coase theorem applies only when the interested parties have no trouble reaching and enforcing an agreement. In the real world, however, bargaining does not always work, even when a mutually beneficial agreement is possible.

Sometimes the interested parties fail to solve an externality problem because of **transaction costs**, the costs that parties incur in the process of agreeing and following through on a bargain. In our example, imagine that Fred and Barney speak different languages so that, to reach an agreement, they will need to hire a translator. If the benefit of solving the barking problem is less than the cost of the translator, Fred and Barney might choose to leave the problem unsolved. In more realistic examples, the transaction costs are the expenses not of translators but of the lawyers required to draft and enforce contracts.

transaction costs
the costs that parties incur in the process of agreeing and following through on a bargain

At other times, bargaining simply breaks down. The recurrence of wars and strikes shows that reaching agreement can be difficult and that failing to reach agreement can be costly. The problem is often that each party tries to hold out for a better deal. For example, suppose that Fred gets a $500 benefit from the dog and Barney bears an $800 cost from the barking. Although it is efficient for Barney to pay Fred to get rid of the dog, there are many prices that could lead to this outcome. Fred might demand $750 and Barney might offer only $550. As they haggle over the price, the inefficient outcome with the barking dog persists.

Reaching an efficient bargain is especially difficult when the number of interested parties is large because coordinating everyone is costly. For example, consider a factory that pollutes the water of a nearby river. The pollution confers a negative externality on the local fishermen. According to the Coase theorem, if the pollution is inefficient, then the factory and the fishermen could reach a bargain in which the fishermen pay the factory not to pollute. If there are many fishermen, however, trying to coordinate all of them in order to bargain with the factory may be almost impossible.

When private bargaining does not work, the government can sometimes play a role. The government is an institution designed for collective action. In this example, the government can act on behalf of the fishermen, even when it is impractical for the fishermen to act for themselves. In the next section, we examine how the government can try to remedy the problem of externalities.

Give an example of a private solution to an externality. What is the Coase theorem? Why are private economic actors sometimes unable to solve the problems caused by an externality?

Public policies on externalities

When an externality causes a market to reach an inefficient allocation of resources, the government can respond in one of two ways. Command-and-control policies regulate behaviour directly. Market-based policies provide incentives so that private decision makers will choose to solve the problem on their own.

Command-and-control policies: Regulation

The government can remedy an externality by making certain activities either required or forbidden. For example, it is a crime to dump poisonous chemicals into the water supply. In this case, the external costs to society far exceed the benefits to the polluter. The government therefore institutes a command-and-control policy that prohibits this act altogether.

In most cases of pollution, however, the situation is not this simple. Despite the stated goals of some environmentalists, it would be impossible to prohibit all polluting activity. For example, virtually all forms of transport – even the horse – produce some undesirable polluting by-products. But it would not be sensible for the government to ban all transport. Thus, instead of trying to eradicate pollution altogether, society has to weigh the costs and benefits in order to decide the kinds and quantities of pollution it will allow. The environment protection agencies in each state are the government agencies with the task of regulating, auditing and monitoring activities that might damage the environment.

Environmental regulations can take many forms. Sometimes a government regulator, like an environment protection agency, dictates a maximum level of pollution that factories may emit. At other times the government regulator requires that firms adopt a particular technology to reduce emissions. In all cases, to design good rules, the regulators need to know the details about specific industries and about the alternative technologies that those industries could adopt. This information is often difficult for government regulators to obtain.

IN THE NEWS . . .

EXTERNALITY HAPPENS . . .

The following article shows how local governments in Australia are trying to stamp out one externality.

From the people who put the P into parks and gardens
by Claire Hunter

At this Brighton park, dog excrement litters the grass, marked by flags placed by *The Age*.

Source: FairfaxPhotos.com/Bruce Postle.

Despite $500 fines, dog toilets and 'pooch patches', some people are still flouting council laws aimed at reducing the amount of dog poo in Melbourne's parks and reserves.

Ms Anne Burch, the manager of local laws and administration at Boroondara Council, said even with $500 fines for people who did not clean up their dog's droppings on council land or public places, and the trial of 'pooch patches', which resemble a sandpit for dogs, 'there is still a lot of dog poo out there'.

This week, *The Age* conducted a poo-in-a-park experiment to see how successful local laws were in combating the problem. Six of the seven parks visited were clean of dog droppings, but as the picture with its marker flags shows, the park at the North Road boat ramp in Brighton was not. Several dogs had clearly missed the dog toilet provided, and their owners had failed to clean up after them.

Mr Russell McMurray, regulator of the Bayside City Council, said the park showed that although council efforts to rid parks and reserves of dog poo were working, there was still room for improvement. Dog owners in the area will soon be legally required to carry a 'pooper scooper', defined as a paper or plastic bag or a device for picking up dog poo.

A local woman who walks her two dogs along the Brighton foreshore regularly says visitors cause the problem. 'It's annoying, the regulars do the right thing, it's the idiots who come down and you never see them again,' she said.

To help people clean up after their pooches, the council provides plastic bags in 10 of its 60 reserves and parks, as well as two dog toilets where people can deposit the waste into a hole in the ground, which contains a chemical to break down the dog poo.

Ms Burch said fines were difficult to enforce. A council officer or ranger has to witness the event and be able to say the offending dog poo definitely came from a certain dog. 'Dogs don't leave a piece of paper with their owners' name and address in their poo,' she said. Ms Burch said that although there were many responsible pet owners who did the right thing, there were still a lot who did not care: 'It's not the poor dog that's the problem, it's the owner,' she said.

Source: Claire Hunter/*The Age*.

Market-based policy 1: Corrective taxes and subsidies

Instead of regulating behaviour in response to an externality, the government can use market-based policies to align private incentives with social efficiency. For instance, as we saw earlier, the government can internalise the externality by taxing activities that have negative externalities and

▸ corrective tax

subsidising activities that have positive externalities. Taxes enacted to correct the effects of negative externalities are called **corrective taxes**. They are also called *Pigovian taxes* after economist Arthur Pigou (1877–1959), an early advocate of their use.

An ideal corrective tax would equal the external cost from an activity with externalities and an ideal corrective subsidy would equal the external benefit from an activity with positive externalities.

Economists usually prefer corrective taxes over regulations as a way to deal with pollution because they can reduce pollution at a lower cost to society. To see why, let us consider an example.

Suppose that two factories – a paper mill and a steel mill – are each emitting 5000 tonnes of carbon dioxide into the atmosphere every year. The government decides that it wants to reduce the amount of these greenhouse gases. It considers two solutions:

- Regulation – the government could tell each factory to reduce its pollution to 3000 tonnes of carbon dioxide per year.
- Corrective tax – the government could levy a tax on each factory of $50 for each tonne of carbon dioxide it emits.

The regulation would dictate a level of pollution, whereas the tax would give factory owners an economic incentive to reduce pollution. Which solution do you think is better?

Most economists would prefer the tax. They would first point out that a tax is just as effective as a regulation in reducing the overall level of pollution. The government can achieve whatever level of pollution it wants by setting the tax at the appropriate level. The higher the tax, the larger the reduction in pollution. Indeed, if the tax is high enough, the factories will close down altogether, reducing pollution to zero.

Although regulation and corrective taxes are both capable of reducing pollution, the tax accomplishes this goal more efficiently. The regulation requires each factory to reduce pollution by the same amount, but an equal reduction is not necessarily the least expensive way to reduce greenhouse gases. It is possible that the paper mill can reduce pollution at a lower cost than the steel mill. If so, the paper mill would respond to the tax by reducing pollution substantially in order to avoid the tax, whereas the steel mill would respond by reducing pollution less and paying the tax.

In essence, the corrective tax places a price on the right to pollute. Just as markets allocate goods to those buyers who value them most highly, a corrective tax allocates pollution to those factories that face the highest cost of reducing it. Whatever the level of pollution the government chooses, it can achieve this goal at the lowest total cost using a tax.

Economists also argue that corrective taxes are better for the environment. Under the command-and-control policy of regulation, the factories have no reason to reduce emissions further once they have reached the target of 3000 tonnes of carbon dioxide. In contrast, the tax gives the factories an incentive to develop cleaner technologies, since a cleaner technology would reduce the amount of tax the factory has to pay.

Corrective taxes are unlike most other taxes. As we discussed in chapter 8, most taxes distort incentives and move the allocation of resources away from the social optimum. The reduction in economic wellbeing – that is, in consumer and producer surplus – exceeds the amount of revenue the government raises, resulting in a deadweight loss. In contrast, when externalities are present, society also cares about the wellbeing of the bystanders who are affected. Corrective taxes alter incentives to account for the presence of externalities and thereby move the allocation of resources closer to the social optimum. Thus, while corrective taxes raise revenue for the government, they enhance economic efficiency.

In many places in the world, the collection of household garbage is a free service. Although it is funded from local rates or taxes, you do not pay any extra when you put out more garbage. To an economist, this means that you face a zero price for your use of the garbage service. As a result, it is likely you will produce too much garbage. By recycling and donating old clothing and the like to charity, you could reduce the amount of garbage. But while the price of garbage collection is zero and recycling or donating takes more time, there will be a tendency for residents as a whole to produce too much rubbish.

The discussion in this chapter suggests a solution to this problem – put a price on the amount of garbage collected and give residents an incentive to reduce the amount of garbage they put out by encouraging them towards alternatives such as recycling and donation. However, as two US economists, Don Fullerton and Thomas Kinnaman, show in a 1996 article in the *American Economic Review*, this simple solution is not so easy to implement in practice.

In the United States, many towns have established prices for each bin of garbage collected. They have done this by requiring residents to purchase stickers that they must place on their garbage bin if they want it to be collected when they put it out. However, when this scheme was implemented in the town of Charlottesville in 1992, Fullerton and Kinnaman found that the scheme had some undesirable consequences.

By putting a price on garbage bins, the number of bins put out for collection dropped substantially (by 37 per cent). However, in each bin, there was much more garbage (about 40 per cent more on average). Why? Because residents would cram more into each bin. If you have ever tried stomping your foot on the garbage in the bin to fit more in, this should not come as a surprise. You would also realise that such compacting is probably better done by garbage trucks than by individuals.

The actual drop in garbage collected was very little, but the bins bulged. What's more, there was far more garbage dumped on roadsides. There was an increase in recycling although there had been a general trend in this direction anyway.

The conclusion is that using Pigovian methods to reduce some activities can be difficult. In the case of garbage collection, it might simply be that the supply of garbage is relatively inelastic. So even high prices and fines might not do the job. And if recycling is the goal, perhaps making it easier for residents to recycle is a better policy. For instance, by providing a recycling collection service, the government can lower the relative cost of recycling compared with throwing stuff out.

Market-based policy 2: Tradeable pollution permits

Returning to our example of the paper mill and the steel mill, let us suppose that, despite the advice of its economists, the government adopts the regulation and requires each factory to reduce carbon dioxide emissions to 3000 tonnes per year. Then one day, after the regulation is in place and both mills have complied, the two firms go to the government with a proposal. The steel mill wants to increase its emissions by 1000 tonnes. The paper mill has agreed to reduce its emissions by the same amount if the steel mill pays it $5 million. Should the government allow the two factories to make this deal?

From the standpoint of economic efficiency, allowing the deal is good policy. The deal must make the owners of the two factories better off, because they are voluntarily agreeing to it. Moreover, the deal does not have any external effects because the total amount of pollution remains the same. Thus, social welfare is enhanced by allowing the paper mill to sell its right to pollute to the steel mill.

The same logic applies to any voluntary transfer of the right to pollute from one firm to another. If the government allows firms to make these deals, it will, in essence, have created a new scarce resource – pollution permits. A market to trade these permits will eventually develop and that market will be governed by the forces of supply and demand. The invisible hand will ensure that this new market efficiently allocates the right to pollute. That is, the permits will end up in the hands of those firms that value them most highly, as judged by their willingness to pay. A firm's willingness to pay for the right to pollute, in turn, will depend on its cost of reducing pollution: The more costly it is for a firm to cut back on pollution, the more it will be willing to pay for a permit.

One advantage of allowing a market for pollution permits is that the initial allocation of pollution permits among firms does not matter from the standpoint of economic efficiency. The logic behind this conclusion is similar to that behind the Coase theorem. Those firms that can reduce pollution most easily would be willing to sell whatever permits they get and those firms that can reduce pollution only at high cost would be willing to buy whatever permits they need. As long as there is a free market for the pollution rights, the final allocation will be efficient whatever the initial allocation.

Reducing pollution using pollution permits may seem quite different from using corrective taxes, but the two policies have much in common. In both cases, firms pay for their pollution. With corrective taxes, polluting firms must pay a tax to the government. With pollution permits, polluting firms must pay to buy the permit. (Even firms that already own permits must pay to pollute; the opportunity cost of polluting is what they could have received by selling their permits on the open market.) Both corrective taxes and pollution permits internalise the externality of pollution by making it costly for firms to pollute.

The similarity of the two policies can be seen by considering the market for pollution. Both panels in Figure 10.5 show the demand curve for the right to pollute. This curve shows that the lower the price of polluting, the more firms will choose to pollute. In panel (a), the government uses a corrective tax to set a price for pollution. In this case, the supply curve for pollution rights is perfectly elastic (because firms can pollute as much as they want by paying the tax), and the position of the demand curve determines the quantity of pollution. In panel (b), the government sets a quantity of pollution by issuing pollution permits. In this case, the supply curve for pollution rights is perfectly inelastic (because the quantity of pollution is fixed by the number of permits), and the position of the

Figure 10.5   The equivalence of corrective taxes and pollution permits

(a) Pigovian tax

(b) Pollution permits

In panel (a), the government sets a price on pollution by levying a corrective tax and the demand curve determines the quantity of pollution. In panel (b), the government limits the quantity of pollution by limiting the number of pollution permits and the demand curve determines the price of pollution. The price and quantity of pollution are the same in the two cases.

demand curve determines the price of pollution. Hence, for any given demand curve for pollution, the government can achieve any point on the demand curve either by setting a price with a corrective tax or by setting a quantity with pollution permits.

In some circumstances, however, selling pollution permits may be better than levying a corrective tax. Suppose the government wants no more than 6000 tonnes of carbon dioxide to be emitted by the steel and paper mills. But because the government does not know the demand curve for pollution, it is not sure what size tax would achieve that goal. In this case, it can simply auction off 6000 pollution permits. The auction price would yield the appropriate size of the corrective tax.

The idea of the government auctioning off the right to pollute may at first sound like the creature of some economist's imagination. And, in fact, that is how the idea began. But tradeable pollution permits are used in the United States for sulphur dioxide and in Europe for greenhouse gases.

In Australia in 2008, the Garnaut report – a 600-page report commissioned by the federal government – recommended the use of tradeable pollution permits to cut greenhouse gas emissions. The report called the permits an emission trading scheme, or ETS. Pollution permits, like corrective taxes, are widely viewed as a cost-effective way to keep the environment clean. Indeed, as this book goes to press, Australia is in the process of introducing a carbon tax as a first step to establishing an ETS.

IN THE NEWS ...

TAXES OR TRADING TO DEAL WITH GLOBAL WARMING?

In this chapter we noted how a market for pollution permits may be better than corrective taxes. In the following article Tim Harford notes that corrective taxes and pollution permits have both similarities and differences. But he argues that the differences mean that corrective taxes are a better way to deal with the threat of global warming.

Undercover economist: Emission impossible?

byTim Harford

A lot of people think it a good idea to reduce the amount of carbon dioxide we pump into the atmosphere. But not many have sensible ideas about the correct way to do that.

One contributor to the FT recently asserted that, 'An individual carbon trading scheme is more equitable and effective than carbon taxation as it reduces consumption quickly and dramatically.' All that carbon dioxide has clearly addled his thinking. It isn't possible to work out whether rationing would reduce emissions more than a tax until you know what the tax might be, or how generous the ration.

When it comes to reducing carbon emissions, the question 'How much?' is separate from the equally important question 'How?' The sensible choice is between a carbon tax and some kind of scheme to trade pollution permits. (Politicians prefer to bung cash at favoured

initiatives; it's in their nature, but makes environmental gains harder to come by.) And for any level of environmental tax you can get the same carbon price and emissions reduction by using a permit quota instead.

That doesn't mean the two systems are equivalent. One difference is the cost of administering the system. Matt Prescott, the director of a Royal Society for the encouragement of Arts (RSA) research project into personal carbon allowances, paints an exciting picture of cheaply loading your carbon permits onto a credit card. I think it would be simpler just to administer a tax.

A second difference is where the revenue goes. A tax directs cash to the government levying it. A lot then depends on how the revenue is used: If it's distributed more heavily towards the poor, taxes are more progressive than a personal carbon allowance.

Permits enrich whoever starts with the permit: The government again, if the permits are auctioned off; or each person in society, if

>>

everybody gets an equal ration. The current vogue is to give permits to highly polluting corporations, which is handy for buying off the energy lobby but otherwise not much use.

A third difference is perhaps the most important but rarely discussed. A carbon tax gives us certainty about the price of carbon but not the quantity of emissions. A tradable permit scheme gives us certainty about the quantity of emissions, but not the price.

The question, then, is where the uncertainty is most damaging. Say we impose a tax, hoping for a 15 per cent reduction in emissions but getting only a 5 per cent fall. Is that less serious than a tradable permit scheme where we expected a carbon price of £25 a tonne but got a price of £75 a tonne?

It is indeed. The uncertainty about next year's emissions is not very worrying, because climate change is caused not by what happens next year, but by the accumulation of emissions since the industrial revolution. If we get the tax wrong and emit too much one year, it will be easy to fix. The economy, on the other hand, is more vulnerable to short-term shocks: Get the permit quota wrong, even for one year, and you could cause lasting damage.

Those environmentalists currently yelling that I am an idiot and am not committed to saving the planet have missed the point. The more you fear climate change, the more stringent the tax or quota should be. What I am saying is that whatever you decide about that, it is less risky to use a tax. The government expends so much effort taxing good things, such as saving and spending money. It would be a shame if it lacked the courage to tax something bad for a change.

Source: Tim Harford/*The Age*, 13 April 2007.

CASE STUDY

Using markets to solve climate change

While a market in tradeable pollution permits might sound fanciful, it exists in Europe, and is helping to limit global warming. The European Emissions Trading Scheme (ETS) was launched on 1 January 2005. Pollution permits are traded between companies in Europe. If a company wants to pollute then it needs to buy a permit. The permits are denominated in terms of tonnes of carbon dioxide, but apply to all greenhouse gases according to their contribution to global warming.

The ETS means that there is now a market price for pollution – between about $10 and $40 per tonne of carbon dioxide. The Scheme applies to over 10 000 large emitters of greenhouse gases.

Climate change is a global problem and the ETS shows how a market can be used to help solve this problem. A European firm that wants to emit carbon dioxide has two choices. It can buy a permit. Alternatively it can participate in a United Nations scheme to reduce greenhouse gases in developing countries. As a result, European firms have sponsored the disposal of the gas HFC-23 in China. This gas is cheap to dispose of and, tonne for tonne, has a global warming effect almost 12 000 times greater than carbon dioxide. As economics predicts, the ETS has given European polluters the incentive to reduce global emissions of greenhouse gases in the cheapest possible way.

The ETS has also provided incentives for companies to invent new ways to limit carbon dioxide pollution. For example, in Holland, carbon dioxide from an oil refinery is being used to help farmers grow fruit and vegetables in greenhouses, reducing emissions by 170 000 tonnes per year.

The ETS has had some problems. The price has been volatile, particularly as companies learn about the permit system and how they might be able to reduce emissions. It is widely agreed that too many permits were issued in 2005 and these permits were initially given away to companies rather than being auctioned. There have been high costs of setting up systems to monitor levels of greenhouse gas emissions. Also, some industries, such as airlines, have been exempt from the Scheme. Many of these problems will be addressed when the third phase of the ETS is launched in 2013.

Some economists, such as one of the authors of this textbook (Greg Mankiw) and Tim Harford in his *In the News* article in this chapter, argue that a system of corrective taxes would work better than a permit market. Others believe that a modified market that uses floors and ceilings to reduce price volatility would be better. Many economists, however, argue that some form of tradeable permit market is the best way to address the problem of global warming.

Objections to the economic analysis of pollution

Some environmentalists argue that clean air and clean water are fundamental human rights that should not be debased by considering them in economic terms. How can you put a price on clean air and clean water? The environment is so important, they say, that we should protect it as much as possible, regardless of the cost.

Economists have little sympathy with this type of argument. To economists, good environmental policy begins by acknowledging the first of the *Ten Lessons from Economics* in chapter 1 – people face trade-offs. Certainly, clean air and clean water have value. But their value must be compared with their opportunity cost – that is, with what one must give up to obtain them. Eliminating all pollution is impossible. Trying to eliminate all pollution would reverse many of the technological advances that allow us to enjoy a high standard of living. Few people would be willing to accept poor nutrition, inadequate medical care or shoddy housing in order to make the environment as clean as possible.

Economists argue that some environmental activists hurt their own cause by not thinking in economic terms. A clean environment can be viewed as simply another good. Like all normal goods it has a positive income elasticity: Rich countries can afford a cleaner environment than poor ones and, therefore, usually have more rigorous environmental protection. Further, like most other goods, clean air and clean water obey the law of demand: The lower the price of environmental protection, the more the public will want. The economic approach of using pollution permits and corrective taxes reduces the cost of environmental protection. It should, therefore, increase the public's demand for a clean environment.

A glue factory and a steel mill emit smoke containing a chemical that is harmful if inhaled in large amounts. Describe three ways a government might respond to this externality. What are the pros and cons of each of your solutions?

Conclusion

The invisible hand is powerful but not omnipotent. A market's equilibrium maximises the sum of producer and consumer surplus. When the buyers and sellers in the market are the only interested parties, this outcome is efficient from the standpoint of society as a whole. But when there are external effects, such as pollution, evaluating a market outcome requires taking into account the wellbeing of third parties as well. In this case, the invisible hand of the marketplace may fail to allocate resources efficiently.

In some cases, people can solve the problem of externalities on their own. The Coase theorem suggests that the interested parties can bargain among themselves and agree on an efficient solution. Sometimes, however, an efficient outcome cannot be reached, perhaps because the large number of interested parties makes bargaining difficult.

When people cannot solve the problem of externalities privately, the government often steps in. Yet, even now, society should not abandon market forces entirely. Rather, the government can confront the problem by requiring decision makers to bear the full costs of their actions. Corrective taxes on emissions and pollution permits, for instance, are designed to internalise the externality of pollution. More and more, they are the policy of choice for those interested in protecting the environment. Market forces, properly redirected, are often the best remedy for market failure.

IN THE NEWS . . .

CHILDREN AS EXTERNALITIES

This tongue-in-cheek editorial from the *Economist*, an international news-magazine, calls attention to a common externality that is not fully appreciated.

Mum's the word: When children should be screened and not heard

A negative externality

Source: iStockphoto/Katrina Brown.

We live in increasingly intolerant times. Signs proliferate demanding no smoking, no spitting, no parking, even no walking … Posh clubs and restaurants have long had 'no jeans' rules, but these days you can be too smart. Some London hostelries have 'no suits' policies, for fear that boisterous city traders in suits might spoil the atmosphere. Environmentalists have long demanded all sorts of bans on cars. Mobile telephones are the latest target: Some trains, airline lounges, restaurants, and even golf courses are being designated 'no phone' areas.

If intolerance really has to be the spirit of this age, the *Economist* would like to suggest restrictions on another source of noise pollution: Children. Lest you dismiss this as mere prejudice, we can even produce a good economic argument for it. Smoking, driving, and mobile phones all cause what economists call 'negative externalities'. That is, the costs of these activities to other people tend to exceed the costs to the individuals of their proclivities. The invisible hand of the market fumbles, leading resources astray. Thus, because a driver's private motoring costs do not reflect the costs he imposes on others

in the form of pollution and congestion, he uses the car more than is socially desirable. Likewise, it is argued, smokers take too little care to ensure that their acrid fumes do not damage other people around them.

Governments typically respond to such market failures in two ways. One is higher taxes, to make polluters pay the full cost of their anti-social behaviour. The other is regulation, such as emission standards or bans on smoking in public places. Both approaches might work for children.

For children, just like cigarettes or mobile phones, clearly impose a negative externality on people who are near them. Anybody who has suffered a 12-hour flight with a bawling baby in the row immediately ahead, or a bored youngster viciously kicking their seat from behind, will grasp this as quickly as they would love to grasp the youngster's neck. Here is a clear case of market failure: Parents do not bear the full costs (indeed young babies travel free), so they are too ready to take their noisy brats with them. Where is the invisible hand when it is needed to administer a good smack?

The solution is obvious. All airlines, trains, and restaurants should create child-free zones. Put all those children at the back of the plane and parents might make more effort to minimize their noise pollution. And instead of letting children pay less and babies go free, they should be charged (or taxed) more than adults, with the revenues used to subsidize seats immediately in front of the war-zone.

Passengers could then request a no-children seat, just as they now ask for a no-smoking one. As more women choose not to have children and the number of older people without young children increases, the demand for childfree travel will expand. Well, yes, it is a bit intolerant – but why shouldn't parents be treated as badly as smokers? And at least there is an obvious airline to pioneer the scheme: Virgin.

Source: *The Economist*, 5 December 1998. © The Economist Newspaper Limited, London 1998.

Summary

- When a transaction between a buyer and a seller directly affects a third party, that effect is called an externality. Negative externalities, such as pollution, cause the socially desirable quantity in a market to be less than the equilibrium quantity. Positive externalities, such as technology spillovers, cause the socially desirable quantity to be greater than the equilibrium quantity.

- Those affected by externalities can sometimes solve the problem privately. For instance, when one business confers an externality on another business, the two businesses can internalise the externality by merging. Alternatively, the interested parties can solve the problem by signing a contract. According to the Coase theorem, if people can bargain without cost, then they can always reach an agreement in which resources are allocated efficiently. In many cases, however, reaching a bargain among the many interested parties is difficult, so the Coase theorem does not apply.

- When private parties cannot adequately deal with external effects, such as pollution, the government often steps in. Sometimes the government prevents socially inefficient activity by regulating behaviour. Other times it internalises an externality using corrective taxes. Another way to protect the environment is for the government to issue a limited number of pollution permits. The end result of this policy is largely the same as imposing corrective taxes on polluters.

Key concepts

Coase theorem
corrective tax
externality

internalising an
externality

transaction costs

Questions for review

1   Give an example of a negative externality and of a positive externality.
2   Use a supply-and-demand diagram to explain the effect of a negative externality in production.
3   List some of the ways that the problems caused by externalities can be solved without government intervention.
4   Imagine that you are a non-smoker sharing a room with a smoker. According to the Coase theorem, what determines whether your room-mate smokes in the room? Is this outcome efficient? How do you and your room-mate reach this solution?
5   Why do economists prefer corrective taxes to regulations as a way of protecting the environment from pollution?

Problems and applications

1   Do you agree with the following statements? Why or why not?
    a   'The benefits of corrective taxes as a way of reducing pollution have to be weighed against the deadweight losses that these taxes cause.'
    b   'A negative production externality calls for a corrective tax on producers, whereas a negative consumption externality calls for a corrective tax on consumers.'

2 Consider the market for fire extinguishers.
   a Why might fire extinguishers exhibit positive externalities in consumption?
   b Draw a graph of the market for fire extinguishers, labelling the demand curve, the social-value curve, the supply curve and the social-cost curve.
   c Indicate the market equilibrium level of output and the efficient level of output. Give an explanation for why these quantities differ.
   d If the external benefit is $10 per extinguisher, describe a government policy that would result in the efficient outcome.

3 Contributions to charitable organisations are tax-deductible. In what way does this government policy encourage private solutions to externalities?

4 Kylie loves to play loud dance music. Paul loves opera and hates dance music. Unfortunately, they are next-door neighbours in an apartment building with paper-thin walls.
   a What is the externality here?
   b What command-and-control policy might the landlord impose? Could such a policy lead to an inefficient outcome?
   c Suppose the landlord lets the tenants do whatever they want. According to the Coase theorem, how might Kylie and Paul reach an efficient outcome on their own? What might prevent them from reaching an efficient outcome?

5 Smoke from wood fires is a major source of air pollution in southern Canberra. Suppose the ACT government is considering banning the use of wood fires because of the pollution they create. In making this decision, the government cares only about efficiency. Use a graph to illustrate the situation in which wood fires should be banned entirely. Now use a graph to illustrate the situation in which the use of wood fires should be reduced from the free-market level but not banned.

6 Greater consumption of alcohol leads to more motor vehicle accidents and, thus, imposes costs on people who do not drink and drive.
   a Illustrate the market for alcohol, labelling the demand curve, the social-value curve, the supply curve, the social-cost curve, the market equilibrium level of output and the efficient level of output.
   b On your graph, shade the area corresponding to the deadweight loss of the market equilibrium. (*Hint:* The deadweight loss occurs because some units of alcohol are consumed for which the social cost exceeds the social value.) Explain.

7 The former premier of Victoria, Sir Henry Bolte, is reported to have stated: 'We care about pollution, but it isn't as important as a $100 million factory'. Do you agree with this statement? If our aim is to maximise economic efficiency, discuss when we would prefer to build the factory and when we would prefer not to build the factory.

8 Many observers believe that the levels of pollution in our economy are too high.
   a If society wishes to reduce overall pollution by a certain amount, why is it efficient to have different amounts of reduction at different firms?
   b Command-and-control approaches often rely on uniform reductions among firms. Why are these approaches generally unable to target the firms that should undertake bigger reductions?
   c Economists argue that appropriate corrective taxes or tradeable pollution rights will result in efficient pollution reduction. How do these approaches target the firms that should undertake bigger reductions?

9 The Pristine River has two polluting firms on its banks. Acme Industrial and Creative Chemicals each dump 100 tonnes of glop into the river each year. The cost of reducing glop emissions per

tonne equals $10 for Acme and $100 for Creative. The local government wants to reduce overall pollution from 200 tonnes to 50 tonnes.

    a   If the government knew the cost of reduction for each firm, what reductions would it impose in order to reach its overall goal? What would be the cost to each firm and the total cost to the firms together?

    b   In a more typical situation, the government would not know the cost of pollution reduction at each firm. If the government decided to reach its overall goal by imposing uniform reductions on the firms, calculate the reduction made by each firm, the cost to each firm and the total cost to the firms together.

    c   Compare the total cost of pollution reduction in parts (a) and (b). If the government does not know the cost of reduction for each firm, is there still some way for it to reduce pollution to 50 tonnes at the total cost you calculated in part (a)? Explain.

10 Figure 10.5 shows that for any given demand curve for the right to pollute, the government can achieve the same outcome either by setting a price with a corrective tax or by setting a quantity with pollution permits. Suppose there is a sharp improvement in the technology for controlling pollution.

    a   Using graphs similar to those in Figure 10.5, illustrate the effect of this development on the demand for pollution rights.

    b   What is the effect on the price and quantity of pollution under each regulatory system? Explain.

11 Suppose that the government decides to issue tradeable permits for a certain form of pollution.

    a   Does it matter for economic efficiency whether the government distributes or auctions the permits? Does it matter in any other ways?

    b   If the government chooses to distribute the permits, does the allocation of permits among firms matter for efficiency? Does it matter in any other ways?

12 The main cause of global warming is carbon dioxide, which enters the atmosphere in varying amounts from different countries but is distributed equally around the globe within a year. Economists Martin and Kathleen Feldstein argue that the correct approach to global warming is not to ask individual countries to stabilise their emissions of carbon dioxide at current levels, as some have suggested. Instead, they argue that carbon dioxide emissions should be reduced in countries where the costs are least and the countries that bear that burden should be compensated by the rest of the world.

    a   Why is international cooperation necessary to reach an efficient outcome?

    b   Is it possible to devise a compensation scheme such that all countries would be better off than under a system of uniform emission reductions? Explain.

13 Some people object to market-based policies to reduce pollution, claiming that they place a dollar value on cleaning our air and water. Economists reply that society implicitly places a dollar value on environmental clean-up even under command-and-control policies. Discuss why this is true.

14 (This problem is challenging.) There are three industrial firms in Happy Valley.
The government wants to reduce pollution to 120 units, so it gives each firm 40 tradeable pollution permits.

Firm	Initial pollution level	Cost of reducing pollution by 1 unit
A	70 units	$20
B	80	25
C	50	10

231

a Who sells permits and how many do they sell? Who buys permits and how many do they buy? Briefly explain why the sellers and buyers are each willing to do so. What is the total cost of pollution reduction in this situation?

b How much higher would the costs of pollution reduction be if the permits could not be traded?

Search me!

When accessing information about economics use the following keywords in any combinations you require:
- conference presentation
- corrective tax
- Coase theorem

CourseMate

For more multimedia resources and activities on economics, visit the Economics CourseMate website.

11

Public goods and common resources

Learning objectives

In this chapter you will:

- learn the defining characteristics of public goods and common resources

- examine why private markets fail to provide public goods

- consider some of the important public goods in our economy

- see why the cost–benefit analysis of public goods is both necessary and difficult

- examine why people tend to use common resources too much

- consider some of the important common resources in our economy.

An old song lyric maintains that 'the best things in life are free'. A moment's thought reveals a long list of goods that the songwriter could have had in mind. Nature provides some of them, such as rivers, mountains, beaches, lakes and oceans. The government provides others, such as playgrounds, libraries and bikepaths. In each case, people do not pay a fee when they choose to enjoy the benefit of the good.

Goods without prices provide a special challenge for economic analysis. Most goods in our economy are allocated in markets, where buyers pay for what they receive and sellers are paid for what they provide. For these goods, prices are the signals that guide the decisions of buyers and sellers. When goods are available free of charge, however, the market forces that normally allocate resources in our economy are absent.

In this chapter we examine the problems that arise for goods without market prices. Our analysis will shed light on one of the *Ten Lessons from Economics* in chapter 1 – governments can sometimes improve market outcomes. When a good does not have a price attached to it, private markets cannot ensure that the good is produced and consumed in the proper amounts. In such cases, government policy can potentially remedy the market failure and raise economic wellbeing.

The different kinds of goods

How well do markets work in providing the goods that people want? The answer to this question depends on the good being considered. As we discussed in chapter 7, we can rely on the market to provide the efficient number of ice-creams; the price of ice-creams adjusts to balance supply and demand, and this equilibrium maximises the sum of producer and consumer surplus. Yet, as we discussed in chapter 10, we cannot rely on the market to prevent aluminium manufacturers from polluting the air we breathe; buyers and sellers in a market typically do not take account of the external effects of their decisions. Thus, markets work well when the good is ice-cream, but they work badly when the good is clean air.

In thinking about the various goods in the economy, it is useful to group them according to two characteristics:

excludable
the property of a good whereby a person can be prevented from using it

- Is the good **excludable**? That is, can people be prevented from using the good?

rival in consumption
the property of a good whereby one person's use diminishes other people's use

- Is the good **rival in consumption**? That is, does one person's use of the good diminish another person's ability to use it?

Using these two characteristics, Figure 11.1 divides goods into four categories:

private goods
goods that are both excludable and rival in consumption

1 **Private goods** are both excludable and rival in consumption. Consider an ice-cream, for example. An ice-cream is excludable because it is possible to prevent someone from eating an ice-cream – you just don't give it to him. An ice-cream is rival in consumption because if one person eats an ice-cream, another person cannot eat the same ice-cream. Most goods in the economy are private goods like ice-creams: You don't get one unless you pay for it and once you get it you are the only person who benefits. When we analysed supply and demand in chapters 4, 5 and 6 and the efficiency of markets in chapters 7, 8 and 9, we implicitly assumed that goods were both excludable and rival in consumption.

public goods
goods that are neither excludable nor rival in consumption

2 **Public goods** are neither excludable nor rival in consumption. That is, people cannot be prevented from using a public good and one person's enjoyment of a public good does not reduce another person's enjoyment of it. For example, national defence is a public good. Once the country is defended from foreign aggressors, it is impossible to prevent any single person from enjoying the benefit of this defence (so it is not excludable). Moreover, when one person enjoys the benefit of defence, he does not reduce the benefit to anyone else (so it is not rival in consumption).

Figure 11.1	Four types of goods

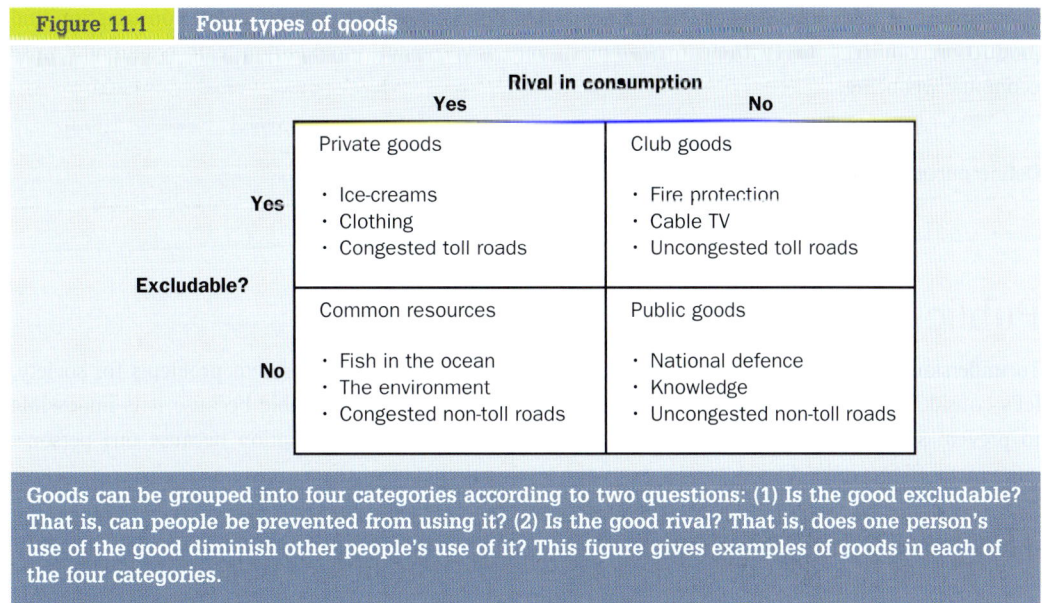

Rival in consumption

	Yes	No
Excludable? Yes	Private goods • Ice-creams • Clothing • Congested toll roads	Club goods • Fire protection • Cable TV • Uncongested toll roads
Excludable? No	Common resources • Fish in the ocean • The environment • Congested non-toll roads	Public goods • National defence • Knowledge • Uncongested non-toll roads

Goods can be grouped into four categories according to two questions: (1) Is the good excludable? That is, can people be prevented from using it? (2) Is the good rival? That is, does one person's use of the good diminish other people's use of it? This figure gives examples of goods in each of the four categories.

3 **Common resources** are rival in consumption but not excludable. For example, fish in the ocean are rival in consumption: When one person catches fish, there are fewer fish for the next person to catch. Yet these fish are not an excludable good because, given the vast size of the ocean, it is difficult to stop fishermen taking fish out of it.

4 **Club goods** are excludable but not rival in consumption. For example, consider fire protection in a small town. It is easy to exclude people from enjoying this good; the fire brigade can just let their houses burn down. Yet fire protection is not rival in consumption. Firefighters spend much of their time waiting for a fire, so protecting an additional household is unlikely to reduce the protection available to others. In other words, once a town has set up a fire brigade, the extra cost of protecting one more household is small. We discuss club goods again in chapter 15, where we see that they are one type of a *natural monopoly*.

Although Figure 11.1 offers a clean separation of goods into four categories, the boundaries between the categories are sometimes fuzzy. Whether goods are excludable or rival in consumption is often a matter of degree. Fish in an ocean may not be excludable because monitoring fishing is so difficult, but a large enough coast guard could make fish at least partly excludable. Similarly, although fish are generally rival in consumption, this would be less true if the population of fishermen were small relative to the population of fish. For purposes of our analysis, however, it will be helpful to group goods into these four categories.

In this chapter, we examine goods that are not excludable and, therefore, are available to everyone free of charge – public goods and common resources.

The study of public goods and common resources is closely related to the study of externalities. For both public goods and common resources, externalities arise because something of value has no price attached to it. If one person were to provide a public good, such as defence, other people would be better off and yet they could not be charged for this benefit. Similarly, when one person uses a common resource, such as the fish in the ocean, other people are worse off and yet they are not

common resources
goods that are rival in consumption but not excludable

club goods
goods that are excludable but not rival in consumption

compensated for this loss. Because of these external effects, private decisions about consumption and production can lead to inefficient outcomes, and government intervention can potentially raise economic wellbeing.

> Define *public goods* and *common resources* and give an example of each.

Public goods

To understand how public goods differ from other goods and why they present problems for society, let's consider an example – a fireworks display. This good is not excludable because it is impossible to prevent someone from seeing fireworks and it is not rival in consumption because one person's enjoyment of fireworks does not reduce anyone else's enjoyment of them.

The free-rider problem

The citizens of Smalltown like seeing fireworks on New Year's Eve. Each of the town's 500 residents places a $10 value on the experience. The cost of putting on a fireworks display is $1000. Because the $5000 of benefits exceeds the $1000 of costs, it is efficient for Smalltown residents to see fireworks on New Year's Eve.

Would the private market produce the efficient outcome? Probably not. Imagine that Ellen, a Smalltown entrepreneur, decided to put on a fireworks display. Ellen would have trouble selling tickets to the event because her potential customers would quickly figure out that they could see the fireworks even without a ticket. Fireworks are not excludable, so people have an incentive to be free riders. A **free rider** is a person who receives the benefit of a good but avoids paying for it. Because people would have an incentive to be free riders rather than ticket buyers, the market would fail to provide the efficient outcome.

free rider
a person who receives the benefit of a good but avoids paying for it

▶ free-rider problem

One way to view this market failure is that it arises because of an externality. If Ellen did put on the fireworks display, she would confer an external benefit on those who saw the display without paying for it. When deciding whether to put on the display, Ellen ignores these external benefits. Even though a fireworks display is socially desirable, it is not privately profitable. As a result, Ellen makes the socially inefficient decision not to put on the display.

Although the private market fails to supply the fireworks display demanded by Smalltown residents, the solution to Smalltown's problem is obvious – the local government can sponsor a New Year's Eve celebration. The town council can raise everyone's taxes by $2 and use the revenue to hire Ellen to produce the fireworks. Everyone in Smalltown is better off by $8 – the $10 at which residents value the fireworks minus the $2 tax bill. Ellen can help Smalltown reach the efficient outcome as a public employee even though she could not do so as a private entrepreneur.

The story of Smalltown is stylised, but it is also realistic. In fact, many local governments in Australia and throughout the world do pay for New Year fireworks. Moreover, the story shows a general lesson about public goods; because public goods are not excludable, the free-rider problem prevents the private market from supplying them. The government, however, can potentially remedy the problem. If the government decides that the total benefits exceed the costs, it can provide the public good and pay for it with tax revenue, making everyone better off.

IN THE NEWS . . .

FREE RIDING ON THE INTERNET

An uncongested home wireless Internet connection is not rival in consumption. And if the homeowner doesn't secure the network with a password, it is also not excludable. As the following article shows, the growth of unprotected wireless Internet networks has resulted in a free-rider problem.

Hey neighbour, stop piggybacking on my wireless

by Michel Marriott

For a while, the wireless Internet connection Christine and Randy Brodeur installed last year seemed perfect. They were able to sit in their sunny Los Angeles backyard working on their laptop computers.

But they soon began noticing that their high-speed Internet access had become as slow as rush-hour traffic on the 405 freeway.

'I didn't know whether to blame it on the Santa Ana winds or what,' recalled Mrs. Brodeur, the chief executive of Socket Media, a marketing and public relations agency.

The 'what' turned out to be neighbors who had tapped into their system. The additional online traffic nearly choked out the Brodeurs, who pay a $40 monthly fee for their Internet service, slowing their access until it was practically unusable.

Piggybacking, the usually unauthorized tapping into someone else's wireless Internet connection, is no longer the exclusive domain of pilfering computer geeks or shady hackers cruising for unguarded networks. Ordinarily upstanding people are tapping in. As they do, new sets of Internet behaviors are creeping into America's popular culture.

'I don't think it's stealing,' said Edwin Caroso, a 21-year-old student at Miami Dade College, echoing an often-heard sentiment.

'I always find people out there who aren't protecting their connection, so I just feel free to go ahead and use it,' Mr. Caroso said. He added that he tapped into a stranger's network mainly for Web surfing, keeping up with e-mail, text chatting with friends in foreign countries and doing homework.

Many who piggyback say the practice does not feel like theft because it does not seem to take anything away from anyone. One occasional piggybacker recently compared it to 'reading the newspaper over someone's shoulder'.

Piggybacking, makers of wireless routers say, is increasingly an issue for people who live in densely populated areas like New York City or Chicago, or for anyone clustered in apartment buildings in which Wi-Fi radio waves, with an average range of about 200 feet, can easily bleed through walls, floors and ceilings. Large hotels that offer the service have become bubbling brooks of free access that spill out into nearby homes and restaurants.

'Wi-Fi is in the air, and it is a very low curb, if you will, to step up and use it,' said Mike Wolf of ABI Research, a high-technology market research company in Oyster Bay, N.Y.

This is especially true, Mr. Wolf said, because so many users do not bother to secure their networks with passwords or encryption programs. The programs are usually shipped with customers' wireless routers, devices that plug into an Internet connection and make access to it wireless. Many home network owners admit that they are oblivious to piggybackers …

David Cole, director of product management for Symantec Security Response, a unit of Symantec, a maker of computer security software, said consumers should understand that an open wireless network invites greater vulnerabilities than just a stampede of 'freeloading neighbors'.

He said savvy users could piggyback into unprotected computers to peer into files containing sensitive financial and personal information, release malicious viruses and worms that could do irreparable damage, or use the computer as a launching pad for identity theft or the uploading and downloading of child pornography.

'The best case is that you end up giving a neighbor a free ride,' Mr. Cole said. 'The worst case is that someone can destroy your computer, take your files and do some really nefarious things with your network that gets you dragged into court.'

Mr. Cole said Symantec and other companies had created software that could not only lock out most network intruders but also protect computers and their content if an intruder managed to gain access.

Some users say they have protected their computers but have decided to keep their networks open as a passive protest of what they consider the exorbitant cost of Internet access.

'I'm sticking it to the man,' said Elaine Ball, an Internet subscriber who lives in Chicago. She complained that she paid $65 a month for Internet access until she recently switched to a $20-a-month promotion plan that would go up to $45 a month after the first three months.

'I open up my network, leave it wide open for anyone to jump on,' Ms. Ball said.

For the Brodeurs in Los Angeles, a close reading of their network's manual helped them to finally encrypt their network. The Brodeurs told their neighbors that the network belonged to them and not to the neighborhood. While apologetic, some neighbors still wanted access to it.

'Some of them asked me, "Could we pay?" But we didn't want to go into the Internet service provider business,' Mrs. Brodeur said. 'We gave some weird story about the network imposing some sort of lockdown protocol.'

Some important public goods

There are many examples of public goods. Here we consider three of the most important.

National defence

The defence of a country is a classic example of a public good. It is also one of the most expensive. In 2010–11 the Australian government spent almost $21 billion on defence, or about $930 per person. People disagree about whether this amount is too small or too large, but almost no one doubts that some government spending for defence is necessary. Even those economists who advocate small government agree that defence is a public good the government should provide.

Basic research

Knowledge is created through research. In evaluating, the appropriate public policy towards knowledge creation, it is important to distinguish general knowledge from specific technological knowledge. Specific technological knowledge, such as the invention of a longer-lasting battery, a smaller microchip or a better digital music player, can be patented. The patent gives the inventor the exclusive right to the knowledge she has created for a period of time. Anyone else who wants to use the patented information has to pay the inventor for the right to do so. In other words, the patent makes the knowledge created by the inventor excludable.

By contrast, general knowledge is a public good. For example, a mathematician cannot patent a theorem. Once a theorem is proved, the knowledge is not excludable: The theorem enters society's general pool of knowledge that anyone can use without charge. The theorem is also not rival in consumption: One person's use of the theorem does not prevent any other person from using the theorem.

Profit-seeking firms spend a lot of research trying to develop new products that they can patent and sell, but they do not spend much on basic research. Their incentive, instead, is to free ride on the general knowledge created by others. As a result, in the absence of any public policy, society would devote too few resources to creating new knowledge.

The government tries to provide the public good of general knowledge in various ways. Government agencies, such as the Australian Research Council and the National Health and Medical Research Council, subsidise basic research in medicine, mathematics, physics, chemistry, biology and even economics. Some people justify government funding of space programs on the grounds that it adds to society's pool of knowledge. Certainly, many private goods, including bullet-proof vests and satellite communications systems, use materials that were first developed by scientists and engineers trying to land a person on the moon. Determining the appropriate level of governmental support for basic research is difficult because the benefits are hard to measure. Moreover, the politicians who allocate funds for research usually have little expertise in science and, therefore, are not in the best position to judge what lines of research will produce the largest benefits.

Fighting poverty

Many government programs are aimed at helping the poor. Unemployment benefits provide a basic income for individuals and families who do not have adequate alternative income. The old-age pension and disability support pension benefit specific low-income groups. Those with low incomes may also receive subsidised medical services. These benefit programs are financed by taxes on people who are financially more successful.

Economists disagree among themselves about what role the government should play in fighting poverty. Although we will discuss this debate more fully in chapter 21, here we note one important argument – advocates of anti-poverty programs claim that fighting poverty is a public good. Even if everyone prefers living in a society without poverty, fighting poverty is not a 'good' that private actions will adequately provide.

To see why, suppose someone tried to organise a group of wealthy individuals to try to eliminate poverty. They would be providing a public good. This good would not be rival in consumption: One person's enjoyment of living in a society without poverty would not reduce anyone else's enjoyment of it. The good would not be excludable: Once poverty is eliminated, no one can be prevented from taking pleasure in this fact. As a result, there would be a tendency for people to free ride on the generosity of others, enjoying the benefits of poverty elimination without contributing to the cause.

Because of the free-rider problem, eliminating poverty through private charity will probably not work. Yet government action can solve this problem. Taxing the wealthy to raise the living standards of the poor can potentially make everyone better off. The poor are better off because they now enjoy a

---

CASE STUDY

Are lighthouses public goods?

Some goods can switch between being public goods and being private goods depending on the circumstances. For example, a fireworks display is a public good if performed in a town with many residents. Yet if performed at a private amusement park, such as Luna Park or Disneyland, a fireworks display is more like a private good because visitors to the park pay for admission.

Another example is a lighthouse. Economists have long used lighthouses as an example of a public good. Lighthouses are used to mark specific locations along the coast so that passing ships can avoid treacherous waters. The benefit that the lighthouse provides to ships' captains is neither excludable nor rival, so each captain has an incentive to free ride by using the lighthouse to

>>

Use of the lighthouse is free to boat owners. Does this make the lighthouse a public good?

Source: iStockphoto/Neta Degany.

In some cases, however, lighthouses may be closer to private goods. On the coast of England in the nineteenth century, some lighthouses were privately owned and operated. The owner of the local lighthouse did not try to charge ships' captains for the service but did charge the owner of the nearby port. If the port owner did not pay, the lighthouse owner turned off the light and ships avoided that port.

In deciding whether something is a public good, one must determine the number of beneficiaries and whether these beneficiaries can be excluded from enjoying the good. A free-rider problem arises when the number of beneficiaries is large and exclusion of any one of them is impossible. If a lighthouse benefits many ships' captains, it is a public good. Yet if it primarily benefits a single port owner, it is more like a private good.

navigate without paying for the service. Because of this free-rider problem, private markets usually fail to provide the lighthouses that ships' captains need. As a result, most lighthouses today are operated by the government.

higher standard of living, and those paying the taxes are better off because they enjoy living in a society with less poverty.

The difficult job of cost–benefit analysis

So far we have seen that the government provides public goods because the private market on its own will not produce an efficient quantity. Yet deciding that the government must play a role is only the first step. The government must then determine what kinds of public goods to provide and in what quantities.

Suppose that the government is considering a public project, such as building a new highway. To judge whether to build the highway, it must compare the total benefits of all those who would use it with the costs of building and maintaining it. To make this decision, the government might hire a team of economists and engineers to conduct a study, called a **cost–benefit analysis**, the goal of which is to estimate the total costs and benefits of the project to society as a whole.

cost–benefit analysis
a study that compares the costs and benefits to society of providing a public good

Cost–benefit analysts have a tough job. Because the highway will be available to everyone free of charge, there is no price with which to judge the value of the highway. Simply asking people how much they would value the highway is not reliable. First, quantifying benefits is difficult using the results from a questionnaire. Second, respondents have little incentive to tell the truth. Those who would use the highway have an incentive to exaggerate the benefit they would receive in order to get the highway built. Those who would be harmed by the highway have an incentive to exaggerate the costs to them in order to prevent the highway from being built.

The efficient provision of public goods is, therefore, intrinsically more difficult than the efficient provision of private goods. Private goods are provided in the market. Buyers of a private good reveal the value they place on it by the prices they are willing to pay. Sellers reveal their costs by the prices they are willing to accept. In contrast, cost–benefit analysts do not observe any price signals when evaluating whether the government should provide a public good. Their findings on the costs and benefits of public projects are, therefore, rough approximations at best.

Imagine that you have been elected to serve as a member of your local council. The town engineer comes to you with a proposal – the council can spend $10 000 to build and operate a traffic light at an intersection that now has only a stop sign. The benefit of the traffic light is increased safety. The engineer estimates, based on data from similar intersections, that the traffic light would reduce the risk of a fatal traffic accident over the lifetime of the traffic light from 1.6 per cent to 1.1 per cent. Should you spend the money for the new light?

Everyone would like to avoid the risk of this, but at what cost?

Source: FairfaxPhotos.com/Patrick Cummins.

To answer this question, you turn to cost–benefit analysis. But you quickly run into an obstacle – the costs and benefits must be measured in the same units if you are to compare them meaningfully. The cost is measured in dollars, but the benefit – the possibility of saving a person's life – is not directly monetary. In order to make your decision, you have to put a dollar value on a human life.

At first, you may be tempted to conclude that a human life is priceless. After all, there is probably no amount of money that you could be paid to voluntarily give up your life or that of a loved one. This suggests that a human life has an infinite dollar value.

For the purposes of cost benefit analysis, however, this answer leads to nonsensical results. If we truly placed an infinite value on human life, we should be placing traffic lights on every street corner. Similarly, we should all be driving large cars with all the latest safety features, instead of smaller ones with fewer safety features. Yet traffic lights are not at every corner and people sometimes choose to buy small cars without air bags or anti-lock braking systems. In both our public and private decisions, we are at times willing to risk our lives in order to save some money.

Once we have accepted the idea that a person's life does have an implicit dollar value, how can we determine what that value is? One approach, sometimes used by courts to award compensation for injury or death, is to look at the total amount of money a person would have earned if that person had lived. Economists are often critical of this approach. It has the bizarre implication that the life of a retired person has no value.

A better way to value human life is to look at the risks that people are voluntarily willing to take and how much they must be paid for taking them. Mortality risk varies across jobs, for example, construction workers in high-rise buildings face greater risk of death than office workers. By comparing wages in risky and less risky occupations, controlling for education, experience and other determinants of wages, economists can get some sense about what value people put on their own lives. North American studies using this approach conclude that the value of a human life is about $10 million.

We can now return to our original example and respond to the town engineer. The traffic light reduces the risk of fatality by 0.5 per cent. Thus, the expected benefit from having the traffic light is 0.005 x $10 million, or $50 000. This estimate of the benefit well exceeds the cost of $10 000, so you should approve the project.

What is the *free-rider problem*? Why does the free-rider problem induce the government to provide public goods? How should the government decide whether to provide a public good?

Common resources

Common resources, like public goods, are not excludable; they are available free of charge to anyone who wants to use them. Common resources are, however, rival; one person's use of the common resource reduces other people's enjoyment of it. Thus, common resources give rise to a new problem. Once the good is provided, policymakers need to be concerned about how much it is used. This problem is best understood from the classic parable called the **Tragedy of the Commons**.

The Tragedy of the Commons

Consider life in a small medieval English town. Of the many economic activities that take place in the town, one of the most important is raising sheep. Many of the town's families own flocks of sheep and support themselves by selling the sheep's wool, which is used to make clothing.

As our story begins, the sheep spend much of their time grazing on the land surrounding the town, called the Town Common. No family owns the land. Instead, the town residents own the land collectively and all the residents are allowed to graze their sheep on it. Collective ownership works well because land is plentiful. As long as everyone can get all the good grazing land they want, the Town Common is not a rival good, and allowing residents' sheep to graze for free causes no problems. Everyone in the town is happy.

As the years pass, the population of the town grows and so does the number of sheep grazing on the Town Common. With a growing number of sheep and a fixed amount of land, the land starts to lose its ability to replenish itself. Eventually, the land is grazed so heavily that it becomes barren. With no grass left on the Common, raising sheep is impossible and the town's once prosperous wool industry disappears. Many families lose their source of livelihood.

What causes the tragedy? Why do the shepherds allow the sheep population to grow so large that it destroys the Town Common? The reason is that social and private incentives differ. Avoiding the destruction of the grazing land depends on the collective action of the shepherds. If the shepherds could act together, they would reduce the sheep population to a size that the Common can support. Yet no single family has an incentive to reduce the size of its own flock because each flock represents only a small part of the problem.

In essence, the Tragedy of the Commons arises because of an externality. When one family's flock grazes on the common land, it reduces the quality of the land available for other families. Because people neglect this negative externality when deciding how many sheep to own, the result is an excessive number of sheep.

If the tragedy had been foreseen, the town could have solved the problem in various ways. It could have regulated the number of sheep in each family's flock, internalised the externality by taxing sheep or auctioned off a limited number of sheep-grazing permits. That is, the medieval town could have dealt with the problem of overgrazing in the way that modern society deals with the problem of pollution.

In the case of land, however, there is a simpler solution. The town can divide up the land among town families. Each family can enclose its parcel of land with a fence and then protect it from excessive grazing. In this way, the land becomes a private good rather than a common resource. This outcome in fact occurred during the enclosure movement in England in the seventeenth century.

Tragedy of the Commons
a parable that illustrates why common resources get used more than is desirable from the standpoint of society as a whole

▸ Tragedy of the Commons

The Tragedy of the Commons is a story with a general lesson – when one person uses a common resource, other people's enjoyment of it is diminished. Because of this negative externality, common resources tend to be used excessively. The government can solve the problem by reducing use of the common resource through regulation or taxes. Alternatively, the government can sometimes turn the common resource into a private good.

IN THE NEWS . . .

THE TRAGEDY OF THE COD FISH

The Tragedy of the Commons still occurs with fishing today. Although individual countries own the rights to fish in their coastal waters, in the open ocean there is competition between fishing fleets to catch the available fish stocks. As this article shows, disputes over fishing have led to conflict between countries and almost the eradication of a fish which was once abundant in the Atlantic Ocean. Despite a ban on fishing off Newfoundland since 2003, fish stocks have not recovered.

Fished out
by Margaret Visser

'A species of fish too well known to require any description' reads the entry for cod in the *Cyclopedia of Commerce and Commercial Navigation* (1858). 'It is amazingly prolific' the article continues …

People have long enjoyed marvelling at the sheer amount, the endlessness of cod. The vast cod-grazing grounds off the American Atlantic coast may well have drawn the first Europeans to the continent … Reports … came back from America during the 16th century, of so many cod that there was scarcely room enough for the sea to hold them, so many that they could be fished by scooping with baskets … Today, cod at the once teeming Grand Banks off Newfoundland is considered an endangered species. Disaster struck very recently, and within a terrifyingly short time. In South Bay, for example, there were over a million cod in 1986; in 1996 it could be excitedly reported that the numbers had increased to fifteen thousand. What fish are left are small …

Cod, once they reach adulthood, have almost no enemies, except for humankind … We, as cod predators, have almost wiped out one of the richest resources of fish ever known …

Icelanders discovered earlier than anybody that, despite human determination to perceive cod as everlasting, cod-stocks were in fact diminishing as the 20th century progressed. This led to three Cod Wars (1958–61, 1971–72 and 1975–76), in which Britain, with the help of Germany, refused to accept Iceland's declaration of ownership of the seas 19 km around its coast. Iceland felt that it needed to control its waters in order to conserve the cod; Britain had overfished the North Sea, and sought fresh pastures …

All the practices of global merchandising are exemplified by the strategies of modern cod fishing. Desirable fish are kept; the rest are tossed back overboard, dead. Radio keeps the ships up to date as to what fish are wanted and not wanted.

If a fishing ground yields no more, the ships simply leave for somewhere not yet exhausted … The warnings of fishermen that the cod stocks were reducing went unheard, as factory ships continued hauling in their catch …

Fish farming can help us undo some of the damage we have done, but farmed fish need to be fed from resources of mackerel, herring and capelin which are expensive and themselves not in endless supply …

The great cod catastrophe may teach the required lessons – or it may not … Dare we hope that, as New Foundlanders put it, the cod 'come back'? – that, having learned something, we may yet be let off this particular hook?

Source: Copyright © 1997 by Mark Kurlansky.
From: *COD: A biography of the Fish That Changed the World* by Mark Kurlansky.
Reprinted by permission of Bloomsbury USA.

This lesson has been known for thousands of years. The ancient Greek philosopher Aristotle pointed out the problem: 'What is common to many is taken least care of, for all men have greater regard for what is their own than for what they possess in common with others'.

Some important common resources

There are many examples of common resources. In almost all cases, the same problem arises as in the Tragedy of the Commons – private decision makers use the common resource too much. Governments often regulate behaviour or impose fees in order to lessen the problem of overuse.

Clean air and global warming

As we discussed in chapter 10, markets do not adequately protect the environment. Pollution, such as greenhouse gas emissions, is a negative externality that can be remedied with regulations, corrective taxes or an emissions trading scheme. One can view this market failure as an example of a common-resource problem. The atmosphere is a common resource like open grazing land and excessive pollution is like excessive grazing. Environmental degradation and global warming are like a modern Tragedy of the Commons.

Oil deposits

Consider an oilfield so large that it lies under many properties with different owners. Any of the owners can drill and extract the oil, but when one owner extracts oil, less is available for the others. The oil is a common resource.

Just as the number of sheep grazing on the Town Common was inefficiently large, the number of wells drawing from the oilfield will be inefficiently large. Because each owner who drills a well imposes a negative externality on the other owners, the benefit to society of drilling a well is less than the benefit to the owner who drills it. That is, drilling a well can be privately profitable even when it is socially undesirable. If owners of the properties decide individually how many oil wells to drill, they will drill too many.

To ensure that the oil is extracted at lowest cost, some type of joint action among the owners is necessary to solve the common-resource problem. The Coase theorem, which we discussed in chapter 10, suggests that a private solution might be possible. The owners could reach an agreement among themselves about how to extract the oil and divide the profits. In essence, the owners would then act as if they were in a single business. Companies that own the right to drill for oil or gas from a single field often form production joint ventures. The companies jointly determine the total amount of oil or gas that is extracted and internalise the negative externality.

Congested roads

Roads can be either public goods or common resources. If a road is not congested, then one person's use does not affect anyone else. In this case, use is not rival in consumption, and the road is a public good. Yet if a road is congested, then use of that road yields a negative externality. When one person drives on the road, it becomes more crowded, and other people must drive more slowly. In this case, the road is a common resource.

One way for the government to overcome the problem of road congestion is to charge drivers a toll. A toll is, in essence, a corrective tax on the externality of congestion. Sometimes, as in the case of suburban roads, tolls are not a practical solution because the cost of collecting them is too high.

But several major cities, including London and Singapore, have found increasing tolls to be a very effective way to reduce congestion.

Sometimes congestion is a problem only at certain times of day. If a bridge is heavily travelled only during rush hour, for instance, the congestion externality is larger during this time than during other times of day. The efficient way to deal with these externalities is to charge higher tolls during rush hour. This toll would provide an incentive for drivers to alter their schedules in order to reduce traffic when congestion is greatest.

Another policy that responds to the problem of road congestion is the tax on petrol. Petrol is a complementary good to driving; an increase in the price of petrol tends to reduce the quantity of driving demanded. Therefore, a petrol tax reduces road congestion.

A petrol tax, however, is an imperfect solution to road congestion. The problem is that the petrol tax affects other decisions besides the amount of driving on congested roads. For example, the petrol tax discourages driving on uncongested roads, even though there is no congestion externality for these roads.

IN THE NEWS . . .

THE CASE FOR TOLL ROADS

Many economists think that drivers should be charged for the congestion that they create on our roads. This article explains why.

Why you'll love paying for roads that used to be free

by Eric A. Morris

To end the scourge of traffic congestion, Julius Caesar banned most carts from the streets of Rome during daylight hours. It didn't work – traffic jams just shifted to dusk. Two thousand years later, we have put a man on the moon and developed garments infinitely more practical than the toga, but we seem little nearer to solving the congestion problem.

If you live in a city, particularly a large one, you probably need little convincing that traffic congestion is frustrating and wasteful. According to the Texas Transportation Institute, the average American urban traveler lost 38 hours, nearly one full work week, to congestion in 2005. And congestion is getting worse, not better; urban travelers in 1982 were delayed only 14 hours that year.

Americans want action, but unfortunately there aren't too many great ideas about what that action might be. As Anthony Downs's excellent book *Still Stuck in Traffic: Coping With Peak-Hour Traffic Congestion* chronicles,

most of the proposed solutions are too difficult to implement, won't work, or both.

Source: Shutterstock/Zhu Difeng.

Fortunately, there is one remedy which is both doable and largely guaranteed to succeed. In the space of a year or two we could have you zipping along the 405 or the LIE at the height of rush hour at a comfortable 55 miles per hour.

There's just one small problem with this silver bullet for congestion: many people seem to prefer the werewolf. Despite its merits, this policy, which is known as 'congestion pricing',

>>

'value pricing', or 'variable tolling', is not an easy political sell.

For decades, economists and other transportation thinkers have advocated imposing tolls that vary with congestion levels on roadways. Simply put, the more congestion, the higher the toll, until the congestion goes away.

To many people, this sounds like a scheme by mustache-twirling bureaucrats and their academic apologists to fleece drivers out of their hard-earned cash. Why should drivers have to pay to use roads their tax dollars have already paid for? Won't the remaining free roads be swamped as drivers are forced off the tolled roads? Won't the working-class and poor be the victims here, as the tolled routes turn into 'Lexus lanes'?

And besides, adopting this policy would mean listening to economists, and who wants to do that?

There's a real problem with this logic, which is that, on its own terms, it makes perfect sense (except for the listening to economists part). Opponents of tolls are certainly not stupid, and their arguments deserve serious consideration. But in the end, their concerns are largely overblown, and the benefits of tolling swamp the potential costs.

Unfortunately, it can be hard to convey this because the theory behind tolling is somewhat complex and counterintuitive. This is too bad, because variable tolling is an excellent public policy. Here's why: the basic economic theory is that when you give out something valuable – in this case, road space – for less than its true value, shortages result.

Ultimately, there's no free lunch; instead of paying with money, you pay with the effort and time needed to acquire the good. Think of Soviet shoppers spending their lives in endless queues to purchase artificially low-priced but exceedingly scarce goods. Then think of Americans who can fulfill nearly any consumerist fantasy quickly but at a monetary cost. Free but congested roads have left us shivering on the streets of Moscow.

To consider it another way, delay is an externality imposed by drivers on their peers. By driving onto a busy road and contributing to congestion, drivers slow the speeds of others – but they never have to pay for it, at least not

directly. In the end, of course, everybody pays, because as we impose congestion on others, others impose it on us. This degenerates into a game that nobody can win.

Markets work best when externalities are internalized: i.e., you pay for the hassle you inflict on others ... Using tolls to help internalize the congestion externality would somewhat reduce the number of trips made on the most congested roads at the peak usage periods; some trips would be moved to less congested times and routes, and others would be foregone entirely. This way we would cut down on the congestion costs we impose on each other.

Granted, tolls cannot fully cope with accidents and other incidents, which are major causes of delay. But pricing can largely eliminate chronic, recurring congestion. No matter how high the demand for a road, there is a level of toll that will keep it flowing freely.

To make tolling truly effective, the price must be right. Too high a price drives away too many cars and the road does not function at its capacity. Too low a price and congestion isn't licked.

The best solution is to vary the tolls in real time based on an analysis of current traffic conditions. Pilot toll projects on roads (like the I-394 in Minnesota and the I-15 in Southern California) use sensors embedded in the pavement to monitor the number and speeds of vehicles on the facility.

A simple computer program then determines the number of cars that should be allowed in. The computer then calculates the level of toll that will attract that number of cars – and no more. Prices are then updated every few minutes on electronic message signs. Hi-tech transponders and antenna arrays make waiting at toll booths a thing of the past.

The bottom line is that speeds are kept high (over 45 m.p.h.) so that throughput is higher than when vehicles are allowed to crowd all at once onto roadways at rush hour, slowing traffic to a crawl.

To maximize efficiency, economists would like to price all travel, starting with the freeways. But given that elected officials have no burning desire to lose their jobs, a more realistic option, for now, is to toll just some freeway lanes that are either new capacity or underused carpool lanes. The other lanes would be left free – and congested. Drivers will then have a choice: wait or pay. Granted, neither is ideal. But right now drivers have no choice at all.

What's the bottom line here? The state of Washington recently opened congestion-priced lanes on its State Route 167. The peak toll in the first month of operation (reached on the evening of Wednesday, May 21) was $5.75. I know, I know, you would never pay such an exorbitant amount when America has taught you that free roads are your birthright. But that money bought Washington drivers a 27-minute time savings. Is a half hour of your time worth $6?

I think I already know the answer, and it is 'it depends'. Most people's value of time varies widely depending on their activities on any given day. Late for picking the kids up from daycare? Paying $6 to save a half hour is an incredible bargain. Have to clean the house? The longer your trip home takes, the better. Tolling will introduce a new level of flexibility and freedom into your life, giving you the power to tailor your travel costs to fit your schedule.

Source: Eric A. Morris/Freakonomics blog, 6 January 2009.

Fish, whales and other wildlife

Many species of animals are common resources. As discussed above, fish, for instance, have commercial value, and anyone can go to the ocean and catch whatever is available. Each person has little incentive to maintain the species for the next year. Just as excessive grazing can destroy the Town Common, excessive fishing can destroy commercially valuable marine populations.

Oceans remain one of the least regulated common resources. Two problems prevent an easy solution. First, many countries have access to the oceans, so any solution would require international cooperation among countries that hold different values. Second, because the oceans are so vast, enforcing any agreement is difficult. As a result, fishing rights have been a frequent source of international tension among normally friendly countries.

Within Australia, various laws aim to protect wildlife. For example, the government restricts duck hunting to a limited season each year. It also restricts the types of duck that may be hunted. These laws regulate the use of a common resource and help maintain the duck population.

Throughout history, many species of animals have been threatened with extinction. When Europeans first arrived in North America, more than 60 million buffalo roamed the continent. Yet hunting the buffalo was so popular during the nineteenth century that by 1900 the animal's population fell to about 400 before the government stepped in to protect the species. In some African countries today, the elephant faces a similar challenge, as poachers kill the animals for the ivory in their tusks.

Yet not all animals with commercial value face this threat. The cow, for example, is a valuable source of food, but no one worries that the cow will soon be extinct. Indeed, the great demand for beef seems to ensure that the species will continue to thrive.

Why is the commercial value of ivory a threat to the elephant, and the commercial value of beef a guardian of the cow? The reason is that elephants are a common resource, whereas cows are a private good. Elephants roam freely without any owners. Each poacher has a strong incentive to kill as many elephants as he can find. Because poachers are numerous, each poacher has only a slight incentive to preserve the elephant population. In contrast, cows live on cattle stations that are privately owned. Station owners take great care to maintain the cow population on their stations because they reap the benefit of their efforts.

>>

Will the market protect me?

Source: photos.com/Getty Images.

Governments have tried to solve the elephant's problem in two ways. Some countries, such as Kenya, Tanzania and Uganda, have made it illegal to kill elephants and sell their ivory. Yet these laws have been hard to enforce, and elephant populations have continued to dwindle. In contrast, other countries, such as Botswana, Malawi, Namibia and Zimbabwe, have made elephants a private good by allowing people to kill elephants, but only those on their own property. Landowners now have an incentive to preserve the species on their own land and, as a result, elephant populations have started to rise. With private ownership and the profit motive now on its side, the African elephant might someday be as safe from extinction as the cow.

Why do governments try to limit the use of common resources?

Conclusion: The importance of property rights

In this chapter and the previous one, we have seen there are some 'goods' that the market does not provide adequately. Markets do not ensure that the air we breathe is clean or that our country is defended from foreign aggressors. Instead, societies rely on the government to protect the environment and to provide defence.

Although the problems we considered in these chapters arise in many different markets, they share a common theme. In all cases, the market fails to allocate resources efficiently because property rights are not well established. That is, some item of value does not have an owner with the legal authority to control it. For example, although no one doubts that the 'good' of clean air or defence is valuable, no one has the right to attach a price to it and profit from its use. A factory pollutes too much because no one charges the factory for the pollution it emits. The market does not provide for defence because no one can charge those who are defended for the benefit they receive.

When the absence of property rights causes a market failure, the government can potentially solve the problem. Sometimes, as in the sale of pollution permits, the solution is for the government to help define property rights and thereby unleash market forces. At other times, as in the restriction on hunting seasons, the solution is for the government to regulate private behaviour. At still other times, as in the provision of defence, the solution is for the government to supply a good that the market fails to supply. In all cases, if the policy is well planned and well run, it can make the allocation of resources more efficient and thus raise economic wellbeing.

Summary

- Goods differ in whether they are excludable and whether they are rival in consumption. A good is excludable if it is possible to prevent someone from using it. A good is rival in consumption if one person's enjoyment of the good prevents other people from enjoying the same good. Markets work best for private goods, which are both excludable and rival. Markets do not work as well for other types of goods.
- Public goods are neither rival nor excludable. Examples of public goods include fireworks displays, defence and the creation of fundamental knowledge. Because people are not charged for their use of the public good, they have an incentive to free ride when the good is provided privately. Therefore, governments provide public goods, making their decision about the quantity based on cost–benefit analysis.
- Common resources are rival but not excludable. Some examples are common grazing land, clean air and congested roads. Because people are not charged for their use of common resources, they tend to use them excessively. Therefore, governments try to limit the use of common resources.

Key concepts

club goods	excludable	public goods
common resources	free rider	rival in consumption
cost–benefit analysis	private goods	Tragedy of the Commons

Questions for review

1. Explain what is meant by a good being 'excludable'. Explain what is meant by a good being 'rival in consumption'. Is a pizza excludable? Is it rival in consumption?
2. Define and give an example of a public good. Can the private market provide this good on its own? Explain.
3. What is cost–benefit analysis of public goods? Why is it important? Why is it hard?
4. Define and give an example of a common resource. Without government intervention, will people use this good too much or too little? Why?

Problems and applications

1. The text says that both public goods and common resources involve externalities.
   a. Are the externalities associated with public goods generally positive or negative? Use examples in your answer. Is the free-market quantity of public goods generally greater or less than the efficient quantity?
   b. Are the externalities associated with common resources generally positive or negative? Use examples in your answer. Is the free-market use of common resources generally greater or less than the efficient use?
2. Think about the goods and services provided by your local government.

a Using the classification in Figure 11.1, explain what category each of the following goods falls into:
  i police protection
  ii garbage collection
  iii education
  iv rural roads
  v city streets.
b Why do you think the government provides items that are not public goods?
3 The text states that private firms will not undertake the efficient amount of basic scientific research.
  a Explain why this is so. In your answer, classify basic research into one of the categories shown in Figure 11.1.
  b What sort of policy has Australia adopted in response to this problem?
  c It is often argued that this policy increases the technological capability of Australian producers relative to that of foreign firms. Is this argument consistent with your classification of basic research in part (a)? (*Hint:* Can excludability apply to some potential beneficiaries of a public good and not others?)
4 Why is there litter along most highways but rarely in people's yards?
5 The public transport systems in some cities charge higher fares during rush hour than during the rest of the day. Why might they do this?
6 Timber companies in Australia cut down many trees on publicly owned land and on privately owned land. Discuss the likely efficiency of logging on each type of land in the absence of government regulation. How do you think the government should regulate logging on publicly owned lands? Should similar regulations apply to privately owned land?
7 An *Economist* article (19 March 1994) states: 'In the past decade, most of the rich world's fisheries have been exploited to the point of near-exhaustion'. The article continues with an analysis of the problem and a discussion of possible private and government solutions:
  a 'Do not blame fishermen for overfishing. They are behaving rationally, as they have always done.' In what sense is 'overfishing' rational for fishermen?
  b 'A community, held together by ties of obligation and mutual self-interest, can manage a common resource on its own.' Explain how such management can work in principle, and what obstacles it faces in the real world.
  c 'Until 1976 most world fish stocks were open to all comers, making conservation almost impossible. Then an international agreement extended some aspects of [national] jurisdiction from 12 to 200 miles offshore.' Using the concept of property rights, discuss how this agreement reduces the scope of the problem.
  d The article notes that many governments come to the aid of suffering fishermen in ways that encourage increased fishing. How do such policies encourage a vicious cycle of overfishing?
  e 'Only when fishermen believe they are assured a long-term and exclusive right to a fishery are they likely to manage it in the same far-sighted way as good farmers manage their land.' Defend this statement.
  f What other policies to reduce overfishing might be considered?
8 In a market economy, information about the quality or function of goods and services is a valuable good in its own right. How does the private market provide this information? Can you think of any way in which the government plays a role in providing this information?
9 Do you think that the Internet is a public good? Why or why not?

10 High-income people are willing to pay more than low-income people to avoid the risk of death. For example, they are more likely to pay for safety features on cars. Do you think cost benefit analysts should take this fact into account when evaluating public projects? Consider, for instance, a rich town and a poor town, both of which are considering the installation of a traffic light. Should the rich town use a higher dollar value for a human life in making this decision? Why or why not?

Search me!

When accessing information about economics use the following keywords in any combinations you require:
- free rider problem
- Tragedy of the Commons

CourseMate

For more multimedia resources and activities on economics, visit the Economics CourseMate website.

12

The design of the tax system

Learning objectives

In this chapter you will:

- get an overview of how the Australian government raises and spends money
- examine the efficiency costs of taxes
- learn alternative ways to judge the equity of a tax system
- see why studying tax incidence is crucial for evaluating tax equity
- consider the trade-off between efficiency and equity in the design of a tax system.

Benjamin Franklin, the great eighteenth-century American statesman, once noted that 'in this world nothing is certain but death and taxes'. But perhaps *Time* magazine better summarised popular opinion: 'There is one difference between a tax collector and a taxidermist – the taxidermist leaves the hide'.

Taxes are inevitable because we, as citizens, expect our government to provide us with various goods and services. The last two chapters have started to shed light on one of the *Ten Lessons from Economics* in chapter 1 – the government can sometimes improve market outcomes. When the government remedies an externality (such as air pollution), provides a public good (such as defence) or regulates the use of a common resource (such as fish in our rivers and streams), it can raise economic wellbeing. Yet the benefits of government come with costs. For the government to perform these and its many other functions, it needs to raise revenue through taxation.

We began our study of taxation in previous chapters, where we saw how a tax on a good affects supply and demand for that good. In chapter 6 we saw that a tax reduces the quantity sold in a market, and we examined how the burden of a tax is shared by buyers and sellers, depending on the elasticities of supply and demand. In chapter 8 we examined how taxes affect economic wellbeing. We learned that taxes cause deadweight losses; the reduction in consumer and producer surplus resulting from a tax exceeds the revenue raised by the government.

In this chapter we build on these lessons to discuss the design of a tax system. We begin with a financial overview of Australian government. When we think about the tax system, it is useful to know some basic facts about how Australian governments raise and spend money. We then consider the fundamental principles of taxation. Most people agree that taxes should impose as small a cost on society as possible and that the burden of taxes should be distributed fairly. That is, the tax system should be both *efficient* and *equitable*. As we will see, however, stating these goals is easier than achieving them.

A financial overview of Australian government

How much of the nation's income does the government take as taxes? Aggregate tax revenue for 2008–09 was approximately $339 billion, or around 28 per cent of the total Australian income. This was divided between the three levels of government. The federal government collected 82 per cent of all taxes, and state governments collected 15 per cent of taxes. Local governments directly collected only 3 per cent of tax revenue.

Tax revenue, as a percentage of total Australian income, has remained relatively constant over the last 20 years. In other words, government tax income has grown at about the same rate as the income of the rest of the economy. Australians pay relatively low tax overall when compared with most other developed nations. Although taxation revenues as a percentage of total income are lower in the United States, Japan and Korea than in Australia, they are higher in Canada, New Zealand and most Western European countries. Traditionally, Australia has relied more heavily on income taxes than other developed countries. This reliance increased steadily between 1950 and 2000. Income tax made up just over half of federal government tax revenue in the late 1950s. By the late 1990s, income tax accounted for almost 75 per cent of federal tax revenue. In July 2000, the federal government introduced a goods and services tax (GST). This tax on consumption reduced the federal government's dependence on income tax revenue and in 2008–09 income tax made up about 72 per cent of total federal government tax revenue.

The overall size of government tells only part of the story. Behind the total lie thousands of individual decisions about taxes and spending. To understand the government's finances more fully, let's look at the breakdown of the total into some broad categories.

The federal government

The federal government collects about four-fifths of the taxes in our economy. It raises this money in a number of ways and it finds even more ways to spend it.

Receipts

Figure 12.1 shows federal government receipts as a percentage of total Australian income since 1970. Revenue grew in the early 1970s but has since remained relatively stable at between 22 per cent and 27 per cent of income. Table 12.1 shows the expected tax receipts of the federal government in the 2010–11 financial year. Total tax receipts in this year were $302.5 billion, a number so large that it is hard to comprehend. To bring this astronomical number down to earth, we can divide it by the size of the Australian population, which was approximately 22.5 million at the end of 2010. We then find that the average Australian paid $13 444 to the federal government.

The largest source of revenue for the federal government is the individual income tax. By 31 October each year, Australian residents who earned more than $6000 over the previous 12 months must fill out a tax form to determine how much income tax they owe the government. People are

| Figure 12.1 | Federal government receipts as a percentage of GDP |

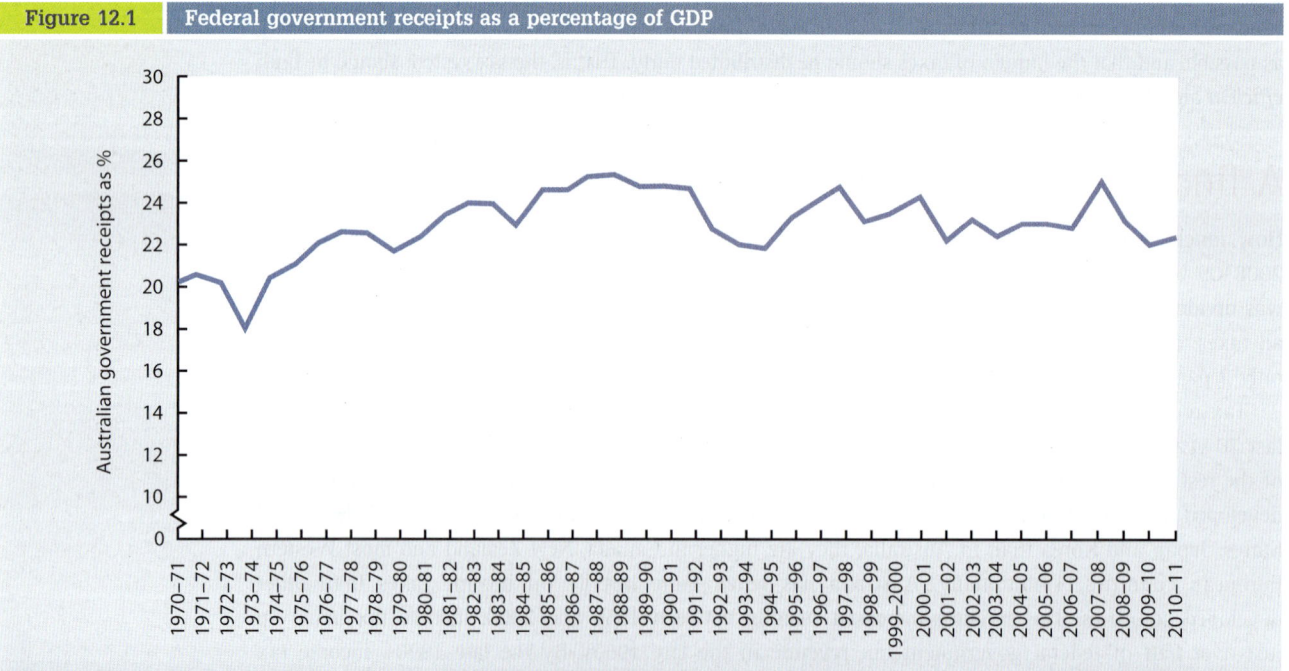

This figure shows the total receipts of the federal government as a percentage of gross domestic product (GDP), which measures total income in the economy. The figure shows that the federal government plays a large role in the Australian economy and that its role has remained fairly stable over the past 40 years.

Source: 2010–11 *Budget Paper No. 1*, statement 10, table 2 and equivalent table from previous years.

Table 12.1 Estimated tax receipts of the federal government, 2010–11			
Tax	Amount ($ billions)	Amount per person ($)	% of tax receipts
Individual income taxes	137	6088	45
Company income taxes	66.5	2956	22
Goods and services tax	50	2222	17
Excise on petroleum products	13.1	582	4
Other excises	18.9	840	6
Other taxes	17	756	6
Total	302.5	13 444	100

Source: 2010–11 *Budget Paper No. 1*, statement 5, various tables.

required to report their income from all sources: wages from working, interest on savings, dividends from companies in which they own shares, profits from any small businesses they operate and so on. People's *tax liability* (how much they owe) is then based on their total income.

A person's income tax liability is not simply proportional to that person's income. Instead, the law requires a more complicated calculation. Taxable income is calculated by subtracting deductible expenses from total income. These expenses are usually related to earning income. For example, some travel expenses related to work are deductible. Some other expenses, such as donations of more than $2 to charitable organisations, are also deductible. An individual's tax liability may also be reduced, for example, if that person is a sole parent.

Once a person has calculated taxable income, the person's tax liability is calculated using the schedule shown in Table 12.2. This table presents the marginal tax rate – the tax rate applied to each additional dollar of income. Because the marginal tax rate rises as income rises, people with higher income pay a larger percentage of their income in taxes. (We discuss the concept of marginal tax rate more fully later in this chapter.)

Table 12.2 shows the marginal income tax rates from 2010–11. These rates have slowly declined over time, particularly for 'middle income' earners. For example, in 2007, the 30 per cent marginal

Table 12.2 Federal income tax rates: 2010–11	
On taxable income …	The tax rate is …
Up to $6000	0%
From $6001 to $37 000	15
From $37 001 to $80 000	30
From $80 001 to $180 000	37
Over $180 001	45

tax rate began at an income of $34 000 rather than $37 000, while the marginal tax rate for people earning $80 000 to $180 000 per year has fallen from 40 per cent to 37 per cent.

In addition to the tax rates shown in Table 12.2, the federal government also charges people a levy of 1.5 per cent of their income. This levy partially offsets the cost of the government's universal health care program, Medicare. In the 1997–98 financial year, the federal government also introduced an extra surcharge of 1 per cent on high-income individuals and families. This surcharge is waived if the individual or family has private medical insurance and is intended to encourage high-income earners to take out this insurance.

Individual income tax made up almost half of all federal government tax revenue in 2006–07. In contrast, company income tax only makes up about 22 per cent of federal government tax revenue. The government taxes each company based on its profit – the amount the company receives for the goods or services it sells minus the costs of producing those goods or services. The company tax rate is set at 30 per cent.

Note that the federal government risks taxing company profits twice – once by company income tax when the business earns the profits and a second time by individual income tax when the company uses its profits to pay dividends to its shareholders. To limit this double taxation, the federal government allows people who receive dividend income to claim a credit for the amount of taxation already paid by the company.

In 2010–11, the GST raised about three-quarters as much revenue as company income tax. The GST applies to most of the things we buy or sell every day. The GST tax rate is set at 10 per cent and sellers must send the tax they collect to the federal government either every month or every three months, depending on the size of their business. The federal government, however, does not get to spend this revenue – the federal government passes it through to the state governments.

The federal government also receives revenue from other taxes on what we buy or sell. These taxes are called excises. The most important excise is on petroleum products, but the federal government also charges excise tax on alcoholic drinks, such as beer, and on tobacco. The government also taxes some international trade (approximately $6.7 billion). Together, excise taxes make up about one-tenth of federal government tax revenue. The 'other taxes' category in Table 12.1 is made up of a variety of taxes, including the fringe benefits tax (approximately $4 billion) and taxes on superannuation funds (approximately $7 billion). The fringe benefits tax applies when employees are given a non-monetary benefit by their employer. Superannuation funds help individuals save for retirement. While the federal government receives some revenue from taxes on these funds, the government also provides tax benefits to people if they save their income in a superannuation fund.

In addition to tax revenue, the federal government receives revenue from interest payments and from sales of products such as government publications. In 2010–11 the federal government received $19.4 billion in non-tax revenue.

Spending

Table 12.3 shows the spending of the federal government in 2010–11. Total spending was $285.8 billion, or $12 702 per person. This table also shows how the federal government's spending was divided among major categories.

The largest category in Table 12.3 is 'social security and welfare'. This involves a variety of programs including age pensions, disability support pensions and family allowances. Almost 40 per

Table 12.3 Budgeted spending of the federal government 2010–11

Category	Amount ($ billions)	Amount per person ($)	% of spending
Social security and welfare	115	5111	40.2
Health	56.9	2529	20.0
Defence	21	933	7.3
Education	32.9	1462	11.5
General public services	20.1	893	7.0
Other economic affairs	9	401	3.2
Other spending	30.9	1373	10.8
Total	$285.8	$12 702	100.0

Source: 2010–11 *Budget Paper No. 1*, statement 6.

cent of social security and welfare payments involve assistance to the aged. Another quarter of payments involve assistance to families with children.

The second largest category of spending is 'health'. The two main federal government health costs are medical benefits paid under the Medicare program and the cost of public hospitals, which the state governments operate with the help of money provided by the federal government. The federal government, using a 'stick and carrot' approach, has been trying to reduce Medicare costs by encouraging people to take out private health insurance. Middle-income earners receive the carrot – some of their private health insurance costs are reimbursed by the government. High-income earners receive the stick – if they do not take out private health insurance, they pay more income tax to the federal government.

Education makes up the next largest category of federal government expenditure. The main recipients of education funds are universities and schools. Most Australian universities are owned by government and the federal government pays over $8.1 billion to these institutions. But the process of funding higher education has changed since the late 1980s; we discuss these changes below.

Defence and 'General public services' each account for about $20 billion of federal government spending. Defence spending includes both the salaries of military personnel and the purchases of military equipment such as guns, planes and ships. Spending on defence fluctuates over time as international tensions and the political climate change. Not surprisingly, spending on defence rises substantially during wars.

'General public services' includes a variety of expenditures. The costs of operating parliament and some government departments are included in this category, as is foreign economic aid and Commonwealth-sponsored research, such as funding by the Australian Research Council.

'Other economic affairs', the sixth category in Table 12.3, includes tourist promotion, some employment training schemes and payments to economic regulators. As we will see later in this book, the federal government has passed laws to allow fair competition between firms. The organisations that enforce these laws are funded under this category of spending.

The federal government spends money in many other areas – on roads, communications, land management, national parks and so on. Rather than list all these areas, they are bundled under the final category in Table 12.3.

The federal government shares some of its tax revenue with the states. The revenue from the GST is passed on to the states. The states also receive money from the federal government that is tied to specific projects. These 'specific purpose payments' are included in Table 12.3. For example, the federal government helps pay for state-owned primary and secondary schools, and this is part of 'education' in the table. In 2010–11, the federal government paid approximately $16.3 billion to state and local governments.

In total, including GST payments to the states, the estimated spending of the federal government in 2010–11 was $354.6 billion. Total tax and non-tax receipts were lower, at $321.9 billion. This shortfall of receipts compared to spending is called a **budget deficit**. When receipts exceed spending, the government is said to run a **budget surplus**. The government finances a budget deficit by borrowing from the public. That is, it sells government debt to the private sector, including both investors in Australia and those abroad. When the government runs a budget surplus, it uses the excess receipts to reduce its outstanding debts.

budget deficit
an excess of government spending over government receipts

budget surplus
an excess of government receipts over government spending

State and local governments

State and local governments collect about 18 per cent of all taxes paid. Let's look at how they obtain tax revenue and how they spend it.

Receipts

The biggest source of revenue for state and local governments is transfers from the federal government, in particular the revenue from the GST. For example, federal government payments accounted for 46.4 per cent of Queensland state government revenue and about 50 per cent of Victorian state government revenue in 2010–11.

State governments also have their own taxes. The two most important taxes for state governments are payroll taxes and stamp duties. A payroll tax is a tax on the wages that a firm pays its workers. State governments have levied payroll taxes since 1971. Firms are usually liable for payroll tax only if their total wage bill is above a minimum threshold. For example, in New South Wales a firm pays payroll tax only if its monthly wages bill is above $50 000. Since July 2002, the payroll tax rate in New South Wales has been 6 per cent. In 2008–09, state governments raised $17 billion in payroll taxes.

Stamp duty was originally introduced in England in 1694 as a tax on certain legal documents. It is now a tax charged by the state governments on some transactions, most notably when someone buys or sells land. It raised $17 billion in total for state governments in 2008–09.

State governments also receive revenue from a variety of other taxes, such as taxes on insurance and motor vehicles. Gambling taxes are important to state governments. In 2010–11, gambling taxes raised about $1.7 billion for the Victorian state government, around 12.6 per cent of total tax revenue. In Queensland, gambling taxes raised about $0.96 billion in 2010–11, or just over 9 per cent of total tax revenue.

The main local government tax is municipal rates, which is a tax on property in the local government's area. In 2008–09 this tax totalled almost $11 billion. Local governments also receive small amounts of revenue from fees such as dog licences.

Spending

The largest expenditures for state and local governments are health and education. State governments pay much of the cost of public schools and hospitals. In total, state and local governments spend almost as much as the federal government on health and substantially more than the federal government on education.

State governments provide most of the funds to operate the public transport systems in our cities. Many of these systems operate at a loss – the amount we pay in fares does not cover the operating expense of the public transport system. State governments also fund most of our roads and the state police forces are paid for by the state governments. In addition, both state and local governments provide a variety of welfare services as well as many of our local amenities: libraries, garbage removal and park maintenance.

What are the two most important sources of tax revenue for the federal government?
What are the two most important sources of tax revenue for state and local governments?

Taxes and efficiency

Now that we have seen how Australian governments at various levels raise and spend money, let's consider how one might evaluate tax policy. Obviously, the aim of a tax system is to raise revenue for the government. But there are many ways to raise any given amount of money. In designing a tax system, policymakers have two objectives: efficiency and equity.

One tax system is more efficient than another if it raises the same amount of revenue at a smaller cost to taxpayers. What are the costs of taxes to taxpayers? The most obvious cost is the tax payment itself. This transfer of money from the taxpayer to the government is an inevitable feature of any tax system. Yet taxes also impose two other costs, which well-designed tax policy tries to avoid or, at least, minimise:

* the deadweight losses that result when taxes distort the decisions that people make
* the administrative burdens that taxpayers bear as they comply with the tax laws.

An efficient tax system is one that imposes small deadweight losses and small administrative burdens.

Deadweight losses

Taxes affect the decisions that people make. If the government taxes ice-cream, people eat less ice-cream and more frozen yoghurt. If the government taxes housing, people live in smaller houses and spend more of their income on other things. If the government taxes labour earnings, people work less and enjoy more leisure.

Because taxes distort incentives, they entail deadweight losses. As we first discussed in chapter 8, the deadweight loss of a tax is the reduction in economic wellbeing of taxpayers in excess of the amount of revenue raised by the government. The deadweight loss is the inefficiency that a tax creates as people allocate resources according to the tax incentive rather than according to the true costs and benefits of the goods and services that they buy and sell.

To recall how taxes cause deadweight losses, consider an example. Suppose that Joe places an $8 value on a pizza and Jane places a $6 value on it. If there is no tax on pizza, the price of pizza will reflect the cost of making it. Let's suppose that the price of pizza is $5, so both Joe and Jane choose to buy one. Both consumers get some surplus of value over the amount paid. Joe gets consumer surplus of $3 and Jane gets consumer surplus of $1. Total surplus is $4.

Now suppose that the government levies a $2 tax on pizza and the price of pizza rises to $7. (This occurs if supply is perfectly elastic.) Joe still buys a pizza, but now he has consumer surplus of only $1. Jane now decides not to buy a pizza because its price is higher than its value to her. The government collects tax revenue of $2 on Joe's pizza. Total consumer surplus has fallen by $3 (from $4 to $1). Because total surplus has fallen by more than the tax revenue, the tax has a deadweight loss. In this case, the deadweight loss is $1.

Notice that the deadweight loss comes not from Joe, the person who pays the tax, but from Jane, the person who doesn't. The reduction in Joe's surplus of $2 exactly offsets the amount of revenue the government collects. The deadweight loss arises because the tax causes Jane to alter her behaviour. When the tax raises the price of pizza, Jane is worse off, and yet there is no offsetting revenue to the government. This reduction in Jane's welfare is the deadweight loss of the tax.

CASESTUDY

The goods and services tax

On 1 July 2001, the Australian government introduced a new goods and services tax (GST). The GST was accompanied by a change in individual income taxes and the reduction or elimination of some other taxes, such as wholesale sales tax. These were the biggest changes in the design of Australia's tax system for at least 30 years.

The GST is a type of consumption tax. Rather than taxing the amount of income that people earn, with a consumption tax the government taxes the amount that people spend. A consumption tax can be applied just to retail sales (called a retail sales tax) or can be levied at each stage of the production process. This multistage tax is known as a value-added tax (VAT) or, as in Australia, a goods and services tax (GST).

Most developed countries have a VAT or GST. New Zealand and Canada both introduced a GST in the 1990s, before Australia. The GST in Australia is set at 10 per cent, so when you buy a pizza or hire a video, the seller has to add 10 per cent onto the price as government tax. This tax level is low by international standards. The GST in New Zealand is set at 15 per cent, while European countries such as Germany and the United Kingdom have a GST of 17.5 per cent or higher. In Denmark, the GST is 25 per cent.

The debate in Australia leading up to the introduction of the GST focused on the costs of the tax system. As we noted earlier in this chapter, in the 1990s the Australian government relied heavily on revenue from individual income tax. One of the inefficiencies caused by this tax is that it can discourage saving. A GST avoids this distortion.

Spend?

Or save?

Source: © photos.com/Getty Images.

Suppose that 25-year-old Anne is considering saving $100. If she put this money in a savings account that earns 8 per cent and leaves it there, she would have $2172 when she reaches the age of 65. Yet if the government taxes a quarter of the interest income each year, the effective interest rate is only

6 per cent. After 40 years of earning 6 per cent, the $100 grows to only $1029, less than half of what it would have been without taxation. Thus, because interest income is taxed, saving is much less attractive.

In contrast, suppose that rather than taxing income, the government taxes a quarter of consumption expenditure. Then at the age of 65, Anne has $2172 and when she spends this money one-quarter goes to the government. This leaves Anne with $1629 to spend on anything she likes, compared with $1029 under the income tax. The shift from an income tax to a consumption tax has made saving more attractive to Anne.

It was also argued that the GST would help reduce tax evasion. With a multistage tax, like the GST, it is easier for tax officials to track transactions and to check that everyone is paying the correct level of tax. But a multistage tax also requires a lot of paperwork, and some economists argued that the increase in paperwork under the GST would increase business costs and help tax evasion. Overall, the evidence on tax evasion and a GST is mixed. In India, some states have a GST while others do not. A 2010 Indian government report found that tax evasion was higher following the introduction

of a GST. However, some of the state taxes were poorly designed, making evasion relatively easy.

The introduction of the GST in Australia was strongly opposed by welfare groups who believe that a consumption tax will benefit the rich and harm the poor. If the marginal income tax rate is rising, like in Table 12.2, then those who have more income will on average pay more tax per dollar than those who have less income. But under a 10 per cent GST, rich and poor alike pay the same amount of tax when they buy a particular good or service. To reduce potential harm to the poor, the government lowered the income tax rates for people earning less than $60 000 per year. It also allowed some products to be exempt from the GST. The GST does not apply to all goods and services. Some goods and services, such as fresh food, medicine, education and child care, do not have GST included in their price. These products are exempt from GST because they are often important for the poorest people in society. The range of exemptions from a GST differs between countries. For example, in New Zealand, the GST applies to all goods and services except rental of residential property and some financial services.

Administrative burden

If you ask the typical person on 31 October for an opinion about the tax system, you might hear about the headache of filling out tax forms. The administrative burden of any tax system is part of the inefficiency it creates. This burden includes not only the time spent filling out tax return forms but also the time spent throughout the year keeping records for tax purposes and the resources the government has to use to enforce the tax laws.

More than three-quarters of individual taxpayers hire tax consultants and accountants to help them with their taxes and complete their tax return forms. This number has doubled since the late 1980s. Tax agents also help their clients arrange their affairs in a way that reduces the amount of taxes owed. This behaviour is legal tax avoidance, which is different from illegal tax evasion.

Critics of our tax system say that these advisers help their clients avoid taxes by abusing some of the detailed provisions of the tax code, often dubbed 'loopholes'. In some cases, loopholes are legislative mistakes; they arise from ambiguities or omissions in the tax laws. More often, they arise because the government has chosen to give special treatment to specific types of behaviour.

The resources devoted to complying with the tax laws are a type of deadweight loss. The government gets only the amount of taxes paid. In contrast, the taxpayer loses not only this amount but also the time and money spent documenting, calculating and avoiding taxes.

The compliance costs of the tax system involve companies as well as individuals. Companies must hire extra staff to calculate and pay income, GST and payroll taxes. Because of the complexity of the Australian tax system, the total administrative burden is likely to be very high compared with some other countries. In a 1997 article in the *Economic Record*, John Freebairn showed that the total administrative burden of the Australian tax system might be two or three times larger than that in the United Kingdom and the Netherlands, when measured as a percentage of tax revenue.

Marginal tax rates versus average tax rates

average tax rate
total taxes paid divided by total income

marginal tax rate
the extra taxes paid on an additional dollar of income

When discussing the efficiency and equity of income taxes, economists distinguish between two notions of the tax rate: the average and the marginal. The **average tax rate** is total taxes paid divided by total income. The **marginal tax rate** is the extra taxes paid on an additional dollar of income.

For example, suppose that the government taxes 20 per cent of the first $50 000 of income and 50 per cent of all income above $50 000. Under this system, a person who makes $60 000 pays a tax of $15 000 (the tax equals 0.20 × $50 000 plus 0.50 × $10 000). For this person, the average tax rate is $15 000/$60 000, or 25 per cent. But the marginal tax rate is 50 per cent because the amount of the tax would rise by $0.50 if the taxpayer earned an additional dollar.

The marginal and average tax rates each contain a useful piece of information. If we are trying to gauge the sacrifice made by a taxpayer, the average tax rate is more appropriate because it measures the fraction of income paid in taxes. In contrast, if we are trying to gauge how much the tax system distorts incentives, the marginal tax rate is more meaningful. One of the *Ten Lessons from Economics* in chapter 1 is that rational people think at the margin. A corollary to this lesson is that the marginal tax rate measures how much the tax system discourages people from working hard. If you are thinking of working an extra few hours, the marginal tax rate determines how much the government takes of your additional earnings. It is the marginal tax rate, therefore, that determines the deadweight loss of an income tax.

---

fyi

Tax avoidance and tax evasion

It is understandable that people will want to minimise their tax payments. Like the free-rider problem we encountered in chapter 11, if people can reduce their personal tax bill then this will make them better off without significantly reducing the benefits they receive from government spending.

Tax minimisation falls into two broad categories – avoidance and evasion. Tax avoidance involves taxpayers using legal loopholes in the tax system to reduce their tax payments. Tax evasion is illegal and involves taxpayers deliberately misreporting their income or expenditures.

Sometimes the line between avoidance and evasion is unclear. In seventeenth-century England, taxes were levied on the number of windows in a dwelling. The idea was that this tax would better target the wealthy who could afford better housing with more windows. To avoid paying the tax, people would block up their windows when they knew the tax collector was coming. After the tax collector left, they would then unblock the windows. Whether this practice could be classified as avoidance or evasion is debatable. Either way, it created a deadweight loss as people spent time and energy blocking and unblocking windows.

IN THE NEWS . . .

USING THE INTERNET TO AVOID TAXES

Australia has a 10 per cent Goods and Services Tax (GST). When you buy something in Australia, the price includes the GST. But when you buy the same thing from overseas, you do not pay this tax to the Australian government. So the GST raises the incentive for individuals to buy overseas and transport their purchases to Australia. When the GST was introduced in 2001, such purchases were difficult for most consumers. But the Internet has now made them easy. We can buy music, books, clothing – pretty much anything that can be transported – from overseas via the Internet. This has started to affect the sales of local retailers. As the article below shows, some of those retailers are threatening to also set up overseas Internet outlets to avoid the GST.

Myer floats tax-free website
by Eli Greenblat and Clancy Yates

The boss of Australia's biggest department store, Myer, is investigating the merits of a China-based retail website to allow customers to shop GST-free.

Bernie Brookes told a business lunch in Melbourne yesterday other leading Australian businesses such as Woolworths and Bunnings could follow Myer's plan to operate a website from China that takes orders from Australian consumers as the sector grows increasingly angry over the leakage of sales to online stores. There has been frustration with the federal government's failure to act on an estimated $20 billion in sales on overseas sites that is not taxed.

'If we can't beat them we will join them,' Mr Brookes warned. 'We just want a level playing field. We will take jobs offshore and we will ship product out of China through our internet site, it's a bloody shame.'

Mr Brookes joins other retailers demanding government action, including Harvey Norman executive chairman Gerry Harvey who last week called for the current $1000 GST-free threshold to be lowered to curb shoppers buying online from overseas suppliers.

Online shopping's popularity has increased this year as the Australian dollar hit parity with the US dollar, making millions of items on American websites significantly cheaper than here.

Mr Brookes said a motivation to look at a China-based model for Myer's department store operations was the inaction and seeming lack of interest from federal Treasurer Wayne Swan. Assistant Treasurer Bill Shorten said the government was looking at the issue, but had no plans to put the GST on online shopping.

Mr Brookes said Myer's China-based website could be up and running by February, attracting a significant portion of the company's estimated $5 million a year in existing internet sales. Goods ordered from the site, such as dresses, jeans or coats, would be packed and shipped from its hub in Shenzhen, southern China, and avoid GST charges.

A spokeswoman for David Jones said it had no plans to create an offshore website.

Source: Eli Greenblat and Clancy Yates/*The Age*, 4 December 2010.

As Table 12.2 shows, the top marginal income tax rate in Australia at present is 45 per cent and only people who earn over $180 000 per year pay this rate. But these figures are misleading. In fact some poor people pay much higher marginal tax rates, as high as 80 per cent or more. These people are effectively taxed at a very high marginal rate because when they earn an extra dollar they lose some of the benefits that the government provides to people on low incomes. Earning more money may mean lower unemployment benefits, family allowance or rent assistance.

To see how effective marginal tax rates might be very high, suppose that Tom is receiving unemployment benefits. Tom has found a small amount of work – 5 hours per week at $10 per hour.

CASESTUDY

Marginal tax rates and the poverty trap

>>

Tom's total income is the $50 per week he earns plus unemployment benefits and rent assistance worth $150 per week. His total income per week is $200 and he pays no income tax. What if Tom is offered additional work for one hour per week? If he accepts the additional work, he is paid an extra $10. Tom's income is still too low for income tax so he receives the entire $10. However, because his income has increased, Tom's unemployment benefits are reduced. For example, unemployment benefits may fall by $1 for every extra $2 that a person earns. In this case, if Tom accepts the additional work he loses $5 in unemployment benefits. Rent assistance also depends on income, so that if Tom earns an extra $10 per week he may lose $3 in rent assistance. Overall, if Tom works for an extra hour he earns $10 but loses $8 – $5 in unemployment benefits and $3 in rent assistance. Working an extra hour raises his weekly income from $200 to only $202. His effective marginal tax rate is 80 per cent.

Although the figures given in the above example are only illustrative, they reflect a general problem for the poor – the more they earn the more their government benefits are reduced. Overall, the extra work may not be worthwhile. For example, research at the University of New South Wales shows how a family with one working parent and four children, whose private income rises by $200 per week, from $500 to $700, may receive a net gain of only $20 per week because of the loss of benefits. In such circumstances, the poor are trapped by the high effective marginal tax rates.

In the 1980s, Iceland changed its tax system in a way that, as a side effect, provided a natural experiment to show how taxes affect an economy. Before the reform, people paid taxes based on their *previous* year's income. After the reform, people paid taxes based on their *current* income. Thus, taxes in 1987 were based on 1986 income, but taxes in 1988 were based on 1988 income. Income earned in 1987 was never taxed. For this one year of transition, the marginal income tax rate fell to zero.

As reported in a December 2001 article in the *American Economic Review*, the citizens of Iceland took advantage of this tax holiday. Total hours worked rose by about 3 per cent in 1987 and then fell back to the normal level in 1988. The production of goods and services in 1987 (as measured by real GDP) was 4 per cent higher than the average of the years before and the years after. This episode confirms one of the *Ten Lessons from Economics* – that people respond to incentives.

The fall in the Icelandic marginal tax rate was for one year only and this fact surely influenced the response. On the one hand, some people may have put off vacations and worked overtime to take advantage of the temporary incentive. On the other hand, no one would alter career plans, and no business would restructure its work environment, in response to an incentive that would soon disappear. A permanent change in the marginal tax rate could have either a larger or a smaller incentive effect than a temporary change.

Lump-sum taxes

lump-sum tax
a tax that is the same amount for every person

Suppose the government imposes a tax of $4000 on everyone; that is, everyone owes the same amount, regardless of earnings or any actions that a person might take. Such a tax is called a **lump-sum tax**.

A lump-sum tax shows clearly the difference between average and marginal tax rates. For a taxpayer with income of $20 000, the average tax rate of a $4000 lump-sum tax is 20 per cent; for a taxpayer with income of $40 000, the average tax rate is 10 per cent. For both taxpayers, the marginal tax rate is zero because an additional dollar of income would not change the amount of tax owed.

A lump-sum tax is the most efficient tax possible. Because a person's decisions do not alter the amount owed, the tax does not distort incentives and, therefore, does not cause deadweight losses.

IN THE NEWS . . .

REFORMING THE TAX SCHEME TO ALLEVIATE POVERTY

In the text we saw how poor people could face very high effective marginal tax rates due to the loss of benefits as their income rises. This is unfair. It also increases unemployment. For people caught in a poverty trap, it is better not to work or to work less hours. In this article, ANU economist Andrew Leigh argues that this could be avoided with some good old-fashioned targeted policies.

Help the poor, and cut taxes
by Andrew Leigh

This week's Treasury tussle featured an unusual moment, in which the debate turned to past reforms, and Peter Costello acknowledged the benefits of the macroeconomic reforms undertaken by previous Labor governments. But missed in the discussion was a chance to also consider another major shift of that era – from universal welfare to a carefully-targeted social safety net.

During the 1980s and early-1990s, means-tested public pensions, childcare benefits, and housing benefits meant that we could be proud of the way we looked after our poorest, while maintaining one of the lowest tax burdens in the developed world.

Unfortunately, the past decade has seen a steady slide away from that philosophy. With a few exceptions (such as the improved targeting of private school funding), much of the increased social spending in Australia has been devoted to universal benefits. The First Home Owner Grant, Private Healthcare Rebate, and Family Tax Benefit Part B are just three examples of policies that have enormous budgetary costs, but minimal social impact. By international standards, Australia's welfare system is still reasonably well targeted, but we're headed in the wrong direction.

Peter Saunders, from the Centre for Independent Studies, calls middle-class benefits the 'tax/welfare churn'. But this implies that the problem is simply one of moving money around. In fact, because taxes have an efficiency cost, each dollar raised in taxes reduces economic output. Estimates of the efficiency cost varies, but the best recent estimate for the 'deadweight burden' in Australia is around 20 cents in the dollar. Perhaps 'tax, burn and churn' would be a better description.

Since most middle-class welfare benefits would probably fail an economic cost-benefit test, why does a government that touts its economic credentials support it? Because middle-class welfare always passes the political cost–benefit test. The well-hewn median voter theorem has a simple prediction: Two parties competing for office will focus most of their energies on winning the support of the voter in the middle of the distribution. Targeted welfare may be good economics, but middle-class welfare is good politics. (As John Howard said last year, 'People like getting a cheque from the government.')

For its part, the Labor Party have raised questions in parliament about the wisdom of universal benefits, but have resisted calls to scrap such programs. Part of the explanation lies in the belief that universal programs are likely to be more politically robust than targeted ones: If we can put in place a program that will endure, why not accept a little waste? Yet the evidence for this argument is mixed. When the next recession hits, and the 'razor gang' comes to scrutinise at government spending, will they really preserve all those low-impact universal programs?

Moreover, there is a strong progressive argument in favour of targeted spending over universal benefits: It is more likely to reduce inequality. Rather than giving a flat education credit for two-thirds of families, why not pour more resources into improving the life chances of the neediest children?

Perhaps what we need is a new campaign advertisement, paid for by 'Australians for Helping the Poor *and* Lowering Taxes'. The commercial could start with a simple visual depiction of how middle class welfare works. A taxpayer hands over five $20 notes. The government representative calmly burns one of them, and hands back the remaining four.

>>

The voiceover could then point out that people enjoy getting the Baby Bonus, but there's little evidence that scrapping it would affect fertility rates or the wellbeing of new parents (camera shows new parents installing a plasma television). By contrast, an Indigenous child born today can expect to live as long as a non-Indigenous child born at the time of Federation (camera shows scenes from one of a dozen disadvantaged communities). If we scrapped the $1.1 billion Baby Bonus, we could put half the proceeds into tax cuts, and the other half into a series of randomised policy trials of programs designed to improve Indigenous health. Fade to black.

What is striking about middle-class welfare is that it offends values that both right and left should hold dear. Since our first major tax uprising at Eureka, Australians have resisted oppressive levels of taxation, and demanded that governments take no more from us than they need. At the same time, we have supported the underdog, reaching out a generous helping hand to those who need it most. A targeted welfare state fulfils both these principles. Middle-class welfare offends them both.

Commentators have long derided politicians who 'spin' the truth. But maybe the ones we need to watch for are those who spin our tax dollars out of our wallets and back in again – wasting 20 cents in the dollar along the way.

Source: Andrew Leigh/*Australian Financial Review*, 1 November 2007.

Because everyone can easily calculate the amount owed and because there is no benefit in hiring tax agents and accountants, the lump-sum tax imposes a minimal administrative burden on taxpayers.

If lump-sum taxes are so efficient, why do we rarely observe them in the real world? The reason is that efficiency is only one goal of the tax system. A lump-sum tax would take the same amount from the poor and the rich, an outcome most people would view as unfair. To understand the tax systems that we observe, we must therefore consider the other major goal of tax policy – equity.

 What is meant by the efficiency of a tax system? What can make a tax system inefficient?

Taxes and equity

Taxes have often been at the centre of heated (and sometimes violent) debate. Taxes contributed to the outbreak of the English civil wars in the 1640s. The Boston Tea Party in 1773, when American colonists dumped imported tea into Boston harbour, was a protest against high British taxes. The Eureka Stockade rebellion at Ballarat in 1854 was sparked by discontent over miners' licence fees.

Debate over tax policy is rarely fuelled by questions of efficiency. Instead, debate arises from disagreements over how the tax burden should be distributed. A US senator once mimicked the public debate with this rhyme:

> Don't tax you.
> Don't tax me.
> Tax that fella behind the tree.

Of course, if we are to rely on the government to provide some of the goods and services we want, taxes must fall on someone. In this section we consider the equity of a tax system. How should the burden of taxes be divided among the population? How do we evaluate whether a tax system is fair?

Everyone agrees that the tax system should be equitable, but there is much disagreement about what equity means and how the equity of a tax system can be judged.

The benefits principle

One principle of taxation, called the **benefits principle**, states that people should pay taxes based on the benefits they receive from government services. This principle tries to make public goods similar to private goods. It seems fair that a person who often goes to the pictures pays more in total for picture tickets than a person who rarely goes. Similarly, a person who gets great benefit from a public good should pay more for it than a person who gets little benefit.

Petrol tax, for instance, is sometimes justified using the benefits principle. Road construction and maintenance are expensive and it seems only fair that those who use the roads should pay these costs. Because those who buy petrol are the same people who use the roads, a petrol tax might be viewed as a fair way to pay for this government service.

The benefits principle can also be used to argue that wealthy citizens should pay higher taxes than poorer ones. Why? Simply because the wealthy benefit more from public services. Consider, for example, the benefits of police protection from theft. Citizens with much to protect get greater benefit from police than do those with less to protect. Therefore, according to the benefits principle, the wealthy should contribute more than the poor to the cost of maintaining the police force. The same argument can be used for many other public services, such as fire protection, national defence and the court system.

It is even possible to use the benefits principle to argue for anti-poverty programs funded by taxes on the wealthy. As we discussed in chapter 11, people may prefer living in a society without poverty, suggesting that anti-poverty programs are a public good. If the wealthy place a greater dollar value on this public good than the middle class do, perhaps just because they have more to spend, then, according to the benefits principle, they should be taxed more heavily to pay for these programs.

The benefits principle is sometimes called 'user pays'. For government-provided services such as water, sewerage and, in some states, electricity, it seems fair that those who use relatively more of the service pay relatively more for the service.

The ability-to-pay principle

Another way to evaluate the equity of a tax system is called the **ability-to-pay principle**, which states that taxes should be levied on a person according to how well that person can shoulder the burden. This principle is sometimes justified by the claim that all citizens should make an 'equal sacrifice' to support the government. The magnitude of a person's sacrifice, however, depends not only on the size of the individual's tax payment but also on that person's income and other circumstances. A $1000 tax paid by a poor person may require a larger sacrifice than a $10 000 tax paid by a rich person.

The ability-to-pay principle leads to two corollary notions of equity: **vertical equity** and **horizontal equity**. Vertical equity states that taxpayers with a greater ability to pay taxes should contribute a larger amount. Horizontal equity states that taxpayers with similar abilities to pay should contribute the same amount. Although these notions of equity are widely accepted, applying them to evaluate a tax system is rarely straightforward.

Vertical equity

If taxes are based on ability to pay, then richer taxpayers should pay more than poorer taxpayers. But how much more should the rich pay? Much of the debate over tax policy concerns this question.

benefits principle
the idea that people should pay taxes based on the benefits they receive from government services

ability-to-pay principle
the idea that taxes should be levied on a person according to how well that person can shoulder the burden

vertical equity
the idea that taxpayers with a greater ability to pay taxes should pay larger amounts

horizontal equity
the idea that taxpayers with similar abilities to pay taxes should pay the same amount

Table 12.4 **Three tax systems**						
	Proportional tax		Regressive tax		Progressive tax	
Income	Amount of tax	Percentage of income	Amount of tax	Percentage of income	Amount of tax	Percentage of income
$50 000	$12 500	25	$15 000	30	$10 000	20
100 000	25 000	25	25 000	25	25 000	25
200 000	50 000	25	40 000	20	60 000	30

proportional tax
a tax for which high-income and low-income taxpayers pay the same fraction of income

regressive tax
a tax for which high-income taxpayers pay a smaller fraction of their income than do low-income taxpayers

progressive tax
a tax for which high-income taxpayers pay a larger fraction of their income than do low-income taxpayers

▸ regressive tax

▸ progressive tax

Consider the three tax systems in Table 12.4. In each case, taxpayers with higher incomes pay more. Yet the systems differ in how quickly taxes rise with income. The first system is called **proportional** because all taxpayers pay the same fraction of income. The second system is called **regressive** because high-income taxpayers pay a smaller fraction of their income, even though they pay a larger amount. The third system is called **progressive** because high-income taxpayers pay a larger fraction of their income.

Which of these three tax systems is most fair? There is no obvious answer and economic theory does not offer any help in trying to find one. Equity, like beauty, is in the eye of the beholder.

Horizontal equity

If taxes are based on ability to pay, then similar taxpayers should pay similar amounts of taxes. But what determines if two taxpayers are similar? People differ in many ways. To evaluate whether a tax code is horizontally equitable, one must determine which differences are relevant to a taxpayer's ability to pay and which differences are not.

Suppose the Smith and Jones families each have an income of $100 000. The Smiths have no children, but Mr Smith has an illness that causes medical expenses of $10 000. The Joneses are in good health, but they have four children. Two of the Jones children are in private secondary schools, generating school fees of $20 000. Would it be fair for these two families to pay the same tax because they have the same income? Would it be fairer to give the Smiths a tax break to help them offset their high medical expenses? Would it be fairer to give the Joneses a tax break to help them with their education expenses?

CASESTUDY

How the burden of taxes is distributed

Much of the debate over tax policy concerns whether the wealthy pay their fair share of taxes. There is no purely objective way to make this judgement. In evaluating this issue for yourself, however, it is useful to know how much families with different incomes pay under the current tax system.

Table 12.5 shows how some selected taxes are distributed among income classes. To construct this table, people were ranked according to their household's income and placed into five groups of equal size, called quintiles. The first row of the table shows the average weekly income of each person's household, which includes private income and direct social security payments. The poorest one-fifth had an average income of $295.00 per week; the richest one-fifth had an average income of $2063.60 per week.

The other rows compare the distribution of personal income taxes and selected indirect taxes among these five groups. The poorest group paid 1.4 per cent of their income as personal income tax

Table 12.5 The burden of selected Australian taxes, 2001–02

	Persons by quintile of equivalent household disposable income				
	Lowest 20%	Second	Third	Fourth	Highest 20%
Gross household income ($ per week)	295.0	609.1	929.6	1288.9	2063.6
Taxes paid as share of gross income (%):					
Personal income tax	1.4	8.5	15.8	19.9	26.0
Selected indirect taxes	20.5	14.1	12.3	10.3	8.9

Calculated from: National Centre for Social and Economic Modelling, *The Distribution of Taxes and Government Benefits in Australia.* Ann Harding, Rachel Lloyd and Neil Warren. 2004. www.natsem.canberra.edu.au/publications/papers/cps/cp04/2004_008/cp2004_008.pdf

on average, but paid 20.5 per cent of their income on indirect taxes. The richest group paid 26.0 per cent of their income as personal income tax on average, but only 8.9 per cent of their income went to pay indirect taxes.

The table shows that personal income tax payments are progressive. Richer households tend to pay more of their income as personal income tax. But the degree of progressivity is less than we would expect simply by looking at the personal income tax rates. This suggests that higher income earners are able to use various loopholes in the tax system to reduce income tax payments.

Although income tax payments are progressive, the table shows that indirect taxes are regressive when expressed as a share of income. Poor households tend to spend most of their income and save little and indirect taxes apply to consumption. As a result, the poor pay a relatively larger share of their income on indirect taxes than do the rich.

There are no easy answers to these questions. In practice, the Australian income tax system is filled with special provisions that alter an individual's tax based on specific circumstances.

When Gough Whitlam's Labor government was elected in 1972, one of its main policies was to remove university fees. Instead of students or their families paying for university education, the state would pay through tax revenue.

Supporters of state-paid university education argued that it would help the poor and disadvantaged. If they had to pay fees, students from poor families might be excluded from university even if they had achieved excellent results at secondary school. In addition, they argued that education was like a public good. Society gains from having more doctors, architects and engineers, so it is only fair that society pays.

Opponents of state-paid university education argued that most students going to university are from relatively well-off families. Having the government pay university fees would be inequitable because poor families would be paying through their taxes to educate well-off students. They also disputed the public good argument. Society may gain from having trained professionals, but this is a private benefit that we pay for when we visit the doctor or employ an engineer. As university graduates tend to earn high wages, it seems unfair that taxpayers should pay twice for this private benefit.

CASESTUDY

Who should pay for higher education?

>>

In 1989, the Hawke Labor government introduced an innovative program to share the costs of university education between the student and the taxpayer. To avoid disadvantaging poor students, no student would have to pay fees before beginning university. Instead, the government would 'lend' the student the money. Further, to make sure that those students who received mainly private benefits from university education paid more of the costs of this education, loan repayments would be based on income that students earn after completing their studies.

This higher education contribution scheme, or HECS, was a world first. It has been modified since its introduction. For example, under the original HECS, students' future payments per course did not depend on which courses they enrolled in each year. The Howard Coalition government altered this in 1997 so that students in Law and Medicine paid more HECS than students in Computing and Economics, who themselves paid more than Arts and Nursing students. Under the original HECS scheme, students repaid their HECS loan only when their annual income exceeded the Australian average –

approximately $32 000. This threshold has been changed a number of times and in 2004 students had to begin to repay their HECS debt even if their income was only $25 348 per year. From 2005, each university had the discretion to set higher HECS charges, subject to government limitations, but the HECS income repayment threshold was raised to $35 000 per year. The repayment threshold rises over time. In 2011–12 it is $44 912.

The success of the HECS scheme has led to its imitation in other countries. England introduced a similar scheme for university funding in 1998. The HECS scheme has also been extended in Australia, and is now part of the broader higher education loan program (HELP). The original scheme only applied to undergraduate degrees, but in 2002 the government introduced a similar scheme for postgraduate students. Although there is argument over the policy details of the HECS/ HELP scheme, most economists would agree that it has created a more equitable split of the burden of higher education between the student and the taxpayer.

Tax incidence and tax equity

Tax incidence – the study of who bears the burden of taxes – is central to evaluating tax equity. As we first saw in chapter 6, the person who bears the burden of a tax is not always the person who gets the tax bill from the government. Because taxes alter supply and demand, they alter equilibrium prices. As a result, they affect people beyond those who, according to statute, actually pay the tax. When evaluating the vertical and horizontal equity of any tax, it is important to take account of these indirect effects.

Many discussions of tax equity ignore the indirect effects of taxes and are based on what economists derisively call the *flypaper theory* of tax incidence. According to this theory, the burden of a tax, like a fly on flypaper, sticks wherever it first lands. That assumption, however, is rarely valid.

For example, a person not trained in economics might argue that a tax on sports cars is vertically equitable because most buyers of sports cars are wealthy. Yet if these buyers can easily substitute other luxuries for sports cars, then a tax on sports cars might reduce only the sale of these cars. In the end, the burden of the tax will fall more on those who make and sell sports cars than on those who buy them. Because most workers who make and sell cars are not wealthy, the equity of a tax on sports cars could be quite different from what the flypaper theory indicates.

IN THE NEWS . . .

THE HECS EXPERIENCE

Australia was a world leader in using government income-contingent loans to pay for higher education. In this article, Ross Gittins looks at plans by Bruce Chapman, one of the designers of the HECS scheme and a Professor at the Australian National University, to extend it beyond higher education.

One HECS of a broader solution

by Ross Gittins

Has it ever occurred to you that one of the main roles of government is to help you manage some of the many risks you face in living your life? It probably hasn't. But when you think about it, it's obvious. That's what the welfare state is for.

There's a risk, for instance, of you being suddenly struck down by a major illness or accident. In a developing country, such an eventuality could reduce you and your family to penury. For us, however, a public ambulance whips you off to hospital, where Medicare ensures you get fixed up without charge.

Were the accident to have happened at work, of course, your expenses – including living expenses – are covered by the workers' compensation insurance the government obliges your employer to take out. Were some other accident to leave you physically or mentally incapacitated, the welfare state ensures you don't starve by providing you with a disability support pension.

Say you can't find a job to support yourself and your family. The welfare state keeps you off the breadline by giving you the dole. At least until WorkChoices, permanent employees who found their services no longer needed could expect a redundancy payment to help tide them over.

Or, say you just become too old to keep working. The government manages the problem by giving you the age pension to live on. Too frugal for your taste? That's why, of late, the government has made it compulsory for 9 per cent of your salary to be put away for you in superannuation savings.

All these things – and many more – are examples of the way governments are ready to manage the risks we run in everyday life. You could also say governments have road rules and speed limits to minimise the risk in crossing the road.

In his book *Government Managing Risk*, published by Routledge, Professor Bruce Chapman, of the Australian National University, expounds on a relatively new instrument governments can use to manage risk, 'income-contingent loans'. These are particularly useful for providing default insurance and consumption smoothing.

Never heard of it? Of course you have. You know it as HECS – the higher education contribution scheme. If you've always thought of HECS as just an impost on our young people you haven't understood its subtleties. The impost is the government's requirement that uni students make a contribution towards the cost of their tuition.

In some other countries, most would have to take out a commercial loan to pay their tuition fees. But not here – here they're able to pay with HECS. One advantage of HECS is that the interest rate charged is no higher than the inflation rate – usually only 2 or 3 per cent a year.

But the other great attraction of HECS is that repayments are income-contingent. That is, they vary with your income. You don't have to make any repayments until your income exceeds about $38 000 a year and thereafter the size of your repayments rises with your income according to a sliding scale.

With an ordinary commercial loan, you're required to make fixed, predetermined repayments come hell or high water. With HECS, if your income falls for any reason, the size of your repayments falls, too. If you lost your job and couldn't find another, so that your income fell back below $38 000, your repayments would cease for as long as you remained below the threshold.

This is why income-contingent loans are said to involve default insurance. Being unable to make repayments doesn't put you in default of the loan contract. And you can see how

>>

repayments that vary with your income help to smooth your consumption spending.

In these ways HECS, being a form of income-contingent loan, turns out to be an instrument government uses to help students manage the risks they run in incurring debts to pay their tuition fees.

One of the great practical advantages of HECS from the Government's perspective is that repayments are collected compulsorily through the tax system, thus reducing collection costs and bad debts.

HECS is an Australian invention. Since we introduced it in 1989 it has been copied in six other countries, including New Zealand, South Africa, Chile, Thailand and Britain.

With help from various contributors, Chapman makes the point that income-contingent loans could be used for many purposes beside tuition fees.

One possible use is for drought assistance. Rather than being given grants, farmers could receive income-contingent loans. The speed with which their incomes recovered after the drought would determine the speed with which the loan was repaid.

Shifting from grants to loans would be fairer. Why? Because the average owner of a drought-stricken property is a lot wealthier than the average taxpayer is. The farmers' problem isn't poverty, it is lack of ready capital to tide them over. Income-contingent loans would give help when it was needed while allowing repayment when it could be afforded.

Income-contingent loans would reduce the risk of farmers defaulting on their commercial loans and allow them to smooth their consumption between the good years and the bad.

Income-contingent loans could also be used to help people pay fines imposed on them by criminal courts. Courts can be reluctant to impose fines – or reluctant to impose fines as high as they should be – because they know the offenders don't have the money to pay.

So the court knows it will probably end up having to jail the offender for non-payment. But not if an income-contingent loan were available.

Another, highly pertinent application would be to use income-contingent loans to help low-income households facing eviction or mortgage default because of a temporary shortage of income due to job loss. As they found employment and their income recovered they could begin repaying the loan.

You see how these various applications involve tiding people over when they're hit by sudden but temporary shocks. You see, too, how much of what governments do involves helping people manage and minimise the risks attendant on daily life.

It would help for all of us – politicians and bureaucrats, voters and taxpayers – to see more clearly that this is what governments do. It then becomes easier to see how much use we could be making of assistance by means of income-contingent loans.

Source: Ross Gittins/*Sydney Morning Herald*,
28 March 2007.

CASESTUDY

Who pays company income tax?

Company income tax provides a good example of the importance of tax incidence for tax policy. Company taxes are popular among voters. After all, a company is not a person. Voters are always eager to have their taxes reduced and have some impersonal corporation pick up the tab.

But before deciding that the company tax is a good way for the government to raise revenue, we should consider who bears the burden of the tax. This is a difficult question on which economists disagree, but one thing is certain – *people pay all taxes*. When the government levies a tax on a company, the company is more like a tax collector than a taxpayer. The burden of the tax ultimately falls on people – the owners, customers or workers of the firm.

Many economists believe that workers and customers bear much of the burden of company tax. To see why, consider an example. Suppose that the Australian government decides to raise the tax on the income earned by car companies. At first, this tax hurts the owners of the car companies, who receive less profit. But, over time, these owners will respond to the tax. Because producing cars is less profitable, they invest less in building new car factories.

Instead, they invest their wealth in other ways – for example, by buying larger houses or by building factories in other industries or other countries. With fewer car factories, the supply of cars declines, as does the demand for car workers. Thus, a tax on companies making cars causes the price of cars to rise and the wages of car workers to fall.

The company tax shows how dangerous the flypaper theory of tax incidence can be. Company tax is popular in part because it appears to be paid by rich corporations. Yet those who bear the ultimate burden of the tax – the customers and workers of firms – are often not rich. If the true incidence of the company tax were more widely known, this tax might be less popular among voters.

Explain the benefits principle and the ability-to-pay principle. What are vertical equity and horizontal equity? Why is studying tax incidence important for determining the equity of a tax system?

Conclusion: The trade-off between equity and efficiency

Almost everyone agrees that equity and efficiency are the two most important goals of a tax system. But these two goals often conflict. Many proposed changes to the tax laws increase efficiency while reducing equity, or increase equity while reducing efficiency. People disagree about tax policy often because they attach different weights to these two goals.

Over the past decade, Australia has experienced a major change in its tax system. The introduction of the GST has changed the way tax is collected in Australia. It has also changed the relationship between state and federal governments. While the federal government collects the GST revenue, it passes it on to the state governments. The old Australian tax system had many problems. It relied too heavily on income taxation, it was complex and had high compliance costs, and it was unfair and inequitable. At the same time, it has also been claimed that the new tax system is too complex, has even higher compliance costs and is even more inequitable.

Economics alone cannot determine the best way to balance the goals of efficiency and equity. This issue involves political philosophy as well as economics. But economists do have an important role in the political debate over tax policy; they can shed light on the trade-offs that society faces and can help us avoid policies that sacrifice efficiency without any benefit in terms of equity.

Summary

- Australian governments raise revenue using various taxes. The most important taxes for the federal government are individual and company income taxes. The federal government also collects the goods and services tax (GST), and passes the revenue from this tax to the state governments. The most important taxes for state and local governments are payroll taxes and municipal rates.
- The efficiency of a tax system refers to the costs it imposes on taxpayers. There are two costs of taxes beyond the transfer of resources from the taxpayer to the government. The first is the distortion in the allocation of resources that arises as taxes alter incentives and behaviour. The second is the administrative burden of complying with the tax laws.
- The equity of a tax system concerns whether the tax burden is distributed fairly among the population. According to the benefits principle, it is fair for people to pay taxes based on the benefits they receive from the government. According to the ability-to-pay principle, it is fair for people to pay taxes based on their capacity to handle the financial burden. When evaluating the equity of a tax system, it is important to remember a lesson from the study of tax incidence – the distribution of tax burdens is not the same as the distribution of tax bills.
- When considering changes in the tax laws, policymakers often face a trade-off between efficiency and equity. Much of the debate over tax policy arises because people give different weights to these two goals.

Key concepts

ability-to-pay principle	budget surplus	progressive tax
average tax rate	horizontal equity	proportional tax
benefits principle	lump-sum tax	regressive tax
budget deficit	marginal tax rate	vertical equity

Questions for review

1 Over the past several decades, has the federal government grown more or less slowly than the rest of the economy?

2 What are the two most important sources of revenue for the federal government?

3 Explain how the federal government avoids taxing company profits twice.

4 Why is the burden of a tax to taxpayers greater than the revenue received by the government?

5 Why might a GST lead to less distortion than an income tax? Could it lead to more distortion? How?

6 Give two arguments why wealthy taxpayers should pay more taxes than poor taxpayers.

7 What is the concept of horizontal equity and why is it hard to apply?

Problems and applications

1 When debating the merits of the GST, welfare groups like ACOSS argued that necessities, such as food and clothing, should be excluded from the new tax. When the tax was introduced, fresh food was excluded. Discuss the merits of this exclusion. Consider both efficiency and equity.

2 Federal government spending in Australia grew in the years between the 1950s and the 1980s, but has remained relatively constant as a share of GDP since the early 1980s. What changes in our economy and our society might explain this trend?

3 Each year the Federal Treasurer and the Minister for Finance circulate the budget papers. Using a recent issue of the budget papers at your library, answer the following questions and provide some numbers to support your answers.

   a Table 12.3 is based on the federal government's budget for 2010–11. It shows the budgeted spending for the 2010–11 financial year. Some types of spending are a larger part of total budget spending today than in the past. One example is social security and welfare. What other types of spending have been increasing as a percentage of total federal government spending? What types of spending have fallen as a percentage of total spending?

   b We noted that governments operate either a budget surplus or a budget deficit. How has the federal government deficit/surplus changed over recent years? How does this compare with the state governments?

   c The budget papers present figures on a wide range of social security programs. Look at three programs and analyse how spending on these programs has changed over recent years. Why might spending on individual programs change?

4 Explain how people's behaviour is affected by the following features of the tax laws.

   a Contributions to charity are tax-deductible.

   b Sales of beer are taxed.

   c Realised capital gains are taxed, but accrued gains are not (when people own shares that rise in value, they have an 'accrued' capital gain – if they sell the shares, they have a 'realised' gain).

   d State governments charge stamp duty on the sale and purchase of houses – the tax increases with the sale price of the house.

5 In 1997, the federal government changed the HECS charge for university courses. Before 1997, Arts courses were the same price as Economics courses. Since 1997, Arts courses have been cheaper than Economics courses. Explain how this change might affect enrolments in Arts and Economics courses.

6 We noted in the chapter how low-income earners could face effective marginal tax rates of 80 per cent or more. Consider people on unemployment benefits. If they accept an extra hour's work, they lose some of their benefits. What do you think is the effect of this feature of the unemployment benefit scheme on the labour supply of people on unemployment benefits? Explain.

7 Under Australian tax laws, interest payments on home mortgages are not tax-deductible. Under US tax laws, these interest payments are tax-deductible. How would this difference in tax laws alter consumer behaviour between the United States and Australia? Explain.

8 Categorise each of the following funding schemes as examples of the benefits principle or the ability-to-pay principle.

   a Visitors to some national parks pay an entrance fee.

   b Local property taxes support the maintenance of local roads.

   c The Victorian government charged a lump-sum tax on each household in the early 1990s to help reduce state debt.

9 Goods that are necessities often have highly inelastic demands. However, poor people spend relatively more of their income on necessities. What are the efficiency implications of introducing a tax on necessities? What are the equity implications? Would such a tax be progressive or regressive?

10 Any income tax schedule embodies two types of tax rates – average tax rates and marginal tax rates.

    a The average tax rate is defined as total taxes paid divided by income. For the proportional tax system presented in Table 12.4, what are the average tax rates for people earning $50 000, $100 000 and $200 000? What are the corresponding average tax rates in the regressive and progressive tax systems?

    b The marginal tax rate is defined as the extra taxes paid on additional income divided by the increase in income. Calculate the marginal tax rate for the proportional tax system as income rises from $50 000 to $100 000. Calculate the marginal tax rate as income rises from $100 000 to $200 000. Calculate the corresponding marginal tax rates for the regressive and progressive tax systems.

    c Describe the relationship between average tax rates and marginal tax rates for each of the three tax systems. In general, which rate is relevant for someone deciding whether to accept a job that pays slightly more than her current job? Which rate is relevant for judging the vertical equity of a tax system?

11 What is the efficiency justification for taxing consumption rather than income? Is a consumption tax likely to be more or less progressive than an income tax? Explain your answer.

12 Under Australian tax law, the employer pays a payroll tax on employee wages. Does this legal obligation for payment indicate the true incidence of these taxes? Explain.

13 In the 1980s the government introduced a 'fringe benefits tax'. If employees received personal benefits from their employer, such as restaurant meals, then the company had to pay tax on this benefit. Advocates of the fringe benefits tax argued that it would stop relatively wealthy people avoiding tax by receiving benefits rather than money income. But the tax was strongly opposed by restaurant owners and employees. Explain.

Search me!

When accessing information about economics use the following keywords in any combinations you require:

- progressive tax
- regressive tax

CourseMate

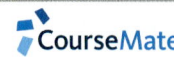

For more multimedia resources and activities on economics, visit the Economics CourseMate website.

PART FIVE
Firm behaviour and the organisation of industry

13

The costs of production

In this chapter you will:

- examine what items are included in a firm's costs of production
- analyse the link between a firm's production process and its total costs
- learn the meaning of average total cost and marginal cost and how they are related
- consider the shape of a typical firm's cost curves
- examine the relationship between short-run and long-run costs.

The goods and services you enjoy every day are produced by firms. You might drive a car produced by Toyota with tyres produced by Bridgestone, while listening to a radio produced by Sony. The economy is made up of thousands of firms. Some firms, such as these three companies, are large; they employ thousands of workers and have thousands of shareholders who share in the firms' profits. Other firms, such as the local hairdresser or newsagent, are small; they employ only a few workers and are owned by a single person or family.

In previous chapters we used the supply curve to summarise firms' production decisions. According to the law of supply, firms are willing to produce and sell a greater quantity of a good when the price of the good is high and this response leads to a supply curve that slopes upwards. For analysing many questions, the law of supply is all you need to know about firm behaviour.

In this chapter and the ones that follow, we examine firm behaviour in more detail. This topic will give you a better understanding of what decisions lie behind the supply curve in a market. In addition, it will introduce you to a part of economics called *industrial organisation* – the study of how firms' decisions regarding prices and quantities depend on the market conditions they face. The suburb in which you live, for instance, may have several fish and chip shops but only one electricity retailer. How does this difference in the number of firms affect the prices in these markets and the efficiency of the market outcomes? The field of industrial organisation considers exactly this question.

Before we turn to these issues, however, we need to discuss the costs of production. All firms, from Virgin Blue airlines to your local café, incur costs as they make the goods and services they sell. As we will see in the coming chapters, a firm's costs are a key determinant of its production and pricing decisions. In this chapter, we define some of the variables that economists use to measure a firm's costs and we consider the relationships among them.

What are costs?

We begin our discussion of costs at Poh's Cake Factory. Poh, the owner of the firm, buys flour, sugar and other cake ingredients. She also buys the mixers and ovens, and she hires workers to run this equipment. She then sells the resulting cakes to consumers. By examining some of the issues that Poh faces in her business, we can learn some lessons about costs that apply to all firms in the economy.

Total revenue, total cost and profit

We begin with the firm's objective. To understand what decisions a firm makes, we must understand what it is trying to do. It is conceivable that Poh started her firm because of an altruistic desire to provide the world with cakes or, perhaps, out of love for the cake business. More likely, however, Poh started her business to make money. Economists normally assume that the goal of a firm is to maximise profit and they find that this assumption works well in most cases.

What is a firm's profit? The amount that the firm receives for the sale of its output (cakes) is called its **total revenue (for a firm)**. The amount that the firm pays to buy inputs (flour, sugar, workers, ovens etc.) is called its **total cost**. Poh gets to keep any revenue that is not needed to cover costs. **Profit** is a firm's total revenue minus its total cost. That is:

$$\text{Profit} = \text{Total revenue} - \text{Total cost}$$

Poh's objective is to make her firm's profit as large as possible.

To see how a firm goes about maximising profit, we must consider fully how to measure its total revenue and its total cost. Total revenue is the easy part – it equals the quantity of output the firm

total revenue (for a firm)
the amount a firm receives for the sale of its output

total cost
the amount a firm pays to buy the inputs into production

profit
total revenue minus total cost

produces times the price at which it sells its output. If Poh produces 10 000 cakes and sells them at $2 a cake, her total revenue is $20 000. In contrast, the measurement of a firm's total costs is more subtle.

Costs as opportunity costs

When measuring costs at Poh's Cake Factory or any other firm, it is important to keep in mind one of the *Ten Lessons from Economics in* chapter 1 – the cost of something is what you give up to get it. Recall that the *opportunity cost* of an item refers to all those things that must be forgone to acquire that item. When economists speak of a firm's cost of production, they include all the opportunity costs of making its output of goods and services.

A firm's opportunity costs of production are sometimes obvious and sometimes less so. When Poh pays $1000 for flour, that $1000 is an opportunity cost because Poh can no longer use that $1000 to buy something else. Similarly, when Poh hires workers to make the cakes, the wages she pays are part of the firm's costs. These costs are *explicit*. In contrast, some of a firm's opportunity costs are *implicit*. Imagine that Poh is a skilled painter and could earn $100 per hour from her artwork. For every hour that Poh works at her cake factory she gives up $100 in income and this forgone income is also part of her costs. The total cost of Poh's business is the sum of the explicit costs and the implicit costs.

This distinction between explicit and implicit costs highlights an important difference between how economists and accountants analyse a business. Economists are interested in studying how firms make production and pricing decisions, so they include all opportunity costs when measuring costs. In contrast, accountants have the job of keeping track of the money that flows into and out of firms. As a result, they measure the explicit costs but often ignore the implicit costs.

The difference between economists and accountants is easy to see in the case of Poh's Cake Factory. When Poh gives up the opportunity to earn money by painting, her accountant will not count this as a cost of her cake business. Because no money flows out of the business to pay for this cost, it never shows up on the accountant's financial statements. An economist, however, will count the forgone income as a cost because it will affect the decisions that Poh makes in her cake business. For example, if Poh's earnings from her artwork rose from $100 to $500 per hour, she might decide that running her cake business is too costly and choose to shut down the factory in order to become a full-time artist.

The cost of capital as an opportunity cost

An important implicit cost of almost every business is the opportunity cost of the financial capital that has been invested in the business. Suppose, for instance, that Poh used $300 000 of her savings to buy her cake factory from the previous owner. If Poh had instead left this money deposited in a savings account that pays an interest rate of 5 per cent, she would have earned $15 000 per year. To own her cake factory, therefore, Poh has given up $15 000 a year in interest income. This $15 000 is one of the opportunity costs of Poh's business.

As we have already noted, economists and accountants treat costs differently and this is especially true in their treatment of the cost of capital. An economist views the $15 000 in interest income that Poh gives up every year as a cost of her business, even though it is an implicit cost. Poh's accountant, however, will not show this $15 000 as a cost because no money flows out of the business to pay for it.

To explore further the difference between economists and accountants, let's change the example slightly. Suppose now that Poh did not have the entire $300 000 to buy the factory but, instead, used

$100 000 of her own savings and borrowed $200 000 from a bank at an interest rate of 5 per cent. Poh's accountant, who measures only explicit costs, will now count the $10 000 interest paid on the bank loan every year as a cost because this amount of money now flows out of the firm. In contrast, according to an economist, the opportunity cost of owning the business is still $15 000. The opportunity cost equals the interest on the bank loan (an explicit cost of $10 000) plus the forgone interest on savings (an implicit cost of $5000).

Economic profit versus accounting profit

Now let's return to the firm's objective – profit. Because economists and accountants measure costs differently, they also measure profit differently. An economist measures a firm's *economic profit* as the firm's total revenue minus all the opportunity costs of producing the goods and services sold. An accountant measures the firm's *accounting profit* as the firm's total revenue minus only the firm's explicit costs.

Figure 13.1 summarises this difference. Notice that, because the accountant ignores the implicit costs, accounting profit is larger than economic profit. For a business to be profitable from an economist's standpoint, total revenue must cover all the opportunity costs, both explicit and implicit.

Economic profit is an important concept because it is what motivates the firms that supply goods and services. As we will see, a firm making positive economic profit will stay in business. It is covering all its opportunity costs and has some revenue left to reward the firm owners. When a firm is making economics losses (that is, when economic profits are negative), the business owners are failing to make enough to cover all the costs of production. Unless conditions change, the firm owners will eventually close the business down and exit the industry. To understand how industries evolve, we need to keep an eye on economic profit.

Figure 13.1	Economists versus accountants

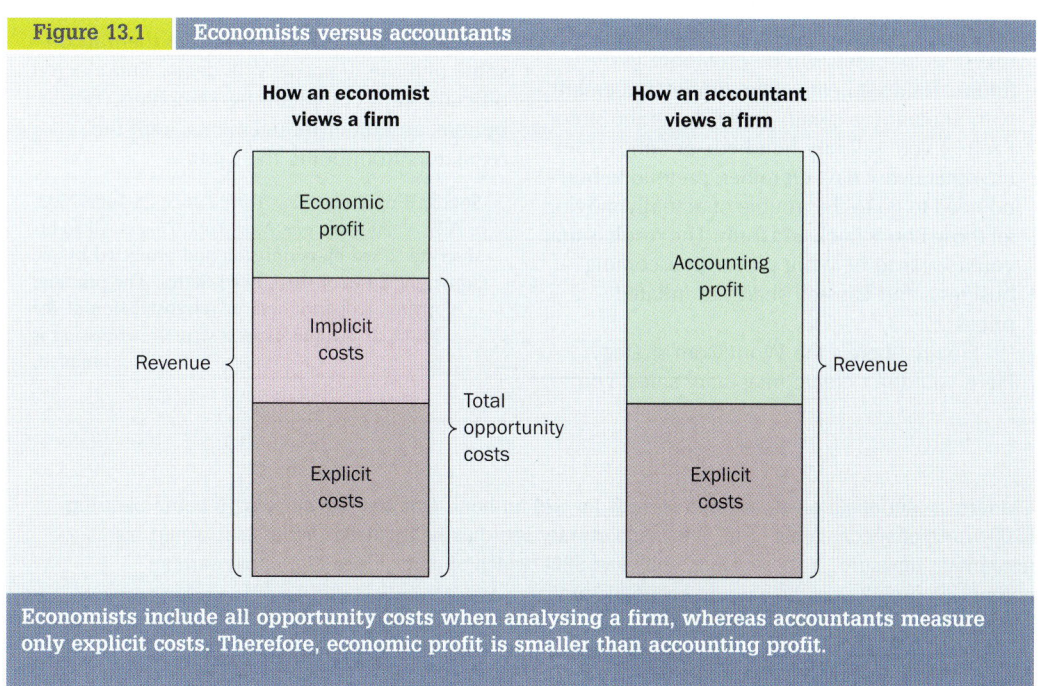

Economists include all opportunity costs when analysing a firm, whereas accountants measure only explicit costs. Therefore, economic profit is smaller than accounting profit.

IN THE NEWS …

TRUE PROFIT VERSUS FICTITIOUS PROFIT

The analysis of firm behaviour begins with the measurement of revenue, costs and profits. In the early 2000s, this topic made the news when several major companies were revealed to have lied about these key measures of performance. This article outlines how accounting measures can be manipulated by an unscrupulous business.

Flavors of fraud

by Paul Krugman

So you're the manager of an ice cream parlor. It's not very profitable, so how can you get rich? Each of the big business scandals uncovered so far suggests a different strategy for executive self-dealing.

First there's the Enron strategy. You sign contracts to provide customers with an ice cream cone a day for the next 30 years. You deliberately underestimate the cost of providing each cone; then you book all the projected profits on those future ice cream sales as part of this year's bottom line. Suddenly you appear to have a highly profitable business, and you can sell shares in your store at inflated prices.

Then there's the Dynegy strategy. Ice cream sales aren't profitable, but you convince investors that they will be profitable in the future. Then you enter into a quiet agreement with another ice cream parlor down the street: Each of you will buy hundreds of cones from the other every day. Or rather, pretend to buy – no need to go to the trouble of actually moving all those cones back and forth. The result is that you appear to be a big player in a coming business, and can sell shares at inflated prices …

Finally, there's the WorldCom strategy. Here you don't create imaginary sales; you make real costs disappear, by pretending that operating expenses – cream, sugar, chocolate syrup – are part of the purchase price of a new refrigerator. So your unprofitable business seems, on paper, to be a highly profitable business that borrows money only to finance its purchases of new equipment. And you can sell shares at inflated prices.

Oh, I almost forgot: How do you enrich yourself personally? The easiest way is to give yourself lots of stock options, so that you benefit from those inflated prices … I'm not saying that all U.S. corporations are corrupt. But it's clear that executives who want to be corrupt have faced few obstacles. Auditors weren't interested in giving a hard time to companies that gave them lots of consulting income; bank executives weren't interested [in] giving a hard time to companies that, as we learned in the Enron case, let them in on some of those lucrative side deals. And elected officials, kept compliant by campaign contributions and other inducements, kept the regulators from doing their job.

Old farmer McDonald gives bagpipe lessons for $20 an hour. One day, he spends 10 hours planting $100 worth of seeds on his farm. What opportunity cost has he incurred? What cost would his accountant measure? If these seeds will yield $200 worth of crops, does McDonald earn an accounting profit? Does he earn an economic profit?

Production and costs

Firms incur costs when they buy inputs to produce the goods and services that they plan to sell. In this section we examine this link between the firm's production process and its total cost. Once again, we consider Poh's Cake Factory.

In the analysis that follows, we make an important simplifying assumption: We assume that the size of Poh's factory is fixed and that Poh can vary the quantity of cake produced only by changing the number of workers. This assumption is realistic in the short run, but not in the long run. That is, Poh cannot build a larger factory overnight, but she can do so within a year or so. This analysis, therefore, should be viewed as describing the production decisions that Poh faces in the short run. We examine the relationship between costs and time horizon more fully later in the chapter.

The production function

Table 13.1 shows how the quantity of cakes Poh's factory produces per hour depends on the number of workers. If there are no workers in the factory, Poh produces no cakes. When there is one worker, she produces 50 cakes. When there are two workers, she produces 90 cakes, and so on. Figure 13.2 presents a graph of these two columns of numbers. The number of workers is on the horizontal axis, and the number of cakes produced is on the vertical axis. This relationship between the quantity of inputs (workers) and quantity of output (cakes) is called the **production function**.

One of the *Ten Lessons from Economics* introduced in chapter 1 is that rational people think at the margin. As we will see in future chapters, this idea is the key to understanding how firms decide how many workers to hire and how much output to produce. To take a step towards these decisions, the third column in Table 13.1 gives the marginal product of a worker. The **marginal product** of any input into production is the increase in the quantity of output obtained from an additional unit of that input. When the number of workers goes from one to two, cake production increases from 50 to 90, so the marginal product of the second worker is 40 cakes. And when the number of workers goes from two to three, cake production increases from 90 to 120, so the marginal product of the third worker is 30 cakes.

Notice that, as the number of workers increases, the marginal product declines. The second worker has a marginal product of 40 cakes, the third worker has a marginal product of 30 cakes, and the

production function
the relationship between quantity of inputs used to make a good and the quantity of output of that good

marginal product
the increase in output that arises from an additional unit of input

Table 13.1 A production function and total cost: Poh's Cake Factory					
Number of workers	Output (quantity of cakes produced per hour)	Marginal product of labour	Cost of factory ($)	Cost of workers ($)	Total cost of inputs (cost of factory + cost of workers) ($)
0	0	—	30	$0	30
1	50	50	30	10	40
2	90	40	30	20	50
3	120	30	30	30	60
4	140	20	30	40	70
5	150	10	30	50	80

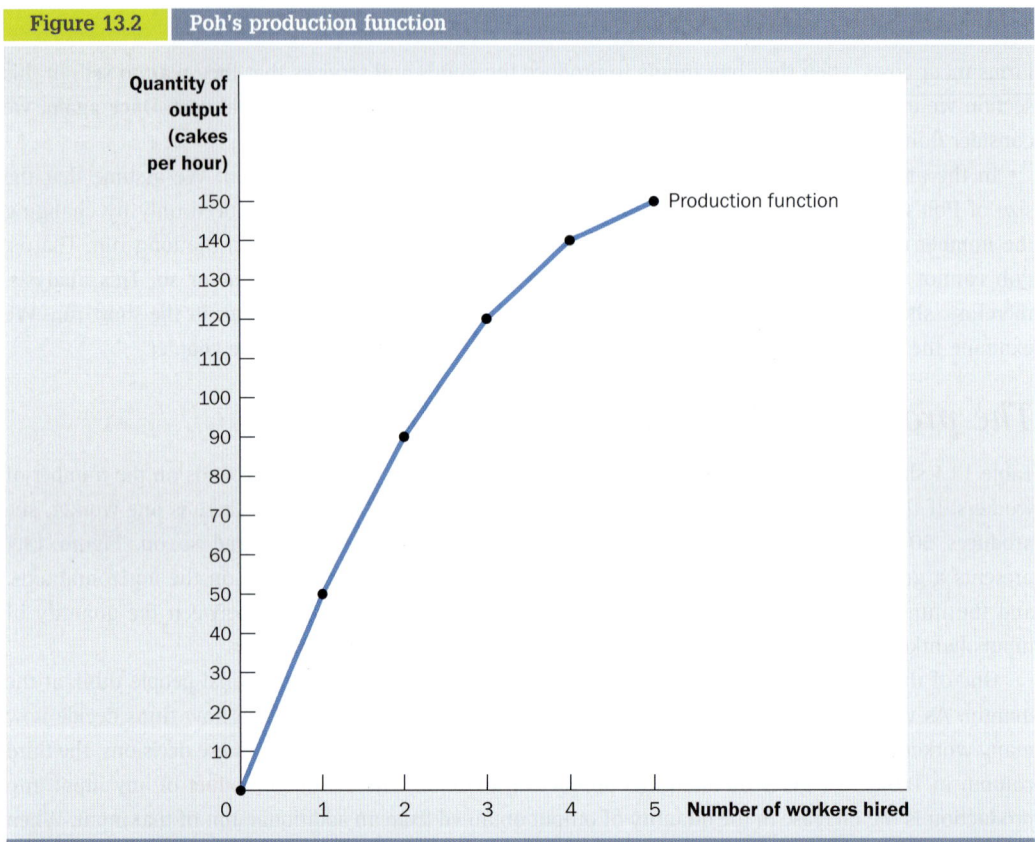

Figure 13.2 | Poh's production function

A production function shows the relationship between the number of workers hired and the quantity of output produced. Here the number of workers hired (on the horizontal axis) is from the first column in Table 13.1, and the quantity of output produced (on the vertical axis) is from the second column. The production function gets flatter as the number of workers increases, which reflects diminishing marginal product.

fourth worker has a marginal product of 20 cakes. This property is called **diminishing marginal product**. At first, when only a few workers are hired, they have easy access to Poh's kitchen equipment. As the number of workers increases, additional workers have to share equipment and work in more crowded conditions. Hence, as more and more workers are hired, each additional worker contributes less to the production of cakes.

diminishing marginal product
the property whereby the marginal product of an input declines as the quantity of the input increases

Diminishing marginal product is also apparent in Figure 13.2. The production function's slope ('rise over run') tells us the change in Poh's output of cakes ('rise') for each additional input of labour ('run'). That is, the slope of the production function measures the marginal product of a worker. As the number of workers increases, the marginal product declines, and the production function becomes flatter.

From the production function to the total-cost curve

The last three columns of Table 13.1 show Poh's cost of producing cakes. In this example, the cost of Poh's factory is $30 per hour and the cost of a worker is $10 per hour. If she hires one worker, her total cost is $40. If she hires two workers, her total cost is $50, and so on. The information in this table shows how the number of workers Poh hires is related to the quantity of cakes she produces and to her total cost of production.

Our goal in the next several chapters is to study firms' production and pricing decisions. For this purpose, the most important relationship in Table 13.1 is between quantity produced (in the second column) and total costs (in the sixth column). Figure 13.3 graphs these two columns of data with the quantity produced on the horizontal axis and total cost on the vertical axis. This graph is called the *total-cost curve*.

Now compare the total-cost curve in Figure 13.3 with the production function in Figure 13.2. These two curves are opposite sides of the same coin. The total-cost curve gets steeper as the amount produced rises, whereas the production function gets flatter as production rises. These changes in slope occur for the same reason. High production of cakes means that Poh's kitchen is crowded with many workers. Because the kitchen is crowded, each additional worker adds less to production, reflecting diminishing marginal product. Therefore, the production function is relatively flat. But now turn this logic around: When the kitchen is crowded, producing an additional cake requires a lot of additional labour and is thus very costly. Therefore, when the quantity produced is large, the total-cost curve is relatively steep.

Figure 13.3	Poh's total-cost curve

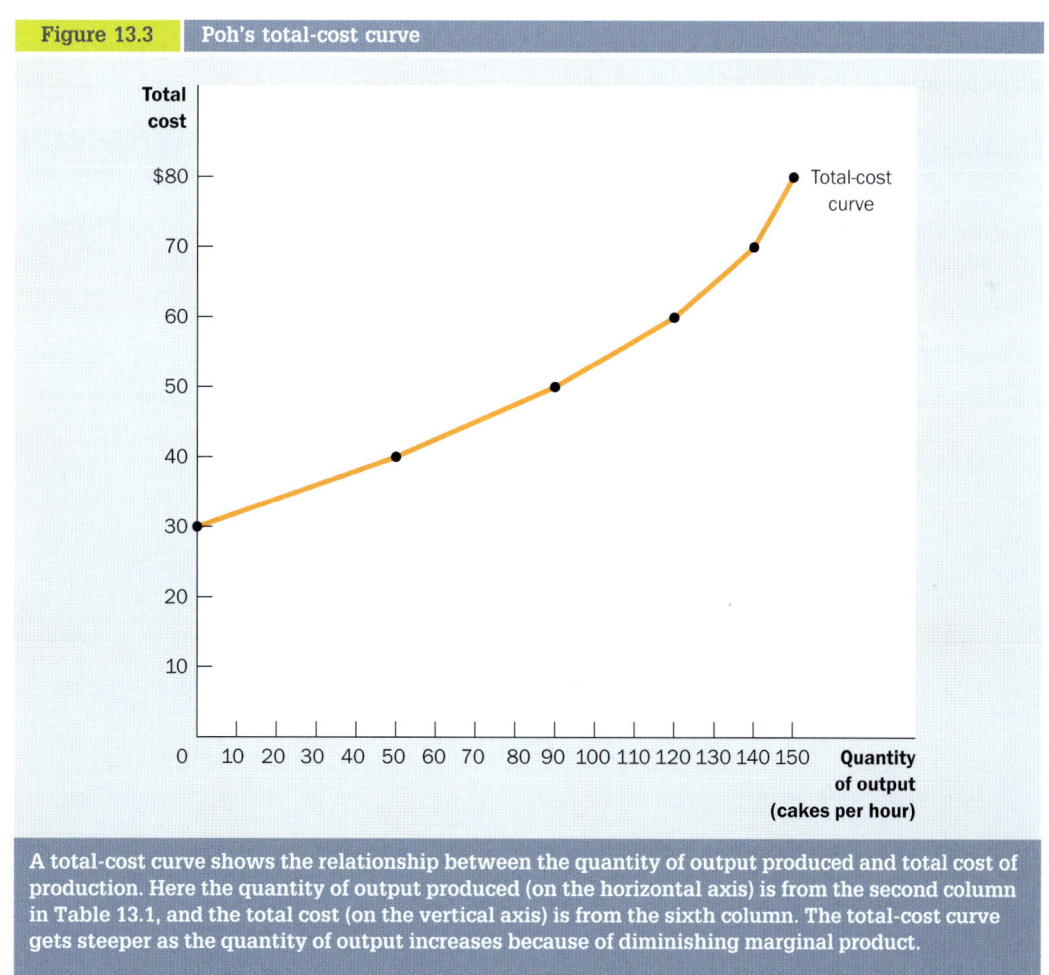

A total-cost curve shows the relationship between the quantity of output produced and total cost of production. Here the quantity of output produced (on the horizontal axis) is from the second column in Table 13.1, and the total cost (on the vertical axis) is from the sixth column. The total-cost curve gets steeper as the quantity of output increases because of diminishing marginal product.

If Farmer Jones plants no seeds on his farm, he gets no crop. If he plants one bag of seeds, he gets 5 kg of wheat. If he plants two bags, he gets 8 kg. If he plants three bags, he gets 10 kg. A bag of seeds costs $10 and seeds are his only cost. Use these data to graph the farmer's production function and total-cost curve. Explain their shapes.

The various measures of cost

Our analysis of Poh's Cake Factory demonstrated how a firm's total cost reflects its production function. From data on a firm's total cost, we can derive several related measures of cost, which will turn out to be useful when we analyse production and pricing decisions in future chapters. To see how these related measures are derived, we consider the example in Table 13.2. This table presents cost data on Poh's neighbour – George's Coffee Shop.

The first column of the table shows the number of cups of coffee that George might produce, ranging from 0 to 10 cups per hour. The second column shows George's total cost of producing coffee. Figure 13.4 plots George's total-cost curve. The quantity of coffee (from the first column) is on the horizontal axis, and total cost (from the second column) is on the vertical axis. George's total-cost curve has a shape similar to Poh's. In particular, it becomes steeper as the quantity produced rises, which (as we have discussed) reflects diminishing marginal product.

Table 13.2 The various measures of cost: George's Coffee Shop							
Quantity of coffee (cups per hour)	Total cost ($)	Fixed cost ($)	Variable cost ($)	Average fixed cost ($)	Average variable cost ($)	Average total cost ($)	Marginal cost ($)
0	3.00	3.00	0.00	—	—	—	—
1	3.30	3.00	0.30	3.00	0.30	3.30	0.30
2	3.80	3.00	0.80	1.50	0.40	1.90	0.50
3	4.50	3.00	1.50	1.00	0.50	1.50	0.70
4	5.40	3.00	2.40	0.75	0.60	1.35	0.90
5	6.50	3.00	3.50	0.60	0.70	1.30	1.10
6	7.80	3.00	4.80	0.50	0.80	1.30	1.30
7	9.30	3.00	6.30	0.43	0.90	1.33	1.50
8	11.00	3.00	8.00	0.38	1.00	1.38	1.70
9	12.90	3.00	9.90	0.33	1.10	1.43	1.90
10	15.00	3.00	12.00	0.30	1.20	1.50	2.10

Figure 13.4 | George's total-cost curve

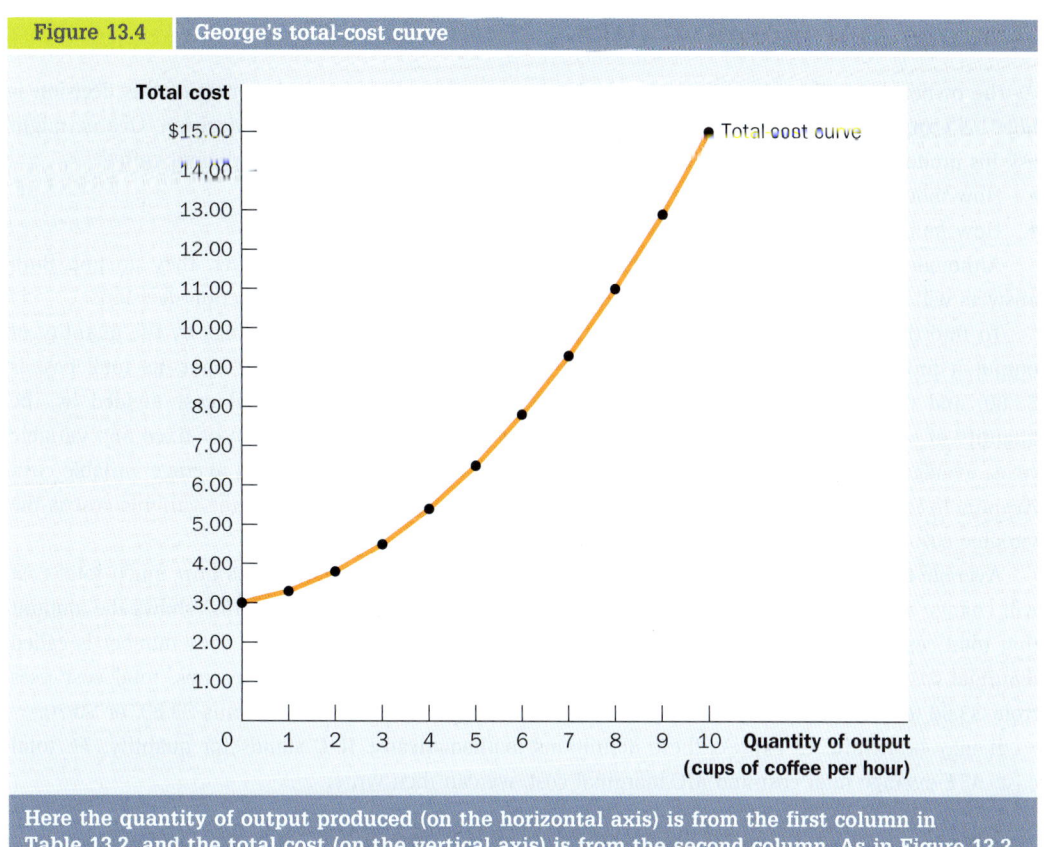

Here the quantity of output produced (on the horizontal axis) is from the first column in Table 13.2, and the total cost (on the vertical axis) is from the second column. As in Figure 13.3, the total-cost curve gets steeper as the quantity of output increases because of diminishing marginal product.

Fixed and variable costs

George's total cost can be divided into two types. Some costs, called **fixed costs**, do not vary with the quantity of output produced. They are incurred even if the firm produces nothing at all. George's fixed costs include the rent he pays because this cost is the same regardless of how much coffee he produces. Similarly, if George needs to hire a full-time bookkeeper to pay bills, regardless of the quantity of coffee produced, the bookkeeper's salary is a fixed cost. The third column in Table 13.2 shows George's fixed cost, which in this example is $3.00 per hour.

Some of the firm's costs, called **variable costs**, change as the firm alters the quantity of output produced. George's variable costs include the cost of coffee beans, milk and sugar. The more coffee George makes, the more of these items he needs to buy. Similarly, if George has to hire more workers to make more coffee, the salaries of these workers are variable costs. The fourth column of the table shows George's variable cost. The variable cost is 0 if he produces nothing, $0.30 if he produces one cup of coffee, $0.80 if he produces two cups of coffee, and so on.

A firm's total cost is the sum of fixed and variable costs. In Table 13.2, total cost in the second column equals fixed cost in the third column plus variable cost in the fourth column.

fixed costs
costs that do not vary with the quantity of output produced

variable costs
costs that vary with the quantity of output produced

Average and marginal cost

As the owner of his firm, George has to decide how much to produce. A key part of this decision is how his costs will vary as he changes the level of production. In making this decision, George might ask his production supervisor the following two questions about the cost of producing coffee:

- How much does it cost to make the typical cup of coffee?
- How much does it cost to increase production of coffee by one cup?

Although at first these two questions might seem to have the same answer, they do not. Both answers will turn out to be important for understanding how firms make production decisions.

To find the cost of the typical unit produced, we would divide the firm's costs by the quantity of output it produces. For example, if the firm produces two cups of coffee per hour, its total cost is $3.80, and the cost of the typical cup of coffee is $3.80/2, or $1.90. Total cost divided by the quantity of output is called **average total cost**. Because total cost is just the sum of fixed and variable costs, average total cost can be expressed as the sum of average fixed cost and average variable cost. **Average fixed cost** is the fixed cost divided by the quantity of output and **average variable cost** is the variable cost divided by the quantity of output.

Average total cost tells us the cost of the typical unit, but it does not tell us how much total cost will change as the firm alters its level of production. The last column in Table 13.2 shows the amount that total cost rises when the firm increases production by one unit of output. This number is called **marginal cost**. For example, if George increases production from two to three cups, total cost rises from $3.80 to $4.50, so the marginal cost of the third cup of coffee is $4.50 minus $3.80, or $0.70.

It may be helpful to express these definitions mathematically. If Q stands for quantity, TC total cost, ATC average total cost and MC marginal cost, we can then write:

$$\text{Average Total Cost} = \text{Total cost/Quantity}$$
$$ATC = TC \,/\, Q$$

and

$$\text{Marginal Cost} = (\text{Change in total cost})/(\text{Change in quantity})$$
$$MC = \triangle TC/\triangle Q$$

Here Δ, the Greek letter delta, represents the change in a variable. These equations show how average total cost and marginal cost are derived from total cost. *Average total cost tells us the cost of a typical unit of output if total cost is divided evenly over all the units produced. Marginal cost tells us the increase in total cost that arises from producing an additional unit of output.* As we will see more fully in the next chapter, business managers like George need to keep in mind the concepts of average total cost and marginal cost when deciding how much of their product to supply to the market.

Cost curves and their shapes

Just as in previous chapters we found graphs of supply and demand useful when analysing the behaviour of markets, we will find graphs of average and marginal cost useful when analysing the behaviour of firms. Figure 13.5 graphs George's costs using the data from Table 13.2. The horizontal axis measures the quantity the firm produces, and the vertical axis measures marginal and average costs. The graph shows four curves: average total cost (*ATC*), average fixed cost (*AFC*), average variable cost (*AVC*) and marginal cost (*MC*).

average total cost
total cost divided by the quantity of output

average fixed cost
fixed costs divided by the quantity of output

average variable cost
variable costs divided by the quantity of output

marginal cost
the increase in total cost that arises from an extra unit of production

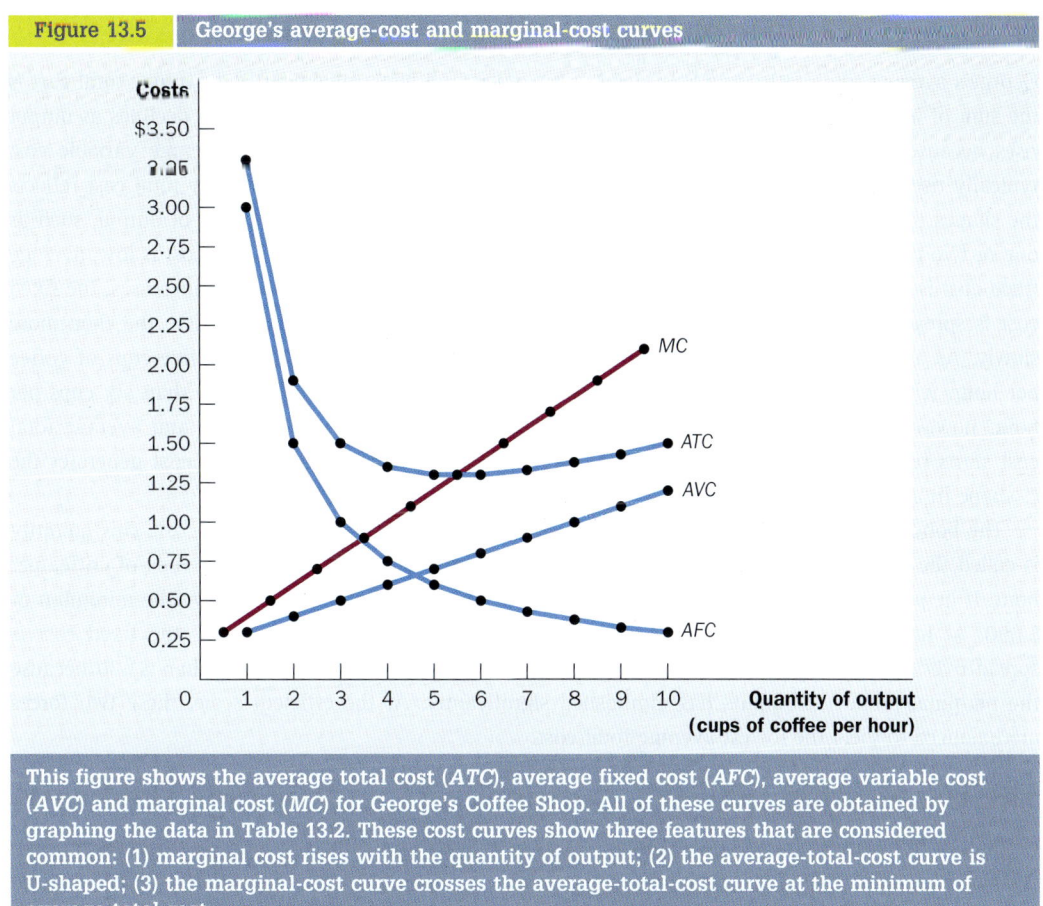

Figure 13.5 | George's average-cost and marginal-cost curves

This figure shows the average total cost (*ATC*), average fixed cost (*AFC*), average variable cost (*AVC*) and marginal cost (*MC*) for George's Coffee Shop. All of these curves are obtained by graphing the data in Table 13.2. These cost curves show three features that are considered common: (1) marginal cost rises with the quantity of output; (2) the average-total-cost curve is U-shaped; (3) the marginal-cost curve crosses the average-total-cost curve at the minimum of average total cost.

The cost curves shown here for George's Coffee Shop have shapes that are common to the cost curves of many firms in the economy. Let's examine three features of these curves in particular: the shape of marginal cost, the shape of average total cost and the relationship between marginal and average total cost.

Rising marginal cost

George's marginal cost rises with the quantity of output produced. This reflects the property of diminishing marginal product. When George produces a small quantity of coffee he has few workers and much of his equipment is not being used. Because he can easily put these idle resources to use, the marginal product of an extra worker is high and the marginal cost of an extra cup of coffee is small. In contrast, when George is producing large quantities of coffee, his shop is crowded with workers and most of his equipment is fully utilised. George can produce more coffee by adding workers, but these new workers have to work in crowded conditions and may have to wait to use the equipment. Therefore, when the quantity of coffee produced is already high, the marginal product of an extra worker is low and the marginal cost of an extra cup of coffee is large.

U-shaped average total cost

George's average-total-cost curve is U-shaped. To understand why, remember that average total cost is the sum of average fixed cost and average variable cost. Average fixed cost always declines as output rises because the fixed cost is getting spread over a larger number of units. Average variable cost typically rises as output increases because of diminishing marginal product. Average total cost reflects the shapes of both average fixed cost and average variable cost. At very low levels of output, such as one or two cups per hour, average total cost is high. Even though average variable cost is low, average fixed cost is high because the fixed cost is spread over only a few units. As output increases, the fixed cost is spread over more units of output. Average fixed cost declines, rapidly at first and then more slowly. As a result, average total cost also declines until the firm's output reaches five cups of coffee per hour, when average total cost is $1.30 per cup. When the firm produces more than six cups per hour, however, the increase in average variable cost becomes the dominant force and average total cost starts rising. The tug of war between average fixed cost and average variable cost generates the U-shape in average total cost.

The bottom of the U-shape occurs at the quantity that minimises average total cost. This quantity is called the **efficient scale** of the firm. For George, the efficient scale is five or six cups of coffee per hour. If he produces more or less than this amount, his average total cost rises above the minimum of $1.30. At lower levels of output, average total cost is higher than $1.30 because the fixed cost is spread over so few units. At higher levels of output, average total cost is higher than $1.30 because the marginal product of inputs has diminished significantly. At the efficient scale, these two forces are balanced to yield the lowest average total cost.

efficient scale
the quantity of output that minimises average total cost

▸ efficient scale

The relationship between marginal cost and average total cost

If you look at Figure 13.5 (or back at Table 13.2), you will see something that may be surprising at first. *Whenever marginal cost is less than average total cost, average total cost is falling. Whenever marginal cost is greater than average total cost, average total cost is rising.* This feature of George's cost curves is not a coincidence from the particular numbers used in the example – it is true for all firms.

To see why, consider an analogy to the game of cricket. Average total cost is like a batting average. Marginal cost is like the score that a player makes in the next game. If a player scores below his average in the next game, then his batting average will fall. If a player scores above his average in the next game, this high marginal score will raise his batting average. If a player scores exactly his average in the next game, his batting average will not change. The mathematics of average and marginal costs is exactly the same as the mathematics of average and marginal scores in cricket or any other sport.

This relationship between average total cost and marginal cost has an important corollary – *the marginal-cost curve crosses the average-total-cost curve at its minimum.* Why? At low levels of output, marginal cost is below average total cost, so average total cost is falling. But after the two curves cross, marginal cost rises above average total cost. For the reason we have just discussed, average total cost must start to rise at this level of output. Hence, this point of intersection is the minimum of average total cost. As you will see in the next chapter, this point of minimum average total cost plays a key role in the analysis of competitive firms.

Typical cost curves

In the examples we have examined so far, the firms exhibit diminishing marginal product and, therefore, rising marginal cost at all levels of output. In many firms, however, diminishing marginal product does

Table 13.3 The various measures of cost: Big Bob's Bagel Bin

Quantity of bagels (per hour)	Total cost ($)	Fixed cost ($)	Variable cost ($)	Average fixed cost ($)	Average variable cost ($)	Average total cost ($)	Marginal cost ($)
0	2.00	2.00	0.00	—	—	—	—
1	3.00	2.00	1.00	2.00	1.00	3.00	1.00
2	3.80	2.00	1.80	1.00	0.90	1.90	0.80
3	4.40	2.00	2.40	0.67	0.80	1.47	0.60
4	4.80	2.00	2.80	0.50	0.70	1.20	0.40
5	5.20	2.00	3.20	0.40	0.64	1.04	0.40
6	5.80	2.00	3.80	0.33	0.63	0.96	0.60
7	6.60	2.00	4.60	0.29	0.66	0.95	0.80
8	7.60	2.00	5.60	0.25	0.70	0.95	1.00
9	8.80	2.00	6.80	0.22	0.76	0.98	1.20
10	10.20	2.00	8.20	0.20	0.82	1.02	1.40
11	11.80	2.00	9.80	0.18	0.89	1.07	1.60
12	13.60	2.00	11.60	0.17	0.97	1.14	1.80
13	15.60	2.00	13.60	0.15	1.05	1.20	2.00
14	17.80	2.00	15.80	0.14	1.13	1.27	2.20

Figure 13.6 Big Bob's cost curves

(a) Total-cost curve

(b) Marginal- and average-cost curves

Many firms, like Big Bob's Bagel Bin, experience increasing marginal product before diminishing marginal product and, therefore, have cost curves like those in this figure. Panel (a) shows how total cost (*TC*) depends on the quantity produced. Panel (b) shows how average total cost (*ATC*), average fixed cost (*AFC*), average variable cost (*AVC*) and marginal cost (*MC*) depend on the quantity produced. These curves are derived by graphing the data from Table 13.3. Note that marginal cost and average variable cost fall for a while before starting to rise.

not start to occur immediately after the first worker is hired. Depending on the production process, the second or third worker might have higher marginal product than the first because a team of workers can divide tasks and work more productively than a single worker. Such firms would first experience increasing marginal product for a while before diminishing marginal product sets in.

Table 13.3 shows the cost data for such a firm, called Big Bob's Bagel Bin. These data are graphed in Figure 13.6. Panel (a) shows how total cost (*TC*) depends on the quantity produced, and panel (b) shows average total cost (*ATC*), average fixed cost (*AFC*), average variable cost (*AVC*) and marginal cost (*MC*). In the range of output from zero to four bagels per hour, the firm experiences increasing marginal product and the marginal-cost curve falls. After five bagels per hour, the firm starts to experience diminishing marginal product and the marginal-cost curve starts to rise. This combination of increasing and diminishing marginal product also makes the average-variable-cost curve U-shaped.

Despite these differences from our previous example, the cost curves shown here share the three properties that are most important to remember:

- Marginal cost eventually rises with the quantity of output.
- The average-total-cost curve is U-shaped.
- The marginal-cost curve crosses the average-total-cost curve at the minimum of average total cost.

Suppose Honda's total cost of producing four cars is $225 000 and its total cost of producing five cars is $250 000. What is the average total cost of producing five cars? What is the marginal cost of the fifth car?

Draw the marginal-cost curve and the average-total-cost curve for a typical firm and explain why these curves cross where they do.

Costs in the short run and in the long run

We noted at the beginning of this chapter that a firm's costs might depend on the time horizon under consideration. Let's examine more precisely why this might be the case.

The relationship between short-run and long-run average total cost

For many firms, the division of total costs between fixed and variable costs depends on the time horizon being considered. Consider, for instance, a car manufacturer, such as Ford. Over a period of only a few months, Ford cannot adjust the number or size of its car factories. The only way it can produce additional cars is to hire more workers at the factories it already has. The cost of these factories is, therefore, a fixed cost in the short run. In contrast, over a period of several years, Ford can expand the size of its factories, build new factories or close old ones. Thus, the cost of its factories is a variable cost in the long run.

Because many costs are fixed in the short run but variable in the long run, a firm's long-run cost curves differ from its short-run cost curves. Figure 13.7 shows an example. The figure presents three short-run average-total-cost curves – for a small, medium and large factory. It also presents the long-run average-total-cost curve. As the firm moves along the long-run curve, it is adjusting the size of the factory to the quantity of production.

This graph shows how short-run and long-run costs are related. The long-run average-total-cost curve is a much flatter U-shape than the short-run average-total-cost curve. In addition, the

Figure 13.7 Average total cost in the short and long run

Because fixed costs are variable in the long run, the average-total-cost curve in the short run differs from the average-total-cost curve in the long run.

long-run curve lies below all of the short-run curves. These properties arise because of the greater flexibility firms have in the long run. In essence, in the long run, the firm gets to choose which short-run curve it wants to use. But in the short-run, it has to use whatever short-run curve it chose in the past.

The figure shows an example of how a change in production alters costs over different time horizons. Suppose that Ford currently uses a medium-sized factory and produces 1000 cars per day. If Ford wants to increase production from 1000 to 1200 cars per day, it has no choice in the short run but to hire more workers at its existing medium-sized factory. Because of diminishing marginal product, average total cost rises from $20 000 to $22 000 per car. In the long run, however, Ford can expand both the size of the factory and its workforce, and average total cost remains at $20 000.

How long does it take for a firm to get to the long run? The answer depends on the firm. It can take a year or longer for a major manufacturing firm, such as a car company, to expand its existing factory or to build a larger factory. By contrast, a person operating a stall at the local Trash and Treasure market can increase or decrease the size of their stall on a week-by-week basis. There is no single answer for how long it takes a firm to adjust its production facilities.

Economies and diseconomies of scale

The shape of the long-run average-total-cost curve conveys important information about the technology for producing a good. When long-run average total cost declines as output increases, there are said to be **economies of scale**. When long-run average total cost rises as output increases,

economies of scale
the property whereby long-run average total cost falls as the quantity of output increases

diseconomies of scale
the property whereby long-run average total cost rises as the quantity of output increases

constant returns to scale
the property whereby long-run average total cost stays the same as the quantity of output changes

▸ economies of scale

there are said to be **diseconomies of scale** . When long-run average total cost does not vary with the level of output, there are said to be **constant returns to scale**. In this example, Ford has economies of scale at low levels of output, constant returns to scale at intermediate levels of output and diseconomies of scale at high levels of output.

What might cause economies or diseconomies of scale? Economies of scale often arise because higher production levels allow specialisation among workers, which permits each worker to become better at his or her assigned tasks. For instance, modern assembly-line production requires a large number of workers, each specialising in a particular task. If Ford were producing only a small quantity of cars, it could not take advantage of this approach and would have higher average total cost. Diseconomies of scale can arise because of coordination problems that are inherent in any large organisation. The more cars Ford produces the more stretched its management team becomes and the less effective the managers become at keeping costs down.

The analysis shows why long-run average-total-cost curves are often U-shaped. At low levels of production, the firm benefits from increased size because it can take advantage of greater specialisation. Coordination problems, meanwhile, are not yet acute. By contrast, at high levels of production, the benefits of specialisation have already been realised and coordination problems become more severe as the firm grows larger. Thus, long-run average total cost is falling at low levels of production because of increasing specialisation and rising at high levels of production because of increasing coordination problems.

If Boeing produces nine jets per month, its long-run total cost is $9.0 million per month. If it produces 10 jets per month, its long-run total cost is $9.5 million per month. Does Boeing exhibit economies or diseconomies of scale?

Conclusion

The purpose of this chapter has been to develop some tools that we can use to study how firms make production and pricing decisions. You should now understand what economists mean by the term costs and how costs vary with the quantity of output a firm produces. To refresh your memory, Table 13.4 summarises some of the definitions we have encountered.

By themselves, a firm's cost curves do not tell us what decisions the firm will make. But, as you will begin to see in the next chapter, they are an important component of that decision.

Table 13.4 The many types of cost: A summary

Term	Definition	Mathematical description
Explicit costs	Costs that require an outlay of money by the firm	—
Implicit costs	Costs that do not require an outlay of money by the firm	—
Fixed costs	Costs that do not vary with the quantity of output produced	FC
Variable costs	Costs that do vary with the quantity of output produced	VC
Total cost	The market value of all the inputs that a firm uses in production	$TC = FC + VC$
Average fixed cost	Fixed costs divided by the quantity of output	$AFC = FC/Q$
Average variable cost	Variable costs divided by the quantity of output	$AVC = VC/Q$
Average total cost	Total cost divided by the quantity of output	$ATC = TC/Q$
Marginal cost	The increase in total cost that arises from an extra unit of production	$MC = \Delta TC/\Delta Q$

fyi

Lessons from a pin factory

'Jack of all trades, master of none.' This well-known saying helps explain why firms sometimes experience economies of scale. A person who tries to do everything usually ends up doing nothing very well. If a firm wants its workers to be as productive as they can be, it is often best to give them a limited task that they can master. But this is possible only if a firm employs a large number of workers and produces a large quantity of output.

In his celebrated book, *An Inquiry into the Nature and Causes of the Wealth of Nations*, Adam Smith described an example of this based on a visit he made to a pin factory. Smith was impressed by the specialisation among the workers that he observed and the resulting economies of scale. He wrote:

> One man draws out the wire, another straightens it, a third cuts it, a fourth points it, a fifth grinds it at the top for receiving the head; to make the head requires two or three distinct operations; to put it on is a peculiar business; to whiten it is another; it is even a trade by itself to put them into paper.

Smith reported that because of this specialisation, the pin factory produced thousands of pins per worker every day. He conjectured that if the workers had chosen to work separately, rather than as a team of specialists, 'they certainly could not each of them make twenty, perhaps not one pin a day'. In other words, because of specialisation, a large pin factory could achieve higher output per worker and lower average cost per pin than a small pin factory.

The specialisation that Smith observed in the pin factory is prevalent in the modern economy. If you want to build a house, for instance, you could try to do all the work yourself. But most people turn to a builder, who in turn hires carpenters, plumbers, electricians, painters and many other types of worker. These workers specialise in particular jobs, and this allows them to become better at their jobs than if they were generalists. Indeed, the use of specialisation to achieve economies of scale is one reason modern societies are as prosperous as they are.

Summary

- The goal of firms is to maximise profit, which equals total revenue minus total cost.
- When analysing a firm's behaviour, it is important to include all the opportunity costs of production. Some of the opportunity costs, such as the wages a firm pays its workers, are explicit. Other opportunity costs, such as the wages the firm owner gives up by working in the firm rather than taking another job, are implicit. Economic profit takes both explicit and implicit costs into account, whereas accounting profit considers only explicit costs.
- A firm's costs reflect its production process. A typical firm's production function gets flatter as the quantity of an input increases, displaying the property of diminishing marginal product. As a result, a firm's total-cost curve gets steeper as the quantity produced rises.
- A firm's total costs can be divided between fixed costs and variable costs. Fixed costs are costs that do not change when the firm alters the quantity of output produced. Variable costs are costs that do change when the firm alters the quantity of output produced.
- From a firm's total cost, two related measures of cost are derived. Average total cost is total cost divided by the quantity of output. Marginal cost is the amount by which total cost would rise if output were increased by one unit.
- When analysing firm behaviour, it is often useful to graph average total cost and marginal cost. For a typical firm, marginal cost rises with the quantity of output. Average total cost first falls as output increases and then rises as output increases further. The marginal-cost curve always crosses the average-total-cost curve at the minimum of average total cost.
- A firm's costs often depend on the time horizon being considered. In particular, many costs are fixed in the short run but variable in the long run. As a result, when the firm changes its level of production, average total cost may rise more in the short run than in the long run.

Key concepts

average fixed cost	diseconomies of scale	production function
average total cost	economies of scale	profit
average variable cost	efficient scale	total cost
constant returns to scale	fixed costs	total revenue (for a firm)
diminishing marginal	marginal cost	variable costs
product	marginal product	

Questions for review

1. What is the relationship between a firm's total revenue, profit and total cost?
2. Give an example of an opportunity cost that an accountant might not count as a cost. Why would the accountant ignore this cost?
3. Define total cost, average total cost and marginal cost. How are they related?
4. Draw the marginal-cost and average-total-cost curves for a typical firm. Explain why the curves have the shapes that they do and why they cross where they do.
5. How and why does a firm's average-total-cost curve differ in the short run and in the long run?
6. Define *economies of scale* and explain why they might arise. Define *diseconomies of scale* and explain why they might arise.

Problems and applications

1   This chapter discusses many types of costs: opportunity cost, total cost, fixed cost, variable cost, average total cost and marginal cost. Fill in the type of cost that best completes the phrases below:

   a   The true cost of taking some action is its _____ .

   b   _____ is falling when marginal cost is below it, and rising when marginal cost is above it.

   c   A cost that does not depend on the quantity produced is a _____ .

   d   In the ice-cream industry in the short run, _____ includes the cost of cream and sugar, but not the cost of the factory.

   e   Profits equal total revenue less _____ .

   f   The cost of producing an extra unit of output is _____ .

2   Your aunt is thinking about opening a hardware store. She estimates that it would cost $500 000 per year to rent the store and buy the stock. In addition, she would have to quit her $50 000 per year job as an accountant.

   a   Define opportunity cost.

   b   What is your aunt's opportunity cost of running a hardware store for a year? If your aunt thought she could sell $510 000 worth of merchandise in a year, should she open the store? Explain.

3   Suppose you go to university and live in a residential college on campus. You pay the college for your room and board.

   a   What is a cost of going to university that is not an opportunity cost?

   b   What is an explicit opportunity cost of attending university?

   c   What is an implicit opportunity cost of attending university?

4   A commercial fisherman notices the following relationship between hours spent fishing and the quantity of fish caught:

Hours	Quantity of fish (kg)
0	0
1	10
2	18
3	24
4	28
5	30

   a   What is the marginal product of each hour spent fishing?

   b   Use these data to graph the fisherman's production function. Explain its shape.

   c   The fisherman has a fixed cost of $10 (his rod). The opportunity cost of his time is $5 per hour. Graph the fisherman's total-cost curve. Explain its shape.

5   Nimbus Ltd, makes brooms and then sells them door-to-door. Here is the relationship between the number of workers and Nimbus's output in a given day.

Workers	Output	Marginal product	Total cost ($)	Average total cost ($)	Marginal cost ($)
0	0				
1	20				
2	50				
3	90				
4	120				
5	140				
6	150				
7	155				

a   Fill in the column of marginal products. What pattern do you see? How might you explain it?
b   A worker costs $100 a day and the firm has fixed costs of $200. Use this information to fill in the column for total cost.
c   Fill in the column for average total cost. (Recall that $ATC = TC/Q$.) What pattern do you see?
d   Now fill in the column for marginal cost. (Recall that $MC = DTC/DQ$.) What pattern do you see?
e   Compare the column for marginal product and the column for marginal cost. Explain the relationship.
f   Compare the column for average total cost and the column for marginal cost. Explain the relationship.

6   Suppose that you and your room-mate have started a hot dog delivery service on campus. List some of your fixed costs and describe why they are fixed. List some of your variable costs and describe why they are variable.

7   Consider the following cost information for a pie shop.

Q (dozens)	Total cost ($)	Variable cost ($)
0	300	0
1	350	50
2	390	90
3	420	120
4	450	150
5	490	190
6	540	240

   a What is the pie shop's fixed cost?
   b Construct a table in which you calculate the marginal cost per dozen pies using the information on total cost. Also calculate the marginal cost per dozen pies using the information on variable cost. What is the relationship between these sets of numbers? Comment.

8 You are thinking about setting up a doughnut van. The van itself costs $200. The ingredients for each doughnut cost $0.50.
   a What is your fixed cost of doing business? What is your variable cost per doughnut?
   b Construct a table showing your total cost, average total cost and marginal cost for output levels varying from 0 to 10 doughnuts. Draw the three cost curves.

9 Your cousin Vinnie owns a painting company with a total fixed cost of $200 and the following schedule for total variable cost:

Total variable cost ($)	Quantity of houses painted per month
10	1
20	2
40	3
80	4
160	5
320	6
640	7

   Calculate average fixed cost, average variable cost and average total cost for each quantity. What is the efficient scale of the painting company?

10 Healthy Harry's Juice Bar has the following cost schedules:

Q (vats)	Variable cost ($)	Total cost ($)
0	0	30
1	10	40
2	25	55
3	45	75
4	70	100
5	100	130
6	135	165

   a Calculate average variable cost, average total cost and marginal cost for each quantity.
   b Graph all three curves. What is the relationship between the marginal-cost curve and the average-total-cost curve? Between the marginal-cost curve and the average-variable-cost curve? Explain.

299

11   Consider the following table of long-run total cost for three different firms:

Quantity	Firm A	Firm B	Firm C
1	$60	$11	$21
2	70	24	34
3	80	39	49
4	90	56	66
5	100	75	85
6	110	96	106
7	120	119	129

Does each of these firms experience economies of scale or diseconomies of scale?

Search me!

When accessing information about economics use the following keywords in any combinations you require:
- economies of scale
- efficient scale

CourseMate

For more multimedia resources and activities on economics, visit the Economics CourseMate website.

14

Firms in competitive markets

Learning objectives

In this chapter you will:

- learn what characteristics make a market competitive

- examine how competitive firms decide how much output to produce

- examine how competitive firms decide when to shut down production temporarily

- examine how competitive firms decide whether to exit or enter a market

- see how firm behaviour determines a market's short-run and long-run supply curves.

If your local petrol station raised the price it charges for petrol by 20 per cent, it would see a large drop in the amount of petrol it sold. Its customers would quickly switch to buying their petrol at other petrol stations. In contrast, if your local water company raised the price of water by 20 per cent, it would see only a small decrease in the amount of water it sold. People might water their lawns less often and buy more water-efficient shower heads, but they would be hard-pressed to reduce water consumption greatly. The difference between the petrol market and the water market is obvious – there are many firms selling petrol, but there is only one firm selling water. As you might expect, this difference in market structure shapes the pricing and production decisions of the firms that operate in these markets.

In this chapter we examine the behaviour of competitive firms, such as your local petrol station. You may recall that a market is competitive if each buyer and seller is small compared with the size of the market and, therefore, has little ability to influence market prices. In contrast, if a firm can influence the market price of the good it sells, it is said to have market power. In the four chapters that follow this one, we examine the behaviour of firms with market power, such as your local water company.

Our analysis of competitive firms in this chapter will shed light on the decisions that lie behind the supply curve in a competitive market. Not surprisingly, we will find that a market supply curve is tightly linked to firms' costs of production. (Indeed, this general insight should be familiar to you from our analysis in chapter 7.) Less obvious, however, is the question of which among a firm's many types of costs – fixed, variable, average and marginal – are most relevant for its supply decisions. We will see that all these measures of cost play important and interrelated roles.

What is a competitive market?

Our goal in this chapter is to examine how firms make production decisions in competitive markets. As a background for this analysis, we begin by considering what a competitive market is.

The meaning of competition

Although we have already discussed the meaning of competition in chapter 4, let's review the lesson briefly. A *competitive market*, sometimes called a *perfectly competitive market*, has two characteristics:

▶ competitive market

* There are many buyers and many sellers in the market.
* The goods offered by the various sellers are largely the same.

As a result of these conditions, the actions of any single buyer or seller in the market have a negligible impact on the market price. Each buyer and seller takes the market price as given.

An example is the market for mowing. Each person offering to mow your lawn for a price has limited control over that price because many other sellers are offering mowing services that are essentially identical. Similarly, no single buyer of mowing services can influence the price of mowing because each buyer purchases a small amount relative to the size of the market. Because sellers can sell all they want at the going price, they have little reason to charge less and if an individual seller charges more, buyers will go elsewhere. Buyers and sellers in competitive markets must accept the price the market determines and, therefore, are said to be price takers.

In addition to the above two conditions for competition, there is a third condition sometimes thought to characterise perfectly competitive markets:

* Firms can freely enter or exit the market.

If, for instance, anyone can decide to start a lawn-mowing business and anyone currently operating a lawn-mowing business can decide to stop, then the lawn-mowing industry would satisfy this condition. Note that much of the analysis of competitive firms does not rely on the assumption of free entry and exit because this condition is not necessary for firms to be price takers. However, as we will see later in this chapter, entry and exit are often powerful forces shaping the long-run outcome in competitive markets.

The revenue of a competitive firm

A firm in a competitive market, like most other firms in the economy, tries to maximise profit, which equals total revenue minus total cost. To see how it does this, we first consider the revenue of a competitive firm. To keep matters concrete, let's consider a specific firm: The Lee Family Lawn-Mowing Business.

The Lee family mows a quantity of lawns Q and receives the market price of P for each lawn mown. The family's total revenue is $P \times Q$. For example, if the market price of mowing a lawn is $20 and the Lee family mows 100 lawns, its total revenue is $2000.

Because the Lee Family Lawn-Mowing Business is only a small part of the total market for mowing, it takes the price as given by market conditions. This means, in particular, that the price of mowing a lawn does not depend on the quantity of lawns that the Lee family mows. If the Lees double the number of lawns they mow, the price of mowing a lawn remains the same and their total revenue doubles. As a result, total revenue is proportional to the amount of output.

Table 14.1 shows the revenue for the Lee Family Lawn-Mowing Business. The first two columns show the amount of output the business produces and the price at which it sells its output. The third column is the total revenue of the business. The table assumes that the price of mowing a lawn is $20, so total revenue is simply $20 times the number of lawns mown.

Just as the concepts of *average* and *marginal* were useful in the last chapter when analysing costs, they are also useful when analysing revenue. To see what these concepts tell us, consider these two questions:

- How much revenue does the business receive for the typical lawn mown?
- How much additional revenue does the business receive if it increases production by mowing one extra lawn?

The last two columns in Table 14.1 answer these questions.

Table 14.1 Total, average and marginal revenue for a competitive firm

Quantity	Price	Total revenue	Average revenue	Marginal revenue
(Q)	(P)	($TR = P \times Q$)	($AR = TR/Q$)	($MR = \Delta TR/\Delta Q$)
1 lawn	$20	$20	$20	—
2	20	40	20	$20
3	20	60	20	20
4	20	80	20	20
5	20	100	20	20
6	20	120	20	20
7	20	140	20	20
8	20	160	20	20

average revenue
total revenue divided by
the quantity sold

marginal revenue
the change in total revenue
from an additional unit sold

The fourth column in the table shows **average revenue**, which is total revenue (from the third column) divided by the amount of output (from the first column). Average revenue tells us how much revenue a firm receives for the typical unit sold. In Table 14.1, you can see that average revenue equals $20, the price of mowing a lawn. This illustrates a general lesson that applies not only to competitive firms but to other firms as well. Total revenue is the price times the quantity ($P \times Q$), and average revenue is total revenue ($P \times Q$) divided by the quantity (Q). Therefore, for all firms, average revenue equals the price of the good.

The fifth column shows **marginal revenue**, which is the change in total revenue from the sale of each additional unit of output. In Table 14.1, marginal revenue equals $20, the price of mowing a lawn. This result illustrates a lesson that applies only to competitive firms. Total revenue is $P \times Q$, and P is fixed for a competitive firm. Therefore, when Q rises by one unit, total revenue rises by P dollars. *For competitive firms, marginal revenue equals the price of the good.*

When a competitive firm doubles the amount it sells, what happens to the price of its output and its total revenue?

Profit maximisation and the competitive firm's supply curve

The goal of a competitive firm is to maximise profit, which equals total revenue minus total cost. We have just discussed the firm's revenue and in the last chapter we discussed the firm's costs. We are now ready to examine how the firm maximises profit and how that decision leads to its supply curve.

A simple example of profit maximisation

Let's begin our analysis of the firm's supply decision with the example in Table 14.2. In the first column of the table is the number of lawns mown by the Lee Family Lawn-Mowing Business. The second column shows the family's total revenue, which is $20 times the number of lawns. The third column shows the family's total cost. Total cost includes fixed costs, which are $10 in this example, and variable costs, which depend on the quantity produced.

The fourth column shows the family's profit, which is calculated by subtracting total cost from total revenue. If the family business produces nothing, it has a loss of $10. If it mows one lawn, it has a profit of $6. If it mows two lawns, it has a profit of $18 and so on. To maximise profit, the business chooses the quantity that makes profit as large as possible. In this example, profit is maximised when the Lees mow either four or five lawns, for a profit of $30.

There is another way to look at the business's decision. The Lees can find the profit-maximising quantity by comparing the marginal revenue and marginal cost from each unit produced. The last two columns in Table 14.2 calculate marginal revenue and marginal cost from total revenue and total cost. The first lawn the business mows has a marginal revenue of $20 and a marginal cost of $4; hence, mowing that lawn increases profit by $16 (from negative $10 to positive $6). The second lawn mown has a marginal revenue of $20 and a marginal cost of $8, so that lawn increases profit by $12 (from $6 to $18). As long as marginal revenue exceeds marginal cost, increasing the quantity raises profit. Once the Lee family has reached five lawns, however, the situation is very different. The sixth lawn would have marginal revenue of $20 and marginal cost of $24, so mowing it would reduce profit by $4 (from $30 to $26). As a result, the Lees would not mow more than five lawns.

Table 14.2 Profit maximisation – a numerical example

Quantity (Q)	Total revenue (TR)	Total cost (TC)	Profit (TR – TC)	Marginal revenue (MR = ΔTR/ΔQ)	Marginal cost (MC = ΔTC/ΔQ)
0 lawns	$0	$10	–$10	—	—
1	20	14	6	$20	$4
2	40	22	18	20	8
3	60	34	26	20	12
4	80	50	30	20	16
5	100	70	30	20	20
6	120	94	26	20	24
7	140	122	18	20	28
8	160	154	6	20	32

One of the *Ten Lessons from Economics* in chapter 1 is that rational people think at the margin. We now see how the Lee Family Lawn-Mowing Business can apply this principle. If marginal revenue is greater than marginal cost – as it is if the family mows only one, two or three lawns – the Lees should increase the number of lawns they mow. If marginal revenue is less than marginal cost – as it is for six, seven or eight lawns – the Lees should decrease production. If the Lees think at the margin and make incremental adjustments to the level of production, they are naturally led to produce the profit-maximising quantity.

The marginal-cost curve and the firm's supply decision

To extend this analysis of profit maximisation, consider the cost curves in Figure 14.1. These cost curves have the three features that, as we discussed in chapter 13, are considered typical: The marginal-cost curve (*MC*) is upward-sloping; the average-total-cost curve (*ATC*) is U-shaped; and the marginal-cost curve crosses the average-total-cost curve at the minimum of average total cost. The figure also shows a horizontal line at the market price (*P*) of the firm's output, which equals the firm's average revenue (*AR*) and its marginal revenue (*MR*). The price line is horizontal because the firm is a price taker – the price is the same regardless of the quantity that the firm decides to produce.

We can use Figure 14.1 to find the quantity of output that maximises profit. Imagine that the firm is producing at Q_1. At this level of output, marginal revenue is greater than marginal cost. That is, if the firm raised its level of production and sales by one unit, the additional revenue (MR_1) would exceed the additional costs (MC_1). Profit, which equals total revenue minus total cost, would increase. Hence, if marginal revenue is greater than marginal cost, as it is at Q_1, the firm can increase profit by raising production.

A similar argument applies when output is at Q_2. In this case, marginal cost is greater than marginal revenue. If the firm reduced production by one unit, the costs saved (MC_2) would exceed the

Figure 14.1 Profit maximisation for a competitive firm

The firm maximises profit by producing the quantity at which marginal cost equals marginal revenue.

This shows the marginal-cost curve (*MC*), the average-total-cost curve (*ATC*) and the average-variable-cost curve (*AVC*). It also shows the market price (*P*), which equals marginal revenue (*MR*) and average revenue (*AR*). At the quantity Q_1, marginal revenue MR_1 exceeds marginal cost MC_1, so raising production increases profit. At the quantity Q_2, marginal cost MC_2 is above marginal revenue MR_2, so reducing production increases profit. The profit-maximising quantity Q_{MAX} is found where the horizontal price line intersects the marginal-cost curve.

revenue lost (MR_2). Therefore, if marginal revenue is less than marginal cost, as it is at Q_2, the firm can increase profit by reducing production.

Where do these marginal adjustments to level of production end? Regardless of whether the firm begins with production at a low level (such as Q_1) or at a high level (such as Q_2), the firm will eventually adjust production until the quantity produced reaches Q_{MAX}. This analysis shows a general rule for profit maximisation:

- If marginal revenue is greater than marginal cost, the firm should increase its output.
- If marginal cost is greater than marginal revenue, the firm should decrease its output.
- At the profit-maximising level of output, marginal revenue and marginal cost are exactly equal.

These rules are the key to rational decision making by a profit-maximising firm. They apply not only to competitive firms but, as we will see in the next chapter, to other firms as well.

We can now see how the competitive firm decides the quantity of its good to supply to the market. Because a competitive firm is a price taker, its marginal revenue equals the market price. For any given price, the competitive firm's profit-maximising quantity of output is found by looking at the intersection of the price with the marginal-cost curve. In Figure 14.1, that quantity is Q_{MAX}.

Figure 14.2 shows how a competitive firm responds to an increase in the price. When the price is P_1, the firm produces quantity Q_1, which is the quantity that equates marginal cost to the price. When the price rises to P_2, the firm finds that marginal revenue is now higher than marginal cost at the previous level of output, so the firm increases production. The new profit-maximising quantity is Q_2, at which marginal cost equals the new higher price. *In essence, because the firm's*

Figure 14.2 Marginal cost as the competitive firm's supply curve

An increase in the price from P_1 to P_2 leads to an increase in the firm's profit-maximising quantity from Q_1 to Q_2. Because the marginal-cost curve shows the quantity supplied by the firm at any given price, it is the firm's supply curve.

marginal-cost curve determines how much the firm is willing to supply at any price, it is the competitive firm's supply curve. There are, however, some caveats to that conclusion, which we examine next.

The firm's short-run decision to shut down

So far we have been analysing the question of how much a competitive firm will produce. In some circumstances, however, the firm will decide to shut down and not produce anything at all.

Here we need to distinguish between a temporary shutdown of a firm and the permanent exit of a firm from the market. A *shutdown* refers to a short-run decision not to produce anything during a specific period of time because of current market conditions. *Exit* refers to a long-run decision to leave the market. The long-run and short-run decisions differ because most firms cannot avoid their fixed costs in the short run but are able to do so in the long run. That is, a firm that shuts down temporarily still has to pay its fixed costs, whereas a firm that exits can save both its fixed and its variable costs.

For example, consider the production decision that a farmer faces. The cost of the land is one of the farmer's fixed costs. If the farmer decides not to produce any crops one season, the land lies fallow and he cannot recover this cost. When making the short-run decision whether to shut down for a season, the fixed cost of land is said to be a *sunk cost*. In contrast, if the farmer decides to leave farming altogether he can sell the land. When making the long-run decision whether to exit the market, the cost of land is not sunk. (We return to the issue of sunk costs shortly.)

Now let's consider what determines a firm's shutdown decision. If the firm shuts down, it loses all revenue from the sale of its product. At the same time, it saves the variable costs of making its product (but still pays the fixed costs). Thus, *the firm shuts down if the revenue that it would earn from producing is less than the variable costs of production.*

A bit of mathematics can make this shutdown criterion more useful. If *TR* stands for total revenue, and *VC* stands for variable costs, then the firm's decision can be written as:

Shut down if $TR < VC$

The firm shuts down if total revenue is less than variable cost. By dividing both sides of this inequality by the quantity *Q*, we can write it as:

Shut down if $TR/Q < VC/Q$

Notice that this can be further simplified. *TR/Q* is total revenue divided by quantity, which is average revenue. As we discussed previously, average revenue for any firm is simply the good's price *P*. Similarly, *VC/Q* is average variable cost *AVC*. Therefore, the firm's shutdown criterion can be restated as:

Shut down if $P < AVC$

That is, a firm chooses to shut down if the price of the good is less than the average variable cost of production. This criterion makes sense – when choosing to produce, the firm compares the price it receives for the typical unit with the average variable cost that it must incur to produce the typical unit. If the price does not cover the average variable cost, the firm is better off stopping production altogether. The firm still loses money (because it has to pay fixed costs) but it would lose even more money by staying open. The firm can reopen in the future if conditions change so that price exceeds average variable cost.

We now have a full description of a competitive firm's profit-maximising strategy. If the firm produces anything, it produces the quantity at which marginal cost equals the price of the good. Yet if the price is less than average variable cost at that quantity, the firm is better off shutting down and not producing anything. These results are illustrated in Figure 14.3. *The competitive firm's short-run supply curve is the portion of its marginal-cost curve that lies above average variable cost.*

Figure 14.3 **The competitive firm's short-run supply curve**

In the short run, the competitive firm's supply curve is its marginal-cost curve (*MC*) above average variable cost (*AVC*). If the price falls below average variable cost, the firm is better off shutting down.

Have you ever walked into a restaurant for lunch and found it almost empty? Why, you might have asked, does the restaurant even bother to stay open? It might seem that the revenue from the few customers could not possibly cover the cost of running the restaurant.

Source: Shutterstock/Rade Kovac.

In making the decision whether to open for lunch, a restaurant owner must keep in mind the distinction between fixed and variable costs. Many of a restaurant's costs – the rent, kitchen equipment, tables, plates, cutlery and so on – are fixed. Shutting down during lunch would not reduce these costs. When the owner is deciding whether to serve lunch, only the variable costs – the price of the additional food and the wages of the extra staff – are relevant. The owner shuts down the restaurant at lunchtime only if the revenue from the few lunchtime customers fails to cover the restaurant's variable costs.

An operator of a miniature-golf course in a summer resort faces a similar decision. Because revenue varies substantially from season to season, the firm must decide when to open and when to close. Once again, the fixed costs – the costs of buying the land and building the course – are irrelevant. The miniature-golf course should be open for business only during those times of year when its revenue exceeds its variable costs.

---

fyi

Spilt milk and sunk costs

Sometime in your life, you have probably been told, 'Don't cry over spilt milk', or 'Let bygones be bygones'. These sayings hold a deep truth about rational decision making. Economists say that a cost is a sunk cost when it has already been committed and cannot be recovered. In a sense, a sunk cost is the opposite of an opportunity cost: An opportunity cost is what you have to give up if you choose to do one thing instead of another, whereas a sunk cost is one that cannot be avoided, regardless of the choices you make. Because nothing can be done about sunk costs, you can ignore them when making decisions about various aspects of life, including business strategy.

Our analysis of the firm's shutdown decision is one example of the irrelevance of sunk costs. We assume that the firm cannot recover its fixed costs by temporarily stopping production. As a result, the firm's fixed costs are sunk in the short run and the firm can safely ignore these costs when deciding how much to produce. The firm's short-run supply curve is the part of the marginal-cost curve that lies above average variable cost, and the size of the fixed cost does not matter for this supply decision.

The irrelevance of sunk costs explains how real businesses make decisions. In September 2001, following the terrorist attacks in the United States and the collapse of Ansett Airlines in Australia, demand for accommodation in many of Australia's tourist regions declined sharply. Cairns, Port Douglas and other regions that relied on international tourists and air transport were particularly hard hit, and hotels in these areas were operating at a loss. Despite the losses, however, these hotels kept their doors open and continued to serve customers. At first, this decision might seem surprising – if a hotel is losing money by renting rooms, why don't the owners of the hotel just shut down their business?

To understand this behaviour, we must acknowledge that many hotel costs are sunk in the short run. If a hotel owns its building and cannot resell it, then the cost of the building is sunk. Alternatively, if the hotel has a fixed term lease for the building then the cost of the building is sunk until the lease expires. The opportunity cost of a night's accommodation includes only the variable costs such as the wages of the cleaning and administrative staff. As long as the total revenue from renting rooms exceeds these variable costs, the hotels should continue operating. And, in fact, they did.

The irrelevance of sunk costs is also important for personal decisions. Imagine, for instance, that you place a $15 value on seeing a newly released film. You buy a ticket for $10, but before entering the theatre, you lose the ticket. Should you buy another ticket? Or should you now go home and refuse to pay a total of $20 to see the film? The answer is that you should buy another ticket. The benefit of seeing the film ($15) still exceeds the opportunity cost (the $10 for the second ticket). The $10 you paid for the lost ticket is a sunk cost. As with spilt milk, there is no point in crying about it.

310

The firm's long-run decision to exit or enter a market

The firm's long-run decision to exit a market is similar to its shutdown decision. If the firm exits, it again will lose all revenue from the sale of its product, but now it saves on both fixed and variable costs of production. Thus, *the firm exits if the revenue it would get from producing is less than its total costs.*

We can again make this criterion more useful by writing it mathematically. If *TR* stands for total revenue and *TC* stands for total cost, then the firm's criterion can be written as:

$$\text{Exit if } TR < TC$$

The firm exits if total revenue is less than total cost. By dividing both sides of this inequality by quantity Q, we can write it as:

$$\text{Exit if } TR/Q < TC/Q$$

We can simplify this further by noting that TR/Q is average revenue, which equals the price P, and that TC/Q is average total cost ATC. Therefore, the firm's exit criterion is:

$$\text{Exit if } P < ATC$$

That is, a firm chooses to exit if the price of the good is less than the average total cost of production.

A parallel analysis applies to an entrepreneur who is considering starting a firm. The firm will enter a market if such an action would be profitable, which occurs if the price of the good exceeds the average total cost of production. The entry criterion is:

$$\text{Enter if } P > ATC$$

The criterion for entry is exactly the opposite of the criterion for exit.

We can now describe a competitive firm's long-run profit-maximising strategy. If the firm is in the market, it produces the quantity at which marginal cost equals the price of the good. Yet if the price is less than the average total cost at that quantity, the firm chooses to exit (or not enter) the market. These results are illustrated in Figure 14.4. *The competitive firm's long-run supply curve is the portion of its marginal-cost curve that lies above average total cost.*

Measuring profit in our graph for the competitive firm

As we study exit and entry, it is useful to analyse the firm's profit in more detail. Recall that profit equals total revenue (*TR*) minus total cost (*TC*):

$$\text{Profit} = TR - TC$$

We can rewrite this definition by multiplying and dividing the right-hand side by Q:

$$\text{Profit} = (TR/Q - TC/Q) \times Q$$

But note that TR/Q is average revenue, which is the price P, and TC/Q is average total cost ATC. Therefore:

$$\text{Profit} = (P - ATC) \times Q$$

This way of expressing the firm's profit allows us to measure profit in our graphs.

Panel (a) of Figure 14.5 shows a firm earning positive profit. As we have already discussed, the firm maximises profit by producing the quantity at which price equals marginal cost. Now look at the

Figure 14.4 The competitive firm's long-run supply curve

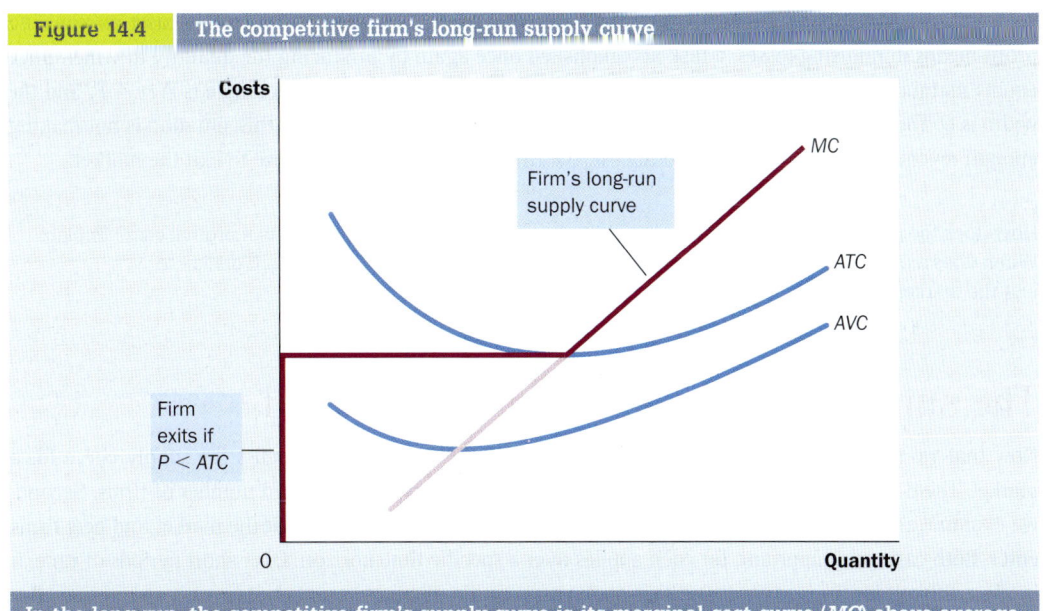

In the long run, the competitive firm's supply curve is its marginal-cost curve (*MC*) above average total cost (*ATC*). If the price falls below average total cost, the firm is better off exiting the market.

Figure 14.5 Profit as the area between price and average total cost

The area of the shaded box between price and average total cost represents the firm's profit. The height of this box is price minus average total cost ($P - ATC$), and the width of the box is the quantity of output (Q). In panel (a), price is above average total cost, so the firm has positive profit. In panel (b), price is less than average total cost, so the firm has losses.

shaded rectangle. The height of the rectangle is $P - ATC$, the difference between price and average total cost. The width of the rectangle is Q, the quantity produced. Therefore, the area of the rectangle is $(P - ATC) \times Q$, which is the firm's profit.

Similarly, panel (b) of this figure shows a firm with losses (negative profit). In this case, maximising profit means minimising losses, a task accomplished once again by producing the quantity at which price equals marginal cost. Now consider the shaded rectangle. The height of the rectangle is $ATC - P$, and the width is Q. The area is $(ATC - P) \times Q$, which is the firm's loss. Because a firm in this situation is not making enough revenue to cover its average total cost, the firm would eventually choose to exit the market.

How does the price faced by a profit-maximising competitive firm compare with its marginal cost? Explain. When does a profit-maximising competitive firm decide to shut down? When does it decide to exit the market?

The supply curve in a competitive market

Now that we have examined the supply decision of a single firm, we can discuss the supply curve for a market. There are two cases to consider. First, we examine a market with a fixed number of firms. Second, we examine a market in which the number of firms can change as old firms exit the market and new firms enter. Both cases are important, for each applies over a specific time horizon. Over short periods of time, it is often difficult for firms to enter and exit, so the assumption of a fixed number of firms is appropriate. But over long periods of time, the number of firms can adjust to changing market conditions.

The short run: Market supply with a fixed number of firms

Consider first a market with 1000 identical firms. For any given price, each firm supplies a quantity of output so that its marginal cost equals the price, as shown in panel (a) of Figure 14.6. That is, as long

Figure 14.6   Market supply with a fixed number of firms

(a) Individual firm supply

(b) Market supply

When the number of firms in the market is fixed, the market supply curve, shown in panel (b), reflects the individual firms' marginal-cost curves, shown in panel (a). Here, in a market of 1000 firms, the quantity of output supplied to the market is 1000 times the quantity supplied by each firm.

as price is above average variable cost, each firm's marginal-cost curve is its supply curve. The quantity of output supplied to the market equals the sum of the quantities supplied by each of the individual firms. Thus, to derive the market supply curve, we add the quantity supplied by each firm in the market. As panel (b) of Figure 14.6 shows, because the firms are identical, the quantity supplied to the market is 1000 times the quantity supplied by each firm.

The long run: Market supply with entry and exit

Now consider what happens if firms are able to enter or exit the market. Let's suppose that everyone has access to the same technology for producing the good and access to the same markets to buy the inputs into production. Therefore, all current and potential firms have the same cost curves.

Decisions about entry and exit in a market of this type depend on the incentives facing the owners of existing firms and the entrepreneurs who could start new firms. If firms already in the market are profitable, then new firms will have an incentive to enter the market. This entry will expand the number of firms, increase the quantity of the good supplied and drive down prices and profits. Conversely, if firms in the market are making losses, then some existing firms will exit the market. Their exit will reduce the number of firms, decrease the quantity of the good supplied and drive up prices and profits. *At the end of this process of entry and exit, firms that remain in the market must be making zero economic profit.*

Recall that we can write a firm's profits as:

$$\text{Profit} = (P - ATC) \times Q$$

This equation shows that an operating firm has zero profit if and only if the price of the good equals the average total cost of producing that good. If price is above average total cost, profit is positive, which encourages new firms to enter. If price is less than average total cost, profit is negative, which encourages some firms to exit. *The process of entry and exit ends only when price and average total cost are driven to equality.*

This analysis has a surprising implication. We noted earlier in the chapter that competitive firms produce so that price equals marginal cost. We just noted that free entry and exit forces price to equal average total cost. But if price is to equal both marginal cost and average total cost, these two measures of cost must equal each other. Marginal cost and average total cost are equal, however, only when the firm is operating at the minimum of average total cost. Recall from the preceding chapter that the level of production with lowest average total cost is called the firm's *efficient scale*. Therefore, *in the long-run equilibrium of a competitive market with free entry and exit, firms must be operating at their efficient scale.*

Panel (a) of Figure 14.7 shows a firm in such a long-run equilibrium. In this figure, price *P* equals marginal cost *MC*, so the firm is maximising profits. Price also equals average total cost *ATC*, so profits are zero. New firms have no incentive to enter the market and existing firms have no incentive to leave the market.

From this analysis of firm behaviour, we can determine the long-run supply curve for the market. In a market with free entry and exit, there is only one price consistent with zero profit – the minimum of average total cost. As a result, the long-run market supply curve must be horizontal at this price, as in panel (b) of Figure 14.7. Any price above this level would generate profit, leading to entry and an increase in the total quantity supplied. Any price below this level would generate losses, leading to exit and a decrease in the total quantity supplied. Eventually, the number of firms in the market

Figure 14.7 | **Market supply with entry and exit**

(a) Firm's zero-profit condition

(b) Market supply

Firms will enter or exit the market until profit is driven to zero. Thus, in the long run, price equals the minimum of average total cost, as shown in panel (a). The number of firms adjusts to ensure that all demand is satisfied at this price. The long-run market supply curve is horizontal at this price, as shown in panel (b).

adjusts so that price equals the minimum of average total cost and there are enough firms to satisfy all the demand at this price.

A shift in demand in the short run and long run

Now that we have a more complete understanding of how firms make supply decisions, we can better explain how markets respond to changes in demand. Because firms can enter and exit a market in the long run but not in the short run, changes in demand have different effects over different time horizons. To see this, let's trace the effects of a shift in demand over time.

Suppose the market for milk begins in long-run equilibrium. Firms are earning zero profit, so price equals the minimum of average total cost. Panel (a) of Figure 14.8 shows this situation. The long-run equilibrium is point A, the quantity sold in the market is Q_1, and the price is P_1.

Now suppose scientists discover that milk has miraculous health benefits. As a result, the demand curve for milk shifts outwards from D_1 to D_2, as in panel (b). The short-run equilibrium moves from point A to point B; as a result, the quantity rises from Q_1 to Q_2, and the price rises from P_1 to P_2. All of the existing firms respond to the higher price by raising the amount produced. Because each firm's supply curve reflects its marginal-cost curve, how much they each increase production is determined by the marginal-cost curve. In the new, short-run equilibrium, the price of milk exceeds average total cost, so the firms are making positive profit.

Over time, the profit generated in this market encourages new firms to enter. Some farmers may switch to milk from other farm products, for example. As the number of firms grows, the short-run supply curve shifts to the right from S_1 to S_2, as in panel (c), and this shift causes the price of milk to fall. Eventually, the price is driven back down to the minimum of average total cost, profits are zero and firms stop entering. Thus, the market reaches a new long-run equilibrium, point C. The price of

Figure 14.8 An increase in demand in the short run and long run

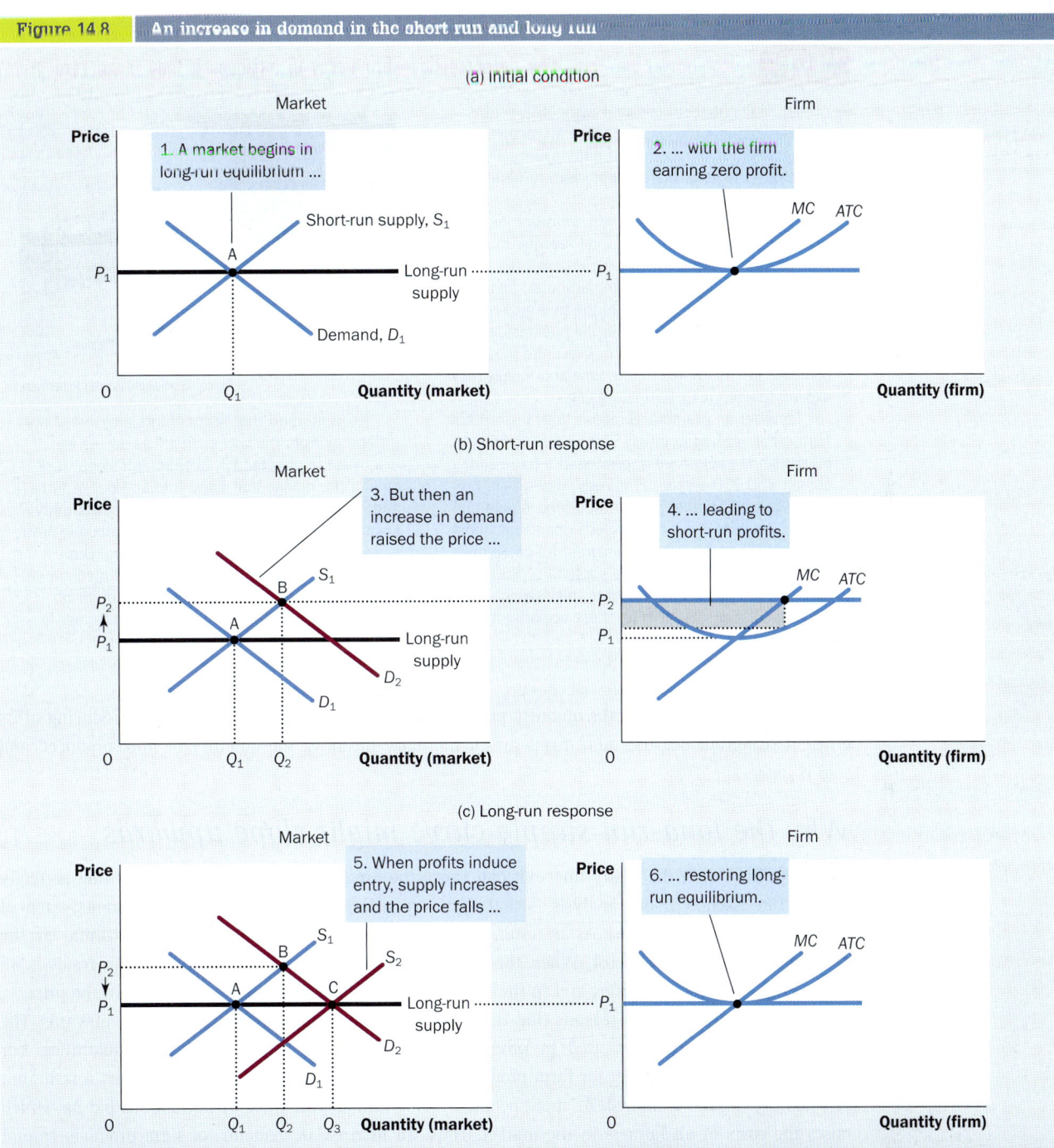

(a) Initial condition

Market

Price

1. A market begins in long-run equilibrium ...

Short-run supply, S_1

A

P_1 — Long-run supply

Demand, D_1

0   Q_1 **Quantity (market)**

Firm

Price

2. ... with the firm earning zero profit.

MC   ATC

P_1

0   **Quantity (firm)**

(b) Short-run response

Market

Price

3. But then an increase in demand raised the price ...

S_1

B

P_2

A

P_1 — Long-run supply

D_2

D_1

0   Q_1 Q_2 **Quantity (market)**

Firm

Price

4. ... leading to short-run profits.

MC   ATC

P_2

P_1

0   **Quantity (firm)**

(c) Long-run response

Market

Price

5. When profits induce entry, supply increases and the price falls ...

S_1 S_2

B

P_2

A   C

P_1 — Long-run supply

D_2

D_1

0   Q_1 Q_2 Q_3 **Quantity (market)**

Firm

Price

6. ... restoring long-run equilibrium.

MC   ATC

P_1

0   **Quantity (firm)**

The market starts in a long-run equilibrium, shown as point A in panel (a). In this equilibrium, each firm makes zero profit, and the price equals the minimum average total cost. Panel (b) shows what happens in the short run when demand rises from D_1 to D_2. The equilibrium goes from point A to point B, price rises from P_1 to P_2, and the quantity sold in the market rises from Q_1 to Q_2. Because price now exceeds average total cost, firms make profits, which over time encourage new firms to enter the market. This entry shifts the short-run supply curve to the right from S_1 to S_2, as shown in panel (c). In the new long-run equilibrium, point C, price has returned to P_1, but the quantity sold has increased to Q_3. Profits are again zero, price is back to the minimum of average total cost, but the market has more firms to satisfy the greater demand.

Why do competitive firms stay in business if they make zero profit?

At first, it might seem odd that competitive firms earn zero profit in the long run. After all, people start businesses to make a profit. If entry eventually drives profit to zero, there might seem to be little reason to stay in business.

To understand the zero-profit condition more fully, recall that profit equals total revenue minus total cost, and that total cost includes all the opportunity costs of the firm. In particular, total cost includes the opportunity cost of the time and money that the firm's owners devote to the business. In the zero-profit equilibrium, the firm's revenue must compensate the owners for the time and money they expend to keep their business going.

Consider an example. Suppose that, to start his farm, a farmer had to invest $1 million, which otherwise he could have deposited in a bank and earned $50 000 a year in interest. In addition, he had to give up another job that would have paid him $30 000 a year. Then the farmer's opportunity cost of farming includes both the interest he could have earned and the forgone wages – a total of $80 000. Even if his profit is driven to zero, his revenue from farming compensates him for these opportunity costs.

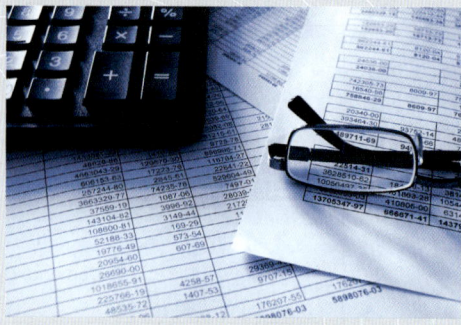

Source: iStockphoto/George Pchemyan.

Keep in mind that accountants measure costs differently from the way economists do. As we discussed in chapter 13, accountants keep track only of the money that flows into and out of firms and, therefore, do not include all the opportunity costs. In the zero-profit equilibrium, economic profit is zero, but accounting profit is positive. Our farmer's accountant, for instance, would conclude that the farmer earned an accounting profit of $80 000, which is enough to keep the farmer in business.

milk has returned to P_1, but the quantity produced has risen to Q_3. Each firm is again producing at its efficient scale, but because more firms are in the dairy business, the quantity of milk produced and sold is higher.

Why the long-run supply curve might slope upwards

So far we have seen that entry and exit can cause the long-run market supply curve to be perfectly elastic. The essence of our analysis is that there are a large number of potential entrants, each of which faces the same costs. As a result, the long-run market supply curve is horizontal at the minimum of average total cost. When the demand for the good increases, the long-run result is an increase in the number of firms and in the total quantity supplied, without any change in the price.

There are, however, two reasons that the long-run market supply curve might slope upwards. The first is that some resources used in production may be available only in limited quantities. For example, consider the market for farm produce. Anyone can choose to buy land and start a farm, but the quantity of land is limited. As more people become farmers, the price of farmland is bid up, which raises the costs of all farmers in the market. Thus, an increase in demand for farm products cannot induce an increase in quantity supplied without also inducing a rise in farmers' costs, which in turn means a rise in price. The result is a long-run market supply curve that is upward-sloping, even with free entry into farming.

A second reason for an upward-sloping supply curve is that firms may have different costs. For example, consider the market for painters. Anyone can enter the market for painting services, but not everyone has the same costs. Costs vary in part because some people work faster than others and in part because some people have better alternative uses of their time than others. For any given price, those with lower costs are more likely to enter than those with higher costs. To increase the quantity of painting services supplied, additional entrants must be encouraged to enter the market. Because these new entrants have higher costs, the price must rise to make entry profitable for them. Thus, the market supply curve for painting services slopes upwards even with free entry into the market.

Notice that if firms have different costs, some firms earn profit even in the long run. In this case, the price in the market reflects the average total cost of the marginal firm – the firm that would exit the market if the price were any lower. This firm earns zero profit, but firms with lower costs earn positive profit. Entry does not eliminate this profit because would-be entrants have higher costs than firms already in the market. Higher cost firms will enter only if the price rises, making the market profitable for them.

Thus, for these two reasons, the long-run supply curve in a market may be upward-sloping rather than horizontal, indicating that a higher price is necessary to induce a larger quantity supplied. Nonetheless, the basic lesson about entry and exit remains true. *Because firms can enter and exit more easily in the long run than in the short run, the long-run supply curve is typically more elastic than the short-run supply curve.*

In the long run with free entry and exit, is the price in a market equal to marginal cost, average total cost, both or neither? Explain with a diagram.

Conclusion: Behind the supply curve

We have been discussing the behaviour of profit-maximising firms that supply goods in perfectly competitive markets. You may recall from chapter 1 that one of the *Ten Lessons from Economics* is that rational people think at the margin. This chapter has applied this idea to the competitive firm. Marginal analysis has given us a theory of the supply curve in a competitive market and, as a result, a deeper understanding of market outcomes.

We have learned that when you buy a good from a firm in a competitive market, you can be assured that the price you pay is close to the cost of producing that good. In particular, if firms are competitive and profit-maximising, the price of a good equals the marginal cost of making that good. In addition, if firms can freely enter and exit the market, the price also equals the lowest possible average total cost of production.

Although we have assumed throughout this chapter that firms are price takers, many of the tools developed here are also useful for studying firms in less competitive markets. In the next three chapters we will examine the behaviour of firms with market power. Marginal analysis will again be useful in analysing these firms, but it will have quite different implications.

Summary

- Because a competitive firm is a price taker, its revenue is proportional to the amount of output it produces. The price of the good equals both the firm's average revenue and its marginal revenue.
- To maximise profit, a firm chooses a quantity of output such that marginal revenue equals marginal cost. Because marginal revenue for a competitive firm equals the market price, the firm chooses quantity so that price equals marginal cost. Thus, the firm's marginal-cost curve is its supply curve.
- In the short run when a firm cannot recover its fixed costs, the firm will choose to shut down temporarily if the price of the good is less than average variable cost. In the long run when the firm can recover both fixed and variable costs, it will choose to exit if the price is less than average total cost.
- In a market with free entry and exit, profits are driven to zero in the long run. In this long-run equilibrium, all firms produce at the efficient scale, price equals the minimum of average total cost, and the number of firms adjusts to satisfy the quantity demanded at this price.
- Changes in demand have different effects over different time horizons. In the short run, an increase in demand raises prices and leads to profits, and a decrease in demand lowers prices and leads to losses. But if firms can freely enter and exit the market, then in the long run the number of firms adjusts to drive the market back to the zero-profit equilibrium.

Key concepts

average revenue marginal revenue

Questions for review

1. What is meant by a competitive firm?
2. Explain the difference between a firm's revenue and its profit. Which do firms maximise?
3. Draw the cost curves for a typical firm. For a given price, explain how the firm chooses the level of output that maximises profit. At that level of output, show on your graph the firm's total revenue and total costs.
4. Under what conditions will a firm shut down temporarily? Explain.
5. Under what conditions will a firm exit a market? Explain.
6. Does a firm's price equal marginal cost in the short run, in the long run or both? Explain.
7. Does a firm's price equal the minimum of average total cost in the short run, in the long run or both? Explain.
8. Are market supply curves typically more elastic in the short run or in the long run? Explain.

Problems and applications

1. What are the characteristics of a competitive market? Which of the following drinks do you think is best described by these characteristics? Why aren't the others?
   a. Tap water
   b. Bottled mineral water
   c. Cola
   d. Beer

2 Your room-mate's long hours in the chemistry lab finally paid off – she discovered a secret formula that lets people do an hour's worth of studying in five minutes. So far, she's sold 200 doses and faces the following average-total-cost schedule:

Q	Average total cost
199	$199
200	200
201	201

If a new customer offers to pay her $300 for one dose, should she make one more? Explain.

3 You are thinking of starting a fishing business. The fixed cost of the business is the cost of a fishing rod, which is $15. (The rod cannot be used for anything except fishing.) The variable costs are bait, which is $1 per fish caught, and your time. The opportunity cost of your time is $10 per hour. The following table shows the relationship between hours spent fishing and number of fish caught.

Hours	1	2	3	4	5
Number of fish caught	10	18	24	28	30

a What is the marginal product of each hour spent fishing? Explain why this number changes as the number of fish you catch increases.

b What is the total cost of catching 10 fish? What about the total cost of catching 18 fish? Draw your total cost curve.

c What is the average cost of 10 fish? How about 18 fish? Draw the average-cost curve and explain its shape.

d What is (approximately) the marginal cost of catching the twentieth fish? What about the marginal cost of the twenty-ninth fish? Explain why the marginal cost changes as the number of fish you catch changes.

e Suppose that you can sell fish for $5 each. How many fish will you catch in order to maximise profit? What is the maximum level of profits that you can make?

f Suppose that you purchase your rod and begin fishing. Suddenly, the price of fish drops to $2.10 each. If you continue to fish, how many fish will you catch in order to maximise your profit? What is the maximum level of profit you can make?

g Suppose, as in part (f), that the price of fish has suddenly dropped to $2.10, but you have already bought your fishing rod. The resale price of fishing rods is zero. Will you continue to fish? Why?

h How would your answer to part (g) change (if at all) if you could resell your rod at $5?

4 The licorice industry is competitive. Each firm produces 2 million straps of licorice per year. The straps have an average total cost of $0.20 each and they sell for $0.30.

a What is the marginal cost of a strap?

b Is the industry in long-run equilibrium? Why or why not?

5 You go out to the best restaurant in town and order a lobster dinner for $140. After eating half of the lobster, you realise that you are quite full. Your date wants you to finish your dinner, because you can't take it home and because 'you've already paid for it'. What should you do? Relate your answer to the material in this chapter.

6 'Strong prices traditionally cause expansion in an industry, eventually bringing an end to high prices and manufacturers' prosperity.' Explain, using appropriate diagrams.

7 Many small boats are made of fibreglass, which is derived from petroleum. Suppose that the price of oil rises.

   a Using diagrams, show what happens to the cost curves of an individual boatbuilding firm and to the market supply curve.

   b What happens to the profits of boatbuilders in the short run? What happens to the number of boatbuilders in the long run?

8 Suppose that the Australian textile industry is competitive and there is no international trade in textiles. In long-run equilibrium, the price per unit of cloth is $30.

   a Describe the equilibrium using graphs for the entire market and for an individual producer.

   b Now suppose that textile producers in other countries are willing to sell large quantities of cloth in Australia for only $25 per unit. Assuming that Australian textile producers have large fixed costs, what is the short-run effect of these imports on the quantity produced by an individual producer? What is the short-run effect on profits? Illustrate your answer with a graph.

   c What is the long-run effect on the number of Australian firms in the industry?

9 Suppose there are 100 ice-cream shops operating in Brisbane. Each shop has the usual U-shaped average-total-cost curve. The market demand curve for ice-cream slopes downwards and the market for ice-cream is in long-run competitive equilibrium.

   a Draw the current equilibrium, using graphs for the entire market and for an individual ice-cream shop.

   b Now the city decides to restrict the number of ice-cream shops. The council passes a law that reduces the number of shops to only 80. What effect will this action have on the market and on an individual shop that is still operating? Use graphs to illustrate your answer.

   c Suppose that the council decides to charge the 80 ice-cream shops a licence fee. How will this affect the number of ice-creams sold by an individual shop and the shop's profit? The council wants to raise as much revenue as possible and also wants to ensure that 80 ice-cream shops remain in the city. At what level should the council set the licence fee? Show the answer on your graph.

10 Assume that the gold-mining industry is competitive.

   a Illustrate a long-run equilibrium using diagrams for the gold market and for a representative gold mine.

   b Suppose that an increase in jewellery demand induces a surge in the demand for gold. Using your diagrams, show what happens in the short run to the gold market and to each existing gold mine.

   c If the demand for gold remains high, what would happen to the price over time? Specifically, would the new long-run equilibrium price be above, below or equal to the short-run equilibrium price in part (b)? Is it possible for the new long-run equilibrium price to be above the original long-run equilibrium price? Explain.

Search me!

 Search me!

When accessing information about economics use the following keywords in any combinations you require:

- competitive market

CourseMate

CourseMate

For more multimedia resources and activities on economics, visit the Economics CourseMate website.

15

Monopoly

Learning objectives

In this chapter you will:

- learn why some markets have only one seller
- analyse how a monopoly determines the quantity to produce and the price to charge
- see how the monopoly's decisions affect economic wellbeing
- see why monopolies try to charge different prices to different customers.

If you own a personal computer, it probably uses some version of Windows, the operating system sold by the Microsoft Corporation. When Microsoft first designed Windows many years ago, it applied for and received a copyright from the government. The copyright gives Microsoft the exclusive right to make and sell copies of the Windows operating system. So if a person wants to buy a copy of Windows, he or she has little choice but to give Microsoft the approximately $250 that the firm has decided to charge for its product. Microsoft is said to have a *monopoly* in the market for Windows.

Microsoft's competitive environment look very different to the description of the market we developed in chapter 14. In that chapter, we analysed competitive markets, in which there are many firms offering essentially identical products, so each firm has little influence over the price it receives. In contrast, a monopoly such as Microsoft has no close competitors and, therefore, can influence the market price of its product. Whereas a competitive firm is a *price taker*, a monopoly firm is a *price maker*.

In this chapter we examine the implications of this market power. We will see that market power alters the relationship between a firm's price and its costs. A competitive firm takes the price of its output as given and then chooses the quantity supplied so that price equals marginal cost. In contrast, the price charged by a monopoly exceeds marginal cost. This result is clearly true in the case of Microsoft's Windows. The marginal cost of Windows – the extra cost that Microsoft incurs when another buyer downloads a copy of the program – is probably less than a dollar. The market price of Windows is many times the marginal cost.

It is perhaps not surprising that monopolies charge high prices for their products. Customers of monopolies might seem to have little choice but to pay whatever the monopoly charges. But, if so, why does a copy of Windows not cost $1000? Or $10 000? The reason, of course, is that if Microsoft sets the price that high, fewer people would buy the product. People would buy fewer computers, switch to other operating systems (like Android or Apple), or make illegal copies. A monopoly firm can control the price of the good it sells, but because high prices reduce the amount that its customers buy, the monopoly's profits are not unlimited.

As we examine the production and pricing decisions of monopolies, we also consider the implications of monopoly for society as a whole. Monopoly firms, like competitive firms, aim to maximise profit. But this goal has very different ramifications for competitive and monopoly firms. In competitive markets, self-interested consumers and producers behave as if they are guided by an invisible hand to promote general economic wellbeing. By contrast, because monopoly firms are unchecked by competition, the outcome in a market with a monopoly is often not in the best interest of society.

Our study of monopoly firms will have many parallels with competitive firms. As we saw in chapter 14, a competitive firm maximises its profit by setting its output so that marginal revenue equals marginal cost. In this chapter, we show that this same profit-maximisation rule applies to a monopoly firm. However, unlike a competitive firm, a monopoly's marginal revenue is not the same as the market price.

Perfect competition and monopoly provide two ends of a competitive spectrum. For a perfectly competitive firm, competition is so fierce that it has no discretion over the price it charges for its product. It is a price taker. In contrast, a monopoly faces no competition. It sets its output and prices so that output is only subject to market demand. Most firms operate in markets where the level of competition is between these two extremes: they face some (but not perfect) competition. In this respect, our study of perfect competition and monopoly are a first step towards understanding how most firms price their goods and services. As we introduce strategic elements in chapter 16 and product differentiation in chapter 18, the picture will be completed.

Why monopolies arise

A firm is a **monopoly** if it is the sole seller of its product and if its product does not have close substitutes. The fundamental cause of monopoly is barriers to entry – a monopoly remains the only seller in its market because other firms cannot enter the market and compete with it. Barriers to entry, in turn, have three main sources:

- *Monopoly resources:* A key resource is owned by a single firm.
- *Government regulation:* The government gives a single firm the exclusive right to produce some good or service.
- *The production process:* A single firm can produce output at a lower cost than can a larger number of producers.

  Let's briefly discuss each of these.

Monopoly resources

The simplest way for a monopoly to arise is for a single firm to own a key resource. For example, consider the market for water in a small town in the outback. If dozens of town residents can pump and sell underground bore water, the competitive model discussed in chapter 14 describes the behaviour of sellers. As a result, the price of a litre of water is driven to equal the marginal cost of pumping an extra litre. But if there is only one resident in town who can pump out underground water and it is impossible to get water from anywhere else, then that resident has a monopoly on water. Not surprisingly, the monopolist has much greater market power than any single firm in a competitive market. In the case of a necessity like water, the monopolist could command quite a high price, even if the marginal cost of pumping an extra litre is low.

Although exclusive ownership of a key resource is a potential cause of monopoly, in practice monopolies rarely arise for this reason. Economies are large and resources are owned by many people. Indeed, because many goods are traded internationally, the natural scope of their markets is often world-wide. There are, therefore, few examples of firms that own a resource for which there are no close substitutes.

CASESTUDY

The gas industry in south-eastern Australia

For a firm to be a monopoly, it must be the only seller of a product that does not have any close substitutes. Traditionally, in Victoria, New South Wales and South Australia, single sellers provided almost all natural gas. Natural gas for Victoria came from fields in the Bass Strait, controlled by a joint venture between Esso and BHP Billiton. Gas for New South Wales and South Australia came from the Cooper Basin, which is also controlled by a single joint venture. Although these firms were the only sellers of gas, were they monopolists? In particular, were the prices set by these gas producers constrained by the ability of consumers to substitute other energy sources (such as electricity, coal and oil) for natural gas?

In Victoria, most natural gas is purchased for domestic use such as cooking, central heating and hot water. Although consumers are unlikely to give up their gas stoves or hot-water systems in the short term if the price of gas rises, there will probably be significant substitution of alternative fuels in the longer term. With higher gas prices, households may decide to buy an electric or solar hot-water system rather than a gas system when their current hot-water system needs replacing. Household demand for natural gas may be fairly inelastic over the short term but is likely to be elastic over a five-year or 10-year period. The Esso–BHP Billiton joint venture may have had little ability to raise prices to monopoly levels except in the short term.

In contrast, natural gas in New South Wales is largely used by industry. Many of the firms that rely on natural gas, such as steel smelters and fertiliser companies, have spent large amounts of money building their factories. These factories cannot be easily moved or adapted to other fuels. Often, electricity cannot be used as a substitute for gas and environmental restrictions prevent firms from using oil or coal as a fuel source, particularly if they are located near a major city such as Sydney. These firms are likely to have few alternatives other than to continue to purchase gas even if the price of gas rises significantly. Indeed, a study by the Australian Bureau of Agricultural and Resource Economics found that industrial users of natural gas have a less-elastic demand curve than domestic users. This suggests that the Cooper Basin Partners, who were the only suppliers of gas to New South Wales, may have had more market power than Victorian gas producers.

The ability of electricity and other fuel sources to constrain the price setting of gas producers was a key issue in the reform of the gas sector. Concerns about the monopoly power of gas producers led the state and federal governments to try to introduce more competition into gas supply. In 1998, the Victorian and NSW gas networks were joined by a pipeline between Albury and Wagga Wagga, while in August 2000 a major pipeline linking Sydney to the Bass Strait gas fields was opened. More recently, coal-seam gas has been discovered in Queensland and more gas pipelines have been built connecting Victoria, South Australia, New South Wales and Queensland. As a result, there is now competition in the supply of gas in south-eastern Australia.

Government-created monopolies

In many cases, monopolies arise because the government has given one person or firm the exclusive right to sell some good or service. Sometimes the monopoly arises from the sheer political clout of the would-be monopolist. Kings, for example, once granted exclusive business licences to their friends and allies. In England, this power was taken away from the monarch by parliament in 1624. At other times, the government grants a monopoly because doing so is in the public interest. For instance, until October 2001, the Australian government had given a monopoly to a company called Melbourne IT to issue .com.au Internet addresses. Since then, the monopoly licence has been given to another company, AusRegistry. Having a single company maintain the address database avoids problems such as issuing the same name twice.

Patent and copyright laws are one example of how the government creates a monopoly to serve the public interest. When a pharmaceutical company discovers a new medicine, it can apply to the government for a patent. If the government deems the medicine to be truly original, it approves the patent, which gives the company the exclusive right to manufacture and sell the medicine for a certain number of years. In Australia, patents for medicine last for 20 years. Similarly, when a novelist finishes a book, she can copyright it. The copyright is a government guarantee that no one can print and sell the work without the author's permission. The copyright makes the novelist a monopolist in the sale of her novel.

The effects of patent and copyright laws are easy to see. Because these laws give one producer a monopoly, they lead to higher prices than would occur under competition. But by allowing these monopoly producers to charge higher prices and earn higher profits, the laws also encourage some desirable behaviour. Pharmaceutical companies are allowed to be monopolists in the medicines they discover in order to encourage research by these companies. Authors are allowed to be monopolists in the sale of their books in order to encourage them to write more and better books.

Thus, the laws governing patents and copyrights have both benefits and costs. The benefits of the patent and copyright laws are the increased incentives for creative activity. These benefits are offset, to some extent, by the costs of monopoly pricing, which we examine fully later in this chapter.

Natural monopolies

An industry is a **natural monopoly** when a single firm can supply a good or service to an entire market at a lower cost than could two or more firms. For example, an industry is a natural monopoly when there are economies of scale over the relevant range of output. Figure 15.1 shows the average total costs of a firm with economies of scale. In this case, a single firm can produce any amount of output at least cost. That is, for any given amount of output, a larger number of firms leads to less output per firm and higher average total cost.

An example of a natural monopoly is the distribution of water. To provide water to residents of a town, a firm must build a network of pipes throughout the town. If two or more firms were to compete in the provision of this service, each firm would have to pay the fixed cost of building a network. Thus, the average total cost of water is lowest if a single firm serves the entire market.

We saw other examples of natural monopolies when we discussed public goods and common resources in chapter 11. We noted that club goods are excludable but not rival in consumption. An example is a bridge used so infrequently that it is never congested. The bridge is excludable because a toll collector can prevent someone from using it. The bridge is not rival in consumption because use of the bridge by one person does not diminish the ability of others to use it. Because there is a fixed cost of building the bridge and a negligible marginal cost of additional users, the average total cost of a trip across the bridge (the total cost divided by the number of trips) falls as the number of trips rises. Therefore, the bridge is a natural monopoly.

When a firm is a natural monopoly, it is less concerned about new entrants eroding its monopoly power. Normally, a firm has trouble maintaining a monopoly position without ownership of a key

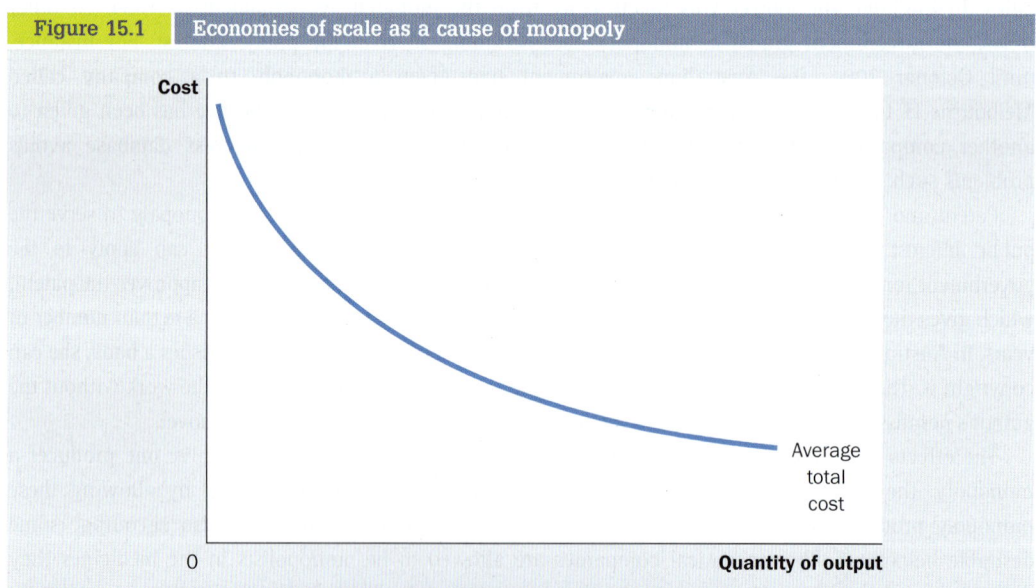

Figure 15.1 | **Economies of scale as a cause of monopoly**

When a firm's average-total-cost curve continually declines, the firm has what is called a natural monopoly. In this case, when production is divided among more firms, each firm produces less, and average total cost rises. As a result, a single firm can produce any given amount at the smallest cost.

resource or protection from the government. The monopolist's profit attracts entrants into the market and these entrants make the market more competitive. In contrast, entering a market in which another firm has a natural monopoly is unattractive. Would-be entrants know that they cannot achieve the same low costs that the monopolist enjoys because, after entry, each firm would have a smaller piece of the market.

In some cases, the size of the market is one determinant of whether an industry is a natural monopoly. Again, consider a bridge across a river. When the population is small, the bridge may be a natural monopoly. A single bridge can satisfy the entire demand for trips across the river at lowest cost. Yet, as the population grows and the bridge becomes congested, satisfying the entire demand may require two or more bridges across the same river. Thus, as a market expands, a natural monopoly can evolve into a competitive market.

What are three reasons a market might have a monopoly? Give two examples of monopolies and explain the reason for each.

How monopolies make production and pricing decisions

Now that we know how monopolies arise, we can consider how a monopoly firm decides how much of its product to make and what price to charge for it. The analysis of monopoly behaviour in this section is the starting point for evaluating whether monopolies are desirable and what policies the government might pursue in monopoly markets.

Monopoly versus competition

The key difference between a competitive firm and a monopoly is the monopoly's ability to influence the price of its output. A competitive firm is small relative to the market in which it operates and, therefore, takes the price of its output as given by market conditions. In contrast, because a monopoly is the sole producer in its market, it can alter the price of its good by adjusting the quantity it supplies to the market.

One way to view this difference between a competitive firm and a monopoly is to consider the demand curve that each firm faces. When we analysed profit maximisation by competitive firms in chapter 14, we drew the market price as a horizontal line. Because a competitive firm can sell as much or as little as it wants at this price, the competitive firm faces a horizontal demand curve, as in panel (a) of Figure 15.2. In effect, because the competitive firm sells a product with many perfect substitutes (the products of all the other firms in its market), the demand curve that any one firm faces is perfectly elastic.

In contrast, because a monopoly is the sole producer in its market, its demand curve is the market demand curve. Thus, the monopolist's demand curve slopes downwards for all the usual reasons, as in panel (b) of Figure 15.2. If the monopolist raises the price of its good, consumers buy less of it. In other words, if the monopolist reduces the quantity of output it sells, the price of its output increases.

The market demand curve provides a constraint on a monopoly's ability to profit from its market power. A monopolist would prefer, if it were possible, to charge a high price and sell a large quantity at that high price. The market demand curve makes that outcome impossible. In particular, the market

Figure 15.2 Demand curves for competitive and monopoly firms

(a) A competitive firm's demand curve

(b) A monopolist's demand curve

Because competitive firms are price takers, in effect they face horizontal demand curves, as in panel (a). Because a monopoly firm is the sole producer in its market, it faces the downward-sloping market demand curve as in panel (b). As a result, the monopoly has to accept a lower price if it wants to sell more output.

demand curve describes the combinations of price and quantity that are available to a monopoly firm. By adjusting the quantity produced (or, equivalently, the price charged), the monopolist can choose any point on the demand curve, but it cannot choose a point off the demand curve.

What price and quantity of output will the monopolist choose? As with competitive firms, we assume that the monopolist's goal is to maximise profit. Because profit is total revenue minus total costs, our next task in explaining monopoly behaviour is to examine a monopolist's revenue.

A monopoly's revenue

Consider a town with a single producer of water. Table 15.1 shows how the monopoly's revenue might depend on the amount of water produced.

The first two columns show the monopolist's demand schedule. If the monopolist produces 1 litre of water, it can sell that litre for $10; if it produces 2 litres, it must lower the price to $9 in order to sell both litres; if it produces 3 litres, it must lower the price to $8, and so on. If you graphed these two columns of numbers, you would get a typical downward-sloping demand curve.

The third column of the table presents the monopolist's total revenue. It equals the quantity sold (from the first column) times the price (from the second column). The fourth column calculates the firm's average revenue, the amount of revenue the firm receives per unit sold. We calculate average revenue by taking the number for total revenue in the third column and dividing it by the quantity of output in the first column. As we discussed in chapter 14, average revenue always equals the price of the good. This is true for monopolists as well as for competitive firms.

The last column of Table 15.1 calculates the firm's marginal revenue, the amount of revenue that the firm receives for each additional unit of output. We calculate marginal revenue by taking the change in total revenue when output increases by one unit. For example, when the firm is producing

Quantity of water	Price	Total revenue	Average revenue	Marginal revenue
(Q)	(P)	(TR = P× Q)	(AR = TR/Q)	(MR = △TR/△Q)
0 litres	$11	$0	—	—
1	10	10	$10	$10
2	9	18	9	8
3	8	24	8	6
4	7	28	7	4
5	6	30	6	2
6	5	30	5	0
7	4	28	4	−2
8	3	24	3	−4

Table 15.1 A monopoly's total, average and marginal revenue

3 litres of water, it receives total revenue of $24. Raising production to 4 litres increases total revenue to $28. Thus, marginal revenue is $28 minus $24, or $4.

Table 15.1 shows a result that will be important for understanding monopoly behaviour – *a monopolist's marginal revenue is always less than the price of its good.* For example, if the firm raises production of water from 3 to 4 litres, it will increase total revenue by only $4, even though it will be able to sell each litre for $7. For a monopoly, marginal revenue is lower than price because a monopoly faces a downward-sloping demand curve. To increase the amount sold, a monopoly firm must lower the price of its good. Hence, to sell the fourth litre of water, the monopolist must get less revenue for each of the first 3 litres.

Marginal revenue is very different for monopolies than it is for competitive firms. When a monopoly increases the amount it sells, it has two effects on total revenue (P × Q):

- *The output effect:* more output is sold, so Q is higher, which tends to increase total revenue.
- *The price effect:* the price falls, so P is lower, which tends to decrease total revenue.

Because a competitive firm can sell all it wants at the market price, there is no price effect. When it increases production by one unit, it receives the market price for that unit, and it does not receive any less for the amount it was already selling. That is, because the competitive firm is a price taker its marginal revenue equals the price of its good. In contrast, when a monopoly increases production by one unit, it must reduce the price it charges for every unit it sells, and this cut in price reduces revenue on the units it was already selling. As a result, a monopoly's marginal revenue is less than its price.

Figure 15.3 graphs the demand curve and the marginal-revenue curve for a monopoly firm. (Since the firm's price equals its average revenue, the demand curve is also the average-revenue curve.) These two curves always start at the same point on the vertical axis because the marginal revenue of the first unit sold equals the price of the good. But, for the reason we just discussed, the monopolist's marginal

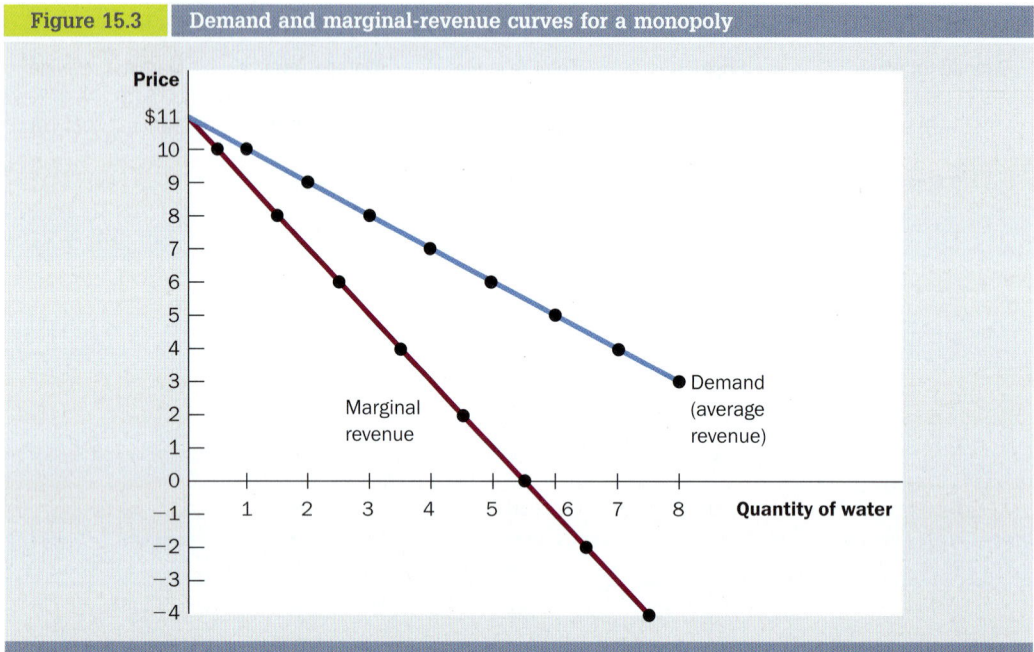

Figure 15.3 Demand and marginal-revenue curves for a monopoly

The demand curve shows how the quantity affects the price of the good. The marginal-revenue curve shows how the firm's revenue changes when the quantity increases by one unit. Because the price on all units sold must fall if the monopoly increases production, marginal revenue is always less than the price.

revenue is less than the price of the good. Thus, a monopoly's marginal-revenue curve lies below its demand curve.

You can see in the figure (as well as in Table 15.1) that marginal revenue can even become negative. Marginal revenue is negative when the price effect on revenue is greater than the output effect. In this case, when the firm produces an extra unit of output, the price falls by enough to cause the firm's total revenue to decline, even though the firm is selling more units.

Profit maximisation

Now that we have considered the revenue of a monopoly firm, we are ready to examine how such a firm maximises profit. Recall that one of the *Ten Lessons from Economics* discussed in chapter 1 is that rational people think at the margin. This lesson is as true for monopolists as it is for competitive firms. Here we apply the logic of marginal analysis to the monopolist's problem of deciding how much to produce.

Figure 15.4 graphs the demand curve, the marginal-revenue curve and the cost curves for a monopoly firm. All these curves should seem familiar. The demand and marginal-revenue curves are like those in Figure 15.3, and the cost curves are like those we introduced in chapter 13 and used to analyse competitive firms in chapter 14. These curves contain all the information we need to determine the level of output that a profit-maximising monopolist will choose.

Suppose, first, that the firm is producing at a low level of output, such as Q_1. In this case, marginal cost is less than marginal revenue. If the firm increased production by one unit, the additional revenue

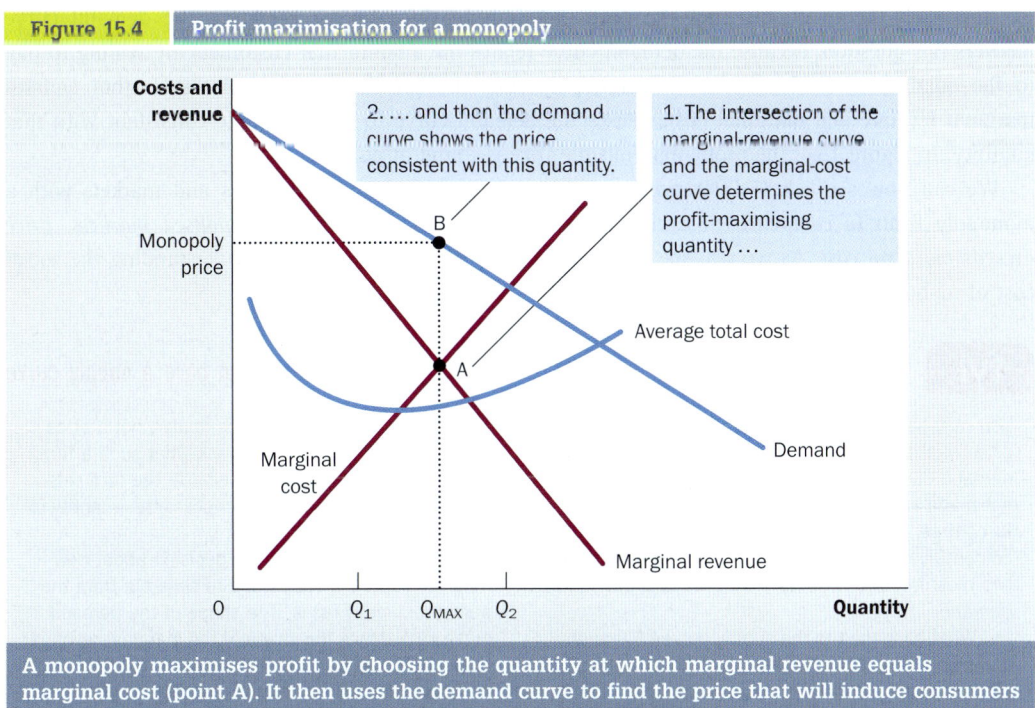

Figure 15.4   Profit maximisation for a monopoly

2. ... and then the demand curve shows the price consistent with this quantity.

1. The intersection of the marginal-revenue curve and the marginal-cost curve determines the profit-maximising quantity ...

A monopoly maximises profit by choosing the quantity at which marginal revenue equals marginal cost (point A). It then uses the demand curve to find the price that will induce consumers to buy that quantity (point B).

would exceed the additional costs, and profit would rise. Thus, when marginal cost is less than marginal revenue, the firm can increase profit by producing more units.

A similar argument applies at high levels of output, such as Q_2. In this case, marginal cost is greater than marginal revenue. If the firm reduced production by one unit, the costs saved would exceed the revenue lost. Thus, if marginal cost is greater than marginal revenue, the firm can raise profit by reducing production.

In the end, the firm adjusts its level of production until the quantity reaches Q_{MAX}, at which marginal revenue equals marginal cost. Thus, *the monopolist's profit-maximising quantity of output is determined by the intersection of the marginal-revenue curve and the marginal-cost curve*. In Figure 15.4, this intersection occurs at point A.

You might recall from chapter 14 that competitive firms also choose the quantity of output at which marginal revenue equals marginal cost. In following this rule for profit maximisation, competitive firms and monopolies are alike. But there is also an important difference between these types of firms – the marginal revenue of a competitive firm equals its price, whereas the marginal revenue of a monopoly is less than its price. That is:

$$\text{For a competitive firm: } P = MR = MC$$

$$\text{For a monopoly firm: } P > MR = MC$$

The equality of marginal revenue and marginal cost at the profit-maximising quantity is the same for both types of firm. What differs is how the price is related to marginal revenue and marginal cost.

How does the monopoly find the profit-maximising price for its product? The demand curve answers this question, because the demand curve relates the amount that customers are willing to pay to the quantity sold. Thus, after the monopoly firm chooses the quantity of output that equates marginal revenue and marginal cost, it uses the demand curve to find the price consistent with that quantity. In Figure 15.4, the profit-maximising price is found at point B.

We can now see a key difference between markets with competitive firms and markets with a monopoly firm: *In competitive markets, price equals marginal cost; in monopolised markets, price exceeds marginal cost.* As we will see in a moment, this finding is crucial to understanding the social cost of monopoly.

A monopoly's profit

How much profit does the monopoly make? To see the monopoly's profit, recall that profit equals total revenue (*TR*) minus total costs (*TC*):

$$\text{Profit} = TR - TC$$

We can rewrite this as:

$$\text{Profit} = (TR/Q - TC/Q) \times Q$$

TR/Q is average revenue, which equals the price *P*, and *TC/Q* is average total cost *ATC*. Therefore:

$$\text{Profit} = (P - ATC) \times Q$$

This equation for profit (which is the same as the profit equation for competitive firms) allows us to measure the monopolist's profit in our graph.

Consider the shaded box in Figure 15.5. The height of the box (the segment BC) is price minus average total cost, *P – ATC*, which is the profit on the typical unit sold. The width of the box (the segment DC) is the quantity sold Q_{MAX}. Therefore, the area of this box is the monopoly firm's total profit.

Figure 15.5 The monopolist's profit

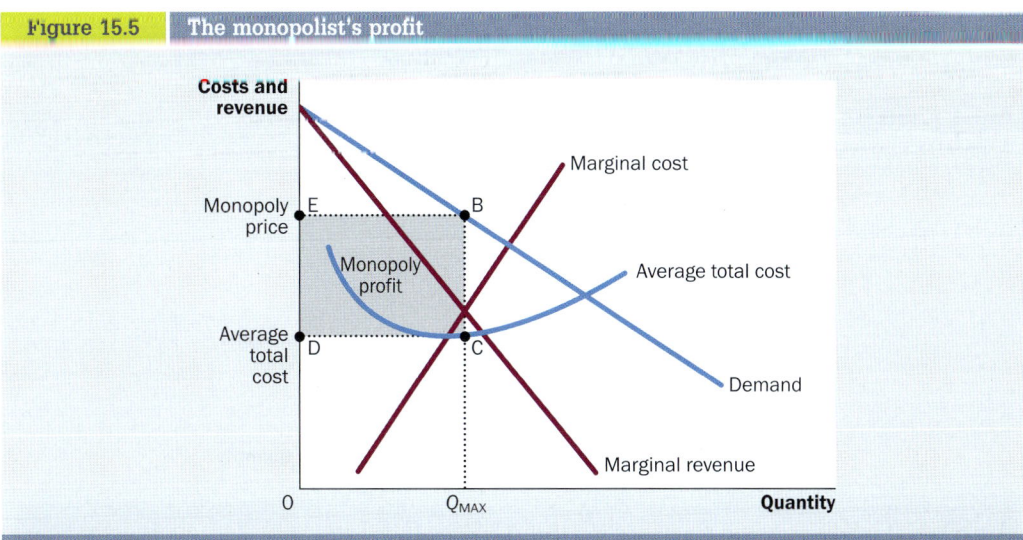

The area of the box BCDE equals the profit of the monopoly firm. The height of the box (BC) is price minus average total cost, which equals profit per unit sold. The width of the box (DC) is the number of units sold.

CASE STUDY

Bell's monopoly and the price of telephone calls

According to our analysis, prices are determined quite differently in monopolised markets from the way they are in competitive markets. A natural way to test this theory is to see what happens when a patent ends. When a company invents a new product, patent law gives the company a monopoly over the sale of that product. But eventually the firm's patent runs out and any company can make and sell the product. At that time, the market switches from being monopolistic to being competitive. By observing what happens to price and output both before and after the patent ends, we can compare monopoly and competitive behaviour.

A good example is provided by the telephone. Alexander Graham Bell invented the telephone and made the first successful transmission on 10 March 1876. Bell's patents over the telephone were held by the American Telephone and Telegraph Company (AT&T) until the patents ended in 1893. When the patents expired, many new firms entered the US telephone industry and it became highly competitive.

What should have happened to the price of telephone calls when the patents ran out? Figure 15.6 shows the market for telephone calls. In this figure, the marginal cost of producing each call is constant. (This is approximately true for many telephone calls.) During the life of the patent, the monopoly firm maximises profit by producing the quantity at which marginal revenue equals marginal cost and charging a price well above marginal cost. But when the patent runs out, the monopoly profit should encourage new firms to enter the market. As the market becomes more competitive, the price should fall to equal marginal cost.

Experience is, in fact, consistent with our theory. While the telephone was protected by a patent, AT&T charged high prices and restricted service to larger towns and cities. In 1893, only 270 000 telephones were installed in the United States. After the patents expired, competition became fierce and prices fell. Within 13 years the number of telephone subscribers had risen to six million. AT&T's profits were reduced by competition and in some states competition was so fierce that AT&T was reported to be making a loss. Just as our analysis predicts, the price of the competitively produced telephone calls was well below the price that the monopolist was charging.

>>

Figure 15.6 | **Prices and patents**

When a patent gives a firm a monopoly over the sale of a product, the firm charges the monopoly price, which is well above the marginal cost. When the patent runs out, new firms enter the market, making it more competitive. As a result, the price falls from the monopoly price to marginal cost.

 Explain how a monopolist chooses the quantity of output to produce and the price to charge.

The welfare cost of monopoly

Is monopoly a good way to organise a market? We have seen that a monopoly, in contrast to a competitive firm, charges a price above marginal cost. From the standpoint of consumers, this high price makes monopoly undesirable. At the same time, however, the monopoly is earning profit from charging this high price. From the standpoint of the owners of the firm, the high price makes monopoly very desirable. Is it possible that the benefits to the firm's owners exceed the costs imposed on consumers, making monopoly desirable from the standpoint of society as a whole?

We can answer this question using the type of analysis we first saw in chapter 7. As in that chapter, we use total surplus as our measure of economic wellbeing. Recall that total surplus is the sum of consumer surplus and producer surplus. Consumer surplus is consumers' willingness to pay for a good minus the amount they actually pay for it. Producer surplus is the amount producers receive for a good minus their costs of producing it. In this case, there is a single producer – the monopolist.

You might already be able to guess the result of this analysis. In chapter 7 we concluded that the equilibrium of supply and demand in a competitive market is not only a natural outcome but a desirable one. In particular, the invisible hand of the market leads to an allocation of resources that makes total surplus as large as it can be. Because a monopoly leads to an allocation of resources different from that in a competitive market, the outcome must, in some way, fail to maximise total economic wellbeing.

The deadweight loss

We begin by considering what the monopoly firm would do if it were run by a benevolent social planner. The social planner cares not only about the profit earned by the firm's owners but also about the benefits received by the firm's consumers. The planner tries to maximise total surplus, which equals producer surplus (profit) plus consumer surplus. Keep in mind that total surplus equals the value of the good to consumers minus the costs of making the good incurred by the monopoly producer.

Figure 15.7 analyses what level of output a benevolent social planner would choose. The demand curve reflects the value of the good to consumers, as measured by their willingness to pay for it. The marginal-cost curve reflects the costs of the monopolist. Thus, *the socially efficient quantity is found where the demand curve and the marginal-cost curve intersect.* Below this quantity, the value to consumers exceeds the marginal cost of providing the good, so increasing output would raise total surplus. Above this quantity, the marginal cost exceeds the value to consumers, so decreasing output would raise total surplus. At the optimal quantity, the value of an extra unit to consumers exactly equals the marginal cost of production.

If the social planner were running the monopoly, the firm could achieve this efficient outcome by charging the price found at the intersection of the demand and marginal-cost curves. Thus, like a

Figure 15.7	The efficient level of output

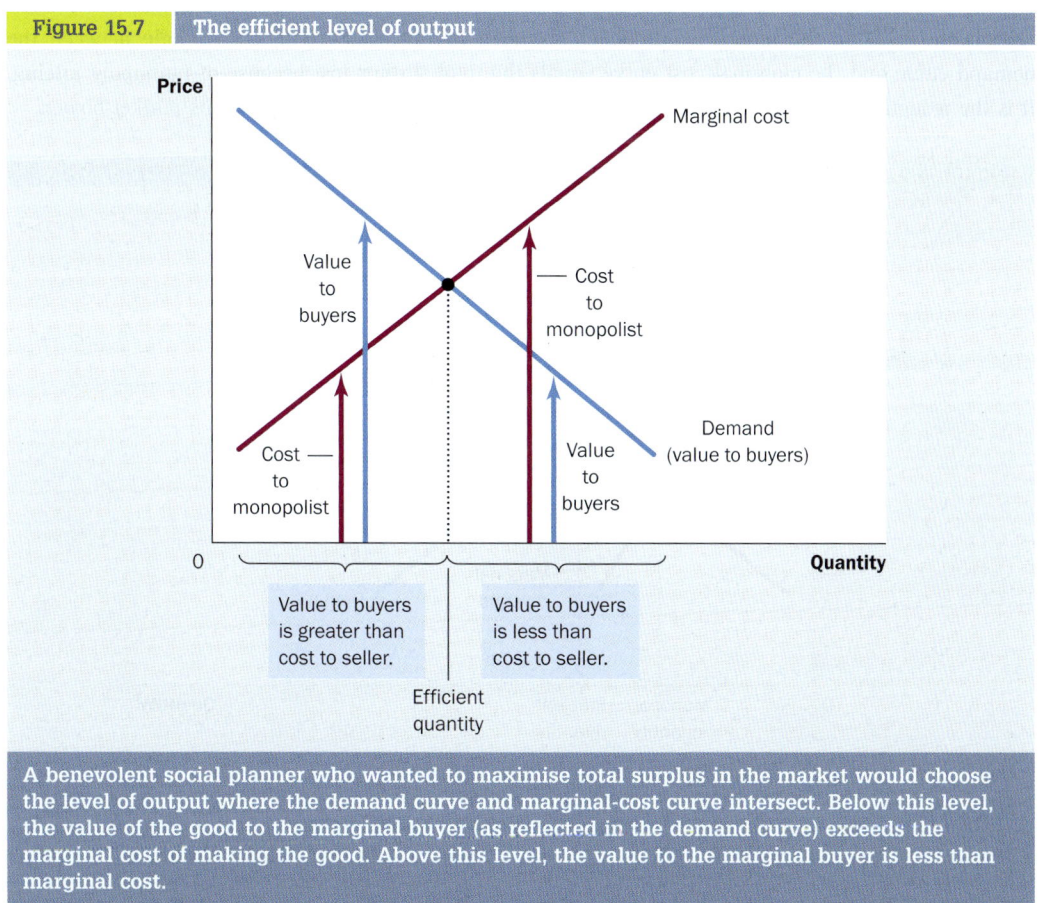

A benevolent social planner who wanted to maximise total surplus in the market would choose the level of output where the demand curve and marginal-cost curve intersect. Below this level, the value of the good to the marginal buyer (as reflected in the demand curve) exceeds the marginal cost of making the good. Above this level, the value to the marginal buyer is less than marginal cost.

competitive firm and unlike a profit-maximising monopoly, a social planner would charge a price equal to marginal cost. Because this price would give consumers an accurate signal about the cost of producing the good, consumers would buy the efficient quantity.

We can evaluate the welfare effects of monopoly by comparing the level of output that the monopolist chooses with the level of output that a social planner would choose. As we have seen, the monopolist chooses to produce and sell the quantity of output at which the marginal-revenue and marginal-cost curves intersect; the social planner would choose the quantity at which the demand and marginal-cost curves intersect. Figure 15.8 shows the comparison. *The monopolist produces less than the socially efficient quantity of output.*

We can also view the inefficiency of monopoly in terms of the monopolist's price. Because the market demand curve describes a negative relationship between the price and quantity of the good, a quantity that is inefficiently low is equivalent to a price that is inefficiently high. When a monopolist charges a price above marginal cost, some potential consumers value the good at more than its marginal cost but less than the monopolist's price. These consumers do not buy the good. Because the value these consumers place on the good is greater than the cost of providing it to them, this result is inefficient. Thus, monopoly pricing prevents some mutually beneficial trades from taking place.

The inefficiency of monopoly can be measured with a deadweight loss triangle, as illustrated in Figure 15.8. Because the demand curve reflects the value to consumers and the marginal-cost curve reflects the costs to the monopoly producer, the area of the deadweight-loss triangle between the demand curve and the marginal-cost curve equals the total surplus lost because of monopoly pricing. It is the reduction in economic wellbeing that results from the monopoly's use of its market power.

Figure 15.8	The inefficiency of monopoly

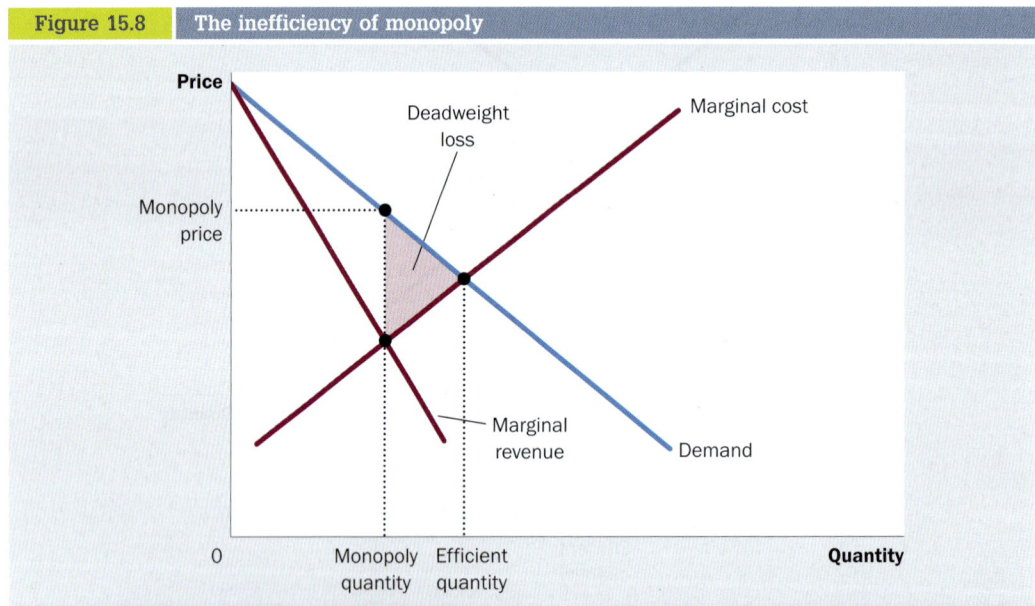

Because a monopoly charges a price above marginal cost, not all consumers who value the good at more than its cost buy it. Thus, the quantity produced and sold by a monopoly is below the socially efficient level. The deadweight loss is represented by the area of the triangle between the demand curve (which reflects the value of the good to consumers) and the marginal-cost curve (which reflects the costs of the monopoly producer).

The deadweight loss caused by monopoly is similar to the deadweight loss caused by a tax. Indeed, a monopolist is like a private tax collector. As we saw in chapter 0, a tax on a good places a wedge between consumers' willingness to pay (as reflected in the demand curve) and producers' costs (as reflected in the supply curve). Because a monopoly exerts its market power by charging a price above marginal cost, it creates a similar wedge. In both cases, the wedge causes the quantity sold to fall short of the social optimum. The difference between the two cases is that the government gets the revenue from a tax, whereas a private firm gets the monopoly profit.

The monopoly's profit: A social cost?

It is tempting to decry monopolies for 'profiteering' at the expense of the public. And, indeed, a monopoly firm does earn a higher profit by virtue of its market power. According to the economic analysis of monopoly, however, the firm's profit is not in itself necessarily a problem for society.

Welfare in a monopolised market, like all markets, includes the welfare of both consumers and producers. Whenever a consumer pays an extra dollar to a producer because of a monopoly price, the consumer is worse off by a dollar, and the producer is better off by the same amount. This transfer from the consumers of the good to the owners of the monopoly does not affect the market's total surplus – the sum of consumer and producer surplus. In other words, the monopoly profit itself does not represent a reduction in the size of the economic pie; it merely represents a bigger slice for producers and a smaller slice for consumers. Unless consumers are for some reason more deserving than producers – a judgement that goes beyond the realm of economic efficiency – the monopoly profit is not a social problem.

The problem in a monopolised market arises because the firm produces and sells a quantity of output below the level that maximises total surplus. The deadweight loss measures how much the economic pie shrinks as a result. This inefficiency is inextricably connected to the monopoly's high price – consumers buy fewer units when the firm raises its price above marginal cost. But keep in mind that the profit earned on the units that continue to be sold is not the problem. The problem stems from the inefficiently low quantity of output. Put differently, if the high monopoly price did not discourage some consumers from buying the good, it would raise producer surplus by exactly the amount it reduced consumer surplus, leaving total surplus the same as could be achieved by a benevolent social planner.

There is, however, a possible exception to this conclusion. Suppose that a monopoly firm has to incur additional costs to maintain its monopoly position. For example, a firm with a government-created monopoly might need to hire lobbyists to convince politicians to continue its monopoly. In this case, the monopoly may use up some of its monopoly profits paying for these additional costs. If so, the social loss from monopoly includes both these costs and the deadweight loss resulting from a price above marginal cost.

---

fyi

Measuring the cost of monopoly

How large is the social cost from monopoly? A number of studies have tried to measure the size of monopoly deadweight loss, but the results from this research have been inconclusive. US researchers, for example, have argued that monopoly deadweight loss represents as little as 0.1 per cent or as much as 6 per cent of total US production. Robert Dixon and John Creedy, at the University of Melbourne, estimate that the size of monopoly deadweight loss in Australia is approximately 1 per cent of total production. Dixon and Creedy also look at how the burden of monopoly deadweight loss is shared over society. They conclude that monopoly has a greater impact on lower-income households. Not only does abuse of monopoly power lead to a general social cost, it also tends to increase social inequality.

How does a monopolist's quantity of output compare with the quantity of output that maximises total surplus?

Price discrimination

So far we have been assuming that the monopoly firm charges the same price to all customers. Yet in many cases firms try to sell the same good to different customers for different prices. This practice is called **price discrimination**.

Before discussing the behaviour of a price-discriminating monopolist, we should note that price discrimination is not possible when a good is sold in a competitive market. In a competitive market, there are many firms selling the same good at the market price. No firm is willing to charge a lower price to any customer because the firm can sell all it wants at the market price. And if any firm tried to charge a higher price to a customer, that customer would buy from another firm. For a firm to price discriminate, it must have some market power.

price discrimination
the business practice of selling the same good at different prices to different customers

▸ price discrimination

A parable about pricing

To understand why a monopolist would want to price discriminate, let's consider a simple example. Imagine that you are the managing director of Readalot Publishing Company. Readalot's best-selling author has just written her latest novel. To keep things simple, let's imagine that you pay the author a flat $2 million for the exclusive rights to publish the book. Let's also assume that the cost of printing the book is zero. Readalot's profit, therefore, is the revenue it gets from selling the book minus the $2 million it has paid to the author. Given these assumptions, how would you, as Readalot's managing director, decide what price to charge for the book?

Your first step in setting the price is to estimate what the demand for the book is likely to be. Readalot's marketing department tells you that the book will attract two types of readers. The book will appeal to the author's 100 000 loyal fans. These fans will be willing to pay as much as $30 for the book. In addition, the book will appeal to about 400 000 less-enthusiastic readers who will be willing to pay up to $5 for the book.

What price maximises Readalot's profit? There are two natural prices to consider: $30 is the highest price Readalot can charge and still get the 100 000 loyal fans, and $5 is the highest price it can charge and still get the entire market of 500 000 potential readers. It is a matter of simple arithmetic to solve Readalot's problem. At a price of $30, Readalot sells 100 000 copies, has revenue of $3 million and makes a profit of $1 million. At a price of $5, it sells 500 000 copies, has revenue of $2.5 million and makes a profit of $500 000. Thus, Readalot maximises profit by charging $30 and forgoing the opportunity to sell to the 400 000 less-enthusiastic readers.

Notice that Readalot's decision causes a deadweight loss. There are 400 000 readers willing to pay $5 for the book and the marginal cost of providing it to them is zero. Thus, $2 million of total surplus is lost when Readalot charges the higher price. This deadweight loss is the usual inefficiency that arises whenever a monopolist charges a price above marginal cost.

Now suppose that Readalot's marketing department makes an important discovery – these two groups of readers are in separate markets. All the loyal fans live in Australia and all the other readers live in the United States. Moreover, it is difficult for readers in one country to buy books in the other.

In response to this discovery, Readalot can change its marketing strategy and increase profits. To the 100 000 Australian readers, it can charge $30 for the book. To the 400 000 American readers, it can charge $5 for the book. In this case, revenue is $3 million in Australia and $2 million in the United States, for a total of $5 million. Profit is then $3 million, which is substantially greater than the $1 million the company could earn charging the same $30 price to all customers. Not surprisingly, Readalot chooses to follow this strategy of price discrimination.

Although the story of Readalot Publishing is hypothetical, it describes accurately the business practice of many publishing companies. Textbooks, for example, are often sold at a lower price in Indonesia than in Australia. Even more important is the price differential between hardcover books and paperbacks. When a publisher has a new novel, it initially releases an expensive hardcover edition and later releases a cheaper paperback edition. The difference in price between these two editions far exceeds the difference in printing costs. The publisher's goal is just as in our example. By selling the hardcover to loyal fans and the paperback to less-enthusiastic readers, the publisher price discriminates and raises its profit.

The moral of the story

Like any parable, the story of Readalot Publishing is stylised. Yet, also like any parable, it teaches some important and general lessons. In this case, there are three lessons to be learned about price discrimination.

The first and most obvious lesson is that price discrimination is a rational strategy for a profit-maximising monopolist. In other words, by charging different prices to different customers, a monopolist can increase its profit. In essence, a price-discriminating monopolist charges each customer a price closer to his or her willingness to pay than is possible with a single price.

The second lesson is that price discrimination requires the ability to separate customers according to their willingness to pay. In our example, customers were separated geographically. But sometimes monopolists choose other differences, such as age or income, to distinguish among customers.

A corollary to this second lesson is that certain market forces can prevent firms from price discriminating. In particular, one such force is *arbitrage*, the process of buying a good in one market at a low price and selling it in another market at a higher price in order to profit from the price difference. In our example, suppose that Australian bookstores could buy the book in the United States and resell it to Australian readers. This arbitrage would prevent Readalot from price discriminating because no Australian would buy the book at the higher price.

The third lesson from our parable is the most surprising – price discrimination can raise economic welfare. Recall that a deadweight loss arises when Readalot charges a single $30 price, because the 400 000 less-enthusiastic readers do not end up with the book, even though they value it at more than its marginal cost of production. In contrast, when Readalot price discriminates, all readers end up with the book and the outcome is efficient. Thus, price discrimination can eliminate the inefficiency inherent in monopoly pricing.

Note that the increase in welfare from price discrimination shows up as higher producer surplus rather than higher consumer surplus. In our example, consumers are no better off for having bought the book, because the price they pay exactly equals the value they place on the book. The entire increase in total surplus from price discrimination accrues to Readalot Publishing in the form of higher profit.

IN THE NEWS . . .

MONOPOLIES AND GOVERNMENT POLICY

In the 1990s and 2000s, Australia privatised many government-owned infrastructure monopolies with the hope of opening up competition or relying on regulation to keep prices in check. This included Telstra, Australia's main telephone company. In this article from 2006, John Quiggin makes the case for reversing this process. And it is now occurring. As this chapter is being written, the government is re-buying part of Telstra in order to build a National Broadband Network (NBN). The NBN will be a new, government-owned telecommunications monopoly.

Make Telstra public again
by John Quiggin

Following Australian telecommunications policy is like watching one of those horror movies where the protagonist insists on going down the staircase into the cellar, even though everyone in the audience can see that disaster awaits. Or perhaps it's more like *Groundhog Day*, where the hero relives the same bad day over and over again. Looking at the current crisis over Telstra, it's striking that, despite the massive technological changes of the past decade, the same policy issues are being debated and the same mistakes are made.

The most salient example is the protracted saga of Telstra's proposed privatisation. It was obvious to anyone who cared to look that the idea of partial privatisation, commenced by the Howard government in 1997 (in emulation of previous privatisations on this model undertaken by Labor) was a recipe for conflicts of interest, and for the creation of a regulatory nightmare.

As Treasurer Peter Costello said in early 2000, barely two years after the T1 sale,

> If Telstra is going to be caught in a position where it is half privately owned and half government-owned, I don't think that is going to be a good outcome. Telstra should all be either privately owned, or if people really think that nationalisation and government ownership is necessary they ought to have the courage of their convictions and nationalise it.

More than six years later, Telstra is still half-private and half-public and it seems inevitable that, even if a sale goes ahead, a substantial share of Telstra will remain in public ownership through the future fund. Certainly, there is nothing in the record of regulatory policy to suggest that full privatisation would work well. So Costello's own logic would suggest that he should be advocating renationalisation.

But the debate over Telstra's ownership is of secondary importance compared to the more fundamental problem that telecommunications policy has failed to meet the needs of telecommunications consumers of Australia as a nation. We lagged badly in the initial provision and take-up of broadband, and now seem certain to fall even further behind as other countries move to high-speed Internet technologies based on optical fibre all the way to the home.

More than ten years and several communications ministers ago, it was evident that poorly designed telecommunications policy was promoting investment decisions driven by considerations of corporate and regulatory strategy, yielding outcomes that were not in the national interest. The biggest example then was the race between Telstra and Optus to roll out duplicate hybrid-fibre coax cable networks, covering half the country, leaving everyone else to wait a decade or more for decent broadband access.

As I wrote at the time, the future of communications, and most notably the rapidly developing Internet, lies in digital networks based on optical fibre … the more progressive telecommunications companies in the United States are already discarding HFC in favor of building optical fibre 'up to the curb … The resources being wasted in providing duplicate analog networks could have made Australia a world leader in the development of digital telecommunications networks.' ('Pay TV's wasted billions', *Australian Financial Review*, 8 January 1996.)

A decade later, with Japan and other countries already delivering fibre to the home, allowing high-speed Internet traffic for both uploads and downloads, Telstra finally came up with a proposal to roll fibre out, but only as far as local nodes. But, this was a mere bargaining chip in Telstra's corporate regulatory strategy, to be withdrawn when the regulator did not give the right outcome.

So, apparently, we are supposed to rely on the second-class option of stretching ADSL technology to its limits, in the hope (contradicted by Telstra's own statements on the subject) that the copper-wire network will stand up to the strain.

It's time for the government to face up to its responsibilities for our national infrastructure. Telstra should be brought back into public ownership, and required to construct telecommunications infrastructure to meet national needs.

The first step in this process is that the government should take its role as majority owner seriously, and appoint a board and CEO committed to acting in the national interest. Peripheral assets like the Foxtel stake should be sold off. And the Future Fund could be used to buy out shareholders who would prefer a company more focused on short-term profits.

Australian telecommunications policy has been stuck in the same endless loop for a decade or more. If the horror movie we've seen so far is to have a happy ending, we need to turn around and head back upstairs.

Source: John Quiggin/*Australian Financial Review*, 17 August 2006.

The analytics of price discrimination

Let's consider a bit more formally how price discrimination affects economic welfare. We begin by assuming that the monopolist can price discriminate perfectly. *Perfect price discrimination* describes a situation in which the monopolist knows exactly each customer's willingness to pay and can charge each customer a different price. In this case, the monopolist charges each customer exactly his or her willingness to pay and the monopolist gets the entire surplus in every transaction.

Figure 15.9 shows producer and consumer surplus with and without price discrimination. Without price discrimination, the firm charges a single price above marginal cost, as shown in panel (a). Because some potential customers who value the good at more than marginal cost do not buy it at this high price, the monopoly causes a deadweight loss. Yet when a firm can perfectly price discriminate, as shown in panel (b), customers who value the good at more than marginal cost buy the good and are charged their willingness to pay. All mutually beneficial trades take place, there is no deadweight loss, and the entire surplus derived from the market goes to the monopoly producer in the form of profit.

In reality, of course, price discrimination is not perfect. Customers do not walk into shops with signs displaying their willingness to pay. Instead, firms price discriminate by dividing customers into groups: young versus old, weekday versus weekend shoppers, Australians versus Americans and so on. Unlike those in our parable of Readalot Publishing, customers within each group differ in their willingness to pay for the product, making perfect price discrimination impossible.

How does this imperfect price discrimination affect welfare? The analysis of these pricing schemes is quite complicated and it turns out that there is no general answer to this question. Compared with

Figure 15.9 | Welfare with and without price discrimination

(a) Monopolist with single price

Price

Consumer surplus

Monopoly price

Deadweight loss

Profit

Marginal cost

Marginal revenue

Demand

0   Quantity sold   **Quantity**

(b) Monopolist with perfect price discrimination

Price

Profit

Marginal cost

Demand

0   Quantity sold   **Quantity**

Panel (a) shows a monopolist that charges the same price to all customers. Total surplus in this market equals the sum of profit (producer surplus) and consumer surplus. Panel (b) shows a monopolist that can perfectly price discriminate. Because consumer surplus equals zero, total surplus now equals the firm's profit. Comparing these two panels, you can see that perfect price discrimination raises profit, raises total surplus and lowers consumer surplus.

the monopoly outcome with a single price, imperfect price discrimination can raise, lower or leave unchanged total surplus in a market. The only certain conclusion is that price discrimination raises the monopoly's profit – otherwise the firm would choose to charge all customers the same price.

Examples of price discrimination

Firms in our economy use various business strategies aimed at charging different prices to different customers. Now that we understand the economics of price discrimination, let's consider some examples.

Movie tickets

Many movie theatres charge a lower price for children, students and senior citizens than for other patrons. This fact is hard to explain in a competitive market. In a competitive market, price equals marginal cost, and the marginal cost of providing a seat for a child, student or senior citizen is the same as the marginal cost of providing a seat for anyone else. Yet this fact is easily explained if movie theatres have some local monopoly power and if children, students and senior citizens have a lower willingness to pay for a ticket. In this case, movie theatres raise their profit by price discriminating.

Airline prices

Seats on aeroplanes are sold at many different prices. Most airlines charge a lower price for a ticket if it has less flexible conditions, such as limits on the ability to change flights or cancel the booking at the last minute. The difference in prices generally is far higher than the difference in cost to the airline of the flexible conditions. So why do airlines price in this way? The reason is that charging a higher price for a flexible ticket provides a way to separate business travellers and personal travellers. A passenger on a business trip has a high willingness to pay and, most likely, wants the flexibility to change their flight at the last minute, for example, if a meeting is rescheduled or runs over time. In contrast, a passenger travelling for personal reasons has a lower willingness to pay and is less likely to need to vary their flight at the last minute. Thus, the airlines can successfully price discriminate by charging a higher price for passengers who want a ticket with flexible conditions.

'Would it bother you to hear how little I paid for this flight?'

Source: © William Hamilton

Store brands

Many large shops have a store brand. The store-brand products are shelved next to well-known brands and are often cheaper than these well-known products. In some cases the store brand and the well-known brand are essentially the same product, produced by the same firm. Why would shops stock the same product but in two different packages with two different prices?

The answer is that store brands allow shops to price discriminate. Some customers are willing to pay a premium to buy a product produced by a well-known manufacturer. These customers are willing to pay more for a product sold with the manufacturer's brand. Other customers do not care about the brand of the product and are simply interested in buying the cheapest product available. By offering a store-brand product as well as the product with the manufacturer's brand, shops are able to price discriminate between these two types of buyers.

Quantity discounts

So far in our examples of price discrimination, the monopolist charges different prices to different customers. Sometimes, however, monopolists price discriminate by charging different prices to the same customer for different units that the customer buys. For example, many firms offer lower prices to customers who buy large quantities. A bakery might charge $0.50 for each doughnut, but $5 for a dozen. This is a form of price discrimination because the customer pays a higher price for the first unit bought than for the twelfth. Quantity discounts are often a successful way of price discriminating because a customer's willingness to pay for an additional unit declines as the customer buys more units.

Telephone and Internet line rentals are often more expensive in rural areas than in urban areas. Is that enough information to conclude that telecommunication firms price discriminate rural consumers?

IN THE NEWS ...

PRICE DISCRIMINATION ON BROADWAY

Theatre producers often use price discrimination to try and raise profits. But how well do they go? This article looks at a study of price discrimination on Broadway by Hal R. Varian. His conclusion is that the producers price discriminate pretty well.

The dynamics of pricing tickets for Broadway shows

by Hal R. Varian

Every night in New York, about 25 000 people, on average, attend Broadway shows.

As avid theatregoers know, ticket prices have been rising inexorably. The top ticket price for Broadway shows has risen 31 per cent since 1998. But the actual price paid has gone up by only 24 per cent.

The difference is a result of discounting. Savvy fans know that there are deals available for even the most popular shows, with the most popular discounts being offered through coupons, two-for-one deals, special prices for students, and through the TKTS booth in Times Square.

Why so much discounting? The value of a seat in a theatre, like a seat on an airplane, is highly perishable. Once the show starts or the plane takes off, a seat is worth next to nothing.

In both industries, sellers use a variety of strategies to try to ensure that the seats are sold to those who are willing to pay the most. This phenomenon was examined by a Stanford economist, Phillip Leslie, in an article, 'Price Discrimination in Broadway Theater', published in the autumn 2004 issue of the *RAND Journal of Economics*.

Mr. Leslie was able to collect detailed data on a 1996 Broadway play, 'Seven Guitars'. Over 140 000 people saw this play, and they bought tickets in 17 price categories. Some price variation was due to the quality of the seats – orchestra, mezzanine, balcony and so on – while other price differences were a result of various forms of discounting.

The combination of quality variation and discounts led to widely varying ticket prices. The average difference of two tickets chosen at random on a given night was about 40 per cent of the average price. This is comparable to the price variation in airline tickets ...

The ticket promotions also varied over the 199 performances of the show. Targeted direct mail was used early on, while two-for-one tickets were not introduced until about halfway through the run.

The tickets offered for sale at the TKTS booth in Times Square are typically orchestra seats, the best category of seats available. But the discounted tickets at TKTS tend to be the lower-quality orchestra seats. They sell at a fixed discount of 50 per cent, but are offered only for performances that day.

Mr. Leslie's goal was primarily to model the behavior of the theatregoer. The audience for Broadway shows is highly diverse. About 10 per cent, according to a 1991 survey conducted by Broadway producers, had household incomes of $25 000 or $35 000 while an equal number had incomes over $150 000 (in 1990 dollars).

The prices and discounting policy set by the producers of Broadway shows try to use this heterogeneity to get people to sort themselves by their willingness to pay for tickets.

You probably will not see Donald Trump waiting in line at TKTS; presumably, those in his income class do not mind paying full price. But a lot of students, unemployed actors and tourists do use TKTS.

Yes, it is inconvenient to wait in line at TKTS. But that is the point. If it weren't inconvenient, everyone would do it, and this would result in substantially lower revenues for Broadway shows.

Mr. Leslie uses some advanced econometric techniques to estimate the values that different income groups put on the various categories of tickets. He finds that Broadway producers do a pretty good job, in general, at maximizing revenue …

We are likely to see more and more goods and services sold using the same sort of differential pricing. As more and more transactions become computer-mediated, it becomes easier for sellers to collect data, to experiment with pricing and to analyze the results of those experiments.

This, of course, makes life more complicated for us consumers. The flip side is that pricing variations make those good deals more likely.

Last time I was in New York, I was pleased that I managed to get a ticket to 'The Producers' for half price. It almost made up for the fact that I had to book my airline ticket two weeks in advance and stay over a Saturday night.

Give two examples of price discrimination. How does perfect price discrimination affect consumer surplus, producer surplus and total surplus?

Conclusion: The prevalence of monopoly

This chapter has discussed the behaviour of firms who have control over the prices they charge. We have seen that these firms behave very differently from the competitive firms studied in the previous chapter. Table 15.2 summarises some of the key similarities and differences between competitive and monopoly markets.

From the standpoint of public policy, a crucial result is that monopolists produce less than the socially efficient quantity and charge prices above marginal cost. As a result, they cause deadweight losses. In some cases, these inefficiencies can be mitigated through price discrimination by the monopolist, but other times they call for policymakers to take an active role. What actions policymakers might take is the subject of chapter 17.

Table 15.2 Competition versus monopoly: A summary comparison	Competition	Monopoly
Similarities		
Goals of firms	Maximise profits	Maximise profits
Rule for maximising profit	$MR = MC$	$MR = MC$
Can earn economic profits in the short run?	Yes	Yes
Differences		
Number of firms	Many	One
Marginal revenue	$MR = P$	$MR < P$
Price	$P = MC$	$P > MC$
Produce welfare-maximising level of output	Yes	No
Entry in the long run?	Yes	No
Can earn economic profits in the long run?	No	Yes
Price discrimination profitable	No	Yes

How prevalent are the problems of monopoly? There are two answers to this question.

In one sense, monopolies are common. Most firms have some control over the prices they charge. They are not forced to charge the market price for their goods, because their goods are not exactly the same as those offered by other firms. A Toyota Camry is not the same as a Ford Falcon. Heinz tomato soup is not the same as Campbell's. Each of these goods has a downward-sloping demand curve, which gives each producer some degree of monopoly power.

Yet firms with substantial monopoly power are quite rare. Few goods are unique. Most have substitutes that, even if not exactly the same, are very similar. Heinz can raise the price of its tomato soup a little without losing all its sales, but if it raises it very much, sales will fall substantially.

In the end, monopoly power is a matter of degree. It is true that many firms have some monopoly power. It is also true that their monopoly power is usually quite limited. In these cases, we will not go far wrong assuming that firms operate in competitive markets, even if that is not precisely the case.

Summary

- A monopoly is a firm that is the sole seller in its market. A monopoly arises when a single firm owns a key resource, when the government gives a firm the exclusive right to produce a good, or when a single firm can supply the entire market at a smaller cost than many firms could.
- Because a monopoly is the sole producer in its market, it faces a downward-sloping demand curve for its product. When a monopoly increases production by one unit, it causes the price of its good to fall, which reduces the amount of revenue earned on all units produced. As a result, a monopoly's marginal revenue is always below the price of its good.
- Like a competitive firm, a monopoly firm maximises profit by producing the quantity at which marginal revenue equals marginal cost. The monopoly then chooses the price at which that quantity is demanded. Unlike a competitive firm, a monopoly firm's price exceeds its marginal revenue, so its price exceeds marginal cost.
- A monopolist's profit-maximising level of output is below the level that maximises the sum of consumer and producer surplus. That is, when the monopoly charges a price above marginal cost, some consumers who value the good more than its cost of production do not buy it. As a result, monopoly causes deadweight losses similar to the deadweight losses caused by taxes.
- Monopolists often can raise their profits by charging different prices for the same good based on a buyer's willingness to pay. This practice of price discrimination can raise economic welfare by getting the good to some consumers who otherwise would not buy it. In the extreme case of perfect price discrimination, the deadweight losses of monopoly are completely eliminated. More generally, when price discrimination is imperfect, it can either raise or lower welfare compared with the outcome with a single monopoly price.

Key concepts

monopoly   natural monopoly   price discrimination

Questions for review

1   Give an example of a government-created monopoly. Is creating this monopoly necessarily bad public policy? Explain.
2   Define natural monopoly. What does the size of a market have to do with whether an industry is a natural monopoly?
3   Why is a monopolist's marginal revenue less than the price of its good?
4   Draw the demand, marginal-revenue and marginal-cost curves for a monopolist. Show the profit-maximising level of output. Show the profit-maximising price.
5   In your diagram from the previous question, show the level of output that maximises total surplus. Show the deadweight loss from the monopoly. Explain your answer.
6   Give two examples of price discrimination. In each case, explain why the monopolist chooses to follow this business strategy.

347

Problems and applications

1   Define a firm's marginal revenue. If the price of a good is always greater than zero, can a monopolist's marginal revenue ever be negative? Explain.

2   Does a monopolist or a competitive firm face a more elastic demand curve? What characteristic of the good being sold leads to a larger elasticity? Explain.

3   Suppose that a natural monopolist were required by law to charge average total cost. On a diagram, label the price charged and the deadweight loss to society relative to marginal-cost pricing.

4   Max is a magazine monopolist. His marginal cost of production (per magazine) is constant at $5. His demand information is as follows:

Price ($)	Q^D
50	0
40	5
30	10
20	20
15	30
10	50
5	102
2.50	200

a   Calculate the total revenue for Max at each price.

b   Calculate the (approximate) marginal revenue for Max at each price.

c   What is Max's profit-maximising output level and price? Compare this with the perfectly competitive equilibrium level of output and price.

5   Consider the delivery of mail. In general, what is the shape of the average-total-cost curve? How might the shape differ between isolated rural areas and densely populated urban areas? How might the shape have changed over time? Explain.

6   Suppose the Go-for-it Gas company has a monopoly on natural gas sales. If the price of electricity increases, what is the change in Go-for-it's profit-maximising levels of output, price and profit? Explain in words and with a graph.

7   A small town is served by many competing supermarkets, which have constant marginal cost.

a   Using a diagram of the market for groceries, show the consumer surplus, producer surplus and total surplus.

b   Now suppose that the independent supermarkets combine to form one chain. Using a new diagram, show the new consumer surplus, producer surplus and total surplus. Relative to the competitive market, what is the transfer from consumers to producers? What is the deadweight loss?

8 Ted Grunge has just finished recording his latest CD. His record company's marketing department determines that the demand for the CD is as follows:

Price ($)	Number of CDs
24	10 000
22	20 000
20	30 000
18	40 000
16	50 000
14	60 000

The company can produce the CD with no fixed cost and a variable cost of $5 per CD.
a Find total revenue for quantity equal to 10 000, 20 000 and so on. What is the marginal revenue for each 10 000 increase in the quantity sold?
b What quantity of CDs would maximise profit? What would the price be? What would the profit be?
c If you were Ted's agent, what recording fee would you advise Ted to demand from the record company? Why?

9 A company is considering building a bridge across a river. The bridge would cost $2 million to build and nothing to maintain. The following table shows the company's anticipated demand over the lifetime of the bridge:

P (per crossing)	Q (number of crossings, in thousands)
$8	0
7	100
6	200
5	300
4	400
3	500
2	600
1	700
0	800

a If the company were to build the bridge, what would be its profit-maximising price? Would that be the efficient level of output? Why or why not?
b If the company is interested in maximising profit, should it build the bridge? What would be its profit or loss?

     c   If the government were to build the bridge, what price should it charge?

     d   Should the government build the bridge? Explain.

10   The Placebo Drug Company holds a patent on one of its discoveries.

     a   Assuming that the production of the drug involves rising marginal cost, illustrate Placebo's profit-maximising price and quantity. Also show Placebo's profits.

     b   Now suppose that the government imposes a tax on each bottle of the drug produced. On a new diagram, illustrate Placebo's new price and quantity. How does each compare with your answer in part (a)?

     c   Although it is not easy to see in your diagrams, the tax reduces Placebo's profit. Explain why this must be true.

     d   Instead of the tax per bottle, suppose that the government imposes a tax on Placebo of $10 000 regardless of how many bottles are produced. How does this tax affect Placebo's price, quantity and profits? Explain.

11   Larry, Curly and Moe run the only pub in town. Larry wants to sell as many drinks as possible without losing money. Curly wants the pub to bring in as much revenue as possible. Moe wants to make the largest possible profits. Using a single diagram of the pub's demand curve and cost curves, show the price and quantity combinations favoured by each of the three partners. Explain.

12   The Best Computer Company just developed a new computer chip, on which it immediately acquires a patent.

     a   Draw a diagram that shows the consumer surplus, producer surplus and total surplus in the market for this new chip.

     b   What happens to these three measures of surplus if the firm can perfectly price discriminate? What is the change in deadweight loss? What transfers occur?

13   Explain why a monopolist will always produce a quantity at which the demand curve is elastic. (*Hint:* If demand is inelastic and the firm raises its price, what happens to total revenue and total costs?)

14   Many schemes for price discriminating involve some cost. For example, discount coupons in newspapers and magazines take time to cut out. Impatient buyers who cannot afford the time end up paying a higher price. But the coupons also take up time and resources from both the buyers who do cut them out and the seller. This question considers the implications of costly price discrimination. To keep things simple, let's assume that our monopolist's production costs are simply proportional to output, so that average total cost and marginal cost are constant and equal to each other.

     a   Draw the cost, demand and marginal-revenue curves for the monopolist. Show the price the monopolist would charge without price discrimination.

     b   In your diagram, mark the area equal to the monopolist's profit and call it X. Mark the area equal to consumer surplus and call it Y. Mark the area equal to the deadweight loss and call it Z.

     c   Now suppose that the monopolist can perfectly price discriminate. What is the monopolist's profit? (Give your answer in terms of X, Y and Z.)

     d   What is the change in the monopolist's profit from price discrimination? What is the change in total surplus from price discrimination? Which change is larger? Explain. (Give your answer in terms of X, Y and Z.)

     e   Now suppose that there is some cost of price discrimination. To model this cost, let's assume that the monopolist has to pay a fixed cost C in order to price discriminate. How would a monopolist make the decision whether to pay this fixed cost? (Give your answer in terms of X, Y, Z and C.)

     f   How would a benevolent social planner, who cares about total surplus, decide whether the monopolist should price discriminate? (Give your answer in terms of X, Y, Z and C.)

     g   Compare your answers to parts (e) and (f). How does the monopolist's incentive to price discriminate differ from the social planner's? Is it possible that the monopolist will price discriminate even though it is not socially desirable?

Search me!

  Search me!

When accessing information about economics use the following keywords in any combinations you require:

- monopoly
- price discrimination
- natural monopoly

CourseMate

CourseMate

For more multimedia resources and activities on economics, visit the Economics CourseMate website.

16

Business strategy

Learning objectives

In this chapter you will:

- see what market structures lie between monopoly and competition
- examine what outcomes are possible when a market is an oligopoly
- learn about the prisoners' dilemma and how it applies to oligopoly and other issues.

If you go to a shop to buy tennis balls, it is likely that you will come home with one of four brands: Wilson, Penn, Dunlop or Spalding. These four companies make almost all of the tennis balls sold in Australia. Together these firms determine the quantity of tennis balls produced and, given the market demand curve, the price at which they are sold.

How can we describe the market for tennis balls? The previous two chapters discussed two types of market structure. In a competitive market, each firm is so small compared with the market that it cannot influence the price of its product and, therefore, takes the price as given by market conditions. In a monopolised market, a single firm supplies the entire market for a good, and that firm can choose any price and quantity on the market demand curve.

The market for tennis balls fits neither the competitive nor the monopoly model. Competition and monopoly are extreme forms of market structure. Competition occurs when there are many firms in a market offering essentially identical products; monopoly occurs when there is only one firm in a market. It is natural to start the study of industrial organisation with these polar cases, for they are the easiest cases to understand. Yet many industries, including the tennis ball industry, fall somewhere between these two extremes. Firms in these industries have competitors but, at the same time, do not face so much competition that they are price takers. Economists call this situation *imperfect competition.*

In this chapter we discuss the types of imperfect competition and examine a particular type called **oligopoly**. The essence of an oligopolistic market is that there are only a few sellers. As a result, the actions of any one seller in the market can have a large impact on the profits of all the other sellers. Oligopolistic firms are interdependent in a way that competitive firms are not. Our goal in this chapter is to see how this interdependence shapes firms' behaviour.

The analysis of oligopoly offers an opportunity to introduce **game theory**, the study of how people behave in strategic situations. By 'strategic' we mean a situation in which a person, when choosing among alternative courses of action, must consider how others might respond to the action he takes. Strategic thinking is crucial not only in checkers, chess and noughts-and-crosses but in many business decisions. Because oligopolistic markets have only a small number of firms, each firm must act strategically. Each firm knows that its profit depends not only on how much it produces but also on how much the other firms produce. In making its production decision, each firm in an oligopoly should consider how its decision might affect the production decisions of all the other firms.

Game theory is not necessary for understanding competitive or monopoly markets. In a market that is either perfectly competitive or monopolistically competitive, each firm is so small compared to

oligopoly
a market structure in which only a few sellers offer similar or identical products

▸ oligopoly

game theory
the study of how people behave in strategic situations

the market that strategic interactions with other firms are not important. In a monopolised market, strategic interactions are absent because the market has only one firm. But, as we will see, game theory is useful for understanding oligopolies and many other situations in which a small number of players interact with one another. Game theory helps explain the strategies that people choose, whether they are playing tennis or selling tennis balls.

Between monopoly and perfect competition

The previous two chapters analysed markets with many competitive firms and markets with a single monopoly firm. In chapter 14, we saw that the price in a perfectly competitive market always equals the marginal cost of production. We also saw that, in the long run, entry and exit drive economic profit to zero, so the price also equals average total cost. In chapter 15, we saw how monopoly firms can use their market power to keep prices above marginal cost, leading to a positive economic profit for the firm and a deadweight loss for society.

The cases of perfect competition and monopoly illustrate some important ideas about how markets work. Most markets in the economy, however, include elements of both these cases and, therefore, are not completely described by either of them. The typical firm in the economy faces competition, but the competition is not so rigorous as to make the firm exactly fit the description of the price-taking firm analysed in chapter 14. The typical firm also has some degree of market power, but its market power is not so great that the firm can exactly fit the description of the monopoly firm analysed in chapter 15. In other words, the typical firm in our economy is imperfectly competitive.

One type of imperfect competition is an oligopoly, which is a market with only a few sellers, each offering a product similar or identical to the others. One example is the market for tennis balls. Another is the market for retail groceries. Two large sellers, Coles and Woolworths, together supply around 70 per cent of all dry groceries sold to Australian consumers.

A second type of imperfectly competitive market is called *monopolistic competition*. This describes a market structure in which there are many firms selling products that are similar but not identical. Examples include the markets for novels, films, CDs and computer games. In a monopolistically competitive market, each firm has a monopoly over the product it makes, but many other firms make similar products that compete for the same customers.

Figure 16A. summarises the four types of market structure. The first question to ask about any market is how many firms there are. If there is only one firm, the market is a monopoly. If there are only a few firms, the market is an oligopoly. If there are many firms, we need to ask another question: Do the firms sell identical or differentiated products? If the many firms sell differentiated products, the market is monopolistically competitive. If the many firms sell identical products, the market is perfectly competitive.

Because reality is never as simple as theory, at times you may find it hard to decide what structure best describes a market. There is, for instance, no single number that separates 'few' from 'many' when counting the number of firms. (Do the dozen or so companies that sell cars in Australia make this market an oligopoly or more competitive? The answer is open to debate.) Similarly, there is no sure way to determine when products are differentiated and when they are identical. (Are different brands of milk really the same? Again, the answer is debatable.) When analysing actual markets, economists have to keep in mind the lessons learned from studying all types of market structure and then apply each lesson as it seems appropriate.

Figure 16.1   The four types of market structure

Economists who study industrial organisation divide markets into four types – monopoly, oligopoly, monopolistic competition and perfect competition.

Now that we understand how economists define the various types of market structure, we can continue our analysis of them. In chapter 18, we analyse monopolistic competition. In this chapter we examine the business strategy of oligopolists.

Define oligopoly and monopolistic competition and give an example of each.

Markets with only a few sellers

Because an oligopolistic market has only a small group of sellers, a key feature of oligopoly is the tension between cooperation and self-interest. The oligopolists are best off when they cooperate and act like a monopolist – producing a small quantity of output and charging a price above marginal cost. Yet because each oligopolist cares about only its own profit, there are powerful incentives at work that hinder a group of firms from maintaining the monopoly outcome.

A duopoly example

To understand the behaviour of oligopolies, let's consider an oligopoly with only two members, called a duopoly. Duopoly is the simplest type of oligopoly. Oligopolies with three or more members face the same problems as oligopolies with only two members, so we do not lose much by starting with the case of duopoly.

Table 16.1 The demand schedule for water		
Quantity (in litres)	Price ($)	Total revenue (and total profit) ($)
0	120	0
10	110	1100
20	100	2000
30	90	2700
40	80	3200
50	70	3500
60	60	3600
70	50	3500
80	40	3200
90	30	2700
100	20	2000
110	10	1100
120	0	0

Imagine a town in which only two residents – Jack and Jill – own wells that produce water safe for drinking. Each Saturday, Jack and Jill decide how many litres of water to pump, bring the water to town and sell it for whatever price the market will bear. To keep things simple, suppose that Jack and Jill can pump as much water as they want without cost; that is, the marginal cost of water equals zero.

Table 16.1 shows the town's demand schedule for water. The first column shows the total quantity demanded and the second column shows the price. If the two well owners sell a total of 10 litres of water, water goes for $110 a litre. If they sell a total of 20 litres, the price falls to $100 a litre. And so on. If you graphed these two columns of numbers, you would get a standard downward-sloping demand curve.

The last column in Table 16.1 shows the total revenue from the sale of water. It equals the quantity sold times the price. Because there is no cost to pumping water, the total revenue of the two producers equals their total profit.

Let's now consider how the organisation of the town's water industry affects the price of water and the quantity of water sold.

Competition, monopolies and cartels

Before considering the price and quantity of water that would result from the duopoly of Jack and Jill, let's discuss briefly what the outcome would be if the water market were either perfectly competitive or a monopoly. These two polar cases are natural benchmarks.

If the market for water were perfectly competitive, the production decisions of each firm drive price equal to marginal cost. Because we have assumed that the marginal cost of pumping additional water is zero, the equilibrium price of water under perfect competition would be zero as well. The equilibrium quantity would be 120 litres. The price of water would reflect the cost of producing it and the efficient quantity of water would be produced and consumed.

Now consider how a monopoly would behave. Table 16.1 shows that total profit is maximised at a quantity of 60 litres and a price of $60 a litre. A profit-maximising monopolist, therefore, would produce this quantity and charge this price. As is standard for monopolies, price would exceed marginal cost. The result would be inefficient, for the quantity of water produced and consumed would fall short of the socially efficient level of 120 litres.

What outcome should we expect from our duopolists? One possibility is that Jack and Jill get together and agree on the quantity of water to produce and the price to charge for it. Such an agreement among firms over production and price is called **collusion** and the group of firms acting in unison is called a **cartel**. Once a cartel is formed, the market is in effect served by a monopoly and we can apply our analysis from chapter 15. That is, if Jack and Jill were to collude, they would agree on the monopoly outcome because that outcome maximises the total profit that the producers can get from the market. Our two producers would produce a total of 60 litres, which would be sold at a price of $60 a litre. Once again, price exceeds marginal cost and the outcome is socially inefficient.

A cartel must agree not only on the total level of production but also on the amount produced by each member. In our case, Jack and Jill must agree how to split between themselves the monopoly production of 60 litres. Each member of the cartel will want a larger share of the market because a larger market share means larger profit. If Jack and Jill agreed to split the market equally, each would produce 30 litres, the price would be $60 a litre and each would get a profit of $1800.

collusion
an agreement among firms in a market about quantities to produce or prices to charge

cartel
a group of firms acting in unison

▸ cartel

The equilibrium for an oligopoly

Oligopolists would like to form cartels and earn monopoly profits, but that is often impossible. As we discuss in the next chapter, competition laws prohibit explicit agreements among oligopolists as a matter of public policy. In addition, squabbling among cartel members over how to divide the profit in the market can make agreement among members difficult. Let's therefore consider what happens if Jack and Jill decide separately how much water to produce.

At first, one might expect Jack and Jill to reach the monopoly outcome on their own, because this outcome maximises their joint profit. In the absence of a binding agreement, however, the monopoly outcome is unlikely. To see why, imagine that Jack expects Jill to produce only 30 litres (half of the monopoly quantity). Jack would reason as follows:

'I could produce 30 litres as well. In this case, a total of 60 litres of water would be sold at a price of $60 a litre. My profit would be $1800 (30 litres × $60 a litre). Alternatively, I could produce 40 litres. In this case, a total of 70 litres of water would be sold at a price of $50 a litre. My profit would be $2000 (40 litres × $50 a litre). Even though total profit in the market would fall, my profit would be higher, because I would have a larger share of the market.'

Of course, Jill might reason the same way. If so, Jack and Jill would each bring 40 litres to town. Total sales would be 80 litres and the price would fall to $40. Thus, if the duopolists individually pursue their own self-interest when deciding how much to produce, they produce a total quantity greater than the monopoly quantity, charge a price lower than the monopoly price and earn total profit less than the monopoly profit.

Although the logic of self-interest increases the duopoly's output above the monopoly level, it does not push the duopolists to reach the competitive allocation. Consider what happens when each duopolist is producing 40 litres. The price is $40, and each duopolist makes a profit of $1600. In this case, Jack's self-interested logic leads to a different conclusion:

'Right now, my profit is $1600. Suppose I increase my production to 50 litres. In this case, a total of 90 litres of water would be sold, and the price would be $30 a litre. Then my profit would be only $1500. Rather than increasing production and driving down the price, I am better off keeping my production at 40 litres.'

The outcome in which Jack and Jill each produce 40 litres looks like some sort of equilibrium. In fact, this outcome is called a **Nash equilibrium** (named after mathematician John Nash, whose life was portrayed in the book and movie *A Beautiful Mind*). A Nash equilibrium is a situation in which economic actors interacting with one another each choose their best strategy given the strategies the others have chosen. In this case, given that Jill is producing 40 litres, the best strategy for Jack is to produce 40 litres. Similarly, given that Jack is producing 40 litres, the best strategy for Jill is to produce 40 litres. Once they reach this Nash equilibrium, neither Jack nor Jill has an incentive to make a different decision.

This example illustrates the tension between cooperation and self-interest. Oligopolists would be better off cooperating and reaching the monopoly outcome. Yet because they pursue their own self-interest, they do not end up reaching the monopoly outcome and maximising their joint profit. Each oligopolist is tempted to raise production and capture a larger share of the market. As each of them tries to do this, total production rises and the price falls.

At the same time, self-interest does not drive the market all the way to the competitive outcome. Like monopolists, oligopolists are aware that increases in the amount they produce reduce the price of their product. Therefore, they stop short of following the competitive firm's rule of producing up to the point where price equals marginal cost.

In summary, *when firms in an oligopoly individually choose production to maximise profit, they produce a quantity of output greater than the level produced by monopoly and less than the level produced by competition. The oligopoly price is less than the monopoly price but greater than the competitive price (which equals marginal cost).*

Nash equilibrium
a situation in which economic actors interacting with one another each choose their best strategy given the strategies that all the other actors have chosen

▶ Nash equilibrium

How the size of an oligopoly affects the market outcome

We can use the insights from this analysis of duopoly to discuss how the size of an oligopoly is likely to affect the outcome in a market. Suppose, for instance, that John and Joan suddenly discover water sources on their property and join Jack and Jill in the water oligopoly. The demand schedule in Table 16.1 remains the same, but now more producers are available to satisfy this demand. How would an increase in the number of sellers from two to four affect the price and quantity of water in the town?

If the sellers of water could form a cartel, they would once again try to maximise total profit by producing the monopoly quantity and charging the monopoly price. Just as when there were only two sellers, the members of the cartel would need to agree on production levels for each member and find some way to enforce the agreement. As the cartel grows larger, however, this outcome is less likely. Reaching and enforcing an agreement become more difficult as the size of the group increases.

If the oligopolists do not form a cartel – perhaps because the competition laws prohibit it – they must each decide on their own how much water to produce. To see how the increase in the number of sellers affects the outcome, consider the decision facing each seller. At any time, each well owner has the option to raise production by one litre. In making this decision, the well owner weighs two effects:

- *the output effect* – because price is above marginal cost, selling one more litre of water at the going price will raise profit
- *the price effect* – raising production will increase the total amount sold, which will lower the price of water and lower the profit on all the other litres sold.

If the output effect is larger than the price effect, the well owner will increase production. If the price effect is larger than the output effect, the owner will not raise production. (In fact, in this case, it is profitable to reduce production.) Each oligopolist continues to increase production until these two marginal effects exactly balance, taking the other firms' production as given.

Now consider how the number of firms in the industry affects the marginal analysis of each oligopolist. The larger the number of sellers, the less concerned each seller is about its own impact on the market price. That is, as the oligopoly grows in size, the magnitude of the price effect falls. When the oligopoly grows very large, the price effect disappears altogether. The production decision of an individual firm no longer affects the market price. In this extreme case, each firm takes the market price as given when deciding how much to produce. It increases production as long as price is above marginal cost.

We can now see that a large oligopoly is essentially a group of competitive firms. A competitive firm considers only the output effect when deciding how much to produce – because a competitive firm is a price taker, the price effect is absent. Thus, *as the number of sellers in an oligopoly grows larger, an oligopolistic market looks more and more like a competitive market. The price approaches marginal cost and the quantity produced approaches the socially efficient level.*

This analysis of oligopoly offers a new perspective on the effects of international trade. Imagine that Toyota and Honda are the only car makers in Japan, Volkswagen and Mercedes-Benz are the only car makers in Germany, and Ford and Holden are the only car makers in Australia. If these nations prohibited international trade in cars, each would have a car oligopoly with only two members, and the market outcome would be likely to depart substantially from the competitive ideal. With international trade, however, the car market is a world market, and the oligopoly in this example has six members. Allowing free trade increases the number of producers from which each consumer can choose and this increased competition keeps prices closer to marginal cost. Thus, the theory of oligopoly provides another reason, in addition to the theory of comparative advantage discussed in chapter 3, that all countries can benefit from free trade.

CASESTUDY

OPEC and the world oil market

Our story about the town's market for water is fictional, but if we change water to crude oil, and Jack and Jill to Iran and Iraq, the story is quite close to being true. Much of the world's oil is produced by a few countries, mostly in the Middle East. These countries together make up an oligopoly. Their decisions about how much oil to pump are much the same as Jack and Jill's decisions about how much water to pump.

The countries that produce most of the world's oil have formed a cartel, called the Organization of Petroleum Exporting Countries (OPEC). As originally formed in 1960, OPEC included Iran, Iraq, Kuwait, Saudi Arabia and Venezuela. By 1973, eight other nations had joined: Qatar, Indonesia, Libya, the United Arab Emirates, Algeria, Nigeria, Ecuador and Gabon. These countries control about three-quarters of the world's oil reserves. Like any cartel, OPEC tries to raise the price of its product through a coordinated reduction in quantity produced. OPEC tries to set production levels for each of the member countries.

The problem that OPEC faces is much the same as the problem that Jack and Jill face in our story.

>>

The OPEC countries would like to maintain a high price for oil. But each member of the cartel is tempted to increase production in order to get a larger share of the total profit. OPEC members frequently agree to reduce production but then cheat on their agreements.

OPEC was most successful at maintaining cooperation and high prices in the period from 1973 to 1985. The price of crude oil rose from US$2.64 a barrel in 1972 to US$11.17 in 1974 and then to US$35.10 in 1981. But in the early 1980s member countries began arguing about production levels, and OPEC became ineffective at maintaining cooperation. By 1986 the price of crude oil had fallen back to US$12.52 a barrel.

During the 1990s, the members of OPEC met about twice a year, but the cartel failed to reach and enforce agreement. The members of OPEC made production decisions largely independent of one another and the world market for oil was fairly competitive. Throughout most of the decade, the price of crude oil, adjusted for overall inflation, remained less than half the level OPEC had achieved in 1981. In 1999, however, cooperation among oil-exporting nations started to pick up. Prices soared in early 2001 but then fell rapidly late in 2001. Prices rose again in 2004 above US$50 per barrel but this was triggered by the war in Iraq rather than OPEC.

Since then prices have remained relatively high driven by both demand from the rapidly growing economies of China and India and by restrictions on supply from OPEC countries. In 2008, oil prices reached US$147 per barrel, before falling back due to slower economic growth in Europe and the US. As this book goes to press, oil prices are around US$85 per barrel. Only time will tell how effective OPEC is at keeping oil prices up in the future.

If the members of an oligopoly could agree on a total quantity to produce, what quantity would they choose? If the oligopolists do not act together but instead make production decisions individually, do they produce a total quantity more or less than in your answer to the previous question? Why?

Game theory and the economics of cooperation

As we have seen, oligopolies would like to reach the monopoly outcome, but doing so requires cooperation, which at times is difficult to maintain. In this section we look more closely at the problems that people face when cooperation is desirable but difficult. To analyse the economics of cooperation, we need to learn a little about game theory.

prisoners' dilemma
a particular 'game' between two captured prisoners that illustrates why cooperation is difficult to maintain even when it is mutually beneficial

In particular, we focus on an important 'game' called the **prisoners' dilemma**. This game provides insight into why cooperation is difficult. In many situations, people fail to cooperate with one another even when cooperation would make them all better off. An oligopoly is just one example. The story of the prisoners' dilemma contains a general lesson that applies to any group trying to maintain cooperation among its members.

The prisoners' dilemma

The prisoners' dilemma is a story about two criminals who have been captured by the police. Let's call them Ned and Kelly. The police have enough evidence to convict both Ned and Kelly of the minor crime of possessing an unlicensed gun, so that each would spend a year in jail. The police also suspect that the two criminals have committed a bank robbery together, but they lack hard evidence to convict them of this major crime. The police question Ned and Kelly in separate rooms and they offer each of them the following deal:

> Right now, we can lock you up for one year. If you confess to the bank robbery and implicate your partner, however, we'll give you immunity, and

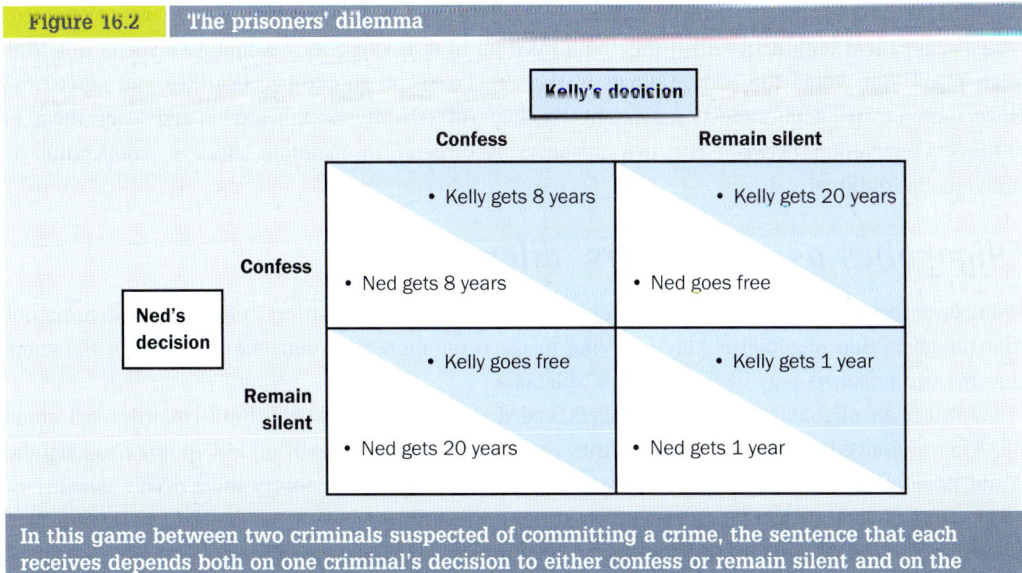

Figure 16.2 The prisoners' dilemma

In this game between two criminals suspected of committing a crime, the sentence that each receives depends both on one criminal's decision to either confess or remain silent and on the decision made by the other criminal.

you can go free. Your partner will get 20 years in jail. But if you both confess to the crime, we won't need your testimony and we can avoid the cost of a trial, so you will each get an intermediate sentence of eight years.

If Ned and Kelly, heartless bank robbers that they are, care only about their own sentences, what would you expect them to do? Would they confess or remain silent? Figure 16.2 shows their choices. Each prisoner has two strategies: Confess or remain silent. The sentence each prisoner gets depends on the strategy he or she chooses and the strategy chosen by his or her partner in crime.

Consider first Kelly's decision. She reasons as follows:

I don't know what Ned is going to do. If he remains silent, my best strategy is to confess, since then I'll go free rather than spending a year in jail. If he confesses, my best strategy is still to confess, since then I'll spend eight years in jail rather than 20. So, regardless of what Ned does, I am better off confessing.

In the language of game theory, a strategy is called a **dominant strategy** if it is the best strategy for a player to follow regardless of the strategies pursued by other players. In this case, confessing is a dominant strategy for Kelly. She spends less time in jail if she confesses, regardless of whether Ned confesses or remains silent.

dominant strategy
a strategy that is best for a player in a game regardless of the strategies chosen by the other players

Now consider Ned's decision. He faces exactly the same choices as Kelly and he reasons in much the same way. Regardless of what Kelly does, Ned can reduce his time in jail by confessing. In other words, confessing is also a dominant strategy for Ned.

In the end, both Ned and Kelly confess and both spend eight years in jail. Yet, from their standpoint, this is a terrible outcome. If they had both remained silent, both of them would have been better off, spending only one year in jail on the gun charge. By each pursuing his or her own interests, the two prisoners together reach an outcome that is worse for each of them.

You might have thought that Ned and Kelly would have foreseen this situation and planned ahead. But even with advance planning, they would still run into problems. Imagine that, before the police captured Ned and Kelly, the two criminals had made a pact not to confess. Clearly, this agreement would make them both better off if they both lived up to it, because they would each spend only one year in jail. But would the two criminals in fact remain silent, simply because they had agreed to? Once they are being questioned separately, the logic of self-interest takes over and leads them to confess. Cooperation between the two prisoners is difficult to maintain, because cooperation is individually irrational.

Oligopolies as a prisoners' dilemma

What does the prisoners' dilemma have to do with markets and imperfect competition? It turns out that the game that oligopolists play in trying to reach the monopoly outcome is similar to the game that the two prisoners play in the prisoners' dilemma.

Consider an oligopoly with two members, called Oilania and Slickland. Both countries sell crude oil. After prolonged negotiation, the countries agree to keep production of oil low in order to keep the world price of oil high. After they agree on production levels, each country must decide whether to cooperate and live up to this agreement or to ignore it and produce at a higher level. Figure 16.3 shows how the profits of the two countries depend on the strategies they choose.

Suppose you are the prime minister of Slickland. You might reason as follows:

> I could keep production low as we agreed, or I could raise my production and sell more oil on world markets. If Oilania lives up to the agreement and keeps its production low, then my country earns profit of $60 billion with high production and $50 billion with low production. In this case, Slickland is better off with high production. If Oilania fails to live up to the agreement and produces at a high level, then my country earns $40 billion with high production and $30 billion with low production. Once again, Slickland is better off with high production. So, regardless of what Oilania chooses to do, my country is better off reneging on our agreement and producing at a high level.

Figure 16.3	An oligopoly game

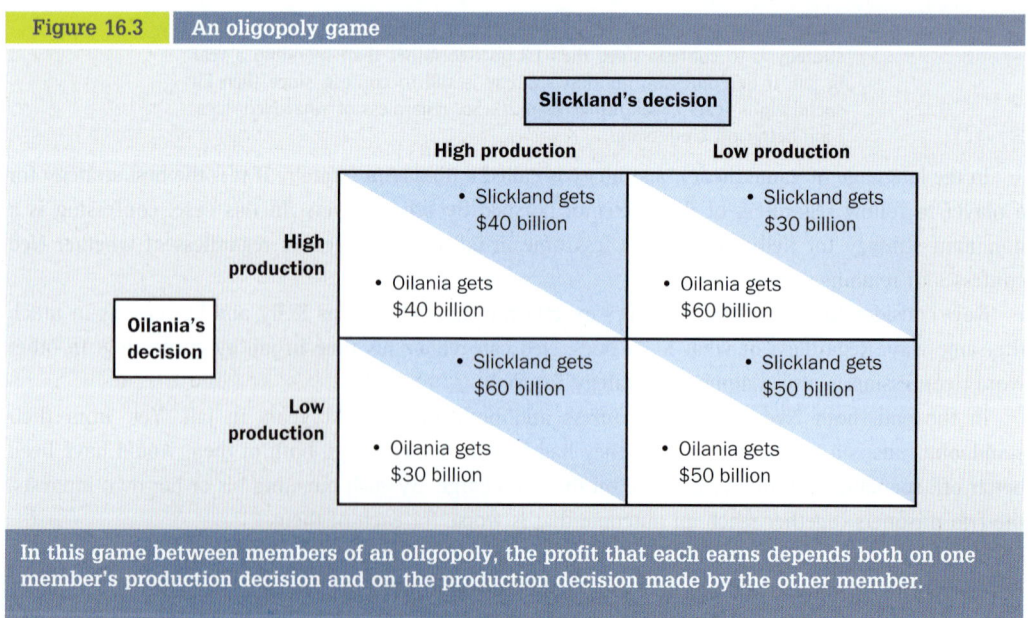

In this game between members of an oligopoly, the profit that each earns depends both on one member's production decision and on the production decision made by the other member.

Producing at a high level is a dominant strategy for Slickland. Of course, Ollania reasons in exactly the same way and so both countries produce at a high level. The result is the inferior outcome (from Ollania's and Slickland's standpoints) with low profits for each country.

This example illustrates why oligopolies have trouble maintaining monopoly profits. The monopoly outcome is jointly rational for the oligopoly, but each oligopolist has an incentive to cheat. Just as self-interest drives the prisoners in the prisoners' dilemma to confess, self-interest makes it difficult for the oligopoly to maintain the cooperative outcome with low production, high prices and monopoly profits.

Other examples of the prisoners' dilemma

We have seen how the prisoners' dilemma can be used to understand the problem facing oligopolies. The same logic applies to many other situations as well. Here we consider three examples in which self-interest prevents cooperation and leads to an inferior outcome for the parties involved.

Arms races

In the decades after the Second World War, the world's two superpowers – the United States and the Soviet Union – were engaged in a prolonged competition over military power. This topic motivated some of the early work on game theory. The game theorists pointed out that an 'arms race' is much like the prisoners' dilemma.

To see why, consider the decisions of the United States and the Soviet Union about whether to build new weapons or to disarm. Each country prefers to have more arms than the other because a larger arsenal gives it more influence in world affairs. But each country also prefers to live in a world safe from the other country's weapons.

Figure 16.4 shows the deadly game. If the Soviet Union chooses to arm, the United States is better off doing the same to prevent the loss of power. If the Soviet Union chooses to disarm, the

Figure 16.4 An arms-race game

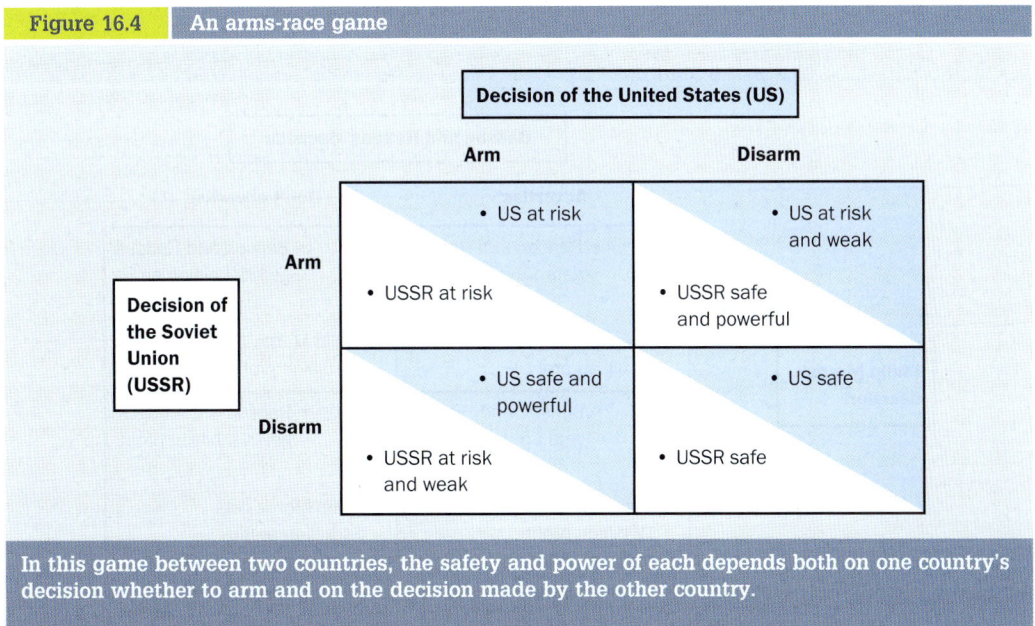

In this game between two countries, the safety and power of each depends both on one country's decision whether to arm and on the decision made by the other country.

United States is better off arming because doing so would make it more powerful. For each country, arming is a dominant strategy. Thus, each country chooses to continue the arms race, resulting in the inferior outcome in which both countries are at risk.

Throughout the era of the Cold War, from the late 1940s through to about 1990, the United States and the Soviet Union attempted to solve this problem through negotiation and agreements over arms control. The problems that the two countries faced were similar to those that oligopolists encounter in trying to maintain a cartel. Just as oligopolists argue over production levels, the United States and the Soviet Union argued over the amount of arms that each country would be allowed. And just as cartels have trouble enforcing production levels, the United States and the Soviet Union each feared that the other country would cheat on any agreement. In both arms races and oligopolies, the relentless logic of self-interest drives the participants toward a non-cooperative outcome that is worse for each party.

Advertising

When two firms advertise to attract the same customers, they face a problem similar to the prisoners' dilemma. For example, consider the decisions facing two cigarette companies, Benson and Hedges and Philip Morris. If neither company advertises, the two companies split the market. If both advertise, they again split the market, but profits are lower, since each company must bear the cost of advertising. Yet if one company advertises while the other does not, the one that advertises attracts customers from the other.

Figure 16.5 shows how the profits of the two companies depend on their actions. You can see that advertising is a dominant strategy for each firm. Thus, both firms choose to advertise, even though both firms would be better off if neither firm advertised.

A test of this theory of advertising occurred in the 1970s, when a number of countries, including Australia, passed laws banning cigarette advertisements on television. When these laws went into effect, cigarette advertising fell and the profits of cigarette companies rose. The law did for the cigarette companies what they could not do on their own – it solved the prisoners' dilemma by enforcing the cooperative outcome with low advertising and high profit.

Figure 16.5 **An advertising game**

In this game between firms selling similar products, the profit that each earns depends both on one firm's advertising decision and on the advertising decision of the other firm.

Common resources

In chapter 11 we saw that people tend to overuse common resources. One can view this problem as an example of the prisoners' dilemma.

Imagine that two gas companies – Queensland Gas Company (QGC) and Santos – own adjacent gas fields. Under the fields is a common reserve of gas worth $12 million. Drilling a well to recover the gas costs $1 million. If each company drills one well, each will get half of the oil and earn a $5 million profit ($6 million in revenue minus $1 million in costs).

Because the oil deposit is a common resource, the companies will not use it efficiently. Suppose that either company could drill a second well. If one company has two of the three wells, that company gets two-thirds of the oil, which yields a profit of $6 million. Yet if each company drills a second well, the two companies again split the oil. In this case, each bears the cost of a second well, so profit is only $4 million for each company.

Figure 16.6 shows the game. Drilling two wells is a dominant strategy for each company. Once again, the self-interest of the two players leads them to an inferior outcome.

The prisoners' dilemma and the welfare of society

The prisoners' dilemma describes many of life's situations and it shows that cooperation can be difficult to maintain, even when cooperation would make both players in the game better off. Clearly, this lack of cooperation is a problem for those involved in these situations. But is lack of cooperation a problem from the standpoint of society as a whole? The answer depends on the circumstances.

In some cases, the non-cooperative equilibrium is bad for society as well as the players. In the arms-race game in Figure 16.4, both the United States and the Soviet Union end up at risk. In the common-resources game in Figure 16.6, the extra wells dug by QGC and Santos are pure waste. In both cases, society would be better off if the two players could reach the cooperative outcome.

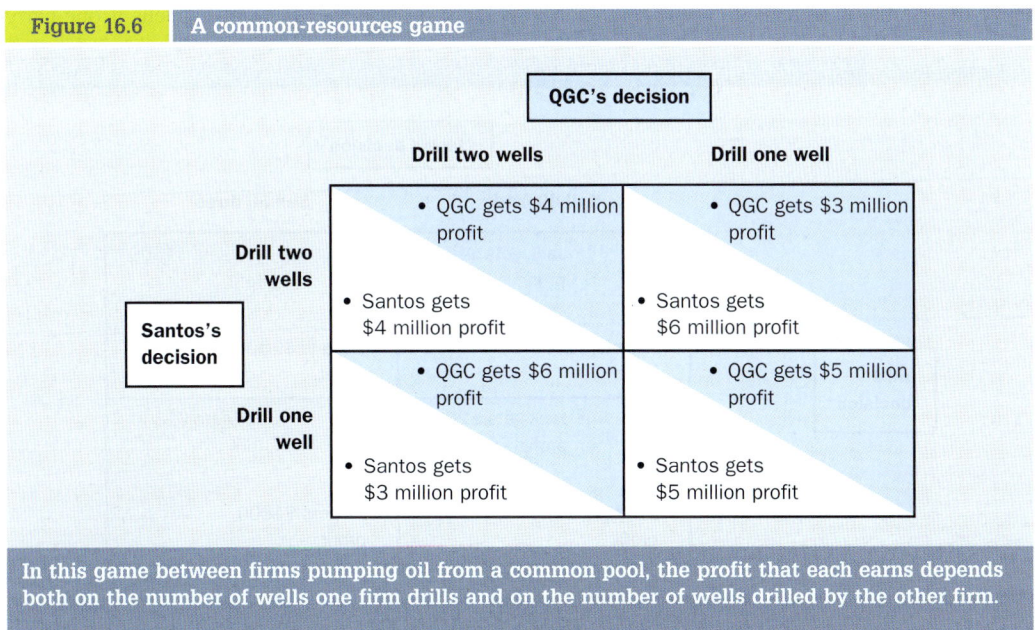

Figure 16.6   A common-resources game

In this game between firms pumping oil from a common pool, the profit that each earns depends both on the number of wells one firm drills and on the number of wells drilled by the other firm.

In contrast, in the case of oligopolists trying to maintain monopoly profits, lack of cooperation is desirable from the standpoint of society as a whole. The monopoly outcome is good for the oligopolists, but it is bad for the consumers of the product. As we first saw in chapter 7, the competitive outcome is best for society because it maximises total surplus. When oligopolists fail to cooperate, the quantity they produce is closer to this optimal level. Put differently, the invisible hand guides markets to allocate resources efficiently only when markets are competitive, and markets are competitive only when firms in the market fail to cooperate with one another.

Similarly, consider the case of the police questioning two suspects. Lack of cooperation between the suspects is desirable, for it allows the police to convict more criminals. The prisoners' dilemma is a dilemma for the prisoners, but it can be a boon to everyone else.

Why people sometimes cooperate

The prisoners' dilemma shows that cooperation is difficult. But is it impossible? Not all prisoners, when questioned by the police, decide to turn in their partners in crime. Cartels sometimes do manage to maintain collusive arrangements, despite the incentive for individual members to defect. Very often, the reason that players can solve the prisoners' dilemma is that they play the game not once but many times.

To see why cooperation is easier to enforce in repeated games, let's return to our duopolists, Jack and Jill. Recall that Jack and Jill would like to maintain the monopoly outcome in which each produces 30 litres, but self-interest drives them to an equilibrium in which each produces 40 litres. Figure 16.7 shows the game they play. Producing 40 litres is a dominant strategy for each player in this game.

Imagine that Jack and Jill try to form a cartel. To maximise total profit, they would agree to the cooperative outcome in which each produces 30 litres. Yet, if Jack and Jill are to play this game only once, neither has any incentive to live up to this agreement. Self-interest drives each of them to renege and produce 40 litres.

Now suppose that Jack and Jill know that they will play the same game every week. When they make their initial agreement to keep production low, they can also specify what happens if one party

Figure 16.7   Jack and Jill's oligopoly game

Jack's decision

		Sell 40 litres	**Sell 30 litres**
Jill's decision	**Sell 40 litres**	• Jack gets $1600 profit • Jill gets $1600 profit	• Jack gets $1500 profit • Jill gets $2000 profit
	Sell 30 litres	• Jack gets $2000 profit • Jill gets $1500 profit	• Jack gets $1800 profit • Jill gets $1800 profit

In this game between Jack and Jill, the profit that each earns from selling water depends both on the quantity one chooses to sell and on the quantity the other chooses to sell.

reneges. They might agree, for instance, that once one of them reneges and produces 40 litres, both of them will produce 40 litres forever after. This penalty is easy to enforce, for if one party is producing at a high level, the other has every reason to do the same.

The threat of this penalty may be all that is needed to maintain cooperation. Each person knows that defecting would raise his or her profit from $1800 to $2000. But this benefit would last for only one week. Thereafter, profit would fall to $1600 and stay there. As long as the players care enough about future profits, they will choose to forgo the one-time gain from defection. Thus, in a game of repeated prisoners' dilemma, the two players may well be able to reach the cooperative outcome.

Imagine that you are playing a game of prisoners' dilemma with a person being 'questioned' in a separate room. Moreover, imagine that you are going to play not once but many times. Your score at the end of the game is the total number of years in jail. You would like to make this score as small as possible. What strategy would you play? Would you begin by confessing or remaining silent? How would the other player's actions affect your subsequent decisions about confessing?

Repeated prisoners' dilemma is quite a complicated game. To encourage cooperation, players must penalise each other for not cooperating. Yet the strategy described earlier for Jack and Jill's water cartel – defect forever as soon as the other player defects – is not very forgiving. In a game repeated many times, a strategy that allows players to return to the cooperative outcome after a period of non-cooperation may be preferable.

To see what strategies work best, political scientist Robert Axelrod held a tournament. People entered by sending computer programs designed to play repeated prisoners' dilemma. Each program then played the game against all the other programs. The 'winner' was the program that received the fewest total years in jail.

The winner turned out to be a simple strategy called tit-for-tat. According to tit-for-tat, a player should start by cooperating and then do whatever the other player did last time. Thus, a tit-for-tat player cooperates until the other player defects; he then defects until the other player cooperates again. In other words, this strategy starts out friendly, penalises unfriendly players and forgives them if warranted. To Axelrod's surprise, this simple strategy did better than all the more complicated strategies that people had sent in.

The tit-for-tat strategy has a long history. It is essentially the biblical strategy of 'an eye for an eye, a tooth for a tooth'. The prisoners' dilemma tournament suggests that this may be a good rule of thumb for playing some of the games of life.

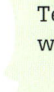

Tell the story of the prisoners' dilemma. Write down a table showing the prisoners' choices and explain what outcome is likely. What does the prisoners' dilemma teach us about oligopolies?

Conclusion

Oligopolies would like to act like monopolies, but self-interest drives them closer to competition. Thus, oligopolies can end up looking either more like monopolies or more like competitive markets, depending on the number of firms in the oligopoly and how cooperative the firms are. The story of the prisoners' dilemma shows why oligopolies can fail to maintain cooperation, even when cooperation is in their best interest.

Of course, as the chapter shows, while firms may benefit from cooperation, such cooperation causes deadweight losses. This provides a motive for policymakers to regulate the behaviour of oligopolists through competition laws. In the next chapter, we look at the types of behaviour that concern policymakers and the tools they use to regulate oligopolists.

Summary

- Oligopolists maximise their total profits by forming a cartel and acting like a monopolist. Yet, if oligopolists make decisions about production levels individually, the result is a greater quantity and a lower price than under the monopoly outcome. The larger the number of firms in the oligopoly, the closer the quantity and price will be to the levels that would prevail under competition.
- The prisoners' dilemma shows that self-interest can prevent people from maintaining cooperation, even when cooperation is in their mutual interest. The logic of the prisoners' dilemma applies in many situations, including arms races, advertising, common-resource problems and oligopolies.

Key concepts

cartel   game theory   prisoners' dilemma
collusion   Nash equilibrium
dominant strategy   oligopoly

Questions for review

1   If a group of sellers could form a cartel, what quantity and price would they try to set?
2   Compare the quantity and price of an oligopoly with those of a monopoly.
3   Compare the quantity and price of an oligopoly with those of a competitive market.
4   How does the number of firms in an oligopoly affect the outcome in its market?
5   What is the prisoners' dilemma and what does it have to do with oligopoly?
6   Give two examples other than oligopoly to show how the prisoners' dilemma helps to explain behaviour.

Problems and applications

1   *The New York Times* (30 November 1993) reported: 'The inability of OPEC to agree last week to cut production has sent the oil market into turmoil … [leading to] the lowest price for domestic crude oil since June 1990'.
    a   Why were the members of OPEC trying to agree to cut production?
    b   Why do you suppose OPEC was unable to agree on cutting production? Why did the oil market go into 'turmoil' as a result?
    c   The newspaper also noted OPEC's view 'that producing nations outside the organization, like Norway and Britain, should do their share and cut production'. What does the phrase 'do their share' suggest about OPEC's desired relationship with Norway and Britain?
2   A large share of the world's supply of diamonds comes from Russia and South Africa. Suppose that the marginal cost of mining diamonds is $1000 per diamond, and the demand for diamonds is described by the following schedule:

Price ($)	Quantity
8000	5000
7000	6000
6000	7000
5000	8000
4000	9000
3000	10 000
2000	11 000
1000	12 000

  a If there were many suppliers of diamonds, what would be the price and quantity?
  b If there were only one supplier of diamonds, what would be the price and quantity?
  c If Russia and South Africa formed a cartel, what would be the price and quantity? If the countries split the market evenly, what would be South Africa's production and profit? What would happen to South Africa's profit if it increased its production by 1000 while Russia stuck to the cartel agreement?
  d Use your answer to part (c) to explain why cartel agreements are often not successful.
3 This chapter discusses companies that are oligopolists in the market for the goods they sell. Many of the same ideas apply to companies that are oligopolists in the market for the inputs they buy.
  a If sellers who are oligopolists try to increase the price of goods they sell, what is the goal of buyers who are oligopolists?
  b Australian football teams have an oligopoly in the market for football players. What is the teams' goal regarding players' salaries? Why is this goal difficult to achieve?
  c Football leagues often decide to set a salary cap for each football team in their league. This limits the amount each team can pay its players. If football teams are already colluding over salaries, why might they still feel the need for a salary cap?
4 Why is game theory helpful for understanding markets with a few firms, but not markets with many firms?
5 Describe several activities in your life in which game theory could be useful. What is the common link among these activities?
6 Consider trade relations between Australia and New Zealand. Assume that the leaders of the two countries believe the pay-offs to alternative trade policies are as follows:

		Australia's decision	
		High tariffs	Low tariffs
New Zealand's decision	Low tariffs	• Australia gains $10 billion • New Zealand gains $10 billion	• Australia gains $20 billion • New Zealand gains $2 billion
	High tariffs	• Australia gains $2 billion • New Zealand gains $20 billion	• Australia gains $4 billion • New Zealand gains $4 billion

     a   What is the dominant strategy for Australia? For New Zealand? Explain.

     b   Define *Nash equilibrium*. What is the Nash equilibrium for trade policy?

     c   Under the Closer Economic Relations agreement, Australia and New Zealand both agreed to allow free trade in goods and services between the two countries. Do the perceived pay-offs as shown here justify this move to a bilateral free trade policy?

     d   Based on your understanding of the gains from trade (discussed in chapters 3 and 9), do you think that these pay-offs actually reflect a nation's welfare under the four possible outcomes?

7   Suppose that you and a classmate are assigned a project on which you will receive one combined mark. You each want to receive a good mark, but you also want to do as little work as possible. The decision box and pay-offs are as follows:

		Your decision	
		Work	Shirk
Classmate's decision	Work	• You: 85%, no fun • Classmate: 85%, no fun	• You: 65%, fun • Classmate: 65%, no fun
	Shirk	• You: 65%, no fun • Classmate: 65%, fun	• You: 40%, fun • Classmate: 40%, fun

     Assume that having fun is your normal state, but having no fun is as unpleasant as a reduction in your assignment mark of 40 per cent.

     a   Write out the decision box that combines the mark and the amount of fun you have into a single pay-off for each outcome.

     b   If neither you nor your classmate knows how much work the other person is doing, what is the likely outcome? Does it matter whether you are likely to work with this person again? Explain your answer.

8   The chapter states that the ban on cigarette advertising on television increased the profits of cigarette companies. Could the ban still be good public policy? Explain your answer.

9   Farmer Jones and Farmer Smith graze their cattle on the same field. If there are 20 cows grazing in the field, each cow produces $4000 of milk over its lifetime. If there are more cows in the field, then each cow can eat less grass and its milk production falls. With 30 cows on the field, each produces $3000 of milk; with 40 cows, each produces $2000 of milk. Cows cost $1000 each.

     a   Assume that Farmer Jones and Farmer Smith can each purchase either 10 or 20 cows, but that neither knows how many the other is buying when she makes her purchase. Calculate the pay-offs of each outcome.

     b   What is the likely outcome of this game? What would be the best outcome? Explain.

     c   There used to be more common grazing land than there is today. Why? (For more discussion of this topic, re-read chapter 11.)

10 Little Kona is a small coffee company that is considering entering a market dominated by Big Brew. Each company's profit depends on whether Little Kona enters and whether Big Brew sets a high price or a low price:

		Big Brew	
		High price	Low price
Little Kona	Enter	Brew makes $3 million Kona makes $2 million	Brew makes $1 million Kona loses $1 million
	Don't enter	Brew makes $7 million Kona makes zero	Brew makes $2 million Kona makes zero

Big Brew threatens Little Kona by saying, 'If you enter, we're going to set a low price, so you had better stay out'. Do you think Little Kona should believe the threat? Why or why not? What do you think Little Kona should do?

11 Jeff and Steve are playing tennis. Every point comes down to whether Steve guesses correctly whether Jeff will hit the ball to Steve's left or right. The outcomes are:

		Steve guesses	
		Left	Right
Jeff hits	Left	Steve wins point Jeff loses point	Steve loses point Jeff wins point
	Right	Steve loses point Jeff wins point	Steve wins point Jeff loses point

Does either player have a dominant strategy? If Jeff chooses a particular strategy (Left or Right) and sticks with it, what will Steve do? So, can you think of a better strategy for Jeff to follow?

Search me!

 Search me!

When accessing information about economics use the following keywords in any combinations you require:

- cartel
- Nash equilibrium
- oligopoly

CourseMate

CourseMate

For more multimedia resources and activities on economics, visit the Economics CourseMate website.

APPENDIX

Types of oligopolistic competition

In the chapter, we described oligopolistic competition in relatively simple terms. Rival firms could choose between colluding or competing, or between advertising and not advertising. In reality, competition in an oligopoly is more complex. This is because firms can choose from a wide range of prices and production decisions.

Game theory is equipped to handle these more complex situations. This appendix will introduce you to two game-theoretic models that capture the interaction between firms in an oligopoly.

Anticipating your competitor's response

To understand the behaviour of a firm in an oligopoly, consider our water duopolists, Jack and Jill. Suppose they are initially producing 40 litres each, so that the market price is $40 per litre. Jack is considering producing more.

However, this will be profitable only if price does not fall by too much. This depends on how Jill might react to Jack's increased production. Jack conjectures that there are two ways Jill may react:

- *Reducing price to maintain quantity sold.* Jill might be concerned about the reduction in her sales quantity as a result of Jack's increased production. In order to maintain her existing volume, Jill could reduce her price.
- *Reducing production to maintain market price.* Alternatively, Jill might be worried about the potential drop in the market price of water when Jack increases his output. She realises that if she cuts back production, she can maintain the existing price in the market.

It is possible that Jill's reactions might be more complicated. Economists, however, have found that focusing on reactions that maintain price or quantity simplifies the analysis of oligopoly. In effect, they define two distinct theories of competition – *Cournot quantity competition* and *Bertrand price competition*. We will examine each in turn. As we will see, because Jack anticipates price matching by Jill under Cournot competition but not Bertrand competition, the former results in higher equilibrium prices than does the latter.

Cournot quantity competition

Suppose that Jack believes that Jill will always maintain her current level of output. That is, he believes that Jill will let the price of water fall rather than reduce her output.

This belief is the basis of Cournot quantity competition. This competition is named after Augustin Cournot who, in 1838, was the first person to attempt to model oligopolistic competition. It is called

Table 16A.1 Jack's profit maximisation decision when Jill produces 20 litres

Market quantity	Jill's quantity	Jack's quantity	Price ($)	Jack's total revenue (and total profit) ($)
20 litres	20 litres	0 litres	100	0
30	20	10	90	900
40	20	20	80	1600
50	20	30	70	2100
60	20	40	60	2400
70	20	50	50	2500
80	20	60	40	2400
90	20	70	30	2100
100	20	80	20	1600
110	20	90	10	900
120	20	100	0	0

quantity competition because each firm believes that its rivals will always act to maintain their current quantity.

When we talked about oligopolistic competition between Jack and Jill in the chapter, we were really talking about Cournot quantity competition. To see this, let's modify the demand schedule for water given in Table 16.1 to focus on Jack's behaviour, given his belief about Jill's output.

Table 16A.1 highlights the decision facing Jack. If Jill is producing 20 litres of water, then Jack knows that demand for his water is simply the market demand less a quantity of 20 litres. This is because for every level of production he chooses, Jill will adjust her price so that the difference between market demand at that price and Jack's production is exactly 20 litres. The individual demand schedule for Jack's water is simply the market schedule less 20 litres.

To maximise profits, Jack will follow the same rule we discussed in chapter 15 for a monopolist – he will choose a quantity that equates his marginal revenue and marginal cost. As Jack's marginal cost is zero in this example, he will maximise profits by maximising total revenue. From Table 16A.1, if Jill is producing 20 litres, Jack will produce 50 litres to maximise his profit.

What if Jack believes that Jill will produce 60 litres of water? This is shown in Table 16A.2. Because Jill is producing more, Jack has to produce less to maintain a given market price. The individual demand schedule facing Jack is lower and Jack's profit-maximising output level is now only 30 litres of water.

Notice that, when Jack believes that Jill is going to produce more, he will react by producing less. The more Jill is going to produce, the smaller the share of the market available to Jack. So Jack reacts by limiting his own output to maintain the market price and maximise his own profits. Figure 16A.1

Table 16A.2 Jack's profit maximisation decision when Jill produces 60 litres

Market quantity	Jill's quantity	Jack's quantity	Price ($)	Jack's total revenue (and total profit) ($)
60 litres	60 litres	0 litres	60	0
70	60	10	50	500
80	60	20	40	800
90	60	30	30	900
100	60	40	20	800
110	60	50	10	500

shows how Jack's output choice will alter with Jill's production decision. The upper part shows how Jack's individual demand curve depends on Jill's output choice. If Jill produces 20 litres then Jack's individual demand curve is given by D_1 – the market demand shifted left by 20 litres. Jack will maximise profits by producing 50 litres of water. This is where the relevant marginal revenue curve MR_1 intersects with marginal cost. Remember that marginal cost is zero in this example. The lower part then plots this decision. Jack produces 50 litres when Jill produces 20 litres.

If Jill increases production to 60 litres, then this reduces Jack's individual demand curve. This is shown by curve D_2. Again Jack maximises profits by producing where marginal revenue equals marginal cost. But because Jill is producing more, Jack's marginal revenue at each level of output is less. This is shown by the curve MR_2. Jack's profit-maximising response to Jill's production is then shown in the lower part. When Jill produces 60 litres of water Jack wants to produce only 30 litres.

Jack's reaction curve, shown in the lower part of Figure 16A.1, shows Jack's profit-maximising level of output for every output level chosen by Jill. If Jill produces nothing, then Jack is a monopolist and will produce the monopoly output, 60 litres. If Jack expects Jill to flood the market and sell 120 litres, then it is not worthwhile for Jack to produce anything. In between, if Jill produces 20 litres, Jack will produce 50, and if Jill produces 60 litres, Jack will produce 30.

If Jill holds similar beliefs to Jack – that is, that Jack will always act to maintain his existing output level – then she will have a reaction curve with a similar property to Jack's. That is, Jill will always want to decrease (increase) her output as Jack increases (decreases) his.

We can place Jack's and Jill's reaction curves on the same diagram. This is done in Figure 16A.2. This allows us to determine the Nash equilibrium in Cournot quantity competition. Recall that the choice of strategies for two players is a Nash equilibrium if neither player can gain by changing to another strategy. In this case, in the choice of quantities, a Nash equilibrium occurs if neither Jack nor Jill wishes to change his or her output, assuming that the other acts to keep his or her output the same.

In Figure 16A.2, the only Nash equilibrium is where Jack and Jill both choose 40 litres of water each. This is the same equilibrium as we found by trial and error in the chapter. If Jack were to choose 20 litres, Jill will want to choose 50 litres – the corresponding point on her reaction curve. These choices of output are not a Nash equilibrium, however, because, while Jill is happy with her

| Figure 16A.1 | Jack's output choice will alter with Jill's production decision |

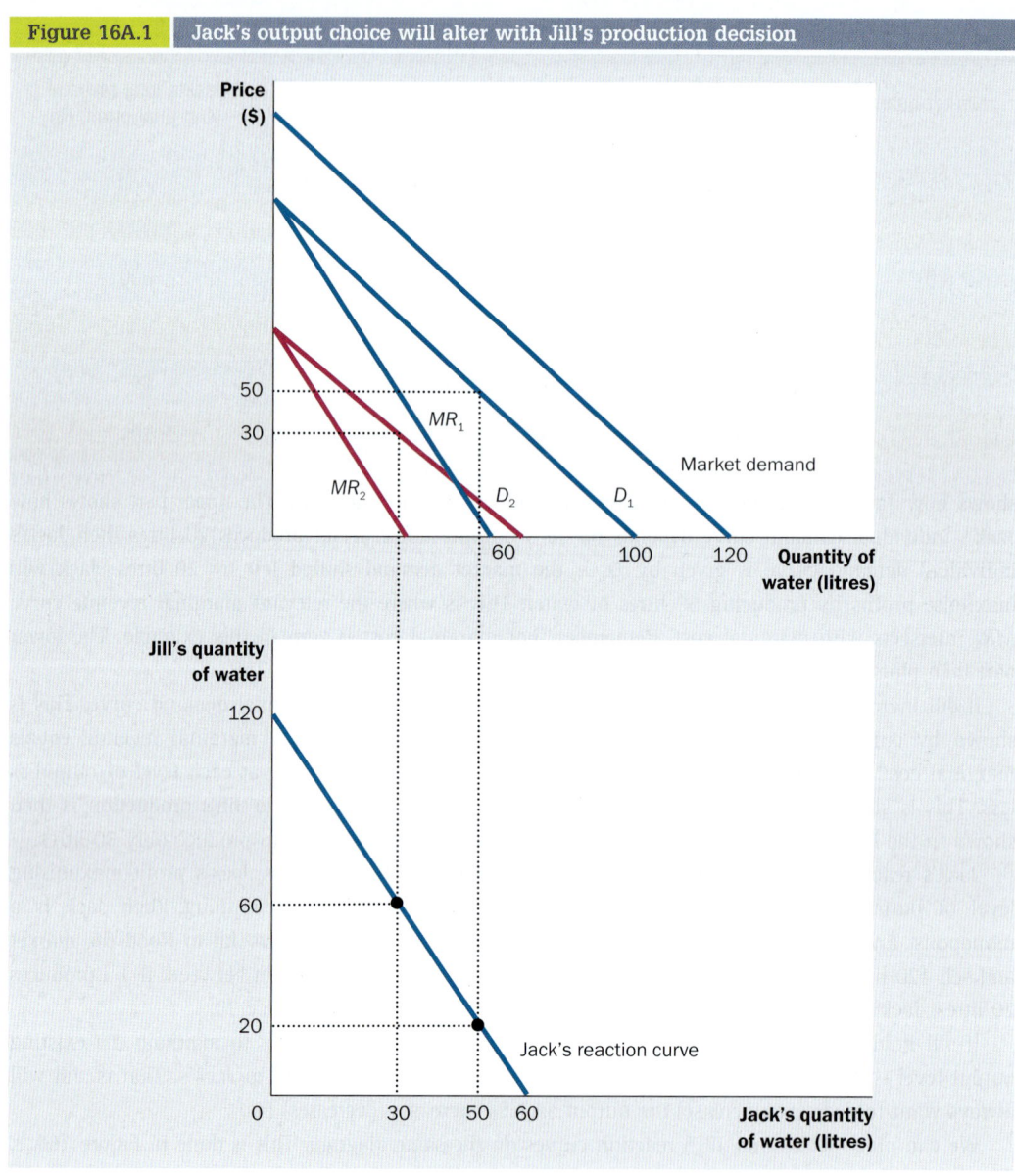

choice, Jack can improve his profits by choosing an output of 35 litres. This corresponds to a point on his reaction curve. Unless both Jack and Jill are choosing outputs on their reaction curves, each is not maximising profits given the choice of the other. Hence, only points where reaction curves coincide represent a Nash equilibrium.

As we noted in the chapter, the Cournot equilibrium involves total production of 80 litres, more than the monopoly output of 60 litres. It also involves less production than under perfect

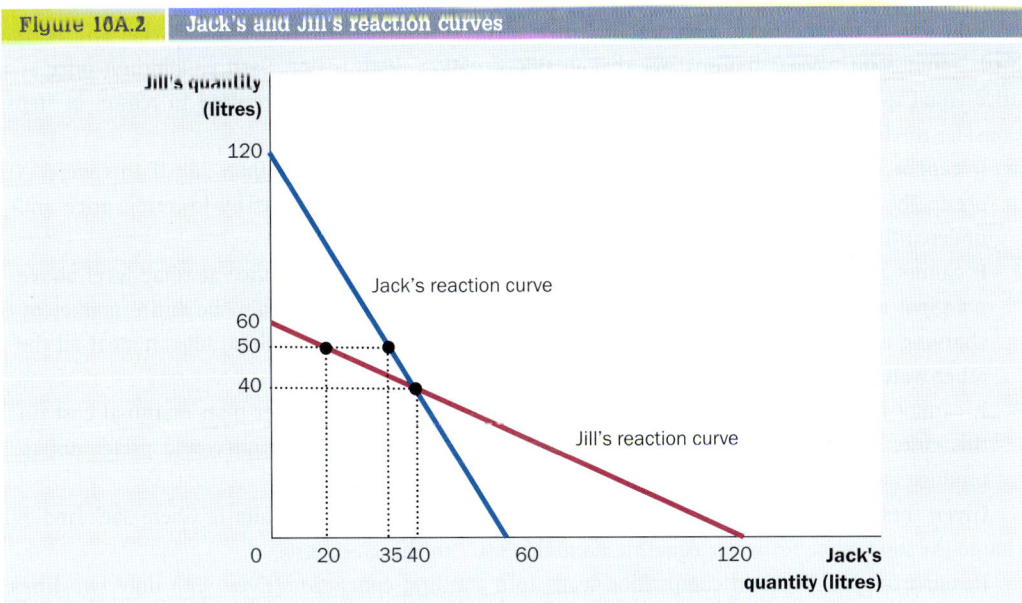

competition. In this example, the perfectly competitive output would be 120 litres with a price equal to the marginal cost of zero.

Bertrand price competition

What if Jack believes that Jill will always act to maintain her price rather than her quantity of sales? This situation is illustrated by Bertrand price competition. Joseph Bertrand, when reviewing Cournot's work in 1883, noticed that a different conclusion could arise when firms believe that rivals will act to maintain price rather than output. It is called price competition for this reason. Indeed, it is easier to analyse Bertrand price competition by examining firms' pricing choices rather than their output choices.

To see what happens in price competition, imagine that Jill currently sells water for $50 per litre. She will sell as much or as little as she needs to maintain this price. Now if Jack sets his price at, say, $60, he will find himself unable to sell any water. This is because water, from the point of view of consumers, is a homogeneous product. Hence, consumers will purchase from the firm that sells at the lowest price. With Jack setting his price at $60, Jill is able to capture the entire market (a quantity of 70 litres). Jack earns no profits.

Can Jack do better than this by changing his price, given that he believes that Jill will maintain her price at $50? Suppose that Jack lowers his price and undercuts Jill. For example, Jack could lower his price to $40. As Jack is selling water more cheaply than Jill, he will capture the entire market. Jack will sell 800 litres and make $3200 in profit. Jill, in contrast, will make no sales and earn no profit. Jack is better off undercutting Jill than by pricing above her.

What is true for Jack is true for Jill. If she prices below Jack, she earns more than if she prices above him. What this means is that both Jack and Jill will find it advantageous to react to the other's price by lowering their own price.

When Jack and Jill have reactions that involve undercutting each other's price, what will be the Nash equilibrium prices? It turns out that in this situation there is one Nash equilibrium price – a price equal to marginal cost which is zero. To see why this is the case, we need to reason in steps. Consider the following:

1   It cannot be a Nash equilibrium for Jack to charge a different price than Jill. If this were to occur, the person with the higher price could always earn more profits by lowering price and undercutting rivals.

2   It cannot be a Nash equilibrium for Jack and Jill to charge the same price at some level above marginal cost. If this were to happen, then either Jack or Jill could gain the entire market by charging a slightly lower price. By making a small price cut, either Jack or Jill can steal all the other water seller's customers and increase his or her own profit.

3   It cannot be a Nash equilibrium for Jack or Jill to charge a price lower than marginal cost (in this case, zero). They would make a loss by selling at such a price and would prefer not to produce at all.

Given these three steps, we must conclude that the only Nash equilibrium is where Jack and Jill charge the same price for water equal to marginal cost – in this case, zero.

In our example, Bertrand competition leads to a startling conclusion. Even with only two firms, each firm in equilibrium will set a price equal to marginal cost – the same as under perfect competition. This result holds whenever production involves constant marginal costs. Bertrand price competition will always lead to the same outcome as perfect competition in this case.

Comparing Cournot and Bertrand competition

Cournot and Bertrand competition yield markedly different outcomes. Bertrand price competition leads to outcomes close to those of perfect competition. In contrast, Cournot pricing outcomes are in between perfect competition and monopoly pricing.

Both types of competition are theoretical possibilities. Which one is more applicable depends on the situation. Remember that each involves firms having a different type of belief about their competitors. In Cournot, firms believe rivals will act to maintain output, whereas in Bertrand, they believe that their rivals' price will remain fixed.

Cournot beliefs will be more appropriate in industries where it is difficult for firms to actually change their output levels. This could occur when firms have limited production capacities, face rigid production technologies or manufacture to maintain an inventory stock rather than to supply customers' orders.

Bertrand competition is more likely when firms compete directly over price before setting output. For example, when tendering for a one-off project, like building a major highway in Melbourne or Sydney, competitors face a situation like Bertrand price competition. The firm with the lowest bid wins the tender and gets to build the project and the losers get nothing.

17

Competition policy

Learning objectives

In this chapter you will:

- consider the various public policies aimed at solving the problem of monopoly

- consider how competition laws try to foster competition in oligopolistic markets

- examine various business strategies such as resale price maintenance and tying

- consider why competition laws are often controversial.

One of the *Ten Lessons from Economics* presented in chapter 1 is that governments can sometimes improve market outcomes. We have already seen how this idea can work when there are externalities or public goods. In this chapter, we show how governments can sometimes improve market outcomes when there is either monopoly or oligopoly.

Monopoly firms, like competitive firms, aim to maximise profit. But this goal has very different ramifications for competitive and monopoly firms. As we first saw in chapter 7, self-interested buyers and sellers in competitive markets are unwittingly led by an invisible hand to promote general economic wellbeing. In contrast, because monopoly firms are unchecked by competition, the outcome in a market with a monopoly is often not in the best interest of society. As we saw in chapter 15, a monopoly will increase its profit by restricting output and raising the price that it charges above marginal cost. This results in a deadweight loss because the monopolist produces less than the socially efficient quantity of output.

Oligopoly can also lead to a deadweight loss. However, oligopoly can lead to a range of market outcomes. If there are many oligopolists then competition can be intense. As we noted in chapter 16, as the number of sellers in an oligopoly grows, an oligopolistic market looks more and more like a competitive market. The price approaches marginal cost and the quantity produced approaches the socially efficient level. In contrast, if there are few oligopolists or if the firms in an oligopoly cooperate and form a cartel, then the market outcome will look like a monopoly. The oligopoly raises profits by producing less and charging more.

Governments around the world have responded by enacting laws that restrict the behaviour of monopolies and oligopolies. In extreme situations, governments have nationalised monopoly and oligopoly firms in the belief that direct government control will lead to a more efficient market outcome. In other situations, governments have acted to break up monopolies. For example, in 1984, the US telephone monopolist, AT&T, was broken into a number of smaller companies due to government action. Similarly, as part of the development of a government-owned National Broadband Network (NBN) in Australia, the main telecommunications company, Telstra, will be broken up. The NBN will use some assets that are separated from Telstra and the break up aims to improve competition in telecommunications.

competition laws
laws that restrict the behaviour of firms with market power, such as monopolies or firms in a small oligopoly

More generally, firms that are either monopolies or oligopolies face a variety of **competition laws** that restrict their behaviour. These laws, which are also called antitrust laws in the US, prevent one firm buying another firm if it is likely to lead to a monopoly or a small oligopoly. They also make it illegal for firms to form a cartel or to use certain tactics to undermine competitors and force them out of the market. In Australia, the key competition regulator, the Australian Competition and Consumer Commission (ACCC), keeps a close eye on firms that either are monopolies or compete in a small oligopoly. For example, in 2009 the ACCC objected to the petrol retailer Caltex buying another petrol retailer, Mobil. Caltex and Mobil were two of the main petrol retailers in Australia at the time and, while there were a number of other major retailers, the ACCC argued that petrol retailing was an oligopoly. The ACCC argued that if Caltex was allowed to purchase Mobil, then competition would be significantly harmed As a result, Caltex decided to pull out of the deal.

competition policy
the laws and procedures that aim to improve social efficiency in oligopolistic and monopolistic markets

Government policies, including competition laws, that aim to improve the efficiency of oligopolistic and monopoly markets are called **competition policy**. In this chapter we consider some of these policies, and look at how they can improve market efficiency.

▸ competition policy

Public policy towards monopolies

We have seen that monopolies, in contrast to competitive markets, fail to allocate resources efficiently. Monopolies produce less than the socially desirable quantity of output and, as a result, charge prices above marginal cost.

Policymakers in the government can respond to the problem of monopoly in one of four ways:

- by trying to make monopolised industries more competitive
- by regulating the behaviour of the monopolies
- by turning some private monopolies into public enterprises
- by doing nothing at all.

Using the law to increase competition

If the two largest Australian banks wanted to merge, the deal would be closely examined by the federal government before it went into effect. The lawyers and economists at the ACCC might well decide that a merger between two large banking corporations would make the Australian banking market substantially less competitive and, as a result, would reduce the economic wellbeing of the country as a whole. If so, the ACCC would challenge the merger in court and, if the judge agreed, the two companies would not be allowed to merge. The main competition law in Australia to control mergers and prevent monopolists from abusing their market power is the **Competition and Consumer Act**. This law, previously called the *Trade Practices Act*, was enacted by parliament in 1974. It has been added to and amended since 1974 to broaden the government's power to prevent anti-competitive behaviour.

The *Competition and Consumer Act* gives the government various ways to promote competition. The Act allows the government to prevent a merger that will substantially lessen competition. The government has used this law in recent years to challenge mergers in the petrol, banking, retail groceries and paint industries. The Act also makes it illegal for a firm with substantial market power to use that power to restrict or harm competition. In one case, BHP Billiton, the big steel and mining company, was found to have breached this section of the Act when it refused to sell a crucial input to a competitor, Queensland Wire Industries.

Amendments to the Act in the 1990s extended the federal government's ability to control firms with market power. Local telephone services are often viewed as a natural monopoly and new sections were added to the Act in 1997 to regulate telecommunications. Part IIIA of the Act was added in 1995 to regulate firms that control important monopoly facilities, such as a pipeline or a rail track.

Competition laws, like the *Competition and Consumer Act*, have costs as well as benefits. Sometimes companies merge not to reduce competition but to lower costs through more efficient joint production. These benefits from mergers are sometimes called *synergies*. By merging, two banks may be able to economise on branch and electronic networks such as EFTPOS and ATMs.

If competition laws are to raise social welfare, the government must be able to determine which mergers are desirable and which are not. That is, it must be able to measure and compare the social benefit from synergies with the social costs of reduced competition. Critics of competition laws are sceptical that governments, through agencies such as the ACCC, can perform the necessary cost–benefit analysis to get it right every time. As an example, in 2003 Qantas and Air New Zealand wanted to form a joint venture that would allow them to cooperate on flight schedules and pricing.

Competition and Consumer Act
Australia's main competition laws (formerly the *Trade Practices Act*)

▸ *Competition and Consumer Act*

Both the ACCC and the Commerce Commission, the competition regulator in New Zealand, decided that the joint venture would result in a loss of social welfare. The airlines appealed this decision to the courts in both Australia and New Zealand. In 2004, the New Zealand High Court upheld the Commerce Commission's decision. The High Court recognised that the joint venture would result in some benefits but concluded that the social loss from reduced competition between the airlines would more than outweigh any benefits. In contrast, the Australian Competition Tribunal upheld the appeal by the airlines. The Tribunal believed that growing competition from other airlines, such as Virgin and Emirates, flying between Australia and New Zealand, would be adequate to prevent the joint venture from reducing competition.

"BUT IF WE DO MERGE WITH AMALGAMATED, WE'LL HAVE ENOUGH RESOURCES TO FIGHT THE ANTI-TRUST VIOLATION CAUSED BY THE MERGER."

Source: ScienceCartoonsPlus.com.

Regulation

Another way in which the government deals with the problem of monopoly is by regulating the behaviour of monopolists. This solution is common in the case of natural monopolies, such as privately owned gas and electric companies. These companies are not allowed to charge any price they want. Instead, government agencies regulate their prices.

What price should the government set for a natural monopoly? This question is not as easy as it might at first appear. One might conclude that the price should equal the monopolist's marginal cost. If price equals marginal cost, customers will buy the quantity of the monopolist's output that maximises total surplus and the allocation of resources will be efficient.

Figure 17.1   Marginal-cost pricing for a natural monopoly

Because a natural monopoly usually has declining average total cost, marginal cost is less than average total cost. Therefore, if regulators require a natural monopoly to charge a price equal to marginal cost, price will be below average total cost and the monopoly will lose money.

There are, however, two practical problems with marginal-cost pricing as a regulatory system. The first is illustrated in Figure 17.1. Natural monopolies usually have declining average total cost. As we discussed in chapter 13, when average total cost is declining, marginal cost is less than average total cost. If regulators are to set a price equal to marginal cost, that price will be less than the firm's average total cost and the firm will lose money. Instead of charging such a low price, the monopoly firm would just exit the industry.

Regulators can respond to this problem in various ways, none of which is perfect. One way is to subsidise the monopolist. In essence, the government picks up the losses inherent in marginal-cost pricing. Yet to pay for the subsidy, the government needs to raise money through taxation, which involves its own deadweight losses. Alternatively, the regulators can allow the monopolist to charge a price higher than marginal cost. If the regulated price equals average total cost, the monopolist earns exactly zero profit. Yet average-cost pricing leads to deadweight losses, because the monopolist's price no longer reflects the marginal cost of producing the good. In essence, average-cost pricing is like a tax on the good the monopolist is selling.

The second problem with marginal-cost pricing as a regulatory system (and with average-cost pricing as well) is that it gives the monopolist no incentive to reduce costs. Each firm in a competitive market tries to reduce its costs because lower costs mean higher profits. But if a regulated monopolist knows that regulators will reduce prices whenever costs fall, the monopolist will not benefit from any reduction in costs and so will not work to reduce costs. The monopolist's failure to reduce costs hurts total welfare.

In practice, regulators deal with both problems by allowing monopolists to keep some of the benefits from lower costs in the form of higher profit, a practice that requires some departure from marginal-cost pricing. Price cap regulation allows the regulated firm to keep all the benefits from lower costs for a fixed period of time. This regulation is used to control market power in the electricity, gas and telecommunications industries in Australia.

Public ownership and privatisation

The third policy used by the government to deal with monopoly is public ownership. That is, rather than regulating a natural monopoly that is run by a private firm, the government can run the monopoly itself. This solution has been common in Australia, New Zealand and some Asian and European countries. In these countries, the government has, at times, owned and operated telephone, water, electricity and rail companies.

When choosing between public and private ownership of a natural monopoly, the government must consider how ownership alters incentives. Private owners have an incentive to minimise costs as long as they reap part of the benefit in the form of higher profit. If the firm's managers are doing a bad job of keeping costs down, the firm's owners will fire them. However, private owners also have an incentive to abuse market power if this raises profits. In contrast, public bureaucrats who operate a government-owned monopoly may have little incentive to lower costs. If the bureaucrat does a bad job the losers are the customers and taxpayers, whose only recourse is the political system. The bureaucrat also has little incentive to abuse market power.

Reducing costs raises economic wellbeing but using market power to increase prices leads to an economic loss. The government's ownership choice will depend on which incentives are stronger and have the biggest effect on economic wellbeing. The best form of ownership will also depend on whether the government can effectively control the actions of a private owner or a public bureaucrat. If a private firm can be effectively regulated to avoid abuse of market power, then private ownership with regulation may be preferred to public ownership. However, as noted above, regulation of natural monopolies often creates a deadweight loss and may reduce the owner's incentives to keep costs low.

Public bureaucrats may be given incentives to lower costs. The government can set cost targets for a public manager and the manager may face demotion or dismissal if these targets are not met. This process of providing incentives to public managers to make them behave more like private owners is called corporatisation.

privatisation
the sale of a government-owned business to private owners

In recent years, governments in Australia and around the world have been relying more on private ownership and regulation and less on public ownership to control natural monopolies. In Australia, the New South Wales government recently sold some of their publicly owned electricity companies to private firms, while the Queensland government privatised QR National, the state's main railway company. The federal government sold Telstra, Australia's largest telecommunications company, to private owners in the 1990s and 2000s. Critics of **privatisation** argue that the motive behind these public sell-offs is to raise funds to control government debt (rather than resorting to unpopular tax increases). Although there is significant debate about the motives behind privatisation, the trend from public to private ownership in part reflects the view that the profit motive is the best way to guarantee that firms are well run.

Doing nothing

Each of the foregoing policies aimed at reducing the problem of monopoly has drawbacks. As a result, some economists argue that it is often best for the government not to try to remedy the inefficiencies of monopoly pricing. Here is the assessment of economist George Stigler, who won the Nobel Prize for his work in industrial organisation, writing in the *Fortune Encyclopedia of Economics*:

> A famous theorem in economics states that a competitive enterprise economy will produce the largest possible income from a given stock of resources. No real economy meets the exact conditions of the theorem, and all real economies will fall short of the ideal economy – a difference called 'market failure'. In my view, however, the degree of 'market failure' for the American economy is much smaller than the 'political failure' arising from the imperfections of economic policies found in real political systems.

As this quotation makes clear, determining the proper role of the government in the economy requires judgements about politics as well as economics.

CASE**STUDY**

*The ACCC –
Australia's
competition
regulator*

There is no general law in Australia that prevents monopoly pricing. If a firm has a lot of market power and might abuse this power by raising its prices to monopoly levels, then state or federal governments may intervene to control the firm's prices. For example, there are price controls in Australia covering telephone calls and electricity prices. Generally, however, the law is aimed at preventing firms from becoming monopolies by mergers or takeovers and stopping firms that have a lot of market power from harming their competitors. These laws make up part of the *Competition and Consumer Act*, and the regulator with the responsibility of upholding these laws is the Australian Competition and Consumer Commission (ACCC).

The ACCC, which was formed in November 1995, has a wide range of responsibilities. Roughly speaking, its tasks fall into two categories – consumer protection and competition protection. Consumer protection laws punish firms if they mislead consumers over products. To give one example, it is the ACCC that protects customers from false claims or omissions in advertisements. In November 2010, following an ACCC investigation, the Federal Court ordered Optus, a telecommunications company, to stop advertising its Internet services in a way that was likely to mislead customers. Consumer protection laws also make certain undesirable selling practices illegal and protect consumers from shoddy goods and defective products.

The competition protection laws prevent firms from agreeing not to compete and stop firms from writing contracts that might limit competition. We discuss these laws in more detail below. It is also illegal under the *Competition and Consumer Act* for firms with market power to use this power to undermine competition. In 1994 and 1995, for example, Woolworths stores in Victoria retaliated against bakers who supplied cheap bread to Woolworth's retail competitors by removing the bakers' bread from Woolworths stores and refusing to accept any further deliveries. Woolworths argued that their actions were simply an attempt to negotiate a better deal from the bakers. The ACCC believed that Woolworth's real motive was to force the bakers to raise their supply prices to competitor stores, making it harder for those stores to compete against Woolworths. In 2004, the Full Federal Court handed down its decision, agreeing with the ACCC that Woolworth's actions were anti-competitive.

One of the most important laws deals with the creation of monopoly. As we noted earlier in this chapter, the *Competition and Consumer Act* prevents mergers or takeovers that will substantially lessen competition. The ACCC plays an important part in determining which mergers are legal and which are illegal. Before firms merge, they can approach the ACCC for 'approval'. The ACCC can grant this approval if they believe that the merger is legal or if they believe that there are public benefits from the merger that more than outweigh any likely anti-competitive effects. Sometimes, the ACCC will require the merging firms to undertake to reduce their market power before the merger is approved. This might include selling some assets to another competitor, such as when Macquarie Media purchased Southern Cross Broadcasting in 2007. Macquarie was required to sell some of its radio stations around Australia to prevent a reduction in competition.

It is sometimes argued that Australia's merger laws are too restrictive. See for example the 'In the news' article on 'Should merging be easier' in this chapter. Most mergers, however, pass the eye of the ACCC with no problems. Around 3 per cent to

>>

5 per cent of mergers involve the firms making undertakings that offset any competition concerns while only about 2 per cent of mergers are opposed outright by the ACCC.

The ACCC, and its chairman Rod Sims, are often unpopular with firms – particularly those that it is investigating. But, if the competition regulator is doing its job then it should be unpopular with business. The aim of a competition regulator is to prevent firms from acting in ways that raise their own profits but, overall, lower the welfare of society. As a previous head of the ACCC noted, unpopularity goes with the job.

IN THE NEWS ...

SHOULD MERGING BE EASIER?

Business often argues that Australia's merger laws are too strict and that the *Competition and Consumer Act* (formally the *Trade Practices Act*) needs to be updated. In this article, Ross Gittins considers the argument for relaxing merger laws in Australia – and finds that the main arguments have poor foundations.

CEOs hanker for a hand-up
by Ross Gittins

With the Howard Government on the ropes in an election year, don't think it's only small business and the bush that are getting in for their chop. Big business has just presented its own log of claims.

The Business Council of Australia held its annual 'strategy forum' last week and addressed this grand question: What does Australia need to do to ensure the country remains relevant and vital with an economy capable of growing and delivering work and better living standards into the future?

After deep deliberation, it came up with five issues it claimed were fundamental to achieving that aim: e-transformation, education and training, modernisation of the *Trade Practices Act*, tax breaks for companies with overseas operations and a 'balanced' approach to greenhouse gas emissions.

Not bad, eh? Two parts trendy motherhood to three parts straight self-interest. What's the best we can do to keep Australia wonderful? Make life easier for big business.

When the CEOs of our biggest companies can come up with nothing more inspiring than that in the way of further economic reform, it suggests they're riven by conflicting interests. All they can agree on is tax cuts all round and open slather on company takeovers.

Huh? Yes, that's right. When they talk about the need for 'a regulatory system which is consistent with international trends' and the need to 'modernise' the *Trade Practices Act*, that's what they're on about: making it easier for them to keep playing the takeover game.

See if you can deduce that from this coded message: 'the forum recognised that the existing *Trade Practices Act*, which was enacted in the early 1970s in very different circumstances, had failed to take account of international trends and needed to be modernised to ensure Australian companies are able to compete'.

If you can't quite see how allowing Australian companies to swallow their competitors will 'ensure they are able to compete', you're obviously not up with the latest 'international trends'.

This is an allusion to a CEOs' special, the National Champion argument. It says that if we want our big companies to be able to expand abroad, we have to allow them to become near-monopolies in our market so they can attain critical mass.

It's a silly argument that will always be more appealing to a CEO than to the rest of us. Why should we put up with an uncompetitive local market just so NAB or Pioneer Concrete can be big in North America? What's in it for us?

And how is allowing our biggest companies to become fat and lazy monopolists in their local market going to make them fit enough to compete in other people's markets?

As for the line that the *Trade Practices Act*, having been passed in 1974, is now terribly out of date, it's nonsense too. The merger provisions of the act were amended in 1993, following two public inquiries.

From the way the CEOs are carrying on, you'd think the present law was greatly inhibiting their takeover plans – but it isn't (more's the pity). Only about 5 per cent of the takeover proposals notified to the ACCC are blocked – and about half of those are subsequently approved after the proposal's been modified to reduce its anti-competitive elements.

The main area where restrictions on takeovers could be contrary to the public interest is in markets for internationally 'tradable' goods (mainly manufactures), where domestic producers may need to consolidate their activities so as to gain the economies of scale needed to compete effectively against imports or on export markets.

But the ACCC has long acknowledged the merits of this case. Domestic consumers' interests are protected by competition from imports, so where imports have at least 10 per cent of the local market, merger proposals are given the tick.

No, the main area of contention is in markets for 'non-tradable' goods or services, where there's no possibility of competition from imports and little likelihood that achieving scale economies in the local market could assist the merged companies' attempts to gain a foothold in overseas markets.

But whereas the economic rationalists' opposition to such mergers assumes the companies' motive is to gain monopoly power in the domestic market, experience suggests motives are often far less rational.

For CEOs who're finding it hard going to gain market share or increase profits by being better than their competitors, taking over other firms is a lazy way of giving the appearance of progress, growth and general busyness. And expanding the empire always justifies an executive pay rise.

The wealth of research showing that shareholders rarely end up benefiting from takeovers lends support to this more cynical interpretation.

Be that as it may, it's clear that while One Nation is attacking national competition policy from one end, the Business Council is now attacking it from the other. A most unedifying spectacle.

Source: Ross Gittins/*Sydney Morning Herald*, 26 February 2001.

Describe the ways policymakers can respond to the inefficiencies caused by monopolies. Give a potential problem with each of these policy responses.

Public policy towards oligopolies

As we saw in chapter 16, cooperation among oligopolists is undesirable from the standpoint of society as a whole, because it leads to production that is too low and prices that are too high. To move the allocation of resources closer to the socially desirable level, policymakers should try to induce firms in an oligopoly to compete rather than cooperate. Let's consider how policymakers do this and then examine the controversies that arise in this area of public policy.

388

Restraint of trade and competition laws

One way that policy discourages cooperation is through the common law. Normally, freedom of contract is an essential part of a market economy. Businesses and households use contracts to arrange mutually advantageous trades. In doing this, they rely on the court system to enforce contracts. Yet, for many centuries, judges in England and Australia have deemed agreements among competitors to reduce quantities and raise prices to be contrary to the public good. They therefore refused to enforce such agreements.

Australia's competition laws reinforce this policy. The *Competition and Consumer Act* makes it illegal for corporations to make a contract or arrangement that would substantially lessen competition. It is also illegal for firms to form a cartel so that they can agree to set prices above a competitive level. This law means that oligopolists cannot agree to act together and make their markets less competitive. The law has been used to prevent collusive behaviour in a number of industries including pre-mixed concrete, steel products and car windscreens. In 2007, Visy Industries was fined $36 million for its role in a cartel with Amcor, the two main suppliers of cardboard boxes in Australia.

IN THE NEWS . . .

HOW TO FORM A CARTEL

In 2007, the Australian Competition and Consumer Commission (ACCC) successfully prosecuted Visy for its part in a cartel that fixed the price of cardboard boxes. The court fined Visy $36 million with individual executives also being fined a total of $4 million. This was the largest cartel fine in Australia's history and one of the largest for a domestic cartel anywhere in the world. This article looks at how the cartel was formed.

Cartel's dirty box of tricks
by Blair Speedy and Cameron Stewart

It was a chance meeting during a lazy beach walk in early 2000 that sowed the seeds of Australia's largest cartel scandal. Walking in one direction along the beach on Queensland's Sunshine Coast was Peter Brown, the manager of the Australian and New Zealand divisions of packaging group Amcor, one of the country's best-known and oldest public companies. Walking the other way was Harry Debney, who ran the cardboard division of arch-rival Visy, owned by billionaire Richard Pratt.

'My wife went to the same school originally that Harry went to, so there was a sort of connection,' Brown recalls. 'We met each other on a beach walk one day and arranged to meet in Melbourne.'

It was to be the last accidental encounter between these two men. Seven years on, these two architects of the cartel are in disgrace,

Amcor, Visy and Pratt have been shamed, and Australians are an estimated $700 million poorer as a result of a ruthless price-fixing deal in the nation's $2 billion box market …

According to Brown's testimony, [in early 2000] Debney called his home and 'had a chat to my wife' and then asked Brown if he could drop by in the morning.

'It wasn't some sort of spur-of-the-moment thing,' he told the ACCC. 'It was planned and he laid out what he would like to do in terms of managing the marketplace.'

In the agreed statement of facts between the ACCC and Visy, tendered to the Federal Court last month, Debney is portrayed as the prime proposer of the cartel, a position at odds with Pratt's public claim that Amcor was the initiator of the illegal deal.

The transcripts show that far from being shocked by Debney's approach, Brown embraced it, believing it to be a lifeline for Amcor as well as for his own future.

>>

'At about that time Russell Jones started to put a lot of pressure on me about the performance of the business in terms of price levels, and I certainly felt I had no alternative but to enter into some sort of pricing arrangement, and I wasn't unenthusiastic,' Brown told the ACCC. 'I mean, I don't think I complained bitterly about the process because I could see that, if it worked, it would lead to better outcomes.'

And it did. Brown said that once prices started to rise under the cartel arrangement, the Amcor board was pleased: 'They said they held me in high regard.'

If Brown's motivation to enter the cartel was to save his ailing company and his career, Visy's motivation – at a time when it was already trouncing Amcor – appears to be a blend of naked greed and Machiavellian intent. Pratt has claimed the cartel agreement was a ruse by Visy to make Amcor relax and then go behind its back to steal market share.

In handing down a record $36 million fine last month to Visy, and through it to Pratt, Federal Court judge Peter Heerey ridiculed this claim, describing it as a 'John le Carré defence'. However, the transcripts reveal Amcor believed Pratt was trying to double-cross it even while setting up the cartel.

'All the advice I was getting from people within Amcor was, "Look, these guys will talk peace with you and then turn around and take a great slab of business from you overnight",' Brown told the ACCC. He revealed that Debney kept warning him he wouldn't be able to control Pratt.

'He (Debney) would make a commitment and something would go wrong and he would say, "Well, you know Richard Pratt, nobody controls Richard".'

Brown revealed that Pratt tried to swipe an Arnott's contract from Amcor despite the cartel agreement forbidding the conspirators from poaching each other's customers.

'The CEO of Arnott's rang me up and said, "I have just had Richard Pratt in here telling me he wants all the business", and I said, "Well, that is a bit of a worry."'

'The guy (Pratt) is a loose cannon: When it suited him, he would go and do what he wanted to do. I mean, when you are worth $3 billion or whatever it is, you can do what you like, pretty well, can't you?'

It was the suspicion that Visy was double-crossing Amcor on the cartel that led Brown to ask Jones to meet Pratt at the All Nations Hotel in Melbourne in May 2001 to reaffirm Visy's commitment to the illegal deal.

According to the transcripts, Jones knew what he was doing was illegal. He said the meeting with Pratt lasted 75 minutes but they talked about the cartel for only about 60 seconds. He took notes of the meeting but made no mention of the cartel discussions in those notes. However, it is Jones's claim about what took place in these crucial 60 seconds that would lead to Pratt's undoing and directly contradict his public claim that he did not know the details of the cartel arrangement with Amcor.

In his ACCC interview, Jones said his cartel discussion with Pratt, though brief, was detailed, with specific contracts being discussed.

'Just to be clear, the matter of the contracts was discussed on the first meeting with Mr Pratt, and Mr Pratt alone,' Jones said. 'I referred to these lists of three or four (contracts). He was aware of them and aware that they were under some sort of negotiation, or likely to be.'

Jones said Pratt 'clearly understood the contents of the discussion' and agreed it 'should be adhered to by both parties'.

Jones told the ACCC he realised the gravity of the game that was being played between two of the country's most powerful companies.

'I was asked to do something which clearly I should not have done,' he said. Later on in the interview, Jones conceded that 'my mistake was that I didn't stop it'.

Source: Blair Speedy & Cameron Stewart/
The Australian, 16 November 2007.

Controversies over competition policy

Over time, much controversy has centred on the question of what kinds of behaviour competition laws should prohibit. Most economists agree that price-fixing agreements among competing firms should be illegal. Yet competition laws have been used to condemn some business practices whose effects are not obvious. Competition laws, if poorly designed, may also harm rather than help competition. Here we consider three examples of controversial competition laws.

Resale price maintenance

One example of a controversial business practice is **resale price maintenance**. Imagine that Superduper Electronics sells DVD players to retail stores for $300. If Superduper requires the retailers to charge customers $350, it is said to engage in resale price maintenance. Any retailer that charged less than $350 would have violated its contract with Superduper.

At first, resale price maintenance might seem anti-competitive and, therefore, detrimental to society. Like an agreement among members of a cartel, it prevents the retailers from competing on price. For this reason, resale price maintenance is illegal under the *Competition and Consumer Act*. Yet some economists have defended resale price maintenance on two grounds.

First, they deny that it is aimed at reducing competition. To the extent that Superduper Electronics has any market power, it can exert that power through the wholesale price, rather than through resale price maintenance. Moreover, Superduper has no incentive to discourage competition among its retailers. Indeed, because a cartel of retailers sells less than a group of competitive retailers, Superduper would be worse off if its retailers were a cartel.

Second, economists have argued that resale price maintenance has a legitimate goal. Superduper may want its retailers to provide customers with a pleasant showroom and a knowledgeable sales force. Yet, without resale price maintenance, some customers would take advantage of one store's service to learn about the DVD player's special features and then buy the DVD player at a discount retailer that does not provide this service. To some extent, good service is a public good among the retailers that sell Superduper DVD players. As we discussed in chapter 11, when one person provides a public good, others are able to enjoy it without paying for it. In this case, discount retailers would free ride on the service provided by other retailers, leading to less service than is desirable. Resale price maintenance is one way for Superduper to solve this free-rider problem.

The example of resale price maintenance illustrates an important principle – *business practices that appear to reduce competition may in fact have legitimate purposes*. This principle makes the application of the competition laws all the more difficult. The economists, lawyers and judges in charge of enforcing these laws must determine what kinds of behaviour public policy should prohibit as impeding competition and reducing economic wellbeing. Often that job is not easy.

Predatory pricing

Firms with market power normally use that power to raise prices above the competitive level. But should policymakers ever be concerned that firms with market power might charge prices that are too low? This question is at the heart of a second debate over competition policy.

Imagine a large airline, call it Aussie Air, has a monopoly on some route. Then Rural Express enters and takes 20 per cent of the market, leaving Aussie with 80 per cent. In response to this competition, Aussie starts slashing its fares. Some competition analysts argue that Aussie's move

resale price maintenance when a wholesaler requires that its retailers do not sell its products to their customers below a specified retail price could be anti-competitive: The price cuts may be intended to drive Rural Express out of the market so Aussie can recapture its monopoly and raise prices again. Such behaviour is called **predatory pricing**.

predatory pricing
when a firm sells its product at an artificially low price in order to drive out an efficient competitor and reduce long-run competition

▸ predatory pricing

Predatory pricing is a common claim in airlines, groceries and other industries. However, some economists are sceptical of this argument and believe that predatory pricing is rarely, and perhaps never, a profitable business strategy. Why? For a price war to drive out a rival, prices have to be driven below cost. Yet if Aussie starts selling cheap tickets at a loss, it had better be ready to fly more planes, because low fares will attract more customers. Rural Express, meanwhile, can respond to Aussie's predatory move by cutting back on flights. As a result, Aussie ends up bearing more than 80 per cent of the losses, putting Rural Express in a good position to survive the price war. If the 'predator' suffers more than the 'prey' then using predatory pricing to harm competition makes no sense.

Economists continue to debate whether predatory pricing should be a concern for competition policymakers. Various questions remain unresolved. Is predatory pricing ever a profitable business strategy? If so, when? Are the courts capable of telling which price cuts are competitive and thus good for consumers and which are predatory? There are no easy answers.

Tying

tying
when a firm will only sell customers one product if they also buy another product

Another example of a controversial business practice is **tying** or bundling. Suppose that Makemoney Movies produces two new films – *Spiderman* and *Hamlet*. If Makemoney offers theatres the two films together at a single price, rather than separately, the studio is said to be tying (or bundling) its two products.

Some tying arrangements can violate competition laws. The reasoning behind the laws against tying – or, as the legal profession calls it, full-line forcing – is as follows. Imagine that *Spiderman* is a blockbuster, whereas *Hamlet* is an unprofitable art film. Then the studio could use the high demand for *Spiderman* to force theatres to buy *Hamlet*. It seemed that the studio could use tying as a mechanism for expanding its market power.

Economists have been sceptical of this argument. Imagine that theatres are willing to pay $20 000 for *Spiderman* and nothing for *Hamlet*. Then the most that a theatre would pay for the two movies together is $20 000 – the same as it would pay for *Spiderman* by itself. Forcing the theatre to accept a worthless movie as part of the deal does not increase the theatre's willingness to pay. Makemoney cannot increase its market power simply by bundling the two movies together.

Why, then, does tying exist? One possibility is that it is a form of price discrimination. Suppose there are two theatres. City Theatre is willing to pay $16 000 for *Spiderman* and $5000 for *Hamlet*. Country Theatre is willing to pay $14 000 for *Spiderman* and $6000 for *Hamlet*. If Makemoney charges separate prices for the two films, its best strategy is to charge $14 000 for *Spiderman* and $5000 for *Hamlet*, for a total of $19 000 from each theatre. Yet if Makemoney offers the two movies as a bundle, it can charge each theatre $20 000 for the movies. Thus, if different theatres value the films differently, tying allows the studio to increase profit by charging a combined price closer to the buyers' total willingness to pay.

Tying remains a controversial business practice. The argument that tying allows a firm to extend its market power to other goods is not well founded, at least in its simplest form. Yet economists have proposed more elaborate theories for how tying can impede competition. Given our current economic knowledge, it is unclear whether tying has adverse effects for society as a whole.

Between 1998 and 2001, Baxter Healthcare, a major pharmaceutical company, offered the following deal to state hospitals. If the hospitals purchased two products, called 'sterile fluids' and 'PD products', separately from Baxter, then each product would have a high price. But if the hospitals bought both products as a bundle, exclusively from Baxter, then they would receive a significant price discount.

Baxter was the only Australian manufacturer of sterile fluids at the time and the cost of importing these fluids was high. In contrast, other pharmaceutical companies could supply PD products. However, hospitals need both of these products and Baxter won all of the contracts.

The ACCC commenced legal action against Baxter in 2002, arguing that Baxter's bundling was a deliberate attempt by the company to use its market power in sterile fluids to reduce competition in the supply of PD products. The court proceedings were controversial, raising difficult economic and legal questions.

The economists who gave evidence in the case, including Barry Nalebuff, from Yale University, provided very different interpretations of Baxter's behaviour. Economists for Baxter argued that the bundled price was simply a legitimate competitive attempt by the company to win as much business as possible. The low bundled price benefitted the hospitals that purchased the products. In contrast, the economists for the ACCC considered that the bundled price was below a competitive level. Baxter was attempting to damage its competitors by setting such a low bundled price.

On the legal side, Baxter argued that it could not violate Australia's competition laws because it was selling products to the government, and these laws do not cover government transactions. The ACCC argued that, while the government could not itself breach the competition laws, the laws still applied when the government was a consumer and the seller engaged in anticompetitive behaviour.

The legal dispute went all the way to the High Court before, in 2008, the Full Federal Court ruled that Baxter's bundling was anti-competitive and illegal. The proceedings were finalised in 2010 with Baxter being fined $4.9 million.

Transparent pricing

Competition authorities in many countries support laws that make prices more transparent. Before July 1997, the dominant telecommunications company in Australia, Telstra, was required by law to report its prices to a regulator. Telstra's competitors could see this price list and it was illegal for Telstra to charge any customer a price that differed from the list price.

These laws were supposed to help competition in telecommunications by making prices clear. If customers know the prices being charged then it makes it easier for them to shop around for the cheapest deal.

Economists were sceptical of this argument. Rather than encouraging competition, requiring firms to list their prices may make it easier for firms to collude. Consider our example from chapter 16 of Jack and Jill, the water duopolists. One reason Jack and Jill might find it difficult to form a cartel is that each producer has an incentive to cheat on any cartel agreement, raise output and push down the price. If the law requires them to list their output level or price in advance then this makes it harder for any firm to successfully cheat on the cartel. As soon as Jack tries to increase his output and lower his price, Jill is informed of this cheating by the competition authorities. Jill can then immediately respond, raising her output and lowering her price. This reduces the short-term benefit Jack gets from cheating. Because Jill is able to immediately detect any attempt by Jack to cheat on the cartel, cheating becomes unprofitable for Jack. The competition laws have helped the cartel to sustain high prices.

A test of the effects of transparent pricing rules comes from experience in Denmark. In 1993, the Danish Competition Council decided to collect and publish the prices that different firms were charging in the ready-mixed concrete industry. By publishing this information, the Council hoped to make prices more transparent for customers. The Council believed that this would make the market more competitive by making it easier for customers to shop around. When economists analysed the Council's action they showed that, rather than making the market more competitive, publishing price data helped the firms to cooperate and set higher prices. Before the Council published the price information, different companies charged different prices for ready-mixed concrete. After the Council began to publish information about prices, however, each company quickly moved to set a price almost identical to that of its competitors. Most importantly, companies that initially charged a low price quickly raised their price to match the high price set by competitors. The Council's attempt to help competition by publishing prices helped the firms to avoid competition. As a result, the Council stopped publishing the price information in December 1996.

IN THE NEWS . . .

DO LOW PRICES HURT OR HELP COMPETITION?

Applying competition laws is never easy. What to one person looks like reasonable competitive behaviour may look to another like an attempt to harm competition. Laws which make low prices illegal are particularly controversial. Competition reduces prices to the benefit of society. But if a firm sets prices too low, it may be viewed as a deliberate attempt to bankrupt competitors and reduce competition. In many countries this 'predatory pricing' is illegal. But rules aimed at preventing predatory pricing may stifle socially desirable competition. This article shows how rules aimed at preventing predatory pricing in Ireland acted like a resale price maintenance scheme. It is argued that this led to higher prices for consumers, without any offsetting benefits.

Competition authority faults grocery order

by Sean MacCarthaigh

The Competition Authority has ... called on the Government not to renew the Groceries Order, which bans all below-cost selling by food retailers. In a discussion paper, the authority said its new powers allowed it to stop predatory pricing, which would include all below-cost selling that was damaging to the consumer, whereas the Groceries Order actually contributed to stifling real competition.

The suggestion met with strong criticism from retailers, who said allowing below-cost selling would put smaller shops out of business. The grocery and dairy lobby group ... said the authority was irresponsible and remote from commercial reality. The business lobby IBEC said a change could mean 23 000 job losses ...

'The Groceries Order has had its day,' said the chairman of the authority, Professor McNutt.

In its submission to the Government, the authority says the ban on below-cost selling in effect allows suppliers to set the minimum price at which retailers can sell their goods, a practice prohibited under the competition laws of virtually all developed countries. Under the Groceries Order, the Competition Authority argues, supermarket chains get significant discounts on goods, but keep these off the invoice sheet. This allows them not to pass the savings on to customers.

'The view of the authority is that the order actually has anticompetitive effects,' said Mr Pat Massey, the body's chief executive. Professor McNutt rejected IBEC's suggestion that 23 000 people could lose their jobs in the grocery sector if the laws were changed, adding 'there was no evidence for this and that competition was usually good for employment'.

Source: Sean MacCarthaigh/*The Irish Times*, 9 July 1997.

What kind of agreement is illegal for businesses to make? Why are competition laws controversial?

Conclusion

Policymakers regulate the behaviour of oligopolists and monopolists through competition laws. While some of these policies are relatively uncontroversial, such as laws that prevent mergers that create a monopoly and laws that break up cartels, other parts of competition policy are the subject of ongoing debate.

Since first enacted in 1974, Australia's competition laws have been the subject of five major reviews, the most recent being the 'Dawson Review' in 2003. This review recommended a number of changes to the laws which fit in with our discussion above. For example, the review recognised that tying can be a legitimate business strategy and recommended that it should only be illegal when it can be shown that the tying leads to a substantial reduction in competition.

The debate on competition policy will continue in the future, reflecting the economic issues presented in this chapter. Some business practices that appear to reduce competition may have legitimate if subtle business purposes. As a result, policymakers need to be careful when using the substantial powers of competition laws to place limits on firm behaviour.

Summary

- Policymakers can respond to the inefficiency of monopoly behaviour in four ways. They can use the competition laws to try to make the industry more competitive. They can regulate the prices that the monopoly charges. They can turn the monopolist into a government-run enterprise. Or, if the market failure is deemed small compared with the inevitable imperfections of policies, they can do nothing at all.
- Policymakers use competition laws to prevent oligopolies from engaging in behaviour that reduces competition. If firms in an oligopoly form a cartel to reduce competition and raise profits, then authorities, such as the ACCC, can prosecute those firms under the competition laws.
- The application of these competition laws and competition policy more generally can be controversial. Some behaviour that may seem to reduce competition may in fact have legitimate business purposes.

Key concepts

Competition and
  Consumer Act
competition laws

competition policy
predatory pricing
privatisation

resale price maintenance
tying

Questions for review

1   What gives the government the power to regulate mergers between firms? From the standpoint of the welfare of society, give a good reason and a bad reason that two firms might want to merge.
2   Describe the two problems that arise when regulators tell a natural monopoly that it must set a price equal to marginal cost.
3   What is resale price maintenance and why is it controversial?
4   Describe the problems facing a firm if it decides to use predatory pricing to eliminate a competitor.
5   How can tying or bundling be used by a firm to raise its profits? Why is this business strategy controversial?
6   Explain how rules that create transparent pricing might also encourage cartels.

Problems and applications

1   Natural monopoly firms are often regulated so that they can only charge prices set by the authorities. Under one approach, prices are based on the monopolist's costs so that for any given quantity of sales, the monopolist can only set prices equal to its average costs.
    a   Why might regulators believe that forcing the monopoly to charge a price equal to average cost is a good outcome? Does this price regulation maximise social welfare? What problems do you see with this form of price regulation?
    b   Suppose the monopolist can undertake innovation that will lower its average cost. If the monopolist faces average-cost price regulation, does it face strong or weak incentives to innovate?
    c   An alternative to average-cost price regulation is to set a 'price cap' for the natural monopoly firm. With a price cap, the regulator does not adjust the regulated price as soon as monopolist's costs change but keeps the same regulated prices for a number of years. It is argued that price-cap regulation encourages innovation. Do you agree with this and why?

396

2   The singer Pink has a monopoly over a scarce resource: herself. She is the only person who can produce a Pink concert. Does this fact imply that the government should regulate the prices of her concerts? Why or why not?

3   While cartels are illegal, companies often have big incentives to form a cartel and raise prices. To understand these incentives, let's analyse a game between the two competing companies. Suppose that each company can charge either a high price for its product or a low price. If one company charges $100, it earns low profits if the other company charges $100 also, and high profits if the other company charges $200. On the other hand, if the company charges $200, it earns very low profits if the other company charges $100, and medium profits if the other company charges $200 also. (You may need to refer to chapter 16 and the prisoners' dilemma to complete this activity.)

   a   Draw the decision box for this game.
   b   What is the Nash equilibrium in this game? Explain.
   c   Is there an outcome that would be better than the Nash equilibrium for both companies? How could it be achieved? Who would lose if it were achieved?

4   Suppose that there are currently four producers of tyres in Australia – Allcar, Bootstone, Carstuff and Duddos. There are no imported tyres in Australia and there are significant barriers to new entry. Allcar has 25 per cent of all tyre sales, Bootstone has 10 per cent of all tyre sales, Carstuff has 40 per cent of all tyre sales and Duddos has 25 per cent of all tyre sales. The marginal cost of producing a tyre is constant and equal to $20 per tyre. The current market price of a tyre is $50. One million tyres are sold each year. Industry estimates suggest that a $10 increase in the market price of tyres will result in a reduction of sales by 100 000 each year. Allcar and Bootstone wish to merge. They claim that their merger will lead to a $10 reduction in the marginal cost of each tyre that they produce (i.e., the marginal cost for the merged firm will fall from $20 per tyre to $10 per tyre). Assume that Allcar and Bootstone are making a correct claim about the reduction in marginal cost but that the merger will also lead to a $10 rise in the market price of tyres.

   a   Draw a diagram showing the deadweight loss associated with the oligopoly in the Australian tyre market before any merger between Allcar and Bootstone.
   b   Show how the deadweight loss will change if Allcar and Bootstone are allowed to merge. Give an estimate of the size of the change in the deadweight loss.
   c   What are the cost savings that will be created by the merger? What factors might affect the total size of these cost savings?
   d   Do you think that the merger between Allcar and Bootstone will increase or decrease social surplus? Why?

5   Businesses are often accused of engaging in predatory pricing. However, competition regulators often have difficulties separating predatory pricing from vigorous competition. The Areeda–Turner test for predatory pricing states that if a firm sets its price above its marginal cost then it is probably not predatory pricing, but if it sets its price below marginal cost then it is probably predatory. Remembering our analysis of profit-maximising firms from chapters 14 and 15, explain why pricing below marginal cost might be viewed as a deliberate attempt to drive out a competitor rather than vigorous competitive pricing. Can you think of any situations where a firm might set a price below marginal cost but not be predatory pricing?

6   The Baxter case study presented in this chapter discussed how Baxter Healthcare was prosecuted under Australian competition laws for bundling two types of pharmaceutical products. But many products come as bundles. Car bodies and engines are sold as a bundle. Mobile phones and calling plans are often sold as a package. Even shoes and shoe laces are usually sold together. Think of reasons why bundling might be good for consumers and business. Under what circumstances could bundling create competition concerns? In particular, why might government be concerned if the firm that bundles the products has a monopoly in part of the bundle?

7   In 2004, the ACCC successfully prosecuted a number of petrol sellers in a Victorian town for collusion. These petrol sellers advertised their prices on boards outside their petrol stations. When one of the sellers wanted to raise petrol prices in the town, they would increase the price on their own board and then ring the other sellers suggesting that they 'go for a drive'.

   a Why was it important for the cartel to have the petrol prices easily visible on boards outside their petrol stations?

   b Should the government prevent this type of collusion by banning the advertising of petrol prices?

   c What would be the costs and benefits of such a policy?

   d More recently, some politicians have been concerned about banks telling their customers about plans to raise the interest rates on home loans. The politicians have argued that these statements allow the banks to signal rate increases to each other, helping them to collude and maintain higher interest rates. Do you think that banks should be banned from telling customers about planned interest rate changes? Why or why not?

Search Me!

When accessing information about economics use the following keywords in any combinations you require:

- *Competition and Consumer Act*
- competition policy
- predatory pricing

CourseMate

For more multimedia resources and activities on economics, visit the Economics CourseMate website.

18

Monopolistic competition

Learning objectives

In this chapter you will:

- analyse competition among firms that sell differentiated products
- compare the outcome under monopolistic competition and under perfect competition
- consider the desirability of outcomes in monopolistically competitive markets
- examine the debate over the effects of advertising
- examine the debate over the role of brand names.

You walk into a bookshop to buy a book to read during your next holiday. On the shelves you find a Sue Grafton mystery, a Stephen King thriller, a Meg Cabot romance, a Stephenie Meyer fantasy and many other choices. When you pick out a book and buy it, what kind of market are you participating in?

On the one hand, the market for books seems quite competitive. As you look over the shelves at your bookshop, you find many authors and many publishers vying for your attention. A buyer in this market has thousands of competing products from which to choose. And because anyone can enter the industry by writing and publishing a book, the book business is not very profitable. For every highly paid novelist, there are hundreds of struggling ones.

On the other hand, the market for books seems quite monopolistic. Because each book is unique, publishers have some latitude in choosing what price to charge. The sellers in this market are price makers rather than price takers. And, indeed, the price of books greatly exceeds marginal cost. The price of a typical hardcover novel, for instance, is about $35, whereas the cost of printing one additional copy of the novel is less than $10.

monopolistic competition
a market structure in which many firms sell products that are similar but not identical

▸ monopolistic competition

In this chapter we examine markets that have some features of competition and some features of monopoly. This market structure is called **monopolistic competition**. In a monopolistically competitive market, each firm has a monopoly over the product it makes, but many other firms make similar products that compete for the same customers. To be more precise, monopolistic competition describes a market with the following attributes:

- *Many sellers:* There are many firms competing for the same group of customers.
- *Product differentiation:* Each firm produces a product that is at least slightly different from those of other firms. Thus, rather than being a price taker, each firm faces a downward-sloping demand curve.
- *Free entry:* Firms can enter (or exit) the market without restriction. Thus, the number of firms in the market adjusts until economic profits are driven to zero.

A moment's thought reveals a long list of markets with these attributes – books, CDs, films, computer games, restaurants, piano lessons, furniture and so on.

Monopolistic competition, like oligopoly, is a market structure that lies between the extreme cases of competition and monopoly. But oligopoly and monopolistic competition are quite different. Oligopoly departs from the perfectly competitive ideal of chapter 14 because there are only a few sellers in the market. The small number of sellers makes vigorous competition less likely and it makes strategic interactions among them vitally important. In contrast, under monopolistic competition, there are many sellers, each of which is small compared with the market. A monopolistically competitive market departs from the perfectly competitive ideal because each of the sellers offers a somewhat different product.

Competition with differentiated products

To understand monopolistically competitive markets, we first consider the decisions facing an individual firm. We then examine what happens in the long run as firms enter and exit the industry. Next, we compare the equilibrium under monopolistic competition with the equilibrium under perfect competition that we examined in chapter 14. Finally, we consider whether the outcome in a monopolistically competitive market is desirable from the standpoint of society as a whole.

The monopolistically competitive firm in the short run

Each firm in a monopolistically competitive market is, in many ways, like a monopoly. Because its product is different from those offered by other firms, it faces a downward-sloping demand curve. (In contrast, a perfectly competitive firm faces a horizontal demand curve at the market price.) Thus, the monopolistically competitive firm follows a monopolist's rule for profit maximisation – it chooses the quantity at which marginal revenue equals marginal cost and then uses its demand curve to find the price consistent with that quantity.

Figure 18.1 shows the cost, demand and marginal-revenue curves for two typical firms, each in a different monopolistically competitive industry. In both panels of this figure, the profit-maximising quantity is found at the intersection of the marginal-revenue and marginal-cost curves. The two panels in this figure show different outcomes for the firm's profit. In panel (a), price exceeds average total cost, so the firm makes a profit. In panel (b), price is below average total cost. In this case, the firm is unable to make a positive profit, so the best the firm can do is to minimise its losses.

All this should seem familiar. A monopolistically competitive firm chooses its quantity and price just as a monopoly does. In the short run, these two types of market structure are similar.

The long-run equilibrium

The situations depicted in Figure 18.1 do not last long. When firms are making profits, as in panel (a), new firms have an incentive to enter the market. This entry increases the number of products from which customers can choose and, therefore, reduces the demand faced by each firm already in the market. In other words, profit encourages entry, and entry shifts the demand curves faced by the

Figure 18.1 Monopolistic competitors in the short run

(a) Firm makes profit

(b) Firm makes losses

Monopolistic competitors, like monopolists, maximise profit by producing the quantity at which marginal revenue equals marginal cost. The firm in panel (a) makes a profit because, at this quantity, price is above average total cost. The firm in panel (b) makes losses because, at this quantity, price is less than average total cost.

| Figure 18.2 | A monopolistic competitor in the long run |

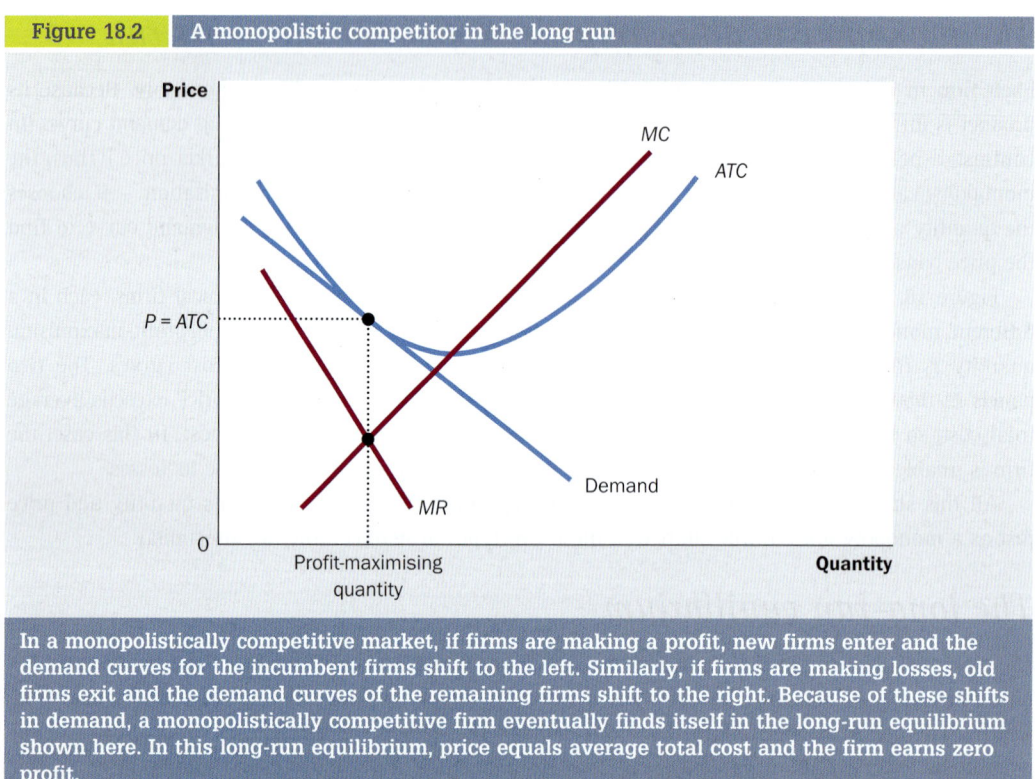

In a monopolistically competitive market, if firms are making a profit, new firms enter and the demand curves for the incumbent firms shift to the left. Similarly, if firms are making losses, old firms exit and the demand curves of the remaining firms shift to the right. Because of these shifts in demand, a monopolistically competitive firm eventually finds itself in the long-run equilibrium shown here. In this long-run equilibrium, price equals average total cost and the firm earns zero profit.

incumbent firms to the left. As the demand for incumbent firms' products fall, these firms experience declining profit.

Conversely, when firms are making losses, as in panel (b), firms in the market have an incentive to exit. As firms exit, customers have fewer products from which to choose. This decrease in the number of firms expands the demand faced by those firms that stay in the market. In other words, losses encourage exit, and exit shifts the demand curves of the remaining firms to the right. As the demand for the remaining firms' products rises, these firms experience rising profit (that is, declining losses).

This process of entry and exit continues until the firms in the market are making exactly zero economic profit. Figure 18.2 depicts the long-run equilibrium. Once the market reaches this equilibrium, new firms have no incentive to enter and existing firms have no incentive to exit.

Notice that the demand curve in this figure just barely touches the average-total-cost curve. Mathematically, we say the two curves are tangent to each other. These two curves must be tangent once entry and exit have driven profit to zero. Because profit per unit sold is the difference between price (found on the demand curve) and average total cost, the maximum profit is zero only if these two curves touch each other without crossing. Also note that this point of tangency occurs at the same quantity where marginal revenue equals marginal cost. That these two points line up is not a coincidence. It is required because this particular quantity maximises profit and the maximum profit is exactly zero in the long run.

To sum up, two characteristics describe the long-run equilibrium in a monopolistically competitive market.

- As in a monopoly market, price exceeds marginal cost. This conclusion arises because profit maximisation requires marginal revenue to equal marginal cost and because the downward-sloping demand curve makes marginal revenue less than the price.
- As in a competitive market, price equals average total cost. This conclusion arises because free entry and exit drive economic profit to zero.

The second characteristic shows how monopolistic competition differs from monopoly. Because a monopoly is the sole seller of a product without close substitutes, it can earn positive economic profit, even in the long run. In contrast, because there is free entry into a monopolistically competitive market, the economic profit of a firm in this type of market is driven to zero.

'Given the downward slope of our demand curve, and the ease with which other firms can enter the industry, we can strengthen our profit position only by equating marginal cost and marginal revenue. Order more jelly beans.'

Source: ScienceCartoonsPlus.com.

Monopolistic versus perfect competition

Figure 18.3 compares the long-run equilibrium under monopolistic competition with the long-run equilibrium under perfect competition. (Chapter 14 discussed the equilibrium with perfect competition.) There are two noteworthy differences between monopolistic and perfect competition – excess capacity and the mark-up.

Excess capacity

As we have just seen, entry and exit drive each firm in a monopolistically competitive market to a point of tangency between its demand and average-total-cost curves. Panel (a) of Figure 18.3 shows that the quantity of output at this point is smaller than the quantity that minimises average total cost. Thus, under monopolistic competition, firms produce on the downward-sloping portion of their average-total-cost curves. In this way, monopolistic competition contrasts starkly with perfect competition. As panel (b) of Figure 18.3 shows, free entry in competitive markets drives firms to produce at the minimum of average total cost.

The quantity that minimises average total cost is called the *efficient scale* of the firm. In the long run, perfectly competitive firms produce at the efficient scale, whereas monopolistically competitive firms produce below this level. Firms are said to have *excess capacity* under monopolistic competition. In other words, a monopolistically competitive firm, unlike a perfectly competitive firm, could increase the quantity it produces and lower the average total cost of production. The firm forgoes this

| Figure 18.3 | Monopolistic versus perfect competition |

Panel (a) shows the long-run equilibrium in a monopolistically competitive market and panel (b) shows the long-run equilibrium in a perfectly competitive market. Two differences are notable: (1) the perfectly competitive firm produces at the efficient scale, where average total cost is minimised – in contrast, the monopolistically competitive firm produces at less than the efficient scale; (2) price equals marginal cost under perfect competition, but price is above marginal cost under monopolistic competition.

opportunity because it would need to cut its price to sell the additional output. It is more profitable for a monopolistic competitor to continue operating with excess capacity.

Mark-up over marginal cost

A second difference between perfect competition and monopolistic competition is the relationship between price and marginal cost. For a competitive firm, such as that shown in panel (b) of Figure 18.3, price equals marginal cost. For a monopolistically competitive firm, such as that shown in panel (a), price exceeds marginal cost, because the firm always has some market power.

How is this mark-up over marginal cost consistent with free entry and zero profit? The zero-profit condition ensures only that price equals average total cost. It does not ensure that price equals marginal cost. Indeed, in the long-run equilibrium, monopolistically competitive firms operate on the declining portion of their average-total-cost curves, so marginal cost is below average total cost. Thus, for price to equal average total cost, price must be above marginal cost.

In this relationship between price and marginal cost, we see a key behavioural difference between perfect competitors and monopolistic competitors. Imagine that you were to ask a firm the following question: Would you like to see another customer come through your door ready to buy from you at your current price? A perfectly competitive firm would answer that it didn't care. Because price exactly equals marginal cost, the profit from an extra unit sold is zero. In contrast, a monopolistically competitive firm is always eager to get another customer. Because its price exceeds marginal cost, an extra unit sold at the posted price means more profit.

Monopolistic competition and the welfare of society

Is the outcome in a monopolistically competitive market desirable from the standpoint of society as a whole? Can policymakers improve on the market outcome? In previous chapters we evaluated markets from the standpoint of efficiency – that is, whether society is getting the most it can out of its scarce resources. We learned that competitive markets lead to efficient outcomes, unless there are externalities, and that monopoly markets lead to deadweight losses. Monopolistically competitive markets are more complex than either of these polar cases, so evaluating welfare in these markets is a more subtle exercise.

One source of inefficiency is the mark-up of price over marginal cost. Because of the mark-up, some consumers who value the good at more than the marginal cost of production (but less than the price) will be deterred from buying it. Thus, a monopolistically competitive market has the normal deadweight loss of monopoly pricing.

Although this outcome is clearly undesirable compared with the first-best outcome of price equal to marginal cost, there is no easy way for policymakers to fix the problem. To enforce marginal-cost pricing, policymakers would need to regulate all firms that produce differentiated products. Because such products are so common in the economy, the administrative burden of such regulation would be overwhelming.

Moreover, regulating monopolistic competitors would entail all the problems of regulating natural monopolies. In particular, because monopolistic competitors are making zero profits already, requiring them to lower their prices to equal marginal cost would cause them to make losses. To keep these firms in business, the government would need to help them cover these losses. Rather than raising taxes to pay for these subsidies, policymakers may decide it is better to live with the inefficiency of monopolistic pricing.

Another way in which monopolistic competition may be socially inefficient is that the number of firms in the market may not be 'ideal'. That is, there may be too much or too little entry. One way to think about this problem is in terms of the externalities associated with entry. Whenever a new firm considers entering the market with a new product, it considers only the profit it would make. Yet its entry would also have two effects that are external to the firm:

- *The product-variety externality:* Because consumers get some consumer surplus from the introduction of a new product, entry of a new firm conveys a positive externality on consumers.
- *The business-stealing externality:* Because other firms lose customers and profits from the entry of a new competitor, entry of a new firm imposes a negative externality on existing firms.

Thus, in a monopolistically competitive market, there are both positive and negative externalities associated with the entry of new firms. Depending on which externality is larger, a monopolistically competitive market could have either too few or too many products.

Both of these externalities are closely related to the conditions for monopolistic competition. The product-variety externality arises because a new firm would offer a product different from those of the existing firms. The business-stealing externality arises because firms post a price above marginal cost and, therefore, are always eager to sell additional units. Conversely, because perfectly competitive firms produce identical goods and charge a price equal to marginal cost, neither of these externalities exists under perfect competition.

In the end, we can conclude only that monopolistically competitive markets do not have all the desirable welfare properties of perfectly competitive markets. That is, the invisible hand does not ensure that total surplus is maximised under monopolistic competition. Yet because the inefficiencies are subtle, hard to measure and hard to fix, there is no easy way for public policy to improve the market outcome.

List the three key attributes of monopolistic competition. Draw and explain a diagram to show the long-run equilibrium in a monopolistically competitive market. How does this equilibrium differ from that in a perfectly competitive market?

Advertising

It is nearly impossible to go through a typical day in a modern economy without being bombarded with advertising. Whether you are reading a newspaper, watching television, surfing the Internet or driving down the highway, some firm will try to convince you to buy its product. Such behaviour is a natural feature of monopolistic competition (as well as some oligopolistic industries). When firms sell differentiated products and charge prices above marginal cost, each firm has an incentive to advertise in order to attract more buyers to its particular product.

The amount of advertising varies substantially across products. Firms that sell highly differentiated consumer goods, such as over-the-counter medicines, perfumes, soft drinks, razor blades, breakfast cereals and dog food, typically spend between 10 and 20 per cent of revenue for advertising. Firms that sell industrial products, such as drill presses and communications satellites, typically spend very little on advertising. And firms that sell homogeneous products, such as wheat, peanuts or crude oil, spend nothing at all.

For the economy as a whole, about 1 to 2 per cent of total firm revenue is spent on advertising. This spending takes many forms, including commercials on television and radio, space in newspapers and magazines, direct mail, the yellow pages, billboards and the Internet.

The debate about advertising

Is society wasting the resources it devotes to advertising? Or does advertising serve a valuable purpose? Assessing the social value of advertising is difficult and often generates heated argument among economists. Let's consider both sides of the debate.

The critique of advertising

Critics of advertising argue that firms advertise in order to manipulate people's tastes. Much advertising is psychological rather than informational. Consider, for example, the typical television commercial for some brand of soft drink. The commercial probably does not tell the viewer about the product's price or quality. Instead, it might show a group of happy people at a party on a beach on a beautiful sunny day. In their hands are cans of the soft drink. The goal of the commercial is to convey a subconscious (if not subtle) message: 'You too can have many friends and be happy, if only you drink our product'. Critics of advertising argue that such a commercial creates a desire that otherwise might not exist.

Critics also argue that advertising impedes competition. Advertising often tries to convince consumers that products are more different than they truly are. By increasing the perception of product differentiation and fostering brand loyalty, advertising makes buyers less concerned with price differences among similar goods. With a less elastic demand curve, each firm charges a larger mark-up over marginal cost.

The defence of advertising

Defenders of advertising argue that firms use advertising to provide information to customers. Advertising conveys the prices of the goods being offered for sale, the existence of new products and the locations of retail outlets. This information allows customers to make better choices about what to buy and, thus, enhances the ability of markets to allocate resources efficiently.

Defenders also argue that advertising fosters competition. Because advertising allows customers to be more fully informed about all the firms in the market, customers can more easily take advantage of price differentials. Thus, each firm has less market power. In addition, advertising allows new firms to enter more easily, because it gives entrants a means of attracting customers from existing firms.

CASESTUDY

Advertising and the price of glasses

What effect does advertising have on the price of a good? On the one hand, advertising might make consumers view products as being more different than they otherwise would. If so, it would make markets less competitive and firms' demand curves less elastic, and this would lead firms to charge higher prices. On the other hand, advertising might make it easier for consumers to find the firms offering the best prices. In this case, it would make markets more competitive and firms' demand curves more elastic, and this would lead to lower prices.

In an article published in the *Journal of Law and Economics* in 1972, economist Lee Benham tested these two views of advertising. In the United States during the 1960s, the various state governments had vastly different rules about advertising by optometrists. Some states allowed advertising for glasses and eye examinations. Many states, however, prohibited it. For example, the Florida law read as follows:

It is unlawful for any person, firm, or corporation to ... advertise either directly or indirectly by any

>>

means whatsoever any definite or indefinite price or credit terms on prescriptive or corrective lens, frames, complete prescriptive or corrective glasses, or any optometric service ... This section is passed in the interest of public health, safety, and welfare, and its provisions shall be liberally construed to carry out its objects and purposes.

Professional optometrists enthusiastically endorsed these restrictions on advertising.

Benham used the differences in US state laws as a natural experiment to test the two views of advertising. The results were striking. In those states that prohibited advertising, the average price paid for a pair of glasses was $33. (This was 1963, when prices were much lower than they are today.) In those states that did not restrict advertising, the average price was $26. Thus, advertising reduced average prices by more than 20 per cent. In the market for glasses, and probably in many other markets as well, advertising fosters competition and leads to lower prices for consumers.

fyi

Galbraith versus Hayek

Two great economists of the twentieth century were John Kenneth Galbraith (bottom left) and Friedrich Hayek. They held very different views about advertising, which reflected their views about the capitalist system more broadly.

John Kenneth Galbraith's most famous book was *The Affluent Society*, published in 1958. In it, he argued that corporations use advertising to create demand for products that people otherwise do not want or need. The market system should not be applauded, he believed, for satisfying desires that it has itself created. Galbraith was sceptical that economic growth was leading to higher levels of wellbeing, because people's aspirations were being made to keep pace with their increased material prosperity. He worried that as advertising and salesmanship artificially enhanced the desire for private goods, public spending on such items as better schools and better parks suffered. The result, according to Galbraith, was 'private opulence and public squalor'. Galbraith's policy recommendation was clear: increase the size of government.

Friedrich Hayek's most famous book was *The Road to Serfdom*, published in 1944. It argued that an expansive government inevitably means a sacrifice of personal freedoms. Hayek also wrote a well-known critique of Galbraith in 1961, addressing specifically Galbraith's view of advertising. Hayek observed that advertising was merely one example of a larger phenomenon: Our social environment creates many of our preferences. Literature, art and music are all acquired tastes. A person's demand for hearing a Mozart concerto may have been created in a music appreciation class, but this fact does not make the desire less legitimate or the music professor a sinister influence. Hayek concluded, 'It is because each individual producer thinks that the consumers can be persuaded to like his products that he endeavors to influence them. But though this effort is part of the influences which shape consumers' taste, no producer can in any real sense "determine" them'.

These two economists disagreed about the roles of advertising, markets and government, but they did have one thing in common: great acclaim. In 1974, Hayek won the Nobel Prize in economics. In 2000, Galbraith won the US National Medal of Freedom. And even though their books are now many decades old, they are still well worth reading. The issues that Hayek and Galbraith addressed are timeless and their insights apply as well to our economy as to their own.

Source: Getty Images.

Source: Corbis Australia.

Advertising as a signal of quality

Many types of advertising contain little apparent information about the product being advertised. Consider a firm introducing a new breakfast cereal. A typical advertisement might have some highly paid actor eating the cereal and exclaiming how wonderful it tastes. How much information does the advertisement really provide?

The answer is: more than you might think. Defenders of advertising argue that even advertising that appears to contain little hard information may, in fact, tell consumers something about product quality. The willingness of the firm to spend a large amount of money on advertising can itself be a signal to consumers about the quality of the product being offered.

Consider the problem facing two firms – SuperGrain and Sunshine Wheat Co. Each company has just come up with a recipe for a new cereal, which it would sell for $5 a box. To keep things simple, let's assume that the marginal cost of making cereal is zero, so the $5 is all profit. Each company knows that if it spends $10 million on advertising, it will get one million consumers to try its new cereal. And each company knows that if consumers like the cereal, they will buy it not once but many times.

Consider first SuperGrain's decision. Based on market research, SuperGrain knows that its cereal is only mediocre. Although advertising would sell one packet to each of one million consumers, the consumers would quickly learn that the cereal is not very good and stop buying it. SuperGrain decides it is not worth paying $10 million in advertising to get only $5 million in sales. So it does not bother to advertise. It sends its cooks back to the drawing board to find another recipe.

Sunshine Wheat, on the other hand, knows that its cereal is great. Each person who tries it will buy a box a month for the next year. Thus, the $10 million in advertising will bring in $60 million in sales. Advertising is profitable here because Sunshine Wheat has a good product that consumers will buy repeatedly. Thus, Sunshine Wheat chooses to advertise.

Now that we have considered the behaviour of the two firms, let's consider the behaviour of consumers. We began by asserting that consumers are inclined to try a new cereal that they see advertised. But is this behaviour rational? Should a consumer try a new cereal just because the seller has chosen to advertise it?

In fact, it may be completely rational for consumers to try new products that they see advertised. In our story, consumers decide to try Sunshine Wheat's new cereal because Sunshine Wheat advertises. Sunshine Wheat chooses to advertise because it knows that its cereal is quite good, whereas SuperGrain chooses not to advertise because it knows that its cereal is only mediocre. By its willingness to spend money on advertising, Sunshine Wheat signals to consumers the quality of its cereal. Each consumer thinks, quite sensibly: 'If Sunshine Wheat is willing to spend so much money advertising this new cereal, it must be really good'.

What is most surprising about this theory of advertising is that the content of the advertisement is irrelevant. Sunshine Wheat signals the quality of its product by its willingness to spend money on advertising. What the advertisements say is not as important as the fact that consumers know ads are expensive. In contrast, cheap advertising cannot be effective at signalling quality to consumers. In our example, if an advertising campaign costs less than $5 million, both SuperGrain and Sunshine Wheat would use it to market their new cereals. Because both good and mediocre cereals would be advertised, consumers could not infer the quality of a new cereal from the fact that it is advertised. Over time, consumers would learn to ignore such cheap advertising.

This theory can explain why firms pay famous actors large amounts of money to make advertisements that, on the surface, appear to convey no information at all. The information is not in the advertisement's content, but simply in its existence and expense.

Brand names

Advertising is closely related to the existence of brand names. In many markets, there are two types of firms. Some firms sell products with widely recognised brand names and other firms sell generic substitutes. For example, in a typical pharmacy, you can find Panadol headache tablets on the shelf next to a generic tablet. In a typical grocery store, you can find Pepsi next to less familiar colas. Most often, the firm with the brand name spends more on advertising and charges a higher price for its product.

Just as there is disagreement about the economics of advertising, there is disagreement about the economics of brand names. Let's consider both sides of the debate.

Critics of brand names argue that brand names cause consumers to perceive differences that do not really exist. In many cases, the generic good is almost indistinguishable from the brand-name good. Consumers' willingness to pay more for the brand-name good, these critics assert, is a form of irrationality fostered by advertising. Economist Edward Chamberlin, one of the early developers of the theory of monopolistic competition, concluded from this argument that brand names were bad for the economy. He proposed that governments discourage their use by refusing to enforce the exclusive trademarks that companies use to identify their products.

More recently, economists have defended brand names as a useful way for consumers to ensure that the goods they buy are of high quality. There are two related arguments. First, brand names provide consumers with information about quality when quality cannot be easily judged in advance of purchase. Second, brand names give firms an incentive to maintain high quality, since firms have a financial stake in maintaining the reputation of their brand names.

To see how these arguments work in practice, consider a famous brand name, McDonald's hamburgers. Imagine that you are driving through an unfamiliar town and want to stop for lunch. You see a McDonald's and a local restaurant next to it. Which do you choose? The local restaurant may in fact offer better food at lower prices, but you have no way of knowing that. In contrast, McDonald's offers a consistent product across many cities. Its brand name is useful to you as a way of judging the quality of what you are about to buy.

The McDonald's brand name also ensures that the company has an incentive to maintain quality. For example, if some customers were to become ill from bad food sold at a McDonald's, the news would be disastrous for the company. McDonald's would lose much of the valuable reputation that it has built up with years of expensive advertising. As a result, it would lose sales and profit not just in the outlet that sold the bad food but in its many outlets throughout the country. In contrast, if some customers were to become ill from bad food at a local restaurant, that restaurant might have to close down, but the lost profits would be much smaller. Hence, McDonald's has a greater incentive to ensure that its food is safe.

The debate over brand names thus centres on the question of whether consumers are rational in preferring brand names over generic substitutes. Critics of brand names argue that brand names are the result of an irrational consumer response to advertising. Defenders of brand names argue that consumers have good reason to pay more for brand-name products because they can be more confident in the quality of these products.

How might advertising make markets less competitive? How might it make markets more competitive? Give the arguments for and against brand names.

Conclusion

Monopolistic competition is true to its name; it is a hybrid of monopoly and competition. Like a monopoly, each monopolistic competitor faces a downward-sloping demand curve and, as a result, charges a price above marginal cost. As in a competitive market, however, there are many firms, and entry and exit drive the profit of each monopolistic competitor towards zero. Table 18.1 summarises these lessons.

Because monopolistically competitive firms produce differentiated products, each firm advertises in order to attract customers to its own brand. To some extent, advertising manipulates consumers' tastes,

Table 18.1 Monopolistic competition: Between perfect competition and monopoly

	Market structure		
	Perfect competition	Monopolistic competition	Monopoly
Features that all three market structures share			
Goal of firms	Maximise profits	Maximise profits	Maximise profits
Rule for maximising	$MR = MC$	$MR = MC$	$MR = MC$
Can earn economic profits in the short run?	Yes	Yes	Yes
Features that monopoly and monopolistic competition share			
Price take?	Yes	No	No
Price	$P = MC$	$P > MC$	$P > MC$
Produces welfare-maximising level of output?	Yes	No	No
Features that perfect competition and monopolistic competition share			
Number of firms	Many	Many	One
Entry in long run?	Yes	Yes	No
Can earn economic profits in long run?	No	No	Yes

promotes irrational brand loyalty and impedes competition. To a larger extent, advertising provides information, establishes brand names of reliable quality and fosters competition.

The theory of monopolistic competition seems to describe many markets in the economy. It is somewhat disappointing, therefore, that the theory does not yield simple and compelling advice for public policy. From the standpoint of the economic theorist, the allocation of resources in monopolistically competitive markets is not perfect. Yet, from the standpoint of a practical policymaker, there may be little that can be done to improve it.

Summary

- A monopolistically competitive market is characterised by three attributes: many firms, differentiated products and free entry.
- The equilibrium in a monopolistically competitive market differs from that in a perfectly competitive market in two related ways. First, each firm has higher average costs; that is, it operates on the downward-sloping portion of the average-total-cost curve. Second, each firm charges a price above marginal cost.
- Monopolistic competition does not have all the desirable properties of perfect competition. There is the standard deadweight loss of monopoly caused by the mark-up of price over marginal cost. In addition, the number of firms (and thus the variety of products) can be too large or too small. In practice, the ability of policymakers to correct these inefficiencies is limited.
- The product differentiation inherent in monopolistic competition leads to the use of advertising and brand names. Critics of advertising and brand names argue that firms use them to take advantage of consumer irrationality and to reduce competition. Defenders of advertising and brand names argue that firms use them to inform consumers and to compete more vigorously on price and product quality.

Key concept

monopolistic competition

Questions for review

1 Describe the three attributes of monopolistic competition. How is monopolistic competition like monopoly? How is it like perfect competition?
2 Draw a diagram of the long-run equilibrium in a monopolistically competitive market. How is price related to average total cost? How is price related to marginal cost?
3 Does a monopolistic competitor produce too much or too little output compared with the most efficient level? What practical considerations make it difficult for policymakers to solve this problem?
4 How might advertising reduce economic wellbeing? How might advertising increase economic wellbeing?
5 How might advertising with no apparent informational content in fact convey information to consumers?
6 Explain two benefits that might arise from the existence of brand names.

Problems and applications

1 Classify the following markets as perfectly competitive, monopolistic or monopolistically competitive, and explain your answer:
   a wooden HB pencils
   b bottled mineral water
   c copper
   d local telephone calls

    e   peanut butter

    f   lipstick.

2 What feature of the product being sold distinguishes a monopolistically competitive firm from a monopolistic firm?

3 The chapter states that monopolistically competitive firms could increase the quantity they produce and lower the average total cost of production. Why don't they do so?

4 Sparkle is one firm of many in the market for toothpaste, which is in long-run equilibrium.

    a   Draw a diagram showing Sparkle's demand curve, marginal-revenue curve, average-total-cost curve and marginal-cost curve. Label Sparkle's profit-maximising output and price.

    b   What is Sparkle's profit? Explain.

    c   On your diagram, show the consumer surplus derived from the purchase of Sparkle toothpaste. Also show the deadweight loss relative to the efficient level of output.

    d   If the government forced Sparkle to produce the efficient level of output, what would happen to the firm? What would happen to Sparkle's customers?

5 Do monopolistically competitive markets typically have the socially desirable number of products? Explain.

6 If you were thinking of entering the ice-cream business, would you try to make ice-cream that is just like one of the existing brands? Explain your decision using the ideas of this chapter.

7 Describe three commercials that you have seen on television. In what ways, if any, were each of these commercials socially useful? In what ways were they socially wasteful? Did the commercials affect the likelihood of your buying the product? Why?

8 For each of the following pairs of firms, explain which firm would be more likely to engage in advertising:

    a   a family-owned farm or a family-owned restaurant

    b   a manufacturer of forklifts or a manufacturer of cars

    c   a company that invented a very reliable watch or a company that invented a less-reliable watch that costs the same amount to make.

9 The makers of Aspro pain reliever do a lot of advertising and have very loyal customers. In contrast, the makers of generic aspirin do no advertising and their customers shop only for the lowest price. Assume that the marginal costs of Aspro and generic aspirin are the same and constant.

    a   Draw a diagram showing Aspro's demand, marginal-revenue and marginal-cost curves. Label Aspro's price and mark-up over marginal cost.

    b   Repeat part (a) for a producer of generic aspirin. How do the diagrams differ? Which company has the bigger mark-up? Explain.

    c   Which company has the bigger incentive for careful quality control? Why?

10 In 2010, newspapers reported that Lavazza coffee paid the actress Julia Roberts around $1.5 million for an Italian advertisement where she drank a cup of coffee, smiled, but said nothing. This was a payment of around $33 000 per second. Why would Lavazza pay Ms Roberts such a high amount for an advertisement? Can such a payment be consistent with rational consumer behaviour? Do you think that this payment is justified?

Search me!

  Search me!

When accessing information about economics use the following keywords in any combinations you require:

- monopolistic competition

CourseMate

For more multimedia resources and activities on economics, visit the Economics CourseMate website.

PART SIX
The economics of labour markets

19

The markets for the factors of production

Learning objectives

In this chapter you will:

- analyse the labour demand of competitive, profit-maximising firms
- consider the household decisions that lie behind labour supply
- learn why equilibrium wages equal the value of the marginal product of labour
- consider how the other factors of production – land and capital – are compensated
- examine how a change in the supply of one factor alters the earnings of all the factors.

When you finish university, your income will be determined largely by what kind of job you take. If you become a computer programmer, you will earn more than if you become a petrol station attendant. This fact is not surprising, but it is not obvious why it is true. No law requires that computer programmers be paid more than petrol station attendants. No ethical principle says that programmers are more deserving. What, then, determines which job will pay you the higher wage?

Your income, of course, is a small piece of a larger economic picture. In 2009–10, the total income of all Australian residents was about $1284 billion. People earned this income in various ways. Workers earned over half of it in the form of wages and fringe benefits. The rest went to landowners and to the owners of capital – the economy's stock of equipment and structures – in the form of rent, profit and interest. What determines how much goes to workers? To landowners? To the owners of capital? Why do some workers earn higher wages than others, some landowners higher rental income than others and some capital owners greater profit than others? Why, in particular, do computer programmers earn more than petrol station attendants?

The answers to these questions, like most in economics, hinge on supply and demand. The supply of and demand for labour, land and capital determine the prices paid to workers, landowners and capital owners. To understand why some people have higher incomes than others, therefore, we need to look more deeply at the markets for the services they provide. That is our job in this and the next two chapters.

This chapter provides the basic theory for the analysis of factor markets. As you may recall from chapter 2, the **factors of production** are the inputs used to produce goods and services. Labour, land and capital are the three most important factors of production. When a computer firm produces a new software program, it uses programmers' time (labour), the physical space on which its offices sit (land) and an office building and computer equipment (capital). Similarly, when a petrol station sells petrol, it uses attendants' time (labour), the physical space (land) and the petrol tanks and pumps (capital).

In many ways factor markets resemble the goods markets we have analysed in previous chapters, but they are different in one important way – the demand for a factor of production is a *derived demand*. That is, a firm's demand for a factor of production is derived from its decision to supply a good in another market. The demand for computer programmers is inextricably tied to the supply of computer software, and the demand for petrol station attendants is inextricably tied to the supply of petrol.

In this chapter we analyse factor demand by considering how a competitive, profit-maximising firm decides how much of any factor to buy. We begin our analysis by examining the demand for labour. Labour is the most important factor of production, because workers receive most of the total income earned in the economy. Later in the chapter, we see will see that our analysis of the labour market also applies to the markets for the other factors of production.

The basic theory of factor markets developed in this chapter takes a large step towards explaining how the income of the economy is distributed among workers, landowners and owners of capital. Chapter 20 builds on this analysis to examine in more detail why some workers earn more than others. Chapter 21 examines how much income inequality results from the functioning of factor markets and considers what role the government should and does play in altering the distribution of income.

factors of production
the inputs used to produce goods and services

▸ factors of production

The demand for labour

Labour markets, like other markets in the economy, are governed by the forces of supply and demand. This is illustrated in Figure 19.1. In panel (a) the supply of and demand for apples determine the price of apples. In panel (b) the supply of and demand for apple pickers determine the price, or wage, of apple pickers.

As we have already noted, however, labour markets are different from most other markets because labour demand is a derived demand. Most labour services, rather than being final goods ready to be enjoyed by consumers, are inputs into the production of other goods. To understand labour demand, we need to focus on the firms that hire the labour and use it to produce goods for sale. By examining the link between the production of goods and the demand for labour, we gain insight into the determination of equilibrium wages.

The competitive profit-maximising firm

Let's look at how a typical firm, such as an apple producer, decides the quantity of labour to demand. The firm owns an apple orchard and each week must decide how many apple pickers to hire to harvest its crop. After the firm makes its hiring decision, the workers pick as many apples as they can. The firm then sells the apples, pays the workers and keeps what is left as profit.

We make two assumptions about our firm. First, we assume that our firm is *competitive* both in the market for apples (where the firm is a seller) and in the market for apple pickers (where the firm is a buyer). Recall from chapter 14 that a competitive firm is a price taker. Because there are many other firms selling apples and hiring apple pickers, a single firm has little influence over the price it gets for apples or the wage it pays apple pickers. The firm takes the price and the wage as given by market

| Figure 19.1 | The versatility of supply and demand |

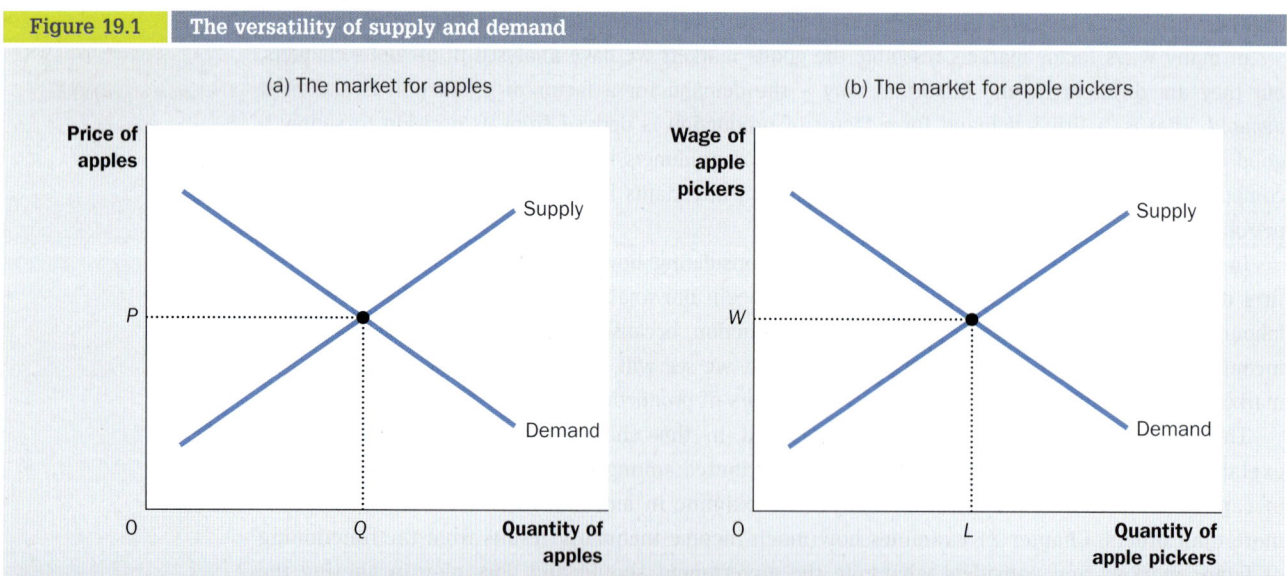

The basic tools of supply and demand apply to goods and to labour services. Panel (a) shows how the supply of and demand for apples determine the price of apples. Panel (b) shows how the supply of and demand for apple pickers determine the wage of apple pickers.

conditions. It only has to decide how many workers to hire and how many apples to sell. (In the appendix, we will consider what happens in the case of monopoly and imperfect competition.)

Second, we assume that the firm is *profit maximising*. Thus, the firm does not directly care about the number of workers it has or the number of apples it produces. It cares only about profit, which equals the total revenue from the sale of apples minus the total cost of producing them. The firm's supply of apples and its demand for workers are derived from its primary goal of maximising profit.

The production function and the marginal product of labour

To make its hiring decision, the firm must consider how the size of its workforce affects the amount of output produced. In other words, it must consider how the number of apple pickers affects the quantity of apples it can harvest and sell. Table 19.1 gives a numerical example. In the first column is the number of workers. In the second column is the quantity of apples the workers harvest each week.

These two columns of numbers describe the firm's ability to produce. As we noted in chapter 13, economists use the term *production function* to describe the relationship between the quantity of the inputs used in production and the quantity of output from production. Here the 'input' is the apple pickers and the 'output' is the apples. The other inputs – the trees themselves, the land, the firm's trucks and tractors, and so on – are held fixed for now. This firm's production function shows that if the firm hires one worker, that worker will pick 100 boxes of apples per week. If the firm hires two workers, the two workers together will pick 180 boxes per week and so on.

Figure 19.2 graphs the data on labour and output presented in Table 19.1. The number of workers is on the horizontal axis and the amount of output is on the vertical axis. This figure illustrates the production function.

One of the *Ten Lessons from Economics* introduced in chapter 1 is that rational people think at the margin. This idea is the key to understanding how firms decide what quantity of labour to hire. To take a step towards this decision, the third column in Table 19.1 gives the **marginal product of labour**, the increase in the amount of output from an additional unit of labour. When the firm increases the number of workers from one to two, for example, the amount of apples produced rises from 100 to 180 boxes. Therefore, the marginal product of the second worker is 80 boxes.

Notice that as the number of workers increases, the marginal product of labour declines. That is, the production process exhibits *diminishing marginal product*. At first, when only a few workers are hired, they can pick the low-hanging fruit. As the number of workers increases, additional workers have to climb higher up the ladders to find apples to pick. Hence, as more and more workers are hired, each additional worker contributes less to the production of apples. For this reason, the production function in Figure 19.2 becomes flatter as the number of workers rises.

The value of the marginal product and the demand for labour

Our profit-maximising firm is concerned more with money than with apples. As a result, when deciding how many workers to hire, the firm considers how much profit each worker would bring in. Because profit is total revenue minus total cost, the profit from an additional worker is the worker's contribution to revenue minus the worker's wage.

To find the worker's contribution to revenue, we must convert the marginal product of labour (which is measured in boxes of apples) into the value of the marginal product (which is measured in dollars). We do this using the price of apples. To continue our example, if a box of apples sells for $10 and if an additional worker produces 80 boxes of apples, then the worker produces $800 of revenue.

marginal product of labour
the increase in the amount of output from an additional unit of labour

Figure 19.2   The production function

The production function is the relationship between the inputs into production (apple pickers) and the output from production (apples). As the quantity of the input increases, the production function gets flatter, reflecting the property of diminishing marginal product.

Table 19.1 How the competitive firm decides how much labour to hire

Labour (number of workers)	Output (boxes per week)	Marginal product of labour	Value of the marginal product of labour	Wage	Marginal profit
(L)	(Q)	(MPL = ΔQ/ΔL)	(VMPL = P × MPL)	(W)	(ΔProfit = VMPL − W)
0	0	—	—	—	—
1	100	100	$1000	$500	$500
2	180	80	800	500	300
3	240	60	600	500	100
4	280	40	400	500	−100
5	300	20	200	500	−300

value of the marginal product
the marginal product of an input times the price of the output

The **value of the marginal product** of any input is the marginal product of that input multiplied by the market price of the output. The fourth column in Table 19.1 shows the value of the marginal product of labour in our example, assuming the price of apples is $10 per box. Because the market price is constant for a competitive firm, the value of the marginal product (like the marginal product itself) diminishes as the number of workers rises. Economists sometimes call this column of numbers the firm's *marginal revenue product*. It is the extra revenue the firm gets from hiring an additional unit of a factor of production.

Now consider how many workers the firm will hire. Suppose that the market wage for apple pickers is $500 per week. In this case, the first worker that the firm hires is profitable; the first worker yields $1000 in revenue or $500 in profit. Similarly, the second worker yields $800 in additional revenue or $300 in profit. The third worker produces $600 in additional revenue or $100 in profit. After the third worker, however, hiring workers is unprofitable. The fourth worker would yield only $400 of additional revenue. Because the worker's wage is $500, hiring the fourth worker would mean a $100 reduction in profit. Thus, the firm hires only three workers.

It is instructive to consider the firm's decision graphically. Figure 19.3 graphs the value of the marginal product. This curve slopes downwards because the marginal product of labour diminishes as the number of workers rises. The figure also includes a horizontal line at the market wage. To maximise profit, the firm hires workers up to the point where these two curves cross. Below this level of employment, the value of the marginal product exceeds the wage, so hiring another worker would increase profit. Above this level of employment, the value of the marginal product is less than the wage, so the marginal worker is unprofitable. Thus, *a competitive, profit-maximising firm hires workers up to the point where the value of the marginal product of labour equals the wage.*

Having explained the profit-maximising hiring strategy for a competitive firm, we can now offer a theory of labour demand. Recall that a firm's labour demand curve tells us the quantity of labour that a firm demands at any given wage. We have just seen in Figure 19.3 that the firm makes that decision

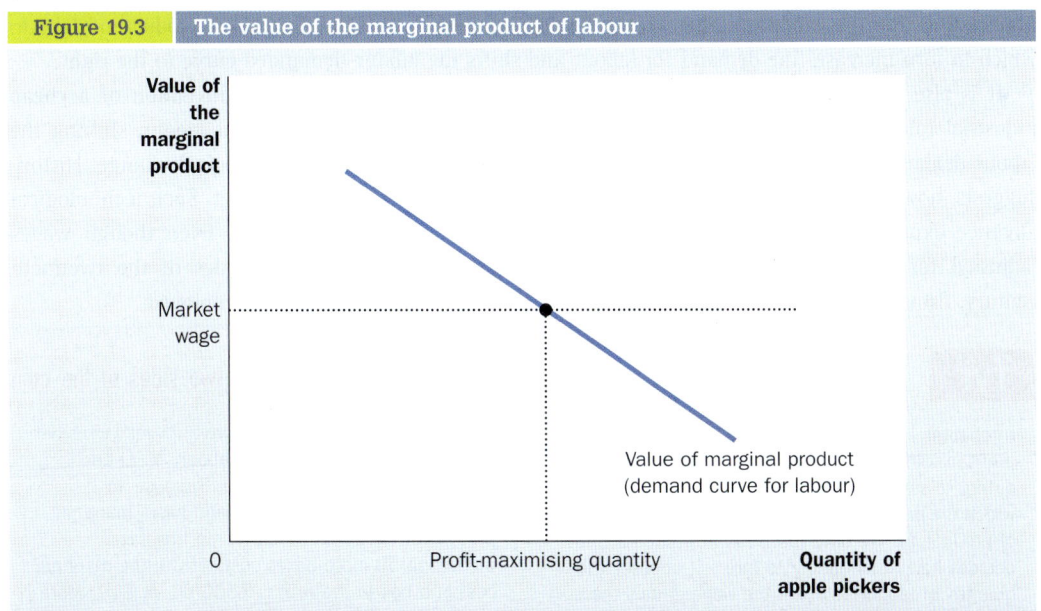

Figure 19.3   The value of the marginal product of labour

This shows how the value of the marginal product (the marginal product times the price of the output) depends on the number of workers. The curve slopes downwards because of diminishing marginal product. For a competitive, profit-maximising firm, this value-of-marginal-product curve is also the firm's labour demand curve.

by choosing the quantity of labour at which the value of the marginal product equals the wage. As a result, *the value-of-marginal-product curve is the labour demand curve for a competitive, profit-maximising firm.*

What causes the labour demand curve to shift?

We now understand the labour demand curve: It reflects the value of marginal product of labour. With this insight in mind, let's consider a few of the things that might cause the labour demand curve to shift.

The output price

The value of the marginal product is marginal product times the price of the firm's output. Thus, when the output price changes, the value of the marginal product changes and the labour demand curve shifts. An increase in the price of apples, for instance, raises the value of the marginal product of each worker that picks apples and, therefore, increases labour demand from the firms that supply apples. Conversely, a decrease in the price of apples reduces the value of the marginal product and decreases labour demand.

Technological change

Between 2001–02 and 2009–10, the amount of output a typical Australian worker produced in an hour increased by about one-third. Why? The most important reason is technological progress: Scientists and engineers are constantly figuring out new and better ways of doing things. This has profound implications for the labour market. Technological advance raises the marginal product of labour, which in turn increases the demand for labour and shifts the labour-demanded curve to the right.

It is also possible for technological change to reduce labour demand. The invention of a cheap industrial robot, for instance, could conceivably reduce the marginal product of labour, shifting the labour-demanded curve to the left. Economists call this labour-saving technological change. History suggests, however, that most technological progress is instead labour-augmenting. Such technological advance explains persistently rising employment in the face of rising wages. Even though wages (adjusted for inflation) increased by 131 per cent during the last four decades of the twentieth century, firms nonetheless increased by 80 per cent the amount of labour they employed.

---

fyi

Input demand and output supply – two sides of the coin

In chapter 14 we discussed how a competitive, profit-maximising firm decides how much of its output to sell – it chooses the quantity of output at which the price of the good equals the marginal cost of production. We have just seen how such a firm decides how much labour to hire – it chooses the quantity of labour at which the wage equals the value of the marginal product. Because the production function links the quantity of inputs to the quantity of output, you should not be surprised to learn that the firm's decision about input demand is closely linked to its decision about output supply. In fact, these two decisions are two sides of the same coin.

To see this relationship more fully, let's consider how the marginal product of labour (MPL) and marginal cost (MC) are related. Suppose an additional worker costs $500 and has a marginal product of 50 boxes of apples. In this case, producing 50 more boxes costs $500; the marginal cost of a box to the firm is $500/50, or $10. More generally, if W is the wage and an extra unit of labour produces MPL units of output, then the marginal cost of a unit of output is $MC = W/MPL$.

This analysis shows that diminishing marginal product is closely related to increasing marginal cost. When our apple orchard grows crowded with workers, each additional worker adds less to the production of apples (*MPL* falls). Similarly, when the apple firm is producing a large quantity of apples, the orchard is already crowded with workers, so it is more costly to produce an additional box of apples (*MC* rises).

Now consider our criterion for profit maximisation. We determined earlier that a profit-maximising firm chooses the quantity of labour so that the value of the marginal product ($P \times MPL$) equals the wage (*W*). We can write this mathematically as:

$$P \times MPL = W$$

If we divide both sides of this equation by *MPL*, we obtain:

$$P = W/MPL$$

We just noted that W/MPL equals marginal cost *MC*. Therefore, we can substitute to obtain:

$$P = MC$$

This equation states that the price of the firm's output is equal to the marginal cost of producing a unit of output. Thus, when a competitive firm hires labour up to the point at which the value of the marginal product equals the wage, it also produces up to the point at which the price equals marginal cost. Our analysis of labour demand in this chapter is just another way of looking at the production decision we first saw in chapter 14.

The supply of other factors

The quantity available of one factor of production can affect the marginal product of other factors. A fall in the supply of ladders, for instance, will reduce the marginal product of apple pickers and thus the demand for apple pickers. We consider this linkage among the factors of production more fully later in the chapter.

---

fyi   **The Luddite revolt**

Over the long span of history, technological progress has been the worker's friend. It has increased productivity, labour demand and wages. Yet there is no doubt that workers sometimes see technological progress as a threat to their standard of living.

The Luddites

Source: Photolibrary.

One famous example occurred in England in the early nineteenth century, when skilled knitters saw their jobs threatened by the invention and spread of machines that could produce textiles using less skilled workers and at much lower cost. The displaced workers organised violent revolts against the new technology. They smashed the weaving machines used in the wool and cotton mills and, in some cases, set the homes of the mill owners on fire. Because the workers claimed to be led by General Ned Ludd (who may have been a legendary figure rather than a real person), they were called Luddites.

The Luddites wanted the British government to save their jobs by restricting the spread of the new technology. Instead, the Parliament took action to stop the Luddites. Thousands of troops were sent to suppress the Luddite riots. The Parliament eventually made destroying machines a capital crime. After a trial in York in 1813, 17 men were hanged for the offence. Many others were convicted and sent to Australia, as prisoners.

Today, the term *Luddite* refers to anyone who opposes technological progress.

Define marginal product of labour and value of the marginal product of labour. Describe how a competitive, profit-maximising firm decides how many workers to hire.

The supply of labour

Having analysed labour demand in detail, let's turn to the other side of the market and consider labour supply. A formal model of labour supply is included in chapter 22, where we develop the theory of household decision making. Here we discuss briefly and informally the decisions that lie behind the labour supply curve.

The trade-off between work and leisure

One of the *Ten Lessons from Economics* in chapter 1 is that people face trade-offs. Probably no trade-off is more obvious or more important in a person's life than the trade-off between work and leisure. The more hours you spend working, the fewer hours you have to watch television, enjoy dinner with friends or pursue your favourite hobby. The trade-off between labour and leisure lies behind the labour supply curve.

Another one of the *Ten Lessons from Economics* is that the cost of something is what you give up to get it. What do you give up to get an hour of leisure? You give up an hour of work, which in turn means an hour of wages. Thus, if your wage is $15 per hour, the opportunity cost of an hour of leisure is $15. And when you get a raise to $20 per hour, the opportunity cost of enjoying leisure goes up.

The labour supply curve reflects how workers' decisions about the labour–leisure trade-off respond to a change in that opportunity cost. An upward-sloping labour supply curve means that an increase in the wage induces workers to increase the quantity of labour they supply. Because time is limited, more hours of work means that workers are enjoying less leisure. That is, workers respond to the increase in the opportunity cost of leisure by taking less of it.

It is worth noting that the labour supply curve need not be upward sloping. Imagine you got that raise from $15 to $20 per hour. The opportunity cost of leisure is now greater, but you are also richer than you were before. You might decide that with your extra wealth you can now afford to enjoy more leisure; in this case, your labour supply curve would slope backwards. In chapter 22, we discuss this possibility in terms of conflicting effects on your labour supply decision (called income and substitution effects). For now, we ignore the possibility of backward-sloping labour supply and assume that the labour supply is upward sloping.

What causes the labour supply curve to shift?

The labour supply curve shifts whenever people change the amount they want to work at a given wage. Let's now consider some of the events that might cause such a shift.

Changes in tastes

In 1954, 29 per cent of women aged 15 to 64 were employed at paid jobs or looking for work. In 2009, the number had risen to 59 per cent. There are, of course, many explanations for this development, but one of them is changing tastes, or attitudes towards work. A generation or two ago, it was the norm for women to stay at home while raising children. Today, family sizes are smaller and more mothers choose to work. The result is an increase in the supply of labour.

Changes in alternative opportunities

The supply of labour in any one labour market depends on the opportunities available in other labour markets. If the wage earned by pear pickers suddenly rises, some apple pickers may choose to switch occupations. The supply of labour in the market for apple pickers falls.

Immigration

Movement of workers from region to region, or country to country, is an obvious and often important source of shifts in labour supply. When immigrants come to Australia, for instance, the supply of labour in Australia increases and the supply of labour in immigrants' home countries contracts. In fact, much of the policy debate about immigration centres on its effect on labour supply and, thereby, on equilibrium in the labour market.

IN THE NEWS . . .

THE ECONOMY NEEDS YOU

This article shows that in times of low unemployment, immigrants play a critical role in keeping the economy going.

You can come in now

Sydney: The Japanese-owned abattoir at Oakey, in south-east Queensland, seems to have everything going for it. There is no shortage of cattle to feed a booming market that has made Australia the world's biggest beef exporter by value. Yet it has been unable to find enough skilled workers to process the beasts. By June, it expects to import workers from Brazil, Australia's main competitor.

After 14 years of boom, the story of scarce skills is being repeated all over Australia. Under pressure from business leaders, John Howard's conservative coalition government has decided to look beyond Australia to curb the crisis. On April 14th Amanda Vanstone, the immigration minister, said that Australia would take in 140 000 immigrants in 2005–06, 20 000 more than last year and the biggest number for 35 years. Rules on ages and English proficiency will be relaxed. Backpackers who spend at least three months picking fruit or working on farms will qualify automatically for a second year's visa.

From a government that cut immigration sharply in its earlier years, and has since been noted for its tough approach to asylum-seekers, the latest increase suggests how much the economy needs immigration. To a list of 38 skills the country says it is short of, including those of doctors, chefs and hairdressers, Ms Vanstone added 18, including the trades of bricklayers, plumbers, electricians and carpenters.

Official figures show that almost 150 000 jobs cannot be filled for lack of the right skills. A recent survey by the Australian Chamber of Commerce and Industry found that almost 80 per cent of employers were worried about finding people with the needed skills. More than half the firms surveyed last year by two of the country's biggest banks said that a shortage of suitable recruits was hampering their growth.

With unemployment hovering just above 5 per cent, these trends have worried the central bank because of inflationary pressures stoked by higher wage demands. But not everyone is welcoming the new recruits. The opposition Labor Party, and the trade unions, say boosting immigration is no substitute for spending more on equipping Australians themselves with the skills they need to find work more readily.

Source: *The Economist*, 28 April 2008.
© The Economist Newspaper Limited, London 2008.

Who has a greater opportunity cost of enjoying leisure – a cleaner or a brain surgeon? Explain. Can this help explain why doctors work such long hours?

Equilibrium in the labour market

So far we have established two facts about how wages are determined in competitive labour markets:

- the wage adjusts to balance the supply and demand for labour
- the wage equals the value of the marginal product of labour.

At first, it might seem surprising that the wage can do both these things at once. In fact, there is no real puzzle here, but understanding why there is no puzzle is an important step to understanding wage determination.

Figure 19.4 shows the labour market in equilibrium. The wage and the quantity of labour have adjusted to balance supply and demand. When the market is in this equilibrium, each firm has bought as much labour as it finds profitable at the equilibrium wage. That is, each firm has followed the rule for profit maximisation – it has hired workers until the value of the marginal product equals the wage. Hence, the wage must equal the value of the marginal product of labour once it has brought supply and demand into equilibrium.

This brings us to an important lesson: *any event that changes the supply of labour or demand for labour must change the equilibrium wage and the value of the marginal product by the same amount, because these must always be equal.* To see how this works, let's consider some events that shift these curves.

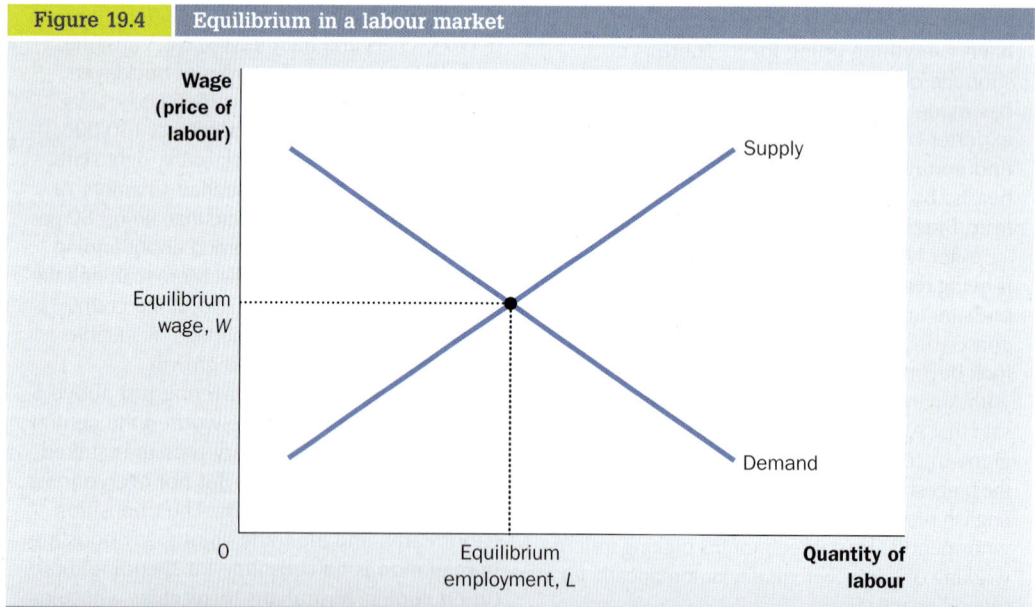

Figure 19.4 | **Equilibrium in a labour market**

Like all prices, the price of labour (the wage) depends on supply and demand. Because the demand curve reflects the value of the marginal product of labour, in equilibrium workers receive the value of their marginal contribution to the production of goods and services.

Shifts in labour supply

Suppose that immigration increases the number of workers willing to pick apples. As Figure 19.5 shows, the supply of labour shifts to the right from S_1 to S_2. At the initial wage W_1, the quantity of labour supplied now exceeds the quantity demanded. This surplus of labour puts downward pressure on the wage of apple pickers and the fall in the wage in turn makes it profitable for firms to hire more workers. As the number of workers employed in each apple orchard rises, the marginal product of a worker falls and so does the value of the marginal product. In the new equilibrium, both the wage and the value of the marginal product of labour are lower than they were before the influx of new workers.

An episode from Israel illustrates how a shift in labour supply can alter the equilibrium in a labour market. During most of the 1980s, many thousands of Palestinians regularly commuted from their homes in the Israeli-occupied West Bank and Gaza Strip to jobs in Israel, primarily in the construction and agriculture industries. In 1988, however, political unrest in these occupied areas induced the Israeli government to take steps that, as a by-product, reduced this supply of workers. Curfews were imposed, work permits were checked more thoroughly and a ban on overnight stays of Palestinians in Israel was enforced more rigorously. The economic impact of these steps was exactly as theory predicts – the number of Palestinians with jobs in Israel fell by half and those who continued to work in Israel enjoyed wage increases of about 50 per cent. With a reduced number of Palestinian workers in Israel, the value of the marginal product of the remaining workers was much higher.

Figure 19.5	A shift in labour supply

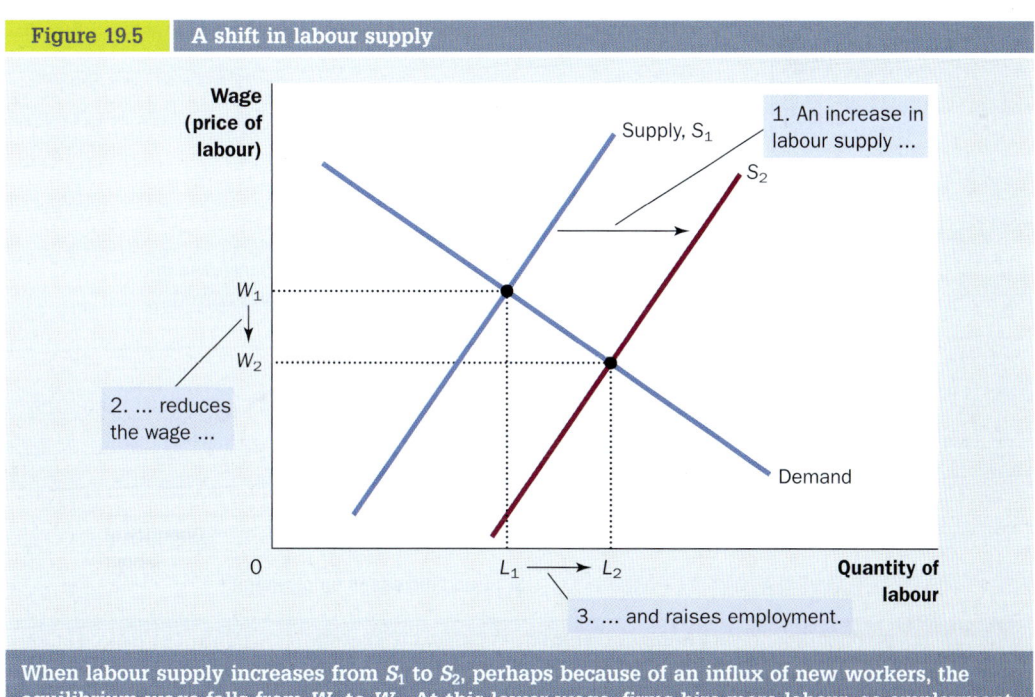

When labour supply increases from S_1 to S_2, perhaps because of an influx of new workers, the equilibrium wage falls from W_1 to W_2. At this lower wage, firms hire more labour, so employment rises from L_1 to L_2. The change in the wage reflects a change in the value of the marginal product of labour; with more workers, the added output from an extra worker is smaller.

Shifts in labour demand

Now suppose that an increase in the popularity of apples causes their price to rise. This price increase does not change the marginal product of labour for any given number of workers, but it does raise the value of the marginal product. With a higher price for apples, hiring more apple pickers is now profitable. As Figure 19.6 shows, when the demand for labour shifts to the right from D_1 to D_2, the equilibrium wage rises from W_1 to W_2, and equilibrium employment rises from L_1 to L_2. Once again, the wage and the value of the marginal product of labour move together.

This analysis shows that prosperity for firms in an industry is often linked to prosperity for workers in that industry. When the price of apples rises, apple producers make greater profit and apple pickers earn higher wages. When the price of apples falls, apple producers earn smaller profit and apple pickers earn lower wages. This lesson is well known to workers in industries with highly volatile prices. Workers in oilfields, for instance, know from experience that their earnings are closely linked to the world price of crude oil.

From these examples, you should now have a good understanding of how wages are set in competitive labour markets. Labour supply and labour demand together determine the equilibrium wage and shifts in the supply or demand curve for labour cause the equilibrium wage to change. At the same time, profit maximisation by the firms that demand labour ensures that the equilibrium wage always equals the value of the marginal product of labour.

| Figure 19.6 | A shift in labour demand |

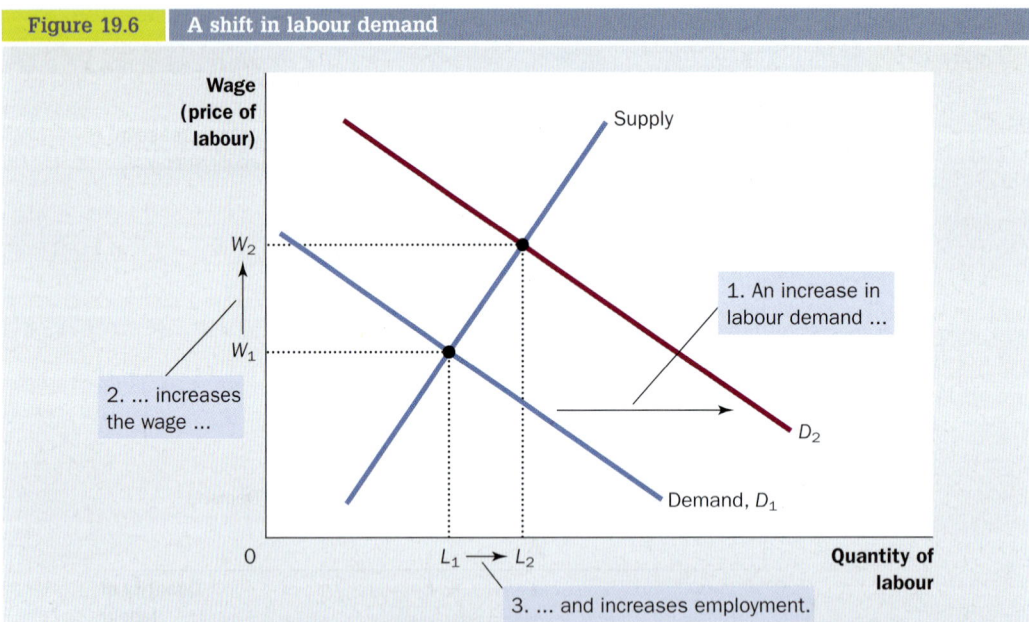

When labour demand increases from D_1 to D_2, perhaps because of an increase in the price of the firms' output, the equilibrium wage rises from W_1 to W_2, and employment rises from L_1 to L_2. Again, the change in the wage reflects a change in the value of the marginal product of labour; with a higher output price, the added output from an extra worker is more valuable.

How does an influx of workers affect labour supply, labour demand, the marginal product of labour and the equilibrium wage?

One of the *Ten Lessons from Economics* in chapter 1 is that our standard of living depends on our ability to produce goods and services. We can now see how this principle works in the market for labour. In particular, our analysis of labour demand shows that wages equal productivity as measured by the value of the marginal product of labour. Put simply, highly productive workers are highly paid, and less-productive workers are less highly paid.

This lesson is key to understanding why workers today are better off than workers in previous generations. In Australia, up until the early 1970s, productivity growth was relatively high (3 per cent per annum). However, after this time there was a decline in the rate of growth in productivity (to 1 per cent per annum during the 1980s). Corresponding to this slowdown in productivity was a reduction in the growth rate in wages (adjusted for inflation) from about 3 per cent per annum to less than 0.5 per cent per annum growth during the 1980s. Australia's productivity growth then rose to over 2 per cent per annum in the 1990s before falling back to about 1.5 per cent in the 2000s. Wages followed the same pattern.

The link between productivity and wages also sheds light on international experience. Table 19.2 presents some data on productivity growth and wage growth for a representative group of countries between 1950 and 1990, ranked in order of their productivity growth. Although these international data are far from precise, a close link between the two variables is apparent. In South Korea, Hong Kong and Singapore, productivity has grown rapidly and so have wages. In Mexico and Argentina, productivity has fallen and so have wages. Australia falls in the middle of the distribution. So over the longer term, by international standards, Australian productivity growth and wage growth have been neither exceptionally bad nor exceptionally good.

Table 19.2 Productivity and wage growth around the world		
Country	Growth rate of productivity (%)	Growth rate of wages (%)
South Korea	6.9	7.9
Hong Kong	6.0	4.9
Singapore	4.9	5.0
Japan	3.0	2.0
Indonesia	2.3	4.4
United Kingdom	2.7	2.4
United States	2.3	0.5
Australia	1.6	0.3
New Zealand	0.9	−0.3
Malaysia	0.8	2.4
Brazil	−0.2	−2.4
Argentina	−1.7	−1.3
Mexico	−1.8	−3.0

Source: Robert Summers and Alan Heston, 'The Penn World Tables (Mark 5): an expanded set of international comparisons, 1950–88', *Quarterly Journal of Economics,* vol. 106, no. 2, 1991, pp. 327–68, and *World Development Report 1994,* Table 7, pp. 174–5. Growth in productivity is measured here as the annualised rate of change in gross national product per person from 1980 to 1988. Growth in wages is measured as the annualised change in earnings per employee in manufacturing from 1980 to 1991.

The other factors of production: Land and capital

We have seen how firms decide how much labour to hire and how these decisions determine workers' wages. At the same time that firms are hiring workers, they are also deciding about other inputs to

432

production. For example, our apple-producing firm might have to choose the size of its apple orchard and the number of ladders to make available to its apple pickers. We can think of the firm's factors of production as falling into three categories: labour, land and capital.

The meaning of the terms *labour* and *land* is clear, but the definition of *capital* is somewhat tricky. Economists use the term **capital** to refer to the stock of equipment and structures used for production. That is, the economy's capital represents the accumulation of goods produced in the past that are being used in the present to produce new goods and services. For our apple firm, the capital stock includes the ladders used to climb the trees, the trucks used to transport the apples, the buildings used to store the apples and even the trees themselves.

capital
the equipment and structures used to produce goods and services

▸ capital

Equilibrium in the markets for land and capital

What determines how much the owners of land and capital earn for their contribution to the production process? Before answering this question, we need to distinguish between two prices, the purchase price and the rental price. The *purchase price* of land or capital is the price a person pays to own that factor of production indefinitely. The *rental price* is the price a person pays to use that factor for a limited period of time. It is important to keep this distinction in mind because, as we will see, these prices are determined by somewhat different economic forces.

Having defined these terms, we can now apply the theory of factor demand we developed for the labour market to the markets for land and capital. The wage is, after all, simply the rental price of labour. Therefore, much of what we have learned about wage determination applies also to the rental prices of land and capital. As Figure 19.7 illustrates, the rental price of land, shown in panel (a), and the rental price of capital, shown in panel (b), are determined by supply and demand. Moreover, the demand for land and capital is determined just like the demand for labour. That is, when our

Figure 19.7 | **The markets for land and capital**

Supply and demand determine the compensation paid to the owners of land, as shown in panel (a), and the compensation paid to the owners of capital, as shown in panel (b). The demand for each factor, in turn, depends on the value of the marginal product of that factor.

apple-producing firm is deciding how much land and how many ladders to rent, it follows the same logic as when deciding how many workers to hire. For both land and capital, the firm increases the quantity hired until the value of the factor's marginal product equals the factor's price. Thus, the demand curve for each factor reflects the marginal productivity of that factor.

We can now explain how much income goes to labour, how much goes to landowners and how much goes to the owners of capital. As long as the firms using the factors of production are competitive and profit-maximising, each factor's rental price must equal the value of the marginal product for that factor. *Labour, land and capital each earn the value of their marginal contribution to the production process.*

Now consider the purchase price of land and capital. The rental price and the purchase price are obviously related; buyers are willing to pay more to buy a piece of land or capital if it produces a valuable stream of rental income. And, as we have just seen, the equilibrium rental income at any point in time equals the value of that factor's marginal product. Therefore, the equilibrium purchase price of a piece of land or capital depends on both the current value of the marginal product and the value of the marginal product expected to prevail in the future.

fyi

What is capital income?

Labour income is an easy concept to understand: it is the pay cheque that workers get from their employers. The income earned by capital, however, is less obvious.

In our analysis, we have been implicitly assuming that households own the economy's stock of capital – ladders, drill presses, warehouses, etc. – and rent it to the firms that use it. Capital income, in this case, is the rent that households receive for the use of their capital. This assumption simplified our analysis of how capital owners are compensated, but it is not entirely realistic. In fact, firms usually own the capital they use and, therefore, they receive the profits from this capital.

These earnings from capital, however, eventually get paid to households. Some of it gets paid in the form of interest to those households who have lent money to firms. Bond holders and bank depositors are two examples of recipients of interest. Thus, when you receive interest on your bank account, that income is part of the economy's capital income.

In addition, some of the profits from capital are paid to households in the form of dividends.

Dividends are payments by a firm to the firm's shareholders. A shareholder is a person who has bought a share in the ownership of the firm and, therefore, is entitled to share in the firm's profits.

A firm does not have to pay out all of its earnings to households in the form of interest and dividends. Instead, it can retain some earnings within the firm and use these earnings to buy additional capital. Although these retained earnings do not get paid to the firm's shareholders, the shareholders benefit from them nonetheless. Because retained earnings increase the amount of capital the firm owns, they tend to increase future earnings and, thereby, the value of the firm's shares.

These institutional details are interesting and important, but they do not alter our conclusion about the income earned by the owners of capital. Capital is paid according to the value of its marginal product, regardless of whether this income gets transmitted to households in the form of interest or dividends or whether it is kept within firms as retained earnings.

Linkages among the factors of production

We have seen that the price paid to any factor of production – labour, land or capital – equals the value of the marginal product of that factor. The marginal product of any factor, in turn, depends on the quantity of that factor that is available. Because of diminishing returns, a factor in abundant supply has a low marginal product and thus a low price, and a factor in scarce supply has a high marginal product and a high price. As a result, when the supply of a factor falls, its equilibrium factor price rises.

When the supply of any factor changes, however, the effects are not limited to the market for that factor. In most situations, factors of production are used together in a way that makes the productivity of each factor dependent on the quantities of the other factors available to be used in the production process. As a result, a change in the supply of any one factor alters the earnings of all the factors.

For example, suppose that a storm destroys many of the ladders that workers use to pick apples from the orchards. What happens to the earnings of the various factors of production? Most obviously, the supply of ladders falls and, therefore, the equilibrium rental price of ladders rises. Those owners who were lucky enough to avoid damage to their ladders now earn a higher return when they rent out their ladders to the firms that produce apples.

Yet the effects of this event do not stop at the ladder market. Because there are fewer ladders with which to work, the workers who pick apples have a smaller marginal product. Thus, the reduction in the supply of ladders reduces the demand for apple pickers and this causes the equilibrium wage to fall.

This story shows a general lesson – an event that changes the supply of any factor of production can alter the earnings of all the factors. The change in earnings of any factor can be found by analysing the impact of the event on the value of the marginal product of that factor.

CASE STUDY

The economics of the Black Death

In fourteenth-century Europe, the bubonic plague wiped out about one-third of the population within a few years. This event, called the Black Death, provides a grisly natural experiment to test the theory of factor markets that we have just developed. Consider the effects of the Black Death on those who were lucky enough to survive. What do you think happened to the wages earned by workers and the rents earned by landowners?

To answer this question, let's examine the effects of a reduced population on the marginal product of labour and the marginal product of land. With a smaller supply of workers, the marginal product of labour rises. (This is simply diminishing marginal product working in reverse.) Thus, we would expect the Black Death to raise wages.

Because land and labour are used together in production, a smaller supply of workers also affects the market for land, the other major factor of production in medieval Europe. With fewer workers available to farm the land, an additional unit of land produced less additional output. In other words, the marginal product of land fell. Thus, we would expect the Black Death to lower rents.

The surviving workers were lucky in more ways than one.

Source: © photos.com/Getty Images.

In fact, both predictions are consistent with the historical evidence. Wages approximately doubled during this period and rents declined 50 per cent or more. The Black Death led to economic prosperity for the peasant classes and reduced incomes for the landed classes.

What determines the income of the owners of land and capital? How would an increase in the quantity of capital affect the incomes of those who already own capital? How would it affect the incomes of workers?

Conclusion

This chapter explained how labour, land and capital are compensated for the roles they play in the production process. The theory developed here is called the *neoclassical theory of distribution*. According to the neoclassical theory, the amount paid to each factor of production depends on the supply of and demand for that factor. The demand, in turn, depends on that particular factor's marginal productivity. In equilibrium, each factor of production earns the value of its marginal contribution to the production of goods and services.

The neoclassical theory of distribution is widely accepted. Most economists begin with the neoclassical theory when trying to explain how the Australian economy's $854 billion of income is distributed among the economy's various members. In the following two chapters, we consider the distribution of income in more detail. As you will see, the neoclassical theory provides the framework for this discussion.

Even at this point you can use the theory to answer the question that began this chapter: Why are computer programmers paid more than petrol station attendants? It is because programmers can produce a good of greater market value than can a petrol station attendant. People are willing to pay dearly for a good computer game, but they are willing to pay little to have their petrol pumped and their windscreens washed. The wages of these workers reflect the market prices of the goods they produce. If people suddenly got tired of using computers and decided to spend more time driving, the prices of these goods would change and so would the equilibrium wages of these two groups of workers.

Summary

- The economy's income is distributed in the markets for the factors of production. The three most important factors of production are labour, land and capital.
- The demand for factors is a derived demand that comes from firms that use the factors to produce goods and services. Competitive, profit-maximising firms hire each factor up to the point at which the value of the marginal product of the factor equals its price.
- The supply of labour arises from individuals' trade-off between work and leisure. An upward-sloping labour supply curve means that people respond to an increase in the wage by enjoying less leisure and working more hours.
- The price paid to each factor adjusts to balance the supply and demand for that factor. Because factor demand reflects the value of the marginal product of that factor, in equilibrium each factor is compensated according to its marginal contribution to the production of goods and services.
- Because factors of production are used together, the marginal product of any one factor depends on the quantities of all factors that are available. As a result, a change in the supply of one factor alters the equilibrium earnings of all the factors.

Key concepts

capital
factors of production

marginal product of
labour

value of the marginal
product

Questions for review

1 Explain how a firm's production function is related to its marginal product of labour, how a firm's marginal product of labour is related to the value of its marginal product, and how a firm's value of marginal product is related to its demand for labour.
2 Give two examples of events that could shift the demand for labour.
3 Give two examples of events that could shift the supply of labour.
4 Explain how wages can adjust to balance the supply and demand for labour while simultaneously equalling the value of the marginal product of labour.
5 If the population of Australia suddenly grew because of a large immigration, what would happen to wages? What would happen to the rents earned by the owners of land and capital?

Problems and applications

1 Suppose that the government proposes a new law aimed at reducing health-care costs – all Australians are to be required to eat one apple daily.
    a How would this apple-a-day law affect the demand for and equilibrium price of apples?
    b How would the law affect the marginal product and the value of the marginal product of apple pickers?
    c How would the law affect the demand and equilibrium wage for apple pickers?
2 Henry Ford once said: 'It is not the employer who pays wages – he only handles the money. It is the product that pays wages'. Explain.

3   Show the effect of each of the following events on the market for labour in the computer manufacturing industry.
    a   The federal government buys personal computers for all Australian university students.
    b   More university students study engineering and computer science.
    c   Computer firms build new manufacturing plants.

4   Your uncle opens a sandwich shop that employs seven people. The employees are paid $6 per hour and a sandwich sells for $3. If your uncle is maximising his profit, what is the value of the marginal product of the last worker he hired? What is that worker's marginal product?

5   Imagine a firm that hires two types of workers – some with computer skills and some without. If technology advances, so that computers become more useful to the firm, what happens to the marginal product of the two types? What happens to equilibrium wages? Explain, using appropriate diagrams.

6   During the 1980s Australia experienced a significant inflow of capital from other countries. For example, Japanese car makers Toyota and Mitsubishi invested in new and upgraded factories in Australia.
    a   Using a diagram of the Australian capital market, show the effect of this inflow on the rental price of capital in Australia and on the quantity of capital in use.
    b   Using a diagram of the Australian labour market, show the effect of the capital inflow on the average wage paid to Australian workers.

7   Suppose that labour is the only input used by a perfectly competitive firm that can hire workers for $50 per day. The firm's production function is as follows:

Days of labour	Units of output
0	0
1	7
2	13
3	19
4	25
5	28

    Each unit of output sells for $10. Plot the firm's demand for labour. How many days of labour should the firm hire? Show this point on your graph.

8   (This question requires knowledge of the appendix to this chapter.) Using the production function described in the previous question, suppose that the firm is a monopolist. Its demand schedule is as follows:

Price	Units of output
20	0
15	7
12	13
10	19
9	25
8	28
7	29

Plot the firm's demand for labour. How many days of labour should the firm hire? Show this point on your graph.

9 (This question is challenging.) In recent years, some policymakers have proposed requiring firms to improve safety standards. For example, there are laws requiring additional safety training and equipment to be provided to each worker. Let's consider the effects of such a policy on the labour market.

   a Suppose that a law required firms to give each worker $3 of safety-related training for every hour that the worker is employed by the firm. How does this law affect the marginal profit that a firm earns from each worker? How does the law affect the demand curve for labour? Draw your answer on a graph with the cash wage on the vertical axis.

   b If there is no change in labour supply, how would this law affect employment and wages?

   c Why might the labour supply curve shift in response to this law? Would this shift in labour supply raise or lower the impact of the law on wages and employment?

   d As chapter 6 discussed, the wages of some workers, particularly the unskilled and inexperienced, are kept above the equilibrium level by minimum-wage laws. What effect would such an occupational safety policy have for these workers?

Search me!

When accessing information about economics use the following keywords in any combinations you require:

- capital
- factors of production

CourseMate

CourseMate

For more multimedia resources and activities on economics, visit the Economics CourseMate website.

APPENDIX

The demand for labour under imperfect competition and monopoly

In the chapter, we demonstrated how the demand for labour was determined in a perfectly competitive market. A competitive, profit-maximising firm hires workers up to the point where the value of the marginal product of labour equals the wage. As we will see here, a similar rule applies when market conditions are not perfectly competitive. However, in this case, firms hire workers up to the point where the marginal revenue product of labour equals the wage. This involves reasoning akin to the competitive firm case. The firm evaluates the effect of an additional worker on total revenue when making its labour quantity choice.

To consider this, let us re-examine the case of the water producer in chapter 15. It was the only producer of water in its town – a monopoly. We learnt in chapter 15 that the monopolist faces demand conditions identical to market demand for water in the town. This demand schedule is reproduced in Table 19A.1. Also listed in that table is the firm's total and marginal revenue.

Recall that the critical feature of the monopolist's demand that distinguishes it from demand faced by a perfectly competitive firm is that it is less elastic. Whereas the demand curve for a firm under perfect competition is perfectly elastic and equal to price, under monopoly (and, indeed, oligopoly and monopolistic competition), price falls as the firm produces more output. This is the price effect we discussed in chapter 15. So as output is increased, marginal revenue is not simply equal to price. As depicted in Table 19A.1, as output rises from, say, 1 to 2 litres per day, total revenue rises by $8. Although the firm sells more litres, it receives less per litre.

Table 19A.1 A monopoly's total and marginal revenue

Quantity of water (Q)	Price (P)	Total revenue ($TR = P \times Q$)	Marginal revenue ($MR = \triangle TR / \triangle Q$)
0 litres	$11	$0	—
1	10	10	$10
2	9	18	8
3	8	24	6

Quantity of water (Q)	Price (P)	Total revenue ($TR = P \times Q$)	Marginal revenue ($MR = \triangle TR / \triangle Q$)
4	7	28	4
5	6	30	2
6	5	30	0
7	4	28	−2
8	3	24	−4

By adding more workers, the firm can supply more water to the town. However, each additional worker causes output to rise by a diminished amount – that is, the marginal product of labour declines with output. This is depicted in Table 19A.2. Note that although output is 4 litres per day when there is a single worker, it is 6 litres per day when there are two workers. Thus, the marginal product of the second worker is 2 litres per day.

To calculate whether it should put the second worker on, however, the firm must calculate the effect on firm profits. In particular, what happens to total revenue? As output rises from 4 to 6 litres per day, price falls from $7 to $5 and revenue rises from $28 to $30. So the addition to revenue from employing a second worker is $2. This is the marginal revenue product of labour for two workers. Table 19A.2 makes this calculation for all quantities of labour employed by the firm. Marginal revenue product is the addition to total revenue created by the addition of another worker.

Suppose that, unlike the market for water, the labour market is competitive and that the prevailing wage is $1 per day. Then a firm will improve its profits by adding another worker if and only if the marginal revenue product of labour from that worker exceeds the worker's wage. For the firm in Table 19A.2, this condition holds true for two workers but not for three. Hence, the firm will choose

Table 19A.2 How a monopolistic firm decides how much labour to hire						
Labour (number of workers) (L)	Output (litres per day) (Q)	Total revenue	Marginal product of labour ($MPL = \triangle Q / \triangle L$)	Marginal revenue product of labour ($MRPL = \triangle TR / \triangle L$)	Wage (W)	Marginal profit ($\triangle Profit = MRPL - W$)
0	0	$0	-	$28	$1	-
1	4	28	4	2	1	$27
2	6	30	2	−2	1	1
3	7	28	1	−4	1	−3
4	8	24	1			−5

to employ two workers and produce an output of 6 litres per day. Thus, any profit-maximising firm hires workers up to the point where the marginal revenue product of labour equals the wage.

Notice that this same rule guides the labour-hiring decision for a competitive firm. In that case, when an additional worker produces more output, each new unit sold earns the prevailing market price. That price is the marginal revenue for each additional unit of output produced. So the value of the marginal product is the same as the marginal revenue product for a competitive firm.

For the monopolist, however, when it adds another worker, that worker produces more output (its marginal product) but earns the firm additional revenue of an amount less than price. The firm must consider this price effect as well as the output effect when deciding to hire another worker. For each extra unit produced, the additional revenue the firm earns is its marginal revenue. Therefore, the marginal revenue product of labour ($\Delta TR/\Delta L$) is the additional revenue over all of the additional output that worker produces or marginal revenue times its marginal product ($\Delta TR/\Delta Q \times \Delta Q/\Delta L$). This is the value an additional worker adds to the firm.

As we mentioned in the chapter, the idea that the firm hires up until the point where the value of the marginal product of labour equals the wage is just another way of looking at the firm's profit-maximising output decision. Recall from chapter 15 that a monopolist wishes to produce an output quantity such that marginal revenue equals marginal cost. In the chapter we demonstrated that marginal cost is the wage divided by the marginal product of labour. Because the value of the marginal product of labour equals marginal revenue multiplied by marginal product, then mathematically we have:

$$MR \times MPL = W \text{ or } MR = W/MPL = MC$$

So when a firm hires labour up to the point where the marginal revenue product equals the wage, it is choosing output such that marginal revenue equals marginal cost.

Thus, the theory of labour demand we introduced in the chapter remains essentially unchanged for situations where markets are not perfectly competitive. In general, the firm chooses its quantity of labour by looking at the point at which the marginal revenue product of labour equals the wage. Hence, *the marginal revenue product curve is the labour demand curve for any firm.*

20

Earnings, unions and discrimination

Learning objectives

In this chapter you will:

- examine how wages compensate for differences in job characteristics

- learn about and compare the human-capital and signalling theories of education

- examine why in some occupations a few superstars earn tremendous incomes

- evaluate the role of unions in labour markets

- examine how information asymmetries might result in efficiency wages

- consider why it is difficult to measure the impact of discrimination on wages

- see when market forces can and cannot provide a natural remedy for discrimination.

Sports stars and musicians can earn incomes in the millions of dollars per year. Most surgeons earn salaries over $250 000 and the average person working in manufacturing earns about $35 000 per year. This illustrates the large differences in earnings that are so common in our economy. These differences explain why some people live in mansions, drive BMWs and holiday on the French Riviera, and other people live in small flats, take the bus and holiday in their own backyards.

What causes earnings to vary so much from person to person? Chapter 19, which developed the basic neoclassical theory of the labour market, offers an answer to this question. There we saw that wages are governed by labour supply and labour demand. Labour demand, in turn, reflects the marginal productivity of labour. In equilibrium, each worker is paid the value of his or her marginal contribution to the economy's production of goods and services.

This theory of the labour market, though widely accepted by economists, is only the beginning of the story. To understand the wide variation in earnings that we observe, we must go beyond this general framework and examine more precisely what determines the supply and demand for different types of labour. That is our goal in this chapter.

Some determinants of equilibrium wages

Workers differ from one another in many ways. Jobs also have differing characteristics – both in terms of the wages they pay and in terms of their non-monetary attributes. In this section we consider how the characteristics of workers and jobs affect labour supply, labour demand and equilibrium wages.

Compensating differentials

When a worker is deciding whether to take a job, the wage is only one of many job attributes that the worker takes into account. Some jobs are easy, fun and safe; others are hard, dull and dangerous. The better the job as gauged by these non-monetary characteristics, the more people there are who are willing to do the job at any given wage. In other words, the supply of labour for easy, fun and safe jobs is greater than the supply of labour for hard, dull and dangerous jobs. As a result, 'good' jobs will tend to have lower equilibrium wages than 'bad' jobs.

For example, imagine you are looking for a job during university orientation week. Two kinds of jobs are available. You can take a job as a new-student assistant, or you can take a job as a cleaner. The assistants leisurely stroll around the campus during the day and help any new students who need directions or other assistance. The cleaners must report to work at 4.30 each morning and clean up the mess left after orientation week parties. Which job would you want? Most people would prefer to be a new-student assistant if the wages were the same. In order to get people to become campus cleaners, the university has to offer higher wages to cleaners than to student assistants.

Economists use the term **compensating differential** to refer to a difference in wages that arises from non-monetary characteristics of different jobs. Compensating differentials are prevalent in the economy. Here are some examples:

compensating differential
a difference in wages that arises to offset the non-monetary characteristics of different jobs

- Coalminers are paid more than other workers with similar levels of education. Their higher wage compensates them for the dirty and dangerous nature of coalmining, as well as the long-term health problems that coalminers experience.
- Workers who work the night shift at factories are paid more than similar workers who work the day shift. The higher wage compensates them for having to work at night and sleep during the day, a lifestyle that most people find undesirable.

- University lecturers are paid less than lawyers and doctors, who have similar amounts of education. Lecturers' lower wages compensate them for the great intellectual and personal satisfaction that their jobs offer. (Indeed, teaching economics is so much fun that it is surprising that economics lecturers get paid anything at all!)

'On the one hand, I know I could make more money if I left public service for the private sector, but, on the other hand, I couldn't chop off heads.'

Source: Fradon, Dana © 1985 Dana Fradon/The New Yorker Collection/www.cartoonbank.com.

CASE STUDY

Paying for work quality

It is sometimes difficult to tell whether wages employees receive are driven by productivity (implying high wages) or job satisfaction (implying lower wages). This is true of some scientific professions where people like to be able to publish their work while their employers may or may not approve of this. One reason for disapproval is that publication gives their competitors an insight into their strategy. But against this are suggestions that publication may make a firm's scientists more connected and able to absorb developments elsewhere, increasing productivity.

So does job satisfaction drive a scientist's wage? It is hard to tell because a high-quality employee will command both a high wage because of productivity reasons and also potentially be able to insist on work conditions. Scott Stern, in a paper published in *Management Science* in 2004, surveyed job candidates to tease all of this out. To take into account the quality of the candidate, Stern not only compared candidates but also compared the group of job offers each received. He showed that candidates with multiple job offers (some with publication rights and others without), would accept 20 per cent lower salaries for the jobs where they could publish. This suggested that personal job satisfaction rather than productivity was driving those rights. People really do 'pay' for job satisfaction.

Human capital

As we discussed in the previous chapter, the word *capital* usually refers to the economy's stock of equipment and structures. The capital stock includes the farmer's tractor, the manufacturer's factory and the teacher's blackboard. The essence of capital is that it is a factor of production that itself has been produced.

There is another type of capital that, although less tangible than physical capital, is just as important to the economy's production. **Human capital** is the accumulation of investments in people. The most important type of human capital is education. Like all forms of capital, education represents an expenditure of resources at one point in time to raise productivity in the future. But, unlike an investment in other forms of capital, an investment in education is tied to a specific person and this linkage is what makes it human capital.

Not surprisingly, workers with more human capital on average earn more than those with less human capital. University graduates in Australia, for example, earn about 36 per cent more than those workers who end their education with a secondary school certificate. This large difference has been documented in many countries around the world. It tends to be even larger in less-developed countries, where educated workers are in scarce supply.

It is easy to see why education raises wages from the perspective of supply and demand. Firms – the demanders of labour – are willing to pay more for the highly educated because highly educated workers have higher marginal products. Workers – the suppliers of labour – are willing to pay the cost of becoming educated only if there is a reward for doing so. In essence, the difference in wages between highly educated workers and less-educated workers may be considered a compensating differential for the cost of becoming educated.

human capital
the accumulation of investments in people, such as education and on-the-job training

▸ human capital

CASESTUDY

The changing value of skills

In Australia, consistent with human capital theory, workers with skills command higher salaries than those without. A 2010 study by the Productivity Commission looked at how wages change with an individual's level of education. Their results showed that, compared with a worker who finished school at or before year 11, a university degree led to around a 38 per cent increase in wages. The relative wage increase was slightly higher for men than for women. Compared to a worker whose education finished at the end of high school, a worker with a university degree earned around 26 per cent higher wages.

While higher education typically leads to higher earnings, the size of the wage premium changes over time. In Australia, the wage premium for a worker with a university degree relative to a worker with just a high school education fell in the 1970s and early 1980s. The premium then rose in the 1990s and early 2000s before falling again in the late 2000s.

What explains these patterns? A study by Jeff Borland, published in the *Economic Record* in 1996, identifies shifts in both the relative demand and relative supply of skilled to unskilled workers. Increased access to education and higher labour force participation rates for women have raised the proportion of workers with university education in the workforce. On the other hand, the relative demand for skilled workers has also been growing.

When both demand and supply increase in a market, the result is an increase in quantity although price may increase or decrease. In the case of the market for skilled workers in Australia, in the 1970s the relative number of skilled workers employed increased and the relative earnings of those workers decreased. Since then, the relative number of skilled workers employed has continued to increase and strong growth in demand for these workers has meant that their relative earnings have also increased. The mining boom in Australia in the late 2000s reversed this trend, at least temporarily.

The value of an education is not simply measured by the earnings of workers in full-time employment. Their employment prospects must also be taken into account. In 1997, for instance,

>>

male workers with a degree were 50 per cent less likely to find themselves without a job compared with those with secondary school education. For women, the improvement in employment prospects from education was even greater.

Taking both relative earnings and the relative likelihood of finding employment into account, there is probably an increasing value to having skills in the workforce.

Ability, effort and chance

Why do top sporting professionals get paid more than minor players? Certainly, the higher wages are not a compensating differential. Playing in top-level sporting competitions is not necessarily a less pleasant task than playing in minor competitions; in fact, the opposite is often true. Top sporting professionals do not require more years of schooling and are not always more experienced. To a large extent, top sporting professionals earn more just because they have greater natural ability.

Natural ability is important for workers in all occupations. Because of heredity and upbringing, people differ in their physical and mental attributes. Some people are strong, others weak. Some people are smart, others less so. Some people are outgoing, others awkward in social situations. These and many other personal characteristics determine how productive workers are and, therefore, play a role in determining the wages they earn.

Closely related to ability is effort. Some people work hard, others are lazy. We should not be surprised to find that those who work hard are more productive and earn higher wages. To some extent, firms reward workers directly by paying people on the basis of what they produce. Salespeople, for instance, are often paid a percentage of the sales they make. At other times, hard work is rewarded less directly in the form of a higher annual salary or a bonus.

Chance also plays a role in determining wages. If a person attended a trade school to learn how to repair televisions with vacuum tubes and then found this skill made obsolete by the invention of solid-state electronics, this worker would end up earning a low wage compared with others with similar years of training. The low wage of this worker is due to chance – a phenomenon that economists recognise but do not shed much light on.

How important are ability, effort and chance in determining wages? It is hard to say, because ability, effort and chance are hard to measure. But indirect evidence suggests that they are very important. When labour economists study wages, they relate a worker's wage to those variables that can be measured – years of schooling, years of experience, age and job characteristics. Although all of these measured variables affect a worker's wage as theory predicts, they account for less than half of the variation in wages in our economy. Because so much of the variation in wages is left unexplained, omitted variables, including ability, effort and chance, must play an important role.

CASESTUDY

The benefits of beauty

People differ in many ways. One difference is how attractive they are. The actor Brad Pitt, for instance, is good-looking. In part for this reason, his films attract large audiences. Not surprisingly, the large audiences mean a large income for him.

How prevalent are the economic benefits of beauty? Labour economists Daniel Hamermesh and

Jeff Biddle tried to answer this question in a study published in the December 1994 issue of the *American Economic Review*. Hamermesh and Biddle examined data from surveys of individuals in the United States and Canada. The interviewers who conducted the survey were asked to rate each respondent's physical appearance. Hamermesh and

Biddle then examined how much the wages of the respondents depended on the standard determinants – education, experience and so on – and how much they depended on physical appearance.

Hamermesh and Biddle found that beauty pays. People who are deemed to be more attractive than average earn 5 per cent more than people of average looks. People of average looks earn 5 per cent to 10 per cent more than people considered less attractive than average. Similar results were found for men and women.

What explains these differences in wages? There are several ways to interpret the 'beauty premium'.

One interpretation is that good looks are themselves a type of innate ability determining productivity and wages. Some people are born with the attributes of a movie star; other people are not. Good looks are useful in any job in which workers present themselves to the public – such as acting, sales and waiting on tables. In this case, an attractive worker is more valuable to the firm than an unattractive worker. The firm's willingness to pay more to attractive workers reflects its customers' preferences.

A second interpretation is that reported beauty is an indirect measure of other types of ability. How

Good looks pay.

Source: iStockphoto/Jacob Wackerhausen.

attractive a person appears depends on more than just heredity. It also depends on dress, hairstyle, personal conduct and other attributes that a person can control. Perhaps a person who successfully projects an attractive image in a survey interview is more likely to be an intelligent person who succeeds at other tasks as well.

A third interpretation is that the beauty premium is a type of discrimination, a topic to which we return later.

An alternative view of education: Signalling

Earlier we discussed the human-capital view of education, according to which schooling raises workers' wages because it makes them more productive. Although this view is widely accepted, some economists have proposed an alternative theory, which emphasises that firms use educational attainment as a way of differentiating between high-ability and low-ability workers. According to this alternative view, when people get a university degree, for instance, they do not become more productive, but they do *signal* their high ability to prospective employers. Because it is easier for high-ability people to get a degree than it is for low-ability people, more high-ability people get degrees. As a result, it is rational for firms to interpret a degree as a signal of ability.

The signalling theory of education is similar to the signalling theory of advertising discussed in chapter 18. In the signalling theory of advertising, the advertisement itself contains no real information, but the firm signals the quality of its product to consumers by its willingness to spend money on advertising. In the signalling theory of education, schooling has no real productivity benefit, but the worker signals innate productivity to employers by being willing to spend years at university. In both cases, an action is being taken not for its intrinsic benefit but because the willingness to take that action conveys private information to someone observing it.

Thus, we now have two views of education: the human-capital theory and the signalling theory. Both views can explain why better educated workers tend to earn more than less-educated workers. According to the human-capital view, education makes workers more productive; according to the signalling view, education is correlated with natural ability. But the two views have radically different predictions for the effects of policies that aim to increase educational attainment. According to the human-capital view, increasing educational levels for all workers would raise all workers' productivity and thereby their wages. According to the signalling view, education does not enhance productivity, so raising all workers' educational levels would not affect wages.

Most likely, the truth lies somewhere between these two extremes. The benefits to education are probably a combination of productivity-enhancing effects of human capital and the productivity-revealing effects of signalling. The open question is the relative size of these two effects.

The superstar phenomenon

Although most actors earn very little and often have to take jobs as waiters to support themselves, actor Sandra Bullock earned just over $60 million in 2009–10. Similarly, while most people who play tennis do it for free as a hobby, Roger Federer professionally earned over $60 million in 2009–10. Sandra Bullock and Roger Federer are superstars in their fields and their great public appeal is reflected in astronomical incomes.

Why do Bullock and Federer earn so much? It is not surprising that there are differences in incomes within occupations. Good carpenters earn more than mediocre carpenters and good plumbers earn more than mediocre plumbers. People vary in ability and effort, and these differences lead to differences in income. Yet the best carpenters and plumbers do not earn the millions that are common among the best actors and athletes. What explains the difference?

To understand the tremendous incomes of Bullock and Federer, we must examine the special features of the markets in which they sell their services. Superstars arise in markets that have two characteristics:

- Every customer in the market wants to enjoy the good supplied by the best producer.
- The good is produced with a technology that makes it possible for the best producer to supply every customer at low cost.

If Sandra Bullock is the finest actor around, then everyone will want to see her next film; seeing twice as many films by an actor half as talented is not a good substitute. Moreover, it is possible for everyone to enjoy a performance by Sandra Bullock. Because it is easy to make multiple copies of a film, Bullock can provide her service to millions of people simultaneously. Similarly, because tennis tournaments are broadcast on television, millions of fans can enjoy the extraordinary athletic skills of Roger Federer.

We can now see why there are no superstar carpenters and plumbers. Other things being equal, everyone may prefer to employ the best carpenter, but a carpenter, unlike a film actor, can provide his services to only a limited number of customers. Although the best carpenter will be able to command a somewhat higher wage than the average carpenter, the average carpenter will still be able to earn a good living.

Source: Getty Images.

Source: Getty Image.

Define *compensating differential* and give an example. Give two reasons why better educated workers earn more than less-educated workers.

Unions and imperfect competition in labour markets

In some industries, labour markets do not operate according to the simple principles of supply and demand. In industries such as transport, teaching and mining, wages are determined by negotiations between unions and employers. A **union** is a type of cartel. Like any cartel, a union is a group of sellers acting together in the hope of exerting their joint market power. Many workers in the economy discuss their wages, benefits and working conditions with their employers as individuals. In contrast, workers in a union do so as a group. The process by which unions and firms agree on the terms of employment is called **collective bargaining**.

Unions are an example of imperfect competition in labour markets. But large employers can also exercise market power. Like product markets, these imperfections in competition in labour markets have an effect on prices and quantity – in this case, wages and levels of employment.

The role of unions has been the source of considerable debate in Australia. Every year it seems that workers and employers in another industry, whether it be air transport, brewing or the ports, are in a dispute. Unionisation was partly a response to very poor working conditions in those industries. There was a time when being a member of a union was seen as very important to maintaining better work conditions. Recently, however, economic changes have altered this pattern. As depicted in Table 20.1, trade union membership rates have been declining in Australia.

Here we will look at how an economist might analyse union behaviour. This will allow us to pinpoint employer concerns about unions and to also evaluate their overall economic impact.

union
a worker association that bargains with employers over wages and working conditions

collective bargaining
the process by which unions and firms agree on the terms of employment

Table 20.1 Unionisation rate – union members as a percentage of employees	
Year	Unionisation rate (%)
1976	53
1982	54
1986	46
1990	41
1994	35
1998	28
2000	25
2003	23
2006	20
2009	20

Source: Anne Hawke and Mark Wooden, 'The changing face of Australian industrial relations', *Economic Record*, vol. 74, no. 224, 1998, pp. 74–88; Australian Bureau of Statistics, Cat. No. 310.0, 6325.0 and 6310.0 (various years).

Unions as monopolists

One way to view a union is as a wage-setting monopolist. To see this, consider the hypothetical example of the strawberry picking industry in the region of Bargainland. For decades, strawberry picking had been one of the lowest paid jobs in the region. Strawberry picking did not require many specialised skills so it could be performed by many workers in Bargainland.

One day, one particularly savvy strawberry picker decided to think more carefully about the market for strawberry pickers. She reasoned that strawberry pickers may be paid so little because owners of strawberry patches could play them off against one another. Pickers who want higher wages have little bargaining power with a patch owner who can simply fire them and hire other pickers at the prevailing wage. To this person, it is not strawberry pickers' lack of skills that is the problem but their lack of market power.

Our smart strawberry picker was skilled in the economics of chapter 15. She reckoned that if all the strawberry pickers in Bargainland were to get together and form an organisation – the Bargainland Strawberry Pickers' Union (BSPU) – they could act more like a monopolist and, hence, increase their wages. 'Pickers need not be at the bottom of the heap in Bargainland', proclaimed the new leader of the union. 'Join the BSPU and together we will ensure a decent income and better working conditions.' All the strawberry pickers in Bargainland agreed to join. In addition, the BSPU ensured that only workers who were members could pick strawberries. This created an entry barrier into strawberry picking. This was an important condition that would allow the union to exercise market power.

But here the union leader found a problem. Although the BSPU could choose a wage, it was constrained to choose a point on the market demand curve for strawberry pickers. Remember that this curve was determined by the value of the marginal product of strawberry pickers. This had not changed, so the BSPU through its actions could only move along this curve.

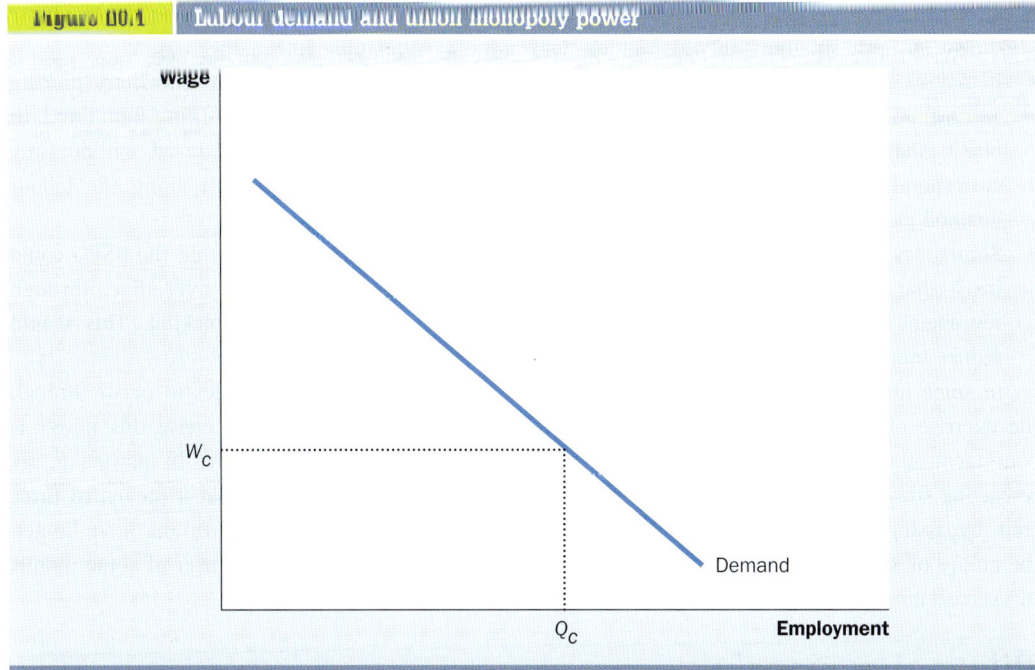

Figure 20.1 **Labour demand and union monopoly power**

Unions might wish to increase the wages of their members. However, when firms in the industry are perfectly competitive, their demand for labour will be represented by a curve such as the one in the diagram. If the union wishes to raise wages above the competitive wage of W_C, it must accept an employment level lower than Q_C. A union that cares about both wage and employment levels faces a dilemma and may not wish to exercise its monopoly power.

In Figure 20.1, you can see that for the wages of strawberry pickers to rise, the number of pickers employed has to fall. For the BSPU leader this was a dilemma; the idea of the BSPU was to raise wages of all of its members, not send them to unemployment or a lower paid job.

This illustrates our first point regarding the interpretation of unions as monopolists – they can raise wages but only at the expense of employment levels. Our examination of monopoly behaviour in chapter 15 was based on the assumption that these firms attempted to maximise profits. They did not care if they sold less, if this led to higher profits. For a union, however, such choices are not so easy. It faces a different set of objectives than does a monopolist in a product market. A union can restrict employment and raise wages and, thereby, raise total income received by workers in the industry. However, in order to do this, the union must also restrict access to employment in the industry. This must harm some workers.

Unions face the same dilemma in asking for better working conditions – such as improved safety, better working hours, annual leave and a healthier work environment. Better working conditions usually mean more costs associated with employing workers. Firms will take such costs into account when determining the quantity of labour they hire. For them, every dollar spent per worker on improved conditions is equivalent to another dollar in wages. Hence, the union, in asking for better working conditions, is constrained by the market demand curve for labour.

Therefore, the union's ability to extract better pay or working conditions is limited by industry conditions. Whether unionised labour is paid more is contingent upon union objectives. If the union is concerned about keeping all its members employed, this will limit its ability to raise wages. There are, however, some situations in which union goals may be compatible with higher wages:

- It may be possible for the workers to agree to shorter working hours. In our strawberry picking story, the union leader could propose that all workers agree to limit their working hours and, in effect, share work. The total quantity of hours worked could then be reduced without any corresponding reduction in employment. The result would be a movement along the labour demand curve to a point where each worker received a higher hourly wage.

- Sometimes it is argued that unions favour members over outsiders. Suppose that the BSPU could insist that no new workers were employed as strawberry pickers. Then, over time, through retirement or other circumstances, some workers will leave strawberry picking. This would reduce total employment and increase wages earned by 'insiders'.

In some industries, it is conceivable that union goals will allow higher wages to occur through the exercise of monopoly power. Recall, however, that a union's ability to exercise this power is contingent upon the same conditions underlying a product market monopoly. In particular, by restricting strawberry pickers to union members, the BSPU was able to ensure that it prevented firms from bypassing the union's attempts at wage setting. In recent times, laws in Australia have limited the ability of unions to insist on compulsory membership. This has eroded the power of some unions to exercise monopoly power.

Bilateral monopoly

monopsony
a market situation where there is a single buyer for a product

In many industries, employers have the ability to negotiate and influence wages. An extreme example of this is called **monopsony**, that is, where there is a single employer in an industry. For instance, mines in outlying towns, steelworks and other firms in large-scale manufacturing industries could be considered monopsonists. When a union confronts a monopsonist, the outcomes can be very different from those for a union whose workers are employed by competitive firms.

Returning to our hypothetical example of the Bargainland strawberry industry, suppose that strawberry-patch owners become concerned about the monopoly power of the BSPU. This is not surprising as higher wages might cause some patches to go out of business. The patches decide to merge and form a single company. This gives them a monopoly over strawberry production in Bargainland and also allows them to negotiate directly with the BSPU over wages and employment. The managing director of the new company is known for tough negotiating.

bilateral monopoly
a market situation where there are both a single buyer and a single seller for a product

The union leader and employer meet to negotiate directly with one another on behalf of their respective organisations. This situation is referred to as a **bilateral monopoly**. We want to consider the type of agreements they might arrive at. Both parties realise one very important thing – any deal that does not maximise industry profit (after considering labour costs) will not be in either party's interests. For instance, suppose that the union leader was concerned that, during harvest season before unionisation, pickers were required to work on weekends. This loss of leisure time had a high opportunity cost to the strawberry pickers. The employer could explain that it was efficient to harvest strawberries quickly. If harvesting did not continue over weekends, this would cost the company a sizeable amount of money in lost strawberries. So the employer proposes to increase weekend wages and share the increased profits created by a speedy harvest with the workers. If the increase in wages is worth the loss of a few weekends' worth of leisure, the union leader accepts the proposal. If adequate compensation is offered, it would not be sensible for the union leader to insist on a work practice that raises production costs.

However, when it comes to negotiations over total wages, both parties are at an impasse. An increase in wages does not itself influence the strawberry company's ability to earn additional revenue. It is simply a transfer from company shareholders to employees. The union leader digs her heels in on this issue and threatens to take industrial action, such as a **strike**, if total wages are not increased. But the BSPU cannot demand too much. If the strawberry company fails to make any profits above total wages paid, its owners might shut it down. Eventually, however, the employer advocate considers the losses from a strike and makes the BSPU a wage offer – lucrative enough so that a strike really is not worthwhile.

strike
the organised withdrawal of labour from a firm by a union

These outcomes, over working time and wages, reflect the type of agreements that can arise in bilateral monopoly. The issue of wages is purely distributional. In fact, there are many agreements that can arise that give workers more or less money relative to shareholders. These agreements can be depicted using a **possibilities frontier**. One such frontier is depicted in Figure 20.2. The possibilities frontier depicts all agreements that can be made that maximise the strawberry industry's profits. At some agreements (such as point A), the union is ineffectual and receives a minimal wage payout. There are others (such as point B) in which the union has all of the bargaining power and so shareholders earn a minimal profit level – just enough to make it worthwhile to continue the business. Finally, there are agreements (such as point C) where both the union and company can be better off by agreeing to a point closer to the possibilities frontier. An example of this was the decision over whether to work weekends during harvest season. By agreeing to do that, both the workers and shareholders were better off.

possibilities frontier
a graph depicting all the outcomes that maximise the sum of profits plus wages to workers

Figure 20.2	Possibilities frontier between a union and employer

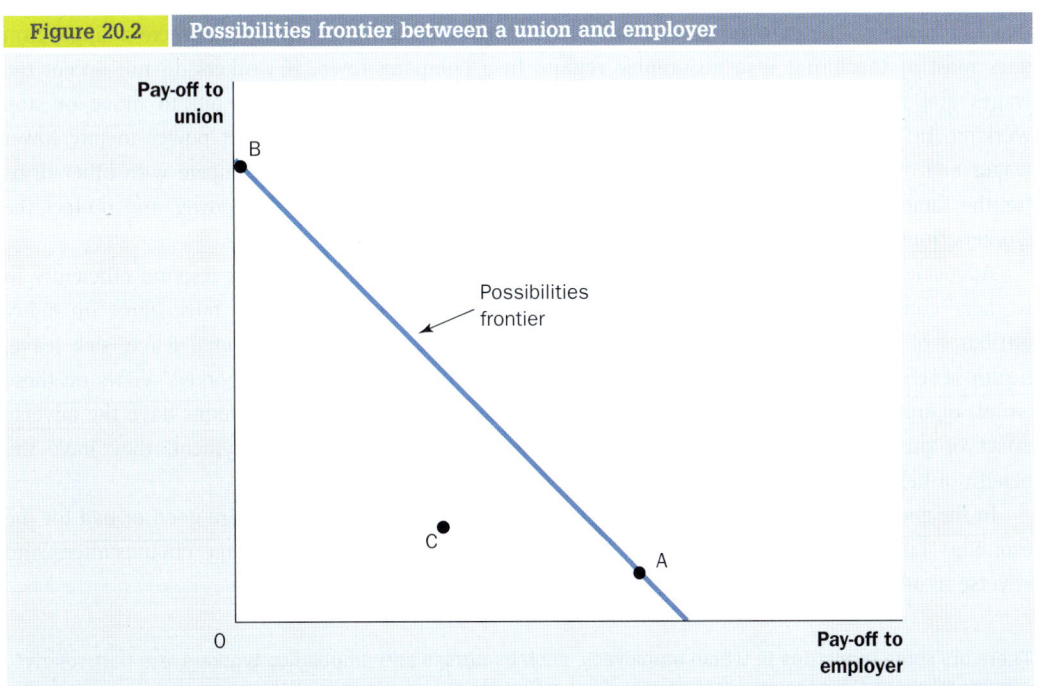

This figure depicts the possibilities frontier between a union and a single industry-wide employer. The figure depicts the pay-offs that the employer and union receive from any given agreement. Only pay-off combinations inside the possibilities frontier can actually be achieved. Both the union and employer will prefer to come to agreements that lie on the possibilities frontier. If they agree to a point such as C, each could be made better off by moving closer to the frontier.

Reasonable negotiators will agree to points on the possibilities frontier. Any point outside the frontier is simply not possible. Any point within the frontier can be improved on to the benefit of both parties, so there is no inherent conflict. The actual point on the frontier where negotiators, such as the union leader and the employer, end up depends on their relative bargaining power. For example, if the BSPU can hold out for a long strike, this improves its bargaining position. However, if the strawberry company can easily find other workers who can pick during the strike, this reduces the union's bargaining position. There are many factors that influence bargaining power, so the earnings of unionised workers will differ from industry to industry.

Are unions good or bad for the economy?

Economists disagree about whether unions are good or bad for the economy as a whole. Let's consider both sides of the debate.

Critics argue that unions are merely a type of cartel. When unions raise wages above the level that would prevail in competitive markets, they reduce the quantity of labour demanded, cause some workers to be unemployed and reduce the wages in the rest of the economy. The resulting allocation of labour is, critics argue, both inefficient and inequitable. It is inefficient because high union wages reduce employment in unionised firms below the efficient, competitive level. It is inequitable because some workers benefit at the expense of other workers.

Advocates of unions contend that unions are a necessary antidote to the market power of the firms that hire workers. The extreme case of this market power is the 'company town', where a single firm does most of the hiring in a geographic region. In a company town, if workers do not accept the wages and working conditions that the firm offers, they have little choice but to move or stop working. In the absence of a union, therefore, the firm could use its market power to pay lower wages and offer worse working conditions than would prevail if it had to compete with other firms for the same workers. In this case, a union may balance the firm's market power and protect the workers from being at the mercy of the firm owners.

Advocates of unions also claim that unions are important for helping firms respond efficiently to workers' concerns. Whenever a worker takes a job, the worker and the firm must agree on many attributes of the job in addition to the wage – hours of work, overtime, annual leave, sick leave, health benefits, promotion schedules, job security and so on. By representing workers' views on these issues, unions allow firms to provide the right mix of job attributes. Even if unions have the adverse effect of pushing wages above the equilibrium level and causing unemployment, they have the benefit of helping firms keep a happy and productive workforce.

In the end, there is no consensus among economists about whether unions are good or bad for the economy. Like many institutions, their influence is probably beneficial in some circumstances and adverse in others.

There are some industries in which employees, such as nurses and ambulance workers, are particularly concerned about the consequences of industrial action on others. How does this concern influence their bargaining power?

The theory of efficiency wages

One explanation for different earnings might come from different practices designed to improve workplace performance. Firms may set wages high so as to motivate workers to perform well in their jobs. This wage is called an **efficiency wage**. Efficiency wages are wages above the equilibrium wages that would result when supply equals demand. Thus, efficiency wages can potentially explain unemployment as well as earnings.

Why should firms want to keep wages high? In some ways, this decision seems odd, for wages are a large part of firms' costs. Normally, we expect profit-maximising firms to want to keep costs – and therefore wages – as low as possible. The novel insight of efficiency-wage theory is that paying high wages might be profitable because they might raise the efficiency of a firm's workers.

There are several types of efficiency-wage theory. Each type suggests a different explanation for why firms may want to pay high wages. Let's now consider four of these theories.

efficiency wages
above-equilibrium wages paid by firms in order to increase worker productivity

▸ efficiency wages

Worker health

The first and simplest type of efficiency-wage theory emphasises the link between wages and worker health. Better paid workers eat a more nutritious diet and workers who eat a better diet are healthier and more productive. A firm may find it more profitable to pay high wages and have healthy, productive workers than to pay lower wages and have less-healthy, less-productive workers.

This type of efficiency-wage theory is not relevant for firms in rich countries such as Australia. In these countries, the equilibrium wages for most workers are well above the level needed for an adequate diet. Firms are not concerned that paying equilibrium wages would place their workers' health in jeopardy.

Paying higher wages to raise worker health is more relevant for firms in less-developed countries where inadequate nutrition is a more common problem. Unemployment is high in the cities of many poor African countries, for example. In these countries, firms may fear that cutting wages would adversely influence their workers' health and productivity. Concern over nutrition may explain why firms do not cut wages despite a surplus of labour.

---

fyi

Why do strikes occur?

Strikes are costly to both firms and workers. To firms they represent lost output; to workers, lost income. The longer the strike, the more costly to both parties. So why do they occur?

Our discussion of bilateral monopoly contended that if unions and management were reasonable, they would see the harm from costly actions and agree to outcomes on the possibilities frontier. The threat of a strike might influence the eventual outcome negotiated, but the strikes themselves should not occur for this would not be in the interests of unions or management.

In reality, strikes occur because negotiations do not always run so smoothly. Negotiations break down. During times of disagreement, unions wish to demonstrate their resolve by striking and being

willing to forgo income. Management also wants to demonstrate to the union that it can weather a strike and hold out as well. In this case, disagreements are the result of 'brinkmanship' – an attempt by both parties to temporarily use threats to demonstrate the value of their work to the firm.

If both unions and management had a better understanding of the costs of strike action, brinkmanship might not occur. In this way, strikes can be seen as the result of a lack of information. Unions might believe that a company does not appreciate their full value. Management might believe that unions do not appreciate the willingness of their company's shareholders to hold out and earn high profits.

>>

Nonetheless, in the past – whether because of simple misunderstandings or differences in information – many workdays were lost to industrial action in Australia. Australia has always had government involvement in the resolution of industrial disputes. At its core is a dispute resolution body – the Industrial Relations Commission. Whenever a union contemplated strike action, the Commission's task was to step in and arbitrate the dispute. Its rulings were binding.

The arbitration system was strengthened considerably during the 1980s. Also during that time, the Labor government struck an Accord with the trade unions to agree to wage restraint. The result of this was a dramatic reduction in strike action. As depicted in Figure 20.3, this resulted in a reduction in workdays lost due to industrial disputes.

Figure 20.3 Industrial disputes in Australia

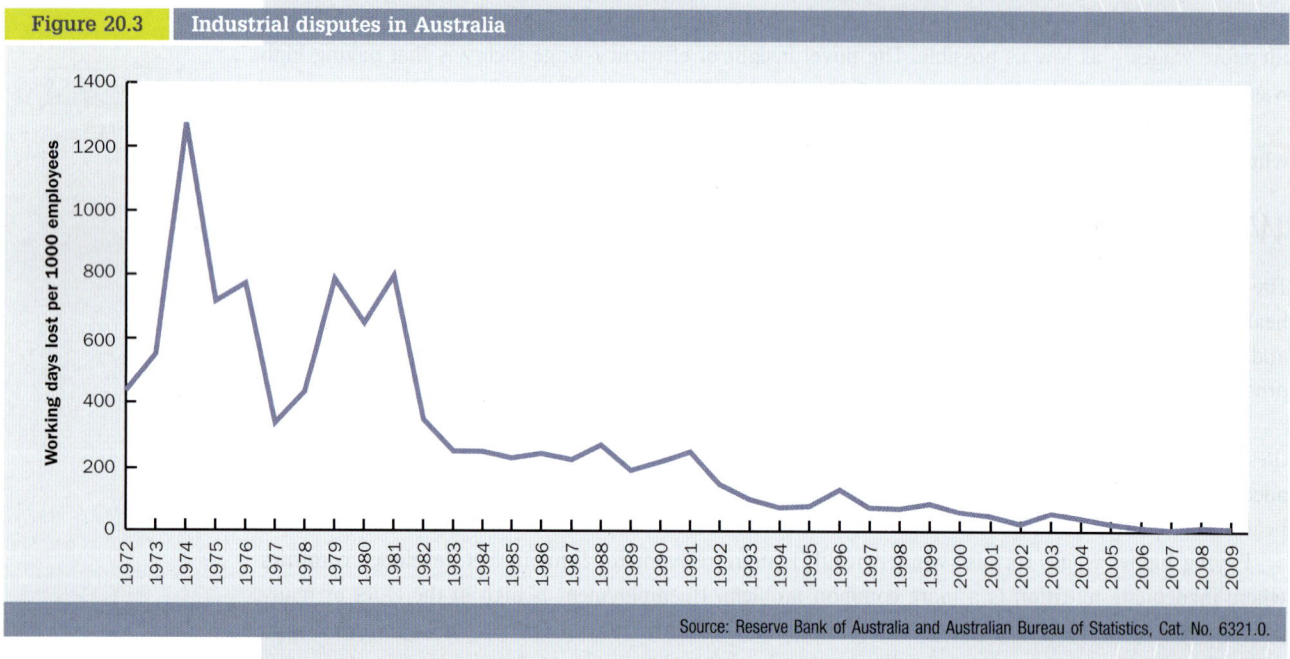

Source: Reserve Bank of Australia and Australian Bureau of Statistics, Cat. No. 6321.0.

Worker turnover

A second type of efficiency-wage theory emphasises the link between wages and worker turnover. Workers quit jobs for many reasons – to take jobs in other firms, to move to other parts of the country, to leave the labour force and so on. The frequency with which they quit depends on the entire set of incentives they face, including the benefits of leaving and the benefits of staying with their current employer. The more a firm pays its workers, the less often its workers will choose to leave. Thus, a firm can reduce turnover among its workers by paying them a high wage.

Why do firms care about turnover? The reason is that it is costly for firms to hire and train new workers. Moreover, even after they are trained, newly hired workers are not as productive as experienced workers. Firms with higher turnover, therefore, will tend to have higher production costs. Firms may find it profitable to pay wages above the equilibrium level in order to reduce turnover.

Worker effort

A third type of efficiency-wage theory emphasises the link between wages and worker effort. In many jobs, workers have some discretion over how hard to work. As a result, firms monitor the efforts of their workers and workers caught shirking their responsibilities are fired. But not all shirkers are caught immediately because monitoring workers is costly and imperfect. A firm can respond to this problem by paying wages above the equilibrium level. High wages make workers more eager to keep their jobs and, thereby, give workers an incentive to put forward their best effort.

This particular type of efficiency-wage theory is similar to the old Marxist idea of the 'reserve army of the unemployed'. Marx thought that employers benefited from unemployment because the threat of unemployment helped to discipline those workers who had jobs. In the worker-effort variant of efficiency-wage theory, unemployment fills a similar role. If the wage were at the level that balanced supply and demand, workers would have less reason to work hard, because if they were fired they could quickly find new jobs at the same wage. Therefore, firms find it profitable to raise wages above the equilibrium level. This causes unemployment while providing an incentive for workers not to shirk their responsibilities.

Worker quality

A fourth and final type of efficiency-wage theory emphasises the link between wages and worker quality. When a firm hires new workers, it cannot perfectly gauge the quality of the applicants. By paying a high wage, the firm attracts a better pool of workers to apply for its jobs.

To see how this might work, consider a simple example. Waterwell Company owns one well and needs one worker to pump water from the well. Two workers, Bill and Ben, are interested in the job. Bill, a proficient worker, is willing to work for $10 per hour. Below that wage, he would rather start his own lawn-mowing business. Ben, a complete incompetent, is willing to work for anything above $2 per hour. Below that wage, he would rather sit on the beach. Economists say that Bill's *reservation wage* – the lowest wage he would accept – is $10, and Ben's reservation wage is $2.

What wage should the firm set? If the firm were interested in minimising labour costs, it would set the wage at $2 per hour. At this wage, the quantity of workers supplied (one) would balance the quantity demanded. Ben would take the job, and Bill would not apply for it. Yet suppose Waterwell knows that only one of these two applicants is competent, but it does not know whether it is Bill or Ben. If the firm hires the incompetent worker, he will damage the well, causing the firm huge losses. In this case, the firm has a better strategy than paying the equilibrium wage of $2 and hiring Ben. It can offer $10 per hour, inducing both Bill and Ben to apply for the job. By choosing randomly between these two applicants and turning the other away, the firm has a fifty-fifty chance of hiring the competent worker. In contrast, if the firm offers any lower wage, it is sure to hire the incompetent worker.

This story illustrates a general phenomenon. When a firm has an excess supply of workers, it might seem profitable to reduce the wage it is offering. But by reducing the wage, the firm induces an adverse change in the mix of workers. In this case, at a wage of $10, Waterwell has two workers applying for one job. But if Waterwell responds to this excess supply by reducing the wage, the competent worker (who has better alternative opportunities) will not apply. Thus, it is profitable for the firm to pay a wage above the level that balances supply and demand.

458

CASESTUDY

Henry Ford and the generous $5-a-day wage

Henry Ford was an industrial visionary. As founder of the Ford Motor Company, he was responsible for introducing modern techniques of production. Rather than building cars with small teams of skilled craftsmen, Ford built cars on assembly lines in which unskilled workers were taught to perform the same simple tasks over and over again. The output of this assembly process was the Model T Ford, one of the most famous early cars.

In 1914, Ford introduced another innovation – the $5 workday. This might not seem like much today, but back then $5 was about twice the going wage. It was also far above the wage that balanced supply and demand. When the new $5-a-day wage was announced, long lines of job seekers formed outside the Ford factories. The number of workers willing to work at this wage far exceeded the number of workers Ford needed.

Ford's high-wage policy had many of the effects predicted by efficiency-wage theory. Staff turnover fell, absenteeism fell and productivity rose. Workers were so much more efficient that Ford's production costs were lower even though wages were higher. Thus, paying a wage above the equilibrium level was profitable for the firm. Henry Ford himself called the $5-a-day wage 'one of the finest cost-cutting moves we ever made'.

Historical accounts of this episode are also consistent with efficiency-wage theory. A historian of the early Ford Motor Company wrote:

> Ford and his associates freely declared on many occasions that the high-wage policy turned out to be good business. By this they meant that it had improved the discipline of the workers, given them a more loyal interest in the institution, and raised their personal efficiency.

An early Ford assembly line

Source: Library of Congress Prints and Photographs Division, Washington D.C. 20540 USA.

Why did it take Henry Ford to introduce this efficiency wage? Why were other firms not already taking advantage of this seemingly profitable business strategy? According to some analysts, Ford's decision was closely linked to his use of the assembly line. Workers organised in an assembly line are highly interdependent. If one worker is absent or works slowly, other workers are less able to complete their own tasks. Thus, while assembly lines made production more efficient, they also raised the importance of low worker turnover, high worker quality and high worker effort. As a result, paying efficiency wages may have been a better strategy for the Ford Motor Company than for other businesses at the time.

Give four explanations for why firms might find it profitable to pay wages above the level that balances quantity of labour supplied and quantity of labour demanded.

The economics of discrimination

Another source of differences in wages is discrimination. **Discrimination** occurs when the marketplace offers different opportunities to similar individuals who differ only by race, ethnic group, sex, age or other personal characteristics. Discrimination reflects some people's prejudice against certain groups in society. Although discrimination is an emotionally charged topic that often generates heated debate, economists try to study the topic objectively in order to separate myth from reality.

discrimination
the offering of different opportunities to similar individuals who differ only by race, ethnic group, sex, age or other personal characteristics

Measuring labour-market discrimination

How much does discrimination in labour markets affect the earnings of different groups of workers? This question is important, but answering it is not easy.

It might seem natural to gauge the amount of discrimination in labour markets by looking at the average wages of different groups. For instance, in recent years the income of the average Indigenous worker in Australia has been about 55 per cent to 65 per cent of the income of the average worker in the rest of the population. The wage of the average female worker has been about 25 per cent less than the wage of the average male worker. These wage differentials are sometimes presented in political debate as evidence that many employers discriminate against Indigenous people and women.

Yet there is an obvious problem with this approach. Even in a labour market free of discrimination, different people have different wages. People differ in the amount of human capital they have and in the kinds of work they are able and willing to do. The wage differences we observe in the economy are, to a large extent, attributable to the determinants of equilibrium wages we discussed in the last section. Simply observing differences in wages among broad groups says little about the prevalence of discrimination.

Consider, for example, the role of human capital. A study by Alison Preston, published in the *Economic Record* in 1997, estimated that about 27 per cent of the wage gap could be explained by human capital factors such as qualifications and experience. That is, part of the reason men appeared to earn more than women was due to the fact that women were less likely to gain higher education qualifications. Similar gaps in education have been reported for Aborigines.

Human capital acquired in the form of job experience also leads to wage differences. Women tend to have less job experience on average compared to men. One reason is that female labour force participation has increased over the past few decades. Because of this historic change, the average female worker today is younger than the average male worker. In addition, women are more likely to interrupt their careers to raise children. For both reasons, the experience of the average female worker is less than the experience of the average male worker.

Yet another source of wage differences is compensating differentials. Men and women do not always choose the same type of work and this fact may help explain some of the earnings differential between men and women. For example, women are more likely to be secretaries and men are more likely to be truck drivers. The relative wages of secretaries and truck drivers depend in part on the working conditions of each job. Because these non-monetary aspects are hard to measure, it is difficult to gauge the practical importance of compensating differentials in explaining the wage differences that we observe.

In the end, the study of wage differences among groups does not establish any clear conclusion about the prevalence of discrimination in Australian labour markets. Most economists believe that some of the observed wage differentials are attributable to discrimination, but there is no consensus about how much. The only conclusion about which economists are in consensus is a negative one – because the differences in average wages among groups in part reflect differences in human capital and job characteristics, they do not by themselves say anything about how much discrimination there is in the labour market.

Of course, differences in human capital among groups of workers may themselves reflect discrimination. The inferior schooling historically available to Indigenous students, for instance, may be traced to prejudice on the part of governments and to regional funding differences. But this kind of discrimination occurs long before the worker enters the labour market. In this case, the disease is political, even if the symptom is economic.

Discrimination by employers

Let's now turn from measurement to the economic forces that lie behind discrimination in labour markets. If one group in society receives a lower wage than another group, even after controlling for human capital and job characteristics, who is to blame for this differential?

The answer is not obvious. It might seem natural to blame employers for discriminatory wage differences. After all, employers make the hiring decisions that determine labour demand and wages. If some groups of workers earn lower wages than we would otherwise expect, then it seems that employers are responsible. Yet many economists are sceptical of this easy answer. They believe that competitive market economies provide a natural antidote to employer discrimination. That antidote is called the profit motive.

Imagine an economy in which workers are differentiated by their hair colour. Blondes and brunettes have the same skills, experience and work ethic. Yet, because of discrimination, employers prefer not to hire workers with blonde hair. Thus, the demand for blondes is lower than it otherwise would be. As a result, blondes earn a lower wage than brunettes.

How long can this wage differential persist? In this economy, there is an easy way for a firm to beat its competitors – it can hire blonde workers. By hiring blondes, a firm pays lower wages and thus has lower costs than firms that hire brunettes. Over time, more and more 'blonde' firms enter the market to take advantage of this cost advantage. The existing 'brunette' firms have higher costs and, therefore, begin to lose money when faced with the new competitors. These losses induce the brunette firms to go out of business. Eventually, the entry of blonde firms and the exit of brunette firms cause the demand for blonde workers to rise and the demand for brunette workers to fall. This process continues until the wage differential disappears.

Put simply, business owners who care only about making money are at an advantage when competing against those who also care about discriminating. As a result, firms that do not discriminate tend to replace those that do. In this way, competitive markets have a natural remedy for employer discrimination.

In the early twentieth century, streetcars in many southern US cities were segregated by race. White passengers sat in the front of the streetcars, and black passengers sat in the back. What do you suppose caused and maintained this discriminatory practice? And how was this practice viewed by the firms that ran the streetcars?

In a 1986 article in the *Journal of Economic History*, economic historian Jennifer Roback looked at these questions. Roback found that the segregation of races on streetcars was the result of laws that required such segregation. Before these laws were passed, racial discrimination in seating was rare. It was far more common to segregate smokers and non-smokers.

Moreover, the firms that ran the streetcars often opposed the laws requiring racial segregation. Providing separate seating for different races raised the firms' costs and reduced their profit. One railroad company manager complained to the city council that, under the segregation laws, 'the company has to haul around a good deal of empty space'.

Here is how Roback describes the situation in one southern US city:

> The railroad company did not initiate the segregation policy and was not at all eager to abide by it. State legislation, public agitation, and a threat to arrest the president of the railroad were all required to induce them to separate the races on their cars ... There is no indication that the management was motivated by belief in civil rights or racial equality. The evidence indicates their primary motives were economic; separation was costly ... Officials of the company may or may not have disliked blacks, but they were not willing to forgo the profits necessary to indulge such prejudice.

The story of southern streetcars illustrates a general lesson – business owners are usually more interested in making profit than in discriminating against a particular group. When firms engage in discriminatory practices, the ultimate source of the discrimination often lies not with the firms themselves but elsewhere. In this particular case, the streetcar companies segregated whites and blacks because discriminatory laws, which the companies opposed, required them to do so.

Discrimination by customers and governments

Although the profit motive is a strong force acting to eliminate discriminatory wage differentials, there are limits to its corrective abilities. Here we consider two of the most important limits: *customer preferences* and *government policies*.

To see how customer preferences for discrimination can affect wages, consider again our imaginary economy with blondes and brunettes. Suppose that restaurant owners discriminate against blondes when hiring waiters. As a result, blonde waiters earn lower wages than brunette waiters. In this case, a restaurant could open up with blonde waiters and charge lower prices. If customers cared only about the quality and price of their meals, the discriminatory firms would be driven out of business and the wage differential would disappear.

On the other hand, it is possible that customers prefer being served by brunette waiters. If this preference for discrimination is strong, the entry of blonde restaurants need not succeed in eliminating the wage differential between brunettes and blondes. That is, if customers have discriminatory preferences, a discriminatory wage differential is consistent with a competitive market. An economy with such discrimination would contain two types of restaurants. Restaurants that hire blonde-haired waiters have lower costs and charge lower prices, and restaurants that hire brunettes have higher costs and charge higher prices. Customers who did not care about the hair colour of their waiters would be attracted to the lower prices at the blonde restaurants. Bigoted customers would go to the brunette restaurants. They would pay for their discriminatory preference in the form of higher prices.

Another way for discrimination to persist in competitive markets is for the government to prescribe discriminatory practices. If, for instance, the government passed a law stating that blondes could wash dishes in restaurants but could not work as waiters, then a wage differential could persist in a competitive market. The example of segregated streetcars in the forgoing case study is one example of government-decreed discrimination. More recently, before South Africa abandoned its system of apartheid, blacks were prohibited from working in some jobs. Discriminatory governments pass such laws in order to suppress the normal equalising force of free and competitive markets.

To sum up – *competitive markets contain a natural remedy for employer discrimination. The entry of firms that care only about profit tends to eliminate discriminatory wage differentials. These wage differentials persist in competitive markets only when customers are willing to pay to maintain the discriminatory practice or when the government mandates it.*

CASESTUDY

Can asymmetric information explain discrimination?

Economic theorists have argued that asymmetric information can sometimes explain discrimination. For instance, employers might be uncertain about the quality of workers. In the absence of other information, employers might use the worker's sex, ethnicity or racial group as an indicator of ability. For instance, an employer might believe workers from a minority group have a lower education level and pay them less. Workers from that group considering investing in more education are deterred from so doing because of this discrimination. They refrain from education, thus reinforcing the negative stereotype.

In a 1998 article in the *Journal of Public Economics*, Patrick Francois argued that such statistical discrimination may explain gender-based earning differences. He supposes that when men and women form households they can either reap the benefits of household trade with one person staying at home while the other works, or hire outsiders to do those jobs, for example, a nanny or cleaning service. The question he then examines is: How does this affect efficiency wages that might be paid to men or women? Suppose that employers believe (rightly or wrongly) that women's partners are more likely to be working as

well. When those employers set wages, they set them high enough to make those workers wish to expend effort in their jobs rather than shirk and risk being fired. However, for a person with a partner at home, the costs of being fired are greater – the family loses all its household income. This means that an employer can pay that worker a lower efficiency wage.

The consequence of this is that, if employers believe that it is more likely that men have partners at home than women do, and it is hard for them to observe this for individuals prior to hiring, then men will be less risky to hire than women. This means that women will have less chance of being hired in high-paying efficiency-wage jobs.

Statistical discrimination based on asymmetric information can explain why earnings differentials between different groups arise, even if there is competition between firms and there are no intrinsic differences between workers from distinct groups. As such, it can rationalise policies of affirmative action designed to redress negative stereotypes.

Problems of asymmetric information occur in a variety of markets. We discuss asymmetric information and the economic issues that it raises in detail in chapter 23.

Why is it hard to establish whether a group of workers is being discriminated against? Explain how profit-maximising firms tend to eliminate discriminatory wage differentials. How might a discriminatory wage differential persist?

Conclusion

In competitive markets, workers earn a wage equal to the value of their marginal contribution to the production of goods and services. There are, however, many things that affect the value of the marginal product. Firms pay more for workers who are more talented, more diligent, more experienced and more educated because these workers are more productive. Firms might also pay more to workers who are members of unions. In the absence of complete information, firms may give workers more pay to attract those of high ability or motivate them to work hard. Firms pay less to those workers against whom customers discriminate. They pay them less because these workers contribute less to revenue.

The theory of the labour market we have developed in the last two chapters explains why some workers earn higher wages than other workers. The theory does not say that the resulting distribution of income is equitable, fair or desirable in any way. That is the topic we take up in chapter 21.

Summary

- Workers earn different wages for many reasons. To some extent, wage differentials compensate workers for job attributes. Other things being equal, workers in hard, unpleasant jobs get paid more than workers in easy, pleasant jobs.

- Workers with more human capital get paid more than workers with less human capital. The return to accumulating human capital is high and has increased over the past decade.

- Although years of education, experience and job characteristics affect earnings as theory predicts, there is much variation in earnings that cannot be explained by things that economists can measure. The unexplained variation in earnings is largely attributable to natural ability, effort and chance.

- Some economists have suggested that better educated workers earn higher wages not because education raises productivity but because workers with high natural ability use education as a way to signal their high ability to employers. If this signalling theory were correct, then increasing the educational attainment of all workers would not raise the overall level of wages.

- Whether a workforce is unionised or not can have an impact on wages. Unions can act like a monopolist in the labour market, restricting employment to raise wages. However, unlike product market monopolists, unions might be concerned about the lost employment. Such concern limits their ability to control wages.

- When a union negotiates with a single firm – a monopsonist – we have a situation called bilateral monopoly. Resulting negotiations over wages and work conditions are likely to lead to agreements on the possibilities frontier. However, where on the frontier the union and management end up depends on their relative bargaining power.

- Efficiency wages can explain why workers earn above-equilibrium wages. According to this theory, firms find it profitable to pay wages above the equilibrium level. High wages can improve worker health, lower worker turnover, increase worker effort and raise worker quality.

- Some differences in earnings are attributable to discrimination on the basis of race, sex or other factors. Measuring the amount of discrimination is difficult, however, because one must correct for differences in human capital and job characteristics.

- Competitive markets tend to limit the impact of discrimination on wages. If the wages of a group of workers are lower than those of another group for reasons not related to marginal productivity, then non-discriminatory firms will be more profitable than discriminatory firms. Profit-maximising behaviour, therefore, can act to reduce discriminatory wage differentials. Discrimination can persist in competitive markets if customers are willing to pay more to discriminatory firms or if the government passes laws requiring firms to discriminate.

Key concepts

bilateral monopoly	discrimination	possibilities frontier
collective bargaining	efficiency wages	strike
compensating differential	human capital	union
	monopsony	

Questions for review

1 Why do coalminers get paid more than other workers with similar amounts of education?
2 In what sense is education a type of capital?
3 How might education raise a worker's wage without raising the worker's productivity?
4 What limits a union's ability to exercise monopoly power over wages?
5 Why is it unlikely the parties in a bilateral monopoly will agree to outcomes inside the possibilities frontier?
6 What claims do advocates of unions make to argue that unions are good for the economy?
7 Explain four ways in which a firm might increase its profits by raising the wages it pays.
8 What difficulties arise in deciding whether a group of workers has a lower wage because of discrimination?
9 Do the forces of economic competition tend to intensify or reduce discrimination on the basis of race?
10 Give an example of how discrimination might persist in a competitive market.

Problems and applications

1 University students sometimes work during their holidays for private firms or the government in areas relating to their chosen careers. Many of these positions are menial and pay little.
  a What is the opportunity cost of taking such a job?
  b Explain why students are willing to take these low-paying jobs.
  c If you were to compare the earnings later in life of workers who as students had worked at menial jobs in the industry that interested them and those who had taken holiday jobs that paid more, what would you expect to find?
2 A basic finding of labour economics is that workers who have more experience in the labour force are paid more than workers who have less experience but the same amount of formal education. Why might this be so? Some studies have also found that experience at the same job has an extra positive influence on wages. Explain.
3 The wages of university-educated workers dropped during the 1970s, rose in the early 1980s, and then dropped and rose again towards the end of the 1980s. Yet economists believe that the demand for university-educated workers increased fairly steadily during this time. What could explain the pattern of wage changes?
4 Relative to the industrialised countries, developing countries have more unskilled workers and fewer skilled workers. Would you expect the value of skills to be relatively higher or lower in developing countries than in industrialised countries? Explain.
5 At some universities, academics in business-related disciplines receive higher salaries than academics in some other fields.
  a Why might this be true?
  b Some other universities have a policy of paying equal salaries to academics in all fields. At some of these universities, academics in business-related disciplines have lighter teaching loads than academics in some other fields. What role do the differences in teaching loads play?
6 Sara works for Steve, whom she hates because of his snobbish attitude. Yet when she looks for other jobs, the best she can do is find a job paying $10 000 less than her current salary. Should she take the job? Analyse Sara's situation from an economic point of view.

7 When recording devices were first invented almost 100 years ago, musicians could suddenly supply their music to large audiences at low cost. How do you suppose this event affected the income of the best musicians? How do you suppose it affected the income of average musicians?

8 A union and a mining company are negotiating over wages and conditions. The mining company would like to run the mine over a longer period of the day. This would require 10 miners to work at night. The company argues that the increased productivity would result in $100 000 additional yearly profits for the firm. The miners, however, believe that being able to work during the day rather than at night is worth about $8000 a year to each. This is the value of being able to spend more time with their families.

   a What will happen in negotiations over night work? Can the company convince the union to accept this?

   b How would your answer change if the relative value of day work was $12 000 for each miner?

9 Do you think that firms in small towns or cities have more market power in hiring? Do you think that firms generally have more market power in hiring today than 50 years ago or less? How do you think this change over time has affected the role of unions in the economy? Explain.

10 Alan runs a management consulting firm. He hires primarily female economists because, he says, 'they will work for less than comparable men because women have fewer job options'. Is Alan's behaviour admirable or despicable? If more employers were like Alan, what would happen to the wage differential between men and women?

11 Suppose that all of the difference in earnings between Indigenous workers and other Australian workers could be attributed to the difference in years of schooling and school quality. Would this imply that discrimination plays no role in the difference in earnings across racial groups? Why or why not?

12 Suppose that all young women were channelled into careers as secretaries, nurses and teachers; at the same time, young men were encouraged to consider these three careers and many others as well.

   a Draw a diagram showing the combined labour market for secretaries, nurses and teachers. Draw a diagram showing the combined labour market for all other fields. In which market is the wage higher? Do men or women receive higher wages on average?

   b Now suppose that society changed and encouraged both young women and young men to consider a wide range of careers. Over time, what effect would this change have on the wages in the two markets you illustrated in part (a)? What effect would the change have on the average wages of men and women?

13 This chapter considers the economics of discrimination by employers, customers and governments. Now consider discrimination by workers. Suppose that some brunette workers did not like working with blonde workers. Do you think this worker discrimination could explain lower wages for blonde workers? If such a wage differential existed, what would a profit-maximising entrepreneur do? If there were many such entrepreneurs, what would happen over time?

Search me!

When accessing information about economics use the following keywords in any combinations you require:

- efficiency wages
- human capital

CourseMate

For more multimedia resources and activities on economics, visit the Economics CourseMate website.

21

Income inequity and poverty

Learning objectives

In this chapter you will:

- examine the degree of economic inequality in our society
- consider some problems that arise when measuring economic inequality
- see how political philosophers view the government's role in redistributing income
- consider the various policies aimed at helping poor families escape poverty.

'The only difference between the rich and other people is that the rich have more money', Mary Colum the Irish critic and short-story writer, once said to novelist Ernest Hemingway. Maybe so. But this claim leaves many questions unanswered. The gap between rich and poor is a fascinating and important topic of study – for the comfortable rich, for the struggling poor and for the aspiring and worried middle class.

From the previous two chapters you should have some understanding about why different people have different incomes. A person's earnings depend on the supply of and demand for that person's labour, which in turn depend on natural ability, human capital, compensating differentials, union membership, incentive effects, discrimination and so on. Because wages and salaries make up about two-thirds of the total income in the Australian economy, the factors that determine wages are also largely responsible for determining how the economy's total income is distributed among the various members of society. In other words, they determine who is rich and who is poor.

In this chapter we discuss the distribution of income. As we shall see, this topic raises some fundamental questions about the role of economic policy. One of the *Ten Lessons from Economics* in chapter 1 is that governments can sometimes improve market outcomes. This possibility is particularly important when considering the distribution of income. The invisible hand of the marketplace acts to allocate resources efficiently, but it does not necessarily ensure that resources are allocated fairly. As a result, many economists – though not all – believe that the government should redistribute income to achieve greater equality. In doing so, however, the government runs into another of the *Ten Lessons from Economics* – people face trade-offs. When the government introduces policies to make the distribution of income more equitable, it distorts incentives, alters behaviour and makes the allocation of resources less efficient.

Our discussion of the distribution of income proceeds in three steps. First, we assess how much inequality there is in our society. Second, we consider some different views about what role the government should play in altering the distribution of income. Third, we discuss various public policies aimed at helping society's poorest members.

The measurement of inequality

We begin our study of the distribution of income by considering four questions of measurement:

- How much inequality is there in our society?
- How many people live in poverty?
- What problems arise in measuring the amount of inequality?
- How often do people move among income classes?

These measurement questions are the natural starting point from which to discuss public policies aimed at changing the distribution of income.

Australian income inequality

There are various ways to describe the distribution of income in the economy. Table 21.1 presents a particularly simple way. It shows the percentage of households that fall into each of nine income categories. You can use this table to find where your household lies in the income distribution.

For examining differences in the income distribution over time or across countries, economists find it more useful to present the income data as in Table 21.2. To see how to interpret this table, consider

Table 21.1 Distribution of income in Australia, 2007–08	
Gross weekly income	% of households
Under $199	2.15
$200–$399	10.70
$400–$599	10.18
$600–$799	9.10
$800–$999	7.43
$1000–$1199	7.32
$1200–$1599	13.73
$1600–$1999	11.03
$2000–$2499	10.20
$2500 and over	18.16

Source: Australian Bureau of Statistics, Cat. No. 6523.0, 2007–08.

Table 21.2 Income inequity in Australia					
Year	Bottom fifth	Second fifth	Third fifth	Fourth fifth	Top fifth
1999–2000	3.8	9.0	15.0	23.8	48.5
1994–95	3.6	9.3	15.2	24.0	47.9
1990	4.8	9.7	15.5	23.9	46.2
1986	4.8	9.7	15.9	24.4	45.3
1981–82	4.6	9.8	16.6	24.8	44.2

This table shows the percentage of total before-tax income received by families in each fifth of the income distribution.

Sources: *Income Distribution, Australia, 1999–2000*, ABS 6523.0; Income Distribution, Australia, various (ABS 6523.0) in 'Are incomes becoming more unequal? Are real incomes rising?' Parliament of Australia, Current Issues Brief 15, 1999–2000, and United Nations University, World Institute for Development Economics Research (2004).

the following thought experiment. Imagine that you lined up all the families in the economy according to their annual income. Then you divided the families into five equal groups: the bottom fifth, the second fifth, the middle fifth, the fourth fifth and the top fifth. Next you calculated the share of total income that each group of families received. In this way, you could produce the numbers in Table 21.2.

These numbers give us a way of gauging how the economy's total income is distributed. If income were equally distributed across all families, each one-fifth of families would receive one-fifth

(20 per cent) of income. If all income were concentrated among just a few families, the top fifth would receive 100 per cent and the other fifths would receive 0 per cent. The actual economy, of course, is between these two extremes. The table shows that in 1999–2000 the bottom fifth of all families received 3.8 per cent of all income and the top fifth of all families received 48.5 per cent of all income. In other words, even though the top and bottom fifths include the same number of families, the top fifth has more than 10 times as much income as the bottom fifth.

Table 21.2 also shows the distribution of income in various years beginning in 1981–82. At first glance, the distribution of income appears to have been stable. Over this time, the bottom fifth of families has received about 4 per cent to 5 per cent of income and the top fifth has received about 40 per cent to 44 per cent of income. Closer inspection of the table reveals a trend in the degree of inequality. From 1981 to 2000, the share of the bottom fifth fell from 4.6 per cent to 3.8 per cent and the share of the top fifth rose from 44.2 per cent to 48.5 per cent.

In chapter 20 we discussed some of the reasons for this increase in inequality. Increases in international trade with low-wage countries and changes in technology have tended to reduce the demand for unskilled labour and raise the demand for skilled labour. As a result, the wages of unskilled workers have fallen relative to the wages of skilled workers and this change in relative wages has increased inequality in family incomes.

IN THE NEWS . . .

EMPLOYMENT PROSPECTS FOR INDIGENOUS AUSTRALIANS

Indigenous Australians are one of our most disadvantaged groups. Official unemployment among Indigenous Australians is approximately three times higher than for the rest of the population. But research from the 1990s showed that unofficial unemployment is much higher. This article looks at the gap between official and real unemployment. While the research is almost 20 years old, and the CDEP scheme discussed in the article has been operating for more than 30 years, there has been little (if any) improvement since the article was written.

Indigenous and invisible
by Mark Davis

Aborigines are the most disadvantaged group in the Australian labour market. Their real rate of unemployment is 34 per cent – and expected to rise to 48 per cent by 2006.

It has been called a demographic time bomb ticking away in Australia's Aboriginal and Torres Strait Islander communities.

While the Australian population as a whole is rapidly ageing, the reverse is true for the country's indigenous population, a fact with profound implications for the welfare of Aboriginal Australians.

Aborigines are already the most disadvantaged group in the Australian labour market.

In 1996, the latest available statistics, Aboriginal unemployment stood at 23 per cent.

But the real unemployment rate for the indigenous population – when those in work-for-the-dole programs were included – was 34 per cent.

It was figures like these which prompted the Workplace Relations Minister, Peter Reith, to warn the Prime Minister, John Howard, last December that Aborigines were in danger of being permanently marginalised from the labour market, with high social costs.

Yet as bad as the current Aboriginal unemployment numbers are, on the Federal Government's own policy settings for indigenous labour market programs they are set to get much worse.

Recent demographic research shows that the Aboriginal working-age population is growing more than twice as fast as the non-indigenous working-age population.

>>

And with the Government winding back growth in the main Aboriginal labour market program, the number of new jobs created for Aborigines is not expected to keep pace with population growth.

A report by the Australian National University's Centre for Aboriginal Economic Policy Research estimates that 64 000 young Aborigines will reach working age over the decade from 1996 to 2006.

This will boost the size of the indigenous workforce by 28 per cent, compared with expected growth in the entire labour force of 11.6 per cent over the same period.

The authors of the ANU report – Dr John Taylor and Dr Boyd Hunter, two of the country's leading experts on Aboriginal labour-market programs – forecast that on current trends the official Aboriginal unemployment rate will reach 28 per cent by 2006.

They estimate that the real unemployment rate will reach a chilling 48 per cent in 2006 (when Aborigines in work-for-the-dole programs are classed as unemployed, consistent with the treatment of non-Aborigines in similar programs).

These are difficult figures to comprehend. To grasp the magnitude of the unemployment problem in Australia's 390 000-strong indigenous population, project the statistics across the whole of the Australian population – then the jobless figure would stand at around 4.5 million.

The grim outlook for Aboriginal labour-market outcomes stems from three factors: Demographics, disadvantage and discrimination.

The demographic trend reflects their relatively high birth rates, coupled with a relatively low life expectancy.

According to demographers Dr Habtemariam Tesfaghiorghis and Dr Alan Gray, virtually all population growth in the Aboriginal community from the 1980s into the new millennium will be concentrated in the 15- to 64-year-old working-age bracket.

'The implications in terms of employment have been shown to be enormous,' they wrote in one of the first research papers to identify the looming demographic shift in the Aboriginal population.

And while demography boosts the number of Aborigines entering the workforce, disadvantage makes it difficult for them to find jobs.

Aborigines are disadvantaged on virtually all the dimensions affecting people's chances of prospering in the labour market – health, education, training, vocational skills and work experience, all the elements making up what economists call the 'human capital' that individuals bring to the labour market.

In labour-market terms, Aborigines also suffer from so-called 'locational disadvantage' – they are relatively concentrated in remote areas and country towns where there are few jobs.

The 1996 census shows that only 30 per cent of the indigenous population live in major urban areas, compared with 63 per cent of the total Australian population.

Then there is the reality of discrimination against Aborigines.

Sophisticated econometric analysis has shown that locational and human-capital disadvantages do not fully account for the poor labour-market outcomes experienced by Aborigines.

A University of Canberra economist, Dr Anne Daly, analysed data from the 1986 census and found that the probability of working-age Aboriginal males being in jobs was 35 percentage points lower than for non-Aboriginal males.

However, her statistical analysis showed that only 7 percentage points of this 35-point gap could be explained by the differences between the two groups in education, age, marital status, location and language.

In a second study, using data from the 1991 census, Daly compared earnings of Aborigines and non-Aborigines in full-time jobs. After allowing for the effect of differences in 'human capital', she still found that Aboriginal males earned 9 per cent less than their non-Aboriginal counterparts.

A recent paper by ANU's Jeff Borland and Boyd Hunter, using data collected in 1994, found that some of the unexplained disparity in labour-market outcomes could be accounted for by the higher arrest rates among Aborigines.

But Borland and Hunter's statistical analysis still concluded that about two-thirds of the difference in employment-to-population rates resulted from different treatment rather than different attributes.

Peter Reith is concerned about the ability of labour-market 'insiders' – people already in secure jobs – to negotiate wages and employment costs up to levels that bar unemployed 'outsiders' from getting jobs.

Aborigines may well be the ultimate labour-market outsiders in Australia.

Yet despite the magnitude of the problem, Aborigines have been largely invisible in the public debate over unemployment. This is because the monthly 'headline' labour-force statistics do not measure labour-market outcomes for Aborigines, leaving the five-yearly census as the only reliable source of data.

In a letter to Howard in December, Reith identified Aborigines as one of the groups needing tailored government assistance.

'It is clear that the present labour-market programs are not providing satisfactory outcomes,' Reith wrote of indigenous unemployment.

He plans to visit Aboriginal communities to discuss the issue and has asked his department to prepare a report on indigenous employment initiatives.

Whether this produces any shift in the Government's approach to indigenous labour-market issues remains to be seen. The reality is that since coming to office, the Government's main policy change in this area has worsened the indigenous employment problem.

Since 1996 the Government has significantly slowed down the rate of expansion in a key Aboriginal labour-market program, the Community Development Employment Projects (CDEP).

CDEP is a work-for-the-dole or 'workfare' scheme in which unemployment and welfare benefits formerly paid to individual Aborigines are instead pooled and paid to local Aboriginal community groups. These funds are then used to pay wages to individuals for working on projects such as infrastructure construction and in ventures including tourism, contracting, retailing, and textile and artefact production.

CDEP was established by the Fraser Government in 1977. It grew dramatically in the late 1980s and early 1990s. At the time of the 1996 census it accounted for around 12 000 of the 82 000 Aborigines officially classified as being in employment.

But once the Howard Government came to office in 1996, it halted the expansion of CDEP and only funded so-called 'natural growth' in the number of places in the scheme.

In last year's Budget, the Government rejected calls by the Aboriginal and Torres Strait Islander Commission to fund an extra 3200 places by 2001–02.

The Government's lack of enthusiasm defies a glowing report on the program by the former chief of Australia's peak employer group, Ian Spicer.

Commissioned by the Government to review CDEP, Spicer concluded: 'Across Australia CDEP has been critical to developing an improved sense of pride in community and culture, and has provided the basis for acquiring greater skills, employment and enterprise development resulting in ongoing social and economic growth.

'In each of the regions where CDEP exists it has made a significant contribution to addressing the unemployment situation of indigenous people. It has, in recent years, been responsible for two-thirds of the jobs created for indigenous Australians.'

The Government's attitude, together with the secular trend for reduced employment growth in the public sector, throws the burden of Aboriginal job creation onto the private sector.

ATSIC has recently forged new links between its labour-market and training programs and private sector employers such as Rio Tinto and Pasminco.

But ANU's John Taylor and Boyd Hunter argue that the major policy hurdle in promoting private-sector employment of Aborigines is geography.

'This is because the majority of indigenous people remain widely scattered across non-metropolitan regions, while new business activity and growth in private-sector employment is increasingly focused on a few mega-metropolitan areas.'

Source: Mark Davis/*Australian Financial Review*,
29 March 1999.

474

Over the past several decades, there has been a dramatic change in women's roles in the Australian economy. The percentage of married women who hold jobs has risen from about 12 per cent in the 1950s to around 70 per cent in the late 2000s. As full-time homemakers have become less common, a woman's earnings have become a more important determinant of the total income of a typical family.

Although the women's movement has led to more equality between men and women regarding access to education and jobs, it has also led to less equality in family incomes. The reason is that the rise in women's labour force participation has not been the same across all income groups. In particular, the women's movement has had its greatest impact on younger women and women from high-income households. Married women over 50 years old are much less likely to have a job than younger married women. Women from low-income households have long had high rates of participation in the labour force, even in the 1950s, and their behaviour has changed much less.

In this sense, the women's movement has changed the behaviour of the partners of high-income men. In the 1950s, a male executive or doctor was likely to marry a woman who would stay at home and raise the children. Today, the partner of a male executive or doctor is more likely to be an executive or doctor herself. The result is that rich households have become even richer, a pattern that raises inequality in family incomes.

As this example shows, there are social as well as economic determinants of the distribution of

Equality for women has meant less equality for family incomes

Source: iStockphoto/Jacob Wackerhausen.

income. Moreover, the simplistic view that 'income inequality is bad' can be misleading. Increasing the opportunities available to women was a good change for society, even if one effect was greater inequality in family incomes. When evaluating any change in the distribution of income, policymakers must look at the reasons for that change before deciding whether it presents a problem for society.

How does the amount of income inequality in Australia compare with that in other countries? This question is interesting, but answering it is problematic. Not every country in the world collects data in the same way; for example, some countries collect data on individual incomes, whereas other countries collect data on family incomes. As a result, data from one country may not be strictly comparable with data from another. Whenever we find a difference between two countries, we can never be sure whether it reflects a true difference in the economies or merely a difference in the way data are collected.

With this warning in mind, consider Table 21.3, which compares the income distribution of

Australia with that of eight other countries. The countries are ranked from the most equitable to the most inequitable. On the top of the list is Japan, where the richest fifth of the population has income only about three times that of the poorest fifth. On the bottom of the list is Brazil, where the richest fifth has income more than 25 times that of the poorest fifth. Although all countries have substantial inequality in income, the degree of inequality is not the same everywhere.

When countries are ranked by inequality, Australia ends up in the middle of the pack. The poorest fifth of the Australian population earns 3.8 per cent of total income, compared with 10.6 per cent in Japan and 2.45 per cent in Brazil.

The income distribution of Australia is almost the same as the income distribution in the United States. The similarity in the economic systems of these two countries is reflected in a similar distribution of income.

Table 21.3 Income inequality around the world

Country	Bottom fifth	Second fifth	Third fifth	Fourth fifth	Top fifth
Japan	10.6	14.2	17.6	22.0	35.7
South Korea	7.5	12.9	17.4	22.9	39.3
United Kingdom	6.6	11.3	15.9	22.4	43.8
China	5.9	10.2	15.1	22.2	46.6
New Zealand	2.7	10.0	16.3	24.1	46.9
Australia	3.8	9.0	15.0	23.8	48.5
United States	3.6	8.9	14.8	23.0	49.6
Malaysia	4.2	8.0	12.4	20.1	55.3
Brazil	2.4	5.6	9.4	16.8	65.7

This shows the percentage of total before-tax income received by families in each fifth of the income distribution.

Source: United Nations University, World Institute for Development Economics Research, World Income Inequality Database (WIID2 beta).

The poverty rate

A commonly used gauge of the distribution of income is the **poverty rate**. The poverty rate is the percentage of the population whose family income falls below an absolute level called the **poverty line**. Although there are many ways of measuring the poverty line, the most commonly used approach in Australia is that defined by the Commission of Inquiry into Poverty – or Henderson Commission – conducted in 1975. This measure was initially set at 56.5 per cent of average weekly earnings. This line is adjusted every year to account for changes in average earnings and it depends on family size. For instance, in 1973, the poverty line was set at $62.70 for a family consisting of two adults and two children. In 2008, the poverty line for such families was $710.14 per week.

To get some idea about what the poverty rate tells us, consider the data for 1972–73. In that year, the typical family had an income of about $111 per week and the poverty line for a family of four was $62.70. The poverty rate was 8.2 per cent. In other words, 8.2 per cent of the population were members of families with incomes below the poverty line for their family size.

The poverty rate has been rising over time. In 1981–82, the poverty rate was 9.2 per cent, rising to 12.8 per cent in 1989–90. Despite continued growth in average income, the poverty rate has drifted

poverty rate
the percentage of the population whose family income falls below an absolute level called the poverty line

poverty line
an absolute level of income set by the federal government for each family size below which a family is deemed to be in poverty

▸ poverty line

Table 21.4 Poverty rates for income units, 1990 and 2000		
	Below the before-housing half average income poverty line (Henderson equivalence scale)	
Income unit type	1990	2000
All units	11.3%	13.0%
Single people	13.7	18.3
Aged 15–24	16.2	15.9
25–49	9.2	11.5
50–64	10.6	11.5
65+	7.3	11.2
Couples without children	6.6	6.4
Couples with children	10.4	12.2
Sole one-parents with children	28.0	21.4

Source: Ann Harding, Rachel Lloyd & Harry Greenwell, Financial Disadvantage in Australia 1990 to 2000: The persistence of poverty in a decade of growth, NATSEM National Centre for Social and Economic Modelling, University of Canberra.

upwards to some extent. This lack of progress in reducing poverty in recent years is closely related to the increasing inequality we saw in Table 21.2. Although economic growth has raised the income of the typical family, the increase in inequality has prevented the poorest families from gaining an equal share in this greater economic prosperity.

Poverty is an economic malady that affects all groups within the population, but it does not affect all groups with equal frequency. Table 21.4 shows the poverty rates for types of family units. It reveals that poverty is related to the number of earners in a household and to age. In addition, it is well known that Indigenous Australians are much more likely to be poor, as are single mothers.

Problems in measuring inequality

Although data on the income distribution and the poverty rate help to give us some idea about the degree of inequality in our society, interpreting these data is not as straightforward as it might first appear. The data are based on households' annual incomes. What people care about, however, is not their incomes but their ability to maintain a good standard of living. For various reasons, data on the income distribution and the poverty rate give an incomplete picture of inequality in living standards. We examine these reasons below.

Expenditure-based versus income-based measures

In Australia, the poverty line is based on income. A better measure, some say, would be expenditure-based, providing a direct measure of living standards. This is done in the United States. There the poverty line is set at roughly three times the cost of providing an adequate diet. This line is adjusted every year to account for changes in the level of prices and, as in Australia, it is based on family size. However, the collection of data on expenditure is a difficult exercise and its use is the subject of considerable controversy.

The economic life cycle

Incomes vary predictably over people's lives. A young worker, especially one at university, has a low income. Income rises as the worker gains maturity and experience, peaks at around age 50, and then falls sharply when the worker retires at around age 65. This regular pattern of income variation is called the **life cycle**.

Because people can borrow and save to smooth out life cycle changes in income, their standard of living in any year depends more on lifetime income than on that year's income. The young often borrow, perhaps to buy a house or car, and then repay the majority of the loan later when their incomes rise. People have their highest saving rates when they are middle-aged. Because people can save in anticipation of retirement, for example, through superannuation, the large declines in incomes at retirement need not lead to similar declines in the standard of living.

This normal life cycle pattern causes inequality in the distribution of annual income, but it does not represent true inequality in living standards. To gauge the inequality of living standards in our society, the distribution of lifetime incomes is more relevant than the distribution of annual incomes. Unfortunately, data on lifetime incomes are not readily available. When looking at any data on inequality, however, it is important to keep the life cycle in mind. Because a person's lifetime income smoothes out the highs and lows of the life cycle, lifetime incomes are more evenly distributed across the population than are annual incomes.

life cycle
the regular pattern of income variation over a person's life

Transitory versus permanent income

Incomes vary over people's lives not only because of predictable life cycle variation but also because of random and transitory forces. One year disease kills off the South Australian grape crop and South Australian vineyards see their incomes fall temporarily. At the same time, the South Australian disease drives up the price of wine and Victorian vineyards see their incomes temporarily rise. The next year the reverse might happen.

Just as people can borrow and lend to smooth out life cycle variation in income, they can also borrow and lend to smooth out transitory variation in income. When Victorian vineyards experience a good year, they would be foolish to spend all of their additional income. Instead, they save some of it, knowing that their good fortune is unlikely to persist. Similarly, the South Australian vineyards respond to their temporarily low incomes by drawing on their savings or by borrowing. To the extent that a family saves and borrows to buffer itself from transitory changes in income, these changes do not affect its standard of living. A family's ability to buy goods and services depends largely on its **permanent income**, which is its normal, or average, income.

permanent income
a person's normal income

To gauge inequality of living standards, the distribution of permanent income is more relevant than the distribution of annual income. Although permanent income is hard to measure, it is an important concept. Because permanent income excludes transitory changes in income, permanent income is more evenly distributed than is current income.

Economic mobility

People sometimes speak of 'the rich' and 'the poor' as if these groups consisted of the same families year after year. In fact, this is not at all the case. Economic mobility, the movement of people among income classes, is substantial in modern economies. Movements up the income ladder can be due to good luck or hard work and movements down the ladder can be due to bad luck or laziness. Some of this mobility reflects transitory variation in income, while some reflects more persistent changes in income.

Because economic mobility is so great, many of those below the poverty line are there only temporarily. Poverty is a long-term problem for relatively few families. In a typical 10-year period, about one in four families falls below the poverty line in at least one year. Yet fewer than 3 per cent of families are poor for eight or more years. Because it is likely that the temporarily poor and the persistently poor face different problems, policies that aim to combat poverty need to distinguish between these groups.

Another way to gauge economic mobility is the persistence of economic success from generation to generation. Andrew Leigh, who has studied this topic in Australia, finds substantial mobility. If a father earns 10 per cent above his generation's average income, his son will most likely earn 2–3 per cent above his generation's average income. Australia appears to be more socially mobile than the United States, but not as socially mobile as the Scandinavian countries.

What does the poverty rate measure? Describe three potential problems in interpreting the measured poverty rate.

The political philosophy of redistributing income

We have just seen how the economy's income is distributed and have discussed some of the problems encountered in interpreting measured inequality. We now turn to the policy question: What should the government do about economic inequality?

This question is not just about economics. Economic analysis alone cannot tell us whether policymakers should try to make our society more egalitarian. Our views on this question are, to a large extent, a matter of political philosophy. Yet because the government's role in redistributing income is central to so many debates over economic policy, here we digress from economic science to consider a bit of political philosophy.

Utilitarianism

utilitarianism
the political philosophy according to which the government should choose policies to maximise the total utility of everyone in society

A prominent school of thought in political philosophy is **utilitarianism**. The founders of utilitarianism are the English philosophers Jeremy Bentham (1748–1832) and John Stuart Mill (1806–73). To a large extent, the goal of utilitarians is to apply the logic of individual decision making to questions concerning morality and public policy.

utility
a measure of happiness or satisfaction

The starting point of utilitarianism is the notion of **utility** – the level of happiness or satisfaction that people receive from their circumstances. Utility is a measure of wellbeing and, according to utilitarians, is the ultimate objective of all public and private actions. The proper goal of the government, they claim, is to maximise the sum of utility of everyone in society.

The utilitarian case for redistributing income is based on the assumption of *diminishing marginal utility*. It seems reasonable that an extra dollar of income to a poor person provides that person with more additional utility than does an extra dollar to a rich person. In other words, as a person's income rises, the extra wellbeing derived from an additional dollar of income falls. This plausible assumption, together with the utilitarian goal of maximising total utility, implies that the government should try to achieve a more equitable distribution of income.

The argument is simple. Imagine that Peter and Paul are the same, except that Peter earns $80 000 and Paul earns $20 000. In this case, taking a dollar from Peter to pay Paul will reduce Peter's utility and raise Paul's utility. But, because of diminishing marginal utility, Peter's utility falls by less than Paul's utility rises. Thus, this redistribution of income raises total utility, which is the utilitarian's objective.

At first, this utilitarian argument might seem to imply that the government should continue to redistribute income until everyone in society has exactly the same income. Indeed, that would be the case if the total amount of income – $100 000 in our example – were fixed. But, in fact, it is not. Utilitarians reject complete equalisation of incomes because they accept one of the *Ten Lessons from Economics* presented in chapter 1 – people respond to incentives.

To take from Peter to pay Paul, the government must pursue policies that redistribute income, such as the Australian income tax and social security system. Under these policies, people with high incomes pay high taxes and people with low incomes receive income transfers. Yet, as we have seen in chapters 8 and 12, taxes distort incentives and cause deadweight losses. If the government takes away additional income a person might earn through higher income taxes or reduced transfers, both Peter and Paul have less incentive to work hard. As they work less, society's income falls and so does total utility. The utilitarian government has to balance the gains from greater equality against the losses from distorted incentives. To maximise total utility, therefore, the government stops short of making society fully egalitarian.

A famous parable sheds light on the utilitarian's logic. Imagine that Peter and Paul are thirsty travellers trapped at different places in the desert. Peter's oasis has much water; Paul's has little. If the government could transfer water from one oasis to the other without cost, it would maximise total utility from water by equalising the amount in the two places. But suppose that the government has only a leaky bucket. As it tries to move water from one place to the other, some of the water is lost in transit. In this case, a utilitarian government might still try to move some water from Peter to Paul, depending on how thirsty Paul is and how leaky the bucket is. But, with only a leaky bucket at its disposal, a utilitarian government will not try to reach complete equality.

Liberalism

A second way of thinking about inequality might be called *liberalism*. American philosopher John Rawls develops this view in his book *A Theory of Justice*. This book was first published in 1971 and it quickly became a classic in political philosophy.

Rawls begins with the premise that a society's institutions, laws and policies should be just. He then takes up the natural question: How can we, the members of society, ever agree on what justice means? It might seem that every person's point of view is inevitably based on his or her particular circumstances – whether he or she is talented or less talented, diligent or lazy, educated or less educated, born to a wealthy family or a poor one. Could we ever objectively determine what a just society would be?

To answer this question, Rawls proposes the following thought experiment. Imagine that before any of us is born, we all get together for a meeting to design the rules that govern society. At this point, we are all ignorant about the station in life each of us will end up filling. In Rawls's words, we are sitting in an 'original position' behind a 'veil of ignorance'. In this original position, Rawls argued, we can choose a just set of rules for society because we must consider how those rules will affect every person. As Rawls puts it: 'Since all are similarly situated and no one is able to design principles to favor his particular conditions, the principles of justice are the result of fair agreement or bargain'. Designing public policies and institutions in this way allows us to be objective about what policies are just.

Rawls then considers what public policy designed behind this veil of ignorance would try to achieve. In particular, he considers what income distribution a person would consider just if that person did not know whether he or she would end up at the top, bottom or middle of the distribution. Rawls argues that a person in the original position would be especially concerned about the possibility of being at the bottom of the income distribution. In designing public policies, therefore, we should aim to raise the welfare of the worst-off person in society. That is, rather than maximising the sum of everyone's utility, as a utilitarian would do, Rawls would maximise the minimum utility. Rawls's rule is called the **maximin criterion**.

Because the maximin criterion emphasises the least fortunate person in society, it justifies public policies aimed at equalising the distribution of income. By transferring income from the rich to the poor, society raises the wellbeing of the least fortunate. The maximin criterion would not, however, lead to a completely egalitarian society. If the government promised to equalise incomes completely, people would have no incentive to work hard, society's total income would fall substantially and the least fortunate person would be worse off. Thus, the maximin criterion still allows disparities in income, because such disparities can improve incentives and thereby raise society's ability to help the poor. Nonetheless, because Rawls's philosophy puts weight on only the least fortunate members of society, it calls for more income redistribution than does utilitarianism.

Rawls's views are controversial, but the thought experiment he proposes has much appeal. In particular, this thought experiment allows us to consider the redistribution of income as a form of social insurance. That is, from the perspective of the original position behind the veil of ignorance, income redistribution is like an insurance policy. Homeowners insure their houses to protect themselves from the risk of their houses burning down. Similarly, when we as a society choose policies that tax the rich to supplement the incomes of the poor, we are all insuring ourselves against the possibility that we might have been a member of a poor family. Because people dislike risk, we should be happy to have been born into a society that provides us with this insurance.

It is not at all clear, however, that rational people behind the veil of ignorance would truly be so averse to risk as to follow the maximin criterion. Indeed, because a person in the original position might end up anywhere in the distribution of outcomes, he or she might treat all possible outcomes equally when designing public policies. In this case, the best policy behind the veil of ignorance would be to maximise the average utility of members of society and the resulting notion of justice would be more utilitarian than **Rawlsianism** suggests.

Libertarianism

A third view of inequality is called **libertarianism**. The two views we have considered so far – utilitarianism and the maximin criterion – both view the total income of society as a shared resource that a social planner can freely redistribute to achieve some social goal. In contrast, libertarians argue that society itself earns no income – only individual members of society earn income. According to

maximin criterion
the claim that the government should aim to maximise the wellbeing of the worst-off person in society

Rawlsianism
the political philosophy according to which the government should choose policies deemed to be just, as evaluated by an impartial observer behind a 'veil of ignorance'

libertarianism
the political philosophy according to which the government should punish crimes and enforce voluntary agreements but not redistribute income

libertarians, the government should not take from some individuals and give to others in order to achieve any particular distribution of income

For instance, philosopher Robert Nozick writes the following in his famous 1974 book, *Anarchy, State and Utopia*:

> We are not in the position of children who have been given portions of pie by someone who now makes last minute adjustments to rectify careless cutting. There is no central distribution, no person or group entitled to control all the resources, jointly deciding how they are to be doled out. What each person gets, he gets from others who give to him in exchange for something, or as a gift. In a free society, diverse persons control different resources, and new holdings arise out of the voluntary exchanges and actions of persons.

Whereas utilitarians and supporters of Rawls try to judge what amount of inequality is desirable in a society, Nozick denies the validity of this very question.

The libertarian alternative to evaluating economic outcomes is to evaluate the process by which these outcomes arise. When the distribution of income is achieved unfairly – for instance, when one person steals from another – the government has the right and duty to remedy the problem. But, as long as the process determining the distribution of income is just, the resulting distribution is fair, no matter how unequal.

Nozick criticises Rawls's maximin criterion by drawing an analogy between the distribution of income in society and the distribution of marks in a course. Suppose you were asked to judge the fairness of the marks in the economics course you are now taking. Would you imagine yourself behind a veil of ignorance and choose a distribution without knowing the talents and efforts of each student? Or would you ensure that the process of assigning marks to students is fair without regard for whether the resulting distribution is equal or unequal? In the case of marks at least, the libertarian emphasis on process over outcomes is compelling.

Libertarians conclude that equality of opportunities is more important than equality of incomes. They believe that the government should enforce individual rights to ensure that everyone has the same opportunity to use their talents and achieve success. Once these rules of the game are established, the government has no reason to alter the resulting distribution of income.

Pam earns more than Pauline. Someone proposes taxing Pam in order to supplement Pauline's income. How would a utilitarian, a supporter of Rawls and a libertarian evaluate this proposal?

Policies to reduce poverty

As we have just seen, political philosophers hold various views about what role the government should take in altering the distribution of income. Political debate among the larger population of voters reflects a similar disagreement. Despite these continuing debates, however, most people believe that, at the very least, the government should try to help those most in need. According to a popular metaphor, the government should provide a 'safety net' to prevent any citizen from falling too far.

Poverty is one of the most difficult problems that policymakers face. Poor families are more likely than the overall population to experience homelessness, drug dependency, domestic violence, health problems, teenage pregnancy, illiteracy, unemployment and low educational attainment. Members of poor families are both more likely to commit crimes and more likely to be victims of crimes.

Although it is hard to separate the causes of poverty from the effects, there is no doubt that poverty is associated with various economic and social ills.

Suppose that you were a policymaker in the government and your goal was to reduce the number of people living in poverty. How would you achieve this goal? Here we consider some of the policy options that you might consider. As we shall see, although each of these options does help some people escape poverty none of them is perfect and deciding which is best is not easy.

Minimum-wage laws

Laws setting a minimum or award wage that employers can pay workers are a perennial source of debate. Advocates view the minimum wage as a way of helping the working poor without any cost to the government. Critics view it as hurting those it is intended to help.

The minimum wage is easily understood using the tools of supply and demand, as we first saw in chapter 6. For workers with low levels of skill and experience, a high award wage forces the wage above the level that balances supply and demand. It therefore raises the cost of labour to firms and reduces the quantity of labour that those firms demand. The result is higher unemployment among those groups of workers affected by the award wage. Although those workers who remain employed benefit from a higher wage, those who might have been employed at a lower wage are worse off.

The magnitude of these effects depends crucially on the elasticity of demand. Advocates of a high minimum wage argue that the demand for unskilled labour is relatively inelastic, so that a high minimum wage depresses employment only slightly. Critics of the minimum wage argue that labour demand is more elastic, especially in the long run when firms can adjust employment and production more fully. They also note that many minimum-wage workers are teenagers from middle-class families so that a high minimum wage is imperfectly targeted as a policy for helping the poor. In Australia, several studies have shown that the typical minimum wage worker lives in a household in about the middle of the income distribution.

Social security

One way to raise the living standards of the poor is for the government to supplement their incomes. The primary way in which the government does this is through the social security system. **Social security** is a broad term that encompasses various government programs. It includes unemployment benefits, the aged pension, family assistance allowances and disability payments.

social security
government programs that supplement the incomes of the needy

A common criticism of social security programs is that they create incentives for people to become 'needy'. For example, some of these programs may encourage families to break up, for many families qualify for financial assistance only if one parent is absent. In the United States, critics of the US welfare system argue that some programs may encourage illegitimate births, for many poor, single women qualify for assistance only if they have children. Poor, single-parent households are an important part of the poverty problem in many developed countries. To the extent that some social security programs seem to raise the number of single-parent families, critics of the welfare system assert that these policies exacerbate the very problems they are supposed to cure.

How severe are these potential problems with the social security system? No one knows for sure. Proponents of the social security system point out that being a poor, single parent on unemployment or other benefits is a difficult existence at best and they are sceptical that many people would be encouraged to pursue such a life if it were not thrust upon them. Moreover, trends over time do not support the view that the decline of the two-parent family is a symptom of the social security system, as the system's critics sometimes claim. Since the early 1970s, benefits (adjusted for inflation) have declined, yet the percentage of children living with only one parent has risen.

Negative income tax

Whenever the government chooses a system to collect taxes, it affects the distribution of income. This is clearly true in the case of a progressive income tax, whereby high-income families pay a larger percentage of their income in taxes than do low-income families. As we discussed in chapter 12, equity across income groups is an important criterion in the design of a tax system.

Many economists have advocated supplementing the income of the poor using a **negative income tax**. It has been supported by economists generally identified with the political right, such as Milton Friedman in the United States, as well as economists associated with the political left, such as Nicholas Kaldor in the United Kingdom. According to this policy, every family would report its income to the government. High-income families would pay a tax based on their incomes. Low-income families would receive a subsidy. In other words, they would 'pay' a 'negative tax'.

For example, suppose the government used the following formula to calculate the tax liability of a family:

$$\text{Taxes owed} = (1/3 \text{ of income}) - \$10\,000$$

In this case, a family that earned \$60 000 would pay \$10 000 in taxes and a family that earned \$90 000 would pay \$20 000 in taxes. A family that earned \$30 000 would owe nothing. And a family that earned \$15 000 would 'owe' –\$5000. In other words, the government would send this family a cheque for \$5000.

Under a negative income tax, poor families would receive financial assistance without having to demonstrate need. The only qualification required to receive assistance would be a low income. Depending on one's point of view, this feature can be either an advantage or a disadvantage. On the one hand, a negative income tax does not encourage illegitimate births and the break-up of families, as critics of the social security system believe current policy does. On the other hand, a negative income tax would subsidise those who are just lazy and, in some people's eyes, undeserving of government support.

negative income tax
a tax system that collects revenue from high-income households and gives transfers to low-income households

▸ negative income tax

IN THE NEWS . . .

THINKING INNOVATIVELY ABOUT INCOME REDISTRIBUTION

Housing is a big part of the problems facing families in poverty. But how do you provide housing assistance without creating poverty traps? Two of the authors of this textbook give their suggestion.

Housing lifelines would rescue many
by Joshua Gans and Stephen King

The announcement of a Productivity Commission inquiry into housing affordability

should be welcomed by all. It is precisely because there is a 'blame game' surrounding what makes housing unaffordable that an independent inquiry is needed.

In that regard, media attention has focused on the plight of the first home buyer as housing

>>

prices rise. The image is of a young couple, likely contemplating children, with little savings, staring down the face of a debt burden for the rest of their lives. To them the issue is how to purchase a cheaper home. And, as a matter of simple economics, the only sustainable way to achieve that is to find a way of expanding the housing stock. Working out what governments can do in this regard is clearly worthwhile.

But, outside the gaze of media attention, there are other real affordability problems. One such class is for those households who have never been able to become homeowners. For them, the problem is as much low income as it is a lack of housing.

But affordability can be an issue for households who have already opted for a large mortgage. When incomes and house prices fluctuate, households with a temporary change in circumstances – such as income loss or the need to move cities to find work – find themselves in immediate housing stress. A primary income earner could lose their job or suffer illness and the danger would be that the whole household would have to sell up and move. The loss of income hopefully would only be temporary, but the effect on housing and lifestyle choices, credit rating and family stress would be longer term. Put simply, a short term loss of income could mean foreclosure or eviction, forcing the household to 'start again'. For those households, the issue is how to afford their current home.

Dealing with this type of affordability problem necessitates new thinking beyond issues of the housing stock per se. In our report to the Prime Minister, we proposed a housing lifeline to deal with this. The idea is that when there is a temporary loss of income the government would step into the breach and offer eligible households (with eligibility based on nothing more than an assets means test) a payment to their housing provider – be it a landlord or a lender – to tide them over the rough patch. When the household's income rose again, they would face a slightly higher marginal tax rate for as long as it took to repay the loan. This would operate in much the same way as the HECS system operates today for higher education.

The housing lifeline has several advantages over traditional social security. For one, its main benefit is the removal of anxiety. Even a household that never uses the lifeline knows that it is there and faces less risk as a result. Accessing the lifeline is a choice that rests with the household itself, so that the people best placed to judge the need for temporary assistance are the ones who choose whether or not to use the lifeline. Also, remember that the lifeline is not a handout – it is a debt that has to be repaid. But this avoids any stigma and uncertainty associated with working out eligibility or waiting for rent assistance and other programs aimed at long-term assistance. Only if a household has persistent difficulties is a more interventionist long-term approach desired. Under the housing lifeline, households are empowered by having the option to access temporary assistance that it can use if need be.

The hope is that a policy like the housing lifeline might actually prevent households from turning what was a short-run loss of income into a long-term social security liability. Income-based handouts can have undesirable outcomes, creating high levels of taxation for subsequent income earned. The housing lifeline, by being based on long-term lifetime income avoids such poverty and incentive traps. Thus, it should reduce the number of households who need to access basic social security and public housing programs.

For landlords and investors in housing, the existence of a lifeline changes the risk calculation when providing housing for those with low incomes and high risk. This will open up housing markets to households who are currently excluded due to income variations and risk. Ultimately, the lifeline will alleviate the problems of housing affordability for a wide range of the community.

Source: Joshua Gans & Stephen King/ *Australian Financial Review*, 6 August 2003.

In-kind transfers

Another way to help the poor is to provide them directly with some of the goods and services they need to raise their living standards. For example, charities provide the needy with food, shelter and toys at Christmas. Indeed, in the United States, the government itself is involved in direct provision of goods. For instance, it gives poor families food stamps, which are government vouchers that can be used to buy food at shops; the shops then redeem these vouchers for money.

Is it better to help the poor with these in-kind transfers or with direct cash payments? There is no clear answer.

Advocates of in-kind transfers argue that such transfers ensure that the poor get what they need most. Among the poorest members of society, alcohol and drug addiction is more common than it is in society as a whole. By providing the poor with food and shelter, society can be more confident that it is not helping to support such addictions. This is one reason that in-kind transfers are more politically popular than cash payments to the poor.

Advocates of cash payments argue that in-kind transfers are inefficient and disrespectful. The government does not know what goods and services the poor need most. Many of the poor are ordinary people down on their luck. Despite their misfortune, they are in the best position to decide how to raise their own living standards. Rather than giving the poor in-kind transfers of goods and services that they may not want, it may be better to give them cash and allow them to buy what they think they need most.

Anti-poverty programs and work incentives

Many policies aimed at helping the poor can have the unintended effect of discouraging the poor from escaping poverty on their own. To see why, consider the following example. Suppose that a family needs an income of $15 000 to maintain a reasonable standard of living. And suppose that, out of concern for the poor, the government promises to guarantee every family that income. Whatever a family earns, the government makes up the difference between that income and $15 000. What effect would you expect this policy to have?

The incentive effects of this policy are obvious – any person who would make under $15 000 by working has no incentive to find and keep a job. For every dollar that the person would earn, the government would reduce the income supplement by a dollar. In effect, the government taxes

100 per cent of additional earnings. An effective marginal tax rate of 100 per cent is surely a policy with a large deadweight loss.

The adverse effects of this high effective tax rate can persist over time. People discouraged from working lose the on-the-job training that jobs might offer. In addition, their children miss the lessons learned by observing parents with a full-time job and this may adversely affect their own ability to find and hold a job.

Although the anti-poverty program we have been discussing is hypothetical, it is not as unrealistic as it might first appear. Unemployment benefits and other social security payments are tied to family income as are payments for health insurance through the government's Medicare program. As a family's income rises, the family becomes ineligible for these programs. When all the government programs are taken together, it is common for families to face effective marginal tax rates that are very high. Sometimes the effective marginal tax rates even exceed 100 per cent, so that poor families are worse off when they earn more. By trying to help the poor, the government discourages those families from working. According to critics of anti-poverty programs, these programs alter work attitudes and create a 'culture of poverty'.

It might seem that there is an easy solution to this problem – reduce benefits to poor families more gradually as their incomes rise. For example, if a poor family loses 30 cents of benefits for every dollar it earns, then it faces an effective marginal tax rate of 30 per cent. This effective tax reduces work effort to some extent, but it does not eliminate the incentive to work completely.

The problem with this solution is that it greatly increases the cost of programs to combat poverty. If benefits are phased out gradually as a poor family's income rises, then families just above the poverty level will also be eligible for substantial benefits. The more gradual the phase-out, the greater the number of eligible families and the greater the cost of the program. Thus, policymakers face a trade-off between burdening the poor with high effective marginal tax rates and burdening taxpayers with costly programs to reduce poverty.

List three policies aimed at helping the poor and discuss the pros and cons of each.

Conclusion

People have long reflected on the distribution of income in society. The ancient Greek philosopher Plato concluded that in an ideal society the income of the richest person would be no more than four times the income of the poorest person. Although the measurement of inequality is difficult, it is clear that our society has much more inequality than Plato recommended.

One of the *Ten Lessons from Economics* discussed in chapter 1 is that governments can sometimes improve market outcomes. There is little consensus, however, about how this idea should be applied to the distribution of income. Philosophers and policymakers today do not agree on how much income inequality is desirable, or even whether public policy should aim to alter the distribution of income. Much of public debate reflects this disagreement. Whenever taxes are raised, for instance, lawmakers argue over how much of the tax hike should fall on the rich, the middle class and the poor.

Another of the *Ten Lessons from Economics* is that people face trade-offs. This lesson is important to keep in mind when thinking about economic inequality. Policies that penalize the successful and reward the unsuccessful may reduce the incentive to succeed. Thus, policymakers face a trade-off between equality and efficiency. As the pie is divided more equitably, the smaller it may become. This is the one lesson concerning the distribution of income about which almost everyone agrees.

IN THE NEWS ...

SCHOOL VOUCHERS

One aim of universal education is to shrink the gap between rich and poor. But government-financed education does not require government-run schools.

The market can transform our schools

by *Milton Friedman*

The Supreme Court's voucher decision clears the way for a major expansion of parental school choice. Opponents of choice can no longer use the First Amendment's religious Establishment Clause to attack voucher programs, now that the Supreme Court has declared the Cleveland program constitutionally acceptable even though most voucher recipients went to parochial schools.

The state of Ohio provided vouchers worth up to $2250 to low-income parents in Cleveland who chose to send their children to private schools that charge them tuition of no more than $2500 per child. The voucher was offered as an alternative to government schooling costing nearly three times as much per student. Yet some 4000 low-income parents still found the private alternative preferable – enough so to pay 10 per cent of private school tuition out of their own pockets. What an indictment of government schools.

Most schools that accept vouchers are religious for a simple reason, and one that is easily corrected. That reason is the low value of the voucher. It is not easy, perhaps not possible, to provide a satisfactory education for $2500 per student. Most private schools spend more than that. But parochial schools are able to accept that low voucher amount because they are subsidized by their churches.

Raise the voucher amount to $7000 – the sum that Ohio state and local governments now spend per child in government schools – and make it available to all students, not simply to students from low-income families, and most private schools accepting vouchers would no longer be religious. A host of new nonprofit and for-profit schools would emerge. Voucher-bearing students would then be less dependent on low-tuition parochial schools.

Parents would then truly have a choice, and the quality of schooling – in both public and private schools – would soar as competition worked its magic. This has happened in Milwaukee, where the voucher program has evolved over the past 10 years. Since that program's creation, 37 new schools have opened, nearly two-thirds of them nonreligious.

Assumption of responsibility by government for educating all children does not require that schooling be delivered in government-run institutions – just as government food stamps need not be spent in government grocery stores.

Besides, an emphasis on school choice is not new, even in public programs. The G.I. Bill enacted at the end of World War II demonstrates how well choice can work. That program provided vouchers for higher education – for use in religious and nonreligious institutions – to millions of veterans; it transformed higher education and provided the educational leadership that has

>>

played a major role in political and economic change in the postwar period.

When the G.I. Bill was enacted, doubts were expressed that the colleges could expand rapidly enough to handle the flood of new students. Yet the number of students enrolled in colleges nearly doubled in the two years after the end of the war. The supply expanded to meet the surge in demand.

The market will respond as fully and rapidly to the increased demand for private schools generated by the expansion of vouchers for elementary and secondary education. Private voucher programs, financed by foundations and individuals, plus the limited government programs so far enacted have already brought forth a market response.

School vouchers can push elementary and secondary education out of the 19th century and into the 21st by introducing market competition on a broad scale, just as

competition has made progress possible in every other area of economic and civic life.

The biggest winner from such an educational revolution would be American society as a whole. A better schooled work force promises higher productivity and more rapid economic growth. Even more important, improved education could help narrow the income gap between the less skilled and more skilled workers and would fend off the prospect of a society divided between the haves and have-nots, of a society in which an educated elite provides for a permanent class of unemployables.

Summary

- Data on the distribution of income show wide disparity in our society. The richest fifth of families earns about 10 times as much income as the poorest fifth.
- Because the economic life cycle, transitory income and economic mobility are so important for understanding variation in income, it is difficult to gauge the degree of inequality in our society using data on the distribution of income in a single year. When these factors are taken into account, they tend to suggest that economic wellbeing is more evenly distributed than is annual income.
- Political philosophers differ in their views about the role of government in altering the distribution of income. Utilitarians (such as John Stuart Mill) would choose the distribution of income to maximise the sum of utility of everyone in society. Followers of John Rawls would determine the distribution of income as if we were behind a 'veil of ignorance' that prevented us from knowing our own stations in life. Libertarians (such as Robert Nozick) would have the government enforce individual rights to ensure a fair process but then not be concerned about inequality in the resulting distribution of income.
- Various policies aim to help the poor – minimum-wage laws/award wages, social security and negative income taxes. Although each of these policies helps some families escape poverty, they also have unintended side effects. Because financial assistance declines as income rises, the poor often face effective marginal tax rates that are very high. Such high effective tax rates discourage poor families from escaping poverty on their own.

Key concepts

libertarianism	permanent income	social security
life cycle	poverty line	utilitarianism
maximin criterion	poverty rate	utility
negative income tax	Rawlsianism	

Questions for review

1 Does the richest fifth of the Australian population earn two, four or 10 times the income of the poorest fifth?
2 What groups in the population are most likely to live in poverty?
3 When gauging the amount of inequality, why do transitory and life cycle variations in income cause difficulties?
4 How would a utilitarian, a supporter of John Rawls and a libertarian determine how much income inequality is permissible?
5 What are the pros and cons of in-kind (rather than cash) transfers to the poor?

Problems and applications

1 Table 21.2 shows that income inequality in Australia has increased during the past 20 years. Some factors contributing to this increase were discussed in chapter 20. What are they?

2   Economists often view life cycle variation in income as one form of transitory variation in income around people's lifetime, or permanent, income. In this sense, how does your current income compare with your permanent income? Do you think your current income accurately reflects your standard of living?

3   The chapter suggests that people can use saving and borrowing to smooth out transitory variation in income in order to maintain steady consumption.

   a   What obstacles might prevent such smoothing?

   b   What does this tell you about whether it is appropriate to base measures of income inequality purely on permanent income?

4   Consider two communities. In one community, 10 families have incomes of $100 each and 10 families have incomes of $20 each. In the other community, 10 families have incomes of $200 each and 10 families have incomes of $22 each.

   a   In which community is the distribution of income more inequitable? In which community is the problem of poverty likely to be worse?

   b   Which distribution of income would Rawls prefer? Explain.

   c   Which distribution of income do you prefer? Explain.

5   The chapter uses the analogy of a 'leaky bucket' to explain one constraint on the redistribution of income.

   a   What elements of the Australian system for redistributing income create the leaks in the bucket? Be specific.

   b   In your opinion, which political party, Liberal or Labor, generally has a stronger belief that the bucket used for redistributing income is leaky? How does that belief affect the party's views about the amount of income redistribution that the government should undertake?

6   Suppose there are two possible income distributions in a society of 10 people. In the first distribution, nine people have incomes of $30 000 and one person has an income of $10 000. In the second distribution, all 10 people have incomes of $25 000.

   a   If the society had the first income distribution, what would be the utilitarian argument for redistributing income?

   b   Which income distribution would Rawls consider more equitable? Explain.

   c   Which income distribution would Nozick consider more equitable? Explain.

7   Do you think a person who believes that the government should help poor children but not poor adults would be more likely to advocate cash welfare payments or in-kind transfers?

8   Suppose that a family's tax liability equalled half its income minus $10 000. Under this system, some families would pay taxes to the government and some families would receive money from the government through a 'negative income tax'.

   a   Consider families with pre-tax incomes of $0, $10 000, $20 000, $30 000 and $40 000. Draw up a table showing pre-tax income, taxes paid to the government or money received from the government, and after-tax income for each family.

   b   What is the marginal tax rate in this system? (See chapter 12 if you need to review the definition of marginal tax rate.) What is the maximum amount of income at which a family receives money from the government?

   c   Now suppose that the tax schedule is changed, so that a family's tax liability equals a quarter of its income minus $10 000. What is the marginal tax rate in this new system? What is the maximum amount of income at which a family receives money from the government?

   d   What is the main advantage of each of the tax schedules discussed here?

9   John and Jeremy are both utilitarians. John believes that labour supply is highly elastic, whereas Jeremy believes that labour supply is quite inelastic. How do you suppose their views about income redistribution differ?

10   Consider each of the following statements. Do you agree or disagree? What do your views imply for public policies, such as taxes on inheritance?

   a 'All parents have the right to work hard and save in order to give their children a better life.'

   b 'Children should not be disadvantaged by the sloth or bad luck of their parents.'

Search me!

When accessing information about economics use the following keywords in any combinations you require:

- negative income tax
- poverty line

CourseMate

CourseMate

For more multimedia resources and activities on economics, visit the Economics CourseMate website.

PART SEVEN
Topics for further study

22

The theory of consumer choice

Learning objectives

In this chapter you will:

- see how a budget constraint represents the choices a consumer can afford
- learn how indifference curves can be used to represent a consumer's preferences
- analyse how a consumer's optimum choices are determined
- see how a consumer responds to changes in income and changes in prices
- break down the impact of a price change into an income effect and a substitution effect
- apply the theory of consumer choice to four questions about household behaviour.

When you walk into a shop, you are confronted with thousands of goods that you might buy. Of course, because your financial resources are limited, you cannot buy everything that you want. You therefore consider the prices of the various goods being offered for sale and buy a bundle of goods that, given your resources, best suits your needs and desires.

In this chapter we develop the theory that describes how consumers make decisions about what to buy. So far throughout this book, we have summarised consumers' decisions with the demand curve. As we discussed in chapters 4 to 7, the demand curve for a good reflects consumers' willingness to pay for it. When the price of a good rises, consumers are willing to pay for fewer units, so the quantity demanded falls. We now look more deeply at the decisions that lie behind the demand curve. The theory of consumer choice presented in this chapter provides a more complete understanding of demand, just as the theory of the competitive firm in chapter 14 provides a more complete understanding of supply.

One of the *Ten Lessons from Economics* discussed in chapter 1 is that people face trade-offs. The theory of consumer choice examines the trade-offs that people face in their role as consumers. A consumer who buys more of one good can afford less of other goods. A consumer who spends more time enjoying leisure and less time working has a lower income and can afford less consumption. A consumer who spends more income in the present and saves less of it must accept a lower level of consumption in the future. The theory of consumer choice examines how consumers facing these trade-offs make decisions and how they respond to changes in their environment.

After developing the basic theory of consumer choice, we apply it to several questions about household decisions. In particular, we ask:
- Do all demand curves slope downwards?
- How do wages affect labour supply?
- How do interest rates affect household savings?
- Do the poor prefer to receive cash or in-kind transfers?

At first, these questions might seem unrelated. But, as we will see, we can use the theory of consumer choice to consider each of them.

The budget constraint: What the consumer can afford

Most people would like to increase the quantity or quality of the goods they consume – to take longer holidays, drive fancier cars or buy better clothes. People consume less than they desire because their spending is constrained, or limited, by their income. We begin our study of consumer choice by examining this link between income and spending.

To keep things simple, we examine the decision facing a consumer (Natalie) who buys only two goods – Pepsi and pizza. Of course, real people buy thousands of different kinds of goods. Yet assuming there are only two goods greatly simplifies the problem without altering the basic insights about consumer choice.

We first consider how Natalie's income constrains the amount she spends on Pepsi and pizza. Suppose that Natalie has an income of $1000 per month and spends that entire income each month on Pepsi and pizza. The price of a litre of Pepsi is $2 and the price of a pizza is $10.

Table 22.1 shows some of the many combinations of Pepsi and pizza that Natalie can buy. The first line in the table shows that if all income is spent on pizza, Natalie can eat 100 pizzas during the month, but would not be able to buy any Pepsi at all. The second line shows another possible

Table 22.1 The consumer's opportunities

Litres of Pepsi	Number of pizzas	Spending on Pepsi	Spending on pizza	Total spending
0	100	$0	$1000	$1000
50	90	100	900	1000
100	80	200	800	1000
150	70	300	700	1000
200	60	400	600	1000
250	50	500	500	1000
300	40	600	400	1000
350	30	700	300	1000
400	20	800	200	1000
450	10	900	100	1000
500	0	1000	0	1000

This table shows what our consumer, Natalie, can afford if income is $1000, the price of Pepsi is $2 and the price of a pizza is $10.

consumption bundle – 90 pizzas and 50 litres of Pepsi. And so on. Each consumption bundle in the table costs exactly $1000.

Figure 22.1 graphs the consumption bundles that Natalie can choose. The vertical axis measures the number of litres of Pepsi, and the horizontal axis measures the number of pizzas. Three points are marked on this figure. At point A, Natalie buys no Pepsi and consumes 100 pizzas. At point B, Natalie buys no pizzas and consumes 500 litres of Pepsi. At point C, Natalie buys 50 pizzas and 250 litres of Pepsi. Point C, which is exactly at the middle of the line from A to B, is the point at which Natalie spends an equal amount ($500) on Pepsi and pizza. Of course, these are only three of the many combinations of Pepsi and pizza that Natalie can choose. All the points on the line from A to B are possible. This line, which is called the **budget constraint**, shows the consumption bundles that Natalie can afford. In this case, it shows Natalie's trade-off between Pepsi and pizza.

budget constraint
the limit on the consumption bundles that a consumer can afford

The slope of the budget constraint measures the rate at which Natalie can trade one good for the other. Recall from the appendix to chapter 2 that the slope between two points is calculated as the change in the vertical distance divided by the change in the horizontal distance ('rise over run'). From point A to point B, the vertical distance is 500 litres and the horizontal distance is 100 pizzas. Thus, the slope is 5 litres per pizza. (Actually, because the budget constraint slopes downwards, the slope is a negative number. But for our purposes we can ignore the minus sign.)

Notice that the slope of the budget constraint equals the *relative price* of the two goods – the price of one good compared with the price of the other. A pizza costs five times as much as a litre of Pepsi.

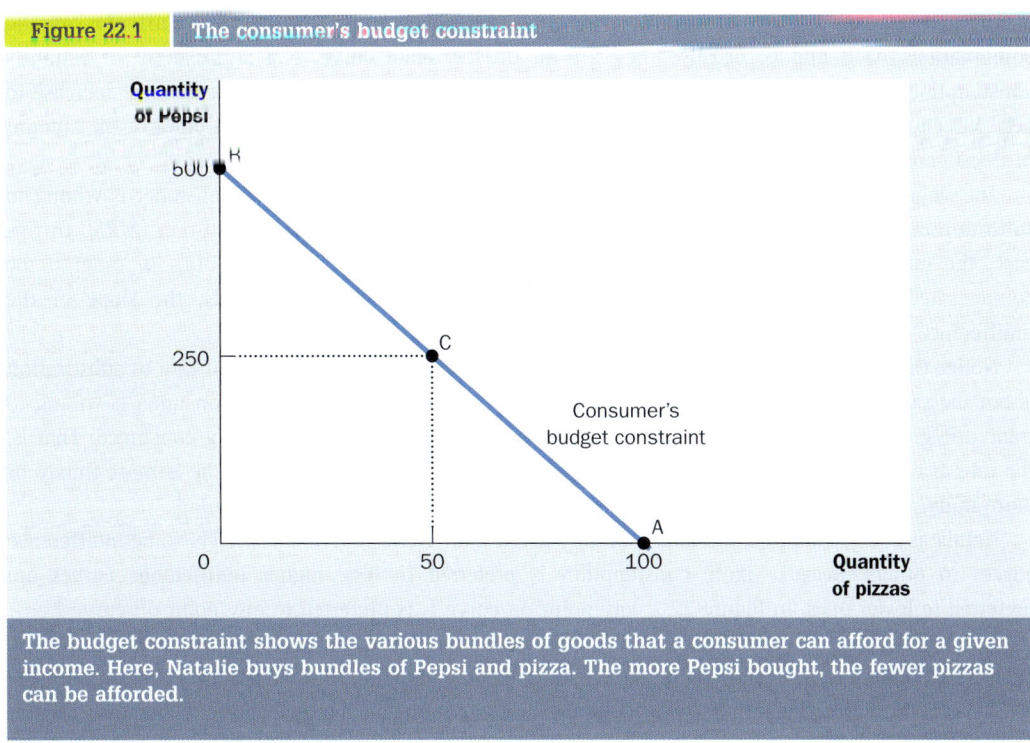

Figure 22.1 The consumer's budget constraint

The budget constraint shows the various bundles of goods that a consumer can afford for a given income. Here, Natalie buys bundles of Pepsi and pizza. The more Pepsi bought, the fewer pizzas can be afforded.

Draw the budget constraint for a person with an income of $1000 if the price of Pepsi is $5 and the price of a pizza is $10. What is the slope of this budget constraint?

Thus, the opportunity cost of a pizza is five litres of Pepsi. The budget constraint's slope of 5 reflects the trade-off the market is offering the consumer: 1 pizza for 5 litres of Pepsi.

Preferences: What the consumer wants

Our goal in this chapter is to see how consumers make choices. Budget constraints are one piece of the analysis – they show what combinations of goods consumers can afford given their incomes and the prices of the goods. Consumers' choices, however, depend not only on this budget constraint but also on their preferences for certain goods. Therefore, a consumer's preferences are the next piece of our analysis.

Representing preferences with indifference curves

Natalie's (the consumer's) preferences allow a choice among different bundles of Pepsi and pizza. If two different bundles are offered, Natalie chooses the bundle to best suit her tastes. If the two bundles suit her tastes equally well, we say that Natalie is *indifferent* between the two bundles.

Just as we have represented Natalie's budget constraint graphically, we can also represent her preferences graphically. We do this with indifference curves. An **indifference curve** shows the bundles of consumption that make a consumer equally happy. In this case, the indifference curves show the combinations of Pepsi and pizza with which Natalie is equally satisfied.

indifference curve
a curve that shows consumption bundles that give the consumer the same level of satisfaction

▸ indifference curve

Figure 22.2 shows two of Natalie's many indifference curves. Natalie is indifferent among combinations A, B and C, because they are all on the same curve. Not surprisingly, if Natalie's consumption of pizza is reduced, say from point A to point B, consumption of Pepsi must increase to keep her equally happy. If consumption of pizza is reduced again, from point B to point C, the amount of Pepsi consumed must increase yet again.

The slope at any point on an indifference curve equals the rate at which a consumer is willing to substitute one good for the other. This rate is called the **marginal rate of substitution** (*MRS*). In this case, the marginal rate of substitution measures how much Pepsi Natalie requires in order to be compensated for a one-unit reduction in pizza consumption. In other words, the slope of the indifference curve shows the marginal rate *of* substitution of Pepsi *for* pizza.

Notice that, because the indifference curves are not straight lines, the marginal rate of substitution is not the same at all points on a given indifference curve. The rate at which a consumer is willing to trade one good for the other depends on the amounts of the goods already being consumed. That is, the rate at which Natalie is willing to trade Pepsi for pizza depends on whether she is more thirsty or more hungry, which in turn depends on how much Pepsi and pizza she is consuming.

Natalie is equally happy at all points on any given indifference curve, but prefers some indifference curves to others. Because more consumption is preferred to less, higher indifference curves are preferred to lower ones. In Figure 22.2, any point on curve I_2 is preferred to any point on curve I_1.

A consumer's set of indifference curves gives a complete ranking of the consumer's preferences. That is, we can use the indifference curves to rank any two bundles of goods. For example, the indifference curves tell us that point D is preferred to point A because point D is on a higher

marginal rate of substitution
the rate at which a consumer is willing to trade one good for another

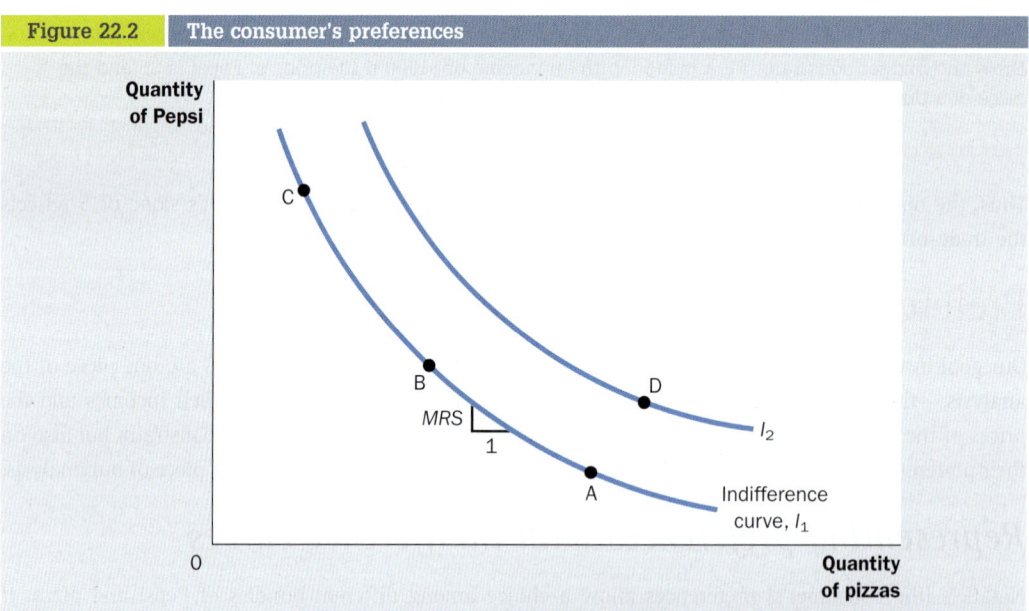

Figure 22.2   The consumer's preferences

The consumer's preferences are represented with indifference curves, which show the combinations of Pepsi and pizza that make Natalie equally satisfied. Because Natalie prefers more of a good, points on a higher indifference curve (I_2 here) are preferred to points on a lower indifference curve (I_1). The marginal rate of substitution (*MRS*) shows the rate at which Natalie is willing to trade Pepsi for pizza.

indifference curve than point A (That conclusion may be obvious, however, because point D offers Natalie both more pizza and more Pepsi.) The indifference curves also tell us that point D is preferred to point C because point D is on a higher indifference curve. Even though point D has less Pepsi than point C, it has more than enough extra pizza to make Natalie prefer it. By seeing which point is on the higher indifference curve, we can use the set of indifference curves to rank any combinations of Pepsi and pizza.

Four properties of indifference curves

Because indifference curves represent a consumer's preferences, they have certain properties that reflect those preferences. Here we consider four properties that describe most indifference curves.

- *Property 1: Higher indifference curves are preferred to lower ones.* A consumer usually prefers more of something to less of it. This preference for greater quantities is reflected in the indifference curves. As Figure 22.2 shows, higher indifference curves represent larger quantities of goods than lower indifference curves. Thus, a consumer prefers being on a higher indifference curve.
- *Property 2: Indifference curves are downward-sloping.* The slope of an indifference curve reflects the rate at which a consumer is willing to substitute one good for the other. In most cases, the consumer likes both goods. Therefore, if the quantity of one good is reduced, the quantity of the other good must increase in order for the consumer to be equally happy. For this reason, most indifference curves slope downwards.
- *Property 3: Indifference curves do not cross.* To see why this is true, suppose that two indifference curves did cross, as in Figure 22.3. Then, because point A is on the same indifference curve as point B, the two points would make the consumer (Natalie) equally happy. In addition, because point B is on the same indifference curve as point C, these two points would make Natalie equally

Figure 22.3	The impossibility of intersecting indifference curves

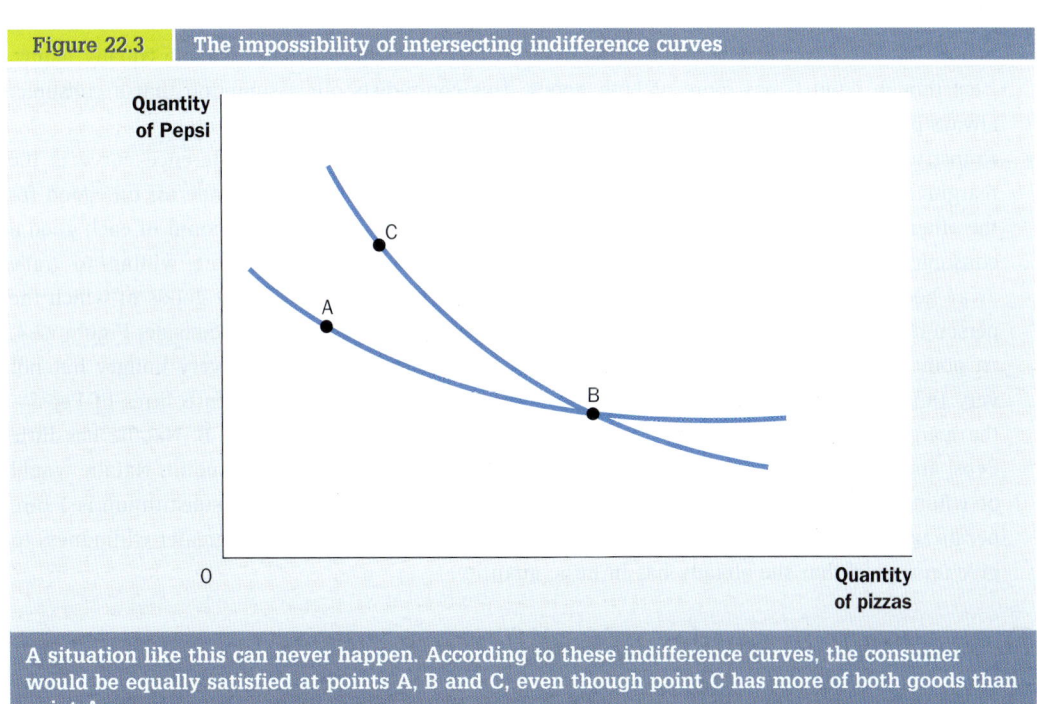

A situation like this can never happen. According to these indifference curves, the consumer would be equally satisfied at points A, B and C, even though point C has more of both goods than point A.

500

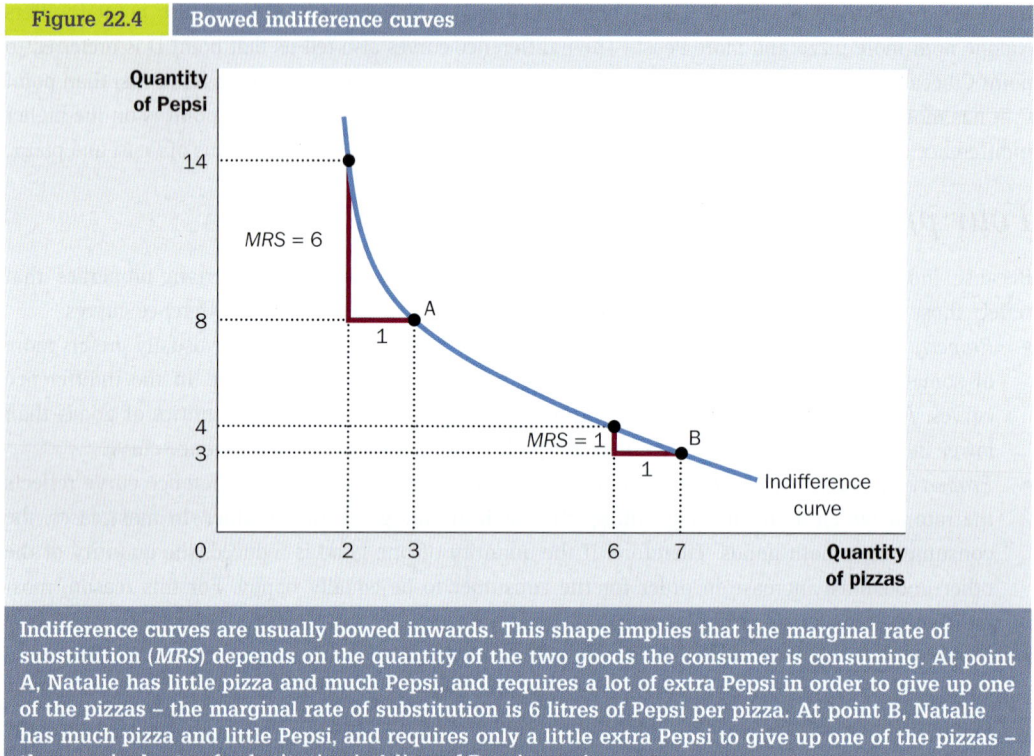

Figure 22.4 | **Bowed indifference curves**

Indifference curves are usually bowed inwards. This shape implies that the marginal rate of substitution (*MRS*) depends on the quantity of the two goods the consumer is consuming. At point A, Natalie has little pizza and much Pepsi, and requires a lot of extra Pepsi in order to give up one of the pizzas – the marginal rate of substitution is 6 litres of Pepsi per pizza. At point B, Natalie has much pizza and little Pepsi, and requires only a little extra Pepsi to give up one of the pizzas – the marginal rate of substitution is 1 litre of Pepsi per pizza.

happy. But these conclusions imply that points A and C would also make Natalie equally happy, even though point C has more of both goods. This contradicts our assumption that a consumer always prefers more of both goods to less. Thus, indifference curves cannot cross.

- *Property 4: Indifference curves are bowed inwards.* The slope of an indifference curve is the marginal rate of substitution – the rate at which a consumer is willing to trade off one good for the other. The marginal rate of substitution (*MRS*) usually depends on the amount of each good a consumer is currently consuming. In particular, because a person is more willing to trade away goods that he or she has in abundance and less willing to trade away goods of which the person has little, the indifference curves are bowed inwards. As an example, consider Figure 22.4. At point A, Natalie has a lot of Pepsi and only a little pizza, making her very hungry but not very thirsty. To induce Natalie to give up one pizza, Natalie has to be given 6 litres of Pepsi – the marginal rate of substitution is 6 litres per pizza. In contrast, at point B, Natalie has little Pepsi and a lot of pizza, and so is very thirsty but not very hungry. At this point, Natalie would be willing to give up one pizza to get 1 litre of Pepsi – the marginal rate of substitution is 1 litre per pizza. Thus, the bowed shape of the indifference curve reflects Natalie's greater willingness to give up a good that she already has in large quantity.

Two extreme examples of indifference curves

The shape of an indifference curve tells us about a consumer's willingness to trade one good for the other. When the goods are easy to substitute for each other, the indifference curves are less bowed;

when the goods are hard to substitute, the indifference curves are very bowed. To see why this is true, let's consider the extreme cases.

Perfect substitutes

Suppose that someone offered you bundles of 10-cent and 20-cent coins. How would you rank the different bundles?

Most likely, you would care only about the total monetary value of each bundle. If so, you would judge a bundle based on the number of 20-cent coins plus twice the number of 10-cent coins. In other words, you would always be willing to trade one 20-cent coin for two 10-cent coins, regardless of the number of 10- and 20-cent coins in the bundle. Your marginal rate of substitution of 10-cent coins for 20-cent coins would be a fixed number – two.

We can represent your preferences regarding 10- and 20-cent coins with the indifference curves in panel (a) of Figure 22.5. Because the marginal rate of substitution is constant, the indifference curves are straight lines. In this extreme case of straight indifference curves, we say that the two goods are **perfect substitutes**.

perfect substitutes
two goods with straight-line indifference curves

Perfect complements

Suppose now that someone offered you bundles of shoes. Some of the shoes fit your left foot, others your right foot. How would you rank these different bundles?

In this case, you might care only about the number of pairs of shoes. In other words, you would judge a bundle based on the number of pairs you could assemble from it. A bundle of five left shoes and seven right shoes yields only five pairs. Getting one more right shoe has no value if there is no left shoe to go with it.

We can represent your preferences for right and left shoes with the indifference curves in panel (b) of Figure 22.5. In this case, a bundle with five left shoes and five right shoes is just as good as a

| Figure 22.5 | Perfect substitutes and perfect complements |

When two goods are easily substitutable, such as 10- and 20-cent coins, the indifference curves are straight lines, as shown in panel (a). When two goods are strongly complementary, such as left shoes and right shoes, the indifference curves are right angles, as shown in panel (b).

bundle with five left shoes and seven right shoes. It is also just as good as a bundle with seven left shoes and five right shoes. The indifference curves, therefore, are right angles. In this extreme case of right-angle indifference curves, we say that the two goods are **perfect complements**.

perfect complements
two goods with right-angle indifference curves

In the real world, of course, most goods are neither perfect substitutes (like 10- and 20-cent coins) nor perfect complements (like right shoes and left shoes). More typically, the indifference curves are bowed inwards, but not so bowed as to become right angles.

Draw some indifference curves for Pepsi and pizza. Explain the four properties of these indifference curves.

Optimisation: What the consumer chooses

The goal of this chapter is to understand how a consumer makes choices. We have the two pieces necessary for this analysis – the consumer's budget constraint (how much she can *afford* to buy) and the consumer's preferences (what she would *like* to buy). Now we put these two pieces together and consider the consumer's decision about what to buy.

The consumer's optimum choices

Consider once again our Pepsi and pizza example. Our consumer, Natalie, would like to end up with the best possible combination of Pepsi and pizza – that is, the combination on the highest possible indifference curve. But Natalie must also end up on or below her budget constraint, which measures the total resources available to her.

fyi

Utility – an alternative way to describe preferences and optimisation

We have used indifference curves to represent a consumer's preferences. Another common way to represent preferences is with the concept of *utility*. Utility is an abstract measure of the satisfaction or happiness that a consumer receives from a bundle of goods. Economists say that a consumer prefers one bundle of goods to another if one provides more utility than the other.

Indifference curves and utility are closely related. Because the consumer prefers points on higher indifference curves, bundles of goods on higher indifference curves provide higher utility. Because the consumer is equally happy with all points on the same indifference curve, all these bundles provide the same utility. You can think of an indifference curve as an 'equal-utility' curve.

The *marginal utility* of any good is the increase in utility that the consumer gets from an additional unit of that good. Most goods are assumed to exhibit *diminishing marginal utility*. The more of the good the consumer already has, the lower the marginal utility provided by an extra unit of that good.

The marginal rate of substitution between two goods depends on their marginal utilities. For example, if the marginal utility of good X is twice the marginal utility of good Y, then a person would need two units of good Y to compensate for losing one unit of good X and the marginal rate of substitution equals two. More generally, the marginal rate of substitution (and thus the slope of the indifference curve) equals the marginal utility of one good divided by the marginal utility of the other good.

Utility analysis provides another way to describe consumer optimisation. Recall that at the consumer's optimum, the marginal rate of substitution equals the ratio of prices. That is:

$$MRS = P_X/P_Y$$

Because the marginal rate of substitution equals the ratio of marginal utilities, we can write this condition for optimisation as:

$$MU_X/MU_Y = P_X/P_Y$$

Now rearrange this expression to become:

$$MU_X / P_X = MU_Y / P_Y$$

This equation has a simple interpretation. At the optimum, the marginal utility per dollar spent on good X equals the marginal utility per dollar spent on good Y. (Why? If this equality did not hold, the consumer could increase utility by spending less on the good that provided lower marginal utility per dollar and more on the good that provided higher marginal utility per dollar.)

When economists discuss the theory of consumer choice, they might express the theory using different words. One economist might say that the goal of the consumer is to maximize utility. Another might say that the goal of the consumer is to end up on the highest possible indifference curve. The first economist would conclude that at the consumer's optimum, the marginal utility per dollar is the same for all goods, whereas the second would conclude that the indifference curve is tangent to the budget constraint. In essence, these are two ways of saying the same thing.

Figure 22.6 shows the budget constraint and three of Natalie's many indifference curves. The highest indifference curve that Natalie can reach (I_2 in the figure) is the one that just barely touches the budget constraint. The point at which this indifference curve and the budget constraint touch is called the *optimum*. Natalie would prefer point A, but cannot afford that point because it lies above the budget constraint. Natalie can afford point B, but that point is on a lower indifference curve and, therefore, provides Natalie less satisfaction. The optimum point represents the best combination of consumption of Pepsi and pizza available to Natalie.

Figure 22.6 The consumer's optimum

The consumer chooses the point on her budget constraint that lies on the highest indifference curve. At this point, called the optimum, the marginal rate of substitution equals the relative price of the two goods. Here the highest indifference curve Natalie can reach is I_2. Natalie prefers point A, which lies on indifference curve I_3, but cannot afford this bundle of Pepsi and pizza. In contrast, point B is affordable, but because it lies on a lower indifference curve, Natalie does not prefer it.

Notice that, at the optimum, the slope of the indifference curve equals the slope of the budget constraint. We say that the indifference curve is tangent to the budget constraint. The slope of the indifference curve is the marginal rate of substitution between Pepsi and pizza, and the slope of the budget constraint is the relative price of Pepsi and pizza. Thus, *a consumer chooses consumption of the two goods so that the marginal rate of substitution equals the relative price.*

In chapter 7 we saw how market prices reflect the marginal value that consumers place on goods. This analysis of consumer choice shows the same result in another way. In making consumption choices, a consumer takes as given the relative price of the two goods and then chooses an optimum at which the marginal rate of substitution equals this relative price. The relative price is the rate at which the *market* is willing to trade one good for the other, whereas the marginal rate of substitution is the rate at which a *consumer* is willing to trade one good for the other. At a consumer's optimum, the consumer's valuation of the two goods (as measured by the marginal rate of substitution) equals the market's valuation (as measured by the relative price). As a result of this consumer optimisation, market prices of different goods reflect the value that consumers place on those goods.

How changes in income affect a consumer's choices

Now that we have seen how a consumer makes the consumption decision, let's examine how consumption responds to changes in income. To be specific, suppose that income increases. With a higher income, Natalie can afford more of both goods. The increase in income, therefore, shifts the budget constraint outwards, as in Figure 22.7. Because the relative price of the two goods has not

Figure 22.7   An increase in income

Quantity of Pepsi

New budget constraint

1. An increase in income shifts the budget constraint outwards …

New optimum

3. … and Pepsi consumption.

Initial optimum

Initial budget constraint

I_2

I_1

0

2. … raising pizza consumption…

Quantity of pizzas

When the consumer's income rises, the budget constraint shifts out. If both goods are normal goods, the consumer responds to the increase in income by buying more of both goods. Here, Natalie buys more pizza and more Pepsi.

changed, the slope of the new budget constraint is the same as the slope of the initial budget constraint. That is, an increase in income leads to a parallel shift in the budget constraint.

The expanded budget constraint allows our consumer, Natalie, to choose a better combination of Pepsi and pizza. In other words, Natalie can now reach a higher indifference curve. Given the shift in the budget constraint and Natalie's preferences as represented by the indifference curves, Natalie's optimum moves from the point labelled 'initial optimum' to the point labelled 'new optimum'.

Notice that, in Figure 22.7, Natalie chooses to consume more Pepsi and more pizza. Although the logic of the model does not require increased consumption of both goods in response to increased income, this situation is the most common one. As you may recall from chapter 4, if consumers want more of a good when their incomes rise, economists call it a *normal good*. The indifference curves in Figure 22.7 are drawn under the assumption that both Pepsi and pizza are normal goods.

Figure 22.8 shows an example in which an increase in income induces our consumer, Natalie, to buy more pizzas but less Pepsi. If a consumer buys less of a good when income rises, economists call it an *inferior good*. Figure 22.8 is drawn under the assumption that pizza is a normal good and Pepsi is an inferior good.

Although most goods are normal goods, there are some inferior goods in the world. One example is second-hand clothes. High-income consumers are more likely to buy new clothes and less likely to buy second-hand clothes than are low-income consumers. Second-hand clothes, therefore, are an inferior good.

▸ inferior good

Figure 22.8 | **An inferior good**

A good is an inferior good if the consumer buys less of it when income rises. Here Pepsi is an inferior good – when Natalie's income increases and the budget constraint shifts outwards, she buys more pizzas but less Pepsi.

How changes in prices affect a consumer's choices

Let's now use this model of consumer choice to consider how a change in the price of one of the goods alters a consumer's choices. Suppose, in particular, that the price of Pepsi falls from $2 to $1 a litre. It is no surprise that the lower price expands the consumer's set of buying opportunities. In other words, a fall in the price of any good shifts the budget constraint outwards.

Figure 22.9 considers more specifically how the fall in price affects the budget constraint. If our consumer, Natalie, spends the entire $1000 income on pizza, then the price of Pepsi is irrelevant. Thus, point A in the figure stays the same. Yet Natalie, by spending the entire income of $1000 on Pepsi, can now buy 1000 rather than only 500 litres. Thus, the end point of the budget constraint moves from point B to point D.

Notice that, in this case, the outward shift in the budget constraint changes the slope of the budget constraint. (This differs from what happened previously when prices stayed the same but the consumer's income changed.) As we have discussed, the slope of the budget constraint reflects the relative price of Pepsi and pizza. Because the price of Pepsi has fallen to $1 from $2 and the price of a pizza has remained $10, our consumer can now trade a pizza for 10 rather than 5 litres of Pepsi. As a result, the new budget constraint is more steeply sloped.

How such a change in the budget constraint alters the consumption of both goods depends on a consumer's preferences. For the indifference curves drawn in this figure, Natalie buys more Pepsi and fewer pizzas.

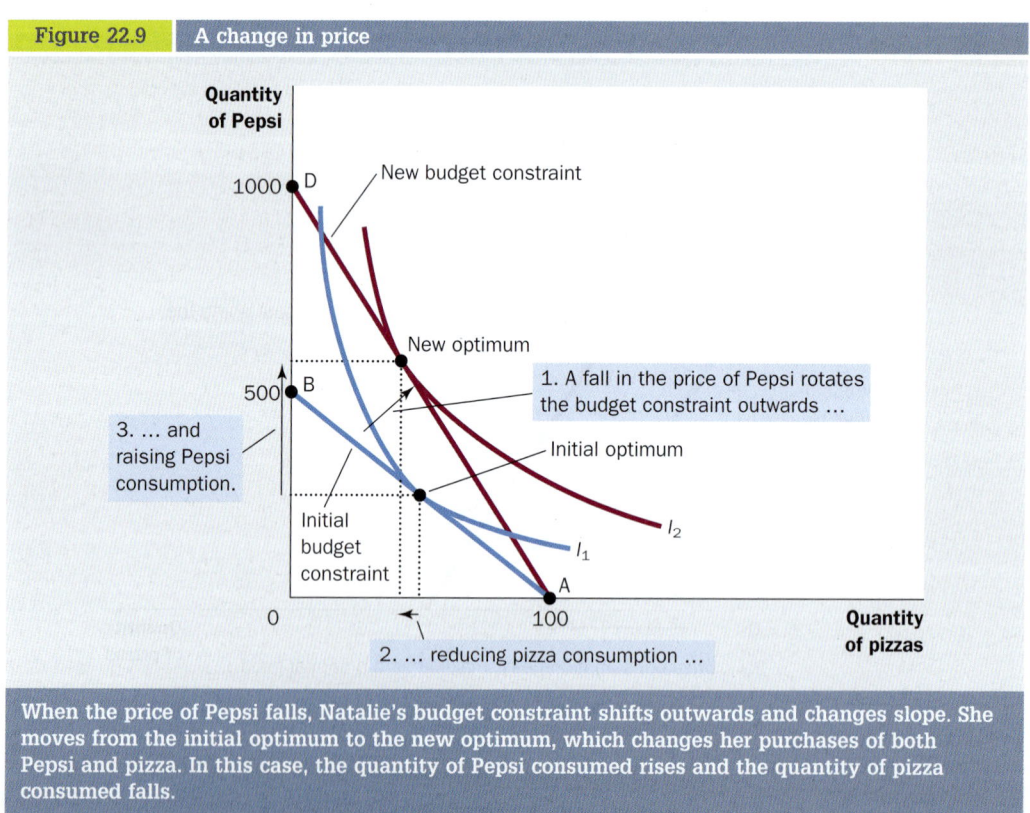

| Figure 22.9 | A change in price |

When the price of Pepsi falls, Natalie's budget constraint shifts outwards and changes slope. She moves from the initial optimum to the new optimum, which changes her purchases of both Pepsi and pizza. In this case, the quantity of Pepsi consumed rises and the quantity of pizza consumed falls.

Income and substitution effects

The impact of a change in the price of a good on consumption can be divided into two effects – an **income effect** and a **substitution effect**. To see what these two effects are, consider how our consumer might respond upon learning that the price of Pepsi has fallen. Natalie might reason in the following ways:

- 'Great news! Now that Pepsi is cheaper, my income has greater purchasing power. I am, in effect, richer than I was. Because I am richer, I can buy both more Pepsi and more pizza.' (This is the income effect.)

- 'Now that the price of Pepsi has fallen, I get more litres of Pepsi for every pizza that I give up. Because pizza is now relatively more expensive, I should buy fewer pizzas and more Pepsi.' (This is the substitution effect.)

Which statement do you find more compelling?

In fact, both of these statements make sense. The decrease in the price of Pepsi makes Natalie better off. If Pepsi and pizza are both normal goods, Natalie will want to spread this improvement in purchasing power over both goods. This income effect tends to make Natalie buy more pizzas and more Pepsi. Yet, at the same time, consumption of Pepsi has become less expensive relative to consumption of pizzas. This substitution effect tends to make Natalie choose more Pepsi and fewer pizzas.

Now consider the end result of these two effects. Natalie certainly buys more Pepsi, because the income and substitution effects both act to raise purchases of Pepsi. But it is ambiguous whether Natalie buys more pizzas, because the income and substitution effects work in opposite directions. This conclusion is summarised in Table 22.2.

We can interpret the income and substitution effects using indifference curves. The income effect is the change in consumption that results from the movement to a higher indifference curve. The substitution effect is the change in consumption that results from being at a point on an indifference curve with a different marginal rate of substitution.

Figure 22.10 shows graphically how to divide the change in a consumer's decision into the income effect and the substitution effect. When the price of Pepsi falls, Natalie moves from the initial optimum, point A, to the new optimum, point C. We can view this change as occurring in two steps. First, Natalie moves along the initial indifference curve I_1 from point A to point B. Natalie is equally happy at these two points, but at point B, the marginal rate of substitution reflects the new relative price. Next, Natalie shifts to the higher indifference curve I_2 by moving from point B to point C. Even though point B and point C are on different indifference curves, they have the same marginal rate of substitution – that is, the slope of the indifference curve I_1 at point B equals the slope of the indifference curve I_2 at point C.

income effect
the change in consumption that results when a price change moves the consumer to a higher or lower indifference curve

substitution effect
the change in consumption that results when a price change moves the consumer along a given indifference curve to a point with a new marginal rate of substitution

Table 22.2	Income and substitution effects when the price of Pepsi falls		
Good	Income effect	Substitution effect	Total effect
Pepsi	Natalie is richer, so she buys more Pepsi	Pepsi is relatively cheaper, so Natalie buys more Pepsi	Income and substitution effects act in the same direction, so Natalie buys more Pepsi
Pizza	Natalie is richer, so she buys more pizza	Pizza is relatively more expensive, so Natalie buys fewer pizzas	Income and substitution effects act in opposite directions, so the total effect on pizza is ambiguous

Figure 22.10 Income and substitution effects

The effect of a change in price can be broken down into an income effect and a substitution effect. The substitution effect – the movement along an indifference curve to a point with a different marginal rate of substitution – is shown here as the change from point A to point B along indifference curve I_1. The income effect – the shift to a higher indifference curve – is shown here as the change from point B on indifference curve I_1 to point C on indifference curve I_2.

Although a consumer never actually chooses point B, this hypothetical point is useful to clarify the two effects that determine a consumer's decision. Notice that the change from point A to point B represents a pure change in the marginal rate of substitution without any change in the consumer's welfare. Similarly, the change from point B to point C represents a pure change in welfare without any change in the marginal rate of substitution. Thus, the movement from A to B shows the substitution effect and the movement from B to C shows the income effect.

Deriving the demand curve

We have just seen how changes in the price of a good alter a consumer's budget constraint and, therefore, the quantities of the two goods bought. The demand curve for any good reflects these consumption decisions. As you should recall, a demand curve shows how the price of a good affects the quantity demanded. We can view a consumer's demand curve as a summary of the optimum decisions that arise from the consumer's budget constraint and indifference curves.

For example, Figure 22.11 considers the demand for Pepsi. Panel (a) shows that when the price of a litre falls from $2 to $1, Natalie's budget constraint shifts outwards. Because of both income and substitution effects, Natalie increases purchases of Pepsi from 50 to 150 litres. Panel (b) shows the demand curve that results from Natalie's decisions. In this way, the theory of consumer choice provides the theoretical foundation for a consumer's demand curve.

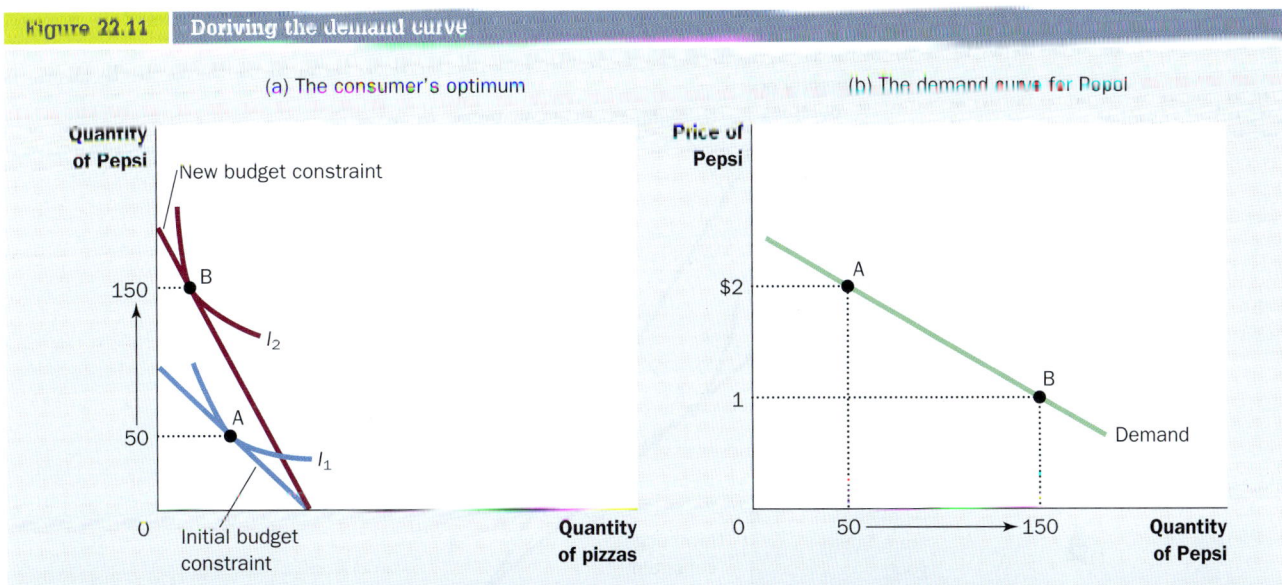

Figure 22.11   **Deriving the demand curve**

(a) The consumer's optimum

(b) The demand curve for Pepsi

Panel (a) shows that when the price of Pepsi falls from $2 to $1, Natalie's optimum moves from point A to point B and the quantity of Pepsi consumed rises from 50 to 150 litres. The demand curve in panel (b) reflects this relationship between the price and the quantity demanded.

It may be comforting to know that the demand curve arises naturally from the theory of consumer choice, but this exercise by itself does not justify developing the theory. There is no need for a rigorous, analytic framework just to establish that people respond to changes in prices. The theory of consumer choice is, however, useful in studying the various decisions people make as they go about their lives, as we see in the next section.

Draw a budget constraint and indifference curves for Pepsi and pizza. Show what happens to the budget constraint and the consumer's optimum when the price of pizza rises. In your diagram, divide the change into an income effect and a substitution effect.

Four applications

Now that we have developed the basic theory of consumer choice, let's use it to shed light on four questions about how the economy works. These four questions might at first seem unrelated. But because each question involves household decision making, we can consider it using the model of consumer behaviour we have just developed.

Do all demand curves slope downwards?

Normally, when the price of a good rises, people buy less of it. Chapter 4 called this usual behaviour the *law of demand*. This law is reflected in the downward slope of the demand curve.

As a matter of economic theory, however, demand curves can sometimes slope upwards. In other words, consumers can sometimes violate the law of demand and buy *more* of a good when

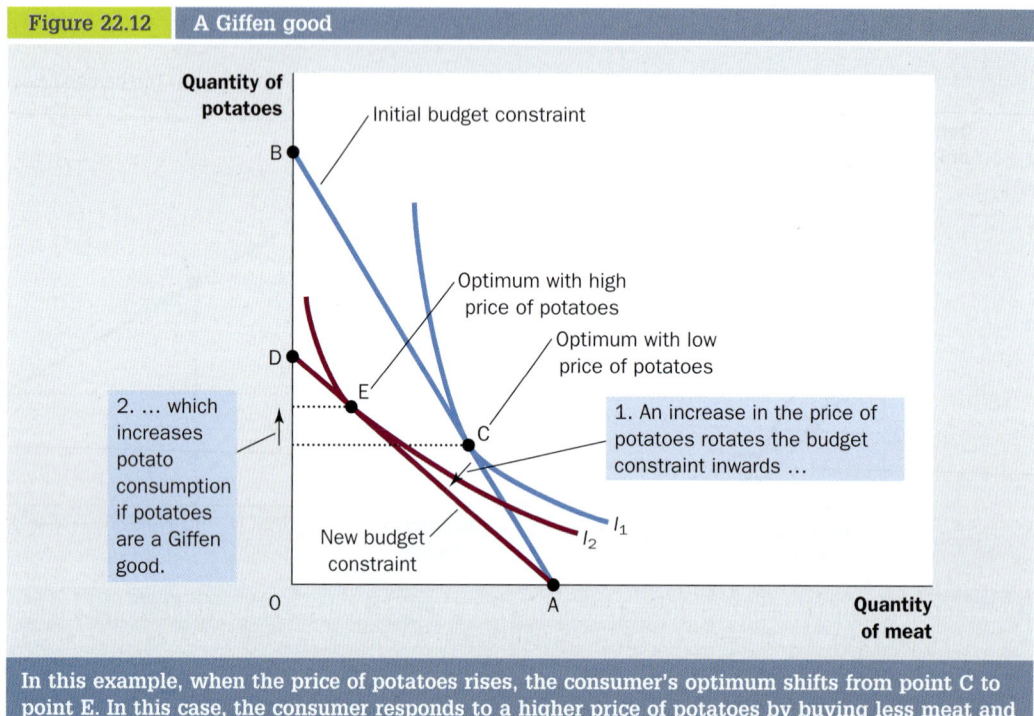

Figure 22.12 A Giffen good

In this example, when the price of potatoes rises, the consumer's optimum shifts from point C to point E. In this case, the consumer responds to a higher price of potatoes by buying less meat and more potatoes.

the price rises. To see how this can happen, consider Figure 22.12. In this example, a consumer buys two goods – meat and potatoes. Initially, the consumer's budget constraint is the line from point A to point B. The optimum is point C. When the price of potatoes rises, the budget constraint shifts inwards and is now the line from point A to point D. The optimum is now point E. Notice that a rise in the price of potatoes has led the consumer to buy a larger quantity of potatoes.

Why is the consumer responding in a seemingly perverse way? The reason is that potatoes here are a strongly inferior good. When the price of potatoes rises, the consumer is poorer. The income effect makes the consumer want to buy less meat and more potatoes. At the same time, because potatoes have become more expensive relative to meat, the substitution effect makes the consumer want to buy more meat and less potatoes. In this particular case, however, the income effect is so strong that it exceeds the substitution effect. In the end, the consumer responds to the higher price of potatoes by buying less meat and more potatoes.

Giffen good
a good for which an increase in the price raises the quantity demanded

Economists use the term **Giffen good** to describe a good that violates the law of demand. (The term is named for economist Robert Giffen, who first noted this possibility.) In this example, potatoes are a Giffen good. Giffen goods are inferior goods for which the income effect dominates the substitution effect. Therefore, they have demand curves that slope upwards.

Have any actual Giffen goods ever been observed? Some historians suggest that potatoes were a Giffen good during the Irish potato famine of the nineteenth century. Potatoes were such a large part of people's diet that when the price of potatoes rose, it had a large income effect. People responded to their reduced living standard by cutting back on the luxury of meat and buying more of the staple food of potatoes. Thus, it is argued that a higher price of potatoes actually raised the quantity of potatoes demanded.

A recent study by Robert Jensen and Nolan Miller has produced similar but more concrete evidence for the existence of Giffen goods. These two economists conducted a field experiment for five months in the Chinese province of Hunan. They gave randomly selected households vouchers that subsidised the purchase of rice, a staple in local diets, and used surveys to measure how consumption of rice responded to changes in the price. They found strong evidence that poor households exhibited Giffen behavior. Lowering the price of rice with the subsidy voucher caused households to reduce their consumption of rice and removing the subsidy had the opposite effect. Jensen and Miller wrote, 'To the best of our knowledge, this is the first rigorous empirical evidence of Giffen behavior'.

Thus, the theory of consumer choice allows demand curves to slope upward and sometimes that strange phenomenon actually occurs. As a result, the law of demand we first saw in Chapter 4 is not completely reliable. It is safe to say, however, that Giffen goods are very rare.

How do wages affect labour supply?

So far we have used the theory of consumer choice to analyse how a person decides to allocate income between two goods. We can use the same theory to analyse how a person allocates time. People spend some of their time enjoying leisure and some of it working so they can afford to buy consumption goods. The essence of the time-allocation problem is the trade-off between leisure and consumption.

Consider the decision facing Sally, a freelance software designer. Sally is awake for 100 hours per week. She spends some of this time enjoying leisure – riding her bike, watching television, studying economics and so on. She spends the rest of this time at her computer developing software. For every hour she spends developing software, she earns $50, which she spends on consumption goods. Thus, her wage ($50) reflects the trade-off Sally faces between leisure and consumption. For every hour of leisure she gives up, she works one more hour and gets $50 of consumption.

Figure 22.13 shows Sally's budget constraint. If she spends all 100 hours enjoying leisure, she has no consumption. If she spends all 100 hours working, she earns a weekly consumption of $5000 but has no time for leisure. If she works 40 hours a week, she enjoys 60 hours of leisure and has weekly consumption of $2000.

Figure 22.13 uses indifference curves to represent Sally's preferences for consumption and leisure. Here consumption and leisure are the two 'goods' that Sally is choosing between. Because Sally always prefers more leisure and more consumption, she prefers points on higher indifference curves to points on lower ones. At a wage of $50 per hour, Sally chooses a combination of consumption and leisure represented by the point labelled 'optimum'. This is the point on the budget constraint that is on the highest possible indifference curve, which is curve I_2.

Now consider what happens when Sally's wage increases from $50 to $60 per hour. Figure 22.14 shows two possible outcomes. In each case, the budget constraint, shown in the left-hand graph, shifts outwards from BC_1 to BC_2. In the process, the budget constraint becomes steeper, reflecting the change in relative price – at the higher wage, Sally gets more consumption for every hour of leisure that she gives up.

Sally's preferences, as represented by her indifference curves, determine how her choice regarding consumption and leisure responds to the higher wage. In both panels, consumption rises. Yet the

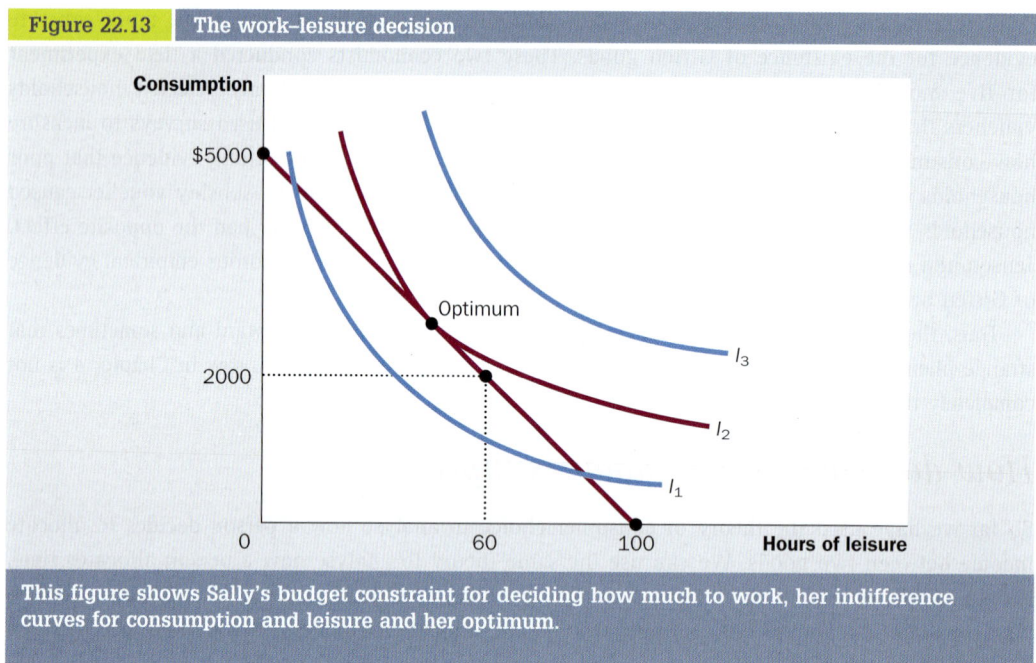

Figure 22.13 | **The work–leisure decision**

This figure shows Sally's budget constraint for deciding how much to work, her indifference curves for consumption and leisure and her optimum.

response of leisure to the change in the wage is different in the two cases. In panel (a), Sally responds to the higher wage by enjoying less leisure. In panel (b), Sally responds by enjoying more leisure.

Sally's decision between leisure and consumption determines her supply of labour, for the more leisure she enjoys the less time she has left to work. In each panel, the right-hand graph in Figure 22.14 shows the labour supply curve implied by Sally's decision. In panel (a), a higher wage induces Sally to enjoy less leisure and work more, so the labour supply curve slopes upwards. In panel (b), a higher wage induces Sally to enjoy more leisure and work less, so the labour supply curve slopes 'backward'.

At first, the backward-sloping labour supply curve is puzzling. Why would a person respond to a higher wage by working less? The answer comes from considering the income and substitution effects of a higher wage.

Consider first the substitution effect. When Sally's wage rises, leisure becomes more costly relative to consumption and this encourages Sally to substitute consumption for leisure. In other words, the substitution effect induces Sally to work harder in response to higher wages, which tends to make the labour supply curve slope upward.

Now consider the income effect. When Sally's wage rises, she moves to a higher indifference curve. She is now better off than she was. As long as consumption and leisure are both normal goods, she tends to want to use this increase in wellbeing to enjoy both higher consumption and greater leisure. In other words, the income effect induces her to work less, which tends to make the labour supply curve slope backward.

In the end, economic theory does not give a clear prediction about whether an increase in the wage induces Sally to work more or less. If the substitution effect is greater than the income effect for Sally, she works more. If the income effect is greater than the substitution effect, she works less. The labour supply curve, therefore, could be either upward- or backward-sloping.

Figure 22.14 An increase in the wage

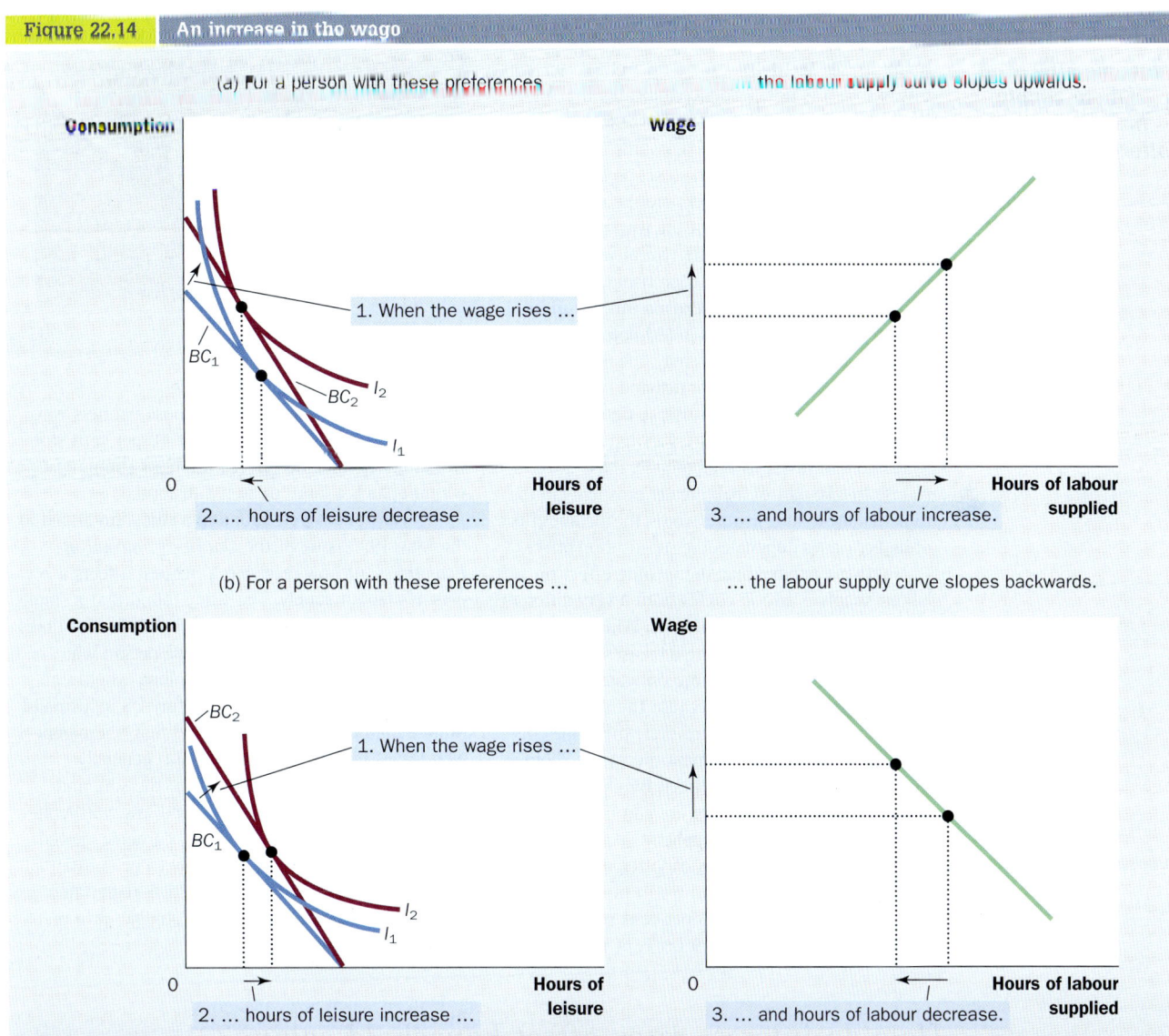

The two panels of this figure show how a person might respond to an increase in the wage. The graphs on the left show the consumer's initial budget constraint BC_1 and new budget constraint BC_2, as well as the consumer's optimum choices between consumption and leisure. The graphs on the right show the resulting labour supply curve. Because hours worked equal total hours available minus hours of leisure, any change in leisure implies an opposite change in the quantity of labour supplied. In panel (a), when the wage rises, consumption rises and leisure falls, resulting in a labour supply curve that slopes upwards. In panel (b), when the wage rises, both consumption and leisure rise, resulting in a labour supply curve that slopes backwards.

514

CASESTUDY

Income effects on labour supply – historical trends, lottery winners and the Carnegie conjecture

The idea of a backward-sloping labour supply curve might at first seem like a mere theoretical curiosity, but in fact it is not. Evidence indicates that the labour supply curve, considered over long periods of time, does in fact slope backwards. A hundred years ago many people worked six days a week. Today five-day working weeks are the norm. At the same time that the length of the working week has been falling, the wage of the typical worker (adjusted for inflation) has been rising.

Here is how economists explain this historical pattern. Over time, advances in technology raise workers' productivity and, thereby, the demand for labour. The increase in labour demand raises equilibrium wages. As wages rise, so does the reward for working. Yet rather than responding to this increased incentive by working more, most workers choose to take part of their greater prosperity in the form of more leisure. In other words, the income effect of higher wages dominates the substitution effect.

Further evidence that the income effect on labour supply is strong comes from a very different kind of data – winners of lotteries. Winners of large prizes in the lottery see large increases in their incomes and, as a result, large outward shifts in their budget constraints. Because the winners' wages have not changed, however, the slopes of their budget constraints remain the same. There is, therefore, no substitution effect. By examining the behaviour of lottery winners, we can isolate the income effect on labour supply.

The results from studies of lottery winners are striking. Of those winners who win more than a total of $50 000, almost 25 per cent quit working within a year, and another 9 per cent reduce the

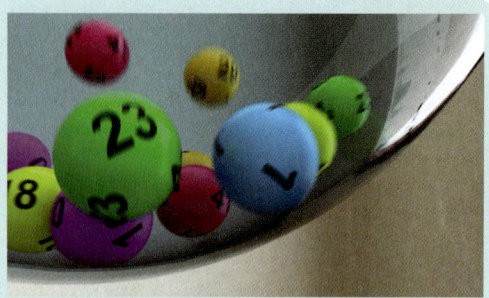

'No more 9 to 5 for me.'

Source: iStockphoto/Mark Evans.

number of hours they work. Of those winners who win more than $1 million, almost 40 per cent stop working. The income effect on labour supply of winning such a large prize is substantial.

Similar results were found in a study, published in the May 1993 issue of the *Quarterly Journal of Economics*, of how receiving a bequest affects a person's labour supply. The study found that a single person who inherits more than $150 000 is four times as likely to stop working as a single person who inherits less than $25 000. This finding would not have surprised the nineteenth-century US industrialist Andrew Carnegie. Carnegie warned that 'the parent who leaves his son enormous wealth generally deadens the talents and energies of the son, and tempts him to lead a less useful and less worthy life than he otherwise would'. That is, Carnegie viewed the income effect on labour supply to be substantial and, from his paternalistic perspective, regrettable. During his life and at his death, Carnegie gave much of his vast fortune to charity.

How do interest rates affect household saving?

An important decision that every person faces is how much income to consume today and how much to save for the future. We can use the theory of consumer choice to analyse how people make this decision and how the amount they save depends on the interest rate their savings will earn.

Consider the decision facing Sam, a worker planning ahead for retirement. To keep things simple, let's divide Sam's life into two periods. In the first period, Sam is young and working. In the second period, he is old and retired. When young, Sam earns $100 000. He divides this income between current consumption and saving. When he is old, Sam will consume what he has saved, including the interest that his savings have earned.

Suppose that the interest rate is 10 per cent. Then for every dollar that Sam saves when young, he can consume $1.10 when old. We can view 'consumption when young' and 'consumption when old' as the two goods that Sam must choose between. The interest rate determines the relative price of these two goods.

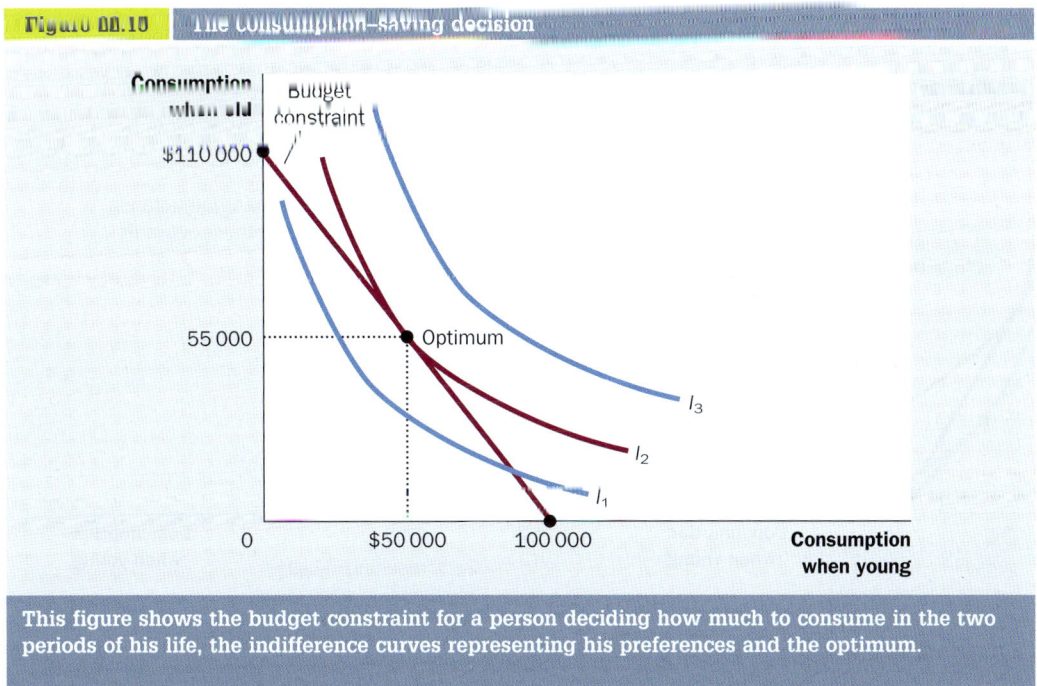

Figure 22.15   The consumption–saving decision

This figure shows the budget constraint for a person deciding how much to consume in the two periods of his life, the indifference curves representing his preferences and the optimum.

Figure 22.15 shows Sam's budget constraint. If he saves nothing, he consumes $100 000 when young and nothing when old. If he saves everything, he consumes nothing when young and $110 000 when old. The budget constraint shows these and all the intermediate possibilities.

Figure 22.15 uses indifference curves to represent Sam's preferences for consumption in the two periods. Because Sam prefers more consumption in both periods, he prefers points on higher indifference curves to points on lower ones. Given his preferences, Sam chooses the optimum combination of consumption in both periods of life, which is the point on the budget constraint that is on the highest possible indifference curve. At this optimum, Sam consumes $50 000 when young and $55 000 when old.

Now consider what happens when the interest rate increases from 10 per cent to 20 per cent. Figure 22.16 shows two possible outcomes. In both cases, the budget constraint shifts outwards and becomes steeper. At the new higher interest rate, Sam gets more consumption when old for every dollar of consumption that he gives up when young.

The two panels show different preferences for Sam and the resulting response to the higher interest rate. In both cases, consumption when old rises. Yet the response of consumption when young to the change in the interest rate is different in the two cases. In panel (a), Sam responds to the higher interest rate by consuming less when young. In panel (b), Sam responds by consuming more when young.

Sam's saving, of course, is his income when young minus the amount he consumes when young. In panel (a), consumption when young falls when the interest rate rises, so saving must rise. In panel (b), Sam consumes more when young, so saving must fall.

The case shown in panel (b) might at first seem odd – Sam responds to an increase in the return on savings by saving less. Yet this behaviour is not as peculiar as it might seem. We can understand it by considering the income and substitution effects of a higher interest rate.

Consider first the substitution effect. When the interest rate rises, consumption when old becomes less costly relative to consumption when young. Therefore, the substitution effect induces Sam to consume more when old and less when young. In other words, the substitution effect induces Sam to save more.

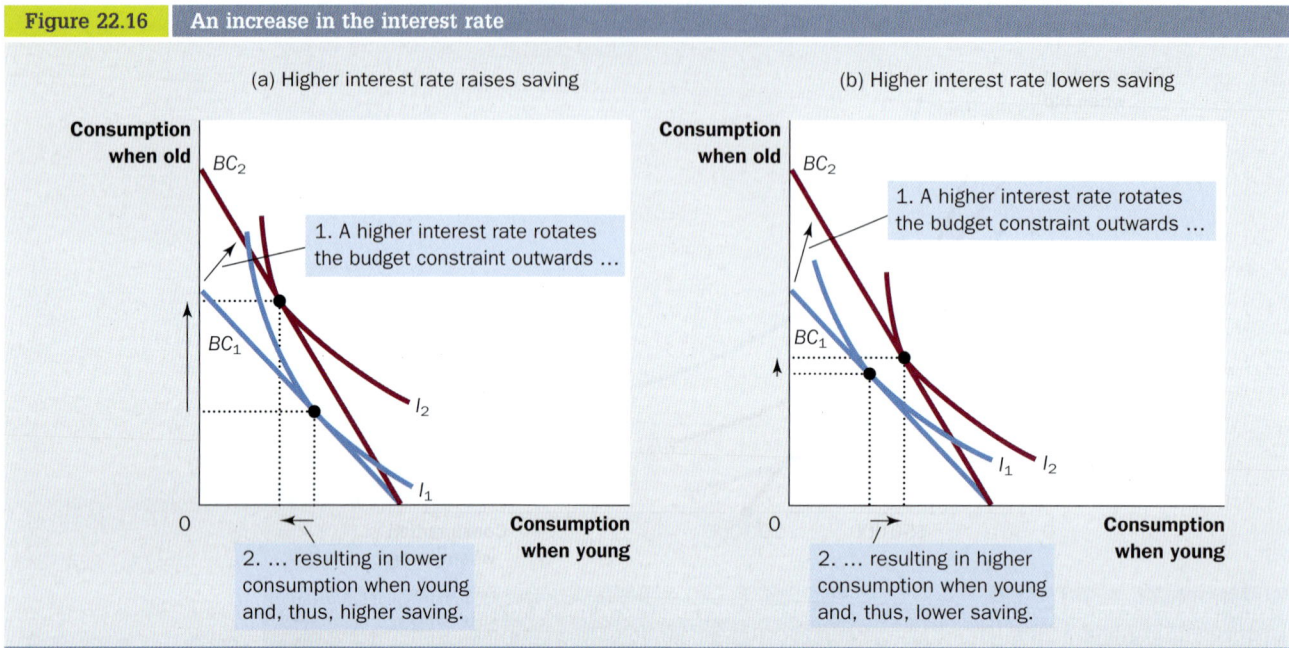

Figure 22.16   An increase in the interest rate

(a) Higher interest rate raises saving

(b) Higher interest rate lowers saving

In both panels, an increase in the interest rate shifts the budget constraint outwards. In panel (a), consumption when young falls, and consumption when old rises. The result is an increase in saving when young. In panel (b), consumption in both periods rises. The result is a decrease in saving when young.

Now consider the income effect. When the interest rate rises, Sam moves to a higher indifference curve. He is now better off than he was. As long as consumption in both periods consists of normal goods, he tends to want to use this increase in wellbeing to enjoy higher consumption in both periods. In other words, the income effect induces him to save less.

The end result, of course, depends on both the income and substitution effects. If the substitution effect of a higher interest rate is greater than the income effect, Sam saves more. If the income effect is greater than the substitution effect, Sam saves less. Thus, the theory of consumer choice says that an increase in the interest rate could either encourage or discourage saving.

Although this ambiguous result is interesting from the standpoint of economic theory, it is disappointing from the standpoint of economic policy. It turns out that an important issue in tax policy hinges in part on how saving responds to interest rates. Some economists have advocated reducing the tax on interest and other capital income, arguing that such a policy change would raise the after-tax interest rate that savers can earn and would thereby encourage people to save more. Other economists have argued that because of offsetting income and substitution effects, such a tax change might not increase saving and could even reduce it. Unfortunately, research has not led to a consensus about how interest rates affect saving. As a result, there remains disagreement among economists about whether changes in tax policy aimed to encourage saving would, in fact, have the intended effect.

Do the poor prefer to receive cash or in-kind transfers?

Paul is poor. Because of his low income, he has a meagre standard of living. The government wants to help. It can either give Paul $1000 worth of food or simply give him $1000 in cash.

What does the theory of consumer choice have to say about the comparison between these two policy options?

Figure 22.17 shows how the two options might work. If the government gives Paul cash, then the budget constraint shifts outwards. He can divide the extra cash between food and non-food consumption however he pleases. In contrast, if the government gives Paul an in-kind transfer of

Figure 22.17   Cash versus in-kind transfers

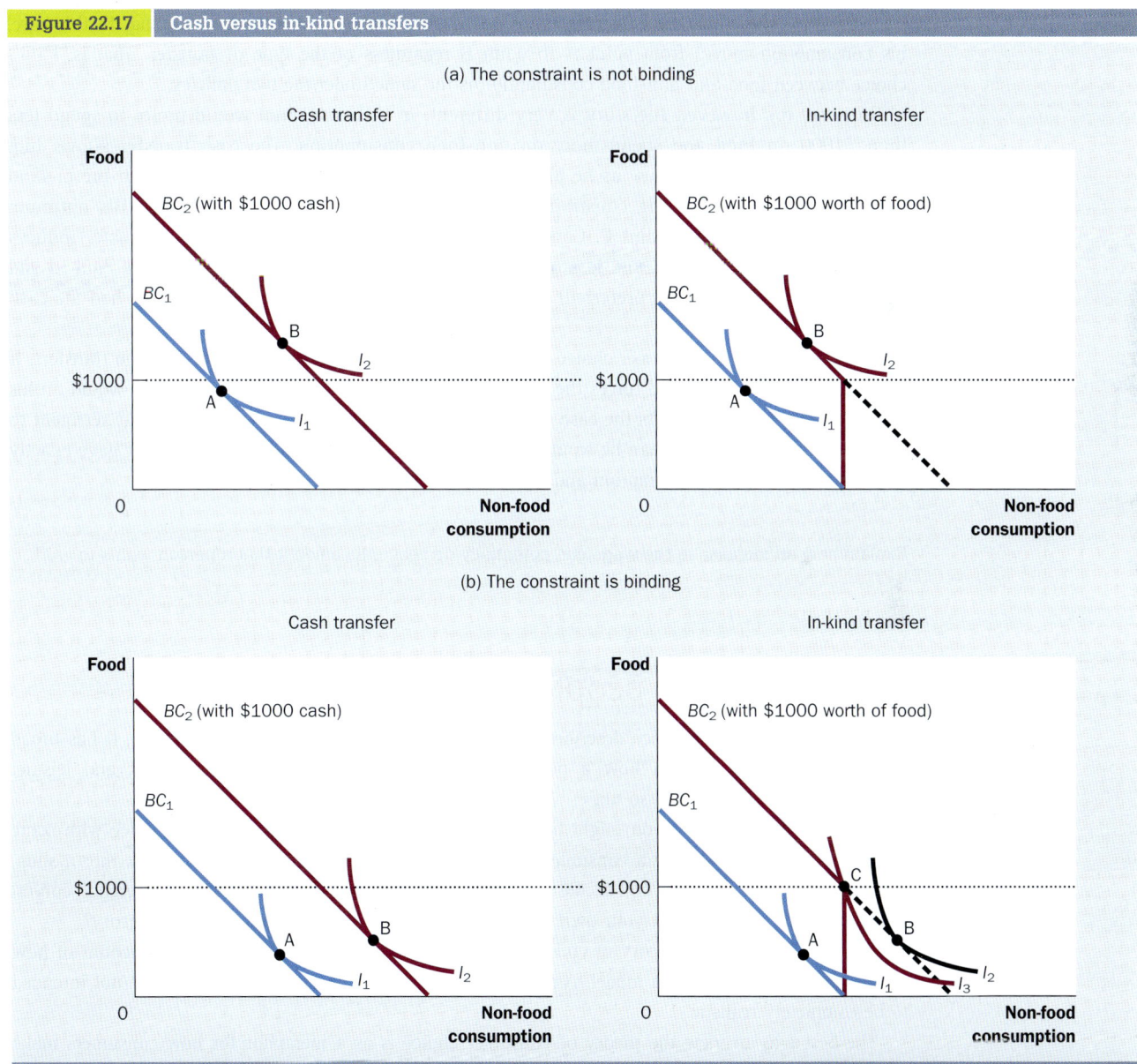

(a) The constraint is not binding

Both panels compare a cash transfer and a similar in-kind transfer of food. In panel (a), the in-kind transfer does not impose a binding constraint and the consumer ends up on the same indifference curve under the two policies. In panel (b), the in-kind transfer imposes a binding constraint and the consumer ends up on a lower indifference curve with the in-kind transfer than with the cash transfer.

food, then his new budget constraint is more complicated. The budget constraint has again shifted out. But now the budget constraint has a kink at $1000 of food, for Paul must consume at least that amount in food. That is, even if Paul spends all his money on non-food consumption, he still consumes $1000 in food.

The ultimate comparison between the cash transfer and in-kind transfer depends on Paul's preferences. In panel (a), Paul would choose to spend at least $1000 on food even if he receives a cash transfer. Therefore, the constraint imposed by the in-kind transfer is not binding. In this case, his consumption moves from point A to point B regardless of the type of transfer. That is, Paul's choice between food and non-food consumption is the same under the two policies.

In panel (b), however, the story is very different. In this case, Paul would prefer to spend less than $1000 on food and spend more on non-food consumption. The cash transfer allows him discretion to spend the money as he pleases and he consumes at point B. In contrast, the in-kind transfer imposes the binding constraint that he consume at least $1000 of food. His optimum allocation is at the kink, point C. Compared with the cash transfer, the in-kind transfer induces Paul to consume more food and less of other goods. The in-kind transfer also forces Paul to end up on a lower (and thus less preferred) indifference curve. Paul is worse off than if he had the cash transfer.

Thus, the theory of consumer choice teaches a simple lesson about cash versus in-kind transfers. If an in-kind transfer of a good forces the recipient to consume more of the good than he would on his own, then the recipient prefers the cash transfer. If the in-kind transfer does not force the recipient to consume more of the good than he would on his own, then the cash and in-kind transfer have exactly the same effect on the consumption and welfare of the recipient.

Explain how an increase in the wage can potentially decrease the amount that a person wants to work.

Conclusion: Do people really think this way?

The theory of consumer choice describes how people make decisions. As we have seen, it has broad applicability. It can explain how a person chooses between Pepsi and pizza, work and leisure, consumption and saving and so on.

At this point, however, you might be tempted to treat the theory of consumer choice with some scepticism. After all, you are a consumer. You decide what to buy every time you walk into a shop. And you know that you do not decide by writing down budget constraints and indifference curves. Doesn't this knowledge about your own decision making provide evidence against the theory?

The answer is no. The theory of consumer choice does not try to present a literal account of how people make decisions. It is a model. And, as we first discussed in chapter 2, models are not intended to be completely realistic.

The best way to view the theory of consumer choice is as a metaphor for how consumers make decisions. No consumer (except an occasional economist) goes through the explicit optimisation envisioned in the theory. Yet consumers are aware that their choices are constrained by their financial resources. And, given those constraints, they do the best they can to achieve the highest level of satisfaction. The theory of consumer choice tries to describe this implicit psychological process in a way that permits explicit economic analysis.

The proof of the pudding is in the eating. And the test of a theory is in its applications. In the last section of this chapter we applied the theory of consumer choice to four practical issues about the economy. If you take more advanced courses in economics, you will see that this theory provides the framework for much additional analysis.

Source: PEARLS BEFORE SWINE © 2003 Stephan Pastis. Reprinted by permission of Universal Uclick for UFS. All rights reserved.

Summary

- A consumer's budget constraint shows the possible combinations of different goods that can be bought given his/her income and the prices of the goods. The slope of the budget constraint equals the relative price of the goods.

- A consumer's indifference curves represent his or her preferences. An indifference curve shows the various bundles of goods that make a consumer equally happy. Points on higher indifference curves are preferred to points on lower indifference curves. The slope of an indifference curve at any point is the consumer's marginal rate of substitution – the rate at which the consumer is willing to trade one good for the other.

- A consumer optimises by choosing the point on the budget constraint that lies on the highest indifference curve. At this point, the slope of the indifference curve (the marginal rate of substitution between the goods) equals the slope of the budget constraint (the relative price of the goods).

- When the price of a good falls, the impact on a consumer's choices can be broken down into an income effect and a substitution effect. The income effect is the change in consumption that arises because a lower price makes the consumer better off. The substitution effect is the change in consumption that arises because a price change encourages greater consumption of the good that has become relatively cheaper. The income effect is reflected in the movement from a lower to a higher indifference curve, whereas the substitution effect is reflected by a movement along an indifference curve to a point with a different slope.

- The theory of consumer choice can be applied in many situations. It can explain why demand curves can potentially slope upwards, why higher wages could either increase or decrease the quantity of labour supplied, why higher interest rates could either increase or decrease saving, and why the poor prefer cash to in-kind transfers.

Key concepts

budget constraint

Giffen good

income effect

indifference curve

marginal rate of substitution

perfect complements

perfect substitutes

substitution effect

Questions for review

1   A consumer has income of $3000. Wine costs $3 a glass and cheese costs $6 a kilogram. Draw the consumer's budget constraint. What is the slope of this budget constraint?

2   Draw a consumer's indifference curves for wine and cheese. Describe and explain four properties of these indifference curves.

3   Pick a point on an indifference curve for wine and cheese and show the marginal rate of substitution. What does the marginal rate of substitution tell us?

4   Show a consumer's budget constraint and indifference curves for wine and cheese. Show the optimum consumption choice. If the price of wine is $3 a glass and the price of cheese is $6 a kilogram, what is the marginal rate of substitution at this optimum?

5   A person who consumes wine and cheese gets a raise, so his income increases from $3000 to $4000. Show what happens if both wine and cheese are normal goods. Now show what happens if cheese is an inferior good.

6 The price of cheese rises from $6 to $10 a kilogram and the price of wine remains $3 a glass. For a consumer with a constant income of $3000, show what happens to consumption of wine and cheese. Divide the change into income and substitution effects.

7 Can an increase in the price of cheese possibly induce a consumer to buy more cheese? Explain.

Problems and applications

1 Jennifer divides her income between coffee and croissants. An early frost in Brazil causes a large increase in the price of coffee in Australia.
   a Show the effect of the frost on Jennifer's budget constraint.
   b Show the effect of the frost on Jennifer's optimum consumption bundle assuming that the substitution effect outweighs the income effect for croissants.
   c Show the effect of the frost on Jennifer's optimum consumption bundle assuming that the income effect outweighs the substitution effect for croissants.

2 Compare the following two pairs of goods:
   a Coke and Pepsi
   b skis and ski bindings.
      In which case do you expect the indifference curves to be fairly straight and in which case do you expect the indifference curves to be very bowed? In which case will the consumer respond more to a change in the relative price of the two goods?

3 Mario consumes only cheese and crackers.
   a Could cheese and crackers both be inferior goods for Mario? Explain.
   b Suppose that cheese is a normal good for Mario whereas crackers are an inferior good. If the price of cheese falls, what happens to Mario's consumption of crackers? What happens to his consumption of cheese? Explain.

4 Jim buys only milk and biscuits.
   a In 2004, Jim earns $100, milk costs $2 per litre and biscuits cost $4 per dozen. Draw Jim's budget constraint.
   b Now suppose that all prices increase by 10 per cent in the year 2005 and that Jim's salary increases by 10 per cent as well. Draw Jim's new budget constraint. How would Jim's optimum combination of milk and biscuits in 2005 compare with his optimum combination in 2004?

5 Consider your decision about how many hours to work.
   a Draw your budget constraint assuming that you pay no taxes on your income. On the same diagram, draw another budget constraint assuming that you pay a 15 per cent tax.
   b Show how the tax might lead to more hours of work, fewer hours or the same number of hours. Explain.

6 Sarah is awake for 100 hours per week. Using one diagram, show Sarah's budget constraints if she earns $6 per hour, $8 per hour and $10 per hour. Now draw indifference curves such that Sarah's labour supply curve is upward-sloping when the wage is between $6 and $8 per hour, and backward-sloping when the wage is between $8 and $10 per hour.

7 Draw the indifference curve for someone deciding how much to work. Suppose the wage increases. Is it possible that the person's consumption would fall? Is this plausible? Discuss. (*Hint:* Think about income and substitution effects.)

8 The labour force participation rate of married women has more than doubled over the past 50 years. One economic influence on this rate was the increase in women's wages over this period. Another economic influence was the increase in men's wages, which raised the standard of living for most married women.

    a Using an indifference-curve diagram, show and then explain how a rise in the income of a husband can lead to a fall in the number of hours worked by his wife. What assumption do you need to make about leisure to get this result?

    b Using another indifference-curve diagram, show and then explain how a rise in female wages affects a woman's decision about how many hours to work.

9 Suppose you take a job that pays $30 000 and set some of this income aside in a savings account that pays an annual interest rate of 5 per cent. Use a diagram with a budget constraint and indifference curves to show how your consumption changes in each of the following situations. To keep things simple, assume that you pay no taxes on your income.

    a Your salary increases to $40 000.

    b The interest rate on your bank account rises to 8 per cent.

10 As discussed in the text, we can divide an individual's life into two hypothetical periods – 'young' and 'old'. Suppose that the individual earns income only when young and saves some of that income to consume when old. If the interest rate on savings falls, can you tell what happens to consumption when young? Can you tell what happens to consumption when old? Explain.

11 Suppose that your state gives each town $5 million in aid per year. The way in which the money is spent is currently unrestricted, but the premier has proposed that towns be required to spend the entire $5 million on education. You can illustrate the effect of this proposal on your town's spending on education using a budget constraint and indifference-curve diagram. The two goods are education and non-education spending.

    a Draw your town's budget constraint under the existing policy, assuming that your town's only source of revenue besides the state aid is a property tax that yields $10 million. On the same diagram, draw the budget constraint under the premier's proposal.

    b Would your town spend more on education under the premier's proposal than under the existing policy? Explain.

    c Now compare two towns – Youngton and Oldton – with the same revenue and the same state aid. Youngton has a large school-age population and Oldton has a large elderly population. In which town is the premier's proposal most likely to increase education spending? Explain.

12 (This problem is challenging.) The social security system provides income to some needy families. Typically, the maximum payment goes to families that earn no income; then, as families begin to earn income, the social security payment declines gradually and eventually disappears. Let's consider the possible effects of this program on a family's labour supply.

    a Draw a budget constraint for a family assuming that the social security system did not exist. On the same diagram, draw a budget constraint that reflects the existence of the social security system.

    b Adding indifference curves to your diagram, show how the social security system could reduce the number of hours worked by the family. Explain, with reference to both the income and substitution effects.

    c Using your diagram from part (b), show the effect of the social security system on the wellbeing of the family.

13 (This problem is challenging.) Suppose that an individual owed no taxes on the first $10 000 she earned and 15 per cent of any income she earned over $10 000. Now suppose that the federal government is considering two ways to reduce the tax burden – a reduction in the tax rate and an increase in the amount on which no tax is owed.

    a What effect would a reduction in the tax rate have on the individual's labour supply if she earned $30 000 to start? Explain in words using the income and substitution effects. You do not need to use a diagram.

b What effect would an increase in the amount on which no tax is owed have on the individual's labour supply? Again, explain in words using the income and substitution effects.

14 (This problem is challenging.) Consider a person deciding how much to consume and how much to save for retirement. This person has particular preferences – her lifetime utility depends on the lowest level of consumption during the two periods of her life. That is:

Utility = Minimum {consumption when young, consumption when old}

a Draw this person's indifference curves. (*Hint*: Recall that indifference curves show the combinations of consumption in the two periods that yield the same level of utility.)
b Draw the budget constraint and the optimum.
c When the interest rate increases, does this person save more or less? Explain your answer using income and substitution effects.

Search me!

When accessing information about economics use the following keywords in any combinations you require:

- indifference curve
- inferior good

CourseMate

For more multimedia resources and activities on economics, visit the Economics CourseMate website.

23

Frontiers of microeconomics

Learning objectives

In this chapter you will:

- consider what happens when economic agents have private information

- understand how political institutions impact on economic policymaking

- learn how economic agents really behave.

Economics is a study of the choices that people make and the resulting interactions they have with one another. This study has many facets, as we have seen in the preceding chapters. Yet it would be a mistake to think that all the facets we have seen make up a finished jewel, perfect and unchanging. Like all scientists, economists are always on the lookout for new areas to study and new phenomena to explain. This final chapter on microeconomics offers an assortment of three topics at the discipline's frontier to see how economists are trying to expand their understanding of human behaviour and society.

The first topic is the economics of *asymmetric information*. Many times in life, some people are better informed than others and this difference in information can affect the choices they make and how they deal with one another. Thinking about this asymmetry can shed light on many aspects of the world, from the market for used cars to the custom of gift giving.

The second topic we examine in this chapter is *political economy*. Throughout this book we have seen many examples where markets fail and government policy can potentially improve matters. But 'potentially' is a needed qualifier: Whether this potential is realised depends on how well our political institutions work. The field of political economy applies the tools of economics to understand the functioning of government.

The third topic in this chapter is *behavioural economics*. This field brings some of the insights from psychology into the study of economic issues. It offers a view of human behaviour that is more subtle and complex than that found in conventional economic theory, but this view may also be more realistic.

This chapter covers a great deal of ground. To do so, it offers not a full helping of these three topics but, instead, a taste of each. One goal is to show a few of the directions in which economists are heading in their effort to expand knowledge of how the economy works. Another goal is to whet your appetite for more courses in economics.

Asymmetric information

'I know something that you don't know.' This statement is a common taunt among children, but it also conveys a deep truth about how people sometimes interact with one another. Many times in life, one person knows more about what is going on than another. A difference in access to relevant knowledge is called an *information asymmetry*.

Examples abound. As we saw in chapter 20, workers know more than their employers about how much effort they put into their jobs. A seller of a used car knows more than the buyer about the car's condition. The first is an example of a *hidden action,* whereas the second is an example of a *hidden characteristic*. In each case, the party in the dark (the employer, the car buyer) would like to know the relevant information, but the informed party (the worker, the car seller) may have an incentive to conceal it.

Because asymmetric information is so prevalent, economists have devoted much effort in recent decades to studying its effects. And, indeed, the 2001 Nobel Prize in economics was awarded to three economists (George Akerlof, Michael Spence and Joseph Stiglitz) for their pioneering work on this topic. Let's discuss some of the insights that this study has revealed.

Hidden actions: Principals, agents and moral hazard

Moral hazard is a problem that arises when one person, called the **agent**, is performing some task on behalf of another person, called the **principal**. If the principal cannot perfectly monitor the agent's

moral hazard
the tendency of a person who is imperfectly monitored to engage in dishonest or otherwise undesirable behaviour

agent
a person who is performing an act for another person, called the principal

principal
a person for whom another person, called the agent, is performing some act

behaviour, the agent tends to undertake less effort than the principal considers desirable. The phrase *moral hazard* refers to the risk, or 'hazard', of inappropriate or otherwise 'immoral' behaviour by the agent. In such a situation, the principal tries various ways to encourage the agent to act more responsibly.

The employment relationship is the classic example. The employer is the principal and the worker is the agent. The moral-hazard problem is the temptation of imperfectly monitored workers to shirk their responsibilities. Employers can respond to this problem in various ways:

- *Better monitoring:* Parents hiring babysitters have been known to plant hidden video cameras in their homes to record the sitter's behaviour when the parents are away. The aim is to catch irresponsible behaviour.

- *Higher wages:* According to *efficiency-wage theories* (discussed in chapter 20), some employers may choose to pay their workers a wage that is above the level of equilibrium of supply and demand in the labour market. A worker who earns an above-equilibrium wage is less likely to shirk, because being caught and fired makes it very hard to find another high-paying job.

- *Delayed payment:* Firms can delay part of a worker's compensation, so if the worker is caught shirking and is fired, a larger penalty is suffered. One example of delayed compensation is the year-end bonus. Similarly, a firm may choose to pay its workers more later in their lives. Thus, the wage increases that workers get as they age may reflect not just the benefits of experience but also a response to moral hazard.

- *Employee stock ownership:* Firms can give worker's stocks or stock options that allow them to share in the profitability of the company directly. This is common in smaller firms but also in legal and accounting partnerships. The ownership stake aligns incentives so long as employees understand the impact of their actions on the firm as a whole.

These various mechanisms to reduce the problem of moral hazard need not be used alone. Employers can use a combination of them.

There are also many other examples of moral hazard beyond the workplace. A homeowner with fire insurance will likely buy too few fire extinguishers because the homeowner bears the cost of the extinguisher while the insurance company receives much of the benefit. A family may live near a river with a high risk of flooding because the family enjoys the scenic views, while the government bears the cost of disaster relief after a flood. Many regulations are aimed at addressing the problem: An insurance company may require homeowners to buy extinguishers and the government may prohibit building homes on land with high risk of flooding. But the insurance company does not have perfect information about how cautious homeowners are and the government does not have perfect information about the risk that families undertake when choosing where to live. As a result, the problem of moral hazard persists.

Search me!
▸ moral hazard

CASESTUDY

Corporate management

Much production in the modern economy takes place within corporations. Like other firms, corporations buy inputs in markets for the factors of production and sell their output in markets for goods and services. Also like other firms, they are guided in their decisions by the objective of profit maximisation. But a large corporation has to deal with some issues that do not arise in, say, a small family-owned business.

What is distinctive about a corporation? From a legal standpoint, a corporation is an organisation that is granted a charter recognising it as a separate legal entity, with its own rights and responsibilities distinct from those of its owners and employees. From an economic standpoint, the most important feature of the corporate form of organisation is the separation of ownership and control. One group of people, called the shareholders, own the corporation's resources.

The separation of ownership and control creates a principal–agent problem. In this case, the shareholders are the principals and the managers are the agents. The chief executive officer and other managers are in the best position to know how to maximise profit for the shareholders. But ensuring that they carry out this task is not always easy. The managers may have goals of their own, such as taking life easy, having a plush office and a private jet, throwing lavish parties or presiding over a large business empire. The managers' goals may not always coincide with the goal of profit maximisation.

The corporation's board of directors is responsible for hiring and firing the top management. The board monitors the managers' performance and it designs their compensation packages. These packages often include incentives aimed at aligning the interest of shareholders with the interest of management. Managers might be given bonuses based on performance or options to buy the company's stock, which are more valuable if the company performs well.

Note, however, that the directors are themselves agents of the shareholders. The existence of a board overseeing management only shifts the principal–agent problem. The issue then becomes how to ensure that the board of directors fulfils its own legal obligation of acting in the best interest of the shareholders. If the directors become too friendly with management, they may not provide the required oversight.

The corporation's principal–agent problem has been in the news in recent years. The top managers of several prominent companies, such as Enron, Tyco and WorldCom, were found to be engaging in activities that enriched themselves at the expense of their shareholders. In these cases, the actions were so extreme as to be criminal and the corporate managers were not just fired but also sent to prison. Some shareholders sued directors for failing to monitor management sufficiently.

Fortunately, criminal activity by corporate managers is rare. But in some ways, it is only the tip of the iceberg. Whenever ownership and control are separated, as they are in most large corporations, there is an inevitable tension between the interests of shareholders and the interests of management.

IN THE NEWS . . .

REAL ESTATE AGENTS ARE FREAKONOMISTS

Real estate agents know more about buying and selling houses than their customers. But how much more? This article documents a study by Steven Levitt and Chad Syverson that featured in the popular book *Freakonomics*. It turns out that when they come to selling their own houses, estate agents don't hold back.

Why a real estate agent may skip the extra mile

by Daniel Gross

As housing prices keep rising year after year, real estate has become a national obsession – and a more powerful economic engine. Sales of homes and condominiums totaled an estimated $2.17 trillion in 2004, said Lawrence Yun, senior economist at the National Association of Realtors.

The industry couldn't function without the armies of agents who help buyers and sellers reach mutually agreeable terms on those four-bedroom, center-hall colonials, and who generally collect hefty 6 per cent commissions for their trouble. But a recent study by two University of Chicago economists suggests that home sellers should regard agents with some caution. The study does not suggest that agents are inherently untrustworthy. Rather, it says, the housing market remains inefficient, and the incentives for agents to maximize profits for their clients aren't powerful enough.

The study was instigated by Steven D. Levitt, a self-described 'rogue economist' who has applied the analytical tools of his trade to everything from sumo wrestlers to drug-dealing

>>

gangs; his work is cataloged in the forthcoming book *Freakonomics*, written with Stephen J. Dubner.

Professor Levitt had fixed up and sold several houses in Oak Park, Ill., a suburb of Chicago. When working with real estate agents, he said, 'I got the impression they weren't working solely in their clients' best interest.'

Along with a colleague, Chad Syverson, Professor Levitt set out to prove it by comparing data on homes that agents sold on behalf of others with those that they owned and sold for themselves. They analyzed sales from 1992 to 2002 of 98 000 homes in suburban Chicago, of which 3300 were owned by real estate agents. When the economists constructed an analysis that controlled for amenities, location and the adjectives used to describe the houses, they found that agent-owned homes, on average, stayed on the market 9.5 days longer and commanded median prices that were 3.7 per cent higher than comparable homes owned by clients.

Of course, agents may just know how to position homes for sale better than other people do. It's their job, after all. And, being human, they may work harder selling their own homes, the way a dentist may take extra care cleaning her own child's teeth. But these explanations don't square with the data. 'If that were the case, you'd expect the clients' homes to stay on the market longer than the brokers' homes,' Professor Levitt said.

The two professors conclude that poorly designed incentives bear some of the blame. 'You have to keep in mind that the agent's incentives don't line up perfectly with your own,' Professor Syverson said.

Real estate agents have a better sense than others of the best price a home can command. But when they work for others, they don't have the financial incentive to pursue it. Most home sales generate a 6 per cent commission, split between the brokerage firms representing the buyer and seller. The agent generally receives half of the firm's draw, or 1.5 per cent of the sale. So if a home sells for $500 000, the agent personally receives $7500. Not bad for what may be just a few days of work. If the agent works for an additional week and urges the seller to hold out for $515 000, that's an extra $15 000 for the seller, but only an extra $225 for the agent. Because every additional dollar throws only a penny and a half into the pocket of the agent, the economists reason, the agent may push clients to accept lowball offers.

Of course, price is just one factor motivating sellers to accept offers. Many are in a hurry, may be because they are relocating for new jobs, or want to be in their new city by the time the next school year starts. So they may feel compelled to accept the first offer. Most agents who sell their own homes, by contrast, aren't leaving the area. 'The brokers may be in a situation where they can be more patient,' said Mr Yun of the National Association of Realtors.

Armed with this knowledge, what should home sellers do? 'You cannot completely trust the advice your broker gives you,' said Christopher J. Mayer, a professor of real estate at Columbia Business School. 'You have to become more educated as a buyer.'

In fact, the economists concluded that sellers, empowered by the Internet, are already eroding agents' advantage. Sites like Realtor.com and domania.com allow anyone to survey the market and check out neighborhood price histories. From 1992 to 1995, in the days before such sites existed, agents' homes commanded prices that were 4.9 per cent higher and stayed on the market more than 14 days longer than equivalent other homes. But from 2000 to 2002, a period when such sites came into popular use, the margins shrank to 2.9 per cent and 2.5 days.

'As consumers become more comfortable with the idea that they can price their own properties, times will get tougher and tougher for real estate agents,' Professor Levitt said.

Hidden characteristics: Adverse selection and the lemons problem

Adverse selection is a problem that arises in markets where the seller knows more about the attributes of the good being sold than the buyer does. As a result, the buyer runs the risk of being sold a good of low quality. That is, the 'selection' of goods being sold may be 'adverse' from the standpoint of the uninformed buyer.

The classic example of adverse selection is the market for used cars. Sellers of used cars know their vehicles' defects while buyers often do not. Because owners of the worst cars are more likely to sell them than are the owners of the best cars, buyers are apprehensive about getting a 'lemon'. As a result, many people avoid buying vehicles in the used car market. This lemons problem can explain why a used car only a few weeks old sells for thousands of dollars less than a new car of the same type. A buyer of the used car might surmise that the seller is getting rid of the car quickly because the seller knows something about it that the buyer does not.

A second example of adverse selection occurs in the labour market. According to another efficiency-wage theory, workers vary in their abilities and they may know their own abilities better than do the firms that hire them. When a firm cuts the wage it pays, the more talented workers are more likely to quit, knowing they are better able to find other employment. Conversely, a firm may choose to pay an above-equilibrium wage to attract a better mix of workers.

A third example of adverse selection occurs in markets for insurance. For example, buyers of health insurance know more about their own health problems than do insurance companies. Because people with greater hidden health problems are more likely to buy health insurance than are other people, the price of health insurance reflects the costs of a sicker-than-average person. As a result, people in average health may observe the high price of insurance and decide not to buy it.

When markets suffer from adverse selection, the invisible hand does not necessarily work its magic. In the used car market, owners of good cars may choose to keep them rather than sell them at the low price that sceptical buyers are willing to pay. In the labour market, wages may be stuck above the level that balances supply and demand, resulting in unemployment. In insurance markets, buyers with low risk may choose to remain uninsured, because the policies they are offered fail to reflect their true characteristics. Advocates of government-provided health insurance sometimes point to the problem of adverse selection as one reason not to trust the private market to provide the right amount of health insurance on its own.

adverse selection
the tendency for the mix of unobserved attributes to become undesirable from the standpoint of an uninformed party

▸ adverse selection

Signalling to convey private information

Although asymmetric information is sometimes a motivation for public policy, it also motivates some individual behaviour that otherwise might be hard to explain. Markets respond to problems of asymmetric information in many ways. One of them is **signalling**, which refers to actions taken by an informed party for the sole purpose of credibly revealing their private information.

We have seen examples of signalling in previous chapters. As we saw in chapter 18, firms may spend money on advertising to signal to potential customers that they have high quality products. As we saw in chapter 20, students may earn university and postgraduate degrees to signal to potential employers that they are high-ability individuals. Recall that the signalling theory of education contrasts with the human-capital theory, which asserts that education increases a person's productivity, rather than merely conveying information about innate talent. These two examples of

signalling
an action taken by an informed party to reveal private information to an uninformed party

signalling (advertising, education) may seem very different, but below the surface they are much the same: In both cases, the informed party (the firm, the student) is using the signal to convince the uninformed party (the customer, the employer) that the informed party is offering something of high quality.

What does it take for an action to be an effective signal? Obviously, it must be costly. If a signal were free, everyone would use it and it would convey no information. For the same reason, there is another requirement: The signal must be less costly, or more beneficial, to the person with the higher-quality product. Otherwise, everyone would have the same incentive to use the signal and the signal would reveal nothing.

Consider again our two examples. In the advertising case, a firm with a good product reaps a larger benefit from advertising because customers who try the product once are more likely to become repeat customers. Thus, it is rational for the firm with the good product to pay for the cost of the signal (advertising), and it is rational for the customer to use the signal as a piece of information about the product's quality. In the education case, a talented person can get through school more easily than a less talented one. Thus, it is rational for the talented person to pay for the cost of the signal (education) and it is rational for the employer to use the signal as a piece of information about the person's talent.

The world is replete with instances of signalling. Magazine ads sometimes include the phrase 'as seen on TV'. Why does a firm selling a product in a magazine choose to stress this fact? One possibility is that the firm is trying to convey its willingness to pay for an expensive signal (a spot on television) in the hope that you will infer that its product is of high quality. For the same reason, graduates of elite universities are always sure to put that fact on their résumés.

CASESTUDY
Gifts as signals

A man is debating what to give his girlfriend for her birthday. 'I know,' he says to himself, 'I'll give her cash. After all, I don't know her tastes as well as she does, and with cash, she can buy anything she wants'. But when he hands her the money, she is offended. Convinced he doesn't really love her, she breaks off the relationship.

'Now we'll see how much he loves me.'

Source: photos.com/Getty Images.

What's the economics behind this story?

In some ways, gift giving is a strange custom. As the man in our story suggests, people typically know their own preferences better than others do, so we might expect everyone to prefer cash to in-kind transfers. If your employer substituted merchandise for your pay cheque, you would likely object to the means of payment. But your reaction is very different when someone who (you hope) loves you does the same thing.

One interpretation of gift giving is that it reflects asymmetric information and signalling. The man in our story has private information that the girlfriend would like to know: Does he really love her? Choosing a good gift for her is a signal of his love. Certainly, picking out a gift has the right characteristics to be a signal. It is costly (it takes time), and its cost depends on the private information (how much he loves her). If he really loves her, choosing a good gift is easy because he is thinking about her all the time. If he doesn't love her, finding the right gift is more difficult. Thus, giving a gift that suits the girlfriend is one way for him to convey the private information of his love for her. Giving cash shows that he isn't even bothering to try.

The signalling theory of gift giving is consistent with another observation: People care most about the custom when the strength of affection is most in question. Thus, giving cash to a girlfriend or boyfriend is usually a bad move. But when college students receive a cheque from their parents, they are less often offended. The parents' love is less likely to be in doubt, so the recipient probably won't interpret the cash gift as a signal of lack of affection.

Screening to induce information revelation

When an informed party takes actions to reveal private information, the phenomenon is called signalling. When an uninformed party takes actions to induce the informed party to reveal private information, the phenomenon is called **screening**.

Some screening is commonsense. A person buying a used car may ask that it be checked by a mechanic before the sale. A seller who refuses this request reveals his private information that the car is a lemon. The buyer may decide to offer a lower price or to look for another car.

Other examples of screening are more subtle. For example, consider a firm that sells car insurance. The firm would like to charge a low premium to safe drivers and a high premium to risky drivers. But how can it tell them apart? Drivers know whether they are safe or risky, but the risky ones won't admit to it. A driver's history is one piece of information (which insurance companies in fact use), but because of the intrinsic randomness of car accidents, history is an imperfect indicator of future risks.

The insurance company might be able to sort out the two kinds of drivers by offering different insurance policies that would induce them to separate themselves. One policy would have a high premium and cover the full cost of any accidents that occur. Another policy would have low premiums but would have, say, $1000 deductible. (That is, the driver would be responsible for the first $1000 of damage and the insurance company would cover the remaining risk.) Notice that the deductible is more of a burden for risky drivers because they are more likely to have an accident. Thus, with a large enough deductible, the low-premium policy with a deductible would attract the safe drivers, while the high-premium policy without a deductible would attract the risky drivers. Faced with these two policies, the two kinds of drivers would reveal their private information by choosing different insurance policies.

screening
an action taken by an uninformed party to induce an informed party to reveal information

Asymmetric information and public policy

We have examined two kinds of asymmetric information – moral hazard and adverse selection. And we have seen how individuals may respond to the problem with signalling or screening. Now let's consider what the study of asymmetric information suggests about the proper scope of public policy.

The tension between market success and market failure is central in microeconomics. We learned in chapter 7 that the equilibrium of supply and demand is efficient in the sense that it maximises the total surplus that society can obtain in a market. Adam Smith's invisible hand seemed to reign supreme. This conclusion was then tempered with the study of externalities (chapter 10), public goods (chapter 11), imperfect competition (chapters 15 to 18) and poverty (chapter 21). These examples of market failure showed that government can sometimes improve market outcomes.

The study of asymmetric information gives us new reason to be wary of markets. When some people know more than others, the market may fail to put resources to their best use. People with high-quality used cars may have trouble selling them because buyers will be afraid of getting a lemon. People with few health problems may have trouble getting low-cost health insurance because insurance companies lump them together with those who have significant (but hidden) health problems.

Although asymmetric information may call for government action in some cases, three facts complicate the issue. First, as we have seen, the private market can sometimes deal with information asymmetries on its own using a combination of signalling and screening. Second, the government rarely has more information than the private parties. Even if the market's allocation of resources is not efficient, when there are information asymmetries, policymakers may find it hard to improve upon the market's admittedly imperfect outcome. Third, the government is itself an imperfect institution – a topic we take up in the next section.

A person who buys a life insurance policy pays a certain amount per year and receives for their family a much larger payment in the event of their death. Would you expect buyers of life insurance to have higher or lower death rates than the average person? How might this be an example of moral hazard? Of adverse selection? How might a life insurance company deal with these problems?

Political economy

As we have seen, markets left on their own do not always reach a desirable allocation of resources. When we judge the markets' outcome to be either inefficient or inequitable, there may be a role for the government to step in and improve the situation. Yet before we embrace an activist government, we need to consider one more fact: The government is also an imperfect institution. The field of *political economy* (sometimes called the field of *public choice*) applies the methods of economics to study how government works.

The Condorcet voting paradox

Most advanced societies rely on democratic principles to set government policy. When a city is deciding between two locations to build a new park, for example, we have a simple way to choose – the majority gets its way. Yet, for most policy issues, the number of possible outcomes far exceeds two. A new park, for instance, could be placed in many possible locations. In this case, as the eighteenth-century French political theorist Marquis de Condorcet famously noted, democracy might run into some problems trying to choose one of the outcomes.

Condorcet paradox
the failure of majority rule to produce transitive preferences for society

To illustrate the **Condorcet paradox**, imagine that three people – Kirk, Spock and McCoy – are choosing what DVD – *Star Wars Episode V: The Empire Strikes Back*, *Harry Potter and the Order of the Phoenix* and *Police Academy 5: Assignment Miami Beach* – to watch. Their individual preferences are shown in Table 23.1.

Table 23.1 Individual preferences			
Rank	Kirk's preferences	Spock's preferences	McCoy's preferences
1st choice	Star Wars	Harry Potter	Police Academy
2nd choice	Harry Potter	Police Academy	Star Wars
3rd choice	Police Academy	Star Wars	Harry Potter

They want to aggregate these individual preferences into preferences for society as a whole. How should they do it?

At first, they might try some pairwise votes. If they started with a comparison of *Star Wars* and *Harry Potter*, they would choose *Star Wars* (both Kirk and McCoy prefer this to *Harry Potter*). Then turning to *Star Wars* and *Police Academy*, they would choose *Police Academy* (Spock's and McCoy's preferences). As *Police Academy* beats *Star Wars*, and *Star Wars* beats *Harry Potter*, they appear to have a clear choice.

But wait, suppose instead that they had begun with *Star Wars* and *Police Academy* – choosing *Police Academy* – and then voted on *Harry Potter* and *Police Academy*, they would have chosen *Harry Potter*! (Kirk and Spock prefer *Harry Potter* to *Police Academy*.) Normally, we expect preferences to exhibit a property called *transitivity*: If A is preferred to B, and B is preferred to C, then we would expect A to be preferred to C. The Condorcet paradox is that democratic outcomes do not always obey this property. Pairwise voting might produce transitive preferences for a society, depending on the pattern of individual preferences, but as our example in the table shows, it cannot be counted on to do so.

One implication of the Condorcet paradox is that the order on which things are voted can affect the result. If they decide by choosing between *Star Wars* and *Harry Potter* and then compare the winner to *Police Academy*, they end up choosing *Police Academy*. But if the voters choose first between *Star Wars* and *Police Academy* and then compare the winner to *Harry Potter*, the town ends up with *Harry Potter*. And if the voters choose first between *Harry Potter* and *Police Academy* and then compare the winner to *Star Wars*, the trio ends up with *Star Wars*.

The Condorcet paradox has two lessons. The narrow lesson is that when there are more than two options, setting the agenda (that is, deciding the order in which items are voted) can have a powerful impact on the outcome of a democratic election. The broad lesson is that majority voting by itself does not tell us what outcome a society really wants.

Arrow's impossibility theorem

Since political theorists first noticed Condorcet's paradox, they have spent much energy studying voting systems and proposing new ones. For example, as an alternative to pairwise majority voting, each person could be asked to rank the possible outcomes – a preference system used as we do for elections in Australia. Of course, in this case, it would not be much help; there would be a three-way tie.

Is there a perfect voting system? Economist Kenneth Arrow took up this question in his 1951 book *Social Choice and Individual Values*. Arrow started by defining what a perfect voting system would be. He assumes that individuals in society have preferences over the various possible outcomes: A, B, C and so on. He then assumes that society wants a voting scheme to choose among these outcomes that satisfies several properties:

- *Unanimity*: If everyone prefers A to B, then A should beat B.
- *Transitivity*: If A beats B, and B beats C, then A should beat C.
- *Independence of irrelevant alternatives*: The ranking between any two outcomes A and B should not depend on whether some third outcome C is also available.
- *No dictators*: There is no person that always gets his way, regardless of everyone else's preferences.

	Voter type		
Table 23.2 A Borda count			
	Type 1	Type 2	Type 3
% of electorate	35	45	20
1st choice	A	B	C
2nd choice	B	C	A
3rd choice	C	A	B

These all seem like desirable properties for a voting system to have. Yet Arrow proved, mathematically and incontrovertibly, that *no voting system can satisfy all of these properties*. This amazing result is called **Arrow's impossibility theorem**.

Arrow's impossibility theorem
a mathematical result showing that, under certain assumed conditions, there is no scheme for aggregating individual preferences into a valid set of social preferences

The mathematics needed to prove Arrow's theorem is beyond the scope of this book, but we can get some sense of why the theorem is true from a couple of examples. We have already seen the problem with the method of majority rule. The Condorcet paradox shows that majority rule fails to produce a ranking among the outcomes that always satisfies transitivity.

Consider a new situation. Suppose that a town is to vote on three possible locations for a new theatre: A, B or C. The preferences are in Table 23.2. Suppose that the mayor decides on the following voting: For each option, we could give one point for last place, two points for second to last, three points for third to last, and so on. The outcome that receives the most total points wins. With the preferences in the table, outcome B is the winner. (You can do the arithmetic yourself.) This voting method is called a *Borda count*, for the eighteenth-century French mathematician and political scientist who devised it. It is often used in polls that rank sports teams.

Notice that the Borda count fails to satisfy the independence of irrelevant alternatives. Recall that outcome B wins with a Borda count. But suppose that suddenly C disappears as an alternative. If the Borda count method is applied only to outcomes A and B, then A wins. (Once again, you can do the arithmetic on your own.) Thus, eliminating alternative C changes the ranking between A and B. The reason for this change is that the result of the Borda count depends on the number of points that A and B receive, and the number of points depends on whether the irrelevant alternative, C, is also available.

Arrow's impossibility theorem is a deep and disturbing result. It doesn't say that we should abandon democracy as a form of government. But it does say that, no matter what voting scheme society adopts for aggregating the preferences of its members, in some way it will be flawed as a mechanism for social choice.

The median voter is king

Despite Arrow's theorem, voting is how most societies choose their leaders and public policies, often by majority rule. The next step in studying government is to examine how governments run by majority

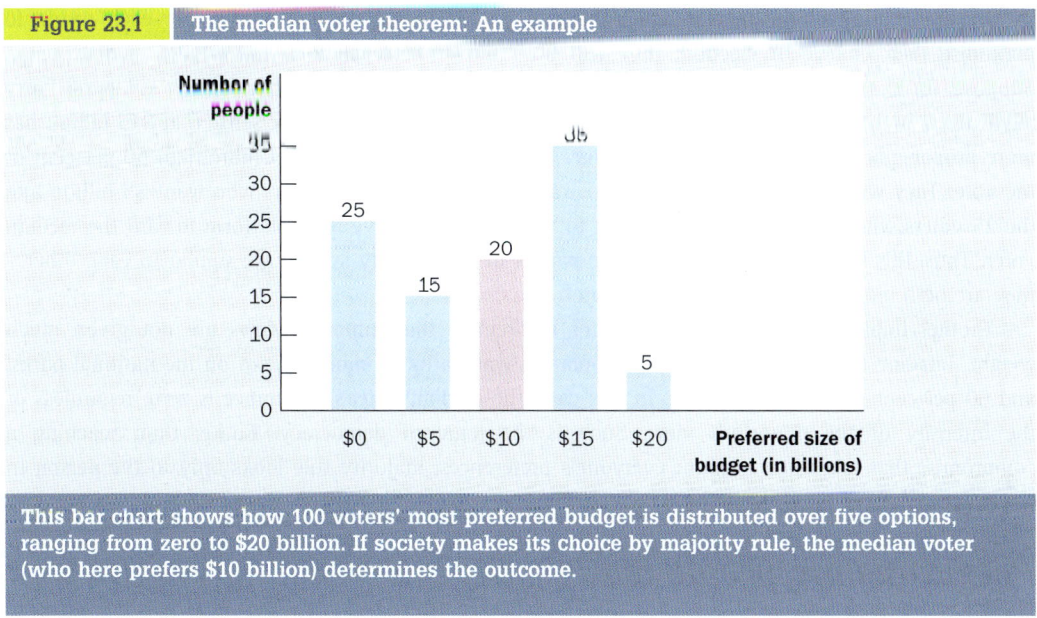

Figure 23.1 The median voter theorem: An example

This bar chart shows how 100 voters' most preferred budget is distributed over five options, ranging from zero to $20 billion. If society makes its choice by majority rule, the median voter (who here prefers $10 billion) determines the outcome.

rule work. That is, in a democratic society, who determines what policy is chosen? In some cases, the theory of democratic government yields a surprisingly simple answer.

Let's consider an example. Imagine that society is deciding on how much money to spend on some public good, such as the army or the national parks. Each voter has his own most preferred budget and he always prefers outcomes closer to his most preferred value to outcomes further away. Thus, we can line up voters from those who prefer the smallest budget to those who prefer the largest. Figure 23.1 is an example. Here there are 100 voters and the budget size varies from zero to $20 billion. Given these preferences, what outcome would you expect democracy to produce?

According to a famous result called the **median voter theorem**, majority rule will produce the outcome most preferred by the median voter. The *median voter* is the voter exactly in the middle of the distribution. In this example, if you take the line of voters ordered by their preferred budgets and count 50 voters from either end of the line, you will find that the median voter wants a budget of $10 billion. By contrast, the average preferred outcome (calculated by adding the preferred outcomes and dividing by the number of voters) is $9 billion, and the modal outcome (the one preferred by the greatest number of voters) is $15 billion.

The median voter rules the day because his or her preferred outcome beats any other proposal in a two-way race. In our example, more than half the voters want $10 billion or more, and more than half want $10 billion or less. If someone proposes, say, $8 billion instead of $10 billion, everyone who prefers $10 billion or more will vote with the median voter. Similarly, if someone proposes $12 billion instead of $10 billion, everyone who wants $10 billion or less will vote with the median voter. In either case, the median voter has more than half the voters on his or her side.

What about the Condorcet voting paradox? It turns out that when the voters are picking a point along a line and each voter aims for his or her own most preferred point, the Condorcet paradox cannot arise. The median voter's most preferred outcome beats all comers.

median voter theorem
a mathematical result showing that if voters are choosing a point along a line and each voter wants the point closest to their most preferred point, then majority rule will pick the most preferred point of the median voter

▸ median voter theorem

One implication of the median voter theorem is that if two political parties are each trying to maximise their chance of election, they will both move their positions toward the median voter. Suppose, for example, that the Labor Party advocates a budget of $15 billion, while the Liberal Party advocates a budget of $10 billion. The Labor position is more popular in the sense that $15 billion has more proponents than any other single choice. Nonetheless, the Liberals get more than 50 per cent of the vote: They will attract the 20 voters who want $10 billion, the 15 voters who want $5 billion and the 25 voters who want zero. If Labor want to win, they will move their platform toward the median voter. Thus, this theory can explain why the parties in a two-party system are similar to each other – they are both moving toward the median voter.

Another implication of the median voter theorem is that minority views are not given much weight. Imagine that 40 per cent of the population want a lot of money spent on the national parks, and 60 per cent want nothing spent. In this case, the median voter's preference is zero, regardless of the intensity of the minority's view. Such is the logic of democracy. Rather than reaching a compromise that takes into account everyone's preferences, majority rule looks only to the person in the exact middle of the distribution.

Politicians are people too

When economists study consumer behaviour, they assume that consumers buy the bundle of goods and services that gives them the greatest level of satisfaction. When economists study firm behaviour, they assume that firms produce the quantity of goods and services that yields the greatest level of profits. What should they assume when they study people involved in the practice of politics?

Politicians also have objectives. It would be nice to assume that political leaders are always looking out for the wellbeing of society as a whole, that they are aiming for an optimal combination of efficiency and equity. Nice, perhaps, but not realistic. Self-interest is as powerful a motive for political actors as it is for consumers and firm owners. Some politicians are motivated by desire for re-election and are willing to sacrifice the national interest when doing so solidifies their base of voters. Other politicians are motivated by simple greed. If you have any doubt, you should look at the world's poor nations, where corruption among government officials is a common impediment to economic development.

This book is not the place to develop a theory of political behaviour. That topic is best left to the political scientists. But when thinking about economic policy, remember that this policy is made not by a benevolent king, but by real people with their own all-too-human desires. Sometimes they are motivated to further the national interest, but sometimes they are motivated by their own political and financial ambitions. We shouldn't be surprised when economic policy fails to resemble the ideals derived in economics textbooks.

A school council is voting on the school budget and the resulting student–teacher ratio. A poll finds that 35 per cent of the voters want a ratio of 9:1, 25 per cent want a ratio of 10:1 and 40 per cent want a ratio of 12:1. What outcome would you expect the school to end up with?

Behavioural economics

Economics is a study of human behaviour, but it is not the only field that can make that claim. The social science of psychology also sheds light on the choices that people make in their lives. The fields of economics and psychology usually proceed independently, in part because they address a different range of questions. But recently a field called *behavioural economics* has emerged in which economists are making use of basic psychological insights. Let's consider some of these insights here.

People aren't always rational

Economic theory is populated by a particular species of organism, sometimes called *homo economicus*. Members of this species are always rational. As firm managers, they maximise profits. As consumers, they maximise utility (or, equivalently, pick the point on the highest indifference curve). Given the constraints they face, they rationally weigh all the costs and benefits and always choose the best possible course of action.

Real people, however, are *homo sapiens*. Although in many ways they resemble the rational, calculating people assumed in economic theory, they are far more complex. They can be forgetful, impulsive, confused, emotional and shortsighted. These imperfections of human reasoning are the bread-and-butter of psychologists, but until recently, economists have neglected them.

Herbert Simon, one of the first social scientists to work at the boundary of economics and psychology, suggested that humans should be viewed not as rational maximisers but as *satisficers*. Rather than always choosing the best course of action, they make decisions that are merely good enough. Similarly, other economists have suggested that humans are only 'near rational' or that they exhibit 'bounded rationality'.

Studies of human decision making have tried to detect systematic mistakes that people make. Here are a few of the findings:

- *People are overconfident*: Imagine that you were asked some numerical questions, such as the number of African countries in the United Nations, the height of the tallest mountain in North America, and so on. Instead of being asked for a single estimate, however, you were asked to give a 90 per cent confidence interval – a range such that you were 90 per cent confident the true number falls within it. When psychologists run experiments like this, they find that most people give ranges that are too small: The true number falls within their intervals far less than 90 per cent of the time. That is, most people are too sure of their own abilities.

- *People give too much weight to a small number of vivid observations*: Imagine that you are thinking about buying a car of brand X. To learn about its reliability, you read *Consumer Reports*, which has surveyed 1000 owners of car X. Then you run into a friend who owns car X, and she tells you that her car is a lemon. How do you treat your friend's observation? If you think rationally, you will realise that she has only increased your sample size from 1000 to 1001, which does not provide much new information. But because your friend's story is so vivid, you may be tempted to give it more weight in your decision making than you should.

- *People are reluctant to change their minds*: People tend to interpret evidence to confirm beliefs they already hold. In one study, subjects were asked to read and evaluate a research report on whether capital punishment deters crime. After reading the report, those who initially favoured the death penalty said they were more sure in their view and those who initially opposed the death penalty also said they were more sure in their view. The two groups interpreted the same evidence in exactly opposite ways.

Think about decisions you have made in your own life. Do you exhibit some of these traits?

A hotly debated issue is whether deviations from rationality are important for understanding economic phenomena. An intriguing example arises in the study of tax-advantaged retirement savings accounts that some firms in the United States offer their workers. In some firms, workers can choose to participate in the plan by filling out a simple form. In other firms, workers are automatically enrolled and can opt out of the plan by filling out a simple form. It turns out many more workers participate in the second case than in the first. If workers were perfectly rational maximisers, they would choose the optimal amount of retirement saving, regardless of the default offered by their employer. In fact, workers' behaviour appears to exhibit substantial inertia. Understanding their behaviour seems easier once we abandon the model of perfect rationality.

Why, you might ask, is economics built on the rationality assumption when psychology and commonsense cast doubt on it? One answer is that the assumption, even if not exactly true, is still a good approximation. For example, when we studied the differences between competitive and monopoly firms, the assumption that firms rationally maximise profit yielded many important and valid insights. Recall from chapter 2 that economic models are not meant to replicate reality but are supposed to show the essence of the problem at hand as an aid to understanding.

Another reason that economists so often assume rationality may be that economists are themselves not rational maximisers. Like most people they are overconfident and they are reluctant to change their minds. Their choice among alternative theories of human behaviour may exhibit excessive inertia. Moreover, economists may be content with a theory that is not perfect but is good enough. The model of rational man may be the theory of choice for a satisficing social scientist.

IN THE NEWS . . .

USE MONEY TO COMMIT TO A DIET

It is tough to commit to a diet. Even when you know it will pay off in the long term, behavioural economics has demonstrated that the short term looms. Two economists imagine bringing the pain forward in the form of money.

Skin in the game
by Ian Ayres and Barry Nalebuff

In 1519 Hernán Cortés scuttled his ships upon arrival in Veracruz, Mexico. Vastly outnumbered, his 600 soldiers decided that they would either defeat the Aztecs or perish trying. By making defeat worse, Cortés increased his chance of victory. And conquer he did.

While we can't all scuttle our ships, we can use this same type of commitment strategy to help us lose weight, stop smoking, exercise more or achieve just about any goal.

Imagine a Commitment Store that offered a financial incentive to lose weight. You promise to lose a pound a week for the next 20 weeks

and then keep the 20 pounds off for the remainder of the year. You back up the promise with a $1000 weight-loss bond. Weigh-ins are biweekly. Every time you meet your goal, you get back $60. Over the course of the year you could earn back $1560. Of course, each time you miss, that costs you $60.

Here's a diet system that literally pays you to lose the weight. If you miss your goal weight one week, you still have an incentive to get back on track to collect the next payout. If $60 a weigh-in isn't enough to get your attention, then buy two or more bonds.

The 56 per cent interest rate might seem high, but the fact is that more than 95 per cent of dieters fail to keep their weight off for a year. Even if half the dieters succeed under this new regime, the store can still turn a healthy profit. Putting aside the interest it could earn on deposited funds (and the overhead costs), it would be taking in $2000 from a pair of dieters and paying out $1560 to one of them.

We're not the first to suggest the idea of financial incentives. This season's edition of NBC's *The Biggest Loser* will pay $250 000 to the person who loses the largest percentage of his or her body weight. We tried something like this ourselves with ABC's *Primetime*. Five volunteers were photographed in bikinis. Unless they lost 15 pounds in two months, those photographs would be splashed on *Primetime* and the Web. As one of the dieters, Cynthia Nacson-Schechter, explained, she knew all about the dangers of being overweight – the increased risk of diabetes, heart attack and death – and yet that wasn't enough to scare her into action. What she feared most was the possibility that her ex-boyfriend would see her hanging out of a bikini on national TV. She lost the weight and then some.

The stick is mightier than the carrot. People hate losing their own money even more than they love gaining a windfall of the same amount. Psychologists call this phenomenon loss aversion. The great thing about the weight-loss bonds is that the overweight investors have put their own skin in the game.

You might be worried that it's unethical to profit from people's failure to lose weight. But the Commitment Store would publish detailed statistics on the distribution of results. You'd know going in the chance of losing money. And you might rationally decide that getting halfway to your goal is not a bad outcome – you'd lose some of your principal but lose

some pounds, too. Even if weight-loss bond buyers lose $200 on average, if the dieters lose 10 pounds this would be a bargain. And those buyers who lose the full 20 make out like bandits, earning interest rates that would make loan sharks proud.

Of course, financial incentives aren't for everyone. The idea of putting a dollar price on every morsel of food that you put in your mouth might ruin the pleasure of eating. (For some people that might be the point.) The store can serve people who react better to financial incentives than to other types of encouragement. Indeed, financial incentives have been shown to help drug addicts abstain. Prizes of cash, computers and even iPods are being used in Vacaville, Calif. and elsewhere to reward school attendance.

This needn't be a question of either financial incentives or nonfinancial weight-loss support. It can be both. Right now people spend about $10 a week to attend Weight Watchers weigh-ins. Weight Watchers should offer people the option of paying $1000 up front and then to be paid $15 a week for every time they come over the next year.

The commitment idea isn't just about weight loss. Any action that can be monitored can be subject to commitment contracts. The American Cancer Society should offer non-smoking bonds. You invest $10 000 and agree to have your hair tested for nicotine over the course of the year. If your hair is nicotine free, you get your money back with interest; if not, your money is forfeited to the charity. The Cancer Society is a winner either way.

Source: *Forbes*, 13 November 2006. Reprinted by permission of Forbes Media LLC © 2011.

People care about fairness

Another insight about human behaviour is best illustrated with an experiment called the *ultimatum game*. The game works like this: Two volunteers (who are otherwise strangers to each other) are told that they are going to play a game and could win a total of $100. Before they play, they learn the rules. The game begins with a coin flip, which is used to assign the volunteers to the roles of player A and player B. Player A's job is to propose a division of the $100 prize between himself and the other player. After player A makes his proposal, player B decides whether to accept or reject it.

If he accepts it, both players are paid according to the proposal. If player B rejects the proposal, both players walk away with nothing. In either case, the game then ends.

Before proceeding, stop and think about what you would do in this situation. If you were player A, what division of the $100 would you propose? If you were player B, what proposals would you accept?

Conventional economic theory assumes in this situation that people are rational wealth-maximisers. This assumption leads to a simple prediction: Player A should propose that he gets $99 and player B gets $1, and player B should accept the proposal. After all, once the proposal is made, player B is better off accepting it as long as he gets something out of it. Moreover, because player A knows that accepting the proposal is in player's B interest, player A has no reason to offer him more than $1. In the language of game theory (discussed in chapter 16), the 99-1 split is the Nash equilibrium.

Yet when experimental economists ask real people to play the ultimatum game, the results are very different from this prediction. People in the role of player B usually reject proposals that give them only $1 or a similarly small amount. Knowing this, people in the role of player A usually propose giving player B much more than $1. Some people will offer a 50-50 split, but it is more common for player A to propose giving player B an amount such as $30 or $40, keeping the larger share for himself. In this case, player B usually accepts the proposal.

What's going on here? The natural interpretation is that people are driven in part by some innate sense of fairness. A 99-1 split seems so wildly unfair to many people that they reject it, even to their own detriment. By contrast, a 70-30 split is still unfair, but it is not so unfair that it induces people to abandon their normal self-interest.

Throughout our study of household and firm behaviour, the innate sense of fairness has not played any role. But the results of the ultimatum game suggest that perhaps it should. For example, in chapters 19 and 20 we discussed how wages were determined by labour supply and labour demand. Some economists have suggested that the perceived fairness of what a firm pays its workers should also enter the picture. Thus, when a firm has an especially profitable year, workers (like player B) may expect to be paid a fair share of the prize, even if the standard equilibrium does not dictate it. The firm (like player A) might well decide to give workers more than the equilibrium wage for fear that the workers might otherwise try to punish the firm with reduced effort, strikes or even vandalism.

People are inconsistent over time

Imagine some dreary task, such as doing your laundry, mowing the lawn or filling out your income tax forms. Now consider the following questions:

1 Would you prefer (A) to spend 50 minutes doing the task immediately or (B) to spend 60 minutes doing the task tomorrow?

2 Would you prefer (A) to spend 50 minutes doing the task in 90 days or (B) to spend 60 minutes doing the task in 91 days?

When asked questions like these, many people choose B to question 1 and A to question 2. When looking ahead to the future (as in question 2), they minimise the amount of time spent on the dreary task. But faced with the prospect of doing the task immediately (as in question 1), they choose to put it off.

In some ways, this behaviour is not surprising – everyone procrastinates from time to time. But from the standpoint of the theory of rationality, it is puzzling. Suppose that, in response to question 2, a person chooses to spend 50 minutes in 90 days. Then, when the 90th day arrives, we allow them to change their mind. In effect, they then face question 1, so they opt for doing the task the next day. But why should the mere passage of time affect the choices made?

Many times in life, people make plans for themselves, but then they fail to follow through. Smokers promise themselves that they will quit, but within a few hours of smoking their last cigarette, they crave another and break their promise. People trying to lose weight promise that they will stop eating dessert, but when the waiter brings the dessert menu, the promise is forgotten. In both cases, the desire for instant gratification induces the decision maker to abandon their own past plans.

Some economists believe that the consumption–saving decision is an important instance where people exhibit this inconsistency over time. For many people, spending provides a type of instant gratification. Saving, like passing up the cigarette or the dessert, requires a sacrifice in the present for a reward in the distant future. And just as many smokers wish they could quit and many overweight individuals wish they ate less, many consumers wish they saved more. According to one survey, 76 per cent of Americans said they were not saving enough for retirement and figures for Australia and New Zealand are believed to be similar.

An implication of this inconsistency over time is that people should try to find ways to commit their future selves to following through on their plans. A smoker trying to quit may throw away his cigarettes and a person on a diet may put a lock on the refrigerator. What can a person who saves too little do? He should find some way to lock up his money before he spends it. Some retirement accounts, like superannuation, do exactly that. Workers can agree to have some money taken out of their pay cheque before they ever see it. The money is deposited in an account that can be used before retirement only with a tax penalty. In effect these plans protect people from their own desires for instant gratification.

Describe at least three ways in which human decision making differs from that of the rational individual of conventional economic theory.

Conclusion

This chapter has examined the frontier of microeconomics. You may have noticed that we have sketched out ideas rather than fully developing them. This is no accident. One reason is that you might study these topics in more detail in advanced courses. Another reason is that these topics remain active areas of research and, therefore, are still being fleshed out.

To see how these topics fit into the broader picture, recall the *Ten Lessons from Economics* in chapter 1. One lesson states that markets are usually a good way to organise economic activity. Another lesson states that governments can sometimes improve market outcomes. As you study economics, you can more fully appreciate the truth of these principles as well as the caveats that go with them. The study of asymmetric information should make you more wary of market outcomes. The study of political economy should make you more wary of government solutions. And the study of behavioural economics should make you wary of any institution that relies on human decision making – including both the market and the government.

If there is a unifying theme to these topics, it is that life is messy. Information is imperfect, government is imperfect and people are imperfect. Of course, you knew this long before you started studying economics, but economists need to understand these imperfections as precisely as they can if they are to explain, and perhaps even improve, the world around them.

Summary

- In many economic transactions, information is asymmetric. When there are hidden actions, principals may be concerned that agents suffer from the problem of moral hazard. When there are hidden characteristics, buyers may be concerned about the problem of adverse selection among the sellers. Private markets sometimes deal with asymmetric information with signalling and screening.

- Although government policy can sometimes improve market outcomes, governments are themselves imperfect institutions. The Condorcet paradox shows that majority rule fails to produce transitive preferences for society and Arrow's impossibility theorem shows that no voting scheme will be perfect. In many situations, democratic institutions will produce the outcome desired by the median voter, regardless of the preferences of the rest of the electorate. Moreover, the individuals who set government policy may be motivated by self-interest rather than the national interest.

- The study of psychology and economics reveals that human decision making is more complex than is assumed in conventional economic theory. People are not always rational, they care about the fairness of economic outcomes (even to their own detriment) and they can be inconsistent over time.

Key concepts

adverse selection	Condorcet paradox	screening
agent	median voter theorem	signalling
Arrow's impossibility theorem	moral hazard	
	principal	

Questions for review

1 What is moral hazard? List three things an employer might do to reduce the severity of this problem.
2 What is adverse selection? Give an example of a market in which adverse selection might be a problem.
3 Define *signalling* and *screening*, and give an example of each.
4 What unusual property of voting did Condorcet notice?
5 Explain why majority rule respects the preferences of the median voter rather than the average voter.
6 Describe the ultimatum game. What outcome from this game would conventional economic theory predict? Do experiments confirm this prediction? Explain.

Problems and applications

1 Each of the following situations involves moral hazard. In each case, identify the principal and the agent, and explain why there is asymmetric information. How does the action described reduce the problem of moral hazard?
   a Landlords require tenants to pay security deposits.
   b Firms compensate top executives with options to buy company stock at a given price in the future.
   c Car insurance companies offer discounts to customers who install anti-theft devices in their cars.

2   Suppose that the Live-Long-and-Prosper Health Insurance Company charges $5000 annually for a family insurance policy. The company's president suggests that the company raise the annual price to $6000 in order to increase its profits. If the firm followed this suggestion, what economic problem might arise? Would the firm's pool of customers tend to become more or less healthy on average? Would the company's profits necessarily increase?

3   The case study in this chapter describes how a boyfriend can signal to a girlfriend that he loves her by giving an appropriate gift. Do you think saying 'I love you' can also serve as a signal? Why or why not?

4   Some AIDS activists believe that health insurance companies should not be allowed to ask applicants if they are infected with the HIV virus that causes AIDS. Would this rule help or hurt those who are HIV-positive? Would it help or hurt those who are not HIV-positive? Would it exacerbate or mitigate the problem of adverse selection in the market for health insurance? Do you think it would increase or decrease the number of people without health insurance? In your opinion, would this be a good policy?

5   The government is considering two ways to help the needy: giving them cash, or giving them free meals at soup kitchens. Give an argument for giving cash. Give an argument, based on asymmetric information, for why the soup kitchen may be better than the cash handout.

6   Ken walks into an ice-cream parlour.

Waiter: We have vanilla and chocolate today.

Ken: I'll take vanilla.

Waiter: I almost forgot. We also have strawberry.

Ken: In that case, I'll take chocolate.

   What standard property of decision making is Ken violating? (*Hint:* Re-read the section on Arrow's impossibility theorem.)

7   Why might a political party in a two-party system choose not to move toward the median voter? (*Hint:* Think about abstentions from voting and political contributions.)

8   Two ice-cream stands are deciding where to locate along a 3-km beach. The people sitting on the beach buy exactly one ice-cream cone each per day from the stand nearest to them. Each ice-cream seller wants the maximum number of customers. Where along the beach will the two stands locate?

9   After a widely reported earthquake in California, many people call their insurance company to apply for earthquake insurance. Might this reaction reflect some deviation from rationality? Discuss.

Search me!

When accessing information about economics use the following keywords in any combinations you require:

- adverse selection
- median voter theorem
- moral hazard

CourseMate

For more multimedia resources and activities
on economics, visit the Economics
CourseMate website.

PART EIGHT
The data of macroeconomics

24

Measuring a nation's income

Learning objectives

In this chapter you will:

- consider why an economy's total income equals its total expenditure
- learn how gross domestic product (GDP) is defined and calculated
- see the breakdown of GDP into its four major components
- learn the distinction between real GDP and nominal GDP
- consider whether GDP is a good measure of economic wellbeing.

When you finish university and start looking for a full-time job, your experience will, to a large extent, be shaped by prevailing economic conditions. In some years, firms throughout the economy are expanding their production of goods and services, employment is rising and jobs are easy to find. In other years, firms are cutting back on production, employment is declining and finding a good job takes a long time. Not surprisingly, any university graduate would rather enter the labour force in a year of economic expansion than in a year of economic contraction.

Because the condition of the overall economy profoundly affects all of us, changes in economic conditions are widely reported by the media. Indeed, it is hard to pick up a newspaper without seeing some newly reported statistic about the economy. The statistic might measure the total income of everyone in the economy (GDP), the rate at which average prices are rising (inflation), the percentage of the labour force that is out of work (unemployment), total spending at stores (retail sales), or the imbalance of trade between Australia and the rest of the world (the trade balance). All these statistics are macroeconomic. Rather than telling us about a particular household or firm, they tell us something about the entire economy.

As you may recall from chapter 2, economics is divided into two branches – microeconomics and macroeconomics. *Microeconomics* is the study of how individual households and firms make decisions and how they interact with one another in markets. *Macroeconomics* is the study of the economy as a whole. The goal of macroeconomics is to explain the economic changes that affect many households, firms and markets at once. Macroeconomists consider diverse questions: Why is average income high in some countries and low in others? Why do prices rise rapidly in some periods of time but are more stable in other periods? Why do production and employment expand in some years and contract in others? These diverse questions are all macroeconomic because they concern the workings of the entire economy.

Because the economy as a whole is just a collection of many households and many firms interacting in many markets, microeconomics and macroeconomics are closely linked. The basic tools of supply and demand, for instance, are as central to macroeconomic analysis as they are to microeconomic analysis. Yet studying the economy in its entirety raises some new and intriguing challenges.

In this chapter and the next one, we discuss some of the data that economists and policymakers use to monitor the overall economy. These data reflect the economic changes that macroeconomists try to explain. This chapter considers *gross domestic product*, or simply GDP, which measures the total income of a nation. GDP is the most closely watched economic statistic because it is thought to be the best single measure of a society's economic wellbeing.

The economy's income and expenditure

If you were to judge how a person is doing economically, you might first look at his or her income. A person with a high income can more easily afford life's necessities and luxuries. It is no surprise that people with higher incomes enjoy higher standards of living – better housing, better health care, fancier cars, more opulent holidays and so on.

The same logic applies to a nation's overall economy. When judging whether the economy is doing well or poorly, it is natural to look at the total income that everyone in the economy is earning. That is the task of gross domestic product (GDP).

GDP measures two things at once – the total income of everyone in the economy and the total expenditure on the economy's output of goods and services. The reason that GDP can perform the trick of measuring both total income and total expenditure is that these two things are really the same. *For an economy as a whole, income must equal expenditure.*

Why is this true? The reason that an economy's income is the same as its expenditure is simply that every transaction has two parties: a buyer and a seller. Every dollar of spending by some buyer is a dollar of income for some seller. Suppose, for instance, that Karen pays Doug $100 to mow her lawn. In this case, Doug is a seller of a service and Karen is a buyer. Doug earns $100 and Karen spends $100. Thus, the transaction contributes equally to the economy's income and to its expenditure. GDP, whether measured as total income or total expenditure, rises by $100.

Another way to see the equality of income and expenditure is with the circular-flow diagram in Figure 24.1. (You may recall this circular-flow diagram from chapter 2.) This diagram describes all the transactions between households and firms in a simple economy. In this economy, households buy goods and services from firms; these expenditures flow through the markets for goods and services. The firms in turn use the money they receive from sales to pay workers' wages, landowners' rent and firm owners' profit; this income flows through the markets for the factors of

Figure 24.1	The circular-flow diagram

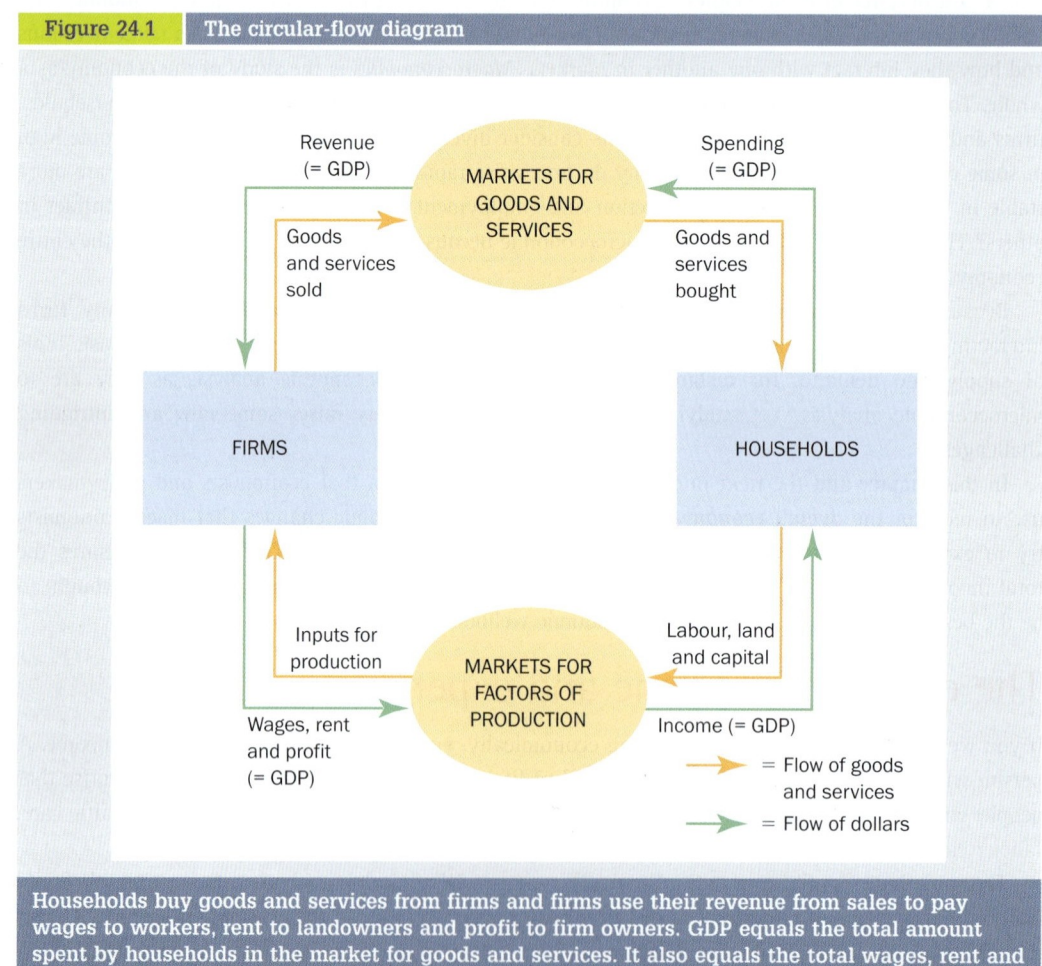

Households buy goods and services from firms and firms use their revenue from sales to pay wages to workers, rent to landowners and profit to firm owners. GDP equals the total amount spent by households in the market for goods and services. It also equals the total wages, rent and profit paid by firms in the markets for the factors of production.

production. In this economy, money continuously flows from households to firms and then back to households.

We can calculate GDP for this economy in one of two ways – by adding up the total expenditure by households or by adding up the total income (wages, rent and profit) paid by firms. Because all expenditure in the economy ends up as someone's income, GDP is the same regardless of how we calculate it.

The real economy is, of course, more complicated than the one illustrated in Figure 24.1. In particular, households do not spend all of their income. Households pay some of their income to the government in taxes, and they save and invest some of their income for use in the future. In addition, households do not buy all goods and services produced in the economy. Some goods and services are bought by governments and some are bought by firms that plan to use them in the future to produce their own output. Yet, regardless of whether a household, government or firm buys a good or service, the transaction has a buyer and seller. Thus, for the economy as a whole, expenditure and income are always the same.

What two things does gross domestic product measure? How can it measure two things at once?

The measurement of gross domestic product

Now that we have discussed the meaning of gross domestic product in general terms, let's be more precise about how this statistic is measured. Here is a definition of GDP:

- **Gross domestic product (GDP)** is the market value of all final goods and services produced within a country in a given period of time.

This definition might seem simple enough. But, in fact, many subtle issues arise when calculating an economy's GDP. Let's therefore consider each phrase in this definition with some care.

gross domestic product (GDP)
the market value of all final goods and services produced within a country in a given period of time

'*GDP is the market value ...*'

You have probably heard the adage 'You can't compare apples and oranges'. Yet GDP does exactly that. GDP adds together many different kinds of products into a single measure of the value of economic activity. To do this, it uses market prices. Because market prices measure the amount people are willing to pay for different goods, they reflect the value of those goods. If the price of an apple is twice the price of an orange, then an apple contributes twice as much to GDP as does an orange.

'*... of all ...*'

GDP tries to be comprehensive. It includes all items produced in the economy and sold legally in markets. GDP measures the market value of not just apples and oranges, but also pears and grapefruit, books and films, haircuts and health care and so on.

GDP also includes the market value of the housing services provided by the economy's stock of housing. For rental housing, this value is easy to calculate – the rent equals both the tenant's expenditure and the landlord's income. Yet many people own the place where they live and, therefore, do not pay rent. The government includes this owner-occupied housing in GDP by estimating its rental value. In essence, GDP is based on the assumption that the owners pay themselves this imputed rent, so the rent is included both in their expenditure and in their income.

There are some products, however, that GDP excludes because measurement of them is so difficult. GDP excludes items produced and sold illicitly, such as illegal drugs. It also excludes most items that are produced and consumed at home and, therefore, never enter the marketplace. Vegetables you buy at the supermarket are part of GDP; vegetables you grow in your garden are not.

These exclusions from GDP can at times lead to paradoxical results. For example, when Karen pays Doug to mow her lawn that transaction is part of GDP. If Karen were to marry Doug, the situation would change. Even though Doug may continue to mow Karen's lawn, the value of the mowing is now left out of GDP because Doug's service is no longer sold in a market. Thus, when Karen and Doug marry, GDP falls (assuming, of course, that Karen no longer pays Doug to mow the lawn).

'... final ...'

When Australian Paper makes paper which Hallmark uses to make a greeting card, the paper is called an *intermediate good* and the card is called a *final good*. GDP includes only the value of final goods. The reason is that the value of intermediate goods is already included in the prices of the final goods. Adding the market value of the paper to the market value of the card would be double counting. That is, it would (incorrectly) count the paper twice.

An important exception to this principle arises when an intermediate good is produced and, rather than being used, is added to a firm's inventory to be used or sold at a later date. In this case, the intermediate good is taken to be 'final' for the moment and its value as inventory investment is added to GDP. When the inventory of the intermediate good is later used or sold, the firm's inventory investment is negative and GDP for the later period is reduced accordingly.

'... goods and services ...'

GDP includes tangible goods (food, clothing, cars) and intangible services (haircuts, house cleaning, doctors' visits). When you buy a song from iTunes by your favourite band or a T-shirt with your favourite band's name on it, you are buying a good and the purchase price is part of GDP. When you pay to hear a concert by the same group, you are buying a service and the ticket price is also part of GDP.

'... produced ...'

GDP includes goods and services currently produced. It does not include transactions involving items produced in the past. When Ford produces and sells a new car, the value of the car is included in GDP. When one person sells a used car to another person, the value of the used car is not included in GDP.

'... within a country ...'

GDP measures the value of production within the geographic confines of a country. When Japanese residents work temporarily in Australia, their production is part of Australian GDP. When an Australian resident owns a factory in Malaysia, the profit from production at that factory is not part of Australian GDP, it is part of Malaysia's GDP. Thus, items are included in a nation's GDP if they are produced domestically, regardless of the nationality of the producer.

Another statistic, called **gross national product (GNP)**, takes a different approach to dealing with the goods and services produced by foreigners. GNP is the value of the production of a nation's permanent residents. When Japanese residents work temporarily in Australia, their production is not part of Australian GNP, it is part of Japan's GNP. When an Australian resident owns a factory in Malaysia, the profit from production at the factory is part of Australian GNP. Thus, income is included in a nation's GNP if it is earned by the nation's permanent residents (called *nationals*), regardless of where they earn it.

Throughout this book, we follow the standard practice of using GDP to measure the value of economic activity. For most purposes, however, the distinction between GDP and GNP is not very important. In Australia and most other countries, domestic residents are responsible for most domestic production, so GDP and GNP are quite close.

gross national product (GNP)
the market value of all final goods and services produced by permanent residents of a nation within a given period of time

'... in a given period of time'

GDP measures the value of production that takes place within a specific interval of time. Usually that interval is a year or a quarter (three months). GDP measures the economy's flow of income and expenditure during that interval.

When the government reports the GDP for a quarter, it usually presents GDP 'at an annual rate'. This means that the figure reported for quarterly GDP is the amount of income and expenditure during the quarter multiplied by 4. The government uses this convention so that quarterly and annual figures on GDP can be compared more easily.

In addition, when the government reports quarterly GDP, it presents the data after they have been modified by a statistical procedure called *seasonal adjustment*. The unadjusted data show clearly that the economy produces more goods and services during some times of the year than during others. (As you might guess, December's Christmas shopping season is a high point.) When monitoring the condition of the economy, economists and policymakers often want to look beyond these regular seasonal changes. Therefore, government statisticians adjust the quarterly data to take out the seasonal cycle. The GDP data reported in the news are always seasonally adjusted.

Now let's repeat the definition of GDP:

- Gross domestic product (GDP) is the market value of all final goods and services produced within a country in a given period of time.

It should now be apparent that GDP is a sophisticated measure of the value of economic activity. In advanced courses in macroeconomics, you will learn more of the subtleties that arise in its calculation. But even now you can see that each phrase in this definition is packed with meaning.

Which contributes more to GDP – the production of a kilogram of mince or the production of a kilogram of king prawns? Why?

The components of GDP

Spending in the economy takes many forms. At any moment, the Tan family may be having lunch at Pizza Hut; Ford may be building an engine factory; the Royal Australian Air Force (RAAF) may be procuring new jet fighters; and Qantas may be buying an aeroplane from Airbus. GDP accounts for all of these various forms of spending on goods and services.

552

To understand how the economy is using its scarce resources, economists are often interested in studying the composition of GDP among various types of spending. To do this, GDP (which we denote as Y) is divided into four components: consumption (C), investment (I), government purchases (G) and net exports (NX):

$$Y = C + I + G + NX$$

This equation is an *identity* – an equation that must be true by the way the variables in the equation are defined. In this case, because each dollar of expenditure included in GDP is placed into one of the four components of GDP, the total of the four components must be equal to GDP.

We have just seen an example of each component. **Consumption** is spending by households on goods and services, such as the Tan's lunch at Pizza Hut. **Investment** is the purchase of new capital equipment, inventories and structures, such as the Ford factory. Investment also includes expenditure on new housing. (By convention, expenditure on new housing is the one form of household spending categorised as investment rather than consumption.) **Government purchases** include spending on goods and services by local, state and federal governments, such as the RAAF's purchase of new jet fighters. **Net exports** equal the purchases of domestically produced goods by foreigners (exports) minus the domestic purchases of foreign goods (imports). A domestic firm's purchase from a producer in another country, such as the Qantas purchase of a plane from Airbus, decreases net exports.

The 'net' in 'net exports' refers to the fact that imports are subtracted from exports. This subtraction is made because imports of goods and services are included in other components of GDP. For example, suppose that a household buys a $50 000 car from Audi, the German car-maker. That transaction increases consumption by $50 000 because car purchases are part of consumer spending. It also reduces net exports by $50 000 because the car is an import. In other words, net exports include goods and services produced abroad (with a minus sign) because these goods and services are included in consumption, investment and government purchases (with a plus sign). Thus, when a domestic household, firm or government buys a good or service from abroad, the purchase reduces net exports – but because it also raises consumption, investment or government purchases, it does not affect GDP.

The meaning of 'government purchases' also requires clarification. When the government pays the salary of an Army general, that salary is part of government purchases. But what happens when the government pays a pension benefit to one of the elderly? Such government spending is called a *transfer payment* because it is not made in exchange for a currently produced good or service. From a macroeconomic standpoint, transfer payments are like a tax rebate. Like taxes, transfer payments alter household income, but they do not reflect the economy's production. No new goods or services are produced in the process of the government giving a transfer payment to an individual. Because GDP is intended to measure the income from (and expenditure on) the production of goods and services, transfer payments are not counted as part of government purchases.

Table 24.1 shows the composition of Australian GDP in 2010. In this year, the GDP of Australia was about $1302 billion. If we divide this number by the 2010 Australian population of just over 21.5 million, we find that GDP per person – the amount of expenditure for the average Australian – was $57 846. Consumption made up 54.8 per cent of GDP, or $31 710 per person. Investment was $12 674 per person. Government purchases were $13 705 per person. Net exports were –$243 per person. This number is negative because Australians spent more on foreign goods than we earned

consumption
spending by households on goods and services, with the exception of purchases of new housing

investment
spending on new capital equipment, inventories and structures, including household purchases of new housing

government purchases
spending on goods and services by local, state and federal governments

net exports
spending on domestically produced goods by foreigners (exports) minus spending on foreign goods by domestic residents (imports) – also called the trade balance

from selling goods to foreigners. In seven of the 10 years from 2000 to 2010, this number was positive – indicating that the value of our exports was greater than the value of our imports in those years.

Table 24.1 GDP and its components

GDP 2010	Total (in $ billion)	Per person ($)	Per cent of total
Consumption	713	31 710	54.8
Investment	285	12 674	21.9
Government expenditures	308	13 705	23.7
Net exports	−5	−243	−0.4
Total GDP	1302	57 846	100

This table shows total GDP for the Australian economy in 2010 and the breakdown of GDP into its four components.

Source: ABS, Cat. No. 52064.0, Table 3.

fyi

Three measures of income

When the Australian Bureau of Statistics (ABS) calculates the nation's GDP every three months, it uses three approaches to calculate the value of national output. The first measure, GDP(E), uses the expenditure approach to calculate national income. This is the approach described in the text. The other measures are GDP(I), the income approach, and GDP(P), the production approach. Conceptually, the three measures are the same but, in practice, they can differ because of the different data sources for each measure. They also differ more in the short run. Over time, more accurate estimates of the data become available, which allow the ABS to update its calculation of GDP. The ABS also calculates various other measures of income for the economy. These other measures differ from GDP by excluding or including certain categories of income. What follows is a brief description of the other two measures of GDP. Figure 24.2 shows the relationship between other income measures.

- *Gross domestic product income approach (GDP(I))* is the sum of factor incomes, consumption of fixed capital (depreciation) and net indirect taxes. Factor incomes include wages, salaries and supplements paid to labour and profit received by both private and public businesses. Depreciation is the wear and tear on the economy's stock of equipment and structures, such as trucks rusting and lightbulbs

burning out. In the national income accounts prepared by the ABS, depreciation is called the 'consumption of fixed capital'.

- *Gross domestic product production approach (GDP(P))* involves taking the market value of goods and services produced by an industry and deducting the cost of goods and services used up by the industry in the productive process, or what is referred to by the ABS as 'intermediate consumption'. This approach uses a concept called **value added** to calculate GDP. When a firm produces a good, it must buy inputs. In the process of production, the firm transforms the inputs into something else. The additional value which is added to the value of the inputs is referred to as the 'value added'. When the ABS uses this approach to calculate GDP, the value of the inputs must be subtracted from the value of the final product to avoid double counting because GDP is the value of final goods and services.

Although the various measures of income differ in detail, they almost always tell the same story about economic conditions. When GDP is growing rapidly, these other measures of income are usually growing rapidly. And when GDP is falling, these other measures are usually falling as well. For monitoring fluctuations in the overall economy, it does not matter much which measure of income we use.

value added
the value of a firm's output minus the value of its inputs

Figure 24.2 **Relationships among other income measures**

National turnover of goods and services	Imports of goods and services	Imports of goods and services	Imports of goods and services	Imports of goods and services	Imports of goods and services	Imports of goods and services	Exports of goods and services
	Gross domestic product			Net income paid overseas	Net income paid overseas	Net income paid overseas	
					Net transfers to overseas	Net transfers to overseas	
						Net lending to overseas	
		Gross domestic product at factor cost	Domestic factor incomes	National income	National disposable income		
						Gross national expenditure	Gross national expenditure
			Indirect taxes less subsidies				
		Indirect taxes less subsidies	Consumption of fixed capital	Consumption of fixed capital	Consumption of fixed capital		

The figure shows the relationships among various measures of expenditure, income and output. National turnover is the total of expenditure on all goods and services, including expenditure on imports. Gross domestic product subtracts imports from national turnover to get a value of goods and services produced within the domestic economy. The value of domestic production can also be obtained by adding up the incomes of domestic factors of production. The figure shows how taxes and subsidies, payments to and receipts from overseas, and borrowing and lending are accounted for in the national income accounts.

Source: Constructed from ABS, Cat. No. 5216.0, 2000.

Q List the four components of expenditure. Which is the largest?

If you go to the ABS website and look at the annual GDP figures (as you are asked to do in question 8 in Problems and applications at the end of the chapter) you'll wonder where we got the figures we've presented in Table 24.1. But some simple additions will get you the same results we've shown. The ABS presents the information in a slightly different way – they show:
- Final consumption expenditure – which includes both household *and* government consumption
- Total gross fixed capital formation – both business *and* government investment
- Exports less imports.

So the published data lumps all consumption together, whether household or government, and all investment together, whether business or government. That's because some government expenditure is consumption (like the purchase of paper clips by a government department) and some government expenditure is investment (like building a new bridge or road). Sometimes we're interested in private sector spending vs public sector (so we would use the $C + I + G + NX$ approach) and sometimes we're interested in how much of GDP is being generated for current consumption and how much for investment in future production capabilities (when we would be happy with the approach that the ABS presents). No matter which approach we use, when we add it all up, it should be the same!

Real versus nominal GDP

As we have seen, GDP measures the total spending on goods and services in all markets in the economy. If total spending rises from one year to the next, one of two things must be true: (1) the economy is producing a larger output of goods and services, or (2) goods and services are being sold at higher prices. When studying changes in the economy over time, economists want to separate these two effects. In particular, they want a measure of the total quantity of goods and services the economy is producing that is not affected by changes in the prices of those goods and services.

To do this, economists use a measure called real GDP. Real GDP answers a hypothetical question: What would be the value of the goods and services produced this year if we valued these goods and services at prices that prevailed in some specific year in the past? By evaluating current production using prices that are fixed at past levels, real GDP shows how the economy's overall production of goods and services changes over time.

To see more precisely how real GDP is constructed, let's consider an example.

A numerical example

Table 24.2 shows some data for an economy that produces only two goods – pizza and packets of instant noodles. The table shows the quantities of the two goods produced and their prices in the years 2011, 2012 and 2013.

To calculate total spending in this economy, we multiply the quantities of pizzas and instant noodles by their prices. In the year 2011, 100 pizzas are sold at a price of $5 per pizza, so expenditure on pizza equals $500. In the same year, 75 packets of instant noodles are sold for $3 per packet of instant noodles and so expenditure on instant noodles is $225. Total expenditure in the economy – the sum of expenditure on pizzas and expenditure on instant noodles – is $725. This amount, the production of goods and services valued at current prices, is called **nominal GDP**.

The table shows the calculation of nominal GDP for these three years. Total spending rises from $725 in 2011 to $1300 in 2012 and then to $2150 in 2013. Part of this rise is attributable to the increase in the quantities of pizzas and instant noodles, and part is attributable to the increase in prices of pizzas and instant noodles.

To obtain a measure of the amount produced that is not affected by changes in prices, we use **real GDP**, which is the production of goods and services valued at constant prices. We calculate real GDP by first choosing one year as a base year. We then use the prices of pizza and instant noodles in the base year to calculate the value of goods and services in all of the years. In other words, the prices in the base year provide the basis for comparing quantities in different years.

Suppose that we choose 2011 to be the base year in our example. We can then use the prices of pizza and instant noodles in 2011 to calculate the value of goods and services produced in 2011, 2012 and 2013. Table 24.2 shows these calculations. To calculate real GDP for 2011, we use the prices of pizza and instant noodles in 2011 (the base year) and the quantities of pizza and instant noodles produced in 2011. (Thus, for the base year, real GDP always equals nominal GDP.) To calculate real GDP for 2012, we use the prices of pizza and instant noodles in 2011 (the base year) and the quantities of pizza and instant noodles produced in 2012. Similarly, to calculate real GDP for 2013, we use the prices in 2011 and the quantities in 2013. When we find that real GDP has risen from $725 in 2011 to $1050 in 2012 and then to $1450 in 2013, we know that the increase is attributable to an increase in the quantities produced, because the prices are held fixed at base-year levels.

nominal GDP
the production of goods and services valued at current prices

▸ nominal GDP

real GDP
the production of goods and services valued at constant prices

▸ real GDP

Table 24.2 Real and nominal GDP

Year	Price and quantities			
	Price of pizza	Quantity of pizza	Price of instant noodles	Quantity of instant noodles
2011	$5	100	$3	75
2012	6	150	4	100
2013	7	200	5	150
Year	**Calculating nominal GDP**			**Nominal GDP ($)**
2011	($5 per pizza × 100 pizza) + ($3 per packet of instant noodles × 75 packets) = $725			725
2012	($6 per pizza × 150 pizza) + ($4 per packet of instant noodles × 100 packets) = $1300			1300
2013	($7 per pizza × 200 pizza) + ($5 per packet of instant noodles × 150 packets) = $2150			2150
Year	**Calculating real GDP (base year 2011)**			**Real GDP ($)**
2011	($5 per pizza × 100 pizza) + ($3 per packet of instant noodles × 75 packets) = $725			725
2012	($5 per pizza × 150 pizza) + ($3 per packet of instant noodles × 100 packets) = $1050			1050
2013	($5 per pizza × 200 pizza) + ($3 per packet of instant noodles × 150 packets) = $1450			1450
Year	**Calculating the GDP deflator**			**GDP deflator**
2011	($725/$725) × 100 = 100			100
2012	($1300/$1050) × 100 = 124			124
2013	($2150/$1450) × 100 = 148			148

This table shows how to calculate real GDP, nominal GDP and the GDP deflator for a hypothetical economy that produces only pizza and instant noodles.

To sum up – *nominal GDP uses current prices to place a value on the economy's production of goods and services; real GDP uses constant base-year prices to place a value on the economy's production of goods and services.* Because real GDP is not affected by changes in prices, changes in real GDP reflect only changes in the amounts being produced. Thus, real GDP is a measure of the economy's production of goods and services.

Our goal in calculating GDP is to gauge how well the overall economy is performing. Because real GDP measures the economy's production of goods and services, it reflects the economy's ability to satisfy people's material needs and desires. Thus, real GDP is a better gauge of economic wellbeing than nominal GDP. When economists talk about the economy's GDP, they usually mean real rather than nominal GDP. And when they talk about growth in the economy, they measure that growth using the percentage change in real GDP from an earlier period.

The GDP deflator

From nominal GDP and real GDP, we can calculate a third useful statistic – the GDP deflator. The GDP deflator measures the current level of prices relative to the level of prices in the base year. In other words, the GDP deflator tells us the rise in nominal GDP that is attributable to a rise in prices rather than a rise in the quantities produced.

The **GDP deflator** is calculated as follows:

$$\text{GDP deflator} = \frac{\text{Nominal GDP}}{\text{Real GDP}} \times 100$$

GDP deflator
A measure of the price level calculated as the ratio of nominal GDP to real GDP times 100

This formula shows why the GDP deflator measures the level of prices in the economy. A change in the price of some good or service, without any change in the quantity produced, affects nominal GDP but not real GDP. This price change, therefore, is reflected in the GDP deflator.

The GDP deflator in our example is calculated at the bottom of Table 24.2. For the year 2011, nominal GDP is $725 and real GDP is $725, so the GDP deflator is 100. (The GDP deflator is always 100 in the base year.) For the year 2012, nominal GDP is $1300 and real GDP is $1050, so the GDP deflator is 124. Because the GDP deflator rose in year 2012 from 100 to 124, we can say that the price level increased by 24 per cent.

The GDP deflator is one measure that economists use to monitor the average level of prices in the economy. We examine another – the consumer price index – in the next chapter.

CASESTUDY

Real GDP over recent history

Now that we know how real GDP is defined and measured, let's look at what this macroeconomic variable tells us about the recent history of Australia. Figure 24.3 shows quarterly data on real GDP for the Australian economy since 1970.

The most obvious feature of these data is that real GDP grows over time. Real GDP of the Australian economy in 2010 was almost four times its level in 1970. Put differently, the output of goods and services produced in Australia has grown on average about 3.5 per cent per year. This continued growth in real GDP enables the typical Australian to enjoy greater economic prosperity than his or her parents and grandparents did.

A second feature of the GDP data is that growth is not steady. The upward climb of real GDP is occasionally interrupted by periods of decline, called recessions. Figure 24.3 marks recessions with shaded vertical bars. Recessions are associated not only with lower incomes but also with other forms of economic distress – rising unemployment, falling profits, increased bankruptcies and so on.

The third thing to notice about GDP growth in Australia is that we have had an extremely long, some would say unprecedented, period of growth in GDP. For the last 18 years, we have not had a recession. Even though many other economies suffered recessions as a result of the global financial crisis, Australia's GDP only dipped in one quarter, at the end of 2008. This could be due to good economic management, to the stimulus package put in place by the Rudd government, to the resources boom, to the demand for our minerals by growing economies like China and India. One thing is certain – it won't last forever.

Much of macroeconomics is aimed at explaining these long-run growth and short-run fluctuations in real GDP. As we will see in the coming chapters, we need different explanatory frameworks or 'models' for these two purposes. Because short-run fluctuations represent deviations from the long-run trend, we first examine the behaviour of the economy in the long run. In particular, chapters 26 to 32 examine how key macroeconomic variables, including real GDP, are determined in the long run. We then build on this analysis to explain short-run fluctuations in chapters 33 to 35.

Figure 24.3 Real GDP in Australia

This figure shows quarterly data on real GDP for the Australian economy since 1970. Recessions – periods of falling real GDP – are marked with the shaded vertical bars.

Source: ABS, Cat. No. 5206.0, 2010.

Q Define real and nominal GDP. Which is a better measure of economic wellbeing? Why?

GDP and economic wellbeing

Earlier in this chapter, GDP was called the best single measure of the economic wellbeing of a society. Now that we know what GDP is, we can evaluate this claim.

As we have seen, GDP measures both the economy's total income and the economy's total expenditure on goods and services. Thus, GDP per person tells us the income and expenditure of the average person in the economy. Because most people prefer to receive higher income and enjoy higher expenditure, GDP per person seems a natural measure of the economic wellbeing of the average individual.

Yet some people dispute the validity of GDP as a measure of welfare. When he was running for president in 1968, US Senator Robert Kennedy gave a moving critique of such economic measures.

> [Gross domestic product] does not allow for the health of our children, the quality of their education, or the joy of their play. It does not include the beauty of our poetry or the strength of our marriages, the intelligence of our public debate or the integrity of our public officials. It measures neither our courage, nor our wisdom, nor our devotion to our country. It measures everything, in short, except that which makes life worthwhile, and it can tell us everything about America except why we are proud that we are Americans.

Much of what Robert Kennedy said is correct and applies equally well to Australia. Why, then, do we care about GDP?

The answer is that a large GDP does in fact help us to lead enjoyable lives. GDP does not measure the health of children, but nations with larger GDP can afford better health care for their children. GDP does not measure the quality of education, but nations with larger GDP can afford better educational systems. GDP does not measure the beauty of poetry, but nations with larger GDP can afford to teach more of their citizens to read and to enjoy poetry. GDP does not take account of our intelligence, integrity, courage, wisdom or devotion to country, but all of these laudable attributes are easier to foster when people are less concerned about being able to afford the material necessities of life. In short, GDP does not directly measure those things that make life worthwhile, but it does measure our ability to satisfy material needs and these are essential ingredients of comfortable, enjoyable and worthwhile lives.

GDP is not, however, a perfect measure of wellbeing. Some things that contribute to a good life are left out of GDP. One is leisure. Suppose, for instance, that everyone in the economy suddenly started working every day of the week, rather than enjoying leisure on weekends. More goods and services would be produced and GDP would rise. Yet, despite the increase in GDP, we should not conclude that everyone would be better off. The welfare loss from reduced leisure would offset the welfare gain from producing and consuming a greater quantity of goods and services.

Another item that GDP excludes is the quality of the environment. Imagine that the government eliminated all environmental regulations. Firms could then produce goods and services without considering the pollution they create and GDP might rise. Yet it is most likely that wellbeing would fall. The deterioration in the quality of air and water would more than offset the welfare gain from greater production. (See the FYI box 'Excerpt from the *Human Development Report 2007/2008*' later in this chapter.)

Because GDP uses market prices to value goods and services, it also excludes the value of almost all activity that takes place outside of markets. Child-rearing and volunteer work, for instance, contribute to the wellbeing of those in society, but GDP does not reflect these contributions. If parents decided to spend fewer hours at their jobs in order to spend more time with their children, the economy might produce fewer goods and services, and GDP might fall, but that change would not necessarily reflect a lower quality of life.

In the end, we conclude that GDP is a good measure of welfare for most – but not all – purposes. It is important to keep in mind what GDP includes as well as what it leaves out.

Although data on other aspects of the quality of life are less complete, they tell a similar story. Countries with low GDP per person tend to have more infants with low birthweight, higher rates of infant mortality, higher rates of maternal mortality, higher rates of child malnutrition and less common access to safe drinking water. In countries with low GDP per person, fewer school-age

CASE STUDY

International differences in GDP and the quality of life

One way to gauge the usefulness of GDP as a measure of economic wellbeing is to examine international data. Rich and poor countries have vastly different levels of GDP per person. If a large GDP leads to a higher standard of living, then we should observe GDP to be strongly correlated with measures of the quality of life. And, in fact, we do.

Table 24.3 shows 12 countries around the world, including Australia and New Zealand, listed in order of their Human Development Index (HDI) ranking. Note that GDP and HDI rankings are not identical, though. The USA has the second-highest GDP ranking of those countries shown, but a slightly lower life expectancy, which lowers its overall HDI ranking. The countries shaded in blue are considered to have high human development, the countries in green have medium human development and Afghanistan, in pink, is considered to have a low level of human development.

Table 24.3 GDP, life expectancy and literacy

Country	HDI rank*	Real GDP per person (2001)	Life expectancy	Adult literacy (%)
Norway	1	$53 433	80.5 years	99
Australia	2	34 923	81.4	99
Japan	10	33 632	82.7	99
USA	13	45 592	79.1	99
New Zealand	20	27 336	80.1	99
UK	21	35 130	79.3	99
Thailand	87	8 135	68.7	94.1
China	92	5 383	72.59	93.3
Indonesia	111	3 712	70.5	92
India	134	2 753	63.4	66.7
Papua New Guinea	148	2 084	60.7	57.8
Afghanistan	181	1 054	43.6	28

The table shows GDP per person and two measures of the quality of life for 12 countries.
* HDI ranking is based on life expectancy, education and real GDP.

Source: *2007/2008 Human Development Report* © 2008 UNDP reproduced with permission of Palgrave Macmillan.

children are in school and those who are in school must learn with fewer teachers per student. These countries also tend to have fewer radios, fewer televisions, fewer telephones, fewer paved roads and fewer households with electricity. International data leave no doubt that a nation's GDP is closely associated with its citizens' standard of living.

Why should policymakers care about GDP?

Excerpt from the *2007/2008 Human Development Report*

The following excerpt from the *Human Development Report*, published by the United Nations Development Programme, illustrates the importance of looking at other measures of economic wellbeing.

Climate change is the defining human development issue of our generation. All development is ultimately about expanding human potential and enlarging human freedom. It is about people developing the capabilities that empower them to make choices and to lead lives that they value. Climate change threatens to erode human freedoms and limit choice. It calls into question the Enlightenment principle that human progress will make the future look better than the past.

The early warning signs are already visible. Today, we are witnessing at first hand what could be the onset of major human development reversal in our lifetime. Across developing countries, millions of the world's poorest people are already being forced to cope with the impacts of climate change. These impacts do not register as apocalyptic events in the full glare of world media attention. They go unnoticed in financial markets and in the measurement of world gross domestic product (GDP). But increased exposure to drought, to more intense storms, to floods and environmental stress is holding back the efforts of the world's poor to build a better life for themselves and their children.

Climate change will undermine international efforts to combat poverty. Seven years ago, political leaders around the world gathered to set targets for accelerated progress in human development. The Millennium Development Goals (MDGs) defined a new ambition for 2015. Much has been achieved, though many countries remain off track. Climate change is hampering efforts to deliver the MDG promise. Looking to the future, the danger is that it will stall and then reverse progress built up over generations not just in cutting extreme poverty, but in health, nutrition, education and other areas. How the world deals with climate change today will have a direct bearing on the human development prospects of a large section of humanity. Failure will consign the poorest 40 percent of the world's population – some 2.6 billion people – to a future of diminished opportunity. It will exacerbate deep inequalities within countries. And it will undermine efforts to build a more inclusive pattern of globalization, reinforcing the vast disparities between the 'haves' and the 'have nots'.

Even though Australia does not include the impact of climate change in the national income accounts, it does measure Australia's greenhouse gas emissions. To see how Australia has performed on greenhouse gas emissions, go to the government climate change website: www.climatechange.gov.au/en/climate-change/emissions.aspx. Over the year from March 2009 to March 2010, Australia's emissions declined by 1 per cent.

Source: *2007/2008 Human Development Report*, © 2008 UNDP reproduced with permission of Palgrave Macmillan.

Conclusion

This chapter has discussed how economists measure the total income of a nation. Measurement is, of course, only a starting point. Much of macroeconomics is aimed at revealing the long-run and short-run determinants of a nation's gross domestic product. Why, for example, is GDP higher in Australia and Japan than in India and Afghanistan? What can the governments of the poorest countries do to promote more rapid growth in GDP? Why does GDP in Australia rise rapidly in some years and fall in others? What can Australian policymakers do to reduce the severity of these fluctuations in GDP? These are the questions we will take up shortly.

At this point, it is important to acknowledge the importance of just measuring GDP. We all get some sense of how the economy is doing as we go about our lives. But economists who study changes in the economy and policymakers who formulate economic policies need more than this vague sense – they need concrete data on which to base their judgements. Quantifying the behaviour of the economy with statistics such as GDP is, therefore, the first step in developing a science of macroeconomics.

Summary

- Because every transaction has a buyer and a seller, the total expenditure in the economy must equal the total income in the economy.
- Gross domestic product (GDP) measures an economy's total expenditure on newly produced goods and services and the total income earned from the production of these goods and services. More precisely, GDP is the market value of all final goods and services produced within a country in a given period of time.
- GDP is divided among four components of expenditure – consumption, investment, government purchases and net exports. Consumption includes spending on goods and services by households, with the exception of purchases of new housing. Investment includes spending on new equipment and structures, including households' purchases of new housing. Government purchases include spending on goods and services by local, state and federal governments. Net exports equal the value of goods and services produced domestically and sold abroad (exports) minus the value of goods and services produced abroad and sold domestically (imports).
- Nominal GDP uses current prices to value the economy's production of goods and services. Real GDP uses constant base-year prices to value the economy's production of goods and services. The GDP deflator – calculated from the ratio of nominal to real GDP – measures the level of prices in the economy.
- GDP is a good measure of economic wellbeing because people prefer higher to lower incomes. But it is not a perfect measure of wellbeing. For example, GDP excludes the value of leisure and the value of a clean environment.

Key concepts

consumption
GDP deflator
government purchases
gross domestic product (GDP)

gross national product (GNP)
investment
net exports
nominal GDP

real GDP
value added

Questions for review

1   Explain why an economy's income must equal its expenditure.
2   Which contributes more to GDP – the production of a tonne of wheat or the production of a tonne of coal? Why?
3   A farmer sells wheat to a baker for $3. The baker uses the wheat to make bread, which is sold for $5. What is the contribution to GDP?
4   Over the last three years, Lynn paid $3000 to put together her wardrobe. Today she sold most of her clothes at a garage sale for $200. How does this sale affect current GDP?
5   List the four components of GDP. Give an example of each.
6   In the year 2011, the economy produces 100 serves of fish and chips for $8 each. In the year 2012, the economy produces 200 serves of fish and chips for $10 each. Calculate nominal GDP, real GDP and the GDP deflator for each year. (Use 2011 as the base year.) By what percentage does each of these three statistics rise from one year to the next? Why is it desirable for a country to have a large GDP? Give an example of something that would raise GDP and yet be undesirable.

Problems and applications

1 What components of GDP (if any) would each of the following transactions affect? Explain.
   a A family buys a new air conditioner
   b Uncle Marco buys a new house
   c Kia sells a Rio from its inventory
   d You buy a pizza
   e The government of New South Wales creates a bike path around Sydney
   f Your parents buy a bottle of South African wine
   g Toyota expands its factory in Altona, Victoria.

2 The 'government purchases' component of GDP does not include spending on transfer payments such as pension benefits. Thinking about the definition of GDP, explain why transfer payments are excluded.

3 Why do you think households' purchases of new housing are included in the investment component of GDP rather than the consumption component? Can you think of a reason that households' purchases of new cars should also be included in investment rather than in consumption? To what other consumption goods might this logic apply?

4 As the chapter states, GDP does not include the value of used goods that are resold. Why would including such transactions make GDP a less informative measure of economic wellbeing?

5 What is the advantage of measuring GDP using the prices, rather than the sizes or weights, of different goods?

6 Consider the following data on Australian GDP:

Year	Nominal GDP (in millions)	GDP deflator (base year 2007–08)
2009	$1 250 474	102.9
2010	1 301 551	109.6

   a What was the growth rate of nominal income between 2009 and 2010? (*Note:* The growth rate is the percentage change from one period to the next. The ABS calculates annual GDP on a financial year basis, from July one year to June the next. The GDP deflator is equal to 100 in the middle of the financial year.)
   b What was the growth rate of the GDP deflator between 2009 and 2010?
   c What was real income in 2009 measured in 2008 prices?
   d What was real income in 2010 measured in 2008 prices?
   e What was the growth rate of real income between 2009 and 2010?
   f Was the growth rate of nominal income higher or lower than the growth rate of real income? Explain.

7 If prices rise, people's income from selling goods increases. Why do economists prefer using real GDP as a measure of economic wellbeing rather than using nominal GDP?

8 Revised estimates of Australian GDP are usually released by the government near the end of each month. Look it up on the ABS website, www.abs.gov.au, or go to a library and find a newspaper article that reports on the most recent release. Discuss the recent changes in real and nominal GDP and in the components of GDP.

9 If a farmer sells the same amount of milk as last year, but at a higher price per litre, her income has increased. Can you tell whether she is better off? Explain.

10 A friend tells you that the GDP of China is three times the GDP of Switzerland. Does this imply that China is better off economically than Switzerland? Why or why not?

11   Goods and services that are sold in black markets, such as illegal drugs, are generally not included in GDP. Does this lead to a misleading comparison between countries, such as in the second column of Table 24.3, comparing Australia and India? Explain. Should these activities be included as a positive or negative in GDP?

12   Australia's underground economy is estimated at 13 per cent of GDP, while Thailand's is estimated at 54 per cent of GDP. Do you think these figures should change the rankings of the countries in the Human Development Index? Why or why not? (*Source:* Friedrich Schneider. Figures are for 2002.)

13   'As merely a gross measure of market activity, GDP only counts money transactions and thus leaves out many "goods" that people provide for each other free. This means that … [t]he crucial economic functions performed in the household and volunteer sectors go entirely unreckoned. The more things are excluded, such as care for the elderly and for children, home maintenance and cleaning, food preparation, and voluntary service for neighborhood, church, and civic groups, the more our families and communities decline and a monetized service sector takes their place, the more the GDP goes up.' (Julian Dautremont-Smith, World Student Community for Sustainable Development.)

Suppose you were asked to devise a way to include the effects of climate change on GDP. What information would you need? Do you think your measure would increase or decrease Australia's GDP? Explain.

14   The participation of women in the Australian labour force has risen dramatically since 1965.

   a   How do you think this rise affected GDP?

   b   Now imagine a measure of wellbeing that includes time spent working in the home and taking leisure. How would the change in this measure of wellbeing compare with the change in GDP?

   c   Can you think of other aspects of wellbeing that are associated with the rise in women's labour-force participation? Would it be practical to construct a measure of wellbeing that includes these aspects?

   d   In the last two decades, there has been an increase in the numbers of fathers staying home to look after their children. How would this affect GDP?

Search me!

When accessing information about economics use the following keywords in any combinations you require:

- nominal GDP
- real GDP

CourseMate

For more multimedia resources and activities on economics, visit the Economics CourseMate website.

25

Measuring the cost of living

Learning objectives

In this chapter you will:

- learn how the consumer price index (CPI) is constructed
- consider why the CPI is an imperfect measure of the cost of living
- compare the CPI and the GDP deflator as measures of the overall price level
- see how to use a price index to compare dollar amounts from different times
- learn the distinction between real and nominal interest rates.

In 1930, as the Australian economy was suffering through the Great Depression, famed racehorse Phar Lap earned £9429 at the Melbourne Cup. At the time, these earnings were extraordinary, even for great racehorses. The prime minister, James Scullin, received a parliamentary allowance of about £1000. When Australia switched from pounds to decimal currency in 1966, a pound was designated to be worth $2, so in dollar terms, these earnings would have been $19 000 and $2000 respectively. (See the 'FYI' box, 'The change to decimal currency' below.) Phar Lap may be more famous than Prime Minister Scullin, but neither amount seems much when compared with the winnings for the present-day Melbourne Cup.

Today the Melbourne Cup pays $3.3 million to the winning horse, over 150 times what Phar Lap won. And Phar Lap is still considered one of the greatest racehorses ever to have lived. At first, this fact might lead you to think that horseracing has become much more lucrative over the past seven decades. But, as everyone knows, the prices of goods and services have also risen. In 1930, an ice-cream would have cost about 2 cents and a ticket to the local picture theatre about 5 cents. Because these prices were so much lower in Phar Lap's day than they are in ours, it is not clear whether Phar Lap's owners enjoyed a higher or lower standard of living than today's horse owners.

In the preceding chapter we looked at how economists use gross domestic product (GDP) to measure the quantity of goods and services that the economy is producing. This chapter examines how economists measure the overall cost of living. To compare Phar Lap's earnings of $19 000 with prize money of today, we need to find some way of turning dollar figures into meaningful measures of purchasing power. That is exactly the job of a statistic called the *consumer price index*. After seeing how the consumer price index is constructed, we discuss how we can use such a price index to compare dollar figures from different points in time.

The consumer price index is used to monitor changes in the cost of living over time. When the consumer price index rises, the typical family has to spend more dollars to maintain the same standard of living. Economists use the term *inflation* to describe a situation in which the economy's overall price level is rising. The *inflation rate* is the percentage change in the price level from the previous period. As we will see in the coming chapters, inflation is a closely watched aspect of macroeconomic performance and is a key variable guiding macroeconomic policy. This chapter provides the background for that analysis by showing how economists measure the inflation rate using the consumer price index.

The consumer price index

consumer price index (CPI)
a measure of the overall cost of the goods and services bought by a typical consumer

The **consumer price index (CPI)** is a measure of the overall cost of the goods and services bought by a typical consumer. Each month the Australian Bureau of Statistics (ABS) calculates and reports the consumer price index. In this section, we discuss how the consumer price index is calculated and what problems arise in its measurement. We also consider how this index compares with the GDP deflator, another measure of the overall level of prices, which we examined in the last chapter.

▶ consumer price index

fyi

The change to decimal currency

Imagine that, instead of the name 'dollar', the currency in Australia was called the 'inflato'. That was one of the names suggested to Prime Minister Holt for the new decimal currency introduced in 1966. The 'royal' was the most favoured name, but others suggested were 'austral', 'A.B.C.D.', 'aborroo', 'anzac', 'centimate', 'deci-cur', 'dollauster', 'kanoala', 'howzat', 'macquarie', 'oz' and 'sheepsback'. It's hard to imagine a shopkeeper saying 'That'll be five sheepsbacks, please'!

The day Australia changed to decimal currency was 14 February 1966. The currency used before the change was the pound (£). One pound was worth 20 shillings, and 1 shilling was worth 12 pence. The

>>

conversion rate was $2 for every pound. A shilling became 10 cents, and 1 penny was equivalent to 5/6 of a cent. This is not an exchange rate, though. It is simply the rate chosen for converting old currency to new. If you found a pound in your attic, it would still be equivalent to $2. How much that pound would buy today compared with how much it would have bought 50 years ago is another matter. What we are discussing in this chapter is what happens to the purchasing power of a unit of currency over time as a result of inflation; that is, a rise in the prices of goods and services.

At the time of the conversion, people predicted that inflation would result from the change. For example, a box of matches sold for 2 pence in the old currency. At the standard conversion rate of 1 penny to 5/6 of a cent, the price in the new currency would be 1.67 cents, but because there were no units of currency smaller than a cent, this would be rounded up to 2 cents, a price increase of roughly 20 per cent. However, these increases would have occurred only for goods that were very low in price and an insignificant part of anyone's budget, so the predicted inflationary effects did not occur.

Other costs of the conversion included changing accounting machines, cash registers and electronic data processing machines to handle decimal currency. There was a government compensation scheme to help business people with the costs of the changeover. Despite concerns that conversion would be costly and inflationary, the transition to decimal currency was made with relatively little fuss.

How the consumer price index is calculated

When the ABS calculates the consumer price index and the inflation rate, it uses data on the prices of thousands of goods and services. To see exactly how these statistics are constructed, let's consider a simple economy in which consumers buy only two goods – movie tickets and apples. Table 25.1 shows the five steps that the ABS follows.

1 *Fix the basket.* The first step in calculating the consumer price index is to determine which prices are most important to the typical consumer. If the typical consumer buys more apples than movie tickets, then the price of apples is more important than the price of movie tickets and, therefore, should be given greater weight in measuring the cost of living. The ABS sets these weights by surveying consumers and finding the basket of goods and services that the typical consumer buys. In the example in the table, the typical consumer buys a basket of four apples and two movie tickets.

2 *Find the prices.* The second step in calculating the consumer price index is to find the prices of each of the goods and services in the basket for each point in time. The table shows the prices of movie tickets and apples for three different years.

3 *Calculate the basket's cost.* The third step is to use the data on prices to calculate the cost of the basket of goods and services at different times. The table shows this calculation for each of the three years. Notice that only the prices in this calculation change. By keeping the basket of goods the same (four apples and two movie tickets), we are isolating the effects of price changes from the effect of any quantity changes that might be occurring at the same time.

4 *Choose a base year and calculate the index.* The fourth step is to designate one year as the base year, which is the benchmark with which other years are compared. To calculate the index, the price of the basket of goods and services in each year is divided by the price of the basket in the base year and this ratio is then multiplied by 100. The resulting number is the consumer price index.

Table 25.1 Calculating the consumer price index and the inflation rate: An example

Step 1: Survey consumers to determine a fixed basket of goods

Four apples, two movie tickets

Step 2: Find the price of each good in each year

Year	Price of apples	Price of movie tickets
2011	$1.50	$6
2012	2.50	8
2013	3.00	10

Step 3: Calculate the cost of the basket of goods in each year

Year	Cost of basket	Calculations
2011	($1.50 per apple × 4 apples) + ($6 per movie ticket × 2 movie tickets) = $18	$18
2012	($2.50 per apple × 4 apples) + ($8 per movie ticket × 2 movie tickets) = $26	$26
2013	($3 per apple × 4 apples) + ($10 per movie ticket × 2 movie tickets) = $32	$32

Step 4: Choose one year as a base year (2011) and calculate the consumer price index in each year

Year	Consumer price index	
2011	($18/$18) × 100 = 100	100
2012	($26/$18) × 100 = 144	144
2013	($32/$18) × 100 = 178	178

Step 5: Use the consumer price index to calculate the inflation rate from previous year

Year	Inflation rate	
2012	(144 − 100)/100 × 100 = 44%	44
2013	(178 − 144)/144 × 100 = 23%	23

This table shows how to calculate the consumer price index and the inflation rate for a hypothetical economy in which consumers buy only movie tickets and apples.

In the example in the table, the year 2011 is the base year. In this year, the basket of movie tickets and apples costs $18. Therefore, the price of the basket in all years is divided by $18 and multiplied by 100. The consumer price index is 100 in 2011. (The index is always 100 in the base year.) The consumer price index is 144 in 2012. This means that the price of the basket in 2012 is 144 per cent of its price in the base year. Put differently, a basket of goods that costs $100 in the base year costs $144 in 2012. Similarly, the consumer price index is 178 in 2013, indicating that the price level in 2013 is 178 per cent of the price level in the base year.

5 *Calculate the inflation rate.* The fifth and final step is to use the consumer price index to calculate the **inflation rate**, which is the percentage change in the price index from the preceding period. In our example, the consumer price index rose by 44 per cent from 2011 to 2012 and by 23 per cent from 2012 to 2013. The inflation rate is said to be 44 per cent in 2012 and 23 per cent in 2013.

inflation rate
the percentage change in the price index from the preceding period

Although this example simplifies the real world by including only two goods, it shows how the ABS calculates the consumer price index and the inflation rate. The ABS collects and processes data on the prices of around 100 000 goods and services at least once each quarter and, by following the five steps described above, determines how quickly the cost of living for the typical consumer is rising. When the ABS makes its quarterly announcement of the inflation rate calculated from the consumer price index, you can usually hear the number on the evening television news, see it in the next day's newspaper or look it up on the ABS website.

In addition to the consumer price index for the overall economy, the ABS calculates several other price indexes. It reports the index for the capital cities (Sydney, Melbourne, Perth, Adelaide, Brisbane, Hobart, Darwin) and Canberra as well as for some narrow categories of goods and services (such as food, clothing and housing). It also calculates the **producer price index**, which measures the cost of a basket of goods and services bought by firms rather than by consumers. Because firms eventually pass on their costs to consumers in the form of higher consumer prices, changes in the producer price index are often thought to be useful in predicting changes in the consumer price index.

producer price index
a measure of the cost of a basket of goods and services bought by firms

---

fyi

What is in the CPI's basket?

When constructing the consumer price index, the ABS tries to include all the goods and services that the typical consumer buys. Moreover, it tries to weight these goods and services according to how much consumers buy of each item.

Figure 25.1 shows the breakdown of consumer spending into the major categories of goods and services for the 14th series, last updated in 2005. (It is updated about every five years and was under review in 2010. See 'In the news' below.) The basics of living are the most significant categories. Housing and household contents and services make up the largest component of the typical consumer's budget, at 30 per cent. Housing (20 per cent) includes rent, utilities, property rates and repairs and maintenance. Household contents and services include furniture, large and small appliances, and household supplies such as laundry soaps and garbage bags. The next largest category at 15 per cent is food and beverages; this includes food at home (10 per cent) and food away from home (5 per cent). Alcoholic beverages and tobacco products are in a separate category (7 per cent). The next category, at 13 per cent, is transport, which includes spending on cars, petrol, buses, trains and so on. Next are recreation (12 per cent), clothing and footwear (4 per cent), and health (5 per cent). Education makes up just 3 per cent of the basket, as does communication. In the last updating of the CPI basket, a new category has been added that includes financial and insurance services (9 per cent).

Problems in measuring the cost of living

The consumer price index is a measure of the aggregate price level in the economy. The goal of the index is to measure changes in the cost of living. In other words, the consumer price index can be used to gauge how much incomes must rise in order to maintain a constant standard of living. The consumer price index, however, is not a perfect measure of the cost of living. Three problems with the index are widely acknowledged but difficult to solve.

Figure 25.1   The basket of goods and services

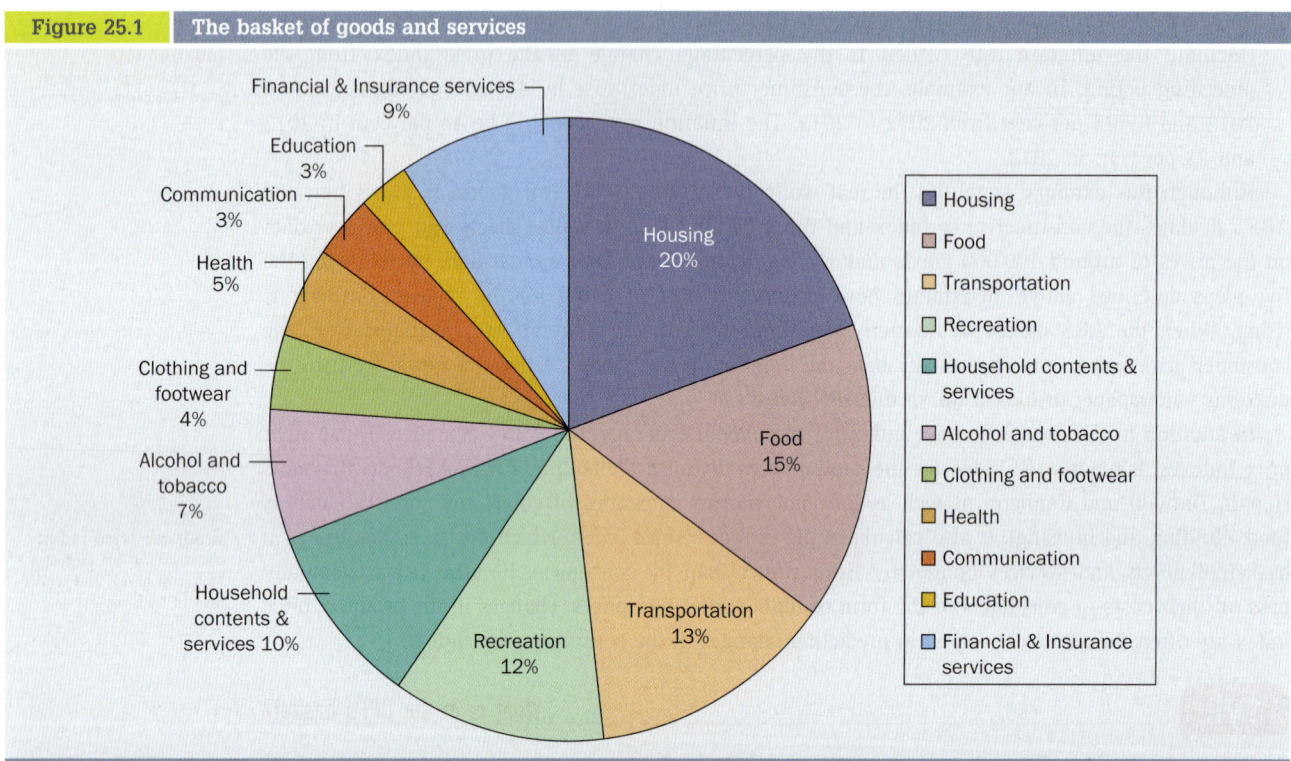

This figure shows how the typical consumer divides his or her spending among various categories of goods and services. The ABS calls each percentage the 'relative importance' of the category.

Source: ABS, Cat. No. 6461.0.

The first problem is called *substitution bias*. When prices change from one year to the next, they do not all change proportionately – some prices rise by more than others. Consumers respond to these differing price changes by buying less of the goods whose prices have risen by large amounts and by buying more of the goods whose prices have risen less or have even fallen. That is, consumers substitute goods that have become relatively less expensive. Yet the consumer price index is calculated assuming a fixed basket of goods. By not taking into account the possibility of consumer substitution, the index overstates the increase in the cost of living from one year to the next.

IN THE NEWS . . .

CHANGING OUR MEASURE OF INFLATION

In the 2007 federal election, the two major parties argued over whether inflation was on the rise or holding steady. The debate was about whether the appropriate measure of inflation was the 'headline' rate (the CPI) or the 'core' or 'underlying' rate of inflation that excludes highly volatile items like food and energy prices. In the first article below, Ross Gittins explains what the difference between these two measures is. The second article discusses whether the CPI is actually a measure of the cost of living at all and what the goals of the ABS's review are.

Forget the headlines: RBA looks at core inflation

by Ross Gittins

With the inflation rate now at 4 per cent – well above the Reserve Bank's 2 to 3 per cent target range – surely it will require more than just this week's interest rate rise to get it back under control?

Well, maybe, but not necessarily. There are a few things to remember. For a start, it is too soon to expect to see the effects of the rate rise in May. So the Reserve already has two rises working their way through the system.

For another thing, the Reserve's target requires it to keep the inflation rate between 2 and 3 per cent *on average* over the business cycle. So it is not required to hit the panic button every time inflation goes outside the range, provided it is confident it has done enough to get inflation within the range before too long.

And finally, as everyone knows, the 1.6 per cent rise in the consumer price index during the June quarter, which took the annual inflation rate to 4 per cent, was heavily influenced by two special factors: a 52 per cent increase in the price of fruit, mainly bananas, and an 11 per cent increase in the price of petrol.

Those two special factors accounted for almost a third each of the 1.6 per cent increase. So, clearly, the underlying inflation position is not as bad as the headline inflation rate suggests.

'Headline' inflation is the inflation rate as measured by the CPI, which is the thing the media focuses on. 'Underlying' (or 'core') inflation is any measure of inflation that tries to identify the *trend* in inflation by removing irregular or volatile, rather than ongoing, influences.

Remember that, for the purposes of managing the economy and deciding the appropriate level of interest rates, we are not interested in the cost of living. We are looking for evidence of the strength of inflation pressures in the economy.

So the leap in the price of bananas is a textbook example of a volatile item. It tells us nothing about the strength of inflation pressures throughout the economy. All it tells us is that a cyclone wiped out most of the nation's banana crop. As soon as another crop grows, banana prices will go back where they were.

The case of petrol prices is not quite as simple. We know petrol prices are volatile because of the ebb and flow of price discounting, and also because they move in line with the always-changing world price of oil.

But petrol prices have been on an uptrend for several years. That is not mere volatility. The latest quarter's increase may or may not prove lasting, but we should not just ignore such a significant medium-term trend.

Be that as it may, Friday's statement on monetary policy makes it clear the Reserve 'abstracted' from the 'temporary influences' of banana and fuel prices in deciding to raise the official interest rate this week.

Rather, its decision was based on the gradual increase in underlying inflation this year. It says the underlying rate has picked up to 'just under 3 per cent' and its new forecast is for the underlying rate over the next two years to stay around 3 per cent.

But how do you actually measure underlying inflation? Well, there are various ways you can do it and in recent years the Reserve has changed its preferred measures.

The method we are most familiar with is the 'exclusion' approach. The Bureau of Statistics calculates the 'CPI excluding volatile items', which is all the prices of the goods and services in the CPI basket except those for fruit, vegetables and petrol. Over the year to June, this measure rose by 2.4 per cent.

The bureau also calculates a measure of the prices of 'market goods and services excluding volatile items', which excludes in addition the prices of goods and services that are provided largely by the public sector, such as urban transport fares, health service fees and state and local government rates and charges. This measure rose by 2 per cent over the year to June.

>>

The trouble with these exclusion measures is that the decision about what to exclude is rather arbitrary, and they can still be affected by temporary movements in the prices of items that are not excluded. So they can retain a fair bit of volatility.

The less familiar, newer way to calculate underlying inflation is the 'statistical' approach. Here you are trying to measure the 'central tendency' of prices by abstracting from the most extreme price changes during the quarter.

Under the 'trimmed mean' method you rank all the price changes from largest to smallest, including price falls, then ignore (trim off) the top 15 per cent and the bottom 15 per cent, leaving only the middle 70 per cent.

Under the 'weighted median' method you rank the price changes, then take as the inflation rate the increase in the item that is in the middle of the distribution, so that half the weighted price changes are above it and half below.

The virtue of these statistical approaches is that they exclude from the calculation *all* the extreme changes, not just an arbitrarily determined list, and they exclude the largest price falls as well as the largest price increases. They do not exclude small movements in fruit, vegetable and petrol prices.

The two statistical measures are calculated by the Reserve and shown with the exclusion measures on its website (click on 'statistics' then 'statistics by frequency' then 'measures of consumer price inflation'). The CPI itself is not seasonally adjusted, but the two statistical measures are, for greater accuracy.

The trimmed mean measure shows underlying inflation of 2.8 per cent over the year to June, while the weighted median measure shows 3 per cent.

The Reserve's current practice is to take the average of these two as its preferred measure, which explains why it says underlying inflation is estimated to have picked up to a rate of 'just under 3 per cent'.

I have probably given you more detail than you need about how the Reserve assesses what is happening to inflation and makes its decisions about whether to raise or lower interest rates, but it was needed to counter all the silliness we have been hearing about the price of bananas.

Source: Ross Gittens/*The Sydney Morning Herald*, 5 August 2006.

If you think there's something wrong with the way we measure inflation, you're quite right. The Australian Bureau of Statistics is reviewing how our measures of inflation are calculated. Mark Colvin, of ABC radio, discusses the review, in the transcript below. To listen to the full interview, go to http://abc.com.au/pm/archives.html.

CPI under review
PM with Mark Colvin

MARK COLVIN: Australia's core measure of inflation, the Consumer Price Index, is under review. In a series of public hearings around the country the Bureau of Statistics is investigating what the community thinks of the CPI and whether it should be changed. At issue: should price rises be measured monthly, rather than quarterly? And should the bureau change it to reflect the full cost of living better? Economics correspondent Stephen Long has this report.

STEPHEN LONG: It's big news.
FEMALE NEWS READER 1: A hike in the cost of living puts more pressure on...
MALE NEWS READER: The CPI number yesterday, the bond market, how did they read it?
FEMALE NEWS READER 2: The latest CPI, the Consumer Price Index figure is out.
STEPHEN LONG: The CPI is a key set of numbers for politicians, bankers, investors and consumers. It's even the stuff of satire.
JOHN CLARKE: What I'm describing Brian is that prices are trending northward going forward.

BRIAN DAWE: What does trending northward going forward mean exactly?

JOHN CLARKE: It means that prices are going up and they're likely to bloody well keep going up.

STEPHEN LONG: But some of the facts about the consumer price index might surprise you. For a start, it's not meant to measure the cost of living.

Jason Russo from the Australian Bureau of Statistics:

JASON RUSSO: No, it's not designed to be a measure of the cost of living.

STEPHEN LONG: So it doesn't include interest payments on mortgages, other loans, or credit cards. Nor does it include the price of established houses. And aside from New Zealand, Australia is the only country in the developed world that doesn't measure changes in consumer prices each month, only every quarter. But all that's up for grabs. Because the make-up of the CPI, the core measure of inflation, is under review.

JASON RUSSO: This is a major review. It's comprehensive so we look across the whole of the CPI, the concepts and the way we construct the statistics.

STEPHEN LONG: The last time a root and branch review took place 12 years ago, the whole nature of the Consumer Price Index changed. Before 1997, it was designed to measure the cost of living, and it took account broad household outlays, including interest payments. That was seen as the best approach for an era when wage rates for most workers were set by arbitration, taking into account the cost of living. Since then it's been designed as an inflation gauge to guide monetary policy. But critics say on that score, the CPI isn't adequate.

IAN MCAULEY: It's not a measure of inflation.

STEPHEN LONG: Ian Mcauley from the University of Canberra.

IAN MCAULEY: It's a measure of changes in consumer prices in the average household. We can have very big asset price inflation as we did say leading up to the global financial crisis, where prices of stocks and of housing rose and that wasn't picked up. What was happening was there was inflation in the economy, but it certainly wasn't showing up in household cost of living. The CPI has been kept low in Australia because of the huge influence of much cheaper consumer, what some would call, luxury goods, flat-screen television, new motor cars –

STEPHEN LONG: Computer equipment and the like?

IAN MCAULEY: Yeah, all of those things. And of course, without being too judgemental, I think you could say that these are not perhaps the necessity of life, say that fresh food, fresh vegetables, rent, which certainly is a strong component of the expenditure of low-income people. These are the things which have been rising steeply and although they're picked up in the CPI they are offset by what you might call luxury items.

STEPHEN LONG: But if you haven't got a lot of disposable income, you might be scratching your head and saying well how can the CPI be 2 per cent, or 2.5 per cent?

IAN MCAULEY: And people are indeed scratching their head. I mean the typical response is, the CPI may have gone up by 2 per cent but that's not my CPI.

STEPHEN LONG: That's a problem if the CPI is used to set wages for the lower paid, as the Howard government's Fairpay Commission appeared to do, or to set benefits. The ABS has created some alternative measures to gauge the cost of living for pensioners and low-income groups. And it's thinking of changing the way it collects data.

JASON RUSSO: We have trained field officers that go out and actually collect the prices first hand. I understand that we collect something like 100 000 prices per quarter.

STEPHEN LONG: Wouldn't it be a lot simpler just to commandeer the scanner data from the retailers?

JASON RUSSO: I guess in the longer term this is one of the issues we have to look at. Are there new ways to capture price data to build a better CPI?

Let's consider a simple example. Imagine that, in the base year, bananas are much cheaper than apples and so consumers buy more bananas than apples. When the ABS constructs the basket of goods, it will include more bananas than apples. But think about what happens when the price of bananas rises dramatically due to storms, like they did in 2007 and 2010. Consumers will naturally respond to the price changes by buying more apples and fewer bananas. Yet, when calculating the consumer price index, the ABS uses a fixed basket, which in essence assumes that consumers continue buying the now-expensive bananas in the same quantities as before. For this reason, the index will measure a much larger increase in the cost of living than consumers actually perceive.

The second problem with the consumer price index is the *introduction of new goods*. When a new good is introduced, consumers have more variety from which to choose. Greater variety, in turn, makes each dollar more valuable, so consumers need fewer dollars to maintain any given standard of living. Yet because the consumer price index is based on a fixed basket of goods, it does not reflect this change in the purchasing power of the dollar.

Again, let's consider an example. When smartphones like the Blackberry and iPhone were introduced, consumers could access the Internet and their email from their phones no matter where they were. This new good increased consumers' wellbeing by expanding their consumption choices. A perfect cost-of-living index would reflect this change as a decrease in the cost of living. The consumer price index, however, did not decrease in response to the introduction of smartphones. The ABS has revised the basket of goods to include such devices and subsequently the index reflected changes in smartphone prices and in the price of mobile Internet and phone connection services. But the reduction in the cost of living associated with the initial introduction of the smartphone never showed up in the index.

The third problem with the consumer price index is *unmeasured quality change*. If the quality of a good deteriorates from one year to the next, the value of a dollar falls, even if the price of the good stays the same. (A dollar buys a good of lower quality.) Similarly, if the quality rises from one year to the next, the value of a dollar rises. The ABS does its best to account for quality change. When the quality of a good in the basket changes – for example, when a car model has more horsepower or gets better petrol consumption per kilometre from one year to the next – the ABS adjusts the price of the good to account for the quality change. It is, in essence, trying to calculate the price of a basket of goods of constant quality. Nonetheless, changes in quality remain a problem, because quality is so hard to measure.

There is still much debate among economists about how severe these measurement problems are and what should be done about them. The issue is important because many government programs use the consumer price index to adjust for changes in the overall level of prices. Some economists have suggested modifying these programs to correct for the measurement problems. For example, most studies conclude that the consumer price index overstates inflation by 0.5 to 2.0 percentage points per year. In response to these findings, the federal government could change benefits programs so that benefits increased every year by the measured inflation rate minus one percentage point. Such a change would provide a crude way of offsetting the measurement problems and, at the same time, reduce benefits outlays significantly.

The GDP deflator versus the consumer price index

In the preceding chapter, we saw another measure of the overall level of prices in the economy — the GDP deflator. The GDP deflator is the ratio of nominal GDP to real GDP. Because nominal GDP is current output valued at current prices and real GDP is current output valued at base-year prices, the GDP deflator reflects the current level of prices relative to the level of prices in the base year.

Economists and policymakers monitor both the GDP deflator and the consumer price index to gauge how quickly prices are rising. Usually, these two statistics tell a similar story. Yet there are two important differences that can cause them to diverge.

The first difference is that the GDP deflator reflects the prices of all goods and services *produced domestically*, whereas the consumer price index reflects the prices of all goods and services *bought by consumers*. For example, suppose that the price of a ship produced by Australian shipbuilders and sold to the Navy rises. Even though the ship is part of GDP, it is not part of the basket of goods and services bought by a typical consumer. Thus, the price increase shows up in the GDP deflator but not in the consumer price index.

As another example, suppose that Subaru raises the price of its cars. Because Subarus are made in Japan, the car is not part of Australian GDP. But some Australian consumers do buy Subarus and so the car is part of the typical consumer's basket of goods. Hence, a price increase in an imported consumption good, such as a Subaru, shows up in the consumer price index but not in the GDP deflator.

This first difference between the consumer price index and the GDP deflator is particularly important if a country imports a significant proportion of its oil. As a result, oil and oil products such as petrol and heating oil are a much larger share of consumer spending than they are of GDP. When the price of oil rises, the consumer price index rises by much more than does the GDP deflator. This is more significant in some countries than others. Australia is a net exporter of oil products, so a change in the price of oil is reflected both in the GDP deflator *and* the consumer price index.

The second and more subtle difference between the GDP deflator and the consumer price index concerns how various prices are weighted to yield a single number for the overall level of prices. The consumer price index compares the price of a *fixed* basket of goods and services with the price of the basket in the base year. The ABS changes the basket of goods once every four or five years. In contrast, the GDP deflator compares the price of *currently produced* goods and services with the price of the same goods and services in the base year. Thus, the group of goods and services used to calculate the GDP deflator changes automatically over time. This difference is not important when all prices are changing proportionately. But if the prices of different goods and services are changing by varying amounts, the way we weight the various prices matters for the overall inflation rate.

Figure 25.2 shows the inflation rate as measured by both the GDP deflator and the consumer price index for each year since 1970. You can see that sometimes the two measures diverge. When they do diverge, it is possible to go behind these numbers and explain the divergence with the two differences we have discussed. The figure shows, however, that divergence between these two measures is the exception rather than the rule. In the mid-1970s, both the GDP deflator and the consumer price index show high rates of inflation. In the mid-1980s and mid-1990s, both measures showed low rates of inflation.

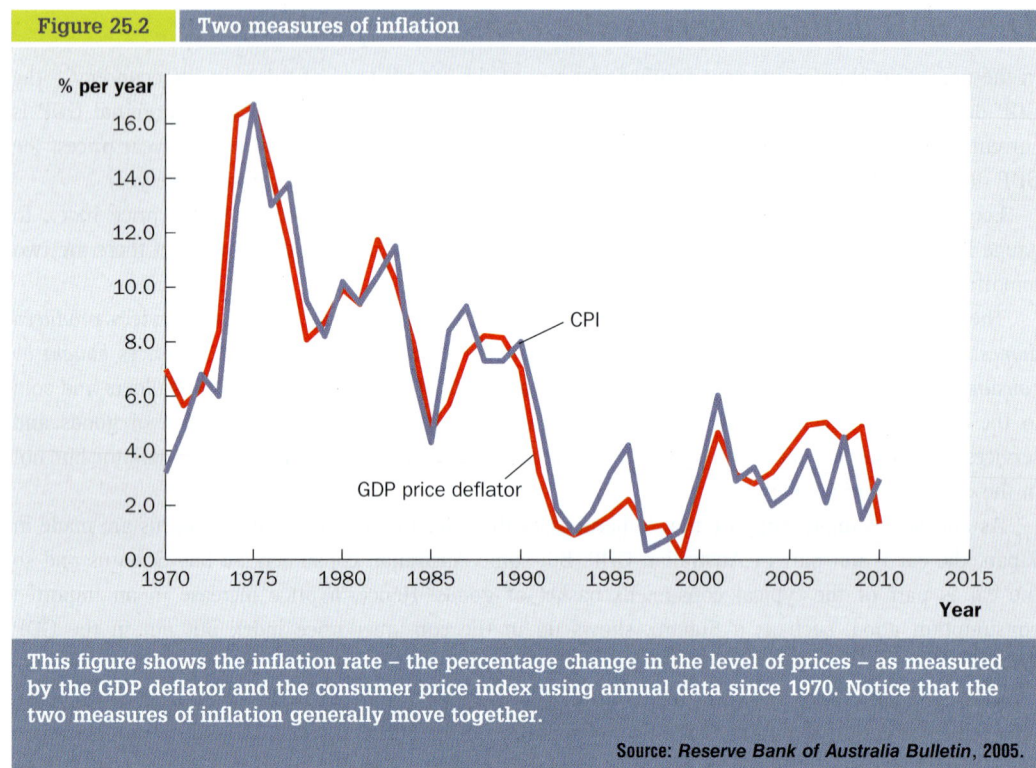

Figure 25.2 Two measures of inflation

This figure shows the inflation rate – the percentage change in the level of prices – as measured by the GDP deflator and the consumer price index using annual data since 1970. Notice that the two measures of inflation generally move together.

Source: *Reserve Bank of Australia Bulletin*, 2005.

Explain briefly what the consumer price index is trying to measure and how it is constructed.

Correcting economic variables for the effects of inflation

The purpose of measuring the overall level of prices in the economy is to permit comparison between dollar figures from different points in time. Now that we know how price indexes are calculated, let's see how we might use such an index to compare a dollar figure from the past with a dollar figure in the present

Dollar figures from different times

We first return to the issue of Phar Lap's winnings. Were his earnings of $19 000 in 1930 high or low compared with the earnings in today's race?

To answer this question, we need to know the level of prices in 1930 and the level of prices today. Part of the increase in prize money just compensates the owners of racehorses for the higher level of prices today. To compare Phar Lap's winnings with those of today's horses, we need to inflate Phar Lap's winnings to turn 1930 dollars into today's dollars. A price index determines the size of this inflation correction. (Remember that Phar Lap's earnings were in pounds, but we are using the equivalent dollar amounts.)

Government statistics give a price index of 4.7 for 1930 and 172.1 for 2010. (The base year is 1989–90.) Thus, the overall level of prices has risen by a factor of 36.6 (which equals 172.1/4.7). We can use these numbers to measure Phar Lap's winnings in 2010 dollars. The calculation is:

$$\text{Winnings in 2010} = \frac{\text{Winnings in 1930} \times \text{Price level in 2010}}{\text{Price level in 1930}}$$
$$= \frac{19\,000 \times 172.1}{4.7}$$
$$= 695\,723$$

We find that Phar Lap's 1930 winnings are equivalent to winnings today of about $695 723. That is a lot of money for a horse, but nothing like the Melbourne Cup winner's earnings today. It is not even as much as what the second-placed horse receives. The example does show that it is important to make these comparisons using the same dollars. Nearly 700 000 dollars looks much better than $19 000.

Let's also examine Prime Minister Scullin's 1930 salary of £1000, or roughly $2000. To translate that figure into 2010 dollars, we again multiply the ratio of the price levels in the two years. We find that Scullin's salary is equivalent to $2000 × (172.1/4.7), or $73 234 in 2010 dollars. This is well below Julia Gilliard's salary of $354 671. It seems that Prime Minister Scullin did not earn very much compared with the famous racehorse or today's prime minister.

Indexation

As we have just seen, price indexes are used to correct for the effects of inflation when comparing dollar figures from different times. This type of correction shows up in many places in the economy. When some dollar amount is automatically corrected for inflation by law or contract, the amount is said to be indexed for inflation.

For example, for many years, the basic wage in Australia was indexed to the consumer price index. Such a provision automatically raises the wage whenever the consumer price index rises.

Indexation is also a feature of many laws. Pension benefits, for example, are frequently adjusted to compensate the elderly for increases in prices. There are, however, many ways in which the tax system is not indexed for inflation, even when perhaps it should be. For example, the brackets of income tax – the income levels at which the tax rates change – are not indexed for inflation. We discuss these issues more fully when we discuss the costs of inflation later in this book.

indexation
the automatic correction of a dollar amount for the effects of inflation by law or contract

Real and nominal interest rates

Correcting economic variables for the effects of inflation is particularly important, and somewhat tricky, when we look at data on interest rates. When you deposit your savings in a bank account, you will earn interest on your deposit. Conversely, when you borrow from a bank to pay for a car, you will pay interest on your loan. Interest represents a payment in the future for a transfer of money in the past. As a result, interest rates always involve comparing amounts of money at different points in time. To fully understand interest rates, we need to know how to correct for the effects of inflation.

Let's consider an example. Suppose that Sally Saver deposits $1000 in a bank account that pays an annual interest rate of 10 per cent. After a year passes, Sally has accumulated $100 in interest. Sally then withdraws her $1100. Is Sally $100 richer than she was when she made the deposit a year earlier?

The answer depends on what we mean by the word 'richer'. Sally does have $100 more than she had before. In other words, the number of dollars has risen by 10 per cent. But if prices have risen at the same time, each dollar now buys less than it did a year ago. Thus, her purchasing power has not risen by 10 per cent. If the inflation rate was 4 per cent, then the amount of goods she can buy has increased by only 6 per cent. And if the inflation rate was 15 per cent, then the price of goods has increased proportionately more than the number of dollars in her account. In that case, Sally's purchasing power has actually fallen by 5 per cent.

IN THE NEWS . . .

MR INDEX GOES TO HOLLYWOOD

What was the most popular film of all time? As the following article notes, answering this question requires an understanding of price indexes.

Winner and still champ

Rumour has it that when the storyline for the film *Titanic* was suggested, the pitch went something like this. 'I've got this great idea for a movie. Romeo and Juliet on a boat. Oh, and the boat sinks.' The film not only took out seven Academy Awards, it also topped the box office, earning $600 million the year it was released.

But those records are for dollars not adjusted for inflation. The Box Office Mojo website lists the top grossing films of all time using today's dollars. Its list indicates that *Titanic*, even with a take of over US$1 billion, will still fall far short of what Scarlett and Rhett accomplished more than half a century ago.

'Frankly, my dear, I don't give a damn about the effects of inflation.'

Source: Corbis Australia.

Top 20 films, adjusted for inflation

Title	Adjusted gross in 2010 dollars	Year
Gone with the Wind	$1 606 254 800	1939
Star Wars	$1 416 050 800	1977
The Sound of Music	$1 132 202 200	1965
E.T.: The Extra-Terrestrial	$1 127 742 000	1982
The Ten Commandments	$1 041 450 000	1956
Titanic	$1 020 349 800	1997
Jaws	$1 018 226 600	1975
Doctor Zhivago	$986 876 900	1965
The Exorcist	$879 020 900	1973
Snow White and the Seven Dwarfs	$866 550 000	1937
101 Dalmatians	$794 342 100	1961
The Empire Strikes Back	$780 536 100	1980
Ben-Hur	$779 100 000	1959
Avatar	$772 516 600	2009
Return of the Jedi	$747 772 300	1983
The Sting	$708 685 700	1973
Raiders of the Lost Ark	$700 727 700	1981
Jurassic Park	$685 336 400	1993
The Graduate	$680 292 600	1967
Star Wars: Phantom Menace	$674 365 200	1999

Source: Box Office Mojo (www.boxofficemojo.com).

The interest rate that the bank pays is called the **nominal interest rate**, and the interest rate corrected for inflation is called the **real interest rate**. We can write the relationship of the nominal interest rate, the real interest rate and inflation as follows:

$$\text{Real interest rate} = \text{Nominal interest rate} - \text{Inflation rate}$$

nominal interest rate
the interest rate as usually reported without a correction for the effects of inflation

real interest rate
the interest rate corrected for the effects of inflation

The real interest rate is the difference between the nominal interest rate and the rate of inflation. The nominal interest rate tells you how fast the number of dollars in your bank account rises over time. The real interest rate tells you how fast the purchasing power of your bank account rises over time.

Search me!

▸ nominal interest rate
▸ real interest rate

Figure 25.3 shows real and nominal interest rates in Australia since 1970. The nominal interest rate is the interest rate on 90-day bank bills. The real interest rate is calculated by subtracting inflation – the percentage change in the consumer price index – from this nominal interest rate.

You can see that real and nominal interest rates do not always move together. For example, in the mid-1970s, nominal interest rates were high. But since inflation was very high, real interest rates were low. Indeed, in some years, real interest rates were negative, for inflation eroded people's savings more quickly than nominal interest payments increased them. In contrast, in both 1985 and 1990, even though nominal interest rates were high, low inflation meant that real interest rates were relatively high. In the coming chapters, when we study the causes and effects of changes in interest rates, it will be important for us to keep in mind the distinction between real and nominal interest rates.

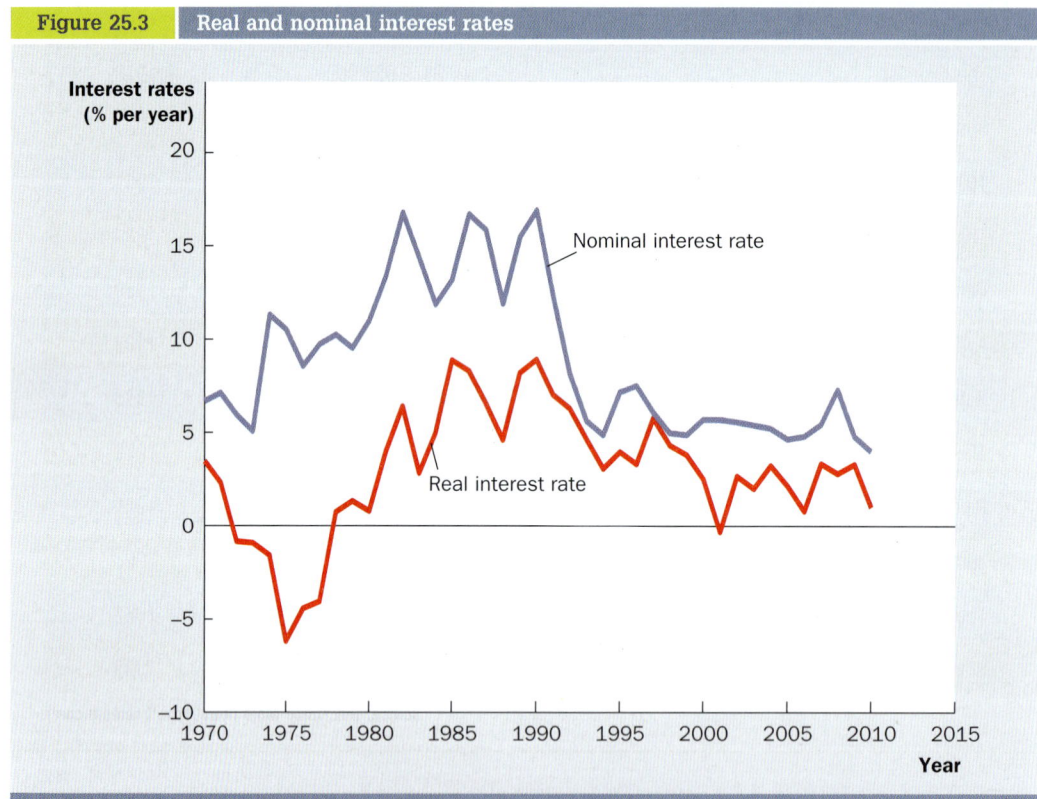

Figure 25.3 **Real and nominal interest rates**

This figure shows nominal and real interest rates using annual data since 1970. The nominal interest rate is the rate on a 90-day bank bill. The real interest rate is the nominal interest rate minus the inflation rate as measured by changes in the consumer price index. Notice the nominal and real interest rates often do not move together.

Source: *Reserve Bank of Australia Bulletin*, 2010.

Henry Ford paid his workers $5 a day in 1914. If a price index was 11 in 1914 and 100 in 2010, how much was the Ford pay cheque worth in 2010 dollars?

Conclusion

When McDonald's was introduced into Australia, a Big Mac, fries and a Coke cost about a dollar. Now the same meal costs $7.75 (if purchased separately). A dollar's not worth what it used to be. Indeed, throughout recent history, the purchasing power of the dollar has not been stable. Persistent increases in the overall level of prices have been the norm. Such inflation reduces the purchasing power of each unit of money over time. When comparing dollar figures from different times, it is important to keep in mind that a dollar today is not the same as a dollar 20 years ago or, most likely, 20 years from now.

This chapter has discussed how economists measure the overall level of prices in the economy and how they use price indexes to correct economic variables for the effects of inflation. This analysis is only a starting point. We have not yet examined the causes and effects of inflation or how inflation interacts with other economic variables. To do that, we need to go beyond issues of measurement. Indeed, that is our next task. Having explained how economists measure macroeconomic quantities and prices in the past chapters, we are now ready to develop the models that explain long-run and short-run movements in these variables.

Summary

- The consumer price index shows the cost of a basket of goods and services relative to the cost of the same basket in the base year. The index is used to measure the overall level of prices in the economy. The percentage change in the consumer price index measures the inflation rate.
- The consumer price index is an imperfect measure of the cost of living for three reasons. First, it does not take into account consumers' ability to substitute goods that become relatively cheaper over time. Second, it does not take into account increases in the purchasing power of the dollar due to the introduction of new goods. Third, it is distorted by unmeasured changes in the quality of goods and services. Because of these measurement problems, the CPI overstates annual inflation by about one percentage point.
- Although the GDP deflator also measures the overall level of prices in the economy, it differs from the consumer price index because it includes goods and services produced rather than goods and services consumed. As a result, imported goods affect the consumer price index but not the GDP deflator. In addition, whereas the consumer price index uses a fixed basket of goods, the GDP deflator automatically changes the group of goods and services over time as the composition of GDP changes.
- Dollar figures from different points in time cannot be used to make valid comparisons of purchasing power. To compare a dollar figure from the past with a dollar figure today, the older figure should be inflated using a price index.
- Various laws and private contracts use price indexes to correct for the effects of inflation. The tax laws, however, are only partially indexed for inflation.
- A correction for inflation is especially important when looking at data on interest rates. The nominal interest rate is the interest rate usually reported; it is the rate at which the number of dollars in a savings account increases over time. In contrast, the real interest rate takes into account changes in the value of the dollar over time. The real interest rate equals the nominal interest rate minus the rate of inflation.

Key concepts

consumer price index (CPI)	inflation rate	producer price index
indexation	nominal interest rate	real interest rate

Questions for review

1 Which do you think has a greater effect on the consumer price index: A 10 per cent increase in the price of an iPod or a 10 per cent increase in the price of petrol? Why?
2 Describe the three problems that make the consumer price index an imperfect measure of the cost of living.
3 If the price of a Royal Australian Air Force fighter jet rises, is the consumer price index or the GDP deflator affected more? Why?
4 If you were a government official deciding on how much to increase the pension, which measure of inflation would you use? If you were a businesswoman trying to decide on a 10-year investment in manufacturing in Australia, would you use the same measure? Why or why not?
5 Explain the meaning of *nominal interest rate* and *real interest rate*. How are they related?

Problems and applications

1 Suppose that people consume only three goods, as shown in this table:

	Tennis balls	Tennis racquets	Gatorade®
2011 price	$9	$125	$3.50
2011 quantity	100	10	200
2012 price	$11	$140	$4
2012 quantity	100	10	200

    a What is the percentage change in the price of each of the three goods? What is the percentage change in the overall price level?

    b Do tennis racquets become more or less expensive relative to Gatorade? Does the wellbeing of some people change relative to the wellbeing of others? Explain.

2 Suppose that the residents of Veggieland spend all of their income on cauliflower, broccoli and carrots. In 2011, they buy 50 heads of cauliflower for $100, 50 bunches of broccoli for $90 and 600 carrots for $75. In 2012 they buy 60 heads of cauliflower for $200, 60 bunches of broccoli for $100 and 600 carrots for $150. If the base year is 2011, what is the CPI in both years? What is the inflation rate in 2012?

3 From 1950 to 2010 the consumer price index in Australia rose around 2310 per cent. Use this fact to adjust each of the following 1950 prices for the effects of inflation. Which items cost less in 2010 than in 1950 after adjusting for inflation? Which items cost more?

Item	1950 price	2010 price
A day at the cricket	$0.25	$36
Woman's Day magazine	$0.05	$4.00
Orange marmalade	$0.12	$4.95
A Holden sedan	$700	$36 000
Sending a package by air from Sydney to the UK	$1.28	$7.20

4 In late 2003, the federal government approved the use of ethanol in petrol (up to 10 per cent). The argument made was that the use of ethanol reduces the amount of greenhouse gases produced by cars, which is good for the environment. Some people argued that it would also be cheaper, because it can be produced from sugar cane, which Australia has in abundance. However, petrol with ethanol is less efficient, so drivers might find their fuel costs *increasing* instead of decreasing. If you were the chief statistician for the ABS, how would you change the CPI to reflect the increased use of ethanol in petrol?

5 Which of the problems in the construction of the CPI might be illustrated by each of the following situations? Explain.

   a The invention of the iPad

   b The introduction of hybrid cars

   c Decreased banana purchases in response to an increase in their price

   d More scoops of sultanas in each package of Sultana Bran®

   e Increased purchases of the Smart Car.

6 The *Sydney Morning Herald* cost $0.05 in 1970 and $1.50 in 2010. The average wage in manufacturing was $3.35 per hour in 1970 and $33.55 in 2010.

   a By what percentage did the price of a newspaper rise?

   b By what percentage did the wage rise?

   c In each year, how many minutes does a worker have to work to earn enough to buy a newspaper?

   d Did workers' purchasing power in terms of newspapers rise or fall?

7 For years, British citizens who are resident in Australia have tried to convince the UK government to index the pensions they receive, just as they would be if they were in the UK. But the UK government has steadfastly refused to index the pensions of British who have settled in Australia for their retirement.

   a If you were a British citizen contemplating retirement in the Aussie sunshine, how would the lack of indexing affect your decisions? What could you do to overcome the disadvantage of having a pension that wasn't indexed?

   b Suppose Australia's inflation rate is 2 per cent per year and the UK's inflation rate is 4 per cent per year. If the UK government indexed all pensions, would British who had migrated to Australia be better or worse off than if they'd stayed in the UK (ignoring the impact of nicer weather in Australia.)

   c Now suppose that inflation and indexing are as suggested in part (b), but Australia has a much higher rate of increase in the price of health care. How does that change your answer to part (b)?

8 Suppose that a borrower and a lender agree on the nominal interest rate to be paid on a loan. Then inflation turns out to be lower than they both expected.

   a Is the real interest rate on this loan higher or lower than expected?

   b Does the lender gain or lose from this unexpectedly high inflation? Does the borrower gain or lose?

   c Inflation since the Global Financial Crisis was much lower than people expected it to be. How would this affect homeowners who obtained fixed-rate mortgages in the mid 2000s? How did it affect the banks that lent them the money?

   d If you were taking out a mortgage today, how would your expectations about inflation in the next 10 years affect your decision about whether to fix your mortgage rate or let it vary?

9 The chapter defines the real interest rate as the nominal interest rate less inflation. Because, under Australian tax laws, nominal interest income is taxed, we can define the after-tax real interest rate as the nominal interest rate after taxes, less inflation.

   a Suppose that the inflation rate is 0 per cent, the nominal interest rate is 6 per cent, and the tax rate is 33 per cent. What is the real interest rate? What is the after-tax real interest rate? What is the effective tax rate on real interest income (the percentage reduction in real interest income due to taxes)?

   b Now suppose that the inflation rate rises to 3 per cent, and the nominal interest rate rises to 9 per cent. What is the real interest rate now? What is the after-tax real interest rate? What is the effective tax rate on real interest income?

c   Some economists argue that because of our tax system, inflation discourages saving. Use your answers to parts (a) and (b) to explain this view.

10   In Australia, income tax brackets are not indexed. When inflation pushed up nominal incomes, what do you think happened to real tax revenue? (*Hint:* This phenomenon is known as 'bracket creep'.)

Search me!

When accessing information about economics use the following keywords in any combinations you require:

- consumer price index
- nominal interest rate
- real interest rate

CourseMate

For more multimedia resources and activities on economics, visit the Economics CourseMate website.

PART NINE
The real economy in the long run

26

Production and growth

Learning objectives

In this chapter you will:

- see how much economic growth differs around the world
- consider why productivity is the key determinant of a country's standard of living
- analyse the factors that determine a country's productivity
- examine how a country's policies influence its productivity growth.

When you travel around the world, you see tremendous variation in the standard of living. The average person in a rich country, such as Australia, the United States or Japan, has an income more than 10 times as high as the average person in a poor country, such as India, Indonesia or Nigeria These large differences in income are reflected in large differences in the quality of life. Richer countries have more cars, more telephones, more televisions, better nutrition, safer housing, better health care and longer life expectancy.

Even within a country, there are large changes in the standard of living over time. In Australia over the past 100 years, average income as measured by real GDP per person has grown by just over 1 per cent per year. Although 1 per cent might seem small, this rate of growth implies that average income doubles about every 70 years. Because of this growth, average income today is nearly five times as high as average income at the beginning of the 1900s. As a result, the typical Australian today enjoys much greater economic prosperity than did an Australian in 1900.

Growth rates vary substantially from country to country. In some East Asian countries, such as Hong Kong, Singapore, South Korea and Taiwan, average income has risen about 7 per cent per year in recent decades. At this rate, average income doubles every 10 years. These countries have, in the length of one generation, gone from being among the poorest countries in the world to being among the richest. In contrast, in some African countries, such as Chad, Ethiopia and Nigeria, average income has been stagnant for many years.

The effects of these differences in growth rates can be seen in Australia. Even though the typical Australian enjoys a greater level of economic prosperity now relative to his or her ancestors in Australia, the Australian standard of living has not increased as rapidly as it has in some other countries. For example, in 1870, GDP per capita in Australia was 1.4 times GDP per capita in the United States. In 2009, Australian GDP per capita was just over three-quarters of US GDP per capita. The fact that Australia has slipped in the rankings of GDP per capita is not necessarily cause for concern, but it does indicate that we are not growing as rapidly as we perhaps could.

What explains these diverse experiences? How can the rich countries be sure to maintain their high standard of living? What policies should the poor countries pursue to promote more rapid growth in order to join the developed world? These are among the most important questions in macroeconomics. As economist Robert Lucas put it: 'The consequences for human welfare in questions like these are simply staggering: Once one starts to think about them, it is hard to think about anything else'.

In the previous two chapters we discussed how economists measure macroeconomic quantities and prices. In this chapter we start studying the forces that determine these variables. As we have seen, an economy's gross domestic product (GDP) measures both the total income earned in the economy and the total expenditure on the economy's output of goods and services. The level of real GDP is a good gauge of economic prosperity and the growth of real GDP is a good gauge of economic progress. Here we focus on the long-run determinants of the level and growth of real GDP. Later in this book we will study the short-run fluctuations of real GDP around its long-run trend.

We proceed here in three steps. First, we examine international data on real GDP per person. These data will give you some sense of how much the level and growth of living standards vary around the world. Second, we examine the role of *productivity* – the amount of goods and services produced for each hour of a worker's time. In particular, we see that a nation's standard of living is determined by the productivity of its workers and we consider the factors that determine a nation's productivity. Third, we consider the link between productivity and the economic policies that a nation pursues.

Economic growth around the world

As a starting point for our study of long-run growth, let's look at the experiences of some of the world's economies. Table 26.1 shows data on real GDP per person for 18 countries. For each country, the data cover nearly 60 years of history. The first and second columns of the table present the countries and time periods. (The time periods differ somewhat from country to country because of differences in data availability.) The third and fourth columns show real GDP per person almost 60 years ago and for a recent year.

Table 26.1	The variety of growth experiences			
Country	Period	Real GDP per capita beginning of period*	Real GDP per capita at end of period	Average growth rate (%)
China	1952–2007	376	8 511	5.73
Japan	1950–2007	2 188	24 661	4.50
Singapore	1960–2007	4 219	29 404	3.59
Thailand	1950–2007	1 109	7 274	3.54
Nigeria	1950–2007	726	1 210	3.15
Indonesia	1960–2007	1 036	5 186	3.01
India	1950–2007	790	3 825	2.76
Brazil	1950–2007	2 108	9 644	2.66
United Kingdom	1950–2007	8 082	26 762	2.20
Australia	1950–2007	10 315	36 303	2.19
Canada	1950–2007	10 410	36 166	2.17
United States	1950–2007	11 233	36 098	2.15
Pakistan	1950–2007	840	2 685	2.14
Mexico	1950–2007	2 699	8 168	2.03
Germany	1970–2007	15 491	31 303	1.87
New Zealand	1950–2007	10 099	22 792	1.49
Argentina	1950–2007	7 814	15 273	1.16
Afghanistan	1970–2007	863	753	0.36

* Real GDP is measured in 2005 dollars.

Source: Alan Heston. *The Penn World Table*. Reproduced with permission.

The data on real GDP per person show that living standards vary widely from country to country. Income per person in Australia, for instance, is about five times that in China and nine times that in India. The poorest countries have average levels of income that have not been seen in Australia for many decades. The typical Argentinian in 2007 had about as much real income as the typical German in 1950. The typical person in India in 2007 had about one-third the real income of a typical Australian 60 years ago.

The last column of the table shows each country's growth rate. The growth rate measures how rapidly real GDP per person grew in the typical year. In Australia, for example, real GDP per person was $10 315 in 1950 and $36 303 in 2007. The growth rate was 2.19 per cent per year. This means that if real GDP per person, beginning at $10 315, were to increase by 2.19 per cent for each of 58 years, it would end up at $36 303. Of course, real GDP per person did not actually rise exactly 2.19 per cent every year – there are short-run fluctuations around the long-run trend. The growth rate of 2.19 per cent represents an average rate of growth for real GDP per person over many years.

The countries in Table 26.1 are ordered by their growth rate from the most to the least rapid. China tops the list with a growth rate of 5.73 per cent per year. China is growing rapidly, but still has a relatively low per capita GDP. Even at its current growth rates, it will still take some time before China's average income is in the top 10.

Fifty-eight years ago, Japan was not a rich country. Japan's average income was higher than Pakistan's and Thailand's average incomes, but it was lower than Mexico's. To put the issue another way, Japan's 1950 income was close to Pakistan's 2007 income. But because of its spectacular growth, Japan is today an economic superpower, with average income about the same as the UK's. Near the bottom of the list of countries is Afghanistan, which has experienced hardly any growth at all over the past century. The typical resident of Afghanistan lives in abject poverty similar to that experienced by his or her great-grandparents.

fyi

The magic of compounding and the rule of 70

It may be tempting to dismiss differences in growth rates as insignificant. If one country grows at 1 per cent while another grows at 3 per cent, so what? What difference can 2 per cent make?

The answer is a big difference. Even growth rates that seem small when written in percentage terms seem large after they are compounded for many years. Compounding refers to the accumulation of a growth rate over a period of time.

Consider an example. Suppose that two university graduates – Delta and Bec – both take their first jobs at the age of 22 earning $30 000 a year. Delta lives in an economy where all incomes grow at 1 per cent per year, whereas Bec lives in one where incomes grow at 3 per cent per year. Straightforward calculations show what happens. Forty years later, when both are 62 years old, Delta earns $45 000 a year, and Bec earns $98 000. Because of that difference of two percentage points in the growth rate, Bec's salary in old age is more than twice Delta's.

An old rule of thumb, called the rule of 70, is helpful in understanding growth rates and the effects of compounding. According to the rule of 70, if some variable grows at a rate of x per cent per year, then that variable doubles in approximately $70/x$ years. In Delta's economy, incomes grow at 1 per cent per year, so it takes about 70 years for incomes to double. In Bec's economy, incomes grow at 3 per cent per year, so it takes about 70/3, or 23, years for incomes to double.

The rule of 70 applies not only to a growing economy but also to a growing savings account. Here is an example. Suppose that when Governor Phillip left office in 1792, he gave $5000 to be invested for a period of 200 years to benefit scientific research into early Australian history. If this money had earned 7 per cent per year (which would, in fact, have been very possible to do), the investment would have doubled in value every 10 years. Over 200 years, it would have doubled 20 times. At the end of 200 years of compounding, the investment would have been worth $2^{20} \times$ $5000, which is about $5 billion.

As these examples show, growth rates compounded over many years can lead to some spectacular results. That is probably why Albert Einstein once called compounding 'the greatest mathematical discovery of all time'.

Because of differences in growth rates, the ranking of countries by income changes substantially over time. As we have seen, Japan is a country that has risen relative to others. Two countries that have fallen behind are New Zealand and Argentina. In 1950, New Zealand was one of the richest countries in the world, with average income nearly as high as the United States and well above the United Kingdom. Today, average income in New Zealand is well below average income in the US and the UK. In 1950, Argentina had almost four times the income of its South American neighbour, Brazil. Today, Argentina's average income is only 1.5 times its neighbour, Brazil. Australia's story is somewhere in between these two. In 1900, Australia had the highest per capita income in the world, but by 1970 it had fallen to around seventh in the rankings. By 1991, Australia was no longer in the top 10 and had fallen behind most western European countries in relative terms. Australia's relatively strong economic growth during a period when other countries have been in recession has seen Australia's ranking rise, to about number 12.

These data show that the world's richest countries have no guarantee that they will stay the richest and that the world's poorest countries are not doomed forever to remain in poverty. But what explains these changes over time? Why do some countries zoom ahead while others lag behind? These are precisely the questions that we take up next.

> **Q** What is the approximate growth rate of real GDP per person in Australia? Name a country that has had faster growth and a country that has had slower growth.

Productivity: Its role and determinants

Explaining the large variation in living standards around the world is, in one sense, very easy. As we will see, the explanation can be summarised in a single word – *productivity*. But, in another sense, the international variation is deeply puzzling. To explain why incomes are so much higher in some countries than in others, we must look at the many factors that determine a nation's productivity.

Why productivity is so important

Let's begin our study of productivity and economic growth by developing a simple model based loosely on Daniel Defoe's famous novel, *Robinson Crusoe*. Robinson Crusoe, as you may recall, is a sailor stranded on a desert island. Because Crusoe lives alone, he catches his own fish, grows his own vegetables and makes his own clothes. We can think of Crusoe's activities – his production and consumption of fish, vegetables and clothing – as being a simple economy. By examining Crusoe's economy, we can learn some lessons that also apply to more complex and realistic economies.

What determines Crusoe's standard of living? The answer is obvious. If Crusoe is good at catching fish, growing vegetables and making clothes, he lives well. If he is bad at doing these things, he lives poorly. Because Crusoe gets to consume only what he produces, his living standard is tied to his productive ability.

productivity
the amount of goods and services produced from each hour of a worker's time

The term **productivity** refers to the quantity of goods and services that a worker can produce for each hour of work. In the case of Crusoe's economy, it is easy to see that productivity is the key determinant of living standards and that growth in productivity is the key determinant of growth in living standards. The more fish Crusoe can catch per hour, the more he eats at dinner. If Crusoe finds a better place to catch fish, his productivity rises. This increase in productivity makes Crusoe better off – he could eat the extra fish, or he could spend less time fishing and devote more time to making other goods he enjoys.

The key role of productivity in determining living standards is as true for nations as it is for stranded sailors. Recall that an economy's gross domestic product (GDP) measures two things at once – the total income earned by everyone in the economy and the total expenditure on the economy's output of goods and services. The reason GDP can measure these two things simultaneously is that, for the economy as a whole, they must be equal. Put simply, an economy's income is the economy's output.

Like Crusoe, a nation can enjoy a high standard of living only if it can produce a large quantity of goods and services. Australians live better than Nigerians because Australian workers are more productive than Nigerian workers. The Japanese have enjoyed more rapid growth in living standards than Argentinians because Japanese workers have experienced more rapidly growing productivity. Indeed, one of the *Ten Lessons from Economics* in chapter 1 is that a country's standard of living depends on its ability to produce goods and services.

Hence, to understand the large differences in living standards we observe across countries or over time, we must focus on the production of goods and services. But seeing the link between living standards and productivity is only the first step. It leads naturally to the next question: Why are some economies so much better at producing goods and services than others?

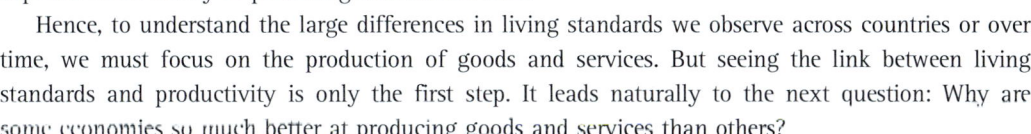

How productivity is determined

Although productivity is uniquely important in determining Robinson Crusoe's standard of living, many factors determine Crusoe's productivity. Crusoe will be better at catching fish, for instance, if he has more fishing rods, if he has been trained in the best fishing techniques, if his island has a plentiful fish supply, and if he has figured out the best places on his island to fish. Each of these determinants of Crusoe's productivity – which we can call *physical capital, human capital, natural resources* and *technological knowledge* – has a counterpart in more complex and realistic economies. Let's consider each of these factors in turn.

Physical capital

Workers are more productive if they have tools with which to work. The stock of equipment and structures that are used to produce goods and services is called **physical capital**, or just *capital*. For example, when woodworkers make furniture, they use saws, lathes and drill presses. More tools allow work to be done more quickly and more accurately. That is, a worker with only basic hand tools can make less furniture each week than a worker with sophisticated and specialised woodworking equipment.

physical capital
the stock of equipment and structures that are used to produce goods and services

As you may recall from chapter 2, the inputs used to produce goods and services – labour, capital and so on – are called the *factors of production*. An important feature of capital is that it is a *produced* factor of production. That is, capital is an input into the production process that in the past was an output from the production process. The woodworker uses a lathe to make the leg of a table. Earlier, the lathe itself was the output of a firm that manufactures lathes. The lathe manufacturer in turn used other equipment to make its product. Thus, capital is a factor of production used to produce all kinds of goods and services, including more capital.

Human capital

A second determinant of productivity is human capital. **Human capital** is the economist's term for the knowledge and skills that workers acquire through education, training and experience. Human capital includes the skills accumulated in early childhood programs, primary school, secondary school, university and on-the-job training for adults in the labour force.

human capital
the knowledge and skills that workers acquire through education, training and experience

Although education, training and experience are less tangible than lathes, bulldozers and buildings, human capital is like physical capital in many ways. Like physical capital, human capital raises a nation's ability to produce goods and services. Also like physical capital, human capital is a produced factor of production. Producing human capital requires inputs in the form of teachers, libraries and student time. Indeed, students can be viewed as 'workers' who have the important job of producing the human capital that will be used in future production.

Natural resources

natural resources
the inputs into the production of goods and services that are provided by nature, such as land, rivers and mineral deposits

A third determinant of productivity is natural resources. **Natural resources** are inputs into production that are provided by nature, such as land, rivers and mineral deposits. Natural resources take two forms – renewable and non-renewable. A forest is an example of a renewable resource. When one tree is cut down, a seedling can be planted in its place to be harvested in the future. Oil is an example of a non-renewable resource. Because oil is produced by nature over many thousands of years, there is only a limited supply. Once the supply of oil is depleted, it is impossible to create more.

Differences in natural resources are responsible for some of the differences in standards of living around the world. The historical success of Australia was driven in part by the large supply of land well suited to agriculture. Today, some countries in the Middle East, such as Kuwait and Saudi Arabia, are rich because they are on top of some of the largest pools of oil in the world.

Although natural resources can be important, they are not necessary for an economy to be highly productive in producing goods and services. Japan, for instance, is one of the richest countries in the world, despite having few natural resources. International trade makes Japan's success possible. Japan imports many of the natural resources it needs, such as oil, and exports its manufactured goods to economies rich in natural resources.

CASESTUDY

Are natural resources a limit to growth?

The world's population is far larger today than it was a century ago and many people are enjoying a much higher standard of living. A perennial debate concerns whether this growth in population and living standards can continue in the future.

Many commentators have argued that natural resources provide a limit to how much the world's economies can grow. At first, this argument might seem hard to ignore. If the world has only a fixed supply of non-renewable natural resources, how can population, production and living standards continue to grow over time? Eventually, won't supplies of oil and minerals start to run out? When these shortages start to occur, won't they stop economic growth and, perhaps, even force living standards to fall?

Despite the apparent appeal of such arguments, most economists are less concerned about such limits to growth than one might guess. They argue that technological progress often yields ways to avoid these limits. If we compare the economy today with the economy of the past, we see various ways in which the use of natural resources has improved.

What happens when these wells run dry?

Source: iStockphoto/Allen Tobey.

Modern cars, particularly hybrids, require fewer litres per kilometre. New houses have better insulation and require less energy to heat and cool them. Recycling allows some non-renewable resources to be reused. The development of alternative fuels, such as ethanol instead of petrol, allows us to substitute renewable for non-renewable resources.

Fifty years ago, some conservationists were concerned about the excessive use of tin and copper.

At the time, these were crucial commodities – tin was used to make many food containers, and copper was used to make telephone wire. Some people advocated mandatory recycling and rationing of tin and copper so that supplies would be available for future generations. Today, however, plastic has replaced tin as a material for making many food containers, and phone calls often travel over fibre-optic cables, which are made from sand. Technological progress has made once-crucial natural resources less necessary.

But are all these efforts enough to permit continued economic growth? One way to answer this question is to look at the prices of natural resources. In a market economy, scarcity is reflected in market prices. If the world were running out of natural resources, then the prices of those resources would be rising over time. But, in fact, the opposite

is more nearly true. The prices of most natural resources (adjusted for overall inflation) are stable or falling. It appears that our ability to conserve these resources is growing more rapidly than their supplies are dwindling. Market prices for most resources give no reason to believe that natural resources are a limit to economic growth. Even the recent large increases in the price of oil may not reflect limits to future economic growth. We saw a significant increase in the demand for oil and the addition of a 'fear premium' to oil prices in the early days of the conflict in Iraq. Recently, oil prices have dropped back. We are driving more fuel-efficient cars and becoming more conscious of our energy consumption. Should the price of oil rise significantly again, this will be a powerful signal from the market that we should look at alternative sources of energy.

Technological knowledge

A fourth determinant of productivity is **technological knowledge** – the understanding of the best ways to produce goods and services. A hundred years ago, most Australians worked on farms, because farm technology required a high input of labour in order to feed the entire population. Today, thanks to advances in the technology of farming, a small fraction of the population can produce enough food to feed the entire country. This technological change made labour available to produce other goods and services.

Technological knowledge takes many forms. Some technology is common knowledge – after it becomes used by one person, everyone becomes aware of it. For example, once Henry Ford successfully introduced production in assembly lines, other car-makers quickly followed suit. Other technology is proprietary – it is known only by the company that discovers it. Only the Coca-Cola Company, for instance, knows the secret recipe for making its famous soft drink. Still other technology is proprietary for a short time. When a drug company discovers a new drug, the patent system gives that company a temporary right to be the exclusive manufacturer of this particular drug. When the patent expires, however, other companies are allowed to make the drug. All these forms of technological knowledge are important for the economy's production of goods and services.

It is worthwhile to distinguish between technological knowledge and human capital. Although they are closely related, there is an important difference. Technological knowledge refers to society's understanding about how the world works. Human capital refers to the resources expended transmitting this understanding to the labour force. To use a relevant metaphor, knowledge is the quality of society's textbooks, whereas human capital is the amount of time that the population has devoted to reading them. Workers' productivity depends on both the quality of textbooks they have available and the amount of time they have spent studying them.

technological knowledge
society's understanding of the best ways to produce goods and services

The production function

Economists often use a *production function* to describe the relationship between the quantity of inputs used in production and the quantity of output from production. For example, suppose Y denotes the quantity of output, L the quantity of labour, K the quantity of physical capital, H the quantity of human capital and N the quantity of natural resources. Then we might write:

$$Y = A\,F(L,\ K,\ H,\ N)$$

where $F(\ )$ is a function that shows how the inputs are combined to produce output. A is a variable that reflects the available production technology. As technology improves, A rises, so the economy produces more output from any given combination of inputs.

Many production functions have a property called *constant returns to scale*. If a production function has constant returns to scale, then a doubling of all the inputs causes the amount of output to double as well. Mathematically, we write that a production function has constant returns to scale if, for any positive number x:

$$xY = A\,F(xL,\ xK,\ xH,\ xN)$$

A doubling of all inputs is represented in this equation by $x = 2$. The right-hand side shows the inputs doubling and the left-hand side shows outputs doubling.

Production functions with constant returns to scale have an interesting implication. To see what it is, set $x = 1/L$. Then the equation above becomes:

$$Y/L = A\,F(1, K/L, H/L, N/L)$$

Notice that Y/L is output per worker, which is a measure of productivity. This equation says that productivity depends on physical capital per worker (K/L), human capital per worker (H/L) and natural resources per worker (N/L). Productivity also depends on the state of technology, as reflected by the variable A. Thus, this equation provides a mathematical summary of the four determinants of productivity we have just discussed.

Q List and describe four determinants of a country's productivity.

Economic growth and public policy

So far, we have determined that a society's standard of living depends on its ability to produce goods and services and that its productivity depends on physical capital, human capital, natural resources and technological knowledge. Let's now turn to the question faced by policymakers around the world: What can government policy do to raise productivity and living standards?

The importance of saving and investment

Because capital is a produced factor of production, a society can change the amount of capital it has. If today the economy produces a large quantity of new capital goods, then tomorrow it will have a larger stock of capital and be able to produce more of all types of goods and services. Thus, one way to raise future productivity is to invest more current resources in the production of capital.

One of the *Ten Lessons from Economics* presented in chapter 1 is that people face trade-offs. This principle is especially important when considering the accumulation of capital. Because resources are scarce, devoting more resources to producing capital requires devoting fewer resources to producing goods and services for current consumption. That is, for society to invest more in capital, it must consume less and save more of its current income. The growth that arises from capital accumulation is not a free lunch – it requires that society sacrifice consumption of goods and services in the present in order to enjoy higher consumption in the future.

The next chapter examines in more detail how the economy's financial markets coordinate saving and investment. It also examines how government policies influence the amount of saving and investment that takes place. At this point it is important to note that encouraging saving and investment is one way that a government can encourage growth and, in the long run, raise the economy's standard of living.

To see the importance of investment for economic growth, consider Figure 26.1, which displays data on 18 countries. Panel (a) shows each country's growth rate over a 58-year period. The countries are ordered by their growth rates, from most to least rapid. Panel (b) shows the percentage of GDP that each country devotes to investment. The correlation between growth and investment, although not perfect, is strong. Countries that devote a large share of GDP to investment, such as Singapore and Japan, tend to have high growth rates. Countries that devote a small share of GDP to investment, such as Nigeria, tend to have low growth rates. Studies that examine a more comprehensive list of countries confirm this strong correlation between investment and growth.

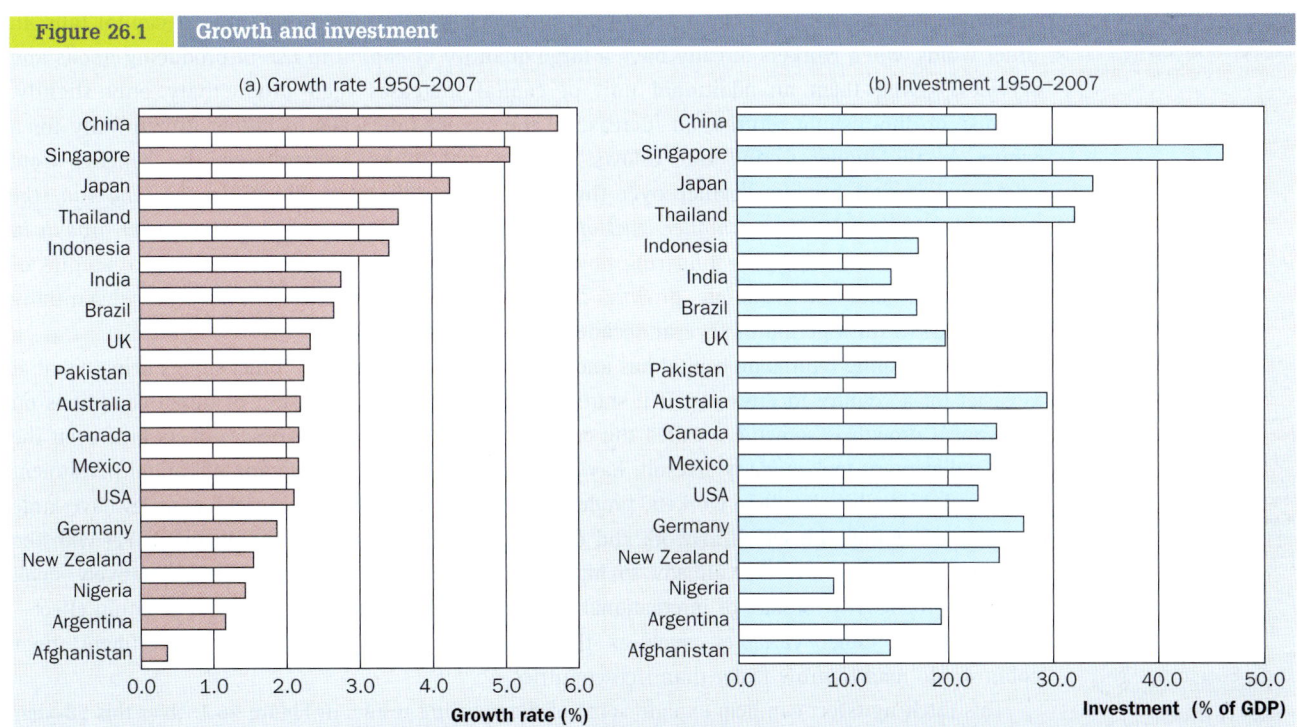

Figure 26.1 Growth and investment

Panel (a) shows the average annual growth rate of GDP per person for 18 countries over the period 1950–2007. Panel (b) shows the percentage of GDP that each country devoted to investment over this period. High growth countries generally have high rates of investment.

Source: *The Penn World Table* (Mark 6.3).

There is, however, a problem in interpreting these data. As the appendix to chapter 2 discussed, a correlation between two variables does not establish which variable is the cause and which is the effect. It is possible that high investment causes high growth, but it is also possible that high growth causes high investment. (Or, perhaps, high growth and high investment are both caused by a third variable that has been omitted from the analysis.) The data by themselves cannot tell us the direction of causation. Nonetheless, because capital accumulation affects productivity so clearly and directly, many economists interpret these data as showing that high investment leads to more rapid economic growth.

Diminishing returns and the catch-up effect

Suppose that a government, convinced by the evidence in Figure 26.1, pursues policies that raise the nation's saving rate – the percentage of GDP devoted to saving rather than consumption. What happens? With the nation saving more, fewer resources are needed to make consumption goods, and more resources are available to make capital goods. As a result, the capital stock increases, leading to rising productivity and more rapid growth in GDP. But how long does this higher rate of growth last? Assuming that the saving rate remains at its new higher level, does the growth rate of GDP stay high indefinitely or only for a period of time?

diminishing returns
the property whereby the benefit from an extra unit of an input declines as the quantity of the input increases

The traditional view of the production process is that capital is subject to **diminishing returns** – as the stock of capital rises, the extra output produced from an additional unit of capital falls. In other words, when workers already have a large quantity of capital to use in producing goods and services, giving them an additional unit of capital increases their productivity only slightly. Because of diminishing returns, an increase in the saving rate leads to higher growth only for a while. As the higher saving rate allows more capital to be accumulated, the benefits from additional capital become smaller over time and so growth slows down. *In the long run, the higher saving rate leads to a higher level of productivity and income, but not to higher growth in these variables.* Reaching this long run, however, can take quite a while. According to studies of international data on economic growth, increasing the saving rate can lead to substantially higher growth for a period of several decades.

catch-up effect
the property whereby countries that start off poor tend to grow more rapidly than countries that start off rich

The diminishing returns on capital has another important implication – other things being equal, it is easier for a country to grow fast if it starts out relatively poor. This effect of initial conditions on subsequent growth is sometimes called the **catch-up effect**. In poor countries, workers lack even the most rudimentary tools and, as a result, have low productivity. Small amounts of capital investment would substantially raise these workers' productivity. In contrast, workers in rich countries have large amounts of capital with which to work and this partly explains their high productivity. Yet with the amount of capital per worker already so high, additional capital investment has a relatively small effect on productivity. Studies of international data on economic growth confirm this catch-up effect – controlling for other variables, such as the percentage of GDP devoted to investment, poor countries do tend to grow faster than rich countries.

▸ catch-up effect
▸ production function

This catch-up effect can help explain some of the puzzling results in Figure 26.1. Over this 58-year period, Australia and Japan devoted a similar share of GDP to investment. Yet Australia experienced only moderate growth of just over 2 per cent, whereas Japan experienced high growth of over 4 per cent. The explanation is the catch-up effect. In 1950, Japan had GDP per person around one-fifth the Australian level, in part because previous investment had been so low. With a small initial capital stock, the benefits to capital accumulation were much greater in Japan, and this gave Japan a higher subsequent growth rate.

This catch-up effect shows up in other aspects of life. When a school gives an end-of-year award to the 'most improved' student, that student is usually one who began the year with relatively poor performance. Students who began the year not studying find improvement easier than students who always worked hard. Note that it is good to be 'most improved', given the starting point, but it is even better to be 'best student'. Similarly, economic growth over the last several decades has been much more rapid in Japan than in Australia, but GDP per person is still higher in Australia.

Investment from abroad

So far we have discussed how policies aimed at increasing a country's saving rate can increase investment and, thereby, long-term economic growth. Yet saving by domestic residents is not the only way for a country to invest in new capital. The other way is investment by foreigners.

Investment from abroad takes several forms. An Australian university might build a university in Thailand. A capital investment that is owned and operated by a foreign entity is called *foreign direct investment*. Alternatively, an Australian might buy shares in a Thai corporation (that is, buy a share of the ownership of the corporation); the Thai corporation can use the proceeds from the sale of shares to build a new factory. An investment that is financed with foreign money but operated by domestic residents is called *foreign portfolio investment*. In both cases, Australians provide the resources necessary to increase the stock of capital in Thailand. That is, Australian saving is being used to finance Thai investment.

When foreigners invest in a country, they do so because they expect to earn a return on their investment. If the University of Melbourne were to open a Thai campus, that would increase the Thai capital stock and, therefore, increase Thai productivity and Thai GDP. Yet, in this case, the university takes some of this additional income back to Australia in the form of profit. Similarly, when an Australian investor buys shares in a Thai corporation, the investor has a right to a portion of the profit that the Thai corporation earns.

Investment from abroad, therefore, affects GDP and GNP differently. Recall that gross domestic product is the income earned within a country by both residents and non-residents, whereas gross national product is the income earned by residents of a country both at home and abroad. If the University of Melbourne opens a campus in Thailand, some of the income the university generates accrues to people who do not live in Thailand. As a result, this investment raises Thailand's GDP more than it raises Thailand's GNP.

Investment from abroad is one way for a country to grow. Even though some of the benefits from this investment flow back to the foreign owners, this investment does increase the economy's stock of capital, leading to higher productivity and higher wages. Moreover, investment from abroad is one way for poor countries to learn the state-of-the-art technologies developed and used in richer countries. For these reasons, many economists who advise governments in less developed economies advocate policies that encourage investment from abroad. Often this means removing restrictions that governments have imposed on foreign ownership of domestic capital.

An organisation that tries to encourage the flow of investment to poor countries is the World Bank. This international organisation obtains funds from the world's advanced countries, such as Australia, and uses these resources to make loans to less developed countries so that they can invest in roads,

IN THE NEWS ...

THE ECONOMIC IMPACT OF NATURAL DISASTERS

In this chapter we have been discussing the importance of investment to achieving economic growth. But sometimes things happen that can diminish a country's growth. One such event was the flooding that occurred in Pakistan in 2010. The impact of these floods was widespread – villages were destroyed and lives disrupted throughout the region. Not only has infrastructure, such as bridges, roads and electricity generators, been destroyed, but hundreds of thousands of homes, significant proportions of crops and livestock have also been lost. This leads to increases in the prices of basics such as food and shelter. The article below explains the impact.

Floods threaten to sink teetering economy

by Matt Wade

The worst floods in Pakistan's history are devastating its already fragile economy, adding further instability to the troubled nation.

The biggest city and commercial hub, Karachi, is in danger of being hit by the floodwaters. Hundreds of thousands of homes, crops and livestock have been washed away and huge damage has been caused to infrastructure including bridges, roads, government buildings and electricity. The United Nations says reconstruction is likely to cost billions.

Further heavy monsoon rains are forecast and the meteorological department has warned of 'flooding in Karachi, Hyderabad and other urban areas'.

At least 1600 people have been killed, but there are warnings the final toll could rise well above 2000. At the weekend about 30 bodies were reportedly recovered following landslides in two flood-hit villages in the north, while 25 more people were believed missing.

About 15 million people have been directly affected by the floods, but the consequences are being felt across the country as food prices rise. There are reports the cost of basics like onions, potatoes and tomatoes has quadrupled following the inundation of huge tracts of prime farming land.

The Prime Minister, Yousuf Raza Gilani, has appealed to the world for help, saying the needed response to the disaster is 'beyond our capacity'. He said 'our country has gone back several years'.

The UN's special envoy, Jean-Maurice Ripert, told the Associated Press that the emergency phase 'will require hundreds of millions of dollars and the recovery and reconstruction part will require billions of dollars'.

Dr Faisal Bari, a Pakistani economist and adviser to the Open Society Institute, said that while the full extent of destruction to public infrastructure would not be known until the floodwaters receded, the 'scale is going to be very large'.

The rescue effort is sapping the government's budget, which had been under serious strain before the floods. But Dr Bari said it was unlikely the international donations would cover the massive cost of rehabilitation, putting additional pressure on domestic finances.

'This is going to be fairly hard for Pakistan to manage,' he said. The UN has said the disaster is 'on par' with the earthquake that hit Kashmir in 2005, killing more than 70 000 people.

While the loss of life has been much lower, the flood has affected a vast area and the economic cost will be significant. It has reportedly wiped out 30 per cent of the cotton crop and damaged a significant proportion of food crops in the breadbasket provinces of Punjab and Sindh.

Every main bridge in the Swat Valley, in the north, has reportedly been destroyed and it could take months to get electricity back to the region.

The Sarhad Chamber of Commerce and Industry in Khyber Pakhtunkhwa (formerly North-West Frontier Province) has put losses in that province at about 200 billion rupees ($2.33 billion). 'The flooding is definitely going to have a growth impact,' Dr Bari said.

In late 2000 Pakistan was forced to borrow from the International Monetary Fund to avoid defaulting on its foreign loans and economists say it remains dependent on the fund.

The economic problems have been blamed for stoking militancy in the country and security experts have warned that the floods could play into the hands of extremist groups if infrastructure and livelihoods are not restored quickly

Source: Matt Wade/*The Sydney Morning Herald*, 10 August 2010.

sewer systems, schools and other types of capital. It also offers the countries advice about how the funds might best be used. The World Bank, together with its sister organisation, the International Monetary Fund (IMF), was set up after the Second World War. One lesson from the war was that economic distress often leads to political turmoil, international tensions and military conflict. Thus, every country has an interest in promoting economic prosperity around the world. The World Bank and the IMF aim to achieve that common goal.

Education

Education – investment in human capital – is at least as important as investment in physical capital for a country's long-run economic success. In Australia, each year of schooling raises a person's wage on average by about 8 per cent. In less developed countries, where human capital is especially scarce, the gap between the wages of educated and uneducated workers is even larger. Thus, one way in which government policy can enhance the standard of living is to provide good schools and to encourage the population to take advantage of them.

Investment in human capital, like investment in physical capital, has an opportunity cost. When students are in school or university, they forgo the wages they could have earned. In less developed countries, children often drop out of school at an early age, even though the benefit of additional schooling is very high, simply because their labour is needed to help support the family.

Some economists have argued that human capital is particularly important for economic growth because human capital conveys positive externalities. An *externality* is the effect of one person's actions on the wellbeing of a bystander. An educated person, for instance, might generate new ideas about how best to produce goods and services. If these ideas enter society's pool of knowledge so everyone can use them, then the ideas are an external benefit of education. In this case, the return on schooling is even greater for society than for the individual. This argument would justify the large subsidies for human-capital investment that we observe in the form of public education.

One problem facing some countries is the *brain drain* – the emigration of many of the most highly educated workers to rich countries, where these workers can enjoy a higher standard of living. This is particularly a problem for poor countries, but Australia also suffers from brain drain. If human capital does have positive externalities, then this brain drain makes those people left behind poorer than they otherwise would be. This problem offers policymakers a dilemma. On the one hand, Australia and the United States and other rich countries have better systems of higher education, and it would seem natural for poor countries to send their best students abroad to earn higher degrees. On the other hand, those students who have spent time abroad may choose not to return home and this brain drain will reduce the poor nation's stock of human capital even further.

Health and nutrition

The term *human capital* usually refers to education, but it can also be used to describe another type of investment in people: expenditures that lead to a healthier population. Other things equal, healthier workers are more productive. The right investments in the health of the population provide one way for a nation to increase productivity and raise living standards.

Economic historian Robert Fogel has suggested that a significant factor in long-run economic growth is improved health from better nutrition. He estimates that in Great Britain in 1780, about one in five people were so malnourished that they were incapable of manual labour. Among those who could work, insufficient caloric intake substantially reduced the work effort they could put forth. As nutrition improved, so did workers' productivity.

Fogel studies these historical trends in part by looking at the height of the population. Short stature can be an indicator of malnutrition, especially during gestation and the early years of life. Fogel finds that as nations develop economically, people eat more and the population gets taller. From 1775 to 1975, the average caloric intake in Great Britain rose by 26 per cent and the height of the average man rose by 3.6 inches (9.1 cm). Similarly, during the spectacular economic growth in South Korea from 1962 to 1995, caloric consumption rose by 44 per cent and average male height rose by 2 inches (5.1 cm). Of course, a person's height is determined by a combination of genetic predisposition and environment. But because the genetic make-up of a population is slow to change, such increases in average height are most likely due to changes in the environment – nutrition being the obvious explanation.

Moreover, studies have found that height is an indicator of productivity. Looking at data on a large number of workers at a point in time, researchers have found that taller workers tend to earn more. Because wages reflect a worker's productivity, this finding suggests that taller workers tend to be more productive. The effect of height on wages is especially pronounced in poorer countries, where malnutrition is a bigger risk.

Fogel won the Nobel Prize in Economics in 1993 for his work in economic history. He concluded that 'improved gross nutrition accounts for roughly 30 per cent of the growth of per capita income in Britain between 1790 and 1980'.

Today, malnutrition is fortunately rare in developed nations such as Australia, the UK and the United States. (Obesity is a more widespread problem.) But for people in developing nations, poor health and inadequate nutrition remain obstacles to higher productivity and improved living standards. The United Nations estimates that almost a third of the population in sub-Saharan Africa is undernourished.

The causal link between health and wealth runs in both directions. Poor countries are poor in part because their populations are not healthy, and their populations are not healthy in part because they are poor and cannot afford adequate health care and nutrition. It is a vicious circle. But this fact opens the possibility of a virtuous circle: Policies that lead to more rapid economic growth would naturally improve health outcomes, which in turn would further promote economic growth.

Property rights and political stability

Another way in which policymakers can foster economic growth is by protecting property rights and promoting political stability. As we first noted when we discussed economic interdependence in chapter 2, production in market economies arises from the interactions of millions of individuals and firms. When you buy a car, for instance, you are buying the output of a car dealer, a car manufacturer, a steel company, an iron ore mining company and so on. This division of production among many firms allows the economy's factors of production to be used as effectively as possible. To achieve this outcome, the economy has to coordinate transactions among these firms, as well as between firms and consumers. Market economics achieve this coordination through market prices. That is, market prices are the instrument with which the 'invisible hand of the marketplace' brings supply and demand into balance. (In his 1776 landmark book, *The Wealth of Nations*, economist Adam Smith referred to the seemingly undirected operation of the marketplace as being guided by an 'invisible hand'.)

An important prerequisite for the price system to work is an economy-wide respect for *property rights*. Property rights refer to the ability of people to exercise authority over the resources they own. A mining company will not make the effort to mine iron ore if it expects the ore to be stolen. The company mines the ore only if it is confident that it will benefit from the ore's subsequent sale. For this reason, courts serve an important role in a market economy – they enforce property rights. Through the criminal justice system, the courts discourage direct theft. In addition, through the civil justice system, the courts ensure that buyers and sellers live up to their contracts.

Although people in developed countries tend to take property rights for granted, those living in less developed countries understand that lack of property rights can be a major problem. In many countries, the system of justice does not work well. Contracts are hard to enforce and fraud often goes unpunished. In more extreme cases, the government not only fails to enforce property rights but actually infringes upon them. To do business in some countries, firms are expected to bribe powerful government officials. Such corruption impedes the coordinating power of markets. It also discourages domestic saving and investment from abroad.

One threat to property rights is political instability. When revolutions and coups are common, there is doubt about whether property rights will be respected in the future. If a revolutionary government might confiscate the capital of some businesses, as was often true after communist revolutions,

A recurring problem facing the world's poorest countries is famine. Every few years, haunting pictures of starving people in an underdeveloped country show up on the nightly news. Such tragedies are surely among the most serious economic problems the world's nations face.

It is tempting to think that the problem of famine is simply due to excessive population. After all, if there were fewer people, then each person could get a larger share of the available food supply. Reducing population growth would seem to be the natural remedy for recurrent famine. It turns out, however, that this straightforward logic is not correct.

In many cases, famine is caused not by an inadequate *supply* of food but by an inadequate *distribution* of food. That is, food is available, but it is not getting to the people who need it. The failure of distribution, in turn, is caused by political instability and poor enforcement of property rights. An example is the famine in Papua New Guinea in 1998. A lack of funding for transport and poor government control over resources prevented food

Papua New Guinea – too many people was not the problem.

Source: AAP Image/AP Photo/David Gray.

supplies from being distributed to outer provinces. Eventually, Australian troops coordinated the relief effort to allow the available food to be distributed properly.

domestic residents have less incentive to save, invest and start new businesses. At the same time, foreigners have less incentive to invest in the country. Even the threat of revolution can act to depress a nation's standard of living.

Thus, economic prosperity depends in part on political prosperity. A country with an efficient court system, honest government officials and a stable political system will enjoy a higher economic standard of living than a country with a poor court system, corrupt officials and frequent revolutions and coups.

Free trade

Some of the world's poorest countries have tried to achieve more rapid economic growth by pursuing *inward-oriented policies*. These policies are aimed at raising productivity and living standards within the country by avoiding interaction with the rest of the world. Domestic firms sometimes claim they need protection from foreign competition in order to compete and grow. This 'infant industry' argument, together with a general distrust of foreigners, has at times led policymakers in less developed countries to impose tariffs and other trade restrictions.

Most economists today believe that poor countries are better off pursuing *outward-oriented policies* that integrate these countries into the world economy. Chapter 3 showed how international trade can improve the economic wellbeing of a country's citizens. Trade is, in some ways, a type of technology. When a country exports wheat and imports steel, the country benefits in the same way as if it had invented a technology for turning wheat into steel. A country that eliminates trade restrictions will, therefore, experience the same kind of economic growth that would occur after a major technological advance.

The adverse impact of inward orientation becomes clear when one considers the small size of many less-developed economies. The total GDP of Fiji, for instance, is about that of Sydney. Imagine what would happen if Sydney residents were prohibited from trading with people living outside the city. Without being able to take advantage of the gains from trade, Sydney would need to produce all the goods it consumes. It would also have to produce all its own capital goods, rather than importing state-of-the-art equipment from other cities. Living standards in Sydney would fall immediately and the problem would be likely to get worse over time. This is precisely what happens when countries pursue inward-oriented policies, such as Argentina did throughout much of the twentieth century. In contrast, countries pursuing outward-oriented policies, such as South Korea, Singapore and Taiwan, have enjoyed high rates of economic growth.

The amount that a nation trades with others is determined not only by government policy but also by geography. Countries with good natural seaports find trade easier than countries without this resource. It is not a coincidence that many of the world's major cities, such as New York, Singapore and Hong Kong, are located next to oceans. Similarly, because landlocked countries find international trade more difficult, they tend to have lower levels of income than countries with easy access to the world's waterways.

IN THE NEWS . . .

THE MILLENNIUM DEVELOPMENT GOALS

In September 2000, world leaders came together at United Nations Headquarters in New York to adopt the United Nations Millennium Declaration, committing their nations to specific targets on eight key issues that perpetuate poverty, with a deadline of 2015. These have become known as the Millennium Development Goals (http://www.un.org/millenniumgoals/bkgd.shtml). With two-thirds of the time gone, the following report discusses progress towards the eight goals.

Source: © United Nations/United Nations Development Programme (UNDP).

Global targets, local ingenuity

In ten years, the living conditions of the poor have been improving – but not necessarily because of the UN's goals

Even at 70, Jiyem, an Indonesian grandmother, gets up in the small hours to cook and collect firewood for her impoverished household. Her three-year-old grandson is malnourished. Nobody in her family has ever finished primary school. Her ramshackle house lacks electricity; the toilet is a hole in the ground; the family drinks dirty water. Asked about her notion of well-being by researchers from Oxford University, Jiyem said, 'I cannot picture what well-being means.'

The sort of deprivation Jiyem describes remains widespread. The United Nations reckons that in 2008 over a quarter of children in the developing world were underweight, a sixth of people lacked access to safe drinking water, and just under half used insanitary toilets or none at all. But while these figures are disquieting, a smaller fraction of people were affected than was the case two decades ago. So such data also indicate the world's progress towards meeting the Millennium Development Goals (MDGs), a set of targets adopted by world leaders at the UN ten years ago.

Millennium Development Goals
Selected targets to be met by 2015
Halve the proportion of people living on less than $1.25 a day (at purchasing-power parity)
Ensure all children complete primary school
Educate boys and girls equally
Reduce the mortality rate among children under five by two-thirds
Reduce the maternal mortality rate by three-quarters
Halt and begin to reverse the spread of HIV/AIDS, malaria and other major diseases
Halve the proportion of people without access to safe water and sanitation
Increase aid and improve governance

Source: © United Nations/United Nations Development Programme (UNDP).

The leaders gave themselves 15 years to reach the goalposts set in 2000. Two-thirds of that time is up. This week they returned to the UN for another meeting. Few, if any, of them

>>

have close experience of poverty. So the MDG exercise has at least made them spend three days discussing matters they might prefer to ignore. It has also helped to shift the debate away from how much is being spent on development towards how much is being achieved.

But few go as far as Ban Ki-Moon, the UN secretary-general, who recently called the goals 'a milestone in international co-operation' that had helped 'hundreds of millions of people around the world'. Talking up the MDGs is, of course, part of Mr Ban's job. And there has indeed been progress on many fronts (see the box below). But it is hard to assign much credit to the exercise itself.

Take the goal of halving the poverty rate from its 1990 level by 2015. The World Bank reckons that in 1990 46% of the developing world's population fell below the internationally accepted poverty line of $1.25 a day at purchasing-power parity. By 2005 the rate had fallen to 27% and, despite a slowdown in progress in the past couple of years, it is now probably lower still. A global halving by 2015 seems well within reach. Yet this 'victory' is mainly due to a drop in China's poverty rate from 60% in 1990 to 16% in 2005. Because China and India accounted for over 62% of the planet's poor in 1990, changes to the world's poverty rate depend heavily on their performance. A global goal is therefore a poor way to give the governments of smaller countries an incentive to tackle poverty.

Alison Evans of Britain's Overseas Development Institute (ODI) reckons that the MDGs have come to be seen as applying to each developing country. But it is hard to track performance at country level: 28 of the poorest countries have recorded poverty rates for only one year between 1990 and 2008, according to a tally by researchers at the Centre for Global Development, a think-tank in Washington, DC. This makes any judgments about their progress mere guesswork. (This caveat does not apply with equal force to the global target, because China and India have enough data to make their progress measurable.)

The ODI reckons that 15 poor countries have already met the goal of halving the poverty rate. And perennial pessimists about Africa's prospects may be surprised to know that the list of the top ten countries ranked by the average annual decline in the poverty rate includes six in Africa: the Gambia, Mali, Senegal, Ethiopia, the Central African Republic and Guinea.

But lack of data aside, there is something odd about setting uniform targets such as 'cutting child mortality by two-thirds', which means that some countries must do much more to avoid being classed as failures than others. Niger is a case in point. Between 1990 and

Moving the right way
Progress on Millennium Development Goals in developing countries

	1990	2008	2015 target
Population living on less than $1.25 a day, % of total	46	27*	23
Undernourished population, % of total	20[†]	16[‡]	10
Deaths of children under five as % of live births	10	7.2	3.3
Primary-school enrolment, % of all primary-school-age children	82[§]	89**	100
Pregnant women attended at least once by skilled medical personnel, % of all pregnant women	64	80	100
Population with access to an improved water source, % of total	71	84	85.5

*2005 [†]1990-92 [‡]2005-07 [§]1998 **2007-08

Source: © United Nations/United Nations Development Programme (UNDP).

2007 it cut the number of children per 1,000 who died before their fifth birthday from 304 to 176. This was the biggest absolute reduction of any country in the world. But Niger is still judged 'off-track' to meet its target, because continuing at the current rate will still result in a reduction of slightly below two-thirds. Its government may well find the MDG exercise mildly discouraging.

Money's limits

The goal-setting exercise has further pitfalls. Too often, the goals are reduced to working out how much money is needed to meet a particular target and then berating governments for not spending enough. Yet the countries that have made most progress in cutting poverty have largely done so not by spending public money, but by encouraging faster economic growth. China is the most obvious example. The best performers in Africa, too, are those that have managed to speed up growth. As Shanta Devarajan, the World Bank's chief economist for Africa, points out, growth does not just make more money available for social spending. It also increases the demand for such things as schooling, and thus helps meet other development goals. Yet the goals, as drawn up, made no mention of economic growth.

Of course, as India's dismal record on child malnutrition demonstrates, growth by itself does not solve all the problems of the poor. It is also clear that while money helps, how it is spent and what it is spent on are enormously important. For instance, campaigners often ask for more to be spent on primary education. But throughout the developing world teachers on the public payroll are often absent from school. Teacher-absenteeism rates are around 20% in rural Kenya, 27% in Uganda and 14% in Ecuador. In Rajasthan in northern India, nurses who were supposed to be staffing primary health clinics were found to be at work only 12% of the time over an 18-month period.

In any case, money that is allocated for such services rarely reaches its intended recipients. A study found that 70% of the money allocated for drugs and supplies by the Ugandan government in 2000 was lost to 'leakage'; in Ghana, 80% was siphoned off. Montek Ahluwalia, of India's Planning Commission, said last year that he reckoned only 16% of the resources earmarked for the poor under the country's subsidised food distribution scheme ever reached them. Money needs to be spent, therefore, not merely on building more schools or hiring more teachers, but on getting them to do what they are paid for, and preventing resources from disappearing somewhere between the central government and their supposed destination.

The good news is that policy experiments carried out by governments, NGOs, academics and international institutions are slowly building up a body of evidence about methods that work. A large-scale evaluation in Andhra Pradesh in southern India has shown, for example, that performance pay for teachers is three times as effective at raising pupils' test scores as the equivalent amount spent on school supplies. In Rajasthan, teachers were paid only on showing a date-stamped photograph to prove they had been in class on a given day. This led not just to a massive decline in absenteeism, but also to better pupil performance.

And in Uganda the government, appalled that money meant for schools was not reaching them, took to publicising how much was being allotted, using radio and newspapers. Leakage was dramatically reduced. The World Bank hopes to bring such innovations to the notice of other governments during the summit, if it can. For if the drive against poverty is to succeed, it will owe more to such ideas and their wider use than to targets set at UN-sponsored summits.

Source: *The Economist*, 23 September 2010.
© The Economist Newspaper Limited, London 2010.

The control of population growth

A country's productivity and living standard are determined in part by its population growth. Obviously, population is a key determinant of a country's labour force. It is no surprise, therefore, that countries with large populations (such as the United States and Japan) tend to produce greater GDP than countries with small populations (such as Australia and New Zealand). But *total* GDP is not a good measure of economic wellbeing. For policymakers concerned about living standards, GDP *per person* is more important, for it tells us the quantity of goods and services available for the typical individual in the economy.

How does growth in the number of people affect the amount of GDP per person? The answer is that high population growth reduces GDP per person. The reason is that rapid growth in the number of workers forces the other factors of production to be spread more thinly. In particular, when population growth is rapid, equipping each worker with a large quantity of capital is more difficult. A smaller quantity of capital per worker leads to lower productivity and lower GDP per worker.

This problem is most apparent in the case of human capital. Countries with high population growth have large numbers of school-age children. This places a larger burden on the educational system. It is not surprising, therefore, that educational attainment tends to be low in countries with high population growth.

The differences in population growth around the world are large. In developed countries, such as Australia, the United States and countries in western Europe, the population has risen about 1 per cent per year in recent decades, and it is expected to rise even more slowly in the future. In contrast, in many poor African countries population growth is about 3 per cent per year. At this rate, the population doubles every 23 years.

Reducing the rate of population growth is widely thought to be one way less developed countries can try to raise their standards of living. In some countries, this goal is accomplished directly with laws regulating the number of children families may have. China, for instance, allows only one child per family; couples who violate this rule are subject to substantial fines. In countries with greater freedom, the goal of reduced population growth is accomplished less directly by increasing awareness of birth control techniques.

The final way in which a country can influence population growth is to apply one of the *Ten Lessons from Economics* – people respond to incentives. Bearing a child, like any decision, has an opportunity

IN THE NEWS . . .

DOES MIGRATION HELP OR HINDER ECONOMIC GROWTH?

Governments all around the globe struggle with how many people from other countries they will allow to migrate to their nations. As the following article from the *Economist* explains, one source of economic growth for many nations is the increase in productivity that occurs when migrants are allowed to work in another country's economy.

Of bedsheets and bison grass vodka
Rich economies gain from high levels of migration, but the benefits are unevenly spread

For the past two decades or so, high rates of immigration into OECD countries have coincided with prolonged economic growth in much of the Western world. Consider Cobh, a bustling tourist town in southern Ireland which used to be famous for exporting people. Some 2.5m Irishmen and women embarked for America from its quayside, and its great and gloomy neo-gothic cathedral was paid for by remittances.

Now, like the rest of Ireland, Cobh heaves with foreign workers. There are Poles on building sites, Latvians who own a shop selling dumplings, *sauerkraut* and other continental delicacies, a South African in the tourist office and another driving a taxi, Chinese in restaurants, a Bangladeshi managing a fishing business, and so on. A hotel owner says that he could not do without the migrants: when he recently advertised for a receptionist, none of the 200 applicants was Irish.

Migration can be both a consequence and a cause of economic well-being, but many people in host countries with lots of migrants have yet to be convinced of the economic benefits. A poll in November 2007, for France 24, found that 55% of Spaniards consider migrants a boon for their economy, and so do 50% of Italians, but only 42% of Britons and Germans and a mere 30% of French respondents.

Some of the hostility towards immigration seems linked to worries about the economy. If recession looms, locals are more afraid that outsiders will take their jobs or scrounge on their welfare systems. The last time that immigration in America was as high as it is now, just under a century ago, xenophobia rose as recession took hold. Today, amid concerns that a housing slide could lead to a general economic slump, American anxiety about migration is rising again. But the poor worry about immigration even when the economy is thriving.

Legal migrants usually have better job prospects than illegal ones, and the more educated outdo the rest. Not all of them stay. Nearly a third of those who crossed the Atlantic to America between 1890 and 1914 – and as many as half the Spaniards and Italians – re-emigrated. Similarly, surveys today show that a majority of Poles in Britain plan to go home within a few years.

Some migrants do better not only than those left behind but also than those in their destination countries. The Institute for Public Policy Research, a British think-tank, found in 2007 that the foreign-born of many ethnic groups are both more likely to have a job and to be better paid than the average Briton. In America, over the past century, studies have shown migrants' wages catching up with, and then often surpassing, those of average Americans. Migrants' children do well too. This is not surprising. Migrants need health, skills, determination, a willingness to take risks and some entrepreneurial nous to take the plunge, which marks them out as special people.

Assuming that migrants are in work, they are bound to benefit the economy of the host country as a whole. Most simply, an expanding workforce permits faster growth. More people can do more work, and many migrants are young adults who are particularly productive. Moreover, migrants increasingly alleviate specific labour shortages in rich economies. Some economies could not function without

foreign workers. In the United Arab Emirates, for instance, they make up an astonishing 85% of the population.

For the moment few other countries rely so heavily on outsiders (see graph), but in a number of rich countries, including Britain and America, foreigners typically make up 10–15% of the labour force and their share is rising. Around half of the new jobs created in Britain today are filled by migrants, often because they have skills that locals lack (from plumbing to banking) or because natives scorn the work (from picking fruit to caring for the elderly).

Low jobless rates in Ireland, Sweden, Britain, America and other countries with high migration suggest that, so far, foreigners are not squeezing out natives. Migrants also help to create jobs, because a good supply of labour encourages those with capital to invest more. For example, the hotel owner in Cobh, knowing he can find affordable staff, has added an extension with extra rooms. In contrast, countries where migrants have been kept at arm's length, such as Germany, complain about a chronic shortage of skilled workers such as engineers, scientists or programmers.

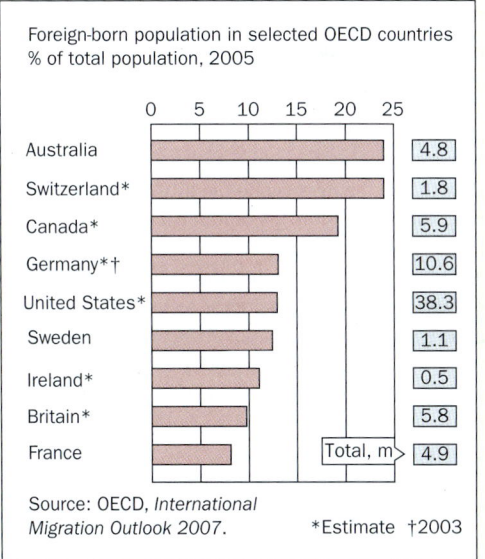

Foreign-born population in selected OECD countries
% of total population, 2005

	Total, m
Australia	4.8
Switzerland*	1.8
Canada*	5.9
Germany*†	10.6
United States*	38.3
Sweden	1.1
Ireland*	0.5
Britain*	5.8
France	4.9

Source: OECD, *International Migration Outlook 2007.*   *Estimate †2003

Source: *The Economist*, 3 January 2008.
© The Economist Newspaper Limited, London 2008.

cost. When the opportunity cost rises, people will choose to have smaller families. In particular, women with the opportunity to receive good education and desirable employment tend to want fewer children than those with fewer opportunities outside the home. Hence, policies that foster equal treatment of women are one way for less developed economies to reduce the rate of population growth.

Research and development

The main reason that living standards are higher today than they were a century ago is that technological knowledge has advanced. The telephone, the silicon chip, the computer and the internal combustion engine are among the thousands of innovations that have improved the ability to produce goods and services.

Although most technological advances come from private research by firms and individual inventors, there is also a public interest in promoting these efforts. To a large extent, knowledge is a *public good* – once one person discovers an idea, the idea enters society's pool of knowledge, and other people can use it freely. Just as government has a role in providing a public good such as national defence, it also has a role in encouraging the research and development of new technologies.

The Australian government has long played a major role in the creation and dissemination of technological knowledge. The government funds research in organisations such as the CSIRO (the Commonwealth Scientific and Industrial Research Organisation). It also provides funding for research in universities across the country through research grants from the Australian Research Council and the National Health and Medical Research Council, and with tax breaks for firms engaging in research and development.

Yet another way in which government policy encourages research is through the patent system. When a person or firm invents a new product, such as a new drug, the inventor can apply for a patent. If the product is deemed truly original, the government awards the patent, which gives the inventor the exclusive right to make the product for a specified number of years. In essence, the patent gives the inventor a property right over the invention, turning the new idea from a public good into a private good. By allowing inventors to profit from their inventions – even if only temporarily – the patent system enhances the incentive for individuals and firms to engage in research.

CASESTUDY

Promoting technological progress

Some economists have argued that rapid population growth may depress economic prosperity by reducing the amount of capital each worker has, but it may also have some benefits. Other economists have suggested that world population growth has been an engine of technological progress and economic prosperity. The mechanism is simple: If there are more people, then there are more scientists, inventors and engineers to contribute to technological advances, which benefits everyone.

Economist Michael Kremer has provided some support for this hypothesis in an article titled 'Population Growth and Technological Change: One Million B.C. to 1990', which was published in the *Quarterly Journal of Economics* in 1993. Kremer begins by noting that over the broad span of human history, world growth rates have

increased with world population. For example, world growth was more rapid when the world population was 1 billion (which occurred around the year 1800) than when the population was only 100 million (around 500 BC). This fact is consistent with the hypothesis that a larger population induces more technological progress.

Kremer's second piece of evidence comes from comparing regions of the world. The melting of the polar icecaps at the end of the Ice Age around 10 000 BC flooded the land bridges and separated the world into several distinct regions that could not communicate with one another for thousands of years. If technological progress is more rapid when there are more people to discover things, then larger regions should have experienced more rapid growth.

According to Kremer, that is exactly what happened. The most successful region of the world in 1500 (when Columbus re-established technological contact) comprised the 'Old World' civilizations of the large Eurasia–Africa region. Next in technological development were the Aztec and Mayan civilizations in the Americas, followed by the hunter-gatherers of Australia, and then the primitive people of Tasmania, who lacked even fire-making and most stone and bone tools.

The smallest isolated region was Flinders Island, a tiny island between Tasmania and Australia. With the smallest population, Flinders Island had the fewest opportunities for technological advance and, indeed, seemed to regress. Around 3000 BC, human society on Flinders Island died out completely. A large population, Kremer concludes, is a prerequisite for technological advance.

Describe three ways a government policymaker can try to raise the growth in living standards in a society. Are there any drawbacks to these policies?

IN THE NEWS . . .

ONE ECONOMIST'S ANSWER

Economist Daron Acemoglu, currently the Charles P. Kindleberger Professor of Applied Economics at MIT, considers why some nations thrive while others do not.

What makes a nation rich? One economist's big answer

by Daron Acemoglu

We are the rich, the haves, the developed. And most of the rest – in Africa, South Asia, and South America, the Somalias and Bolivias and Bangladeshes of the world – are the nots. It's always been this way, a globe divided by wealth and poverty, health and sickness, food and famine, though the extent of inequality across nations today is unprecedented: The average citizen of the United States is ten times as prosperous as the average Guatemalan, more than twenty times as prosperous as the average North Korean, and more than forty times as prosperous as those living in Mali, Ethiopia, Congo, or Sierra Leone.

The question social scientists have unsuccessfully wrestled with for centuries is, Why? But the question they should have been asking is, How? Because inequality is not predetermined. Nations are not like children – they are not born rich or poor. Their governments make them that way.

You can chart the search for a theory of inequality to the French political philosopher Montesquieu, who in the mid-eighteenth century came up with a very simple

explanation: People in hot places are inherently lazy. Other no less sweeping explanations soon followed: Could it be that Max Weber's Protestant work ethic is the true driver of economic success? Or perhaps the richest countries are those that were former British colonies? Or maybe it's as simple as tracing which nations have the largest populations of European descent? The problem with all of these theories is that while they superficially fit some specific cases, others radically disprove them.

It's the same with the theories put forth today. Economist Jeffrey Sachs, director of Columbia University's Earth Institute, attributes the relative success of nations to geography and weather: In the poorest parts of the world, he argues, nutrient-starved tropical soil makes agriculture a challenge, and tropical climates foment disease, particularly malaria. Perhaps if we were to fix these problems, teach the citizens of these nations better farming techniques, eliminate malaria, or at the very least equip them with artemisinin to fight this deadly disease, we could eliminate poverty. Or better yet, perhaps we just move these people and abandon their inhospitable land altogether.

Jared Diamond, the famous ecologist and best-selling author, has a different theory: The

>>

origin of world inequality stems from the historical endowment of plant and animal species and the advancement of technology. In Diamond's telling, the cultures that first learned to plant crops were the first to learn how to use a plow, and thus were first to adopt other technologies, the engine of every successful economy. Perhaps then the solution to world inequality rests in technology – wiring the developing world with Internet and cell phones.

And yet while Sachs and Diamond offer good insight into certain aspects of poverty, they share something in common with Montesquieu and others who followed: They ignore incentives. People need incentives to invest and prosper; they need to know that if they work hard, they can make money and actually keep that money. And the key to ensuring those incentives is sound institutions – the rule of law and security and a governing system that offers opportunities to achieve and innovate. That's what determines the haves from the have-nots – not geography or weather or technology or disease or ethnicity.

Put simply: Fix incentives and you will fix poverty. And if you wish to fix institutions, you have to fix governments.

How do we know that institutions are so central to the wealth and poverty of nations? Start in Nogales, a city cut in half by the Mexican-American border fence. There is no difference in geography between the two halves of Nogales. The weather is the same. The winds are the same, as are the soils. The types of diseases prevalent in the area given its geography and climate are the same, as is the ethnic, cultural, and linguistic background of the residents. By logic, both sides of the city should be identical economically.

And yet they are far from the same.

On one side of the border fence, in Santa Cruz County, Arizona, the median household income is $30 000. A few feet away, it's $10 000. On one side, most of the teenagers are in public high school, and the majority of the adults are high school graduates. On the other side, few of the residents have gone to high school, let alone college. Those in Arizona enjoy relatively good health and Medicare for those over sixty-five, not to mention an efficient road

network, electricity, telephone service, and a dependable sewage and public-health system. None of those things are a given across the border. There, the roads are bad, the infant-mortality rate high, electricity and phone service expensive and spotty.

The key difference is that those on the north side of the border enjoy law and order and dependable government services – they can go about their daily activities and jobs without fear for their life or safety or property rights. On the other side, the inhabitants have institutions that perpetuate crime, graft, and insecurity.

Nogales may be the most obvious example, but it's far from the only one. Take Singapore, a once-impoverished tropical island that became the richest nation in Asia after British colonialists enshrined property rights and encouraged trade. Or China, where decades of stagnation and famine were reversed only after Deng Xiaoping began introducing private-property rights in agriculture, and later in industry. Or Botswana, whose economy has flourished over the past forty years while the rest of Africa has withered, thanks to strong tribal institutions and farsighted nation building by its early elected leaders.

Now look at the economic and political failures. You can begin in Sierra Leone, where a lack of functioning institutions and an overabundance of diamonds have fueled decades of civil war and strife and corruption that continue unchecked today. Or take communist North Korea, a geographical, ethnic, and cultural mirror of its capitalist neighbor to the south, yet ten times poorer. Or Egypt, cradle of one of the world's great civilizations yet stagnant economically ever since its colonization by the Ottomans and then the Europeans, only made worse by its post-independence governments, which have restricted all economic activities and markets. In fact, the theory can be used to shed light on the patterns of inequality for much of the world.

If we know why nations are poor, the resulting question is what can we do to help them? Our ability to impose institutions from the outside is limited, as the recent U. S. experiences in Afghanistan and Iraq demonstrate. But we are not helpless, and in many instances, there is a lot to be done. Even the most repressed citizens of the world will stand up to tyrants when given the opportunity. We saw this recently in Iran and a few years ago in Ukraine during the Orange Revolution.

The U. S. must not take a passive role in encouraging these types of movements. Our foreign policy should encourage them by punishing repressive regimes through trade embargoes and diplomacy... At the microlevel, we can help foreign citizens by educating them and arming them with the modern tools of activism, most notably the Internet, and perhaps even encryption technology and

cell phone platforms that can evade firewalls and censorship put in place by repressive governments, such as those in China or Iran, that fear the power of information.

There's no doubt that erasing global inequality, which has been with us for millennia and has expanded to unprecedented levels over the past century and a half, won't be easy. But by accepting the role of failed governments and institutions in causing poverty, we have a fighting chance of reversing it.

Source: *What makes a nation rich?*
By Daron Acemoglu, 18 November 2009.
© *Esquire*. Reproduced with permission.

Figure 26.2 | **The growth in real GDP per person**

This figure shows the average growth rate of real GDP per person for 16 advanced economies including the major countries of Europe, and Canada, the United States, Japan and Australia. Notice that the growth rate rose substantially after 1950 and then fell after 1970.

Source: Adapted from *The Penn World Table*.

Conclusion: The importance of long-run growth

In this chapter we have discussed what determines the standard of living in a nation and how policymakers can endeavour to raise the standard of living through policies that promote economic growth. Most of this chapter is summarised in one of the *Ten Lessons from Economics* – a country's standard of living depends on its ability to produce goods and services. Policymakers who want to encourage growth in standards of living must aim to increase their nation's productive ability by encouraging rapid accumulation of the factors of production and ensuring that these factors are employed as effectively as possible.

Economists differ in their views of the role of government in promoting economic growth. At the very least, government can lend support to the invisible hand by maintaining property rights and political stability. More controversial is whether government should target and subsidise specific industries that might be especially important for technological progress. There is no doubt that these issues are among the most important in economics. The success of one generation's policymakers in learning and heeding the fundamental lessons about economic growth determines what kind of world the next generation will inherit.

Summary

- Economic prosperity, as measured by GDP per person, varies substantially around the world. The average income in the world's richest countries is more than 10 times that in the world's poorest countries. Because growth rates of real GDP also vary substantially, the relative positions of countries can change dramatically over time.
- The standard of living in an economy depends on the economy's ability to produce goods and services. Productivity, in turn, depends on the amounts of physical capital, human capital, natural resources and technological knowledge available to workers.
- Government policies can influence the economy's growth rate in many ways – encouraging saving and investment, encouraging investment from abroad, fostering education, maintaining property rights and political stability, allowing free trade, controlling population growth, and promoting the research and development of new technologies.
- The accumulation of capital is subject to diminishing returns – the more capital an economy has, the less additional output the economy gets from an extra unit of capital. Because of diminishing returns, higher saving leads to higher growth for a period of time, but growth eventually slows down as the economy approaches a higher level of capital, productivity and income. Also because of diminishing returns, the return on capital is especially high in poor countries. Other things being equal, these countries can grow faster because of the catch-up effect.

Key concepts

catch-up effect
diminishing returns
human capital

natural resources
physical capital

productivity
technological knowledge

Questions for review

1. What two things does GDP measure? What does this dual meaning tell us about the determinants of the standard of living in a society?
2. List and describe four determinants of productivity.
3. In what way is a university degree a form of capital?
4. Explain how higher saving leads to a higher standard of living. How might a higher savings rate lead to a lower standard of living?
5. Does a higher rate of saving lead to higher growth temporarily or indefinitely?
6. How does good health and nutrition contribute to the rate of the nation's GDP growth?
7. How does the rate of immigration influence the level of GDP per person? Does it matter what educational level the immigrants have achieved before they come here?
8. Describe two ways in which the Australian government tries to encourage advances in technological knowledge.

Problems and applications

1 Most countries, including Australia, import substantial amounts of goods and services from other countries. Yet the chapter says that a nation can enjoy a high standard of living only if it can produce a large quantity of goods and services itself. Can you reconcile these two facts?

2 Suppose that society decided to reduce consumption and increase investment.
   a How would this change affect economic growth?
   b Would it matter what type of investment was undertaken?
   c What groups in society would benefit from this change? What groups might be hurt?

3 Australian income per person today is roughly four times what it was a century ago. Many other countries have also experienced significant growth over that period. What are some specific ways in which your standard of living differs from that of your great-grandparents? Is your standard of living higher in every regard?

4 The chapter discusses how employment has declined relative to output in the farm sector. Can you think of another sector of the economy where the same phenomenon has occurred more recently? Would you consider the change in employment in this sector to represent a success or a failure from the standpoint of society as a whole?

5 Ten years ago, government expenditure on research and development (R&D) was greater than business expenditure on R&D. In 2008–09, business expenditure on R&D was much greater than the government's.
   a What changes in government policy could have led to this change?
   b Does it matter whether the investment in R&D is undertaken by the government or by business? Explain.
   c Sweden, Finland, Japan and Korea all had business expenditure on R&D of over 2.5 per cent of GDP, whereas Australia's business expenditure on R&D was 1.3 per cent. What would you expect the differences to be in the growth rates of the five countries? Explain.

6 What is the opportunity cost of investing in capital? Do you think a country can 'over-invest' in capital? What is the opportunity cost of investing in human capital? Do you think a country can 'over-invest' in human capital? Explain.

7 Suppose that a car manufacturing company owned entirely by German citizens opens a new factory in Chengdu, China.
   a What sort of foreign investment would this represent?
   b What would be the effect of this investment on Chinese GDP? Would the effect on Chinese GNP be larger or smaller?
   c Many productive resources were destroyed in the earthquake in Chengdu, China in April 2008. What would this do to Chinese GDP in 2008? What would it do to Chinese GDP in the years following 2008?

8 In the past decade, China has become the biggest recipient of foreign direct investment among developing economies. In other words, more foreign investment flows into China than into any other developing (and more than many developed) economies.
   a Would the Chinese government be pleased at these developments? Why or why not?
   b What are the long-term benefits to the Chinese economy of receiving investment from overseas companies?

616

9 When the Taliban were in power in Afghanistan, there were many restrictions on girls receiving an education. There has been some relaxation of restrictions since 2002, but some provinces still won't allow girls to be taught by men. What is the economic impact of policies such as these? How do they affect Afghanistan's economic development potential?

10 Different governments grant patents for different numbers of years. How do you think this affects in which countries multinational corporations conduct their research? Suppose governments everywhere reduced the number of years a patent lasts. What would be the effect of this change on the incentive to do research? Could this change produce a decline in the growth rate of GDP? Explain.

11 International data show a positive correlation between political stability and economic growth.
   a Through what mechanism could political stability lead to strong economic growth?
   b Through what mechanism could strong economic growth lead to political stability?

Search me!

  Search me!

When accessing information about economics use the following keywords in any combinations you require:

• catch-up effect
• production function

CourseMate

 CourseMate

For more multimedia resources and activities on economics, visit the Economics CourseMate website.

27

Saving, investment and the financial system

Learning objectives

In this chapter you will:

- learn about some of the important financial institutions in the Australian economy

- consider how the financial system is related to key macroeconomic variables

- develop a model of the supply of and demand for loanable funds in financial markets

- use the loanable funds model to analyse various government policies

- consider how government budget deficits affect the Australian economy.

Imagine that you have just graduated from university (with a degree in economics, of course) and you decide to start your own business – an economic forecasting firm. Before you make any money selling your forecasts, you have to incur substantial costs to set up your business. You have to buy computers with which to make your forecasts, as well as desks, chairs and filing cabinets to furnish your new office. Each of these is a type of capital that your firm will use to produce and sell its services.

How do you obtain the funds to invest in these capital goods? Perhaps you are able to pay for them out of your past savings. More likely, however, like most entrepreneurs, you do not have enough money of your own to finance the start of your business. As a result, you have to get the money you need from other sources.

There are various ways for you to finance these capital investments. You could borrow the money, perhaps from a bank or from a friend or relative. In this case, you would promise not only to return the money at a later date but also to pay interest for the use of the money. Alternatively, you could convince someone to provide the money you need for your business in exchange for a share of your future profits, whatever they might happen to be. In either case, your investment in computers and office equipment is being financed by someone else's saving.

The **financial system** consists of those institutions in the economy that help to match one person's saving with another person's investment. As we discussed in the previous chapter, saving and investment are key ingredients to economic growth. When a country saves a large portion of its GDP, more resources are available for investment in capital, and higher capital raises a country's productivity and living standard. But that chapter did not explain how the economy coordinates saving and investment. At any time, some people want to save some of their income for the future and others want to borrow in order to finance investments in new and growing businesses. What brings these two groups of people together? What ensures that the supply of funds from those who want to save balances the demand for funds from those who want to invest?

financial system
the group of institutions in the economy that help to match one person's saving with another person's investment

This chapter examines how the financial system works. First, we discuss the large variety of institutions that make up the financial system in our economy. Second, we discuss the relationship between the financial system and some key macroeconomic variables – notably saving and investment. Third, we develop a model of the supply of and demand for funds in financial markets. In the model, the interest rate is the price that adjusts to balance supply and demand. The model shows how various government policies affect the interest rate and, thereby, society's allocation of scarce resources.

Financial institutions in the Australian economy

At the broadest level, the financial system moves the economy's scarce resources from savers (people who spend less than they earn) to borrowers (people who spend more than they earn). Savers save for various reasons – to put a child through university in several years or to retire comfortably in several decades. Similarly, borrowers borrow for various reasons – to buy a house in which to live or to start a business with which to make a living. Savers supply their money to the financial system with the expectation that they will get it back with interest at a later date. Borrowers demand money from the financial system with the knowledge that they will be required to pay it back with interest at a later date.

The financial system is made up of various financial institutions that help coordinate savers and borrowers. As a prelude to analysing the economic forces that drive the financial system, let's discuss the most important of these institutions. Financial institutions can be grouped into two categories – financial markets and financial intermediaries. We consider each category in turn.

Financial markets

financial markets
financial institutions through which savers can directly provide funds to borrowers

Financial markets are the institutions through which a person who wants to save can directly supply funds to a person who wants to borrow. The two most important financial markets in our economy are the bond market and the stock market.

▶ Australian financial institutions

bond (security)
a certificate of indebtedness

The bond market

When BHP Billiton, the big international resources company, wants to borrow to finance construction of a new coal mine, it can borrow directly from the public. It does this by selling bonds. A **bond (security)** is a certificate of indebtedness that specifies the obligations of the borrower to the holder of the bond. Put simply, a bond is just an IOU. It identifies the time at which the loan will be repaid, called the *date of maturity*, and the rate of interest that will be paid periodically until the loan matures. Buyers of bonds give their money to BHP Billiton in exchange for the promise of interest and eventual repayment of the amount borrowed (called the principal). Buyers can hold the bonds until maturity or sell them at an earlier date to someone else.

There are literally hundreds of different kinds of bonds in the Australian economy. When large corporations or the federal or state governments need to borrow to finance the purchase of a new factory or a new jet fighter, they usually do so by issuing bonds. If you look at the *Australian Financial Review* or the Australian Securities Exchange website (www.asx.com.au), you will find a listing of the prices and interest rates on some of the most important bond issues. Although these bonds differ in many ways, three characteristics of bonds are most important.

The first characteristic is a bond's *term* – the length of time until the bond matures. Some bonds have short terms, such as a few months, and others have terms as long as 100 years. (The British government has even issued a bond that never matures, called a *perpetuity*. This bond pays interest forever, but the principal is never repaid.) The interest rate on a bond depends, in part, on its term. Long-term bonds are riskier than short-term bonds because holders of long-term bonds have to wait longer for repayment of principal. If a holder of a long-term bond needs the money earlier than the distant date of maturity, the buyer has no choice but to sell the bond to someone else, perhaps at a reduced price. To compensate for this risk, long-term bonds usually pay higher interest rates than short-term bonds.

The second important characteristic of a bond is its *credit risk* – the probability that the borrower will fail to pay some of the interest or principal. Such a failure to pay is called a *default*. Borrowers can (and sometimes do) default on their loans by declaring bankruptcy. When bond buyers perceive that the probability of default is high, they demand a higher interest rate to compensate them for this risk. Because the Australian government is considered a safe credit risk, government bonds tend to pay low interest rates. In contrast, financially shaky corporations raise money by issuing *junk bonds*, which pay very high interest rates. Buyers of bonds can judge credit risk by checking with various private credit-rating agencies, such as Standard & Poor's or Moody's, which rate the credit risk of different bonds.

The third important characteristic of a bond is its *tax treatment* – the way in which the tax laws treat the interest earned on the bond. The interest on most bonds is taxable income, so the bond owner has to pay a portion of the interest in income taxes. In some countries, state and local governments issue bonds. When state and local governments issue bonds in the United States, called *municipal bonds*, the bond owners are not required to pay federal income tax on the interest income. Because of this tax advantage, bonds issued by state and local governments in the United States pay a lower interest rate than bonds issued by corporations or the federal government. However, in Australia, interest earned on bonds is treated as any other type of income and taxed at the normal rate.

The stock market

Another way for BHP Billiton to raise funds to build a new coal mine is to sell shares in the company. Shares represent ownership in a firm and are, therefore, a claim to the profits that the firm makes. For example, if BHP Billiton sells a total of 1 000 000 shares, then each share represents ownership of 1/1 000 000 of the business.

share
a claim to partial ownership in a firm

The sale of shares to raise money is called *equity finance*, whereas the sale of bonds is called *debt finance*. Although corporations use both equity and debt finance to raise money for new investments, shares and bonds are very different. The owner of shares in BHP Billiton is a part-owner of BHP Billiton; the owner of a BHP Billiton bond is a creditor of the corporation. If BHP Billiton is very profitable, the shareholders enjoy the benefits of these profits, whereas the bondholders get only the interest on their bonds. And if BHP Billiton runs into financial difficulty, the bondholders are paid what they are due before shareholders receive anything at all. Compared with bonds, shares offer the holder both higher risk and potentially higher return.

After a corporation sells shares to the public, these shares trade among shareholders on organised stock exchanges. In these transactions, the corporation itself receives no money when its shares change hands. The most important stock exchange in the Australian economy is the Australian Stock Exchange (ASX), but our stock market is also influenced by stock markets overseas. Some of the important overseas markets are the New York Stock Exchange, the American Stock Exchange, and NASDAQ (National Association of Securities Dealers Automated Quotation system) in the United States, the Tokyo Stock Exchange, the Stock Exchange of Hong Kong and the London Stock Exchange. Most of the world's countries have their own stock exchanges on which the shares of local companies trade.

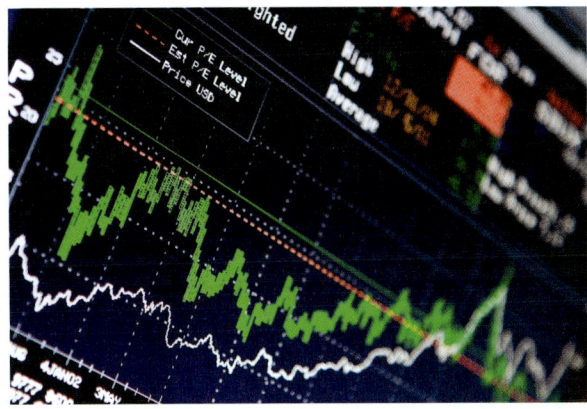

Source: iStockphoto/Tom Fewster.

The prices at which shares trade on stock exchanges are determined by the supply of and demand for the shares in these companies. Because shares represent ownership in a corporation, the demand for a share (and thus its price) reflects people's perception of the corporation's future profitability. When people become optimistic about a company's future, they raise their demand for its shares and thereby bid up the price of a share. Conversely, when people come to expect a company to have little profit or even losses, the price of a share falls.

Various share indexes are available to monitor the overall level of share prices. A share index is calculated as an average of a group of share prices. The Australian share index is the All Ordinaries, which is an index of common shares listed on the Australian Stock Exchange. One of the world's most famous share indexes is the Dow Jones Industrial Average in the United States, which has been

How to read the newspaper's share tables

Most daily newspapers include share tables, which contain information about recent trading in the shares of several thousand companies. Many websites also contain this information. For example, the Australian Stock Exchange website, www.asx.com.au, provides share prices for all its listed companies. Here is the kind of information these tables usually provide.

- *Price.* The single most important piece of information about a share is its price. The newspaper usually presents several prices. The 'last' or 'closing' price is the price of the last transaction that occurred before the stock exchange closed the previous day. Many newspapers also give the 'high' and 'low' prices over the past day of trading and, sometimes, over the past year as well.

- *Volume.* Most newspapers present the number of shares sold during the past week of trading. This figure is called the *weekly volume.*

- *Dividend.* Corporations pay out some of their profits to their shareholders; this amount is called the *dividend.* (Profits not paid out are called *retained profits* and are used by the corporation for additional investment.) Newspapers often report the dividend paid over the previous year for each share. They sometimes report the *dividend yield,* which is the dividend

expressed as a percentage of the share's price.

- *Price–earnings ratio.* A corporation's profit is the amount of revenue it receives for the sale of its products minus its costs of production as measured by its accountants. Some of the profits are used to pay dividends; the rest is kept in the firm to make new investments. The price–earnings ratio, often called the P/E ratio, is the price of a corporation's share divided by the amount the corporation earned per share over the past year. Historically, the typical price–earnings ratio is about 15. A higher P/E indicates that a corporation's shares are expensive relative to its recent earnings; this might indicate either that people expect earnings to rise in the future or that the shares are overvalued. Conversely, a lower P/E indicates that a corporation's shares are cheap relative to its recent earnings; this might indicate either that people expect earnings to fall or that the shares are undervalued.

Why does the newspaper report all these data every day? Many people who invest their savings in shares follow these numbers closely when deciding which shares to buy and sell. In contrast, other shareholders follow a buy-and-hold strategy – they buy the shares of well-run companies, hold them for long periods of time and do not respond to the daily fluctuations reported in the newspaper.

Symbol for company's shares	Name of company	Total value of all shares traded		Highest and lowest price of the shares over the past year		Increase or decrease in price in the last week		Dividend yield	
ASX Code	Stock	Market Capital $m	Last Sale Price	12 Months		%	Price/ Earnings Ratio	Div Yield %	Daily Volumes (000s)
				High	Low				
ANZ	ANZ Banking Group	61.611	23.76	26.23	19.95	2.33	16.6	4.49	4 063
BHP	BHP Billiton Ltd	137.599	41.54	44.93	35.58	3.76	15.3	2.32	3 291
CBA	Commonwealth Bank	79.178	51.02	60.00	47.05	0.43	14.8	5.67	1 035
FGL	Foster's Group Ltd	11.855	6.03	6.44	5.11	-0.16	–	1.95	4 531
NAB	National Australia Bank	54.934	25.46	32.37	22.23	2.91	12.9	5.71	1 760
RIO	Rio Tinto Ltd	48.273	82.47	81.25	58.86	3.12	17.1	1.27	1 240
TLS	Telstra Corp	33.099	2.68	3.55	2.60	0.75	8.5	10.53	12 884
WBC	Westpac Banking Group	69.291	22.9	28.43	20.56	1.08	16.7	5.39	3 356
WES	Wesfarmers	34.176	32.95	34.83	25.80	3.24	25.1	3.68	349
WOW	Woolworths Ltd	36.711	28.96	30.57	25.19	2.53	18.1	3.87	991

calculated regularly since 1896. It is now based on the prices of the shares of 30 major US companies, such as General Motors, General Electric, Coca-Cola, AT&T and IBM. Other well-known share indexes include the Nikkei in Tokyo, the Hang Seng in Hong Kong, the FTSE in London and Standard & Poor's 500 Index in the United States. Because share prices reflect expected profitability, these share indexes are watched closely as possible indicators of future economic conditions.

Financial intermediaries

Financial intermediaries are financial institutions through which savers can indirectly provide funds to borrowers. The term *intermediary* reflects the role of these institutions in standing between savers and borrowers. Here we consider two of the most important financial intermediaries – banks and managed funds.

financial intermediaries
financial institutions through which savers can indirectly provide funds to borrowers

Banks

Chris owns a small grocery store and wants to finance a business expansion. The strategy taken is probably quite different from that of BHP Billiton. Unlike BHP Billiton, Chris would find it difficult to raise funds in the bond and stock markets. Most buyers of shares and bonds prefer to buy those issued by larger, more familiar companies. Chris, a small grocer, therefore, is most likely to finance his business expansion with a loan from a local bank.

Banks are the financial intermediaries with which people are most familiar. One of the main jobs of banks is to take in deposits from people who want to save and use these deposits to make loans to people who want to borrow. Banks pay depositors interest on their deposits and charge borrowers slightly higher interest on their loans. The difference between these rates of interest covers the banks' costs and returns some profit to the owners of the banks.

Besides being financial intermediaries, banks play a second important role in the economy – they facilitate purchases of goods and services by allowing people to write cheques against their deposits. In other words, banks help create a special asset that people can use as a *medium of exchange*. A medium of exchange is an item that people can easily use to make payments. A bank's role in providing a medium of exchange distinguishes it from many other financial institutions. Shares and bonds, like bank deposits, are a possible *store of value* for the wealth that people have accumulated in past saving, but access to this wealth is not as easy, cheap and immediate as just writing a cheque. For now, we ignore this second role of banks, but we will return to it when we discuss the monetary system in a later chapter.

Managed funds

A financial intermediary of increasing importance in the Australian economy is the managed fund. A **managed fund** is a type of financial investment that allows investors to own a selection, or *portfolio*, of various types of shares, bonds, or both shares and bonds without buying them individually. When an individual investor puts money into a managed fund, a manager or trustee makes the decisions about which shares or bonds to purchase. However, the individual investor in the managed fund accepts all the risk and return associated with the portfolio. If the value of the portfolio rises, the investor benefits; if the value of the portfolio falls, the investor suffers the loss.

managed fund
a type of financial investment that allows investors to own a portfolio of various types of shares and/or bonds

The main advantage of managed funds is that they allow people with small amounts of money to diversify. Buyers of shares and bonds are well advised to heed the adage 'don't put all your eggs in one basket'. Because the value of any single share or bond is tied to the fortunes of one company, holding a single kind of share or bond is very risky. In contrast, people who hold a diverse portfolio of shares and bonds face less risk because they have only a small stake in each company. Managed funds make this diversification easy. With only a few hundred dollars, a person can buy shares in a managed fund and, indirectly, become the part owner or creditor of hundreds of major companies. For this service, the company operating the managed fund charges shareholders a fee, usually between 0.5 per cent and 2.0 per cent of assets each year.

A second advantage claimed by managed fund companies is that managed funds give ordinary people access to the skills of professional money managers. The managers of most managed funds pay close attention to the developments and prospects of the companies in which they buy shares. These managers buy the shares of those companies that they view as having a profitable future and sell the shares of companies with less promising prospects. This professional management, it is argued, should increase the return that managed fund depositors earn on their savings.

Financial economists, however, are often sceptical of this second argument. With thousands of money managers paying close attention to each company's prospects, the price of a company's share is usually a good reflection of the company's true value. As a result, it is hard to 'beat the market' by buying good shares and selling bad ones. In fact, managed funds called *index funds*, which buy all the shares in a given share index, perform somewhat better on average than managed funds that engage the services of professional money managers. The explanation for the superior performance of index funds is that they keep costs low by buying and selling very rarely and by not having to pay the salaries of the professional money managers.

Summing up

The Australian economy contains a large variety of financial institutions. In addition to the bond market, the stock market, banks and managed funds, there are also credit unions, insurance companies, and even the local loan shark. These institutions differ in many ways. When analysing the macroeconomic role of the financial system, however, it is more important to keep in mind the similarities of these institutions rather than the differences. These financial institutions all serve the same goal – directing the resources of savers into the hands of borrowers.

What are shares? What are bonds? How are they different? How are they similar?

IN THE NEWS . . .

TO BAIL OR LET THEM SINK?

In 2008, a New York-based global financial services company, Lehman Brothers, failed. This was a shock to the financial system, as there had not been a major financial house bankruptcy since the savings and loan failures of the late 1980s and early 1990s. Many commentators at the time predicted a collapse in the global financial system. While there have been major bank failures in the UK and Europe and several European economies have been in danger of defaulting on their loans, the global financial system has been remarkably resilient in the two years since Lehman Brothers collapsed. The US government undertook to stabilise the US financial system (and by extension, the global financial system) by providing liquidity to those banks who were in danger of failing in late 2008. There is ongoing debate about whether or not the government should have done this. In the following two articles, we hear both sides – the 'teach them a lesson and let them sink' school of thought and the 'liquidity and confidence are crucial to the smooth operation of the economy, so bail them out' point of view.

Don't reward bad behaviour

U.S. bank bailout encourages risky behavior – watchdog

Washington, Jan 30 (Reuters) – The U.S. taxpayer-funded rescue program set up to save banks from collapse during the financial crisis makes future reckless behavior more likely, the government's bailout watchdog said in a quarterly report.

A quarterly report to Congress on the $700 billion Troubled Asset Relief Program, or TARP, made available in draft form late on Saturday, said financial firms seen as too big to fail before 2008 have only grown larger as they feasted on subsidies from the bailout program.

'To the extent that institutions were previously incentivized to take reckless risks through a "heads I win, tails the government will bail me out" mentality, the market is more convinced than ever that the government will step in as necessary to save systemically significant institutions,' the report from the Office of the Special Inspector General for the Troubled Asset Relief Program, said.

The office, headed by Neil Barofsky, acts as a watchdog for taxpayers over how TARP money the Treasury Department administers is used.

The report said little has been achieved in terms of correcting underlying problems that helped create the financial crisis.

'Even if TARP saved our financial system from driving off a cliff in 2008, absent meaningful reform, we are still driving on the same winding mountain road, but this time in a faster car,' it warned.

The report noted that TARP, which was originally pitched to Congress as a way to help banks by buying toxic or unwanted assets and then, when Congress approved it, turned into a plan for injecting capital into banks, is changing again.

'Treasury has stated that, going forward, TARP will focus on foreclosure mitigation efforts, small-business lending, and a continuation of support for the asset-backed securities markets,' the report said.

With some banks already repaying TARP capital, it appears that taxpayers' ultimate costs may be less than initially feared but many of the program's goals are not being met.

The report noted, for example, that while TARP was supposed to encourage banks to increase financing for U.S. businesses and consumers, lending is actually decreasing on a month-by-month basis.

Source: Reported by Glenn Somerville, edited by Leslie Adler, 1 February 2010, Thomson Reuters.

In favour of the bank bailout:

The fire next time
by Paul Krugman

On Tuesday, Mitch McConnell, the Senate minority leader, called for the abolition of municipal fire departments.

Firefighters, he declared, 'won't solve the problems that led to recent fires. They will make them worse.' The existence of fire departments, he went on, 'not only allows for taxpayer-funded bailouts of burning buildings; it institutionalizes them.' He concluded,

'The way to solve this problem is to let the people who make the mistakes that lead to fires pay for them. We won't solve this problem until the biggest buildings are allowed to burn.'

O.K., I fibbed a bit. Mr. McConnell said almost everything I attributed to him, but he was talking about financial reform, not fire reform. In particular, he was objecting not to the existence of fire departments, but to legislation that would give the government the power to seize and restructure failing financial institutions.

But it amounts to the same thing.

Now, Mr. McConnell surely isn't sincere; while pretending to oppose bank bailouts, he's actually doing the bankers' bidding. But before I get to that, let's talk about why he's wrong on substance.

In his speech, Mr. McConnell seemed to be saying that in the future, the U.S. government should just let banks fail. We 'must put an end to taxpayer funded bailouts for Wall Street banks.' What's wrong with that?

The answer is that letting banks fail – as opposed to seizing and restructuring them – is a bad idea for the same reason that it's a bad idea to stand aside while an urban office building burns. In both cases, the damage has a

tendency to spread. In 1930, U.S. officials stood aside as banks failed; the result was the Great Depression. In 2008, they stood aside as Lehman Brothers imploded; within days, credit markets had frozen and we were staring into the economic abyss.

So it's crucial to avoid disorderly bank collapses, just as it's crucial to avoid out-of-control urban fires.

Saving and investment in the national income accounts

Events that occur within the financial system are central to understanding developments in the overall economy. As we have just seen, the institutions that make up this system – the bond market, the stock market, banks and managed funds – have the role of coordinating the economy's saving and investment. And as we saw in the previous chapter, saving and investment are important determinants of long-run growth in GDP and living standards. As a result, macroeconomists need to understand how financial markets work and how various events and policies affect them.

As a starting point for an analysis of financial markets, we discuss in this section the key macroeconomic variables that measure activity in these markets. Our emphasis here is not on behaviour but on accounting. *Accounting* refers to how various numbers are defined and added up. A personal accountant might help individuals add up their income and expenses. A national income accountant does the same thing for the economy as a whole. The national income accounts include, in particular, GDP and the many related statistics.

The rules of national income accounting include several important identities. Recall that an *identity* is an equation that must be true because of the way the variables in the equation are defined. Identities are useful to keep in mind, for they clarify how different variables are related to one another. Here we consider some accounting identities that shed light on the macroeconomic role of financial markets.

Some important identities

Recall that gross domestic product (GDP) is both total income in an economy and the total expenditure on the economy's output of goods and services in a given period of time. GDP (denoted as Y) is divided into four components of expenditure: consumption (C), investment (I), government purchases (G) and net exports (NX). We write:

$$Y = C + I + G + NX$$

This equation is an identity because every dollar of expenditure that shows up on the left-hand side also shows up in one of the four components on the right-hand side. Because of the way each of the variables is defined and measured, this equation must always hold.

In this chapter, we simplify our analysis by assuming that the economy we are examining is closed. A *closed economy* is one that does not interact with other economies. In particular, a closed economy does not engage in international trade in goods and services, nor does it engage in international borrowing and lending. Of course, actual economics are *open economies*, that is, they interact with other economies around the world. (We will examine the macroeconomics of open economies later in this book.) Nonetheless, assume a closed economy is a useful simplification with which we can learn some lessons that apply to all economies. Moreover, this assumption applies perfectly to the world economy (since interplanetary trade is not yet common).

Because a closed economy does not engage in international trade, imports and exports are exactly zero. Therefore, net exports (*NX*) are also zero. In this case, we can write:

$$Y = C + I + G$$

This equation states that GDP is the sum of consumption, investment and government purchases. Each unit of output sold in a closed economy is consumed, invested or bought by the government.

To see what this identity can tell us about financial markets, subtract *C* and *G* from both sides of this equation. We obtain:

$$Y - C - G = I$$

The left-hand side of this equation ($Y - C - G$) is the total income in the economy that remains after paying for consumption and government purchases. This amount is called **national saving**, or just **saving**, and is denoted *S*. Substituting *S* for $Y - C - G$, we can write the last equation as:

$$S = I$$

This equation states that saving equals investment.

To understand the meaning of national saving, it is helpful to manipulate the definition a bit more. Let *T* denote the amount that the government collects from households in taxes minus the amount it pays back to households in the form of transfer payments (such as pension benefits or social security payments). We can then write national saving in either of two ways:

$$S = Y - C - G$$

or

$$S = (Y - T - C) + (T - G)$$

These equations are the same, since the two *T*s in the second equation cancel each other, but each reveals a different way of thinking about national saving. In particular, the second equation separates national saving into two pieces: Private saving ($Y - T - C$) and public saving ($T - G$).

Consider each of these two pieces. **Private saving** is the amount of income that households have left after paying their taxes and paying for their consumption. In particular, because households receive income of *Y*, pay taxes of *T* and spend *C* on consumption, private saving is $Y - T - C$. **Public saving** is the amount of tax revenue that the government has left after paying for its spending. The government receives *T* in tax revenue and spends *G* on goods and services. If *T* exceeds *G*, the government runs a **budget surplus** because it receives more money than it spends. This surplus of $T - G$ represents public saving. If the government spends more than it receives in tax revenue (as has

national saving (saving)
the total income in the economy that remains after paying for consumption and government purchases

private saving
the income that households have left after paying for taxes and consumption

public saving
the tax revenue that the government has left after paying for its spending

budget surplus
an excess of tax revenue over government spending

628

budget deficit
when government spending
exceeds tax revenue

been the case for the most part until relatively recently), then *G* is larger than *T*. In this case, the government runs a **budget deficit**, and public saving *T – G* is a negative number.

Now consider how these accounting identities are related to financial markets. The equation *S = I* reveals an important fact – *for the economy as a whole, saving must be equal to investment.* Yet this fact raises some important questions. What mechanisms lie behind this identity? What coordinates those people who are deciding how much to save and those people who are deciding how much to invest? The answer is the financial system. The bond market, the stock market, banks, managed funds and other financial markets and intermediaries stand between the two sides of the *S = I* equation. They take in the nation's saving and channel it to the nation's investors.

The meaning of saving and investment

The terms *saving* and *investment* can sometimes be confusing. Most people use these terms casually and sometimes interchangeably. In contrast, the macroeconomists who put together the national income accounts use these terms carefully and distinctly.

Consider an example. Suppose that Larry earns more than he spends and deposits his unspent income in a bank or uses it to buy a bond or some shares from a corporation. Because Larry's income exceeds his consumption, he adds to the nation's saving. Larry might think of himself as 'investing' his money, but a macroeconomist would call Larry's act 'saving' rather than 'investment'.

In the language of macroeconomics, investment refers to the purchase of new capital, such as equipment or buildings. When Moe borrows from the bank to build himself a new house, he adds to the nation's investment. Similarly, when the Curly Corporation sells some shares and uses the proceeds to build a new factory, it also adds to the nation's investment.

Although the accounting identity *S = I* shows that saving and investment are equal for the economy as a whole, this does not have to be true for every individual household or firm. Larry's saving can be greater than his investment, and he can deposit the excess in a bank. Moe's saving can be less than his investment and he can borrow the shortfall from a bank. Banks and other financial institutions make these individual differences between saving and investment possible by allowing one person's saving to finance another person's investment.

Define private saving, public saving, national saving and investment. How are they related?

The market for loanable funds

market for loanable funds
the market in which those who want to save supply funds and those who want to borrow to invest demand funds

Having discussed some of the important financial institutions in our economy and the macroeconomic role of these institutions, we are ready to build a model of financial markets. Our purpose in building this model is to explain how financial markets coordinate the economy's saving and investment. The model also gives us a tool with which we can analyse various government policies that influence saving and investment.

▸ market for loanable funds

To keep things simple, we assume that the economy has only one financial market, called the **market for loanable funds**. All savers go to this market to deposit their savings and all borrowers go to this market to get their loans. In this market there is one interest rate, which is both the return on saving and the cost of borrowing.

The assumption of a single financial market, of course, is not literally true. As we have seen, the economy has many types of financial institutions. But, as we discussed in chapter 2, the art in building an economic model is simplifying the world in order to explain it. For our purposes here, we can ignore the diversity of financial institutions and assume that the economy has a single financial market.

Supply of and demand for loanable funds

The economy's market for loanable funds, like other markets in the economy, is governed by supply and demand. To understand how the market for loanable funds operates, therefore, we first look at the sources of supply and demand in that market.

The supply of loanable funds comes from those people who have some extra income they want to save and lend out, and from the government when government revenue is in excess of government expenditure. This lending can occur directly, such as when a household buys a bond from a firm, or it can occur indirectly, such as when a household makes a deposit in a bank which in turn uses the funds to make loans. In both cases, saving is the source of the supply of loanable funds.

The demand for loanable funds comes from households and firms who wish to borrow to make investments. This demand includes families taking out mortgages to buy homes. It also includes firms borrowing to buy new equipment or build factories. In both cases, investment is the source of the demand for loanable funds.

The interest rate is the price of a loan. It represents the amount that borrowers pay for loans and the amount that lenders receive on their saving. Because a high interest rate makes borrowing more expensive, the quantity of loanable funds demanded falls as the interest rate rises. Similarly, because a high interest rate makes saving more attractive, the quantity of loanable funds supplied rises as the interest rate rises. In other words, the demand curve for loanable funds slopes downwards and the supply curve for loanable funds slopes upwards.

Figure 27.1 shows the interest rate that balances the supply of and demand for loanable funds. In the equilibrium shown, the interest rate is 5 per cent, and the quantity of loanable funds demanded and the quantity of loanable funds supplied both equal $1200 million. The adjustment of the interest rate to the equilibrium level occurs for the usual reasons. If the interest rate were lower than the equilibrium level, the quantity of loanable funds supplied would be less than the quantity of loanable funds demanded. The resulting shortage of loanable funds would encourage lenders to raise the interest rate they charge. Conversely, if the interest rate were higher than the equilibrium level, the quantity of loanable funds supplied would exceed the quantity of loanable funds demanded. As lenders competed for the scarce borrowers, interest rates would be driven down. In this way, the interest rate approaches the equilibrium level at which the supply of and demand for loanable funds exactly balance.

Recall that economists distinguish between the real interest rate and the nominal interest rate. The nominal interest rate is the interest rate as usually reported – the monetary return on saving and the cost of borrowing. The real interest rate is the nominal interest rate corrected for inflation; it equals the nominal interest rate minus the inflation rate. Because inflation erodes the value of money over time, the real interest rate more accurately reflects the real return on saving and the cost of borrowing. Therefore, the supply of and demand for loanable funds depend on the real (rather than nominal) interest rate, and the equilibrium in Figure 27.1 should be interpreted as determining the real interest rate in the economy. For the rest of this chapter, when you see the term *interest rate*, you should remember that we are talking about the real interest rate.

This model of the supply of and demand for loanable funds shows that financial markets work much like other markets in the economy. In the market for milk, for instance, the price of milk

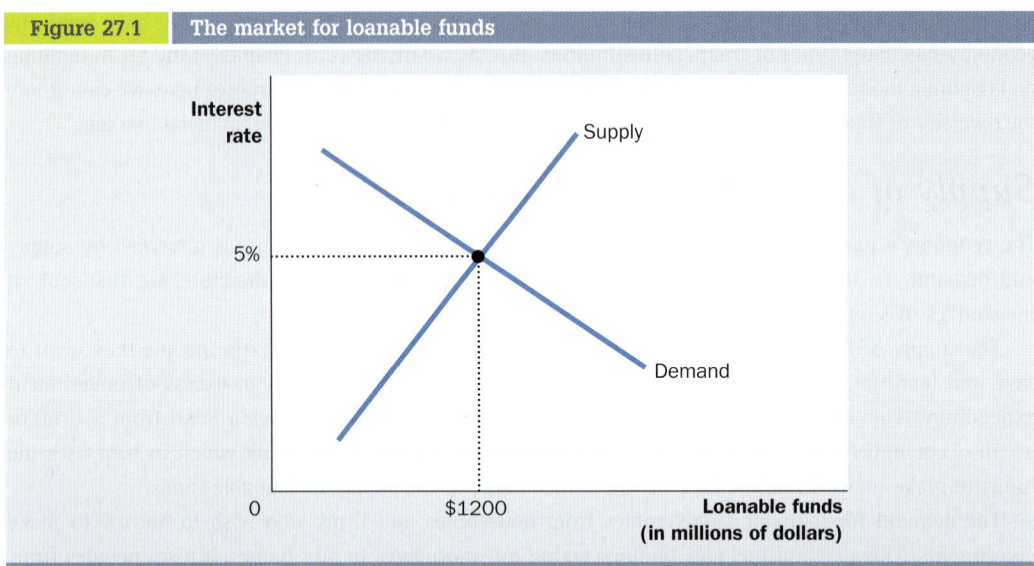

Figure 27.1 | The market for loanable funds

The interest rate in the economy adjusts to balance the supply of and demand for loanable funds. The supply of loanable funds comes from national saving, including both private saving and public saving. The demand for loanable funds comes from firms and households who want to borrow for purposes of investment. Here the equilibrium interest rate is 5 per cent and $1200 million of loanable funds are supplied and demanded.

adjusts so that the quantity of milk supplied balances the quantity of milk demanded. In this way, the invisible hand coordinates the behaviour of dairy farmers and the behaviour of milk drinkers. Once we realise that saving represents the supply of loanable funds and investment represents the demand, we can see how the invisible hand coordinates saving and investment. When the interest rate adjusts to balance supply and demand in the market for loanable funds, it coordinates the behaviour of people who want to save (the suppliers of loanable funds) and the behaviour of people who want to invest (the demanders of loanable funds).

We can now use this analysis of the market for loanable funds to examine various government policies that affect the economy's saving and investment. Because this model is just supply and demand in a particular market, we analyse any policy using the three steps discussed in chapter 4. First, we decide whether the policy shifts the supply curve or the demand curve. Second, we determine the direction of the shift. Third, we use the supply-and-demand diagram to see how the equilibrium changes.

Policy 1: Taxes and saving

Australian families save a smaller fraction of their incomes than their counterparts in many other countries, such as Japan and Germany. Although the reasons for these international differences are unclear, many Australian policymakers view the low level of Australian saving as a major problem. One of the *Ten Lessons from Economics* in chapter 1 is that a country's standard of living depends on its ability to produce goods and services. And, as we discussed in the last chapter, saving is an important long-run determinant of a nation's productivity. If Australia could somehow raise its saving rate to the level that prevails in other countries, the growth rate of GDP would increase and, over time, Australian citizens would enjoy a higher standard of living.

Another of the *Ten Lessons from Economics* is that people respond to incentives. Many economists have used this principle to suggest that the low saving rate in Australia is at least partly attributable to tax laws that discourage saving. The Australian government collects revenue by taxing income, including interest and dividend income. To see the effects of this policy, consider a 25-year-old who saves $1000 and buys a 30-year bond that pays an interest rate of 9 per cent. In the absence of taxes, the $1000 grows to $13 268 when the individual reaches age 55. Yet if that interest is taxed at a rate of, say, 33 per cent, then the after-tax interest rate is only 6 per cent. In this case, the $1000 grows to only $5743 after 30 years. The tax on interest income substantially reduces the future payoff from current saving and, as a result, reduces the incentive for people to save.

In response to this problem, many economists and lawmakers have proposed changing the tax laws to encourage greater saving. In 1993, for instance, then Opposition Leader John Hewson proposed replacing the current system of wholesale taxes with a consumption tax or goods and services tax (GST), and lowering income tax rates. Although John Hewson wasn't successful in his bid for the prime minister's job, John Howard was re-elected as prime minister in 1998 with another proposal for a GST. Under the consumption tax that John Howard introduced, income that is saved is not taxed until the saving is later spent. Many countries have something similar to a GST; in Europe it is referred to as a VAT or value-added tax. More modest proposals have included reduced taxes on contributions to superannuation funds that allow people to shelter some of their saving from taxation. Let's consider the effect of such a saving incentive on the market for loanable funds, as illustrated in Figure 27.2.

Figure 27.2   **An increase in the supply of loanable funds**

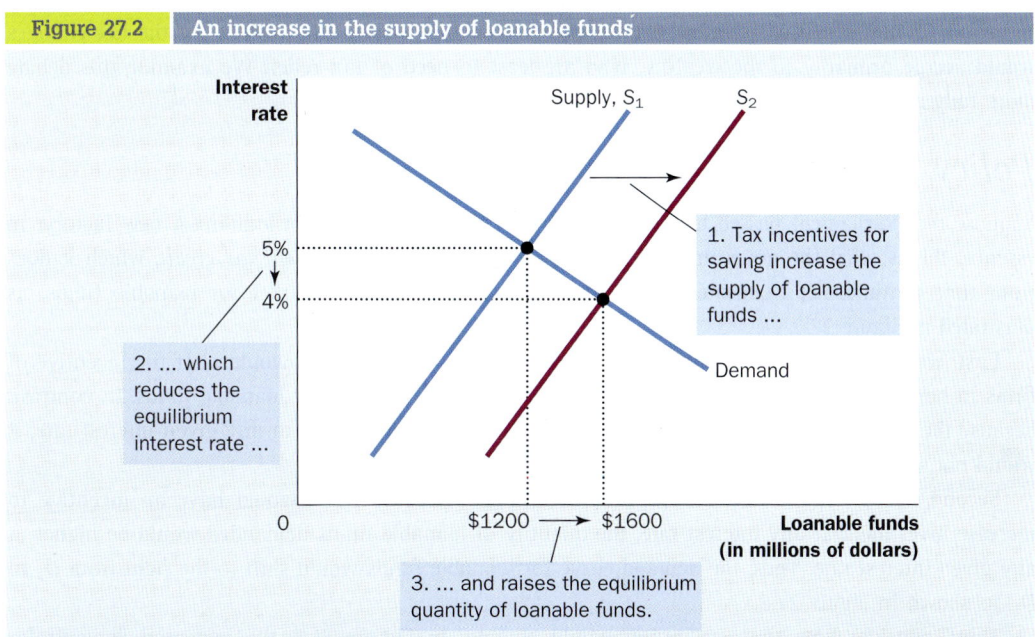

A change in the tax laws to encourage Australians to save more would shift the supply of loanable funds to the right from S_1 to S_2. As a result, the equilibrium interest rate would fall, and the lower interest rate would stimulate investment. Here the equilibrium interest rates falls from 5 per cent to 4 per cent, and the equilibrium quantity of loanable funds saved and invested rises from $1200 million to $1600 million.

First, which curve would this policy affect? Because the tax change would alter the incentive for households to save *at any given interest rate*, it would affect the quantity of loanable funds supplied at each interest rate. Thus, the supply of loanable funds would shift. Because the tax change would not directly affect the amount that borrowers want to borrow at any given interest rate, the demand for loanable funds would be unchanged.

Second, which way would the supply curve shift? Because saving would be taxed less heavily than under current law, households would increase their saving by consuming a smaller fraction of their income. Households would use this additional saving to increase their deposits in banks or to buy more bonds. The supply of loanable funds would increase and the supply curve would shift to the right from S_1 to S_2, as shown in Figure 27.2.

Finally, we compare the old and new equilibria. In the figure, the increased supply of loanable funds reduces the interest rate from 5 per cent to 4 per cent. The lower interest rate raises the quantity of loanable funds demanded from $1200 million to $1600 million. That is, the shift in the supply curve moves the market equilibrium along the demand curve. With a lower cost of borrowing, households and firms are motivated to borrow more to finance greater investment. Thus, *if a change in the tax laws encouraged greater saving, the result would be lower interest rates and greater investment.*

Although this analysis of the effects of increased saving is widely accepted among economists, there is less consensus about what kinds of tax changes should be enacted. Many economists endorse tax reform aimed at increasing saving in order to stimulate investment and growth. Yet others are sceptical that these tax changes would have much effect on national saving. These sceptics also doubt the equity of the proposed reforms. They argue that, in many cases, the benefits of the tax changes would accrue primarily to the wealthy, who are least in need of tax relief. We examine this debate more fully in the final chapter of this book.

Policy 2: Taxes and investment

Suppose that Parliament passed a law giving a tax reduction to any firm building a new factory. In essence, this is what the government does when it institutes an *investment tax credit*, which it does from time to time. Let's consider the effect of such a law on the market for loanable funds, as illustrated in Figure 27.3.

First, would the law affect supply or demand? Because the tax credit would alter the incentive of firms to borrow and invest in new capital, it would alter the demand for loanable funds. In contrast, because the tax credit would not affect the amount that households save at any given interest rate, it would not affect the supply of loanable funds.

Second, which way would the demand curve shift? Because firms would have an incentive to increase investment at any interest rate, the quantity of loanable funds demanded would be higher at any given interest rate. Thus, the demand curve for loanable funds would shift to the right from D_1 to D_2, as shown in Figure 27.3.

Third, consider how the equilibrium would change. In Figure 27.3, the increased demand for loanable funds raises the interest rate from 5 per cent to 6 per cent and the higher interest rate in turn increases the quantity of loanable funds supplied from $1200 million to $1400 million as households respond by increasing the amount they save. This change in household behaviour is represented here as a movement along the supply curve. Thus, *if a change in the tax laws encouraged greater investment, the result would be higher interest rates and greater saving.*

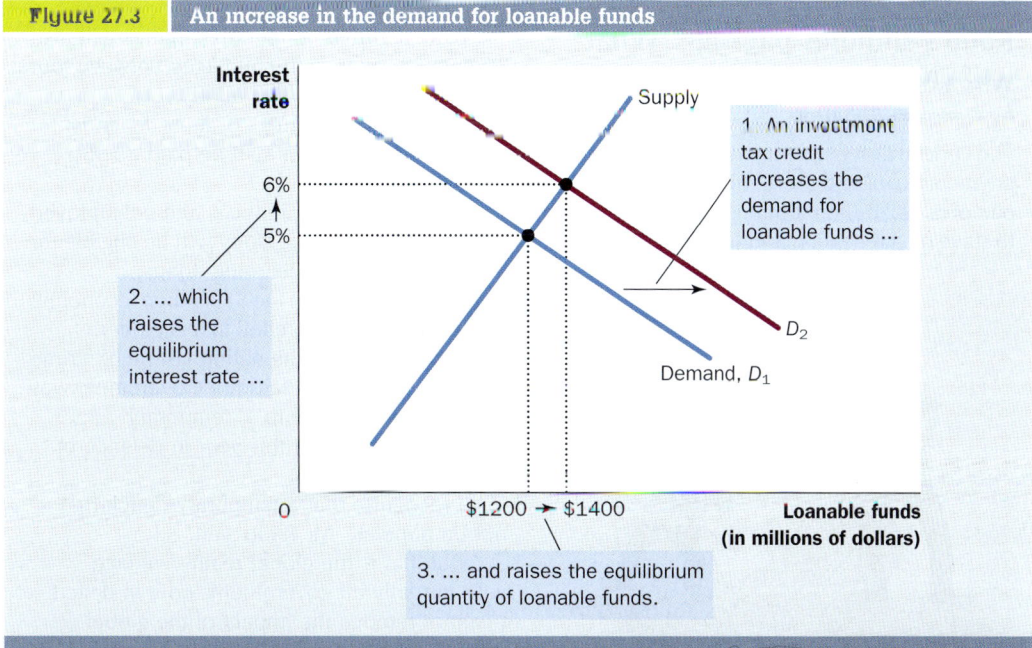

Figure 27.3 An increase in the demand for loanable funds

Interest rate

Supply

6%
5%

1 An investment tax credit increases the demand for loanable funds ...

D_2

Demand, D_1

2. ... which raises the equilibrium interest rate ...

0    $1200 → $1400   Loanable funds (in millions of dollars)

3. ... and raises the equilibrium quantity of loanable funds.

If the passage of an investment tax credit encouraged Australian firms to invest more, the demand for loanable funds would increase. As a result, the equilibrium interest rate would rise and the higher interest rate would stimulate saving. Here, when the demand curve shifts from D_1 to D_2, the equilibrium interest rate rises from 5 per cent to 6 per cent and the equilibrium quantity of loanable funds saved and invested rises from $1200 million to $1400 million.

Policy 3: Government budgets: Surplus or deficit?

One of the most pressing policy issues of the past decade has been the size of the government budget surplus. When the government takes in more revenue than it spends, the excess is called the *budget surplus*. When the government spends more than it receives in tax revenue, the shortfall is called the *budget deficit*. The accumulation of past budget deficits is called *government debt*. When a government runs a budget surplus, it can reduce the size of the accumulated government debt. Up until the global financial crisis (the GFC), the Australian government had run budget surpluses for several years. It had retired a significant proportion of the government's accumulated debt. Having created a surplus, it was in a good position to engage in some pump-priming (injecting expenditure into the economy to kick-start it) when the GFC hit.

IN THE NEWS ...

STIMULATING THE ECONOMY

The Rudd government introduced a stimulus package to boost consumer confidence and increase expenditure in the economy. The following article describes where the money went. Not everyone thought it was a great idea at the time, but 18 months after the initiative, there is some agreement that it helped keep consumers spending and prevented Australia from suffering more of a downturn than many other economies.

>>

Rudd's stimulus package: What will you get?

by Georgina Robinson

The Federal Government will dole out cash payments to more than 13 million Australians as part of its $42 billion stimulus package designed to stave off a recession and limit job losses.

Source: John Shakespeare/*The Sydney Morning Herald*, 2009.

Every one of the estimated 8.7 million Australian workers earning $100 000 or less will receive up to $950 as part of the plan, which also throws $26 billion at road, home and school building projects, the Government said.

From early April, anyone earning $80 000 or less will be paid the full $950; people earning between $80 000 and $90 000 will get $650; and those earning between $90 000 and $100 000 will receive $300.

You must have lodged a 2007–2008 tax return to receive the cash, to be paid from April.

Those who haven't yet lodged a return can do so until the end of June this year and still be eligible for their bonus.

Families will benefit, too. An additional $950 will be paid to an estimated 1.5 million single-income families where the main breadwinner earns up to $150 000.

Low- and middle-income families will also receive $950 for each child aged between four and 18 to help with education costs.

About 21 000 farmers or farm-dependent small business owners will be paid a $950 hardship bonus.

And students, apprentices and unemployed people who undertake study will be eligible for a $950 training and learning bonus.

The plan builds on the $10 billion 'economic security' package unveiled in December.

In an address to the nation last night, Prime Minister Kevin Rudd said the Government was prepared to plunge into a 'temporary' $22.5 billion budget deficit this year in defence of Australian jobs.

'I recognise that a temporary deficit may not be popular,' Mr Rudd said.

'But that is the global reality we face with virtually all governments now in deficit. I cannot remove the impact of the global recession on Australian jobs but by Government action we can reduce it.'

On another key front, 2.7 million homes will receive free ceiling insulation and the solar hot water rebate will be increased from $1000 to $1600 and will not be means-tested.

The Government says the measures will shave $200 a year off household energy bills and kick along a growing industry.

One building in all of the country's 9540 schools will be built or upgraded, 20 000 social housing dwellings will be built and 800 new Defence homes will be constructed.

The package also allocates $890 million to local road and national highway projects.

And small businesses buying eligible assets will receive a 30 cent-in-the-dollar investment tax break in a measure totalling $2.7 billion.

Source: Georgina Robinson/
The Sydney Morning Herald, 4 February 2009.

During national elections, there is always much debate about which party is more fiscally responsible. Let's consider the impact of a government that runs a budget deficit. We can analyse the effects of a budget deficit by following our three steps in the market for loanable funds, which is illustrated in Figure 27.4. First, which curve shifts when the budget deficit rises? Recall that national saving – the source of the supply of loanable funds – is composed of private saving and public

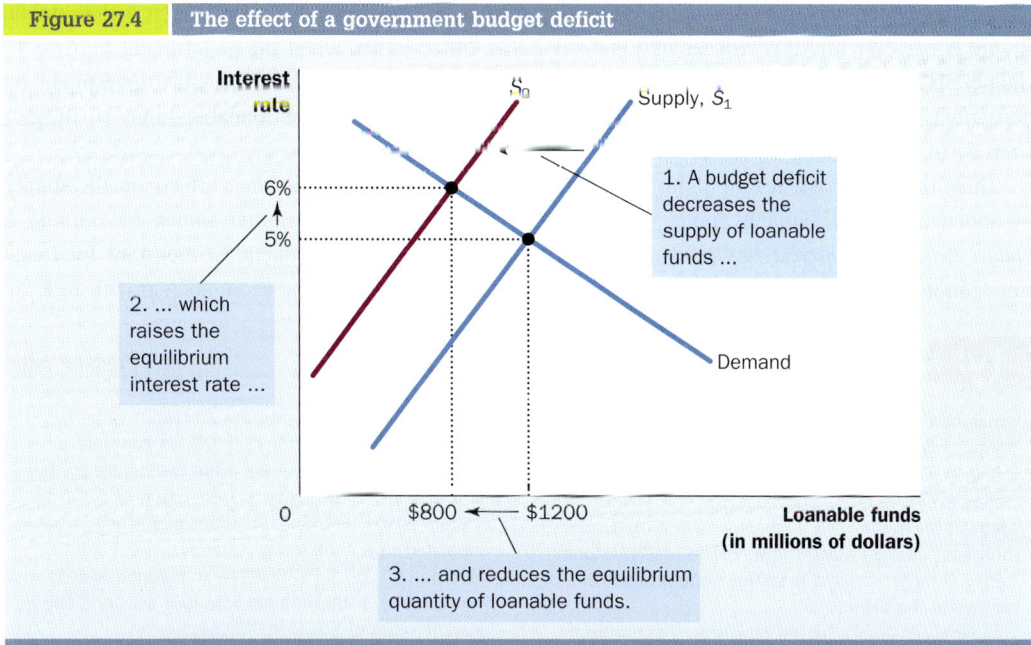

Figure 27.4 The effect of a government budget deficit

1. A budget deficit decreases the supply of loanable funds ...

2. ... which raises the equilibrium interest rate ...

3. ... and reduces the equilibrium quantity of loanable funds.

When the government spends more than it receives in tax revenue, the resulting budget deficit lowers national saving. The supply of loanable funds decreases and the equilibrium interest rate rises. Thus, when the government borrows to finance its budget deficit, it crowds out households and firms who otherwise would borrow to finance investment. Here, when the supply shifts from S_1 to S_2, the equilibrium interest rate rises from 5 per cent to 6 per cent and the equilibrium quantity of loanable funds saved and invested falls from $1200 million to $800 million.

saving. A change in the government budget deficit represents a change in public saving and, thereby, in the supply of loanable funds. Because the budget deficit does not influence the amount that households and firms want to borrow to finance investment at any given interest rate, it does not alter the demand for loanable funds.

CASE**STUDY**

The debate over the budget surplus

Our analysis shows why, other things being the same, budget surpluses are better for economic growth than budget deficits. Making economic policy, however, is not as simple as this observation may make it sound. A good example occurred in the late 1990s, when the Australian government found itself with a budget surplus, and much debate centred on what to do with it.

Many policymakers favoured using the budget surplus to retire government debt, rather than dissipating it with a spending increase or tax cut. They based their conclusion on the analysis we have just seen: Using the surplus to retire some of the government debt would stimulate private investment and economic growth.

Other policymakers took a different view. Some thought the surplus should be used to increase government spending on infrastructure and education because, they argued, the return to these public investments is greater than the typical return to private investment. Some thought taxes should be cut, arguing that lower tax rates would distort decision making less and lead to a more efficient allocation of resources.

The debate over whether we should have a budget surplus continues.

Second, which way does the supply curve shift? When the government runs a budget deficit, public saving is negative and this reduces national saving. In other words, when the government borrows to finance its budget deficit, it reduces the supply of loanable funds available to finance investment by households and firms. Thus, a budget deficit shifts the supply curve for loanable funds to the left from S_1 to S_2, as shown in Figure 27.4.

Thus, the most basic lesson about budget deficits follows directly from their effects on the supply of and demand for loanable funds – *when the government reduces national saving by running a budget deficit, the interest rate rises and investment falls.* Because investment is important for long-run economic growth, long-running government budget deficits reduce the economy's growth rate.

---

fyi   Present value

Imagine that someone offered to give you $100 today or $100 in 10 years. Which would you choose? This is an easy question. Getting $100 today is clearly better, because you can always deposit the money in a bank, still have it in 10 years and earn interest along the way. The lesson: Money today is more valuable than the same amount of money in the future.

Now consider a harder question: Imagine that someone offered you $100 today or $200 in 10 years. Which would you choose? To answer this question, you need some way to compare sums of money from different points of time. Economists do this with a concept called present value. The *present value* of any future sum of money is the amount today that would be needed, at current interest rates, to produce that future sum.

To learn how to use the concept of present value, let's work through a couple of simple problems.

Question: If you put $100 in a bank account today, how much will it be worth in N years? That is, what will be the future value of this $100?

Answer: Let's use r to denote the interest rate expressed in decimal form (so an interest rate of 5 per cent means $r = 0.05$). If interest is paid each year, and if this interest paid remains in the bank account to earn more interest (a process called *compounding*), the $100 will become $(1 + r) \times$ $100 after 1 year, $(1 + r) \times (1 + r) \times$ $100 after 2 years, $(1 + r) \times (1 + r) \times (1 + r) \times$ $100 after 3 years, and so on. After N years, the $100 becomes $(1 + r)^N \times$ $100. For example, if we are investing at an interest rate of 5 per cent for 10 years, then the future value of the $100 will be $(1.05)^{10} \times$ $100, which is $163.

Question: Now suppose you are going to be paid $200 in N years. What is the present value of this future payment? That is, how much would you have had to deposit in a bank right now to yield $200 in N years?

Answer: To answer this question, just turn the previous answer on its head. In the last question, we computed a future value from a present value by *multiplying* by the factor $(1 + r)^N$. To compute a present value from a future value, we divide by the factor $(1 + r)^N$. Thus, the present value of $200 in N years is $200/(1 + r)^N$. If that amount is deposited in a bank today, after N years it would become $(1 + r)^N \times [$200/(1 + r)^N]$, which is $20. For instance, if the interest rate is 5 per cent, the present value of $200 in 10 years is $200/(1.05)^{10}$, which is $123.

This illustrates the general formula: *If r is the interest rate, then the amount X to be received in N years has present value of $X/(1 + r)^N$.*

Let's now return to our earlier question: Should you choose $100 today or $200 in 10 years? We can infer from our calculation of present value that if the interest rate is 5 per cent, you should prefer the $200 in 10 years. The future $200 has a present value of $123, which is greater than $100. You are, therefore, better off waiting for the future sum.

Notice that the answer to our question depends on the interest rate. If the interest rate were 8 per cent, then the $200 in 10 years would have a present value of $200/(1.05)^{10}$, which is only $93. In this case, you should take the $100 today. Why should the interest rate matter for your choice? The answer is that the higher the interest rate, the more you can earn by depositing your money at the bank, so the more attractive getting $100 today becomes.

The concept of present value is useful in many applications, including the decisions that companies face when evaluating investment projects. For instance, imagine that Mitsubishi is thinking about building a new factory. Suppose that the factory will cost $100 million today and will yield the company $200 million in 10 years. Should Mitsubishi undertake the project? You can see that this decision is exactly like the one we have been studying. To make its decision, the company will compare the present value of the $200 million return to the $100 million cost.

The company's decision, therefore, will depend on the interest rate. If the interest rate is 5 per cent, then the present value of the $200 million return from the factory is $123 million, and the company will choose to pay the $100 million cost. By contrast, if the interest rate is 8 per cent, then the present value of the return is only $93 million, and the company will decide to forgo the project. Thus, the concept of present value helps explain why investment – and thus the quantity of loanable funds demanded – declines when the interest rate rises.

Here is another application of present value: Suppose you win a million dollar lottery, but the prize is going to be paid out as $20 000 a year for 50 years. How much is the prize really worth? After performing 50 calculations similar to those above (one calculation for each payment) and adding up the results, you would learn that the present value of this prize at a 7 per cent interest rate is only $276 000. This is one way that lotteries make money – by selling tickets in the present and paying out prizes in the future.

Third, we compare the old and new equilibria. In the figure, when the budget deficit reduces the supply of loanable funds, the interest rate rises from 5 per cent to 6 per cent. This higher interest rate then alters the behaviour of the households and firms that participate in the loan market. In particular, many demanders of loanable funds are discouraged by the higher interest rate. Fewer families buy new homes and fewer firms choose to build new factories. The fall in investment because of government borrowing is called **crowding out** and is represented in the figure by the movement along the demand curve from a quantity of $1200 million in loanable funds to a quantity of $800 million. That is, when the government borrows to finance its budget deficit, it crowds out private borrowers who are trying to finance investment.

crowding out
a decrease in investment that results from government borrowing

Thus, the most basic lesson about budget deficits follows directly from their effects on the supply of and demand for loanable funds – *when the government reduces national saving by running a budget deficit, the interest rate rises and investment falls.* Because investment is important for long-run economic growth, government budget deficits reduce the economy's growth rate.

CASESTUDY

A comparison of government debt in Australia and the United States

Discussions regarding the Australian federal budget are often filled more with rhetoric than with reason. For example, when the Howard government brought down its 1997–98 budget, it was claimed that the government's reversal of the '$10.3 billion deficit black hole' inherited by the government into a $1.6 billion surplus was the 'first ever serious and sustainable attack on public debt by a federal government, which [had] inherited a legacy of endemic overspending, endless deficits and rising debt'. However, a look at the history of Australia's budget position tells a different story.

Figure 27.5 shows the debt of the Commonwealth government expressed as a percentage of Australian GDP. From the 1950s to the early 1980s, the debt–GDP ratio declined. Although the government did run budget deficits during some of these years, the deficits were sufficiently small that the size of the government's debt grew less rapidly than the overall economy. Because GDP is a rough measure of the government's ability to raise tax revenue, a declining debt–GDP ratio indicates the

economy is, in some sense, living within its means. In contrast, when the budget deficits increased in the early 1980s, the government debt started rising more rapidly than the overall economy. As a result, the debt–GDP ratio started to rise. The increase in the debt–GDP ratio was short-lived, though. It rose from 1982 to 1986, but then fell sharply from 1986 to 1991 and then rose again until 1995. The highest level it reached in this period was around 26 per cent. Because the Australian government ran budget surpluses from 1997 to 2001, it has been able to reduce the debt even further. In 2001, government debt was only 5.1 per cent of GDP, compared to the US figure of debt at over 50 per cent of GDP. By 2005–06, the government had eliminated federal government debt and started accumulating government savings. Because of an increase in government expenditure for the GFC stimulus package, the government has once again run a budget deficit and started accumulating debt. But compared to the level of US government debt, it seems insignificant.

>>

Figure 27.5 The Australian government's debt

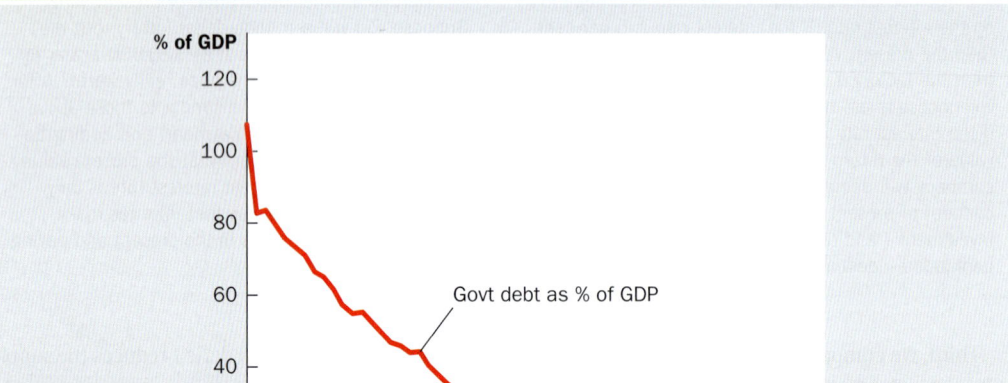

% of GDP

Govt debt as % of GDP

Year

The debt of the federal government, expressed here as a percentage of GDP, was high after the large expenditures of the Second World War but has declined significantly until the 1980s. In the 1980s and 1990s, it fluctuated around 20 per cent of GDP, but is now negative – that is, the government is now accumulating savings.

Source: © Commonwealth of Australia 2010.

Figure 27.6 shows the ratio of US government debt to GDP for the same period. The debt–GDP ratio for the US government rose from the 1970s to the mid-1990s. Even at its lowest levels, it reached levels that Australian policymakers have considered dangerously high, around 25 per cent. The ballooning of debt in the United States led to calls for a balanced budget amendment to the US Constitution. Although there are significant differences in the economies of the two countries and therefore in their abilities to finance budget deficits, it is important to keep Australia's debt position in perspective.

As we saw in the previous chapter, national saving is a key ingredient in long-run economic growth. By using some of the private sector's saving to finance the budget deficit, the government pulls resources away from investment in new capital and, thereby, depresses the living standards of future generations. Policymakers from both political parties accept this basic argument and view persistent budget deficits as an important policy problem.

Why, if there is such unanimity, have Australian governments run budget deficits? Part of the answer is that there is disagreement about how to eliminate

"Our deficit-reduction plan is simple, but it will require a great deal of money."

Source: Day, Robert © Robert Day/The New Yorker Collection/ www.cartoonbank.com.

Figure 27.6 **The US government's debt**

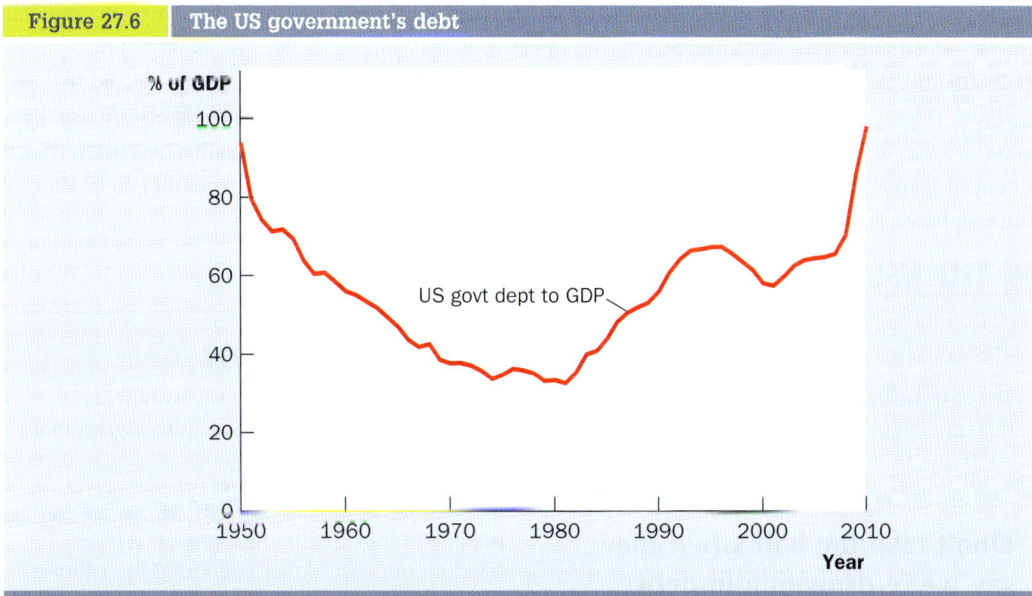

The debt of the US government, expressed here as a percentage of GDP, was high after the large expenditures of the Second World War but then declined throughout the 1950s and 1960s. It began rising again in the early 1980s when President Reagan's tax cuts were not accompanied by similar cuts in government spending.

Source: US Department of the Treasury; US Department of Commerce.

the deficit. The former Coalition government achieved the budget surplus by cutting back on expenditure on social services. Others would like to cut some taxes in order to stimulate private saving. They would balance the budget through deeper cuts in government spending than social welfare groups think is wise. In this way, disagreement over the details of deficit reduction, together with a general reluctance to make hard decisions, has allowed government budget deficits to persist.

Like most policy debates, the debate over government budgets has many facets. We discuss more of these in the final chapter of this book. But the basic elements of this debate should already be clear. Whenever policymakers consider the government's budget deficit and its impact on the economy, foremost in their minds are saving, investment and interest rates.

If more Australians adopted a 'live for today' approach to life, how would this affect saving, investment and the interest rate?

Conclusion

'Neither a borrower nor a lender be,' Polonius advises his son in Shakespeare's *Hamlet*. If everyone followed this advice, this chapter would have been unnecessary.

Few economists would agree with Polonius. In our economy, people borrow and lend often, and usually for good reason. You may borrow one day to start your own business or to buy a home. And people may lend to you in the hope that the interest you pay will allow them to enjoy a more prosperous retirement. The financial system has the job of coordinating all this borrowing and lending activity.

In many ways, financial markets are like other markets in the economy. The price of loanable funds – the interest rate – is governed by the forces of supply and demand, just as other prices in the economy are. And we can analyse shifts in supply or demand in financial markets as we do in other markets. One of the *Ten Lessons from Economics* introduced in chapter 1 is that markets are usually a good way to organise economic activity. This lesson applies to financial markets as well. When financial markets bring the supply of and demand for loanable funds into balance, they help allocate the economy's scarce resources to their most efficient uses.

IN THE NEWS ...

IS GOVERNMENT DEBT A DIRTY WORD?

The last Australian federal election was fought in part on the issue of each party's ability to manage the economy, to be fiscally responsible. In the following article, Ross Gittins argues that we're not doing too badly in the debt department.

Don't take the bait when they say we're drowning in debt
by Ross Gittins

Source: Rocco Fazzari/*The Sydney Morning Herald*, 28 July 2010.

Will there be an election rate rise?
I've had to cut short my leave because of the election campaign, but those who follow the political debate faithfully might be better off taking an overseas holiday for the next three weeks. It's clear they'd miss little but aggravation.

The paradoxical truth is that modern election campaigns are aimed at those who *aren't* much interested in the topic. Swinging voters are assumed to be completely self-interested and short-sighted, driven by emotion rather than intellect, ill-informed and easily conned by slogans and television ads.

Hence all the nonsense we're hearing from both sides. For those of us who do take an intelligent interest, the best response is to conduct our own debate, ignoring the silliness as much as we can.

This election is the battle of the scare campaigns. Pollies are trying to frighten us about big new taxes, the return of WorkChoices, the threat from boat people, and deficits and debt. I've written a lot in recent times about why we don't need to be too worried by budget deficits and public debt. But observing all the trouble the major developed countries are having has caused me to see the matter in a different light.

Many of the European economies and, to a lesser extent the United States, are worried about the huge levels of public debt they have racked up and the risk that the financial markets will begin to doubt their ability to repay those debts.

As a result, the British, German and other governments have embarked on austerity campaigns, cutting government spending and increasing taxes at a time when their economies are weak. To slash budget deficits at such a time is likely to make their economies even weaker, meaning the actual progress they make in reducing their deficits is likely to be small, notwithstanding the pain the austerity measures are inflicting.

How did they get themselves into such a predicament? Well, the global financial crisis left them with no alternative but to borrow heavily to rescue their mismanaged banks, and then borrow again to try to reflate their economies. Had they failed to prop up their banks – as happened in the Great Depression of the 1930s – things would have been much worse. Fortunately, the worst was averted. But it would be wrong to conclude all the borrowing of recent times is what has got the main economies into trouble.

No, the real problem is they went into the crisis with such high budget deficits and levels of public debt. Throughout the long boom that preceded the crisis, most governments were running annual deficits rather than surpluses, thereby adding to accumulated debt rather than paying it off. They had failed to get their houses in order during the good times and so were badly placed when the bad times struck.

Why were they caught out? Because their politicians had been indulging voters who want ever-increasing government services but are most resistant to higher taxes. Rather than forcing their voters to face financial reality, they just went on year after year putting the shortfall on tick.

When you consider the genuine worries of the big countries, you realise how silly it is for us to worry about our tiny budgetary problem. They have levels of public debt up about 80 or 90 per cent of their annual national incomes (gross domestic product). Our present budget deficits and consequent borrowing are expected to leave us with a net public debt that peaks at $94 billion in 2013.

Does that sound a lot? If it does it's because you don't realise how big our government and the Australian economy really are. It will represent just 6 per cent of our annual national income.

Let me ask you a personal question: how big is your mortgage relative to your annual income? If it amounted to just 6 per cent of your annual income, how worried would you be? It's common for people to take out home loans that are three or four times their annual income.

Unlike the rest of the developed economies, we went into the global financial crisis with no net debt. Peter Costello and the Howard government get the credit for this.

They introduced and stuck to a 'medium-term fiscal strategy' of keeping the budget in balance *on average* over the economic cycle. That is, it's OK for the budget to go into deficit during recessions, provided it goes back into surplus during the recovery, thereby eventually paying off the debt incurred during the period when the economy was weak and the budget was propping it up.

The Rudd/Gillard government is following this same strategy. Indeed, so successful has the opposition been in putting the frighteners on the public over deficits and debt that Labor is on its best behaviour, promising to find spending cuts to offset all new spending promises. The usual vote-buying auction has turned into a Dutch auction. Amazing.

As I've argued all along, the Liberals' relatively recent obsession with deficits and debt (it was the creation of Costello, never being part of John Howard's rhetoric when he was treasurer or in opposition) is way overdue. But when you look at the problem the Europeans' and Americans' budgetary laxity has got them into, you realise our antipodean obsession with avoiding public debt has its advantages.

We've been more frugal than we've needed to be, but it has certainly kept us out of trouble.

In economics, however, there are no free lunches. Everything comes at an (opportunity) cost. So successful has Costello been at demonising all government debt – state and federal – that we've failed to invest in enough economic and social infrastructure. Our debt level is minor, but we're living in the worst house in the street.

Source: Ross Gittins/*The Sydney Morning Herald*, 28 July 2010.

In one way, however, financial markets are special. Financial markets, unlike most other markets, serve the important role of linking the present and the future. Those who supply loanable funds – savers – do so because they want to convert some of their current income into future purchasing power. Those who demand loanable funds – borrowers – do so because they want to invest today in order to have additional capital in the future to produce goods and services. Thus, well-functioning financial markets are important not only for current generations but also for future generations who will inherit many of the resulting benefits.

Summary

- The Australian financial system is made up of many types of financial institutions, such as the bond market, the stock market, banks and managed funds. All these institutions act to direct the resources of households who want to save some of their income into the hands of households and firms who want to borrow.
- National income accounting identities reveal some important relationships among macroeconomic variables. In particular, for a closed economy, national saving must equal investment. Financial institutions are the mechanism through which the economy matches one person's saving with another person's investment.
- The interest rate is determined by the supply of and demand for loanable funds. The supply of loanable funds comes from households who want to save some of their income and lend it out. The demand for loanable funds comes from households and firms who want to borrow for investment. To analyse how any policy or event affects the interest rate, one must consider how it affects the supply of and demand for loanable funds.
- National saving equals private saving plus public saving. A government budget deficit represents negative public saving and, therefore, reduces national saving and the supply of loanable funds available to finance investment. When a government budget deficit crowds out investment, it reduces the growth of productivity and GDP.

Key concepts

bond (security)	financial markets	private saving
budget deficit	financial system	public saving
budget surplus	managed fund	share
crowding out	market for loanable funds	
financial intermediaries	national saving (saving)	

Questions for review

1 What is the role of the financial system? Name and describe two markets that are part of the financial system in our economy. Name and describe two financial intermediaries.

2 What is national saving? What is private saving? What is public saving? How are these three variables related?

3 What is investment? How does an economist's definition of investment differ from the ordinary usage of the term 'investment'? How is it related to national saving?

4 Describe a change in the tax laws that might decrease private saving. If this policy were implemented, how would it affect the market for loanable funds?

5 What is a government budget surplus? How does it affect interest rates, investment and economic growth? What happens when the government runs a deficit? How does a deficit affect interest rates, investment and economic growth?

Problems and applications

1 For each of the following pairs, which bond would you expect to pay a higher interest rate? Explain.

  a A bond of the Australian government or a bond of an African government

  b A bond that repays the principal in the year 2010 or a bond that repays the principal in the year 2025

  c A bond from BHP Billiton or a bond from a software company you run in your garage

  d A bond issued by the federal government or a bond issued to finance the construction of a new airport for Brisbane.

2 The 'yield curve' is a graph of the interest rates on bonds of different terms, with the term shown on the horizontal axis and the interest rate shown on the vertical axis.

  a Based on the discussion in the chapter, would you expect the yield curve to be upward-sloping or downward-sloping?

  b Using the business section of a recent newspaper, graph the yield curve for Australian government bonds. Does the curve have the slope you expected?

  c What factors affect the slope of the yield curve?

3 A US president once said: 'There is no moral difference between gambling at cards or in lotteries or on the race track and gambling in the share market'.

  a How important is luck in each of the 'gambling' activities listed by the US president? Do you think investing in the share market is simply a matter of luck?

  b If you are wise and start investing in a pension fund when you graduate from university, it is likely that your superannuation fund will hold a portfolio of shares. Is this a good idea? Explain.

4 During the Global Financial Crisis, most banks in Australia increased their interests for home loans over and above the increases in the cash rate announced by the Reserve Bank of Australia. They argued that their cost of capital, that is, what they had to pay to borrow money on the world's financial markets, had increased. Use the loanable funds model to explain why banks would be justified in doing this.

5 In mid-2010, share markets all over the world increased, including the All Ordinaries in Australia. Why would they all move together? What would such a rise indicate to you about the level of growth in the world economy?

6 The chapter explains that managed funds allow people with small amounts of money to buy a diverse portfolio of shares and bonds. What is the advantage of owning a diverse portfolio rather than holding shares or bonds from a single company?

7 Use the Internet to look at a website for a managed fund, such as the Commonwealth Bank's Internet broker, CommSec, at http://funds.comsec.com.au. Compare the return on an actively managed mutual fund with the return on an index fund. What explains the difference in those returns?

8 In 2009, the governments of Italy and Greece had national debt of nearly 120 per cent of GDP. Other European governments worried about these governments defaulting, so they organised a €750 billion bailout. Why do you suppose other governments would be so worried about Italian or Greek governments failing to repay their debt?

9 Many workers hold large amounts of shares issued by the firms at which they work. Why do you suppose companies encourage this behaviour? Why might people not want to hold shares in the company where they work?

10 Two investors are discussing their investment strategies. One says she always looks for companies that seem to have good prospects, but have low price-earnings ratios. The other says he only invests in shares of companies that are in strongly growing industries. What are the merits of each investment strategy? What are the pitfalls?

11 Explain the difference between saving and investment as defined by a macroeconomist. Which of the following situations represent investment? Saving? Explain.
   a Your family takes out a mortgage and buys a new house
   b You use your $200 pay cheque to buy shares in Boral
   c Your flat-mate earns $100 and deposits it in her account at a bank
   d You borrow $1000 from a bank to buy a car to use in your pizza delivery business.

12 Suppose that BHP Billiton is considering buying its major rival, Rio Tinto.
   a Assuming that BHP Billiton needs to borrow money in the bond market, why would an increase in interest rates affect BHP Billiton's decision about whether to buy Rio Tinto?
   b If BHP Billiton has enough of its own funds to finance the acquisition without borrowing, would an increase in interest rates still affect BHP Billiton's decision about whether to acquire Rio? Explain.

13 Suppose the government borrows $20 million more next year than this year.
   a Use a supply-and-demand diagram to analyse this policy. Does the interest rate rise or fall?
   b What happens to investment? To private saving? To public saving? To national saving? Compare the size of the changes with the $20 million of extra government saving.
   c How does the elasticity of supply of loanable funds affect the size of these changes? (*Hint:* See chapter 5 to review the definition of elasticity.)
   d How does the elasticity of demand for loanable funds affect the size of these changes?
   e Suppose households believe that greater government saving today implies lower taxes since there will be no government debt in the future. What does this belief do to private saving and the supply of loanable funds today? Does it increase or decrease the effects you discussed in parts (a) and (b)?

14 Over the past 10 years, new computer technology has enabled firms to reduce substantially the amount of inventories they hold for each dollar of sales. Illustrate the effect of this change on the market for loanable funds. (*Hint:* Expenditure on inventories is a type of investment.) What do you think has been the effect on investment in factories and equipment?

15 'Some economists worry that the ageing populations of industrial countries are going to start running down their savings just when the investment appetite of emerging economies is growing' (*Economist*, 6 May 1995). Were they right that this is a concern? Illustrate the effect of these phenomena on the world market for loanable funds.

16 This chapter explains that investment can be increased both by reducing taxes on private saving and by reducing the government budget deficit.
   a The current Australian government is trying to implement both of these things at once. Why will it be difficult to implement both of these policies at the same time?
   b What would you need to know about private saving in order to judge which of these two policies would be a more effective way to raise investment?

Search me!

  Search me!

When accessing information about economics use the following keywords in any combinations you require:

- Australian financial institutions
- market for loanable funds

CourseMate

For more multimedia resources and activities on economics, visit the Economics CourseMate website.

28

The natural rate of unemployment

Learning objectives

In this chapter you will:

- learn about the data used to measure the level of unemployment
- consider how unemployment can result from minimum-wage laws
- see how unemployment can arise from union wage bargaining and efficiency wages
- consider how unemployment arises from the process of job search.

Losing a job can be the most distressing economic event in a person's life. Most people rely on their labour earnings to maintain their standard of living and many people get from their work not only income but also a sense of personal accomplishment. A job loss means a lower living standard in the present, anxiety about the future and reduced self-esteem. It is not surprising, therefore, that politicians, campaigning for office, often speak about how their proposed policies will help create jobs.

In the last two chapters, we have seen some of the forces that determine the level and growth of a country's standard of living. A country that saves and invests a high fraction of its income, for instance, enjoys more rapid growth in its capital stock and its GDP than a similar country that saves and invests less. An even more obvious determinant of a country's standard of living is the amount of unemployment it typically experiences. People who would like to work but cannot find a job are not contributing to the economy's production of goods and services. Although some degree of unemployment is inevitable in a complex economy with thousands of firms and millions of workers, the amount of unemployment varies substantially over time and across countries. When a country keeps its workers as fully employed as possible, it achieves a higher level of GDP than it would if it left many of its workers standing idle.

This chapter begins our study of unemployment. The problem of unemployment is usefully divided into two categories – the long-run problem and the short-run problem. The economy's *natural rate of unemployment* refers to the amount of unemployment that the economy normally experiences. *Cyclical unemployment* refers to the year-to-year fluctuations in unemployment around its natural rate and it is closely associated with the short-run ups and downs of economic activity. Cyclical unemployment has its own explanation, which we defer until we study short-run economic fluctuations later in this book. In this chapter we discuss the determinants of an economy's natural rate of unemployment. As we will see, the designation *natural* does not in any way imply that this rate of unemployment is desirable or inevitable. It merely means that this unemployment does not go away on its own, even in the long run.

We begin the chapter by looking at some of the relevant facts that describe unemployment. In particular, we examine three questions: How does the government measure the economy's rate of unemployment? What problems arise in interpreting the unemployment data? How long are the unemployed typically without work?

We then turn to the reasons that economies always experience some unemployment and the ways in which policymakers can help the unemployed. We discuss four potential explanations for the economy's natural rate of unemployment – minimum-wage laws, unions, efficiency wages and job search. As we will see, long-run unemployment does not arise from a single problem that has a single solution. Instead, it reflects a variety of related problems. As a result, there is no easy way for policymakers to reduce the economy's natural rate of unemployment and, at the same time, to alleviate the hardships experienced by the unemployed.

Identifying unemployment

We begin this chapter by examining more precisely what the term *unemployment* means. We consider how the government measures unemployment, what problems arise in interpreting the unemployment data, and how long the typical spell of unemployment lasts.

How is unemployment measured?

Measuring unemployment is the job of the Australian Bureau of Statistics (ABS). Every month the ABS produces data on unemployment and on other aspects of the labour market, such as types of employment, length of the average working week and the duration of unemployment. These data come from a regular survey of 0.45 per cent of Australian households, called the Labour Force Survey.

Based on the answers to survey questions, the ABS places each adult (aged 15 years and older) in each surveyed household into one of three categories:

* employed
* unemployed
* not in the labour force.

A person is considered employed if he or she spent at least one hour of the previous week working at a paid job (including self-employment) or family business. A person is unemployed if he or she is on temporary layoff, is looking for a job, or is waiting to start a new job. A person who fits neither of the first two categories, such as a full-time student, homemaker or retiree, is not in the labour force. Figure 28.1 shows this breakdown for 2010.

Figure 28.1	The breakdown of the population in 2010

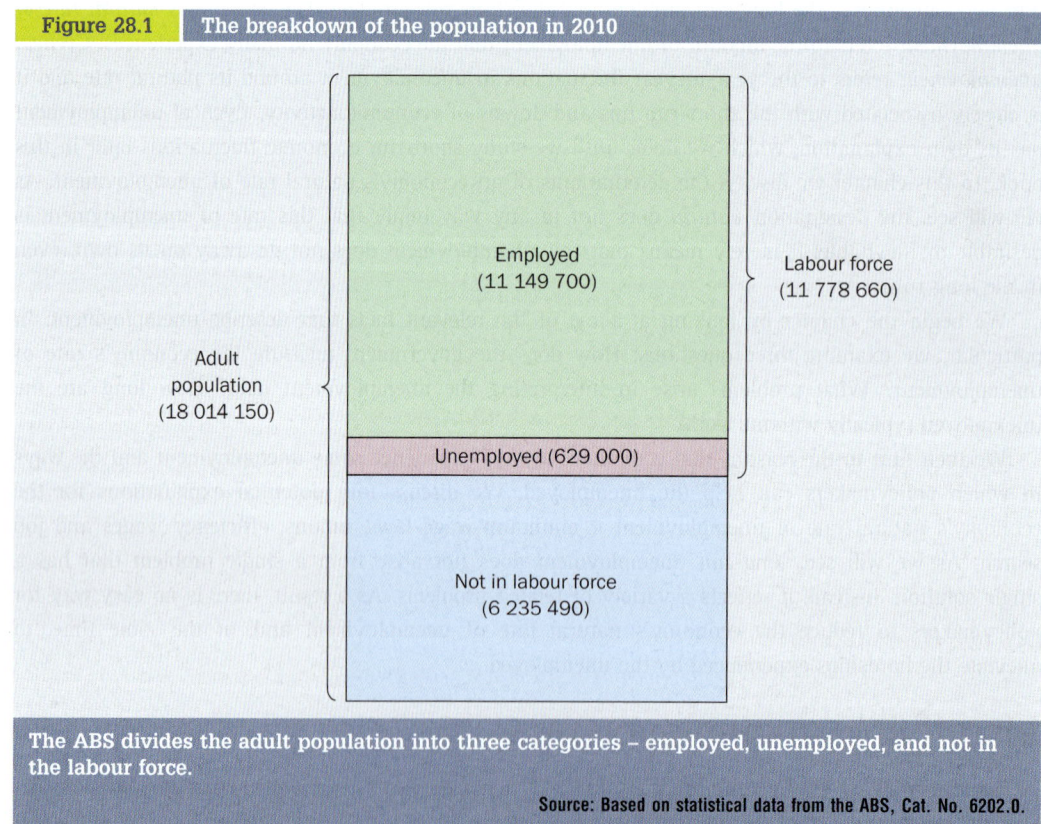

The ABS divides the adult population into three categories – employed, unemployed, and not in the labour force.

Source: Based on statistical data from the ABS, Cat. No. 6202.0.

Once the ABS has placed all the individuals covered by the survey in a category, it calculates various statistics to summarise the state of the labour market. The ABS defines the **labour force** as the sum of the employed and the unemployed:

$$\text{Labour force} = \text{Number of employed} + \text{Number of unemployed}$$

The ABS defines the **unemployment rate** as the percentage of the labour force that is unemployed:

$$\text{Unemployment rate} = \frac{\text{Number of unemployed} \times 100}{\text{Labour force}}$$

The ABS calculates unemployment rates for the entire adult population and for more narrow groups – men, women, youth and so on.

The ABS uses the same survey to produce data on labour-force participation. The **labour-force participation rate** measures the percentage of the total adult population of Australia that is in the labour force:

$$\text{Labour-force participation rate} = \frac{\text{Labour force}}{\text{Adult population}} \times 100$$

This statistic tells us the fraction of the population that has chosen to participate in the labour market. The labour-force participation rate, like the unemployment rate, is calculated both for the entire adult population and for more narrow groups.

To see how these data are calculated, consider the figures for 2010. In that year, about 11.15 million people were employed and about 0.63 million people were unemployed. The labour force was:

$$\text{Labour force} = 11.15 + 0.63 = 11.78 \text{ million}$$

The unemployment rate was:

$$\text{Unemployment rate} = \frac{0.63}{11.78} = 5.3\%$$

Because the adult population was 18.01 million, the labour-force participation rate was:

$$\text{Labour force participation rate} = \frac{11.78}{18.01} = 65.4\%$$

Hence, in 2010, a little less than two-thirds of the Australian adult population were participating in the labour market and 5.3 per cent of those labour-market participants were unemployed.

Table 28.1 shows the statistics on unemployment and labour-force participation for various groups within the Australian population. Three comparisons are most apparent. First, women have lower rates of labour-force participation than men, but once in the labour force women have similar rates of unemployment. Second, migrants to Australia have both lower unemployment rates and lower participation rates than the overall population. Third, teenagers have lower rates of labour-force participation and much higher rates of unemployment than the overall population. More generally, these data show that labour-market experiences vary widely among groups within the economy.

labour force
the total number of workers, including both the employed and the unemployed

unemployment rate
the percentage of the labour force that is unemployed

labour-force participation rate
the percentage of the adult population that is in the labour force

Table 28.1 The labour-market experiences of various demographic groups

Demographic group	Unemployment rate	Labour-force participation rate
Adults (aged 15 and over)		
Total	5.3%	64.9%
Male	5.3	72.1
Female	5.4	57.9
Lone parent with dependants	8.1	60.0
Persons not born in Australia	4.6	59.0
Teenagers (aged 15–19)		
Total	14.1	57.4
Male	14.7	56.5
Female	13.6	59.0

This table shows the unemployment rate and the labour-force participation rate of various groups in the population for August 2010.

Source: ABS, various catalogues, 2011.

In recent years, economists and policy-makers have become concerned about *how much* employed people are working and whether or not the labour force is *underutilised* – that is, working less than they could or would like to. From the ABS publication 6105.0 (October, 2010):

> While it may seem as if Australians are working longer hours than ever, the average actual hours worked per employed person have decreased over the past 32 years. However, the average actual hours worked by full-time and part-time employed people have both increased ... This total decrease, but component increase, can be attributed to the changing full-time to part-time composition of the workforce.

In other words, more and more people are working part-time, so even though some of us are working longer hours, more and more of us are working part-time. The ABS now calculates the underutilisation rate, the number of unemployed plus the *under*employed, as a percentage of the labour force. This has risen from around 9 per cent in 2008 to well over 10 per cent in 2010.

The ABS data on the labour market allow economists and policymakers to monitor changes in the economy over time. Figure 28.2 shows the unemployment rate in Australia since 1978. The figure shows that the economy always has some unemployment and that the amount changes from year to year. The normal rate of unemployment around which the unemployment rate fluctuates is called the **natural rate of unemployment**, and the deviation of unemployment from its natural rate is called **cyclical unemployment**. In the figure, the natural rate is shown as a horizontal line at 5 per cent, which is a rough estimate of the natural rate for the Australian economy during this period. Later in this book, we discuss short-run economic fluctuations, including the year-to-year fluctuations in unemployment around its natural rate. In the rest of this chapter, however, we ignore the short-run fluctuations and examine why unemployment is a chronic problem for market economies.

natural rate of unemployment
unemployment accounted for by structural factors around which the actual unemployment rate fluctuates

cyclical unemployment
the deviation of unemployment from its natural rate

▸ natural rate of unemployment
▸ cyclical unemployment

| Figure 28.2 | Unemployment rate since 1978 |

% of labour force

Annual unemployment

Natural rate of unemployment

1978 1983 1988 1993 1998 2003 2008 2010

Year

This graph uses annual data on the unemployment rate to show the fraction of the labour force without a job.

Source: ABS, various catalogues, 2011.

Women's role in Australian society has changed dramatically over the past century. Social commentators have pointed to many causes for this change. In part, it is attributable to new technologies, such as the washing machine, clothes dryer, refrigerator, freezer and dishwasher, which have reduced the amount of time required to complete routine household tasks. In part, it is attributable to improved birth control, which has reduced the number of children born to the typical family. And, of course, the change in women's role is also partly attributable to changing political and social attitudes. Together, these developments have had a profound impact on society in general and on the economy in particular.

More women are working now than ever before.

Source: iStockphoto/Justin Horrocks.

Nowhere is that impact more obvious than in data on labour-force participation. Just after

CASESTUDY

Labour-force participation of men and women in the Australian economy

>>

the Second World War, men and women had very different roles in society. Only around 30 per cent of women were working or looking for work, in contrast to over 85 per cent of men. Figure 28.3 shows the labour-force participation rates of men and women in Australia since 1978. Over the past several decades, the difference between the participation rates of men and women has gradually diminished as growing numbers of women have entered the labour force and some men have left it. Data for 2010 show that nearly 59 per cent of women were in the labour force, in contrast to 72 per cent of men. Although labour-force participation rates for men and women are converging, male participation rates are still higher.

The increase in women's labour-force participation is easy to understand, but the fall in men's may seem puzzling. There are several reasons for this decline. First, young men now stay in school longer than their fathers and grandfathers did. Second, older men now retire earlier and live longer. Third, with more women employed, more fathers now stay at home to raise their children. Full-time students, retirees and stay-at-home fathers are all counted as out of the labour force. Finally, there is much concern that technological progress and a lack of opportunities and incentives for learning new skills has contributed to the unemployment of older men.

| Figure 28.3 | Labour-force participation rates for men and women since 1978 |

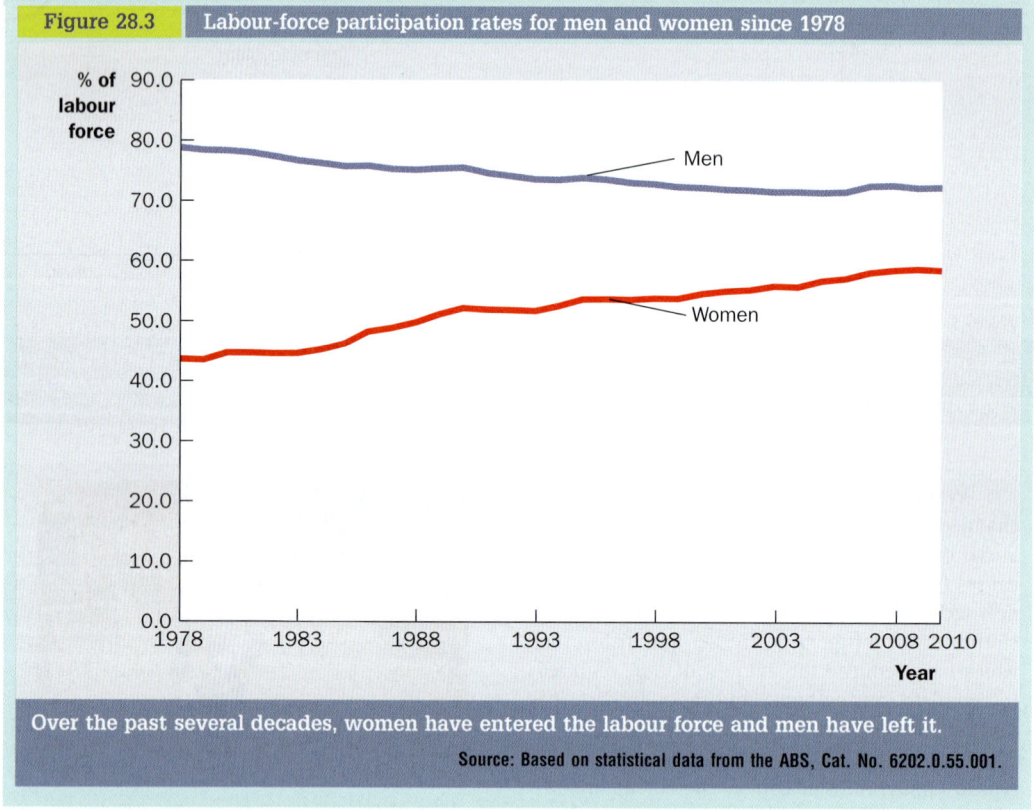

Over the past several decades, women have entered the labour force and men have left it.

Source: Based on statistical data from the ABS, Cat. No. 6202.0.55.001.

Is unemployment measured correctly?

Measuring the amount of unemployment in the economy might seem straightforward. In fact, it is not. Although it is easy to distinguish between a person with a full-time job and a person who is not working at all, it is much harder to distinguish between a person who is unemployed and a person who is not in the labour force.

Movements into and out of the labour force are, in fact, very common. More than one-third of the unemployed are recent entrants into the labour force. These entrants include young workers looking for their first jobs, such as recent university graduates. They also include, in greater numbers, older workers who had previously left the labour force but have now returned to look for work. Moreover, not all unemployment ends with the job seeker finding a job. Almost half of all spells of unemployment end when the unemployed person leaves the labour force.

Because people move into and out of the labour force so often, statistics on unemployment are difficult to interpret. On the one hand, some of those who report being unemployed may not, in fact, be trying hard to find a job. They may be calling themselves unemployed in order to qualify for one of the government programs that provide financial assistance for the unemployed. It would be more realistic to view some of these individuals as out of the labour force. On the other hand, some of those who report being out of the labour force may, in fact, want to work. These individuals may have tried to find a job but have given up after an unsuccessful search. Such individuals, called **discouraged workers**, do not show up in unemployment statistics, even though they are truly workers without jobs.

There is no easy way to fix the unemployment rate as reported by the ABS to make it a more reliable indicator of conditions in the labour market. In the end, it is best to view the reported unemployment rate as a useful but imperfect measure of joblessness.

discouraged workers
individuals who would like to work but have given up looking for a job

How long are the unemployed without work?

In judging how serious the problem of unemployment is, one question to consider is whether unemployment is typically a short-term or long-term condition. If unemployment is short term, one might conclude that it is not a big problem. Workers may require a few weeks between jobs to find the openings that best suit their skills and tastes. Yet if unemployment is long term, one might conclude that it is a serious problem. Workers unemployed for many months are more likely to suffer economic and psychological hardship.

Because the duration of unemployment can affect our view about how big a problem unemployment is, economists have devoted much energy to studying data on the duration of unemployment spells. In this work, they have uncovered a result that is important, subtle and seemingly contradictory – *most spells of unemployment are short and most unemployment observed at any given time is long term.*

To see how this statement can be true, consider an example. Suppose that you visited an unemployment office every week for a year to survey the unemployed. Each week you find that there are four unemployed workers. Three of these workers are the same individuals for the whole year, whereas the fourth person changes every week. Based on this experience, would you say that unemployment is typically short term or long term?

Some simple calculations help answer this question. In this example, you meet a total of 55 unemployed people – 52 of them are unemployed for 1 week and three are unemployed for the full year. Thus, 52/55, or 95 per cent, of unemployment spells end in 1 week. That is, most spells of unemployment are short. Yet consider the total amount of unemployment. The three people unemployed for 1 year (52 weeks) make up a total of 156 weeks of unemployment. Together with the 52 people unemployed for 1 week, this makes 208 weeks of unemployment. In this example, 156/208, or 75 per cent, of unemployment is attributable to those individuals who are unemployed for a full year. Thus, most unemployment observed at any given time is long term.

This subtle conclusion implies that economists and policymakers must be careful when interpreting data on unemployment and when designing policies to help the unemployed. Most people who become unemployed will soon find jobs. Yet most of the economy's unemployment problem is attributable to the relatively few workers who are jobless for long periods of time.

Why is there unemployment?

We have discussed how the government measures the amount of unemployment, the problems that arise in interpreting unemployment statistics and the findings of labour economists on the duration of unemployment. You should now have a good idea about what unemployment is. This discussion, however, has not explained why economies experience unemployment. In most markets in the economy, prices adjust to bring quantity supplied and quantity demanded into balance. In an ideal labour market, wages would adjust to balance the quantity of labour supplied and the quantity of labour demanded. This adjustment of wages would ensure that all workers are always fully employed.

Of course, reality does not resemble this ideal. There are always some workers without jobs, even when the overall economy is doing well. In other words, the unemployment rate never falls to zero; instead, it fluctuates around the natural rate of unemployment. Two types of unemployment help explain why unemployment never falls to zero. One is *frictional unemployment*. This is unemployment associated with job search – when people are temporarily unemployed while they search for a new job. This type of unemployment is usually of a shorter duration. The other type of unemployment is called *structural unemployment*. This is unemployment that results from the mismatch between the skills that businesses require and the skills that workers have. Structural unemployment tends to be longer in duration because it takes time for people to acquire the new skills that the labour market demands.

To understand this natural rate, we now examine four reasons that actual labour markets depart from the ideal of full employment – minimum-wage laws, unions, efficiency wages and job search.

How is the unemployment rate measured? How might the unemployment rate overstate the amount of joblessness? How might it understate it?

IN THE NEWS . . .

WHAT IS THE NATURAL RATE OF UNEMPLOYMENT?

What's so natural about 5 per cent? Ross Gittins of the *Sydney Morning Herald* argues that 5 per cent is still a very big number. He presents two sides of the argument as to why the NAIRU has increased in the last few decades.

Why 600 000 out of work is a magic number
by Ross Gittins

Who would have expected it? A year ago we thought we were headed for a severe recession and this week we learn the rate of unemployment is down to 5.1 per cent. Do you realise that's just a fraction above what economists – and the Gillard government – regard as full employment?

Huh? If 5 per cent of the labour force – 600 000 people – is still looking for work, how on earth can economists say we're at full employment? Good question. Unfortunately, economists don't have a good answer.

This year's budget papers – which seem to have been overtaken by events already – say the unemployment rate is expected to fall to 5 per cent by the middle of next year and to 4.75 per cent by mid-2012, 'around levels consistent with full employment'.

Last month a senior Treasury officer, Dr David Gruen, told a Senate committee it was 'a longstanding practice' to regard full employment as 5 per cent, although there was 'a reasonable band of uncertainty around that number'.

'With the best will in the world, we cannot really tell whether it is 5 per cent or anywhere in the range, say, from about 4.75 per cent to 5.25 per cent,' he told the committee.

I guess the first thing to understand is that, to an economist, 'full employment' does not mean what you and I think it does. It does not mean everyone who wants a job has found one.

Rather, it refers to the lowest *sustainable* rate of unemployment. That is, the lowest rate to which unemployment can fall before shortages of labour lead to excessive wage increases and start pushing up inflation.

In the jargon, this is the 'non-accelerating-inflation rate of unemployment' (NAIRU). So in an economist's mind the NAIRU is synonymous with full employment.

As Gruen implied, no one knows for certain where the NAIRU is, though we do know it can shift over time.

So, though economists do make calculations to estimate where it lies, you really have to discover where it is by real-world experience.

When the unemployment rate got down to 4 per cent in early 2008, most economists would have regarded that as clearly below the NAIRU. The private-sector wage index rose by 4.3 per cent over the following year – hardly a wage explosion, but clearly on the high side, particularly when the productivity of labour has been improving so slowly.

And the underlying rate of inflation has now been above the target range of 2 per cent to 3 per cent for more than three years. So I guess that does confirm that the NAIRU is nearer 5 per cent than 4 per cent.

Economists actually regard 5 per cent as good because, not that long ago, they believed the NAIRU was up somewhere between 7 per cent and 8 per cent. The rest of us, on the other hand, are shocked by the idea that economists could be satisfied with unemployment no lower than 5 per cent.

And oldies can remember the 1950s, '60s and early '70s when full employment (and the NAIRU) was regarded as an unemployment rate no higher than 2 per cent.

The 2 per cent was easily justified as 'frictional unemployment'. At any time, roughly 2 per cent of the labour force are unemployed simply because they are moving between jobs, and thus of no concern. In those days people were unemployed so briefly many did not bother to register for the dole.

But how do economists explain why the lowest point at which inflation pressure can be quiescent has shifted from 2 per cent to 5 per cent over the past 35 years or so? Well, the reason you can get inflationary wage pressure while still having 600 000 people looking for jobs is 'structural mismatch': the remaining unemployed either don't have the skills employers are seeking or don't live in the parts of the country where those workers are being sought.

But that does not explain why structural mismatch is a much greater problem today than it was 40 years ago. So the truth is, economists can't offer a thorough explanation for why the full-employment rate has risen, as many of them will admit.

It is worth noting, however, that since the postwar Golden Age ended with the arrival of stagflation in the mid-1970s, NAIRUs have risen significantly in most developed economies.

And just because economists can prove it, that doesn't stop them having theories – rival theories, naturally.

Economists of a neo-classical disposition incline to the view that the full-employment rate is higher these days because a combination of increased interventions in the economy – minimum wage rates that are too high, unemployment benefits that are too generous and unfair dismissal laws – have

>>

stopped the labour market functioning as efficiently as it used to.

Limits on employers' freedom to dismiss unsatisfactory workers have made them more reluctant to hire those workers at the bottom of the barrel, it's argued.

Or, unduly high minimum wages effectively price unattractive workers out of a job, while generous unemployment benefits reduce the incentive for people to find work.

There may be other reasons why people don't try as hard to find work these days: because the stigma of being unemployed has declined, because dual-income households reduce the pressure on one partner to find work, which may be particularly true of married women.

But these arguments aren't terribly convincing. Relative to average income, our dole payments are very low.

And while it's true our minimum wage is quite high relative to average income, our NAIRU isn't that much higher than America's, even though its minimum wage is terribly low.

So economists of a more Keynesian disposition try to explain the higher full-employment rate more in terms of how the *structure* of the economy has changed (as opposed to how governments have made *prices* more inflexible). When you get down to an unemployment rate of 5 per cent, most of those who have been unemployed for any length of time are unskilled, with a chequered work history. It may be that the kind of jobs suitable for such people no longer exist to the same extent they once did.

And there's a suspicion that where the NAIRU lies is affected by how rapidly you approach it. If unemployment falls rapidly, you may hit the NAIRU at a higher level than if growth is more sedate and it takes a lot longer to get unemployment down.

Sorry, but all this is about the best explanation economists can offer. There is a lot economists do not know.

Source: Ross Gittins/*The Sydney Morning Herald*, 10 July 2010.

Minimum-wage laws

We begin by reviewing how unemployment arises from minimum-wage laws. Although minimum wages are not the predominant reason for unemployment in our economy, they may have an important effect on certain groups with particularly high unemployment rates. Moreover, the analysis of minimum wages is a natural place to start because, as we will see, it can be used to understand some of the more common reasons for unemployment.

Figure 28.4 reviews the basic economics of a minimum wage. When a minimum-wage law forces the wage to remain above the level that balances supply and demand, it raises the quantity of labour supplied and reduces the quantity of labour demanded compared with the equilibrium level. There is a surplus of labour. Because there are more workers willing to work than there are jobs, some workers are unemployed.

Because we discussed minimum-wage laws extensively in chapter 6, we will not discuss them further here. It is, however, important to note why minimum-wage laws are *not* a predominant reason for unemployment – most workers in the economy earn above-award wages. Minimum-wage laws are binding most often for the least skilled and least experienced members of the labour force. It is only among these workers that minimum-wage laws explain the existence of unemployment.

Although Figure 28.4 was drawn to show the effects of a minimum-wage law, it shows a more general lesson – *if the wage is kept above the equilibrium level for any reason, the result is unemployment.* Minimum-wage laws are just one reason that wages may be 'too high'.

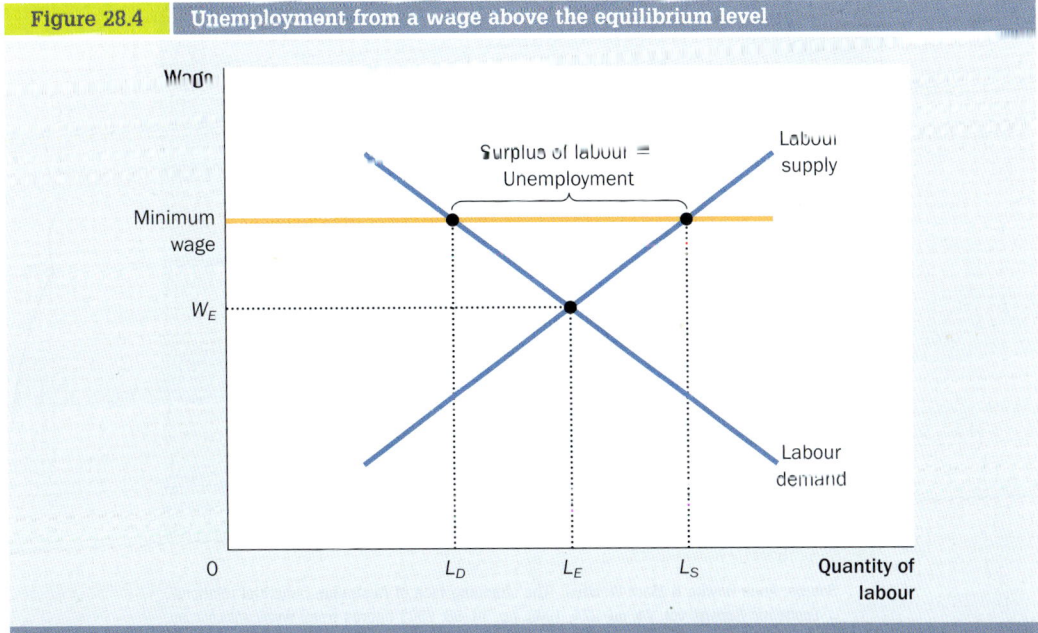

Figure 28.4   **Unemployment from a wage above the equilibrium level**

In this labour market, the wage at which supply and demand balance is W_E. At this equilibrium wage, the quantity of labour supplied and the quantity of labour demanded both equal L_E. In contrast if the wage is forced to remain above the equilibrium level, perhaps because of a minimum-wage law, the quantity of labour supplied rises to L_S, and the quantity of labour demanded falls to L_D. The resulting excess supply of labour, L_S–L_D, represents unemployment.

In the next two sections, we consider two other reasons that wages may be kept above the equilibrium level – unions and efficiency wages. The basic economics of unemployment in these cases is the same as that shown in Figure 28.4, but these explanations of unemployment can apply to many more of the economy's workers.

Draw the supply curve and the demand curve for a labour market in which the wage is fixed above the equilibrium level. Show the quantity of labour supplied, the quantity demanded and the amount of unemployment.

Unions and collective bargaining

In some industries, labour markets do not operate according to the simple principles of supply and demand. In industries such as transport, teaching and mining, wages are determined by negotiations between unions and employers. A **union** is a type of cartel. Like any cartel, a union is a group of sellers acting together in the hope of exerting their joint market power. Many workers in the economy discuss their wages, benefits and working conditions with their employers as individuals. In contrast, workers in a union do so as a group. The process by which unions and firms agree on the terms of employment is called **collective bargaining**.

union
a worker association that bargains with employers over wages and working conditions

collective bargaining
the process by which unions and firms agree on the terms of employment

Table 28.2 Unionisation rate – union members as a percentage of employees	
Year	Unionisation rate (%)
1976	53
1982	54
1986	50
1990	46
1994	38
1996	35
2003	25
2007	19

Source: Anne Hawke & Mark Wooden, 'The changing face of Australian industrial relations', *Economic Record*, vol. 74, no. 224, 1998, pp. 74–88; 2003 figures from: www.actu.asn.au.

The role of unions has been the source of considerable debate in Australia. Every year it seems that workers and employers in some industry, whether it be air transport, meat processing or the waterfront, are in a dispute. Unionisation was partly a response to very poor working conditions in those industries. There was a time when being a member of a union was seen as very important to achieving better work conditions. Recently, however, economic changes have altered this pattern. As depicted in Table 28.2, trade union membership rates are declining in Australia.

The economics of unions

When a union bargains with a firm, it asks for higher wages, better benefits and better working conditions than the firm would offer in the absence of a union. If the union and the firm do not reach agreement, the union can organise a withdrawal of labour from the firm, called a **strike**. Because a strike reduces production, sales and profit, a firm facing a strike threat is likely to agree to pay higher wages than it otherwise would.

When a union raises the wage above the equilibrium level, it raises the quantity of labour supplied and may reduce the quantity of labour demanded, resulting in unemployment. Those workers who remain employed are better off, but those who were previously employed and are now unemployed at the higher wage are worse off. Indeed, unions are often thought to cause conflict between different groups of workers – between the *insiders* who benefit from high union wages and the *outsiders* who do not get the union jobs.

The outsiders can respond to their status in one of two ways. Some of them remain unemployed and wait for the chance to become insiders and earn the high union wage. Others take jobs in firms that are not unionised. Thus, when unions raise wages in one part of the economy, the supply of labour increases in other parts of the economy. This increase in labour supply, in turn, reduces wages in industries that are not unionised. In other words, workers in unions reap the benefit of collective bargaining, whereas workers not in unions bear some of the cost.

strike
the organised withdrawal of labour from a firm by a union

The end result is that the existence of unions can cause wages to be higher and, hence, some workers to be unemployed. However, the ability of unions to exert this control depends on their specific goals. Many unions are explicitly concerned about unemployment levels and are willing to negotiate arrangements that promote existing employment levels. During the 1990s, these negotiations were assisted by the Hawke Labor government, which offered workers tax cuts in order to preserve after-tax real incomes.

CASE**STUDY**

Australian workplace relations past and present

As discussed in chapter 6, Australia has a system of minimum wages that take the form of awards. These are minimum wage levels that are set for certain jobs in broad industry categories. So in contrast to a simple minimum wage, the award system affords some flexibility in the system to take into account differences in industry conditions and job skills.

These awards are still, however, minimum wages. Federal elections have been won and lost over whether workers should bargain over wages and other terms and conditions of employment as individuals or collectively, through representation by a union. In 2005, the Howard government introduced WorkChoices, a significant reform to the way workers and employers bargained with each other. WorkChoices eliminated unfair dismissal laws for smaller companies (laws that prevented companies from arbitrarily dismissing workers), introduced individual bargaining arrangements and diminished the power of unions to bargain on behalf of groups of workers. It also reduced the ability of workers to go on strike legally. Employer groups credited WorkChoices with improving productivity and enhancing Australia's economic growth potential.

Not everyone agreed, though. In 2007, the Labor Party won the election and many commentators said the ill-will created in the workforce by WorkChoices was a major factor in Kevin Rudd, leader of the Labor Party, becoming Prime Minister. In 2009, the Rudd government passed legislation that removed the emphasis on individual bargaining, introduced Fair Work Australia to replace the Australian Industrial Relations Commission, which had previously settled industrial disputes, set wage awards and ruled on unfair dismissal cases. Fair Work Australia's role is to cover all aspects of industrial relations, including determining the system of award wages, setting minimum wages, engaging in dispute resolution, including claims for unfair dismissal, and approving agreements between enterprises and workers or groups of workers.

Historically, the Australian Industrial Relations Commission played an important role in

>>

monitoring the demands for wage increases as a result of increases in inflation. Recall that inflation raises prices across the economy. This reduces the purchasing power of the current income of workers and puts pressure on those incomes to rise. In Australia, this pressure has been recognised and has periodically been a part of the determination of awards (from 1921 to 1952 and from 1975 to 1980). Under wage indexation, wages would rise in line with inflation. If the inflation rate was 8 per cent, award wages would automatically rise by at least 8 per cent.

The problem with this policy is that wages are part of the costs of production. So when wages rise for reasons other than an increase in productivity, production costs rise. This, in turn, leads to higher prices for goods and services and, hence, inflation. If this inflation is again passed through to higher wages, the cycle continues. The result, as occurred during the late 1970s, is an ever-rising inflation rate. In 1980, partial indexation was seen as a way of stopping the 'wage–price spiral'. However, union pressure meant that real wages continued to rise.

In 1983, the Labor Party, under Bob Hawke, decided to use its close relationship with the Australian Council of Trade Unions (ACTU) to break this cycle. As part of their election policy, they entered into a Prices and Incomes Accord (known simply as the Accord). This Accord limited wage increases, guaranteed productivity increases and, at the same time, maintained worker incomes. In return, unions received assurances of the use of macroeconomic policies that would expand employment rather than fight inflation.

The Accord was renegotiated over the next decade to include guarantees of tax cuts in return for wage restraint. As we will see in a later chapter, wages policy became an integral part of macroeconomic stabilisation policy.

IN THE NEWS …

HOW TO DIVIDE UP THE GROWING PIE?

Unions and employer groups disagree who has benefited the most from Australia's continued economic growth. Employers worry that if wages grow too rapidly, it will lead to increases in their costs and reduce their competitiveness. The ACTU counters that wages growth hasn't kept up with the growth in profits.

ACTU profit protest skews facts say employer groups
by Geoff Winestock

The economic pie has grown in the past year but unions say the numbers prove workers are not getting their fair share.

The Australian Council of Trade Unions has seized on data showing that, as a share of total national income, company profits have surged to 39 per cent while wages account for just under 50 per cent.

A decade ago wages accounted for 5 percentage points more of total national income while the Australian Bureau of Statistics' measure of profits was as low as 33 per cent.

ACTU secretary Jeff Lawrence told the Australian Industry Group annual conference in the past week that the profit share percentage was now near the record highs seen in 2008 but 'the wage share of income is the lowest since 1964'. Lawrence said he was only trying to rebut claims from business that Prime Minister Julia Gillard's pro-union Fair Work reforms introduced 18 months ago would cause a wages blowout.

Nevertheless, employer groups including the Australian Mines and Metals Association said Lawrence's rhetoric foreshadowed a 'greedy cash grab' in coming wage claims.

Lawrence's use of the obscure statistics of wage and profit share unsettles some because it conjures up images of a zero-sum game.

Ian Harper, who was chairman of the former Australian Fair Pay Commission, says Lawrence is correct that profit share has grown recently but it does not prove workers are being exploited. He says in the past five years the fastest growing section of the economy has been the mining industry, which is very capital-intensive. Wage costs typically account for just 10 per cent of total revenue in mining.

Harper predicts that as the huge investments in mining plateau, the profit share will fall. 'Once the capital boom starts to ease off we will see a strong response to the productivity of labour and wages,' Harper says.

Mark Wooden, of the Institute of Applied Economic and Social Research at the University of Melbourne, also cautions against reading too much into wage and profit share data, often distorted by tax and statistical blips. For instance, he says part of the growth in profit share in the past 10 years reflects the big cuts in company tax a decade ago, which encouraged small business owners to channel more of their remuneration into dividends rather than salary. Wages as a share of total income at about 56 per cent were much higher during the 1990s before the company tax cuts. He says a rise in the profit share is not necessarily bad for ACTU members because increasingly they share in the profits via their superannuation funds. Wooden adds unions are right to point out that gross operating profits have recovered 17 per cent in the year to end June but says that does not justify a uniform push for higher wages because recovery has not been uniform.

In the mining sector, the ABS measure of gross operating profit jumped 60 per cent over the past year, 15 times faster than wages. But in many sectors, such as financial services and wholesale trade, wages stayed firm while profits fell.

Wooden says wage demands on vulnerable industries or companies will just drive up unemployment.

'If the ACTU is talking about targeting companies making big profits, I have no qualms. That is what unions were put on this earth to do,' he says. '[But] if they are talking about increasing award wages across the board, then it hits companies that cannot afford it.'

As the economy recovers from the global financial crisis, the Reserve Bank of Australia says wage rises are 'relatively moderate'.

The wage price index, which the RBA watches keenly, grew just 3 per cent in the year to the June quarter, which is slightly below inflation and well below the average of the past decade.

In its October board meeting minutes, released during the week, wages did not rate a mention but the RBA scrutinised various measures of labour market tightness for signs that wage pressure might be building.

It said the evidence was mixed. Business surveys suggest workers are still easy to find while one ABS measure of job vacancies was 'somewhat tighter'.

Source: Geoff Winestock/*The Australian Financial Review*, 23 October 2010.

fyi

Why do strikes occur?

Strikes are costly to both firms and workers. To firms they represent lost output; to workers, lost income. The longer the strike, the more costly to both parties. So why do they occur?

In reality, strikes occur because negotiations do not always run so smoothly. Negotiations break down. During times of disagreement, unions wish to demonstrate their resolve by striking and being willing to forgo income. Management also wants to demonstrate to the union that it can weather a strike and hold out as well. In this case, disagreements are the result of 'brinkmanship' – an attempt by both parties to temporarily use threats to demonstrate the value of their work to the firm.

If both unions and management had a better understanding of the costs of strike action, brinkmanship might not occur. In this way, strikes can be seen as the result of a lack of information. Unions might believe that a company does not appreciate their full value. Management might believe that unions do not appreciate the willingness of their company's shareholders to hold out and earn high profits.

Nonetheless, in the past – whether because of simple misunderstandings or differences in information – many workdays were lost to industrial action in Australia. Australia has always had government involvement in the resolution of

>>

industrial disputes. At its core is a dispute resolution body – previously the Industrial Relations Commission, now Fair Work Australia. Whenever a union contemplated strike action, the Commission's task was to step in and arbitrate the dispute. Its rulings were binding. Today, Fair Work Australia performs that role.

The arbitration system was strengthened considerably during the 1980s. Also during that time the Labor government struck an Accord with the trade unions to agree to wage restraint. The result of this was a dramatic reduction in strike action. As depicted in Figure 28.5, this resulted in a reduction in workdays lost due to industrial disputes. Under the Coalition government, there was an initial increase in the number of days lost through disputes, but this number has dropped dramatically, with only a slight increase in 2002.

Figure 28.5   Industrial disputes in Australia

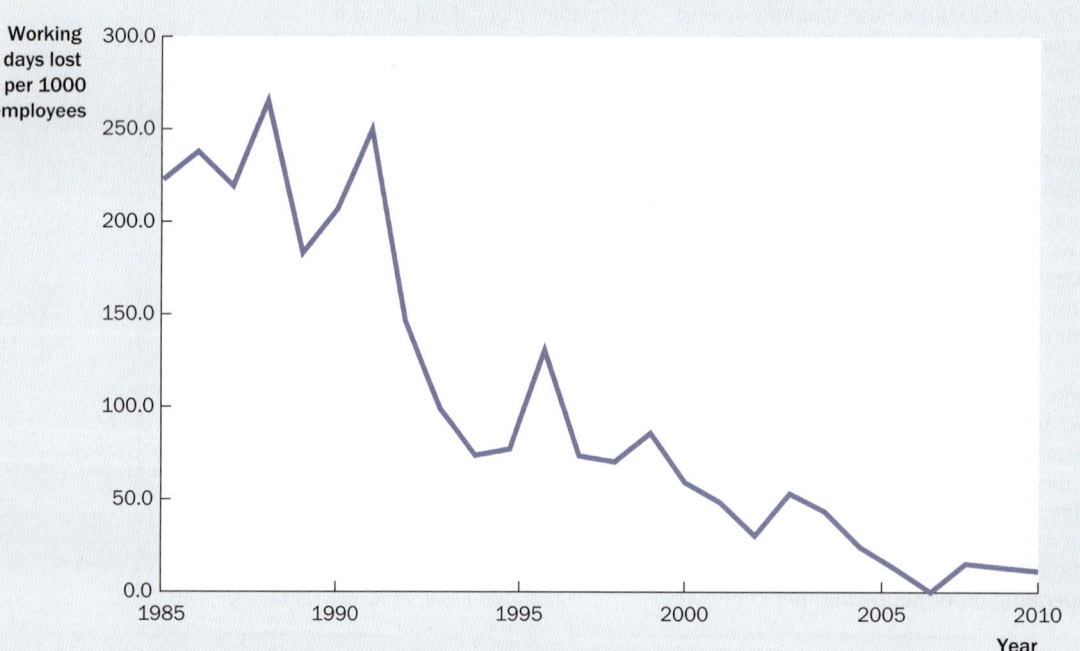

Source: Based on statistical data from the ABS, various years, Cat. Nos 6101.0 and 6321.0.

 How does a union in the car industry affect wages and employment at Holden and Ford? How does it affect wages and employment in other industries?

The theory of efficiency wages

One explanation for different earnings might come from different practices designed to improve workplace performance. Firms may set wages high so as to motivate workers to perform well in their jobs. This wage is called an **efficiency wage**. Efficiency wages are necessarily above-equilibrium wages that would result when supply equals demand. Thus, efficiency wages can potentially explain unemployment as well as earnings.

efficiency wages
above-equilibrium wages paid by firms in order to increase worker productivity

Why should firms want to keep wages high? In some ways, this decision seems odd, for wages are a large part of firms' costs. Normally, we expect profit-maximising firms to want to keep costs – and therefore wages – as low as possible. The novel insight of efficiency-wage theory is that paying high wages might be profitable because it might raise the efficiency of a firm's workers by more than it costs.

There are several types of efficiency-wage theory. Each type suggests a different explanation for why firms may want to pay high wages. Let's now consider four of these theories.

Worker health

The first and simplest type of efficiency-wage theory emphasises the link between wages and worker health. Better paid workers eat a more nutritious diet and workers who eat a better diet are healthier and more productive. A firm may find it more profitable to pay high wages and have healthy, productive workers than to pay lower wages and have less healthy, less productive workers.

This type of efficiency-wage theory is not relevant for firms in rich countries such as Australia. In these countries, the equilibrium wages for most workers are well above the level needed for an adequate diet. Firms are not concerned that paying equilibrium wages would place their workers' health in jeopardy.

Paying higher wages to raise worker health is more relevant for firms in less developed countries where inadequate nutrition is a more common problem. Unemployment is high in the cities of many poor African countries, for example. In these countries, firms may fear that cutting wages would adversely influence their workers' health and productivity. Concern over nutrition may explain why firms do not cut wages despite a surplus of labour.

Worker turnover

A second type of efficiency-wage theory emphasises the link between wages and worker turnover. Workers quit jobs for many reasons – to take jobs in other firms, to move to other parts of the country, to leave the labour force and so on. The frequency with which they quit depends on the entire set of incentives they face, including the benefits of leaving and the benefits of staying with their current employer. The more a firm pays its workers, the less often its workers will choose to leave. Thus, a firm can reduce turnover among its workers by paying them a high wage.

Why do firms care about turnover? The reason is that it is costly for firms to hire and train new workers. Moreover, even after they are trained, newly hired workers are not as productive as experienced workers. Firms with higher turnover, therefore, will tend to have higher production costs. Firms may find it profitable to pay wages above the equilibrium level in order to reduce worker turnover.

Worker effort

A third type of efficiency-wage theory emphasises the link between wages and worker effort. In many jobs, workers have some discretion over how hard to work. As a result, firms monitor the efforts of their workers, and workers caught shirking their responsibilities are fired. But not all shirkers are caught immediately because monitoring workers is costly and imperfect. A firm can respond to this problem by paying wages above the equilibrium level. High wages make workers more eager to keep their jobs and, thereby, give workers an incentive to put forward their best effort.

This particular type of efficiency-wage theory is similar to the old Marxist idea of the 'reserve army of the unemployed'. Marx thought that employers benefited from unemployment because the threat of unemployment helped to discipline those workers who had jobs. In the worker-effort variant of efficiency-wage theory, unemployment fills a similar role. If the wage were at the level that balanced supply and demand, workers would have less reason to work hard because, if they were fired, they could quickly find new jobs at the same wage. Therefore, firms find it profitable to raise wages above the equilibrium level. This causes unemployment while providing an incentive for workers not to shirk their responsibilities.

Worker quality

A fourth and final type of efficiency-wage theory emphasises the link between wages and worker quality. When a firm hires new workers, it cannot perfectly gauge the quality of the applicants. By paying a high wage, the firm attracts a better pool of workers to apply for its jobs.

To see how this might work, consider a simple example. Waterwell Company owns one well and needs one worker to pump water from the well. Two workers, Bill and Ben, are interested in the job. Bill, a proficient worker, is willing to work for $10 per hour. Below that wage, he would rather start his own lawn-mowing business. Ben, a complete incompetent, is willing to work for anything above $2 per hour. Below that wage, he would rather sit on the beach. Economists say that Bill's *reservation wage* – the lowest wage he would accept – is $10, and Ben's reservation wage is $2.

What wage should the firm set? If the firm were interested in minimising labour costs, it would set the wage at $2 per hour. At this wage, the quantity of workers supplied (one) would balance the quantity demanded. Ben would take the job and Bill would not apply for it. Yet suppose Waterwell knows that only one of these two applicants is competent, but it does not know whether it is Bill or Ben. If the firm hires the incompetent worker, he will damage the well, causing the firm huge losses. In this case, the firm has a better strategy than paying the equilibrium wage of $2 and hiring Ben. It can offer $10 per hour, inducing both Bill and Ben to apply for the job. By choosing randomly between these two applicants and turning the other away, the firm has a 50-50 chance of hiring the competent worker. In contrast, if the firm offers any lower wage, it is sure to hire the incompetent worker.

This story illustrates a general phenomenon. When a firm has an excess supply of workers, it might seem profitable to reduce the wage it is offering. But by reducing the wage, the firm induces an adverse change in the mix of workers. In this case, at a wage of $10, Waterwell has two workers applying for one job. But if Waterwell responds to this excess supply by reducing the wage, the competent worker (who has better alternative opportunities) will not apply. Thus, it is profitable for the firm to pay a wage above the level that balances supply and demand.

CASESTUDY

Henry Ford and the generous $5-a-day wage

Henry Ford was an industrial visionary. As founder of the Ford Motor Company, he was responsible for introducing modern techniques of production. Rather than building cars with small teams of skilled craftsmen, Ford built cars on assembly lines in which unskilled workers were taught to perform the same simple tasks over and over again. The output of this assembly process was the Model T Ford, one of the most famous early cars.

In 1914, Ford introduced another innovation – the $5 workday. This might not seem like much today, but back then $5 was about twice the going wage. It was also far above the wage that balanced supply and demand. When the new $5-a-day wage was announced, long lines of job seekers formed outside the Ford factories. The number of workers willing to work at this wage far exceeded the number of workers Ford needed.

Ford's high-wage policy had many of the effects predicted by efficiency wage theory. Turnover fell, absenteeism fell and productivity rose. Workers were so much more efficient that Ford's production costs were lower even though wages were higher. Thus, paying a wage above the equilibrium level was profitable for the firm. Henry Ford himself called the $5-a-day wage 'one of the finest cost-cutting moves we ever made'.

Historical accounts of this episode are also consistent with efficiency-wage theory. A historian of the early Ford Motor Company wrote, 'Ford and his associates freely declared on many occasions that the high-wage policy turned out to be good business. By this they meant that it had improved the discipline of the workers, given them a more loyal interest in the institution, and raised their personal efficiency.'

Why did it take Henry Ford to introduce this efficiency wage? Why were other firms not already taking advantage of this seemingly profitable business strategy? According to some analysts, Ford's decision was closely linked to his use of the assembly line. Workers organised in an assembly line are highly interdependent. If one worker is absent or works slowly, other workers are less able to complete their own tasks. Thus, while assembly lines made production more efficient, they also raised the importance of low worker turnover, high worker quality and high worker effort. As a result, paying efficiency wages may have been a better strategy for the Ford Motor Company than for other businesses at the time.

Give four explanations for why firms might find it profitable to pay wages above the level that balances quantity of labour supplied and quantity of labour demanded.

Job search

A fourth reason economies always experience some unemployment, besides minimum-wage laws, unions and efficiency wages, is job search. **Job search** is the process of matching workers with appropriate jobs. If all workers and all jobs were the same, so that all workers were equally well suited for all jobs, job search would not be a problem. Laid-off workers would quickly find new jobs that were well suited to them. But, in fact, workers differ in their tastes and skills, jobs differ in their attributes, and information about job candidates and job vacancies is disseminated slowly among the many firms and households in the economy.

job search
the process by which workers find appropriate jobs given their tastes and skills

The unemployment that arises because of job search is, in an important sense, different from the unemployment that arises because of minimum-wage laws, unions and efficiency wages. In the previous three cases, the wage is above the equilibrium level, so the quantity of labour supplied exceeds the quantity of labour demanded; workers are unemployed because they are *waiting* for jobs to open up. In contrast, job search is not due to the failure of wages to balance labour supply and labour demand. When job search is the explanation for unemployment, workers are *searching* for the jobs that best suit them.

---

fyi

The economics of asymmetric information

In many situations in life, information is asymmetric – one person in a transaction knows more about what is going on than the other person. This possibility raises a variety of interesting problems for economic theory. We have just seen some of these problems raised in the context of developing the theory of efficiency wages. These problems, however, go beyond the study of unemployment.

The worker-quality variant of efficiency-wage theory illustrates a general principle called *adverse*

>>

selection. Adverse selection arises when one person knows more about the attributes of a good than another and, as a result, the uninformed person runs the risk of being sold a good of low quality. In the worker-quality story, for instance, workers have better information about their own abilities than firms do. When a firm cuts the wage it pays, the selection of workers changes in a way that is adverse to the firm.

Adverse selection arises in many other circumstances. Here are two examples:

- Sellers of used cars know their cars' defects whereas buyers often do not. Because owners of the worst cars are more likely to sell them than are the owners of the best cars, car buyers are correctly apprehensive about getting a 'lemon'. As a result, many people avoid buying cars in the used-car market.

- Buyers of private health insurance know more about their own health problems than do health funds. Because people with greater hidden health problems are more likely to buy private health insurance than are other people, the price of health insurance reflects the costs of a sicker-than-average person. As a result, people with average health problems are discouraged from buying private health insurance.

In each case, the market for the product – used cars or private health insurance – does not work as well as it might because of the problem of adverse selection.

Similarly, the worker-effort variant of efficiency-wage theory illustrates a general phenomenon called *moral hazard*. Moral hazard arises when one person, called the agent, is performing some task on behalf of another person, called the principal. Because the principal cannot perfectly monitor the agent's behaviour, the agent tends to undertake less effort than the principal considers desirable. The term 'moral hazard' refers to the risk of dishonest or otherwise inappropriate behaviour by the agent. In such a situation, the principal tries various ways to encourage the agent to act more responsibly.

In an employment relationship, the firm is the principal and the worker is the agent. The moral-hazard problem is the temptation of imperfectly monitored workers to shirk their responsibilities. According to the worker-effort variant of efficiency-wage theory, the principal can encourage the agent not to shirk by paying a wage above the equilibrium level because then the agent has more to lose if caught shirking. In this way, high wages reduce the problem of moral hazard.

Moral hazard arises in many other situations. Here are some examples:

- A homeowner with fire insurance buys too few fire extinguishers. The reason is that the homeowner bears the cost of the extinguisher whereas the insurance company receives much of the benefit.

- A babysitter allows children to watch more television than the parents of the children prefer. The reason is that more educational activities require more energy from the babysitter, even though they are beneficial for the children.

- A family lives near a river with a high risk of flooding. The reason it continues to live there is that the family enjoys the scenic views and the government will bear part of the cost when it provides disaster relief after a flood.

Can you identify the principal and the agent in each of these situations? How do you think the principal in each case might solve the problem of moral hazard?

The inevitability of search unemployment

Search unemployment is often the result of changes in the demand for labour among different firms. When consumers decide that they prefer iPhones over Blackberrys, Apple increases employment and Research in Motion (the company that makes Blackberrys) lays off workers. The former Research in Motion workers must now search for new jobs and Apple must decide which new workers to hire for the various jobs that have opened up. The result of this transition is temporary unemployment.

Similarly, because different regions of the country produce different goods, employment can rise in one region and fall in another. Consider, for instance, what happens when the world price of coal rises. Coal mines in Western Australia respond to the higher price by increasing production and employment. At the same time, more expensive coal increases electricity costs, so aluminium refineries in Queensland that are electricity-intensive decrease production and employment. Changes in the composition of demand among industries or regions are called sectoral shifts. Because it takes time for workers to search for jobs in the new sectors, *sectoral shifts* temporarily cause unemployment.

Search unemployment is inevitable simply because the economy is always changing. A century ago, the sectors with the largest employment in Australia were primary industries such as agriculture and mining. Today, the largest employers are in services including retail trade and health care services. As this transition took place, jobs were created in some firms and were destroyed in others. The end result of this process has been higher productivity and higher living standards. But, along the way, workers in declining industries found themselves out of work and searching for new jobs.

Public policy and job search

Even if some search unemployment is inevitable, public policy can nonetheless affect its prevalence. To the extent that policy can reduce the time it takes unemployed workers to find new jobs, it can reduce search unemployment.

Government programs try to facilitate job finding in various ways. One way is through government-sponsored employment agencies, which give out information about job vacancies in order to match workers and jobs more quickly. Another way is through public training programs, which aim to ease the transition of workers from declining to growing industries and to help disadvantaged groups escape poverty. The Australian government now spends around 2.5 billion dollars each year on job training and related programs.

Critics of these programs question whether the government should get involved with the process of job search. They argue that it is better to let the private market match workers and jobs. In fact, most job search in our economy takes place without intervention by the government. Newspaper advertisements, job newsletters, university placement offices, headhunters and word of mouth all help spread information about job openings and job candidates. Similarly, much worker education is done privately, either through schools or through on-the-job training. These critics contend that the government is no better – and most likely worse – at disseminating the right information to the right workers and deciding what kinds of worker training would be most valuable. They claim that these decisions are best made privately by workers and employers.

Unemployment benefits

One government program that increases the amount of search unemployment, without intending to do so, is **unemployment benefits**. This program is designed to offer workers partial protection against income loss. Any person who becomes unemployed is eligible for such benefits. However, in recent times, the length of eligibility has been lowered to about six months if a person does not undertake reasonable efforts to regain employment. Regardless, unemployment benefits are usually only a fraction of a worker's previous wage.

unemployment benefits
a government program that partially protects workers' incomes when they become unemployed

Although unemployment benefits reduce the hardship of unemployment, they also increase the amount of unemployment. The explanation is based on one of the *Ten Lessons from Economics* in chapter 1 – people respond to incentives. Because unemployment benefits stop when a worker takes a new job, the unemployed devote less effort to job search and are more likely to turn down unattractive job offers. In addition, because unemployment benefits make unemployment less onerous, workers are less likely to seek guarantees of job security when they negotiate with employers over the terms of employment.

Many studies by labour economists have examined the incentive effects of unemployment benefits. One study examined an experiment run by the US state of Illinois in 1985. When unemployed workers applied to collect unemployment benefits, the state randomly selected some of them and offered each a $500 bonus if they found new jobs within 11 weeks. This group was then compared with a control group not offered the incentive. The average spell of unemployment for the group offered the bonus was 7 per cent shorter than the average spell for the control group. This experiment shows that the design of the unemployment benefits system influences the effort that the unemployed devote to job search.

Several other studies examined search effort by following a group of workers over time. In the United States, rather than lasting for many years (subject to job search requirements), unemployment benefits usually run out after six months or a year. These studies found that when the unemployed become ineligible for benefits, the probability of their finding a new job rises markedly. Thus, receiving unemployment benefits does reduce the search effort of the unemployed.

Even though unemployment benefits reduce search effort and raise unemployment, we should not necessarily conclude that the policy is a bad one. The program does achieve its primary goal of reducing the income uncertainty that workers face. In addition, when workers turn down unattractive job offers, they have the opportunity to look for jobs that better suit their tastes and skills. Some economists have argued that unemployment benefits improve the ability of the economy to match each worker with the most appropriate job.

The study of unemployment benefits shows that the unemployment rate is an imperfect measure of a nation's overall level of economic wellbeing. Most economists agree that eliminating unemployment benefits would reduce the amount of unemployment in the economy. Yet economists disagree on whether economic wellbeing would be enhanced or diminished by this change in policy.

IN THE NEWS . . .

THE LOCATION OF UNEMPLOYMENT

Popular discussions of unemployment rarely consider the composition of the unemployed. Even though unemployment in certain groups is sometimes targeted (for instance, youth or ethnic minority), there is still a tendency to view unemployment in the aggregate around the country. But as the following article demonstrates, not all Australians are benefitting equally from the boom in the mining industry.

Finding a job easier in some places than others

by Mark Davis

The gap between Australia's regional jobless rates is at its widest in almost 20 years.
Far north Queensland may be beautiful one day, perfect the next, but the economic climate in the tropical north has taken on a definite wintry chill.

Unemployment in Cairns and the surrounding region has skyrocketed to 12.3 per cent over the last 12 months – a level which would mean a deep recession if it were replicated nationwide.

For while the Federal Government has taken credit for the Australia-wide unemployment rate not rising as much as feared when the global financial crisis hit, behind the national figures lies a very different story of regional winners and losers.

Cairns is the most extreme case. But local unemployment rates have risen to close to double figures in several jobless hotspots around the country – including swathes of Melbourne's outer suburbs which are home to the battlers who flocked back to Labor at the 2007 election.

By contrast, there is a handful of prosperous regions where the local population is virtually in full employment. Sydney's wealthy lower north shore, for instance, had the country's lowest regional unemployment rate of just 2.6 per cent in the September quarter.

The gap between Australia's highest and lowest regional unemployment rates has doubled since the middle of 2008. At nearly 10 per cent, it is at its widest since the early 1990s.

While a rising economic tide may lift all boats, a receding tide apparently leaves some regions more high and dry than others.

The national unemployment rate stood at 5.7 per cent in September, up 1.4 percentage points over the last 12 months. Economists reckon it will peak next year at around 7 per cent, an outlook considerably better than expected when the global financial crisis struck the economy late last year.

But the ABS also publishes labour force estimates for 66 statistical regions around the country. And these show that almost one in every five regions already had unemployment rates of 7 per cent or higher in the September quarter.

In Melbourne, the hardest hit of the ABS statistical regions is south-eastern Melbourne – covering Dandenong, Narre Warren, Berwick, Cranbourne and Pakenham – where the unemployment rate has jumped more than four percentage points over the year to the September quarter to reach 8.7 per cent.

Other high unemployment regions are north-western Melbourne – taking in areas running north and north-west from Coburg to Broadmeadows, Craigieburn and Sunbury, where unemployment stood at 7.7 per cent in the three months to September – and outer-western Melbourne, which runs from the suburbs of Footscray and Essendon West to Keilor, Melton and Werribee, where unemployment for the quarter was 6.7 per cent.

In country Victoria, the central northern statistical region of Goulburn-Ovens-Murray – which includes Albury, Wangaratta, Shepparton, Mansfield, Strathbogie and Echuca – has an unemployment rate of 6.3 per cent.

The Minister for Employment Participation, Mark Arbib, who, with Deputy Prime Minister Julia Gillard, is responsible for the Federal Government's regional employment strategies,

says the global recession has affected local communities in different ways.

'Some communities have proven extremely resilient and others have felt the full brunt of the recession,' Senator Arbib told The Age.

He says the Government's research suggests there are several common denominators that make local labour markets vulnerable to slower economic growth.

'Areas with high levels of manufacturing have done worst during the downturn. Some areas have a more diversified industry base and don't rely heavily on one sector.

'Areas with low levels of educational attainment are vulnerable because it affects labour mobility, in terms of people's ability to move from one job into another. The less education you have, the more at risk your job is and at the same time the more training is required to move into a new job.'

Melbourne's south-east, he points out, relies heavily on manufacturing, which accounts for about 20 per cent of local employment. There have been more than 2,300 reported redundancies in the south-eastern suburbs over the last year, many in automotive component manufacturing.

Senator Arbib says the Government is tackling the regionally uneven distribution of unemployment by designating 20 'priority employment areas' where there are high levels of unemployment, low employment growth and high proportions of the local population on welfare benefits.

It has hired local employment coordinators for each of these areas. These are convening Keep Australia Working forums and jobs expos to bring together federal, state and local government officials, along with local businesses and community groups, to develop regional employment plans.

Trucking magnate Lindsay Fox and former ACTU secretary Bill Kelty are touring the priority employment areas to promote the process.

Senator Arbib also points to the Government's $650 million Jobs Fund, which is delivering grants for local job creation projects and a boost to government wage subsidies for employers taking on apprentices

>>

over the coming summer months when school leavers will enter the labour market.

But the Opposition's spokesman on employment and workplace relations, Michael Keenan, says there is a fundamental divide between Labor and the Coalition on how to tackle unemployment.

'On the one hand the Government is massively regulating the labour market with its changes to industrial relations legislation, making it harder for the private sector to create employment,' Mr Keenan said.

'Then they are setting up government programs to try to create jobs. They seem to think it is the government's role to provide employment, but history shows that is not a sustainable approach. Surely the way to create jobs is to allow the people that do it best, the employers, to get on with the job.'

Cairns has been especially hard hit by the lack of a diversified local industry employment structure, due to its heavy reliance on tourism.

The local federal MP, Labor's Jim Turnour, says tourism to north Queensland has been hit by the triple whammy of the global recession, swine flu and a stronger Australian dollar.

'When visitor numbers fall it flows right through into construction and other parts of the economy,' Mr Turnour said.

'Some businesses are doing better than others, but in general there is a negative feeling and a real concern in Cairns that, come the end of the year, people will decide there are no jobs and will not re-enrol their kids in school and move on.'

Mr Turnour's far north electorate of Leichhardt is one of many Coalition-held Queensland electorates that fell to Labor in the 2007 election. He holds it by just 3.8 per cent of the two-party preferred vote, making it one of the key marginal seats the Government will defend at the next federal election.

Not surprisingly, then, Mr Turnour is talking up the impact of the Government's regional employment strategy, including initiatives to diversify far north Queensland's tourism base and to encourage investment by mining companies to create jobs.

The Government has been pointing to Australia's relatively small downturn as evidence of the success of its economic policies. So Labor strategists will be concerned at the potential for high local unemployment to generate backlashes in individual electorates at next year's election.

Much of the country's unemployment is concentrated in highly safe Labor electorates such as Banks, Blaxland and Fowler in Sydney, and Calwell, Wills, Gellibrand and Employment Minister Julia Gillard's seat of Lalor in Melbourne.

But there are nine marginal Labor and Liberal electorates in regions with high unemployment. In addition to Leichhardt, these are: Fairfax, Fisher and Flynn along the Queensland central coast; Macarthur in Sydney's south-west and Greenway in the north-west; La Trobe on Melbourne's south-eastern fringes; and Swan and Canning in Perth's south-east.

That means the success of the Government's regional employment strategies will not only have social and economic consequences – but could also have significant political fallout in election 2010.

Source: Mark Davis/*The Age*, 2 November 2009.

How would an increase in the world price of oil affect the amount of search unemployment? Is this unemployment undesirable? What public policies might affect the amount of unemployment caused by this price change?

Conclusion

In this chapter, we discussed the measurement of unemployment and the reasons economies always experience some degree of unemployment. We have seen how minimum-wage laws, unions, efficiency wages and job search can all help explain why some workers do not have jobs. Which of these four explanations for the natural rate of unemployment are the most important for the Australian economy and other economies around the world? Unfortunately, there is no easy way to tell. Economists therefore differ in which of these explanations of unemployment they consider most important.

Unemployment is not a simple problem with a simple solution. Instead, it has various explanations and is affected by various public policies. When politicians debate the minimum wage, the laws regulating collective bargaining, or unemployment benefits, one issue is always the impact of these policies on the economy's natural rate of unemployment.

Summary

- The unemployment rate is the percentage of those who would like to work but do not have jobs. The ABS calculates this statistic monthly based on a survey of thousands of households.
- The unemployment rate is an imperfect measure of joblessness. Some people who call themselves unemployed may actually not want to work and some people who would like to work have left the labour force after an unsuccessful search.
- In the Australian economy, most people who become unemployed find work within a short period of time. Nonetheless, most unemployment observed at any given time is attributable to the few people who are unemployed for long periods of time.
- One reason our economy always has some unemployment is minimum-wage laws. By raising the wage of unskilled and inexperienced workers above the equilibrium level, minimum-wage laws raise the quantity of labour supplied and reduce the quantity demanded. The resulting excess supply of labour represents unemployment.
- A second reason for unemployment is the market power of unions. When unions push the wages in unionised industries above the equilibrium level, they create an excess supply of labour.
- A third reason for unemployment is suggested by the theory of efficiency wages. According to this theory, firms find it profitable to pay wages above the equilibrium level. High wages can improve worker health, lower worker turnover, increase worker effort and raise worker quality.
- A fourth reason for unemployment is the time it takes for workers to search for jobs that best suit their skills and tastes. The unemployment benefit is a government policy that, while protecting workers' incomes, increases the amount of search unemployment.

Key concepts

collective bargaining
cyclical unemployment
discouraged workers
efficiency wages

job search
labour force
labour-force participation rate
natural rate of unemployment

strike
unemployment benefits
unemployment rate
union

Questions for review

1. What are the three categories into which the ABS divides everyone? How does it calculate the labour force, the unemployment rate and the labour-force participation rate?
2. Is all unemployment short term? What factors affect whether it is short term or long term? Explain.
3. Are minimum-wage laws a better explanation for unemployment among teenagers or among university graduates? Why?
4. Why would some people be underemployed? How does this affect the economy's growth prospects if people are underemployed?
5. Why does the level of unemployment vary from region to region within Australia? If you were advising the government about policies to improve unemployment, what would you suggest to improve the distribution of unemployment?

6   Explain four ways in which a firm might increase its profits by raising the wages it pays.

7   Is search unemployment short term or long term? How might the government reduce the amount of search unemployment?

Problems and applications

1   The ABS announced that, in October 2010, of all adult Australians, 11 149 700 were employed, 623 549 were unemployed, and the participation rate was 65.5 per cent. The civilian population over 15 years of age was 18 014 150. How many were not in the labour force? How big was the labour force? What was the unemployment rate?

2   As shown in Figure 28.3, the overall labour-force participation rate of men declined between 1978 and 2010. This overall decline reflects different patterns for different age groups, however, as shown in the following table.

	All men	Men 15–24	Men 25–54	Men 55 and over
1978	78%	80%	92%	54%
2010	72	69	90	40

   a   Which group experienced the largest decline? Given this information, what factor may have played an important role in the decline in overall male labour-force participation over this period?

   b   Why do different groups have different participation rates?

3   The following table show the *underemployment rate* for men, women and all people aged 25-34. The underemployment rate for men in this age bracket has gone up by 3.3 per cent, but for women only by 1.3 per cent. Why is this information useful for policymakers?

	Men 25–34	Women 25–34	All people 25–34
1978	1.3	5.4	2.7
2010	4.6	6.7	5.5

4   Are the following workers more likely to experience short-term or long-term unemployment? Explain.

   a   A construction worker laid off because of a decrease in the number of new building projects

   b   A mining engineer who loses her job at a mine in an isolated area

   c   A fruit picker laid off because of floods

   d   A cook in a fast-food outlet who loses his job when a new restaurant opens across the street

   e   A cleaner with little formal education who loses her job when her cleaning job is outsourced.

5   Using a diagram of the labour market, show the effect of an increase in the minimum wage on the wage paid to workers, the number of workers supplied, the number of workers demanded and the amount of unemployment.

6   Australian Workplace Agreements (AWAs), brought in by the Howard government in 2006, were individual agreements negotiated between an individual and his or her employer. They replaced collective or enterprise bargaining agreements, which were negotiated between a group of

employees, by a union, for example, and an employer. The Rudd and Gillard governments replaced AWAs with enterprise bargaining arrangements, where workers could be represented by someone else and bargain as a group.

a Do you think individual workers would have more or less power under AWAs than under the enterprise bargaining agreements?

b The Rudd Government, elected in late 2007, dismantled the AWA methodology for reaching workplace employment contracts. What are the *economic* arguments for and against AWAs?

7 It has been suggested that Australia has a two-speed economy – that is, some sectors that are doing really well and some sectors that aren't.

a If we had perfectly working labour markets, what would you expect to happen to wages in the two sectors? Explain.

b How would you explain the ongoing existence of high wages in the mining sector and high levels of rural unemployment?

c What government policies would you recommend to overcome the two-speed economy?

8 Each of the following situations involves moral hazard. In each case, identify the principal and the agent, and explain why there is asymmetric information. How does the action described reduce the problem of moral hazard?

a Landlords require tenants to pay security deposits

b Firms compensate top executives with options to buy company shares at a given price in the future

c Car insurance companies offer discounts to older drivers or those who have had fewer accidents.

9 Suppose that the Live-Long-and-Prosper Health Fund charges $8000 annually for family health cover. The fund's managing director suggests that the firm raise the annual price to $10 000 in order to increase its profits. If the firm followed this suggestion, what economic problem might arise? Would the firm's pool of customers tend to become more or less healthy on average? Would the firm's profits necessarily increase?

10 (This problem is challenging.) Suppose that the federal government passes a law requiring employers to provide employees some benefit (such as private health care) that raises the cost of an employee by $4 per hour. (In answering these questions, be quantitative when you can.)

a What effect does this legal requirement have on the demand for labour?

b If employees place a value on this benefit exactly equal to its cost, what effect does this legal requirement have on the supply of labour?

c If the wage is free to balance supply and demand, how does this legal requirement affect the wage and the level of employment? Are employers better or worse off? Are employees better or worse off?

d If a minimum-wage law prevents the wage from balancing supply and demand, how does the legal requirement to provide the benefit affect the wage, the level of employment and the level of unemployment? Are employers better or worse off? Are employees better or worse off?

e Now suppose that workers do not value the benefit at all. How does this alternative assumption change your answers to parts (b), (c) and (d) above?

Search me!

  Search me!

When accessing information about economics use the following keywords in any combinations you require:

- cyclical unemployment
- natural rate of unemployment

CourseMate

For more multimedia resources and activities on economics, visit the Economics CourseMate website.

PART TEN
Money and prices in the long run

29

The monetary system

Learning objectives

In this chapter you will:

- consider what money is and what functions money has in the economy

- learn about the Reserve Bank of Australia

- examine how the banking system influences the amount of money in the economy

- see what tools the Reserve Bank of Australia uses to influence liquidity conditions in the economy.

When you walk into a restaurant to buy a meal, you get something of value – your hunger satisfied. To pay for this service, you might hand the restaurateur several worn-out pieces of coloured plastic decorated with strange symbols, government buildings and the portraits of famous dead Australians. Or you might hand over a plastic card that is used to electronically access your cheque or savings account. Whether you pay by cash or debit card, the restaurateur is happy to work hard to satisfy your gastronomical desires in exchange for these pieces of plastic, which, in and of themselves, are worthless.

To anyone who has lived in a modern economy, this social custom is not at all odd. Even though plastic money has no intrinsic value, the restaurateur is confident that, in the future, some third person will accept it in exchange for something that the restaurateur does value. And that third person is confident that some fourth person will accept the money, with the knowledge that yet a fifth person will accept the money … and so on. To the restaurateur and to other people in our society, your cash represents a claim to goods and services in the future.

The social custom of using money for transactions is extraordinarily useful in a large, complex society. Imagine, for a moment, that there was no item in the economy widely accepted in exchange for goods and services. People would have to rely on *barter* – the exchange of one good or service for another – to obtain the things they need. To get your restaurant meal, for instance, you would have to offer the restaurateur something of immediate value. You could offer to wash some dishes, clean the floor, or give away your family's secret recipe for lamb roast. An economy that relies on barter will have trouble allocating its scarce resources efficiently. In such an economy, trade is said to require the *double coincidence of wants* – the unlikely occurrence that two people each have a good or service that the other wants at the same time.

The existence of money makes trade easier. Our restaurateur, George, does not care whether you can produce a valuable good or service for him. He is happy to accept your money, knowing that other people will do the same for him. Such a convention allows trade to be roundabout – a coincidence of desires to trade is not required. George accepts your money and uses it to pay Ellen, his chef; Ellen uses her pay cheque to send her child to day care; the day care centre uses these fees to pay Tom, a teacher; and Tom hires you to mow his lawn. As money flows from person to person in the economy, it facilitates production and trade, thereby allowing people to specialise in what they do best and raising everyone's standard of living.

In this chapter, we begin to examine the role of money in the economy. We discuss what money is, the various forms that money takes, how the banking system helps create money and how the government influences the quantity of money in circulation. Because money is so important in the economy, we devote much effort in the rest of this book to learning how money is linked to various economic variables, including inflation, interest rates, production and employment. Consistent with our long-run focus in the last three chapters, we will examine the long-run effects of changes in monetary policy in the next chapter. The short-run effects of monetary changes are a more complex topic, which we take up later in the book. This chapter provides the background for all of this further analysis.

The meaning of money

What is money? This might seem like an odd question. When you read that billionaire James Packer has a lot of money, you know what that means – he is so rich that he can buy almost anything he wants. In this sense, the term *money* is used to mean *wealth*.

680

money
the set of assets in an economy that people regularly use to buy goods and services from other people

Economists, however, use the word in a more specific sense. **Money** is the set of assets in the economy that people regularly use to buy goods and services from other people. The cash in your wallet is money because you can use it to buy a meal at a restaurant or a shirt at a clothing shop. In contrast, if you happened to be a major shareholder in Consolidated Press Holdings, as James Packer is, you would be wealthy, but this asset is not considered a form of money. You could not buy a meal or a shirt with this wealth without first obtaining some money. According to the economist's definition, money includes only those few types of wealth that are regularly accepted by sellers in exchange for goods and services.

The functions of money

Money has three functions in the economy – it is a *medium of exchange*, a *unit of account* and a *store of value*. These three functions together distinguish money from other assets.

medium of exchange
an item that buyers give to sellers when they want to purchase goods and services

A **medium of exchange** is an item that buyers give to sellers when they purchase goods and services. When you buy a shirt at a clothing shop, the shop gives you the shirt and you give the shop your money. This transfer of money from buyer to seller allows the transaction to take place. When you walk into a shop, you are confident that the shop will accept your money for the items it is selling because money is the commonly accepted medium of exchange.

unit of account
the yardstick people use to post prices and record debts

A **unit of account** is the yardstick people use to post prices and record debts. When you go shopping, you might observe that a shirt costs $20 and a meat pie costs $2. Even though it would be accurate to say that the price of a shirt is 10 meat pies and the price of a meat pie is 1/10 of a shirt, prices are never quoted in this way. Similarly, if you take out a loan from a bank, the size of your future loan repayments will be measured in dollars, not in a quantity of goods and services. When we want to measure and record economic value, we use money as the unit of account.

store of value
an item that people can use to transfer purchasing power from the present to the future

A **store of value** is an item that people can use to transfer purchasing power from the present to the future. When a seller accepts money today in exchange for a good or service, that seller can hold the money and become a buyer of another good or service at another time. Of course, money is not the only store of value in the economy. A person can also transfer purchasing power from the present to the future by holding shares, bonds, real estate, art or even old stamps. The term *wealth* is used to refer to the total of all stores of value, including both money and non-monetary assets.

liquidity
the ease with which an asset can be converted into the economy's medium of exchange

Economists use the term **liquidity** to describe the ease with which an asset can be converted into the economy's medium of exchange. Because money is the economy's medium of exchange, it is the most liquid asset available. Other assets vary widely in their liquidity. Most shares and bonds can be sold easily at little or no cost, so they are relatively liquid assets. In contrast, selling a house, a Rembrandt painting or a 1948 Don Bradman cricket bat requires more time and effort, so these assets are less liquid.

When people decide in what form to hold their wealth, they have to balance the liquidity of each possible asset against the asset's usefulness as a store of value. Money is the most liquid asset, but it is far from perfect as a store of value. When prices rise, the value of money falls. In other words, when goods and services become more expensive, each dollar in your wallet can buy less. This link between the price level and the value of money will turn out to be important for understanding how money affects the economy.

Kinds of money

commodity money
money that takes the form of a commodity with intrinsic value

When money takes the form of a commodity with intrinsic value, it is called **commodity money**. The term *intrinsic value* means that the item would have value even if it were not used as money.

One example of commodity money is gold. Gold has intrinsic value because it is used in industry and in the making of jewellery. Although today we no longer use gold as money, historically gold has been a common form of money because it is relatively easy to carry, measure and verify for impurities. And in times of great uncertainty, such as in the recent global financial crisis, people hold gold because it is seen as a safer asset. When an economy uses gold as money (or uses plastic or paper money that is convertible into gold on demand), it is said to be operating under a *gold standard*.

Another example of commodity money is cigarettes. In prisoner-of-war camps during the Second World War, prisoners traded goods and services with one another using cigarettes as the store of value, unit of account and medium of exchange. Similarly, as the Soviet Union was breaking up in the late 1980s, cigarettes started replacing the rouble as the preferred currency in Moscow. In both cases, even non-smokers were happy to accept cigarettes in an exchange, knowing that they could use the cigarettes to buy other goods and services. In the early days of the Australian colonies, rum was used as commodity money. Workers were paid in gallons of rum and they then used this as a medium of exchange. It didn't serve as much of a store of value, though – you could say it was a very liquid asset!

Money without intrinsic value is called **fiat money**. A *fiat* is simply an order or decree, and fiat money is established as money by government decree. For example, compare the plastic dollars in your wallet (printed by the Reserve Bank of Australia) and the paper dollars from a game of Monopoly® (printed by the Parker Brothers game company). Why can you use the first to pay your bill at a restaurant but not the second? The answer is that the Australian government has decreed its dollars to be valid money. Each note in your wallet reads 'This Australian note is legal tender throughout Australia and its territories'.

fiat money
money without intrinsic value that is used as money because of government decree

Although the government is central to establishing and regulating a system of fiat money (such as by prosecuting counterfeiters), other factors are also required for the success of such a monetary system. To a large extent, the acceptance of fiat money depends as much on expectations and social convention as on government decree. The Soviet government in the 1980s never abandoned the rouble as the official currency. Yet the people of Moscow preferred to accept cigarettes (or even

Source: *The Economic Rationalist's Guide to Sex*, Harper Collins, Australia 1997. Reproduced with permission.

American dollars) in exchange for goods and services, because they were more confident that these alternative monies would be accepted by others in the future. The same thing happened more recently in Indonesia, where the value of the rupiah dropped dramatically in a short period of time. Some places in Indonesia would accept only American dollars in payment for goods or services.

Money in the Australian economy

money supply
the quantity of money available in the economy

As we will see, the quantity of money circulating in the economy, called the **money supply**, has a powerful influence on important economic variables. We will find out in the next chapter how closely money supply and the level of inflation are linked. But before we consider why that is true, we need to ask a preliminary question. What is the quantity of money? In particular, suppose you were given the task of measuring how much money there is in the Australian economy. What would you include in your measure?

currency
the plastic notes and metal coins in the hands of the public

The most obvious asset to include is **currency** – the plastic notes and metal coins in the hands of the public. Currency is clearly the most widely accepted medium of exchange in our economy. There is no doubt that it is part of the money supply.

Yet currency is not the only asset that you can use to buy goods and services. Most shops today also accept debit cards, or offer EFTPOS facilities. (EFTPOS stands for 'electronic funds transfer at point of sale'.) There is a distinction between the plastic card itself and the funds in savings or cheque accounts that the card allows consumers to access. (See the 'FYI' box 'Credit cards, debit cards, smart cards and money' further below.) Some shops also accept personal cheques. Wealth held in your savings or cheque account is almost as convenient for buying things as wealth held in your wallet. To measure the money supply, therefore, you might want to include **current deposits** – balances in bank accounts that depositors can access on demand simply by using a debit card or writing a cheque.

current deposits
balances in bank accounts that depositors can access on demand by using a debit card or writing a cheque

IN THE NEWS . . .

MONEY ON THE ISLAND OF YAP

The role of social custom in the monetary system is most apparent in foreign cultures with customs very different from our own. The following article describes the money on the island of Yap. As you read the article, ask yourself whether Yap is using a type of commodity money, a type of fiat money, or something in between.

Fixed assets, or why a loan in Yap is hard to roll over
by Art Pine

Yap, Micronesia – On this tiny South Pacific island, life is easy and the currency is hard.

Elsewhere, the world's troubled monetary system creaks along; floating exchange rates wreak havoc on currency markets, and devaluations are commonplace. But on Yap the currency is as solid as a rock. In fact, it is rock. Limestone to be precise.

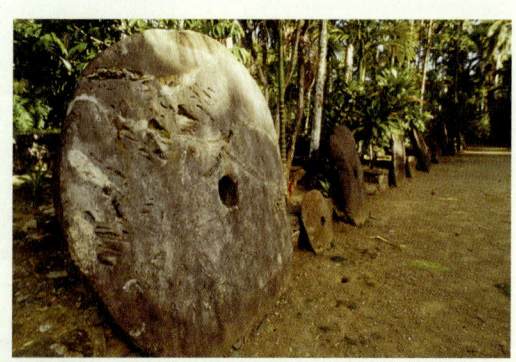

Money on the island of Yap – not exactly small change

Source: iStockphoto/Tammy Paluso.

For nearly 2000 years the Yapese have used large stone wheels to pay for major purchases, such as land, canoes and permissions to marry. Yap is a US trust territory, and the dollar is used in grocery stores and gas stations. But reliance on stone money, like the island's ancient caste system and the traditional dress of loincloths and grass skirts, continues.

Buying property with stones is 'much easier than buying it with US dollars', says John Chodad, who recently purchased a building lot with a 30-inch stone wheel. 'We don't know the value of the US dollar…'

Stone wheels don't make good pocket money, so for small transactions, Yapese use other forms of currency, such as beer. Beer is proffered as payment for all sorts of odd jobs, including construction. The 10 000 people on Yap consume 40 000 to 50 000 cases a year, mostly of Budweiser…

The people of Yap have been using stone money ever since a Yapese warrior named Anagumang first brought the huge stones from limestone caverns on neighboring Palau, some 1500 to 2000 years ago. Inspired by the moon, he fashioned the stone into large circles. The rest is history.

Yapese lean the stone wheels against their houses or prop up rows of them in village 'banks'. Most of the stones are 2½ to 5 feet in diameter, but some are as much as 12 feet across. Each has a hole in the center so it can be slipped onto the trunk of a fallen betel nut tree and carried. It takes 20 men to lift some stones.

By custom, the stones are worthless when broken. You never hear people on Yap musing about wanting a piece of the rock. Rather than risk a broken stone – or back – Yapese tend to leave the larger stones where they are and make a mental accounting that the ownership has been transferred – much as gold bars used in international transactions change hands without leaving the vaults of the New York Federal Reserve Bank…

There are some decided advantages to using massive stones for money. They are immune to black-market trading, for one thing, and they pose formidable obstacles to pickpockets. In addition, there aren't any sterile debates about how to stabilize the Yapese monetary system. With only 6600 stone wheels remaining on the island, the money supply stays put…

Meanwhile, Yap's stone money may be about to take on international significance. Just yesterday, Washington received notice that Tosiho Nakayama, the president of Micronesia, plans to bring a stone disk when he visits the United States next month. It will be flown by Air Force jet…

Officials say Mr Nakayama intends the stone as Micronesia's symbolic contribution toward reducing the US budget deficit.

Source: *Wall Street Journal*, 29 March 1984, p. A1. Reprinted by permission of the *Wall Street Journal*, Copyright © 1984 Dow Jones & Company, Inc. All Rights Reserved Worldwide.

Once you start to consider balances in savings or cheque accounts as part of the money supply, you are led to consider the large variety of other accounts that people hold at banks and other financial institutions. Bank depositors usually cannot write cheques against the balances in their savings accounts, but they can easily transfer funds from other accounts into cheque accounts or use debit cards to access their funds. Thus, these accounts should plausibly be part of the Australian money supply.

In a complex economy such as ours, it is not easy to draw a line between assets that can be called 'money' and assets that cannot. The coins in your pocket are clearly part of the money supply and the Sydney Opera House clearly is not, but there are many assets in between these extremes for which the choice is less clear. Therefore, various measures of the money supply are available for the Australian economy. Table 29.1 shows the three most important monetary aggregates – currency, M3 and broad money. Each of these measures uses a slightly different criterion for distinguishing monetary from non-monetary assets.

For our purposes in this book, we need not dwell on the differences between the various measures of money. The important point is that the money supply for the Australian economy includes not just currency but also deposits in banks and other financial institutions that can be readily accessed and used to buy goods and services.

Table 29.1	Three measures of the money supply for the Australian economy	
Measure	Amount in 2010 ($ million)	What's included
Currency	46 700	Notes and coins
M3	1 254 300	Current deposits with banks Traveller's cheques Savings deposits Certificates of deposit
Broad money	1 295 800	Everything in M3 Deposits in non-bank financial institutions and bank deposits by non-bank financial institutions

Source: *Reserve Bank of Australia Bulletin.*

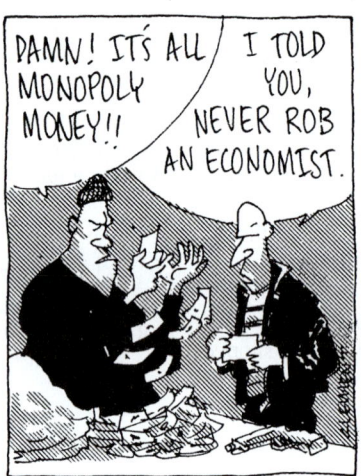

Source: *The Economic Rationalist's Guide to Sex,* Harper Collins, Australia 1997.
Reproduced with permission.

CASESTUDY

Whose currency is the fairest in the land?

For over 50 years, the US dollar has been the currency that everyone wanted. People around the world have been willing to accept US dollars in payment for goods and services in preference to their own currencies. In fact, in 1960, it was estimated that half of all US currency in circulation was held outside the US. Today, it is estimated that up to 70 per cent of US currency is held overseas. So what function is the US dollar serving? Why would foreigners want to hold so much US currency? And will the US dollar continue to be so desirable? This question has been asked a lot more since the global financial crisis showed the US economy to be more vulnerable than most people thought.

The US dollar has been used outside the US for several purposes – as a reserve currency (held by foreign governments as a store of value), as a medium of exchange in countries that don't have a stable monetary system, and as a store of value for tax evaders, drug dealers and other criminals.

For most people in the US economy, currency is not a particularly good way to hold wealth. Currency can be lost or stolen. Moreover, currency does not earn interest, whereas money in a bank account does. Thus, most people in the US hold only small amounts of currency. In contrast, criminals may prefer not to hold their wealth in banks. A bank deposit would give police a paper trail with which to trace their illegal activities. For criminals, currency may be the best store of value available.

But why would other governments hold US dollars? It's not because someone decreed that they should. It's because the US economy is the largest in the world (at least for the time being), it is important in world trade, it has open financial markets, its currency is easily convertible and several countries peg their currency to the US dollar. All of these things make it a good store of value for other governments.

In the 1980s, the Japanese yen was a threat to the dominance of the US dollar, as was the euro throughout most of the 2000s. However, most economists don't see a decline in the significance of the US dollar in the global market any time soon. Even though China is closing in on the US position as the dominant economy in the world, the Chinese government still fixes the rate at which its currency, the yuan or renmimbi, is traded, so it is not likely to replace the US dollar as the preferred reserve currency.

List and describe the three functions of money.

The Reserve Bank of Australia

Whenever an economy relies on a system of fiat money, as the Australian economy does, some agency must be responsible for regulating the system. In Australia, that agency is the **Reserve Bank of Australia (RBA)**. If you look at an Australian note, you will see that it is signed by the Secretary to the Treasury and the Governor of the Reserve Bank of Australia. The RBA is an example of a **central bank** – an institution designed to oversee the banking system and financial conditions of the economy. Other major central banks around the world include the Federal Reserve System of the United States, the Bank of England, the Bank of Japan and the European Central Bank.

Reserve Bank of Australia (RBA)
the central bank of Australia

central bank
an institution designed to oversee the banking system and regulate the quantity of money in the economy

 Search me!

▸ Reserve Bank of Australia

fyi

Credit cards, debit cards, smart cards and money

Is this money?

Source: iStockphoto.

It might seem natural to include credit cards as part of the economy's supply of money. After all, people use credit cards to make many of their purchases. Aren't credit cards, therefore, a medium of exchange?

Although at first this argument may seem persuasive, credit cards are excluded from all measures of the quantity of money. The reason is that credit cards are not really a method of payment but a method of *deferring* payment, like taking out a short-term loan. When you buy a meal with a credit card, the bank that issued the card pays the restaurant what is due. At a later date, you will have to repay the bank (perhaps with interest). When the time comes to pay your credit card bill, you will probably do so by transferring funds from your savings or cheque account electronically or through phone banking. The balance in your savings or cheque account is part of the economy's supply of money.

>>

Notice that credit cards are very different from debit cards, which automatically withdraw funds from a bank account to pay for items bought. Rather than allowing the user to postpone payment for a purchase, a debit card allows the user immediate access to deposits in a bank account. In this sense, a debit card is more similar to a cheque than to a credit card. The account balances that lie behind debit cards are included in measures of the quantity of money.

Smart cards are similar to debit cards in that they aren't a form of loan like credit cards – they either access your cheque or savings account balances or are 'topped up' with transfers from your accounts or with cash. They usually have a set amount transferred to them and then can be used until these balances are drawn down. So they aren't 'money' either because you can't use them unless you have money to transfer to them.

Even though credit cards are not considered a form of money, they are nonetheless important in analysing the monetary system. People who have credit cards can pay many of their bills all at once at the end of the month, rather than sporadically as they make purchases. As a result, people who have credit cards probably carry less money on average than people who do not have credit cards. Thus, the introduction and increased popularity of credit cards may reduce the amount of money that people choose to carry.

Organisation of the RBA

The origins of the RBA are in the Commonwealth Bank of Australia, which was established in 1911 in response to the banking crisis of the 1890s. It combined the roles of a commercial bank and a central bank. Central bank functions developed gradually until the Second World War when the powers of the central banking arm were increased to include control over exchange rates and administration of monetary and banking policy. In 1945, these powers were formalised in the *Commonwealth Bank Act* and the *Banking Act*. The RBA was created in its current form by the *Reserve Bank Act* of 1959, when it was separated from the Commonwealth Bank and given its own Board.

The Reserve Bank Board is responsible for determining the bank's monetary and banking policy. The Board consists of nine members, including the Governor and Deputy Governor and the Secretary to the Treasury. The Governor and Deputy Governor are appointed by the Governor-General on the recommendation of the government. The remaining members of the Board are drawn from industry, universities and, in the past, the trade union movement. Individuals who are employed by banks are not eligible to be members of the Board as this would represent a conflict of interest.

The Reserve Bank Board determines monetary policy after advice from the various departments within the RBA. The Economic Group is responsible for economic analysis of international and domestic markets, forecasting and research relevant to the framing of monetary policy. The Financial Markets Group is responsible for implementation of policy decisions. The RBA operates independently of the government of the day, but in cases of irreconcilable differences over policy, legislation provides for the government to be able to overrule the RBA. However, this is clearly a measure of last resort. The procedures required to do this are politically demanding and thus reinforce the RBA's independence. For the most part, the RBA and the government interact on a consultative basis.

Changes in the RBA's role

The RBA has, historically, had three related jobs. The first is to monitor individual banks and ensure their stability. The RBA monitors each bank's financial condition and makes recommendations to the bank if it is experiencing financial difficulties and is unable to meet depositors' demands. This is known as *prudential supervision*. (This role has been shifted to APRA, the Australian Prudential Regulation Authority, discussed below.) A related role is acting as a guarantor of stability in the banking system. As part of this role, the RBA also facilitates bank transactions by clearing cheques. This helps ensure that the banking system has sufficient liquidity at any one time.

Unlike the Federal Reserve in the United States, the RBA does not act as a lender of last resort. In the United States, when financially troubled banks find themselves short of cash, the Federal Reserve acts as a lender to those who cannot borrow anywhere else – in order to maintain stability in the overall banking system. In Australia, the RBA has not specifically acted in this capacity, although under the new agreement between the Treasurer, Wayne Swan, and the Reserve Bank, the Bank will provide liquidity to the system if not to a specific bank. It will continue to monitor liquidity in the system and assist troubled banks to find a solution to their problems. For instance, the RBA has played a role in facilitating mergers and acquisitions of troubled banks by other banks.

The RBA's third job is to determine monetary policy. **Monetary policy** is the management by the central bank of liquidity conditions in the economy. **Liquidity conditions** refers to the price and availability of funding for the economy's expenditure. According to the RBA's charter, the objectives of monetary policy are to '... contribute to stability of the currency ..., the maintenance of full employment; and the economic prosperity and welfare of the people of Australia'. The RBA's main contribution to these objectives is to control inflation. It has an announced target for monetary policy of keeping inflation to around 2–3 per cent over time.

The long-run objective of monetary policy is to influence the rate of growth in the economy and the level of prices. When overall economic growth is too fast and the economy is overheating this puts upward pressure on prices. The RBA will implement a tightening of monetary policy to slow the economy. On the other hand, when the economy is experiencing slow growth, the RBA will implement expansionary monetary policy. This process is described in detail next.

monetary policy
the management by the central bank of liquidity conditions in the economy

liquidity conditions
the price and availability of funding for the economy's expenditure

IN THE NEWS ...

THE IMPORTANCE OF THE RBA

Most commentators have acknowledged the Reserve Bank's role in ensuring a smoothly operating financial system, but the recent financial crisis has given the RBA a renewed prominence. Because Australia has come through the financial crisis relatively unscathed, many commentators are giving credit to the RBA for steering the ship of the Australian economy smoothly through the disturbed waters of the global financial system. A new agreement makes it very clear what the RBA's role is in stabilising that financial system, particularly in times of crisis. The agreement also affirms the RBA's financial independence. The following articles discuss the RBA's role, what it is responsible for, and what it's not.

Reserve Bank's independence essential to our growth
by Michael Stutchbury, Economics editor

Fifty years after opening its doors, the Reserve Bank of Australia has published a historical declaration of independence: an assertion of the central bank's political legitimacy as it shifts to taming inflation in the wake of the global crisis.

Australia came late to stand-alone central banking. Until 1960, the government-owned Commonwealth Bank combined the nation's central banking alongside its own commercial operations. It was a global oddity, both supporting and competing against the private banks.

Half a century later, the RBA now ranks among the most reputable central banks in the world after guiding the Australian economy through the crisis. It's a historic first for the nation.

On the weekend, this newspaper chose Kevin Rudd as its Australian of the Year for fighting off the global crisis. *Time* magazine chose US Federal Reserve chairman Ben Bernanke as its person of 2009 for cleaning up some of the mess his central bank largely caused.

RBA governor Glenn Stevens avoided a subprime housing boom and banking crisis; moved ahead of any other central bank to aggressively cut interest rates when the crisis hit; but then was the first to twig that Australia's China card would allow us to weather the worst of the storm. Stevens has since quickly lifted official interest rates three times, something the old politician-controlled RBA would never have been allowed to do.

That's evident from *The Evolution of Central Banking in Australia*, a 150-page monograph commissioned by Stevens from economic historian Selwyn Cornish to mark the RBA's first 50 years. It's basically the story of how the high inflation and high-unemployment stagflation of the 1970s was turned into the prolonged low-inflation economic upswing in the early 90s. That also makes it about the RBA's transformation from political subservience that extended to printing money to finance Canberra's budget deficits in the 70s to the political independence that jacked up official interest rates during the 2007 election campaign.

Significantly, the lesson of the RBA's history as told by Cornish is that the central bank has been driven by what works rather than by doctrine or ideology. The pragmatic declaration is that the RBA's monetary policy is more potent with deregulated financial markets and independence from political influence.

Cornish's accounts of the RBA's dealings with the Whitlam government are chilling.

Then governor, John Phillips, told new treasurer Jim Cairns in late 1974 that the board was 'concerned and apprehensive about the current and prospective economic situation. Rapid inflation and high unemployment pose grave threats to our economy and our society.

Moreover, both inflation and unemployment could become much worse and the potential damage could be very severe'. Labor's massive government spending and budget deficits needed to be urgently reined in.

Then there are gems from Cornish's trawling of the Treasury files. Only months earlier, Cairns, the deputy prime minister, had told then treasurer Frank Crean: 'I have come to the conclusion that we should move immediately to float the dollar.' Amid the madness, that didn't happen of course until 1983 under the next Labor government. In the meantime, Cornish details the subterranean battles with the Fraser government.

These disputes intensified as the late 70s resources boom picked up. According to Cornish, treasurer John Howard personally confronted the RBA board in February 1979 after it rejected the government's demand to lower the regulated ceiling on bank lending rates. Governor Harold Knight issued a threat: the RBA would not hesitate to invoke section 11 of the *Reserve Bank Act*, which would make public its unresolved opposition to a government directive. The RBA held sway and to this day section 11 has never been invoked.

As the boom weakened, Howard's 1982 budget speech foreshadowed using the private banks' statutory reserve deposits held at the RBA to boost the housing industry. The board 'objected strongly' to this sectoral 'raid' on its SRD accounts. Amid 'prolonged discussions' with Howard, the RBA again threatened to invoke section 11. Again it held sway.

After the boom turned to bust, the floating currency and financial deregulation strengthened the RBA's leverage over the economy through use of its official cash rate, rather than varying SRD requirements and the like. The problem, exposed by the late 80s boom, was that it lacked a set of rules to effectively operate this price lever. This came after the RBA exploited the pain of the early 1990s recession to entrench low inflation. Thus started the era of explicitly targeting low – 2 to 3 per cent – inflation. Granting the central bank operational independence made the target more credible. That meant it was more likely to anchor low inflation expectations.

The result has been nearly two decades of low-inflation growth. 'There is nothing to compare with this period in Australia's economic history', says Cornish. Hence, the early 90s marked 'a historic turning point – a defining moment – in the bank's history and indeed in the history of Australian monetary policy'.

Importantly, this includes 'perhaps the longest sequence of monetary tightening in the bank's history', from 2002 to the eve of the global financial crisis, as Australia's China boom heated up.

The string of cash rate hikes provided 'an important source of macroeconomic stability'. 'Indeed, for the first time since World War II, an export-led boom was experienced without an accompanying wages break-out and excessive price inflation,' Cornish concludes.

The implication is clear. Today's RBA leadership – Stevens has just posted 30 years' service – suffered many defeats before finally slaying 70s inflation. It is determined to make sure prices growth doesn't become entrenched above its target zone in 2010 as the resources boom picks up steam again. That ensures

Stevens will lift interest rates further, regardless of political pain.

Yet, the central banks we used to look up to – such as the US Fed and the Bank of England – have been monetising their governments' massive budget deficits in the wake of the crisis. That's a recipe for inflation.

And the Asian central banks we will look to more – particularly the People's Bank of China – are fuelling asset price bubbles by keeping their currencies undervalued and their interest rates too low in the face of weak exports.

The Asian central banks are politically controlled, a recipe for instability.

This means the global crisis may have merely postponed the real test of whether the RBA's inflation target regime can withstand a full-blooded resources boom. Stevens has set the test: the RBA's institutional autonomy rests on the pragmatic issue of whether it contributes, in the words of its founding 1959 act, to 'the economic prosperity and welfare of the people of Australia'.

Source: Michael Stutchbury/*The Australian*, 26 January 2010.

RBA officially given a role as stabiliser for financial system
by Eric Johnston

The Reserve Bank's mandate has been broadened to explicitly take into account the stability of the nation's financial system.

A new agreement between the RBA and Treasurer Wayne Swan also spells out, for the first time, that the central bank has no obligation to step in and use its balance sheet to bail out a failing bank.

But the agreement makes clear that, in the event of a financial crisis, the central bank will

be prepared to provide crucial support for the banking sector by pumping in liquidity.

Mr Swan yesterday reaffirmed the independence of the RBA and confirmed support for it to target inflation of 2–3 per cent.

The agreement is the first such statement in three years. Previous agreements have not included explicit reference to the RBA's role in overseeing the financial stability of the economy. But in a bid to avoid moral hazard, the new objective 'does not equate to a guarantee of solvency for financial institutions', the statement says.

Source: Eric Johnston/*The Age*, 1 October 2010.

The functions of the RBA have changed in the last two decades. An inquiry into the financial sector, known as the Wallis Inquiry, recommended the separation of these three roles. A new regulatory body, the Australian Prudential Regulation Authority (APRA), was created in 1998. APRA performs many of the functions of prudential supervision of banks – as well as other financial institutions, such as insurance companies – that the RBA had previously performed and the RBA has been left in charge of monetary policy and operation of the payments system, or the settlement of cheques between banks. In the past, the RBA used its instruments of monetary policy to exercise prudential control over the banking system, but with changes in the implementation of monetary policy and innovations in the financial sector in the last two decades, these controls were no longer considered useful. Under the new regulatory structure, the RBA no longer has an obligation to protect the interests of bank depositors, nor does it supervise any individual financial institution. Instead, it concentrates more broadly on the overall stability of the financial system.

We discuss later in this chapter how the RBA actually influences the amount of cash in the economy, but it is worth noting here that the RBA's main policy target is the cash rate – the interest rate that financial institutions can earn on overnight loans of their currency or reserves. The process that the RBA uses to change the cash rate is explained below. The cash rate is important because it signals whether the Reserve Bank thinks the economy needs stimulating (indicated by a drop in the cash rate) or slowing down (indicated by an increase in the cash rate).

The RBA is an important institution because changes in monetary policy can profoundly affect the economy. One of the *Ten Lessons from Economics* in chapter 1 is that prices rise when the government prints too much money. Another of the *Ten Lessons from Economics* is that society faces a short-run trade-off between inflation and unemployment. The power of the RBA rests on these principles. For reasons we discuss more fully in the coming chapters, the RBA's policy decisions have an important influence on the economy's rate of inflation in the long run and the economy's employment and production in the short run.

What role does the RBA play in the Australian economy?

Banks and the money supply

So far we have introduced the concept of 'money' and discussed how the RBA influences the liquidity or cash in the system by buying and selling government securities in open-market operations. But as we saw in Table 29.1, the amount of 'money' in the system is much greater than the amount of 'cash'. How does this work? We explain this by examining the role that banks play in the monetary system through their acceptance of deposits and issuing of loans.

Recall that the amount of money you hold includes both currency (the notes in your wallet and coins in your pocket) and deposits at banks (the balances in your savings and cheque accounts). Because deposits are held in banks, the behaviour of banks can influence the quantity of deposits in the economy and, therefore, the money supply. This section examines how banks affect the money supply and how they complicate the job of controlling the interest rate and thus the money supply.

The simple case of 100 per cent reserve banking

To see how banks influence the money supply, it is useful to imagine first a world without any banks at all. In this simple world, currency is the only form of money. To be concrete, let's suppose that the total quantity of currency is $100. The supply of money is, therefore, $100.

Now suppose that someone opens a bank, called First State Bank. First State Bank is only a depository institution. That is, the bank accepts deposits but does not make loans. The purpose of the bank is to give depositors a safe place to keep their money. Whenever people deposit some money, the bank keeps the money in its vault until the depositors come to withdraw it or write cheques against their balances. Deposits that banks have received but have not loaned out are called **reserves**. In this imaginary economy, all deposits are held as reserves, so this system is called *100 per cent reserve banking*.

reserves
deposits that banks have received but have not lent out

We can express the financial position of First State Bank with a *T-account*, which is a simplified accounting statement that shows changes in a bank's assets and liabilities. Here is the T-account for First State Bank if the economy's entire $100 of money is deposited in the bank:

First State Bank

Assets		Liabilities	
Reserves	$100.00	Deposits	$100.00

On the left-hand side of the T-account are the bank's assets of $100 (the reserves it holds in its vaults). On the right-hand side of the T-account are the bank's liabilities of $100 (the amount it owes to its depositors). Notice that the assets and liabilities of First State Bank exactly balance.

Now consider the money supply in this imaginary economy. Before First State Bank opens, the money supply is the $100 of currency that people are holding. After the bank opens and people deposit their currency, the money supply is the $100 of current deposits. (There is no longer any currency outstanding, for it is all in the bank vault.) Each deposit in the bank reduces currency and raises current deposits by exactly the same amount, leaving the money supply unchanged. Thus, *if banks hold all deposits in reserve, banks do not influence the supply of money.*

Money creation with fractional-reserve banking

Eventually, the bankers at First State Bank may start to reconsider their policy of 100 per cent reserve banking. Leaving all that money sitting idle in their vaults seems unnecessary. Why not use some of it to make loans? Families buying houses, firms building new factories and students paying for university would all be happy to pay interest to borrow some of that money for a while. Of course, First State Bank has to keep some reserves so that currency is available if depositors want to make withdrawals. But if the flow of new deposits is roughly the same as the flow of withdrawals, First State needs to keep only a fraction of its deposits in reserve. Thus, First State adopts a system called **fractional-reserve banking**.

fractional-reserve banking
a banking system in which banks hold only a fraction of deposits as reserves

Let's suppose that First State decides to keep 10 per cent of its deposits in reserve and to lend the rest. Banks may hold reserves because people may want to withdraw some cash from their accounts. We say that the **reserve ratio** – the fraction of total deposits that the bank holds as reserves – is 10 per cent. Now let's look again at the bank's T-account:

reserve ratio
the fraction of deposits that banks hold as reserves

First State Bank

Assets		Liabilities	
Reserves	$10.00	Deposits	$100.00
Loans	90.00		

First State still has $100 in liabilities because making the loans did not alter the bank's obligation to its depositors. But now the bank has two kinds of assets – it has $10 of reserves in its vault and it has loans of $90. (These loans are liabilities of the people taking out the loans but they are assets of the bank making the loans, because the borrowers will later repay the bank.) In total, First State's assets still equal its liabilities.

Once again consider the supply of money in the economy. Before First State makes any loans, the money supply is the $100 of deposits in the bank. Yet when First State makes these loans, the money supply increases. The depositors still have current deposits totalling $100, but now the borrowers hold $90 in currency. The money supply (which equals currency plus current deposits) equals $190. Thus, *when banks hold only a fraction of deposits in reserve, banks create money.*

At first, this creation of money by fractional-reserve banking may seem too good to be true because it appears that the bank has created money out of thin air. To make this creation of money seem less miraculous, note that when First State Bank lends some of its reserves and creates money, it does not create any wealth. Loans from First State give the borrowers some currency and thus the ability to buy goods and services. Yet the borrowers are also taking on debts, so the loans do not make them any richer. In other words, as a bank creates the asset of money, it also creates a corresponding liability for its borrowers. At the end of this process of money creation, the economy is more liquid in the sense that there is more of the medium of exchange, but the economy is no wealthier than before.

Source: THE BORN LOSER © 2003 Art and Chip Sansom.
Used by permission of UNIVERSAL UCLICK for UFS.
All rights reserved.

The money multiplier

The creation of money does not stop with First State Bank. Suppose the borrower from First State uses the $90 to buy something from someone who then deposits the currency in Second State Bank. Here is the T-account for Second State Bank:

Second State Bank

Assets		Liabilities	
Reserves	$9.00	Deposits	$90.00
Loans	81.00		

After the deposit, this bank has liabilities of $90. If Second State also has a reserve ratio of 10 per cent, it keeps assets of $9 in reserve and makes $81 in loans. In this way, Second State Bank creates an additional $81 of money. If this $81 is eventually deposited in Third State Bank, which also has a reserve ratio of 10 per cent, this bank keeps $8.10 in reserve and makes $72.90 in loans. Here is the T-account for Third State Bank:

Third State Bank

Assets		Liabilities	
Reserves	$8.10	Deposits	$81.00
Loans	72.90		

The process goes on and on. Each time that money is deposited and a bank loan is made, more money is created. The 'money' in the system is in the form of currency plus deposits, which are considered to be part of the money supply. Remember that there is still only $100 of currency in the system.

How much money is eventually created in this economy? Let's add it up:

Original deposit	=	$100.00
First State lending	=	90.00 [= 0.9 × $100.00]
Second State lending	=	81.00 [= 0.9 × $90.00]
Third State lending	=	72.90 [= 0.9 × $81.00]
•		•
•		•
•		•
Total money supply	=	$1000.00

It turns out that even though this process of money creation can continue forever, it does not create an infinite amount of money. If you laboriously add the infinite sequence of numbers in the foregoing example, you find the $100 of reserves generates $1000 of money. The amount of money the banking system generates with each dollar of reserves is called the **money multiplier**. In this imaginary economy, where the $100 of reserves (the currency deposited originally in First State Bank) generates $1000 of money ($900 of which is in the form of deposits), the money multiplier is 10.

What determines the size of the money multiplier? It turns out that the answer is simple – *the money multiplier is the reciprocal of the reserve ratio.* If all banks in the economy had the same reserve ration, R, then each dollar of reserves generates $1/R$ dollars of money. In our example, $R = 1/10$, so the money multiplier is 10.

This reciprocal formula for the money multiplier makes sense. If a bank holds $1000 in deposits, then a reserve ratio of 1/10 (10 per cent) means that the bank must hold $100 in reserves. The money multiplier just turns this idea around – if the banking system holds a total of $100 in reserves, it can have only $1000 in deposits. Similarly, if the reserve ratio were 1/5 (20 per cent), the banking system must have five times as much in deposits as in reserves, implying a money multiplier of 5. The higher the reserve ratio, the less of each deposit banks lend, and the smaller the money multiplier. In the special case of 100 per cent reserve banking, the reserve ratio is 1, the money multiplier is 1 and banks do not create money.

Bank capital, leverage and the financial crisis of 2008–09

In the previous sections, we have seen a very simplified explanation of how banks work. The reality of modern banking, however, is a bit more complicated and this complex reality played a leading role in

money multiplier
the amount of money the banking system generates with each dollar of reserves

the financial crisis of 2008 and 2009. Before looking at that crisis, we need to learn a bit more about how banks actually function.

In the bank balance sheets you have seen so far, a bank accepts deposits and uses those deposits either to make loans or to hold reserves. More realistically, a bank gets financial resources not only from accepting deposits but also, like other companies, from issuing equity and debt. The resources that a bank obtains from issuing equity to its owners are called *bank capital*. A bank uses these financial resources in various ways to generate profit for its owners. It not only makes loans and holds reserves but also buys financial securities, such as stocks and bonds.

Here is a more realistic example of a bank's balance sheet:

More Realistic National Bank

Assets		Liabilities and owners' equity	
Reserves	$200	Deposits	$800
Loans	$700	Debt	$150
Securities	$100	Capital (owners' equity)	$50

On the right side of this balance sheet are the bank's liabilities and capital (also known as *owners' equity*). This bank obtained $50 of resources from its owners. It also took in $800 of deposits and issued $150 of debt. The total of $1000 was put to use in three ways; these are listed on the left side of the balance sheet, which shows the bank's assets. This bank held $200 in reserves, made $700 in bank loans and used $100 to buy financial securities, such as government or corporate bonds. The bank decides how to allocate its resources among asset classes based on their risk and return, as well as on any regulations (such as reserve requirements) that restrict the bank's choices.

By the rules of accounting, the reserves, loans and securities on the left side of the balance sheet must always equal, in total, the deposits, debt and capital on the right side of the balance sheet. There is no magic in this equality. It occurs because the value of the owners' equity is, by definition, the value of the bank's assets (reserves, loans and securities) minus the value of its liabilities (deposits and debt). Therefore, the left and right hand sides of the balance sheet always sum to the same total.

Many businesses in the economy rely on *leverage*, the use of borrowed money to supplement existing funds for investment purposes. Indeed, whenever anyone uses debt to finance an investment project, he is applying leverage. Leverage is particularly important for banks, however, because borrowing and lending are at the heart of what they do. To fully understand banking, therefore, it is crucial to understand how leverage works.

The *leverage ratio* is the ratio of the bank's total assets to bank capital. In this example, the leverage ratio is $1000/$50, or 20. A leverage ratio of 20 means that for every dollar of capital that the bank owners have contributed, the bank has $20 of assets. Of the $20 of assets, $19 are financed with borrowed money – either by taking in deposits or issuing debt.

You may have learned in a science class that a lever can amplify a force: A boulder that you cannot move with your arms alone will move more easily if you use a lever. A similar result occurs with bank leverage. To see how this works, let's continue with this numerical example. Suppose that the bank's assets were to rise in value by 5 per cent because, say, some of the securities the bank was holding rose in price. Then the $1000 of assets would now be worth $1050. Because the depositors and debt holders are still owed $950, the bank capital rises from $50 to $100. Thus, when the leverage rate is 20, a 5 per cent increase in the value of assets increases the owners' equity by 100 per cent.

The same principle works on the downside, but with troubling consequences. Suppose that some people who borrowed from the bank default on their loans, reducing the value of the bank's assets by 5 per cent to $950. Because the depositors and debt holders have the legal right to be paid before the bank owners, the value of the owners' equity falls to zero. Thus, when the leverage ratio is 20, a 5 per cent fall in the value of the bank assets leads to a 100 per cent fall in bank capital. If the value of assets were to fall by more than 5 per cent, the bank's assets would fall below its liabilities. In this case, the bank would be *insolvent* and it would be unable to pay off its debt holders and depositors in full.

Bank regulators require banks to hold a certain amount of capital. The goal of such a *capital requirement* is to ensure that banks will be able to pay off their depositors. The amount of capital required depends on the kind of assets a bank holds. If the bank holds safe assets such as government bonds, regulators require less capital than if the bank holds risky assets such as loans to borrowers whose credit is of dubious quality. In Australia, the Australian Prudential Regulation Authority, APRA, requires institutions that accept deposits, such as banks, to hold 8 per cent of their assets in high-quality, safe form. This is called the prudential capital ratio.

In 2008 and 2009, many banks in the US found themselves with too little capital after they had incurred losses on some of their assets – specifically, mortgage loans and securities backed by mortgage loans. The shortage of capital induced the banks to reduce their lending, a phenomenon sometimes called a *credit crunch,* which in turn contributed to a severe downturn in economic activity. To address this problem, the US Treasury, working together with the Federal Reserve (the US central bank), put many billions of dollars of public funds into the banking system to increase the amount of bank capital. As a result, it temporarily made the US taxpayer a part owner of many banks. The goal of this unusual policy was to recapitalise the banking system so that bank lending could return to a more normal level, which in fact occurred by late 2009.

Monetary policy in Australia today

We can see from our discussion of fractional-reserve banking that banks have a significant influence on the amount of money in the economy – how much the banks decide to keep as reserves and how much they loan out determines the overall level of deposits in the economy. Since deposits are considered to be part of the money supply, banks have a big impact on the money supply. Does this mean the RBA can simply change the amount of reserves banks are required to keep to change the money supply? Not exactly.

Up until 1993, the RBA required banks to keep a fixed percentage of their deposits as reserves, so the RBA could exercise control over the money supply through the money multiplier. (The RBA also used other direct controls over banks prior to 1993.) But APRA no longer requires all banks to have the same level of reserves for prudential purposes. The amount of reserves each bank keeps depends on the riskiness of their loans and their projected demand for cash. In our example in the previous section, all banks kept 10 per cent of their deposits as reserves. But today they are neither required to do so nor do they choose to do so.

So how does the RBA conduct monetary policy if they can't control the money supply? Instead of focusing on the amount of money in the system, the RBA targets the cash rate, as we indicated earlier in this chapter. The RBA uses the cash rate to influence the level of economic activity rather than attempting to control the money supply. The RBA announces a cash rate and then either injects **cash** or removes cash from the short-term money market, the overnight market for cash, to ensure that the

cash
the amount of currency and bank reserves in the economy

target rate is the equilibrium rate in the market. Thus, the RBA allows the money supply to adjust to money demand to ensure that the targeted rate is the actual rate. The cash rate is then used as a benchmark rate from which other interest rates in the economy are determined.

Each bank keeps deposits with the Reserve Bank to facilitate their transactions with each other and with the Government. These deposits are called *exchange settlement (ES)* accounts. The banks use these accounts to resolve any imbalances they have with each other or with the government at the end of the day. This market is known as the overnight money market. The deposits in the ES accounts earn a rate of interest from the RBA just below the cash rate and banks can borrow from the RBA at just above the cash rate if they are short of deposits. This band, or channel, around the cash rate ensures that the target cash rate announced by the RBA is the actual cash rate in the overnight money market, where banks can borrow and lend to each other on a short-term basis. The following examples illustrate how this works:

Suppose Matt gets a notice from the Australian Tax Office (ATO) that he owes them $100. He has an account with the ABC Bank. He does an electronic funds transfer from his account at ABC to the ATO. Since the ATO is a government organisation, its bank is the RBA. So the ATO's account at the RBA goes up by $100.

Now suppose Margie pays for her trip to Bali using her account with the ANB Bank. She does an electronic funds transfer of $500 from her account at the ANB to her travel agent's account at the ABC Bank. These transfers are all handled through the banks' exchange settlement accounts at the RBA.

What's the result of these transactions at the end of the day? The ABC's ES account at the RBA has gone up by $400 – which is equal to the $500 transferred from Margie's account with the ANB minus the $100 that Matt owes to the ATO. The ANB's ES account has gone down by $500. And the ATO's account has gone up by $100.

Suppose that ANB doesn't have the $500 in its ES account. But it 'owes' the money to the ABC. If it is short of money at the end of the day, it can borrow money from the overnight money market to make up the short fall. And the rate that it pays for borrowing this money overnight is essentially the cash rate.

This overnight money market facility gives the RBA great control over the cash rate. If the RBA supplies more funds to the exchange settlement funds than the banks want to hold, they will lend this money out in the overnight money market. This increase in funds leads to a decrease in the cash rate. If the RBA removes funds from the overnight money market, the cash rate will increase, as banks who want to borrow money bid up the rate. Thus, the cash rate, sitting within the channel, is determined in the money market as a result of the interaction between the demand for and supply of overnight funds.

Open-market operations

open-market operations the purchase and sale of Australian government securities by the RBA

The last piece of this picture is how the RBA adds funds to the market or withdraws funds from the market. The RBA uses something called **open-market operations** to guarantee that its target rate is the equilibrium interest rate in the short-term money market. An open-market operation is the purchase or sale of Australian government securities. If the RBA sees that there is an excess supply of funds in the overnight market at the target interest rate, it will withdraw funds from the market by selling government securities. When it sells government securities, it takes in cash from the financial institutions purchasing the government securities by reducing their ES funds, thus reducing the cash

Figure 29.1 The target cash rate and the actual cash rate

The graph shows the cash rate the RBA targets and the overnight rate actually obtained.

Source: Reserve Bank of Australia.

in the system. If there is an excess demand for funds at the target interest rate, the RBA will buy government securities, increasing the ES funds of the financial institutions selling the securities, thus increasing the cash in the system. When the RBA increases or decreases the amount of cash in the system, this changes the price of cash – the **cash rate**. In essence, the RBA is setting the 'price' of money, and allowing the quantity to adjust to achieve that price. (This is explained in greater detail in chapter 34.) In this way, the RBA can ensure that its target cash rate is the actual cash rate in the market.

In practice, the RBA often uses something called a *repo*, or repurchase agreement, to affect the level of exchange settlement funds. These repos are agreements between the RBA and a commercial financial institution that the securities that have been bought or sold will be resold or repurchased, effectively reversing the transaction, at an agreed date and price in the future. Repos increased in use during the late 1990s and 2000s as the number of government securities issued declined due to reductions in government debt and the reduced need of government to borrow from the public to fund its expenditures.

Figure 29.1 shows that the actual cash rate nearly always equals the target rate.

The RBA determines the target cash rate by examining several factors that bear directly on the rate of inflation and the level of economic activity in the short-run. These include aggregate demand, the rate of jobs growth, the change in the level of unemployment, capacity levels in the economy and the impact of international economic conditions. The Board makes a judgement about whether current economic conditions are likely to produce an increase in inflation or whether the economy is slowing down. For example, when the RBA Board announced that the cash rate wouldn't change in September 2010, it put out the following statement to explain its decision.

cash rate
the interest rate that financial institutions can earn on overnight loans of their currency or reserves

▸ cash rate

IN THE NEWS ...

RBA POLICY DECISION

Media Release Statement by Glenn Stevens, Governor: Monetary policy decision

At its meeting today, the Board decided to leave the cash rate unchanged at 4.5 per cent.

The global economy grew faster than trend over the year to mid 2010, but will probably ease back to about trend pace over the coming year. Growth in China is moderating to a more sustainable rate as policies are now less accommodating. Similar adjustments to policies and growth rates are occurring in other countries in the Asian region. In Europe, output has improved significantly so far this year, but prospects for next year are probably for slower growth given planned fiscal contraction. US growth was solid in the first half of 2010 but the pace of expansion in the second half of the year is looking weaker.

Financial markets are functioning more smoothly than they were a few months ago, though caution persists, with equity prices soft and yields on sovereign bonds issued by major countries reaching unusually low levels. Commodity prices are also off their peaks, though those most important for Australia remain at very high levels, and the terms of trade have regained their peak of two years ago.

Recent information suggests that the Australian economy has been growing at around trend pace. This has been helped by high levels of public spending over the past year but private demand has also been firming. The high level of the terms of trade is boosting incomes, which will tend to add to demand over the year ahead, while the effects of earlier expansionary policy measures will be diminishing. Indications are that business investment in particular could increase strongly.

Domestic credit and asset markets present a more balanced picture than six months ago. Business credit has stabilised and while credit conditions for some sectors remain difficult, evidence is slowly emerging of more willingness to lend. Credit outstanding for housing has slowed a little over recent months, and the upward pressure on dwelling prices appears to have abated.

The demand for labour has firmed over the past year in line with improving growth. After the significant decline last year, growth in wages has picked up somewhat, as had been expected. Through to mid 2011, underlying inflation is likely to be in the top half of the target zone, while CPI inflation will probably be just above 3 per cent for a few quarters due to the impact of the tobacco tax changes.

The current setting of monetary policy is resulting in interest rates to borrowers around their average levels of the past decade. With growth in the near term likely to be close to trend, inflation close to target and with the global outlook remaining somewhat uncertain, the Board judged this setting of monetary policy to be appropriate for the time being.

Source: Reserve Bank of Australia, 7 September 2010.

The cash rate is significant because it is the interest rate that is the foundation for all other interest rates in the economy. The cash rate is like a wholesale rate that financial institutions charge one another for borrowing and lending. When financial institutions then decide to lend to businesses or private individuals, they use the cash rate as a basis for determining the interest rates they will charge.

How does the change in the cash rate affect the level of economic activity throughout the economy? If the economy is growing too fast, the RBA will announce a higher target for the cash rate. The RBA will undertake open-market operations to ensure that the cash rate moves up to the higher target level. The higher cash rate tends to push up deposit and borrowing rates at financial institutions in general. For some borrowers, it will now not make sense to borrow money for previously intended purposes, whether it be an investment project, a consumer item or the acquisition of financial assets. Hence there are fewer opportunities for banks and other financial institutions to profitably expand their balance sheets by making more loans. The pace of money and credit creation slows as a result. In addition, the demand for real goods and services falls or grows more slowly and pressure on resource usage in the economy lessens, resulting in a fall in prices or in their rate of increase. This process will be described in more detail in chapter 34, but this brief explanation helps us understand how the RBA's actions in the short-term money market affect the short-run position of the economy.

Open-market operations are easy to conduct. In fact, the RBA's purchases and sales of government securities in the nation's bond markets are similar to the transactions that individuals might undertake for their own portfolios. (Of course, when an individual buys or sells a security, money changes hands, but the amount of money in circulation remains the same.) In addition, the RBA can use open-market operations to effect small or large changes in the cash rate on any day without major changes in laws or banking regulations. (For more information on monetary policy operations, see: www.rba.gov.au/MonetaryPolicy/about_monetary_policy.html.)

Problems in controlling the money supply

The RBA uses the cash rate as its policy instrument because it cannot control the money supply for two reasons, each of which arises because much of the money supply is created by our system of fractional-reserve banking.

The first problem is that the RBA does not control the amount of money that households choose to hold as deposits in banks. The more money that households deposit, the more reserves banks have and the more money the banking system can create. The less money that households deposit, the less reserves banks have and the less money the banking system can create. To see why this is a problem, suppose that one day people begin to lose confidence in the banking system and, therefore, decide to withdraw deposits and hold more currency. When this happens, the banking system loses reserves and creates less money. The money supply falls, even without any RBA action.

This problem is confounded by innovations in the way that people pay for their goods and services. As we've seen, people don't need to have cash to pay for the things that they buy. They can use credit cards, debits cards and smart cards and there are probably even more methods on the way. All of this means that it is harder to predict how much cash people will actually need and how much they will leave as deposits.

The second problem of monetary control is that the RBA does not control the amount that bankers choose to lend. Once money is deposited in a bank, it creates more money only when the bank lends it out. Yet banks can choose the amount of reserves they wish to hold. To see why variations in the amount of reserves complicate control of the money supply, suppose that one day bankers become more cautious about economic conditions and decide to make fewer loans and hold greater reserves. In this case, the banking system creates less money than it otherwise would. Because of the bankers' decision, the money supply falls. We've seen this during the global financial crisis, particularly in the US and in Europe, financial systems that were more affected by the GFC than Australia.

Hence, in a system of fractional-reserve banking, the amount of money in the economy depends in part on the behaviour of depositors and bankers. Because the RBA cannot control or perfectly predict this behaviour, it cannot perfectly control the money supply. Partly for this reason, the RBA chose to shift its emphasis from controlling the money supply to targeting interest rates. The RBA still collects data on deposits and reserves from banks and non-bank financial institutions (NBFIs) every week, so it is quickly aware of any changes in depositor or banker behaviour. However, it has much more control over the cash rate and can implement changes in the cash rate fairly quickly. This can be seen in Figure 29.1, where the target cash rate is graphed against the actual cash rate. This graph shows that when the RBA sets a target cash rate, it is able to achieve this rate fairly precisely.

CASE STUDY

Bank runs and the money supply

Although bank runs are infrequent occurrences, they do happen occasionally. There were bank runs in Victoria in 1990–91. A bank run occurs when depositors suspect that a bank may go bankrupt and, therefore, 'run' to the bank to withdraw their deposits.

Bank runs are a problem for banks under fractional-reserve banking. Because a bank holds only a fraction of its deposits in reserve, it cannot satisfy withdrawal requests from all depositors. Even if the bank is in fact solvent (meaning that its assets exceed its liabilities), it will not have enough cash on hand to allow all depositors immediate access to all of their money. When a run occurs, the bank is forced to close its doors until some bank loans are repaid or until some arrangement is made by the RBA to provide it with the currency it needs to satisfy depositors.

Bank runs complicate the control of the money supply. An important example of this problem occurred during the Great Depression in the early 1930s. After a wave of bank runs and bank closures, households and bankers became more cautious. Households withdrew their deposits from banks, preferring to hold their money in the form of currency. This decision reversed the process of money creation, as bankers responded to falling reserves by reducing bank loans. At the same time, bankers increased their reserve ratios so that they would have enough cash on hand to meet their depositors' demands in any future bank runs. The higher reserve ratio reduced the money multiplier, which also reduced the money supply. This contraction in money supply occurred even though there was no deliberate action by the Commonwealth Bank of Australia.

However, the effects of the contraction in deposits were less severe in Australia than in other countries. Many economists nonetheless point to this fall in the money supply to explain the high unemployment and falling prices that prevailed during this period. (In later chapters we examine the mechanisms by which changes in the money supply affect unemployment and prices.)

Today, bank runs are not a major problem for the banking system or the RBA. Even though the RBA and APRA do not specifically guarantee the safety of deposits at specific banks, they discourage bank runs through ensuring stability of the financial system. (In October 2008, after the collapse of Lehman Brothers in the US, the Australian government issued a guarantee of bank deposits up to $1 million. This guarantee came from the Government, not the RBA.) As a result, most people see bank runs only in films. In some other countries, though, other means are used to prevent people from making runs on banks. During the recent global financial crisis, authorities in different countries imposed controls on various types of financial transactions to prevent people from withdrawing their deposits from the banking system. And we've seen a major bailout of banks in the United States precisely because of fears of runs on the banks in the US.

Q Describe how banks create money.

Conclusion

Several years ago, a book made the best-seller list in the United States with the title *Secrets of the Temple: How the Federal Reserve Runs the Country*. Although no doubt an exaggeration, this title highlights the important role of the monetary system in our daily lives. Whenever we buy or sell anything, we are relying on the extraordinarily useful social convention called 'money'. Now that we know what money is and what determines its supply, we can discuss how money supply and money demand interact to affect interest rates and hence the level of economic activity. We begin to discuss that topic in the next chapter.

Summary

- The term *money* refers to assets that people regularly use to buy goods and services.
- Money serves three functions. As a medium of exchange, it provides the item used to make transactions. As a unit of account, it provides the way in which prices and other economic values are recorded. As a store of value, it provides a way of transferring purchasing power from the present to the future.
- Commodity money, such as gold, is money that has intrinsic value – it would be valued even if it were not used as money. Fiat money, such as plastic dollars, is money without intrinsic value – it would be worthless if it were not used as money.
- In the Australian economy, money takes the form of currency and various types of bank deposits, such as cheque accounts.
- The Reserve Bank of Australia, Australia's central bank, is responsible for regulating the Australian monetary system. The RBA sets interest rates to reach a target range of inflation. It does this through open-market operations – the purchase of government securities increases the amount of cash in the economy, thus lowering the interest rate, and the sale of government securities decreases the amount of cash in the economy, thus increasing the interest rate.
- When banks lend some of their deposits, they increase the quantity of money in the economy. Because of this role of banks in determining the money supply, the RBA's control of the money supply is imperfect.

Key concepts

cash	fractional-reserve banking	money supply
cash rate	liquidity	open-market operations
central bank	liquidity conditions	Reserve Bank of Australia (RBA)
commodity money	medium of exchange	reserve ratio
currency	monetary policy	reserves
current deposits	money	store of value
fiat money	money multiplier	unit of account

Questions for review

1. What distinguishes money from other assets in the economy?
2. What is commodity money? What is fiat money? Which kind do we use?
3. What are current deposits and why should they be included in the supply of money?
4. What is the cash rate? What happens to the money supply when the RBA raises the cash rate?
5. Explain how changes in the cash rate affect other interest rates in the economy.
6. Why would financial institutions say they no longer strictly follow movements in the cash rate to determine the interest rates that they charge people who borrow money from them?
7. What are reserve requirements? Why doesn't the RBA use reserve requirements to control the money supply? Would banks have their own 'reserve requirements'; that is, would they keep some deposits in reserve even if they were not required to?
8. Why can't the RBA control the money supply perfectly?
9. What is meant by 'prudential supervision'? Which agency is now responsible for this function in the Australian financial system?

Problems and applications

1   Which of the following is money in the Australian economy? Which is not? Explain your answers by discussing each of the three functions of money.
   a   An Australian dollar coin
   b   A euro (the currency of the European Union)
   c   A Ferrari
   d   A smart card.

2   In some places, people try to barter goods and services rather than pay for them. Here is an example from a newspaper column: 'Will swap designer wedding gown and up to 3 bridesmaids' gowns for 2 return tickets and 3 nights' lodging in Tasmania'.
   a   Why would it be difficult to run our economy using barter instead of money?
   b   In light of your answer to part (a), why might newspaper notices like the one above exist?

3   Most people's think their house is their biggest asset. Consider the three functions of money. Does your family home perform these three functions well?

4   Consider how the following situations would affect the economy's monetary system.
   a   Suppose that the people on Yap discovered an easy way to make limestone wheels. How would this development affect the usefulness of stone wheels as money? Explain.
   b   Suppose that someone in Australia discovered an easy way to counterfeit $100 notes. How would this development affect the Australian monetary system? Explain.

5   Your aunt repays a $100 loan from Third State Bank (TSB) by writing a $100 cheque on her TSB cheque account. Use T-accounts to show the effect of this transaction on your aunt and on TSB. Has your aunt's wealth changed? Explain.

6   Beleaguered State Bank (BSB) holds $250 million in deposits and maintains a reserve ratio of 10 per cent.
   a   Show a T-account for BSB.
   b   Now suppose that BSB's largest depositor withdraws $10 million from her account in cash. If BSB decides to restore its reserve ratio by reducing the amount of loans outstanding, show its new T-account.
   c   Explain what effect BSB's action will have on other banks.
   d   Why might it be difficult for BSB to take the action described in part (b)? Discuss another way for BSB to return to its original reserve ratio.

7   What would be the impact on the money supply, bank reserves and interest rates if the RBA announced that from tomorrow, coins would no longer be accepted as legal tender (and the RBA did not issue any new notes)?

8   Happy Bank starts with $200 in bank capital. It then takes in $800 in deposits. It keeps 8 per cent (1/12th) of deposits in reserve. It uses the rest of its assets to make bank loans.
   a   Show the balance sheet of Happy Bank.
   b   What is Happy Bank's leverage ratio?
   c   Suppose that 10 per cent of the borrowers from Happy Bank default and these bank loans become worthless. Show the bank's new balance sheet.
   d   By what percentage do the bank's total assets decline? By what percentage does the bank's capital decline? Which change is larger? Why?

9   Suppose that the T-account for First State Bank is as follows:

First State Bank

Assets		Liabilities	
Reserves	$100 000	Deposits	$1 000 000
Loans	900 000		

    a   Suppose a borrower from FSB (First State Bank) pays off their loan and no-one else wants to take out a loan. (Suppose they had a $200 000 loan from FSB.) How does this affect their balance sheet?

    b   If people aren't taking out loans, how does this affect the money supply?

10   Suppose that banks hold reserves of 5 per cent against cheque account deposits.

    a   If the RBA sells $1 million of government securities, what is the effect on the economy's reserves and money supply?

    b   Suppose banks decide to increase their reserves to 10 per cent. Why might banks choose to do so? What effect does this have on the money supply?

11   Suppose MacroComp, a major software company, buys PCGames, a small Australian company that produces computer games. They draw a cheque on their account at WhichBank for $100 million. The owners of PC Games deposit this cheque in their account at That Bank.

    a   Show what happens to the balance sheet of both Which Bank and That Bank.

    b   Show the balance sheet of their exchange settlement accounts at the RBA.

    c   If the sale of the software company is the largest transaction of the day, which of the two banks is more likely to have to borrow money on the short-term money market?

12   (This problem is challenging.) The economy of Elmendyn contains 2000 $1 notes.

    a   If people hold all money as currency, what is the quantity of money?

    b   If people hold all money as current deposits and banks maintain 100 per cent reserves, what is the quantity of money?

    c   If people hold equal amounts of currency and current deposits and banks maintain 100 per cent reserves, what is the quantity of money?

    d   If people hold all money as current deposits and banks maintain a reserve ratio of 10 per cent, what is the quantity of money?

    e   If people hold equal amounts of currency and current deposits and banks maintain a reserve ratio of 10 per cent, what is the quantity of money?

Search me!

When accessing information about economics use the following keywords in any combinations you require:

- cash rate
- Reserve Bank of Australia

CourseMate

For more multimedia resources and activities on economics, visit the Economics CourseMate website.

30

Inflation: Its causes and costs

Learning objectives

In this chapter you will:

- consider the various costs that inflation imposes on society
- learn the meaning of the classical dichotomy and monetary neutrality
- see why some countries experience hyperinflation when they print too much money
- examine the relationship between the nominal interest rate and the inflation rate.

Although today you need more than a dollar or two to buy yourself an ice-cream, life was very different 50 years ago. If you were walking along Bondi Beach on a hot summer's day and wanted to buy an ice-cream, it would have cost you about 5 cents.

You are probably not surprised at the increase in the price of ice-cream. In our economy, most prices tend to rise over time. This increase in the overall level of prices is called *inflation*. Earlier in the book we examined how economists measure the inflation rate as the percentage change in the consumer price index, the GDP deflator or some other index of the overall price level. These price indexes show that, over the past 50 years, prices have risen on average about 5 per cent per year. Accumulated over so many years, a 5 per cent annual inflation rate leads to almost a 15-fold increase in the price level.

Inflation may seem natural and inevitable to a person who grew up in Australia during the second half of the twentieth century, but in fact it is not inevitable at all. There were long periods in the nineteenth century during which most prices fell – a phenomenon called *deflation*. The average level of prices in the Australian economy was 20 per cent lower in 1898 than in 1889. Farmers who had accumulated large debts suffered when the fall in crop prices reduced their incomes and thus their ability to pay off their debts. It was a time of great turmoil in the colonies.

Although inflation has been the norm in more recent history, there has been substantial variation in the rate at which prices rise. From 1990 to 2010, prices rose at an average rate of about 3 per cent per year. In contrast, in the 1970s, prices rose by almost 11 per cent per year, which meant the price level increased by more than 2½ times over the decade. The public often views such high rates of inflation as a major economic problem. In fact, when Malcolm Fraser led the Coalition to victory in the 1975 election, high inflation was one of the major issues of the campaign. Fraser promised to 'fight inflation first'.

International data show an even broader range of inflation experiences. Germany after the First World War experienced a spectacular example of inflation. The price of a newspaper rose from 0.3 of a mark in January 1921 to 70 000 000 marks less than two years later. Other prices rose by similar amounts. An extraordinarily high rate of inflation such as this is called *hyperinflation*. New Zealand had such high inflation in the 1970s and 1980s that the central bank made low inflation its number one priority in the 1990s. In 1996, the Reserve Bank of New Zealand announced an inflation target of between 0 per cent and 3 per cent per year. Other countries, such as Japan, have experienced very low rates of inflation. In 2010, Japan had *negative* inflation – that is, prices declined by 1.4% on average.

What determines whether an economy experiences inflation and, if so, how much? This chapter answers the question by developing the *quantity theory of money*. Chapter 1 summarised this theory as one of the *Ten Lessons from Economics* – prices rise when the government prints too much money. This insight has a long and venerable tradition among economists. The quantity theory was discussed by the famous eighteenth-century philosopher David Hume and has been advocated more recently by the prominent economist Milton Friedman. This theory of inflation can explain both moderate inflations, such as those we have experienced in Australia, and hyperinflations, such as those experienced in interwar Germany and, more recently, in some Latin American and African countries.

After developing a theory of inflation, we turn to a related question: Why is inflation a problem? At first glance, the answer to this question may seem obvious – inflation is a problem because people don't like it. In the 1970s, when Australia experienced relatively high rates of inflation, opinion polls placed inflation as one of the most important issues facing the nation. This sentiment was echoed in other countries as well. In the United States, President Ford called inflation 'public enemy number one'. Ford briefly wore a 'WIN' button on his lapel – for Whip Inflation Now.

But what, exactly, are the costs that inflation imposes on a society? The answer may surprise you. Identifying the various costs of inflation is not as straightforward as it first appears. As a result, although all economists decry hyperinflation, some economists argue that the costs of moderate inflation are not nearly as large as the general public believes.

The causes of inflation

We begin our study of inflation by developing the quantity theory of money. Most economists rely on this theory for explaining the long-run determinants of the price level and the inflation rate.

The level of prices and the value of money

Suppose we observe over some period of time the price of an ice-cream rising from 5 cents to a dollar. What conclusion should we draw from the fact that people are willing to give up so much more money in exchange for an ice-cream? It is possible that people have come to enjoy ice-cream more (perhaps because some celebrity chef has developed a miraculous new flavour). Yet that is probably not the case. It is more likely that people's enjoyment of ice-cream has stayed roughly the same and that, over time, the money used to buy ice-cream has become less valuable. Indeed, the first insight about inflation is that it is more about the value of money than about the value of goods.

This insight helps point the way towards a theory of inflation. When the consumer price index and other measures of the price level rise, commentators are often tempted to look at the many individual prices that make up these price indexes: 'The CPI rose by 3 per cent last month, led by a 20 per cent rise in the price of coffee and a 30 per cent rise in the price of petrol'. Although this approach does contain some interesting information about what's happening in the economy, it also misses a key point – inflation is an economy-wide phenomenon that concerns, first and foremost, the value of the economy's medium of exchange.

The economy's overall price level can be viewed in two ways. So far, we have viewed the price level as the price of a basket of goods and services. When the price level rises, people have to pay more for the goods and services they buy. Alternatively, we can view the price level as a measure of the value of money. A rise in the price level means a lower value of money because each dollar in your wallet now buys a smaller quantity of goods and services.

It may help to express these ideas mathematically. Suppose P is the price level as measured, for instance, by the consumer price index or the GDP deflator. Then P measures the number of dollars needed to buy a basket of goods and services. Now turn this idea around – the quantity of goods and services that can be bought with \$1 equals $1/P$. In other words, if P is the price of goods and services measured in terms of money, $1/P$ is the value of money measured in terms of goods and services. Thus, when the overall price level rises, the value of money falls.

Money supply, money demand and monetary equilibrium

What determines the value of money? The answer to this question, like many in economics, is supply and demand. Just as the supply of and demand for bananas determine the price of bananas, the supply of and demand for money determine the value of money. Thus, our next step in developing the quantity theory of money is to consider the determinants of money supply and money demand.

First consider money demand. There are many determinants of the quantity of money demanded, just as there are many determinants of the quantity demanded of other goods and services. How much money people choose to hold in their wallets, for instance, depends on how much they rely on credit cards and on whether an automatic teller machine is easy to find. And, as we will emphasise in a later chapter, the quantity of money demanded depends on the interest rate that a person could earn by using the money to buy an interest-bearing bond rather than leaving it in a wallet or low-interest cheque account.

Although many variables affect the demand for money, one variable stands out in importance – the average level of prices in the economy. People hold money because it is the medium of exchange. Unlike other assets, such as bonds or shares, people can use money to buy the goods and services on their shopping lists. How much money they choose to hold for this purpose depends on the prices of those goods and services. The higher prices are, the more money the typical transaction requires and the more money people will choose to hold in their wallets and cheque accounts. That is, a higher price level (a lower value of money) increases the quantity of money demanded for transaction purposes.

Now consider the money supply. In the last chapter, we discussed how the Reserve Bank of Australia (RBA), together with the banking system, influences the supply of money. The RBA no longer sets a target for the level of the money supply. Some central banks still do, though. In the following explanation, we begin to see why modern central banks focus on interest rates and inflation rather than targeting the level of the money supply.

To help us understand the relationship between the level of prices and the value of money, let's consider an economy called Zoobooloo. In the land of Zoobooloo, the Central Bank sets the level of money supply. What ensures that the quantity of money the Zoobooloo Central Bank (ZCB) supplies balances the quantity of money people demand? The answer, it turns out, depends on the time horizon being considered. Later in this book we will examine the short-run answer and we will see that interest rates play a key role. In the long run, however, the answer is different and much simpler. *In the long run, the overall level of prices adjusts to the level at which the demand for money equals the supply.* If the price level is above the equilibrium level, people will want to hold more money than the ZCB has created, so the price level must fall to balance supply and demand. If the price level is below the equilibrium level, people will want to hold less money than the ZCB has created and the price level must rise to balance supply and demand. At the equilibrium price level, the quantity of money that people want to hold exactly balances the quantity of money supplied by the ZCB.

Figure 30.1 illustrates these ideas. The horizontal axis of this graph shows the quantity of money. The left-hand vertical axis shows the value of money and the right-hand vertical axis shows the price level. Notice that the price-level axis is inverted – when the value of money is high (as measured on the left axis), the price level is low (as measured on the right axis). The supply curve for money in this figure is vertical, indicating that the ZCB has fixed the quantity of money available. The demand curve for money is downward-sloping, indicating that when the value of money is low, people demand a larger quantity of it to buy goods and services. At the equilibrium, shown in the figure as point A, the quantity of money demanded balances the quantity of money supplied. This equilibrium of money supply and money demand determines the value of money and the price level.

The effects of a monetary injection

Let's see what happens to the value of the Zoobooloo dollar (Z$) when the Zoobooloo Central Bank (ZCB) increases the money supply. To do so, imagine that the economy is in equilibrium and then,

Figure 30.1 **How the supply of and demand for money in Zoobooloo determine the equilibrium price level**

The horizontal axis shows the quantity of money. The left vertical axis shows the value of money and the right vertical axis shows the price level. The supply curve for money is vertical because the quantity of money supplied is fixed by the ZCB. The demand curve for money is downward-sloping because people want to hold a larger quantity of money when each dollar buys less. At the equilibrium, point A, the value of money (on the left axis) and the price level (on the right axis) have adjusted to bring the quantity of money supplied and the quantity of money demanded into balance.

suddenly, the ZCB does as economist Milton Friedman suggested and doubles the supply of money by printing some more and dropping it around the country from helicopters. (Or, less dramatically and more realistically, the ZCB could inject money into the economy by buying some government bonds from the public in open-market operations.) What happens after such a monetary injection? How does the new equilibrium compare with the old one?

Figure 30.2 shows what happens. The monetary injection shifts the supply curve to the right from MS_1 to MS_2, and the equilibrium moves from point A to point B. As a result, the value of money (shown on the left axis) decreases from ½ to ¼, and the equilibrium price level (shown on the right axis) increases from 2 to 4. In other words, when an increase in the money supply makes dollars more plentiful, the result is an increase in the price level that makes each dollar less valuable.

This explanation of how the price level is determined and why it might change over time is called the **quantity theory of money**. According to the quantity theory, the quantity of money available in the economy determines the value of money, and growth in the quantity of money is the primary cause of inflation. As Milton Friedman once put it: 'Inflation is always and everywhere a monetary phenomenon'.

quantity theory of money
a theory asserting that the quantity of money available determines the price level and that the growth rate in the quantity of money available determines the inflation rate

Figure 30.2 An increase in the money supply

When the ZCB increases the supply of money, the money supply curve shifts from MS_1 to MS_2. The value of money (on the left axis) and the price level (on the right axis) adjust to bring supply and demand back into balance. The equilibrium moves from point A to point B. Thus, when an increase in the money supply makes dollars more plentiful, the price level increases, making each dollar less valuable.

CASESTUDY

Printing money

Our example of Zoobooloo shows what happens when a central bank prints more money. Most Western central banks now focus more on interest rates rather than money supply, but the dangers of printing too much money are still very present today. According to Steve Hanke of *Forbes* magazine, in Zimbabwe inflation was estimated at 6.5 quindecillion novemdecillion per cent (65 followed by 107 zeros) in December 2008 because the Zimbabwean Reserve Bank printed too much money. It's hard to even imagine what that means. As Hanke said, it means prices double nearly every 24 hours. There are signs in public toilets that said the Zim dollar wasn't even good for toilet paper! As prices rose, the Zimbabwean Reserve Bank had to print dollars with higher and higher denominations. Finally, in 2009, the Zimbabwean government allowed people to use other currencies, such as the South African rand and the US dollar

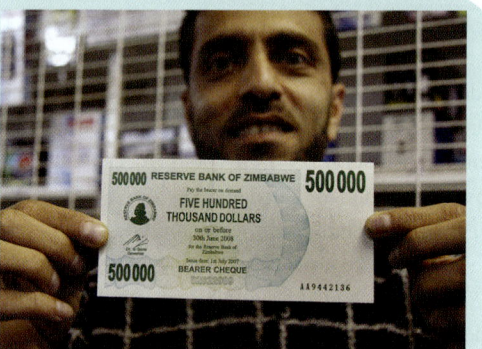

Source: Getty Images.

since no one wanted to use (or were able to even carry that much of) the Zim dollar. This is a clear example of the quantity theory of money in action!

A brief look at the adjustment process

So far we have compared the old equilibrium and the new equilibrium after an injection of money. How does the economy get from the old to the new equilibrium? A complete answer to this question requires an understanding of short-run fluctuations in the economy, which we examine later in this book. Yet, even now, it is instructive to consider briefly the adjustment process that occurs after a change in money supply.

The immediate effect of a monetary injection is to create an excess supply of money. Before the injection, the economy was in equilibrium (point A in Figure 30.2). At the prevailing price level, people had exactly as much money as they wanted. But after the helicopters drop the new money and people pick it up in the streets, people have more dollars in their wallets than they want. At the prevailing price level, the quantity of money supplied now exceeds the quantity demanded.

People try to get rid of this excess supply of money in various ways. They might buy goods and services with their excess holdings of money. Or they might use this excess money to make loans to others by buying bonds or by depositing the money in a bank savings account. These loans allow other people to buy goods and services. In either case, the injection of money increases the demand for goods and services.

Because the economy's ability to produce goods and services has not changed, this greater demand for goods and services causes the prices of goods and services to increase. The increase in the price level, in turn, increases the quantity of money demanded. Eventually, the economy reaches a new equilibrium (point B in Figure 30.2) at which the quantity of money demanded again equals the quantity of money supplied. In this way, the overall price level for goods and services adjusts to bring money supply and money demand into balance.

The classical dichotomy and monetary neutrality

We have seen how changes in the money supply lead to changes in the average level of prices of goods and services. How do these monetary changes affect other important macroeconomic variables, such as production, employment, real wages and real interest rates? This question has long intrigued economists. Indeed, the great philosopher David Hume wrote about it in the 18th century.

Hume and his contemporaries suggested that economic variables should be divided into two groups. The first group consists of **nominal variables** – variables measured in monetary units. The second group consists of **real variables** – variables measured in physical units. For example, the income of corn farmers is a nominal variable because it is measured in dollars, whereas the quantity of corn they produce is a real variable because it is measured in bushels. Nominal GDP is a nominal variable because it measures the dollar value of the economy's output of goods and services; real GDP is a real variable because it measures the total quantity of goods and services produced and is not influenced by the current prices of those goods and services. The separation of real and nominal variables is now called the **classical dichotomy**. (A *dichotomy* is a division into two groups, and *classical* refers to the earlier economic thinkers.)

Applying the classical dichotomy is tricky when we turn to prices. Most prices are quoted in units of money and, therefore, are nominal variables. When we say that the price of corn is $2 a bushel or

nominal variables
variables measured in monetary units

real variables
variables measured in physical units

classical dichotomy
the theoretical separation of nominal and real variables

that the price of wheat is $1 a bushel, both prices are nominal variables. But what about a *relative price* – the price of one thing compared to another? In our example, we could say that the price of a bushel of corn is 2 bushels of wheat. This relative price is not measured in terms of money. When comparing the prices of any two goods, the dollar signs cancel and the resulting number is measured in physical units. Thus, while dollar prices are nominal variables, relative prices are real variables.

This lesson has many applications. For instance, the real wage (the dollar wage adjusted for inflation) is a real variable because it measures the rate at which people exchange goods and services for a unit of labour. Similarly, the real interest rate (the nominal interest rate adjusted for inflation) is a real variable because it measures the rate at which people exchange goods and services today for goods and services in the future.

Why separate variables into these groups? The classical dichotomy is useful because different forces influence real and nominal variables. According to classical analysis, nominal variables are influenced by developments in the economy's monetary system, whereas money is largely irrelevant for explaining real variables.

This idea was implicit in our discussion of the real economy in the long run. In previous chapters, we examined how real GDP, saving, investment, real interest rates and unemployment are determined without mentioning the existence of money. In that analysis, the economy's production of goods and services depends on productivity and factor supplies, the real interest rate balances the supply and demand for loanable funds, the real wage balances the supply and demand for labour and unemployment results when the real wage is for some reason kept above its equilibrium level. These conclusions have nothing to do with the quantity of money supplied.

Changes in the supply of money, according to classical analysis, affect nominal variables but not real variables. When the central bank doubles the money supply, the price level doubles, the dollar wage doubles and all other dollar values double. Real variables, such as production, employment, real wages and real interest rates, are unchanged. This irrelevance of monetary changes for real variables is called **monetary neutrality**.

monetary neutrality
the proposition that changes in the money supply do not affect real variables

An analogy sheds light on the meaning of monetary neutrality. Recall that, as the unit of account, money is the yardstick we use to measure economic transactions. When a central bank doubles the money supply, all prices double and the value of the unit of account falls by half. A similar change would occur if the government were to reduce the length of a metre from 100 cm to 50 cm – as a result of the new unit of measurement, all *measured* distances (nominal variables) would double, but the *actual* distances (real variables) would remain the same. The dollar, like the metre, is merely a unit of measurement, so a change in its value should not have important real effects.

Is this conclusion of monetary neutrality a realistic description of the world in which we live? The answer is 'not completely'. A change in the length of a metre from 100 to 50 cm would not matter much in the long run, but in the short run it would certainly lead to confusion and various mistakes. Similarly, most economists today believe that over short periods of time – within the span of a year or two – there is reason to think that monetary changes do have important effects on real variables. Hume himself also doubted that monetary neutrality would apply in the short run. (We will turn to the study of short-run non-neutrality in a later chapter.)

Yet most economists today accept the classical analysis' conclusion as a description of the economy in the long run. Over the course of a decade, for instance, monetary changes have important effects on nominal variables but only negligible effects on real variables. When studying long-run changes in the economy, the neutrality of money offers a good description of how the world works.

Velocity and the quantity equation

We can obtain another perspective on the quantity theory of money by considering the following question: How many times per year is the typical dollar coin used to pay for a newly produced good or service? The answer to this question is given by a variable called the **velocity of money**. In physics, the term *velocity* refers to the speed (and direction) at which an object travels. In economics, the velocity of money refers to the speed at which the typical note or coin travels around the economy from wallet to wallet.

velocity of money
the rate at which money changes hands

To calculate the velocity of money, we divide the nominal value of output (nominal GDP) by the quantity of money. If P is the price level (the GDP deflator), Y the quantity of output (real GDP) and M the quantity of money (notes and coins), then velocity is:

$$V = \frac{(P \times Y)}{M}$$

To see why this makes sense, imagine a simple economy that produces only pizza. Suppose that the economy produces 100 pizzas in a year, that a pizza sells for $10, and that the quantity of money in the economy is $50 consisting of 50 dollar coins. Then the velocity of money is:

$$V = \frac{(\$10 \times 100)}{\$50}$$
$$= 20$$

In this economy, people spend a total of $1000 per year on pizza. For this $1000 of spending to take place with only $50 of money, each dollar coin must change hands 20 times per year.

With slight algebraic rearrangement, this equation can be rewritten as:

$$M \times V = P \times Y$$

This equation states that the quantity of money (M) times the velocity of money (V) equals the price of output (P) times the amount of output (Y). It is called the **quantity equation** because it relates the quantity of money (M) to the nominal value of output ($P \times Y$). The quantity equation shows that an increase in the quantity of money in an economy must be reflected in one of the other three variables – the price level must rise, the quantity of output must rise, or the velocity of money must fall.

quantity equation
the equation $M \times V = P \times Y$, which relates the quantity of money, the velocity of money and the dollar value of the economy's output of goods and services

If we assume that the velocity of money is relatively stable, we have a clear relationship between money and prices in the long run. We now have all the elements necessary to explain the equilibrium price level and inflation rate. Here they are:

1 Assume the velocity of money is relatively stable over time.
2 Because velocity is stable, if a central bank were to change the quantity of money (M), it would cause proportionate changes in the nominal value of output ($P \times Y$).
3 The economy's output of goods and services (Y) is primarily determined by factor supplies and the available technology. In particular, because money is neutral, money does not affect output.

4 With output (Y) determined by factor supplies and technology, if the central bank alters the money supply (M) and induces parallel changes in the nominal value of output ($P \times Y$), these changes are reflected in changes in the price level (P).

5 Therefore, if the central bank increases the money supply rapidly, the result is a high rate of inflation.

▸ Search me!

▸ hyperinflation

CASESTUDY

Money and prices during four hyperinflations

These five steps are the essence of the quantity theory of money. Although earthquakes can wreak havoc on a society, they have the beneficial by-product of providing much useful data for seismologists. These data can shed light on alternative theories and, thereby, help society predict and deal with future threats. Similarly, hyperinflations offer monetary economists a natural experiment they can use to study the effects of money on the economy.

Hyperinflations are interesting in part because the changes in the money supply and price level are so large. Indeed, hyperinflation is generally defined as inflation that exceeds 50 per cent *per month*. This means that the price level increases more than 100-fold over the course of a year.

The data on hyperinflation show a clear link between the quantity of money and the price level. Figure 30.3 graphs data from four classic hyperinflations that occurred during the 1920s in

Figure 30.3   **Money and prices during four hyperinflations**

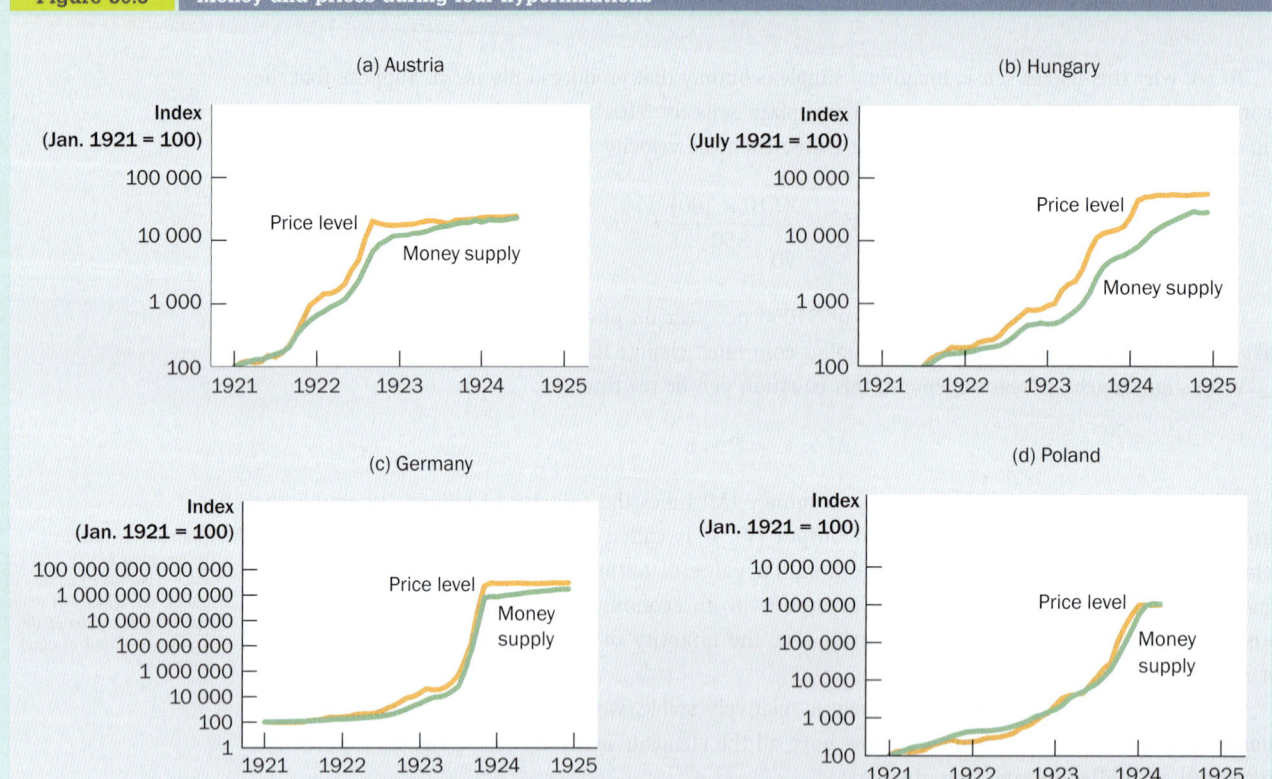

This figure shows the quantity of money and the price level during four hyperinflations. (Note that these variables are graphed on *logarithmic* scales. This means that equal vertical distances on the graph represent equal *percentage* changes in the variable.) In each case, the quantity of money and the price level move closely together. The strong association between these two variables is consistent with the quantity theory of money, which states that growth in the money supply is the primary cause of inflation.

Source: Adapted from Thomas J. Sargent, 'The end of four big inflations' in Robert Hall (ed.), *Inflation* (Chicago: University of Chicago Press, 1983), pp. 41–93.

Austria, Hungary, Germany and Poland. Each graph shows the quantity of money in the economy and an index of the price level. The slope of the money line represents the rate at which the quantity of money was growing and the slope of the price line represents the inflation rate. The steeper the lines, the higher the rates of money growth or inflation.

Notice that in each graph the quantity of money and the price level are almost parallel. In each instance, growth in the quantity of money is moderate at first and so is inflation. But over time the quantity of money in the economy starts growing faster and faster. At about the same time, inflation also takes off. Then when the quantity of money stabilises, the price level stabilises as well. These episodes illustrate well one of the *Ten Lessons from Economics* – prices rise when the government prints too much money.

The inflation tax

If inflation is so easy to explain, why do countries experience hyperinflation? That is, why do the central banks of these countries choose to print so much money that its value is certain to fall rapidly over time?

The answer is that the governments of these countries are using money creation as a way to pay for their spending. When the government wants to build roads, pay salaries to police officers, or give transfer payments to the poor or elderly, it first has to raise the necessary funds. Normally, the government does this by levying taxes, such as income and sales taxes, and by borrowing from the public by selling government bonds. Yet the government can also pay for spending by simply printing the money it needs.

When the government raises revenue by printing money, it is said to levy an **inflation tax**. The inflation tax is not exactly like other taxes, however, because no one receives a bill from the government for this tax. Instead, the inflation tax is more subtle. When the government prints money, the price level rises, and the dollars in your wallet are less valuable. Thus, *the inflation tax is like a tax on everyone who holds money.*

inflation tax
the revenue the government
raises by creating money

The importance of the inflation tax varies from country to country and over time. In Australia in the 1970s, the inflation tax was a significant source of revenue. However, one of the most striking examples was the German hyperinflation after the First World War. The German government was required to pay war reparations to the Allies, but it was unable to collect sufficient tax revenue to meet the debt. It financed the debt by borrowing freshly minted money from the Reichsbank, the German central bank. By 1922, prices were 1475 times their pre-war level.

Almost all hyperinflations follow the same pattern as the hyperinflation following the First World War in Germany. The government has high spending, inadequate tax revenue and limited ability to borrow. As a result, it turns to the printing press to pay for its spending. The massive increases in the quantity of money lead to massive inflation. The inflation ends when the government institutes fiscal reforms – such as cuts in government spending – that eliminate the need for the inflation tax.

The Fisher effect

According to the principle of monetary neutrality, an increase in the rate of money growth raises the rate of inflation but does not affect any real variable. An important application of this principle concerns the effect of money on interest rates. Interest rates are important variables for macroeconomists to understand because they link the economy of the present and the economy of the future through their effects on saving and investment.

To understand the relationship between money, inflation and interest rates, recall the distinction between the nominal interest rate and the real interest rate. The *nominal interest rate* is the interest rate you hear about at your bank. If you have a savings account, for instance, the nominal interest rate tells you how fast the number of dollars in your account will rise over time. The *real interest rate* corrects the nominal interest rate for the effect of inflation in order to tell you how fast the purchasing power of your savings account will rise over time. The real interest rate is the nominal interest rate minus the inflation rate:

$$\text{Real interest rate} = \text{Nominal interest rate} - \text{Inflation rate}$$

For example, if the bank posts a nominal interest rate of 7 per cent per year and the inflation rate is 3 per cent per year, then the real value of the deposits grows by 4 per cent per year.

We can rewrite this equation to show that the nominal interest rate is the sum of the real interest rate and the inflation rate:

$$\text{Nominal interest rate} = \text{Real interest rate} + \text{Inflation rate}$$

This way of looking at the nominal interest rate is useful because different economic forces determine each of the two terms on the right-hand side of this equation. As we discussed in an earlier chapter, the supply of and demand for loanable funds determine the real interest rate. And, according to the quantity theory of money, growth in the money supply determines the inflation rate.

IN THE NEWS . . .

FIGHTING THE WAR ... ON INFLATION?

Of all of the devastating effects of war, the one that is least mentioned is the impact on prices. In Iraq, the war effort has lead to spikes in the prices of most essential items. Complicating the stability of the currency is the prevalence of US dollars in the economy. The first article shows how the war led to price increases and the second article explains how the US government is attempting to improve the stability of the Iraqi dinar by reducing the use of US dollars.

Weary Iraqis face new foe: Rising prices

by Damien Cave

Baghdad, Iraq, Aug. 25 – For Mehdi Dawood, Iraq's failures have leached into the cucumbers, a staple of every meal that now devours a fifth of his monthly pension.

And it is not just the vegetables. Fuel and electricity prices are up more than 270 percent from last year's, according to Iraqi government figures. Tea in some markets has quadrupled, egg prices have doubled, and all over the country the daily routine now includes a new question: What can be done without?

'Meat, I just don't buy it anymore,' said Mr. Dawood, 66, holding half-filled bags at a market in Baghdad. 'It's too expensive.'

'We are all suffering,' he said. 'It's the government's fault. There is no security. There is no stability.'

As if Iraqis did not have enough to worry about. Going to the market already requires courage – after repeated bombings there – and now life's most basic needs are becoming drastically more expensive.

Three months into the administration of Prime Minister Nuri Kamal al-Maliki, the inflation rate has reached 70 percent a year, up from 32 percent last year. Wages are flat, banks are barely functioning and the consensus among many American and Iraqi officials is that inflation is most likely to accelerate.

Violence, corruption and the fallout from decades of government control are kicking up the price of nearly everything, especially fuel, which in turn multiplies the production cost for goods.

'It's a very serious problem,' said Anthony H. Cordesman, a Middle East analyst at the Center for Strategic and International Studies in Washington. 'You don't have stable trucking; you don't have stable distribution. You have a constant protection racket, with security forces who are involved in sectarian fighting often taking bribes to have things operate. All of that builds up pressure on prices.'

Mr. Maliki's office has responded with proposals to spur foreign investment and calls for public patience, even forgiveness. But billions in American aid has already been spent on Iraq with limited impact.

Compared with security problems, which can be addressed to some extent by deploying more troops to the streets, the economy is harder to control, especially since most Iraqi commerce occurs beyond the reach of government policy.

Fuel remains the country's most visible example of economic dysfunction. A gallon of gasoline cost as little as 4 cents in November. Now, after the International Monetary Fund pushed the Oil Ministry to cut its subsidies, the official price is about 67 cents.

The spike has come as a shock to Iraqis, who make only about $150 a month on average – if they have jobs. Estimates of unemployment range from 40 to 60 percent. And with black-market sellers commanding $3.19 a gallon because of shortages, up from about $1.25 a few months ago, the actual price most Iraqis pay is far higher than what is officially sanctioned.

Filling up now requires several days' pay, monastic patience or both.

Three years after fuel shortages led to riots in Basra, tension is often palpable at the pumps. Lines stretch as far as the eye can see, and at least two shootings have been reported in Baghdad this month alone. Near a station downtown this week, bribes and line cutting

appeared to be the norm. At one point a Mercedes and several police vehicles cut ahead of at least 50 cars while a policeman watched.

'Why are you letting people come from outside?' shouted a man who was just a few cars from the station after seven hours of waiting.

The station's manager said the drivers given special treatment must have had a note showing that they were doctors, or attending a funeral. A few hundred yards back, by a beat-up station wagon, Abdul Rehman Qasim had a different theory: the drivers avoiding the wait possessed either money or power. He had neither.

'I'm a poor guy,' he said. 'So I leave some of my children here. They spend the night in the car.'

'Under the government of Maliki, things are getting worse and worse,' he added. 'Only God can save us.'

In Iraq's once-bustling markets, frustration is equally acute. Car bombers have regularly attacked commercial districts, and prices seem to be up at every stall. At markets in a middle-class Shiite area near downtown, chickpeas have doubled in price. Lamb now runs as high as $2.75 a pound, up from $1.50.

Cucumbers, tomatoes and eggplant have all jumped too, while the price of the propane gas cylinders most families use for cooking has quintupled to more than $15.

'We live hand to mouth,' said Mr. Dawood, a retired clerk for Pepsi.

Veiled women shopping nearby agreed. 'We're tired, and the situation is horrible,' said Zakiya Abid Salman, 55, a widow carrying eggplants. 'There are no jobs, and the prices are always rising.'

Merchants said they had no choice but to increase prices because of the increased costs of doing business. And still, they said, their incomes have declined.

Ali Fouad, 27, pushing live fish around a shallow tub of water, said the price of transporting his product from farms south of Baghdad has nearly tripled since last year. A few months ago he sold about 110 pounds of fish a day, earning roughly $50 after expenses. Since he had to raise prices about

60 percent, he said, he sells less and earns only $20 a day.

'What's our life today?' he asked. 'We are working only for gas, ice and electricity. There is no savings.'

Stanching inflation will not be easy. Experts here say they struggle just to collect the data necessary to diagnose the problem, while Iraq largely lacks the usual mechanisms for controlling prices.

The Central Bank of Iraq is only three years old. Though the International Monetary Fund reports that officials have raised interest rates – and accelerated efforts to create a functioning market economy – its most recent study in July also concluded that 'the banking system is largely inert'. As a result, the report said, the effectiveness of such measures would be 'very limited'.

'Increasing the interest rate for business loans and mortgages – if people aren't taking out those loans, how much of an effect can you have?' said Edward W. Kloth, an economic adviser at the American Embassy here. 'The tools that are available are very limited in this kind of a situation.'

Ali al-Dabagh, a spokesman for Prime Minister Maliki, said in an interview that 'the government is working hard to find solutions'. He blamed terrorists for undermining Iraq's elected leaders, but he acknowledged that the country 'needs an administrative revolution'.

For the families trying to survive, time sometimes seems to be running out. Fathi Khalid, 43, a vegetable seller with a mostly empty stall, said obstacles seemed to multiply by the day. Sometimes roads are blocked so harvests never arrive. Sometimes he cannot afford to pay the right bribes. And week after week, his customers purchase less and less.

'Most people buy half what they used to,' he said. 'The vegetables sit here and rot.'

Use of U.S. dollar in Iraq being reduced to stimulate local currency, economy

Contingency Operating Location Basra, Iraq – U.S. currency may soon become difficult to find in Iraq as part of an effort to protect Soldiers and increase the value of the Iraqi dinar.

Sgt. Brittany A. Raimer, a dispersing manager with the 368th Finance Management Company, 36th Sustainment Brigade, 13th Sustainment Command (Expeditionary), said eliminating the use of U.S. currency on the battlefield will help to stimulate the economy of Iraq.

'One of the main focuses of finance is to ultimately eliminate U.S. currency from the battlefield,' said Raimer, a Lake Charles, La.,

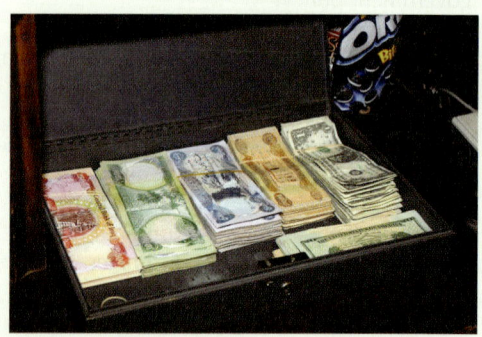

The contents of the cash drawer on 27 January at the finance office at Contingency Operating Location Basra, Iraq, illustrates how the use of US currency is being reduced in Iraq.

native. 'Our government is implementing the use of the Iraqi dinar, to both undermine the dependency the Iraqi nationals have on American currency and to back the Dinar, greatly increasing its weight on the market.'

The use of electronic fund transfers to pay vendors and contractors, and urging servicemembers to rely on the Eagle Cash Card, rather than cash, are two major changes that have been implemented in Iraq to eliminate the use of cash, said Raimer.

'The Eagle Cash Card enables personnel to have a direct link to the bank account without the hassle of hard cash,' said Raimer. 'The stored value card has been instrumental in effectively moving toward a cashless battlefield.'

Sgt. Toni M. Guillery, a dispersing agent with the 368th, said the Eagle Cash Card is designed to help prevent servicemembers from losing money or being robbed while in country.

'Carrying a single card is better than carrying a wad of money in your pocket, but one concern that I do have is…on the kiosks, you have to use a pin number in order to access the money, but when you go to vendors, you do not,' said Guillery. 'If you (fill the card) up to the max, and you lose that card, and somebody picks it up and finds it and they are a dishonest person, they can go and spend that money.'

Guillery said the unit only disburses U.S. currency to servicemembers who are about to go on mid-tour leave or re-deploy.

Guillery said the unit disburses less than $10 000 in U.S. currency per month, but disburses more than IQD351 000 000, the equivalent of roughly $300 000 per month.

The current exchange rate is IQD1,170 to $1, said Guillery.

Raimer said the transition away from the U.S. dollar has aided the progression of the banking industry in Iraq.

Raimer said, 'the progression (away from U.S. currency) has greatly supported the modernization of the banking system, thus improving and instilling trust in the local economy.'

Source: Courtesy of US Army/13th Sustainment Command Expeditionary Public Affairs, 3 February 2010.

Let's go back to Zoobooloo to consider how the growth in the money supply affects interest rates. In the long run, over which money is neutral, a change in money growth should not affect the real interest rate. The real interest rate is, after all, a real variable. For the real interest rate not to be affected, the nominal interest rate must adjust one-for-one to changes in the inflation rate. Thus, *when the ZCB increases the rate of money growth, the result is both a higher inflation rate and a higher nominal interest rate*. This adjustment of the nominal interest rate to the inflation rate is called the **Fisher effect**, after economist Irving Fisher (1867–1947), who first studied it.

The Fisher effect is, in fact, crucial for understanding changes over time in the nominal interest rate. Figure 30.4 shows the nominal interest rate and the inflation rate in the Australian economy since 1970. The close association between these two variables is clear. The nominal interest rate rose from 1973 to 1975 because inflation was also rising during this time. Similarly, the nominal interest rate fell from the early 1980s to the mid-1990s because the RBA finally got inflation under control.

Fisher effect
the one-for-one adjustment of the nominal interest rate to the inflation rate

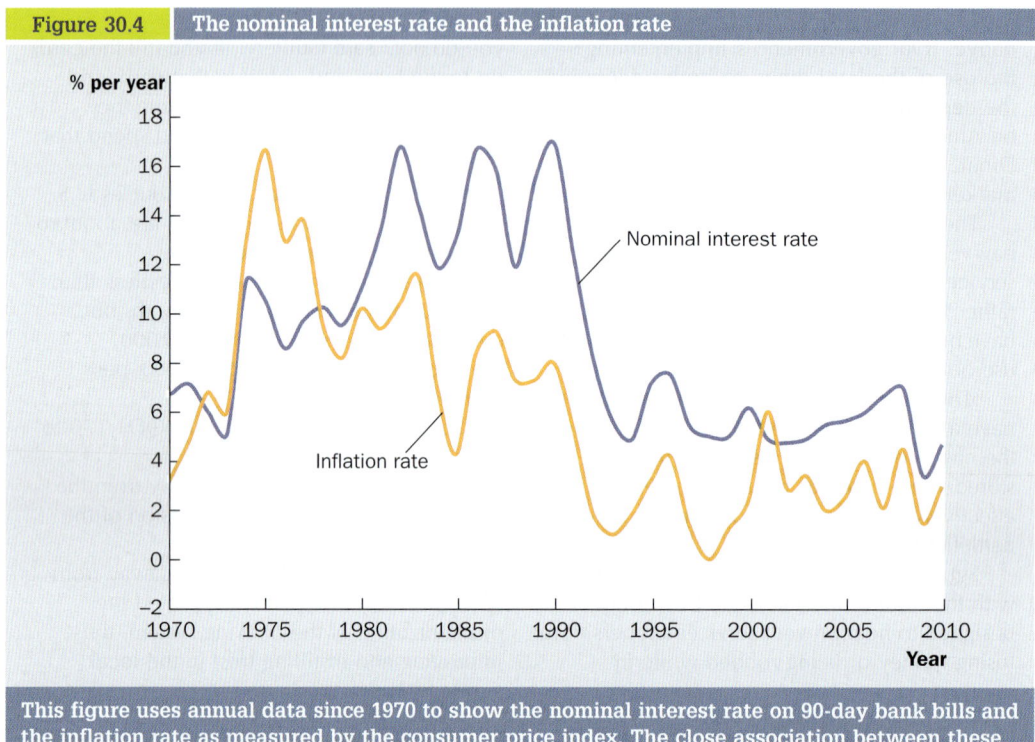

Figure 30.4 | The nominal interest rate and the inflation rate

This figure uses annual data since 1970 to show the nominal interest rate on 90-day bank bills and the inflation rate as measured by the consumer price index. The close association between these two variables is evidence for the Fisher effect – when the inflation rate rises, so does the nominal interest rate.

Source: Reserve Bank of Australia.

The government of a country increases the growth rate of the money supply from 5 per cent per year to 50 per cent per year. What happens to prices? What happens to nominal interest rates? Why might the government be doing this?

The costs of inflation

In the early 1980s, when the Australian inflation rate was above 10 per cent per year, inflation dominated debates over economic policy. Even though inflation dropped significantly during the first half of the 1990s, inflation remained a closely watched macroeconomic variable. One 1996 study found that *inflation* was the economic term mentioned most often in Australian newspapers and magazines.

Inflation is closely watched and widely discussed because it is thought to be a serious economic problem. In fact, its importance has lead to a profound change in the way most central banks, including the RBA, manage monetary policy. But is that true? And if so, why?

A fall in purchasing power? The inflation fallacy

If you ask ordinary people why inflation is bad, they will tell you that the answer is obvious – inflation robs them of the purchasing power of their hard-earned dollars. When prices rise, each dollar of income buys fewer goods and services. Thus, it might seem that inflation directly lowers living standards.

Yet further thought reveals a fallacy in this answer. When prices rise, buyers of goods and services do pay more for what they buy. At the same time, however, sellers of goods and services get more for what they sell. Because most people earn their incomes by selling their services, such as their labour, inflation in incomes goes hand in hand with inflation in prices. Thus, *inflation does not in itself reduce people's real purchasing power.*

People believe the inflation fallacy because they do not appreciate the principle of monetary neutrality. Workers who receive an annual wage increase of 10 per cent tend to view it as a reward for their own talents and efforts. When an inflation rate of 6 per cent reduces the real value of that wage increase to only 4 per cent, workers might feel that they have been cheated of what is rightfully their due. In fact, as we discussed in previous chapters, real incomes are determined by real variables, such as physical capital, human capital, natural resources and the available production technology. Nominal incomes are determined by those factors and the overall price level. If the RBA were to lower the inflation rate from 6 per cent to zero, workers' annual wage increase would fall from 10 per cent to 4 per cent. They might feel less robbed by inflation, but their real income would not rise more quickly.

But if nominal incomes tend to keep pace with rising prices, why then is inflation a problem? It turns out that there is no single answer to this question. Instead, economists have identified several costs of inflation. Each of these costs shows some way in which persistent growth in the money supply does, in fact, have some effect on real variables.

Shoeleather costs

As we have discussed, inflation is like a tax on the holders of money. The tax itself is not a cost to society – it is only a transfer of resources from households to the government. Yet most taxes give people an incentive to alter their behaviour to avoid paying the tax and this distortion of incentives causes efficiency losses for society as a whole. Like other taxes, the inflation tax also causes efficiency losses, as people waste scarce resources trying to avoid it.

How can a person avoid paying the inflation tax? Because inflation erodes the real value of the money in your wallet, you can avoid the inflation tax by holding less money. One way to do this is to go to the bank more often. For example, rather than withdrawing $200 every four weeks, you might withdraw $50 once a week. By making more frequent trips to the bank, you can keep more of your wealth in your interest-bearing savings account and less in your wallet, where inflation erodes its value.

shoeleather costs
the resources wasted when inflation encourages people to reduce their money holdings

The cost of reducing your money holdings is called the **shoeleather cost** of inflation because making more frequent trips to the bank causes your shoes to wear out more quickly. Of course, this term is not to be taken literally – the actual cost of reducing your money holdings is not the wear and tear on your shoes but the time and convenience you must sacrifice to keep less money on hand than you would if there were no inflation.

The shoeleather costs of inflation may seem trivial. And, in fact, they are in the Australian economy, which has had only moderate inflation in recent years. But this cost is magnified in countries experiencing hyperinflation. Here is a description of one person's experience in Bolivia during its hyperinflation (as reported in the 13 August 1985 issue of the *Wall Street Journal*, p. 1):

> When Edgar Miranda gets his monthly teacher's pay of 25 million pesos, he hasn't a moment to lose. Every hour, pesos drop in value. So, while his wife rushes to market to lay in a month's supply of rice and noodles, he is off with the rest of the pesos to change them into black-market dollars.
>
> Mr Miranda is practising the First Rule of Survival amid the most out-of-control inflation in the world today. Bolivia is a case study of how runaway inflation undermines a society. Price increases are so huge that the figures build up almost beyond comprehension. In one six-month period, for example, prices soared at an annual rate of 38 000%. By official count, however, last year's inflation reached 2000%, and this year's is expected to hit 8000% – though other estimates range many times higher. In any event, Bolivia's rate dwarfs Israel's 370% and Argentina's 1100% – two other cases of severe inflation.
>
> It is easier to comprehend what happens to the thirty-eight-year-old Mr Miranda's pay if he doesn't quickly change it into dollars. The day he was paid 25 million pesos, a dollar cost 500 000 pesos. So he received $50. Just days later, with the rate at 900 000 pesos, he would have received $27.

As this story shows, the shoeleather costs of inflation can be substantial. With the high inflation rate, Mr Miranda does not have the luxury of holding the local money as a store of value. Instead, he is forced to convert his pesos quickly into goods or into US dollars, which offer a more stable store of value. The time and effort that Mr Miranda expends to reduce his money holdings are a waste of resources. If the monetary authority pursued a low-inflation policy, Mr Miranda would be happy to hold pesos, and he could put his time and effort to more productive use. In fact, shortly after this article was written, the Bolivian inflation rate was reduced substantially with more restrictive monetary policy.

Menu costs

Most firms do not change the prices of their products every day. Instead, firms often announce prices and leave them unchanged for weeks, months or even years. One survey found that the typical

Australian firm changes its prices about once a year. One very visible exception to this is petrol prices, which are often changed several times during the week.

Firms change prices infrequently because there are costs of changing prices. Costs of price adjustment are called menu costs, a term derived from a restaurant's cost of printing a new menu. Menu costs include the cost of printing new price lists and catalogues, the cost of sending these new price lists and catalogues to dealers and customers, the cost of advertising the new prices, the cost of deciding on new prices and even the cost of dealing with customer annoyance over price changes. (Of course, for some methods of selling, such as web-based sales, the cost of price changes is relatively low, so they can change much more frequently.)

menu costs
the costs of changing prices

Inflation increases the menu costs that firms must bear. In the current Australian economy, with its low inflation rate, annual price adjustment is an appropriate business strategy for many firms. But when high inflation makes firms' costs rise rapidly, annual price adjustment is impractical. During hyperinflations, for example, firms must change their prices daily or even more often just to keep up with all the other prices in the economy.

Relative-price variability and the misallocation of resources

Suppose that the Eatabit Eatery prints a new menu with new prices every January and then leaves its prices unchanged for the rest of the year. If there is no inflation, Eatabit's relative prices – the prices of its meals compared with other prices in the economy – would be constant over the course of the year. In contrast, if the inflation rate is 12 per cent per year, Eatabit's relative prices will automatically fall by 1 per cent each month. The restaurant's prices will be relatively high in the early months of the year, just after it has printed a new menu, and relatively low in the later months. And the higher the inflation rate, the greater this automatic variability. Thus, because prices change only once in a while, inflation causes relative prices to vary more than they otherwise would.

Why does this matter? The reason is that market economies rely on relative prices to allocate scarce resources. Consumers decide what to buy by comparing the quality and prices of various goods and services. Through these decisions, they determine how the scarce factors of production are allocated among industries and firms. When inflation distorts relative prices, consumer decisions are distorted and markets are less able to allocate resources to their best uses.

Inflation-induced tax distortions

Almost all taxes distort incentives, cause people to alter their behaviour and lead to a less efficient allocation of the economy's resources. Many taxes, however, become even more problematic in the presence of inflation. The reason is that lawmakers often fail to take inflation into account when writing the tax laws. Economists who have studied the tax laws conclude that inflation tends to raise the tax burden on income earned from savings.

One example is the tax treatment of interest income. Income tax treats the nominal interest earned on savings as income, even though part of the nominal interest rate merely compensates for inflation. To see the effects of this policy, consider the numerical example in Table 30.1. The table compares two economies, both of which tax interest income at a rate of 25 per cent. In Economy 1, inflation is zero, and the nominal and real interest rates are both 4 per cent. In this case, the 25 per cent tax on interest income reduces the real interest rate from 4 per cent to 3 per cent. In Economy 2, the real interest rate is again 4 per cent, but the inflation rate is 8 per cent. As a result of the Fisher effect, the nominal interest rate is 12 per cent. Because the income tax treats this entire 12 per cent interest as income,

Table 30.1 How inflation raises the tax burden on saving	Economy 1 (price stability)	Economy 2 (inflation)
Real interest rate	4%	4%
Inflation rate	0	8
Nominal interest rate (real interest rate + inflation rate)	4	12
Reduced interest due to 25% tax (0.25 x nominal interest rate)	1	3
After-tax nominal interest rate (0.75 x nominal interest rate)	3	9
After-tax real interest rate (after-tax nominal interest rate − inflation rate)	3	1

In the presence of zero inflation, a 25 per cent tax on interest income reduces the real interest rate from 4 per cent to 3 per cent. In the presence of 8 per cent inflation, the same tax reduces the real interest rate from 4 per cent to 1 per cent.

the government takes 25 per cent of it, leaving an after-tax nominal interest rate of only 9 per cent and an after-tax real interest rate of only 1 per cent. In this case, the 25 per cent tax on interest income reduces the real interest rate from 4 per cent to 1 per cent. Because the after-tax real interest rate provides the incentive to save, saving is much less attractive in the economy with inflation (Economy 2) than in the economy with stable prices (Economy 1).

The taxes on nominal interest income are one example of how tax laws interact with inflation. There are many others. Because of these inflation-induced tax changes, higher inflation tends to discourage people from saving. Recall that the economy's saving provides the resources for investment, which in turn is a key ingredient to long-run economic growth. Thus, when inflation raises the tax burden on saving, it tends to depress the economy's long-run growth rate. There is, however, no consensus among economists about the size of this effect.

One solution to this problem, other than eliminating inflation, is to index the tax system. That is, the tax laws could be rewritten to take account of the effects of inflation. This is already done in the case of capital gains. A capital gain is the profit made by selling an asset for more than its purchase price. For example, if you purchased shares in XYZ Company in 1980 for $10 and then sold the same shares in 1998 for $50, you would have made a capital gain of $40. But if the overall price level had doubled between 1980 and 1998, then the increase in the value of your asset was really only $20. If the tax laws did not take into account the effects of inflation, you would pay tax on the profit of $40 instead of $20. The tax laws in Australia adjust the purchase price using a price index and assess the tax only on the real gain.

In the case of interest income, the government could tax only real interest income by excluding that portion of the interest income that merely compensates for inflation. To some extent, the tax laws have moved in the direction of indexation, as demonstrated above with capital gains. However, the income levels at which marginal income tax rates change are not adjusted automatically for inflation.

In an ideal world, the tax laws would be written so that inflation would not alter anyone's real tax liability. In the world in which we live, however, tax laws are far from perfect. More complete indexation would probably be desirable, but it would further complicate tax laws that many people already consider too complex.

Confusion and inconvenience

Imagine that we took a poll and asked people the following question: 'This year the metre is 100 cm. How long do you think it should be next year?' Assuming we could get people to take us seriously, they would tell us that the metre should stay the same length – 100 cm. Anything else would just complicate life needlessly.

What does this finding have to do with inflation? Recall that money, as the economy's unit of account, is what we use to quote prices and record debts. In other words, money is the yardstick with which we measure economic transactions. The job of the RBA is a bit like the job of Standards Australia – to ensure the reliability of a commonly used unit of measurement. When inflation occurs, it erodes the real value of the unit of account. The RBA's response, as we will see in later chapters, is to limit this erosion.

It is difficult to judge the costs of the confusion and inconvenience that arise from inflation. Earlier we discussed how the tax laws incorrectly measure real incomes in the presence of inflation. Similarly, accountants incorrectly measure firms' profits when prices are rising over time. Because inflation causes dollars at different times to have different real values, calculating a firm's profit – the difference between its revenue and costs – is more complicated in an economy with inflation. Therefore, to some extent, unexpected inflation makes investors less able to sort out successful from unsuccessful firms, which in turn impedes financial markets in their role of allocating the economy's saving to alternative types of investment.

A special cost of unexpected inflation: Arbitrary redistributions of wealth

So far, most of the costs of inflation we have discussed occur even if inflation is steady and predictable. Inflation has an additional cost, however, when it comes as a surprise. Unexpected inflation redistributes wealth among the population in a way that has nothing to do with either merit or need. These redistributions occur because many loans in the economy are specified in terms of the unit of account – money.

Consider an example. Suppose that Sam Student takes out a $20 000 loan at a 7 per cent interest rate from Bigbank to attend university. In 10 years, the loan will come due. After his debt has compounded for 10 years at 7 per cent, Sam will owe Bigbank $40 000. The real value of this debt will depend on inflation over the decade. If Sam is lucky, the economy will have hyperinflation. In this case, wages and prices will rise so high that Sam will be able to pay the $40 000 debt out of small change. In contrast, if the economy goes through a major deflation, then wages and prices will fall and Sam will find the $40 000 debt a greater burden than he anticipated.

This example shows that unexpected changes in prices redistribute wealth among debtors and creditors. Hyperinflation enriches Sam at the expense of Bigbank because it diminishes the real value of the debt; Sam can repay the loan in dollars that are less valuable than he anticipated. Deflation enriches Bigbank at Sam's expense because it increases the real value of the debt; in this case, Sam has to repay the loan in dollars that are more valuable than he anticipated. If inflation were predictable, then Bigbank and Sam could take inflation into account when setting the nominal interest rate. (Recall the Fisher effect.) But if inflation is hard to predict, it imposes risk on Sam and Bigbank that both would prefer to avoid.

This cost of unexpected inflation is important to consider together with another fact – inflation is especially volatile and uncertain when the average rate of inflation is high. This is seen most simply by examining the experience of different countries. Countries with low average inflation, such as Germany in the late twentieth century, tend to have stable inflation. Countries with high average inflation, such as many countries in Latin America, tend also to have unstable inflation. There are no known examples of economies with high, stable inflation. This relationship between the level and volatility of inflation points to another cost of inflation. If a country pursues a high-inflation monetary policy, it will have to bear not only the costs of high expected inflation but also the arbitrary redistributions of wealth associated with unexpected inflation.

CASESTUDY

The Wonderful Wizard of Oz and the free-silver debate

As a child, you may have seen the film *The Wizard of Oz*, based on a children's book written in 1900. The film and book tell the story of a young girl, Dorothy, who finds herself lost in a strange land far from home. You probably did not know, however, that the story is actually an allegory about US monetary policy in the late nineteenth century.

From 1880 to 1896, the price level in the US economy fell by 23 per cent. Because this event was unanticipated, it led to a major redistribution of wealth. Most farmers in the western part of the country were debtors. Their creditors were the bankers in the east. When the price level fell, it caused the real value of these debts to rise, which enriched the banks at the expense of the farmers.

According to populist politicians of the time, the solution to the farmers' problem was the free coinage of silver. During this period, the United States was operating with a gold standard. The quantity of gold determined the money supply and, thereby, the price level. The free-silver advocates wanted silver, as well as gold, to be used as money. If adopted, this proposal would have increased the money supply, pushed up the price level and reduced the real burden of the farmers' debts.

The debate over silver was heated and it was central to the politics of the 1890s. A common election slogan of the populists was 'We are mortgaged; all but our votes'. One prominent advocate of free silver was William Jennings Bryan, the Democrat nominee for president in 1896. He is remembered in part for a speech at the Democratic Party's nominating convention in which he said: 'You shall not press down upon the brow of labor this crown of thorns. You shall not crucify mankind upon a cross of gold.' Rarely since then have politicians waxed so poetic about alternative approaches to monetary policy. Nonetheless, Bryan lost the election to Republican William McKinley, and the United States remained on the gold standard.

L. Frank Baum, the author of *The Wonderful Wizard of Oz*, was a midwestern journalist. When he sat down to write a story for children, he made the characters represent protagonists in the major political battle of his time. Although modern commentators on the story differ somewhat in the interpretation they assign to each character, there is no doubt that the story highlights the debate over monetary policy. Here is how economic historian Hugh Rockoff, writing in the August 1990 issue of the *Journal of Political Economy*, interprets the story:

An early debate over monetary policy

Source: Corbis Australia.

DOROTHY:	Traditional American values
TOTO:	Prohibitionist party, also called the Teetotallers
SCARECROW:	Farmers
TIN WOODSMAN:	Industrial workers
COWARDLY LION:	William Jennings Bryan
	[Democrat nominee for president in 1896]
MUNCHKINS:	Citizens of the east
WICKED WITCH OF THE EAST:	Grover Cleveland [Democrat president 1893–97]
WICKED WITCH OF THE WEST:	William McKinley
	[Republican president 1897–1901]
WIZARD:	Marcus Alonzo Hanna
	[chairman of the Republican party at the time]
OZ:	Abbreviation for ounce of gold
YELLOW BRICK ROAD:	Gold standard

In the end of Baum's story, Dorothy does find her way home, but it is not by just following the yellow brick road. After a long and perilous journey, she learns that the wizard is incapable of helping her or her friends. Instead, Dorothy finally discovers the magical power of her *silver* slippers. (When the book was made into the film *The Wizard of Oz*, in 1939, Dorothy's slippers were changed from silver to ruby. Apparently, the Hollywood filmmakers were not aware that they were telling a story about nineteenth-century monetary policy.)

Although the populists lost the debate over the free coinage of silver, they did eventually get the monetary expansion and inflation that they wanted. In 1898, prospectors discovered gold near the Klondike River in Alaska. Increased supplies of gold also arrived from the Canadian Yukon and the gold mines of South Africa. As a result, the money supply and the price level started to rise in the United States and other countries operating on the gold standard. Within 15 years, prices in the United States were back to the levels that had prevailed in the 1880s, and farmers were better able to handle their debts.

IN THE NEWS . . .

IF INFLATION IS BAD, THEN DEFLATION MUST BE GOOD ... RIGHT?

This chapter has discussed the causes and impact of inflation, but sometimes economies experience deflation. Given everything we've said about inflation being a concern, deflation must be good, right? Well, not exactly. Deflation means economies are experiencing a lack of demand and as we will see in chapter 33, that's not necessarily better than having inflation.

Japan caught in deflation conundrum

by Christopher Johnson

Tokyo – If you live in Southeast Asia and need cheap clothing, come to Tokyo and check out these prices: 700 yen (US$7.45) for jeans,

1,000 yen for women's boots, and 7,800 yen for men's suits – about a third of what they cost a decade ago, when Japanese used to go to Bangkok and Hong Kong to shop.

For 12 straight months, prices in Japan have been falling, the country's Statistics Bureau said last week, and land prices are roughly half

>>

what they were 20 years ago. Prices fell by 1.2% in February from a year earlier. The finance minister and Bank of Japan board members are promising to stem the price slide, and many financial analysts are warning that further 'de-flay' could delay any economic recovery.

Declining prices can encourage consumers, expecting further price falls, to delay purchases. That hits company turnover and profits, prompting further price cuts and factory lay-offs to stem costs – further eroding overall consumer purchasing power and sales. Government income from sales and other taxes is also hit in the downward price spiral.

Yet Eisuke Sakakibara, famous as 'Mr Yen' when he was a top bureaucrat at the Ministry of Finance in the 1990s, argues that Japan's deflation is not necessarily a bad thing. 'We aren't in a deflationary spiral. I do not think mild deflation in Japan is a bad thing,' he said at a forum of financial analysts last week in Tokyo. 'We should enjoy mild deflation, rather than ponder it as a disease.'

Sakakibara says deflation is due to economic integration, as intra-regional trade in East Asia reaches 57% of all the region's trade. 'If you import cheap goods from China, then naturally prices will come down, compared to the conventional prices we're used to in Japan. It's very difficult to avoid deflation by monetary policies, when it's because of structural changes. Relatively slow deflation is something given.'

Yet many others strongly disagree, saying deflation will further dampen economic growth and lead to an eternally greater burden of debt compared with what the country produces, or gross domestic product (GDP).

'Deflation is a bad thing. People don't want to spend money, that is the big problem,' says Masaaki Kanno, a former senior official of the Bank of Japan, currently chief economist at JP Morgan in Tokyo. 'Now deflation and the economy are affecting each other. It's not easy to see what is the egg and what is the chicken. Without ending deflation, the government's target of 3% growth is impossible.'

The Japanese economy grew by 0.9% in the final three months of last year, or 3.8% on an annualized basis.

'Deflation corrodes the health of your economy long term,' says Richard Jerram, head of Asian economics for Macquarie Capital Securities in Tokyo. 'Non-manufacturing companies are more pessimistic than they were a year ago. Deflation means it's impossible to fix the fiscal problems in the economy without some nominal growth. If you have persistent deflation for the next five to 10 years, public finances are going to crash.'

As prices and wages fall, many Japanese are putting off purchases of appliances or cars, since they might be cheaper next year. Yet when chatting in supermarkets about 'de-flay' (deflation) and 'in-flay' (inflation), many Japanese say they are *kowaii* (afraid). After seeing prices spiral too high in the 1980s and subsequently decline, they still don't reflect the real worth of things.

Tokyo consumers, who tend to rent apartments, even when they cost $1,000 for a tiny living space in the suburbs, rather than own homes, are all for cheaper food, clothing and housing in a city where urban parking spots fetch between US$200 to $600 a month. Many feel that prices still have a long way to fall toward 'normal' levels.

Things haven't been normal since the early 1980s, when the Japanese currency stood at 300 yen to the US dollar (compared with 93 this week). Back then, a spartan room in a seaside village bed-and-breakfast (*minshuku*), at 3,000 yen per person, equated to $40 total for a family of four; a fair rate, not unlike a decent motel in America. Since workers could easily afford a 900 yen lunch special of pork on rice with miso soup, thousands of mom-and-pop shops sprouted up to serve them, fostering a culture of full employment, which attracted thousands of foreign workers.

After the 1985 Plaza Accord, major powers intervened in currency markets to weaken the dollar and strengthen the yen. The goal, echoed in present-day international pressures on China, was to open Japan to more imports and slow down its export juggernaut. The yen quickly doubled in value, and property values skyrocketed, to 50 times their 1950s levels in some cases. Even the cramped wooden house where this correspondent lived in the Osaka area in 1989 was worth $1 million at that time.

Expecting Japanese to get wealthier, businesses jacked up their prices to absurd levels, and Japanese kept buying $60 bottles of wine and $100 melons because they feared prices would rise further. But when the bubble burst, and the stock market benchmark index, the Nikkei 225, shrank from 39,000 to 9,000 in the 1990s, prices didn't fall accordingly. Many landlords, farmers, and suppliers stubbornly held their prices firm, believing consumer demand would recover – which it never did.

Today, even amid Japan's worst downturn since the war, minshuku owners still expect a family of four to pay 12,000 yen, despite 25 years of wear and chronic vacancy as city-folk stay home instead of taking weekend breaks.

Any sudden jump in economic growth might not boost prices. During the export boom of 2006, Japanese corporations channeled record profits toward research rather than into rewards for their workers. Employees felt betrayed, and refrained from buying their own company's products. Since wages on average were still 10% lower than 1997 levels, household spending continued to drop.

Suburban property values, meanwhile, have fallen to half of their 1990 peak. Even though home prices are less 'stupid' than before – as many Japanese say – many younger workers are either afraid of losing their jobs, or are waiting for prices to sink to a lower bottom. China's boom can't help, because Chinese can't build cheap houses and bring them to Japan.

Given Japan's declining population, policymakers are faced with tough choices on how to turn things around. The Bank of Japan last month doubled a credit program for commercial lenders to 20 trillion yen. Governor Masaaki Shirakawa said he hoped the move would lower borrowing costs and spur growth and prices. Former BoJ official Kanno says the central bank should lead the way out of deflation.

'The BoJ is responsible for ending deflation,' he says. 'They shouldn't wait for the government. Discussing inflation targeting is simply a waste of time. People's price expectations will not be affected by higher inflation targets.'

Kanno says spending 40 trillion to 50 trillion yen might trigger inflation but wouldn't be sustainable and would increase debt servicing costs. 'All the best policies are going to have short-term pain to get the best long-term results. Without taking these risks, Japan will fall into a trap which we can't find an exit. The government should let people know how bad deflation is. Japanese journalists don't want to tell the truth to the Japanese public. The current public pension system will not be sustained.'

While agreeing with many of Kanno's points, Macquarie Capital's Jerram doubts whether the central bank can fight deflation on its own.

'Deflation everywhere else is a monetary phenomenon, but Japan sees itself as unique, because deflation is due to deregulation,' says Jerram, who has been monitoring Japan for two decades. 'The tolerance of deflation is extremely unorthodox. The United States for example will take extreme measures to avoid going into the deflation hole. The problem with tolerating it is, you wake up one day and feel the need to do something about it. Japan is in such a deep hole, that a little bit of fiddling around the edges, such as what the Bank of Japan is doing, is not going to make that much of a difference.'

Jerram says the politicians should take action instead of telling the BOJ to try harder. 'I think the government doesn't understand it well enough. To be fair to them, they just took office six months ago, and they're starting to see how bad things are. You need to tell the public that the last 10 to 15 years have been a terrible mistake. It's a question of whether you want a crisis now or a crisis later.'

One solution, he says, is to set short-term interest rates at minus 3 or 4%. 'The idea that nothing can be done is a fantasy. If you fight deflation, it appears to hurt pensioners and lower income workers, but it might be better in the long term.'

Yet Sakakibara warns that extreme measures could make things worse.

>>

'Just because prices are coming down doesn't mean Japan is in a recession. We just had a recovery combined with deflation. We shouldn't worry about deflation too much,' says Sakakibara, now a professor at Waseda University. 'Taking actions to solve deflation might have some undesirable side-effect. We need to really worry when deflation comes with a recession.'

Source: *Asia Times Online* (www.atimes.com), 7 April 2010.

List and describe six costs of inflation.

Conclusion

This chapter discussed the causes and costs of inflation. The main cause of inflation is simply growth in the quantity of money. When a central bank creates money in large quantities, the value of money falls quickly over time. To maintain stable prices, the central bank must maintain strict control over interest rates or the money supply.

The costs of inflation are more subtle. They include shoeleather costs, menu costs, increased variability of relative prices, unintended changes in tax liabilities, confusion and inconvenience, and arbitrary redistributions of wealth. Are these costs, in total, large or small? All economists agree that they become huge during hyperinflation. But their size for moderate inflation – when prices rise by less than 10 per cent per year – is more open to debate.

Although this chapter presented many of the most important lessons about inflation, the discussion is incomplete. When a central bank reduces the rate of money growth, prices rise less rapidly, as the quantity theory suggests. Yet as the economy makes the transition to this lower inflation rate, the change in monetary policy will have disruptive effects on production and employment. That is, even though monetary policy is neutral in the long run, it has profound effects on real variables in the short run. Later in this book we will examine the reasons for short-run monetary non-neutrality in order to enhance our understanding of the causes and costs of inflation.

Summary

- If a central bank increases the supply of money, it causes the price level to rise. Persistent growth in the quantity of money supplied leads to continuing inflation.
- The principle of monetary neutrality asserts that changes in the quantity of money influence nominal variables but not real variables. Most economists believe that monetary neutrality approximately describes the behaviour of the economy in the long run.
- A government can pay for some of its spending simply by printing money. When countries rely heavily on this 'inflation tax', the result is hyperinflation.
- One application of the principle of monetary neutrality is the Fisher effect. According to the Fisher effect, when the inflation rate rises, the nominal interest rate rises by the same amount, so that the real interest rate remains the same.
- Many people think that inflation makes them poorer because it raises the cost of what they buy. This view is a fallacy, however, because inflation also raises nominal incomes.
- Economists have identified six costs of inflation: shoeleather costs associated with reduced money holdings; menu costs associated with more frequent adjustment of prices; increased variability of relative prices; unintended changes in tax liabilities due to non-indexation of the tax laws; confusion and inconvenience resulting from a changing unit of account; and arbitrary redistributions of wealth between debtors and creditors. Many of these costs are large during hyperinflation, but the size of these costs for moderate inflation is less clear.

Key concepts

classical dichotomy
Fisher effect
inflation tax
menu costs

monetary neutrality
nominal variables
quantity equation
quantity theory of money

real variables
shoeleather costs
velocity of money

Questions for review

1 Explain how an increase in the price level affects the real value of money.
2 According to the quantity theory of money, what is the effect of a decrease in the quantity of money?
3 Explain the difference between nominal and real variables, and give two examples of each. According to the principle of monetary neutrality, which variables are affected by changes in the quantity of money?
4 In what sense is inflation like a tax? How does thinking about inflation as a tax help explain hyperinflation?
5 According to the Fisher effect, how does an increase in the inflation rate affect the real interest rate and the nominal interest rate?
6 What are the costs of inflation? Which of these costs do you think are most important for the Australian economy?
7 If inflation is less than expected, who benefits – debtors or creditors? Explain.

Problems and applications

1   The United States' Federal Reserve Bank does not have inflation targeting as a monetary policy objective. Make the case for why the US Fed should switch to inflation targeting.

2   The chapter preceding this one showed that there are several different measures of the money stock, with the larger measures including more types of assets than the smaller ones. How can the quantity equation hold for all of these measures?

3   The economist John Maynard Keynes wrote: 'Lenin is said to have declared that the best way to destroy the capitalist system was to debauch the currency. By a continuing process of inflation, governments can confiscate, secretly and unobserved, an important part of the wealth of their citizens.' Justify Lenin's assertion.

4   Suppose that a country's inflation rate increases sharply. What happens to the inflation tax on the holders of money? Why is wealth that is held in savings accounts *not* subject to a change in the inflation tax? Can you think of any way in which holders of savings accounts are hurt by the increase in the inflation rate?

5   In the lead-up to the last federal election, some political parties made the case for increased direction of RBA monetary policy by the government of the day so that monetary policy and fiscal policy were better coordinated. Do you agree or not? If you were writing a policy paper for your political party, which would you argue for – independence of the RBA or direction of monetary policy by the government? Be sure to explain your conclusions thoroughly – the leader of your party wants to make a credible case to the public.

6   Suppose that Bob is a bean farmer and Rita is a rice farmer. Bob and Rita are the only people in the economy and both always consume equal amounts of rice and beans.
    In 2011 the price of beans was $4 and the price of rice was $5.

    a   Suppose that in 2012 the price of beans was $6 and the price of rice was $7.50. What was inflation? Was Bob better off, worse off, or unaffected by the changes in prices? What about Rita?

    b   Now suppose that in 2012 the price of beans was $6 and the price of rice stayed at $5. What was inflation? Was Bob better off, worse off, or unaffected by the changes in prices? What about Rita?

    c   Finally, suppose that in 2012 the price of beans was $4 and the price of rice was $2.50. What was inflation? Was Bob better off, worse off, or unaffected by the changes in prices? What about Rita?

7   Most companies no longer produce 'books' of prices, but have put all of their prices on computer. (Think of companies that produce a wide range of products in different specifications, such as a steel company that produces steel pipes and tubes in a large variety of lengths, diameters and thicknesses.) How does this computerisation affect menu costs? Does computerisation of price lists make firms more or less likely to respond to changes in input prices by changes in their prices? How has this affected inflation?

8   If you lived in a low inflation economy, would you hold your wealth in cash, gold or buy some other asset, such as paintings? Explain.

9   Suppose that Australians expect inflation to equal 6 per cent in 2012, but, in fact, prices rise by only 3 per cent. How would this unexpectedly low inflation rate help or hurt the following?

    a   The federal government
    b   A homeowner with a fixed-rate mortgage
    c   A casual worker who has no labour contract
    d   A private school that has invested some of its endowment in Treasury bonds.

10 Explain one harm associated with unexpected inflation that is *not* associated with expected inflation. Then explain one harm associated with both expected and unexpected inflation.

11 Explain whether the following statements are true, false, or uncertain.

a   'Inflation hurts borrowers and helps lenders, because borrowers must pay a higher rate of interest.'

b   'If prices change in a way that leaves the overall price level unchanged, then no one is made better or worse off.'

c   'Inflation does not reduce the purchasing power of most workers.'

Search me!

 Search me!

When accessing information about economics use the following keywords in any combinations you require:

- hyperinflation

CourseMate

 CourseMate

For more multimedia resources and activities on economics, visit the Economics CourseMate website.

PART ELEVEN
The macroeconomics of open economies

31

Open-economy macroeconomics: Basic concepts

Learning objectives

In this chapter you will:

- learn how net exports measure the international flow of goods and services
- learn how net foreign investment measures the international flow of capital
- consider why net exports must always equal net foreign investment
- see how saving, domestic investment and net foreign investment are related
- learn the meaning of the nominal exchange rate and the real exchange rate
- examine purchasing-power parity as a theory of how exchange rates are determined.

When you graduate from university and decide to buy a car, you may compare the latest models offered by Holden and Hyundai. When you take your next holiday, you may consider spending it on a beach in Queensland or in Tahiti. When you get a job and begin to save for your retirement, you may choose between a managed fund that buys shares in Australian companies and one that buys shares in foreign companies. In all of these cases, you will be participating not just in the Australian economy but in economies around the world.

There are clear benefits to an economy that is open to international trade – trade allows people to produce what they produce best and to consume the great variety of goods and services produced around the world. Indeed, one of the *Ten Lessons from Economics* highlighted in chapter 1 is that trade can make everyone better off. Chapter 3 examined the gains from trade more fully – that international trade can raise living standards in all countries by allowing each country to specialise in producing those goods and services in which it has a comparative advantage.

So far, our development of macroeconomics has largely ignored the economy's interaction with other economies around the world. For some economies, such as that of the United States, many questions in macroeconomics can be discussed without considering international issues. However, for some economies, such as the Australian economy, the effects of international trade are very important. We ignored the effects of international trade when we discussed topics such as the natural rate of unemployment and the causes of inflation to keep our exposition simple and focused. Indeed, to keep their analysis simple, macroeconomists often assume a **closed economy** – an economy that does not interact with other economies.

closed economy
an economy that does not interact with other economies in the world

To build a complete picture of the economy, though, we need to examine an **open economy** – an economy that interacts freely with other economies around the world. This chapter and the next one, therefore, provide an introduction to open-economy macroeconomics. We begin in this chapter by discussing the key macroeconomic variables that describe an open economy's interactions in world markets. You may have noticed mention of the variables exports, imports, the trade balance and exchange rates in newspapers or news bulletins. Our first job is to understand what these data mean. In the next chapter we develop a model to explain how these variables are determined and how they are affected by various government policies.

open economy
an economy that interacts freely with other economies around the world

The international flows of goods and capital

An open economy interacts with other economies in two ways – it buys and sells goods and services in world product markets, and it buys and sells financial assets in world financial markets. Here we discuss these two activities and the close relationship between them.

The flow of goods: Exports, imports and net exports

As noted in chapter 3, *exports* are domestically produced goods and services that are sold abroad, and *imports* are foreign-produced goods and services that are sold domestically. When Boeing, the US aircraft manufacturer, builds a plane and sells it to Qantas, the sale is an export for the United States and an import for Australia. When Holden Australia makes a car and sells it to a New Zealand resident, the sale is an import for New Zealand and an export for Australia.

The *net exports* of any country are the value of its exports minus the value of its imports. The Ford sale raises Australian net exports and the Boeing purchase reduces Australian net exports. Because net exports tell us whether a country is, in total, a seller or a buyer in world markets for

"But we're not just talking about buying a car—we're talking about confronting this country's trade deficit with Japan."

Source: Gerberg, Mort © Mort Gerberg/The New Yorker Collection/www.cartoonbank.com.

trade balance (net exports)
spending on domestically produced goods by foreigners (exports) minus spending on foreign goods by domestic residents (imports)

trade surplus
an excess of exports over imports

trade deficit
an excess of imports over exports

balanced trade
a situation in which exports equal imports

▶ net exports

goods and services, net exports are also called the **trade balance**. If net exports are positive, exports are greater than imports, indicating that the country sells more goods and services abroad than it buys from other countries. In this case, the country is said to run a **trade surplus**. If net exports are negative, exports are less than imports, indicating that the country sells fewer goods and services abroad than it buys from other countries. In this case, the country is said to run a **trade deficit**. If net exports are zero, its exports and imports are exactly equal, and the country is said to have **balanced trade**.

In the next chapter, we develop a theory that explains an economy's trade balance, but even at this early stage it is easy to think of many factors that might influence a country's exports, imports and net exports. Those factors include:

- the tastes of consumers for domestic and foreign goods
- the prices of goods at home and abroad
- the rates at which people can exchange domestic currency for foreign currencies
- the cost of transporting goods from country to country
- the policies of the government towards international trade.

As these variables change over time, so does the amount of international trade.

CASESTUDY

The importance of trade in the Australian economy

International trade has always been a significant part of the Australian economy. Figure 31.1 shows the total value of goods and services exported to other countries and imported from other countries expressed as a percentage of gross domestic product. In the early 1950s, exports of goods and services averaged around 20 per cent of GDP. In the mid-1950s, they levelled off to around 13 per cent and stayed around that level until the mid 1990s, when they began to rise. Imports of goods and services have followed a similar pattern. After the Second World War, the fledgling Australian economy began to develop a

manufacturing base, so more goods were produced in the domestic economy for domestic production. But trade has remained an important part of the national economy.

Because Australia is a small economy, it has always relied on goods produced overseas for both investment and consumption. Many of the goods that Australians need to produce other goods or that Australians like to consume are not produced in the domestic economy. So we import these goods. Since Australia is physically a large country, well endowed with natural resources, for years our most important exports have been minerals and primary products,

Figure 31.1 | **The openness of the Australian economy**

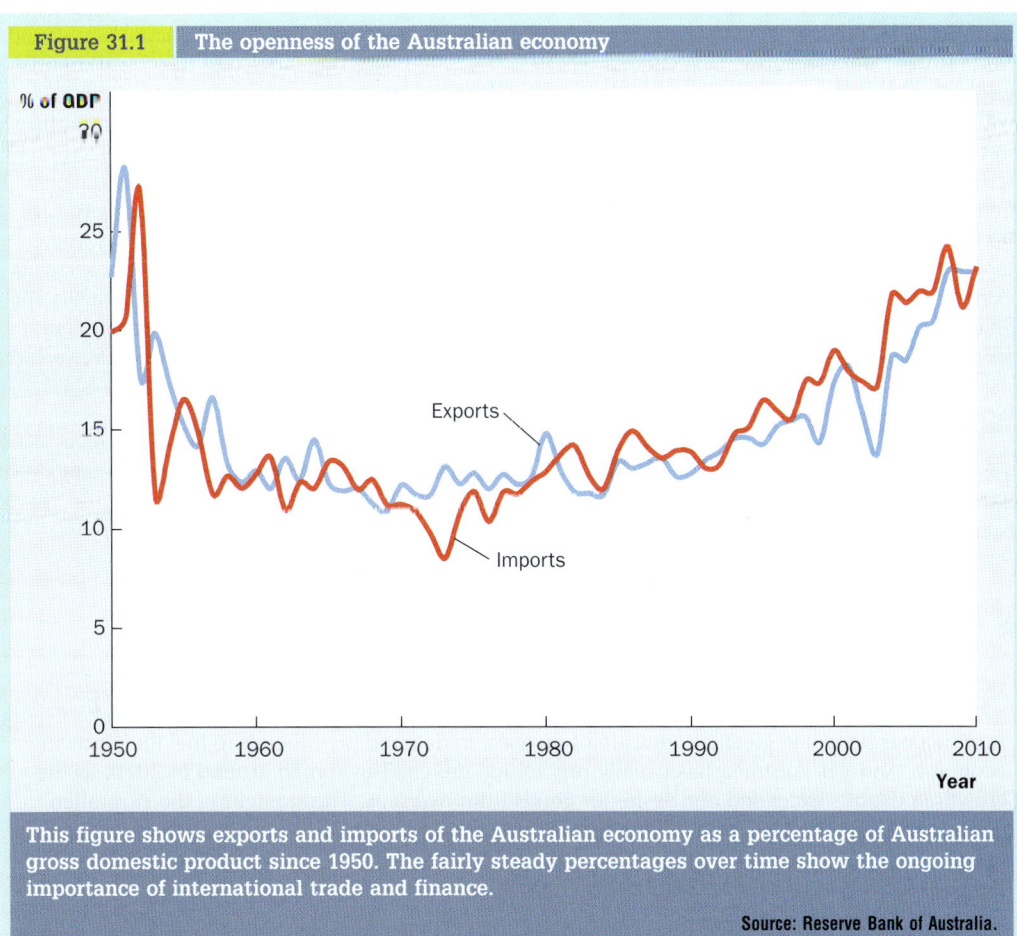

This figure shows exports and imports of the Australian economy as a percentage of Australian gross domestic product since 1950. The fairly steady percentages over time show the ongoing importance of international trade and finance.

Source: Reserve Bank of Australia.

particularly wool, hence the expression 'riding on the sheep's back'.

Even though trade has always been important for Australia, trade has increased in importance globally. This increase in international trade is partly due to improvements in transportation. In 1950, the average merchant ship carried less than 10 000 tonnes of cargo; today, many ships carry more than 100 000 tonnes. The long-distance jet was introduced in 1958 and the wide-bodied jet in 1967, making air transport far cheaper. Because of these developments, goods that once had to be produced and consumed locally can now be traded around the world. Cut flowers, for instance, are now grown in Israel and flown to the United States to be sold. Fresh fruits and vegetables that can grow only in summer can now be eaten by consumers in the Northern Hemisphere in winter as well, because they

can be shipped from countries in the Southern Hemisphere, such as Australia.

The increase in international trade has also been influenced by advances in telecommunications, which have allowed businesses to reach overseas customers more easily. Australia's first intercontinental telephone connection was created in 1902 when a submarine cable was laid across the Pacific, linking Australia with Canada. The first transatlantic telephone cable was not laid until 1956, though. As recently as 1966, the technology allowed only 138 simultaneous conversations between North America and Europe. Today, communications satellites permit more than 1 million conversations to occur at the same time.

Technological progress has also fostered international trade by changing the kinds of goods

>>

that economies produce. When bulky raw materials (such as steel) and perishable goods (such as wheat) were a large part of the world's output, transporting goods was often costly and sometimes impossible. In contrast, goods produced with modern technology are often light and easy to transport. Consumer electronics, for instance, have low weight for every dollar of value, which makes them easy to produce in one country and sell in another. A more extreme example is the film industry. Once Fox Studios in Sydney makes a film, it can send copies of the film around the world at almost zero cost. Indeed, films are an export of many countries including Australia, the United States and India.

The government's trade policies have also been a factor in increasing international trade. As discussed in chapter 3, economists have long believed that free trade between countries is mutually beneficial. Over time, policymakers around the world have come to accept these conclusions. International agreements, such as the North American Free Trade Agreement (NAFTA) and the General Agreement on Tariffs and Trade (GATT), now governed by the World Trade Organization (WTO), have gradually lowered trade barriers, such as tariffs and import quotas. Australia is a leader both in lowering trade barriers and in encouraging other countries to do likewise. In fact, Australia and the United States signed a free-trade agreement in 2004 that will liberalise trade between the two countries. The pattern of increasing trade is a phenomenon that most economists and policymakers endorse and encourage. As trade has always been a significant part of Australia's economy, these changes are to Australia's benefit.

IN THE NEWS ...

AUSTRALIA'S TRADE BALANCE SWITCHES TO POSITIVE

Australia has benefited greatly from China's increase in demand for minerals to fuel their growing economy. And yet, Australia has usually run a trade deficit. This turned around in 2010, as the growth in exports exceeded our desire for goods from overseas. The strength of the Australian economy through the GFC comes largely from these exports, but as the following article discusses, we're also experiencing something some economists have dubbed 'the MasterChef effect' – the desire to eat out more as a result of seeing all that lovely food on TV.

Current account deficit shrinks: Mining surge brings record $74 billion in exports

by Peter Martin, Economics correspondent

A record surge of mining revenue has all but eliminated Australia's current account deficit, long regarded as the country's biggest economic problem.

As high as $16 billion in the March quarter, Australia's current account deficit shrank to $5.6 billion in the June quarter. That is just 1.7 per cent of gross domestic product, the third-lowest result in 30 years and the lowest in about 10 years.

A measure of the amount of money leaving the nation each quarter over and above that coming in, it climbed as high as 6 per cent of GDP in the 1980s, prompting the then treasurer Paul Keating to observe that 'the world doesn't owe us a living' and that unless we made changes we would become a 'banana republic'.

Australia's trade balance has moved from 'negative', where spending on imports exceeded income from exports, to strongly positive, with a record high $74 billion in export income exceeding imports by $6.5 billion, the widest margin since the 1970s.

Export prices jumped 14 per cent with metal ore and mineral prices up 39 per cent and coal prices up 25 per cent. Export volumes surged 12 per cent.

'This is a much bigger rise in volumes than what we saw during the 2006-08 commodity price boom,' said ANZ economist Katie Dean.

'Rural exports are also climbing, with wheat prices hitting record highs.'

Separately released retail figures show consumers further opening their wallets in July, cautiously in most cases, with overall spending up a fraction of 1 per cent, but up dramatically at restaurants and cafes where the figures show spending climbing 8.5 per cent.

'It could be a MasterChef effect,' said Deutsche Bank economist Adam Boyton.

'They jump clear across all states. It is consistent with reports from late July that restaurants had benefited from a surge in interest stemming from the TV program.

'Media reports suggest that the final of this show drew just under 4 million viewers, making it Australia's single most popular non-sport show since ratings began.

'While it is very difficult to isolate the true effect of the show, a positive influence on 'restaurant-quality' dining makes some sense.'

Caretaker Treasurer Wayne Swan said the news showed 'despite increased global uncertainty, Australia's economy is strong and continues to benefit from the sound management that saw us fight off recession'.

He said the economy could face the global challenges ahead from a position of strength and stability.

Asked at a Sydney seminar whether a second 'double dip' global recession was possible, Reserve Bank assistant governor Guy Debelle said he thought it was a risk before adding that it was 'a somewhat unquantifiable risk'.

Other news released yesterday showed building approvals up for the first time in four months, rising 2.3 per cent in July. An RP Data measure of house prices was relatively flat, increasing by just 0.4 per cent.

Economic growth figures, due to be released today, are expected to show the economy growing strongly by about 1 per cent in the June quarter after analysts lifted forecasts in response to the trade figures.

We're in the money…

In the three months to June:
– Record $74 billion export income
– Largest trade surplus since 1970s
– Decade-low current account deficit
  And starting to spend…
  In July
– Spending at cafes & restaurant 8.5%
– Building approvals 2.3%
– House prices 0.4%

Source: Peter Martin/*The Sydney Morning Herald*, 1 September 2010, p. 7.

The flow of financial resources: Net foreign investment

So far we have been discussing how residents of an open economy participate in world markets for goods and services. In addition, residents of an open economy participate in world financial markets. An Australian resident with $20 000 could use that money to buy a car from Hyundai, but she could instead use that money to buy shares in the Hyundai corporation. The first transaction would represent a flow of goods, whereas the second would represent a flow of capital.

The term **net foreign investment** (sometimes referred to as *net capital outflow*) refers to the purchase of foreign assets by domestic residents minus the purchase of domestic assets by foreigners. When an Australian resident buys shares in British Telecom, the British phone company, the purchase raises Australian net foreign investment. When a Japanese resident buys a bond issued by the Australian government, the purchase reduces Australian net foreign investment.

Recall that foreign investment takes two forms. When the Australian Pie Company opens up a bakery in Moscow, that is an example of *foreign direct investment*. Alternatively, if an Australian buys shares in a Russian corporation, that is an example of *foreign portfolio investment*. In the first case, the Australian owner is actively managing the investment, whereas in the second case the Australian owner has a more passive role. So the distinction is the degree of control. In both cases, Australian residents are buying assets located in another country, so both purchases increase Australian net foreign investment.

net foreign investment
the purchase of foreign assets by domestic residents minus the purchase of domestic assets by foreigners

▸ net foreign investment

We develop a theory to explain net foreign investment in the next chapter. Here, let's consider briefly some of the more important variables that influence net foreign investment:

- the real interest rates being paid on foreign assets
- the real interest rates being paid on domestic assets
- the perceived economic and political risks of holding assets abroad
- the government policies that affect foreign ownership of domestic assets.

For example, consider Australian investors deciding whether to buy Japanese government bonds or Australian government bonds. (Recall that a bond is, in effect, an IOU of the issuer.) To make this decision, Australian investors compare the real interest rates offered on the two bonds. The higher a bond's real interest rate, the more attractive it is. While making this comparison, however, Australian investors must also take into account the risk that one of these governments might *default* on its debt (that is, not pay interest or principal when it is due), as well as any restrictions that the Japanese government has imposed, or might impose in the future, on foreign investors in Japan.

IN THE NEWS . . .

AN APPLE A DAY … BUT WHAT IF IT'S FROM TOO FAR AWAY?

There is much debate about whether globalisation is good or not. One of the issues that has increased in prominence is how many miles our food travels. It's great to be able to eat strawberries in the northern winter or to have apples from Tasmania in the spring, but does it make sense to ship food half way around the world? The concept of 'food miles' – how far our food has travelled – was coined in an attempt to measure the greenhouse gas emissions created by shipping food from one country to another. But it's not always a good measure of whether that asparagus from Argentina creates a higher level of emissions or not, as the following article discusses.

The true cost of our daily bread
by Ben Cubby

'Food mile' labels don't always tell the whole story, writes Ben Cubby

When the British supermarket giant Tesco decided to start labelling its produce with 'food miles' to let people know how far it travelled before reaching the shelf, the move was greeted with a bizarre mixture of fear, derision and relief.

The fear came from the global food industry and many primary producers, who remain worried that people will be put off by finding out how far their food has come.

The derision arose because Tesco had wandered blithely into the labyrinth of attempting to accurately measure greenhouse gas emissions. It is so fantastically complicated that a team of Oxford University climate experts commissioned by the supermarket chain to do the maths described their own findings as 'highly contentious'.

The relief stemmed from the many consumer groups, farmers and other advocates of local produce who had been crying out for more information for years. Food labelling fed a general belief in the community that people have a right to know where their food comes from and what impact it has had on the environment.

'You can't expect somebody to stand in the aisle with their mobile phone and surf the net to find the right information,' says Jeff Angel, the director of Sydney's Total Environment Centre. 'Mostly the right information isn't there yet.'

Australia is about to start treading the food labelling path. The federal government is undertaking a comprehensive review of labelling standards, and for the first time this includes the environmental impact of food. Findings are said to be available early next year. A few supermarkets in Australia, such as Aldi, have pledged to start labelling their products with an estimated carbon footprint by next year.

The US giant Walmart plans to have 'eco-labels' on its products within the year. In Britain, Marks & Spencer followed Tesco and has a sticker on all products that arrive by air. Coca-Cola and Pepsi are working with England's Carbon Trust to measure reductions in CO_2 in their bottling process.

What we eat makes up about one-third of the total greenhouse gas emissions from an average Australian household, according to the CSIRO. This means that, in theory, a solar panel on your roof could be cancelled out by a lifetime preference for imported Italian pasta and sun-dried tomatoes. A high protein diet can be a useful for losing weight, but eating beef three times a week means about 1.5 tonnes of methane emissions a year, the CSIRO says, which could be more than the entire food footprint of a dedicated vegetarian.

To test the food miles concept in Australian conditions, the *Herald* mapped the journey of an unremarkable basket of groceries and found that it had, collectively, travelled further than some of its consumers.

Even though most of the produce was Australian, the most conservative estimates, using methodology and data being experimented with by the CSIRO and the Department of Climate Change, showed the food had travelled at least 80 919 kilometres before it reached the shelves of its central Sydney supermarket.

The lightweight basket can easily be carried in one hand, yet simply getting it to the shop burnt enough fuel to run a heavily loaded car for 30 kilometres. This is the most conservative food miles figure possible, with all distances rounded down and assumptions that transport vehicles were well-maintained, fuel efficient and encountered minimal traffic on their way to market.

If the energy cost of refrigeration, snap-freezing, pre-cooking and storage are factored in, the carbon footprint of the food basket soars to alarming levels. This is without the emissions from plastic packaging, which has risen in the past five years despite signs of consumer resistance, together with the smelting of metal for canned food and the production and printing of paper labels and the manufacture of adhesives.

Sydney's food supply network is a bit like an ant colony, with a constant stream of workers fanning out across the surrounding landscape and bringing in food. Ants have solved the problem of supplying a static colony with sustenance by deploying the majority of their workforce as fetchers and carriers, whereas humans have done it by mechanisation.

It is an intricate, invisible web that is in most respects a masterpiece of commerce and logistics, in that it delivers healthy, fresh and nutritious food to the overwhelming majority of people at prices they can afford.

While most citizens are asleep, about 4600 refrigerated trucks are on the move early each morning, bringing produce from regional centres to the city's main food distribution points at Wetherill Park, Bankstown, Silverwater, Blacktown and Flemington. A fleet of smaller, diesel-burning commercial vehicles collects produce and delivers it to shop shelves.

The IGA supermarket chain has two main distribution centres at Blacktown and Silverwater, but where its produce comes from before that is a trickier proposition.

It's the suppliers job as to where they source the food from, said a spokesman for Metcash, the owner of the IGA brand and distributor of its products.

'They have to comply with our policy of sourcing produce locally. We can trace back to wholesale, then the distributors can trace back to their suppliers from there. If there is a problem with one product, we can source it from somewhere else.' Essentially, where the supermarkets fresh food comes from is a day-to-day proposition, depending on price and availability.

For instance, even though Australia produces 12 000 tonnes of fresh garlic a year, none was available when the *Herald* visited to buy its sample grocery basket. The garlic was from Mexico, and using the most conservative assumptions about freight travel it had travelled about 10 160 kilometres by sea and road before it arrived at IGA.

>>

On the assumption the garlic's nautical voyage went smoothly and there was minimal traffic congestion and no mechanical trouble by road in Mexico or Sydney, the single head of Mexican garlic generated about 940 grams of carbon dioxide emissions from the fuels used to get it to the shelf.

IGA isn't the only supermarket to rely heavily on imported garlic; about 9000 tonnes are imported annually from China, according to data compiled by Australian Garlic Producers, an industry group. This accounts for half the garlic on supermarket shelves.

When tracing the food from the IGA basket, the *Herald* used the methods deployed by the Australian Greenhouse Office, which has since been absorbed into the Department of Climate Change and Energy. It was also informed by calculations used in a study of a basket of groceries sampled in Melbourne by staff at CERES Community Environment Park, which found that 29 common food items had travelled 70 803 kilometres. The fresh produce in the IGA basket was impossible to trace to the farm gate in every case, so average transport figures from the most likely production areas, based on trucking times and fuel use, were used.

Essentially, the distance and fuel efficiency of the type of transport to get food from A to B was divided by the weight of the food involved. As well as showing how far food has actually come, it highlights some of the shortcomings of food miles, because the weight of a particular product becomes the key determining factor. Vegetables can have a heavier food miles footprint than meat, even though meat production generally uses more energy.

It also downplays the fuel used to generate electricity for the refrigeration of food, which most analysts believe is probably more important than how far the food has travelled.

Keeping food cool generates an estimated 18 million tonnes of greenhouse gas in Australia, the equivalent of putting an extra 4.3 million cars on the road each year, according to a Food Science Australia submission to a Senate inquiry into food in 2008.

The cereal products in the food basket fared relatively well in terms of food miles, with the Sanitarium Weet-Bix and loaf of Tip Top bread

generating less carbon dioxide than their own weight.

Both used Australian wheat, milled locally and mostly trucked by road, with the breakfast cereals more simple range of ingredients giving it the edge in food miles. The loaf of bread required small quantities of gluten, yeast, salt, sugar and vegetable oil in the baking process, lifting its carbon dioxide emissions to about 425 grams of CO_2 for the shipping of one 650-gram loaf.

Most of the fresh vegetables were traced to their most likely sources within a 400-kilometre radius of Sydney and they also had relatively petite carbon footprints. Half a kilo of Black & Gold frozen peas required about 315 grams of carbon dioxide emissions from fuel to get it to the supermarket, while a bag of brushed potatoes took a more circuitous route from the south-west of Sydney, generating just over half a kilogram of carbon.

A bunch of broccollini, with a relatively straightforward road journey to Flemington markets and then the IGA distribution centre, came in at just 92 grams of CO_2 but mandarins from just north of Gympie in Queensland travelled an estimated 1247 kilometres down the coast to Sydney, generating 448 grams of emissions from an articulated lorry.

Imported produce stood out for its lengthy journeys and relatively high emissions, though in the absence of access to a ship's log the number of nautical miles actually covered can only be based on standard shipping routes.

A 280-gram jar of Sacla brand sundried tomatoes travelled an estimated 14 680 nautical miles in a container vessel before being unloaded at Port Botany, leading to a carbon footprint of 2.72 kilograms of greenhouse gas on the way. A 100-gram wedge of Castello blue cheese managed the journey with a slightly less polluting 1.34 kilograms of CO_2, not including refrigeration.

By comparison, a wedge of King Island camembert crossed the Bass Strait and completed the voyage to Sydney while managing to emit 138 grams of carbon dioxide, according to the Department of Climate Change model.

A porterhouse steak, believed to be from the northern tablelands in NSW although this could not be directly confirmed by IGA, would have travelled a minimum of 670 kilometres if the truck driver took the fastest route, generating about 225 grams of CO$_2$ from transport.

Sourcing fish products is more complex, because trawlers cruise different fishing grounds chasing a worthwhile catch, but the swordfish fillet purchased at IGA was probably from the Brisbane grounds off the east coast. Based on average trawling practices, discussed in a Bureau of Rural Sciences report into fisheries in 2004, the unlucky swordfish could have been on a 1300 nautical mile round trip before arriving at market, its weight burning up 450 grams of carbon dioxide fuel on the way. Like the red meat, though, refrigeration costs

would add significantly to the food's greenhouse burden

Even advocates of local produce agree that food miles is only one tool among many for measuring the true impact of food. It can be useful but doesn't show the full picture, said Holly Vyner of the organic produce group, Biological Farmers of Australia. In general it is much more important to look at how the food is processed. There are exceptions, but less packaging, less chemical fertiliser and less travel generally leaves a lighter footprint.

Source: Ben Cubby/*The Sydney Morning Herald*, 19 June 2010.

The equality of the current account and the capital and financial accounts

We have seen that an open economy interacts with the rest of the world in two ways – in world markets for goods and services and in world financial markets. The current account and the capital and financial accounts (usually considered together) each measure a type of imbalance in these markets. The current account measures an imbalance between a country's exports and its imports of goods and services – its *net exports* (NX) – as well as the flow of income and current transfers. Income and current transfers are important to the Australian economy because many Australians own property overseas or earn income from overseas companies and many foreigners own property in Australia or earn income from Australian companies. The net flow of income to and from Australia is referred to as *net income* (NY). Current transfers include items such as Australian aid to other countries (such as food aid provided to the victims of the tsunami) or pensions paid to foreign citizens now resident in Australia. We call the net flow of transfers *net transfers* (NT).

We can now write our current account balance (*CAB*) as:

$$CAB = NX + NY + NT$$

The capital and financial accounts measure an imbalance between the amount of foreign assets bought by domestic residents and the amount of domestic assets bought by foreigners. Following international convention, Australia separates this into capital transfers (which happen when Australia gives aid to another country to build a bridge) and financial transactions that represent a transfer of ownership of Australia's assets between Australians and foreigners. (You might have noticed a similarity between current transfers and consumption expenditure in GDP – both are for current consumption and not for longer term investments. Just as investment in GDP is a measure of how much of national income is used to build things that help us produce more in the future, so are capital transfers – they represent Australia's contribution to investment in other countries.) To simplify our analysis, we will combine the capital and financial accounts together and refer to them as *net foreign investment*.

An important but subtle fact of accounting states that, for an economy as a whole, these two imbalances must offset each other. That is, net foreign investment (*NFI*) always equals the current account balance (*CAB*):

$$NFI = CAB$$

This equation holds because every transaction that affects one side of this equation must also affect the other side by exactly the same amount. This equation is an *identity* – an equation that must hold by the way the variables in the equation are defined and measured.

To see why this accounting identity is true, consider an example. Suppose that Fisher & Paykel, the New Zealand white goods manufacturer, sells some refrigerators to a Japanese hotel. In this sale, a New Zealand company gives fridges to a Japanese company, and a Japanese company gives yen to a New Zealand company. Notice that two things have occurred simultaneously. New Zealand has sold to a foreigner some of its output (the refrigerators), and this sale increases New Zealand net exports. In addition, New Zealand has acquired some foreign assets (the yen) and this acquisition increases New Zealand net foreign investment.

Although Fisher & Paykel most likely will not hold onto the yen it has acquired in this sale, any subsequent transaction will preserve the equality of net exports and net foreign investment. For example, Fisher & Paykel may exchange its yen for New Zealand dollars with a New Zealand stockbroker that wants the yen to buy shares in Sony Corporation, the Japanese maker of consumer electronics. In this case, Fisher & Paykel's net export of refrigerators equals the stockbroker's net foreign investment in Sony shares. Hence, *NX* and *NFI* rise by an equal amount.

Alternatively, Fisher & Paykel may exchange its yen for New Zealand dollars with another New Zealand company that wants to buy computers from Toshiba, the Japanese computer maker. In this case, New Zealand imports (of computers) exactly offset New Zealand exports (of refrigerators). The sales by Fisher & Paykel and Toshiba together affect neither New Zealand net exports nor New Zealand net foreign investment. That is, *NX* and *NFI* are the same as they were before these transactions took place.

The equality of the current account and net foreign investment follows from the fact that every international transaction is an exchange. When a seller country transfers a good or service to a buyer country, the buyer country gives up some asset to pay for this good or service. The value of that asset equals the value of the good or service sold. When we add everything up, the net value of goods and services sold by a country and the net income it earns from overseas (*CAB*) must equal the net value of assets acquired (*NFI*). The international flow of goods and services and income and the international flow of capital are two sides of the same coin.

IN THE NEWS . . .

FLOWS BETWEEN THE DEVELOPING AND DEVELOPED COUNTRIES

When capital flows between the rich and poor countries, this might be seen as a good thing, providing the funds for developing nations to build the infrastructure they need to grow. But sometimes these flows are not such a good thing – as we see below, the global crisis was a contagion no one was immune from.

The global crisis and the poor
A downturn that began in the rich world is hurting those who can least afford it

'POOR countries are innocent,' says Ngozi Okonjo-Iweala, the Nigerian managing director of the World Bank. They did not contribute one jot to the global credit crunch, and their banks and firms have few links to global capital markets. For a while, it seemed as if the rich world's mess might even pass them by. The oil-price fall of 2008 benefited oil-importing developing countries to the tune of 2% of their national incomes. As recently as January, the IMF thought emerging and developing countries would grow 3.3% this year, compared with a predicted fall of 2% for rich economies.

But innocence, it seems, will not protect anyone. A financial crisis that began in New York and London and spread to manufacturing in rich, then industrialising countries, has now hit the 'bottom billion': the poorest people in 60-odd countries who have seen only halting gains from globalisation, but will feel its reverse, perhaps precipitously.

Many live in sub-Saharan Africa, where the IMF has just cut its forecast for growth this year to 3.3% from an original 6.7%. The figure may fall further. Dominique Strauss-Kahn, the IMF's managing director, told a conference in Tanzania that millions could be thrown back into poverty by the crisis. Piling on gloom, he saw a 'threat of civil unrest, perhaps even of war' as a result.

The poor are being hit not by the financial tsunami itself but by second-order waves of trouble. So the impact has been delayed – but it may also be prolonged.

The global meltdown affects poor countries in three ways. First, capital: as investors in the West rebuild balance sheets, private capital flows dry up, hurting marginal borrowers like the poor. According to the Institute of International Finance, a think-tank in Washington, DC, net private capital flows to poor countries will slump from almost $1 trillion in 2007 to $165 billion in 2009. The main victims are big emerging markets in East Asia and eastern Europe. But African countries have been turning to private capital too. In 2007 they raised $6.5 billion in international bonds, trivial in global terms but not to Africa. In 2008, they raised nothing.

For the poor, the other kind of external capital is aid. Britain's Overseas Development Institute reckons that official aid may fall by about a fifth, or $20 billion, this year, after being more or less flat in 2005–07. The fall is partly a product of the recession in donor countries (some give a certain share of their GDP as aid) and partly a result of currency changes which make aid in pounds and euros worth less in local terms. Italy and Ireland are cutting their aid effort. Others are 'front-loading' it (borrowing from future years to keep steady now), so aid could fall further after 2009.

As capital flows dry up, investment is being slashed. ArcelorMittal has mothballed an iron-ore project in Liberia. The World Bank estimates that new private activity in infrastructure was 40% lower in August–November of 2008 than a year before.

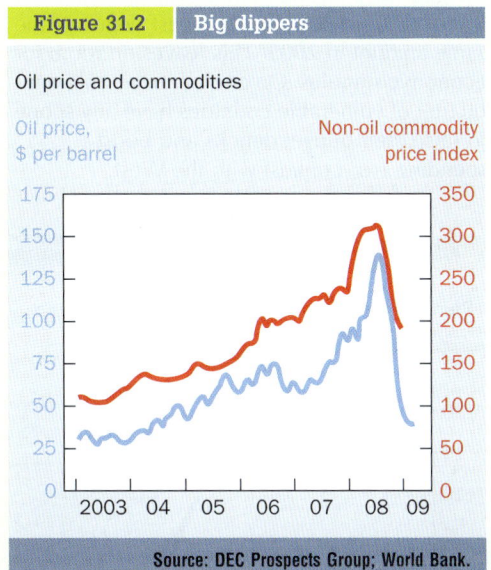

Figure 31.2 | **Big dippers**

Oil price and commodities

Source: DEC Prospects Group; World Bank.

The second effect of the meltdown is the dive in commodity prices (see chart above). Most poor states still rely on commodities for big shares of their foreign exchange and tax revenues. Cocoa generates a fifth of Côte d'Ivoire's revenues, for instance.

For such places, price volatility has been a curse. The drop in oil and commodity prices in 2008 benefited oil- and food-importers. But this

>>

followed a sharp price rise and, for many, relief has come too late. The food crisis of 2007–08 increased the number of people suffering from malnutrition by 44m. Farmers and oil exporters benefited then. No longer.

Now, falling export earnings are exacerbating poor countries' woes. In theory, the poorest should be cushioned from declining world trade. Even so, the latest data look dire. American imports from middle-income countries fell 3% in the year to November 2008. But imports from poor countries fell 6%; those from sub-Saharan Africa, 12%. The African Development Bank says African current accounts, in surplus by 3.8% of GDP in 2007, will be 6% in the red this year.

The fall in commodity prices puts further pressure on budgets, already hit by declining aid (which can substitute for taxes). African budgets have swung from a healthy surplus of 3% of GDP in 2007 to a forecast deficit of the same amount in 2009. This leaves no room for economic stimulus. On one estimate, only one-quarter of vulnerable countries have any scope to raise their budget deficits and boost spending – in contrast with the West.

Figure 31.3 | **Fewer happy returns**

Remittance flows to developing countries
% change on year earlier

Source: World Bank.

The third area where the meltdown is being felt is labour. Those poor countries that do

make things for export are suffering from the fall in world trade. India lost 500 000 export jobs in the last quarter of 2008, for example. Many countries also export workers who send back remittances. These were worth $300 billion in 2008, more than aid. Some countries depend on them. They account for 45% of GDP in Tajikistan, 38% in Moldova and 24% in Lebanon and Guyana. Remittances had been rising fast in 2005–07; now they are falling (see chart above). Malaysia recently revoked work visas for 55 000 Bangladeshis in order to boost job prospects for locals. Countries which send workers to Russia are doubly hit: many work in the crisis-affected oil industry and send money back in fast-depreciating roubles.

The overall picture is dire. As capital inflows and export earnings vanish, poor countries face a mountain of debt: $2.5 trillion–3 trillion of emerging-market debt falls due in 2009 – as much as the American and European budget deficits, plus Europe's bank bail-out costs. The World Bank puts emerging markets' financing shortfall between $270 billion and $700 billion.

Tragically, these problems follow a decade of growth that has lifted millions out of poverty. According to Martin Ravallion of the World Bank, roughly one person in six in emerging markets had raised themselves above the $2-a-day poverty line in 2005, though they still got less than $3 a day. Many may now slip back. Mr Ravallion thinks that 65m people will fall below the $2-a-day poverty line this year, 12m more than he had expected a month ago; 53m will fall below the level of absolute poverty, which is $1.25 a day – compared with 46m expected last month.

The consequence will be dreadful. The World Bank reckons that between 200 000 and 400 000 more children will die every year between now and 2015 than would have perished without the crisis. Progress towards a richer, more equitable world has been set back years.

Source: *The Economist*, 12 March 2009.
© The Economist Newspaper Limited, London 2009.

Saving, investment and their relationship to the international flows

A nation's saving and investment are, as we have seen in previous chapters, crucial to its long-run economic growth. Let's therefore consider how these variables are related to the international flows of goods and capital, as measured by the current account and net foreign investment. We can do this most easily with the help of some simple mathematics.

As you may recall, when we discussed the components of gross domestic product earlier in the book, we didn't account for the fact that not only do we earn income from our exports and spend some of that income on imports, but we also earn income from our overseas investments. We need to adjust our definition of income to reflect this. If you recall, the economy's gross domestic product (Y) is divided among four components: consumption (C), investment (I), government purchases (G) and net exports (NX). To take account of our earnings from overseas investments, we define our gross national disposable income (what we have to spend or save) as:

$$GNDY = GDP + NY + NT$$

Total income available for expenditure on the economy's output is the sum of gross domestic product (GDP) and what we earn from investments overseas (net income, NY) and gifts and grants from overseas (net transfers, NT). Recall that 'national saving' is the income of the nation that is left after paying for current consumption and government purchases. Gross national saving (S) equals $GNDY - C - G$. If we rearrange the equation to reflect this fact, we obtain:

$$S = GNDY - C - G$$

If we substitute in our definition of disposable income, we find:

$$\begin{aligned}
S &= C + I + G + NX + NY + NT - C - G \\
&= I + NX + NY + NT \\
&= I + CAB
\end{aligned}$$

Because our current account balance (CAB) also equals net foreign investment (NFI), we can also write this equation as:

$$S = I + NFI$$
Saving = Domestic investment + Net foreign investment

This equation shows that a nation's saving must equal its domestic investment plus its net foreign investment. In other words, when Australian citizens save a dollar of their income for the future, that dollar can be used to finance accumulation of domestic capital or it can be used to finance the purchase of capital abroad.

This equation should look somewhat familiar. Earlier in the book, when we analysed the role of the financial system, we considered this identity for the special case of a closed economy. In a closed economy, net foreign investment is zero ($NFI = 0$), so saving equals investment ($S = I$). In contrast, an open economy has two uses for its saving – domestic investment and net foreign investment.

As before, we can view the financial system as standing between the two sides of this identity. For example, suppose the Barnes family decides to save some of its income for retirement. This decision contributes to national saving, the left-hand side of our equation. If the Barnes family deposits their saving in a managed fund, the managed fund may use some of the deposit to buy shares issued by BHP Billiton, which uses the proceeds to build a processing factory in Victoria. In addition, the managed fund may use some of the Barnes family's deposit to buy shares issued by Toyota, which uses the proceeds to build a factory in Osaka. These transactions show up on the right-hand side of the equation. From the standpoint of Australian accounting, the BHP Billiton expenditure on a new factory is domestic investment and the purchase of Toyota shares by an Australian resident is net foreign investment. Thus, all saving in the Australian economy shows up as investment in the Australian economy or as Australian net foreign investment.

CASESTUDY

Saving, investment and net foreign investment of Australia

Since the late 1970s, Australia has relied in part on foreign investment to fund its domestic investment. We can use our macroeconomic accounting identities to help us understand why this would be so. In panel (a) of Figure 31.4, we show national saving and domestic investment for the Australian economy as a percentage of GDP since 1960. Panel (b) shows net foreign investment as a percentage of GDP. Notice that, as the identities require, domestic investment plus net foreign investment always equals national saving.

The figure shows a change beginning in the late 1970s. Before 1975, national saving and domestic investment were very close and so net foreign investment was small. After 1976, however,

national saving fell dramatically. (This decline was due in part to increased government budget deficits and in part to a fall in private saving.) Yet the Australian economy did not experience a similar fall in domestic investment. As a result, net foreign investment became a large negative number, indicating that foreigners were buying more assets in Australia than Australians were buying abroad.

One of the consequences of having a high level of foreign investment in Australia is that Australia must then pay interest and dividend payments on that investment. Australians pay much more in dividends and interest than they receive in dividends and interest from overseas. This difference, what we've called net income and net transfers, is added to

| Figure 31.4 | National saving, domestic investment and net foreign investment |

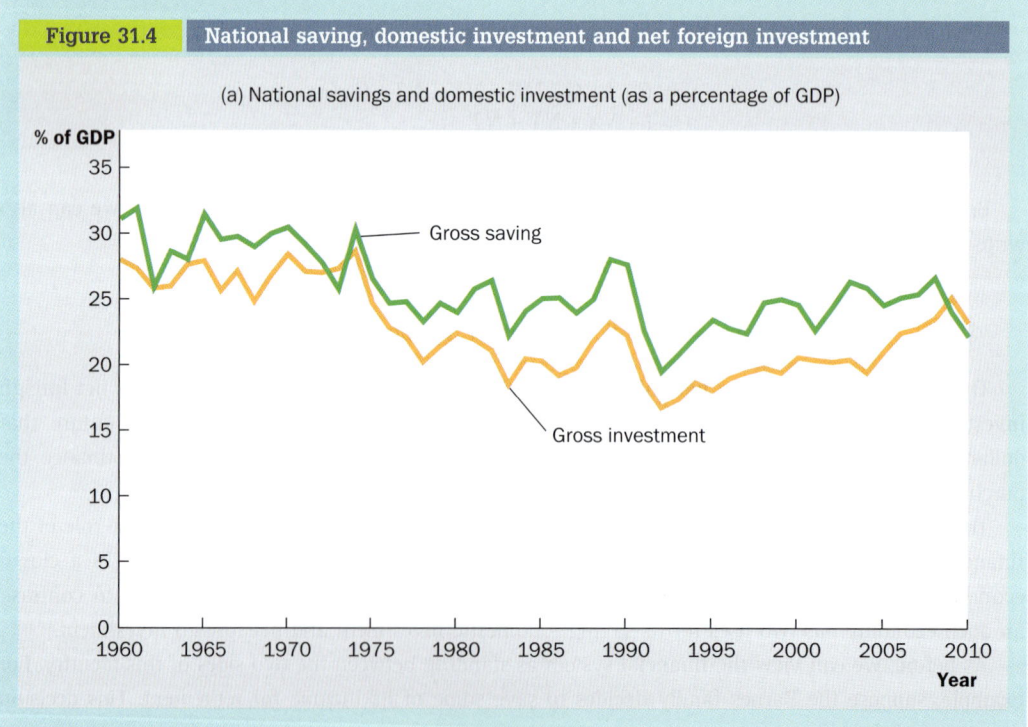

(a) National savings and domestic investment (as a percentage of GDP)

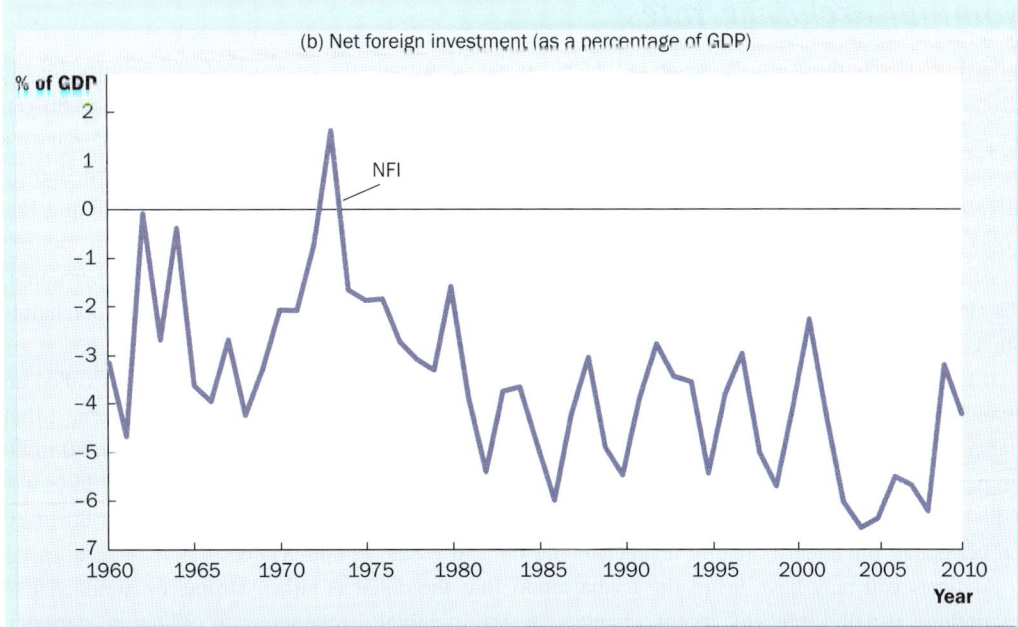

(b) Net foreign investment (as a percentage of GDP)

Panel (a) shows national saving and domestic investment as a percentage of GDP. Panel (b) shows net foreign investment as a percentage of GDP. You can see from the figure that national saving has been lower since 1976 than it was before 1976. This fall in national saving has been reflected mainly in reduced net foreign investment rather than in reduced domestic investment.

Source: ABS, various catalogues, 2010.

net exports to come up with the *current account* (*CAB* in our model). For example, in 2010, Australia's net exports were –$3775 million, but income and transfers were –$50 072 million, which meant that our current account balance was –$54 072 million. The total on the capital and financial accounts was $54 186. This amount is positive because we have had a net inflow of capital. Another way of saying this is that our net lending to non-residents (*NFI* in our model) was negative, –54 186. The difference between the current account and the capital account, –114, is the statistical discrepancy.

Define *net exports* and *net foreign investment*. Explain how they are related.

The prices for international transactions:
Real and nominal exchange rates

So far we have discussed measures of the flow of goods and services and the flow of capital across a nation's border. In addition to these quantity variables, macroeconomists also study variables that measure the prices at which these international transactions take place. Just as the price in any market serves the important role of coordinating buyers and sellers in that market, international prices help coordinate the decisions of consumers and producers as they interact in world markets. Here we discuss the two most important international prices – the nominal and real exchange rates.

Nominal exchange rates

nominal exchange rate
the rate at which a person can trade the currency of one country for the currency of another

The **nominal exchange rate** is the rate at which a person can trade the currency of one country for the currency of another. For example, if you go to a bank, you might see a posted exchange rate of 80 yen per dollar. If you give the bank one Australian dollar, it will give you 80 Japanese yen; and if you give the bank 80 Japanese yen, it will give you one Australian dollar. (In reality, the bank will post slightly different prices for buying and selling yen. The difference gives the bank some profit for offering this service. For our purposes here, we can ignore these differences.)

An exchange rate can always be expressed in two ways. If the exchange rate is 80 yen per dollar, it is also 1/80 (0.0125) dollar per yen. Throughout this book, we always express the nominal exchange rate as units of foreign currency per Australian dollar, such as 80 yen per dollar.

If the exchange rate changes so that a dollar buys more foreign currency, that change is called an **appreciation** of the dollar. If the exchange rate changes so that a dollar buys less foreign currency, that change is called a **depreciation** of the dollar. For example, when the exchange rate rises from 80 to 90 yen per dollar, the dollar is said to appreciate. At the same time, because a Japanese yen now buys less of the Australia currency, the yen is said to depreciate. When the exchange rate falls from 80 to 70 yen per dollar, the dollar is said to depreciate and the yen is said to appreciate.

appreciation
an increase in the value of a currency as measured by the amount of foreign currency it can buy

depreciation
a decrease in the value of a currency as measured by the amount of foreign currency it can buy

At times you may have heard the media report that the dollar is either 'strong' or 'weak'. These descriptions usually refer to recent changes in the nominal exchange rate. When a currency appreciates, it is said to *strengthen* because it can then buy more foreign currency. Similarly, when a currency depreciates, it is said to *weaken*.

For any country, there are many nominal exchange rates. The Australian dollar can be used to buy Japanese yen, British pounds, euros, Thai baht and so on. When economists study changes in the exchange rate, they often use indexes that average these many exchange rates. Just as the consumer price index turns the many prices in the economy into a single measure of the price level, an exchange rate index turns these many exchange rates into a single measure of the international value of the currency. So when economists talk about the dollar appreciating or depreciating, they often are referring to an exchange rate index that takes into account many individual exchange rates.

Real exchange rates

real exchange rate
the rate at which a person can trade the goods and services of one country for the goods and services of another

The **real exchange rate** is the rate at which a person can trade the goods and services of one country for the goods and services of another. For example, suppose that you go shopping and find that a case of German beer is twice as expensive as a case of Australian beer. We would then say that the real exchange rate is a ½ case of German beer per case of Australian beer. Notice that, like the nominal exchange rate, the real exchange rate is expressed as units of the foreign item per unit of the domestic item. But in this instance the item is a good rather than a currency.

Real and nominal exchange rates are closely related. To see how, consider an example. Suppose that a tonne of Australian rice sells for $100, and a tonne of Japanese rice sells for 18 000 yen. What is the real exchange rate between Australian and Japanese rice? To answer this question, we must first use the nominal exchange rate to convert the prices into a common currency. If the nominal exchange rate is 90 yen per dollar, then a price for Australian rice of $100 per tonne is equivalent to 9000 yen per tonne. Australian rice is half as expensive as Japanese rice. The real exchange rate is a ½ tonne of Japanese rice per tonne of Australian rice.

We can summarise this calculation for the real exchange rate with the following formula:

$$\text{Real exchange rate} = \frac{\text{Nominal exchange rate} \times \text{Domestic price}}{\text{Foreign price}}$$

Using the numbers in our example, the formula applies as follows:

$$
\begin{aligned}
\text{Real exchange rate} &= \frac{(90 \text{ yen per doller}) \times (\$100 \text{ per tonne of Australian rice})}{18\,000 \text{ yen per tonne of Japanese rice}} \\
&= \frac{9\,000 \text{ yen per tonne of Australian rice}}{18\,000 \text{ yen per tonne of Japanese rice}} \\
&= \frac{1}{2} \text{ tonne of Japanese rice per tonne of Australian rice}
\end{aligned}
$$

Thus, the real exchange rate depends on the nominal exchange rate and on the prices of goods in the two countries measured in the local currencies.

Why does the real exchange rate matter? As you might guess, the real exchange rate is a key determinant of how much a country exports and imports. When Woolworths is deciding whether to buy Australian rice or Japanese rice to put on its shelves, for example, it will ask which rice is cheaper. The real exchange rate gives the answer. As another example, imagine that you are deciding whether to take a seaside holiday in Cairns in Queensland or in Phuket in Thailand. You might ask your travel agent the price of a hotel room in Cairns (measured in dollars), the price of a hotel room in Phuket (measured in baht), and the exchange rate between baht and dollars. If you decide where to holiday by comparing costs, you are basing your decision on the real exchange rate.

When studying an economy as a whole, macroeconomists focus on overall prices rather than the prices of individual items. That is, to measure the real exchange rate, they use price indexes, such as the consumer price index. By using a price index for Australia (P), a price index for prices abroad (P^*), and the nominal exchange rate between the Australian dollar and foreign currencies (e), we can calculate the overall real exchange rate between Australia and other countries as follows:

$$\text{Real exchange rate} = \frac{(e \times P)}{P^*}$$

This real exchange rate measures the price of a basket of goods and services available domestically relative to a basket of goods and services available abroad.

As we will see more fully in the next chapter, a country's real exchange rate is a key determinant of its net exports of goods and services. A depreciation (fall) in the Australian real exchange rate means that Australian goods have become cheaper relative to foreign goods. This change encourages consumers both at home and abroad to buy more Australian goods and fewer goods from other countries. As a result, Australian exports rise, and Australian imports fall, and both of these changes raise Australian net exports. Conversely, an appreciation (rise) in the Australian real exchange rate means that Australian goods have become more expensive compared with foreign goods, so Australian net exports fall.

Define *nominal exchange rate* and *real exchange rate*, and explain how they are related. ▪ If the nominal exchange rate goes from 100 to 120 yen per dollar, has the dollar appreciated or depreciated?

IN THE NEWS . . .

A RISING AUSSIE DOLLAR IS ENOUGH TO DRIVE YOU TO DRINK – BUT NOT IF YOU'RE BUYING AUSSIE WINE OVERSEAS

Australian wines are well known around the world. They have beaten some of the best at prestigious wine shows overseas. Australian winemakers have done well in the past 20 years. But economic forces are proving to be more difficult to overcome than the most discerning wine judges. A rising Australian dollar and a glut of grapes is making it hard to sell Australian wine for a decent price overseas, as the following article by Peter van Onselen explains.

If wine industry's a loser, sour grapes won't help

Peter van Onselen

Australia is caught between two world orders and must resist intervening

Spare a thought for the Australian wine industry and what it must be going through at the moment. But once you have done so, don't make the mistake of wanting to help it out. There is a glut of grapes on the market on the back of a bumper season. That's pushing the price of wine considerably down because of the larger than usual competition at the domestic level.

Then there is the impact of the soaring Australian dollar, which is making our wines more expensive for overseas buyers. The dollar has been especially strong against the greenback and the pound, and the US and Britain are our wine industry's two biggest export markets.

On top of the challenges that a rising dollar poses for exports, it makes imported wines cheaper, which means that domestic wine producers must also deal with consumers now attracted to French, Spanish and Italian wines that they otherwise might have been priced out of buying.

Finally, wine producers up and down the Murray-Darling River – one of the key regions for Australia's wine industry – are now facing the prospect of massive cuts to their water entitlements under the Murray-Darling Basin Authority's draft plan for fixing the problems with the river.

In the long run, of course, water cuts will result in water allocation buybacks, which will reduce the number of wine producers in the basin and thereby fix the supply side of the wine industry's problems, at least domestically.

It could also be a way out for unprofitable producers.

Less wine production means higher prices. That's not good for consumers and it's certainly not good for wine exporters, but domestically – despite the challenge of competing with cheaper overseas wines while our dollar is strong – it's a good outcome for winemakers that survive the purge. But in the short term, try explaining that to a wine industry on the brink.

As tempting as it must be for our most interventionist of federal governments to prop up the wine industry (if it can find any votes in doing so), along with many other industries suffering in similar ways, there is nothing it can or more accurately should be doing about the situation. Government can't save every problem free markets and environmental and economic circumstances throw up. Intervention is not always the answer. Sometimes you just have to let the market rip.

Australia's dollar is rising mostly because of global factors. The US economy is weak, its government is doing a certain amount of quantitative easing (printing money). The international community is getting increasingly angry about China's undervalued currency. Unlike most other nations, China hasn't floated its exchange rate and its government has decided it is in China's best interests to slow down the yuan's assent. Protectionist talk is therefore creeping back into the minds of some.

In a weak global economic environment where the old world is slowly being replaced by a new order, which includes China, India and Brazil, Australia is torn between the two sides. Culturally (although less so than was once the case) we are part of the old world – that is, the Western developed collection of nations. However, geographically, we are part of the new order – the rise of Asia and underdeveloped nations in our region.

You could even say that elements of our two-speed economy are explained by this dynamic. Our mining interests are servicing the new order while our ailing manufacturing sectors are part of the old order – hence the divide in fortunes. Australia's problem is a better one to have than those most of the developed nations face, but that doesn't mean we can sit back and let the new order sweep us up and thereby maintain living standards.

We need to embrace reforms to do two things: make sure our most profitable industries for the future are supported and given every chance. Second, we must avoid the pitfalls of pandering to the electorate by saving 'losers'. In other words, no intervention, just facilitation.

Like it or not, the wine industry as it is currently constituted appears to be one of the losers. Our climate in some parts of the country where grape harvesting occurs isn't suited to it, and if climate change is to be believed the Australian climate is only going to become less suited to it. We don't have the domestic population to sustain our rather large wine industry without exports accounting for much of what is produced, yet with our rising dollar the wine industry's export competitiveness is now questionable.

Both major parties during the week have rejected the idea of government getting

involved in curtailing the dollar's rise. That's a good thing, but for exporters it means that one way of trying to do something about the economic pressures they face is removed.

Brazil's Finance Minister, Guido Mantega, was right when he declared last month that a currency war had broken out internationally. However, it isn't something Australia should get involved with. We are too small and our interests are torn between the two sides of the debate. Sometimes market forces have to be left to help shape the new reality. But for that to happen, the public must become accepting of economic liberalism. The reason? Because the political world we live in is voter-driven. The days of courageous political decision-making are behind us – replaced by the poll- and focus group-obsessed MP. Voters need to be courageous enough to let our leaders suggest unpopular but necessary reforms without committing to vote the other way because of it. And the politicians must be constructive enough to debate the merits and pitfalls behind disagreements on action rather than carp about the action itself.

If none of that happens, we won't be the nation we could be in 20 years' time. We would be weighed down by unproductive industries, even if one of the consequences was a wide selection of Australian wines.

Source: Peter van Onselen/*The Australian*, 20 October 2010.

A first theory of exchange-rate determination: Purchasing-power parity

Exchange rates vary substantially over time. In 1974, an Australian dollar could be used to buy 1.49 US dollars, 402 Japanese yen, 0.579 of a British pound, or 618 Indonesian rupiah. In 2010, an Australian dollar bought 0.98 of a US dollar, 82 Japanese yen, 0.63 of a British pound or 8796 Indonesian rupiah. In other words, over this period the value of the dollar fell by 34 per cent compared with the US dollar. The value of the dollar fell by almost 80 per cent relative to the Japanese yen. And yet it appreciated by over 1300 per cent compared with the Indonesian Rupiah.

What explains these large changes? Economists have developed many models to explain how exchange rates are determined, each emphasising some of the many forces at work. Here we develop the simplest theory of exchange rates, called **purchasing-power parity**. This theory states that a unit of any given currency should be able to buy the same quantity of goods in all countries. Many

purchasing-power parity
a theory of exchange rates whereby a unit of any given currency should be able to buy the same quantity of goods in all countries

economists believe that purchasing-power parity describes the forces that determine exchange rates in the long run. We now consider the logic on which this long-run theory of exchange rates is based, as well as the theory's implications and limitations.

The basic logic of purchasing-power parity

The theory of purchasing-power parity is based on a principle called the law of one price. This law asserts that a good must sell for the same price in all locations. Otherwise, there would be opportunities for profit left unexploited. For example, suppose that coffee beans sold for less in Brisbane than in Perth. A person could buy coffee in Brisbane for, say, $20 a kilo and then sell it in Perth for $30 a kilo, making a profit of $10 per kilo from the difference in price. The process of taking advantage of differences in prices in different markets is called *arbitrage*. In our example, as people took advantage of this arbitrage opportunity, they would increase the demand for coffee in Brisbane and increase the supply in Perth. The price of coffee would rise in Brisbane (in response to greater demand) and fall in Perth (in response to greater supply). This process would continue until, eventually, the prices were the same in the two markets, ignoring transaction costs.

Now consider how the law of one price applies to the international marketplace. If a dollar (or any other currency) could buy more coffee in Australia than in Japan, international traders could profit by buying coffee in Australia and selling it in Japan. This export of coffee from Australia to Japan would drive up the Australian price of coffee and drive down the Japanese price. Conversely, if a dollar could buy more coffee in Japan than in Australia, traders could buy coffee in Japan and sell it in Australia. This import of coffee into Australia from Japan would drive down the Australian price of coffee and drive up the Japanese price. In the end, the law of one price tells us that a dollar must buy the same amount of coffee in all countries.

This logic leads us to the theory of purchasing-power parity. According to this theory, a currency must have the same purchasing power in all countries. That is, an Australian dollar must buy the same quantity of goods in Australia and Japan, and a Japanese yen must buy the same quantity of goods in Japan and Australia. Indeed, the name of this theory describes it well. *Parity* means equality, and *purchasing power* refers to the value of money. *Purchasing-power parity* states that one unit of every currency must have the same real value in every country.

Implications of purchasing-power parity

What does the theory of purchasing-power parity say about exchange rates? It tells us that the nominal exchange rate between the currencies of two countries depends on the price levels in those countries. If a dollar buys the same quantity of goods in Australia (where prices are measured in dollars) as in Japan (where prices are measured in yen), then the number of yen per dollar must reflect the prices of goods in Australia and Japan. For example, if a kilo of coffee costs 1500 yen in Japan and $20 in Australia, then the nominal exchange rate must be 75 yen per dollar (1500 yen/ $20 = 75 yen per dollar). Otherwise, the purchasing power of the dollar would not be the same in the two countries.

To see more fully how this works, it is helpful to use just a bit of mathematics. Suppose that P is the price level in Australia (measured in dollars), P^* is the price level in Japan (measured in yen), and e is the nominal exchange rate (the number of yen a dollar can buy). Now consider the quantity of goods a dollar can buy at home and abroad. At home, the price level is P, so the purchasing power of

$1 at home is $1/P$. Abroad, a dollar can be exchanged into e units of foreign currency, which in turn have purchasing power e/P^*. For the purchasing power of a dollar to be the same in the two countries, it must be the case that:

$$1/P = e/P^*$$

With rearrangement, this equation becomes:

$$1 = eP/P^*$$

Notice that the left-hand side of this equation is a constant, and the right-hand side is the real exchange rate. Thus, if the purchasing power of the dollar is always the same at home and abroad, then the real exchange rate – the relative price of domestic and foreign goods – cannot change. To see the implication of this analysis for the nominal exchange rate, we can rearrange the last equation to solve for the nominal exchange rate:

$$e = P^*/P$$

That is, the nominal exchange rate equals the ratio of the foreign price level (measured in units of the foreign currency) to the domestic price level (measured in units of the domestic currency). *According to the theory of purchasing-power parity, the nominal exchange rate between the currencies of two countries must reflect the different price levels in those countries.*

A key implication of this theory is that nominal exchange rates change when price levels change. As we saw in the preceding chapter, the price level in any country adjusts to bring the quantity of money supplied and the quantity of money demanded into balance. Because the nominal exchange rate depends on the price levels, it also depends on the money supply and money demand in each country. When a central bank in any country increases the money supply and causes the price level to rise, it also causes that country's currency to depreciate relative to other currencies in the world. In other words, when the central bank prints large quantities of money, that money loses value both in terms of the goods and services it can buy and in terms of the amount of other currencies it can buy.

IN THE NEWS . . .

PURCHASING-POWER PARITY AND THE BIG MAC

In 1986, the *Economist* devised an ingenious way to evaluate whether a currency is valued at the level predicted by the theory of purchasing power parity. Their approach was to divide the price of a Big Mac in 120 countries by the American price and compare the result with the actual exchange rate. According to the burgernomic approach, the price of a Big Mac in Australia looks pretty good.

Burgernomics
When the chips are down: The latest Big Mac index suggests the euro is still overvalued
Ask Western policymakers how they intend to squeeze growth from their sluggish economies and most pin their hopes on higher exports. That makes exchange rates an especially sensitive topic. A weaker currency improves the competitiveness of a country by making exports cheaper. It also encourages domestic consumers to switch from expensive imports to domestic goods. *The Economist*'s exchange-rate scorecard, the Big Mac index, shows that currencies continue to be cheap in

>>

the developing world but overvalued in Europe.

The index is a lighthearted attempt to gauge how far currencies are from their fair value. It is based on the theory of purchasing-power parity (PPP), which argues that in the long run exchange rates should move to equalise the price of an identical basket of goods between two countries. Our basket consists of a single item, a Big Mac hamburger, produced in nearly 120 countries. The fair-value benchmark is the exchange rate that leaves burgers costing the same in America as elsewhere.

Asia remains the cheapest place to enjoy a burger. China's recent decision to increase the 'flexibility' of the yuan has not made much difference yet. A Big Mac costs $1.95 in China at current exchange rates, against $3.73 in America. Our index suggests that a fair-value rate would be 3.54 yuan to the dollar, compared with the current rate of 6.78. In other words the yuan is undervalued by 48%.

Other Asian currencies such as the Thai baht and the South Korean won are also undervalued. The Brazilian real is one of the few emerging-market currencies that is trading well above its Big Mac benchmark. With interest rates high—the policy rate now stands at 10.75%—Brazil has attracted lots of attention from yield-hungry investors. Burgernomics suggests that the real is overvalued by 31%.

The Big Mac numbers should be taken with a generous pinch of salt. They are not a precise predictor of currency movements. The bulk of a burger's cost depends on local inputs such as rent and wages, which tend to be lower in poor countries. Consequently PPP comparisons are more reliable between countries with similar levels of income.

So it is particularly interesting to see that on a burger basis the euro is still overvalued when compared with many other rich-world currencies. Sovereign-debt worries and soggy growth rates have helped shift the currency towards its fair value over the past 12 months. A year ago the euro was overvalued by 29% on the burger benchmark; that figure is now down to 16%. (Britain's currency has gone

from being mildly overvalued this time last year to slightly undervalued now.) And the single currency has been moving back up again in recent weeks, on hopes that stress-test results, which were due out on July 23rd, will shore up confidence in Europe's banking system.

Other currencies are dearer still. Investors looking for a safe place to put their money have sought refuge in the Swiss franc. Despite

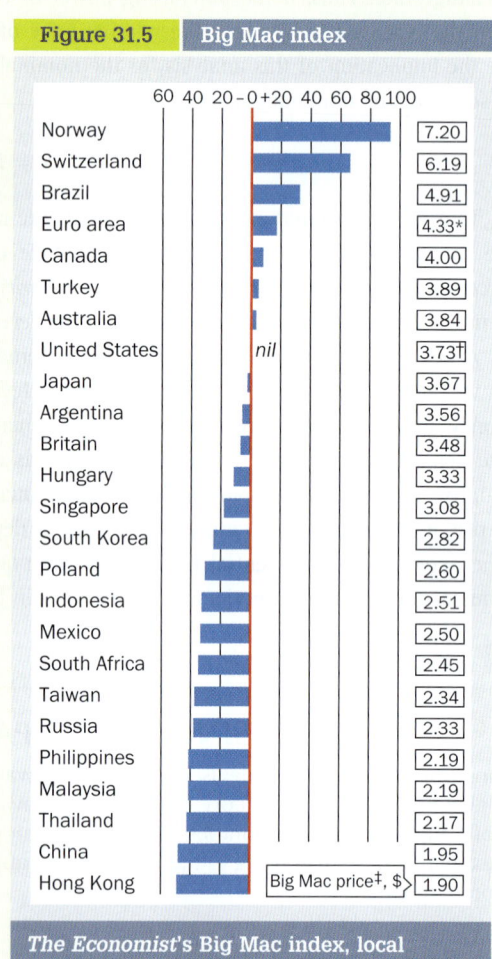

Figure 31.5 | **Big Mac index**

The Economist's Big Mac index, local currency under (–)/over (+) valuation against the US dollar, %
* Weighted average of member countries
† Average of four cities
‡ At market exchange rate (July 21st)

Source: © The Economist, 22 July 2010.

Table 31.1 Big Mac index

| | Big Mac prices* | | Implied PPP[†] of the dollar | Actual dollar exchange rate July 21st | Under (−)/over(+) valuation against the dollar, % |
	In local currency	In dollars			
United States[‡]	$3.73	3.73			
Argentina	Peso 14.0	3.56	3.75	3.93	−5
Australia	A$4.35	3.84	1.17	1.13	3
Brazil	Real 8.71	4.91	2.33	1.77	31
Britain	£2.29	3.48	1.63[§]	1.52[§]	−7
Canada	C$4.17	4.00	1.12	1.04	7
Chile	Peso 1750	3.34	469	524	−10
China	Yuan 13.2	1.95	3.54	6.78	−48
Colombia	Peso 8200	4.39	2196	1868	18
Costa Rica	Colones 2000	3.83	536	522	3
Czech Republic	Koruna 67.6	3.43	18.1	19.7	−8
Denmark	Dk 28.5	4.90	7.63	5.81	31
Egypt	Pound 13.0	2.28	3.48	5.70	−39
Estonia	Kroon 32.0	2.62	8.57	12.2	−30
Euro area	€3.38	4.33	1.10[††]	1.28[††]	16
Hong Kong	HK$14.8	1.90	3.96	7.77	−49
Hungary	Forint 740	3.33	198	222	−11
Indonesia	Rupiah 22 780	2.51	6102	9063	−33
Israel	Shekel 14.9	3.86	3.99	3.86	3
Japan	¥320	3.67	85.7	87.2	−2
Latvia	Lats 1.55	2.80	0.42	0.55	−25
Lithuania	Litas 7.30	2.71	1.96	2.69	−27
Malaysia	Ringgit 7.05	2.19	1.89	3.21	−41
Mexico	Peso 32.0	2.50	8.57	12.8	−33

>>

	Big Mac prices*				
	In local currency	In dollars	Implied PPP† of the dollar	Actual dollar exchange rate July 21st	Under (−)/over(+) valuation against the dollar, %
New Zealand	NZ$5.00	3.59	1.34	1.39	−4
Norway	Kroner 45.0	7.20	12.1	6.25	93
Pakistan	Rupee 210	2.46	56.3	85.5	−34
Peru	Sol 10.0	3.54	2.68	2.83	−5
Philippines	Peso 102	2.19	27.3	46.5	−41
Poland	Zloty 8.30	2.60	2.22	3.20	−30
Russia	Rouble 71.0	2.33	19.0	30.4	−38
Saudi Arabia	Riyal 10.0	2.67	2.68	3.75	−29
Singapore	S$4.23	3.08	1.13	1.37	−18
South Africa	Rand 18.5	2.45	4.94	7.54	−34
South Korea	Won 3400	2.82	911	1204	−24
Sri Lanka	Rupee 210	1.86	56.3	113	−50
Sweden	SKr 48.4	6.56	13.0	7.37	76
Switzerland	SFr 6.50	6.19	1.74	1.05	66
Taiwan	NT$ 75.0	2.34	20.1	32.1	−37
Thailand	Baht 70.0	2.17	18.8	32.3	−42
Turkey	Lira 5.95	3.89	1.59	1.53	4
UAE	Dirhams 11.0	2.99	2.95	3.67	−20
Ukraine	Hryvnia 14.5	1.84	3.88	7.90	−51
Uruguay	Peso 79.0	3.74	21.2	21.1	*nil*

The Economist's Big Mac index provides a rough measure of the purchasing power of a currency
* At current exchange rates
† Purchasing-power parity; local price divided by price in United States
‡ Average of Atlanta, Chicago, New York and San Francisco
§ Dollars per pound
** Weighted average of prices in euro area
†† Dollars per euro

Source: © *The Economist*, 22 July 2010.

attempts by the Swiss central bank to stem the appreciation, the Swiss franc is overvalued by 68%. Those on the hunt for a value meal should also steer clear of Scandinavia. In Norway a Big Mac would set you back by 45 kroner or $7.20, nearly twice the cost in America.

Source: *The Economist*, 22 July 2010,
© The Economist Newspaper Limited, London 2010.

While the Big Mac is a good that can be found worldwide and therefore useful for comparing exchange rates, many economists object to the index because burgers aren't really tradeable goods. Two alternatives have been created that might be more useful. One was created by UBS, a Swiss bank (UBS, Prices and Earnings, 2009). It uses the same burger to measure the purchasing power of local wages. It divides the price of a Big Mac by the average net hourly wage in cities around the world. A worker from Jakarta must toil for almost 2½ hours to buy a Big Mac, but a Moscow wage buys the burger in 21 minutes, a Tokyo salary buys one in just 12 minutes, and in Sydney it takes 14 minutes' work to buy a Big Mac.

IN THE NEWS . . .

PURCHASING-POWER PARITY AND THE IPOD

In 2007, the Commonwealth Bank's online trading company, CommSec, devised an alternative to the Big Mac index – the iPod index. (In 2009, UBS added the iPod to its index as well. See http://www.ubs.com/1/e/wealthmanagement/wealth_management_research/prices_earnings.html.) This index does the same thing that the Big Mac index does, but uses a good that *is* tradeable. Peter Martin, of the *Sydney Morning Herald,* reports on what's happened to the Aussie dollar according to the iPod index.

Tough for buyers, but iPod price signals economic rise
by Peter Martin

What a difference an improving economy makes. Before Christmas heavy discounting made Australia the cheapest place in the world in which to buy iPod nanos.

Now we've slipped to just the 14th cheapest, and have become about the priciest nation in the English-speaking world, outpricing the US, Canada, and Britain. All iPods are made in China, and, in theory, should all be sold at the same price at prevailing exchange rates after taking into account transport costs. But discounting and price gouging can change that.

Like *The Economist* magazine's Big Mac index before it, the Commonwealth Securities iPod index compares worldwide prices in order to get an idea of which economies are weak enough to need discounting and which are so strong retailers can afford to gouge.

The updated index suggests Australia has moved from weak to neutral territory, with retailers in the US, Canada and the UK remaining positively frail.

'Just before Christmas, Myer slashed the price of the top-selling eight-gigabyte iPod nano from $199 to $159. When converted to US dollars it meant Australian consumers could buy here $10 cheaper than in the US and $11 cheaper than in Hong Kong,' said CommSec economist Craig James. 'But right now Australian tourists could save $21 shopping in Singapore, $35 in Hong Kong.'

The less generous approach to discounting reflects improved retail fortunes. The Bureau of Statistics found consumers shunned department stores in the lead-up to Christmas spending an extraordinary 3 per cent less than the December before, the first time in almost two decades one December had not improved on another. In January department store sales rebounded a seasonally adjusted 7 per cent.

>>

Like the Big Mac index, the iPod index can also be used to indicate whether a currency is over or undervalued. With the iPod selling for only $US149 in the United States but $US175 in China, the index suggests the US dollar is 15 per cent undervalued against the Chinese yuan. Put another way, it points to pressure for China to devalue the yuan. But Australia is one of the countries least out of whack against the yuan. The iPod index suggests we are just 4 per cent overvalued.

'Looking at the index, it is hard to conclude that the Aussie dollar is either significantly under or overvalued,' said Mr James.'

Source: Peter Martin/*The Sydney Morning Herald*, 23 March 2010.

CASESTUDY

The nominal exchange rate during hyperinflation

Macroeconomists cannot conduct controlled experiments. Instead, they must glean what they can from the natural experiments that history gives them. One natural experiment is hyperinflation – the high inflation that arises when a government turns to the printing press to pay for large amounts of government spending. Because hyperinflations are so extreme, they illustrate some basic economic principles with clarity.

| Figure 31.6 | Money, prices and the nominal exchange rate during the German hyperinflation |

This figure shows the money supply, the price level and the exchange rate (measured as US cents per mark) for the German hyperinflation from January 1921 to December 1924. Notice how similarly these three variables move. When the quantity of money started growing quickly, the price level followed, and the mark depreciated relative to the dollar. When the German central bank stabilised the money supply, the price level and exchange rate stabilised as well.

Source: Adapted from Thomas J. Sargent, 'The end of four big inflations' in Robert Hall, ed., *Inflation* (Chicago: University of Chicago Press, 1983), pp. 41–93.

Consider the German hyperinflation of the early 1920s. Figure 31.6 shows the German money supply, the German price level and the nominal exchange rate (measured as US cents per German mark) for that period. Notice that these series move closely together. When the supply of money starts growing quickly, the price level also takes off, and the German mark depreciates. When the money supply stabilises, so does the price level and the exchange rate.

The pattern shown in this figure appears during every hyperinflation. It leaves no doubt that there is a fundamental link between money, prices and the nominal exchange rate. The quantity theory of money discussed in the previous chapter explains how the money supply affects the price level. The theory of purchasing-power parity discussed here explains how the price level affects the nominal exchange rate.

We can now answer the question that began this section: Why has the Australian dollar lost value compared with the US dollar and gained value compared with the Indonesian rupiah? The answer is that the US has pursued a less inflationary monetary policy than Australia, and Indonesia has pursued a more inflationary monetary policy. From 1970 to 2010, inflation in Australia was 6 per cent per year. In contrast, inflation was 5 per cent in the United States and over 14 per cent in Indonesia. As Australian prices rose relative to US prices, the value of the Australian dollar fell relative to the US dollar. Similarly, as Australian prices fell relative to Indonesian prices, the value of the Australian dollar rose relative to the rupiah.

Limitations of purchasing-power parity

Purchasing-power parity provides a simple model of how exchange rates are determined. For understanding many economic phenomena, the theory works well. In particular, it can explain many long-term trends, such as the depreciation of the Australian dollar against the US dollar and the appreciation of the Australian dollar against the Indonesian rupiah. It can also explain the major changes in exchange rates that occur during hyperinflations.

Yet the theory of purchasing-power parity is not completely accurate. That is, exchange rates do not always move to ensure that a dollar has the same real value in all countries all the time. There are two reasons that the theory of purchasing-power parity does not always hold in practice.

The first reason is that many goods are not easily traded. Imagine, for instance, that haircuts are more expensive in Paris than in Sydney. International travellers might avoid getting their haircuts in Paris and some hairdressers might move from Sydney to Paris. Yet such arbitrage would probably be too limited to eliminate the differences in prices. Thus, the deviation from purchasing-power parity might persist and a dollar (or euro) would continue to buy less of a haircut in Paris than in Sydney.

The second reason that purchasing-power parity does not always hold is that even tradeable goods are not always perfect substitutes when they are produced in different countries. For example, some consumers prefer German beer and others prefer Australian beer. Moreover, consumer tastes for beer change over time. If German beer suddenly becomes more popular, the increase in demand will drive up the price of German beer. As a result, a dollar (or a euro) might then buy more beer in Australia than in Germany. But despite this difference in prices in the two markets, there might be no opportunity for profitable arbitrage because consumers do not view the two beers as equivalent.

Thus, both because some goods are not tradeable and because some tradeable goods are not perfect substitutes with their foreign counterparts, purchasing-power parity is not a perfect theory of exchange-rate determination. For these reasons, real exchange rates do in fact fluctuate over time. Nonetheless, the theory of purchasing-power parity does provide a useful first step in understanding exchange rates. The basic logic is persuasive – as the real exchange rate drifts from the level predicted by purchasing-power parity, people have greater incentive to move goods across national borders. Even if the forces of purchasing-power parity do not completely fix the real exchange rate, they do provide a reason to expect that changes in the real exchange rate are most often small or temporary. As a result, large and persistent movements in nominal exchange rates typically reflect changes in price levels at home and abroad.

 Over the past 20 years, Argentina has had high inflation and Japan has had low inflation. What do you predict has happened to the number of Argentine pesos a person can buy with a Japanese yen?

Conclusion

The purpose of this chapter has been to develop some basic concepts that macroeconomists use to study open economies. You should now understand why a nation's net exports must equal its net foreign investment and why national saving must equal domestic investment plus net foreign investment. You should also understand the meaning of the nominal and real exchange rates, as well as the implications and limitations of purchasing-power parity as a theory of how exchange rates are determined.

The macroeconomic variables defined here offer a starting point for analysing an open economy's interactions with the rest of the world. In the next chapter, we develop a model that can explain what determines these variables. We can then discuss how various events and policies affect a country's trade balance and the rate at which nations make exchanges in world markets.

Summary

- Net exports are the value of domestic goods and services sold abroad minus the value of foreign goods and services sold domestically. Net foreign investment is the acquisition of foreign assets by domestic residents minus the acquisition of domestic assets by foreigners. Because every international transaction involves an exchange of an asset for a good or service, an economy's net foreign investment always equals its net exports.

- An economy's saving can be used either to finance investment at home or to buy assets abroad. Thus, national saving equals domestic investment plus net foreign investment.

- The nominal exchange rate is the relative price of the currency of two countries and the real exchange rate is the relative price of the goods and services of two countries. When the nominal exchange rate changes so that each dollar buys more foreign currency, the dollar is said to *appreciate* or *strengthen*. When the nominal exchange rate changes so that each dollar buys less foreign currency, the dollar is said to *depreciate* or *weaken*.

- According to the theory of purchasing-power parity, a dollar (or a unit of any other currency) should be able to buy the same quantity of goods in all countries. This theory implies that the nominal exchange rate between the currencies of two countries should reflect the price levels in those countries. As a result, countries with relatively high inflation should have depreciating currencies, and countries with relatively low inflation should have appreciating currencies.

Key concepts

appreciation	net foreign investment	real exchange rate
balanced trade	nominal exchange rate	trade balance (net exports)
closed economy	open economy	trade deficit
depreciation	purchasing-power parity	trade surplus

Questions for review

1 Define net exports and net foreign investment. Explain how and why they are related.
2 Explain the relationship between saving, investment and net foreign investment.
3 Describe the economic logic behind the theory of purchasing-power parity. What are the problems with the theory?
4 If the Reserve Bank of Australia started printing large quantities of Australian dollars, what would happen to the number of Japanese yen a dollar could buy? the number of US dollars an Australian dollar could buy? The number of Chinese RMB an Australian dollar could buy?

Problems and applications

1 How would the following transactions affect Australian exports, imports and net exports?
 a An Australian chef spends the summer touring restaurants in Asia.
 b Department stores in London buy clothes designed by Australian designers Sass & Bide.
 c Your older sister buys an Alfa Romeo.
 d John Butler sells a million CDs in Europe.

    e A New Zealand citizen shops at a store in Melbourne to avoid the New Zealand goods and services tax (assuming that they can get their Australian GST rebated on departure from Australia).

2 Suggest some specific reasons that each of the following products is traded internationally more today than in the past:

    a wheat

    b banking services

    c computer software

    d iron ore.

3 How would the following transactions affect Australian net foreign investment? Also, state whether each involves direct investment or portfolio investment.

    a An Australian mobile phone company establishes an office in Azerbaijan.

    b British pension funds buy shares in Rio Tinto.

    c Toyota closes its factory in Altona.

    d A Westpac mutual fund sells its News Ltd shares to a Chinese investor.

4 Holding national saving constant, does an increase in net foreign investment increase, decrease or have no effect on a country's accumulation of domestic capital?

5 The *Australian Financial Review* contains a table showing Australian exchange rates or you can find exchange rates on the web. Use either source to answer the following questions.

    a Does this table show nominal or real exchange rates? Explain.

    b What are the exchange rates between Australia and the United States and between Australia and Japan? Calculate the exchange rate between the United States and Japan.

    c If Australian inflation exceeds US inflation over the next year, would you expect the dollar to appreciate or depreciate relative to the US dollar?

6 Would each of the following groups be happy or unhappy if the Australian dollar appreciated? Explain.

    a Australian cattle growers who export their beef overseas

    b Australian companies who buy their inputs overseas

    c Australian students planning a study year overseas

    d An Australian firm trying to purchase a plant located overseas that will produce goods to be sent back to Australia.

7 What is happening to the Australian real exchange rate in each of the following situations? Explain.

    a The Australian nominal exchange rate is unchanged, but prices rise faster in Australia than abroad.

    b The Australian nominal exchange rate is unchanged, but prices rise faster abroad than in Australia.

    c The Australian nominal exchange rate declines, and prices are unchanged in Australia and abroad.

    d The Australian nominal exchange rate declines, and prices rise faster abroad than in Australia.

8 List three goods for which the law of one price is likely to hold and three goods for which it is not. Justify your choices.

9 If a Japanese car costs 600 000 yen, if a similar Australian car costs $20 000, and if a dollar can buy 90 yen, what are the nominal and real exchange rates? Does purchasing power parity hold?

10 As the value of the Australian dollar rises, more and more people are buying goods from overseas on the Internet and having them shipped to Australia. Does this mean purchasing power parity is more or less likely to hold for these goods?

11 Assume that Australian coal sells for $45 per tonne, Chinese coal sells for 320 RMB (yuan) per tonne, and the nominal exchange rate is 6 RMB (yuan) per dollar.

    a Explain how you could make a profit from this situation. What would be your profit per tonne of coal? If other people exploit the same opportunity, what would happen to the price of coal in China and the price of coal in Australia?

    b Suppose that coal is the only commodity in the world. What would happen to the real exchange rate between Australia and China?

    c What would prevent the exchange rate from adjusting?

12 As you can see from the 'In the news' item earlier, *The Economist*, an international news magazine, regularly collects data on the price of a McDonald's Big Mac hamburger in different countries in order to examine the theory of purchasing-power parity.

    a Why might the Big Mac be a good product to use for this purpose?

    b Based on the Big Mac data, purchasing-power parity appears to hold roughly across some countries, though not across others. Why might the assumptions underlying the theory of purchasing-power parity not hold exactly for Big Macs?

    c Do you think the UBS index on minutes worked required to buy a Big Mac would be a better measure of purchasing power parity than the simple Big Mac index? Why or why not?

    d Why would the iPod index be a better measure than either Big Mac index?

Search me!

 Search me!

When accessing information about economics use the following keywords in any combinations you require:

- net exports
- net foreign investment

CourseMate

 CourseMate

For more multimedia resources and activities on economics, visit the Economics CourseMate website.

32

A macroeconomic theory of the open economy

Learning objectives

In this chapter you will:

- build a model to explain an open economy's trade balance and exchange rate
- use the model to analyse the effects of government budget deficits
- use the model to analyse the macroeconomic effects of trade policies
- use the model to analyse political instability and capital flight.

Since the 1970s, Australia's trade balance has swung between surplus and deficit. Sometimes we export more goods and services than we import. Sometimes we import more than we export. Despite periods of trade surplus, economists debate whether the trade deficits are a problem for the Australian economy. The nation's business community, however, has a strong opinion. Many business leaders claim that the trade deficits reflect unfair competition – foreign firms are allowed to sell their products in Australian markets, they contend, while foreign governments impede Australian firms selling Australian products abroad.

Imagine that you are the prime minister and you want to end these trade deficits. What should you do? Should you try to limit imports, perhaps by increasing tariffs on the import of cars from Japan? Or should you try to influence the nation's trade deficit in some other way?

To understand what factors determine a country's trade balance and how government policies can affect it, we need a macroeconomic theory of the open economy. The preceding chapter introduced some of the key macroeconomic variables that describe an economy's relationship with other economies – including net exports, net foreign investment and the real and nominal exchange rates. This chapter develops a model that shows what forces determine these variables and how these variables are related to one another.

To develop this macroeconomic model of an open economy, we build on our previous analysis in two important ways. First, the model takes the economy's GDP as given. The economy's output of goods and services, as measured by real GDP, is assumed to be determined by the supplies of the factors of production and by the available production technology that turns these inputs into output. Second, the model takes the economy's price level as given. The price level is assumed to adjust to bring the supply and demand for money into balance. In other words, this chapter takes as a starting point the lessons learned in previous chapters about the determination of the economy's output and price level.

The goal of the model in this chapter is to highlight those forces that determine the economy's trade balance and exchange rate. In one sense, the model is simple – it merely applies the tools of supply and demand to an open economy. Yet the model is also more complicated than others we have seen because it involves looking simultaneously at two related markets – the market for loanable funds and the market for foreign-currency exchange. After we develop this model of the open economy, we use it to examine how various events and policies affect the economy's trade balance and exchange rate. We will then be able to determine the government policies that are most likely to reverse the trade deficits that the Australian economy has experienced from time to time over the past few decades.

Supply of and demand for loanable funds and foreign-currency exchange

To understand the forces at work in an open economy, we focus on supply and demand in two markets. The first is the market for loanable funds, which coordinates the economy's saving and investment (including its net foreign investment). The second is the market for foreign-currency exchange, which coordinates people who want to exchange the domestic currency for the currency of other countries. In this section we discuss supply and demand in each of these markets. In the next section we put these markets together to explain the overall equilibrium for an open economy.

The market for loanable funds

When we first analysed the role of the financial system earlier in this book, we made the simplifying assumption that the financial system consists of only one market, called the *market for loanable funds*. All savers go to this market to deposit their saving and all borrowers go to this market to get their loans. In this market, there is one interest rate, which is both the return on saving and the cost of borrowing.

To understand the market for loanable funds in an open economy, the place to start is the identity discussed in the preceding chapter:

$$S = I + NFI$$

Saving = Domestic investment + Net foreign investment

Whenever a nation saves a dollar of its income, it can use that dollar to finance the purchase of domestic capital or to finance the purchase of an asset abroad. The two sides of this identity represent the two sides of the market for loanable funds. The supply of loanable funds comes from national saving (S). The demand for loanable funds comes from domestic investment (I) and net foreign investment (NFI). Note that the purchase of a capital asset adds to the demand for loanable funds, regardless of whether that asset is located at home or abroad. Because net foreign investment can be either positive or negative, it can either add to or subtract from the demand for loanable funds that arises from domestic investment.

As we learned in our earlier discussion of the market for loanable funds, the quantity of loanable funds supplied and the quantity of loanable funds demanded depend on the real interest rate. A higher real interest rate encourages people to save and, therefore, raises the quantity of loanable funds supplied. A higher interest rate also makes borrowing to finance capital projects more costly; thus, it discourages investment and reduces the quantity of loanable funds demanded.

In addition to influencing national saving and domestic investment, the real interest rate in a country affects that country's net foreign investment. To see why, consider two managed funds – one in Australia and one in Canada – deciding whether to buy an Australian government bond or a Canadian government bond. The managed funds would make this decision in part by comparing the real interest rates in Australia and Canada. When the Australian real interest rate rises, the Australian bond becomes more attractive to both managed funds. Thus, an increase in the Australian real interest rate discourages Australians from buying foreign assets and encourages foreigners to buy Australian assets. For both reasons, a high Australian real interest rate reduces Australian net foreign investment.

We represent the market for loanable funds on the familiar supply-and-demand diagram in Figure 32.1. As in our earlier analysis of the financial system, the supply curve slopes upwards because a higher interest rate increases the quantity of loanable funds supplied and the demand curve slopes downwards because a higher interest rate decreases the quantity of loanable funds demanded. Unlike the situation in our previous discussion, however, the demand side of the market now represents the behaviour of both domestic investment and net foreign investment. That is, in an open economy, the demand for loanable funds comes not only from those who want to borrow funds to buy domestic capital goods but also from those who want to borrow funds to buy foreign assets.

The interest rate adjusts to bring the supply of and demand for loanable funds into balance. If the interest rate were below the equilibrium level, the quantity of loanable funds supplied would be less than the quantity demanded. The resulting shortage of loanable funds would push the interest rate upwards. Conversely, if the interest rate were above the equilibrium level, the quantity of loanable

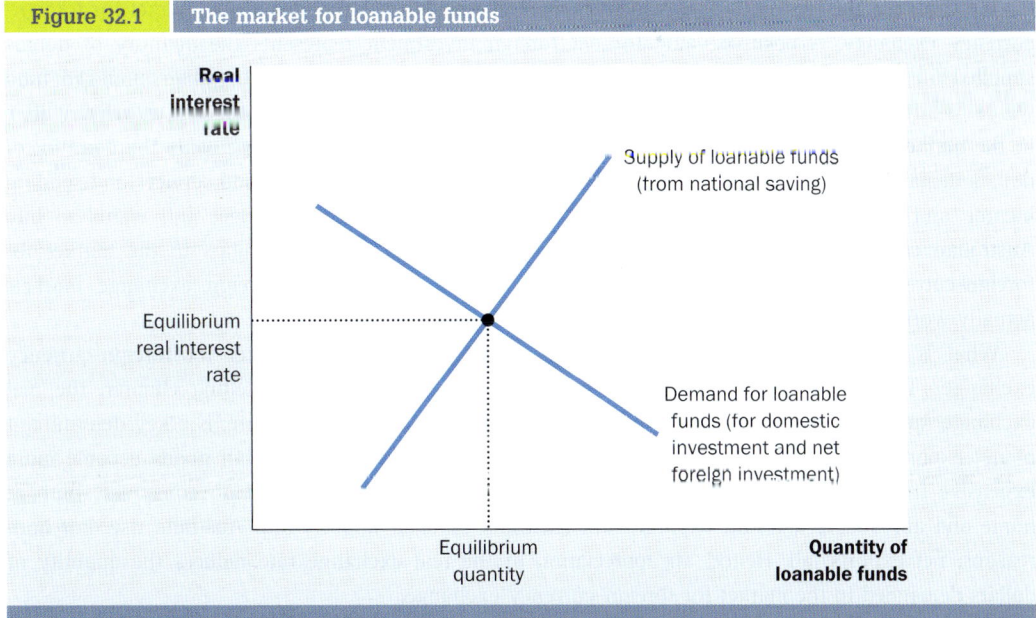

Figure 32.1 The market for loanable funds

The interest rate in a large, open economy, as in a closed economy, is determined by the supply of and demand for loanable funds. National saving is the source of the supply of loanable funds. Domestic investment and net foreign investment are the sources of the demand for loanable funds. At the equilibrium interest rate, the amount that people want to save exactly balances the amount that people want to borrow for the purpose of buying domestic capital and foreign assets.

funds supplied would exceed the quantity demanded. The surplus of loanable funds would drive the interest rate downwards. At the equilibrium interest rate, the supply of loanable funds exactly balances the demand. That is, *at the equilibrium interest rate, the amount that people want to save exactly balances the desired quantities of domestic investment and net foreign investment.*

The market for foreign-currency exchange

The second market in our model of the open economy is the market for foreign-currency exchange. Participants in this market trade Australian dollars in exchange for foreign currencies. To understand the market for foreign-currency exchange, we begin with another identity from the last chapter:

$$NFI = \text{CAB}$$

Net foreign investment = Current account balance

This identity states that the imbalance between the purchase and sale of capital assets abroad (*NFI*) equals the imbalance between exports and imports of goods and services and the net flow of income and transfers (*CAB*). When the current account balance is negative, for instance, we are buying more foreign goods and services than foreigners are buying Australian goods and services, and we are sending more income and transfers overseas than foreigners are sending to Australia. What are foreigners doing with the Australian currency they are getting from this net sale of goods and services and net receipt of income and transfers from Australia? They must be using it to add to their holdings of Australian assets. These purchases of assets abroad are reflected in a negative value of net foreign investment.

▸ loanable funds

We can view the two sides of this identity as representing the two sides of the market for foreign-currency exchange. A positive value for net foreign investment represents the quantity of dollars supplied for the purpose of buying assets abroad. For example, when an Australian managed fund wants to buy a Japanese government bond, it needs to change dollars into yen, so it supplies dollars in the market for foreign-currency exchange. The current account balance represents the quantity of dollars demanded for the purpose of buying Australian net exports of goods and services and sending income and transfers back to Australia. For example, when a Japanese steel mill wants to buy Australian coal, it needs to change its yen into dollars, so it demands dollars in the market for foreign-currency exchange. (This view is a simplification of the way foreign exchange markets actually work. We discuss this in greater detail below.)

What is the price that balances the supply and demand in the market for foreign-currency exchange? The answer is the real exchange rate. As we saw in the preceding chapter, the real exchange rate is the relative price of domestic and foreign goods and, therefore, is a key determinant of net exports. When the Australian real exchange rate appreciates, Australian goods become more expensive relative to foreign goods, making Australian goods less attractive to consumers both at home and abroad. As a result, exports from Australia fall and imports into Australia rise. For both reasons, net exports fall. Hence, an appreciation of the real exchange rate reduces the quantity of dollars demanded in the market for foreign-currency exchange.

Figure 32.2 shows supply and demand in the market for foreign-currency exchange. The demand curve slopes downwards for the reason we just discussed – a higher real exchange rate makes

Figure 32.2   **The market for foreign-currency exchange**

The real exchange rate is determined by the supply of and demand for foreign-currency exchange. The supply of dollars to be exchanged into foreign currency comes from net foreign investment. Because net foreign investment does not depend on the real exchange rate, the supply curve is vertical. The demand for dollars comes from net exports. Because a lower real exchange rate stimulates net exports (and thus increases the quantity of dollars demanded to pay for these net exports), the demand curve is downward-sloping. At the equilibrium real exchange rate, the number of dollars people supply to buy foreign assets exactly balances the number of dollars people demand to buy net exports.

Australian goods more expensive and reduces the quantity of dollars demanded to buy those goods. The supply curve is vertical because the quantity of dollars supplied for net foreign investment does not depend on the real exchange rate. (As discussed earlier, net foreign investment depends on the real interest rate. When discussing the market for foreign currency exchange, we take the real interest rate and net foreign investment as given.)

The real exchange rate adjusts to balance the supply of and demand for dollars, just as the price of any good adjusts to balance supply of and demand for that good. If the real exchange rate were below the equilibrium level, the quantity of dollars supplied would be less than the quantity demanded. The resulting shortage of dollars would push the value of the dollar upwards. Conversely, if the real exchange rate were above the equilibrium level, the quantity of dollars supplied would exceed the quantity demanded. The surplus of dollars would drive the value of the dollar downwards. *At the equilibrium real exchange rate, the demand for dollars to buy net exports exactly balances the supply of dollars to be exchanged into foreign currency to buy assets abroad.*

At this point, it is worth noting that the division of transactions between 'supply' and 'demand' in this model is somewhat artificial. In our model, net exports are the source of the demand for dollars, and net foreign investment is the source of the supply. Thus, when an Australian resident imports a car made in Japan, our model treats that transaction as a decrease in the quantity of dollars demanded (because net exports fall) rather than an increase in the quantity of dollars supplied. Similarly, when a Japanese citizen buys an Australian government bond, our model treats that transaction as a decrease in the quantity of dollars supplied (because net foreign investment falls)

rather than an increase in the quantity of dollars demanded. This use of language may seem somewhat unnatural at first, but it will prove useful when analysing the effects of various policies.

Describe the sources of supply and demand in the market for loanable funds and the market for foreign-currency exchange.

Equilibrium in the open economy

So far we have discussed supply and demand in two markets – the market for loanable funds and the market for foreign-currency exchange. Let's now consider how these markets are related to each other.

Net foreign investment: The link between the two markets

We begin by recapping what we've learned so far in this chapter. We have been discussing how the economy coordinates four important macroeconomic variables: national saving (S), domestic investment (I), net foreign investment (NFI) and the current account balance (CAB).

Keep in mind the following identities:

$$S = I + NFI$$

and

$$NFI = CAB$$

In the market for loanable funds, supply comes from national saving, demand comes from domestic investment and net foreign investment, and the real interest rate balances supply and demand. In the market for foreign-currency exchange, supply comes from net foreign investment, demand comes from the current account balance, and the real exchange rate balances supply and demand.

fyi

Purchasing-power parity as a special case

In the preceding chapter we developed a simple theory of the exchange rate called *purchasing-power parity*. This theory asserts that a dollar (or any other currency) must buy the same quantity of goods and services in every country. As a result, the real exchange rate is fixed and all changes in the nominal exchange rate between two currencies reflect changes in the price levels in the two countries.

How is the model of the exchange rate developed here related to the theory of purchasing-power parity? According to the theory of purchasing-power parity, international trade responds quickly to international price differences. If goods were cheaper in one country than in another, they would

be exported from the first country and imported into the second until the price differential disappeared. In other words, the theory of purchasing-power parity assumes that net exports are highly responsive to small changes in the real exchange rate. If net exports were in fact so responsive, the demand curve in Figure 32.2 would be horizontal.

Thus, the theory of purchasing-power parity is a special case of the model considered here. In that special case, the demand curve for foreign-currency exchange, rather than being downward-sloping, is horizontal at the level of the real exchange rate that ensures parity of purchasing power at home and abroad.

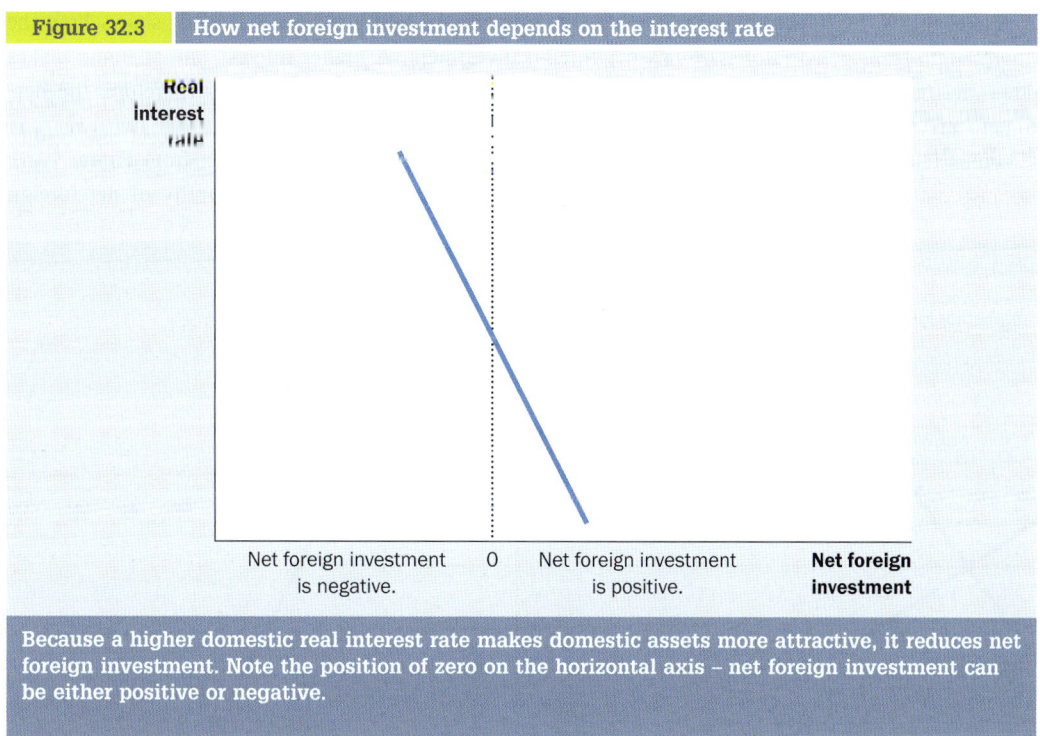

Figure 32.3 How net foreign investment depends on the interest rate

Real interest rate

Net foreign investment is negative.   0   Net foreign investment is positive.   **Net foreign investment**

Because a higher domestic real interest rate makes domestic assets more attractive, it reduces net foreign investment. Note the position of zero on the horizontal axis – net foreign investment can be either positive or negative.

Net foreign investment is the variable that links these two markets. In the market for loanable funds, net foreign investment is a component of demand. A person who wants to buy an asset abroad must finance this purchase by borrowing in the market for loanable funds. In the market for foreign-currency exchange, net foreign investment is the source of supply. A person who wants to buy an asset in another country must supply dollars in order to exchange them for the currency of that country.

The key determinant of net foreign investment, as we have discussed, is the real interest rate. When the Australian interest rate is high, owning Australian assets is more attractive and Australian net foreign investment is low. Figure 32.3 shows this negative relationship between the interest rate and net foreign investment. This net-foreign-investment curve is the link between the market for loanable funds and the market for foreign-currency exchange.

Simultaneous equilibrium in two markets

We can now put all the pieces of our model together in Figure 32.4. This figure shows how the market for loanable funds and the market for foreign-currency exchange jointly determine the important macroeconomic variables of an open economy.

Panel (a) of the figure shows the market for loanable funds (taken from Figure 32.1). As before, national saving is the source of the supply of loanable funds. Domestic investment and net foreign investment are the source of the demand for loanable funds. The equilibrium real interest rate (r_1) brings the quantity of loanable funds supplied and the quantity of loanable funds demanded into balance.

Panel (b) of the figure shows net foreign investment (taken from Figure 32.3). It shows how the interest rate from panel (a) determines net foreign investment. A higher interest rate at home makes domestic assets more attractive and this in turn reduces net foreign investment. Therefore, the net-foreign-investment curve in panel (b) slopes downwards.

Panel (c) of the figure shows the market for foreign-currency exchange (taken from Figure 32.2). Because net foreign investment must be paid for with foreign currency, the quantity of net foreign

Figure 32.4 The real equilibrium in an open economy

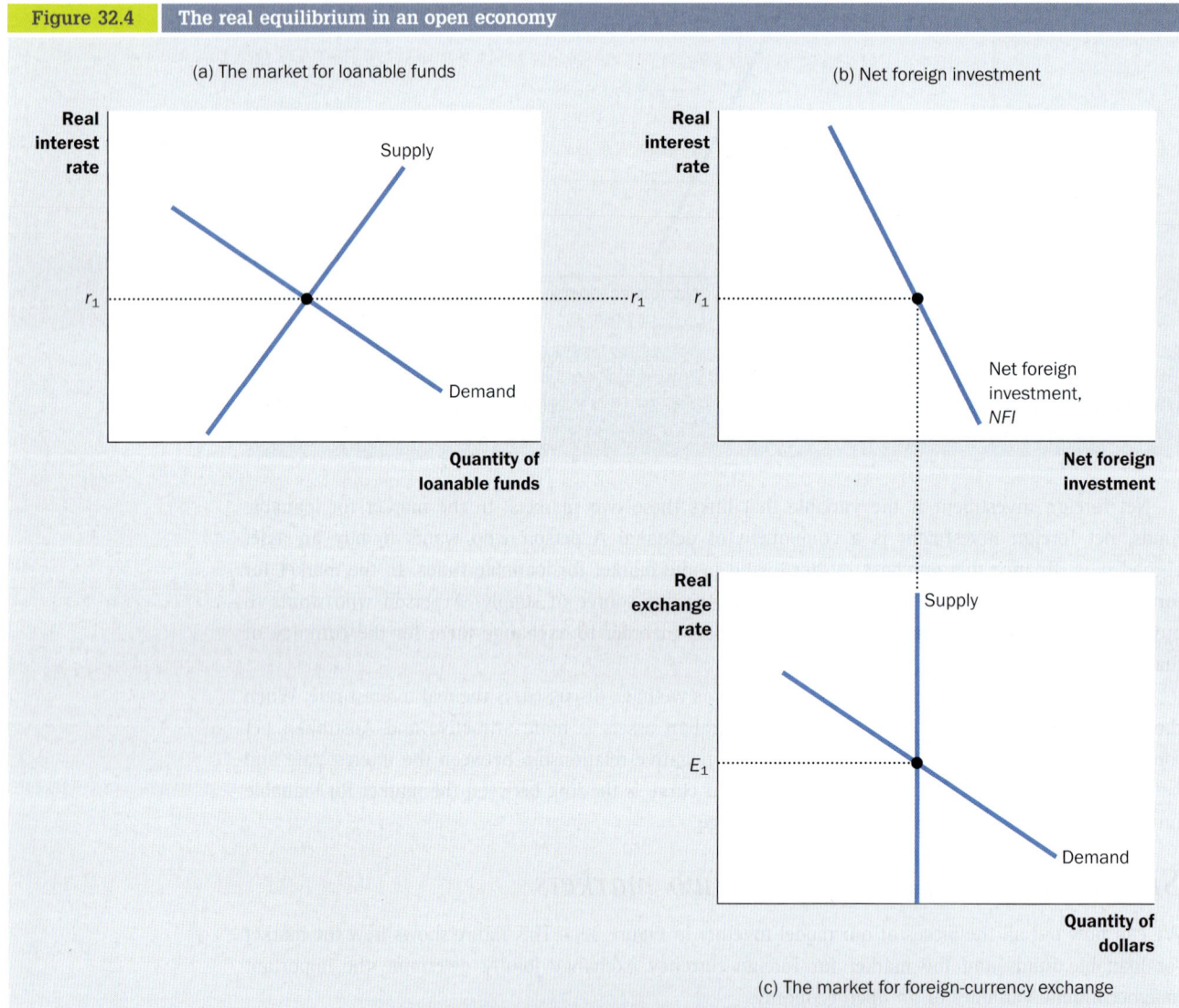

In panel (a), the supply of and demand for loanable funds determine the real interest rate. In panel (b), the interest rate determines net foreign investment, which provides the supply of dollars in the market for foreign-currency exchange. In panel (c), the supply of and demand for dollars in the market for foreign-currency exchange determine the real exchange rate.

investment from panel (b) determines the supply of dollars to be exchanged into foreign currencies. The real exchange rate does not affect net foreign investment, so the supply curve is vertical. The demand for dollars comes from net exports, because a depreciation of the real exchange rate increases net exports, the demand curve for foreign-currency exchange slopes downwards. The equilibrium real exchange rate (E_1) brings into balance the quantity of dollars supplied and the quantity of dollars demanded in the market for foreign-currency exchange.

The two markets shown in Figure 32.4 determine two relative prices – the real interest rate and the real exchange rate. The real interest rate determined in panel (a) is the price of goods and services in the present relative to goods and services in the future. The real exchange rate determined in panel (c) is the price of domestic goods and services relative to foreign goods and services. These two relative prices adjust simultaneously to balance supply and demand in these two markets. As they do so, they determine national saving, domestic investment, net foreign investment and net exports. In a moment, we will use this model to see how all these variables change when some policy or event causes one of these curves to shift.

fyi

The classical dichotomy once again

The macroeconomic theory of the open economy that we have just developed is 'classical'. This term has two related meanings. First, the theory harks back to themes emphasised by economists of centuries past. Second, and more important, the theory uses the classical dichotomy and the assumption of monetary neutrality. Recall that the classical dichotomy is the theoretical separation of real and nominal variables. Our model of the open economy is written completely in terms of real variables, including quantities (saving, investment, net foreign investment and net exports) and relative prices (the real interest rate and the real exchange rate). The model explains these real variables without including a role for money.

How do changes in the money supply affect the economy? The answer is the same as in our analysis in previous chapters. Classical theory posits that the price level adjusts to balance money supply and money demand. If the central bank doubles the money supply, the price level doubles. If the central bank follows a policy of persistent growth in the money supply, the result is persistent inflation.

To ensure that real variables are not affected by monetary changes, all nominal variables must adjust to these changes. In particular, if the real exchange rate is not affected by monetary changes, then the nominal exchange rate (measured in units of foreign currency per dollar) must fall as the domestic price level rises. We first saw this effect of inflation on nominal exchange rates in the preceding chapter when we discussed the theory of purchasing-power parity. Nothing we have said about the open economy in this chapter alters these conclusions.

Recall that the assumption of monetary neutrality is best viewed as applying over the long run. To fully understand year-to-year changes in the economy, we need to incorporate reasons for short-run monetary non-neutrality. We cover that topic beginning in the next chapter. Throughout this chapter, we maintain the assumption of monetary neutrality in order to understand the implications of this classical model.

In the model of the open economy just developed, two markets determine two relative prices. What are the markets? What are the two relative prices?

How policies and events affect an open economy

Having developed a model to explain how key macroeconomic variables are determined in an open economy, we can now use the model to analyse how changes in policy and other events alter the economy's equilibrium. As we proceed, keep in mind that our model is just supply and demand in two markets – the market for loanable funds and the market for foreign-currency exchange. When using the model to analyse any event, we can apply the three steps outlined in chapter 4. First, we determine which of the supply and demand curves the event affects. Second, we determine which way the curves shift. Third, we use the supply-and-demand diagrams to examine how these shifts alter the economy's equilibrium.

Government budget deficits

When we first discussed the supply of and demand for loanable funds earlier in the book, we examined the effects of government budget deficits, which occur when government spending exceeds government revenue. Because a government budget deficit represents *negative* public saving, it reduces national saving (the sum of public and private saving). Thus, a government budget deficit reduces the supply of loanable funds, drives up the interest rate and crowds out investment.

Now let's consider the effects of a budget deficit in an open economy. First, which curve in our model shifts? As in a closed economy, the initial impact of the budget deficit is on national saving and, therefore, on the supply curve for loanable funds. Second, which way does this supply curve shift? Again as in a closed economy, a budget deficit represents *negative* public saving, so it reduces national saving and shifts the supply curve for loanable funds to the left. This is shown as the shift from S_1 to S_2 in panel (a) of Figure 32.5.

Our third and final step is to compare the old and new equilibria. Panel (a) shows the impact of an Australian budget deficit on the Australian market for loanable funds. With fewer funds available for borrowers in Australian financial markets, the interest rate rises from r_1 to r_2 to balance supply and demand. Faced with a higher interest rate, borrowers in the market for loanable funds choose to borrow less. This change is represented in the figure as the movement from point A to point B along the demand curve for loanable funds. In particular, households and firms reduce their purchases of capital goods. As in a closed economy, budget deficits crowd out domestic investment.

In an open economy, however, the reduced supply for loanable funds has additional effects. Panel (b) shows that the increase in the interest rate from r_1 to r_2 reduces net foreign investment. (This fall in net foreign investment is also part of the decrease in the quantity of loanable funds demanded in the movement from point A to point B in panel (a).) Because saving kept at home now earns higher rates of return, investing abroad is less attractive, and domestic residents buy fewer foreign assets. Higher interest rates also attract foreign investors, who want to earn the higher returns on Australian assets. Thus, when budget deficits raise interest rates, both domestic and foreign behaviour cause Australian net foreign investment to fall.

Panel (c) shows how budget deficits affect the market for foreign-currency exchange. Because net foreign investment is reduced, people need less foreign currency to buy foreign assets and this induces a leftward shift in the supply curve for dollars from S_1 to S_2. The reduced supply of dollars causes the real exchange rate to appreciate from E_1 to E_2. That is, the dollar becomes more valuable compared with foreign currencies. This appreciation, in turn, makes Australian goods more expensive compared with foreign goods. Because people both at home and abroad switch their purchases away from the more expensive Australian goods, exports from Australia fall and imports into Australia rise. For both reasons, Australian net exports fall. Hence, *in an open economy, government budget deficits raise real interest rates, crowd out domestic investment, cause the dollar to appreciate and push the trade balance towards deficit.*

| Figure 32.5 | The effects of a government budget deficit |

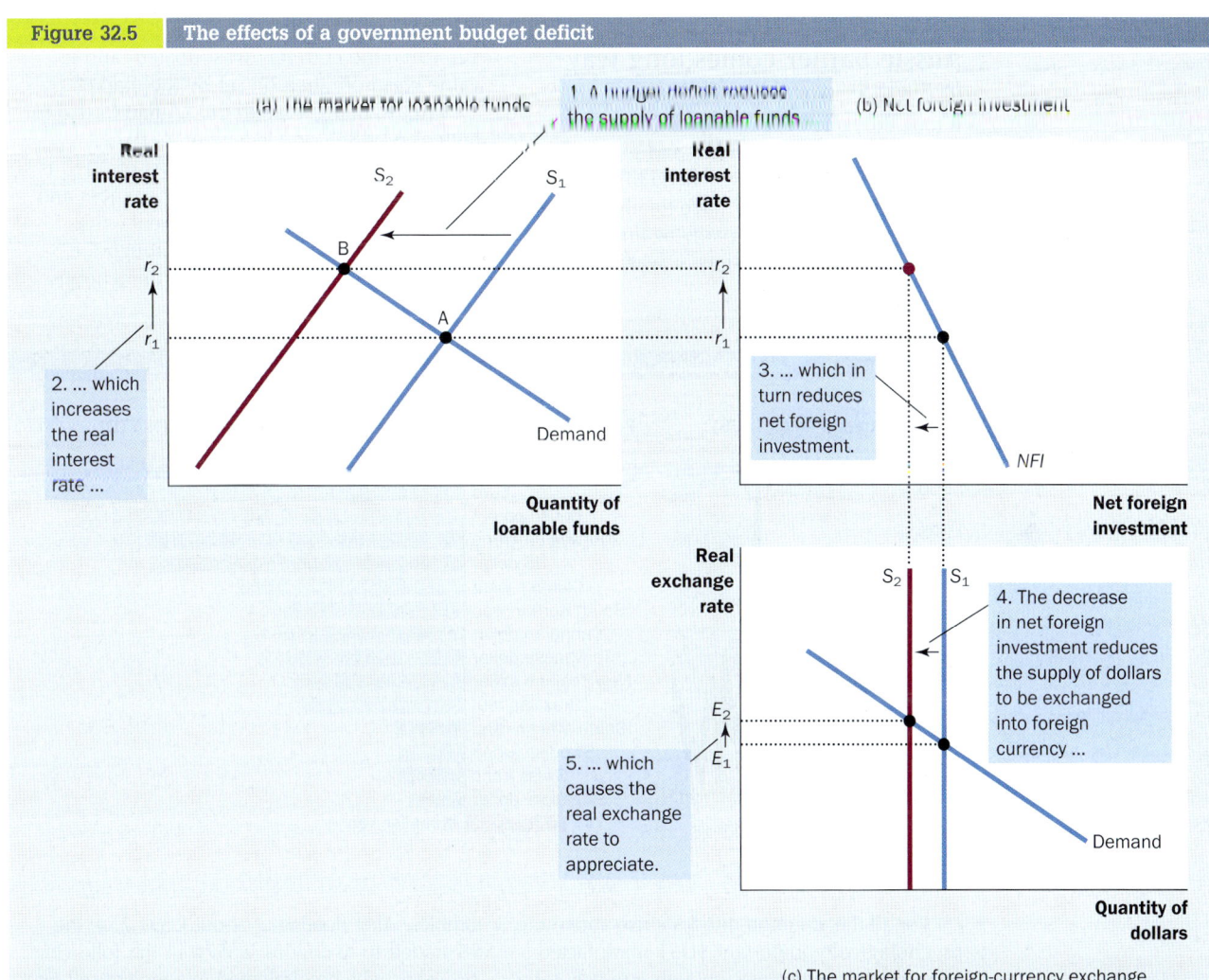

(a) The market for loanable funds

1. A budget deficit reduces the supply of loanable funds

(b) Net foreign investment

2. ... which increases the real interest rate ...

3. ... which in turn reduces net foreign investment.

4. The decrease in net foreign investment reduces the supply of dollars to be exchanged into foreign currency ...

5. ... which causes the real exchange rate to appreciate.

(c) The market for foreign-currency exchange

When the government runs a budget deficit, it reduces the supply of loanable funds from S_1 to S_2 in panel (a). The interest rate rises from r_1 to r_2 to balance the supply of and demand for loanable funds. In panel (b), the higher interest rate reduces net foreign investment. Reduced net-foreign investment, in turn, reduces the supply of dollars in the market for foreign-currency exchange from S_1 to S_2 in panel (c). This fall in the supply of dollars causes the real exchange rate to appreciate from E_1 to E_2. The appreciation of the exchange rate pushes the trade balance towards deficit.

IN THE NEWS ...

AUSSIE DOLLAR HITS PARITY WITH US DOLLAR

There's really nothing special about the Aussie dollar being equal to the US dollar, except ... It is an indication of the strength of the Australian economy at a time when other economies are still coming out of recession. The following article from the *Australian Financial Review* discusses the history of the A$ since it was floated and explains why it's riding high now.

>>

Aussie battler comes long way
by Philip Baker and Pip Freebairn

It took 28 years but soaring commodity prices, rising domestic interest rates and expectations the US Federal Reserve will need to do more to bolster the US economy have finally propelled the Australian dollar to parity against the US dollar for the first time since it was floated in December 1983.

12, 1983, the currency was 'floated' and its value was from then on set by the market.

Prior to being floated, the $A had traded as high as $1.4885 on December 7, 1973.

The $A's strength through most of 2010 is in stark contrast to the bouts of weakness and risk aversion that earned the currency the nickname 'the Aussie battler'. Through the years, the $A has endured some tremendous

| Figure 32.6 | The Australian dollar's performance against other currencies in 2010 |

For all the attention, the $A's rise above the psychologically important $US1 mark lasted only seconds. Strategists, though, are generally upbeat on the outlook for the $A and expect it to remain strong over coming months.

That's a plus for importers and those taking overseas holidays who can buy goods more cheaply, but it is a headache for exporters and manufacturers of locally produced goods.

The last time the $A traded above one US dollar was on July 28, 1982, when the dollar rate was periodically set by the Reserve Bank of Australia against a basket of currencies. The Labor government, led by prime minister Bob Hawke and treasurer Paul Keating, as part of major reforms to the Australian financial landscape, pushed for Australia to adopt a floating exchange rate policy. From December

tumbles. After floating at about US91.25¢, the $A traded to as low as US57¢ in the following 3½ years, which culminated in a violent sell-off in June and July of 1986. Over those two months, investors wiped as much as US16¢ from the local unit. It was during this two-month period that Keating's famous 'banana republic' statement and Moody's Investors Service hit Australia's foreign currency credit rating with a double downgrade.

Keating's warning that Australia was at risk of becoming too reliant on a single industry was a left-field shock to Australian complacency.

It was in stark contrast to the normal 'steady as she goes' rhetoric of the day which most politicians were used to dishing out. It allowed the government to move swiftly to a sounder fiscal policy, and to persuade the unions to accept a significant erosion in real wages. And it also enabled Labor to win the 1987 election on a policy of austerity rather than handouts.

The $A muddled through the recession of the early 1990s and took a beating in 1997 as the Asian financial crisis took hold.

The $A slid to new record lows against the $US during the tech boom, reaching a low of US47.75¢ in April 2001, as Australia was viewed by global investors to be 'old economy' and clearly not the way of the future. Over the past decade, the $A has doubled in value, supported by burgeoning demand for Australia's natural resources.

Accordingly, the $A has often been branded a commodity currency, and is viewed as a proxy for Asian growth.

This unwound spectacularly during the global financial crisis in 2008. The $A was tracking towards parity with the $US, eventually peaking at US98.49¢, but following the bankruptcy of Lehman Brothers, tumbled toward US60¢ as investors fled riskier assets.

Now, though, higher-yielding assets like the $A are back in demand. The still-parlous state of the US economy has the US Federal Reserve poised to undertake another round of government bond purchases in a process known as quantitative easing. This would put downward pressure on the $US, but expectations the financial system will be awash with liquidity and expectations of inflation are also prompting investors to seek out higher-yielding assets, such as the Australian dollar, and gold, which is viewed as a natural hedge against inflation and is trading at record levels above $US1380 an ounce.

The relative strength of the Australian economy is in contrast to those of the US, Europe and Japan, where interest rates are at record lows. The RBA, on the other hand, is more likely to raise interest rates at subsequent meetings, which would further support a strong $A.

The $A is also trading at multi-year highs against the British pound and the euro.

Although there has been talk of 'currency wars' as other countries race to the bottom to keep the value of their currencies low, the $A has performed strongly, and is up against all major currencies in 2010 with the exception of the Japanese yen, which itself is at multi-year highs against the US dollar.

Up 10.4 per cent against the greenback this year, some experts say the $A's run is not over yet. Fuelled by China's growth and a falling US dollar, that is under pressure as the Fed is faced with ongoing structural imbalances in the world's largest economy, economists have been raising their forecasts for the $A.

Westpac Banking Corp has increased its end of year target to US1.02¢, up from US98¢, and the June 2011 target to US1.05¢. 'The $A is a safe haven for global investors right now with central banks around the world looking at ways to stimulate their economies through printing money,' Westpac chief economist Bill Evans says.

He reckons the risk for the $A is that it keeps rising as the Fed ponders the possibility of another round of quantitative easing when the Reserve Bank of Australia is looking to increase interest rates.

'Recent comments from Fed officials have prompted us to raise our estimates that the Fed will have to buy something like $US1.5 trillion in bonds to keep rates down rather than $US800 billion. We doubt whether the currency markets have fully priced such a large task. That means that further US dollar weakness is likely over the course of the remainder of 2010 and through to at least the first half of 2011,' said Mr Evans.

The US dollar last week hit a new low against the Swiss franc, while the yen hit another 15-year high against the greenback as investors seek out safe haven investments.

Other Asian currencies have also surged in recent weeks as investors seek higher yields and growth opportunities in more economically sound countries.

The moves in foreign exchange markers throw out a challenge to exporting nations because high currencies make their products less competitive abroad.

The average exchange rate for the $A this year is about US90.2¢, compared with its long term average since it was floated of US72.3¢.

But experts warn that average rate is set to rise. Commonwealth Bank of Australia chief economist Michael Blythe expects the

>>

Australian dollar will continue to be volatile but around a higher average, and this will lift the post-float average to around US77¢ in the next few years. 'Obviously where we are now there is a cyclical element to it, but it is also a structural element to it,' he says.

'It is a structural step up which is a reflection of the whole China commodity story, which clearly has further to run.'

A strong currency is not good news for everyone – exporters and investors in global sharemarket funds are among those not rejoicing yesterday but the traditional wisdom that a strong currency reflects a strong economy still holds good, while the $A has also been seen as [a] barometer for how good people are feeling.

Blythe says the effect of the higher dollar can be seen in weaker activity in the tourism and education services sectors, and that parts of manufacturing and agricultural sectors are also likely to suffer in the next few years.

On a trade-weighted index, however, the currency has yet to reach the highs of the early 1980s, underscoring the big part the falling US dollar is playing.

Certainly, global investors like this Australian story. Buying the $A is a winner: it gives investors access to both a high interest rate and, via our commodities trade, a stake in the explosive growth in emerging economies.

Disappointment with the pace of the US jobs recovery and fears about sovereign debt have set off renewed financial instability in the world's largest economy, raising doubts as to whether more pain from the credit crisis lies ahead.

The US dollar has slumped against major currencies this year as investors brace themselves for another round of quantitative easing from the US Federal Reserve aimed at kickstarting the economy.

With interest rates already at zero in the US there is no other option open to the Fed but investors are worried that by inflating their way out of trouble the Fed is also delivering a major downgrade to the greenback.

RBA Australia chief currency strategist Greg Gibbs said the negative sentiment towards the greenback is likely to be a theme in markers this year and much of next year.

'It will be around for as long as it takes US quantitative policy easing to bear some fruit and the US economy start to look like it is moving back to trend growth. Most peoples' anticipation of that is that it will be a long drawn-out process,' Mr Gibbs said.

Fears about governments in Europe being able to finance their debts has also sparked a flight to commodity currencies and away from the US dollar as the Obama administration remains under pressure to curb spending as it faces a $US1.6 trillion budget deficit this year.

Investors don't want US dollars and so there is a huge switch into physical assets and currencies backed by resources like the $A.

While the outlook for currency markets is always uncertain, one thing economists agree on is the RBA will not be following the lead of other central banks like the Bank of Japan and Swiss National Bank and intervene in the currency to stem its appreciation.

Access Economics Professor Ian Harper said just as it did in the Asian Financial Crisis, the RBA will allow the $A to act as a stabiliser on the economy, by dampening growth in other export sectors which will help to alleviate inflation pressures and meet its monetary policy target.

Source: Philip Baker and Pip Freebairn/*The Australian Financial Review*, 18 October 2010.

Trade policy

trade policy
a government policy that directly influences the quantity of goods and services that a country imports or exports

A **trade policy** is a government policy that directly influences the quantity of goods and services that a country imports or exports. Trade policy takes various forms. One common trade policy is a *tariff*, a tax on imported goods. Another is an *import quota*, a limit on the quantity of a good that can be produced abroad and sold domestically. Trade policies are common throughout the world, although sometimes they are disguised. For example, the US government has often pressured Japanese car manufacturers to reduce the number of cars they sell in the United States. These so-called voluntary export restrictions are not really voluntary and, in essence, are a form of import quota. In Australia, tariffs and quotas have been used to restrict the import of cars into Australia.

Let's consider the macroeconomic impact of trade policy. Suppose that the Australian car industry, concerned about competition from Japanese car manufacturers, convinces the Australian government to increase tariffs on imported cars. The tariff would affect the number of cars that will be imported from Japan. (This is, in effect, what Australian car manufacturers did in the first term of the Howard government, when they convinced the government to limit planned reductions in tariffs on imported cars.) In making their case, lobbyists for the car industry assert that the trade restriction would shrink the size of the Australian trade deficit. Are they right? Our model, as illustrated in Figure 32.7, offers an answer.

The first step in analysing the trade policy is to determine which curve shifts. The initial impact of the tariff is, not surprisingly, on imports. Because net exports (equal to exports minus imports) are a component of the current account balance, the policy also affects the current account. And because the current account balance is the source of demand for dollars in the market for foreign-currency exchange, the policy affects the demand curve in this market.

The second step is to determine which way this demand curve shifts. Because the tariff reduces the number of Japanese cars sold in Australia, it reduces imports at any given real exchange rate. Net exports, which equal exports minus imports, will therefore rise for any given real exchange rate. This rise in net exports causes the current account balance to rise as well. Because foreigners need dollars to buy Australian net exports, which are a component of the current account balance, there is an increased demand for dollars in the market for foreign-currency exchange. This increase in the demand for dollars is shown in panel (c) as the shift from D_1 to D_2.

The third step is to compare the old and new equilibria. As we can see in panel (c), the increase in the demand for dollars causes the real exchange rate to appreciate from E_1 to E_2. Because nothing has happened in the market for loanable funds in panel (a), there is no change in the interest rate. There is also no change in net foreign investment, shown in panel (b). And because there is no change in net foreign investment, there can be no change in the current account balance, even though the tariff has reduced imports.

The reason that the current account balance can stay the same while imports fall is explained by the change in the real exchange rate – when the dollar appreciates in value in the market for foreign-currency exchange, domestic goods become more expensive relative to foreign goods. This appreciation encourages imports and discourages exports – and both of these changes work to offset the direct increase in the current account balance due to the import quota. In the end, an import quota reduces both imports and exports, but net exports (exports minus imports) are unchanged.

We have thus come to a surprising implication – *trade policies do not affect the trade balance*. That is, policies that directly influence exports or imports do not alter net exports. This conclusion seems less surprising if one recalls the accounting identity:

$$CAB = NFI = S - I$$

The current account balance equals net foreign investment, which equals national saving minus domestic investment. Trade policies do not alter the current account balance because they do not alter national saving or domestic investment. For given levels of national saving and domestic investment,

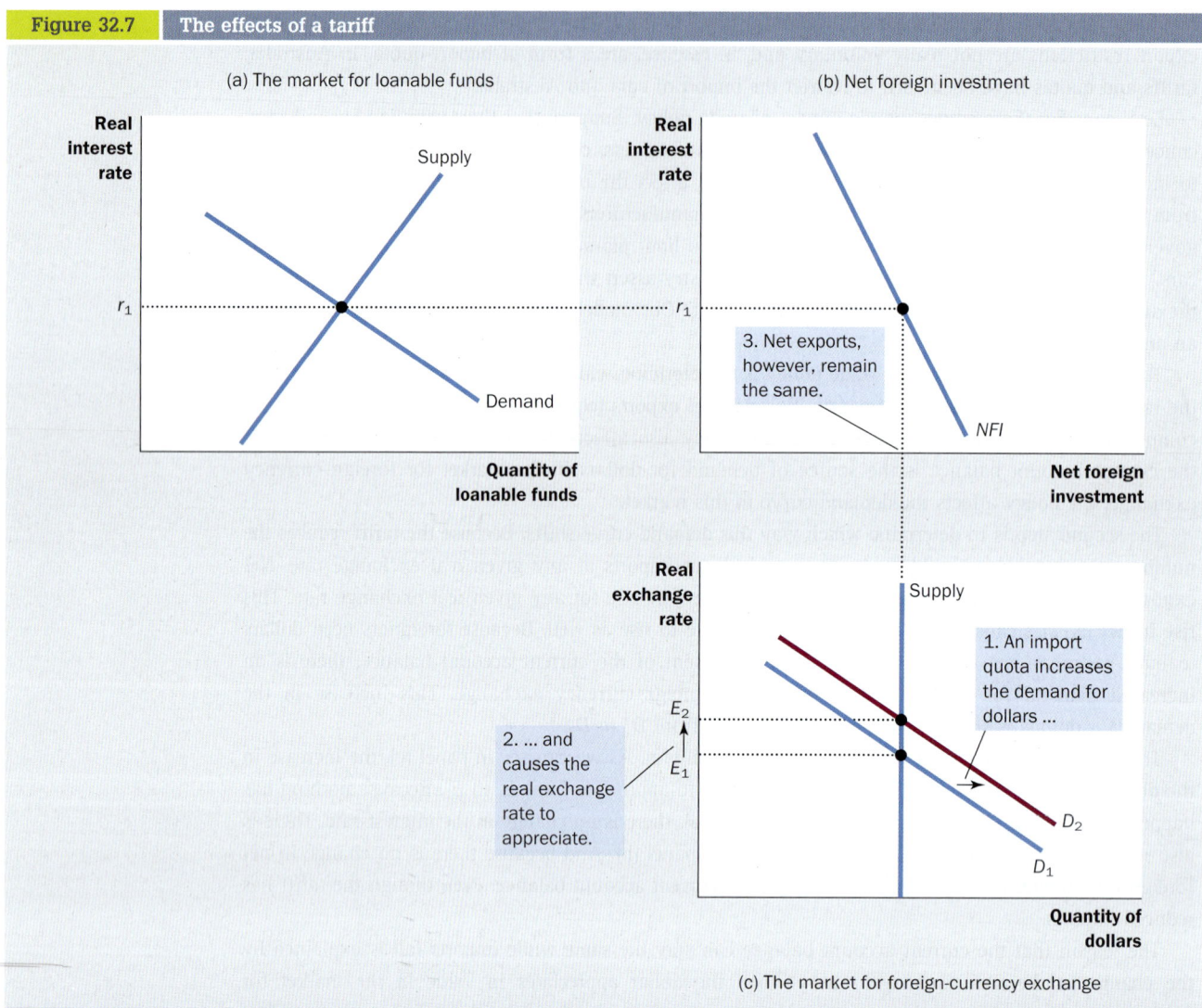

Figure 32.7 The effects of a tariff

(a) The market for loanable funds

(b) Net foreign investment

3. Net exports, however, remain the same.

2. ... and causes the real exchange rate to appreciate.

1. An import quota increases the demand for dollars ...

(c) The market for foreign-currency exchange

When the Australian government imposes a tariff on the import of cars, nothing happens in the market for loanable funds in panel (a) or to net foreign investments in panel (b). The only effect is a rise in the current account balance (exports minus imports plus net income and transfers) for any given real exchange rate. As a result, the demand for dollars in the market for foreign-currency exchange rises, as shown by the shift from D_1 to D_2 in panel (c). This increase in the demand for dollars causes the value of the dollar to appreciate from E_1 to E_2. This appreciation of the dollar tends to reduce the current account balance, offsetting the direct effect of the import quota on the trade balance.

the real exchange rate adjusts to keep the current account balance the same, regardless of the trade policies the government puts in place.

Although trade policies do not affect a country's overall trade balance, these policies do affect specific firms, industries and countries. When the Australian government imposes a tariff on Japanese cars, Holden has less competition from abroad and will sell more cars. At the same time, because the dollar has appreciated in value, Australian beef producers will find it harder to compete with Argentinian beef producers. Australian exports of beef will fall and Australian imports of beef will rise. In this case, the tariff on Japanese cars will increase net exports of cars and decrease net exports of beef. In addition, it will increase net exports from Australia to Japan and decrease net exports from Australia to Argentina. The overall trade balance of the Australian economy, however, stays the same.

The effects of trade policies are, therefore, more microeconomic than macroeconomic. Although advocates of trade policies sometimes claim (incorrectly) that these policies can alter a country's balance of trade, they are usually more motivated by concerns about particular firms or industries. One should not be surprised, for instance, to hear an executive from Holden advocating tariffs on imported cars. Economists almost always oppose such trade policies. As we saw in chapter 3, free trade allows economies to specialise in doing what they do best, making residents of all countries better off. Trade restrictions interfere with these gains from trade and, thus, reduce overall economic wellbeing.

Political instability and capital flight

Political instability in Indonesia and Malaysia in the 1990s made world financial markets nervous. People began to view these countries as much less stable than they had previously thought. They decided to pull some of their assets out of Indonesia and Malaysia in order to move these funds to Australia, the United States and other 'safe havens'. Such a large and sudden movement of funds out of a country is called **capital flight**. To see the implications of capital flight for the Indonesian economy, we again follow our three steps for analysing a change in equilibrium, but this time we apply our model of the open economy from the perspective of Indonesia rather than Australia.

capital flight
a large and sudden reduction in the demand for assets located in a country

Consider first which curves in our model capital flight affects. When investors around the world observe political problems in Indonesia, they decide to sell some of their Indonesian assets and use the proceeds to buy Australian assets. This act increases Indonesian net foreign investment and, therefore, affects both markets in our model. Most obviously, it affects the net-foreign-investment curve and this in turn influences the supply of rupiah in the market for foreign-currency exchange. In addition, because the demand for loanable funds comes from both domestic investment and net foreign investment, capital flight affects the demand curve in the market for loanable funds.

Now consider which way these curves shift. When net foreign investment increases, there is greater demand for loanable funds to finance these purchases. Thus, as panel (a) of Figure 32.8 shows, the demand curve for loanable funds shifts to the right from D_1 to D_2. In addition, because net foreign investment is higher for any interest rate, the net-foreign-investment curve also shifts to the right from NFI_1 to NFI_2, as in panel (b).

To see the effects of capital flight on the economy, we compare the old and new equilibria. Panel (a) of Figure 32.8 shows that the increased demand for loanable funds causes the interest rate in Indonesia to rise from r_1 to r_2. Panel (b) shows that Indonesian net foreign investment increases. (Although the rise in the interest rate does make Indonesian assets more attractive, this only partly offsets the impact of capital flight on net foreign investment.) Panel (c) shows that the increase in net foreign investment raises the supply of rupiah in the market for foreign-currency exchange from S_1 to S_2. That is, as people try to get out of Indonesian assets, there is a large supply of rupiah to be converted into dollars. This increase in supply causes the rupiah to depreciate from E_1 to E_2. Thus, *capital flight from Indonesia increases Indonesian interest rates and decreases the value of the Indonesian rupiah in the market for foreign-currency exchange.* This is exactly what was observed in 1998. From January to May, the interest rate on short-term Indonesian government bonds rose from

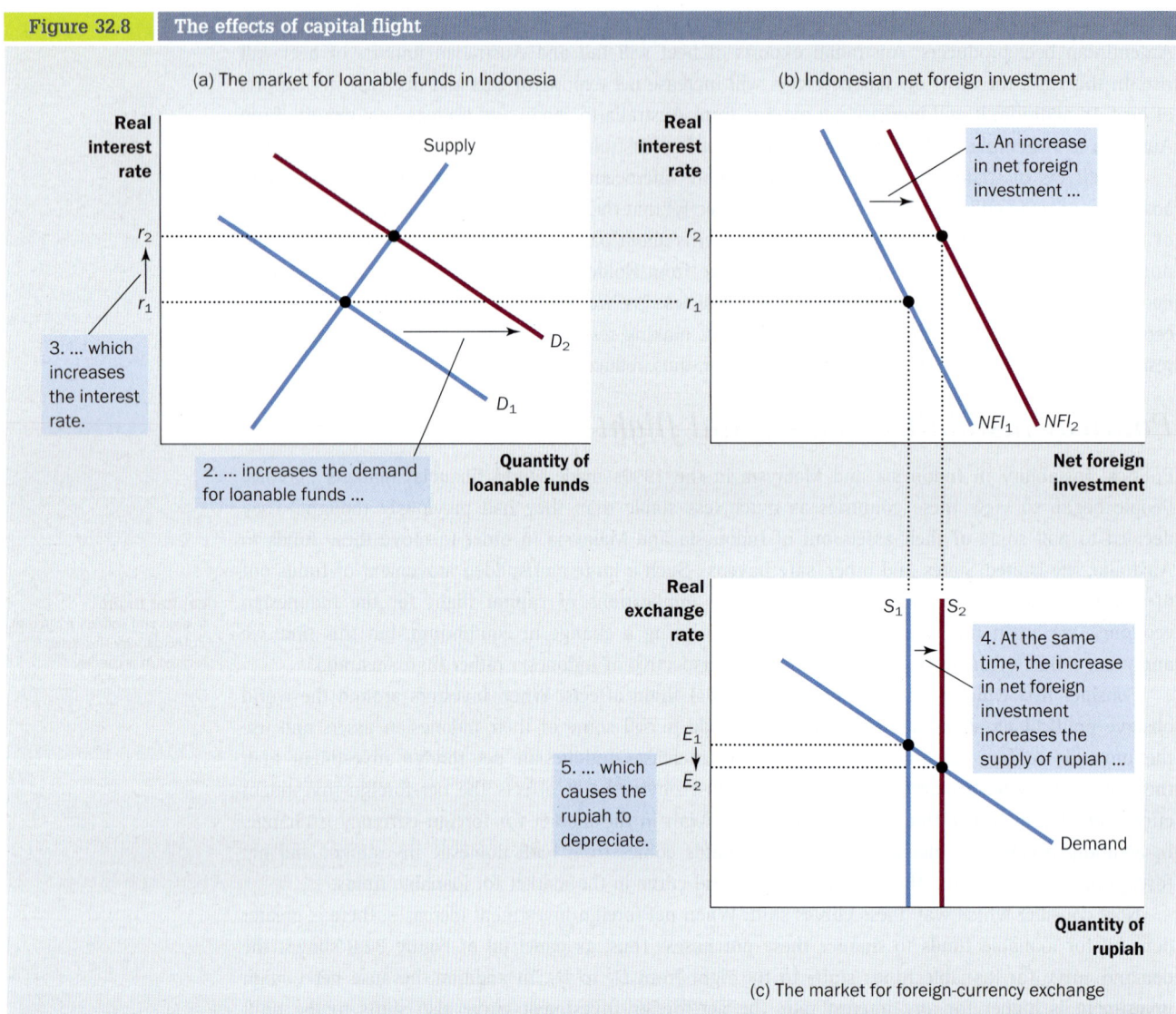

Figure 32.8   The effects of capital flight

(a) The market for loanable funds in Indonesia

Real interest rate

Supply

r_2

r_1

D_2

D_1

3. ... which increases the interest rate.

2. ... increases the demand for loanable funds ...

Quantity of loanable funds

(b) Indonesian net foreign investment

Real interest rate

1. An increase in net foreign investment ...

r_2

r_1

NFI_1 NFI_2

Net foreign investment

Real exchange rate

S_1 S_2

4. At the same time, the increase in net foreign investment increases the supply of rupiah ...

E_1

E_2

5. ... which causes the rupiah to depreciate.

Demand

Quantity of rupiah

(c) The market for foreign-currency exchange

If people in Indonesia decide that Indonesia is a risky place to keep their savings, they will move their capital to safer havens such as Australia, resulting in an increase in Indonesian net foreign investment. Consequently, the demand for loanable funds in Indonesia rises from D_1 to D_2, as shown in panel (a), and this drives up the Indonesian real interest rate from r_1 to r_2. Because net foreign investment is higher for any interest rate, that curve also shifts to the right from NFI_1 to NFI_2 in panel (b). At the same time, in the market for foreign-currency exchange, the supply of rupiah rises from S_1 to S_2 as shown in panel (c). This increase in the supply of rupiah causes the rupiah to depreciate from E_1 to E_2, so the rupiah becomes less valuable compared to other currencies.

19 per cent to 44 per cent, and the rupiah depreciated in value from 5300 to 9000 rupiah per Australian dollar from January to July.

Although capital flight has its largest impact on the country from which capital is fleeing, it also affects other countries. When capital flows out of Indonesia into Australia, for instance, it has the opposite effect on the Australian economy as it has on the Indonesian economy. In particular, the rise in Indonesian net foreign investment coincides with a fall in Australian net foreign investment. As the rupiah depreciates in value and Indonesian interest rates rise, the dollar appreciates in value and Australian interest rates fall. The size of this impact on the Australian economy is small, however, because flows of capital into Australia are relatively limited.

Could the events that occurred in Indonesia ever happen in Australia? Although the Australian economy has long been viewed as a safe economy in which to invest, political developments in Australia have at times induced small amounts of capital flight. For example, when Paul Keating made his now infamous 'banana republic' statement in 1986, the effect of the announcement was, in a small way, similar to that experienced by Indonesia in 1998. Over the course of a single day, the exchange rate fell more than US 5 cents, the largest devaluation in a 24-hour period. Thus, even the stable Australian economy is potentially susceptible to the effects of capital flight.

Suppose that Australians decided to spend a smaller fraction of their incomes. What would be the effect on saving, investment, interest rates, the real exchange rate and the trade balance?

Conclusion

International economics is a topic of growing importance. Australian citizens have always bought goods produced abroad and produced goods to be sold overseas. Through managed funds and other financial institutions, they borrow and lend in world financial markets. As a result, a full analysis of the Australian economy requires an understanding of how the Australian economy interacts with other economies in the world. This chapter has provided a basic model for thinking about the macroeconomics of open economies.

Although the study of international economics is valuable, we should be careful not to exaggerate its importance. Policymakers and commentators are often quick to blame foreigners for problems facing the Australian economy. In contrast, economists more often view these problems as home-grown. For example, politicians often discuss foreign competition as a threat to Australian living standards. Economists are more likely to lament the low level of national saving. Low saving impedes growth in capital, productivity and living standards, regardless of whether the economy is open or closed. Foreigners are a convenient target for politicians because blaming foreigners provides a way to avoid responsibility without insulting any domestic constituency. Whenever you hear popular discussions of international trade and finance, therefore, it is especially important to try to separate myth from reality. The tools you have learned in the past two chapters should help in that endeavour.

IN THE NEWS . . .

THE RISE OF ASIA

There is a saying that gained prominence during the Global Financial Crisis (which perhaps wasn't so global, after all): 'Each of us wakes in the morning and faces a choice: either we can look west and see darkness, or we can turn to the east and see the sun rise'. This is a metaphor for what is happening to the balance of global economic power. As Western economies (mainly European and the US) struggle to overcome the financial crisis, economies in Asia are growing very nicely. But as the following article from *The Economist* cautions, the exchange rate that is used has a big impact on just how much we think Asia is at the centre of the economic universe.

East or famine: The balance of economic power

Asia's economic weight in the world has risen, but by less than commonly assumed

The idea that the world's economic centre of gravity is moving eastward is not new. But the global financial crisis, many argue, has given the shift in economic power from America and western Europe to Asia a big shove. Emerging Asia rebounded from recession much faster than the developed world; its banking systems and debt dynamics … are much healthier. In 2009 China overtook Germany to become the world's biggest exporter. On one measure it now looks likely to become the world's biggest economy within ten years. But just how far has power really tilted towards Asia?

The region has certainly become more important to bankers and businessmen, accounting for a record share of many companies' profits last year. Several senior executives have relocated to Asia, the latest being HSBC's chief executive, Michael Geoghegan, who officially moved from London to Hong Kong on February 1st. Since 1995 Asia's real GDP (even including less sprightly Japan) has grown more than twice as fast as that of America or western Europe. Morgan Stanley forecasts that it will grow by an average of 7% this year and next, compared with 3% for America and 1.2% for western Europe.

Yet a closer look at the figures suggests that the shift in economic power from West to East can be exaggerated. Thanks partly to falling currencies, Asia's total share of world GDP (in nominal terms at market exchange rates) has actually slipped, from 29% in 1995 to 27% last year. In 2009 Asia's total GDP exceeded America's but was still slightly smaller than western Europe's (although it could overtake the latter this year). To put it another way, the output of the rich West is still almost twice as big as that of the East.

As for the popular belief that Asian producers are grabbing an ever-larger slice of exports, the region's 31% share of world exports last year was not much higher than in 1995 (28%) and remains smaller than western Europe's. Indeed, the shift towards Asia appears to have slowed, not quickened. Its share of world output and exports surged during the 1980s and early 1990s. Although China's share has grown since then, this has been largely offset by the decline in Japan, whose share of output and exports has halved.

What about Asia's financial muscle? Asian stockmarkets account for 34% of global market capitalisation, ahead of both America (33%) and Europe (27%). Asian central banks also hold two-thirds of all foreign-exchange reserves. That sounds impressive, but their influence over global financial markets is more modest, because official reserves account for only around 5% of the world's total stash of financial assets. The bulk of private sector wealth still lies in the West. The fact that Asian currencies make up only 3% of total foreign exchange reserves indicates how far Asia still lags in financial matters.

The 'rise of Asia' is no myth, however. GDP figures converted at market exchange rates understate Asia's real expansion. Many currencies tumbled during the Asian financial crisis in the late 1990s, slashing the dollar value of their economies. Japan's nominal GDP has been squeezed by deflation. More importantly, prices of many domestic products, from housing to haircuts, are always cheaper in low-income countries, implying that households' real spending power is bigger.

If GDP is instead measured at purchasing-power parity (PPP) to take account of these lower prices, Asia's share of the world economy has risen more steadily, from 18% in 1980 to 27% in 1995 and 34% in 2009. By this gauge, Asia's economy will probably exceed the combined sum of America's and Europe's within four years. In PPP terms, three of the world's four biggest economies (China, Japan and India) are already in Asia, and Asia has accounted for half of the world's GDP growth over the past decade.

Some economists claim that PPP measures exaggerate Asia's economic clout. What really matters to Western firms is consumer spending in plain dollar terms. Although over three-fifths of the world's population live in Asia, they only account for just over one-fifth of global private consumption, much less than America's 30% share. But official figures almost certainly understate consumer spending in emerging Asia, because of the poor statistical coverage of spending on services. Figures from the Economist Intelligence Unit, a sister company of *The Economist*, suggest that Asia accounts for around one-third of world retail sales. Asia is now the biggest market for many products, accounting for 35% of all car sales last year and 43% of mobile phones. Asia guzzles 35% of the world's energy, up from 26% in 1995. It has accounted for two thirds of the increase in world energy demand since 2000.

Many Western firms are more interested in Asia's capital spending than its consumption, and here Asia is undoubtedly the giant. In 2009, 40% of global investment (at market exchange rates) took place in Asia, as much as in America and Europe combined. In finance, Asian firms launched eight of the ten biggest initial public offerings (IPOs) in 2009 and more than twice as much capital was raised through IPOs in China and Hong Kong last year as in America.

Winston Churchill once said: 'The longer you can look back, the farther you can look forward.' The new economic order is in fact a resurgence of a very old one. Asia accounted for over half of world output for 18 of the past 20 centuries. And its importance will only increase in the coming years. Rich countries' growth rates are likely to be squeezed over the next decade as huge household debts dampen spending, and soaring government debt and higher taxes blunt incentives to work and invest. In contrast, growth in emerging Asia (almost four-fifths of the region's total output) is likely to remain strong. Robust growth should also give governments in emerging Asian economies the confidence to let their currencies rise, which would further boost the relative size of their economies in dollar terms.

By 2020 Asia could well produce half of some big Western multinationals' sales and profits, up from a typical proportion of 20–25% today. Asian staff eagerly await the day when they can fix the times for international conference calls, so Europeans and Americans have to put up with after-midnight discussions with the Beijing office. That may be the best test of whether economic power has really shifted east.

Source: *The Economist*, 27 February 2010.
© The Economist Newspaper Limited, London 2010.

Summary

- To analyse the macroeconomics of open economies, two markets are central – the market for loanable funds and the market for foreign-currency exchange. In the market for loanable funds, the interest rate adjusts to balance the supply of loanable funds (from national saving) and the demand for loanable funds (from domestic investment and net foreign investment). In the market for foreign-currency exchange, the real exchange rate adjusts to balance the supply of dollars (for net foreign investment) and the demand for dollars (for net exports). Because net foreign investment is part of the demand for loanable funds and provides the supply of dollars for foreign-currency exchange, it is the variable that connects these two markets.

- A policy that reduces national saving, such as a government budget deficit, reduces the supply of loanable funds and drives up the interest rate. The higher interest rate reduces net foreign investment, which reduces the supply of dollars in the market for foreign-currency exchange. The dollar appreciates, and net exports fall.

- Although restrictive trade policies, such as a tariff or quota on imports, are sometimes advocated as a way to alter the trade balance, they do not necessarily have that effect. A trade restriction increases net exports for a given exchange rate and, therefore, increases the demand for dollars in the market for foreign-currency exchange. As a result, the dollar appreciates in value, making domestic goods more expensive relative to foreign goods. This appreciation offsets the initial impact of the trade restriction on net exports.

- When investors change their attitudes about holding assets of a country, the ramifications for the country's economy can be profound. In particular, political instability can lead to capital flight, which tends to increase interest rates and cause a country's currency to depreciate.

Key concepts

capital flight   trade policy

Questions for review

1   Describe supply and demand in the market for loanable funds and the market for foreign-currency exchange. How are these markets linked?
2   How does a government budget surplus affect the trade balance?
3   Suppose that Japan decided to ban imports of lobsters from Australia (and that Australia's current exports of lobster to Japan are significant). What would this policy do to the trade balance and the real exchange rate? What is the impact on the lobster industry in Australia?
4   Suppose that Parliament removes all restrictions on foreign direct investment in Australia. How does this policy affect saving, domestic investment, net foreign investment, the interest rate, the exchange rate and the trade balance?

Problems and applications

1   Japan generally runs a significant trade surplus. Do you think this is most related to high foreign demand for Japanese goods, low Japanese demand for foreign goods, a high Japanese saving rate relative to Japanese investment, or structural barriers against imports into Japan? Explain your answer.

2   During the GFC, income of some of Australia's trading partners declined significantly. How did that affect the Australian net exports curve? How would this affect the value of the dollar in the market for foreign-currency exchange?

3   The Australian government has run a budget surplus in recent years. At the same time, the value of the Australian dollar has risen significantly from its low of US$0.49 per A$ in September 2001.
    a   Are these two things related? If so, how?
    b   The Australian government budget returned to deficit due to the stimulus package. And yet, the Aussie dollar reached parity with the US dollar. How would you explain these two facts?

4   Several successive governments in Australia have said they were implementing polices to encourage saving. What would be the effect of increased saving on the value of the dollar?

5   The Australian trade deficit during the 1980s was due largely to the rise in the Australian budget deficit. On the other hand, the popular press sometimes claims that the increased trade deficit resulted from a decline in the quality of Australian products relative to foreign products.
    a   Assume that Australian products did decline in relative quality during the 1980s. How did this affect net exports *at any given exchange rate*?
    b   Use a three-panel diagram to show the effect of this shift in net exports on the Australian real exchange rate and trade balance.
    c   Is the claim in the popular press consistent with the model in this chapter? Does a decline in the quality of Australian products have any effect on our standard of living? (*Hint:* When we sell our goods to foreigners, what do we receive in return?)

6   Economists have argued that removing trade restrictions benefits Australian industries that produce goods for *export*. They say that export industries would find it easier to sell their goods abroad – even if other countries didn't follow our example and reduce their trade barriers. Explain in words why Australian *export* industries would benefit from a reduction in restrictions on *imports* to Australia.

7   Suppose the Americans suddenly develop a strong dislike for Australian wines. Answer the following questions in words and using a diagram.
    a   What happens to the demand for dollars in the market for foreign-currency exchange?
    b   What happens to the value of dollars in the market for foreign-currency exchange?
    c   What happens to the quantity of net exports?

8   Australia has been a strong supporter of world reductions in protectionism. Some people in industry have argued, however, that we should subsidise innovation, particularly for industries that are likely to export. Using a three-panel diagram, show the effect of an innovation investment tax on net exports and the real exchange rate. Do you agree with this strategy?

9   Suppose that real interest rates increase in Australia relative to the rest of the world. Explain how this will affect Australian net foreign investment. Then explain how this change will affect Australian net exports by using a formula from the chapter and by using a diagram. What will happen to the Australian real exchange rate?

10   Suppose that Australians decide to increase their saving.
    a   If the elasticity of Australian net foreign investment with respect to the real interest rate is very high, will this decrease in private saving have a large or small effect on Australian domestic investment?
    b   If the elasticity of Australian exports with respect to the real exchange rate is very low, will this decrease in private saving have a large or small effect on the Australian real exchange rate?

11   Suppose that Europeans suddenly become more interested in investing in New Zealand.
    a   What happens to New Zealand net foreign investment?

    b   What effect does this have on New Zealand private saving and New Zealand domestic investment?

    c   What is the long-run effect on New Zealand capital stock?

12 Over the past decade, an increasing number of Chinese have decided to invest in Australia. That is, Australian net foreign investment in China is negative.

    a   If the Chinese decided they wanted to buy more Australian assets, what would happen in the Australian market for loanable funds? In particular, what would happen to Australian interest rates, Australian saving and Australian investment?

    b   What would happen in the market for foreign-currency exchange? In particular, what would happen to the value of the dollar and the Australian balance of trade?

13 (This problem is challenging.) Most models of open economies show that a decline in national saving leads to a decline in net foreign investment and thus in net exports. This is often referred to as the twin deficits problem – a government budget deficit and a trade deficit. (For much of the last decade, the United States has experienced the twin deficits, with both a trade deficit and a government budget deficit.) At the same time, economists have found that national saving has equalled domestic investment over long time periods in virtually every country.

    a   In what way does this fact seem to contradict the models?

    b   Suppose that investors are unwilling to accumulate too many assets from a single foreign country. How does this behaviour help to reconcile the fact and the models?

    c   If investors are unwilling to accumulate too many assets from the US, what would happen to the US trade deficit over time even if the US budget deficit remained large?

Search me!

When accessing information about economics use the following keywords in any combinations you require:

- foreign currency exchange
- loanable funds

CourseMate

For more multimedia resources and activities on economics, visit the Economics CourseMate website.

PART TWELVE
Short-run economic fluctuations

33

Aggregate demand and aggregate supply

Learning objectives

In this chapter you will:

- learn three key facts about short-run economic fluctuations

- consider how the economy in the short run differs from the economy in the long run

- develop a short-run theory called the model of aggregate demand and aggregate supply

- see how shifts in either aggregate demand or aggregate supply can cause recessions.

Economic activity fluctuates from year to year. In most years, the production of goods and services rises. Because of increases in the labour force, increases in the capital stock and advances in technological knowledge, the economy can produce more and more over time. This growth allows everyone to enjoy a higher standard of living. On average over the past 50 years, the production of the Australian economy as measured by real GDP has grown by about 2 per cent per year.

In some years, however, this normal growth does not occur. Firms find themselves unable to sell all of the goods and services they have to offer, so they cut back on production. Workers are laid off, unemployment rises and factories are left idle. With the economy producing fewer goods and services, real GDP and other measures of income fall. Such a period of falling incomes and rising unemployment is called a **recession** if it is relatively mild and a **depression** if it is more severe.

What causes short-run fluctuations in economic activity? What, if anything, can public policy do to prevent periods of falling incomes and rising unemployment? When recessions and depressions do occur, how can policymakers reduce their length and severity? These are the questions that we take up in this and the next two chapters.

The variables that we study in the coming chapters are largely those we have already seen. They include GDP, unemployment, exchange rates and the rate of inflation. Also familiar are the policy instruments of government spending and taxes and interest rates. What differs in the next few chapters is the time horizon of our analysis. Our focus in the previous seven chapters has been on the behaviour of the economy in the long run. Our focus now is on the economy's short-run fluctuations around its long-run trend.

Although there remains some debate among economists about how to analyse short-run fluctuations, most economists use the model of *aggregate demand and aggregate supply*. Learning how to use this model for analysing the short-run effects of various events and policies is the main task ahead. This chapter introduces the model's two key pieces – the aggregate-demand curve and the aggregate-supply curve. After getting a sense of the overall structure of the model in this chapter, we examine the pieces of the model in more detail in the next two chapters.

recession
a period of declining real incomes and rising unemployment

depression
a severe recession

Three key facts about economic fluctuations

Short-run fluctuations in economic activity occur in all countries. As a starting point for understanding these year-to-year fluctuations, let's discuss some of their most important properties.

Fact 1: Economic fluctuations are irregular and unpredictable

Fluctuations in the economy are often called the *business cycle*. As this term suggests, economic fluctuations correspond to changes in business conditions. When real GDP grows rapidly, business is good. Firms find that customers are plentiful and that profits are growing. On the other hand, when real GDP falls, businesses have trouble. In recessions, most firms experience declining sales and profits.

The term *business cycle* is somewhat misleading, however, because it seems to suggest that economic fluctuations follow a regular, predictable pattern. In fact, economic fluctuations are not at all regular and they are almost impossible to predict with any accuracy. Panel (a) of Figure 33.1 shows the real GDP of the Australian economy since 1970. The shaded areas represent times of recession.

As the figure shows, recessions do not come at regular intervals. Sometimes recessions are close together, such as the recessions of 1974 and sometimes the economy goes many years without a recession. At the end of 2010, by most measures, Australia had not had a recession for over 19 years.

Figure 33.1 A look at short-run economic fluctuations

This figure shows real GDP in panel (a), investment spending in panel (b) and unemployment in panel (c) for the Australian economy using quarterly data since 1970. Recessions are shown as the shaded areas. Notice that real GDP declines during recessions, while unemployment rises. Investment spending usually declines, as can be seen in the recessions of 1982–83 and 1991.

Source: ABS, Cat. No. 5206.

Fact 2: Most macroeconomic quantities fluctuate together

Real GDP is the variable that is most commonly used to monitor short-run changes in the economy because it is the most comprehensive measure of economic activity. Real GDP measures the value in constant prices of all final goods and services produced within a given period of time. It also measures the total income (adjusted for inflation) of everyone in the economy.

It turns out, however, that for monitoring short-run fluctuations, it does not really matter which measure of economic activity one looks at. Most macroeconomic variables that measure some type of income, spending or production fluctuate closely together. When real GDP falls in a recession, so do personal income, corporate profits, consumer spending, investment spending, industrial production, retail sales, home sales, car sales and so on. Because recessions are economy-wide phenomena, they show up in many different types of macroeconomic data.

Although many macroeconomic variables fluctuate together, they fluctuate by different amounts. In particular, as panel (b) of Figure 33.1 shows, investment spending varies greatly over the business cycle. Even though investment averages about one-quarter of GDP, declines in investment account for about two-thirds of the declines in GDP during recessions. In other words, when economic conditions deteriorate, much of the decline is attributable to reductions in spending on new factories, housing and inventories.

Fact 3: As output falls, unemployment rises

Changes in the economy's output of goods and services are strongly correlated with changes in the economy's utilisation of its labour force. In other words, when real GDP declines, the rate of unemployment rises. This fact is hardly surprising – when firms choose to produce a smaller quantity of goods and services, they lay off workers, expanding the pool of unemployed.

Panel (c) of Figure 33.1 shows the unemployment rate in the Australian economy since 1970. Once again, recessions are shown as the shaded areas in the figure. The figure shows clearly the impact of recessions on unemployment. In each of the recessions, the unemployment rate rises substantially. When the recession ends and real GDP starts to expand, the unemployment rate gradually declines. The unemployment rate never approaches zero; instead, it fluctuates around its natural rate. The natural rate in Australia has risen over time and is now about 5 per cent.

Source: DILBERT © 2008 Scott Adams. Used by permission of UNIVERSAL UCLICK. All rights reserved.

fyi

Okun's law

When the real GDP of the economy fluctuates, how much does unemployment typically change? Economists answer this question with Okun's law. This law can be described with the following equation:

$$\text{Change in unemployment rate} = -\frac{1}{2} \times \left(\begin{array}{l} \text{Percentage change} \\ \text{in real GDP} - 3 \text{ per cent} \end{array} \right)$$

According to this equation, when real GDP grows at its average rate of 3 per cent, the unemployment rate remains unchanged. When the economy expands more rapidly than 3 per cent, the unemployment rate falls by about half as much. For example, if real GDP grows by 5 per cent from one year to the next (2 per cent higher than normal), Okun's law predicts a fall in the unemployment rate of one percentage point. When real GDP falls, or rises by less than 3 per cent, the unemployment rate rises. For example, if real GDP falls by 1 per cent from one year to the next, as it might during a recession, Okun's law predicts a rise in unemployment of two percentage points.

Okun's law is named for economist Arthur Okun, who first studied the link between fluctuations in real GDP and fluctuations in unemployment for the US economy. Okun did not claim his law to be a fundamental truth of economic theory. The law is, instead, a simple description of US data on real GDP and unemployment. When economists look at data from other countries, they find that the numbers in the formula for Okun's law differ somewhat. Nonetheless, in all countries, there is a strong correlation between changes in GDP and changes in unemployment.

As we study economic fluctuations in the next few chapters, we should keep Okun's law in mind. This law reminds us that the business cycle concerns related movements in the quantity of goods and services that the economy is producing (as measured by real GDP) and the number of people who cannot find jobs (as measured by the unemployment rate).

List and discuss three key facts about economic fluctuations.

CASE**STUDY**

No recession in Australia during the GFC?

Did Australia have a recession during the GFC? Most economists have said no, but some commentators in the media have pointed to measures other than real GDP and concluded that Australia did experience recessionary conditions during 2008–09. For example, unemployment rose steadily from 5 per cent in January 2008 to a high of 5.8 per cent in September 2009. The value of housing starts went down by over 6 per cent between September 2008 and September 2009. Alterations to existing buildings went down by over 10 per cent during the same period. By these measures, Australia may indeed have experienced a recession during 2008–09. (But whatever measure you use, the GFC appears to have had less of an impact on Australia than on the US and European economies.)

While we have used a fairly standard definition of recession as two quarters of negative growth, not all economists agree that this is an adequate definition of recession. All would agree that a recession is a downturn in economic activity. What this means is a matter of debate. At the National Bureau of Economic Research (the NBER) in the US, a committee to assess economic cycles has been established. They examine several factors to determine whether the US economy is in recession or not. For example, they look at real GDP on both the expenditure and income side, economy-wide employment, real income, measures of industrial production as well as other factors.

Their definition of a business cycle is instructive:

The NBER's Business Cycle Dating Committee maintains a chronology of the U.S. business cycle. The chronology comprises alternating dates of peaks and troughs in economic activity. A recession is a period between a peak and a trough, and an expansion is a period between a trough and a peak. During a recession, a significant decline in economic activity spreads across the economy and can last from a few months to more than a year. Similarly, during an expansion, economic activity rises substantially, spreads across the economy, and usually lasts for several years. (http://www.nber.org/cycles/general_state ent.html)

In Australia, the Reserve Bank looks at a number of variables to determine the state of economic activity. For example, in the November 2010 statement on monetary policy, these variables included: the level of construction, both residential and non-residential; the level of commodity prices; consumer confidence as measured by surveys and the level of consumer debt; the housing market; the labour market and wages growth; and the appreciation of the Australian dollar. While all of these factors might be said to be reflected in the level of real GDP, looking at these factors individually gives a better understanding of what is driving economic conditions and what the near-term future holds for the economy.

Explaining short-run economic fluctuations

Describing the regular patterns that economies experience as they fluctuate over time is easy. Explaining what causes these fluctuations is more difficult. Indeed, compared with the topics we have studied in previous chapters, the theory of economic fluctuations remains controversial. In this and the next two chapters, we develop the model that most economists use to explain short-run fluctuations in economic activity.

How the short run differs from the long run

In previous chapters, we developed theories to explain what determines most important macroeconomic variables. Chapter 26 explained the level and growth of productivity and real GDP.

Chapter 27 explained how the real interest rate adjusts to balance saving and investment. Chapter 28 explained the various causes of unemployment. Chapters 29 and 30 explained the monetary system and how the interest rate, the inflation rate and the level of economic activity are related. Chapters 31 and 32 extended this analysis to open economies in order to explain the trade balance and the exchange rate.

All of this previous analysis was based on two related ideas – the classical dichotomy and monetary neutrality. Recall that the classical dichotomy is the separation of variables into real variables (those that measure quantities or relative prices) and nominal variables (those measured in terms of money). According to classical macroeconomic theory, changes in the money supply (or the nominal interest rate) affect nominal variables but not real variables in the long run. As a result of this monetary neutrality, chapters 26, 27 and 28 were able to examine the determinants of real variables (real GDP, the real interest rate and unemployment) without introducing nominal variables (the money supply and the inflation rate).

Do these assumptions of classical macroeconomic theory apply to the world in which we live? The answer to this question is of central importance to understanding how the economy works – *most economists believe that classical theory describes the world in the long run but not in the short run.* Beyond a period of several years, changes in the nominal interest rate affect the overall level of prices and other nominal variables but do not affect real GDP, unemployment or other real variables. When studying year-to-year changes in the economy, however, the assumption of monetary neutrality is no longer appropriate. Most economists believe that, in the short run, real and nominal variables are highly interrelated.

To understand the economy in the short run, therefore, we need a new model. To build this new model, we rely on many of the tools we have developed in previous chapters, but we have to abandon the classical dichotomy and the neutrality of money.

The basic model of economic fluctuations

Our model of short-run economic fluctuations focuses on two variables. The first variable is the economy's output of goods and services, as measured by real GDP. The second variable is the inflation rate, as measured by the CPI or the GDP deflator. Notice that output is a real variable, whereas the inflation rate is a nominal variable. Hence, by focusing on the relationship between these two variables, we are highlighting the breakdown of the classical dichotomy.

Just as we analyse an individual market with a market demand curve and a market supply curve, we analyse fluctuations in the economy as a whole with the **model of aggregate demand and aggregate supply**. This model is illustrated in Figure 33.2. On the vertical axis is the overall inflation rate in the economy. On the horizontal axis is the overall quantity of goods and services. The **aggregate-demand curve** shows the quantity of goods and services that households, firms and the government want to buy at any inflation rate. The **aggregate-supply curve** shows the quantity of goods and services that firms produce and sell at any inflation rate. According to this model, the inflation rate and the quantity of output adjust to bring aggregate demand and aggregate supply into balance.

It may be tempting to view the model of aggregate demand and aggregate supply as nothing more than a large version of the model of market demand and market supply, which we introduced in chapter 4. Yet, in fact, this model is quite different. When we consider demand and supply in a particular market – ice-cream, for instance – the behaviour of buyers and sellers depends on the

model of aggregate demand and aggregate supply
the model that most economists use to explain short-run fluctuations in economic activity around its long-run trend

aggregate-demand curve
a curve that shows the quantity of goods and services that households, firms and the government want to buy at any inflation rate

aggregate-supply curve
a curve that shows the quantity of goods and services that firms choose to produce and sell at any inflation rate

▶ aggregate demand
▶ aggregate supply

Figure 33.2   Aggregate demand and aggregate supply

Inflation rate

Aggregate supply

Equilibrium inflation rate

Aggregate demand

0   Equilibrium output   **Quantity of output**

Economists use the model of aggregate demand and aggregate supply to analyse economic fluctuations. On the vertical axis is the inflation rate. On the horizontal axis is the economy's total output of goods and services. Output and the inflation rate adjust to the point at which the aggregate-supply and aggregate-demand curves intersect.

ability of resources to move from one market to another. When the price of ice-cream rises, the quantity demanded falls because buyers will use their incomes to buy products other than ice-cream. Similarly, a higher price of ice-cream raises the quantity supplied because firms that produce ice-cream can increase production by hiring workers away from other parts of the economy. This *microeconomic* substitution from one market to another is impossible when we are analysing the economy as a whole. After all, the quantity that our model is trying to explain – real GDP – includes the quantities produced in all of the economy's markets. To understand why the aggregate-demand curve is downward-sloping and why the aggregate-supply curve is upward-sloping, we need a *macroeconomic* theory. Developing such a theory is our next task.

How does the economy's behaviour in the short run differ from its behaviour in the long run? ▪ Draw the model of aggregate demand and aggregate supply. What variables are on the two axes?

The aggregate-demand curve

The aggregate-demand curve tells us the quantity of all goods and services demanded in the economy at any given inflation rate. As Figure 33.3 illustrates, the aggregate-demand curve is downward-sloping. This means that, other things being equal, a fall in the economy's overall inflation rate (from, say, π_1 to π_2) tends to raise the quantity of goods and services demanded (from Y_1 to Y_2).

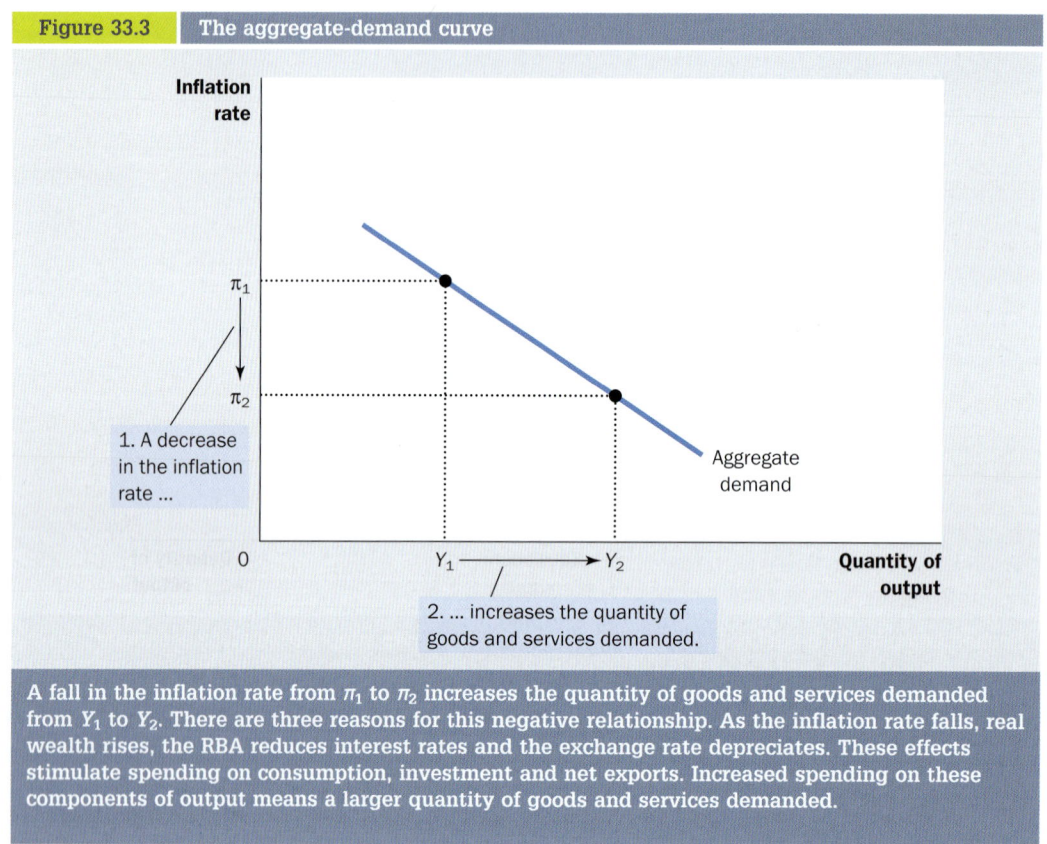

Figure 33.3 | The aggregate-demand curve

A fall in the inflation rate from π_1 to π_2 increases the quantity of goods and services demanded from Y_1 to Y_2. There are three reasons for this negative relationship. As the inflation rate falls, real wealth rises, the RBA reduces interest rates and the exchange rate depreciates. These effects stimulate spending on consumption, investment and net exports. Increased spending on these components of output means a larger quantity of goods and services demanded.

Why the aggregate-demand curve is downward-sloping

What lies behind this negative relationship between the inflation rate and the quantity of goods and services demanded? To answer this question, it is useful to recall that GDP (Y) is the sum of consumption (C), investment (I), government purchases (G) and net exports (NX):

$$Y = C + I + G + NX$$

Each of these four components contributes to the aggregate demand for goods and services. Government spending is assumed to be a fixed policy variable, but the other three components of spending – consumption, investment and net exports – depend on economic conditions and, in particular, on the inflation rate. To understand the downward slope of the aggregate-demand curve, therefore, we must examine how the inflation rate affects the quantity of goods and services demanded for consumption, investment and net exports.

The interest-rate effect

As we discussed in chapter 29, the RBA has a strong policy objective of keeping inflation between 2 and 3 per cent. If inflation is higher than this, the RBA will increase interest rates. If inflation is lower than this, the RBA will lower interest rates. If the RBA lowers interest rates this, in turn, encourages borrowing by firms that want to invest in new plant and equipment and by households who want to invest in new housing. Thus, *a lower inflation rate induces the RBA to reduce the interest rate, which encourages greater spending on investment goods, and thereby increases the quantity of goods and services demanded.*

The wealth effect

Consider the money that you hold in your wallet and your bank account. The nominal value of this money is fixed, but its real value is not. When inflation falls, these dollars are more valuable because they can now be used to buy more goods and services. Thus, *a decrease in the inflation rate makes consumers feel more wealthy, which in turn encourages them to spend more. The increase in consumer spending means a larger quantity of goods and services demanded.* This wealth effect was emphasised by economist Arthur Pigou (1877–1959), and it is sometimes called the *Pigou effect*.

The exchange-rate effect

As we have just discussed, a lower inflation rate in Australia means the RBA lowers the cash rate, leading to lower interest rates in Australia in general. In response, some Australian investors will seek higher returns by investing abroad. For instance, as the interest rate on Australian government bonds falls, a managed fund might sell Australian government bonds in order to buy German government bonds. As the managed fund tries to move assets overseas, it increases the supply of dollars in the market for foreign-currency exchange. The increased supply of dollars causes the dollar to depreciate relative to other currencies. (That is, each dollar buys fewer units of foreign currencies.) As a result of this depreciation, foreign goods become more expensive relative to domestic goods and this change in relative prices increases Australian exports of goods and services and decreases Australian imports of goods and services. Net exports, which equal exports minus imports, increase. Thus, *when a fall in the Australian inflation rate causes Australian interest rates to fall, the real exchange rate depreciates, and this depreciation stimulates Australian net exports and thereby increases the quantity of goods and services demanded.* This exchange-rate effect was emphasised by economists Robert Mundell and Marcus Fleming.

Summary

There are, therefore, three distinct but related reasons that a fall in the inflation rate increases the quantity of goods and services demanded:

1   consumers feel wealthier, which stimulates the demand for consumption goods
2   the RBA reduces interest rates, which stimulates the demand for investment goods
3   the exchange rate depreciates, which stimulates the demand for net exports.

For all three reasons, the aggregate-demand curve slopes downwards.

Why the aggregate-demand curve might shift

The downward slope of the aggregate-demand curve shows that a fall in the inflation rate raises the overall quantity of goods and services demanded. Many other factors beyond the inflation rate, however, affect the quantity of goods and services demanded. When one of these other factors changes, the aggregate-demand curve shifts.

There are many possible examples of events that shift aggregate demand. Here are a few:

- Australians suddenly become more concerned about saving for retirement and, as a result, reduce their current consumption. Because the quantity of goods and services demanded at any inflation rate is lower, the aggregate-demand curve shifts to the left.
- The computer industry introduces a faster line of computers, and many firms decide to invest in new computer systems. Because the quantity of goods and services demanded at any inflation rate is higher, the aggregate-demand curve shifts to the right.
- The government decides that, with the increase in political instability in the region, it will increase purchases of new weapon systems. Because the quantity of goods and services demanded at any inflation rate is higher, the aggregate-demand curve shifts to the right.

The shifts in the aggregate-demand curve in the first two examples arise from changes in spending plans by consumers or firms. The shift in the last example arises from changes in fiscal policy. In fact, shifts in aggregate demand sometimes come from private behaviour and sometimes come from public policy.

In the next chapter, we examine the aggregate-demand curve in more detail. There we examine, in particular, how the tools of monetary and fiscal policy can shift aggregate demand. At this point, however, you should have some idea about why the aggregate-demand curve slopes downwards and what kinds of events and policies can shift this curve.

Explain the three reasons that the aggregate-demand curve slopes downwards. ▪ Give an example of an event that would shift the aggregate-demand curve. Which way would this event shift the curve?

The aggregate-supply curve

The aggregate-supply curve tells us the quantity of goods and services that firms produce and sell at any given inflation rate. The relationship between the inflation rate and the quantity supplied depends on the time horizon. In the long run, the aggregate-supply curve is vertical, whereas in the short run, the aggregate-supply curve is upward-sloping. To understand short-run economic fluctuations and how the short-run behaviour of the economy deviates from its long-run behaviour, we need to examine both the long-run aggregate-supply curve and the short-run aggregate-supply curve.

Why the aggregate-supply curve is vertical in the long run

What determines the quantity of goods and services supplied in the long run? We implicitly answered this question earlier in the book when we analysed the process of economic growth. *In the long run, an economy's supply of goods and services depends on its supplies of capital and labour and on the available production technology used to turn capital and labour into goods and services.* Because the inflation rate does not affect these long-run determinants of real GDP, the long-run aggregate-supply curve is vertical, as in Figure 33.4. In other words, the economy's capital, labour and technology determine the quantity of goods and services supplied, and the quantity supplied is the same regardless of what the inflation rate happens to be.

The vertical long-run aggregate-supply curve is, in essence, just an application of the classical dichotomy and monetary neutrality. As we have already discussed, classical macroeconomic theory is

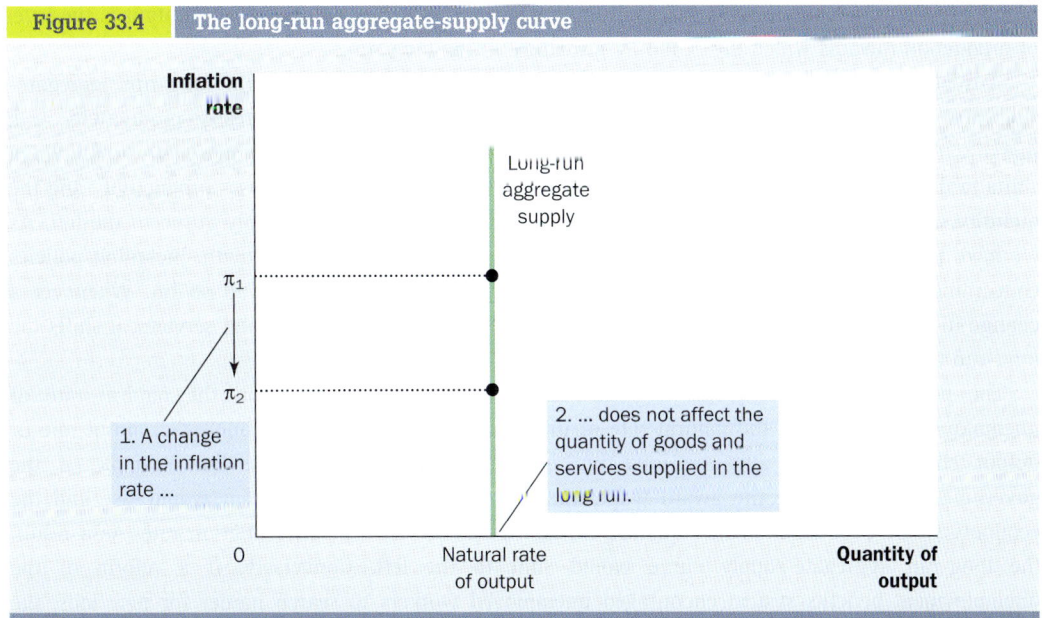

| Figure 33.4 | The long-run aggregate-supply curve |

In the long run, the quantity of output supplied depends on the economy's quantities of capital and labour and on the technology for turning these inputs into output. The quantity supplied does not depend on the overall inflation rate. As a result, the long-run aggregate-supply curve is vertical at the natural rate of output.

based on the assumption that real variables do not depend on nominal variables. The long-run aggregate-supply curve is consistent with this idea because it implies that the quantity of output (a real variable) does not depend on the level of prices (a nominal variable).

As noted earlier, most economists believe that this principle works well when studying the economy over a period of many years, but not when studying year-to-year changes. Thus, the aggregate-supply curve is vertical only in the long run.

One might wonder why supply curves for specific goods and services can be upward-sloping if the long-run aggregate-supply curve is vertical. The reason is that the supply of specific goods and services depends on *relative prices* – the prices of those goods and services compared with other prices in the economy. For example, when the price of ice-cream rises, suppliers of ice-cream increase their production, taking labour, milk, chocolate and other inputs away from the production of other goods, such as cakes. In contrast, the economy's overall production of goods and services is limited by its capital, labour and technology. Thus, when all prices in the economy rise together, there is no change in the overall quantity of goods and services supplied.

Why the long-run aggregate-supply curve might shift

The position of the long-run aggregate-supply curve shows the quantity of goods and services predicted by classical macroeconomic theory. This level of production is sometimes called *potential output* or *full-employment output* or *trend output*. These terms are somewhat misleading, however, because in the short run, output can either fall below or rise above this level. To be more accurate, we will call this level of output the *natural rate of output* because it shows what the economy produces when unemployment is at its natural, or normal, rate. The natural rate of output is the level of production towards which the economy gravitates in the long run.

Any change in the economy that alters the natural rate of output shifts the long-run aggregate-supply curve. An increase in the economy's capital stock, for instance, increases productivity and, thereby, the quantity of goods and services supplied. As a result, the long-run aggregate-supply curve shifts to the right. Conversely, a decrease in the economy's capital stock decreases productivity and the quantity of goods and services supplied, shifting the long-run aggregate-supply curve to the left. As we have previously discussed, many factors influence long-run economic growth, including policies concerning saving, investment, education, technology, international trade and so on. Whenever a change in one of these factors alters the economy's ability to produce goods and services, it shifts the long-run aggregate-supply curve.

The position of the long-run aggregate-supply curve also depends on the natural rate of unemployment. That is, if the natural rate of unemployment changes, the economy's natural rate of output changes as well and the long-run aggregate-supply curve shifts. For example, if the government were to raise the award wage, the natural rate of unemployment would rise and the economy would produce a smaller quantity of goods and services for any inflation rate. As a result, the long-run aggregate-supply curve would shift to the left. Conversely, if a reform of the unemployment benefits system encouraged unemployed workers to search harder for new jobs, the natural rate of unemployment would fall and the long-run aggregate-supply curve would shift to the right.

In sum, the long-run aggregate-supply curve merely provides a new way of describing the classical model of the economy we developed in previous chapters. As discussed in previous chapters, any policy or event that raised real GDP can now be viewed as increasing the quantity of goods and services supplied and shifting the long-run aggregate-supply curve to the right. Similarly, any policy or event that lowered real GDP can now be viewed as decreasing the quantity of goods and services supplied and shifting the long-run aggregate-supply curve to the left.

Why the aggregate-supply curve is upward-sloping in the short run

Although the model of aggregate demand and aggregate supply can be used to describe the economy in the long run, the model is designed to analyse short-run deviations from this long-run equilibrium. The key difference between the short run and the long run is the behaviour of aggregate supply. In the short run, the aggregate-supply curve is upward-sloping, as in Figure 33.5. That is, over a period of a year or two, an increase in the overall level of prices in the economy tends to raise the quantity of goods and services supplied, and a decrease in the level of prices tends to reduce the quantity of goods and services supplied.

What causes this positive relationship between the inflation rate and output? Macroeconomists have proposed three theories for the upward slope of the short-run aggregate-supply curve. In each theory, a specific market imperfection causes the supply side of the economy to behave differently in the short run than in the long run. Although each of the following theories differs in detail, they share a common theme – the quantity of output supplied deviates from its long-run, or 'natural', level when the inflation rate deviates from the inflation rate that people expected. When the inflation rate rises above the expected level, output rises above its natural rate, and when the inflation rate falls below the expected level, output falls below its natural rate.

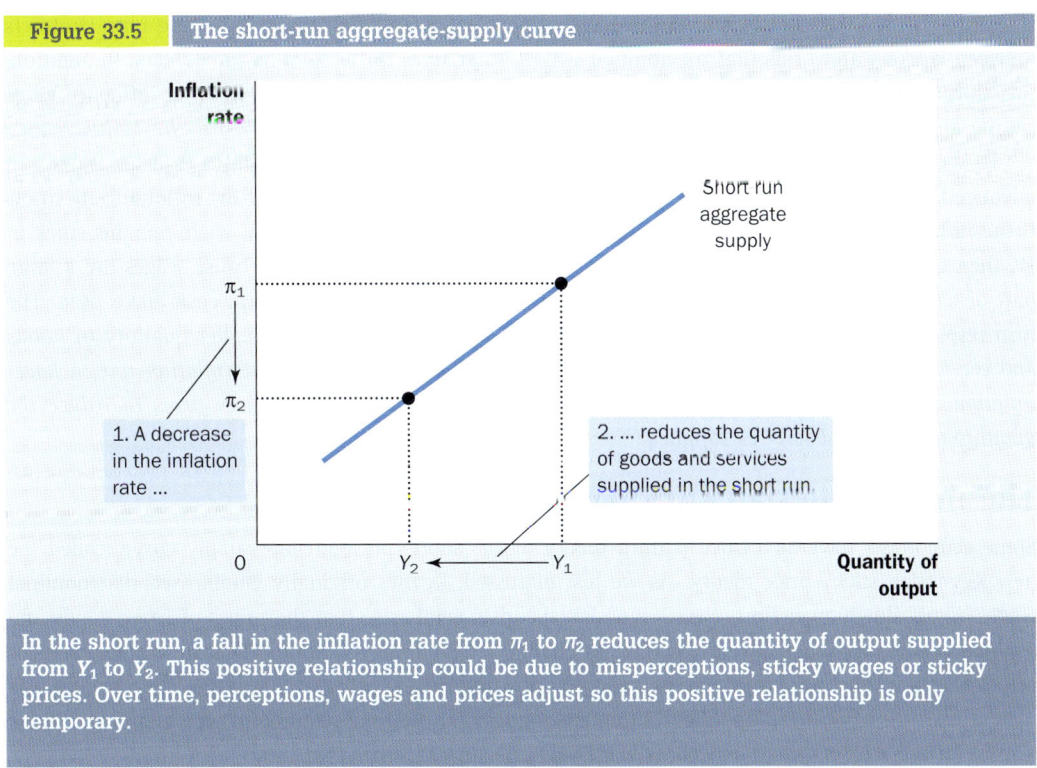

Figure 33.5   The short-run aggregate-supply curve

In the short run, a fall in the inflation rate from π_1 to π_2 reduces the quantity of output supplied from Y_1 to Y_2. This positive relationship could be due to misperceptions, sticky wages or sticky prices. Over time, perceptions, wages and prices adjust so this positive relationship is only temporary.

The new classical misperceptions theory

One theory of the short-run aggregate-supply curve, which is based on the work of economists Milton Friedman and Robert Lucas, is the new classical misperceptions theory. According to this theory, changes in the inflation rate can temporarily mislead suppliers about what is happening in the markets in which they sell their output. As a result of these short-run misperceptions, suppliers respond to changes in the level of prices, and this response leads to an upward-sloping aggregate-supply curve.

To see how this might work, suppose the inflation rate falls below the level that people expected. When suppliers see the prices of their products fall, they may mistakenly believe that their *relative* prices have fallen. For example, wheat farmers may notice a fall in the price of wheat before they notice a fall in the prices of the many items they buy as consumers. They may infer from this observation that the reward for producing wheat is temporarily low and they may respond by reducing the quantity of wheat they supply. Similarly, workers may notice a fall in their nominal wages before they notice a fall in the prices of the goods they buy. They may infer that the reward for working is temporarily low and respond by reducing the quantity of labour they supply. In both cases, *a lower inflation rate causes misperceptions about relative prices and these misperceptions induce suppliers to respond to the lower inflation rate by decreasing the quantity of goods and services supplied.*

The Keynesian sticky-wage theory

Another explanation of the upward slope of the short-run aggregate-supply curve is based on the work of John Maynard Keynes. According to Keynes and many of his followers, the short-run aggregate-supply curve slopes upwards because nominal wages are slow to adjust, or 'sticky', in the short run. To some extent, the slow adjustment of nominal wages is attributable to long-term contracts between workers and firms that fix nominal wages, sometimes for as long as three years. In addition, this slow adjustment may be attributable to social norms and notions of fairness that influence wage setting and that change only slowly over time.

To see what sticky nominal wages mean for aggregate supply, imagine that a firm has agreed in advance to pay its workers a certain nominal wage based on what it expected the inflation rate to be. If the inflation rate π falls below the level that was expected and the nominal wage remains stuck at W, then the real wage W/π rises above the level the firm planned to pay. Because wages are a large part of a firm's production costs, a higher real wage means that the firm's real costs have risen. The firm responds to these higher costs by hiring less labour and producing a smaller quantity of goods and services. In other words, *because wages do not adjust immediately to the inflation rate, a lower inflation rate makes employment and production less profitable, which induces firms to reduce the quantity of goods and services supplied.*

The new Keynesian sticky-price theory

Some economists have advocated a third theory of the short-run aggregate-supply curve, called the new Keynesian sticky-price theory. As we just discussed, Keynes originally emphasised that nominal wages adjust slowly over time. New Keynesian theorists emphasise that the prices of some goods and services also adjust sluggishly in response to changing economic conditions. This slow adjustment of prices occurs in part because there are costs to adjusting prices, called *menu costs*. These menu costs include the cost of printing and distributing catalogues and the time required to change price tags. As a result of these costs, prices as well as wages may be sticky in the short run.

To see the implications of sticky prices for aggregate supply, suppose that each firm in the economy announces its prices in advance based on the economic conditions it expects to prevail. Then, after prices are announced, the economy experiences an unexpected contraction in the money supply due to banks being cautious about making loans, leading to a decline in deposits. This (as we have learned) will reduce the inflation rate in the long run. Although some firms reduce their prices immediately in response to changing economic conditions, other firms may not want to incur additional menu costs and, therefore, may temporarily lag behind. Because these lagging firms have prices that are too high, their sales decline. Declining sales, in turn, cause these firms to cut back on production and employment. In other words, *because not all prices adjust instantly to changing conditions, an unexpected fall in the inflation rate leaves some firms with higher-than-desired prices, and these higher-than-desired prices depress sales and induce firms to reduce the quantity of goods and services they produce.*

Summary

Thus, there are three alternative explanations for the upward slope of the short-run aggregate-supply curve: (1) misperceptions, (2) sticky wages, and (3) sticky prices. Economists debate which of these theories is correct. For our purposes in this book, however, the similarities of the theories are more important than the differences. All three theories suggest that output deviates from its natural rate when the inflation rate deviates from the inflation rate that people expected.

Notice that each of these three theories of short-run aggregate supply emphasises a problem that is likely to be only temporary. Whether the upward slope of the aggregate-supply curve is attributable to misperceptions, sticky wages or sticky prices, these conditions will not persist forever. Eventually, as people adjust their expectations, misperceptions are corrected, nominal wages adjust and prices become unstuck. In the long run, therefore, the aggregate-supply curve is vertical rather than upward-sloping.

Why the short-run aggregate-supply curve might shift

The short-run aggregate-supply curve tells us the quantity of goods and services supplied in the short run for any given level of prices. Many events that shift the long-run aggregate-supply curve shift the short-run aggregate-supply curve as well. For example, when an increase in the economy's capital stock increases productivity, both the long-run and short-run aggregate-supply curves shift to the right. When an increase in the minimum wage raises the natural rate of unemployment, both the long-run and short-run aggregate-supply curves shift to the left.

There is, however, an important new variable that affects the position of the short-run aggregate-supply curve – people's expectation of the inflation rate. As we have discussed, the quantity of goods and services supplied depends, in the short run, on misperceptions, sticky wages and sticky prices. Yet perceptions, wages and prices are set on the basis of expectations of the inflation rate. For example, when people expect the inflation rate to be high, they will tend to set wages high. High wages tend to raise firms' costs and, for any given actual inflation rate, reduce the quantity of goods and services that firms supply. Thus, *a higher expected inflation rate decreases the quantity of goods and services supplied and shifts the short-run aggregate-supply curve to the left. Conversely, a lower expected inflation rate increases the quantity of goods and services supplied and shifts the short-run aggregate-supply curve to the right.*

As we will see, this influence of expectations on the position of the short-run aggregate-supply curve reconciles the economy's behaviour in the short run with its behaviour in the long run. In the short run, expectations are fixed and the economy finds itself at the intersection of the aggregate-demand curve and the short-run aggregate-supply curve. In the long run, expectations adjust and the short-run aggregate-supply curve shifts. This shift ensures that the economy eventually finds itself at the intersection of the aggregate-demand curve and the long-run aggregate-supply curve.

Explain why the long-run aggregate-supply curve is vertical. Explain three theories for why the short-run aggregate-supply curve is upward-sloping.

IN THE NEWS ...

WATER SUPPLY A CRITICAL RESOURCE

Australia has always had a strong agricultural sector. It used to be said that Australia's economic growth 'rode on the sheep's back'. These days, even though the rural sector is still significant, there are concerns about how strong the sector can continue to be if key growing areas don't have access to water. We tend to think of adding to the economy's resources, but as the following article indicates, if nature takes away some of those resources, we may see our long-run aggregate supply curve shifting left instead of right.

>>

Big ideas for our rural lifeblood
by Graham Lloyd, **Environment editor**

There's interest in projects that won't put anyone off the land

It's shearing time for Chris Hewitt, who runs a 5000 ha mixed grazing and wheat property at Warracknabeal in the dry country of western Victoria, about 60km north of Horsham near the South Australian border.

Hewitt keeps his eye on the contractors pulling in the wool, and the wheat and barley takes care of itself in the surrounding landscape. Hewitt's water future is secure. His area is untouched by the Murray-Darling Basin plan to return water to the environment because the work has already been done with the $700 million Wimmera Mallee project covering 10 per cent of Victoria. The project involved laying more than 8000km of piping to secure the region's water and give some back to the environment. It has been so successful that the Murray-Darling Basin Authority's draft plan has not recommended any further water allocation reduction in the region's river system.

The Wimmera Mallee project provides a case study in how large-scale infrastructure projects can transform the water equation without putting anyone off the land. But it also highlights many of the pitfalls that must be faced if similarly ambitious projects are considered in future, and the cost. With rural protests forcing the first signs of a backdown by the federal government over the amount of water it can expect from buybacks from farmers to restore environmental flows in the Murray-Darling, large-scale infrastructure projects are back on the agenda. A $5.8 billion fund has been set aside in the forward estimates, of which only $420m has been spent to date.

As it travels the country holding local meetings with farmers, the MDBA is collecting submissions on alternatives to water buybacks. All sorts of schemes have been put forward. Some are old, others revolutionary, and many attempt to capture the spirit of the Snowy Mountains hydro-electric scheme in ambition.

But engineering feasibility is not the only constraint they face.

A Productivity Commission report into market mechanisms for recovering water in the Murray-Darling Basin found 'subsidising infrastructure is rarely cost-effective in obtaining water for the environment, nor is it likely to be the best way of sustaining irrigation communities'. Rather than having a $5.8bn program focused predominantly on infrastructure upgrades, the Productivity Commission says it would have been more effective and efficient to use the buyback program as the sole means of easing the transition to the set water limits from each region. It says infrastructure projects should only be approved where a properly conducted cost-benefit analysis shows there are net benefits.

Crane Group managing director Greg Sedgwick says the Productivity Commission report conflates different levels of water infrastructure including projects with improvements in on-farm irrigation systems. Crane Group supplied the piping for the Wimmera Mallee project and Sedgwick makes no secret of his commercial self-interest. But independent research by ACIL Tasman, funded by industry, argues there are additional benefits to infrastructure spending over buy-backs. 'While funds acquired through buy-backs are likely to be substantially reinvested within regions, a substantial portion of funds are likely to move outside regions,' the ACIL report says.

'Water efficiency investments in large infrastructure projects tend to lock the incidence of these investments into the regions and to take advantage of existing farm and post-farm facilities.' The report finds that while water infrastructure spending is more expensive than water buy-backs on a per-mega-litre basis, if the economic effect of the loss of water to the regional community is taken into account, these projects generate significant economic benefit and maintain the social fabric of rural Australia.

Based on the Wimmera Mallee project, on a straight per-mega-litre cost, infrastructure spending is roughly double the cost of water buybacks. Unlike buybacks, however, it is possible to quantify the actual water saved and those annual savings continue for centuries.

Sedgwick has no doubt closing in irrigation channels is the best way to spend money to save water and retain rural jobs. 'I can't go past the fact that the most successful project, the Wimmera Mallee pipeline, is the one area that does not have cuts to water allocations under the Murray-Darling Basin plan,' Sedgwick says. 'It is the clear option that saves water and leaves jobs in place. It is a pretty good economic argument...

According to Hewitt, if there is a downside it is that everyone wants a piece of the water savings and 'the cake is not that big'. 'There will always be a debate about how those savings are used,' Hewitt says. 'We went through a huge community consultation process to establish the project and in our case there were benefits for everybody. It is much more difficult for the Murray-Darling Basin Authority because there will be a cost on the community.' Hewitt says the key was to ensure that any environmental gains were clearly defined and easily measured.

The Murray-Darling [is] a $15bn food basket. The Murray-Darling Basin covers about one million square kilometres, 14 per cent of Australia's land mass. The basin contains Australia's three longest rivers: the Darling (2740km); the Murray (2510km), and the Murrumbidgee (1690km). Nearly 85 per cent of the basin is used for agriculture.

It receives an average annual rainfall of 530 618 gigalitres: 94 per cent evaporates or transpires, 2 per cent drains into the ground and 4 per cent becomes run-off. The basin contains 65 per cent of Australia's irrigated land. Just more than two million people live in the basin. About 10 per cent of them are employed in agriculture. Almost two-fifths of Australia's farmers live in the Murray-Darling Basin.

Agriculture and households in the basin consume 52 per cent of Australia's water. Agricultural activities that consume the basin's water are cotton (20 per cent), dairy (17 per cent), other livestock pasture (17 per cent), and rice (16 per cent). In 2005–06 there were 61 000 farms in the basin, accounting for 39 per cent of all Australian farms.

Proportions of food production: rice, 100 per cent; oranges, 95 per cent; pigs, 62 per cent; apples, 54 per cent; and wheat, 48 per cent. In 2005–06, the gross value of agricultural production was worth $15 billion, or 39 per cent of the total Australian value of agricultural commodities.

Source: Graham Lloyd/*The Australian*, 29 October 2010.

Two causes of recession

Now that we have introduced the model of aggregate demand and aggregate supply, we have the basic tools we need to analyse short-run fluctuations in economic activity. In the next two chapters, we will refine our understanding of how to use these tools. But even now we can use what we have learned about aggregate demand and aggregate supply to examine the two basic causes of recession.

Figure 33.6 shows an economy in long-run equilibrium. Equilibrium output and the inflation rate are determined by the intersection of the aggregate-demand curve and the long-run aggregate-supply curve, shown as point A in the figure. At this point, output is at its natural rate. The short-run aggregate-supply curve passes through this point as well, indicating that perceptions, wages and prices have fully adjusted to this long-run equilibrium. That is, when an economy is at its long-run equilibrium, perceptions, wages and prices must have adjusted so that the intersection of aggregate demand with short-run aggregate supply is the same as the intersection of aggregate demand with long-run aggregate supply.

| Figure 33.6 | The long-run equilibrium |

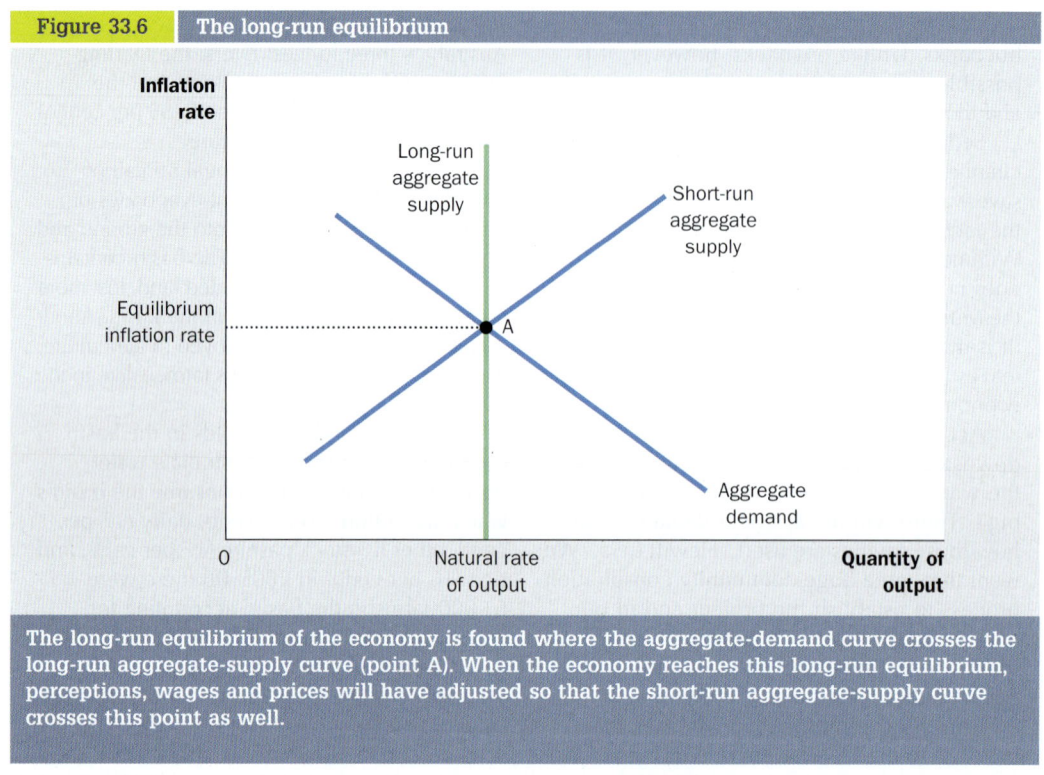

The long-run equilibrium of the economy is found where the aggregate-demand curve crosses the long-run aggregate-supply curve (point A). When the economy reaches this long-run equilibrium, perceptions, wages and prices will have adjusted so that the short-run aggregate-supply curve crosses this point as well.

The effects of a shift in aggregate demand

Suppose that for some reason a wave of pessimism suddenly overtakes the economy. The cause might be a decline in the world economy, a crash in the stock market or the outbreak of a war overseas. Because of this event, many people lose confidence in the future and alter their plans. Households cut back on their spending and delay major purchases, and firms put off buying new equipment.

What is the impact of such a wave of pessimism on the economy? Such an event reduces the aggregate demand for goods and services. That is, for any given inflation rate, households and firms now want to buy a smaller quantity of goods and services. As Figure 33.7 shows, the aggregate-demand curve shifts to the left from AD_1 to AD_2.

In this figure, we can examine the effects of the fall in aggregate demand. In the short run, the economy moves along the initial short-run aggregate-supply curve AS_1, going from point A to point B. As the economy moves from point A to point B, output falls from Y_1 to Y_2, and the inflation rate falls from π_1 to π_2. The falling level of output indicates that the economy is in a recession. Although not shown in the figure, firms respond to lower sales and production by reducing employment. Thus, the pessimism that caused the shift in aggregate demand is, to some extent, self-fulfilling – pessimism about the future leads to falling incomes and rising unemployment.

What should policymakers do when faced with such a recession? One possibility is to take action to increase aggregate demand. As we noted earlier, an increase in government spending would increase the quantity of goods and services demanded at any price and, therefore, would shift the aggregate-demand curve to the right. If policymakers can act with sufficient speed and precision they can offset the initial shift in aggregate demand, return the aggregate-demand curve back to AD_1 and

Figure 33.7 A contraction in aggregate demand

A fall in aggregate demand, which might be due to a wave of pessimism in the economy, is represented with a shift to the left in the aggregate-demand curve from AD_1 to AD_2. The economy moves from point A to point B. Output falls from Y_1 to Y_2 and the inflation rate falls from π_1 to π_2. Over time, as perceptions, wages and prices adjust, the short-run aggregate-supply curve shifts to the right from AS_1 to AS_2 and the economy reaches point C, where the new aggregate-demand curve crosses the long-run aggregate-supply curve. The inflation rate falls to π_3 and output returns to its natural rate Y_1.

bring the economy back to point A. (The next chapter discusses in more detail the ways in which monetary and fiscal policy influence aggregate demand, as well as some of the practical difficulties in using these policy instruments.)

The other option is for the RBA to react to the decline in inflation and output by reducing the cash rate, thus increasing the demand for goods and services. This can be seen in the following figure.

Even without action by policymakers, the recession eventually remedies itself. Over time, people correct the misperceptions, sticky wages and sticky prices that cause aggregate supply to slope upwards in the short run. In particular, as expectations of the inflation rate fall, perceptions, wages and prices are adjusted, and the short-run aggregate-supply curve shifts to the right from AS_1 to AS_2 as in Figure 33.7. In the long run, the economy approaches point C, where the new aggregate-demand curve (AD_2) crosses the long-run aggregate-supply curve.

In the new long-run equilibrium, point C, output is back to its natural rate. Even though the wave of pessimism has reduced aggregate demand, the inflation rate has fallen sufficiently (to π_3) to offset the shift in the aggregate-demand curve. Thus, in the long run, the shift in aggregate demand is reflected fully in the inflation rate and not at all in the level of output. In other words, the long-run effect of a shift in aggregate demand is a nominal change (the inflation rate is lower) but not a real change (output is the same).

IN THE NEWS . . .

POST-GFC: HOW MUCH WILL AUSTRALIA BE AFFECTED BY ECONOMIC CONDITIONS IN EUROPE AND THE US?

Australia has weathered the global economic storm relatively well, but will we continue to thrive? And what should the policy stance be? In the following interview, Frank Gelber, chief economist at BIS Shrapnel, an industry research and forecasting firm, discusses Australia's economic prospects and the importance of China and the minerals sector in our ongoing economic growth.

The dangers in becoming China's quarry

MARK COLVIN: A long-range economic forecaster is warning that Australia's reliance on mineral exports to China has made the nation highly vulnerable.

Frank Gelber is chief economist at the industry research and forecasting firm, BIS Shrapnel. He says that Australia can look forward to strong economic growth in the next five years with 'sectoral booms' in mining and property. But Frank Gelber warns that there is a risk of the economy overheating and crashing if the cycles coincide.

He outlined his views to our economics correspondent, Stephen Long.

FRANK GELBER: Forget about double dips and all that sort of stuff, the economy's growing and will pick up pace from here.

STEPHEN LONG: You're not worried about the situation overseas? The sovereign debt concerns in Europe? The high unemployment rate and weak consumption in the United States?

FRANK GELBER: Yes, I am worried about overseas. I don't think we'll see sovereign debt causing a crisis. The financial system will cope with that but I'm not looking for a quick and strong recovery overseas. They had over investment and they're going to have a protracted period of weak investment until they absorb the excess capacity created during their boom. And so that means they've got 10 to 15 years of patchy growth to contend with.

STEPHEN LONG: So why is the outlook so different here?

FRANK GELBER: Well, we didn't have over investment in Australia but we would have. Had it not been for the financial crisis, we would have over invested and would have crashed like them but the GFC did us a huge favour and, as a result, now we haven't got any substantial over investment. We've got the next round of minerals projects coming forward, we've got business under investing and creating more capacity constraints and so the next phase is an upswing in investment.

Housing, first cab off the rank, and that's already started and it transmits to construction. Mining, we know about; and non-residential building will follow after a few years. And before that we're going to need to see strong rises in rents and property values to under-write new construction.

STEPHEN LONG: Well, here's the dilemma, how are we going to achieve a big upswing in housing investment and, on your analysis and you're not alone, we're massively under invested in new dwelling construction, together with the mining boom? How can we have that without an outbreak of inflation?

FRANK GELBER: We can't.

STEPHEN LONG: So we're facing boom conditions and a response by the Reserve Bank to jack up interest rates?

FRANK GELBER: We're not looking for a god almighty boom coming through here quickly at least but sector by sector we will see an upswing building momentum into what will become a boom in each sector and it will be those rolling investments cycles that drive growth in the Australian economy.

STEPHEN LONG: What happens if the sectoral booms coincide?

FRANK GELBER: If they are synchronised, then we will see boom conditions a little bit like the 1980s where we saw a big boom leading to major oversupply and a subsequent recession. But if we do that, hey it's going to be a wild ride. So hang on to your hats.

STEPHEN LONG: And you think that business should be counting on the upswing and putting money into investment now?

FRANK GELBER: Well, it makes sense.

STEPHEN LONG: How much of a risk is it that we're hitching our little red wagon to the big red engine called China? That we're relying so much on commodity exports and a minerals boom to sustain the economy?

FRANK GELBER: Well, it frightens the hell out of me. Remember, you know, in the old days, what is it, 20, 30 years ago, Rex Connor used to say, we're going to be a massive earth moving operation from Australia to Japan and he only got one thing wrong in that, the destination.

We're running down the rest of the economy, we're specialising in minerals and this is all very nice when we've got very high minerals prices and very strong demand. But minerals prices don't always boom and demand isn't always strong.

The lessons of the last 50 years should have taught us that so that we're setting ourselves up for a huge fall if at some stage we see falls in minerals prices and a demand then perhaps a collapse in the dollar, which would underwrite the competitiveness of our other domestic tradeables investment, but we won't have any domestic industries to invest in. No, it's not going to happen in the very short term. But happens ten years from now?

STEPHEN LONG: In terms of economic policy then, what should we be doing to create an economy that is less vulnerable?

FRANK GELBER: Oh, that was an easy question, was it? Okay. First of all we need to recognise the problem that we're specialising in minerals and then what we need to do is to try to impede the demise of the other tradeables industries.

Does it mean some sort of an industry policy? Again, yes it does.

STEPHEN LONG: Very unfashionable phrase.

FRANK GELBER: Well, we haven't needed it for a long time.

STEPHEN LONG: But we do now?

FRANK GELBER: We do now. And, look there are things that we can and do do even at high dollar but what we need to do is to understand what the world would look like in a lower dollar environment and to protect, no hang on, protect is an even more unfashionable world.

STEPHEN LONG: Very much so.

FRANK GELBER: Okay, so help those industries that do those things survive.

MARK COLVIN: Frank Gelber, chief economist at BIS Shrapnel, speaking to Stephen Long. You can hear more of that interview, where Frank Gelber analyses what should be done to address the housing shortage, on the PM website from this evening.

The effects of a shift in aggregate supply

Imagine once again an economy at its long-run equilibrium. Now suppose that suddenly some firms experience an increase in their costs of production. For example, droughts might reduce yields of some crops, driving up the cost of producing food products. Or an explosion at a gasworks might drastically reduce the supply of natural gas, driving up the cost of production as firms try to switch to alternative energy sources.

What is the macroeconomic impact of such an increase in production costs? For any given inflation rate, firms now want to supply a smaller quantity of goods and services. Thus, as Figure 33.8 shows, the short-run aggregate-supply curve shifts to the left from AS_1 to AS_2. (Depending on the event, the long-run aggregate-supply curve might also shift. To keep things simple, however, we will assume that it does not.)

In this figure, we can trace the effects of the leftward shift in aggregate supply. In the short run, the economy moves along the existing aggregate-demand curve, going from point A to point B. The output of the economy falls from Y_1 to Y_2, and the inflation rate rises from π_1 to π_2. Because

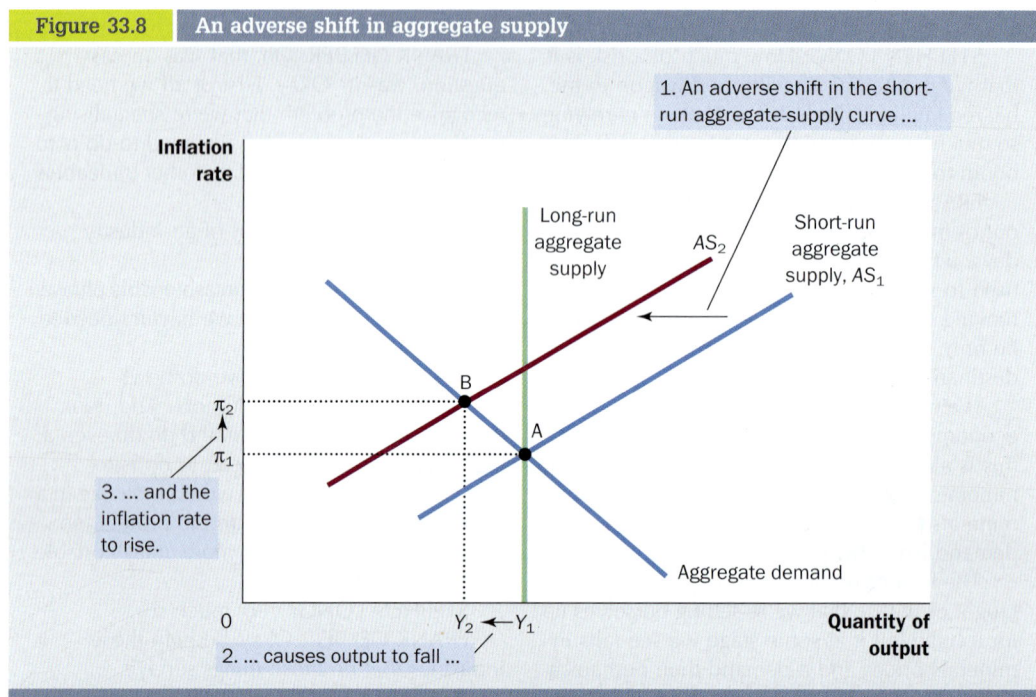

Figure 33.8 An adverse shift in aggregate supply

1. An adverse shift in the short-run aggregate-supply curve ...

Inflation rate

Long-run aggregate supply

AS_2

Short-run aggregate supply, AS_1

B

A

π_2

π_1

3. ... and the inflation rate to rise.

Aggregate demand

0   Y_2 ← Y_1 **Quantity of output**

2. ... causes output to fall ...

When some event increases firms' costs, the short-run aggregate-supply curve shifts to the left from AS_1 to AS_2. The economy moves from point A to point B. The result is stagflation – output falls from Y_1 to Y_2 and the inflation rate rises from π_1 to π_2.

stagflation
a period of falling output and rising prices

the economy is experiencing both *stagnation* (falling output) and *inflation* (rising prices), such an event is sometimes called **stagflation**.

What should policymakers do when faced with stagflation? As we will discuss more fully later in this book, there are no easy choices. One possibility is to do nothing. In this case, the output of goods and services remains depressed at Y_2 for a while. Eventually, however, the recession will remedy itself as perceptions, wages and prices adjust to the higher production costs. A period of low output and high unemployment, for instance, puts downward pressure on workers' wages. Lower wages, in turn, increase the quantity of output supplied. Over time, as the short-run aggregate-supply curve shifts back towards AS_1, the inflation rate falls and the quantity of output approaches its natural rate. In the long run, the economy returns to point A, where the aggregate-demand curve crosses the long-run aggregate-supply curve.

Alternatively, policymakers who control monetary and fiscal policy might attempt to offset some of the effects of the shift in the short-run aggregate-supply curve by shifting the aggregate-demand curve. This possibility is shown in Figure 33.9. In this case, changes in policy shift the aggregate-demand curve to the right from AD_1 to AD_2 – exactly enough to prevent the shift in aggregate supply from affecting output. The economy moves directly from point A to point C. Output remains at its natural rate and the inflation rate rises from π_1 to π_3. In this case, policymakers are said to *accommodate* the shift in aggregate supply because they allow the increase in costs to affect the level of prices permanently. This is unusual in Australia, as the Reserve Bank would typically increase interest rates if it sees the rate of inflation rising by a significant amount. One exception to this is

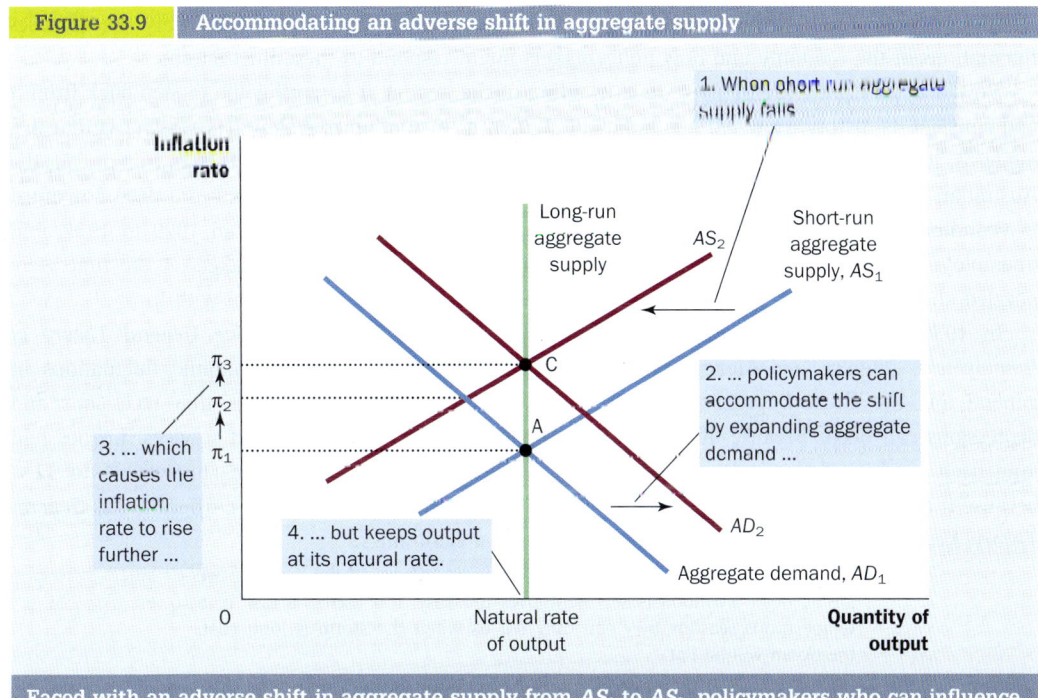

Figure 33.9 Accommodating an adverse shift in aggregate supply

1. When short run aggregate supply falls

Inflation rate

Long-run aggregate supply

AS_2

Short-run aggregate supply, AS_1

2. ... policymakers can accommodate the shift by expanding aggregate demand ...

3. ... which causes the inflation rate to rise further ...

π_3

π_2

π_1

C

A

4. ... but keeps output at its natural rate.

AD_2

Aggregate demand, AD_1

0

Natural rate of output

Quantity of output

Faced with an adverse shift in aggregate supply from AS_1 to AS_2, policymakers who can influence aggregate demand might try to shift the aggregate-demand curve to the right from AD_1 to AD_2. The economy would move from point A to point C. This policy would prevent the supply shift from reducing output in the short run, but the inflation rate would permanently rise from π_1 to π_3.

when the GST was introduced in 2000. There was a one-time jump in inflation to about 6 per cent for the year it was introduced.

To sum up, this story about shifts in aggregate supply has two important implications:

- Shifts in aggregate supply can cause stagflation – a combination of recession (falling output) and inflation (rising prices).
- Policymakers who can influence aggregate demand cannot offset both of these adverse effects simultaneously.

Suppose that the passage of a referendum to make Australia a republic suddenly increases people's confidence in the future. Use the model of aggregate demand and aggregate supply to analyse the effect on the economy.

Conclusion: The origins of aggregate demand and aggregate supply

This chapter has achieved two goals. First, we have discussed some of the important facts about short-run fluctuations in economic activity. Second, we have introduced a basic model to explain those fluctuations, called the model of aggregate demand and aggregate supply. In the next two chapters we look at each piece of this model in more detail in order to understand more fully what causes fluctuations in the economy and how policymakers might respond to these fluctuations.

Now that we have a preliminary understanding of this model, it is worthwhile to step back from it and consider its history. How did this model of short-run fluctuations develop? The answer is that this model is, to a large extent, a by-product of the Great Depression of the 1930s. During this period, the Australian economy and most other major economies around the world experienced a deep downturn in economic activity. In Australia, real GDP fell by more than 10 per cent from 1929 to 1932, and unemployment rose from 6 per cent to 20 per cent. Economists and policymakers at the time were puzzled about what had caused this event and were uncertain about how to deal with it.

In 1936, economist John Maynard Keynes published a book entitled *The General Theory of Employment, Interest, and Money*, which attempted to explain short-run economic fluctuations in general and the Great Depression in particular. Keynes's main message was that recessions and depressions can occur because of inadequate aggregate demand for goods and services. Keynes had long been a critic of classical economic theory – the theory we examined in chapters 26 to 32 – because it could explain only the long-run effects of policies. A few years before offering *The General Theory*, Keynes had written the following about classical economics:

> The long run is a misleading guide to current affairs. In the long run we are all dead. Economists set themselves too easy, too useless a task if in tempestuous seasons they can only tell us when the storm is long past, the ocean will be flat.

Keynes's message was aimed at policymakers as well as economists. As the world's economies suffered from high unemployment, Keynes advocated policies to increase aggregate demand, including government spending on public works. In the next chapter, we examine in detail how policymakers can try to use the tools of monetary and fiscal policy to influence aggregate demand. The analysis in the next chapter, as well as in this one, owes much to the legacy of John Maynard Keynes.

Summary

- All societies experience short-run economic fluctuations around long-run trends. These fluctuations are irregular and largely unpredictable. When recessions do occur, real GDP and other measures of income, spending and production fall, and unemployment rises.
- Economists analyse short-run economic fluctuations using the model of aggregate demand and aggregate supply. According to this model, the output of goods and services and the overall level of prices adjust to balance aggregate demand and aggregate supply.
- The aggregate-demand curve slopes downwards for three reasons. First, a lower inflation rate raises the real value of households' money holdings and other forms of wealth, which stimulates consumer spending. Second, a lower inflation rate reduces the quantity of money that households demand; the RBA, seeing a fall in prices, reduces interest rates, which stimulates investment spending. Third, a lower inflation rate, and thus lower interest rates, means the dollar depreciates in the market for foreign-currency exchange, which stimulates net exports.
- The long-run aggregate-supply curve is vertical. In the long run, the quantity of goods and services supplied depends on the economy's labour, capital and technology, but not on the overall level of prices.
- The short-run aggregate-supply curve is upward-sloping. There are three theories to explain short-run aggregate supply. According to the new classical misperceptions theory, an unexpected fall in the inflation rate leads suppliers to mistakenly believe that their relative prices have fallen, which induces them to reduce production. According to the Keynesian sticky-wage theory, an unexpected fall in the inflation rate temporarily raises real wages, which induces firms to reduce employment and production. According to the new Keynesian sticky-price theory, an unexpected fall in the inflation rate leaves some firms with prices that are temporarily too high, which reduces their sales and causes them to cut back production.
- One possible cause of recession is a fall in aggregate demand. When the aggregate-demand curve shifts to the left, output and prices fall in the short run. Over time, as perceptions, wages and prices adjust, the short-run aggregate-supply curve shifts to the right and the economy returns to its natural rate of output at a new, lower inflation rate.
- A second possible cause of recession is an adverse change in aggregate supply. When the aggregate-supply curve shifts to the left, the short-run effect is falling output and rising prices – a combination called stagflation. Over time, as perceptions, wages and prices adjust, the inflation rate falls back to its original level, and output recovers.

Key concepts

aggregate-demand curve
aggregate-supply curve
depression

model of aggregate demand and
  aggregate supply

recession
stagflation

Questions for review

1   Draw a diagram with aggregate demand, short-run aggregate supply and long-run aggregate supply. Be careful to label the axes correctly.
2   List and explain the three reasons that the aggregate-demand curve is downward-sloping.

3 Explain why the long-run aggregate-supply curve is vertical. What causes the long-run aggregate supply curve to shift?

4 List and explain the three theories for why the short-run aggregate-supply curve is upward-sloping.

5 What might shift the aggregate-demand curve to the right? Use the model of aggregate demand and aggregate supply to trace through the effects of such a shift.

6 What might shift the aggregate-supply curve to the right? Use the model of aggregate demand and aggregate supply to trace through the effects of such a shift.

Problems and applications

1 Why do you think that investment is more variable over the business cycle than consumer spending? Which category of consumer spending do you think would be most volatile: durable goods (such as furniture and car purchases), non-durable goods (such as food and clothing), or services (such as haircuts and restaurant meals)? Why?

2 Suppose that the economy is undergoing a boom because of an increase in aggregate demand.

   a Using an aggregate-demand/aggregate-supply diagram, depict the current state of the economy.

   b If real GDP is now 1 per cent above last year's value, how does the unemployment rate compare with last year's rate? (*Hint:* Review Okun's law.)

   c 'Capacity utilisation' is a measure of how intensively the capital stock is being used. In a boom, is capacity utilisation above or below its long-run average? Explain.

3 Explain whether each of the following events will increase, decrease or have no effect on long-run aggregate supply.

   a Australia experiences a wave of immigration.

   b The Gillard government decides to build new ports in Western Australia, in Queensland and in New South Wales.

   c A lack of waterflow causes farmland along the Murray-Darling River system to become too dry to farm.

   d An earthquake destroys factories in Newcastle and Sydney.

4 Suppose the economy is in long-run equilibrium, as in Figure 33.6. Show the impact on aggregate demand, on short-run aggregate supply or long-run aggregate supply of each of the following, assuming they all happen, in the sequence they are listed:

   a Demand for Australian iron ore and coal increases dramatically as the Indian and Chinese economies expand.

   b New laws make it easier for collective bargaining to occur, leading to an increase in wages in certain key sectors.

   c A new technology is perfected that lowers the cost of geosequestration, the process by which greenhouse gasses are captured and stored deep underground.

5 Explain why the following statements are false.

   a 'The aggregate-demand curve slopes downwards because it is the horizontal sum of the demand curves for individual goods.'

   b 'The long-run aggregate-supply curve is vertical because economic forces do not affect long-run aggregate supply.'

   c 'If firms adjusted their prices every day, then the short-run aggregate-supply curve would be horizontal.'

    d 'Whenever the economy enters a recession, its long-run aggregate-supply curve shifts to the left.'

6 For each of the three theories for the upward slope of the short-run aggregate-supply curve, carefully explain the following:
    a How the economy recovers from a recession and returns to its long-run equilibrium without any policy intervention.
    b What determines the speed of that recovery.

7 The Australian economy is currently experiencing higher than desired levels of inflation. If the RBA did *not* increase interest rates, would the economy adjust to long-run equilibrium? Explain in words and using an aggregate-demand/aggregate-supply diagram what conditions would prevail if the economy did adjust. Why would the RBA *not* want to let the economy adjust on its own?

8 Suppose workers and firms suddenly believe that inflation will be quite low over the coming year. Suppose also that the economy begins in long-run equilibrium and the aggregate-demand curve does not shift.
    a What happens to nominal wages? What happens to real wages?
    b Using an aggregate-demand/aggregate-supply diagram, show the effect of the change in expectations on both the short-run and long-run levels of prices and output.
    c Were the expectations of low inflation accurate? Explain.

9 Suppose there is credible research that discovers that we really are running out of oil faster than we thought (that we're already past the point of 'peak oil'). This causes a significant and permanent increase in the price of oil.
    a How is this reflected in our aggregate-supply and aggregate-demand diagrams.
    b What policies could the government undertake to correct the impact of this increase in the price of oil?
    c Would there be any negative impacts from your recommended government policies?

10 Explain whether each of the following events shifts the short-run aggregate-supply curve, the aggregate-demand curve, both or neither. For each event that does shift a curve, use a diagram to illustrate the effect on the economy.
    a Households decide to save a larger share of their income.
    b A plague of locusts eats the year's wheat crop.
    c The birthrate shoots up nine months after a particularly cold Melbourne winter.
    d Storms in Western Australia destroy Port Hedland, the port through which the largest percentage of iron ore shipped from Australia flows.

11 Suppose that firms become very optimistic about future business conditions and invest heavily in new capital equipment.
    a Use an aggregate-demand/aggregate-supply diagram to show the short-run effect of this optimism on the economy. Label the new levels of prices and real output. Explain in words why the aggregate quantity of output *supplied* changes.
    b Use the diagram from part (a) to show the new long-run equilibrium of the economy. (For now, assume there is no change in the long-run aggregate-supply curve.) Explain in words why the aggregate quantity of output *demanded* changes between the short run and the long run.
    c How might the investment boom affect the long-run aggregate-supply curve? Explain.

12 Suppose the law is changed so that innovation activities by firms are taxed at a much lower rate than other company expenses.
    a How would this affect firms' allocation between different types of investment? Explain.
    b How would this affect the interest rate? Explain.
    c What happens to the quantity of investment overall? Explain.

d   What happens to the short-run aggregates supply curve? Explain.
e   What happens to the long-run aggregate supply curve? Explain.
f   What happens to the value of the dollar? Explain.
g   What happens to the quantity of net exports demanded? Explain.
h   What happens to aggregate demand? Explain.

Search me!

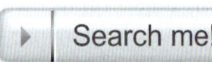

When accessing information about economics use the following keywords in any combinations you require:

- aggregate demand
- aggregate supply

CourseMate

For more multimedia resources and activities on economics, visit the Economics CourseMate website.

34

The influence of monetary and fiscal policy on aggregate demand

Learning objectives

In this chapter you will:

- analyse how fiscal policy affects aggregate demand
- analyse how monetary policy affects aggregate demand through interest rates
- discuss the debate over whether policymakers should try to stabilise the economy
- reconsider how the economy behaves differently in the short run and in the long run.

Imagine that you are a member of the Reserve Bank Board, which sets monetary policy. You observe that the Australian government has increased government spending to such an extent that the budget surplus has been eliminated. You and the other Board members decide what direction you think monetary policy should take. What policy recommendation should you make in response to this change in fiscal policy? Should the Reserve Bank of Australia (RBA) decrease interest rates, increase interest rates or leave them the same?

To answer this question, you need to consider the impact of monetary and fiscal policy on the economy. In the preceding chapter, we saw how to explain short-run economic fluctuations using the model of aggregate demand and aggregate supply. When the aggregate-demand curve or the aggregate-supply curve shifts, the result is fluctuations in the economy's overall output of goods and services, and in its overall level of prices (the inflation rate). As we noted in the previous chapter, monetary and fiscal policy can each influence aggregate demand. Thus, a change in one of these policies can lead to short-run fluctuations in output and the rate of inflation. Policymakers will want to anticipate this effect and, perhaps, adjust the other policy in response.

In this chapter we examine in more detail how the government's tools of monetary and fiscal policy influence aggregate-demand. We have previously discussed the long-run effects of these policies. In chapters 26 and 27 we saw how fiscal policy affects saving, investment and long-run economic growth. In chapters 29 and 30 we saw how the RBA sets the interest rate. We also how the money supply determines the inflation rate in the long run. We now see how these policy tools affect aggregate demand and, in doing so, affect short-run economic fluctuations.

As we have already learned, many factors influence aggregate demand besides monetary and fiscal policy. In particular, desired spending by households and firms determines the overall demand for goods and services. When desired spending changes, aggregate demand shifts. If policymakers do not respond, such shifts in aggregate demand cause short-run fluctuations in output and employment. As a result, monetary and fiscal policymakers sometimes use the policy levers at their disposal to try to offset these shifts in aggregate demand and thereby stabilise the economy. Here we discuss the theory behind these policy actions and some of the difficulties that arise in using this theory in practice.

How monetary policy influences aggregate demand

The aggregate-demand curve shows the quantity of goods and services demanded for any inflation rate. As you may recall from the preceding chapter, the aggregate-demand curve slopes downwards for three reasons:

- *Interest-rate effect:* A lower inflation rate leads to a lower interest rate through Reserve Bank policy and the lower interest rate stimulates investment spending.
- *Wealth effect:* A lower inflation rate raises the real value of households' money holdings and other assets, and higher real wealth stimulates consumer spending.
- *Exchange-rate effect:* When a lower inflation rate leads to lower interest rates, investors move some of their funds overseas and cause the domestic currency to depreciate relative to foreign currencies. This depreciation makes domestic goods cheaper compared with foreign goods and, therefore, stimulates net exports.

These three effects should not be viewed as alternative theories. Instead, they occur simultaneously to increase the quantity of goods and services demanded when the inflation rate falls.

Although all three effects work together in explaining the downward slope of the aggregate-demand curve, they are not of equal importance. Because money holdings are a small part of

▸ monetary policy

Figure 34.1   Monetary policy graph

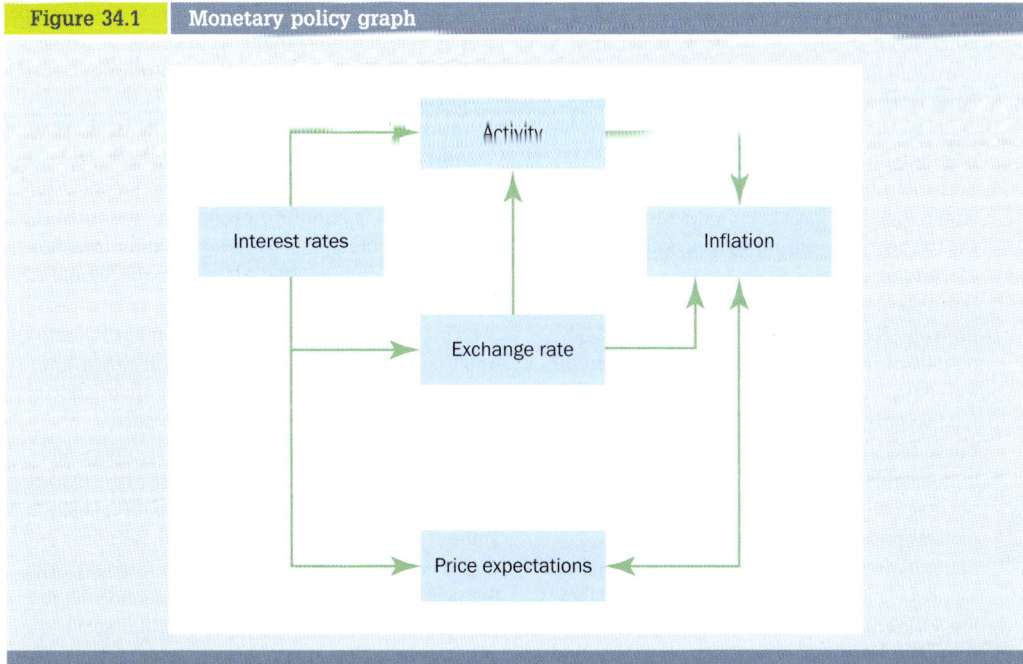

In this diagram, we see the interconnections between interest rates, the level of economic activity in the economy, the exchange rate, inflation and the level of price expectations. The RBA monitors several economic variables to determine whether or not to change interest rates. But its primary objective is to keep inflation in the range of 2–3 per cent. As the case study below from the RBA website explains, the inflation target was developed to facilitate a stable financial system and to assist with stable economic growth.

household wealth, the wealth effect is the least important of the three. Because exports and imports represent a relatively large fraction of Australian GDP, the exchange-rate effect can be significant for the Australian economy. (This effect is much less important for larger countries because larger countries typically export and import a smaller fraction of their GDP.) However, the most important reason for the downward slope of the aggregate-demand curve is the interest-rate effect. Figure 34.1 from the RBA website gives you an overall picture of how monetary policy works to affect aggregate demand.

CASESTUDY

Why 2–3 per cent?

There is considerable international evidence that high inflation is harmful to economic performance. In particular, countries that have had relatively high rates of inflation in the post-war period have tended to experience lower rates of economic growth than low-inflation countries. This is not a mechanical relationship that explains country differences precisely from year to year, but one that is evident in terms of averages over long periods of time.

There are several ways in which inflation causes harmful economic effects, of which three, in particular, are worth highlighting.

- *Interaction with the tax system.* Most tax systems measure income in a way that does not allow for inflation. To give just one example, interest received is fully counted as income for tax purposes, even though it partly represents a compensation for inflation rather than real income. Similarly, interest paid by businesses is fully counted as a cost, when in fact it is partly a transfer to compensate the lender for inflation. As a result, when inflation is high, the tax system tends to overstate the real value of both interest receipts and payments;

>>

consequently, interest income is taxed more heavily than intended and business interest costs receive a bigger-than-intended benefit from tax deductibility. This effect seems to have been important in encouraging excessive borrowing by businesses in the 1980s, and would therefore have been a destabilising factor for the economy during that period.

- *Uncertainty*. Inflation is a source of uncertainty that makes economic decision-making more difficult. Periods of high inflation are usually periods of greater-than-average variability in inflation. They are also periods when individual relative prices and wages become more variable. These facts point to the uncertainty that high and variable inflation can generate, as people become confused about how quickly the general price level is rising and what the appropriate prices are for individual goods and services. That in turn makes the price system less efficient as a mechanism for allocating resources.

- *Distributional effects*. Because inflation erodes the real value of money, it redistributes wealth from those who own monetary assets to those who owe money. The big winners from inflation in the 1970s and 1980s were those who were able to use borrowed money to finance the holding of assets that rose in value; inflation reduced the real value of their debts but pushed up asset prices. Other winners tend to be those who can tailor their tax and other affairs in a way that takes advantage of inflation – often those who are already among the better off. More generally, the expectation of inflation tends to generate private behaviour designed to minimise its effects or to exploit them. This is at

best wasteful of productive resources and may involve significant distortions to private incentives – for example, the incentive to invest in those assets that tend to rise most in value when inflation is high.

These arguments point to a general conclusion that inflation is harmful to economic performance, so policy should aim at keeping inflation low. But how low an inflation rate is low enough? Should we be aiming at zero?

There are several reasons why aiming for zero inflation might not be warranted, and why a low positive target may be the most appropriate. First, the economy is subject to what are called 'downward nominal rigidities'. That is, prices and wages that do not normally fall even when market equilibrium might require that. But with a small amount of inflation in the system, these prices and wages can fall in relative terms (by not rising with the general price level) even if they cannot fall in absolute terms. This is an argument that small amounts of inflation may help to make price systems more flexible. Secondly, there may be biases in the measurement of inflation such that true inflation is on average overstated by standard measures. This can arise, for example, when the rising quality of a good or service is not properly taken into account when measuring its price. To the extent that this is the case, inflation would be overstated and the target would need to make allowance for this by aiming higher than zero. Finally, it is likely to be costly to reduce inflation, so some judgement needs to be made as to how far inflation reduction should be taken, allowing for both the costs and benefits of doing so.

Source: Reserve Bank of Australia.

The downward slope of the aggregate-demand curve

Having seen the connection between the interest rate and inflation, we now consider its implications for the aggregate demand for goods and services. We use the interest-rate effect to explain the downward slope of the aggregate-demand curve. Suppose that the rate of inflation in the economy rises. According to the RBA's policy guidelines, if the RBA sees rising inflation, it would then increase interest rates.

This increase in the interest rate has ramifications for the quantity of goods and services demanded, as shown in Figure 34.2. At a higher interest rate, the cost of borrowing and the return on savings are greater. Fewer households choose to borrow to buy a new house and those who do buy smaller houses, so the demand for residential investment falls. Fewer firms choose to borrow to build

Figure 34.2 The slope of the aggregate-demand curve

1. An increase in the inflation rate ...

2. ... leads to the RBA increasing the interest rate, which in turn reduces the quantity of goods and services demanded.

An increase in the inflation rate from π_1 to π_2 leads to the RBA increasing the interest rate. Because the interest rate is the cost of borrowing, the increase in the interest rate reduces the quantity of goods and services demanded from Y_1 to Y_2. This negative relationship between the inflation rate and quantity demanded is represented with a downward-sloping aggregate-demand curve.

new factories and buy new equipment, so business investment falls. Households choose to save more for the future, so spending on consumption goods falls. For all these reasons, when the inflation rate rises from π_1 to π_2, the RBA raises the interest rate and therefore the quantity of goods and services demanded falls from Y_1 to Y_2.

Hence, this analysis of interest-rate effect can be summarised in two steps:

1 A higher inflation rate induces the RBA to increase interest rates.
2 A higher interest rate reduces the quantity of goods and services demanded.

The end result of this analysis is a negative relationship between the inflation rate and the quantity of goods and services demanded. This relationship is illustrated with a downward-sloping aggregate-demand curve.

To sum up, *changes in the cash rate move us up and down the aggregate demand curve. A reduction in the cash rate induced by a reduction in the inflation rate, a loosening of monetary policy, sees the quantity of goods and services demanded increase. An increase in the cash rate induced by an increase in the inflation rate, a tightening of monetary policy, reduces the quantity of goods and services demanded.*

Explain how an increase in the cash rate affects the aggregate-demand curve.

The theory of liquidity preference

We've just seen how monetary policy affects the level of aggregate demand. In our explanation, the RBA anticipates increases or decreases in the inflation rate and changes the interest rate to slow economic activity down or to give it a boost. The use of the cash rate as the monetary policy instrument reflects our understanding of how modern economies work. Behind this understanding is a model of the money market called the liquidity preference theory. John Maynard Keynes proposed this theory in his classic book *The General Theory of Employment, Interest, and Money*. At the time Keynes was writing, central banks didn't set the interest rate, they conducted monetary policy by changing the supply of money. Keynes wanted to explain what factors determined the economy's interest rate. The theory is, in essence, just an application of supply and demand. According to Keynes, the interest rate adjusts to balance the supply of and demand for money. Even though monetary policy doesn't work the way we describe it in this theory, it helps us understand how people's decisions about how much money to hold influences economic activity in the economy through the interest rate.

You may recall that economists distinguish between two interest rates: The *nominal interest rate* is the interest rate we usually hear about and the *real interest rate* is the interest rate corrected for the effects of inflation. When there is no inflation, the two rates are the same. But when borrowers and lenders expect prices to rise over the course of the loan, they agree to a nominal interest rate that exceeds the real interest rate by the expected rate of inflation. The higher nominal interest rate compensates for the fact that they expect the loan to be repaid in less valuable dollars.

Which interest rate are we now trying to explain with the theory of liquidity preference? The answer is both. In the analysis that follows, we hold constant the expected rate of inflation. This assumption is reasonable for studying the economy in the short run, because expected inflation is typically stable over short periods of time. In this case, nominal and real interest rates differ by a constant. When the nominal interest rate rises or falls, the real interest rate that people expect to earn rises or falls as well. For the rest of this chapter, when we refer to changes in the interest rate, you should envision the real and nominal interest rates moving in the same direction.

Money supply and interest rates in the liquidity preference theory

The first piece of the theory of liquidity preference is the supply of money. Suppose the central bank in our economy used the money supply to conduct monetary policy. The details of how the central bank exercises control over the money supply are not crucial for the analysis in this chapter. We could easily assume that the money falls from the sky when the central bank wants to increase the money supply or that it is sucked up in a big vacuum when they want to decrease money supply. Our goal here is to examine how changes in the money supply affect the aggregate demand for goods and services. For this purpose, we can ignore the details of how central bank policy is implemented and assume that the central bank controls the money supply directly. In other words, the quantity of money supplied in the economy is fixed at whatever level the central bank decides to set it.

Because the quantity of money supplied is fixed by central bank policy, it does not depend on other economic variables. In particular, it does not depend on the interest rate. Once the central bank has made its policy decision, the quantity of money supplied is the same, regardless of the prevailing interest rate. We represent a fixed money supply with a vertical supply curve, as in Figure 34.3.

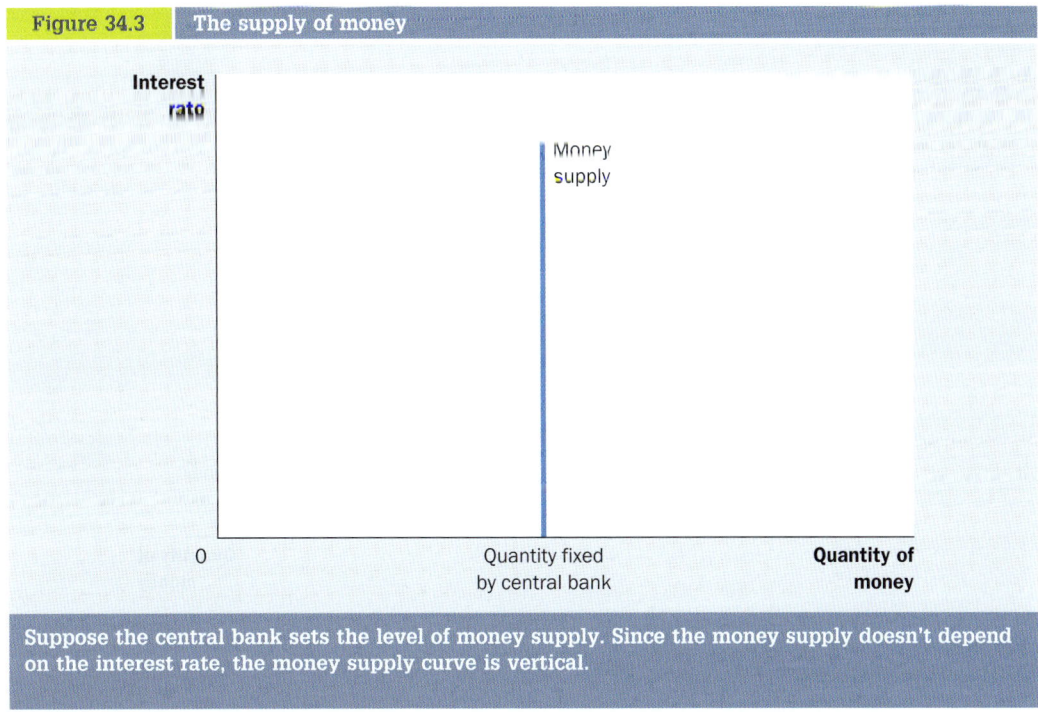

Figure 34.3   The supply of money

Interest rate

Money supply

0

Quantity fixed by central bank

Quantity of money

Suppose the central bank sets the level of money supply. Since the money supply doesn't depend on the interest rate, the money supply curve is vertical.

Money demand

The second piece of the theory of liquidity preference is the demand for money. As a starting point for understanding money demand, recall that any asset's *liquidity* refers to the ease with which that asset is converted into the economy's medium of exchange. Money is the economy's medium of exchange, so it is by definition the most liquid asset available. The liquidity of money explains the demand for it – people choose to hold money instead of other assets that offer higher rates of return because money can be used to buy goods and services.

Although there are many determinants of the quantity of money demanded, the theory of liquidity preference emphasises that one of the most important is the interest rate. The reason is that the interest rate is the opportunity cost of holding money. That is, when you hold wealth as cash in your wallet, instead of as an interest-bearing bond, you lose the interest you could have earned. An increase in the interest rate raises the cost of holding money and, as a result, reduces the quantity of money demanded. Thus, as shown in Figure 34.4, the money-demand curve is downward-sloping.

Equilibrium in the money market

According to the theory of liquidity preference, the interest rate adjusts to balance the supply and demand for money. There is one interest rate, called the equilibrium interest rate, at which the quantity of money demanded exactly balances the quantity of money supplied. If the interest rate is at any other level, people will try to adjust their portfolios of assets and, as a result, drive the interest rate toward the equilibrium.

For example, suppose that the interest rate is above the equilibrium level, such as r_1 in Figure 34.5. In this case, the quantity of money that people want to hold, MD_1, is less than the quantity of money that the central bank has supplied. Those people who are holding the surplus of money will try to get

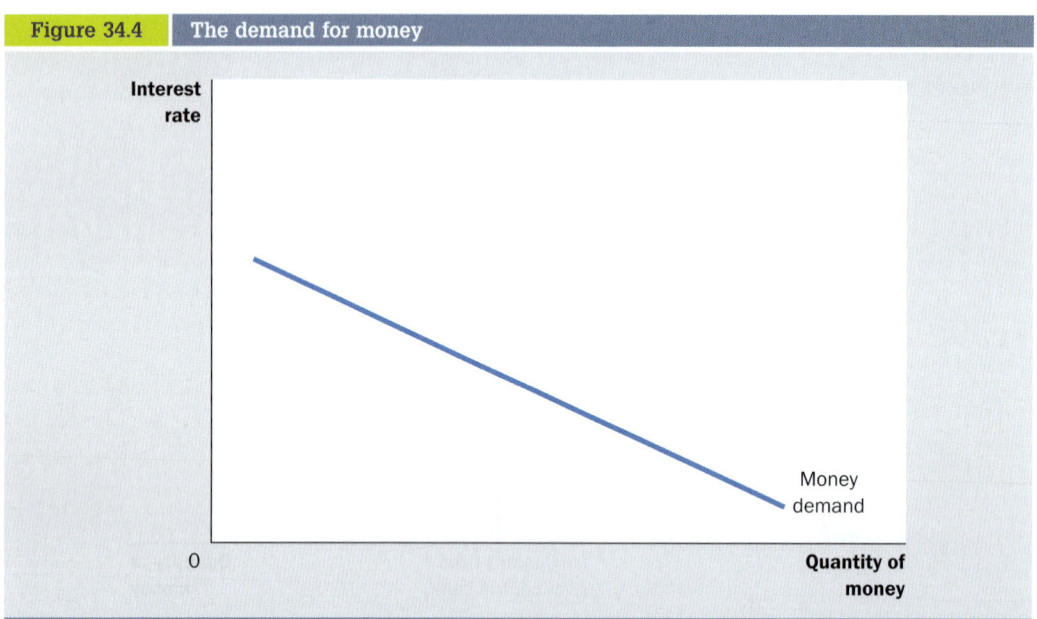

Figure 34.4   The demand for money

Because the interest rate measures the opportunity cost of holding non-interest-bearing money instead of interest-bearing bonds, an increase in the interest rate reduces the quantity of money demanded. A downward-sloping demand curve represents this negative relationship.

Figure 34.5   Equilibrium in the money market

According to the theory of liquidity preference, the interest rate adjusts to ensure that the quantity of money supplied and the quantity of money demanded are in balance.

rid of it by buying interest-bearing bonds or by depositing it in an interest-bearing bank account. Because bond issuers and banks prefer to pay lower interest rates, they respond to this surplus of money by lowering the interest rates they offer. As the interest rate falls, people become more willing to hold money until, at the equilibrium interest rate, people are happy to hold exactly the amount of money the central bank has supplied.

Conversely, at interest rates below the equilibrium level, such as r_2 in Figure 34.5, the quantity of money that people want to hold, MD_2, is greater than the quantity of money that the central bank has supplied. As a result, people try to increase their holdings of money by reducing their holdings of bonds and other interest-bearing assets. As people cut back on their holdings of bonds, bond issuers find that they have to offer higher interest rates to attract buyers. Thus, the interest rate rises and approaches the equilibrium level.

So we can see from the liquidity preference theory and from our description of modern monetary policy in the preceding section that whether the central bank sets the interest rate (the cash rate in Australia) or sets the money supply, the impact on the level of economic activity is the same – the interest rate in the money market has an impact on real economic activity in the short run because prices are sticky in the short run.

How fiscal policy influences aggregate demand

The government can influence the behaviour of the economy not only with monetary policy but also with fiscal policy. Fiscal policy refers to the government's choices regarding the overall level of government purchases or taxes. Earlier in the book we examined how fiscal policy influences saving, investment and growth in the long run. In the short run, however, the main effect of fiscal policy is on the aggregate demand for goods and services.

Changes in government purchases

When the government changes its own purchases of goods and services, it shifts the aggregate-demand curve directly. Suppose, for instance, that the Australian Department of Defence places a $5 billion order for new submarines with the Australian Submarine Corporation, a South Australian company. This order raises the demand for the output produced by Australian Submarine Corporation, which induces the company to hire more workers and increase production. Because Australian Submarine Corporation is part of the economy, the increase in the demand for their submarines is reflected in an increase in the aggregate demand for goods and services. The aggregate-demand curve shifts to the right.

By how much does this $5 billion order from the government shift the aggregate-demand curve? At first, one might guess that the aggregate-demand curve shifts to the right by exactly $5 billion. It turns out, however, that this is not correct. There are two macroeconomic effects that make the size of the shift in aggregate demand differ from the change in government purchases. The first – the multiplier effect – suggests that the shift in aggregate demand could be *larger* than $5 billion. The second – the crowding-out effect – suggests that the increase in aggregate demand could be *smaller* than $5 billion. We now discuss each of these effects in turn.

The multiplier effect

When the government buys $5 billion of goods from Australian Submarine Corporation, that purchase has repercussions. The immediate impact of the higher demand from the government is to raise employment and profits at Australian Submarine Corporation. But as the workers see higher earnings and the firm owners see higher profits, they respond to this increase in income by raising their own spending on consumer goods. As a result, the government purchase from Australian Submarine Corporation raises the demand for the products of many other firms in the economy as well. Because each dollar spent by the government can raise the aggregate demand for goods and services by more than a dollar, government purchases are said to have a **multiplier effect** on aggregate demand.

This multiplier effect continues even after this first round. When consumer spending rises, the firms that produce these consumer goods hire more people and experience higher profits. Higher earnings and profits stimulate consumer spending once again and so on. Thus, there is positive feedback as higher demand leads to higher income, which in turn leads to even higher demand. Once all these effects are added together, the total impact on the quantity of goods and services demanded can be much larger than the initial impulse from higher government spending.

Figure 34.6 illustrates the multiplier effect. The increase in government purchases of $5 billion initially shifts the aggregate-demand curve to the right from AD_1 to AD_2 by exactly $5 billion. But when consumers respond by increasing their spending, the aggregate-demand curve shifts still further to AD_3.

This multiplier effect arising from the response of consumer spending can be strengthened by the response of investment to higher levels of demand. For instance, Australian Submarine Corporation might respond to the higher demand for submarines by deciding to buy more equipment or build another plant. In this case, higher government demand spurs higher demand for investment goods. This positive feedback from demand to investment is sometimes called the *investment accelerator*.

multiplier effect
the additional shifts in aggregate demand that result when expansionary fiscal policy increases income and thereby increases consumer spending

▸ multiplier effect

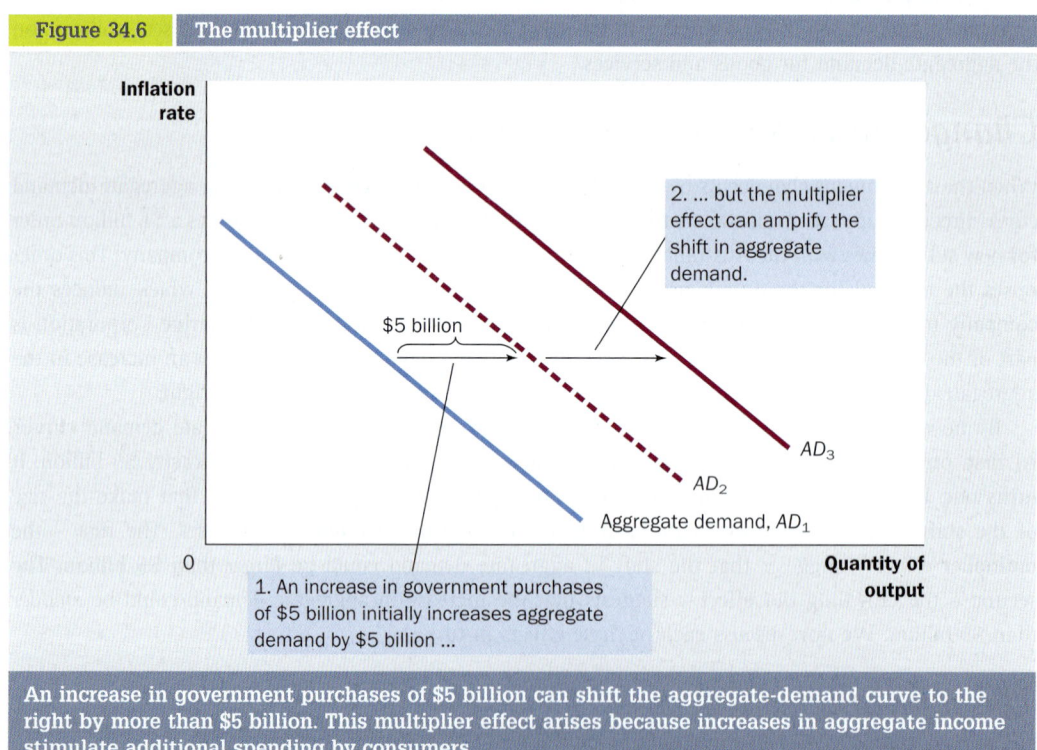

Figure 34.6   The multiplier effect

2. … but the multiplier effect can amplify the shift in aggregate demand.

$5 billion

AD_3

AD_2

Aggregate demand, AD_1

0

Quantity of output

1. An increase in government purchases of $5 billion initially increases aggregate demand by $5 billion …

Inflation rate

An increase in government purchases of $5 billion can shift the aggregate-demand curve to the right by more than $5 billion. This multiplier effect arises because increases in aggregate income stimulate additional spending by consumers.

The crowding-out effect

Although the multiplier effect suggests that the change in demand from fiscal policy can be larger than the change in government purchases, there is another effect that works in the opposite direction. An increase in government purchases stimulates the demand for goods and services, which leads to an increase in the inflation rate. The RBA reacts to the increase in the inflation rate by increasing the cash rate, and a higher interest rate tends to choke off the demand for goods and services. The reduction in demand that results when a fiscal expansion induces a rise in the interest rate by the RBA is called the **crowding-out effect**.

To see why crowding out occurs, let's consider once again what happens when the government buys $5 billion of submarines from Australian Submarine Corporation. As we have discussed, this increase in demand raises the incomes of the workers and owners of this firm (and, because of the multiplier effect, of other firms as well). As incomes rise, households plan to buy more goods and services and, as a result, inflation rises.

The RBA sees the increase in demand leading to an increase in inflation and responds by increasing interest rates. The increase in the interest rate, in turn, reduces the quantity of goods and services demanded. In particular, because borrowing is more expensive, the demand for residential and business investment goods declines. That is, as the increase in government purchases increases the demand for goods and services, it may also crowd out investment. This crowding-out effect partially offsets the impact of government purchases on aggregate demand, as illustrated in Figure 34.7. The initial impact of

crowding-out effect
the offset in aggregate demand that results when expansionary fiscal policy induces the RBA to increase the interest rate and thereby reduce investment spending

| Figure 34.7 | The crowding-out effect |

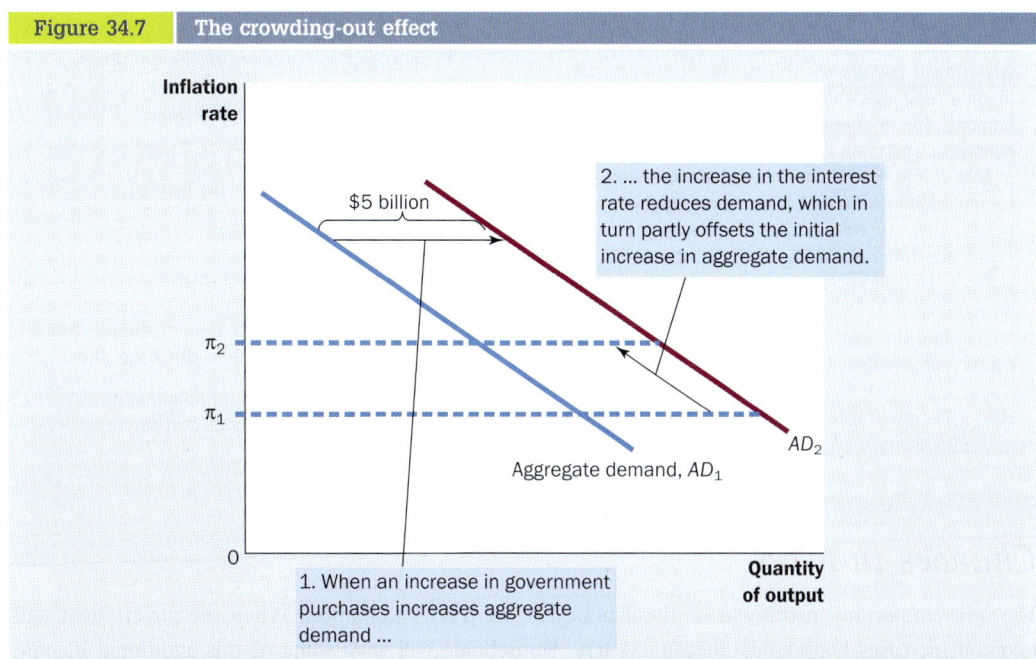

This diagram shows the effects on aggregate demand. The initial impact of the increase in government purchases shifts the aggregate-demand curve from AD_1 to AD_2. Because the interest rate is the cost of borrowing, the increase in the interest rate that results from the RBA increasing the cash rate tends to reduce the quantity of goods and services demanded, particularly for investment goods. This crowding out of investment partially offsets the impact of the fiscal expansion on aggregate demand. In the end, we move up the aggregate-demand curve from π_1 to π_2, so the increase in aggregate demand is less than $5 billion.

the increase in government purchases is to shift the aggregate-demand curve from AD_1 to AD_2, but once crowding out takes place, we move up the aggregate-demand curve AD_2 from π_1 to π_2.

To sum up – *when the government increases its purchases by $5 billion, the aggregate demand for goods and services could rise by more or less than $5 billion, depending on whether the multiplier effect or the crowding-out effect is larger.*

Changes in taxes

The other important instrument of fiscal policy is the level of taxation. When the government cuts taxes, it increases households' take-home pay. Households will save some of this additional income, but they will also spend some of it on consumer goods. Because it increases consumer spending, the tax cut shifts the aggregate-demand curve to the right. Similarly, a tax increase depresses consumer spending and shifts the aggregate-demand curve to the left.

The size of the shift in aggregate demand resulting from a tax change is also affected by the multiplier and crowding-out effects. When the government cuts taxes and stimulates consumer spending, earnings and profits rise, which further stimulates consumer spending. This is the multiplier effect. (The multiplier effect for a tax change will be less than the multiplier effect of an equivalent change in government spending.) At the same time, higher income leads to greater expenditure on goods and services, which leads to higher prices. When the RBA raises the interest rate, this makes borrowing more costly, which reduces investment spending. This is the crowding-out effect. Depending on the size of the multiplier and crowding-out effects, the change in aggregate demand could be larger or smaller than the tax change that causes it.

In addition to the multiplier, there is another important determinant of the size of the shift in aggregate demand that results from a tax change – households' perceptions about whether the tax change is permanent or temporary. For example, suppose that the government announces a tax cut of $1000 per household. In deciding how much of this $1000 to spend, households must ask themselves how long this extra income will last. If households expect the tax cut to be permanent, they will view it as adding substantially to their financial resources and, therefore, increase their spending by a large amount. In this case, the tax cut will have a large impact on aggregate demand. In contrast, if households expect the tax change to be temporary, they will view it as adding only slightly to their financial resources and, therefore, will increase their spending by only a small amount. In this case, the tax cut will have a small impact on aggregate demand.

---

fyi

How fiscal policy might affect aggregate supply

So far our discussion of fiscal policy has stressed how changes in government purchases and changes in taxes influence the quantity of goods and services demanded. Most economists believe that the short-run macroeconomic effects of fiscal policy work mainly through aggregate demand. Yet fiscal policy can potentially also influence the quantity of goods and services supplied.

For instance, consider the effects of tax changes on aggregate supply. One of the *Ten Lessons from Economics* in chapter 1 is that people respond to incentives. When government policymakers cut tax rates, workers get to keep more of each dollar they earn, so they have a greater incentive to work and to produce goods and services. As a result, the quantity of goods and services supplied is greater at any given inflation rate. This is represented by a shift to the right in the aggregate-supply curve. Some economists, called *supply-siders*, have argued that the influence of tax cuts on aggregate supply is very large. Indeed, some supply-siders claim the

influence is so large that a cut in tax rates will actually increase tax revenue by increasing worker effort. Most economists, however, believe that the supply-side effects of tax cuts are much smaller.

Like changes in taxes, changes in government purchases can also potentially affect aggregate supply. Suppose, for instance, that the government increases expenditure on a form of government-provided capital, such as roads. Roads are used by private businesses to make deliveries to their customers; an increase in the quantity of roads increases these businesses' productivity. Hence, when the government spends more on roads, it increases the quantity of goods and services supplied at any given inflation rate and, thus, shifts the aggregate-supply curve to the right. This effect on aggregate supply is probably more important in the long run than in the short run, however, because it would take some time for the government to build the new roads and put them into use.

Suppose that the government reduces spending on highway construction by $10 billion. Which way does the aggregate-demand curve shift? Explain why the shift might be larger than $10 billion. Explain why the shift might be smaller than $10 billion.

Using policy to stabilise the economy

We have seen how monetary and fiscal policy can affect the economy's aggregate demand for goods and services. These theoretical insights raise an important policy question: Should policymakers use these instruments in order to control aggregate demand and stabilise the economy? If so, when? If not, why not?

The case for active stabilisation policy

Let's return to the question that began this chapter. When government spending is cut to maintain the budget surplus, what should the RBA do? As we have seen, government spending is one determinant of the position of the aggregate-demand curve. When the government cuts spending, aggregate demand will fall, which will depress production and employment in the short run. If the RBA is concerned about this adverse effect of the fiscal policy, it can influence an expansion of aggregate demand by reducing the cash rate. A reduction in the interest rate stimulates consumption and investment spending, thus offsetting (at least in part) the decline in aggregate demand resulting from the change in fiscal policy.

This analysis is exactly that followed by members of the Reserve Bank Board. They know that monetary policy is an important determinant of aggregate demand. They also know that there are other important determinants as well, including fiscal policy as set by the government. As a result, the Board watches the debates over fiscal policy with a keen eye.

This response of monetary policy to the change in fiscal policy is an example of a more general phenomenon – the use of policy instruments to stabilise aggregate demand and, as a result, production and employment. Economic stabilisation has been an explicit goal of Australian macroeconomic policy since the *Reserve Bank Act* of 1959. This Act states that the RBA should 'contribute to stability of the currency ..., the maintenance of full employment; and the economic prosperity and welfare of the people of Australia'. In essence, the RBA is required to be accountable for short-run macroeconomic performance.

The Reserve Bank charter has two implications. The first, more modest, implication is that the RBA should avoid being a cause of economic fluctuations. Thus, most economists advise against large and sudden changes in monetary (or fiscal) policy, for such changes are likely to cause fluctuations in aggregate demand. This has been one argument put forward for why the RBA usually only announces small changes in the cash rate, of 0.25 per cent (or 25 basis points, where a basis point is 1/100 of a per cent.) Moreover, when large changes do occur, it is important that monetary and fiscal policymakers be aware of and respond to the other's actions.

The second, more ambitious, implication of the charter is that the RBA should respond to changes in the private economy in order to stabilise aggregate demand. Although recent changes in emphasis of the RBA's responsibilities mean that it is less likely to get involved in management of short-run fluctuations of the economy, there is a strong history of central bank involvement in stabilisation policy.

The *Reserve Bank Act* was passed not long after the publication of John Maynard Keynes's *The General Theory of Employment, Interest, and Money*. As we discussed in the preceding chapter, *The General Theory* has been one of the most influential books ever written about economics. In it, Keynes emphasised the key role of aggregate demand in explaining short-run economic fluctuations. Keynes claimed that the government should actively stimulate aggregate demand when aggregate demand appeared insufficient to maintain production at its full-employment level. Government stimulus could take the form of expansionary fiscal policy or expansionary monetary policy.

Keynes (and his many followers) argued that aggregate demand fluctuates because of largely irrational waves of pessimism and optimism. He used the term *animal spirits* to refer to these arbitrary changes in attitude. When pessimism reigns, households reduce consumption spending, and firms reduce investment spending. The result is reduced aggregate demand, lower production and higher unemployment. Conversely, when optimism reigns, households and firms increase spending. The result is higher aggregate demand, higher production and inflationary pressure. Notice that these changes in attitude are, to some extent, self-fulfilling.

In principle, the government can adjust its monetary and fiscal policy in response to these waves of optimism and pessimism and, thereby, stabilise aggregate demand. So, when people are excessively pessimistic, the RBA can lower the cash rate; when they are excessively optimistic, it can increase the cash rate. A former chairman of the US Federal Reserve described this view of monetary policy very simply: 'The Federal Reserve's job is to take away the punch bowl just as the party gets going'.

CASESTUDY

Keynesian thinking today

Keynesian economics was declared dead and buried by Nobel prize winner Robert Lucas in 1980 when he said: 'One cannot find good, under-forty economists who identify themselves or their work as Keynesian ... At research seminars, people don't take Keynesian theorizing seriously anymore: the audience starts to whisper and giggle to one another'. And yet Keynesian economists have been hiding away in governments around the world for decades, modelling the economy and influencing policy.

Keynes first published his book *The General Theory of Employment, Interest, and Money* in 1936. The height of its influence was in the United States in the 1960s and 1970s. When a reporter in 1961 asked President John F. Kennedy why he advocated a tax cut, Kennedy replied: 'To stimulate the economy. Don't you remember your Economics 101?' Kennedy's policy was, in fact, based on the analysis of taxes we have developed in this chapter. His goal was to increase aggregate demand in order to stimulate production and employment.

John Maynard Keynes

Source: Corbis Australia.

In choosing this policy, Kennedy was relying on his team of economic advisers. This team included such prominent economists as James Tobin and Robert Solow, who later would win Nobel prizes for their contributions to economics. As students in the 1940s, these economists had closely studied John Maynard Keynes's *General Theory*, which was then only a few years old. When the Kennedy advisers proposed cutting taxes, they were putting Keynes's ideas into action.

Although tax changes can have a potent influence on aggregate demand, they have other effects as well. In particular, by changing the incentives that people face, taxes can alter the aggregate supply of goods and services. Part of the Kennedy proposal was an investment tax credit, which gives a tax break to firms that invest in new capital. Higher investment would not only stimulate aggregate demand immediately but would also increase the economy's productive capacity over time. Thus, the short-run goal of increasing production through higher aggregate demand was coupled with a long-run goal of increasing production through higher aggregate supply. The tax cut would help in this because it was an investment tax credit, not simply an across-the-board tax cut. And, indeed, when the tax cut Kennedy proposed was finally enacted in 1964, it helped usher in a period of robust economic growth.

Policymakers in various countries have, from time to time, proposed using fiscal policy as a tool for controlling aggregate demand. For example, some governments in Europe have recently had a decidedly Keynesian outlook. Germany and France have both had finance ministers who have advocated Keynesian-type expansionary fiscal policies to combat European unemployment of over 10 per cent.

The Japanese government boosted government expenditure in 1998 to try to kick-start the Japanese economy. Both private consumption and investment demand were low and exports were

>>

down due to the downturn in the economies of Japan's trading partners in Asia. The Japanese government was urged by its trading partners to make up for the lack of aggregate demand by 'priming the pump'.

Similarly, when President Clinton moved into the White House in 1993, one of his first proposals was a 'stimulus package' of increased government spending. Many economists considered the Clinton proposal too late to be of much help. Moreover, deficit reduction to encourage long-run economic

growth was considered a higher priority than a short-run expansion in aggregate demand. The elimination of the budget deficit reduces crowding out and therefore encourages private sector investment.

And in the recent Global Financial Crisis, governments in the US, Australia and Europe have all used some form of 'stimulus package' to stop their economies from going further into recession. In fact, as the following article by Ross Gittins indicates, Keynes is definitely back in fashion.

IN THE NEWS ...

KEYNES IS FASHIONABLE ONCE AGAIN

As the preceding case study shows, Keynesian economics is certainly popular with policymakers, even if most academic economists haven't embraced him again. Ross Gittins explains why Keynes' ideas are back in vogue.

How economists forgot much of what they knew

by Ross Gittins

When I started as an economics writer in the mid-1970s, the Keynesian ideas that had guided macro-economic policy through the postwar Golden Age were judged a failure and economics was in crisis.

But now, as Professor John Quiggin of the University of Queensland reminds us in his new book, *Zombie Economics*, the global financial crisis and the Great Recession have revealed the ideas that replaced simple Keynesianism as failures that plunged economics back into crisis.

The end of the Golden Age and the loss of faith in Keynesianism were brought about by the advent of 'stagflation' – high inflation despite a stagnant economy. Keynesian theory said you could have high unemployment or high inflation but not at the same time. It could fix one or the other but not both together.

There aren't many new ideas in economics, just old ideas tarted up. Keynes's ideas were new, however. The 'neo-classical' orthodoxy of his day said recessions couldn't happen, so it couldn't explain the Great Depression of the 1930s and had no policies to end it.

Keynes identified various market 'imperfections' that explained the economy's malfunctioning and advocated government spending to stimulate the economy and get it growing again. When economists lost faith in Keynesianism they turned back to the discredited neo-classical orthodoxy. Milton Friedman's 'monetarism', for instance, was based on the old 'quantity theory of money'.

Government policymakers soon gave up on monetarism's targeting of growth in the supply of money – it didn't work – but a lasting consequence of that episode was to switch the primacy in macro-management from fiscal policy (the budget) to monetary policy (interest rates).

Keynesianism was criticised because its approach at the macro (top-down) level didn't fit with the bottom-up approach of micro-economics. Its conclusions about how the whole economy worked didn't fit with the standard conclusions about how individual markets worked.

Building models of the macro economy based on neo-classical micro-economic foundations had various attractions. Giving up Keynesianism's more realistic assumptions about how the world worked made the models more rigorously logical and amenable to mathematics.

Assuming everyone was rational and in possession of perfect information got economics back to its libertarian roots, creating a presumption against government intervention in markets and favouring small government and lower taxes.

One development on the old neo-classical foundation was the 'efficient market hypothesis', which Quiggin says is the central theoretical doctrine of the 'market liberalism' that replaced Keynesianism.

It says financial markets are the best possible guide to the value of economic assets and therefore to decisions about investment and production. And coming after the collapse of the Keynesian Bretton Woods system of fixed exchange rates, it provided a rationale for the era of finance-driven capitalism that's ended so badly.

In its 'weak form', the hypothesis says movements in the prices of assets such as shares can't be predicted from their past movements as claimed by 'technical analysts'. Like a drunk, share prices move in a 'random walk' in reaction to whatever good or bad news next comes along.

In its 'strong form', the hypothesis says the market price of an asset is the best possible estimate of its value, incorporating all the available information.

If this is true, bubbles can't develop in asset markets, causing them to crash when finally the bubble bursts.

You can see how this faith – an amazing triumph of hope over centuries of experience – encouraged the excessive deregulation of banks and the financial system, which had formerly been heavily regulated in response to the banks' key role in the Depression.

At the level of macro-economic theory, monetarism was soon superseded by 'new classical' economics, incorporating mathematically (and ideologically) convenient propositions such as 'rational expectations' and 'Ricardian equivalence'.

Rational expectations assumes people's expectations about future events will always be right; everyone has the same views about how the economy works as the economics professors who built the model.

Ricardian equivalence – named after David Ricardo, the classical economist who first thought of the idea, then dismissed it – assumes that when governments engage in deficit spending during recessions this has no stimulatory effect on the economy because everyone knows taxes will eventually have to rise to pay off the debt, so they start saving.

Between them, these ideas rendered ineffective government efforts to manage the macro economy. In practice, the academics were less damning of monetary policy. Predictably, new classical economics was never popular with politicians and treasuries, but it fed the general mood that the less governments intervened in the economy the better.

These 'new classical' academics developed 'real business cycle' theory to explain why economies move in cycles of boom and bust, even though simple neo-classical theory says they don't and many conservative economists had argued that all unemployment was voluntary. Under this theory all fluctuations in economic activity are caused by 'exogenous shocks' (developments outside the economic system) such as changes in technology, the terms of trade or workers' preferences for leisure.

Eventually academics – including those in the 'new Keynesian' school, which retained remnants of the old Keynesianism – coalesced around the 'dynamic stochastic general equilibrium' model. This did allow for the possibility that wages and prices might be slow to adjust, and for imbalances between supply and demand, but moved the model only a short way towards the real world.

The fact that, following the malfunctioning of the 1970s, the main economies seemed to settle down after 1985 – with inflation back under control and unemployment lower – led many economists to conclude this Great Moderation proved economics was now on the right track and the business cycle had been tamed.

Famous last words. The US housing boom proved to be a giant bubble that eventually burst, we realised what crazy games the global financial markets had been playing, the sharemarket crashed, the banking system tottered on its foundations and the developed world entered by far the worst recession since the Depression, which looks likely to linger for the rest of the decade.

And the people whose unrealistic theories helped to bring the calamity about had no idea it was coming because they were playing 'rigorous' mathematical games at the time.

I haven't done justice to Quiggin's book, so if you're interested in a readable exposition of

the exploits of academic economists over the past 35 years I recommend it highly. It's the story of how economists forgot much of what they knew. Please, guys, don't do that again.

Source: Ross Gittins/*The Sydney Morning Herald*, 13 November 2010.

The case against active stabilisation policy

Some economists argue that the government should avoid using monetary and fiscal policy to try to stabilise the economy. They claim that these policy instruments should be set to achieve long-run goals, such as rapid economic growth and low inflation, and that the economy should be left to deal with short-run fluctuations on its own. Although these economists may admit that monetary and fiscal policy can stabilise the economy in theory, they doubt whether it can do so in practice.

The main argument against active monetary and fiscal policy is that these policies affect the economy with a substantial lag. As we have seen, monetary policy works by changing interest rates, which in turn influence investment spending. But many firms make investment plans far in advance. Thus, changes in monetary policy are thought to take at least six months to have much effect on output and employment, and these effects can last for several years. Critics of stabilisation policy argue that because of this lag, the RBA should not try to fine-tune the economy. They claim that the RBA often reacts too late to changing economic conditions and, as a result, ends up being a cause rather than a cure of economic fluctuations. They advocate a passive monetary policy that simply ensures sufficient liquidity in the system for the level of economic activity.

Fiscal policy also works with a lag but, unlike the lag in monetary policy, the lag in fiscal policy is largely attributable to the political process. In Australia, this is because changes in fiscal policy involve adjustments to the government's spending and taxing behaviour that may not be fully supported by the Senate. So although the government budget is, by convention, usually accepted by the Senate, by the time it has been negotiated, passed and implemented, the condition of the economy may well have changed.

These lags in monetary and fiscal policy are a problem in part because economic forecasting is so imprecise. If forecasters could accurately predict the condition of the economy a year in advance, then monetary and fiscal policymakers could look ahead when making policy decisions. In this case, policymakers could stabilise the economy, despite the lags they face. In practice, however, recessions and depressions arrive without much advance warning. And even when we see them coming, not everyone agrees that government intervention is the right thing to do.

IN THE NEWS . . .

INTEREST RATES CAN'T SOLVE EVERYTHING

In the last section we saw how pro-stabilisation policy advocates made the case for intervention in the economy. In the following article, Gerald O'Driscoll gives the other side of the story – why governments shouldn't intervene to stabilise the economy and when they do, they often do the wrong thing. (Harry S. Truman, a US president in the 1940s and 50s, bemoaned the indecision of economists. He said 'Give me a one-handed economist! All my economists say, "On the one hand… on the other",') To be well-informed, we have to understand both sides of the argument.

The Fed can't solve our economic woes

by Gerald P. O'Driscoll Jr

A policy of low interest rates is a textbook response of monetary authorities to the economic weakness brought on by deficient aggregate demand. The policy is justified by pointing to various ways in which money can promote economic activity – including by stimulating investment, discouraging savings, encouraging consumption spending, and allowing individuals to lower their debt burdens by refinancing existing debt. While these effects are theoretically plausible, this textbook policy does not apply to our present situation.

First, our lingering crisis and economic weakness was brought on not by a Keynesian failure of effective demand, but by a Hayekian asset boom and bust. Second, the textbook case for low interest rates treats the policy as one of benefits without costs. No such policy exists.

The housing boom and bust was a classic asset bubble, such as occurred frequently in the 18th and 19th centuries. Easy money working through cheap credit made long-term investments appear more valuable than would otherwise have been the case.

In most cases, investment booms drive industries with sound fundamentals. When the cheap credit keeps flowing, however, fundamentals are forgotten and the process evolves into a mania (to use the old-fashioned term). What cannot be sustained will not be, so the boom ends in a crisis.

In these scenarios, the collapse of demand is a consequence – not the cause – of the bust. Policies to address crises must get cause and effect right.

When housing prices peaked and then turned down, there were repercussions throughout the financial system and then the broader economy. Mortgage-related securities soured, hitting the balance sheets of the institutions that had purchased them. As that became known, the prices of the securities of these institutions (mainly but not exclusively financial) fell. Credit dried up and the economy tanked. A general rout in the stock market ensued.

The financial panic and ensuing great recession was a classic balance-sheet recession. As balance sheets shrank in value, demand collapsed. There was a liquidity crisis as well, centered around Lehman's collapse, but the driving force was collapsing balance sheets, impaired capital values and, for many, insolvencies.

The declines in home values, investor portfolios and 401(k) plans, and the uncertainties surrounding retirement plans, have all had a big impact. The solution lies in restoring balance sheets. For financial firms, that means raising capital. For consumers and businesses alike, that means saving more of their reduced incomes.

Yet public policy has focused almost exclusively on stimulating spending without much regard to why spending, especially consumption, has flagged. Until balance sheets (corporate and household) are restored, increased spending cannot be sustained.

Temporary spending and tax breaks are always dubious, and especially so now when the rational motivation is to save more and consume less. One-off tax credits for homes, for example, merely borrowed sales from the future. These fiscal programs predictably depressed rather than augmented future consumption.

What is in short supply is not liquidity, but savings. The Fed can supply the former but not the latter. Both fiscal and monetary polices need to shift their focus. The Fed has done the heavy lifting and responded more than adequately to liquidity issues. Now there is little further it can do that is beneficial.

Its move toward Japan-style quantitative easing is a misstep. And historically low interest rates – about which the Bank of International Settlements, the bank for central banks, sounded a warning in its 2009/2010 annual report – will inevitably distort economic

>>

activity, as they did during the housing boom. Low interest rates slow the process of restoring balance sheets by keeping asset prices artificially inflated. They also penalize saving, thus prolonging the process of rebuilding balance sheets.

In the fiscal realm, policy must be reoriented from stimulating consumption to encouraging productive investment (not renewed financial speculation). That means no income-tax increases or costly new mandates. In particular, the Bush tax cuts should not be allowed to expire. No matter how the administration spins it, their expiration would entail a large increase in marginal tax rates in the midst of economic weakness. That would further impede savings and capital accumulation, discouraging firms from expanding and hiring workers. Treasury Secretary Tim Geithner is proposing to repeat the mistake of Herbert Hoover, who persuaded Congress to raise taxes in 1932.

Markets are resilient, but their recovery can be impeded by bad policies. At present, both monetary and fiscal policies are on the wrong track.

Mr. O'Driscoll is a senior fellow at the Cato Institute. He was formerly a vice president at the Federal Reserve Bank of Dallas and later at Citigroup.

Source: *The Wall Street Journal*, 16 August 2010. Reprinted by permission of *The Wall Street Journal*, Copyright © 2010 Dow Jones & Company, Inc. All Rights Reserved Worldwide.

Automatic stabilisers

automatic stabilisers
changes in fiscal policy that stimulate aggregate demand when the economy goes into a recession or rein in aggregate demand when the economy booms without policymakers having to take any deliberate action

All economists – both advocates and critics of stabilisation policy – agree that the lags in the implementation of policy render policy less useful as a tool for short-run stabilisation. The economy would be more stable, therefore, if policymakers could find a way to avoid some of these lags. In fact, they have. **Automatic stabilisers** are changes in fiscal policy that stimulate aggregate demand when the economy goes into a recession without policymakers having to take any deliberate action.

The most important automatic stabiliser is the tax system. When the economy goes into a recession, the amount of taxes collected by the government falls automatically because almost all taxes are closely tied to economic activity. Personal income tax depends on households' incomes, payroll tax depends on workers' earnings, and company income tax depends on firms' profits. Because incomes, earnings and profits all fall in a recession, the government's tax revenue falls as well. This automatic tax cut stimulates aggregate demand and, thereby, reduces the magnitude of economic fluctuations.

Government outlays also act as automatic stabilisers. In particular, when the economy goes into a recession and workers are laid off, more people apply for unemployment benefits and other forms of income support. This automatic increase in government outlays stimulates aggregate demand at exactly the time when aggregate demand is insufficient to maintain full employment. Indeed, when the unemployment benefits system was first introduced in 1945, economists who advocated this policy did so in part because of its power as an automatic stabiliser.

The automatic stabilisers in the Australian economy are not sufficiently strong to prevent recessions completely. Nonetheless, without these automatic stabilisers, output and employment would probably be more volatile than they are. For this reason, many economists oppose any sort of legislated requirement for a balanced budget. When the economy goes into a recession, taxes fall, government spending rises and the government's budget moves towards deficit. If the government faced a strict balanced-budget rule, it would be forced to look for ways to raise taxes or cut spending in a recession. In other words, a strict balanced-budget rule would eliminate the automatic stabilisers inherent in our current system of taxes and government spending.

IN THE NEWS . . .

OPENNESS FROM THE RBA'S GOVERNOR

In 2006, the Deputy Governor of the Reserve Bank of Australia took over from long-serving Governor Ian Macfarlane. He was perceived to be a safe bet – not likely to implement drastic changes. And yet, he has made significant, if quiet, changes in the way Australia's central bank operates. Alan Kohler writes about the openness that Glenn Stephens brought to RBA monetary policy decisions.

The RBA opens its doors
by Alan Kohler

Warm plaudits to the Reserve Bank Governor Glenn Stevens for the bank's new policy of glasnost.

It is a revolution at 65 Martin Place: there is to be a statement each month whatever the decision, the decision will be announced at 2.30pm on the day of the board meeting rather than at 9.30am the next day, and the minutes of each meeting are to be issued two weeks later. The sainted Harry Knight (1975–1982), among other former Governors, would be pursing his lips like crazy.

So the main thing that happened yesterday was the RBA flinging open its doors. Next question: what do we see there?

The decision to keep rates on hold was not a surprise, and nor were the reasons for it: that borrowing costs have already gone up and look like going up some more.

'These developments will help contain private demand over the period ahead,' said Glenn Stevens in his statement.

Thanks for that, Governor. And the November minutes? Well, the most remarkable thing about them, in my view, was what they did not contain – the elephant in the room that was apparently studiously ignored throughout the meeting: the election.

Because they were putting up rates during an election campaign for the first time, that decision was one of the most momentous in the history of the RBA, and all of the members of the board would have been acutely aware of

that. Yet according to the minutes, it was not mentioned. It's a pity minutes were not taken of the conversation during lunch.

What they did talk about was inflation, domestic demand, the world economy and financial markets.

RBA staff were forecasting a rise in underlying inflation to 3.25 per cent and CPI inflation to 3.5 per cent next year. All the data on demand and activity pointed to further pressure on inflation, so board members agreed that on domestic grounds the case for a rate hike was clear.

The world economy was weakening because of the slowdown in the US, but thanks to China, global growth was still expected to be above average in 2008.

As for financial markets, confidence was fragile but conditions had been more settled recently (this was early November – now they're not so settled).

A month is a long time in credit markets. Back then the directors were told that 'although interest costs in wholesale markets were still a little higher than a few months earlier, sound borrowers were still able to obtain finance readily'.

But now, according to yesterday's statement, 'borrowing costs have risen appreciably since mid year, particularly for business borrowers'.

It's a tricky time for central bankers – and a good time to be more open.

Source: Alan Kohler/*Business Spectator*, www.businessspectator.com.au, 5 December 2007.

Suppose firms become pessimistic about the future. What happens to aggregate demand? If the RBA wants to stabilise aggregate demand, how should it alter the money supply? If it does this, what happens to the interest rate?

The economy in the long run and the short run

At this point, we should pause and reflect on a seemingly awkward contradiction. It might appear as if we now have two explanations for how interest rates are determined. Chapter 27 said that the interest rate adjusts to balance the supply of and demand for loanable funds (that is, national saving and desired investment). In contrast, this chapter said that the interest rate is determined by the Reserve Bank of Australia. Which of these theories is right? The answer is 'both'. (See the 'FYI' further on for an algebraic explanation using the liquidity preference theory.)

To understand how this can be true, we must consider the differences between the long-run and short-run behaviour of the economy. Three macroeconomic variables are of central importance – the economy's output of goods and services, the interest rate and the inflation rate. According to the classical macroeconomic theory we developed in chapters 26, 27 and 30, these variables are determined as follows:

1 *Output* is determined by the supplies of capital and labour and the available production technology for turning capital and labour into output.
2 For any given level of output, the *interest rate* adjusts to balance the supply of and demand for loanable funds.
3 The *inflation rate* adjusts to balance the supply of and demand for money in the long run. Changes in the supply of money lead to proportionate changes in the inflation rate.

These are three of the essential propositions of classical economic theory. Most economists believe that these propositions do a good job of describing how the economy works *in the long run*.

Yet these propositions do not hold in the short run. As we discussed in the preceding chapter, many prices are slow to adjust to changes in the money supply. As a result, the rate of inflation cannot, by itself, balance the supply of and demand for money in the short run. This price inflexibility allows interest rate changes to affect the aggregate demand for goods and services. As aggregate demand fluctuates, the economy's output of goods and services moves away from the level determined by factor supplies and technology.

For thinking about the economy in the short run, then, it is best to reverse the order of analysis:

1 The *inflation rate* is stuck at some level and, in the short run, is relatively unresponsive to changing economic conditions.
2 The RBA sets the *interest rate* and money supply adjusts to satisfy money demand at that interest rate.
3 The level of *output* responds to changes in the aggregate demand for goods and services, which is in part determined by the interest rate that the RBA sets.

Figure 34.8 summarises these propositions and highlights the differences between the economy in the long run and the economy in the short run.

Thus, the different theories of the interest rate are useful for different purposes. When thinking about the long-run determinants of interest rates, it is best to keep in mind the loanable-funds

Figure 34.8 How long-run and short-run macroeconomic theories differ

(a) The long run

Output is fixed by factor supplies and technology. → Interest rate balances supply of and demand for loanable funds. → Price level balances supply of and demand for money.

(b) The short run

Price level is predetermined (sticky). → Interest rate balances supply of and demand for money. → Output responds to changes in aggregate demand.

This figure illustrates the differences between the long-run and short-run behaviour of the economy. In the long run, the interest rate and inflation rate adjust to accommodate a fixed level of output. In the short run, the interest rate and output adjust to accommodate a predetermined level of prices.

theory. This theory highlights the importance of an economy's saving propensities and investment opportunities. In contrast, when thinking about the short-run, it is best to keep in mind the interest-rate effect to see how monetary policy affects short-run economic activity.

fyi

The long run and the short run: An algebraic explanation

A few mathematically inclined readers might find the following algebraic explanation helpful for clarifying the difference between the economy's behaviour in the long run and its behaviour in the short run. If you are not so inclined, just skip this box.

We can view the economy as described by two key markets – the money market and the goods market. Supply and demand in the money market are described by the equation:

$$M = L(r)P$$

where M is the money supply, P the inflation rate and r the interest rate. $L(r)$ is a function showing how money demand responds to the interest rate. This is called the LM (liquidity–money) equation. Supply and demand in the goods market are described by the equation:

$$Y = C + I(r) + G$$

where Y is output, C consumption, I investment and G government purchases. (For simplicity, we

assume here a closed economy, so net exports do not enter this equation.) Note that national saving, $Y - C - G$, represents the supply of loanable funds, and investment, $I(r)$, represents the demand for loanable funds, which depends on the interest rate. This is called the IS (investment–saving) equation. The IS and LM equations together describe two relationships among three variables – output Y, the interest rate r and the inflation rate P.

Now let's compare the long run and short run. Over both time horizons, the IS and the LM equations must be satisfied to ensure equilibrium in both the goods market and the money market. But different variables move to maintain equilibrium in the long run and the short run. Here is the difference:

- In the long run, output Y is determined by factor supplies and technology. Given the fixed level of output, the interest rate r adjusts to satisfy the IS equation. Given this interest rate, the inflation rate P adjusts to satisfy the LM equation.
- In the short run, the inflation rate P is stuck at a level set in the past. Given the fixed inflation rate

>>

846

and a nominal interest rate set by the RBA, this means r is determined. This means M changes to satisfy the *LM* equation. The interest rate being determined means the level of output Y adjusts to satisfy the *IS* equation.

The long-run case corresponds to our analysis in chapters 26, 27 and 30. The short-run case corresponds to our analysis of monetary and fiscal policy in this chapter.

Explain the difference between long-run and short-run macroeconomic analysis. What theory of the interest rate is best for analysing the economy in the long run? What theory is best for analysing the economy in the short run?

Conclusion

Before policymakers make any change in policy, they need to consider all the effects of their decisions. Earlier in the book we examined classical models of the economy, which describe the long-run effects of monetary and fiscal policy. There we saw how fiscal policy influences saving, investment, the trade balance and long-run growth, and how monetary policy influences the inflation rate.

In this chapter we examined the short-run effects of monetary and fiscal policy. We saw how these policy instruments can change the aggregate demand for goods and services and, thereby, alter the economy's production and employment in the short run. When governments reduce their spending in order to balance the budget, they need to consider both the long-run effects on saving and growth and the short-run effects on aggregate demand and employment. When the RBA increases the interest rate, it must take into account the long-run effect on inflation as well as the short-run effect on production. In the next chapter we discuss the transition between the short run and the long run more fully and we see that policymakers often face a trade-off between long-run and short-run goals.

Summary

- In developing a theory of short-run economic fluctuations, Keynes proposed the theory of liquidity preference to explain the determinants of the interest rate. According to this theory, the interest rate adjusts to balance the supply of and demand for money.
- An increase in inflation generally leads to the RBA increasing the cash rate. Banks use the cash rate to set other interest rates, including the interest rate for firms borrowing money to undertake investment. Because the interest rate represents the cost of borrowing, a higher interest rate reduces investment and, thereby, the quantity of goods and services demanded. The downward-sloping aggregate-demand curve expresses this negative relationship between the inflation rate and the quantity demanded.
- Policymakers can influence aggregate demand with monetary policy. A decrease in the interest rate stimulates investment spending, represented by a movement down the aggregate-demand curve. Conversely, an increase in the interest rate lowers investment spending, represented by a movement up the aggregate-demand curve.
- Policymakers can also influence aggregate demand with fiscal policy. An increase in government purchases or a cut in taxes shifts the aggregate-demand curve to the right. A decrease in government purchases or an increase in taxes shifts the aggregate-demand curve to the left.
- When the government alters spending or taxes, the resulting shift in aggregate demand can be larger or smaller than the fiscal change. The multiplier effect tends to amplify the effects of fiscal policy on aggregate demand. The crowding-out effect tends to dampen the effects of fiscal policy on aggregate demand.
- Because monetary and fiscal policy can influence aggregate demand, the government sometimes uses these policy instruments in an attempt to stabilise the economy. Economists disagree about how active the government should be in this effort. According to advocates of active stabilisation policy, changes in attitudes by households and firms shift aggregate demand; if the government does not respond, the result is undesirable and unnecessary fluctuations in output and employment. According to critics of active stabilisation policy, monetary and fiscal policy work with such long lags that attempts at stabilising the economy often end up being destabilising.
- The effects of monetary and fiscal policy depend on the time horizon. The aggregate-demand effects on output emphasised in this chapter hold only in the short run, over which prices are sticky. In the long run, output is determined by factor supplies and technology.

Key concepts

automatic stabilisers   crowding-out effect   multiplier effect

Questions for review

1 What is the theory of liquidity preference? How does it help explain the downward slope of the aggregate-demand curve?
2 Why does an increase in interest rates move the economy up the aggregate-demand curve?
3 The government spends $3 billion to build a new road linking Cairns and Adelaide. Explain why aggregate demand might increase by more than $3 billion. Explain why aggregate demand might increase by less than $3 billion.

4   Suppose that survey measures of consumer confidence indicate a wave of pessimism is sweeping the country. If policymakers do nothing, what will happen to aggregate demand? What should the RBA do if it wants to stabilise aggregate demand? If the RBA does nothing, what might the government do to stabilise aggregate demand?

5   Give an example of a government policy that acts as an automatic stabiliser. Explain why this policy has this effect.

6   Why do changes in monetary policy have different effects over different time horizons?

Problems and applications

1   Explain how each of the following developments would affect the demand for money and the interest rate. What would have to happen to the money supply in each case? Illustrate your answers with diagrams.

   a   A wave of optimism boosts business investment.

   b   The RBA is worried about the impact of high housing prices and suggests Australian banks decrease the size of their loans.

   c   An increase in oil prices shifts the short-run aggregate-supply curve upwards.

   d   Households decide to hold more money because of concerns about a reoccurrence of a global financial crisis.

2   Other countries have 'smart cards' – similar to credit or debit cards, but with the added security of an imbedded microprocessor. They have been used as an alternative to debit cards – people purchase a 'smart card' of a certain monetary value and then the card can be topped up when its value is used up, like with a phone card.

   a   How would this affect the velocity of money?

   b   Suppose there is an increase in counterfeiting and shops stop accepting cash in payment for goods and services and instead accept smart cards. How does this affect the money supply?

   c   How would this affect interest rates?

3   Consider two policies – a tax cut that will last for only one year and a tax cut that is expected to be permanent. Which policy will stimulate greater spending by consumers? Which policy will have the greater impact on aggregate demand? Explain. Would it make any difference if the tax cut were a reduction in the GST rate, say from 10 per cent to 5 per cent, or a reduction in income tax rates? Explain.

4   The interest rate in Australia fell sharply during 1991. Many observers believed this decline showed that monetary policy was quite expansionary during the year. Could this conclusion be incorrect? (*Hint:* Australia was in the middle of a recession in 1991.)

5   In 1984, new legislation allowed banks to pay interest on cheque account deposits, which they could not do previously.

   a   If we define money to include cheque account deposits, what effect did this legislation have on money demand? Explain.

   b   If the RBA had maintained a constant money supply in the face of this change, what would have happened to the interest rate? What would have happened to aggregate demand and aggregate output?

   c   If the RBA had maintained a constant market interest rate (the interest rate on non-monetary assets) in the face of this change, what change in the money supply would have been necessary? What would have happened to aggregate demand and aggregate output?

6   Consider two economies – Flimland and Flamland. In Flimland, the central bank uses interest rates to conduct monetary policy. In Flamland, the central bank conducts monetary policy by changing the money supply.

   a   Which country would have a more effective monetary policy? Explain.

   b   Which country would have higher inflation? Explain.

   c   Why can't Flimland and Flamland set both interest rates *and* money supply?

7   This chapter explains that expansionary monetary policy reduces the interest rate and thus stimulates demand for consumption and investment goods. Explain how such a policy also stimulates the demand for net exports. (You may need to refer to chapter 32 to answer this question.)

8   Suppose economists observe that an increase in government spending of $10 billion raises the total demand for goods and services by $30 billion.

   a   Is crowding out occurring in this case? Explain.

   b   If these economists ignore the possibility of crowding out, what would they estimate the marginal propensity to consume (*MPC*) to be?

   c   Now suppose the economists allow for crowding out. Would their new estimate of the *MPC* be larger or smaller than their initial one?

9   Suppose the government reduces taxes by $30 million, that there is no crowding out and that the marginal propensity to consume is ¾.

   a   What is the initial effect of the tax reduction on aggregate demand?

   b   What additional effects follow this initial effect? What is the total effect of the tax cut on aggregate demand?

   c   How does the total effect of this $30 million tax cut compare with the total effect of a $30 million increase in government purchases? Why?

10   Suppose consumers suddenly become less optimistic about their future incomes and decide to purchase $30 million fewer additional goods and services. Will this change have a 'multiplier' effect on total output? Explain.

11   The Gillard government is concerned about the growing budget deficit, so they decide to cut government expenditures by $10 billion. They also decide the economy needs a boost so they decide to cut income taxed by $30 billion. Would this simply mean a net increase in aggregate demand of $20 billion? Why or why not?

12   Suppose that the Commonwealth government decided to *increase* government spending at the same time as the RBA decides to increase interest rates. What is the net effect on aggregate demand? What factors in the economy does your answer depend upon?

13   Assume the economy is in a recession. Explain how each of the following policies would affect consumption and investment. In each case, indicate any direct effects, any effects resulting from changes in total output, any effects resulting from changes in the interest rate and the overall effect. If there are conflicting effects making the answer ambiguous, say so.

   a   An increase in government spending

   b   A reduction in taxes

   c   A lowering of interest rates.

14   For various reasons, fiscal policy changes automatically when output and employment fluctuate.

   a   Explain why tax revenue changes when the economy booms.

   b   Explain why government spending changes when the economy goes into a recession.

   c   If the government were to operate under a strict balanced-budget rule, what would it have to do in a booming economy? Would that make the boom more or less extreme?

15 In response to an increase in interest rates, would the following things be smaller, larger or no different in the long run than in the short run?

   a   Consumer expenditures

   b   The inflation rate

   c   The interest rate

   d   Aggregate output.

16 Suppose that the RBA decides to increase the interest rate.

   a   What will happen to the money supply? Illustrate your answer with an appropriate diagram.

   b   What is the effect of this policy on the interest rate in the long run? How do you know?

   c   What characteristic of the economy makes the short-run effect of monetary policy on the interest rate different from the long-run effect?

Search me!

When accessing information about economics use the following keywords in any combinations you require:

 • monetary policy   • multiplier effect

CourseMate

CourseMate

For more multimedia resources and activities on economics, visit the Economics CourseMate website.

35

The short-run trade-off between inflation and unemployment

Learning objectives

In this chapter you will:

- learn why policymakers face a short-run trade-off between inflation and unemployment

- consider why the inflation–unemployment trade-off disappears in the long run

- see how supply shocks can shift the inflation–unemployment trade-off

- consider the short-run cost of reducing the rate of inflation

- see how policymakers' credibility might affect the cost of reducing inflation.

Two closely watched indicators of economic performance are inflation and unemployment. When the Australian Bureau of Statistics (ABS) releases data on these variables each month, policymakers are eager to hear the news. Some commentators have added together the inflation rate and the unemployment rate to produce a *misery index*, which purports to measure the health of the economy.

How are these two measures of economic performance related to each other? Earlier in the book we discussed the long-run determinants of unemployment and the long-run determinants of inflation. We saw that the natural rate of unemployment depends on various features of the labour market, such as minimum-wage laws, the market power of unions, the role of efficiency wages and the effectiveness of job search. In contrast, the inflation rate depends primarily on growth in the quantity of money, which the central bank influences. In the long run, therefore, inflation and unemployment are largely unrelated problems.

In the short run, just the opposite is true. One of the *Ten Lessons from Economics* discussed in chapter 1 is that society faces a short-run trade-off between inflation and unemployment. If monetary and fiscal policymakers expand aggregate demand, they can lower unemployment in the short run, but only at the cost of higher inflation. If they contract aggregate demand, they can lower inflation, but only at the cost of temporarily higher unemployment.

In this chapter we examine this trade-off more closely. The relationship between inflation and unemployment is a topic that has attracted the attention of some of the most important economists of the last 50 years. The best way to understand this relationship is to see how thinking about it has evolved over time. As we will see, the history of thought regarding inflation and unemployment since the 1950s is inextricably connected to the history of the Australian economy. These two histories will show why the trade-off between inflation and unemployment holds in the short run, why it does not hold in the long run and what issues it raises for economic policymakers.

The Phillips curve

The short-run relationship between inflation and unemployment is often called the *Phillips curve*. We begin with the discovery of the Phillips curve and its migration to Australia.

Origins of the Phillips curve

In 1958, economist A. W. Phillips from New Zealand published an article in the British journal *Economica* that would make him famous. The article was entitled 'The Relationship between Unemployment and the Rate of Change of Money Wages in the United Kingdom, 1861–1957'. In it, Phillips showed a negative correlation between the rate of unemployment and the rate of inflation. That is, Phillips showed that years with low unemployment tend to have high inflation, and years with high unemployment tend to have low inflation. (Phillips examined inflation in nominal wages rather than inflation in prices, but for our purposes that distinction is not important. These two measures of inflation usually move together.) Phillips concluded that two important macroeconomic variables – inflation and unemployment – were linked in a way that economists had not previously appreciated.

Although Phillips's discovery was based on data for the United Kingdom, researchers quickly extended his finding to other countries. Two years after Phillips published his article, economists Paul Samuelson and Robert Solow published an article in the *American Economic Review* called 'Analytics of Anti-Inflation Policy' in which they showed a similar negative correlation between inflation and unemployment in data for the United States. They reasoned that this correlation arose because low

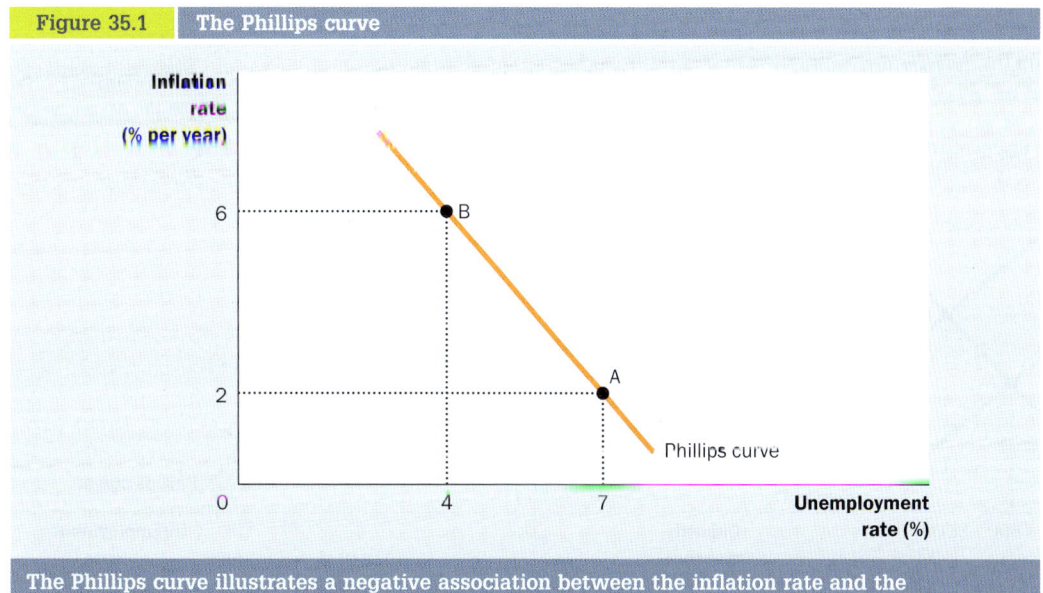

Figure 35.1 The Phillips curve

The Phillips curve illustrates a negative association between the inflation rate and the unemployment rate. At point A, inflation is low and unemployment is high. At point B, inflation is high and unemployment is low.

unemployment was associated with high aggregate demand and because high demand puts upward pressure on wages and prices throughout the economy. Samuelson and Solow dubbed the negative association between inflation and unemployment the **Phillips curve**. Figure 35.1 shows an example of a Phillips curve like the one found by Samuelson and Solow.

    As the title of their paper suggests, Samuelson and Solow were interested in the Phillips curve because they believed that it held important lessons for policymakers. In particular, they suggested that the Phillips curve offers policymakers a menu of possible economic outcomes. By altering monetary and fiscal policy to influence aggregate demand, policymakers could choose any point on this curve. Point A offers high unemployment and low inflation. Point B offers low unemployment and high inflation. Policymakers might prefer both low inflation and low unemployment, but the historical data as summarised by the Phillips curve indicate that this combination is impossible. According to Samuelson and Solow, policymakers face a trade-off between inflation and unemployment, and the Phillips curve illustrates that trade-off.

Phillips curve
the short-term trade-off between inflation and unemployment

▸ Phillips curve

Aggregate demand, aggregate supply and the Phillips curve

The model of aggregate demand and aggregate supply provides an easy explanation for the menu of possible outcomes described by the Phillips curve. *The Phillips curve simply shows the combinations of inflation and unemployment that arise in the short run as shifts in the aggregate-demand curve move the economy along the short-run aggregate-supply curve.* As we discussed in chapter 33, the greater the aggregate demand for goods and services, the greater the economy's output and the higher the overall price level. Okun's law tells us that greater output means a lower rate of unemployment. Thus, an increase in aggregate demand moves the economy along the Phillips curve to a point with lower unemployment and higher inflation.

Figure 35.2 How the Phillips curve is related to the model of aggregate demand and aggregate supply

This figure assumes a price index of 100 for the year 2012 and charts possible outcomes of the year 2013. Panel (a) shows the model of aggregate demand and aggregate supply. If aggregate demand is low, the economy is at point A; output is low (7500) and the price index is low (102). If aggregate demand is high, the economy is at point B; output is high (8000) and the price index is high (106). Panel (b) shows the implications for the Phillips curve. Point A, which arises when aggregate demand is low, has high unemployment (7 per cent) and low inflation (2 per cent). Point B, which arises when aggregate demand is high, has low unemployment (4 per cent) and high inflation (6 per cent).

To see how this works, let's consider an example. To keep the numbers simple, imagine that the price index (as measured, for instance, by the consumer price index) equals 100 in the year 2012. Figure 35.2 shows two possible outcomes that might occur in year 2013. Panel (a) shows the two outcomes using the model of aggregate demand and aggregate supply. Panel (b) illustrates the same two outcomes using the Phillips curve.

In panel (a) of the figure, we can see the implications for output and the price level in the year 2013. If the aggregate demand for goods and services is relatively low, the economy experiences outcome A. The economy produces output of 7500 and the price index is 102. In contrast, if aggregate demand is relatively high, the economy experiences outcome B. Output is 8000 and the price index is 106. Thus, higher aggregate demand moves the economy to an equilibrium with higher output and higher inflation.

In panel (b) of the figure, we can see what these two possible outcomes mean for unemployment and inflation. Because firms need more workers when they produce a greater output of goods and services, unemployment is lower in outcome B than in outcome A. In this example, when output rises from 7500 to 8000, unemployment falls from 7 per cent to 4 per cent. Moreover, because the price index is higher at outcome B than at outcome A, the inflation rate (the percentage change in the price index from the previous year) is also higher. In particular, since the price level was 100 in the year 2012, outcome A has an inflation rate of 2 per cent and outcome B has an inflation rate of 6 per cent. Thus, we can compare the two possible outcomes for the economy either in terms of output and the price level (using the model of aggregate demand and aggregate supply) or in terms of unemployment and inflation (using the Phillips curve).

As we saw in the preceding chapter, fiscal policy can shift the aggregate-demand curve. Therefore, fiscal policy can move the economy along the Phillips curve. Increases in government spending, or cuts in taxes shift the aggregate-demand curve to the right and move the economy to a point on the Phillips curve with lower unemployment and higher inflation. Cuts in government spending, or increases in taxes shift the aggregate-demand curve to the left and move the economy to a point on the Phillips curve with lower inflation and higher unemployment. Or the central bank can alter interest rates to move the economy directly up and down the aggregate demand curve, increasing interest rates when inflation is high and decreasing interest rates when inflation is low. In this sense, the Phillips curve offers policymakers a menu of combinations of inflation and unemployment.

Draw the Phillips curve. Use the model of aggregate demand and aggregate supply to show how policy can move the economy from a point on this curve with high inflation to a point with low inflation.

Shifts in the Phillips curve: The role of expectations

The Phillips curve seems to offer policymakers a menu of possible inflation–unemployment outcomes. But does this menu remain stable over time? Is the Phillips curve a relationship on which policymakers can rely? These are the questions that economists took up in the late 1960s, shortly after Samuelson and Solow had introduced the Phillips curve into the macroeconomic policy debate.

The long-run Phillips curve

In 1968, economist Milton Friedman published a paper in the *American Economic Review*, based on an address he had recently given as president of the American Economic Association. The paper was entitled 'The Role of Monetary Policy'. It contained sections on 'What Monetary Policy Can Do' and 'What Monetary Policy Cannot Do'. Friedman argued that one thing monetary policy cannot do, other than for only a short time, is pick a combination of inflation and unemployment on the Phillips curve. At about the same time, another economist, Edmund Phelps, also published a paper denying the existence of a long-run trade-off between inflation and unemployment.

Friedman and Phelps reasoned from classical principles of macroeconomics, which we discussed in chapters 26 to 32. Recall that classical theory points to growth in the quantity of money as the main determinant of inflation. But classical theory also states that monetary growth does not have real effects – it merely alters all prices and nominal incomes proportionately. In particular, monetary growth does not influence those factors that determine the economy's unemployment rate, such as the market power of unions, the role of efficiency wages or the process of job search. Friedman and Phelps concluded that there is no reason to think the rate of inflation would, *in the long run*, be related to the rate of unemployment.

Here, in his own words, is Friedman's view about what a central bank can hope to accomplish in the long run:

> The monetary authority controls nominal quantities – directly, the quantity of its own liabilities [currency plus bank reserves]. In principle, it can use this control to peg a nominal quantity – an exchange rate, the price level, the nominal level of national income, the quantity of money

by one definition or another – or to peg the change in a nominal quantity – the rate of inflation or deflation, the rate of growth or decline in nominal national income, the rate of growth of the quantity of money. It cannot use its control over nominal quantities to peg a real quantity – the real rate of interest, the rate of unemployment, the level of real national income, the real quantity of money, the rate of growth of real national income, or the rate of growth of the real quantity of money.

Milton Friedman, *American Economic Review*, 1968.

These views have important implications for the Phillips curve. In particular, they imply that monetary policymakers face a long-run Phillips curve that is vertical, as in Figure 35.3. The vertical long-run Phillips curve is, in essence, one expression of the classical idea of monetary neutrality. As you may recall, we expressed this idea in chapter 33 with a vertical long-run aggregate-supply curve. Indeed, the vertical long-run Phillips curve and the vertical long-run aggregate-supply curve are two sides of the same coin.

The easiest way to see this is to consider an economy like the one we discussed in chapter 30 (Zoobooloo) where the central bank controls the money supply. Suppose the Zoobooloo Central Bank increases money supply in order to expand output. All this would do in the long run is create inflation. We can see this in Figure 35.4. In panel (a) of this figure, an increase in the money supply shifts the aggregate-demand curve to the right from AD_1 to AD_2. As a result of this shift, the long-run equilibrium moves from point A to point B. The inflation rate rises from π_1 to π_2, but because the aggregate-supply curve is vertical, output remains the same. In panel (b), the higher growth in the money supply raises the inflation rate by moving the economy from point A to point B. But because the Phillips curve is vertical, the rate of unemployment is the same at these two points. Thus, the vertical long-run aggregate-supply curve and the vertical long-run Phillips curve

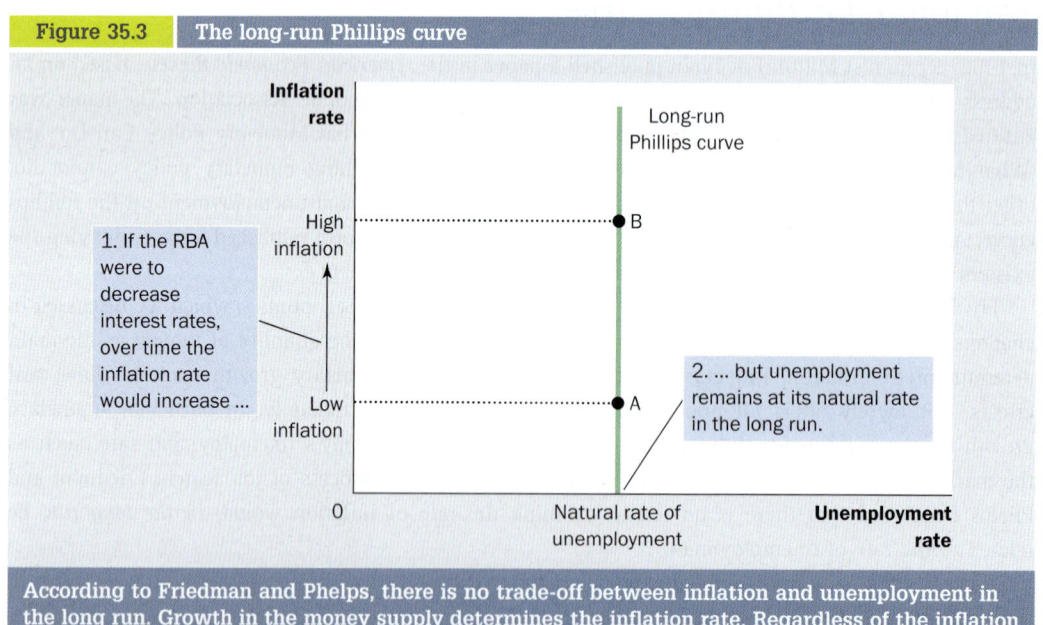

Figure 35.3   **The long-run Phillips curve**

According to Friedman and Phelps, there is no trade-off between inflation and unemployment in the long run. Growth in the money supply determines the inflation rate. Regardless of the inflation rate, the unemployment rate gravitates towards its natural rate. As a result, the long-run Phillips curve is vertical.

Figure 35.4 How the long-run Phillips curve is related to the model of aggregate demand and aggregate supply

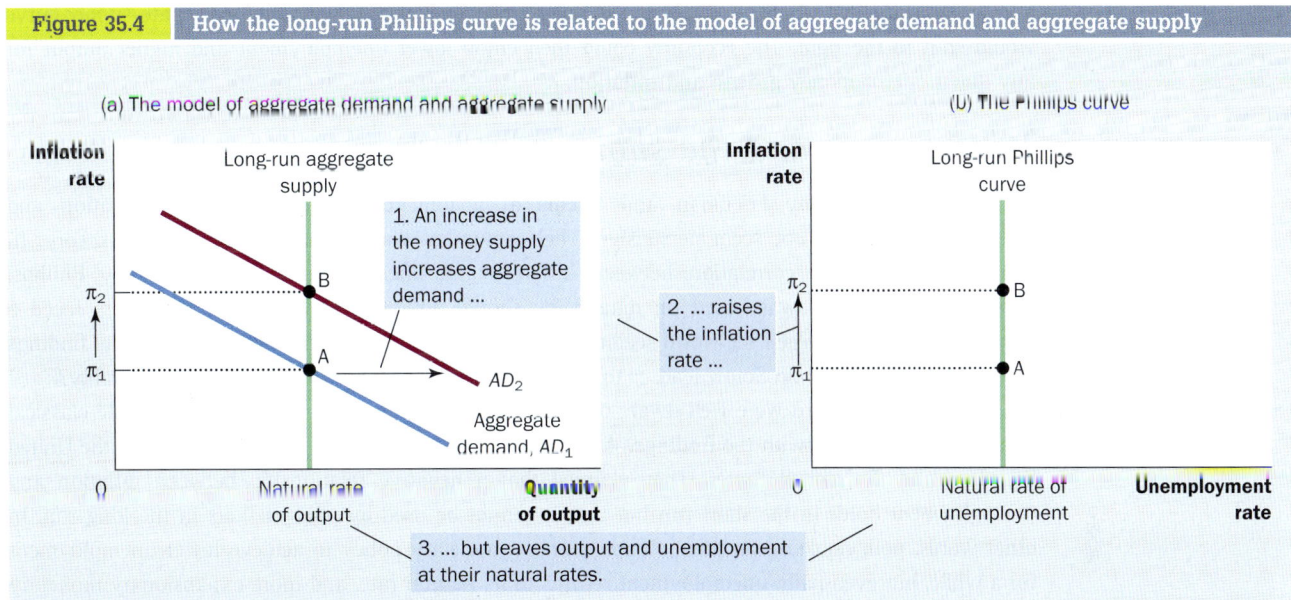

(a) The model of aggregate demand and aggregate supply

(b) The Phillips curve

1. An increase in the money supply increases aggregate demand ...

2. ... raises the inflation rate ...

3. ... but leaves output and unemployment at their natural rates.

Panel (a) shows the model of aggregate demand and aggregate supply with a vertical aggregate-supply curve. When expansionary monetary policy shifts the aggregate-demand curve to the right from AD_1 to AD_2, the equilibrium moves from point A to point B. The inflation rate rises from π_1 to π_2, while output remains the same. Panel (b) shows the long-run Phillips curve, which is vertical at the natural rate of unemployment. Expansionary monetary policy moves the economy from lower inflation (point A) to higher inflation (point B) without changing the rate of unemployment.

both imply that monetary policy influences nominal variables (the inflation rate) but not real variables (output and unemployment). Regardless of the monetary policy pursued by the central bank of Zoobooloo, output and unemployment are, in the long run, at their natural rates.

What is so 'natural' about the natural rate of unemployment? Friedman and Phelps used this adjective to describe the unemployment rate towards which the economy tends to gravitate in the long run. Yet the natural rate of unemployment is not necessarily the socially desirable rate of unemployment. Nor is the natural rate of unemployment constant over time. For example, suppose that a newly formed union uses its market power to raise the real wages of some workers above the equilibrium level. The result is an excess supply of workers and, therefore, a higher natural rate of unemployment. This unemployment is 'natural' not because it is good but because it is beyond the influence of monetary policy. This level of unemployment is often referred to as the **NAIRU (non-accelerating inflation rate of unemployment)**. It is the level of unemployment that does not result in increases in the inflation rate. More rapid money growth would not reduce the market power of unions or the level of unemployment; it would lead only to more inflation.

Although monetary policy cannot influence the natural rate of unemployment, other types of policy can. To reduce the natural rate of unemployment, policymakers should look to policies that improve the functioning of the labour market. Earlier in the book we discussed how various labour-market policies, such as minimum-wage laws, collective-bargaining laws, unemployment benefits and job-training programs, affect the natural rate of unemployment. A policy change that reduced the natural rate of unemployment would shift the long-run Phillips curve to the left. In addition, because lower unemployment means more workers are producing goods and services, the quantity of goods

NAIRU (non-accelerating inflation rate of unemployment) the level of unemployment that does not result in increases in the inflation rate

▶ inflation–unemployment trade-off

and services supplied would be larger at any given price level and the long-run aggregate-supply curve would shift to the right. The economy could then enjoy lower unemployment and higher output for any given rate of money growth and inflation.

Expectations and the short-run Phillips curve

At first, the denial by Friedman and Phelps of a long-run trade-off between inflation and unemployment might not seem persuasive. Their argument was based on an appeal to theory. In contrast, the negative correlation between inflation and unemployment documented by Phillips, Samuelson and Solow was based on data. Why should anyone believe that policymakers faced a vertical Phillips curve when the world seemed to offer a downward-sloping one? Shouldn't the findings of Phillips, Samuelson and Solow lead us to reject the classical conclusion of monetary neutrality?

Friedman and Phelps were well aware of these questions; they offered a way to reconcile classical macroeconomic theory with the findings of a downward-sloping Phillips curve in data from the United Kingdom and the United States. They claimed that a negative relationship between inflation and unemployment holds in the short run but that it cannot be used by policymakers in the long run. In other words, policymakers can pursue expansionary monetary policy to achieve lower unemployment for a while, but eventually unemployment returns to its natural rate, and more expansionary monetary policy leads only to higher inflation.

Friedman and Phelps reasoned as we did in chapter 33 when we explained the difference between the short-run and long-run aggregate-supply curves. (In fact, the discussion in that chapter drew heavily on the legacy of Friedman and Phelps.) As you may recall, the short-run aggregate-supply curve is upward-sloping, indicating that an increase in the inflation rate raises the quantity of goods and services that firms supply. In contrast, the long-run aggregate-supply curve is vertical, indicating that the inflation rate does not influence quantity supplied in the long run. Chapter 33 presented three theories to explain the upward slope of the short-run aggregate-supply curve – misperceptions about relative prices, sticky wages and sticky prices. Because perceptions, wages and prices adjust to changing economic conditions over time, the positive relationship between the inflation rate and quantity supplied applies in the short run but not in the long run. Friedman and Phelps applied this same logic to the Phillips curve. Just as the aggregate-supply curve slopes upwards only in the short run, the trade-off between inflation and unemployment holds only in the short run. And just as the long-run aggregate-supply curve is vertical, the long-run Phillips curve is also vertical.

To help explain the short-run and long-run relationship between inflation and unemployment, Friedman and Phelps introduced a new variable into the analysis – *expected inflation*. Expected inflation measures how much people expect the overall price level to change. As we discussed in chapter 33, the expected price level affects the perceptions of relative prices that people form and the wages and prices that they set. As a result, expected inflation is one factor that determines the position of the short-run aggregate-supply curve. In the short run, the RBA can take expected inflation (and thus the short-run aggregate-supply curve) as already determined. If the RBA were to change the money supply (that is, not follow a rule of inflation targeting), the aggregate-demand curve would shift and the economy would move along a given short-run aggregate-supply curve. In the short run, therefore, monetary changes would lead to unexpected fluctuations in output, prices, unemployment and inflation. In this way, Friedman and Phelps explained the Phillips curve that Phillips, Samuelson and Solow had documented.

Yet the RBA's ability to create unexpected inflation by increasing the money supply exists only in the short run. In the long run, people come to expect whatever inflation rate the RBA chooses to target. Because perceptions, wages and prices will eventually adjust to the inflation rate, the long-run aggregate-supply curve is vertical. In this case, changes in aggregate demand, such as those due to changes in the money supply, do not affect the economy's output of goods and services. Thus, Friedman and Phelps concluded that unemployment returns to its natural rate in the long run.

The analysis of Friedman and Phelps can be summarised in the following equation:

$$\text{Unemployment rate} = \text{Natural rate of unemployment} - a(\text{Actual inflation} - \text{Expected inflation})$$

This equation relates the unemployment rate to the natural rate of unemployment, actual inflation and expected inflation. In the short run, expected inflation is already given. As a result, higher actual inflation is associated with lower unemployment. (How much unemployment responds to unexpected inflation is determined by the size of a, a number that in turn depends on the slope of the short-run aggregate-supply curve.) In the long run, however, people come to expect whatever inflation the RBA targets. Thus, actual inflation equals expected inflation and unemployment is at its natural rate.

According to Friedman and Phelps, it is dangerous to view the Phillips curve as a menu of options available to policymakers. To see why, imagine an economy at its natural rate of unemployment with low inflation and low expected inflation, shown in Figure 35.5 as point A. Now suppose that policymakers try to take advantage of the trade-off between inflation and unemployment by using monetary or fiscal policy to expand aggregate demand. In the short run when expected inflation is given, the economy goes from point A to point B. Unemployment falls below its natural rate and inflation rises above expected inflation. Over time, people get used to this higher inflation rate and they raise their expectations of inflation. When expected inflation rises, the short-run trade-off

| **Figure 35.5** | **How expected inflation shifts the short-run Phillips curve** |

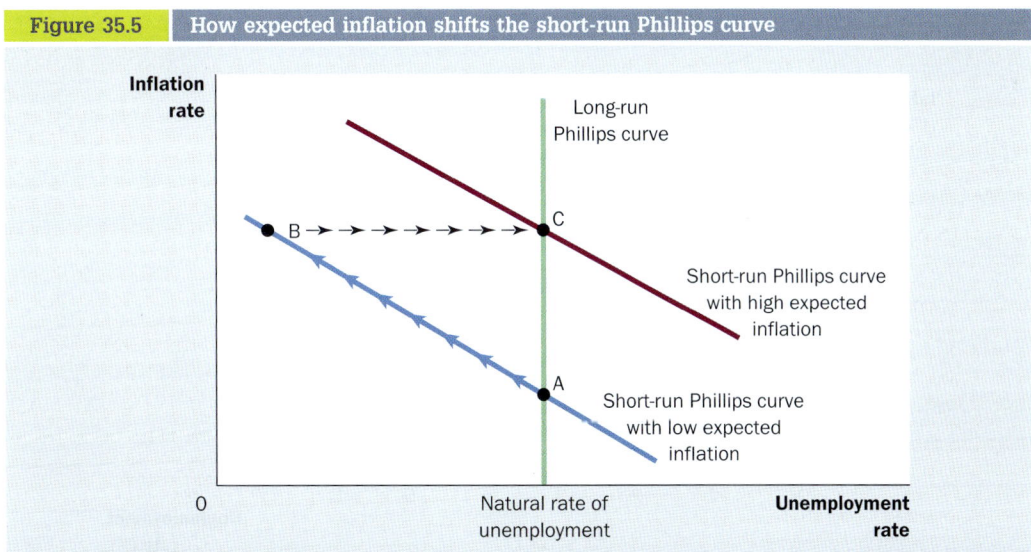

The higher the expected rate of inflation, the higher the short-run trade-off between inflation and unemployment. At point A, expected inflation and actual inflation are both low and unemployment is at its natural rate. If the RBA pursues an expansionary monetary policy, the economy moves from point A to point B in the short run. At point B, expected inflation is still low, but actual inflation is high. Unemployment is below its natural rate. In the long run, expected inflation rises and the economy moves to point C. At point C, expected inflation and actual inflation are both high and unemployment is back to its natural rate.

between inflation and unemployment shifts upwards. The economy ends up at point C, with higher inflation than at point A but with the same level of unemployment.

Thus, Friedman and Phelps concluded that policymakers do face a trade-off between inflation and unemployment, but only a temporary one. If policymakers use this trade-off, they lose it.

CASESTUDY

The US economy as the natural experiment for the natural-rate hypothesis

natural-rate hypothesis
the claim that unemployment eventually returns to its normal, or natural, rate, regardless of the rate of inflation

Friedman and Phelps had made a bold prediction in 1968 – if policymakers try to take advantage of the Phillips curve by choosing higher inflation in order to reduce unemployment, they will succeed at reducing unemployment only temporarily. This view – that unemployment eventually returns to its natural rate, regardless of the rate of inflation – is called the **natural-rate hypothesis**. A few years after Friedman and Phelps proposed this hypothesis, monetary and fiscal policymakers inadvertently created a natural experiment to test it. Their laboratory was the US economy.

Before we see the outcome of this test, however, let's look at the data that Friedman and Phelps had when they made their prediction in 1968. Figure 35.6 shows the unemployment rate and the inflation rate for the period from 1961 to 1968 in the United States. These data trace out a Phillips curve. As inflation rose over these 8 years,

unemployment fell. The economic data from this era seemed to confirm the trade-off between inflation and unemployment.

The apparent success of the Phillips curve in the 1960s made the prediction of Friedman and Phelps all the more bold. In 1958, Phillips had suggested a negative association between inflation and unemployment. In 1960, Samuelson and Solow had shown it in US data. Another decade of data had confirmed the relationship. To some economists at the time, it seemed ridiculous to claim that the Phillips curve would break down once policymakers tried to use it.

But, in fact, that is exactly what happened. Beginning in the late 1960s, the US government followed policies that expanded the aggregate demand for goods and services. In part, this expansion was due to fiscal policy – government spending rose as the Vietnam War heated up. In part, it was due to monetary policy – because the Federal

| Figure 35.6 | The Phillips curve in the 1960s in the United States |

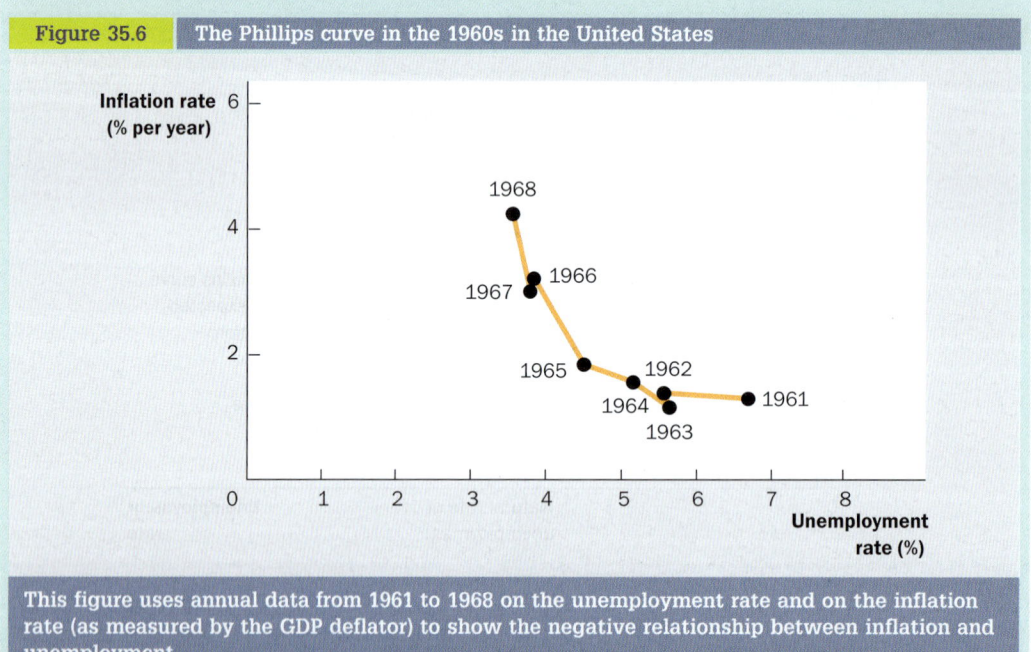

This figure uses annual data from 1961 to 1968 on the unemployment rate and on the inflation rate (as measured by the GDP deflator) to show the negative relationship between inflation and unemployment.

Source: US Department of Labor; US Department of Commerce.

Reserve was trying to hold down interest rates in the face of expansionary fiscal policy, the quantity of money rose about 13 per cent per year during the period from 1970 to 1972, compared with 7 per cent per year in the early 1960s. As a result, inflation stayed high (about 5–6 per cent per year in the late 1960s and early 1970s, compared with about 1–2 per cent per year in the early 1960s). But, as Friedman and Phelps had predicted, unemployment did not stay low.

Figure 35.7 shows the history of inflation and unemployment from 1961 to 1973 in the

---

Figure 35.7 The breakdown of the Phillips curve in the United States

This figure shows annual data from 1961 to 1973 on the unemployment rate and on the inflation rate (as measured by the GDP deflator). Notice that the Phillips curve of the 1960s breaks down in the early 1970s.

Source: US Department of Labor; US Department of Commerce.

Figure 35.8 The Phillips curve in Australia from 1960 to 1970

This figure uses annual data from 1960 to 1970 on the unemployment rate and on the inflation rate (as measured by the implicit price deflator for GDP) to show the negative relationship between inflation and unemployment.

Source: Reserve Bank of Australia, Occasional Paper No. 8.

United States. Notice that the simple negative relationship between these two variables started to break down around 1970. In particular, as inflation remained high in the early 1970s, people's expectations of inflation caught up with reality and the unemployment rate reverted to the 5–6 per cent range that had prevailed in the early 1960s. By 1973, policymakers had learned that Friedman and Phelps were right – there is no trade-off between inflation and unemployment in the long run.

Australia experienced a similar breakdown in the Phillips curve. Figure 35.8 shows the Phillips curve for the 1960s. As you can see, the trade-off between inflation and unemployment is not straightforward. Australia, like the United States, had a fairly stable Phillips curve during the 1960s, but the oil shocks of the 1970s, along with increases in wages due to indexation of wages to inflation, helped shift the Australian Phillips curve to the right (see Figure 35.11 later in this chapter).

Draw the short-run Phillips curve and the long-run Phillips curve. Explain why they are different.

Source: David Messer.

Shifts in the Phillips curve: The role of supply shocks

Friedman and Phelps had suggested in 1968 that changes in expected inflation shift the short-run Phillips curve and the experience of the early 1970s convinced most economists that Friedman and Phelps were right. Within a few years, however, the economics profession would turn its attention to a different source of shifts in the short-run Phillips curve – shocks to aggregate supply.

This time, the shift in focus came not from two American economics professors but from a group of Arab sheiks. In 1974, the Organization of Petroleum Exporting Countries (OPEC) began to exert its market power as a cartel in the world oil market in order to increase its members' profits. The countries of OPEC, such as Saudi Arabia, Kuwait and Iraq, restricted the amount of crude oil they pumped and

Figure 35.9   An adverse shock to aggregate supply

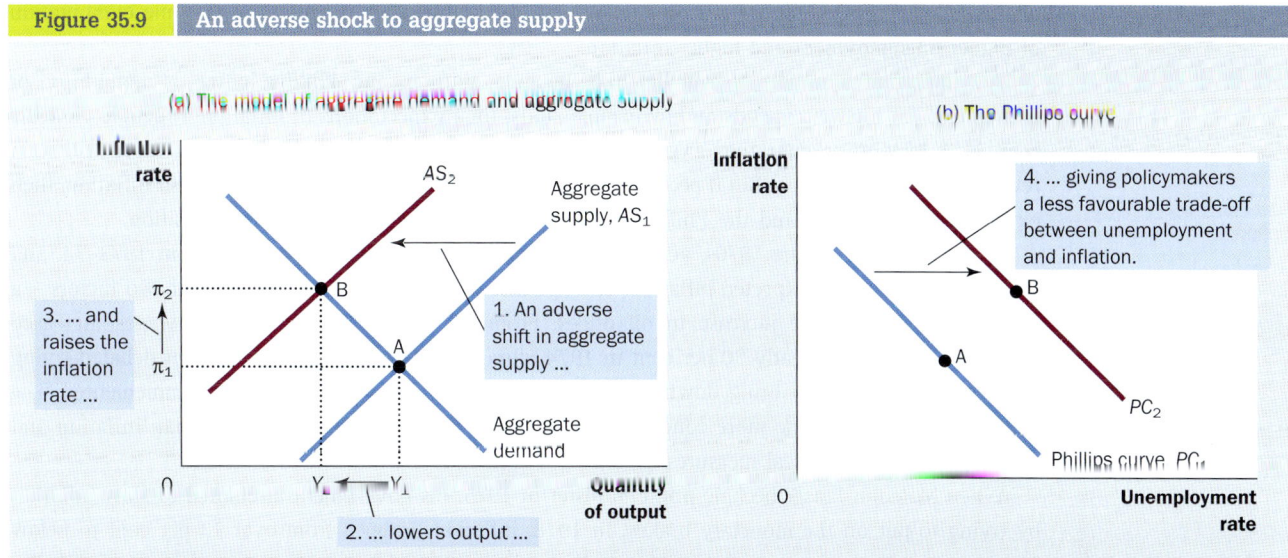

Panel (a) shows the model of aggregate demand and aggregate supply. When the aggregate-supply curve shifts to the left from AS_1 to AS_2, the equilibrium moves from point A to point B. Output falls from Y_1 to Y_2 and the rate of inflation rises from π_1 to π_2. Panel (b) shows the short-run trade-off between inflation and unemployment. The adverse shift in aggregate supply moves the economy from a point with lower unemployment and lower inflation (point A) to a point with higher unemployment and higher inflation (point B). The short-run Phillips curve shifts to the right from PC_1 to PC_2. Policymakers now face a worse trade-off between inflation and unemployment.

sold on world markets. Within a few years, this reduction in supply caused the price of oil to almost double.

This OPEC price increase had major macroeconomic effects in countries around the world. Because an increase in the price of oil raises the cost of producing many goods and services, it reduces the quantity of goods and services supplied at any given price level. (This is true even for a country like Australia that is generally a net exporter of oil. The increase in the price of oil may be good for oil producers, but it still raises the costs of production of just about everything else in the economy.) As panel (a) of Figure 35.9 shows, this reduction in supply is represented by the shift to the left in the aggregate-supply curve from AS_1 to AS_2. The inflation rate rises from π_1 to π_2, and output falls from Y_1 to Y_2. The result is called *stagflation*.

This shift in aggregate supply is associated with a similar shift in the short-run Phillips curve, shown in panel (b). Because firms need fewer workers to produce the smaller output, employment falls and unemployment rises. And the inflation rate – the percentage change in the price level from the previous year – is also higher. Thus, the shift in aggregate supply leads to higher unemployment and higher inflation. The short-run trade-off between inflation and unemployment shifts to the right from PC_1 to PC_2.

Confronted with an adverse shift in aggregate supply, policymakers face a difficult choice. If they contract aggregate demand to fight inflation, they will raise unemployment further. If they expand aggregate demand to fight unemployment, they will raise inflation further. In other words, policymakers face a less favourable trade-off between inflation and unemployment than they did before the shift in aggregate supply – they have to live with a higher rate of inflation for a given rate of unemployment, a higher rate of unemployment for a given rate of inflation, or some combination of higher unemployment and higher inflation.

An important question is whether this adverse shift in the Phillips curve is temporary or permanent. The answer depends on how people adjust their expectations of inflation. If people view the event as a temporary aberration, expected inflation does not change and the Phillips curve will soon revert to its former position. But if people view the shock as leading to a new era of higher inflation, then expected inflation rises and the Phillips curve remains at its new, less desirable position.

In Australia during the 1970s, actual inflation did rise substantially, particularly in 1973–74, and this led to increases in expected inflation. The rise in actual inflation was the result of two factors – a wage explosion and the increase in oil prices. From the late 1960s to 1973–74, wages increased rapidly, increasing by nearly 30 per cent in 1974 alone. Gough Whitlam's government debated trying a 'short, sharp shock' to bring down inflation in 1974, but the policy was never implemented. The Labor government became more concerned about increasing unemployment rather than inflation and reversed its restrictive fiscal measures.

When Malcolm Fraser became prime minister in 1975, his government attempted to slow inflation by trying to put on the monetary brakes. In 1978, inflation dropped from over 13 per cent to below 10 per cent, but the impact of the second oil shock in 1979 and continued increases in commodity prices led to another round of high inflation. In 1983, after an extended period of wage explosion and two OPEC supply shocks, the Australian economy had an inflation rate of more than 11 per cent and an unemployment rate of nearly 10 per cent. This combination of inflation and unemployment was not at all near the trade-off that seemed possible in the 1960s. (In the 1960s, the Phillips curve suggested that an unemployment rate of 6 per cent would be associated with an inflation rate of less than 1 per cent. Inflation of more than 10 per cent was unthinkable in the 1960s.) With the misery index in 1983 near a historic high, the public was widely dissatisfied with macroeconomic performance. Something had to be done, and soon it would be.

IN THE NEWS . . .

THE DREADED 'R' WORD

At the beginning of 2008, the US economy was showing signs of the dreaded 'R' word, recession. (In one episode of 'The West Wing', an American TV show about the White House, everyone is forbidden from using the 'R' word – they call it a 'bagel' instead.) Ben Bernanke, chairman of the Federal Reserve Board, reduced interest rates and the Bush administration pursued tax cuts – both measures to 'pump prime' the economy. But as always, there is tension between short-term measures to get the economy going and long-term stability with low inflation, as indicated in the following article.

Fed chief's reassurance fails to halt stock plunge

by Edmund L. Andrews

Washington – The stock market plunged again on Thursday on bad economic news, taking little comfort from reassuring words by the chairman of the Federal Reserve or an emerging consensus about a stimulus plan that many worry could be too late. On a day when stocks were pushed down another 3 percent on reports of more weakness in housing and manufacturing – bringing the decline this year to a stomach-churning 9 percent – all the major players in Washington agreed on the need for putting extra money into people's hands quickly.

President Bush publicly confirmed for the first time that he would propose a package of emergency measures, outlining its basic principles on Friday, in an effort to restore the eroding confidence of investors and consumers. The package is expected to include more than $100 billion in one-time tax rebates for individuals and an opportunity for businesses to rapidly write off their capital investments.

In a rare sign of his willingness to cut a deal with Democrats in Congress, White House officials said Mr. Bush would not demand that the stimulus package include provisions that permanently extend his signature tax cuts from 2001 and 2003. In a conference call with Democratic leaders on Thursday afternoon, Mr. Bush signaled his eagerness to reach agreement. 'I think there was a collective sense that there was no reason why we can't get something done quickly,' said Tony Fratto, the White House deputy press secretary. 'I think that was a unanimous feeling on the call.'

Despite the rising prospect of a fiscal pump-priming effort from Washington, investors on Wall Street remained in a black mood as data showed that the housing debacle was getting worse and beginning to bring down the rest of the economy.

The Dow Jones industrial average turned down even as the Fed chairman, Ben S. Bernanke, began to deliver his widely anticipated testimony to the House Budget Committee. By the end of the day, the Dow had plunged 307 points; the fall since Jan. 1 is now 9.2 percent. Wall Street started the day with Merrill Lynch reporting that it lost $9.8 billion in the fourth quarter, mainly because of booking $15 billion in losses tied to soured home loans.

Adding to the pessimism, which drowned out the reassurances by Mr. Bernanke that a recession could be averted, were reports that manufacturing activity could be slowing even more than analysts had expected, and that housing starts dropped 14 percent last month and reached their lowest level in 16 years. Mr. Bernanke insisted that despite concerns about 'slowing growth,' the economy remained 'extraordinarily resilient.'

'It has a strong labor force, excellent productivity and technology and a deep and liquid financial market that is in the process of trying to repair itself,' Mr. Bernanke said. 'So I think we need to keep in mind also that the economy does have inherent strengths and that those will certainly surface over a period of time.

But James W. Paulsen, a strategist at Wells Capital Management, reflected the view of many investors that help from Washington would come too late. 'By the time they actually pass anything, it will be past the time we need it,' Mr. Paulsen said.

Mr. Bernanke refused to endorse any specific measures, but he said the key to success would be to act fast and to focus on temporary measures that get extra money into the hands of people within the next 12 months. To do that, he added, Congress would have to pass legislation within the next month or two.

'In order for this to be useful, you would need to act quickly,' Mr. Bernanke told the committee on Thursday morning. 'Stimulus that comes too late will not help support economic activity in the near term, and it could be actively destabilizing.'

For economists and for the Federal Reserve, the big question is which tax cuts or spending measures will produce the biggest and fastest jolt to economic activity. Most economists agree that tax rebates are one of the fastest ways to lift consumer spending. They also agree that stimulus measures are most efficient when aimed at low-income or middle-income people, because they are more likely than affluent people to spend any extra money rather than save it.

According to estimates several years ago by Mark Zandi, chief economist of Moody's Economy.com, the measures that produced the biggest 'bang for the buck' were increases in unemployment benefits, which produced about $1.73 in additional demand for every dollar spent. Tax rebates to all citizens generated about $1.19 for every dollar spent, while reductions in tax rates produced only 59 cents per dollar.

But other economists argue that temporary incentives for business investment have a powerful effect as well.

Oil prices surged past the US$100 a barrel mark in 2007. Is this a supply shock? Explain. Use the model of aggregate demand and aggregate supply to explain the effects of such a shock. How does it affect the Phillips curve?

The cost of reducing inflation

Despite the Fraser government's efforts to bring inflation down, it hovered around 10 per cent until 1983, when Bob Hawke brought a Labor government to power. Inflation in Australia was mostly the result of the rise in wages, but with a Labor government negotiating with the Australian Council of Trade Unions (ACTU), a brake was applied to the wage increases. The government was committed to a Prices and Incomes Accord (known as the Accord) which would limit wage increases and guarantee productivity increases while maintaining worker incomes. The era of the Accords had begun.

To understand the importance of the Accords in bringing down wages, we need to understand how wages were determined before the Accord and why they were allowed to rise so rapidly. From 1921 to 1953, a centrally arbitrated minimum wage was set. A significant component of this wage was indexed to inflation. But as inflation increased to levels of 25 per cent in 1953, this indexation was removed. By the 1970s a system of arbitrated collective bargaining had developed that determined wages in the major industries, such as oil and metal trades, by bargaining between the big unions and employer groups. These wages then formed the benchmark for increases in wages in other industries.

Wage indexation was reintroduced in 1975 as a means of controlling the wages outbreak. The objective was to strictly limit increases in wages that were not based on indexation. But this was not successful – wages continued to rise, although more slowly. Partial indexation was used until 1980, when there was a move back to decentralised wage determination. Strong unions bargained to obtain wage increases in excess of the increase in prices so that workers' real wages would not fall. This led to greater increases in prices, which led to increases in wages and so on. It was this wage–price spiral that the newly elected government intended to change in 1983.

The ACTU had been advocating a centralised wage fixation system based on 'prices and productivity'. This meant that wages should rise in line with inflation to stop the real wage falling and also to reflect productivity gains so that workers would get a share of the increased profit that their productivity helped generate. However, this approach to wage increases was difficult to maintain in the face of rising inflation. The traditional approach to solving inflation problems was to slam on the brakes and slow the economy down. According to accepted thinking on the Phillips curve, this would mean a rise in unemployment, an unpalatable outcome for the unions. As the Australian economy went into recession in 1982–83, there were two possibilities for lowering inflation. One was to lower aggregate demand through a combination of tight monetary policy and restrictive fiscal policy, and the other was to come to some agreement with the unions over wage restraint. We consider these two possibilities in turn.

The sacrifice ratio

To reduce the inflation rate, the RBA could pursue contractionary monetary policy. Figure 35.10 shows some of the effects of such a decision. When the RBA slows the rate of money growth (which was the monetary policy instrument used in the 1980s), it contracts aggregate demand. The fall in aggregate demand, in turn, reduces the quantity of goods and services that firms produce, and this fall in production leads to a fall in employment. The economy begins at point A in the figure and moves along the short-run Phillips curve to point B, which has lower inflation and higher unemployment. Over time, as people come to understand that prices are rising more slowly, expected inflation falls and the short-run Phillips curve shifts downwards. The economy moves from point B to point C. Inflation is lower and unemployment is back at its natural rate.

Thus, if an economy is to reduce inflation, it must endure a period of high unemployment and low output. In Figure 35.10, this cost is represented by the movement of the economy through point B as it travels from point A to point C. The size of this cost depends on the slope of the Phillips curve and how quickly expectations of inflation adjust to the new monetary policy.

Figure 35.10	Disinflation monetary policy in the short run and the long run

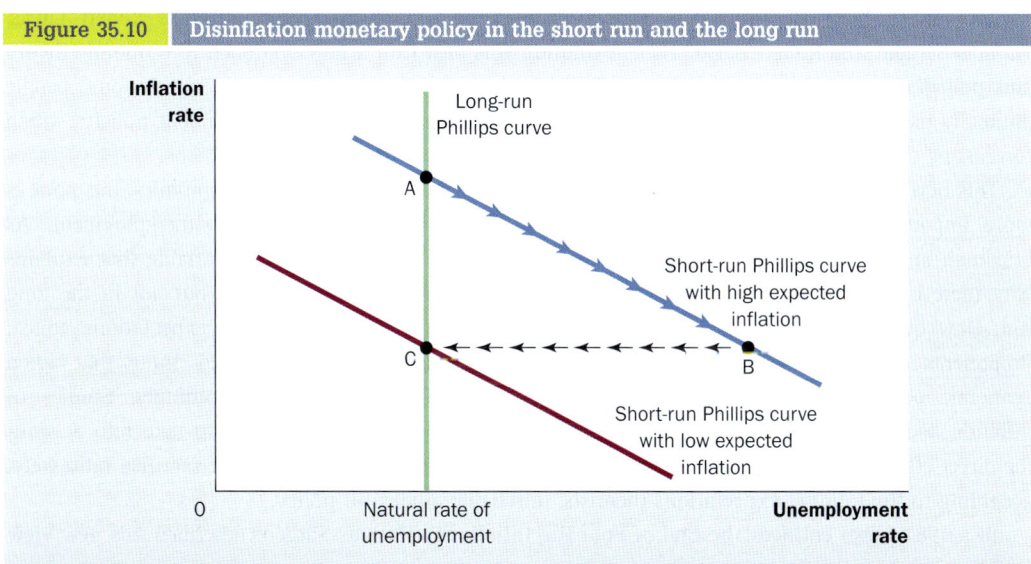

When the RBA pursues contractionary monetary policy to reduce inflation, the economy moves along a short-run Phillips curve from point A to point B. Over time, expected inflation falls and the short-run Phillips curve shifts downwards. When the economy reaches point C, unemployment is back at its natural rate.

sacrifice ratio
the number of percentage
points of annual output lost in
the process of reducing
inflation by one percentage
point

Many studies have examined the data on inflation and unemployment in order to estimate the cost of reducing inflation. The findings of these studies are often summarised in a statistic called the **sacrifice ratio**. The sacrifice ratio is the number of percentage points of annual output lost in the process of reducing inflation by one percentage point. A typical estimate of the sacrifice ratio is 5. That is, for each percentage point that inflation is reduced, 5 per cent of annual output must be sacrificed in the transition.

Such estimates surely must have made the Fraser government apprehensive as it confronted the task of reducing inflation. Inflation was running at almost 10 per cent per year. To reach moderate inflation of, say, 4 per cent per year would mean reducing inflation by six percentage points. If each percentage point cost 5 per cent of the economy's annual output, then reducing inflation by six percentage points would require sacrificing 30 per cent of annual output.

According to studies of the Phillips curve and the cost of disinflation, this sacrifice could be paid in various ways. An immediate reduction in inflation would depress output by 30 per cent for a single year, but that outcome was surely too harsh even for the most ardent inflation 'hawks' in Treasury. It would surely be better to spread out the cost over several years. If the reduction in inflation took place over five years, for instance, then output would have to average only 6 per cent below trend during that period to add up to a sacrifice of 30 per cent. An even more gradual approach would be to reduce inflation slowly over a decade, so that output would have to be only 3 per cent below trend. Whatever path was chosen, however, it seemed that reducing inflation would not be easy.

Rational expectations and the possibility of costless disinflation

Just as the Fraser government was pondering how costly reducing inflation might be, a group of economics professors was leading an intellectual revolution that would challenge the conventional wisdom on the sacrifice ratio. This group included such prominent economists as Robert Lucas, Thomas Sargent and Robert Barro. Their revolution was based on a new approach to economic theory and policy called **rational expectations**. According to the theory of rational expectations, people optimally use all the information they have, including information about government policies, when forecasting the future.

rational expectations
the theory according to which
people optimally use all the
information they have,
including information about
government policies, when
forecasting the future

This new approach has had profound implications for many areas of macroeconomics, but none is more important than its application to the trade-off between inflation and unemployment. As Friedman and Phelps had first emphasised, expected inflation is an important variable that explains why there is a trade-off between inflation and unemployment in the short run but not in the long run. How quickly the short-run trade-off disappears depends on how quickly expectations adjust. Proponents of rational expectations built on the Friedman–Phelps analysis to argue that when economic policies change, people adjust their expectations of inflation accordingly. Studies of inflation and unemployment that tried to estimate the sacrifice ratio had failed to take into account the direct effect of the policy regime on expectations. As a result, estimates of the sacrifice ratio were, according to the rational-expectations theorists, unreliable guides for policy.

In a 1981 paper entitled 'The End of Four Big Inflations', Thomas Sargent described this new view as follows:

> An alternative 'rational expectations' view denies that there is any inherent momentum to the present process of inflation. This view maintains that firms and workers have now come to expect high rates of inflation in the future and that they strike inflationary bargains in light of these expectations. However, it is held that people expect high rates of

inflation in the future precisely because the government's current and prospective monetary and fiscal policies warrant those expectations... An implication of this view is that inflation can be stopped much more quickly than advocates of the 'momentum' view have indicated and that their estimates of the length of time and the costs of stopping inflation in terms of foregone output are erroneous... This is not to say that it would be easy to eradicate inflation. On the contrary, it would require more than a few temporary restrictive fiscal and monetary actions. It would require a change in the policy regime... How costly such a move would be in terms of foregone output and how long it would be in taking effect would depend partly on how resolute and evident the government's commitment was.

According to Sargent, the sacrifice ratio could be much smaller than suggested by previous estimates. Indeed, in the most extreme case, it could be zero. If the government made a credible commitment to a policy of low inflation, people would be rational enough to lower their expectations of inflation immediately. The short-run Phillips curve would shift downwards and the economy would reach low inflation quickly without the cost of temporarily high unemployment and low output.

The Accord approach

Although no one in the Hawke government or the ACTU would have claimed to be advocates of the theory of rational expectations, the idea of reducing inflationary expectations was fundamental to the approach of the Accord. If the government could get the ACTU to accept some form of wage reductions, then prices would not need to increase as much to pay for the wage increases. Wage earners would begin to expect a lower level of inflation and not demand large wage increases in the next round of wage negotiation. Then the cycle of increasing wages and prices could be broken. The first Accord still had full indexation, but by the second round (Accord Mark II), indexation had been removed. In return for productivity gains, workers at all levels would be granted superannuation coverage. So the emphasis had been changed from wage increases to other forms of benefits for workers that would be less inflationary, including tax cuts and reductions in the Medicare levy. Costs of production could be kept low by the productivity gains that were promised in return for these benefits.

Inflation did indeed come down in 1984 and 1985. But in 1986, Australia suffered a significant depreciation of its dollar that caused inflation to rise again. Figure 35.11 shows the inflation rate and unemployment rate during this period, with the Phillips Curve indicated by A. Without the Accord, the inflation rate might have been much higher, but by the late 1980s, fears of escalating inflation were again strong. The government decided to use restrictive monetary policy to bring inflation down, as well as continuing to rely on the Accord to prevent a wages blow-out from the higher inflation rates. This led to the recession of 1990–91, dubbed by the then Treasurer, Paul Keating, as the 'recession we had to have'. This recession did get the inflation rate under control – it was down to 1 per cent by 1993. However, the cost was a significant increase in unemployment. Unemployment reached 10.7 per cent in 1993, its highest level since the Depression.

Does this experience refute the possibility of costless disinflation as suggested by the rational-expectations theorists? Some economists have argued that the answer to this question is a resounding yes. To make the transition from high inflation to low inflation, the economy had to experience a painful period of high unemployment.

Yet there are two reasons not to reject the conclusions of the rational-expectations theorists so quickly. First, even though disinflation did impose a cost of temporarily high unemployment, the cost was not as large as many economists had predicted. Most estimates of the sacrifice ratio based on the

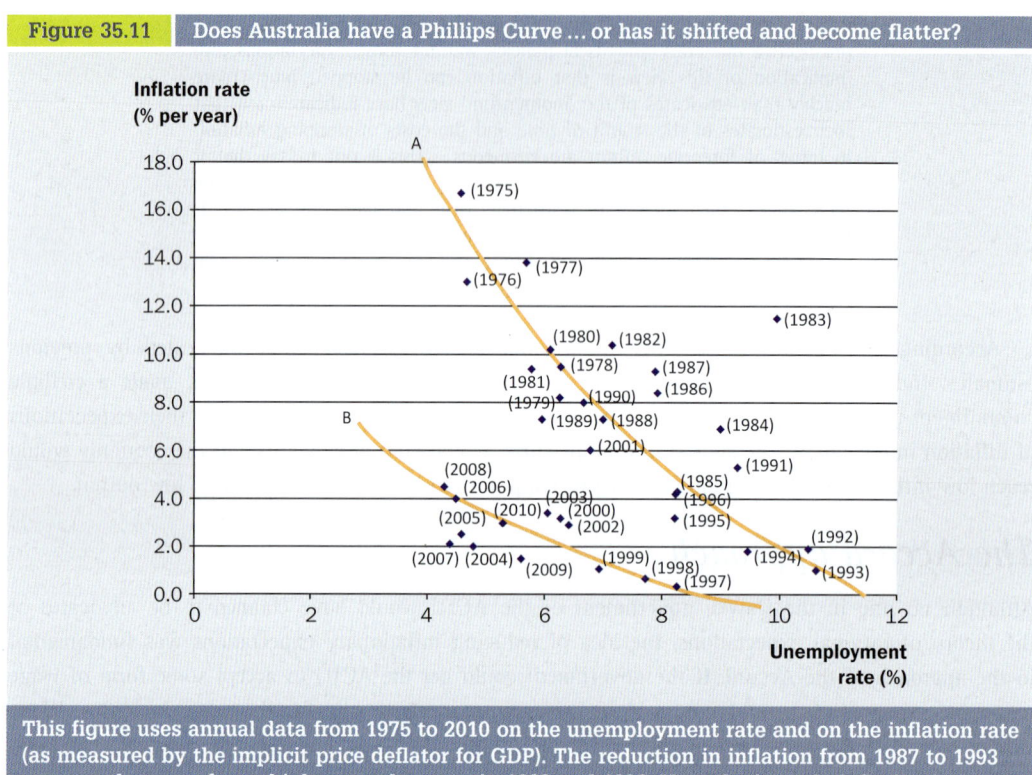

Figure 35.11 | **Does Australia have a Phillips Curve ... or has it shifted and become flatter?**

This figure uses annual data from 1975 to 2010 on the unemployment rate and on the inflation rate (as measured by the implicit price deflator for GDP). The reduction in inflation from 1987 to 1993 came at the cost of very high unemployment in 1992 and 1993. Note the jump in inflation in 2001 due to the introduction of the GST in 2000.

Source: Reserve Bank of Australia, Occasional Paper No. 8 and various ABS tables.

disinflation experienced from 1987 to 1993 are smaller than estimates that had been obtained from previous data. Perhaps Treasurer Keating was right. We did have to have a recession to see some direct effect on expectations, as the rational-expectations theorists claimed.

A low inflation era

Since the wages inflation of the 1970s and the disinflation of the 1990s, the Australian economy has experienced relatively mild fluctuations in inflation, but unemployment stayed fairly high until the end of the 1990s. The high unemployment figure in 1996 was in part responsible for defeating the Keating Labor government and bringing in a Coalition government for the first time in 13 years.

The RBA has been careful to avoid repeating the policy mistakes of the 1960s, when excessive aggregate demand pushed unemployment below the natural rate and raised inflation. When unemployment fell and inflation rose in 1989 and 1990, the RBA contracted aggregate demand, leading to the recession of 1991 and 1992. Unemployment then rose above the natural rate and inflation fell. The economy gradually recovered from this recession in the mid-1990s, and inflation stabilised at about 2 per cent. In 2004, unemployment fell to a 10-year low of around 5 per cent, and has been between 4 and 5 per cent for most of the years between 2004 and 2011. Some economists believe this to be well below Australia's natural rate of unemployment, which had been estimated to be somewhere between 6.5 per cent and 7 per cent. But since unemployment has stayed below 5 per cent for some time, many economists have readjusted their notion of the natural rate to around 5 per cent.

At the same time, inflation has been below 4 per cent for all but five of the last 20 years. The RBA is sufficiently worried about excess demand pressure on inflation with such low unemployment that it has increased interest rates several times in the last decade, even though the global financial crisis created worries about a recession. All of this indicates that the Phillips curve may well have shifted in Australia. We can see a shift in the Phillips curve in Figure 35.11, from A to B, indicating that the high levels of inflation have indeed been tamed.

IN THE NEWS . . .

CAN THE 'ENERGIZER BUNNY ECONOMY' KEEP ON GOING?

Is the Australian economy an 'Energizer bunny economy'? US economist Paul Krugman called the Australian economy a 'miracle economy' and the OECD said Australia was the rich world's best performer. Why all the praise for the wonder (economy) down-under? Australia has had about 20 years of high growth, relatively low inflation and low unemployment. But the good times may be about to end or at least some cold water poured on the party. The following article explains how Australia's continued growth is putting pressure on inflation, which may lead to more interest rate rises.

Outlook stays strong, but...GDP surge hits bump

by Rachel Hewitt

THE ECONOMY

Australia's outperforming economy has hit a speed bump with growth at the slowest pace since the dark days of the global financial crisis but pundits say 'the big picture' is still intact and the outlook remains strong.

The nation's economy grew just 0.2 per cent in the September quarter, which was half what the market was expecting and the lowest reading since the economy went backwards in December 2008.

The Australian dollar dived below US$0.96 after the weaker gross domestic product was revealed, shedding more than half a cent before clawing back some losses in later trade.

Economists acknowledged that the data looked concerning on face value, but stressed that the disappointing result followed a 1.1 per cent growth surge in the June quarter.

'Most importantly, the outlook remains strong, particularly for mining investment, and policy is about the future not the past,' said HSBC chief economist Paul Bloxham.

But he said an interest rate rise in the first three months of next year was now 'perhaps less likely'.

ANZ economists said yesterday's Australian Bureau of Statistics data revealed real national income growth of 7.8 per cent year-on-year – a 22-year high – because of sharply higher commodity prices.

'Given the size of the national income boost and the record level of mining investment in the pipeline, we are confident these factors will drive a re-acceleration in Australian economic growth over 2011–12,' wrote ANZ's Katie Dean, Amber Rabinov and Julie Toth.

They said yesterday's economic 'speed bump' showed higher interest rates were having the desired impact.

TD Securities head of Asia-Pacific research Annette Beacher said the market was not pricing in another interest rate rise until November next year but this was 'overdone' and 'the big picture remains intact'.

'Year-on-year income (growth) is nearly double-digit...and it's the income side of the economy that creates inflationary pressures,' she said.

A quarterly slowdown was expected because of the effects of the withdrawal of public stimulus policy, such as the schools building program, a strong fall in exports and higher interest rates.

The ANZ economists described the result as 'saved by the farm' because the agricultural

>>

sector drove growth with output up 18.5 per cent.

Yesterday's GDP release came as other data revealed that manufacturing activity weakened in November.

The Australian Industry Group–PwC performance of manufacturing index fell

1.8 points – due to the higher dollar, interest rates and skills shortages.

Source: Rachel Hewitt/*The Herald-Sun*, 2 December 2010.

What does the future hold? Macroeconomists are notoriously bad at forecasting, but several lessons of the past are clear. First, as long as the RBA remains vigilant in its control over interest rates and, thereby, aggregate demand, there is no reason for inflation to heat up, as it did in the late 1960s. Second, the possibility always exists for the economy to experience adverse shocks to aggregate supply, as it did in the 1970s. If that unfortunate development occurs, policymakers will have little choice but to confront a less desirable trade-off between inflation and unemployment.

Q What is the sacrifice ratio? How might the credibility of the RBA's commitment to reduce inflation affect the sacrifice ratio?

Conclusion

This chapter has examined how economists' thinking about inflation and unemployment has evolved over time. We have discussed the ideas of many of the best economists of the twentieth century – from the Phillips curve of Phillips, Samuelson and Solow, to the natural-rate hypothesis of Friedman and Phelps, to the rational-expectations theory of Lucas, Sargent and Barro. Four of this group have already won Nobel prizes for their work in economics and more are likely to be so honoured in the years to come.

Although the trade-off between inflation and unemployment has generated much intellectual turmoil over the past 40 years, certain principles have developed that today command consensus. Here is how Milton Friedman expressed the relationship between inflation and unemployment in 1968:

> There is always a temporary tradeoff between inflation and unemployment; there is no permanent tradeoff. The temporary tradeoff comes not from inflation per se, but from unanticipated inflation, which generally means, from a rising rate of inflation. The widespread belief that there is a permanent tradeoff is a sophisticated version of the confusion between 'high' and 'rising' that we all recognize in simpler forms. A rising rate of inflation may reduce unemployment, a high rate will not.
>
> But how long, you will say, is 'temporary'?... I can at most venture a personal judgment, based on some examination of the historical evidence, that the initial effects of a higher and unanticipated rate of inflation last for something like two to five years.

Today, about 40 years later, this statement still summarises the view of most macroeconomists.

Summary

- The Phillips curve describes a negative relationship between inflation and unemployment. By expanding aggregate demand, policymakers can choose a point on the Phillips curve with higher inflation and lower unemployment. By contracting aggregate demand, policymakers can choose a point on the Phillips curve with lower inflation and higher unemployment.
- The trade-off between inflation and unemployment described by the Phillips curve holds only in the short run. In the long run, expected inflation adjusts to changes in actual inflation and the short-run Phillips curve shifts. As a result, the long-run Phillips curve is vertical at the natural rate of unemployment.
- The short-run Phillips curve also shifts because of shocks to aggregate supply. An adverse supply shock, such as the increase in world oil prices during the 1970s, gives policymakers a less favourable trade-off between inflation and unemployment. That is, after an adverse supply shock, policymakers have to accept a higher rate of inflation for any given rate of unemployment, or a higher rate of unemployment for any given rate of inflation.
- When the RBA increases the cash rate to reduce inflation, it moves the economy along the short-run Phillips curve, which results in temporarily high unemployment. The cost of disinflation depends on how quickly expectations of inflation fall. Some economists argue that a credible commitment to low inflation can reduce the cost of disinflation by inducing a quick adjustment of expectations.

Key concepts

natural-rate hypothesis
NAIRU (non-accelerating inflation
  rate of unemployment)

Phillips curve
rational expectations

sacrifice ratio

Questions for review

1 Draw the short-run trade-off between inflation and unemployment. How might the RBA move the economy from one point on this curve to another?
2 Draw the long-run trade-off between inflation and unemployment. Explain how the short-run and long-run trade-offs are related. How can the government affect the long-run trade-off between inflation and unemployment?
3 Why might the natural rate of unemployment differ across countries?
4 The RBA decides to reduce inflation. Use the Phillips curve to show the short-run and long-run effects of this policy. How might the short-run costs be reduced?

Problems and applications

1 Suppose the natural rate of unemployment is 4 per cent. On one graph, draw two Phillips curves that can be used to describe the four situations listed here. Label the point that shows the position of the economy in each case:

    a   actual inflation is 5 per cent and expected inflation is 3 per cent

    b   actual inflation is 3 per cent and expected inflation is 5 per cent

    c   actual inflation is 5 per cent and expected inflation is 5 per cent

    d   actual inflation is 3 per cent and expected inflation is 3 per cent.

2 Illustrate the effects of the following developments on both the short-run and long-run Phillips curves. Give the economic reasoning underlying your answers.

    a   A reduction in the natural rate of unemployment

    b   An increase in the price of imported oil

    c   A reduction in government spending

    d   An increase in expected inflation.

3 Suppose that there is a reduction in people's inflation expectations.

    a   Illustrate the changes in the economy using both an aggregate-supply/aggregate-demand diagram and a Phillips-curve diagram.

    b   What will happen in the long run if expected inflation is lower? What will happen in the long run if expected inflation changes in the same direction that actual inflation changes in the short run? Illustrate your answers using your diagrams from part (a).

4 Suppose the economy is in a long-run equilibrium.

    a   Draw the economy's short-run and long-run Phillips curves.

    b   Suppose a wave of business pessimism reduces aggregate demand. Show the effect of this shock on your diagram from part (a). If the RBA undertakes expansionary monetary policy, can it return the economy to its original inflation rate and original unemployment rate?

    c   Now suppose the economy is back in long-run equilibrium and then the price of imported oil rises. Show the effect of this shock with a new diagram like that in part (a). If the RBA undertakes expansionary monetary policy, can it return the economy to its original inflation rate and original unemployment rate? If the RBA undertakes contractionary monetary policy, can it return the economy to its original inflation rate and original unemployment rate? Explain why this situation differs from that in part (b).

5 Suppose the government passed a law that changed the RBA's charter such that keeping unemployment as its natural rate was its primary focus.

    a   What do you think would happen to inflation?

    b   Suppose the RBA got the natural rate of unemployment wrong and it was actually 4 per cent when the RBA thought it was 6 per cent. If the economy was at 5 per cent unemployment, what would the RBA's policy decision be and what would happen to inflation and unemployment?

6 Suppose the RBA announced that it would pursue contractionary monetary policy in order to reduce the inflation rate. Would the following conditions make the ensuing recession more or less severe? Explain.

    a   Wage contracts have long durations.

    b   There is a great deal of confidence in the RBA's determination to reduce inflation.

    c   Expectations of inflation adjust quickly to actual inflation.

7 What factors determine the slope of the short-run Phillips curve? What factors determine how quickly it shifts in response to changes in the economy?

8 According to one version of Okun's law (discussed in chapter 33), when real GDP is 1 per cent below its trend level, the unemployment rate is half a percentage point above its natural rate. If the sacrifice ratio in Australia is 5, the natural rate of unemployment is 5 per cent, and the RBA wants to reduce inflation by 2 per cent, what rate of unemployment would be necessary for the RBA to reach its goal in five years?

9   Australian Workplace Agreements (AWAs) allowed companies to change workers' pay and conditions more frequently than some of the contracts written under enterprise bargaining, when contracts set terms and conditions for several years. Compare the slope of the Phillips curve under AWAs (with flexible terms and conditions) and under enterprise bargaining (with fixed conditions for three years, for example).

10 Given the unpopularity of inflation, why don't elected leaders always support efforts to reduce inflation? Economists believe that countries can reduce the cost of disinflation by letting their central banks make decisions about monetary policy without interference from politicians. Why might this be so?

Search me!

When accessing information about economics use the following keywords in any combinations you require:

- inflation–unemployment trade-off
- Phillips curve

CourseMate

For more multimedia resources and activities on economics, visit the Economics CourseMate website.

PART THIRTEEN
Final thoughts

Chapter 36 Five debates over macroeconomic policy

36

Five debates over macroeconomic policy

Learning objectives

In this chapter you will:

- consider whether policymakers should try to stabilise the economy
- consider whether monetary policy should be made by rule rather than by discretion
- consider whether the central bank should aim for zero inflation
- consider whether the government should balance its budget
- consider whether the tax laws should be reformed to encourage saving.

It is hard to open a newspaper without finding some politician or editorial writer advocating a change in economic policy. The government should cut government spending to increase the budget surplus, or give the surplus back in the form of tax reductions. The Reserve Bank of Australia (RBA) should cut interest rates to stimulate a flagging economy, or it should avoid such moves in order not to risk higher inflation. Government was right to reform the tax system to promote faster economic growth, or it should revoke the GST tax system to achieve a more equitable distribution of income. Economic issues are central to the continuing political debate in Australia and other countries around the world. Heads of governments around the world should heed the advice of US presidential candidate Bill Clinton's chief strategist in 1992 – he posted a sign to remind the staff of the central campaign issue: 'The economy, stupid'.

The previous dozen chapters have developed the tools that economists use when analysing the behaviour of the economy as a whole and the impact of policies on the economy. This final chapter presents both sides in five leading debates over macroeconomic policy. The knowledge you have accumulated in this course provides the background with which we can discuss these important, unsettled issues. It should help you choose a side in these debates or, at least, help you see why choosing a side is so difficult.

That monetary and fiscal policymakers should try to stabilise the economy

In chapters 33, 34 and 35 we saw how changes in aggregate demand and aggregate supply can lead to short-run fluctuations in production and employment. We also saw how monetary and fiscal policy can shift aggregate demand and, thereby, influence these fluctuations. But even if policymakers *can* influence short-run economic fluctuations, does that mean they *should*? Our first debate concerns whether monetary and fiscal policymakers should use the tools at their disposal in an attempt to smooth the ups and downs of the business cycle.

Pro: Policymakers should try to stabilise the economy

Left on their own, economies tend to fluctuate. When households and firms become pessimistic, for instance, they cut back on spending and this reduces aggregate demand for goods and services. The fall in aggregate demand, in turn, reduces the production of goods and services. Firms lay off workers and the unemployment rate rises. Real GDP and other measures of income fall. Rising unemployment and falling income help confirm the pessimism that initially generated the economic downturn.

Such a recession has no benefit for society – it represents a sheer waste of resources. Workers who become unemployed because of inadequate aggregate demand would rather be working. Business owners whose factories are left idle during a recession would rather be producing valuable goods and services and selling them at a profit.

There is no reason for society to suffer through the booms and busts of the business cycle. The development of macroeconomic theory has shown policymakers how to reduce the severity of economic fluctuations. By 'leaning against the wind' of economic change, monetary and fiscal policy can stabilise aggregate demand and, thereby, production and employment. When aggregate demand is inadequate to ensure full employment, policymakers should boost government spending, cut taxes and lower interest rates. When aggregate demand is excessive, risking higher inflation, policymakers should cut government spending, raise taxes and increase interest rates. Such policy actions put macroeconomic theory to its best use by leading to a more stable economy, which benefits everyone.

Con: Policymakers should not try to stabilise the economy

Although monetary and fiscal policy can be used to stabilise the economy in theory, there are substantial obstacles to the use of such policies in practice.

One problem is that monetary and fiscal policy do not affect the economy immediately but instead work with a substantial lag. Monetary policy affects aggregate demand by changing interest rates, which in turn affects spending, especially residential and business investment. But many households and firms set their spending plans in advance. As a result, it takes time for changes in interest rates to alter the aggregate demand for goods and services. Many studies indicate that changes in monetary policy have little effect on aggregate demand until about six months after the change is made.

Fiscal policy works with a lag because of the long political process that governs changes in spending and taxes.

Because of these long lags, policymakers who want to stabilise the economy need to look ahead to economic conditions that are likely to prevail when their actions will take effect. Unfortunately, economic forecasting is highly imprecise, in part because macroeconomics is such a primitive science and in part because the shocks that cause economic fluctuations are intrinsically unpredictable. Thus, when policymakers change monetary or fiscal policy, they must rely on educated guesses about future economic conditions.

All too often, policymakers trying to stabilise the economy do just the opposite. Economic conditions can easily change between the time when a policy action begins and when it takes effect. Because of this, policymakers can inadvertently exacerbate rather than mitigate the magnitude of economic fluctuations. Some economists have claimed that many of the major economic fluctuations in history, including the Great Depression of the 1930s, can be traced to destabilising policy actions.

One of the first rules taught to doctors is 'do no harm'. The human body has natural restorative powers. Confronted with a sick patient and an uncertain diagnosis, often a doctor should do nothing but leave the patient's body to its own devices. Intervening in the absence of reliable knowledge merely risks making matters worse.

The same can be said about treating an ailing economy. It might be desirable if policymakers could eliminate all economic fluctuations, but that is not a realistic goal given the limits of macroeconomic knowledge and the inherent unpredictability of world events. Economic policymakers should refrain from intervening often with monetary and fiscal policy and be content if they do no harm.

Explain why monetary and fiscal policy work with a lag. Why do these lags matter in the choice between active and passive policy?

That monetary policy should be made by rule rather than by discretion

As we first discussed in chapter 29, the Board of the RBA sets monetary policy in Australia in consultation with the government. The committee meets every month to evaluate the state of the economy. Based on this evaluation and forecasts of future economic conditions, it chooses whether to raise, lower or leave unchanged the level of short-term interest rates. The RBA then allows the money supply to adjust to ensure the target is reached. The target cash rate is re-evaluated at the RBA Board's monthly meeting.

The Board operates with almost complete discretion over how to conduct monetary policy. As we saw, the charter of the RBA gives the institution only vague recommendations about what goals it should pursue; and the Act does not tell the RBA how to pursue whatever goals it might choose. Once members are appointed to the Board, they have little mandate but to 'do the right thing'.

Some economists are critical of this institutional design. Our second debate over macroeconomic policy, therefore, focuses on whether the RBA should have its discretionary powers reduced and, instead, be committed to following a rule in how it conducts monetary policy.

Pro: Monetary policy should be made by rule

Discretion in the conduct of monetary policy has two problems. The first is that it does not limit incompetence and abuse of power. When the government sends police into a community to maintain order, it gives them strict guidelines about how to carry out their job. Because police have great power, allowing them to exercise that power in whatever way they want would be dangerous. Yet when the government gives central bankers the authority to maintain economic order, it gives them no guidelines. Monetary policymakers are allowed undisciplined discretion.

As an example of abuse of power, central bankers are sometimes tempted to use monetary policy to affect the outcome of elections. Suppose that the vote for the government is based on economic conditions at election time. A central banker sympathetic to the incumbent government might be tempted to pursue expansionary policies just before the election to stimulate production and employment, knowing that the resulting inflation will not show up until after the election. Thus, to the extent that central bankers ally themselves with politicians, discretionary policy can lead to economic fluctuations that reflect the electoral calendar. Economists call such fluctuations the *political business cycle*.

One way to avoid this problem with discretionary policy is to commit the central bank to a policy rule. For example, suppose that Parliament passed a law requiring the RBA to set interest rates to target 1 per cent inflation. (Why 1 per cent? Because zero inflation is very hard to achieve and not necessarily desirable. See the second debate below.) Such a law would eliminate incompetence and abuse of power on the part of the RBA and it would make the political business cycle impossible. People would now know exactly what the RBA intended to do each month because it would be legally required to pursue a low-inflation monetary policy. With low expected inflation, the economy would face a more favourable short-run trade-off between inflation and unemployment.

Con: Monetary policy should not be made by rule

Although there may be pitfalls with discretionary monetary policy, there is also an important advantage to it – flexibility. The RBA has to confront various circumstances, not all of which can be foreseen. In the 1930s, banks failed in record numbers. In the 1970s, the price of oil skyrocketed around the world. In October 1987, the stock market fell by 22 per cent in a single day. In the aftermath of 11 September 2001, people expected a collapse of the US economy that would have worldwide effects. The RBA must decide how to respond to these shocks to the economy. In September, 2008, the world saw the collapse of Lehman Brothers Investment Bank in the US and a worldwide recession was feared. A designer of a policy rule could not possibly consider all the contingencies and specify in advance the correct policy response. It is better to appoint good people to conduct monetary policy and then give them the freedom to do the best they can.

Moreover, the alleged problems with discretion are largely hypothetical. The practical importance of the political business cycle, for instance, is far from clear. In some cases, just the opposite seems to occur. For example, Prime Minister Keating appointed Bernie Fraser to head the RBA in 1990. Nonetheless, Fraser continued the contraction of monetary policy initiated in April 1988 in order to combat the high rate of inflation. The predictable result of Fraser's decision was a recession and the predictable result of the recession was a decline in Keating's popularity. Rather than using monetary policy to help the politician who had appointed him, Fraser helped with Keating's defeat in the 1996 election.

Any attempt to replace discretion with a rule must confront the difficult task of specifying a precise rule. Despite much research examining the costs and benefits of alternative rules, economists have not reached a consensus about what a good rule would be. Until there is a consensus, society has little choice but to give central bankers discretion to conduct monetary policy as they see fit.

Give an example of a monetary policy rule. Why might your rule be better than discretionary policy? Why might it be worse?

That the central bank should aim for zero inflation

One of the *Ten Lessons from Economics* discussed in chapter 1 and developed more fully in chapter 30 is that prices rise when the government prints too much money. Another of the *Ten Lessons from Economics* discussed in chapter 1 and developed more fully in chapter 35 is that society faces a short-run trade-off between inflation and unemployment. Put together, these two principles raise a question for policymakers: How much inflation should the central bank be willing to tolerate? Our third debate is whether zero is the correct target for the inflation rate.

Pro: The central bank should aim for zero inflation

Inflation confers no benefit to society, but it does impose several real costs. As we discussed in chapter 30, economists have identified six costs of inflation:

- shoeleather costs associated with reduced money holdings
- menu costs associated with more frequent adjustment of prices
- increased variability of relative prices
- unintended changes in tax liabilities due to non-indexation of the tax laws
- confusion and inconvenience resulting from a changing unit of account
- arbitrary redistributions of wealth associated with dollar-denominated debts.

Some economists argue that these costs are small, at least for moderate rates of inflation, such as the low inflation experienced in Australia during most of the 1990s and 2000s. But other economists claim these costs can be substantial, even for moderate inflation. Moreover, there is no doubt that the public dislikes inflation. When inflation heats up, opinion polls identify inflation as one of the nation's leading problems.

Of course, the benefits of zero inflation have to be weighed against the costs of achieving it. Reducing inflation usually requires a period of high unemployment and low output, as illustrated by the short-run Phillips curve. But this disinflationary recession is only temporary. Once people come to understand that policymakers are aiming for zero inflation, expectations of inflation will fall, which improves the short-run trade-off. Because expectations adjust, there is no trade-off between inflation and unemployment in the long run.

Reducing inflation is, therefore, a policy with temporary costs and permanent benefits. That is, once the disinflationary recession is over, the benefits of zero inflation would persist into the future. If policymakers are farsighted, they should be willing to incur the temporary costs for the permanent benefits. This is precisely the calculation made by Bernie Fraser in the early 1990s, when he reduced inflation from about 8 per cent in 1989 to about 2 per cent in 1992. Fraser was following in the footsteps of Paul Volcker, the Chairman of the US Federal Reserve who performed a similar feat for the US economy in the 1980s. Volcker is considered a hero among central bankers.

Moreover, the costs of reducing inflation need not be as large as some economists claim. If the RBA announces a credible commitment to zero inflation, it can directly influence expectations of inflation. Such a change in expectations can improve the short-run trade-off between inflation and unemployment, allowing the economy to reach lower inflation at a reduced cost. The key to this strategy is credibility – people must believe that the RBA is actually going to carry through its announced policy. Parliament could help in this regard by passing legislation that made price stability the RBA's only goal. Such a law would make it less costly to achieve zero inflation without reducing any of the resulting benefits.

Con: The central bank should not aim for zero inflation

Although price stability may be desirable, the benefits of zero inflation compared with moderate inflation are small, whereas the costs of reaching zero inflation are large. Estimates of the sacrifice ratio suggest that reducing inflation by one percentage point requires giving up about 5 per cent of one year's output. Reducing inflation from, say, 4 per cent to zero requires a loss of 20 per cent of a year's output. At the current level of gross domestic product of about $1301 billion, this cost translates into $260 billion of lost output, which is about $11 569 per person. Although people might dislike inflation, it is not at all clear that they would (or should) be willing to pay this much to get rid of it.

The social costs of disinflation are even larger than this $11 569 figure suggests, for the lost income is not spread equitably over the population. When the economy goes into recession, all incomes do not fall proportionately. Instead, the fall in aggregate income is concentrated on those workers who lose their jobs. The vulnerable workers are often those with the least skills and experience. Hence, much of the cost of reducing inflation is borne by those who can least afford to pay it.

Although economists can list several costs of inflation, there is no professional consensus that these costs are substantial. The shoeleather costs, menu costs and others that economists have identified do not seem great, at least for moderate rates of inflation. It is true that the public dislikes inflation, but the public may be misled into believing the inflation fallacy – the view that inflation erodes living standards. Economists understand that living standards depend on productivity, not monetary policy. Because inflation in nominal incomes goes hand in hand with inflation in prices, reducing inflation would not cause real incomes to rise more rapidly.

Moreover, policymakers can reduce many of the costs of inflation without actually reducing inflation. They can eliminate the problems associated with the non-indexed tax system by rewriting the tax laws to take account of the effects of inflation. They can also reduce the arbitrary redistributions of wealth between creditors and debtors caused by unexpected inflation by issuing indexed government bonds, as in fact the Australian government did in 1985. Such an act insulates holders of government debt from inflation. In addition, by setting an example, it might encourage private borrowers and lenders to write debt contracts indexed for inflation.

Reducing inflation might be desirable if it could be done at no cost, as some economists argue is possible. Yet this trick seems hard to carry out in practice. When economies reduce their rate of inflation, they almost always experience a period of high unemployment and low output. It is risky to believe that the central bank could achieve credibility so quickly as to make disinflation painless.

Indeed, a disinflationary recession can potentially leave permanent scars on the economy. Firms in all industries reduce their spending on new plant and equipment substantially during recessions, making investment the most volatile component of GDP. Even after the recession is over, the smaller stock of capital reduces productivity, incomes and living standards below the levels they otherwise would have achieved. In addition, when workers become unemployed in recessions, they lose valuable job skills. Even after the economy has recovered, their value as workers is diminished. Some economists have argued that the high unemployment in many European economies during the past decade is the aftermath of the disinflations of the 1980s.

Why should policymakers put the economy through a costly, inequitable disinflationary recession to achieve zero inflation, which may have only modest benefits? American economist Alan Blinder argued forcefully in his book *Hard Heads, Soft Hearts* that policymakers should not make this choice:

> The costs that attend the low and moderate inflation rates experienced in the United States and in other industrial countries appear to be quite modest – more like a bad cold than a cancer on society... As rational individuals, we do not volunteer for a lobotomy to cure a head cold. Yet, as a collectivity, we routinely prescribe the economic equivalent of lobotomy (high unemployment) as a cure for the inflationary cold.

Blinder concludes that it is better to learn to live with moderate inflation.

▸ inflation

Explain the costs and benefits of reducing inflation to zero. Which are temporary and which are permanent?

That the government should balance its budget

Perhaps the most persistent macroeconomic debate in recent years has been over the Australian government's budget deficit. As you may recall, a budget deficit is an excess of government spending over government revenue. The government finances a budget deficit by issuing government debt. When we studied financial markets in chapter 27, we saw how budget deficits affect saving, investment and interest rates. But how big a problem are budget deficits? Our fourth debate concerns whether fiscal policymakers should make balancing the government's budget a high priority.

Pro: The government should balance its budget

In 1997, the Australian government debt reached over $96 billion, or about 18 per cent of GDP. Under the Howard government, the level of government debt declined significantly, as the government cut spending and paid off existing debt. In 2006, the government had retired existing debt and had a surplus. In 2008, the size of the surplus was projected to be over $12 billion, or around $571 per person, given Australia's population in 2008. In the Federal election in 2007, Kevin Rudd ran and won the election as a 'fiscal conservative', pledging to keep the Australian government budget in surplus, ensuring that the government would not go into debt again. (However, when the Global

Financial Crisis came along, the Rudd government sent the budget into deficit by announcing a fiscal expansion – giving families up to $900 in 'Ruddy dollars', as the stimulus package was known.)

Why would political parties on either side want to be known as 'fiscal conservatives'? It is because of the direct effect of government debt in placing a burden on future generations of taxpayers. When these debts and accumulated interest come due, future taxpayers will face a difficult choice. They can pay higher taxes, enjoy less government spending, or both, in order to make resources available to pay off the debt and accumulated interest. Or they can delay the day of reckoning and put the government into even deeper debt by borrowing once again to pay off the old debt and interest. In essence, when the government runs a budget deficit, it allows current taxpayers to pass the bill for some of their government spending on to future taxpayers. Inheriting such a large debt cannot help but lower the living standard of future generations.

In addition to this direct effect, budget deficits also have various macroeconomic effects. Because budget deficits represent *negative* public saving, they lower national saving (the sum of private and public saving). Reduced national saving causes real interest rates to rise and investment to fall. Reduced investment leads over time to a smaller stock of capital. A lower capital stock reduces labour productivity, real wages and the economy's production of goods and services. Thus, when the government increases its debt, future generations are born into an economy with lower incomes as well as higher taxes.

There are, nevertheless, situations in which running a budget deficit is justifiable. Throughout history, the most common cause of increased government debt is war. When a military conflict raises government spending temporarily, it is reasonable to finance this extra spending by borrowing. Otherwise, taxes during wartime would have to rise precipitously. Such high tax rates would greatly distort the incentives faced by those who are taxed, leading to large efficiency losses. In addition, such high tax rates would be unfair to current generations of taxpayers, who already have to make the sacrifice of fighting the war.

Similarly, it is reasonable to allow a budget deficit during a temporary downturn in economic activity. When the economy goes into a recession, tax revenue falls automatically, because the income tax and the payroll tax are levied on measures of income. If the government tried to balance its budget during a recession, it would have to raise taxes or cut spending at a time of high unemployment. Such a policy would tend to depress aggregate demand at precisely the time it needed to be stimulated and, therefore, would tend to increase the magnitude of economic fluctuations.

Con: The government should not balance its budget

The problem of the budget deficit is often exaggerated. Although government debt does represent a tax burden on younger generations, it is not large compared with the average person's lifetime income. The Australian government deficit projection for 2010–11 is $40.8 billion or $1813 per person. A person who works 40 years for $25 000 a year will earn $1 million over their lifetime. Their share of the government deficit represents much less than 2 per cent of their lifetime resources.

Moreover, it is misleading to view the effects of budget deficits in isolation. The budget deficit is just one piece of a large picture of how the government chooses to raise and spend money. In making these decisions about fiscal policy, policymakers affect different generations of taxpayers in many ways. The budget deficit should be considered together with these other policies.

For example, suppose the government reduces the budget deficit by cutting spending on education. Does this change in policy make young generations better off? The government debt will be smaller when they enter the labour force, which means a smaller tax burden. Yet if they are less well educated, their productivity and incomes will be lower. Many estimates of the return on education (the increase in a worker's wage that results from an additional year of learning) find that it is quite large. Reducing the budget deficit by cutting education spending could, all things considered, make future generations worse off.

Single-minded concern about the budget deficit is also dangerous because it draws attention away from various other policies that redistribute income across generations. For example, in the 1970s, the Australian government decided not to charge fees for university education. That meant an increase in Commonwealth government spending on education. It financed this higher spending by increasing borrowing, which was a burden on future generations. This policy resulted in a redistribution of income for the generation receiving the benefit of free university education. Instead of paying for their education out of current income, they would pay for it in the future by paying off government debt. This occurred even though the policy did not affect the budget deficit. Thus, the budget deficit is only a small piece of the larger issue of how government policy affects the welfare of different generations.

To some extent, the adverse effects of government budget deficits can be reversed by forward-looking parents. Suppose parents are worried about the impact of the government debt on their children. Parents can offset the impact simply by saving and leaving a larger bequest. The bequest would enhance the children's ability to bear the burden of future taxes. Some economists claim that people do, in fact, behave this way. If this were true, higher private saving by parents would offset the public dis-saving of budget deficits, and deficits would not affect the economy. (As chapter 27 noted, this theory is called *Ricardian equivalence*.) Most economists doubt that parents are so farsighted, but some people probably do act this way, and anyone could. Deficits give people the opportunity to consume at the expense of their children, but deficits do not require them to do so. If the government debt were actually a great problem facing future generations, some parents would help to solve it.

Critics of budget deficits sometimes assert that the government debt cannot continue to rise forever, but in fact it can. Just as a bank evaluating a loan application would compare a person's debts with his income, we should judge the burden of the government debt relative to the size of the nation's income. Population growth and technological progress cause the total income of the Australian economy to grow over time. As a result, the nation's ability to pay the interest on the government debt grows over time as well. As long as the government debt grows more slowly than the nation's income, there is nothing to prevent the government debt from growing forever.

Some numbers can put the budget deficit into perspective. The real output of the Australian economy grows on average about 3 per cent per year. If the inflation rate is 3 per cent per year, then nominal income grows at a rate of 6 per cent per year. The government debt, therefore, can rise by 6 per cent per year without increasing the ratio of debt to income. In 2010–11 the Australian government debt was projected to be $79 billion; 6 per cent of this figure is around $4.76 billion. As long as the budget deficit is smaller than $4.76 billion, the policy is sustainable. Even though the current budget deficit is greater than this, the budget is projected to be in surplus by 2012–13. Unlike other economies that have massive debt to GDP ratios, Australia's government deficits are manageable and have kept the Australian economy from the recessions other economies have experienced in the last few years. There will never be any day of reckoning that forces budget deficits to end or the economy to collapse.

Explain how a budget deficit makes future generations worse off. Explain how reducing the budget deficit might make future generations worse off.

That the tax laws should be reformed to encourage saving

A nation's standard of living depends on its ability to produce goods and services. This was one of the *Ten Lessons from Economics* in chapter 1. As we saw in chapter 26, a nation's productive capability, in turn, is determined largely by how much it saves and invests for the future. Our fifth debate is whether policymakers should reform the tax laws in order to encourage greater saving and investment.

Pro: The tax laws should be reformed to encourage saving

A nation's saving rate is a key determinant of its long-run economic prosperity. When the saving rate is higher, more resources are available for investment in new plant and equipment. A larger stock of plant and equipment, in turn, raises labour productivity, wages and incomes. It is, therefore, no surprise that international data show a strong correlation between national saving rates and measures of economic wellbeing.

Another of the *Ten Lessons from Economics* presented in chapter 1 is that people respond to incentives. This lesson should apply to people's decisions about how much to save. If a nation's laws make saving attractive, people will save a higher fraction of their incomes, and this higher saving will lead to a more prosperous future.

Unfortunately, the Australian tax system discourages saving by taxing the return on saving quite heavily. For example, consider Julie, a 25-year-old worker, who saves $1000 of her income in order to have a more comfortable retirement at the age of 70. If she buys a bond that pays an interest rate of 10 per cent, the $1000 will accumulate at the end of 45 years to $72 900 in the absence of taxes on interest. But suppose she faces a marginal tax rate on interest income of 40 per cent, which is typical for many workers. In this case, her after-tax interest rate is only 6 per cent and the $1000 will accumulate at the end of 45 years to only $13 800. That is, accumulated over this long span of time, the tax rate on interest income reduces the benefit of saving $1000 from $72 900 to $13 800 – or by about 80 per cent.

In addition to the tax laws, many other policies and institutions in our society reduce the incentive for households to save. Some government benefits, such as social welfare, age pensions and sickness benefits, are means-tested; that is, the benefits are reduced for those who, in the past, have been prudent enough to save some of their income. Youth Allowance payments for students are granted as a function of the wealth of the students and their parents. Such a policy is like a tax on wealth and, as such, discourages students and parents from saving.

There are various ways in which the tax laws could provide an incentive to save, or at least reduce the disincentive that households now face. Already the tax laws give preferential treatment to some types of retirement saving. When a taxpayer puts income into a superannuation fund, for instance, that income and the interest it earns are taxed at much lower rates than ordinary earned income, if the funds are not withdrawn until retirement. Because there are penalties for withdrawal before retirement age, these retirement plans provide little incentive for other types of saving, such as saving to pay for education. A small step to encourage greater saving would be to expand the ability of households to use such tax-advantaged savings accounts.

A more comprehensive approach is what the Howard government did in 2000: that is, to reconsider the entire basis upon which the government collects revenue. The centrepiece of the Australian tax system is income tax. A dollar earned is taxed the same whether it is spent or saved. The alternative introduced by the Howard government is a consumption tax, known in Australia as the GST or goods and service tax. Under a consumption tax, a household pays taxes only on the basis of what it spends. Income that is saved is exempt from taxation until the saving is later withdrawn and spent on consumption goods. In essence, a consumption tax puts all saving automatically into a tax-advantaged savings account, much like funds in a superannuation account. A switch from income to consumption taxation greatly increases the incentive to save.

Con: The tax laws should not be reformed to encourage saving

Although increasing saving may be desirable, it is not the only goal of tax policy. Policymakers also must be sure to distribute the tax burden fairly. The problem with proposals to increase the incentive to save is that they increase the tax burden on those who can least afford it.

It is an undeniable fact that high-income households save a higher fraction of their income than low-income households. As a result, any tax change that favours people who save will also tend to favour people with high incomes. Policies such as tax-advantaged retirement accounts may seem appealing, but they lead to a less egalitarian society. By reducing the tax burden on the wealthy who can take advantage of these accounts, they force the government to raise the tax burden on the poor.

The same argument applies to the tax laws governing inheritances. There are no death duties in Australia, so individuals who want to leave their accumulated wealth to their children (or anyone else) rather than consuming it themselves are advantaged. To a large extent, concern about national saving is motivated by a desire to ensure economic prosperity for future generations. The tax laws already encourage the most direct way in which one generation can help the next.

Source: *The Economic Rationalist's Guide to Sex*, Harper Collins, Australia 1997. Reproduced with permission.

Moreover, it is not clear if tax policies designed to encourage saving are effective at achieving that goal. Many studies have found that saving is relatively inelastic – that is, the amount of saving is not very sensitive to the rate of return on saving. If this is indeed the case, then tax provisions that raise the effective return by reducing the taxation of capital income will further enrich the wealthy without inducing them to save more than they otherwise would. A reduction in tax will lower public saving and, on balance, national saving may actually fall.

From the standpoint of economic theory, it is not clear whether a higher rate of return would increase saving. The outcome depends on the relative size of two conflicting effects, called the *substitution effect* and the *income effect*. On the one hand, a higher rate of return raises the benefit of saving – each dollar saved today produces more consumption in the future. This substitution effect tends to raise saving. On the other hand, a higher rate of return lowers the need for saving – a household has to save less to achieve any target level of consumption in the future. This income effect tends to reduce saving. If the substitution and income effects approximately cancel each other, as some studies suggest, then saving will not change when lower taxation of capital income raises the rate of return.

There are other ways to raise national saving than by giving tax breaks to the rich. National saving is the sum of private and public saving. Instead of trying to alter the tax laws to encourage greater private saving, policymakers can simply raise public saving by reducing the budget deficit. Reducing the budget deficit, perhaps by raising taxes on the wealthy, offers a direct way of raising national saving and increasing prosperity for future generations.

Indeed, once public saving is taken into account, it seems that tax provisions to encourage saving might backfire. Tax changes that reduce the taxation of capital income reduce government revenue and, thereby, increase the budget deficit. To increase national saving, such a change in the tax laws must stimulate private saving by more than it increases the budget deficit. If this is not the case, so-called saving incentives can potentially make matters worse.

▸ tax incentives
▸ saving

Give three examples of how our society discourages saving. What are the drawbacks of eliminating these disincentives?

Conclusion

This chapter has considered five debates over macroeconomic policy. For each, it began with a controversial proposition and then offered the arguments pro and con. If you find it hard to choose a side in these debates, you may find some comfort in the fact that you are not alone. The study of economics does not always make it easy to choose among alternative policies. Indeed, by clarifying the inevitable trade-offs that policymakers face, it can make the choice more difficult.

Difficult choices, however, have no right to seem easy. When you hear politicians or commentators proposing something that sounds too good to be true, it probably is. If they sound like they are offering you a free lunch, you should look for the hidden price tag. Few if any policies come with benefits but no costs. By helping you see through the fog of rhetoric so common in political discourse, the study of economics should make you a better informed participant in our national debates.

Summary

- Advocates of active monetary and fiscal policy view the economy as inherently unstable and believe that policy can manage aggregate demand in order to offset the inherent instability. Critics of active monetary and fiscal policy emphasise that policy affects the economy with a lag and that our ability to forecast future economic conditions is quite bad. As a result, attempts to stabilise the economy can end up being destabilising.

- Advocates of rules for monetary policy argue that discretionary policy can suffer from incompetence and abuse of power. Critics of rules for monetary policy argue that discretionary policy is more flexible in responding to changing economic circumstances.

- Advocates of a zero-inflation target emphasise that inflation has many costs and few if any benefits. Moreover, the cost of eliminating inflation – depressed output and employment – is only temporary. Even this cost can be reduced if the central bank announces a credible plan to reduce inflation, thereby directly lowering expectations of inflation. Critics of a zero-inflation target claim that moderate inflation imposes only small costs on society, whereas the recession necessary to reduce inflation is quite costly.

- Advocates of a balanced government budget argue that budget deficits impose an unjustifiable burden on future generations by raising their taxes and lowering their incomes. Critics of a balanced government budget argue that the deficit is only one small piece of fiscal policy. Single-minded concern about the budget deficit can obscure the many ways in which policy, including various spending programs, affects different generations.

- Advocates of tax incentives for saving point out that our society discourages saving in many ways, such as by heavily taxing the income from capital and by reducing benefits for those who have accumulated wealth. They endorse reforming the tax laws to encourage saving, perhaps by switching from an income tax to a consumption tax. Critics of tax incentives for saving argue that many proposed changes to stimulate saving would primarily benefit the wealthy, who do not need a tax break. They also argue that such changes might have only a small effect on private saving. Raising public saving by eliminating the government's budget deficit would provide a more direct and equitable way to increase national saving.

Questions for review

1. What causes the lags in the effect of monetary and fiscal policy on aggregate demand? What are the implications of these lags for the debate over active versus passive policy?
2. Are political business cycles likely in Australia? Why or why not?
3. Explain how credibility might affect the cost of reducing inflation. What has the Reserve Bank of Australia done to improve its credibility?
4. Why are some economists against a target of zero inflation?
5. Explain two ways in which a government budget surplus helps a future worker.
6. What are two situations in which a budget deficit is justifiable?
7. Give an example of how reductions in government debt might hurt current generations.
8. Some economists say that the government can continue running a budget deficit forever. How is that possible?
9. Some income from capital is taxed twice. Explain.
10. Give an example, other than tax policy, of how our society discourages saving. What adverse effect might be caused by tax incentives to increase saving?

Problems and applications

1 The chapter suggests that the economy, like the human body, has 'natural restorative powers'.

   a Illustrate the short-run effect of a fall in aggregate demand using an aggregate-demand/aggregate-supply diagram. What happens to total output, income and employment?

   b If the government does not use stabilisation policy, what happens to the economy over time? Illustrate on your diagram. Does this adjustment generally occur in a matter of months or a matter of years?

   c Does the economy restore itself? How quickly do the economy's restorative powers work?

2 In January 2008, the US Federal Reserve Board decreased interest rates twice in 10 days. Why do you think they needed to have two reductions so close together? What do you think this would do to their credibility?

3 In the text, we said that the RBA could set either the interest rate or the money supply, but not both. Does this make it harder for the RBA to follow a monetary rule? Explain.

4 Time inconsistency refers to a government policy-making body announcing one policy, but pursuing another. It means that policymakers have less credibility than if they did what they said they'd do. It applies to fiscal policy as well as to monetary policy. Suppose the government announced a reduction in taxes on income from capital investments, such as new factories.

   a If investors believed that capital taxes would remain low, how would the government's action affect the level of investment?

   b After investors have responded to the announced tax reduction, does the government have an incentive to renege on its policy? Explain.

   c Given your answer to part (b), would investors believe the government's announcement? What can the government do to increase the credibility of announced policy changes?

   d Explain why this situation is similar to the time inconsistency problem faced by monetary policymakers.

5 Suppose the Gillard government proposes a plan to assist 18-year-olds in establishing their own superannuation plans. Suppose they give people in the lowest tax brackets a $1000 government contribution to their savings account for every $5000 saved during a given year, but will only do so if they don't withdraw the money from their savings accounts for five years. What are the arguments for and against such a plan. What do you think this plan will do to aggregate demand in the short-run? In the long-run? Could the plan lead to an increase in interest rates? Explain.

6 Why are the benefits of reducing inflation permanent and the costs temporary? Why are the costs of increasing inflation permanent and the benefits temporary? Use Phillips-curve diagrams in your answer.

7 Explain how each of the following policies redistributes income across generations. Is the redistribution from young to old, or from old to young?

   a An increase in the budget deficit

   b An increase in fees for certain university courses

   c Payments to people who have lost homes and businesses in the floods in Queensland.

   d Indexation of pension benefits to inflation.

8 We have discussed budget deficits as if they are all the same. Does it matter what the government spends its borrowed funds on? Why might some deficits be good for the economy in the long run?

9 The chapter says that budget deficits reduce the income of future generations, but can boost output and income during a recession. Explain how both of these statements can be true.

10 The chapter says that tax changes that encourage saving will tend to favour people with high incomes. If the government cut taxes on capital income, what could it do at the same time to avoid redistributing income?

11 What is the fundamental trade-off that society faces if it chooses to save more?

12 Suppose the government reduced the tax rate on income from savings.
   a Who would benefit from this tax reduction most directly?
   b What would happen to the capital stock over time? What would happen to the capital available to each worker? What would happen to productivity? What would happen to wages?
   c In light of your answer to part (b), who might benefit from this tax reduction in the long run?

13 For several of the policy debates discussed in this chapter, the costs of certain choices are borne primarily by a narrow segment of the population.
   a Give several examples and explain why the costs are unevenly distributed.
   b How does the uneven distribution of costs affect your view of these debates?

Search me!

When accessing information about economics use the following keywords in any combinations you require:

- inflation
- saving
- tax incentive

CourseMate

For more multimedia resources and activities on economics, visit the Economics CourseMate website.

Glossary

ability-to-pay principle
the idea that taxes should be levied on a person according to how well that person can shoulder the burden

absolute advantage
the comparison among producers of a good according to their productivity

adverse selection
the tendency for the mix of unobserved attributes to become undesirable from the standpoint of an uninformed party

agent
a person who is performing an act for another person, called the principal

aggregate-demand curve
a curve that shows the quantity of goods and services that households, firms and the government want to buy at any inflation rate

aggregate-supply curve
a curve that shows the quantity of goods and services that firms choose to produce and sell at any inflation rate

appreciation
an increase in the value of a currency as measured by the amount of foreign currency it can buy

Arrow's impossibility theorem
a mathematical result showing that, under certain assumed conditions, there is no scheme for aggregating individual preferences into a valid set of social preferences

automatic stabilisers
changes in fiscal policy that stimulate aggregate demand when the economy goes into a recession or rein in aggregate demand when the economy booms without policymakers having to take any deliberate action

average fixed cost
fixed costs divided by the quantity of output

average revenue
total revenue divided by the quantity sold

average tax rate
total taxes paid divided by total income

average total cost
total cost divided by the quantity of output

average variable cost
variable costs divided by the quantity of output

awards
the minimum wage rates that can be paid to particular workers in particular industries

balanced trade
a situation in which exports equal imports

benefits principle
the idea that people should pay taxes based on the benefits they receive from government services

bilateral monopoly
a market situation where there is both a single buyer and a single seller for a product

bond (security)
a certificate of indebtedness

budget constraint
the limit on the consumption bundles that a consumer can afford

budget deficit
an excess of government spending over government receipts

budget surplus
an excess of government receipts over government spending

capital
the equipment and structures used to produce goods and services

capital flight
a large and sudden reduction in the demand for assets located in a country

cartel
a group of firms acting in unison

cash
the amount of currency and bank reserves in the economy

cash rate
the interest rate that financial institutions can earn on overnight loans of their currency or reserves

catch-up effect
the property whereby countries that start off poor tend to grow more rapidly than countries that start off rich

central bank
an institution designed to oversee the banking system and regulate the quantity of money in the economy

ceteris paribus
a Latin phrase, translated as 'other things being equal', used as a reminder that all variables other than the ones being studied are assumed to be constant

circular-flow diagram
a visual model of the economy that shows how dollars flow through markets among households and firms

classical dichotomy
the theoretical separation of nominal and real variables

closed economy
an economy that does not interact with other economies in the world

club goods
goods that are excludable but not rival in consumption

Coase theorem
the proposition that if private parties can bargain without cost over the allocation of resources, they can solve the problem of externalities on their own

collective bargaining
the process by which unions and firms agree on the terms of employment

collusion
an agreement among firms in a market about quantities to produce or prices to charge

commodity money
money that takes the form of a commodity with intrinsic value

common resources
goods that are rival in consumption but not excludable

comparative advantage
the comparison among producers of a good according to their opportunity cost

compensating differential
a difference in wages that arises to offset the non-monetary characteristics of different jobs

Competition and Consumer Act
Australia's main competition laws (formerly the *Trade Practices Act*).

competition laws
laws that restrict the behaviour of firms with market power, such as monopolies or firms in a small oligopoly

competition policy
the laws and procedures that aim to improve social efficiency in oligopolistic and monopolistic markets

competitive market
a market in which there are many buyers and many sellers so that each has a negligible impact on the market price

complements
two goods for which a decrease in the price of one good leads to an increase in the demand for the other good

Condorcet paradox
the failure of majority rule to produce transitive preferences for society

constant returns to scale
the property whereby long-run average total cost stays the same as the quantity of output changes

consumer price index (CPI)
a measure of the overall cost of the goods and services bought by a typical consumer

consumer surplus
a buyer's willingness to pay minus the amount the buyer actually pays

consumption
spending by households on goods and services, with the exception of purchases of new housing

corrective tax
a tax imposed to correct the effects of a negative externality

cost
the value of everything a seller must give up to produce a good

cost–benefit analysis
a study that compares the costs and benefits to society of providing a public good

cross-price elasticity of demand
a measure of how much the quantity demanded of one good responds to a change in the price of another good, computed as the percentage change in quantity demanded of the first good divided by the percentage change in the price of the second good

crowding out
a decrease in investment that results from government borrowing

crowding-out effect
the offset in aggregate demand that results when expansionary fiscal policy induces the RBA to increase

the interest rate and thereby reduce investment spending

currency
the plastic notes and metal coins in the hands of the public

current deposits
balances in bank accounts that depositors can access on demand by using a debit card or writing a cheque

cyclical unemployment
the deviation of unemployment from its natural rate

deadweight loss
the reduction in total surplus that results from a market distortion such as a tax or a monopoly price

demand curve
a graph of the relationship between the price of a good and the quantity demanded

demand schedule
a table that shows the relationship between the price of a good and the quantity demanded

depreciation
a decrease in the value of a currency as measured by the amount of foreign currency it can buy

depression
a severe recession

diminishing marginal product
the property whereby the marginal product of an input declines as the quantity of the input increases

diminishing returns
the property whereby the benefit from an extra unit of an input declines as the quantity of the input increases

discouraged workers
individuals who would like to work but have given up looking for a job

discrimination
the offering of different opportunities to similar individuals who differ only by race, ethnic group, sex, age or other personal characteristics

diseconomies of scale
the property whereby long-run average total cost rises as the quantity of output increases

dominant strategy
a strategy that is best for a player in a game regardless of the strategies chosen by the other players

economics
the study of how society manages its scarce resources

economies of scale
the property whereby long-run average total cost falls as the quantity of output increases

efficiency
the property of society getting the most it can from its scarce resources

efficiency wages
above-equilibrium wages paid by firms in order to increase worker productivity

efficient scale
the quantity of output that minimises average total cost

elasticity
a measure of the responsiveness of quantity demanded or quantity supplied to one of its determinants

equilibrium
a situation in which supply and demand have been brought into balance

equilibrium price
the price that balances supply and demand

equilibrium quantity
the quantity supplied and the quantity demanded when the price has adjusted to balance supply and demand

equity
the property of distributing economic prosperity fairly among the members of society

excludable
the property of a good whereby a person can be prevented from using it

exports
goods and services produced domestically and sold abroad

externality
the uncompensated impact of one person's actions on the wellbeing of a bystander. A positive externality makes the bystander better off. A negative externality makes the bystander worse off.

factors of production
the inputs used to produce goods and services

fiat money
money without intrinsic value that is used as money because of government decree

financial intermediaries
financial institutions through which savers can indirectly provide funds to borrowers

financial markets
financial institutions through which savers can directly provide funds to borrowers

financial system
the group of institutions in the economy that help to match one person's saving with another person's investment

Fisher effect
the one-for-one adjustment of the nominal interest rate to the inflation rate

fixed costs
costs that do not vary with the quantity of output produced

fractional-reserve banking
a banking system in which banks hold only a fraction of deposits as reserves

free rider
a person who receives the benefit of a good but avoids paying for it

game theory
the study of how people behave in strategic situations

GDP deflator
a measure of the price level calculated as the ratio of nominal GDP to real GDP times 100

Giffen good
a good for which an increase in the price raises the quantity demanded

government purchases
spending on goods and services by local, state and federal governments

gross domestic product (GDP)
the market value of all final goods and services produced within a country in a given period of time

gross national product (GNP)
the market value of all final goods and services produced by permanent residents of a nation within a given period of time

horizontal equity
the idea that taxpayers with similar abilities to pay taxes should pay the same amount

human capital
the accumulation of investments in people, such as education and on-the-job training

import quota
a limit on the quantity of a good produced abroad that can be sold domestically

imports
goods and services produced abroad and sold domestically

income effect
the change in consumption that results when a price change moves the consumer to a higher or lower indifference curve

income elasticity of demand
a measure of how much the quantity demanded of a good responds to a change in consumers' income, calculated as the percentage change in quantity demanded divided by the percentage change in income

indexation
the automatic correction of a dollar amount for the effects of inflation by law or contract

indifference curve
a curve that shows consumption bundles that give the consumer the same level of satisfaction

inferior good
a good for which, other things being equal, an increase in income leads to a decrease in quantity demanded

inflation
an increase in the overall level of prices in the economy

inflation rate
the percentage change in the price index from the preceding period

inflation tax
the revenue the government raises by creating money

internalising an externality
altering incentives so that people take into account the external effects of their actions

investment
spending on new capital equipment, inventories and structures, including household purchases of new housing

invisible hand
The idea that buyers and sellers freely interacting in a market economy will create an outcome that allocates goods and services to those people who value them most highly and makes the best use of our scarce resources

job search
the process by which workers find appropriate jobs given their tastes and skills

labour force
the total number of workers, including both the employed and the unemployed

labour-force participation rate
the percentage of the adult population that is in the labour force

law of demand
the claim that, other things being equal, the quantity demanded of a good falls when the price of the good rises

law of supply
the claim that, other things being equal, the quantity supplied of a good rises when the price of the good rises

law of supply and demand
the claim that the price of any good adjusts to bring the supply and demand for that good into balance

libertarianism
the political philosophy according to which the government should punish crimes and enforce voluntary agreements but not redistribute income

life cycle
the regular pattern of income variation over a person's life

liquidity
the ease with which an asset can be converted into the economy's medium of exchange

liquidity conditions
the price and availability of funding for the economy's expenditure

lump-sum tax
a tax that is the same amount for every person

macroeconomics
the study of economy-wide phenomena, including inflation, unemployment and economic growth

managed fund
a type of financial investment that allows investors to own a portfolio of various types of shares and/or bonds

marginal change
a small incremental adjustment to a plan of action

marginal cost
the increase in total cost that arises from an extra unit of production

marginal product
the increase in output that arises from an additional unit of input

marginal product of labour
the increase in the amount of output from an additional unit of labour

marginal rate of substitution
the rate at which a consumer is willing to trade one good for another

marginal revenue
the change in total revenue from an additional unit sold

marginal tax rate
the extra taxes paid on an additional dollar of income

market
a group of buyers and sellers of a particular good or service

market economy
an economy that allocates resources through the decentralised decisions of many firms and households as they interact in markets for goods and services

market failure
a situation in which a market left on its own fails to allocate resources efficiently

market for loanable funds
the market in which those who want to save supply funds and those who want to borrow to invest demand funds

market power
the ability of a single economic actor (or small group of actors) to have a substantial influence on market prices

maximin criterion
the claim that the government should aim to maximise the wellbeing of the worst-off person in society

median voter theorem
a mathematical result showing that if voters are choosing a point along a line and each voter wants the point closest to his most preferred point,

then majority rule will pick the most preferred point of the median voter

medium of exchange
an item that buyers give to sellers when they want to purchase goods and services

menu costs
the costs of changing prices

microeconomics
the study of how households and firms make decisions and how they interact in markets

model of aggregate demand and aggregate supply
the model that most economists use to explain short-run fluctuations in economic activity around its long-run trend

monetary neutrality
the proposition that changes in the money supply do not affect real variables

monetary policy
the management by the central bank of liquidity conditions in the economy

money
the set of assets in an economy that people regularly use to buy goods and services from other people

money multiplier
the amount of money the banking system generates with each dollar of reserves

money supply
the quantity of money circulating in the economy

monopolistic competition
a market structure in which many firms sell products that are similar but not identical

monopoly
a firm that is the sole seller of a product without close substitutes

monopsony
a market situation where there is a single buyer for a product

moral hazard
the tendency of a person who is imperfectly monitored to engage in dishonest or otherwise undesirable behaviour

multiplier effect
the additional shifts in aggregate demand that result when expansionary fiscal policy increases income and thereby increases consumer spending

NAIRU (non-accelerating inflation rate of unemployment)
the level of unemployment that does not result in increases in the inflation rate

Nash equilibrium
a situation in which economic actors interacting with one another each choose their best strategy given the strategies that all the other actors have chosen

national saving (saving)
the total income in the economy that remains after paying for consumption and government purchases

natural monopoly
a monopoly that arises because a single firm can supply a good or service to an entire market at a smaller cost than could two or more firms

natural-rate hypothesis
the claim that unemployment eventually returns to its normal, or natural, rate, regardless of the rate of inflation

natural rate of unemployment
unemployment accounted for by structural factors around which the actual unemployment rate fluctuates

natural resources
the inputs into the production of goods and services that are provided by nature, such as land, rivers and mineral deposits

negative income tax
a tax system that collects revenue from high-income households and

gives transfers to low-income households

net exports (trade balance)
spending on domestically produced goods by foreigners (exports) minus spending on foreign goods by domestic residents (imports) – also called the trade balance

net foreign investment
the purchase of foreign assets by domestic residents minus the purchase of domestic assets by foreigners

nominal exchange rate
the rate at which a person can trade the currency of one country for the currency of another

nominal GDP
the production of goods and services valued at current prices

nominal interest rate
the interest rate as usually reported without a correction for the effects of inflation

nominal variables
variables measured in monetary units

normal good
a good for which, other things being equal, an increase in income leads to an increase in quantity demanded

normative statements
claims that attempt to prescribe how the world should be

oligopoly
a market structure in which only a few sellers offer similar or identical products

open economy
an economy that interacts freely with other economies around the world

open-market operations
the purchase and sale of Australian government securities by the RBA

opportunity cost
whatever must be given up to obtain some item

897

perfect complements
two goods with right-angle indifference curves

perfect substitutes
two goods with straight-line indifference curves

permanent income
a person's normal income

Phillips curve
the short-term trade-off between inflation and unemployment

physical capital
the stock of equipment and structures that are used to produce goods and services

positive statements
claims that attempt to describe the world as it is

possibilities frontier
a graph depicting all the outcomes that maximise the sum of profits plus wages to workers

poverty line
an absolute level of income set by the federal government for each family size below which a family is deemed to be in poverty

poverty rate
the percentage of the population whose family income falls below an absolute level called the poverty line

predatory pricing
when a firm sells its product at an artificially low price in order to drive out an efficient competitor and reduce long-run competition

price ceiling
a legal maximum on the price at which a good can be sold

price discrimination
the business practice of selling the same good at different prices to different customers

price elasticity of demand
a measure of how much the quantity demanded of a good responds to a change in the price of that good, calculated as the percentage change

in quantity demanded divided by the percentage change in price

price elasticity of supply
a measure of how much the quantity supplied of a good responds to a change in the price of that good, calculated as the percentage change in quantity supplied divided by the percentage change in price

price floor
a legal minimum on the price at which a good can be sold

principal
a person for whom another person, called the agent, is performing some act

prisoners' dilemma
a particular 'game' between two captured prisoners that illustrates why cooperation is difficult to maintain even when it is mutually beneficial

private goods
goods that are both excludable and rival in consumption

private saving
the income that households have left after paying for taxes and consumption

privatisation
the sale of a government-owned business to private owners

producer price index
a measure of the cost of a basket of goods and services bought by firms

producer surplus
the amount a seller is paid for a good minus the seller's cost

production function
the relationship between quantity of inputs used to make a good and the quantity of output of that good

production possibilities frontier
a graph that shows the various combinations of output that the economy can possibly produce given the available factors of production and the available production technology

productivity
the quantity of goods and services produced from each hour of a worker's time

profit
total revenue minus total cost

progressive tax
a tax for which high-income taxpayers pay a larger fraction of their income than do low-income taxpayers

proportional tax
a tax for which high-income and low-income taxpayers pay the same fraction of income

public goods
goods that are neither excludable nor rival in consumption

public saving
the tax revenue that the government has left after paying for its spending

purchasing-power parity
a theory of exchange rates whereby a unit of any given currency should be able to buy the same quantity of goods in all countries

quantity demanded
the amount of a good that buyers are willing and able to purchase

quantity equation
the equation $M \times V = P \times Y$, which relates the quantity of money, the velocity of money and the dollar value of the economy's output of goods and services

quantity supplied
the amount of a good that sellers are willing and able to sell

quantity theory of money
a theory asserting that the quantity of money available determines the price level and that the growth rate in the quantity of money available determines the inflation rate

rational expectations
the theory according to which people optimally use all the information they have, including information about government policies, when forecasting the future

Rawlsianism
the political philosophy according to which the government should choose policies deemed to be just, as evaluated by an impartial observer behind a 'veil of ignorance'

real exchange rate
the rate at which a person can trade the goods and services of one country for the goods and services of another

real GDP
the production of goods and services valued at constant prices

real interest rate
the interest rate corrected for the effects of inflation

real variables
variables measured in constant units

recession
a period of declining real incomes and rising unemployment

regressive tax
a tax for which high-income taxpayers pay a smaller fraction of their income than do low-income taxpayers

resale price maintenance
when a wholesaler requires that its retailers do not sell its products to their customers below a specified retail price

Reserve Bank of Australia (RBA)
the central bank of Australia

reserve ratio
the fraction of deposits that banks hold as reserves

reserve requirements
regulations on the minimum amount of reserves that banks must hold against deposits

reserves
deposits that banks have received but have not lent out

rival in consumption
the property of a good where one person's use diminishes other people's use

sacrifice ratio
the number of percentage points of annual output lost in the process of reducing inflation by one percentage point

scarcity
the limited nature of society's resources

screening
an action taken by an uninformed party to induce an informed party to reveal information

share
a claim to partial ownership in a firm

shoeleather costs
the resources wasted when inflation encourages people to reduce their money holdings

shortage
a situation in which quantity demanded is greater than quantity supplied

signalling
an action taken by an informed party to reveal private information to an uninformed party

social security
government programs that supplement the incomes of the needy

stagflation
a period of falling output and rising prices

store of value
an item that people can use to transfer purchasing power from the present to the future

strike
the organised withdrawal of labour from a firm by a union

substitutes
two goods for which a decrease in the price of one good leads to a decrease in the demand for the other good

substitution effect
the change in consumption that results when a price change moves the consumer along a given indifference curve to a point with a new marginal rate of substitution

supply curve
a graph of the relationship between the price of a good and the quantity supplied

supply schedule
a table that shows the relationship between the price of a good and the quantity supplied

surplus
a situation in which quantity supplied is greater than quantity demanded

tariff
a tax on goods produced abroad and sold domestically

tax incidence
the study of who bears the burden of taxation

technological knowledge
society's understanding of the best ways to produce goods and services

total cost
the amount a firm pays to buy the inputs into production

total revenue (for a firm)
the amount a firm receives for the sale of its output

total revenue (in a market)
the amount paid by buyers and received by sellers of a good, calculated as the price of the good times the quantity sold

trade balance
see net exports

trade deficit
an excess of imports over exports

Trade Practices Act
see *Competition and Consumer Act*.

trade policy
a government policy that directly influences the quantity of goods and services that a country imports or exports

899

trade surplus
an excess of exports over imports

Tragedy of the Commons
a parable that illustrates why common resources get used more than is desirable from the standpoint of society as a whole

transaction costs
the costs that parties incur in the process of agreeing and following through on a bargain

tying
when a firm will only sell customers one product if they also buy another product

unemployment benefits
a government program that partially protects workers' incomes when they become unemployed

unemployment rate
the percentage of the labour force that is unemployed

union
a worker association that bargains with employers over wages and working conditions

unit of account
the yardstick people use to post prices and record debts

utilitarianism
the political philosophy according to which the government should choose policies to maximise the total utility of everyone in society

utility
a measure of happiness or satisfaction

value added
the value of a firm's output minus the value of its inputs

value of the marginal product
the marginal product of an input times the price of the output

variable costs
costs that vary with the quantity of output produced

velocity of money
the rate at which money changes hands

vertical equity
the idea that taxpayers with a greater ability to pay taxes should pay larger amounts

welfare economics
the study of how the allocation of resources affects economic wellbeing

willingness to pay
the maximum amount that a buyer will pay for a good

world price
the price of a good that prevails in the world market for that good

Suggestions for reading

If you enjoyed the economics course you have just finished, you might like reading more about economic issues in the following books.

- *Freakonomics: A Rogue Economist Explores the Hidden Side of Everything*, Steven D. Levitt and Stephen J. Dubner (New York: William Morrow, 2005). Economic principles and clever data analysis applied to a wide range of offbeat topics, including drug dealing, online dating and sumo wrestling.

- *The Undercover Economist: Exposing Why the Rich Are Rich, the Poor Are Poor and Why You Can Never Buy A Decent Used Car!*, Tim Harford (Oxford: Oxford University Press, 2006). An easy to read and thought-provoking introduction to the key economic issues of the day.

- *Supercrunchers: Why Thinking-by-Numbers Is the New Way to Be Smart*, Ian Ayres (New York: Bantam, 2007). What happens when you combine economics, statistics and large datasets? The answer is 'answers' and lots of them to issues that drive government and business.

- *Reinventing the Bazaar: A Natural History of Markets*, John McMillan (New York: Norton, 2002). The late, great New Zealand economist provides a deep and nuanced, yet still very readable, analysis of how society can make the best use of market mechanisms.

- *Thinking Strategically: A Competitive Edge in Business, Politics, and Everyday Life*, 2nd edn, Avinash Dixit and Barry Nalebuff (New York: Norton, 2008). This introduction to game theory discusses how all people – from corporate executives to arrested criminals – should and do make strategic decisions that affect themselves and others.

- *Micromotives and Macrobehavior*, rev. edn, Thomas Schelling (New York: Norton, 2006). The Nobel Prize winning game theorist explains how to construct models to explain how seemingly small and meaningless decisions have a big impact on the patterns of large groups.

- *Information Rules: A Strategic Guide to the Network Economy*, Carl Shapiro and Hal R. Varian (Boston: Harvard Business School Press, 1999). Two microeconomists explain how businesses succeed in the modern information-driven economy.

- *Co-opetition*, Adam M. Brandenburger and Barry J. Nalebuff (New York: Doubleday, 1996). This book explains the usefulness of game theory for business decision making in a competitive environment.

- *Capitalism and Freedom*, Milton Friedman (Chicago: University of Chicago Press, 1962). In this classic book, one of the most important economists of the twentieth century argues that society should rely less on the government and more on the free market.

- *The Worldly Philosophers*, Robert L. Heilbroner (New York: Touchstone, 1953). This classic book discusses the lives, times and ideas of the great economic thinkers, including Adam Smith, David Ricardo and John Maynard Keynes.

- *Murder at the Margin*, Marshall Jevons (Princeton, NJ: Princeton University Press, 1993), and *The Fatal Equilibrium*, Marshall Jevons (Cambridge, Mass.: MIT Press, 1985). In each of these two mystery novels, an economist-sleuth applies the principles of economics to figure out who did it. Yes, the books are corny, but they are also fun.

901

- *The Logic of Life,* Tim Harford (Random House, 2009). The best review of how economics can be used to explain aspects of everyday life.
- *The Limits of Organization*, Kenneth J. Arrow (New York: Norton, 1974). A Nobel laureate conducts a thoughtful examination of the foundations of economic decision making and the organisation of society.
- *Core Economics for Managers*, Joshua Gans (Melbourne: Cengage Learning, 2005). Take your economics one step further into bargaining and strategy with this text designed to teach economics to business students.
- *Getting It Right: Markets and Choices in a Free Society*, Robert J. Barro (Cambridge, Mass.: MIT Press, 1996). In this collection of essays based on his *Wall Street Journal* columns, conservative economist Robert Barro offers his view about the workings of the economy and the proper scope of economic policy.
- *Hard Heads, Soft Hearts: Tough-minded Economics for a Just Society*, Alan S. Blinder (Reading, Mass.: Addison-Wesley, 1987). How should government policymakers balance economic efficiency and social compassion? Alan Blinder, who served as an economic adviser to President Clinton, offers his answers in this wide-ranging book.
- *New Ideas from Dead Economists*, Todd G. Buchholz (New York: Penguin Books, 1989). This amusing book provides an overview of the history of economic thought.
- *The Winner-take-all Society: How More and More Americans Compete for Fewer and Bigger Prizes, Encouraging Economic Waste, Income Inequality, and an Impoverished Cultural Life*, Robert H. Frank and Philip J. Cook (New York: The Free Press, 1995). This book examines some of the reasons for, and the effects of, increasing inequality of incomes in the United States.
- *The Age of Diminished Expectations: US Economic Policy in the 1990s*, Paul Krugman (Cambridge, Mass.: MIT Press, 1990). Liberal economist Paul Krugman considers the problems that face the US economy and the policies that might improve economic performance.
- *Peddling Prosperity: Economic Sense and Nonsense in the Age of Diminished Expectations*, Paul Krugman (New York: Norton, 1994). This book examines the evolution of economic ideas and economic policy, with an emphasis on developments over the past 30 years.
- *The Armchair Economist: Economics and Everyday Life*, Steven E. Landsburg (New York: The Free Press, 1993). Why does popcorn cost so much at movie theatres? Steven Landsburg discusses this and other puzzles of economic life in this offbeat yet engaging book.
- *Unlocking the Infrastructure: The Reform of Public Utilities in Australia*, Stephen King and Rodney Maddock (Sydney: Allen & Unwin, 1996). This book looks at competition policy and microeconomic reform in Australia.
- *Great Expectations: Microeconomic Reform and Australia*, John Quiggin (Sydney: Allen & Unwin, 1996). John Quiggin takes a critical look at microeconomic reform in Australia.
- *A Random Walk down Wall Street*, Burton G. Malkiel (New York: Norton, 1973, revised 1996). This introduction to stocks, bonds and financial economics is not a 'get rich quick' book, but it might help you get rich slowly.
- *John Maynard Keynes: Hopes Betrayed, 1883–1920*, Robert Skidelsky (New York: Viking, 1983) and *John Maynard Keynes: The Economist as Saviour, 1920–1937*, Robert Skidelsky (London: Macmillan, 1992). These two books constitute the first two volumes of a biographical

trilogy (the third is not yet published) that covers the life of one of the most important and interesting economists of all time.

- *Nudge*, Richard H. Thaler and Cass R. Sunstein (New Haven [London]: Yale University Press, 2008) and *Sway*, Ori Brafman and Rom Brafman (New York: Doubleday, 2008). Both of these books look at the way our perceptions and biases affect the way we make decisions about economic matters.

Pick of the Economics blogs

- *Marginal Revolution*: www.marginalrevolution.com. The most popular economics blog from two economists at George Mason University.
- *Freakonomics*: freakonomics.com. The two authors of Freakonomics extend their commentary of economics and everyday life.
- *Greg Mankiw*: gregmankiw.blogspot.com. One of the authors of this textbook takes a hard-headed look at macroeconomics and economic policy.
- *Brad DeLong's Semi-Daily Journal*: Delong.typepad.com. The oldest and one of the most influential economics blogs, from a Berkeley professor who grasps reality with both hands.
- *The Becker-Posner Blog*: www.becker-posner-blog.com. One Nobel laureate and a judge debate economic trends and policies.
- *Core Economics*: economics.com.au. Australian academic economists examine policy, economics and strategy.
- *John Quiggin*: johnquiggin.com. Australia's foremost economic commentator looks at the world from a social democratic perspective.

Index